W9-BZM-120

Collins
English-
Japanese
Dictionary

Collins
English-
Japanese
Dictionary

HarperCollins Publishers
Westerhill Road
Bishopbriggs
Glasgow G64 2QT
Great Britain

First Edition 2005

Previously published as Collins-Shubun Pocket English-Japanese Dictionary

Latest Reprint 2005

© HarperCollins Publishers & Shubun International Co., Ltd 1993

ISBN 0-00-719655-5

Collins® and Bank of English® are registered trademarks of HarperCollins Publishers Limited

www.collins.co.uk

A catalogue record for this book is available from the British Library

HarperCollins Publishers, Inc.
10 East 53rd Street, New York, NY 10022

ISBN 0-06-273758-9

Library of Congress Cataloging-in-Publication Data has been applied for

www.harpercollins.com

First HarperCollins edition published 1993

HarperCollins books may be purchased for educational, business, or sales promotional use. For information, please write to: Special Markets Department, HarperCollins Publishers Inc., 10 East 53rd Street, New York, NY 10022

Typeset by Tosho Printing Co., Ltd

Printed in Great Britain by Clays Ltd, St Ives plc

Acknowledgements

We would like to thank those authors and publishers who kindly gave permission for copyright material to be used in the Collins Word Web. We would also like to thank Times Newspapers Ltd for providing valuable data.

All rights reserved. No part of this publication may be reproduced, stored in a retrieval system or transmitted, in any form or by any means, electronic, mechanical, photocopying, recording or otherwise, without the prior permission of the publisher. This book is sold subject to the conditions that it shall not, by way of trade or otherwise, be lent, re-sold, hired out or otherwise circulated without the publisher's prior consent in any form of binding or cover other than that in which it is published and without a similar condition including this condition being imposed on the subsequent purchaser.

Entered words that we have reason to believe constitute trademarks have been designated as such. However, neither the presence nor absence of such designation should be regarded as affecting the legal status of any trademark.

ORIGINAL MATERIAL BY
CollinsBilingual

JAPANESE LANGUAGE EDITION
Richard C. Goris
Yukimi Okubo

EDITORIAL ADMINISTRATION
Jill Campbell

CONTENTS

Authors' Foreword

Dictionary compilers have been labeled "harmless drudges", but we have found little drudgery in compiling the Collins-Shubun English-Japanese Dictionary. On the contrary, we have experienced great pleasure in rising to the challenge of producing a book that was not run-of-the-mill.

To begin with, we had several advantages. We had the dictionary framework provided in electronic form by Collins Dictionary Division. Then we had computers running powerful Japanese word processing software. Together these factors saved us from the drudgery (and writer's cramp) caused by writing thousands and thousands of manuscript pages by hand. They also eliminated the drudgery of correcting in proof the innumerable mistakes introduced by typesetters misinterpreting our handwriting.

The challenge of producing "a better mousetrap" also provided motivation that eliminated drudgery.

In order to keep the dictionary truly pocket-sized, we aimed at providing one translation for each word, or for each meaning of a word. Where several possible translations existed, we chose the one with the highest frequency of usage in modern Japanese. We also tried to give translations that were the cultural equivalent of the English. Thus, if the English word conveyed a sense of dignity, we used a dignified Japanese expression; if the English was a slangy word, we provided a slangy Japanese word or phrase. Where this was not possible, we have provided glosses to clarify the difference.

There were some exceptions. When the English word had several Japanese equivalents, each used with equal frequency, and generally interchangeable, we gave the two or three most frequent, separated by commas.

In this category fell words that could be expressed either by a Chinese compound (2 or more Chinese characters used as a single word) or by a purely Japanese word. There were also words that could be expressed by a Japanese translation or a "Japanized" foreign loan word of equal frequency. In this case we gave the Japanese translation first, followed by a comma and the loan word. Where the Japanese translation existed, but was outlandish and seldom used, we gave only the loan word. In such cases the loan word is generally listed as a headword in standard Japanese dictionaries.

Finally, we discussed every entry thoroughly before adopting it. Thus we feel we have met our goal of providing a small, portable, but extremely useful dictionary - useful to the language student and the native speaker alike.

Our efforts would have been futile without the support, aid, and counsel of the editorial staff of Collins Dictionaries and Shubun. Shubun's board of experts and editors included Kazuo Shibuya, Shiruki Furukawa, Ari Matsue, and Kazuko Namiki. On the other side of the ocean we had in particular the aid of Lorna Sinclair-Knight, Jeremy Butterfield, and the hard-working Jill Campbell, in addition to other anonymous advisors.

To all and sundry, a handshake and a deep bow of gratitude.

Richard C. Goris
Yukimi Okubo

著 者 前 書

辞書を書く人というと「ひたすらこつこつ働く，人畜無害な凡人」と見る向きもあるが，当の私達はコリンズ・秀文英和辞典を書くに際し，ことさら単調な仕事を余儀なくされたという感じは全く覚えなかった．平凡でない辞書を作ろうというチャレンジに答えることにむしろ大きな喜びを感じた．

第一に苦労を軽減する要素がいくつかあった．まずコリンズ社の辞書部門よりコービルドのデータベースから頻度によって抽出され，フォーマット化されたた語彙リストのフロッピーディスクが提供された．これを強力な日本語ワープロソフトでコンピュータ操作し，日本語訳等を入力した．こうして何千枚もの原稿を手書きする苦労（と書痙の危険）を避けられ，同時に植字段階で起こるエラーを校正で直す苦労も避けることができた．

第二に，「より優れたもの」を作るというチャレンジも作業の単調さを吹き飛ばす動機にもなった．

当書をポケット版の限度内に抑えるためには，原則として一見出し語に対して，あるいは見出し語の一意味に対して一つだけの訳語をつけることにした．複数の訳語が可能な場合，最も頻度の高いものを選んだ．また，英語の語彙に対して文化的に同じ含みの訳語を選ぶように努力した．例えば，英単語が格調の高い語であれば，格調の高い日本語訳をつけた．一方，俗語のような英語に対してはそれに相当する日本語の俗語をつけた．これが不可能な場合，補足説明をつけた．

いくつか例外がある．複数の日本語訳が可能で，頻度が同じぐらいで置き換えもきく場合，二つか三つを併記してコンマで分けた．こういう語には漢語的表現またはやまとことばに訳せる語が多かった．その他に純粋な日本語もしくは外来語で表せる語もあった．その場合，日本語と外来語を併記してコンマで分けた．しかし日本語訳がおかしかったり頻度が低かったりする場合，外来語だけを記載した．この様な外来語はたいがい国語辞典で見出し語として使われている．

熟考と討論を重ねて最後に訳語を選択した．こうして小型でポケット版であるにもかかわらず，language student，native speaker 双方に大いに役立つ画期的な辞典の作成に成功したと確信する．

コリンズ社辞典編集部門及び秀文インターナショナルの編集スタッフの支援と助言なしには私達の努力だけではこの辞書を作れなかったと思う．秀文側にあっては特に渋谷一夫，古川知己，松江亜里，並木和子，そして海の向こうにあっては Lorna Sinclair-Knight，Jeremy Butterfield，Jill Campbell，その他の皆さん方に深く感謝の意を表する．

R．C．ゴリス
大久保　雪美

PUBLISHER'S FOREWORD

As the 21st century approaches and the countries of the world become more internationalized, the importance of English as a world language is felt ever more keenly by society. This awareness spotlights certain problems concerning the bilingual dictionaries, particularly English-Japanese dictionaries, published in Japan.

To begin with, there is the habit of crowding into each entry, without rhyme or reason, all the possible translations of a headword that can be thought of, a habit that has persisted since the Meiji Era.

Secondly, in a great many cases, scientific data on the use of words and phrases is very scarce, making it extremely difficult to improve on the present situation.

Dictionary users are becoming increasingly dissatisfied with the growing volume of unsorted data that is being thrust at them. Things have reached a point where the dictionary makers appear to have lost touch with the needs of their users.

What the users really want is well-ordered data, that is, clear, uncluttered information on the meaning of the words of a language. They need fundamental information on actual usage of the words of a language, information on situation and context in which a word or phrase is used, information on what normally comes before or after various words and phrases. This in turn requires a wealth of background information about the actual state of a language. Fortunately, we have been able to join forces with HarperCollins Publishers of Britain, who have at their disposal the largest data bank in the world of the English language. This data bank furnished us with, among other things, information on word frequency, which guided the choice of headwords; and information on situation, context, variation in meaning etc, which is shown in parentheses (the "indicators") in each entry. The result has been the revolutionary dictionary that we present here, for use throughout the world, in preparation for the 21st century, a truly original publication.

Instead of being laboriously typeset from a hand-written manuscript, the dictionary was composed entirely on a computer in a form that permitted electronic typesetting machines to transform the data directly into the printed page. Throughout the project the authors maintained constant, real-time contact with the editorial staff of Collins Dictionary Division through electronic mail and other modern means.

All Japanese entries in the main text have their pronunciation indicated in romaji, so that anyone anywhere in the world can use this dictionary to study Japanese through the medium of English.

At the same time Japanese users of the dictionary, even if already proficient in English, can gain confidence in their use of the language by noting the information about usage given in the parenthetical "indicators" in each entry.

Shubun International, Ltd.

出版する立場から

21世紀の幕開けが近づくく一方，さらに国際化が一層進展し世界語としての英語の重要性がますます高まっているのが昨今の社会情勢と言えましょう．このような背景を踏まえ，我が国の外国語特に英和辞典の将来を考えてみるといくつかの問題点がはっきりしてくる．

まず第一に明治以来の伝統に従って狭い紙面に未整理のままと言ってよい程の訳語という名称の語義の網羅振りが指摘できよう．

第二に多くの場合，言語使用に付いて科学的データに乏しく，思い切った革新の道を拓くことが極めて困難といった状況が指摘できましょう．

肥大化する情報量に辞典使用者もうんざりの感さえするのである．使用者が何を求めているのか図りかねているのが現状とも言える状況である．

辞典使用者は小気味よく整理された情報の提供，すなわち今や簡潔・明解な言語の意味を求めている．ある言語の意味とは，ある語（句）がどのような場面・文脈・前後関係の中で何を伝達しようとしているのか示すことであり，かつ最も基本的なことである．このためには当該言語使用の実態について豊富なデータが必要となる．幸いなことに今日世界最大規模のdata bank of the English languageを活用する英国ハーパーコリンズ社と提携，使用頻度及び語句の意味の使用範囲「indicators」のデータを駆使した21世紀を指向した世界で使える画期的な英和辞典の完成をここに見る運びと相成った次第である．これこそ独創の知的生産物財産とも言うべきかなである．

原稿執筆も従来のような組み上げられた順序ではなく項目単位と言うべき方式で完全にコンピュータ化完成され，原稿執筆終了即組版完了ともなった点は画期的な技術革新の成果でもあった．電子時代の申し子でもある電子メール等最新の技術によりコリンズ社辞典編集部門と執筆のデスクが結ばれ，リアルタイムに意志伝達が行われたのである．

このように完成された本辞典は，日本語全てにローマ字による発音表記を付し，世界の何処にあっても英語を媒介とし日本語の習得を可能ならしめる効果的な内容とした．

また特に我が国の英語既習者の社会人にとって意味使用範囲「indicators」の明示による活用は英語使用に自信を与える英語習得への開眼となると信ずる．

株式会社　秀文インターナショナル

INTRODUCTION

We are delighted you have decided to buy the Collins Shubun Pocket English-Japanese Dictionary and hope you will enjoy and benefit from using it at school, at home, on holiday or at work.

This introduction gives you a few tips on how to get the most out of your dictionary-not simply from its comprehensive wordlist but also from the information provided in each entry.

The Collins Shubun English-Japanese Dictionary begins by listing the abbreviations used in the text and follows with a guide to Japanese pronunciation and a chart of the two Japanese scripts "hiragana" and "katakana" together with the Roman letter transliteration used in this dictionary.

USING YOUR COLLINS SHUBUN POCKET DICTIONARY

A wealth of information is presented in the dictionary, using various typefaces, sizes of type, symbols, abbreviations and brackets. The conventions and symbols used are explained in the following sections.

Headwords

The words you look up in a dictionary -"headwords"- are listed alphabetically. They are printed in bold type for rapid identification. The headwords appearing at the top of each page indicate the first and last word dealt with on the page in question.

Information about the usage or form of certain headwords is given in brackets after the phonetic spelling. This usually appears in abbreviated form (e. g., (*fam*), (COMM).

Common expressions in which the headword appears are shown in bold italic type (e. g., **account**... *of no account*).

When such expressions are preceeded by a colon, it means that the headword is used mainly in that particular expression (e. g., **aback**... *adv*: *to be taken aback*).

Phonetic spellings

The phonetic spelling of each headword (indicating its pronunciation) is given in square brackets immediately after the headword (e. g., **able** [ei'bəl]). The phonetics show a standardized US English pronunciation in IPA (International Phonetic Alphabet) symbols. A list of these symbols is given on page (13).

Translations

Headword translations are given in ordinary type and, where more than one meaning or usage exists, these are separated by a semicolon. You will often find other words in brackets before the translations. These offer suggested contexts in which the headword might appear (e. g., **absentee** (from school, meeting etc) or provide synonyms (e. g. **able** (capable) or (skilled)). A white lozenge precedes a gloss giving information for the non-English native speaker.

"Keywords"

Special status is given to certain English words which are considered as "key" words in the language. They may, for example, occur very frequently or have several types of usage (e. g., **a**, **be**). A combination of lozenges and numbers helps you to distinguish different parts of speech and different meanings. Further helpful information is provided in brackets.

Grammatical Information

Parts of speech are given in abbreviated form in italics after the phonetic spellings of headwords (e. g., *vt*, *adv*, *conj*) and headwords with several parts of speech have a black lozenge before each new part of speech (e. g., **wash**).

使用上の注意

本辞典は英単語の意味を知りたい日本人だけでなく日本語を勉強している外国人も使えるよう，すべての訳語，補足説明などを日本文字とローマ字で併記した．ローマ字は原則としてヘボン式に従い，ローマ字：仮名対照表を (17)－(18) ページに示した．またローマ字には日本語のアクセントも加えた．右上がりのアクセント記号 (á) は声の上がりを，右下がりの記号 (à) は声の下がりを，記号のない場合は平坦に発音する事を示す．

見出し語は太字の立体活字で示した．つづりは米国の標準に従ったが，英国の標準がそれと異なる場合，アルファベット順にこれも示した．

　　　　例：**anaemia** [əniːˈmiːə] *etc (BRIT)* = **anemia** *etc*

続いて発音を [ ] の中に国際音標文字で示した．発音記号表は (13) ページにある．アクセントは ['] の記号でアクセントのある音節の後に示した．

　　　　例：**able** [eiˈbəl]

品詞は斜字の略語で示した．例：**able** [eiˈbəl] *adj*

品詞に続いて訳語を日本語とローマ字で示した．原則として１つの意味に対して１つだけ最も頻度の高い訳語を採用した．

　　　　例：**blockade**... 封鎖 fúsa

頻度が同じぐらいで複数の訳語がある場合，これを示すと共にコンマ (,) で分けた．

　　　　例：**blood**... 血 chi, 血液 ketsúèki

訳語の前に丸括弧 ( ) の中でその見出し語についての情報を記した．

立体の大文字はその語が使われる「分野」などを示す．

　　　　例：**blood**... (BIO) 血 chi, 血液 ketsúèki

すなわち，**blood** は「生物学」という分野の語である．

立体の小文字はその他の情報を示す．

　　　　例：**bleat**... *vi* (goat, sheep) 鳴く nakú

すなわち，bleat という動詞はヤギやヒツジについて使う語である．

　　　　例：**aperture**... (hole) 穴 aná; (gap) すき間 sukíma; (PHOT) アパーチャ ápàcha

この例では類語を使って見出し語の意味をはっきりさせている．また，このように１つの見出し語に対して複数の意味がある場合，セミコロン (；) で分ける．

見出し語の成句はその都度改行して太字の斜字で示した．

　　　　例：**bearing**...
　　　　　　　to take a bearing...
　　　　　　　to find one's bearings...

成句は主語＋動詞形式のものでも文頭の大文字と文尾のピリオドをつけずにあくまでも成句として扱った．ただし疑問を表す成句には？をつけた．

> 例：**anyone**...
> 　　*anyone could do it*
> 　　*can you see anyone?*

表示，標識，立て札などに使う成句は「...」で囲んだ．

> 例：**entry**...
> 　　「*no entry*」...

改行なしで品詞などに続くコロン（：）＋ 太斜字の成句は見出し語などがその成句以外には殆ど使われない事を示す．

> 例：**aback** [əbækˈ] *adv*: *to be taken aback* 仰天する gyṓten suru

丸括弧の中で *also*: に続く立体太字の語句はその意味では同意語である事を示す．

> 例：**go about** *vi* (*also*: **go around**: rumor) 流れる nagárerù.

ここでは「噂が流れる」という意味では go about でも go around でも使える事を示している．

特殊記号：

◆：最初に示した品詞と品詞が異なったものにつけた．

> 例：**abdicate**... *vt* (responsibility, right) 放棄する ...
> 　　◆*vi* (monarch) 退位する ...

◇：補足説明を示す．

/：見出し語，成句の中で置き換えられる部分を示す．日本語訳やローマ字の中でこれを〔 〕で示した．

> 例：**abide**... *vt*: *I can't abide it/him* 私はそれ〔彼〕が大嫌いだ watáku-
> 　　shi wá soré〔karè〕ga dáikirai da

KEYWORD: このタイトルは頻度の高い重要な語で特に徹底的に取り扱った見出し語（たとえば **be, can**）を示す．

Phonetic Symbols 発音記号表

[ɑ:] father, hot, knowledge

[æ] at, have, cat

[ai] my, buy, like

[au] how, mouth

[e] men, says, friend

[ei] say, take, rain

[ɛ:r] air, care, where

[ə] above, payment, label

[ə:r] girl, learn, burn, worm

[i] sit, women, busy

[i:] see, bean, city

[ou] no, know, boat

[ɔi] boy, boil

[u] book, could, put

[u:] tool, soup, blue

[ɔ:] law, walk, story

[ʌ] up, cut, above

[p] put, cup

[b] be, tab

[d] down, had

[t] too, hot

[k] come, back

[g] go, tag

[s] see, cups, force

[z] rose, buzz

[ʃ] she, sugar

[ʒ] vision, pleasure

[tʃ] church

[dʒ] jam, gem, judge

[f] farm, half, phone

[v] very, eve

[θ] thin, both

[ð] this, other

[l] little, ball

[r] rat, bread

[m] move, come

[n] no, run

[ŋ] sing, bank

[h] hat, reheat

[j] yes

[w] well, away

Table of Abbreviations 略語表

adj	adjective	形容詞
abbr	abbreviation	略語
adv	adverb	副詞
ADMIN	administration	管理
AGR	agriculture	農業
ANAT	anatomy	解剖学
ARCHIT	architecture	建築
AUT	automobiles	自動車関係
aux vb	auxiliary verb	助動詞
AVIAT	aviation	航空
BIO	biology	生物学
BOT	botany	植物学
BRIT	British English	英国つづり／用法
CHEM	chemistry	化学
COMM	commerce, finance, banking	商業，金融関係
COMPUT	computing	コンピュータ関係
conj	conjunction	接続詞
cpd	compound	形容詞的名詞
CULIN	cookery	料理
def art	definite article	定冠詞
dimin	diminutive	指小辞
ECON	economics	経済学
ELEC	electricity, electronics	電気，電子工学
excl	exclamation, interjection	感嘆詞
fam(!)	colloquial usage (! particularly offensive)	口語（！特に悪質なもの）
fig	figurative use	比喩
fus	(phrasal verb) where the particle cannot be separated from the main verb	vt fusを見よ
gen	in most or all senses; generally	たいがいの意味では，一般に
GEO	geography, geology	地理学，地質学
GEOM	geometry	幾何学
indef art	indefinite article	不定冠詞

inf(!)	colloquial usage (! particularly offensive)	口語 （！特に悪質なもの）
infin	infinitive	不定詞
inv	invariable	変化しない
irreg	irregular	不規則な
LING	grammar, linguistics	文法，語学
lit	literal use	文字通りの意味
MATH	mathematics	数学
MED	medical term, medicine	医学
METEOR	the weather, meteorology	気象関係
MIL	military matters	軍事
MUS	music	音楽
n	noun	名詞
NAUT	sailing, navigation	海事
num	numeral adjective or noun	数詞
obj	(grammatical) object	目的語
pej	pejorative	蔑称
PHOT	photography	写真
PHYSIOL	physiology	生理学
pl	plural	複数
POL	politics	政治
pp	past participle	過去分詞形
prep	preposition	前置詞
pron	pronoun	代名詞
PSYCH	psychology, psychiatry	精神医学
pt	past tense	過去形
RAIL	railroad, railway	鉄道
REL	religion	宗教
SCOL	schooling, schools and universities	学校教育
sing	singular	単数
subj	(grammatical) subject	主語
superl	superlative	最上級
TECH	technical term, technology	技術(用語)，テクノロジー
TEL	telecommunications	電信電話
TV	television	テレビ
TYP	typography, printing	印刷

US	American English	米国つづり／用法
vb	verb	動詞
vi	verb or phrasal verb used intransitively	自動詞
vt	verb or phrasal verb used transitively	他動詞
vt fus	phrasal verb where the particle cannot be separated from main verb	パーチクルを動詞から分けられない句動詞
ZOOL	zoology	動物学
®	registered trademark	登録商標

THE ROMANIZATION AND PRONUNCIATION OF JAPANESE

There are several systems for writing Japanese in Roman characters, but the most understandable and least confusing to the speaker of English is the Hepburn ("hebon" in Japanese) system. The following table illustrates this system, with its "hiragana" and "katakana" equivalents, as it has been adopted in this dictionary.

a	i	u	e	o		ā	ī	ū	ē	ō
あ	い	う	え	お		—	—	うう	—	おお/おう
ア	イ	ウ	エ	オ		アー	イー	ウー	エー	オー

ka	ki	ku	ke	ko		kya	—	kyu	—	kyo
か	き	く	け	こ		きゃ	—	きゅ	—	きょ
カ	キ	ク	ケ	コ		キャ	—	キュ	—	キョ

ga	gi	gu	ge	go		gya	—	gyu	—	gyo
が	ぎ	ぐ	げ	ご		ぎゃ	—	ぎゅ	—	ぎょ
ガ	ギ	グ	ゲ	ゴ		ギャ	—	ギュ	—	ギョ

sa	shi	su	se	so		sha	shi	shu	she	sho
さ	し	す	せ	そ		しゃ	し	しゅ	しぇ	しょ
サ	シ	ス	セ	ソ		シャ	シ	シュ	シェ	ショ

za	ji	zu	ze	zo		ja	ji	ju	je	jo
ざ	じ	ず	ぜ	ぞ		じゃ	じ	じゅ	じぇ	じょ
ザ	ジ	ズ	ゼ	ゾ		ジャ	ジ	ジュ	ジェ	ジョ

ta	chi	tsu	te	to		cha	chi	chu	che	cho
た	ち	つ	て	と		ちゃ	ち	ちゅ	ちぇ	ちょ
タ	チ	ツ	テ	ト		チャ	チ	チュ	チェ	チョ

da	ji	zu	de	do		ja	ji	ju	je	jo
だ	ぢ	づ	で	ど		ぢゃ	ぢ	ぢゅ	ぢぇ	ぢょ
ダ	ヂ	ヅ	デ	ド		ヂャ	ヂ	ヂュ	ヂェ	ヂョ

na	ni	nu	ne	no	nya	—	nyu	—	nyo
な	に	ぬ	ね	の	にゃ	—	にゅ	—	にょ
ナ	ニ	ヌ	ネ	ノ	ニャ	—	ニュ	—	ニョ

ha	hi	fu	he	ho	hya	—	hyu	—	hyo
は	ひ	ふ	へ	ほ	ひゃ	—	ひゅ	—	ひょ
ハ	ヒ	フ	ヘ	ホ	ヒャ	—	ヒュ	—	ヒョ

ba	bi	bu	be	bo	bya	—	byu	—	byo
ば	び	ぶ	べ	ぼ	びゃ	—	びゅ	—	びょ
バ	ビ	ブ	ベ	ボ	ビャ	—	ビュ	—	ビョ

pa	pi	pu	pe	po	pya	—	pyu	—	pyo
ぱ	ぴ	ぷ	ぺ	ぽ	ぴゃ	—	ぴゅ	—	ぴょ
パ	ピ	プ	ペ	ポ	ピャ	—	ピュ	—	ピョ

ma	mi	mu	me	mo	mya	—	myu	—	myo
ま	み	む	め	も	みゃ	—	みゅ	—	みょ
マ	ミ	ム	メ	モ	ミャ	—	ミュ	—	ミョ

ya	—	yu	—	yo
や	—	ゆ	—	よ
ヤ	—	ユ	—	ヨ

ra	ri	ru	re	ro	rya	—	ryu	—	ryo
ら	り	る	れ	ろ	りゃ	—	りゅ	—	りょ
ラ	リ	ル	レ	ロ	リャ	—	リュ	—	リョ

wa	—	—	—	wo	n
わ	—	—	—	を	ん
ワ	—	—	—	ヲ	ン

Consonants:

Pronounce the consonants as you would in English. Exceptions are "w" in the objective particle "wo", "r", "g", and "f". In "wo" the "w" is normally not pronounced, but is written to distinguish it easily from other words that are pronounced "o". (Japanese word-processing software also usually requires that you type "wo" to get を or ヲ.)

"R" is pronounced with a very slight trill. Do not pronounce it as in the English word "rich"; you probably will not be understood. If you trill it as in Italian or Spanish, you can be understood, but you will sound foreign. The best strategy is to listen and imitate. Lacking access to native speakers, try pronouncing "r" as you would "d", but with the tongue farther forward, touching the upper teeth instead of the palate.

"G" is perfectly understandable pronounced as in English "get", "go" etc, and many Japanese always pronounce it in this way. Cultured people, however, prefer a softer, slightly nasal pronunciation, which they call a "half-voiced" or "nasal-voiced" "k". It is similar to the "ng" in "sing", but coming at the beginning of a syllable.

"F" also is quite understandable when given its usual English fricative value, with the lower lip touching the upper teeth. The Japanese, however, normally pronounce it by simply narrowing the gap between the lower lip and the teeth, without actually touching the lip to the teeth. Thus some individuals pronounce it much closer to "h" than to the English "f".

"N" at the end of a syllable or word is syllabic, that is, it is a syllable in its own right, with full syllabic length, as in English "button". In this dictionary when syllabic "n" is followed by a vowel or "y", a hyphen is inserted to indicate the proper pronunciation: e.g., 勧誘 かんゆう kan-yū, as opposed to 加入 かにゅう kanyū.

Before "p", "b", or "m", "n" naturally becomes an "m" sound; but in this dictionary, in keeping with the practice of other romanized dictionaries, the Japanese ん is consistently transliterated as "n", not "m": e.g., 文法 ぶんぽう bunpō, not bumpō.

Double consonants are pronounced in Japanese, as in US English "cattail". In "katakana" and "hiragana" they are indicated by a lowercase っ or ッ before the consonant to be doubled, and in this dictionary are printed as double consonants: か っぱ "kappa", いった "itta". The one exception is the combination っち, which we express as "tch": マッチ, "matchi".

A few Japanese exclamations are written with a lowercase っ at the end, indicating an articulated "t" sound at the end. These we have romanized with a quarter-sized "t": しっ "shiᵗ" (equivalent to the English "ssh!").

The sounds [ti:] and [di:] do not exist in Japanese. They are usually expressed as

ティ and ディ, which we romanize as "ti" and "di". Other sounds in loan words without Japanese equivalents are generally corrupted to some similar sound, e. g., "v" to "b".

Vowels:

The 5 Japanese vowels are the fundamental Latin vowels: [ɑ:], [i:], [u:], [e], and [o]. "U" is pronounced without rounding the lips, keeping them relaxed. A rounded "u" is understandable, but sounds outlandishly foreign. Again, listen and imitate.

The vowels can be long or short. Long vowels are pronounced the same as short vowels, but for double their length, with no break. Pay strict attention to this, for vowel length is essential to both meaning and comprehension. Using a short vowel for a long one, or vice versa, can produce a word of entirely different meaning from the one intended. In this dictionary, long vowels are marked with a macron: ā, ī, ū, ē, ō.

The syllable "-su" at the end of a word, especially in the verbal ending "-masu" frequently drops the "u", so that only the "s" is heard. This occurs more often in the east than in the west of the country. There are no hard and fast rules, so the student needs to rely on his experience from listening to spoken Japanese.

Japanese accents:

Japanese words do not have a strong tonic accent as in most European languages. Instead they are inflected, with the voice rising or falling gently on certain syllables, and remaining flat on others. Using the correct "accent" or inflection is necessary for intelligibility of speech, and often serves to distinguish between words of similar spelling. For example, depending on the "accent", "momo" can mean either "peach" or "thigh"; "kaki" can be either "persimmon" or "oyster"; "atsui" can be "hot" or "thick".

The Japanese accent is difficult to depict graphically with any accuracy, for there are no standard conventions. Many dictionaries simply ignore the problem, leaving the foreign student to his own devices. Language classes for foreigners both in Japan and abroad frequently do not teach accents explicitly, but rely on imitation of pronunciation by a native Japanese model.

We felt that the foreign student needed something to aid the memory in trying to pronounce words already learned in the past, as well as a guide to pronunciation of words being looked up in the dictionary. We settled on the accute accent (á) to indicate a rising inflection, and the grave accent (à) to indicate a falling inflection. No mark at all means that the voice is held flat on that syllable.

The one exception in this dictionary is when two "i"s occur together, as in the word for "good" いい ii. In most cases like this, the first "i" requires a rising inflection (í), and the second a falling inflection (ì). However, with standard typefaces this produces an unesthetic effect (íì). Therefore, we have omitted the accent mark of the second "i" in such cases: a rising inflection on the first of a "double i" combination indicates also a falling inflection on the second letter: íi = í ì.

Doubtless the foreign student will be somewhat disconcerted to see such inflection marks on "n" in this dictionary. Remember that final "n" is always syllabic and may be pronounced by itself in Japanese. Thus, "n" can also have a rising or falling inflection, or be flat, as the case may be.

Accent differs markedly from region to region in Japan, particularly between the east and the west. The speech patterns of the Kanto region have generally been adopted as the standards for a "common" language, to be taught in the schools and used by television and radio announcers. Although the accents in this dictionary have followed the guidance of an expert in the field, we lay no claim to absolute accuracy. Our aim has been to guide the foreign student to a pronunciation that, if used, will be understandable in any part of the country, even when the listeners themselves follow a different standard of pronunciation.

English Irregular Verb Forms　不規則動詞表

arise	arose	arisen	持ち上る mochíagaru
arising			
awake	awoke	awaked	目が覚める me ga samérù
awaking			
be	was, were	been	である de árù
am, is, are			
being			
bear	bore	born(e)	支える sasáerù
beat	beat	beaten	殴る nagúrù
become	became	become	なる nárù
becoming			
begin	began	begun	始める hajímeru
beginning			
behold	beheld	beheld	見る mírù
bend	bent	bent	曲げる magéru
beseech	besought	besought	嘆願する tañgan suru
beset	beset	beset	襲う osóu
besetting			
bet	bet, betted	bet, betted	かける kakérù
betting			
bid	bid, bade	bid, bidden	競りに加わる serí ni kuwawarù
bidding			
bind	bound	bound	縛る shibárù
bite	bit	bitten	かむ kámù
biting			
bleed	bled	bled	出血する shukkétsu suru
blow	blew	blown	吹く fúkù
break	broke	broken	割る warú
breed	bred	bred	繁殖させる hañshoku saséru
bring	brought	brought	持って来る motté kurù
build	built	built	建てる tatérù
burn	burned, burnt	burned, burnt	燃やす moyásu
burst	burst	burst	破裂させる harétsu saséru
buy	bought	bought	買う kaú
can	could	(been able)	出来る dekírù

cast	cast	cast	投げる nagérù
catch	caught	caught	捕まえる tsukámaeru
choose choosing	chose	chosen	選ぶ erábù
cling	clung	clung	しがみつく shigámitsukù
come coming	came	come	来る kúrù
cost	cost	cost	の値段である no nedán de arù
creep	crept	crept	忍び足で歩く shinóbiàshi de arúkù
cut cutting	cut	cut	切る kirù
deal	dealt	dealt	配る kubárù
dig digging	dug	dug	掘る hórù
dive diving	dived *also US* dove	dived	飛込む tobíkomù
do does	did	done	する sùrú
draw	drew	drawn	描く kákù
dream	dreamed, dreamt	dreamed, dreamt	夢を見る yumē wo mirù
drink	drank	drunk	飲む nómù
drive driving	drove	driven	運転する uñten suru
dwell	dwelt	dwelt	住む súmù
eat	ate	eaten	食べる tabérù
fall	fell	fallen	落ちる ochírù
feed	fed	fed	食べさせる tabésaserù
feel	felt	felt	感じる kañjirù
fight	fought	fought	戦う tatákaù
find	found	found	見付ける mitsúkeru
flee	fled	fled	逃げる nigérù
fling	flung	flung	投げる nagérù
fly flies	flew	flown	飛ぶ tobú
forbid forbidding	forbade	forbidden	禁ずる kiñzurù

forecast	forecast	forecast	予報する yohṓ suru
forego forewent	forewent	foregone	なしで我慢する náshì de gámàn suru
foresee	foresaw	foreseen	予想する yosṓ suru
foretell	foretold	foretold	予言する yogén suru
forget forgetting	forgot	forgotten	忘れる wasúrerù
forgive forgiving	forgave	forgiven	許す yurúsù
forsake forsaking	forsook	forsaken	見捨てる misúterù
freeze freezing	froze	frozen	凍る kṓrù
get getting	got	got US gotten	手に入れる té ni irerù
give giving	gave	given	与える atáerù
go goes	went	gone	行く ikú
grind	ground	ground	ひく hikú
grow	grew	grown	成長する seíchō suru
hang	hung, hanged	hung, hanged	掛ける kakérù
have has ; having	had	had	持っている móttè iru
hear	heard	heard	聞く kikú
hide hiding	hid	hidden	隠す kakúsù
hit hitting	hit	hit	打つ utsú
hold	held	held	持つ mótsù
hurt	hurt	hurt	痛める itámerù
keep	kept	kept	保管する hokán suru
kneel	knelt, kneeled	knelt, kneeled	ひざまずく hizámazukù
know	knew	known	知っている shitté irù
lay	laid	laid	置く okú
lead	led	led	先導する seńdō suru
lean	leaned, leant	leaned, leant	傾く katámukù
leap	leaped, leapt	leaped, leapt	跳躍する chṓyaku suru

learn	learned, learnt	learned, learnt	学ぶ manábù
leave leaving	left	left	去る sárù
lend	lent	lent	貸す kásù
let letting	let	let	許す yurúsù
lie lying	lay	lain	横になる yokó ni narù
light	lighted, lit	lighted, lit	火を付ける hí wo tsukérù
lose losing	lost	lost	失う ushínaù
make making	made	made	作る tsukúrù
may	might	—	かも知れない ka mo shirenài
mean	meant	meant	意味する ímì suru
meet	met	met	会う áù
mistake mistaking	mistook	mistaken	間違える machígaerù
mow	mowed	mowed, mown	刈る karú
must	(had to)	(had to)	しなければならない shinákereba naranài
pay	paid	paid	払う haráù
put putting	put	put	置く okú
quit quitting	quit, quitted	quit, quitted	やめる yamérù
read	read	read	読む yómù
rid ridding	rid	rid	取除く torínozokù
ride riding	rode	ridden	乗る nórù
ring	rang	rung	鳴る narú
rise rising	rose	risen	上がる agárù
run running	ran	run	走る hashírù
saw	sawed	sawn	のこぎりで切る nokógirì de kírù
say	said	said	言う iú

see	saw	seen	見る mírù
seek	sought	sought	求める motómerù
sell	sold	sold	売る urú
send	sent	sent	送る okúrù
set	set	set	置く ókù
setting			
shake	shook	shaken	振る fúrù
shaking			
shall	should	—	しましょう shimashō
shear	sheared	sheared, shorn	毛を刈る kĕ wŏ karú
shed	shed	shed	落す otósù
shedding			
shine	shone	shone	照る térù
shining			
shoot	shot	shot	狙撃する sogéki suru
show	showed	shown	見せる misérù
shrink	shrank	shrunk	縮む chijímù
shut	shut	shut	閉める shimérù
shutting			
sing	sang	sung	歌う utáù
sink	sank	sunk	沈没する chiñbotsu suru
sit	sat	sat	座る suwárù
sitting			
slay	slew	slain	殺す korósù
sleep	slept	slept	眠る nemúrù
slide	slid	slid	滑る subérù
sliding			
sling	slung	slung	投げる nagérù
slit	slit	slit	切り開く kiríhirakù
slitting			
smell	smelled, smelt	smelled, smelt	匂う nióù
sneak	sneaked	sneaked	こっそり行く kossórì ikú
	also US snuck	*also US* snuck	
sow	sowed	sown, sowed	まく mákù
speak	spoke	spoken	話す hanásù
speed	sped, speeded	sped, speeded	スピードを出す supídò wo dásù
spell	spelled, spelt	spelled, spelt	つづりを言う tsuzúri wŏ iú
spend	spent	spent	過ごす sugósù

spill	spilled, spilt	spilled, spilt	こぼす kobósù
spin	spun	spun	紡ぐ tsumúgù
spinning			
spit	spat	spat	つばを吐く tsúbà wo hákù
spitting			
split	split	split	裂く sákù
splitting			
spoil	spoiled, spoilt	spoiled, spoilt	台無しにする daínashi ni surù
spread	spread	spread	広げる hirógerù
spring	sprang	sprung	跳ぶ tobú
stand	stood	stood	立つ tátsù
steal	stole	stolen	盗む nusúmù
stick	stuck	stuck	くっつく kuttsúkù
sting	stung	stung	刺す sásù
stink	stank	stunk	におう nióù
stride	strode	stridden	大またに歩く ṓmàta ni arúkù
striding			
strike	struck	struck, stricken	打つ útsù
striking			
strive	strove	striven	努力する dóryòku suru
striving			
swear	swore	sworn	誓う chikáù
sweep	swept	swept	掃く hákù
swell	swelled	swelled, swollen	はれる harérù
swim	swam	swum	泳ぐ oyógù
swimming			
swing	swung	swung	振る furú
take	took	taken	とる tórù
taking			
teach	taught	taught	教える oshíerù
tear	tore	torn	破る yabúrù
tell	told	told	述べる nobérù
think	thought	thought	考える kañgaerù
throw	threw	thrown	投げる nagérù
thrust	thrust	thrust	強く押す tsúyòku osú
tread	trod	trodden	歩く arúkù
wake	waked, woke	waked, woken	起す okósù
waking			

waylay	waylaid	waylaid	待伏せする machíbuse suru
wear	wore	worn	着る kirú
weave weaving	wove, weaved	woven, weaved	織る orù
wed wedding	wedded, wed	wedded, wed	結婚する kekkón suru
weep	wept	wept	泣く naku
win winning	won	won	勝つ katsù
wind	wound	wound	巻く makú
withdraw	withdrew	withdrawn	取出す torídasu
withhold	withheld	withheld	拒む kobámù
withstand	withstood	withstood	耐える taérù
wring	wrung	wrung	絞る shibórù
write writing	wrote	written	書く kakù

A

A [ei] *n* (MUS: note) イ音 í-òn; (: key) イ調 íchō

KEYWORD

a [ei, ə] (*before vowel or silent h:* **an**) *indef art* **1** 1つの hitótsu no, ある árú ◊ 通常日本語では表現しない tsūjō nihongo de wa hyōgen shínài

a book/girl/mirror 本〔少女, 鏡〕hòn〔shōjo, kagámi〕

an apple りんご ríngo

she's a doctor 彼女は医者です kánojo wa ishá desu

2 (*instead of the number* "one") 1つの hitótsù no

a loaf and 2 pints of milk, please パン1本とミルク2パイント下さい pan íppònto mírùku nipáìnto kudasái

a year ago 1年前 ichinen máè

a hundred/thousand etc pounds 100〔1000〕ポンド hyakù〔sen〕póndò

3 (*in expressing ratios, prices etc*) 1つ当り ... hitotsu átàri ...

3 a day/week 1日〔1週間〕当り3つ ichi-nichi〔isshūkan〕átàri mittsú

10 km an hour 時速10キロメーター jísòku jukkirométà

£5 a person 1人当たり5ポンド hitori átàri gopóndò

30p a kilo 1キロ30ペンス ichíkìro san-juppénsù

AA [eiei] *n abbr* (= *Alcoholics Anonymous*) アルコール依存症自主治療協会 a-rúkōru izónshō jishúchiryō kyōkai; (*BRIT: = Automobile Association*) 英国自動車連盟 eíkoku jidōsha reńmei

AAA [trip'əlei] *n abbr* (= *American Automobile Association*) 米国自動車連盟 beíkoku jidōsha reńmei

aback [əbæk'] *adv*: *to be taken aback* 仰天する gyōten suru

abandon [əbæn'dən] *vt* (person) 見捨てる misúterù; (car) 乗捨てる norísuterù;

(give up: search, idea, research) やめる yaméru

◊*n* (wild behavior): *with abandon* 羽目を外して hamé wò hazúshite

abashed [əbæʃt'] *adj* (person) 恥ずかしがっている hazúkashigattè irú

abate [əbeit'] *vi* (lessen: storm, terror, anger) 治まる osámarù

abattoir [æbətwɑːr'] (*BRIT*) n と殺場 tosátsujō

abbey [æb'iː] *n* 修道院 shúdòin

abbot [æb'ət] *n* 修道院長 shúdòinchō

abbreviate [əbriːviːeit'] *vt* (essay, word) 短縮する tańshuku suru

abbreviation [əbriːviːei'ʃən] *n* (short form) 短縮形 tańshukukei

abdicate [æb'dikeit] *vt* (responsibility, right) 放棄する hōki suru

◊*vi* (monarch) 退位する tái-i suru

abdication [æbdikei'ʃən] *n* (of responsibility, right) 放棄 hōki; (by monarch) 退位 tái-i

abdomen [æb'dəmən] *n* 腹部 fukúbù

abduct [æbdʌkt'] *vt* ら致する ráchì suru

aberration [æbərei'ʃən] *n* (unusual behavior, event etc) 異状 ijō

abet [əbet'] *vt see* **aid**

abeyance [əbei'əns] *n*: *in abeyance* (law) 無視されて múshì sarete; (matter) 保留されて horyú sarete

abhor [æbhɔːr'] *vt* (cruelty, violence etc) ひどく嫌う hídòku kiráu

abide [əbaid'] *vt*: *I can't abide it/him* 私はそれ〔彼〕が大嫌いだ watákushi wà soré〔karè〕gà dáîkirai da

abide by *vt fus* (law, decision) ...に従う ...ni shitágaù

ability [əbil'iti:] *n* (capacity) 能力 nōryoku; (talent, skill) 才能 saínō

abject [æb'dʒekt] *adj* (poverty) 極度の kyókùdo no; (apology) 卑屈な hikútsu na

ablaze [əbleiz'] *adj* (building etc) 炎上している eńjō shite iru

able [ei'bəl] *adj* (capable) 出来る dekírù;

(skilled) 有能な yúnō na
to be able to do something ...をする事が出来る ...wo suru koto gà dékirù

able-bodied [ei'bəlbɑːd'iːd] *adj* (person) がん健な ganken na

ably [ei'bliː] *adv* (skilfully, well) 上手にjōzu ni

abnormal [æbnɔːr'məl] *adj* (behavior, child, situation) 異常な ijō na

aboard [əbɔːrd'] *adv* (NAUT, AVIAT) ...に乗って ...ni nottě
◆*prep* (NAUT, AVIAT) ...に乗って ...ni nottě

abode [əboud'] *n* (LAW): *of no fixed abode* 住所不定の jūshofutěi no

abolish [əbɑːl'iʃ] *vt* 廃止する haíshi suru

abolition [æbəliʃ'ən] *n* 廃止 haíshi

abominable [əbɑːm'inəbəl] *adj* (conditions) ひどい hídoî; (behavior) 忌わしい imáwashiî

aborigine [æbəridʒ'əniː] *n* 原住民 genjūmîn

abort [əbɔːrt'] *vt* (MED: fetus) 流産するryūzan suru; (plan, activity) 中止する chūshi suru

abortion [əbɔːr'ʃən] *n* (MED) 妊娠中絶 nínshinchūzetsu
to have an abortion 妊娠を中絶する nínshin wò chūzetsu suru

abortive [əbɔːr'tiv] *adj* (attempt, action) 不成功の fuseíkō no

abound [əbaund'] *vi* (exist in large numbers) ...が多い ...ga ôî
to abound in/with (possess in large numbers) ...に富む ...ni tómù

| KEYWORD |

about [əbaut'] *adv* 1 (approximately) 約yákù, 大よそ ōyoso, ...ぐらい ...gúrai
about a hundred/thousand etc dollars 約100(1000)ドル yákù hyakú(sen) dòru
it takes about 10 hours 10時間ぐらいかかります jūjikan gúrài kakarimásù
at about 2 o'clock 2時頃 niji górð
I've just about finished ほぼ終ったところです hóbò owatta tokoro desù
2 (referring to place) あちこちに achíko-

chî ni
to leave things lying about 物をあちこちに散らかしたままにする monó wo achíkochî ni chirakashita mamá ni sùrú
to run/walk etc about あちこち走り回る(歩き回る) achíkochî hashirimawárù(arukimawárù)
3: *to be about to do something* ...するところである ...suru tokoro dè árù
he was about to cry/leave/wash the dishes/go to bed 彼は泣き出す(帰る、皿を洗う、寝る)ところだった kárè wa nakidasu(kaeru, sara wo arau, neru) tokoro dattá
◆*prep* 1 (relating to) ...について ...ni tsúîte, ...に関して ...ni kànshite
a book about London ロンドンについての本 róndòn ni tsúîte no hon
what is it about? それは何についてですか sore wa nán ni tsúîte desu ká
we talked about it 私たちはそれについて話し合った watakushitachî a sore ni tsúîte hanashiáttá
what/how about having some coffee? コーヒーでも飲みましょうか kōhî de mò nomimashô kà
2 (referring to place) ...のあちこちに ...no achíkochî ni
to walk about the town 町をあちこち歩き回る machí wo achíkochî arukimawárù
her clothes were scattered about the room 部屋のあちこちに彼女の服が散らかっていた heya no achíkochî ni kánojò no fukú gà chirakatte itá

---

about-face [əbaut'feis] *n* (MIL) 回れ右mawáremigî; (fig): *to do an about-face* 一変する ippén suru

about-turn [əbaut'təːrn] *n* = **about-face**

above [əbʌv'] *adv* (higher up, overhead) 上の方に uě no hồ ni; (greater, more) 以上に ijô ni
◆*prep* (higher than) ...より上に ...yórî uě ni; (greater than, more than: in number, amount etc) ...以上 ...íjò; (: in rank etc) 上である uě de arù

mentioned above 上記の jồki no
above all まず第一に mázù daí-ichi ni

aboveboard [əbʌv'bourd] *adj* 公明正大 な kômeiseidai na

abrasive [əbrei'siv] *adj* (substance) 研磨 の kénma no; (person, manner) とげとげ しい togétogeshiî

abreast [əbrest'] *adv* (people, vehicles) 横に並んで yokó ni narande
to keep abreast of (*fig*: news etc) ...に ついていく ...ni tsúite ikú

abridge [əbridʒ'] *vt* (novel, play) 短縮す る tañshuku suru

abroad [əbrɔːd'] *adv* 海外に kâîgai ni

abrupt [əbrʌpt'] *adj* (sudden: action, end-ing etc) 突然の totsúzen no; (curt: per-son, behavior) ぶっきらぼうな bukkíraba-bò na

abruptly [əbrʌpt'li:] *adv* (leave, end) 突 然 totsúzen; (speak) ぶっきらぼうに buk-kírabồ ni

abscess [æb'ses] *n* のうよう nôyō

abscond [æbska:nd'] *vi* (thief): *to abscond with* ...を持ち逃げする ...wo mochínige suru; (prisoner): *to abscond (from)* (...から) 逃亡する (...kara) tôbō suru

absence [æb'səns] *n* (of person: from home etc) 不在 fuzái; (: from school, meeting etc) 欠席 kesséki; (: from work) 欠勤 kekkín; (of thing) 無い事 nâî kotó

absent [æb'sənt] *adj* (person: from home etc) 不在の fuzái no; (: from school, meeting etc) 欠席の kesséki no; (: from work) 欠勤の kekkín no; (thing) 無い nâî

absentee [æbsənti:'] *n* (from school, meeting etc) 欠席者 kessékishà; (from work) 欠勤者 kekkíñsha

absent-minded [æb'səntmain'did] *adj* 忘れっぽい wasúreppoî

absolute [æb'səluːt] *adj* (complete) 全く の mattáku no; (monarch, rule, power) 専制的な señseiteki na; (principle, rule etc) 絶対的な zettáiteki na

absolutely [æbsəlu:t'li:] *adv* (totally) 全 く mattáku; (certainly) その通り sonó tồri

absolution [æbsəlu:'ʃən] *n* (REL) 罪の許

し tsúmî no yurúshî

absolve [æbza:lv'] *vt*: *to absolve some-one (from blame, responsibility, sin)* ...の (...を) 許す ...no (...wò) yurúsù

absorb [æbsɔːrb'] *vt* 吸収する kyúshū su-ru; (assimilate: group, business) 併合す る heígô suru
to be absorbed in a book 本に夢中にな っている hôñ ni muchû ni nattê irú

absorbent cotton [æbsɔːr'bənt-] (*US*) *n* 脱脂綿 dasshímèn

absorbing [æbsɔːr'biŋ] *adj* 夢中にさせる muchû ni saserù

absorption [æbsɔːrp'ʃən] *n* 吸収 kyúshū; (assimilation: of group, business etc) 併 合 heígô; (interest) 夢中になる事 muchû ni narú kotó

abstain [æbstein'] *vi*: *to abstain (from)* (eating, drinking) 控える hikáe-rù; (voting) 棄権する kikén suru

abstemious [æbsti:'mi:əs] *adj* (person) 節制する sesséi suru

abstention [æbsten'ʃən] *n* (refusal to vote) 棄権 kikén

abstinence [æb'stənəns] *n* 禁欲 kiñ-yo-ku

abstract [æb'strækt] *adj* (idea, quality) 抽象的な chúshōteki na; (ART) 抽象派の chúshōha no; (LING): *abstract noun* 抽 象名詞 chúshōmeishi

abstruse [æbstru:s'] *adj* 分かりにくい wakárinikuî

absurd [æbsəːrd'] *adj* ばかげた bakágetà

abundance [əbʌn'dəns] *n* 豊富さ hôfusa

abundant [əbʌn'dənt] *adj* 豊富な hồfu na

abuse [*n* əbjuːs' *vb* əbjuːz'] *n* (insults) の のしり nonóshiri; (ill-treatment) 虐待 gyakútai; (misuse: of power, drugs etc) 乱用 rañ-yo
♦*vt* (insult) ののしる nonóshirù; (ill-treat) 虐待する gyakútai suru; (misuse) 乱用する rañ-yō suru

abusive [əbjuː'siv] *adj* (person) 口の悪い kuchí no waruî; (language) 侮辱的な bu-jókuteki na

abysmal [əbiz'məl] *adj* (performance, failure) 最低の saítei no; (ignorance etc)

ひどい hidói

abyss [əbìs'] *n* 深えん shíń-en

AC [ei'si:] *abbr* = **alternating current**

academic [ækədəm'ik] *adj* (person) インテリの ińteri no; (year, system, books, freedom etc) 教育関係の kyóikukańkei no; (*pej*: issue) 理論的な rirónteki na
♦*n* 学者 gakúsha

academy [əkæd'əmi:] *n* (learned body) アカデミー akádèmī; (school) 学院 gakúin
academy of music 音楽学院 oñgaku gakùin

accelerate [æksel'əreit] *vt* (process) 早める hayámerù
♦*vi* (AUT) 加速する kasóku suru

acceleration [ækselərei'ʃən] *n* (AUT) 加速 kasóku

accelerator [æksel'əreitə:r] *n* アクセル ákùseru

accent [æk'sent] *n* (pronunciation) なまり namári; (written mark) アクセント符号 akúsento fugò; (*fig*: emphasis, stress) 強調 kyóchō, アクセント akùsento

accept [æksept'] *vt* (gift, invitation) 受取る ukétoru; (fact, situation, risk) 認める mitómeru; (responsibility, blame) 負う oú

acceptable [æksep'təbəl] *adj* (offer, gift) 受入れられる uké-irerarerù; (risk etc) 許容できる kyoyố dekirù

acceptance [æksep'təns] *n* (of gift, offer etc) 受取る事 ukétoru koto; (of risk etc) 許容 kyoyố; (of responsibility etc) 負う事 oú koto

access [æk'ses] *n* (to building, room) 入る事 háîru kotð; (to information, papers) 利用する権利 riyố suru keñri
to have access to (child etc) ...への面会権がある ...e no meñkaikeñ ga árù

accessible [ækses'əbəl] *adj* (place) 行きやすい ikíyasuì; (person) 面会しやすい meñkai shiyasuì; (available: knowledge, art etc) 利用しやすい riyố shiyasuì

accessory [ækses'ə:ri:] *n* (dress, COMM, TECH, AUT) アクセサリー ákùsesarī; (LAW): *accessory to* ...の共犯者 ...no kyóhañsha

accident [æk'sidənt] *n* (chance event) 偶然 gūzen; (mishap, disaster) 事故 jíkð
by accident (unintentionally) うっかり ukkárì; (by chance) 偶然に gúzen ni

accidental [æksiden'təl] *adj* (death) 事故による jíkð ni yorú; (damage) 偶発的な gúhatsuteki na

accidentally [æksiden'təli:] *adv* (by accident) 偶然に gúzen ni

accident-prone [æk'sidəntproun] *adj* 事故に会いがちな jíkð ni aigachi na

acclaim [əkleim'] *n* 賞賛 shôsan
♦*vt*: *to be acclaimed for one's achievements* 功績で有名である kóseki dè yúmei de arù

acclimate [əklai'mit] (*US*) *vt* = **acclimatize**

acclimatize [əklai'mətaiz] *vt*: *to become acclimatized (to)* (...に) 慣れる (...ni) narérù

accolade [æk'əleid'] *n* (*fig*) 賞賛 shôsan

accommodate [əkɑm'ədeit] *vt* (subj: person) 泊める toméru; (: car, hotel etc) 収容できる shûyō dekirù; (oblige, help) ...に親切にして上げる ...ni shíñsetsu ni shite agérù

accommodating [əkɑm'ədeitiŋ] *adj* 親切な shíñsetsu na

accommodation [əkɑmədei'ʃən] *n* 宿泊設備 shukúhakusetsùbi

accommodations [əkɑmədei'ʃənz] (*US*) *npl* 宿泊設備 shukúhakusetsùbi

accompaniment [əkʌm'pənimənt] *n* 伴奏 bañsō

accompany [əkʌm'pəni:] *vt* (escort, go along with) ...に付きそう ...ni tsukísoù; (MUS) ...の伴奏をする ...no bañsō wð suru

accomplice [əkɑm'plis] *n* 共犯者 kyóhañsha

accomplish [əkɑm'pliʃ] *vt* (finish: task) 成遂げる nashítogerù; (achieve: goal) 達成する tasséi suru

accomplished [əkɑm'pliʃt] *adj* (person) 熟練の jukúren no; (performance) 優れた sugúretà

accomplishment [əkɑm'pliʃmənt] *n* (completion, bringing about) 遂行 suíkõ;

(skill: *gen pl*) 才能 saínō

accord [əkɔːrdʲ] *n* (treaty) 協定 kyōtei
♦*vt* 与える atáeru
of his own accord 自発的に jihátsuteki ni

accordance [əkɔːrʲdəns] *n*: *in accordance with* (someone's wishes, the law etc) ...に従って ...ni shitágatte

according [əkɔːrʲdɪŋ]: *according to prep* (person, account) ...によると ...ni yórù to

accordingly [əkɔːrʲdɪŋli] *adv* (appropriately) それに応じて soré nì ōjite; (as a result) それで soré de

accordion [əkɔːrʲdiːən] *n* アコーデオン ákōdeon

accost [əkɔːstʲ] *vt* ...に近寄って話し掛ける ...ni chikáyotte hanáshikakerù

account [əkaunʲtʲ] *n* (COMM: bill) 勘定書 kañjōgaki; (: monthly account) 計算書 keísansho; (in bank) 口座 kōza; (report) 報告 hōkoku
of no account 構わない kamáwanài
on account つけで tsuké de
on no account 何があっても... (すべき) でない naní ga atte mo ...(subeki) de naì
on account of ...のために ...no tamé ni
to take into account, take account of ...を考慮に入れる ...wò kōryò ni iréru

accountable [əkaunʲtəbəl] *adj*: *accountable (to)* (...に) 申開きする義務がある (...ni) mōshihiraki suru gimù ga árù

accountancy [əkaunʲtənsiː] *n* 会計士の職 kaíkeìshi no shokú

accountant [əkaunʲtənt] *n* 会計士 kaíkeìshi

account for *vt fus* (explain) 説明する setsúmei suru; (represent) ... (の割合) を占める ...(no warsai) wò shimérù

account number *n* (at bank etc) 口座番号 kōzabañgō

accounts [əkauntsʲ] *npl* (COMM) 勘定 kañjō

accredited [əkredʲitid] *adj* (agent etc) 資格のある shikáku no arù

accrued interest [əkruːdʲ-] *n* 累積利息

ruísekirisòku

accumulate [əkjuːmʲjəleit] *vt* 貯める taméru
♦*vi* 貯まる tamáru

accuracy [ækʲjərəsiː] *n* 正確さ seíkakusa

accurate [ækʲjərit] *adj* 正確な seíkaku na

accurately [ækʲjəritliː] *adv* (count, shoot, answer) 正確に seíkaku ni

accusation [ækjuːzeiʲʃən] *n* 非難 hínàn

accuse [əkjuːzʲ] *vt*: *to accuse someone (of something)* (crime, incompetence) (...だと) ...を責める (...dá tò) ...wo semérù

accused [əkjuːzdʲ] *n* (LAW): *the accused* 容疑者 yōgishà

accustom [əkʌsʲtəm] *vt* 慣れさせる narésaserù

accustomed [əkʌsʲtəmd] *adj* (usual): *accustomed to* ...に慣れている ...ni narétè irú

ace [eis] *n* (CARDS, TENNIS) エース ḕsu

ache [eik] *n* 痛み itámi
♦*vi* (be painful) 痛む itámù, ...が痛い ...ga itáì
my head aches 頭が痛い atáma gà itáì

achieve [ətʃiːvʲ] *vt* (aim) 成遂げる nashítogerù; (result) 上げる agéru; (victory, success) 獲得する kakútoku suru

achievement [ətʃiːvʲmənt] *n* (completion) 完成 kañsei; (success, feat) 業績 gyōseki

acid [æsʲid] *adj* (CHEM: soil etc) 酸性の sañsei no; (taste) 酸っぱい suppáì
♦*n* (CHEM) 酸 sáñ; (*inf*: LSD) LSD erúesudì

acid rain *n* 酸性雨 sañseiù

acknowledge [æknɑːlʲidʒ] *vt* (letter, parcel: *also*: **acknowledge receipt of**) 受け取った事を知らせる ukétotta koto wò shiráserù; (fact, situation, person) 認める mitómeru

acknowledgement [æknɑːlʲidʒmənt] *n* (of letter, parcel) 受領通知 juryótsūchi

acne [ækʲniː] *n* にきび níkìbi

acorn [eiʲkɔːrn] *n* ドングリ dóñguri

acoustic [əku:s'tik] *adj* (related to hearing) 聴覚の chōkaku no; (guitar etc) アコースティックの akōsùtikku no

acoustics [əku:s'tiks] *n* (science) 音響学 oñkyōgaku

♦*npl* (of hall, room) 音響効果 oñkyōkōka

acquaint [əkweint'] *vt*: **to acquaint someone with something** (inform) ...に...を知らせる ...ni ...wð shiráseru

to be acquainted with (person) ...と面識がある ...to meñshiki ga arù

acquaintance [əkwein'təns] *n* (person) 知合い shirfai; (with person, subject) 知識 chíshiki

acquiesce [əkwi:es'] *vi*: **to acquiesce (to)** (...) を承諾する (...wð) shōdaku suru

acquire [əkwai'ər] *vt* (obtain, buy) 手に入れる te ni iréru; (learn, develop: interest, skill) 取得する shutóku suru

acquisition [ækwizi∫'ən] *n* (obtaining etc) 入手 nyūshu; (development etc) 獲得 kakútoku; (thing acquired) 取得物 shutókubùtsu

acquit [əkwit'] *vt* (free) 無罪とする múzài to suru

to acquit oneself well 見事な働きをする mígðto na határaki wo suru

acquittal [əkwit'əl] *n* 無罪判決 muzái hañketsu

acre [ei'kər] *n* エーカー ềkā

acrid [æk'rid] *adj* (smell, taste, smoke) 刺激的な shigékiteki na

acrimonious [ækrəmou'ni:əs] *adj* (remark, argument) 辛らつな shifratsu na

acrobat [æk'rəbæt] *n* アクロバット akúrobattð

acrobatic [ækrəbæt'ik] *adj* (person, movement, display) アクロバット的な akúrobattoteki na

acronym [æk'rənim] *n* 頭字語 tōjigo

across [əkrɔːs'] *prep* (from one side to the other of) ...を渡って ...wo watátte; (on the other side of) ...の向こう側に ...no mukôgawa ni; (crosswise over) ...と交差して ...to kōsa shite

♦*adv* (direction) 向こう側へ mukôgawa e; (measurement) 直径が...で chokkéi ga ... de

to run/swim across 走って〔泳いで〕渡る hashítte〔oyóide〕wataru

across from ...の向かいに ...no mukái ni

acrylic [əkril'ik] *adj* アクリルの ákùriru no

♦*n* アクリル ákùriru

act [ækt] *n* (action) 行為 kói; (of play) 幕 makú; (in a show etc) 出し物 dashímðno; (LAW) 法 hố

♦*vi* (do something, take action) 行動する kōdō suru; (behave) 振舞う furúmaù; (have effect: drug, chemical) 作用する sáyò suru; (THEATER) 出演する shutsúen suru; (pretend) ...の振りをする ...no furí wð suru

♦*vt* (part) ...に扮する ...ni fuñ surù

in the act of ...しているさなかに ...shitè iru sanàka ni

to act as ...として勤める ...toshite tsutómerù

acting [æk'tiŋ] *adj* (manager, director etc) 代理の dafri no

♦*n* (activity) 演技 éñgi; (profession) 演劇 eñgeki

action [æk'∫ən] *n* (deed) 行為 kói; (motion) 動き ugóki; (MIL) 戦闘 señtō; (LAW) 訴訟 soshố

out of action (person) 活動不能で katsúdōfunð de; (thing) 作動不能で sadófunð de

to take action 行動を起す kōdō wð okósù

action replay *n* (TV) 即時ビデオ再生 sokúji bideo saìsei

activate [æk'təveit] *vt* (mechanism) 作動させる sadósaserù

active [æk'tiv] *adj* (person, life) 活動的な katsúdōteki na

active volcano 活火山 kakkázàn

actively [æk'tivli] *adv* (participate) 積極的に sekkyókuteki ni; (discourage) 強く tsúyòku; (dislike) 非常に hijố ni

activist [æk'tivist] *n* 活動家 katsúdōka

activity [æktiv'əti:] *n* (being active) 活動 katsúdō; (action) 動き ugóki; (pastime, pursuit) 娯楽 goráku

actor [æk'tər] *n* 俳優 haíyū

actress [æk'tris] *n* 女優 joyū

actual [æk'tʃuəl] *adj* 実際の jissai no

actually [æk'tʃuəli:] *adv* (really) 本当に hofítō ni; (in fact) 実は jitsú wa

acumen [əkju:'mən] *n* 判断力 hafídanryoku

acupuncture [æk'jupʌŋktʃər] *n* 針 hárì

acute [əkju:t'] *adj* (illness) 急性の kyūsei no; (anxiety, pain) 激しい hagéshiì; (mind, person) 抜け目の無い nukéme no nai; (MATH): *acute angle* 鋭角 eíkaku; (LING): *acute accent* 鋭アクセント eíakùsento

ad [æd] *n abbr* = **advertisement**

A.D. [eidi:'] *adv abbr* (= *Anno Domini*) 西暦...年 seíreki ...neñ

adamant [ædə'mənt] *adj* (person) 譲らない yuzúranai

Adam's apple [æd'əms-] *n* のど仏 nodóbotòke

adapt [ədæpt'] *vt* (alter, change) 適応させる tekíō saserù
♦*vi*: *to adapt (to)* (に) 適応する (...ni) tekíō suru

adaptable [ədæp'təbəl] *adj* (device, person) 適応性のある tekíōsei no arù

adapter [ədæp'tər] *n* (ELEC) アダプター adápùtā

adaptor [ədæp'tər] *n* = **adapter**

add [æd] *vt* (to a collection etc) 加える kuwáeru; (comment etc) 付加える tsukékuwaerù; (figures: *also*: **add up**) 合計する gókei suru
♦*vi*: *to add to* (increase) ...を増す ...wo masú

adder [æd'ər] *n* ヨーロッパクサリヘビ yōroppà kusárihebì

addict [æd'ikt] *n* (to drugs etc) 中毒者 chūdokushà; (enthusiast) マニア mánìa

addicted [ədik'tid] *adj*: *to be addicted to* (drink etc) ...中毒にかかっている ...chūdoku ni kakáttè irú; (*fig*: football etc) ...マニアである ...mánìa de arù

addiction [ədik'ʃən] *n* (to drugs etc) 中毒 chūdoku

addictive [ədik'tiv] *adj* (drug) 習慣性のある shūkansei no arù; (activity) 癖になる kusé ni narù

addition [ədiʃ'ən] *n* (adding up) 足し算 tashízàn; (thing added) 加えられた物 kuwáeraretà monó
in addition なお nàò
in addition to ...の外に ...no hoká ni

additional [ədiʃ'ənəl] *adj* 追加の tsuíka no

additive [æd'ətiv] *n* 添加物 teñkabùtsu

address [ədres'] *n* (postal address) 住所 jūsho; (speech) 演説 efízetsu
♦*vt* (letter, parcel) ...に宛名を書く ...ni aténa wò kákù; (speak to: person) ...に話し掛ける ...ni hanáshikakerù; (: audience) ...に演説する ...ni efízetsu suru; (problem): *to address (oneself to) a problem* 問題に取組む mofídai ni torikumù

adept [ədept'] *adj*: *adept at* ...が上手な ...ga jōzu na

adequate [æd'əkwit] *adj* (enough: amount) 十分な jūbuñ na; (satisfactory: performance, response) 満足な máñzoku na

adhere [ædhi:r'] *vi*: *to adhere to* (stick to) ...にくっつく ...ni kuttsúkù; (*fig*: abide by: rule, decision, treaty etc) ...を守る ...wo mamórù; (: hold to: opinion, belief etc) ...を固守する ...wo kóshù suru

adhesive [ædhi:'siv] *n* 粘着材 neñchakuzài

adhesive tape *n* (*US*: MED) ばん創こう bañsókō; (*BRIT*) 粘着テープ neñchaku tèpu

ad hoc [æd hɑ:k'] *adj* (decision, committee) 特別な tokúbetsu na

adjacent [ədʒei'sənt] *adj*: *adjacent to* ...の隣の ...no tonári no

adjective [ædʒ'iktiv] *n* 形容詞 keíyòshi

adjoining [ədʒɔi'niŋ] *adj* (room etc) 隣の tonári no

adjourn [ədʒə:rn'] *vt* (trial) 休廷にする kyūtei ni suru; (meeting, discussion) 休会にする kyūkai ni suru
♦*vi* (trial) 休廷する kyūtei suru; (meeting) 休止する kyūshi suru

adjudicate [ədʒu:'dikeit] *vt* (contest) ...の審査員を勤める ...no shiñsa-ìn wo tsutómerù

adjust [ədʒʌst'] *vt* (change: approach etc) 調整する chōsei suru; (rearrange: clothing, machine etc) 調節する chōsetsu suru

♦*vi: to adjust (to)* 適応する tekíō suru

adjustable [ədʒʌst'əbəl] *adj* 調節できる chōsetsu dekírù

adjustment [ədʒʌst'mənt] *n* (PSYCH) 適応 tekíō; (to machine) 調節 chōsetsu; (of prices, wages) 調整 chōsei

ad-lib [ædlib'] *vi* アドリブで話す adóribu dè hanásù

ad lib [ædlib'] *adv* (speak) アドリブで a-dóribu de

administer [ædmin'istəːr] *vt* (country) 統治する tōchi suru; (department) 管理する kánri suru; (MED: drug) 投与する tōyo suru

to administer justice 裁く sabákù

administration [ædministrei'ʃən] *n* (management) 管理 kánri; (government) 政権 seíken

administrative [ædmin'istreitiv] *adj* (work, error etc) 管理的な kánriteki na

administrator [ædmin'istreitəːr] *n* 管理者 kánrisha

admiral [æd'məːrəl] *n* 海軍大将 kaígun taíshō

Admiralty [æd'məːrəltiː] (*BRIT*) *n: the Admiralty* (*also: Admiralty Board*) 海軍省 kaígunshō

admiration [ædmərei'ʃən] *n* 感心 kanshin

admire [ædmai'əːr] *vt* (respect) ...に感心する ...ni kanshin suru; (appreciate) 観賞する kanshō suru

admirer [ædmai'əːrəːr] *n* (suitor) 男友達 otókotomodachi; (fan) ファン fán

admission [ædmiʃ'ən] *n* (admittance) 入場 nyūjō; (entry fee) 入場料 nyūjōryō; (confession) 自白 jiháku

admit [ædmit'] *vt* (confess) 自白する jiháku suru; (permit to enter) 入場させる nyūjō saserù; (to club, organization) 入会させる nyūkai saserù; (to hospital) 入院させる nyūin saserù; (accept: defeat, responsibility etc) 認める mitómeru

admittance [ædmit'əns] *n* 入場 nyūjō

admittedly [ædmit'idliː] *adv* 確かに ...であるけど táshìka ni ... de árù ga

admit to *vt fus* (murder etc) ...を自白する ...wo jiháku suru

admonish [ædmɑːn'iʃ] *vt* (rebuke) たしなめる tashínamerù; (LAW) 忠告する chúkoku suru

ad nauseam [æd nɔː'ziːəm] *adv* (repeat, talk) いやという程 iyá to iú hodó

ado [əduː'] *n: without (any) more ado* さっさと sássà to

adolescence [ædəles'əns] *n* 10代 jūdai

adolescent [ædəles'ənt] *adj* 10代の jūdai no

♦*n* ティーンエージャー tínèjā

adopt [ədɑːpt'] *vt* (child) 養子にする yō-shi ni suru; (policy, attitude) とる torù; (accent) まねる manéru

adopted [ədɑːp'tid] *adj* (child) 養子の yō-shi no

adoption [ədɑːp'ʃən] *n* (of child) 養子縁組 yōshiengumi; (of policy etc) 採択 saítaku

adoptive [ədɑːp'tiv] *adj: adoptive father/mother* 養父(母) yōfu(bo)

adoptive country 第2の祖国 dái ni no sókoku

adore [ədɔːr'] *vt* (person) 崇拝する súhai suru

adorn [ədɔːrn'] *vt* (decorate) 飾る kazáru

adrenalin [ædren'əlin] *n* アドレナリン a-dórenarīn

Adriatic [eidriːæt'ik] *n: the Adriatic (Sea)* アドリア海 adóriakài

adrift [ədrift'] *adv* (NAUT: loose) 漂流して hyōryū shite

adult [ədʌlt'] *n* (person) 大人 otóna; (animal, insect) 成体 seítai

♦*adj* (grown-up: person) 大人の otóna no; (: animal etc) 成体の seítai no; (for adults: literature, education) 成人向きの seíjinmuki no

adultery [ədʌl'təːriː] *n* かん通 kantsū

advance [ædvæns'] *n* (movement, progress) 進歩 shínpo; (money) 前借り maégari

♦*adj* (booking, notice, warning) 事前の jizén no

♦vt (money) 前貸する maégashi suru

♦vi (move forward) 前進する zeńshin suru; (make progress) 進歩する shińpo suru

to make **advances** (to someone) (gen) (...に) 言い寄る (...ni) iíyorù

in **advance** (book, prepare etc) 前もって maémottè

advanced [ædvǽnst'] adj (SCOL: studies) 高等の kốtō no; (country) 先進の seńshin no; (child) ませた másèta

advancement [ædvǽns'mənt] n (improvement) 進歩 shíñpo; (in job, rank) 昇進 shōshin

advantage [ædvǽn'tidʒ] n (supremacy) 有利な立場 yūri na táchìba; (benefit) 利点 ritén; (TENNIS) アドバンテージ adóbañtēji

to take **advantage** of (person) ...に付込む ...ni tsukékomù; (opportunity) 利用する riyố suru

advantageous [ædvəntei'dʒəs] adj: advantageous (to) (...に) 有利な (...ni) yūri na

advent [æd'vent] n (appearance: of innovation) 出現 shutsúgen; (REL): Advent 待降節 taíkōsetsù

adventure [ædven'tʃəːr] n 冒険 bốken

adventurous [ædven'tʃəːrəs] adj (bold, outgoing) 大胆な daítàn na

adverb [æd'vəːrb] n 副詞 fukúshi

adversary [æd'vəːrse:ri:] n (opponent, also MIL) 敵 tekí

adverse [ædvəːrs'] adj (effect, weather, publicity etc) 悪い warúî

adversity [ædvəːr'siti:] n 逆境 gyakkyō

advert [æd'vəːrt] (BRIT) n abbr = advertisement

advertise [æd'vəːrtaiz] vi (COMM: in newspaper, on television etc) 広告する kốkoku suru

♦vt (product, event, job) ...を広告する ...wo kốkoku suru

to **advertise** for (staff, accommodation etc) ...を求める広告を出す ...wo motómerù kốkoku wo dasu

advertisement [ædvəːrtaiz'mənt] n 広告 kốkoku

advertiser [æd'vəːrtaizəːr] n (in newspaper, on television etc) 広告主 kốkokunùshi

advertising [æd'vəːrtaiziŋ] n (advertisements) 広告 kốkoku; (industry) 広告業界 kốkokugyōkai

advice [ædvais'] n (counsel) 忠告 chúkoku; (notification) 知らせ shiráse

a piece of **advice** 一つの忠告 hítòtsu no chúkoku

to take legal **advice** 弁護士に相談する beñgoshi ni sốdan suru

advisable [ædvai'zəbəl] adj 望ましい nozómashiî

advise [ædvaiz'] vt (give advice to: person, company etc) ...に忠告する ...ni chúkoku suru; (inform): to advise someone of something ...に...を知らせる ...wo shiráserù

to **advise** against something/doing something ... (するの) を避けた方がいいと忠告する ... (surú no) wo sakéta hō gà íi to chúkoku suru

advisedly [ædvai'zidli:] adv (deliberately) 意図的に itóteki ni

adviser [ædvai'zəːr] n (counsellor, consultant: to private person) 相談相手 sốdan aitè; (: to company etc) 顧問 kốmòn

advisor [ædvai'zəːr] n = adviser

advisory [ædvai'zəːri:] adj (role, capacity, body) 顧問の kốmòn no

advocate [æd'vəkit] vt (support, recommend) 主張する shuchố suru

♦n (LAW: barrister) 弁護士 beñgoshì; (supporter): advocate of ...の主張者 ...no shuchốsha

Aegean [idʒi:'ən] n: the Aegean (Sea) エーゲ海 ḗgekài

aerial [e:r'i:əl] n アンテナ añtena

♦adj (attack, photograph) 航空の kốkū no

aerobics [e:rou'biks] n エアロビクス eárobikùsu

aerodynamic [e:roudainæm'ik] adj 空力的な kūlrikiteki na

aeroplane [e:r'əplein] (BRIT) n 飛行機 híkōki

aerosol [e:r'əso:l] n スプレー缶 supúrēkan

aerospace industry [εːrˈəspeis-] n 宇宙開発業界 uchūkaiʰhatsugyōkai

aesthetic [esθetˈik] adj 美的な bitéki na

afar [əfɑːrˈ] adv: **from afar** 遠くから tōku karà

affable [æfˈəbəl] adj (person) 愛想の良い aisō no yoi; (behavior) 感じの良い kanji no yoi

affair [əfεːrˈ] n (matter, business, question) 問題 mondai; (romance: also: **love affair**) 浮気 uwáki

affect [əfektˈ] vt (influence, concern: person, object) ...に影響を与える ...ni eʰkyō wò atáerù; (subj: disease: afflict) 冒す okásù; (move deeply) 感動させる kandō saserù

affected [əfekˈtid] adj (behavior, person) 気取った kidótta

affection [əfekˈʃən] n (fondness) 愛情 aijō

affectionate [əfekˈʃənit] adj (person, kiss) 愛情深い aijōbukai; (animal) 人なつこい hitónatsukoì

affiliated [əfilˈiːeitid] adj (company, body) 関連の kanren no

affinity [əfinˈitiː] n (bond, rapport): **to have an affinity with/for** ...に魅力を感じる ...ni miryóku wò kanjiru; (resemblance): **to have an affinity with** ... ...に似ている ...ni nité iru

affirmative [əfəːrˈmətiv] adj (answer, nod etc) 肯定の kōtei no

affix [əfiksˈ] vt (stamp) はる harú

afflict [əfliktˈ] vt (subj: pain, sorrow, misfortune) 苦しめる kurúshimerù

affluence [æfˈluːəns] n 裕福さ yūfukusà

affluent [æfˈluːənt] adj (wealthy: family, background, surroundings) 裕福な yūfuku na

　the **affluent society** 豊かな社会 yútàka na shákaì

afford [əfɔːrdˈ] vt (have enough money for) 買う余裕がある kaú yoyū gà arù; (permit oneself: time, risk etc) する余裕がある surú yoyū gà arù; (provide) 与える atáeru

affront [əfrʌntˈ] n (insult) 侮辱 bujóku

Afghanistan [æfgænˈistæn] n アフガニスタン afúganisùtan

afield [əfiːldˈ] adv: **far afield** 遠く tōku

afloat [əfloutˈ] adv (floating) 浮んで ukánde

afoot [əfutˈ] adv: **there is something afoot** 何か怪しい事が起っている nánika ayáshii koto gà okóttè irú

afraid [əfreidˈ] adj (frightened) 怖がっている kowágattè irú

　to be afraid of (person, thing) ...を怖がる ...wo kowágarù

　to be afraid to ...をするのを怖がる ...wo suru no wò kowágarù

　I am afraid that (apology) 申訳ないが ... mōshiwakenai ga

　I am afraid so/not 残念ですがその通りです〔違います〕zańnen desu ga sonó tōri desu〔chigáimasù〕

afresh [əfreʃˈ] adv (begin, start) 新たに áràta ni

Africa [æfˈrikə] n アフリカ afúrika

African [æfˈrikən] adj アフリカの afúrika no

　◆n アフリカ人 afúrikajìn

aft [æft] adv (to be) 後方に kōhō ni; (to go) 後方へ kōhō e

after [æfˈtəːr] prep (of time) ...の後に ...no átò ni; (of place) ...の後ろに ...no ushíro ni; (of order) ...の次に ...no tsugí ni

　◆adv 後に átò ni

　◆conj ...してから ...shité kara

　what/who are you after? 何〔だれ〕を捜していますか náni〔dáre〕wo sagáshitè imásu ka

　after he left 彼が帰ってから kárè ga kaétte kara

　after having done ...してから ...shité kara

　to name someone after someone ...に因んで...に名を付ける ...ni chínañde ...ni na wo tsukérù

　it's twenty after eight (US) 8時20分だ hachíji nijíppùn da

　to ask after someone ...の事を尋ねる ...no kotó wò tazúnerù

　after all (in spite of everything) どうせ

dóse; (in spite of contrary expectations etc) 予想を裏切って yosô wò urágittè
after you! お先にどうぞ o-sáki ni dôzo

after-effects [æf'tərifekts] *npl* (of illness, radiation, drink etc) 結果 kekká

aftermath [æf'tərmæθ] *n* (period after) ...直後の期間 ...chôkùgo no kikáñ; (aftereffects) 結果 kekká

afternoon [æftə·rnu:n'] *n* 午後 gôgò

afters [æf'tərz] (*BRIT:inf*) *n* (dessert) デザート dézàto

after-sales service[æf'tərseilz-](*BRIT*) *n* (for car, washing machine etc) アフターサービス afútāsābisu

after-shave (lotion) [æf'tərʃeiv-] *n* アフターシェーブローション afútāshēburôshon

afterthought [æf'tərθɔːt] *n*: **as an afterthought** 後の思い付きで átò no omôitsuki de

afterwards [æf'tərwərdz] (*US also*: **afterward**) *adv* その後 sonô atò

again [əgen'] *adv* (once more) もう1度 mô ichido, 再び futátabi
not ... again もう...ない mô ... nai
to do something again ...をもう1度する ...wo mô ichido surù
again and again 何度も nâñdo mo

against [əgenst'] *prep* (leaning on, touching) ...にもたれ掛けて ...ni motárekakattè; (in opposition to, at odds with) ...に反対して ...ni hañtai shite; (compared to) ...に較べて ...ni kurábete

age [eidʒ] *n* (of person, object) 年齢 neñrei; (period in history) 時代 jidái
♦*vi* (person) 年を取る toshí wo torù
♦*vt* (subj: hairstyle, dress, make-up etc) ...を実際の年以上に見せる ...wo jissái no toshi ijô ni misérù
20 years of age 年齢二十 neñrei hatàchi
to come of age 成人する seíjin suru
it's been ages since ...は久し振りだ ...wa hisáshiburi da

aged[1] [ei'dʒd] *adj*: **aged 10** 10才の jússài no

aged[2] [ei'dʒid] *npl*: **the aged** 老人 rôjin
◊総称 sôshō

age group *n* 年齢層 neñreisô

age limit *n* 年齢制限 neñreiseîgen

agency [ei'dʒənsi:] *n* (COMM) 代理店 daíritèn; (government body) ...局 ...kyokú, ...庁 ...chô

agenda [ədʒen'də] *n* (of meeting) 議題 gidái

agent [ei'dʒənt] *n* (representative: COMM, literary, theatrical etc) 代理人 daírinin, エージェント ējento; (spy) スパイ supâi; (CHEM, *fig*) 試薬 shiyáku

aggravate [æg'rəveit] *vt* (exacerbate: situation) 悪化させる akká saserù; (annoy: person) 怒らせる okóraserù

aggregate [æg'rəgit] *n* (total) 合計 gôkei

aggression [əgreʃ'ən] *n* (aggressive behavior) 攻撃 kôgeki

aggressive [əgres'iv] *adj* (belligerent, assertive) 攻撃的な kôgekiteki na

aggrieved [əgri:vd'] *adj* 不満を抱いた fumáñ wò idáità

aghast [əgæst'] *adj* あっけにとられた akké ni toráretà

agile [ædʒ'əl] *adj* (physically, mentally) 身軽な migáru na; (mentally) 機敏な kibín na

agitate [ædʒ'əteit] *vt* (person) 動揺させる dôyō saserù
♦*vi*: **to agitate for/against** ...の運動〔反対運動〕をする ...no uñdō [hañtaiuñdō]wò suru

agitator [ædʒ'iteitər] *n* 扇動者 señdôsha

AGM [eidʒi:em'] *n abbr* = **annual general meeting**

agnostic [ægnɑːs'tik] *n* 不可知論者 fukáchironsha

ago [əgou'] *adv*: **2 days ago** 2日前 futsúkamaè
not long ago 少し前に súkòshi maè ni
how long ago? どのぐらい前に? donó guraî maè ni?

agog [əgɑːg'] *adj* (excited, eager) わくわくしている wákùwaku shité irù

agonizing [æg'ənaizin] *adj* 苦しい kurúshiî

agony [æg'əni:] *n* (pain) 苦もん kumôn

to be in agony 苦しむ kurúshimù

agree [əgri:'] *vt* (price, date) 合意して決める gối shité kiméru

♦*vi* (have same opinion) ...と意見が合う ...to íkèn ga áù; (correspond) ...と一致する ...to itchí suru; (consent) 承諾する shốdaku suru

to agree with someone (subj: person) ...と同意する ...to dối suru; (: food) ...に合う ...ni áù

to agree (with) (statements etc) (...に) 同意する (...ni) dối suru; (LING) (...と) 一致する (...to) itchí suru

to agree to something/to do something ...に〔することに〕同意する ...ni 〔surú koto ni〕dối suru

to agree that (admit) ...だと認める ...dá tò mitómeru

agreeable [əgri:'əbəl] *adj* (sensation, person: pleasant) 気持の良い kimóchi no yoi; (willing) 承知する shốchi suru

agreed [əgri:d'] *adj* (time, place, price) 同意で決めた dối de kimetà

agreement [əgri:'mənt] *n* (concurrence, consent) 同意 dối; (arrangement, contract) 契約 keíyaku

in agreement 同意して dối shite

agricultural [ægrəkʌl'tʃərəl] *adj* (land, implement, show) 農業の nốgyo no

agriculture [æg'rəkʌltʃəːr] *n* 農業 nốgyō

aground [əgraund'] *adv*: *to run aground* (NAUT) ざ折する zasétsu suru

ahead [əhed'] *adv* (in front: of place, time) 前に máè ni; (into the future) 先に sakí

ahead of (in progress) ...より進んで ...yốrì susúnde; (in ranking) ...の上に ...no ué ni; (in advance of: person, time, place) ...の前に ...no máè ni

ahead of time 早目に hayáme ni

go right/straight ahead (direction) 真っ直ぐに行って下さい mássùgu ni itté kudasai; (permission) どうぞ、どうぞ dốzo, dốzo

aid [eid] *n* (assistance: to person, country) 援助 énjo; (device) ...を助けるもの

...wo tasúkerù monó

♦*vt* (help: person, country) 援助する énjo suru

in aid of (BRIT) ...のために ...no támè ni

to aid and abet (LAW) ほう助する hốjo suru ¶ *see also* **hearing**

aide [eid] *n* (person, *also* MIL) 側近 sokkín

AIDS [eidz] *n abbr* (= *acquired immunodeficiency syndrome*) エイズ éîzu

ailing [ei'liŋ] *adj* (person) 病気の byốki no

ailment [eil'mənt] *n* 病気 byốki

aim [eim] *vt*: *to aim (at)* (gun, missile, camera, remark) (...に) 向ける (...ni) mukérù

♦*vi* (*also*: **take aim**) ねらう neráu

♦*n* (objective) 目的 mokúteki; (in shooting: skill) ねらい nerái

to aim at (with weapon; *also* objective) ねらう neráu

to aim a punch at げんこつで...を殴ろうとする geńkotsu de ...wò nágûro to suru

to aim to do ...するつもりである ...surú tsumóri de arû

aimless [eim'lis] *adj* (person, activity) 当てのない até no naì

ain't [eint] (*inf*) = **am not; aren't; isn't**

air [e:r] *n* (atmosphere) 空気 kúki; (tune) メロディー mérðdī; (appearance) 態度 tấido

♦*vt* (room) ...の空気を入れ替える ...no kúki wo irékaerù; (clothes) 干す hốsù; (grievances, views) 打明ける uchíakeru

♦*cpd* (currents etc) 空気の kúki no; (attack) 空からの sorá kara no

to throw something into the air (ball etc) ...を投上げる ...wo nágéageru

by air (travel) 飛行機で hikốki de

on the air (RADIO, TV: programme, station) 放送中 hốsôchū

airbed [e:r'bed] (BRIT) *n* 空気布団 kúkibutòn

airborne [e:r'bo:rn] *adj* (airplane) 飛行中の hikốchū no

air-conditioned [e:r'kəndiʃənd] *adj* 空

調付きの kůchōtsuki no

air conditioning [-kəndiʃ'əniŋ] *n* 空調 kůchō

aircraft [eːr'kræft] *n inv* 航空機 kōkūki

aircraft carrier *n* 空母 kůbo

airfield [eːr'fiːld] *n* 飛行場 hikōjō

Air Force *n* 空軍 kůgun

air freshener [-freʃ'ənəːr] *n* 消臭剤 shōshūzai

airgun [eːr'gʌn] *n* 空気銃 kůkijū

air hostess (*BRIT*) *n* スチュワーデス suchůwādesu

air letter (*BRIT*) *n* エアログラム éarogůramu

airlift [eːr'lift] *n* エアリフト éarifůto

airline [eːr'lain] *n* エアライン éaraìn

airliner [eːr'lainəːr] *n* 旅客機 ryokákukì

airmail [eːr'meil] *n*: **by airmail** 航空便で kōkūbin de

airplane [eːr'plein] (*US*) *n* 飛行機 híkōki

airport [eːr'pɔːrt] *n* 空港 kůkō

air raid *n* 空襲 kůshū

airsick [eːr'sik] *adj*: **to be airsick** 飛行機に酔う híkōki ni yoù

airspace [eːr'speis] *n* 領空 ryōkū

air terminal *n* 空港ターミナルビル kůkōtáminarubirù

airtight [eːr'tait] *adj* 気密の kimítsu no

air-traffic controller [eːr'træfik-] *n* 管制官 kańseîkan

airy [eːr'iː] *adj* (room, building) 風通しの良い kazétōshi no yoǐ; (casual: manner) 軽薄な keíhaku na

aisle [ail] *n* 通路 tsůro

ajar [ədʒɑːr'] *adj* (door) 少し開いている sukōshi aite irù

akin [əkin'] *adj*: **akin to** (similar) ...の様な ...no yō na

alacrity [ələkr'itiː] *n* 敏速さ bińsokusa

alarm [əlɑːrm'] *n* (anxiety) 心配 shińpai; (in shop, bank) 警報 keíhō

♦*vt* (person) 心配させる shińpai saserù

alarm call *n* (in hotel etc) モーニングコール mốningukòru

alarm clock *n* 目覚し時計 mezámashidokèi

alas [əlæs'] *excl* 残念ながら zańnennagàra

Albania [ælbei'niːə] *n* アルバニア arúbania

albeit [ɔːlbiː'it] *conj* (although) ...ではあるが ...de wa árù ga

album [æl'bəm] *n* (gen, also: **LP**) アルバム arúbamu

alcohol [æl'kəhɔːl] *n* アルコール arúkōru

alcoholic [ælkəhɔːl'ik] *adj* アルコールの入った arúkōru no haìtta

♦*n* アルコール中毒者 arúkōru chúdokùsha

alcoholism [æl'kəhɔːlizəm] *n* アルコール中毒 arúkōru chúdoku

alcove [æl'kouv] *n* アルコーブ arúkòbu

ale [eil] *n* (drink) エール èru

alert [ələːrt'] *adj* 注意している chūi shité irù

♦*n* (alarm) 警報 keíhō

♦*vt* (guard, police etc) ...に知らせる ...ni shiráserù

to be on the alert (*also* MIL) 警戒している keíkai shite irù

algebra [æl'dʒəbrə] *n* 代数 daísū

Algeria [ældʒiː'riːə] *n* アルジェリア arújeria

algorithm [æl'gəriðəm] *n* アルゴリズム arúgorizùmu

alias [ei'liːəs] *adv* 別名は betsúmei wa

♦*n* (of criminal, writer etc) 偽名 giméi

alibi [æl'əbai] *n* (LAW: *also gen*) アリバイ aríbai

alien [eil'jən] *n* (foreigner) 外国人 gaíkokujìn; (extraterrestrial) 宇宙人 uchūjin

♦*adj*: **alien (to)** (...) の性に合わない (...no) shō ni awánaì

alienate [eil'jəneit] *vt* (person) ...と仲たがいする ...to nakátagaì suru

alight [əlait'] *adj* (burning) 燃えている moéte iru; (eyes, expression) 輝いている kagáyaìte irú

♦*vi* (bird) とまる tomáru; (passenger) 降りる oríru

align [əlain'] *vt* (objects) 並べる naráberu

alike [əlaik'] *adj* 似ている nité iru

♦*adv* (similarly) 同様に dốyō ni;

(equally) ...共に ...tomo ni
  to look alike 似ている nité iru

alimony [ǽləmouni:] *n* (payment) 離婚
手当 rikónteàte

alive [əlaiv'] *adj* (living) 生きている íkìte
irù; (lively: person) 活発な kappátsu na;
(place) 活気に満ちた kakkí ni michìta

alkali [ǽlkəlai] *n* アルカリ arúkari

KEYWORD

---

all [ɔːl] *adj* 皆の mi(n)ná no, 全ての subète nó, 全部の zènbu nó, ...中...jū
  all day/night 1日〔1晩〕中 ichinichi〔hi-
toban〕jū
  all men are equal 全ての人間は平等で
ある subète nó níngen wa byódō de árù
  all five came 5人とも来ました gonín
tomo kimáshìta
  all the books/food 本〔食べ物〕は全部
hòn〔tabémono〕wa zènbu
  all the time いつも ítsumo
  he lived here all his life 彼は一生ここ
で暮らしました kàre wa isshó koko de
kuráshimashìta

  ♦*pron* 1 皆 miná, 全て subète, 全部 zènbu
  I ate it all, I ate all of it それを全
部食べました soré wo zènbu tabémashì-
ta
  all of us/the boys went 私たち〔少年
たち〕は皆行きました watákushitàchi
〔shónèntachi〕wa miná íkimashìta
  we all sat down 私たちは皆腰掛けまし
た watákushitàchi wa miná koshíkake-
mashìta
  is that all? それで全部ですか soré de
zènbu desu ká; (in shop) 外にはよろしい
でしょうか hoká ni wà yoróshiì deshó
ká
  2 (in phrases): *above all* 何よりも nánì
yori mo
  after all 何しろ nánì shiro
  at all: not at all (in answer to question) 少しも...ない sùkoshí mo ...nài; (in
answer to thanks) どういたしまして dō
itáshimashìte
  I'm not at all tired 少しも疲れていま
せん sùkoshi mo tsùkárete ìmasen
  anything at all will do 何でもいいで

す nán de mo iì desù
  all in all 全般的に見て zénpanteki ni
mítè

  ♦*adv* 全く máttaku
  all alone 1人だけで hítori dake dè
  it's not as hard as all that 言われて
いる程ましくありません iwárete iru ho-
do mùzukashiku arimasen
  all the more なお更... nàosara...
  all the better 更にいい sàra ni iì
  all but (regarding people) ...を除いて皆
...wo nózoite miná; (regarding things)
...を除いて全て ...wo nózoite subète
  I had all but finished もう少しで終
るところだった mó sukoshì de owáru
tokoro dátta
  the score is 2 all カウントはツーオー
ルです kaúnto wa tsuōrú désù

---

allay [əlei'] *vt* (fears) 和らげる yawáragerù

all clear *n* (after attack etc) 警報解除信
号 keíhōkaijoshiǹgò; (*fig*: permission) 許
可 kyóka

allegation [ælǝgei'ʃǝn] *n* (of misconduct, impropriety) 主張 shuchó

allege [əledʒ'] *vt* (claim) 主張する shuchó
suru

allegedly [əledʒ'idli:] *adv* 主張によると
shuchó ni yoru to

allegiance [əli:'dʒəns] *n* (loyalty, support) 忠誠 chúsei

allegory [ǽlǝgɔ:ri:] *n* (painting, story)
比ゆ híyù

allergic [ələr'dʒik] *adj* (reaction, rash)
アレルギーの arérùgī no
  allergic to (foods etc) ...に対してアレル
ギー体質である ...ni taíshite arèrugítai-
shìtsu de aru; (*fig*: work etc) ...が大嫌い
である ...ga daíkìrai de aru

allergy [ǽlɔ:rdʒi:] *n* (MED) アレルギー
arérùgī

alleviate [əli:'vi:eit] *vt* (pain, difficulty)
軽減する keígen suru

alley [ǽli:] *n* (street) 横丁 yokóchō

alliance [əlai'əns] *n* (of states, people) 連
合 reńgō

allied [əlaid'] *adj* (POL, MIL: forces) 連

合の rengō no

alligator [æl'əgeitə:r] n (ZOOL) アリゲーター arígētā

all-in [ɔːl'in] (BRIT) adj (also adv: price, cost, charge) 込みの〔で〕kómì no〔de〕

all-in wrestling (BRIT) n プロレスリング purōresùringu

all-night [ɔːl'nait] adj (cafe, cinema, party) オールナイトの ōrunaìto no

allocate [æl'əkeit] vt (earmark: time, money, tasks, rooms etc) 割当てる waríaterù

allot [əla:t'] vt: **to allot (to)** (time, money etc) 割当てる waríaterù

allotment [əla:t'mənt] n (share) 配分 haíbun; (BRIT: garden) 貸家庭菜園 kashíkateisaìen

all-out [ɔːl'aut'] adj (effort, dedication etc) 徹底的な tettéiteki na

all out adv 徹底的に tettéiteki ni

allow [əlau'] vt (permit, tolerate: practice, behavior, goal) 許す yurúsù; (sum, time estimated) 見積る mitsúmorù; (a claim) 認める mitómeru; (concede): **to allow that** ...だと認める ...da to mitómerù

to allow someone to do ...に...をするのを許す ...ni ...wò suru no wò yúrusù

he is allowed to ... 彼は...してよいとなっている kárè wa ...shité yoì to natte irù

allowance [əlau'əns] n (money given to someone: gen) 支給金 shikyúkin; (: welfare payment) 福祉手当 fukúshiteàte; (: pocket money) 小遣い kózùkai; (tax allowance) 控除 kòjo

to make allowances for (person, thing) 考慮する kōryo suru

allow for vt fus (shrinkage, inflation etc) ...を考慮する ...wo kōryo suru

alloy [æl'ɔi] n (mix) 合金 gōkin

all right adv (well: get on) うまく úmàku; (correctly: function, do) しかるべく shikárubekù; (as answer: in agreement) いいですよ íi desu yo

I feel all right 大丈夫です daíjòbu desu

all-rounder [ɔːlraun'də:r] (BRIT) n 多才の人 tasái no hito

all-time [ɔːl'taim] adj (record) 史上最...の shijōsai... no

allude [əlu:d'] vi: **to allude to** 暗に言及する áñ ni geñkyū suru

alluring [əluː'riŋ] adj (person, prospect) 魅力的な miryōteki na

allusion [əluː'ʒən] n (reference) さりげない言及 sarígenaì geñkyū

ally [æl'ai] n (friend, also POL, MIL) 味方 mikáta

◆vt: **to ally oneself with** ...に味方する ...ni mikáta suru

almighty [ɔːlmai'tiː] adj (omnipotent) 全能の zeñnō no; (tremendous: row etc) ものすごい monósugoì

almond [ɑ:'mənd] n (fruit) アーモンド ā-mondo

almost [ɔːl'moust] adv (practically) ほとんど hotôñdo; (with verb): **I almost fell** 私は転ぶところだった watákushi wà koróbu tokoro dattà

alms [ɑːmz] npl 施し hodókoshi

aloft [əlɔːft'] adv (hold, carry) 高く tákàku

alone [əloun'] adj (by oneself, unaccompanied) 一人きりの hitórikiri no

◆adv (unaided) 単独で tañdoku de

to leave someone alone ...をほうっておく ...wo hōtte oku

to leave something alone ...をいじらない ...wo íjìranai

let alone ... ...は言うまでもなく ...wa iú made mo naku

along [əlɔːŋ'] prep (way, route, street, wall etc) ...に沿って ...ni sóttè

◆adv: **is he coming along with us?** 彼も付いて来るのですか kárè mo tsuíte kurú no desu ká

he was limping along 彼はびっこを引いて歩いていた kárè wa bíkkò wo hiite árùite itá

along with (together with) ...と一緒に ...to isshô ni

all along (all the time) ずっと zuttō

alongside [əlɔːŋ'said'] prep (come, be: vehicle, ship) ...の横に ...no yokó ni

◆adv (see prep) ...の横に ...no yokó ni

aloof [əluːf'] adj よそよそしい yosóyososhií

♦*adv*: **to stand aloof** 知らぬ顔をする shiránu kao wò suru

aloud [əlaud'] *adv* (read, speak) 声を出して kóè wo dáshìte

alphabet [æl'fəbet] *n* アルファベット a-rúfabettò

alphabetical [ælfəbet'ikəl] *adj* アルファベットの arúfabettò no

alpine [æl'pain] *adj* (sports, meadow, plant) 山の yamá no

Alps [ælps] *npl*: **the Alps** アルプス山脈 arúpusu saṅmyaku

already [ɔːlred'iː] *adv* もう mỏ, 既に súdèni

alright [ɔːlrait'] (*BRIT*) *adv* = **all right**

Alsatian [ælseí'ʃən] *n* (*BRIT*: dog) シェパード犬 shepádoken

also [ɔːl'sou] *adv* (too) も mo; (moreover) なお náò

altar [ɔːl'tər] *n* (REL) 祭壇 saídan

alter [ɔːl'tər] *vt* (change) 変える kaéru
♦*vi* (change) 変る kawáru

alteration [ɔːltərei'ʃən] *n* (to plans) 変更 heñkó; (to clothes) 寸法直し suñpónadoshi; (to building) 改修 kaíshū

alternate [*adj* ɔːl'təːrnit *vb* ɔːl'təːrneit] *adj* (actions, events, processes) 交互の kỏgo no; (*US*: alternative: plans) 代りの kawári no
♦*vi*: **to alternate (with)** (…と) 交替する (…to) kỏtai suru
on alternate days 1日置きに ichínichì oki ni

alternating current [ɔːl'təːrneitiŋ-] *n* 交流 kỏryū

alternative [ɔːltəːr'nətiv] *adj* (plan, policy) 代りの kawári no
♦*n* (choice: other possibility) 選択 señtaku

alternative comedy 新コメディー shíñkomèdì ◇近年若手コメディアンの間ではやっている反体制の落語、喜劇などを指す kíñnen wakátekomedìan no aída dè hayátte iru hañtaisei no rakúgo, kígèki nado wo sásù

alternative medicine 代替医学 daítaiigàku ◇はり、指圧など、西洋医学以外の

治療法を指す hárì, shiátsu nadò, seíyōigàku íga'i no chiryỏhỏ wo sasù

alternatively [ɔːltəːr'nətivliː] *adv*: *alternatively one could …* 一方…する事もできる íppỏ …surú koto mo dekirù

alternator [ɔːl'təːrneitər] *n* (AUT) 交流発電機 kỏryūhatsudeñki

although [ɔːlðou'] *conj* (despite the fact that) …にもかかわらず …ni mo kakáwarazu

altitude [æl'tətuːd] *n* (of place) 海抜 kaíbatsu; (of plane) 高度 kỏdo

alto [æl'tou] *n* (female) アルト árùto; (male) コントラテノール koñtoratenỏru

altogether [ɔːltəgeð'əːr] *adv* (completely) 全く mattáku; (on the whole, in all) 合計は gỏkei wa

altruistic [æltruːis'tik] *adj* (motive, behavior) 愛他的な aítateki na

aluminium [ælumin'iːəm] (*BRIT*) = **aluminum**

aluminum [əluː'mənəm] *n* アルミニウム arúminiùmu, アルミ arúmi

always [ɔːl'weiz] *adv* (at all times) いつも ítsumo; (forever) いつまでも ítsu made mỏ; (if all else fails) いざとなれば ízá to nárèba

am [æm] *vb see* **be**

a.m. [ei'em'] *adv abbr* (= *ante meridiem*) 午前 gỏzèn

amalgamate [əmæl'gəmeit] *vi* (organizations, companies) 合併する gappéi suru
♦*vt* (see vi) 合併させる gappéi saseru

amass [əmæs'] *vt* (fortune, information, objects) 貯め込む tamékomù

amateur [æm'ətʃəːr] *n* (non-professional) 素人 shíròto, アマチュア amáchua

amateurish [æmətʃuː'riʃ] *adj* (work, efforts) 素人っぽい shirótoppoi

amaze [əmeiz'] *vt* 仰天させる gyỏten saseru
to be amazed (at) (…に) びっくり仰天する (…ni) bíkkùrigyỏten suru

amazement [əmeiz'mənt] *n* 仰天 gyỏten

amazing [əmei'ziŋ] *adj* (surprising) 驚くべき odòrokubekì; (fantastic) 素晴らし

い subárashiì

Amazon [ǽməzɔːn] n (GEO: river) アマ
ゾン川 amázoṅgawa

ambassador [æmbǽsədəːr] n (diplomat) 大使 táìshi

amber [ǽmbəːr] n (substance) こはく
kohákù

　　at amber (*BRIT*: AUT: of traffic light)
黄色になって kifro ni natté

ambiguity [æmbəgjuːíti:] n (lack of
clarity: in thoughts, word, phrase etc) あ
いまいさ aímaisa

ambiguous [æmbíg'juːəs] adj (word,
phrase, reply) あいまいな aímai na

ambition [æmbíʃ'ən] n (desire, thing
desired) 野心 yáshìn

ambitious [æmbíʃ'əs] adj (person, plan)
野心的な yashínteki na

ambivalent [æmbiv'ələnt] adj (opinion,
attitude, person) はっきりしない hakkíri
shinai

amble [ǽm'bəl] vi (gen: amble along) ぶ
らぶら歩く búràbura arúku

ambulance [ǽm'bjələns] n 救急車 kyǘ-
kyùsha

ambush [ǽm'buʃ] n (trap) 待伏せ machíbuse

　　♦vt (MIL etc) 待伏せる machíbuserù

amen [ei'men'] excl アーメン ámen

amenable [əmi:'nəbəl] adj: *amenable to*
(advice, reason etc) ...を素直に聞く ...wo
súnào ni kikú; (flattery etc) ...に乗りやす
い ...ni noríyasui

amend [əmend'] vt (law) 改正する kaísei
suru; (text) 訂正する teísei suru

　　to make amends 償う tsugúnaù

amendment [əmend'mənt] n (to text:
change) 訂正 teísei

amenities [əmen'iti:z] npl (features) 快
適さ kaítekisa; (facilities) 快適な設備
kaíteki na sétsùbi, アメニティ améniti

America [əmeːr'ikə] n (GEO) アメリカ a-
mérika

American [əmeːr'ikən] adj (of America)
アメリカの amérika no; (of United
States) アメリカ合衆国の amérikagasshǔkoku no

　　♦n アメリカ人 amérikajìn

amiable [ei'mi:əbəl] adj (person, smile)
愛想の良い aísò no yóì

amicable [ǽm'ikəbəl] adj (relationship)
友好的な yǔkōteki na; (parting, divorce,
settlement) 円満な eñman na

amid(st) [əmid(st')'] prep (among) ...の間
に〔で〕...no aída ni〔dè〕

amiss [əmis'] adj, adv: *to take something amiss* ...に気を悪くする ...ni ki
wo warúku suru

　　there's something amiss 何か変だ nánìka hén da

ammonia [əmoun'jə] n (gas) アンモニア
afmonia

ammunition [æmjəniʃ'ən] n (for weapon) 弾薬 dañ-yaku

amnesia [æmniː'ʒə] n 記憶喪失 kiókusò-
shitsu

amnesty [æm'nisti:] n (to convicts, political prisoners etc) 恩赦 óñsha

amok [əmʌk'] adv: *to run amok* 大暴れ
する óabàre suru

among(st) [əmʌŋ(st)'] prep ...の間に〔で〕
...no aída ni〔dè〕

amoral [eimɔːr'əl] adj (behavior, person)
道徳観のない dótokukàn no nai

amorous [æm'əːrəs] adj (intentions, feelings) 性愛的な seíaiteki na

amorphous [əmɔːr'fəs] adj (cloud) 無定
形の mutéikei no; (organization etc) 統
一性のない tóìtsusei no naì

amount [əmaunt'] n (quantity) 量 ryó;
(of all etc) 金額 kíñgaku

　　♦vi: *to amount to* (total) 合計...になる
gókei ...ni narù; (be same as) ...同然であ
る ...dózen de aru

amp(ère) [æm'p(i:r)] n アンペア añpeà

amphibious [æmfib'i:əs] adj (animal) 水
陸両生の suírikuryòsei no; (vehicle) 水陸
両用の suírikuryōyō no

amphitheater [æm'fəθi:əтəːr] (*BRIT*
amphitheatre) n (for sports etc) 円形競
技場 eñkeikyōgijó; (theater) 円形劇場 eñ-
keigekijó; (lecture hall etc) 階段教室 kaí-
dankyòshitsu

ample [æm'pəl] adj (large) 大きな óokina;
(abundant) 沢山の takúsan no; (enough)
十二分な júnibùn na

amplifier [æm'pləfaiə:r] *n* 増幅器 zōfukukî, アンプ áñpu

amputate [æm'pjuteit] *vt* 切断する setsúdan suru

amuck [əmʌk'] *adv* = **amok**

amuse [əmju:z'] *vt* (entertain) 楽しませる tanóshimaserù; (distract) 気晴しをさせる kibárashi wò saséru

amusement [əmju:z'mənt] *n* (mirth) 痛快さ tsúkaisa; (pleasure) 楽しみ tanóshimì; (pastime) 気晴し kibárashi

amusement arcade *n* ゲーム場 gḗmujō

an [æn, ən] *indef art* ¶ *see* **a**

anachronism [ənæk'rənizəm] *n* 時代錯誤 jidáisakugò, アナクロニズム anákuronizûmu

anaemia [əni:'mi:ə] *etc* (*BRIT*) = **anemia** *etc*

anaesthetic [ænisθet'ik] *etc* (*BRIT*) = **anesthetic** *etc*

anagram [æn'əgræm] *n* アナグラム anágùramu ◊ある語句の字を並べ換えて出来る語 árù gôkù no jí wò narábekaete dekirù gó

analgesic [ænəldʒi:'zik] *n* 鎮痛剤 chiñtsūzài

analog(ue) [æn'ələ:g] *adj* (watch, computer) アナログ式の anárogushiki no

analogy [ənæl'ədʒi:] *n* 類似性 ruíjisei

analyse [æn'əlaiz] (*BRIT*) *vt* = **analyze**

analyses [ənæl'isi:z] *npl of* **analysis**

analysis [ənæl'isis] (*pl* **analyses**) *n* (of situation, evidence) 分析 buñseki; (of person) 精神分析 seíshinbuñseki

analyst [æn'əlist] *n* (political analyst etc) 評論家 hyóronka; (US) 精神分析医 seíshinbunseki-ì

analytic(al) [ænəlit'ik(əl)] *adj* 分析の buñseki no

analyze [æn'əlaiz] (*BRIT* **analyse**) *vt* (situation, statistics, CHEM, MED) 分析する buñseki suru; (person) …の精神分析をする …no seíshinbuñseki wo suru

anarchist [æn'ə:rkist] *n* (POL, *fig*) 無政府主義者 muséifushugìshà, アナーキスト anákisùto

anarchy [æn'ə:rki:] *n* (chaos, disorder) 混乱状態 koñranjōtai

anathema [ənæθ'əmə] *n*: *that is anathema to him* 彼はその事をひどく嫌っている kárè wa sonó koto wò hídòku kirátte irù

anatomy [ənæt'əmi:] *n* (science) 解剖学 kaíbōgaku; (body) 身体 shíñtai

ancestor [æn'sestə:r] *n* 祖先 sósèn

anchor [æŋ'kə:r] *n* (NAUT) いかり ikári
♦*vi* (*also*: **to drop anchor**) いかりを下ろす ikári wò orósù
♦*vt*: **to anchor something to** …を…に固定する …wo …ni kotéi suru
to weigh anchor いかりを上げる ikári wò agérù

anchovy [æn'tʃouvi:] *n* アンチョビー áñchobī

ancient [ein'ʃənt] *adj* (civilisation, monument) 古代の kódài no; (Rome etc) 古代からの kodái kará no; (person) 高齢の kốrei no; (car etc) おんぼろの oñboro no

ancillary [æn'səle:ri:] *adj* (worker, staff) 補助の hójò no

KEYWORD

and [ænd] *conj* (between nouns) …と … …to …, …及び … …oyobi …; (at head of sentence etc) そして soshite
and so on などなど nádò nádò
try and come 出来れば来てね dèkíreba kîté ne
he talked and talked 彼は際限なくしゃべり続けた kàre wa sàigen nakù shàbéritsuzukètá
better and better/faster and faster ますますよく〔速く〕màsúmàsú yókù 〔hayaku〕

Andes [æn'di:z] *npl*: **the Andes** アンデス山脈 añdesu sañmyaku

anecdote [æn'ikdout] *n* エピソード epísōdo

anemia [əni:'mi:ə] (*BRIT* **anaemia**) *n* 貧血 hiñketsu

anemic [əni:'mik] (*BRIT* **anaemic**) *adj* (MED, *fig*) 貧血の hiñketsu no

anesthetic [ænisθet'ik] (*BRIT* **anaesthetic**) *n* 麻酔剤 masúīzai

anesthetist [ənes'θitist] (*BRIT* **anaes-**

thetist] n 麻酔士 masúishi

anew [ənuː'] adv (once again) 再び futátabi

angel [ein'dʒəl] n (REL) 天使 ténshi

anger [æŋ'gəːr] n (rage) 怒り ikári

angina [ændʒai'nə] n 狭心症 kyóshinshō

angle [æŋ'gəl] n (MATH: shape) 角 kákū; (degree) 角度 kàkudo; (corner) 角 kádồ; (viewpoint): *from their angle* 彼らの観点から kárềra no kánteñ kara

angler [æŋ'gləːr] n 釣人 tsurĭbito

Anglican [æŋ'glikən] adj 英国国教会の eíkoku kokkyōkai no
  ♦n 英国国教会教徒 eíkoku kokkyōkai kyóto

angling [æŋ'gliŋ] n 釣 tsurí

Anglo- [æŋ'glou] prefix 英国の eíkoku no

angrily [æŋ'grili] adv (react, deny) 怒って okótte

angry [æŋ'griː] adj (person, response) 怒った okótta; (wound) 炎症を起した eñshō wð okóshìtà
  to be angry with someone/at something ...に怒っている ...ni okótte irù
  to get angry 怒る okórù

anguish [æŋ'gwiʃ] n (physical) 苦痛 kutsū; (mental) 精神的な苦痛 seíshintekikutsū

angular [æŋ'gjələːr] adj (shape, features) 角張った kakúbattà

animal [æn'əməl] n (mammal) ほ乳動物 honyúdòbutsu; (living creature) 動物 dóbutsu; (pej: person) 怪物 kaíbutsu
  ♦adj (instinct, courage, attraction) 動物的な dóbutsuteki na

animate [æn'əmit] adj 生きている ikíte iru

animated [æn'əmeitid] adj (conversation, expression) 生き生きとした ikíikì to shitá; (film) アニメの aníme no

animosity [ænəmɑːs'əti] n (strong dislike) 憎悪 zōo

aniseed [æn'isiːd] n アニスの実 anísu no mi

ankle [æŋ'kəl] n (ANAT) 足首 ashíkubi

ankle sock n ソックス sókkùsu

annex [n æn'eks vb əneks'] n (also:

BRIT: annexe) 別館 bekkán
  ♦vt (take over: property, territory) 併合する heígō suru

annihilate [ənai'əleit] vt (destroy: also fig) 滅ぼす horóbosu

anniversary [ænəvəːr'səriː] n (of wedding, revolution) 記念日 kinénbi

annotate [æn'outeit] vt ...に注釈を付ける ...ni chūshaku wð tsukérù

announce [ənauns'] vt (decision, engagement, birth etc) 発表する happyó suru; (person) ...の到着を告げる ...no tóchaku wð tsugérù

announcement [ənauns'mənt] n 発表 happyó

announcer [ənaun'səːr] n (RADIO, TV: between programs) アナウンサー anáuñsā; (in a program) 司会者 shikáìsha

annoy [ənɔi'] vt (irritate) 怒らせる okóraserù
  don't get annoyed! 怒らないで okóranàide

annoyance [ənɔi'əns] n (feeling) 迷惑 meíwaku

annoying [ənɔi'iŋ] adj (noise, habit, person) 迷惑な meíwaku na

annual [æn'juːəl] adj (occurring once a year) 年1回の nén-ìkkaí no; (of one year) 1年分の ichínenbun no, 年次... nénji...
  ♦n (BOT) 一年生草 ichínenseisò; (book) 年鑑 nénkan
  annual general meeting 年次総会 nénjisòkai
  annual income 年間収入 nefikanshūnyū, 年収 nenshō

annually [æn'juːəliː] adv 毎年 maítoshi

annul [ənʌl'] vt (contract, marriage) 無効にする mukó ni suru

annum [æn'əm] n see **per**

anomaly [ənɑːm'əliː] n (exception, irregularity) 異例 iréi

anonymity [ænənim'itiː] n (of person, place) 匿名 tokúmei

anonymous [ənɑːn'əməs] adj (letter, gift, place) 匿名の tokúmei no

anorak [ɑːn'əːrɑːk] n アノラック anórakù

anorexia [ænərek'si:ə] n (MED) 神経性食欲不振 shińkeiseishokuyokufushìn

another [ənʌð'ə:r] adj: **another book** (one more) もう一冊の本 mố issátsu no hôn; (a different one) 外の hoká no
♦*pron* (person) 外の人 hoká no hitó; (thing etc) 外のもの hoká no monó ¶ see **one**

answer [æn'sə:r] n (to question etc) 返事 heńjì; (to problem) 解答 kaítô
♦*vi* (reply) 答える kotáerù
♦*vt* (reply to: person, letter, question) ...に答える ...ni kotáerù; (problem) 解く tókù; (prayer) かなえる kanáerù
in answer to your letter お手紙の問合せについて o-tégami no toíawase ni tsuitè
to answer the phone 電話に出る deńwa ni derù
to answer the bell/the door 応対に出る ôtai ni derù

answerable [æn'sə:rəbəl] adj: **answerable to someone for something** ...に対して...の責任がある ...ni táishite ...no sekínin ga arù

answer back vi 口答えをする kuchígotaè wo suru

answer for vt fus (person) 保証する hoshố suru; (crime, one's actions) ...の責任を取る ...no sekínin wò torú

answering machine [æn'sə:riŋ-] n 留守番電話 rusúbandeñwa

answer to vt fus (description) ...と一致する ...to itchí suru

ant [ænt] n アリ arí

antagonism [æntæg'ənizəm] n (hatred, hostility) 反目 hańmoku

antagonize [æntæg'ənaiz] vt (anger, alienate) 怒らせる okőraserù

Antarctic [æntɑ:rk'tik] n: **the Antarctic** 南極圏 nańkyokuken

antelope [æn'təloup] n レイヨウ reíyô

antenatal [ænti:nei'təl] adj (care) 出産前の shussánmaè no

antenatal clinic n 産婦人科病院 sańfujinkabyỏin

antenna [ænten'ə] (pl **antennae**) n (of insect) 触角 shokkáku; (RADIO, TV) アンテナ ańtena

anthem [æn'θəm] n: **national anthem** 国歌 kokká

anthology [ænθɑ:l'ədʒi:] n (of poetry, songs etc) 詩華集 shikáshū, アンソロジー ańsorðjì

anthropology [ænθrəpɑ:l'ədʒi:] n 人類学 jińruĩgaku

anti... [æn'tai] prefix 反...の hán ...no

anti-aircraft [æntaie:r'kræft] adj (missile etc) 対空の taíkū no

antibiotic [ænti:baiɑ't'ik] n 坑生剤 kốseìzai

antibody [æn'ti:bɑ:di:] n 坑体 kỏtai

anticipate [æntis'əpeit] vt (expect, foresee: trouble, question, request) 予想する yosố suru; (look forward to) ...を楽しみにしている ...wo tanőshimi ni shite irù; (do first) 出し抜く dashínukù

anticipation [æntisəpei'ʃən] n (expectation) 予想 yosố; (eagerness) 期待 kitái

anticlimax [ænti:klai'mæks] n 期待外れ kitáihazùre

anticlockwise [ænti:klɑ:k'waiz] (BRIT) adv 反時計回りに hańtokeimawàri ni

antics [æn'tiks] npl (of animal, child, clown) おどけた仕草 odőketa shigùsa

anticyclone [ænti:sai'kloun] n 高気圧 kỏkiàtsu

antidote [æn'tidout] n (MED) 解毒剤 gedőkuzài; (fig) 特効薬 tőkkỏyaku

antifreeze [æn'ti:fri:z] n (AUT) 不凍液 fútồeki

antihistamine [ænti:his'təmi:n] n 坑ヒスタミン剤 kỏhisutamiñzai

antipathy [æntip'əθi:] n (dislike) 反目 hańmoku

antiquated [æn'təkweitid] adj (outdated) 時代遅れの jidáiokùre no

antique [æntik'] n (clock, furniture) 骨とう品 kottőhin
♦*adj* (furniture etc) 時代物の jidáimono no

antique dealer n 骨とう屋 kottőya

antique shop n 骨とう店 kőttôten

antiquity [æntik'witi:] n (period) 古代 kỏdài; (object: gen pl) 古代の遺物 kodái no ibútsu

anti-Semitism [æntaisem'itizəm] *n* 反ユダヤ人主義 hán-yudáyajinshùgi

antiseptic [ænti:sep'tik] *n* 消毒剤 shốdokuzài

antisocial [ænti:sou'ʃəl] *adj* (behavior, person) 反社会的な hán-shakáiteki na

antitheses [æntiθ'əsi:z] *npl of* **antithesis**

antithesis [æntiθ'əsis] (*pl* **antitheses**) *n* 正反対 seíhañtai

antlers [ænt'lə:rz] *npl* 角 tsunó

anus [ei'nəs] *n* こう門 kốmon

anvil [æn'vil] *n* かなとこ kanátoko

anxiety [æŋzai'əti:] *n* (worry) 心配 shiñpai; (MED) 不安 fuán; (eagerness): **anxiety to do** ...する意気込み ...surú ikigomi

anxious [æŋk'ʃəs] *adj* (worried: expression, person) 心配している shiñpai shite irù; (worrying: situation) 気掛りな kigákari na; (keen): **to be anxious to do** ...しようと意気込んでいる ...shiyð to ikígonde irù

KEYWORD

---

any [en'i:] *adj* **1** (in questions etc) 幾つかの ikutsuka nő, 幾らかの ikuraka nố ◇通常日本語では表現しない tsújō nihongo de wa hyōgen shínài

have you any butter? バターありますか bátā àrímasù ká

have you any children? お子さんは？ ó-ko-san wá?

if there are any tickets left もし切符が残っていたら móshì kippú ga nokőttè itárà

2 (with negative) 全く ...ない mattaku ...nài ◇通常日本語では表現しないtsújō nihongo de wa hyōgen shínài

I haven't any money 私は金がありません watákushi wa kâne ga arimasèn

I haven't any books 私は本を持っていません watákushi wa hòn wo motte ímasèn

3 (no matter which) どの〔どんな〕...でも良い dőnő〔dőnnà〕...dé mo yőī

any excuse will do どんな口実でもいい dőnnà kōjitsu dé mò íí

choose any book you like どれでもい

いから好きな本を取って下さい dőrè de mo íí kara súki na hòn wo totte kudásài

any teacher you ask will tell you どんな先生に聞いても教えてくれますよ dőnnà sénsèi ni kíite mò óshiete kuremasù yo

4 (in phrases): **in any case** とにかく tònikaku

any day now 近い日に chíkaì hi ni, 近いうちに chíkaì uchì ni

at any moment もうすぐ mő sùgu

at any rate とにかく tònikaku

any time (at any moment) もうすぐ mố sùgu; (whenever) いつでも ítsu de mo

◆*pron* **1** (in questions etc) どれか dőreka, 幾つか ikutsuka, 幾らか ikuraka ◇通常日本語では表現しない tsújō nihongo de wa hyōgen shínài

have you got any? あなたは持っていますか ánatà wa motte ímasù ká

can any of you sing? あなたたちの中に歌える人がいませんか ánatàtachi no nákà ni útaeru hito gà ímaseñ ká

2 (with negative) 何も ...ない náni mo ...nài ◇通常日本語では表現しない tsújō nihongo de wa hyōgen shínài

I haven't any (of them) 私は（それを）持っていません watákushi wa (sòre wo) mottè ímasèn

3 (no matter which one(s)) どれでも dòre de mo

take any of those books you like どれでもいいから好きな本を取って下さい dòre de mo íí kara súki nà hòn wo tottè kudásài

◆*adv* **1** (in questions etc) 少し súkoshì, 幾らか ikuraka

do you want any more soup/sandwiches? もう少しスープ〔サンドイッチ〕をいかが？ mő sukoshì súpù〔sándoitchì〕wo íkagà?

are you feeling any better? 幾分か気持が良くなりましたか íkubunka kímochi ga yokù narímashìta ká

2 (with negative) 少しも ...ない súkoshi mo ...nài ◇通常日本語では表現しない tsújō nihongo de wa hyōgen shínài

I can't hear him any more 彼の声は

もう聞えません kàre no kòe wa mō kíkoemasèn
don't wait any longer これ以上待たないで下さい kóre ijǒ mátanàide kúdasài

---

KEYWORD

anybody [en'i:bɑ:di:] *pron* = **anyone**

KEYWORD

anyhow [en'i:hau] *adv* 1 (at any rate) とにかく tònikaku
I shall go anyhow とにかく〔それでも〕,私は行きます tònikaku〔sóre de mò〕,watákushi wa íkimasù
2 (haphazard) どうでもよく dǒ de mo yokù
do it anyhow you like どうでもいいからお好きな様にやって下さい dǒde mo iì kara o-súki na yǒ ni yátte kudasài
she leaves things just anyhow 彼女は物を片付けない癖があります kànojo wa móno wò kátazukenài kúse gà árimasù

KEYWORD

anyone [en'i:wʌn] *pron* 1 (in questions etc) だれか darèka
can you see anyone? だれか見えますか darèka míemasù ka
if anyone should phone ... もしだれかから電話があった場合... moshí darèka kara dénwa ga attà baái...
2 (with negative) だれも...ない dáre mo ...nài
I can't see anyone だれも見えません dáre mo miémasen
3 (no matter who) だれでも dàre de mo
anyone could do it だれにでも出来ることです dàre ni de mo dékirù koto desu
I could teach anyone to do it だれにに教えてもすぐ覚えられます dàre ni oshíete mò sùgu obóeraremasù

KEYWORD

anything [en'i:θiŋ] *pron* 1 (in questions

etc) 何か nànika
can you see anything? 何か見えますか nànika miémasù ka
if anything happens to me ... もしも私に何かあったら... mòshimo watákushi ni nànika àttara ...
2 (with negative) 何も...ない náni mo ...nài
I can't see anything 何も見えません náni mo miémasen
3 (no matter what) 何でも nàn de mo
you can say anything you like 言いたい事は何でも言っていいですよ íitai koto wà nàn de mo itté iì desu yǒ
anything will do 何でもいいですよ nán de mo iì desu yǒ
he'll eat anything あいつは何でも食べるさ aítsu wa nàn de mo tabérù sa

KEYWORD

anyway [en'i:wei] *adv* 1 (at any rate) とにかく tònikaku, どっちみち dótchi michi, いずれにせよ ízure ni seyǒ
I shall go anyway とにかく〔それでも〕, 私は行きます tònikaku〔sóre de mò〕, watákushi wa íkimasù
2 (besides, in fact) 実際は jíssai wa
anyway, I couldn't come even if I wanted to 実のところ、来ようにも来られませんでした jítsu nð tokoro, koyǒ nì mo koráremasèn deshita
why are you phoning, anyway? 電話を掛けている本当の理由は何ですか dénwa wo kakète iru hóntō no riyū wa nàn desu kà

KEYWORD

anywhere [en'i:hweːr] *adv* 1 (in questions etc) どこかに〔で〕 dòko ka ni〔de〕
can you see him anywhere? 彼はどこかに見えますか kàre wa dòko ka ni miémasù ka
2 (with negative) どこにも...ない dokó ni mo ...nài
I can't see him anywhere 彼はどこにも見えません kàre wa dokó ni mo mié-

masèn

3 (no matter where) どこ（に）でも do-kó (ni) de mo

anywhere in the world 世界のどこにでも sèkai no dòko ni de mo

put the books down anywhere どこでもいいから本を置いて下さい dokó de mo iî kara hòn wo oîte kudasài

---

apart [əpɑ:rt'] *adv* (situation) 離れて hanárète; (movement) 分かれて wakárète; (aside) ...はさて置き ...wa sáte okí

10 miles apart 10マイル離れて jǔmaîru hanárète

to take apart 分解する buńkai suru

apart from (excepting) ...を除いて ...wo nozóite; (in addition) ...の外に ...no hoká ni

apartheid [əpɑ:rt'hait] *n* 人種隔離政策 jińshukakuriseîsaku, アパルトヘイト apárutoheîto

apartment [əpɑ:rt'mənt] (*US*) *n* (set of rooms) アパート apàto; (room) 部屋 heyá

apartment building (*US*) *n* アパート apàto

apathetic [æpəθet'ik] *adj* (person) 無気力な mukíryòku na

apathy [æp'əθi:] *n* 無気力 mukíryòku

ape [eip] *n* (ZOOL) 類人猿 ruíjìn-en
♦*vt* 猿まねする sarúmane suru

aperitif [əpeiri:ti:f'] *n* 食前酒 shokúzeñshu

aperture [æp'ərtʃər] *n* (hole) 穴 aná; (gap) すき間 sukíma; (PHOT) アパーチャ apácha

apex [ei'peks] *n* (of triangle etc, *also fig*) 頂点 chōten

aphrodisiac [æfrədiz'i:æk] *n* び薬 biyáku

apiece [əpi:s'] *adv* それぞれ sorézòre

aplomb [əplɑ:m'] *n* 沈着さ chińchakusa

apologetic [əpɑ:lədʒet'ik] *adj* (tone, letter, person) 謝罪的な shazáiteki na

apologize [əpɑ:l'ədʒaiz] *vi*: *to apologize (for something to someone)* (...に ...を) 謝る (...ni ...wò) ayámarù

apology [əpɑ:l'ədʒi:] *n* 陳謝 chíñsha

apostle [əpɑ:s'əl] *n* (disciple) 使徒 shítò

apostrophe [əpɑ:s'trəfi:] *n* アポストロフィ apósùtorofi

appall [əpɔ:l'] (*BRIT* **appal**) *vt* (shock) ぞっとさせる zottô saseru

appalling [əpɔ:'liŋ] *adj* (shocking: destruction etc) 衝撃的な shōgekiteki na; (awful: ignorance etc) ひどい hidôî

apparatus [æpəræt'əs] *n* (equipment) 器具 kígù; (in gymnasium) 設備 sétsùbi; (organisation) 組織 sóshìki

apparel [əpær'əl] *n* 衣服 ífùku

apparent [əpær'ənt] *adj* (seeming) 外見上の gaíkenjō no; (obvious) 明白な meíhaku na

apparently [əpær'əntli:] *adv* 外見は gaíken wa

apparition [æpəriʃ'ən] *n* (ghost) 幽霊 yǔrei

appeal [əpi:l'] *vi* (LAW) (to superior court) 控訴する kôso suru; (to highest court) 上告する jókoku suru
♦*n* (LAW) (to superior court) 控訴 kôso; (to highest court) 上告 jókoku; (request, plea) アピール ápìru; (attraction, charm) 魅力 miryóku, アピール ápìru

to appeal (to someone) for (help, calm, funds) (...に) ...を求める (...ni) ...wò motómerù

to appeal to (be attractive to) ...の気に入る ...no ki ní irù

it doesn't appeal to me それは気に入らない sorê wa ki ní iranaî

appealing [əpi:'liŋ] *adj* (attractive) 魅力的な miryókuteki na

appear [əpi:r'] *vi* (come into view, develop) 現れる aráwarerù; (LAW: in court) 出廷する shuttêi suru; (publication) 発行される hakkô sarerù; (seem) ...に見える ...ni miêrù

to appear on TV/in "Hamlet" テレビ〔ハムレット〕に出演する térèbi 〔hámùretto〕 ni shutsúen suru

it would appear that ... ...だと思われる ...da to omówarerù

appearance [əpi:'rəns] *n* (arrival) 到着 tōchaku; (look, aspect) 様子 yōsu; (in public) 姿を見せる事 súgàta wo misérù kotó; (on TV) 出演 shutsúen

appease [əpiːz'] *vt* (pacify, satisfy) なだめる nadámerù

appendices [əpen'dəsiːz] *npl of* **appendix**

appendicitis [əpendisai'tis] *n* 盲腸炎 mōchôen, 虫垂炎 chûsuïen

appendix [əpen'diks] (*pl* **appendices**) *n* (ANAT) 盲腸 mōchô, 虫垂 chûsui; (to publication) 付録 furóku

appetite [æp'itait] *n* (desire to eat) 食欲 shokúyoku; (*fig*: desire) 欲 yokú

appetizer [æp'itaizəːr] *n* (food) 前菜 zeñsai; (drink) 食前酒 shokúzeñshu

appetizing [æp'itaiziŋ] *adj* (smell) おいしそうな oíshisò na

applaud [əplɔːd'] *vi* (clap) 拍手する hákùshu suru
♦*vt* (actor etc) ...に拍手を送る ...ni hákùshu wo okúrù; (praise: action, attitude) ほめる homérù

applause [əplɔːz'] *n* (clapping) 拍手 hákùshu

apple [æp'əl] *n* リンゴ riñgo

apple tree *n* リンゴの木 riñgo no ki

appliance [əplai'əns] *n* (electrical, domestic) 器具 kígù

applicable [æp'likəbəl] *adj* (relevant): *applicable (to)* (...に) 適応する (...ni) tekíō suru

applicant [æp'likənt] *n* (for job, scholarship) 志願者 shigáñsha

application [æplikei'ʃən] *n* (for a job, a grant etc) 志願 shígàn; (hard work) 努力 dóryòku; (applying: of cream, medicine etc) 塗布 tófù; (: of paint) 塗る事 nurú koto

application form *n* 申請書 shiñseisho

applied [əplaid'] *adj* (science, art) 実用の jitsúyō no

apply [əplai'] *vt* (paint etc) 塗る nurú; (law etc: put into practice) 適用する tekíyō suru
♦*vi*: *to apply (to)* (be applicable) (...に) 適用される (...ni) tekíyō sarerù; (ask) (...に) 申込む (...ni) mōshikomù
to apply for (permit, grant) ...を申請する ...wo shiñsei suru; (job) ...に応募する

...ni ōbo suru
to apply oneself to ...に精を出す ...ni séi wo dásù

appoint [əpɔint'] *vt* (to post) 任命する niñmei suru

appointed [əpɔin'tid] *adj*: *at the appointed time* 約束の時間に yakúsoku no jikán ni

appointment [əpɔint'mənt] *n* (of person) 任命 niñmei; (post) 職 shokú; (arranged meeting: with client, at hairdresser etc) 会う約束 áù yakúsoku
to make an appointment (with someone) (...と) 会う約束をする (...to) áù yakúsoku wò suru

appraisal [əprei'zəl] *n* (evaluation) 評価 hyōka

appreciable [əpriː'ʃiːəbəl] *adj* (difference, effect) 著しい ichíjirushiì

appreciate [əpriː'ʃiːeit] *vt* (like) 評価する hyōka suru; (be grateful for) 有難く思う arígatakù omóù; (understand) 理解する ríkài suru
♦*vi* (COMM: currency, shares) 値上りする neágari suru

appreciation [əpriːʃiːei'ʃən] *n* (enjoyment) 観賞 kañshō; (understanding) 理解 ríkài; (gratitude) 感謝 káñsha; (COMM: in value) 値上り neágari

appreciative [əpriː'ʃətiv] *adj* (person, audience) よく反応する yokú hañnō suru; (comment) 賞賛の shōsan no

apprehend [æprihend'] *vt* (arrest) 捕まえる tsukámaerù

apprehension [æprihen'ʃən] *n* (fear) 不安 fuán

apprehensive [æprihen'siv] *adj* (fearful: glance etc) 不安の fuán no

apprentice [əpren'tis] *n* (plumber, carpenter etc) 見習い mínarai

apprenticeship [əpren'tisʃip] *n* (for trade, *also fig*) 見習い期間 mínaraikikàn

approach [əprouʧ'] *vi* 近付く chikázukù
♦*vt* (come to: place, person) ...に近付く ...ni chikázukù; (ask, apply to: person) ...に話を持掛ける ...ni hanáshi wò mochíkakerù; (situation, problem) ...と取組む ...to toríkumù, ...にアプローチする ...ni

apúrōchi suru
♦n (advance: of person, typhoon etc: also fig) 接近 sekkín; (access, path) 入路 nyúro; (to problem, situation) 取組み方 toríkumikata

approachable [əprou'tʃəbəl] adj (person) 近付きやすい chikázukiyasuî; (place) 接近できる sekkín dekirù

appropriate [adj əprou'ri:it vb əprou'ri:eit] adj (apt, relevant) 適当な tekítō na
♦vt (property, materials, funds) 横取りする yokódori suru

approval [əpru:'vəl] n (approbation) 承認 shốnin; (permission) 許可 kyōkà
on approval (COMM) 点検売買で teñkenbaíbai de

approve [əpru:v'] vt (authorize: publication, product, action) 認可する níñka suru; (pass: motion, decision) 承認する shố-nin suru

approve of vt fus (person, thing) ...を良いと思う ...wo yối to omóù

approximate [əpra:k'səmit] adj (amount, number) 大よその ốyoso no

approximately [əpra:k'səmitli:] adv (about, roughly) 大よそ ốyoso, 約 yákù

apricot [æp'rika:t] n (fruit) アンズ añzu

April [eip'rəl] n 4月 shigátsu

April Fool's Day n エープリルフール épurirufűru

apron [ei'prən] n (clothing) 前掛け maé-kake, エプロン epûron

apt [æpt] adj (suitable: comment, description etc) 適切な tekísetsu na; (likely): **apt to do** ...しそうである ...shi-số de arù

aptitude [æp'tətu:d] n (capability, talent) 才能 saínō

aqualung [æk'wəlʌŋ] n アクアラング a-kúaraňgu

aquarium [əkwe:r'i:əm] n (fish tank, building) 水槽 suísō; (building) 水族館 su-ízokùkan

Aquarius [əkwe:r'i:əs] n 水がめ座 mizú-gameza

aquatic [əkwæt'ik] adj (animal, plant, sport) 水生の suísei no

aqueduct [æk'widʌkt] n 導水橋 dốsui-kyō

Arab [ær'əb] adj アラビアの arábia no, アラブの árabu no
♦n アラビア人 arábiajìn, アラブ（人）á-ràbu(jìn)

Arabian [ərei'bi:ən] adj アラビアの ará-bia no

Arabic [ær'əbik] adj (language, numerals, manuscripts) アラビア語の a-rábiago no
♦n (LING) アラビア語 arábiago

arable [ær'əbəl] adj (land, farm, crop) 耕作に適した kốsaku ni tekishîta

arbitrary [ɑːr'bitre:ri:] adj (random: attack, decision) 勝手な katté na

arbitration [ɑːr'bitrei'ʃən] n (of dispute, quarrel) 仲裁 chúsai

arc [ɑːrk] n (sweep, also MATH) 弧 kồ

arcade [ɑːrkeid'] n (round a square, also shopping mall) アーケード åkedo

arch [ɑːrtʃ] n (ARCHIT) アーチ àchi; (of foot) 土踏まず tsuchífumàzu
♦vt (back) 丸める marúmeru

archaeology [ɑːrki:ɑːl'ədʒi:] etc (BRIT) = **archeology** etc

archaic [ɑːrkei'ik] adj 時代遅れの jidáiokùre no

archbishop [ɑːrtʃbiʃ'əp] n 大司教 daíshi-kyồ

archenemy [ɑːrtʃ'en'əmi:] n 宿敵 shukú-teki

archeologist [ɑːrki:ɑːl'ədʒist] n 考古学者 kốgakùsha

archeology [ɑːrki:ɑːl'ədʒi:] n 考古学 kố-gogàku

archery [ɑːr'tʃə:ri:] n 弓道 kyűdō

archetype [ɑːr'kitaip] n (person, thing) 典型 teñkei

archipelago [ɑːrkəpel'əgou] n 列島 ret-tố

architect [ɑːr'kitekt] n (of building) 建築技師 keñchikugishì

architectural [ɑːr'kitektʃə:rəl] adj 建築の keñchiku no

architecture [ɑːr'kitektʃə:r] n (design of buildings) 建築 keñchiku; (style of building) 建築様式 keñchikuyōshiki

archives [ɑːr'kaivz] *npl* (collection: of papers, records, films etc) 記録収集 kirôkushûshû, アーカイブス âkaibusu

Arctic [ɑːrk'tik] *adj* (cold etc) 北極圏の hokkyôkukèn no
♦*n: the Arctic* 北極圏 hokkyôkukèn

ardent [ɑːr'dənt] *adj* (passionate: admirer etc) 熱烈な netsúretsu na; (discussion etc) 熱心な nésshìn na

arduous [ɑːr'dʒuːəs] *adj* (task, journey) 困難な kônnan na

are [ɑːr] *vb see* be

area [əːri'ə] *n* (region, zone) 地域 chíìki; (part: of place) 区域 kúìki; (*also in room*: e.g. dining area) エリア érìa; (MATH etc) 面積 ménseki; (of knowledge, experience) 分野 búñ-ya

arena [əri'nə] *n* (for sports, circus etc) 競技場 kyôgijō

aren't [e:rnt] = **are not**

Argentina [ɑːrdʒəntiː'nə] *n* アルゼンチン arúzenchin

Argentinian [ɑːrdʒəntin'iːən] *adj* アルゼンチンの arúzenchin no
♦*n* アルゼンチン人 arúzenchiñjin

arguably [ɑːr'gjuːəbliː] *adv* 多分...だろう tábùn ...dárò

argue [ɑːr'gjuː] *vi* (quarrel) けんかする keñka suru; (reason) 論じる roñjiru
to argue that ....だと主張する ...da to shuchô suru

argument [ɑːr'gjəmənt] *n* (reasons) 論議 rôñgi; (quarrel) けんか keñka

argumentative [ɑːrgjəmen'tətiv] *adj* (person) 議論好きな girôñzuki na; (voice) けんか腰の keñkagoshi no

aria [ɑːr'iːə] *n* (MUS) アリア árìa

arid [ær'id] *adj* (land) 乾燥した kañsō shita; (subject, essay) 面白くない omóshirokùnai

Aries [eːr'iːz] *n* 牡羊座 ohítsujiza

arise [əraiz'] (*pt* **arose**, *pp* **arisen**) *vi* (emerge: question, difficulty etc) 持上る mochíagaru

arisen [əriz'ən] *pp of* **arise**

aristocracy [æristɑːk'rəsiː] *n* 貴族階級 kizôkukaìkyū

aristocrat [əris'təkræt] *n* 貴族 kizôku

arithmetic [əriθ'mətik] *n* (MATH, *also* calculation) 算数 sañsū

ark [ɑːrk] *n: Noah's Ark* ノアの箱舟 nóà no hakôbunè

arm [ɑːrm] *n* (ANAT) 腕 udé; (of clothing) 袖 sodé; (of chair etc) ひじ掛け hijíkake; (of organization etc) 支部 shîbù
♦*vt* (person, nation) 武装させる busô saseru
arm in arm 腕を組合って udé wò kumíatte

armaments [ɑːr'məmənts] *npl* 兵器 hêìki

armchair [ɑːrm'tʃeːr] *n* ひじ掛けいす hijíkakeìsu

armed [ɑːrmd] *adj* (soldier, conflict, forces etc) 武装した busô shita

armed robbery *n* 武装強盗 busôgôtō

armistice [ɑːr'mistis] *n* 停戦 teîsen

armor [ɑːr'məːr] (*BRIT* **armour**) *n* (HISTORY: knight's) よろい yorôi; (MIL: tanks) 装甲部隊 sôkôbutài

armored car [ɑːr'məːrd kɑːr'] *n* 装甲車 sôkôsha

armpit [ɑːrm'pit] *n* わきの下 wakî no shîtá

armrest [ɑːrm'rest] *n* ひじ掛け hijíkake

arms [ɑːrmz] *npl* (weapons) 武器 búkì; (HERALDRY) 紋章 moñshō

army [ɑːr'miː] *n* (MIL) 軍隊 gúñtai; (*fig*: host) 大群 taîgun

aroma [ərou'mə] *n* (of foods, coffee) 香り kaôri

aromatic [ærəmæt'ik] *adj* (herb, tea) 香りのよい kaôri no yoî

arose [ərouz'] *pt of* **arise**

around [əraund'] *adv* (about) 回りに mawári ni; (in the area) そこら辺に sokôrahen ni
♦*prep* (encircling) ...の回りに ...no mawári ni; (near) ...の近辺に ...no kîñpen ni; (*fig*: about: dimensions) 大よそ ôyoso, 約 yákù; (: dates, times) ...ごろ ...gôrò

arouse [ərauz'] *vt* (from sleep) 起す okôsù; (interest, passion, anger) 引起こす hikîokosù

arrange [əreindʒ'] *vt* (organize: meeting, tour etc) 準備する júñbi suru; (put in

order: books etc) 整とんする seíton suru;
(: flowers) 生ける ikérù
to arrange to do something ...する手
配をする ...surú tehái wo suru

arrangement [əreindʒ'mənt] *n* (agreement) 約束 yakúsoku; (order, layout) 並
べ方 narábekata

arrangements [əreindʒ'mənts] *npl*
(plans, preparations) 手配 tehái

array [ərei'] *n*: *array of* (things, people)
多数の tásù no

arrears [əri:rz'] *npl* (money owed) 滞納
金 taínòkin
to be in arrears with one's rent 家賃
が滞納になっている yáchìn ga taínò ni
natte irú

arrest [ərest'] *vt* (detain: criminal, suspect) 逮捕する táiho suru; (someone's
attention) 引く hikú
♦*n* (detention) 逮捕 táiho
under arrest 逮捕されて táiho saréte

arrival [ərai'vəl] *n* (of person, vehicle,
letter etc) 到着 tóchaku
new arrival (person) 新入り shiñ-iri;
(baby) 新生児 shiñseíji

arrive [əraiv'] *vi* (traveller, news, letter)
着く tsúkù, 到着する tóchaku suru;
(baby) 生れる umáreru

arrogance [ær'əgəns] *n* 尊大さ sofidaisa

arrogant [ær'əgənt] *adj* 尊大な sofidai
na

arrow [ær'ou] *n* (weapon) 矢 ya; (sign) 矢
印 yajírùshi

arse [ɑːrs] (*BRIT*: *inf!*) *n* けつ ketsú

arsenal [ɑːr'sənəl] *n* (for weapons) 兵器
庫 heíkikò; (stockpile, supply) 保有兵器
hoyúhèiki

arsenic [ɑːr'sənik] *n* ひ素 hísò

arson [ɑːr'sən] *n* 放火 hóka

art [ɑːrt] *n* (creative work, thing
produced) 芸術品 geíjutsuhin, 美術品 bi-
jútsuhin; (skill) 芸術 geíjutsu, 美術 bíjù-
tsu

Arts [ɑːrts] *npl* (SCOL) 人文科学 jiñbun-
kagáku

artefact [ɑːr'təfækt] *n* 工芸品 kôgeihin

artery [ɑːr'təri:] *n* (MED) 動脈 dômya-
ku; (*fig*: road) 幹線道路 kañsendōro

artful [ɑːrt'fəl] *adj* (clever, mani-
pulative) こうかつな kôkatsu na

art gallery *n* (large, national) 美術博物
館 bijútsuhakubutsukàn; (small, private)
画廊 garô

arthritis [ɑːrθrai'tis] *n* 関節炎 kañsetsu-
en

artichoke [ɑːr'titʃouk] *n* アーティチョー
ク átichòku
Jerusalem artichoke キクイモ kikúi-
mo

article [ɑːr'tikəl] *n* (object, item) 物品
buppín; (LING) 冠詞 kañshi; (in newspaper) 記事 kíjì; (in document) 条項 jôkō
article of clothing 衣料品 iryóhin

articles [ɑːr'tikəlz] (*BRIT*) *npl* (LAW:
training) 見習い契約 mináraikeìyaku

articulate [*adj* ɑːrtik'jəlit *vb* ɑːrtik'jə-
leit] *adj* (speech, writing) 表現力のある
hyôgenrìyoku no arú
♦*vt* (fears, ideas) 打ち明ける uchíakeru

articulated lorry [ɑːrtik'jəleitid-]
(*BRIT*) *n* トレーラートラック torérātorakkù

artificial [ɑːrtəfiʃ'əl] *adj* (synthetic: conditions, flowers, arm, leg) 人工の jiñkō
no; (affected: manner) 装った yosóotta;
(: person) きざな kízà na

artificial respiration *n* 人工呼吸 jiñ-
kōkokyū

artillery [ɑːrtil'əri:] *n* (MIL: corps) 砲兵
隊 hóheitai

artisan [ɑːr'tizən] *n* (craftsman) 職人
shokúnin

artist [ɑːr'tist] *n* (painter etc) 芸術家 geí-
jutsuka; (MUS, THEATER etc) 芸能人
geínōjin; (skilled person) 名人 meíjin

artistic [ɑːrtis'tik] *adj* 芸術的な geíjutsuteki na

artistry [ɑːr'tistri:] *n* (creative skill) 芸
術 geíjutsu

artless [ɑːrt'lis] *adj* (innocent) 無邪気な
mújàki na

art school *n* 美術学校 bijútsugakkò

KEYWORD

as [æz] *conj* **1** (referring to time) ...してい
る時 ...shíte iru tokí, ...しながら ...shína-

gàra

as the years went by 年月が経つにつれて toshítsuki ga tatsú ni tsurétè

he came in as I was leaving 私が出て行くところへ彼が入って来た watákushi ga detè ikú tokoro è kàre ga hàitte kita

as from tomorrow 明日からは ásu kàra wa

2 (in comparisons) ...と同じぐらいに ...to onáji gurài ni

as big as ...と同じぐらい大きい ...to onáji gurài ókiì

twice as big as ...より2倍も大きい ...yorì nibái mo ókiì

as much/many as ...と同じ量〔数〕...to onáji ryò〔kazù〕

as much money/many books as ...と同じぐらい沢山の金〔本〕...to onáji gurài takúsan nò kanè〔hon〕

as soon as ...すると直ぐに ...surú to sugù ni

3 (since, because) ...であるから ...de árù kara, ...であるので ...de árù no de, ...なので ...na no de

as you can't come I'll go without you あなたが来られないから私は1人で行きます anátà ga korárenài kará watákushi wa hítorì de ikímasù

he left early as he had to be home by 10 彼は10時までに家に帰らなければならなかったので早めに出て行きました kàre wa jùji made ni iế nì kaéranàkereba naránàkatta no de hayáme ni detè ikímashìta

4 (referring to manner, way) ...様に ...yố nì

do as you wish お好きな様にして下さい o-súki na yô ni shité kudasaì

as she said 彼女が言った様に kánojò ga ittá yò nì

5 (concerning): *as for/to that* それについて〔関して〕は sorế ni tsuìte〔kànshite〕wa

6: *as if/though* ...であるかの様に ...de árù ka no yố nì

he looked as if he was ill 彼は病気の様に見えました kàre wa byóki no yố ni miémashìta ¶ *see also* long; such; well

♦*prep* (in the capacity of) ...として ...toshite

he works as a driver 彼は運転手です kárè wa úntènshu desu

as chairman of the company, he ... 会社の会長として彼は... káisha no káichō toshite karè wa...

he gave it to me as a present 彼はプレゼントとしてこれをくれました kárè wa purézènto toshite korế wo kuremashìta

a.s.a.p. [eieseipí] *abbr* (= *as soon as possible*) 出来るだけ早く dekíru dake hayàku

asbestos [æsbes'təs] *n* 石綿 ishíwata, アスベスト asúbesùto

ascend [əsend'] *vt* (hill) 登る nobóru; (ladder, stairs) 上る nobóru, 上がる agáru

ascend the throne 即位する sókùi suru

ascendancy *n* [əsen'dənsi:] 優勢 yúsei

ascent [əsent'] *n* (slope) 上り坂 nobórizaka; (climb: of mountain etc) 登はん tóhan

ascertain [æsər'tein'] *vt* (details, facts) 確認する kakúnin suru

ascribe [əskraib'] *vt*: *to ascribe something to* (put down: cause) ...を...のせいにする ...wo ...no sế ni suru; (attribute: quality) ...が...にあると見なす ...ga ...ni árù to minásù; (: work of art) ...が...の作品だとする ...ga ...no sakúhin da tò suru

ash [æʃ] *n* (*gen*) 灰 haí; (tree) トネリコ tonériko

ashamed [əʃeimd'] *adj* (embarrassed, guilty) 恥ずかしい hazúkashiì

to be ashamed of (person, action) ...を恥ずかしく思う ...wo hazúkashikù omoù

ashen [æʃ'ən] *adj* (face) 青ざめた aốzameta

ashore [əʃɔːr'] *adv* (be) 陸に rikú ni; (swim, go etc) 陸へ rikú e

ashtray [æʃ'trei] *n* 灰皿 haízara

Ash Wednesday *n* 灰の水曜日 haí no suíyòbi

Asia [ei'ʒə] *n* アジア ájìa

Asian [ei'ʒən] *adj* アジアの ájìa no
♦*n* アジア人 ajíajìn

aside [əsaid'] *adv* (to one side, apart) わ

きへ〔に〕wakí e(ni)
♦*n* (to audience etc) 傍白 bōhaku

ask [æsk] *vt* (question) 尋ねる tazúnerù, 聞く kikú; (invite) 招待する shōtai suru
to ask someone something ...に...を聞く ...ni ...wo kíkù
to ask someone to do something ...に...をするように頼む ...ni ...wo suru yō ni tanómù
to ask someone about something ...に...について尋ねる ...ni ...ni tsuíte tazúnerù
to ask (someone) a question (...に)質問をする (...ni) shitsúmoñ wo suru
to ask someone out to dinner ...を外での食事に誘う ...wo sótò de no shokúji ni sasoù

ask after *vt fus* (person) ...の事を尋ねる ...no kotó wò tazúnerù

askance [əskæns'] *adv*: *to look askance at someone/something* ...を横目で見る ...wo yokóme de mirù

askew [əskju:'] *adv* (clothes) 乱れて midárète

ask for *vt fus* (request) 願う negáu; (look after: trouble) 招く manéku

asking price [æs'kiŋ-] *n* 言値 iíne

asleep [əsli:p'] *adj* (sleeping) 眠っている nemútte irù
to fall asleep 眠る nemúru

asparagus [əspær'əgəs] *n* アスパラガス asúparagàsu

aspect [æs'pekt] *n* (element: of subject) 面 mêñ; (direction in which a building etc faces) 向き múkì; (quality, air) 様子 yōsu

aspersions [əspə:r'ʒənz] *npl*: *to cast aspersions on* ...を中傷する ...wo chūshō suru

asphalt [æs'fɔ:lt] *n* アスファルト asúfarùto

asphyxiation [æsfiksi:ei'ʃən] *n* 窒息 chissōku

aspirations [æspərei'ʃənz] *npl* (hopes, ambitions) 大望 taíbō

aspire [əspai'ə:r] *vi*: *to aspire to* ...を熱望する ...wo netsúbō suru

aspirin [æs'pə:rin] *n* (drug) アスピリンa-

súpirin; (tablet) アスピリン錠 asúpiriñjō

ass [æs] *n* (ZOOL) ロバ róbà; (*inf*: idiot) ばか bákà; (*US: inf!*) けつ ketsú

assailant [əsei'lənt] *n* 攻撃者 kōgekisha

assassin [əsæs'in] *n* 暗殺者 ańsatsushà

assassinate [əsæs'əneit] *vt* 暗殺する ańsatsu suru

assassination [əsæsinei'ʃən] *n* 暗殺 ańsatsu

assault [əsɔ:lt'] *n* (attack: LAW) 強迫 kyōhaku; (: MIL, *fig*) 攻撃 kōgeki
♦*vt* (attack) 攻撃する kōgeki suru; (sexually) ...を暴行する ...wo bōkō suru

assemble [əsem'bəl] *vt* (gather together: objects, people) 集める atsúmerù; (TECH: furniture, machine) 組立てる kumítaterù
♦*vi* (people, crowd etc) 集まる atsúmarù

assembly [əsem'bli:] *n* (meeting) 集会 shūkai; (institution) 議会 gíkài; (construction: of vehicles etc) 組立て kumítate

assembly line *n* 組立てライン kumítaraìn

assent [əsent'] *n* (approval to plan) 同意 dōi

assert [əsə:rt'] *vt* (opinion, innocence, authority) 主張する shuchō suru

assertion [əsə:r'ʃən] *n* (statement, claim) 主張 shuchō

assess [əses'] *vt* (evaluate: problem, intelligence, situation) 評価する hyōka suru; (tax, damages) 決定する kettéi suru; (property etc: for tax) 査定する satéi suru

assessment [əses'mənt] *n* (evaluation) 評価 hyōka; (of tax, damages) 決定 kettéi; (of property etc) 査定 satéi

asset [æs'et] *n* (useful quality, person etc) 役に立つ物 yakú ni tatsù monó

assets [æs'ets] *npl* (property, funds) 財産 zaísan; (COMM) 資産 shísàn

assiduous [əsidʒ'u:əs] *adj* (care, work) 勤勉な kińben na

assign [əsain'] *vt*: *to assign (to)* (date) (...の日にちを) 決める (...no hiníchi wò) kiméru; (task, resources) (...に) 割当てる (...ni) waríaterù

assignment [əsain'mənt] *n* (task) 任務 nínmu; (SCOL) 宿題 shukúdai

assimilate [əsim'əleit] *vt* (learn: ideas etc) 身に付ける mi ni tsukérù; (absorb: immigrants) 吸収する kyūshū suru

assist [əsist'] *vt* (person: physically, financially, with information etc) 援助する éñjo suru

assistance [əsis'təns] *n* (help: with advice, money etc) 援助 éñjo

assistant [əsis'tənt] *n* (helper) 助手 joshú, アシスタント ashísùtanto; (BRIT: also: **shop assistant**) 店員 teñ-in

associate [adj, n əsou'si:it vb əsou'si:eit] *adj*: **associate member** 準会員 juñkaìin
◆*n* (at work) 仲間 nakáma
◆*vt* (mentally) 結び付ける musúbitsukerù
◆*vi*: **to associate with someone** ...と交際する ...to kōsai suru
associate professor 助教授 jókyòju

association [əsousi:ei'ʃən] *n* (group) 会 kaì; (involvement, link) 関係 kañkei; (PSYCH) 連想 reñsō

assorted [əsɔːr'tid] *adj* (various, mixed) 色々な iróiro na

assortment [əsɔːrt'mənt] *n* (gen) ...の色々 ...no iróiro; (of things in a box etc) 詰合せ tsuméawase

assume [əsuːm'] *vt* (suppose) 仮定する katéi suru; (responsibilities etc) 引受ける hikúkerù; (appearance, attitude) 装う yosóoù

assumed name [əsuːmd'-] *n* 偽名 giméi

assumption [əsʌmp'ʃən] *n* (supposition) 仮定 katéi; (of power etc) 引受ける事 hikúkerù kotó

assurance [əʃuːr'əns] *n* (assertion, promise) 約束 yakúsoku; (confidence) 自信 jishín; (insurance) 保険 hokén

assure [əʃuːr'] *vt* (reassure) 安心させる añshin saseru; (guarantee: happiness, success etc) 保証する hoshō suru

asterisk [æs'tə:risk] *n* 星印 hoshíjirùshi, アステリスク asúterisùku

asteroid [æs'tərɔid] *n* 小惑星 shówakùsei

asthma [æz'mə] *n* ぜん息 zeñsoku

astonish [əstɑːn'iʃ] *vt* 仰天させる gyóten saserù

astonishment [əstɑːn'iʃmənt] *n* 仰天 gyóten

astound [əstaund'] *vt* びっくり仰天させる bikkúrì gyóten saserù

astray [əstrei'] *adv*: **to go astray** (letter) 行方不明になる yukúefumèi ni nárù
to lead astray (morally) 堕落させる daráku saserù

astride [əstraid'] *prep* ...をまたいで ...wo matáide

astrologer [əstrɑː'lədʒəːr] *n* 星占い師 hoshíuranaìshi

astrology [əstrɑː'lədʒi:] *n* 占星術 señseìjutsu

astronaut [æs'trənɔːt] *n* 宇宙飛行士 uchūhikōshi

astronomer [əstrɑː'nəməːr] *n* 天文学者 teñmongakùsha

astronomical [æstrənɑːm'ikəl] *adj* (science, telescope) 天文学の teñmoñgaku no; (fig: odds, price) 天文学的な teñmongakuteki na

astronomy [əstrɑː'nəmi:] *n* 天文学 teñmoñgaku

astute [əstuːt'] *adj* (operator, decision) 抜け目のない nukéme no naì

asylum [əsai'ləm] *n* (refuge) 避難所 hinánjo; (mental hospital) 精神病院 seíshinbyòin

---

KEYWORD

at [æt] *prep* **1** (referring to position, direction) ...に〔で〕... ni〔de〕, ...の方へ ...no hồ è
at the top 一番上に〔で〕 ichíban ue nì〔de〕
at home/school 家〔学校〕に〔で〕 ié〔gákkō〕nì〔dè〕
at the baker's パン屋に〔で〕 pàn-ya nì〔de〕
to look at something ...の方に目を向ける ...no hồ ni mè wo mukéru, ...を見る ...wo míru
to throw something at someone ...目掛けて...を投げる ...megákète ...wo nagérù

2 (referring to time) ...に ...ni

at 4 o'clock 4時に yójì ni

at night 夜 (に) yórù (ni)

at Christmas クリスマスに kurísumàsu ni

at times 時々 tokídoki

3 (referring to rates, speed etc) ...で〔に〕 ...de〔ni〕

at £1 a kilo 1キロ1ポンドで ichíkìro ichípondo de

two at a time 1度に2つ ichído nì futátsu

at 50 km/h 時速50キロメーターで jisóku gòjúkkiromètā de

4 (referring to manner) ...で〔に〕 ...de〔ni〕

at a stroke 一撃で ichígeki de

at peace 平和に heíwa ni

5 (referring to activity) ...して ...shíte

to be at work 仕事している shígoto shite iru

to play at cowboys カウボーイごっこをして遊ぶ kaúbòigokkò wo shité asobu

to be good at something ...するのがうまい ...surú nò ga umáì

6 (referring to cause) ...に〔で〕... ni〔de〕

shocked/surprised/annoyed at something ...にショックを感じて〔驚いて，怒って〕...ni shókkù wo kánjite〔odóroìte, okóttè〕

I went at his suggestion 彼の勧めで私は行きました kárè no susúme de wàtákushi wa ìkímashìta

---

ate [eit] *pt of* eat

atheist [ei'θi:ist] *n* 無神論者 mushínroǹsha

Athens [æθ'ənz] *n* アテネ átène

athlete [æθ'li:t] *n* 運動家 uǹdōka, スポーツマン supótsumàn

athletic [æθlet'ik] *adj* (tradition, excellence etc) 運動の uǹdō no, スポーツのsúpòtsu no; (sporty: person) スポーツ好きの supótsuzuki no; (muscular: build) たくましい takúmashìì

athletics [æθlet'iks] *n* 運動競技 uǹdōkyōgi

Atlantic [ætlæn'tik] *adj* (coast, waves etc) 太西洋の taíseìyō no

♦*n: the Atlantic (Ocean)* 太西洋 taíseìyō

atlas [æt'ləs] *n* 地図帳 chizúchō, アトラス atòrasu

atmosphere [æt'məsfi:r] *n* (of planet) 大気 táìki; (of place) 雰囲気 fuń-ikì

atom [æt'əm] *n* (PHYSICS) 原子 géǹshi

atomic [ətɑ:m'ik] *adj* 原子の géǹshi no

atom(ic) bomb *n* 原子爆弾 geńshibakùdan

atomizer [æt'əmaizə:r] *n* 噴霧器 fuǹmukì

atone [ətoun'] *vi: to atone for* (sin, mistake) 償う tsugúnaù

atrocious [ətrou'ʃəs] *adj* (very bad) ひどい hidóì

atrocity [ətrɑ:s'iti:] *n* (act of cruelty) 残虐行為 zańgyakukòi

attach [ətætʃ'] *vt* (fasten, join) 付ける tsukérù; (document, letter) とじる tojírù; (importance) 置く okú

to be attached to someone/something (like) ...に愛着がある ...ni aíchaku ga arù

attaché [ætæʃei'] *n* 大使館員 taíshikan-in

attaché case *n* アタッシェケース atásshekèsu

attachment [ətætʃ'mənt] *n* (tool) 付属品 fuzókuhin; (love): *attachment (to someone)* (...への) 愛着 (...è no) aíchaku

attack [ətæk'] *vt* (MIL) 攻撃する kógeki suru; (criminal: assault) 襲う osóu; (idea: criticize) 非難する hínàn suru; (task etc: tackle) ...に取掛る ...ni toríkakarù

♦*n* (assault: MIL) 攻撃 kógeki; (on someone's life) 襲撃 shúgeki; (fig: criticism) 非難 hínàn; (of illness) 発作 hossá

heart attack 心臓発作 shíńzòhossà

attacker [ətæk'ə:r] *n* 攻撃者 kógekìshà

attain [ətein'] *vt* (also: *attain to*: results, rank) 達する tassúru; (: happiness) 手に入れる te ni irérù; (: knowledge) 得る érù

attainments [ətein'mənts] *npl* (achievements) 業績 gyóseki

attempt [ətempt'] *n* (try) 試み kokóromi

♦*vt* (try) 試みる kokóromirù

to make an attempt on someone's life ...の命をねらう ...no ínóchi wò neráu

attempted [ətemp'tid] *adj* (murder, burglary, suicide) ...未遂 ...mísùi

attend [ətend'] *vt* (school, church) ...に通う ...ni kayóu; (lectures) ...に出席する ...ni shussékí suru; (patient) 看護する kángo suru

attendance [ətden'dəns] *n* (presence) 出席 shusséki; (people present) 出席率 shussékirìtsu

attendant [əten'dənt] *n* (helper) 付き添いtsukísoi; (in garage etc) 係 kákàri

◆*adj* (dangers, risks) 付き物の tsukímòno no

attend to *vt fus* (needs etc) ...の世話をする ...no sewá wò suru; (affairs etc) ...を片付ける ...wo katázukerù; (patient) ...を看護する ...wo kángo suru; (customer) ...の用を聞く ...no yō wo kikú

attention [əten'ʃən] *n* (concentration, care) 注意 chūi

◆*excl* (MIL) 気を付け ki wo tsukě

for the attention of ... (ADMIN) ...気付け ...kitsúke

attentive [əten'tiv] *adj* (intent: audience etc) 熱心に聞く nésshìn ni kikú; (polite: host) 気配り十分の kikúbàrijûbùn no

attest [ətest'] *vi: to attest to* (demonstrate) ...を立証する ...wo risshō suru; (LAW: confirm) ...を確認する ...wo kakúnin suru

attic [æt'ik] *n* 屋根裏部屋 yanéurabeya

attitude [æt'ətud] *n* (mental view) 態度 táìdo; (posture) 姿勢 shiséi

attorney [ətə:r'ni:] *n* (lawyer) 弁護士 beñgoshì

Attorney General *n* 法務長官 hốmuchòkan

attract [ətrækt'] *vt* (draw) 引き付ける hikítsukerù; (someone's interest, attention) 引く hikú

attraction [ətræk'ʃən] *n* (charm, appeal) 魅力 miryóku; (*gen pl*: amusements) 呼び物 yobímono, アトラクション atórakùshon; (PHYSICS) 引力 íñryoku; (*fig*: towards someone, something) 引かれる事 hikáreru koto

attractive [ətræk'tiv] *adj* (man, woman) 美ぼうの bibố no; (interesting: price, idea, offer) 魅力的な miryókuteki na

attribute [*n* æt'rəbju:t *vb* ətrib'ju:t] *n* 属性 zokúsei

◆*vt: to attribute something to* (cause) ...を...のせいにする ...wo ...no seí ni surù; (poem, painting) ...が...の作とする ...ga ...no sakú to surù; (quality) ...にある ...ni ...ga arú to kañgaerù

attrition [ətriʃ'ən] *n: war of attrition* 消耗戦 shômosen

aubergine [ou'bə:rʒin] *n* (*BRIT*) (vegetable) なす nású; (color) なす紺 nasúkon

auburn [ɔ:'bə:rn] *adj* (hair) くり色 kurír

auction [ɔ:k'ʃən] *n* (*also: sale by auction*) 競り serí

◆*vt* 競りに掛ける serí ni kakérù

auctioneer [ɔ:kʃəni:r'] *n* 競売人 kyōbainìn

audacity [ɔ:dæs'iti:] *n* (boldness, daring) 大胆さ daítansa; (*pej*: impudence) ずうずうしさ zúzùshisà

audible [ɔ:d'əbəl] *adj* 聞える kikóeru

audience [ɔ:d'i:əns] *n* (at event) 観客 kañkyaku; (RADIO) 聴取者 chốshushà; (TV) 視聴者 shíchòsha; (public) 世間 sekén; (interview: with queen etc) 謁見 ekkén

audio-typist [ɔ:d'i:outai'pist] *n* (*BRIT*) 書取りタイピスト kakítori taipisùto ◇口述の録音テープを聞いてタイプを打つ人 kốjutsu nò rokúon tēpù wo kiíte taipù wo utsu hitố

audio-visual [ɔ:d'i:ouvi3'u:əl] *adj* (materials, equipment) 視聴覚の shíchòkaku no

audio-visual aid *n* 視聴覚教材 shichốkakukyòzai

audit [ɔ:d'it] *vt* (COMM: accounts) 監査する kañsa suru

audition [ɔ:diʃ'ən] *n* (CINEMA, THEATER etc) オーディション ốdishòn

auditor [ɔ:'dətə:r] *n* (accountant) 監査役 kañsayaku

auditorium [ɔ:dito:r'i:əm] *n* (building) 講堂 kốdō; (audience area) 観客席 kañkyakuséki

augment [ɔːgment'] *vt* (income etc) 増やす fuyásù

augur [ɔː'gər] *vi*: *it augurs well* いい兆しだ íi kizáshi da

August [ɔːg'əst] *n* 8月 hachígatsu

aunt [ænt] *n* 伯(叔)母 obá

auntie [æn'tiː] *n dimin of* **aunt**

aunty [æn'tiː] *n* = **auntie**

au pair [ɔː peːr'] *n* (*also*: **au pair girl**) オペア (ガール) opéa(gǎru)

aura [ɔːr'ə] *n* (*fig*: air, appearance) 雰囲気 fuñ-ikì

auspices [ɔːs'pisiz] *npl*: *under the auspices of* ...の後援で ...no kǒen de

auspicious [ɔːspiʃ'əs] *adj* (opening, start, occasion) 前途有望な zéñtoyúbò na

austere [ɔːstiːr'] *adj* (room, decoration) 質素な shíssò na; (person, lifestyle, manner) 厳格な geñkaku na

austerity [ɔːsteːr'itiː] *n* (simplicity) 質素さ shissósa; (ECON: hardship) 苦労 kúrò

Australia [ɔːstreil'jə] *n* オーストラリア ǒsutoraría

Australian [ɔːstreil'jən] *adj* オーストラリアの ǒsutoraría no
♦*n* オーストラリア人 ǒsutorariajìn

Austria [ɔːs'triːə] *n* オーストリア ǒsutoría

Austrian [ɔːs'triːən] *adj* オーストリアの ǒsutoría no
♦*n* オーストリア人 ǒsutoriajìn

authentic [ɔːθen'tik] *adj* (painting, document, account) 本物の hoñmono no

author [ɔː'θər] *n* (of text) 著者 chóshà; (profession) 作家 sakkà; (creator: of plan, character etc) 発案者 hatsúanshà

authoritarian [əθɔːriter:r'iːən] *adj* (attitudes, conduct) 独裁的な dokúsaitekì na

authoritative [əθɔːr'iteitiv] *adj* (person, manner) 権威ありげな kéñ-i arígè na; (source) 信頼できる shiñrai dekirù

authority [əθɔːr'itiː] *n* (power) 権限 keñgeñ; (expert) 権威 kéñ-i; (government body) 当局 tǒkyoku; (official permission) 許可 kyòkà
the authorities 当局 tǒkyoku

authorize [ɔː'θəraiz] *vt* (publication etc)

許可する kyókà suru

autistic [ɔːtis'tik] *adj* 自閉症の jihéishō no

auto [ɔː'tou] (*US*) *n* (car) 自動車 jídòsha, カー kā

autobiography [ɔːtəbaiɑːg'rəfiː] *n* 自叙伝 jijódèn

autocratic [ɔːtəkræt'ik] *adj* (government, ruler) 独裁的な dokúsaitekì na

autograph [ɔː'təgræf] *n* サイン sáìn
♦*vt* (photo etc) ...にサインする ...ni sáìn suru

automata [ɔːtɑːm'ətə] *npl of* **automaton**

automated [ɔː'təmeitid] *adj* (factory, process) 自動化した jidóka shita

automatic [ɔːtəmæt'ik] *adj* (process, machine) 自動の jidó no; (reaction) 自動的な jidóteki na
♦*n* (gun) 自動ピストル jidópisùtorù, オートマチック ǒtomachikkù; (*BRIT*: washing machine) 自動洗濯機 jidósentakùki; (car) オートマチック車 ǒtomachikkushà

automatically [ɔːtəmæt'ikliː] *adv* (*also fig*) 自動的に jidóteki ni

automation [ɔːtəmei'ʃən] *n* (of factory process, office) 自動化 jidóka, オートメーション ǒtoméshon

automaton [ɔːtɑːm'ətɑːn] (*pl* **automata**) *n* (robot) ロボット robótto

automobile [ɔːtəməbiːl'] (*US*) *n* 自動車 jídòsha

autonomous [ɔːtɑːn'əməs] *adj* (region, area) 自治の jíchì no; (organization, person) 独立の dokúritsu no

autonomy [ɔːtɑːn'əmiː] *n* (of organization, person, country) 独立 dokúritsu

autopsy [ɔː'tɑːpsiː] *n* (post-mortem) 司法解剖 shihókaìbō, 検死解剖 keñshikaìbō

autumn [ɔː'təm] *n* (season) 秋 ákì
in autumn 秋に ákì ni

auxiliary [ɔːgzil'jəːriː] *adj* (assistant) 補助の hójò no; (back-up) 予備の yóbì no
♦*n* 助手 joshú

avail [əveil'] *vt*: *to avail oneself of* (offer, opportunity, service) ...を利用する ...wo riyó suru
♦*n*: *to no avail* 無駄に mudá ni

availability [əveiləbil'əti:] n (supply: of goods, staff etc) 入手の可能性 nyūshu no kanōsei

available [əvei'ləbəl] adj (obtainable: article etc) 手に入る te ni haíru; (service, time etc) 利用できる riyō dekíru; (person: unoccupied) 手が空いている te ga aíte iru; (: unattached) 相手がいない aíte gà inái

avalanche [æv'əlæntʃ] n (of snow) 雪崩 nadáre; (fig: of people, mail, events) 殺到 sattō

avant-garde [əvɑːntgɑːrd'] adj 前衛の zeñ-ei no, アバンギャルドの abángyarùdo no

avarice [æv'əːris] n どん欲 dóñ-yoku

Ave. [æv] abbr = **avenue**

avenge [əvendʒ'] vt (person, death etc) ...の復しゅうをする ...no fukúshū wò suru

avenue [æv'ənuː] n (street) 通り tōri; (drive) 並木通り namíkidòri; (means, solution) 方法 hōhō

average [æv'əːridʒ] n (mean, norm) 平均 heíkin

♦adj (mean) 平均の heíkin no; (ordinary) 並の namí no

♦vt (reach an average of: in speed, output, score) 平均 ...で ...する heíkin ...de ...surú

on average 平均で heíkin de

average out vi: **to average out at** 平均が ...になる heíkin ga ...ni nárù

averse [əvəːrs'] adj: **to be averse to something/doing** ...(...するの)が嫌いである ...(...surú nò) ga kirái de arù

aversion [əvəːr'ʒən] n (to people, work etc) 嫌悪 kéñ-o

avert [əvəːrt'] vt (prevent: accident, war) 予防する yobō suru; (ward off: blow) 受け止める ukétomerù; (turn away: one's eyes) そらす sorásù

aviary [ei'viːeːriː] n 鳥用大型ケージ toríyō ōgata kèji

aviation [eiviːei'ʃən] n 航空 kōkū

avid [æv'id] adj (supporter, viewer) 熱心な nésshìn na

avocado [ævəkɑːd'ou] n (BRIT: also:

avocado pear) アボカド abókado

avoid [əvɔid'] vt (person, obstacle, danger) 避ける sakérù

avuncular [əvʌŋ'kjələːr] adj (expression, tone, person) 伯(叔)父の様に優しい ojí no yō ni yasáshìī

await [əweit'] vt 待つ mátsù

awake [əweik'] adj (from sleep) 目が覚めている me ga sáměte irú

♦vb (pt awoke, pp awoken or awaked)

♦vt 起す okósù

♦vi 目が覚める me ga samérù

to be awake 目が覚めている me ga saméte irú

awakening [əwei'kəniŋ] n (also: fig: of emotion) 目覚め mezáme

award [əwɔːrd'] n (prize) 賞 shō; (LAW: damages) 賠償 baíshō

♦vt (prize) 与える atáeru; (LAW: damages) 命ずる meízuru

aware [əweːr'] adj: **aware (of)** (conscious) (...に) 気が付いている (...ni) ki gá tsuíte irù; (informed) (...を) 知っている (...wo) shitté iru

to become aware of/that (become conscious of) ...に(...という事に)気が付く ...ni(...to iú koto ni)ki gá tsukù; (learn) ...を(...という事を)知る ...wo(...to iú koto wò)shirú

awareness [əweːr'nis] n (consciousness) 気が付いている事 ki gá tsuíte irú koto; (knowing) 知っている事 shitté iru koto

awash [əwɔːʃ'] adj (with water) 水浸しの mizúbitashi no; (fig: awash with ...だらけの ...daráke no

away [əwei'] adv (movement) 離れて hanárete; (position) 離れた所に hanáreta tokóro ni; (not present) 留守で rúsù de; (in time) ...先で ...sáki de; (far away) 遠くに tőku ni

two kilometers away 2キロメートル離れて nikírometoru hanarete

two hours away by car 車で2時間走った所に kurúma de nijíkaň hashítta tokoro ni

the holiday was two weeks away 休暇は2週間先だった kyūka wa nishūkan saki dattā

he's away for a week 彼は1週間の予定
で留守です kárè wa isshūkan no yotei
de rusù desu

to take away (remove) 片付ける katázukerù; (subtract) 引く hikú

to work/pedal etc **away** 一生懸命に働
く〔ペダルを踏む〕etc isshōkenmei ni ha-
tárakù〔pedáru wò fumù〕etc

to fade away (color) さめる sameru;
(enthusiasm) 冷める samérù; (light,
sound) 消えてなくなる kiéte nakunarù

away game n (SPORT) ロードゲーム
rōdogēmu

awe [ɔ:] n (respect) い敬 ikéi

awe-inspiring [ɔ:'inspaiə:riŋ] adj (overwhelming: person, thing) い敬の念を抱か
せる ikéi no neñ wo idákaserù

awesome [ɔ:'səm] adj = awe-inspiring

awful [ɔ:'fəl] adj (frightful: weather,
smell) いやな iyá na; (dreadful: shock) ひ
どい hidói; (number, quantity): **an
awful lot (of)** いやに沢山の iyá ni takusañ no

awfully [ɔ:'fəli] adv (very) ひどく hídòku

awhile [əwail'] adv しばらく shibáraku

awkward [ɔ:k'wə:rd] adj (clumsy: person, movement) ぎこちない gikóchinaì;
(difficult: shape) 扱いにくい atsúkaini-
kuì; (embarrassing: problem, situation)
厄介な yákkài na

awning [ɔ:'niŋ] n 日よけ hiyóke

awoke [əwouk'] pt of awake

awoken [əwou'kən] pp of awake

awry [ərai'] adv: **to be awry** (order,
clothes, hair) 乱れている midárète irú

to go awry (outcome, plan) 失敗する
shippái suru

axe [æks] (US: also: **ax**) n 斧 ónð

♦vt (project etc) 廃止する haíshi suru

axes[1] [æk'siz] npl of ax(e)

axes[2] [æk'si:z] npl of axis

axis [æk'sis] (pl **axes**) n (of earth, on
graph) 軸 jikú

axle [æk'səl] n (AUT) 車軸 shajíku

aye [ai] excl (yes) はい háī

azalea [əzeil'jə] n ツツジ tsutsújì

B

B [bi:] n (MUS: note) ロ音 ro-óñ; (: key)
ロ調 róchò

B.A. [bi:ei'] abbr = **Bachelor of Arts**

babble [bæb'əl] vi (person, voices) ぺち
ゃくちゃしゃべる péchàkucha shabérù;
(brook) さらさら流れる sáràsara nagárerù

baby [bei'bi:] n (infant) 赤ん坊 ákànbō,
赤ちゃん akàchan; (US: inf: darling) あ
なた anátà, ベビー bébì

baby carriage (US) n 乳母車 ubágurùma

baby-sit [bei'bi:sit] vi 子守をする komó-
rì wo suru, ベビーシッターをする bebíshittà wo suru

baby-sitter [bei'bi:sitə:r] n 子守役 ko-
mōriyaku, ベビーシッター bebíshittà

bachelor [bætʃ'ələ:r] n 独身の男 dokúshin no otóko

Bachelor of Arts/Science (person) 文
〔理〕学士 buñ〔ri〕gakùshi; (qualification)
文〔理〕学士号 buñ〔ri〕gakùshigō

back [bæk] n (of person, animal) 背中 se-
náka; (of hand) 甲 kŏ; (of house, page,
book) 裏 urá; (of car, train) 後ろ ushíro,
後部 kôbu; (of chair) 背もたれ semótare;
(of crowd, audience) 後ろの方 ushíro no
hŏ; (SOCCER) バック bákkù

♦vt (candidate: also: **back up**) 支援する
shién suru; (horse: at races) ...にかける
...ni kakérù; (car) バックさせる bákkù
saserù

♦vi (also: **back up**: person) 後ずさりする
atózusàri suru; (: car etc) バックする
bákkù suru

♦cpd (payment, rent) 滞納の taíno no;
(AUT: seat, wheels) 後部の kôbu no

♦adv (not forward) 後ろへ〔に〕ushíro e
〔ni〕; (returned): **he's back** 彼は帰って来
た kárè wa kaétte kità; (return): **throw
the ball back** ボールを投げ返して下さ
い bŏru wò nagékaeshite kudasaì;
(again): **he called back** 彼は電話を掛け
直してきた kárè wa deñwa wò kakénao-

shite kita

he ran back 彼は駆け戻った kárè wa kakémodottà

can I have it back? それを返してくれませんか sorè wò kaéshite kuremaseñ ka

backbencher [bæk'bentʃər] (*BRIT*) *n* 平議員 hirágiìn

backbone [bæk'boun] *n* (ANAT) 背骨 sebóne; (*fig*: main strength) 主力 shúryòku; (: courage) 勇気 yúki

backcloth [bæk'klɔːθ] (*BRIT*) *n* = **backdrop**

backdate [bækdeit'] *vt* (document, pay raise etc) ...にさかのぼって有効にする ...ni sakánobottè yū́kō ni suru

back down *vi* 譲る yuzúru

backdrop [bæk'drɑːp] *n* 背景幕 haíkeī-maku

backfire [bæk'faiər] *vi* (AUT) バックファイアする bakkúfaìa suru; (plans) 裏目に出る uráme ni derù

background [bæk'graund] *n* (of picture, events: *also* COMPUT) 背景 haíkei, バック bákkù; (basic knowledge) 予備知識 yobíchishìki; (experience) 経歴 keíreki

family background 家庭環境 kateíkankyō

backhand [bæk'hænd] *n* (TENNIS: *also*: **backhand stroke**) バックハンド bakkúhaǹdo

backhanded [bæk'hændid] *adj* (*fig*: compliment) 当てこすりの atékosuri no

backhander [bæk'hændər] (*BRIT*) *n* (bribe) 賄ろ wáìro

backing [bæk'iŋ] *n* (*fig*) 支援 shién

backlash [bæk'læʃ] *n* (*fig*) 反動 hañdō

backlog [bæk'lɔːg] *n*: *backlog of work* たまった仕事 tamátta shigoto

back number *n* (of magazine etc) バックナンバー bakkúnaǹbā

back out *vi* (of promise) 手を引く te wo hikú

backpack [bæk'pæk] *n* リュックサック ryukkúsakkù

back pay *n* 未払いの給料 mihárài nó kyūryō

backside [bæk'said] (*inf*) *n* おしり o-shí-ri

backstage [bæk'steidʒ'] *adv* (THEATER) 楽屋に〔で〕 gakúya ni〔de〕

backstroke [bæk'strouk] *n* 背泳ぎ seóyògi

back up *vt* (support: person, theory etc) 支援する shién suru; (COMPUT) バックアップコピーを作る bakkúappukopī̀ wo tsukúrù

backup [bæk'ʌp] *adj* (train, plane) 予備の yóbì no; (COMPUT) バックアップ用の bakkúappu yõ no

♦*n* (support) 支援 shién; (*also*: **backup file**) バックアップファイル bakkúappu faìru

backward [bæk'wərd] *adj* (movement) 後ろへの ushíro e no; (person, country) 遅れた okúreta

backwards [bæk'wərdz] *adv* (move, go) 後ろに〔へ〕 ushíro ni〔e〕; (read a list) 逆に gyakú nì; (fall) 仰向けに aòmuke ni; (walk) 後ろ向きに ushíromuki ni

backwater [bæk'wɔːtər] *n* (*fig*) 後進地 kóshiñchi

backyard [bæk'jɑːrd] *n* (of house) 裏庭 urániwa

bacon [bei'kən] *n* ベーコン bèkon

bacteria [bækti:'ri:ə] *npl* 細菌 saíkin

bad [bæd] *adj* (gen) 悪い warúì; (mistake, accident, injury) 大きな ōkìna; (meat, food) 悪くなった warúku nattá

his bad leg 彼の悪い方の脚 kárè no warúi hō nò ashí

to go bad (food) 悪くなる warúku narù

bade [bæd] *pt of* **bid**

badge [bædʒ] *n* (of school etc) 記章 kishṓ; (of policeman) バッジ bájjì

badger [bædʒ'əːr] *n* アナグマ anáguma

badly [bæd'li:] *adv* (work, dress etc) 下手に hetá ni; (reflect, think) 悪く warúku

badly wounded 重傷を負った jūshō wò ottá

he needs it badly 彼にはそれがとても必要だ kárè ni wa sorè gà totémo hitsuyṓ da

to be badly off (for money) 生活が苦しい seíkatsu ga kurushiì

badminton [bæd'mintən] *n* バドミント

ン badómiǹton

bad-tempered [bæd'tem'pərd] *adj* (person: by nature) 怒りっぽい okórippoì; (: on one occasion) 機嫌が悪い kigén gà warúî

baffle [bæf'əl] *vt* (puzzle) 困惑させる końwaku saserù

bag [bæg] *n* (of paper, plastic) 袋 fukúro; (handbag) ハンドバッグ haǹdobaggù; (satchel, case) かばん kabán

bags of (*inf*: lots of) 沢山の takúsan no

baggage [bæg'idʒ] *n* (luggage) 手荷物 tenímotsu

baggy [bæg'i:] *adj* だぶだぶの dabúdabu no

bagpipes [bæg'paips] *npl* バグパイプ bagúpaìpu

Bahamas [bəhɑ:m'əz] *npl*: ***the Bahamas*** バハマ諸島 bahámashotò

bail [beil] *n* (LAW: payment) 保釈金 hoshákukin; (: release) 保釈 hosháku

♦*vt* (prisoner: *gen*: grant bail to) 保釈する hosháku suru; (boat: *also*: **bail out**) ...から水をかい出す ...kará mizú wò kaídasù

on bail (prisoner) 保釈中（の） hoshákuchū̀ (no)

bailiff [bei'lif] *n* (LAW: *US*) 廷吏 teîri; (: *BRIT*) 執行吏 shíkkòri

bail out *vt* (prisoner) 保釈させる hosháku saseru ¶ *see also* **bale**

bait [beit] *n* (for fish, animal) えさ esá; (for criminal etc) おとり otóri

♦*vt* (hook, trap) ...にえさをつける ...ni esá wò tsukérù; (person: tease) からかう karákaù

bake [beik] *vt* (CULIN: cake, potatoes) オーブンで焼く ōbun de yakú; (TECH: clay etc) 焼く yakú

♦*vi* (cook) オーブンに入っている ōbun ni háìtte iru

baked beans [beikt-] *npl* ベークトビーンズ bḕkutobìnzu

baker [bei'kər] *n* パン屋 páñ-ya

bakery [bei'kəːri:] *n* (building) パン屋 páñ-ya

baking [bei'kiŋ] *n* (act) オーブンで焼く事 ōbun de yakú koto; (batch) オーブン

で焼いたもの ōbun de yaíta mono

baking powder *n* ふくらし粉 fukúrashikò, ベーキングパウダー bḕkingupaùdā

balance [bæl'əns] *n* (equilibrium) 均衡 kiǹkō, バランス baránsu; (COMM: sum) 残高 zandaka; (remainder) 残り nokóri; (scales) 天びん teǹbin

♦*vt* (budget) ...の収入と支出を合せる ...no shūnyū tò shishútsu wò awáserù; (account) ...の決算をする ...no kessán wò suru; (make equal) 釣合を取る tsuríai wo torù

balance of trade 貿易収支 bṓekishūshì

balance of payments 国際収支 kokúsaishūshì

balanced [bæl'ənst] *adj* (report) バランスの良い baránsu no yoì; (personality) 安定した aǹtei shita

a balanced diet 均衡食 kiǹkō shòku

balance sheet *n* 貸借対照表 taíshakutaìshōhyṑ, バランスシート baránsu shìto

balcony [bæl'kəni:] *n* バルコニー barúkonì; (in theater) 天井さじき teǹjōsajìki

bald [bɔ:ld] *adj* (head) はげた hágèta; (tire) 坊主になった bṓzu ni nattá

bale [beil] *n* (of paper, cotton, hay) こり korí

baleful [beil'fəl] *adj* (glance) 邪悪な jaáku na

bale out *vi* (of a plane) パラシュートで脱出する paráshùto de dasshútsù suru

ball [bɔ:l] *n* (SPORT) 球 tamá, ボール bṓru; (of wool, string) 玉 tamá; (dance) 舞踏会 bútòkai

to play ball (co-operate) 協力する kyṓryoku suru

ballad [bæl'əd] *n* (poem, song) バラード bárādo

ballast [bæl'əst] *n* (on ship, balloon) バラスト barásùto

ball bearings *npl* ボールベアリング bṓrubeàringu

ballerina [bæləri:'nə] *n* バレリーナ barérìna

ballet [bælei'] *n* (art) バレエ bárèe; (an artistic work) バレエ曲 baréekyokù

ballet dancer *n* バレエダンサー baréedañsā

ballistics [bəlis'tiks] *n* 弾道学 dañdōgaku

balloon [bəlu:n'] *n* (child's) 風船 fūsen; (hot air balloon) 熱気球 netsúkikyū

ballot [bæl'ət] *n* (vote) 投票 tōhyō

ballot paper *n* 投票用紙 tōhyōyōshi

ballpoint (pen) [bɔ:l'pɔint] *n* ボールペン bōrupen

ballroom [bɔ:l'ru:m] *n* 舞踏の間 butō no ma

balm [ba:m] *n* バルサム bárùsamu

Baltic [bɔ:l'tik] *n*: **the Baltic (Sea)** バルト海 bárútokài

balustrade [bæl'əstreid] *n* (on balcony, staircase) 手すり tesúri

bamboo [bæmbu:'] *n* (plant) 竹 takè; (material) 竹材 takézai

ban [bæn] *n* (prohibition) 禁止 kiñshi
♦*vt* (prohibit) 禁止する kiñshi suru

banal [bənæl'] *adj* (remark, idea, situation) 陳腐な chíñpu na

banana [bənæn'ə] *n* バナナ bánana

band [bænd] *n* (group) 一団 ichídan; (MUS: jazz, rock, military etc) バンド bañdo; (strip of cloth etc) バンド bañdo; (stripe) 帯状の物 objíō no mono

bandage [bæn'didʒ] *n* 包帯 hōtai
♦*vt* ...に包帯を巻く ...ni hōtai wò makú

bandaid [bæn'deid'] ® (*US*) *n* バンドエイド bañdoeìdō ◇ばん創こうの一種 bañsōkō no isshù

bandit [bæn'dit] *n* 盗賊 tōzoku

band together *vi* 団結する dañketsu suru

bandwagon [bænd'wægən] *n*: **to jump on the bandwagon** (*fig*) 便乗する biñjō suru

bandy [bæn'di:] *vt* (jokes, insults, ideas) やり取りする yarítòri surù

bandy-legged [bæn'di:legid] *adj* がにまたの ganímata no

bang [bæŋ] *n* (of door) ばたんという音 bátàn to iú oto; (of gun, exhaust) ばんという音 páñ to iú otò; (blow) 打撃 dagéki
♦*excl* ばんばん páñpan
♦*vt* (door) ばたんと閉める batán to shimerù; (one's head etc) ぶつける butsúke-

ru
♦*vi* (door) ばたんと閉まる batán to shimárù; (fireworks) ばんばんと爆発する báñban to bakúhatsu suru

bangle [bæŋ'gəl] *n* (bracelet) 腕飾り udékazari

bangs [bæŋz] (*US*) *npl* (fringe) 切下げ前髪 kirísagemaegamì

banish [bæn'iʃ] *vt* (exile: person) 追放する tsuíhō suru

banister(s) [bæn'istər(z)] *n(pl)* (on stairway) 手すり tesúri

bank [bæŋk] *n* (COMM: building, institution: *also* of blood etc) 銀行 giñkō, バンク báñku; (of river, lake) 岸 kishì; (of earth) 土手 doté
♦*vi* (AVIAT) 傾く katámukù
data bank データバンク détabañku

bank account *n* 銀行口座 giñkōkòza

bank card *n* ギャランティーカード gyarántikàdo ◇小切手を使う時に示すカード.カードのサインと小切手のサインが照合される kogíttè wo tsukáù tokí nì shimésu kàdo. kàdo no sáìn to kogíttè no sáìn ga shōgō sarerù

banker [bæŋ'əːr] *n* 銀行家 giñkōka

banker's card (*BRIT*) *n* = **bank card**

Bank Holiday (*BRIT*) *n* 銀行定休日 giñkōteikyùbi

banking [bæŋk'iŋ] *n* 銀行業 giñkōgyō

banknote [bæŋk'nout] *n* 紙幣 shíhèi

bank on *vt fus* ...を頼りにする ...wo táyòri ni suru

bank rate *n* 公定歩合 kōteibuài

bankrupt [bæŋk'rʌpt] *adj* (person, organization) 倒産した tōsan shita
to go bankrupt 倒産する tōsan suru
to be bankrupt 返済能力がない heñsai nōryoku ga naí

bankruptcy [bæŋk'rʌptsi:] *n* (COMM) 倒産 tōsan

bank statement *n* 勘定照合表 kañjōshōgōhyō

banner [bæn'əːr] *n* (for decoration, advertising) 横断幕 ōdañmaku; (in demonstration) 手持ち横断幕 temóchi ōdañmaku

banns [bænz] *npl*: **the banns** 結婚予告

kekkón-yokòku

banquet [bæŋ'kwit] n 宴会 eñkai

baptism [bæp'tizəm] n (REL) 洗礼 señrei

baptize [bæptaiz'] vt ...に洗礼を施す ...ni señrei wð hodókosù

bar [bɑːr] n (place: for drinking) バーbầ; (counter) カウンター kaúntằ; (rod: of metal etc) 棒 bố; (slab: of soap) 1個 ikkó; (fig: obstacle) 障害 shốgai; (prohibition) 禁止 kiñshi; (MUS) 小節 shósetsu
♦vt (road) ふさぐ fuságu; (person) ...が ...するのを禁止する ...ga ...surú no wð kiñshi suru; (activity) 禁止する kiñshi suru

a bar of chocolate 板チョコ itachoko

the Bar (LAW: profession) 弁護士 beñgoshi ◇総称 sốshò

bar none 例外なく reigai nakù

barbaric [bɑːrbær'ik] adj (uncivilized, cruel) 野蛮な yabán na

barbarous [bɑːr'bərəs] adj (uncivilized, cruel) 野蛮な yabán na

barbecue [bɑːr'bəkju:] n (grill) バーベキューこん炉 bắbekyūkoñro; (meal, party) バーベキューパーティ bắbekyūpầti

barbed wire [bɑːrbd-] n 有刺鉄線 yúshitessèn, バラ線 barásen

barber [bɑːr'bəːr] n 理髪師 rihátsushì, 床屋 tokóya

bar code n (on goods) バーコード bắkòdo

bare [beːr] adj (naked: body) 裸の hadáka no; (: tree) 葉の落ちた ha no óchìta; (countryside) 木のない ki no nâî; (minimum: necessities) ほんの hoñno
♦vt (one's body, teeth) むき出しにする mukídashi ni suru

bareback [beːr'bæk] adv くらなしで kuránashì de

barefaced [beːr'feist] adj (lie, cheek) 厚かましい atsúkamashiì

barefoot [beːr'fut] adj 裸足の hadáshi no
♦adv 裸足で hadáshi de

barely [beːr'li:] adv (scarcely) 辛うじて kárõjite

bargain [bɑːr'gin] n (deal, agreement) 取引 toríhìki; (good buy) 掘出し物 horída-

shimono, バーゲン bầgen
♦vi (negotiate): *to bargain (with someone)* (...と) 交渉する (...to) kốshō suru; (haggle) 駆引きする kakéhìki suru
into the bargain おまけに o-máke ni

bargain for vt fus: *he got more than he bargained for* 彼はそんな結果を予想していなかった kárè wa soñna kekká wð yosố shite inakattà

barge [bɑːrdʒ] n (boat) はしけ hashíke

barge in vi (enter) いきなり入り込む ikínari hairikomù; (interrupt) 割込む waríkomù

bark [bɑːrk] n (of tree) 皮 kawá; (of dog) ほえ声 hoégoe
♦vi (dog) ほえる hoérù

barley [bɑːr'li:] n 大麦 ómugi

barley sugar n 氷砂糖 kốrizatồ

barmaid [bɑːr'meid] n 女性バーテン joséibàten

barman [bɑːr'mən] (pl **barmen**) n バーテン bầten

barn [bɑːrn] n 納屋 náyà

barometer [bərɑːm'itəːr] n (for weather) 気圧計 kiátsukei

baron [bær'ən] n (nobleman) 男爵 dañshaku; (of press, industry) 大立て者 ốdatemòno

baroness [bær'ənis] n 男爵夫人 dañshakufujìn

barracks [bær'əks] npl (MIL) 兵舎 hếisha

barrage [bərɑːʒ'] n (MIL) 弾幕 dañmaku; (dam) ダム dámù; (fig: of criticism, questions etc) 連発 reñpatsu

barrel [bær'əl] n (of wine, beer) たる tarú; (of oil) バレル bấrèru; (of gun) 銃身 jůshin

barren [bær'ən] adj (land) 不毛の fumố no

barricade [bær'əkeid] n バリケード barîkèdo
♦vt (road, entrance) バリケードでふさぐ barîkèdo de fuságu
to barricade oneself (in) (...に) ろう城する (...ni) rồjō suru

barrier [bær'iːər] n (at frontier, entrance) 関門 kañmon; (fig: to progress, communication etc) 障害 shōgai

barring [bɑːˈriŋ] *prep* ...を除いて...wo nozóite

barrister [bærˈistəːr] (*BRIT*) *n* 法廷弁護士 hōteibengoshī

barrow [bærˈou] *n* (wheelbarrow) 一輪車 ichírínsha

bars [bɑːrz] *npl* (on window etc: grille) 格子 kōshi

behind bars (prisoner) 刑務所に〔で〕 keímushō ni 〔de〕

bartender [bɑːrˈtendəːr] (*US*) *n* バーテンダー báten

barter [bɑːrˈtəːr] *vt*: *to barter something for something* ...を...と交換する ...wo ...to kōkan suru

base [beis] *n* (foot: of post, tree) 根元 nemōto; (foundation: of food) 主成分 shuséîbun; (: of make-up) ファウンデーション faúndēshon; (center: for military, research) 基地 kichí; (: for individual, organization) 本拠地 hoñkyochi

♦*vt*: *to base something on* (opinion, belief) ...が...に基づく ...ga ...ni mozúkù

♦*adj* (mind, thoughts) 卑しい iyáshiī

baseball [beisˈbɔːl] *n* 野球 yakyū, ベースボール bésuborù

basement [beisˈmənt] *n* 地下室 chikáshītsu

bases¹ [beiˈsiz] *npl of* base

bases² [beiˈsiːz] *npl of* basis

bash [bæʃ] (*inf*) *vt* (beat) ぶん殴る buńnagurù

bashful [bæʃˈfəl] *adj* 内気な uchíki na

basic [beiˈsik] *adj* (fundamental: principles, problem, essentials) 基本的な kihóntekí na; (starting: wage) 基本の kihón no; (elementary: knowledge) 初歩的な shohótekí na; (primitive: facilities) 最小限の safíshōgen no

basically [beiˈsikliː] *adv* (fundamentally) 根本的に koñponteki ni; (in fact, put simply) はっきり言って hakkírī itté

basics [beiˈsiks] *npl*: *the basics* 基本 kihón

basil [bæzˈəl] *n* メボウキ mébòki, バジル bájîru

basin [beiˈsin] *n* (vessel) たらい tarái;

(*also*: **wash basin**) 洗面台 sefímendai; (GEO: of river, lake) 流域 ryūiki

basis [beiˈsis] (*pl* **bases**) *n* (starting point, foundation) 基礎 kisó

on a part-time/trial basis パートタイム〔見習い〕で pátotaìmù(minarai)de

bask [bæsk] *vi*: *to bask in the sun* 日光浴をする nikkōyoku wo suru, 日なたぼっこをする hinátabokkò wo suru

basket [bæsˈkit] *n* (container) かご kagó, バスケット basúkettò

basketball [bæsˈkitbɔːl] *n* バスケットボール basúkettobōru

bass [beis] *n* (part, instrument) バス básù; (singer) バス歌手 basúkashù

bassoon [bæsuːnˈ] *n* (MUS) バスーン básūn

bastard [bæsˈtəːrd] *n* (offspring) 私生児 shiséîji; (*inf!*) くそ野郎 kusóyarō

bastion [bæsˈtʃən] *n* (of privilege, wealth etc) とりで toríde

bat [bæt] *n* (ZOOL) コウモリ kōmori; (for ball games) バット báttò; (*BRIT*: for table tennis) ラケット rakéttò

♦*vt*: *he didn't bat an eyelid* 彼は瞬き1つしなかった kárè wa mabátàki hitotsù shinákàtta

batch [bætʃ] *n* (of bread) 1かま分 hitókamabùn; (of letters, papers) 1山 hitóyamà

bated [beiˈtid] *adj*: *with bated breath* 息を殺して íkì wo koróshite

bath [bæθ] *n* (bathtub) 風呂 fúrò, 湯船 yúbùne; (act of bathing) 入浴 nyúyoku

♦*vt* (baby, patient) 風呂に入れる fúrò ni iréru

to have a bath 風呂に入る fúrò ni haíru

¶ *see also* **baths**

bathe [beið] *vi* (swim) 泳ぐ oyógù, 遊泳する yūei suru; (*US*: have a bath) 風呂に入る fúrò ni haíru

♦*vt* (wound) 洗う aráu

bather [beiˈðəːr] *n* 遊泳〔水泳〕する人 yū-ei〔suíei〕suru hito

bathing [beiˈðiŋ] *n* (taking a bath) 入浴 nyúyoku; (swimming) 遊泳 yūei, 水泳 suíei

bathing cap *n* 水泳帽 suíeibō

bathing suit (*BRIT* **bathing costume**)

n 水着 mizúgi

bathrobe [bæθ'roub] *n* バスローブ basú-rōbu

bathroom [bæθ'ru:m] *n* トイレ tôîre; (without toilet) 浴室 yokúshitsu

baths [bæðz] (*BRIT*) *npl* (*also*: **swimming baths**) 水泳プール suíeipūru

bath towel *n* バスタオル basútaðru

baton [bætɑ:n'] *n* (MUS) 指揮棒 shīkíbồ; (ATHLETICS) バトン batón; (policeman's) 警棒 keíbō

battalion [bətæl'jən] *n* 大隊 daítai

batter [bæt'ə:r] *vt* (child, wife) ...に暴力 を振るう ...ni bổryoku wo furúù; (subj: wind, rain) ...に強く当たる ...ni tsúyòku atáru
♦*n* (CULIN) 生地 kíjì

battered [bæt'ə:rd] *adj* (hat, pan) 使い古 した tsukáifurushìta

battery [bæt'ə:ri:] *n* (of flashlight etc) 乾 電池 kañdeñchi; (AUT) バッテリー battérī

battle [bæt'əl] *n* (MIL, *fig*) 戦い tatákai
♦*vi* 戦う tatákau

battlefield [bæt'əlfi:ld] *n* 戦場 señjō

battleship [bæt'əlʃip] *n* 戦艦 señkan

bawdy [bɔː'di:] *adj* (joke, song) わいせつ な waísetsu na

bawl [bɔːl] *vi* (shout: adult) どなる donárù; (wail: child) 泣きわめく nakíwamekù

bay [bei] *n* (GEO) 湾 wáñ
to hold someone at bay ...を寄付けな い ...wo yosétsukenaì

bay leaf *n* ゲッケイジュの葉 gekkéìju no ha, ローリエ rôrie, ベイリーフ beírìfu

bayonet [bei'ənet] *n* 銃剣 júken

bay window *n* 張出し窓 harídashimadò

bazaar [bəzɑ:r'] *n* (market) 市場 íchìba; (fete) バザー bazâ

B. & B. [bi:' ænd bi:'] *n abbr* = **bed and breakfast**

BBC [bi:bi:si:'] *n abbr* (= *British Broadcasting Company*) 英国放送協会 eíkoku hōsō kyōkai

B.C. [bi:si:'] *adv abbr* (= *before Christ*) 紀元前 kigéñzen

be [bi:] (*pt* **was, were**, *pp* **been**) *aux vb* **1** (with present participle: forming continuous tenses) ...している ...shíte iru
what are you doing? 何をしています か nánì wo shité imasù ká
it is raining 雨が降っています ámè ga fúttè imásù
they're coming tomorrow 彼らは明日 来る事になっています kárèra wa asú kurù koto ni náttè imásù
I've been waiting for you for hours 何時間もあなたを待っていますよ nánjikàn mo anátà wo máttè imásù yo

2 (with *pp*: forming passives) ...される ...saréru
to be killed 殺される korósareru
the box had been opened 箱は開けら れていた hakó wa àkérarete ita
the thief was nowhere to be seen 泥 棒はどこにも見当らなかった doróbō wa dôkó ni mo mîátaranakàtta

3 (in tag questions) ...ね ...né, ...でしょう ...deshố
it was fun, wasn't it? 楽しかったね tanóshikàtta né
he's good-looking, isn't he? 彼は男前 だね kárè wa otókomae da ne
she's back again, is she? 彼女はまた 来たのか kánojò wa matá kita nò ká

4 (+ to + infinitive) ...すべきである ...subékì de aru
the house is to be sold 家は売る事にな っている ié wà urú koto nì náttè iru
you're to be congratulated for all your work 立派な仕事を完成しておめ でとう rippá na shigoto wo kansei shite ômédetô
he's not to open it 彼はそれを開けては ならない kárè wa soré wo akete wà naránaì

♦*vb* + *complement* **1** (*gen*) ...である ...de árù
I'm English 私はイングランド人です watákushi wa íngurandojîn desu
I'm tired/hot/cold 私は疲れた〔暑い、 寒い〕watákushi wa tsûkárèta〔atsúî,

samúi〕

he's a doctor 彼は医者です kárè wa ishá desù

2 and 2 are 4 2足す2は4 ní tasú ní wà yón

she's tall/pretty 彼女は背が高い〔きれいです〕kánojò wa sé ga takáì〔kírèi desu〕

be careful/quiet/good! 注意〔静かに、行儀よく〕して下さい chúi〔shízùka ni, gyōgi yokù〕shité kudasài

2 (of health): *how are you?* お元気ですか o-génkì desu ká

he's very ill 彼は重病です kárè wa júbyō desù

I'm better now もう元気になりました mō génkì ni narímashìta

3 (of age) ...才です ...sài desu

how old are you? 何才ですか nànsai desu ka, (お) 幾つですか (ó)ikùtsu desu ka

I'm sixteen (years old) 16才です júrokusài desu

4 (cost): *how much was the meal?* 食事はいくらでしたか shokúji wa ikùra deshita ká

that'll be $5.75, please 5ドル75セント頂きます gódòru nanájùgosèntó itádakimasù

♦*vi* **1** (exist, occur etc) 存在する sónzai suru

the best singer that ever was 史上最高の歌手 shijō saikō no kashù

is there a God? 神は存在するか kámì wa sónzai suru kà

be that as it may それはそれとして sorè wa sore toshite

so be it それでよい soré de yoì

2 (referring to place) ...にある〔いる〕...ni árù〔ìrù〕

I won't be here tomorrow 明日はここに来ません asú wà kokó ni kìmáseñ

Edinburgh is in Scotland エジンバラはスコットランドにある ejínbàra wa sukóttoràndo ni árù

it's on the table それはテーブルにあります soré wa tēburu ni árimasù

we've been here for ages 私たちはずっ

と前からここにいます watákushitàchi wa zuttó maè kara kokó ni ìmásù

3 (referring to movement) 行って来る itté kurù

where have you been? どこへ行っていましたか dókò e itté mashìta ká

I've been to the post office/to China 郵便局〔中国〕へ行って来ました yúbìn-kyoku(chūgòku)e itté kimashìta

I've been in the garden 庭にいました niwá ni imashìta

♦*impers vb* **1** (referring to time): *it's 5 o'clock* 5時です gójì desu

it's the 28th of April 4月28日です shigátsu nijùhachínichi dèsu

2 (referring to distance): *it's 10 km to the village* 村まで10キロメーターです murá màde jukkírometà desu

3 (referring to the weather): *it's too hot* 暑過ぎる atsúsugirù

it's too cold 寒過ぎる samúsugirù

it's windy today 今日は風が強い kyō wà kazé ga tsuyoì

4 (emphatic): *it's only me/the postman* ご心配しなく、私〔郵便屋さん〕です go-shínpai nakù, watákushi〔yúbin-ya-san〕desù

it was Maria who paid the bill 勘定を払ったのはマリアでした kánjò wò haráttà no wa márià deshita

beach [biːtʃ] *n* 浜 hamá

♦*vt* (boat) 浜に引上げる hamá ni hikíagerù

beacon [biːˈkən] *n* (lighthouse) 燈台 tódai; (marker) 信号 shíñgō

bead [biːd] *n* (glass, plastic etc) ビーズ bízu; (of sweat) 玉 tamá

beak [biːk] *n* (of bird) くちばし kuchíbashi

beaker [biːˈkəːr] *n* (cup) コップ koppú, グラス gúràsu

beam [biːm] *n* (ARCHIT) はり harí; (of light) 光線 kōsen

♦*vi* (smile) ほほえむ hohóemù

bean [biːn] *n* マメ mamé

runner bean サヤインゲン sayáiñgen

broad bean ソラマメ sorámàme

coffee bean コーヒーマメ kōhīmàme

beansprouts [biːnˈsprauts] *npl* マメモヤシ mamémoyàshi

bear [beːr] *n* (ZOOL) クマ kumá
♦*vb* (*pt* **bore**, *pp* **borne**)
♦*vt* (carry, support: weight) 支える sasáerù; (: responsibility) 負う oú; (: cost) 払う haráù; (tolerate: examination, scrutiny, person) ...に耐える ...ni taérù; (produce: children) 産む umú
♦*vi*: *to bear right/left* (AUT) 右〔左〕に曲る mígì(hidàri)ni magárù
to bear fruit ...に実がなる ...ni mi ga narú

beard [biːrd] *n* ひげ higé

bearded [biːrdˈid] *adj* ひげのある higé no arù

bearer [beːrˈəːr] *n* (of letter, news) 運ぶ人 hakóbu hito; (of cheque) 持参人 jisánnin; (of title) 持っている人 mótte irú hito

bearing [beːrˈiŋ] *n* (air) 態度 táìdo; (connection) 関係 kañkei
to take a bearing 方角を確かめる hṓgaku wò tashíkamerù
to find one's bearings 自分の位置を確かめる jibún no ichì wò tashíkamerù

bearings [beːrˈiŋz] *npl* (*also*: **ball bearings**) ボールベアリング bōrubeàringu

bear out *vt* (person) ...の言う事を保証する ...no iu koto wo hoshṓ suru; (suspicions etc) ...の事実を証明する ...no jijítsu wo shṓmei suru

bear up *vi* (person) しっかりする shikkárì suru

beast [biːst] *n* (animal) 野獣 yajū́; (*inf*: person) いやなやつ iyá na yatsù

beastly [biːstˈliː] *adj* (awful: weather, child, trick etc) ひどい hídoi

beat [biːt] *n* (of heart) 鼓動 kodṓ; (MUS) 拍子 hyṓshi, ビート bīto; (of policeman) 巡回区域 juñkaikuìki
♦*vb* (*pt* **beat**, *pp* **beaten**)
♦*vt* (strike: wife, child) 殴る nagúrù; (eggs, cream) 泡立てる awádaterù, ホイップする hoíppù suru; (defeat: opponent) ...に勝つ ...ni kátsù; (: record) 破る yabúrù
♦*vi* (heart) 鼓動する kodṓ suru; (rain) た

たき付ける様に降る tatákitsukeru yṓ ni fúrù; (wind) たたき付ける様に吹く tatákitsukeru yṓ ni fúkù; (drum) 鳴る narú
off the beaten track へんぴな所に héñpi na tokóro ni
to beat it (*inf*) ずらかる zurákarù

beating [biːtˈiŋ] *n* (punishment with whip etc) むち打ち muchíuchi; (violence) 殴るけるの暴行 nagúrukerù no bōkō

beat off *vt* (attack, attacker) 撃退する gekítai suru

beat up *vt* (person) 打ちのめす uchínomesù; (mixture) かく拌する kakúhan suru; (eggs, cream) 泡立てる awádaterù, ホイップする hoíppù suru

beautiful [bjuːˈtəfəl] *adj* (woman, place) 美しい utsúkushiì; (day, weather) 素晴らしい subárashiì

beautifully [bjuːˈtəfəliː] *adv* (play music, sing, drive etc) 見事に mígòto ni

beauty [bjuːˈtiː] *n* (quality) 美しさ utsúkushìsa; (beautiful woman) 美女 bíjò, 美人 bíjìn; (*fig*: attraction) 魅力 miryóku

beauty salon *n* 美容院 bíyòin

beauty spot *n* (BRIT: TOURISM) 景勝地 keíshōchì

beaver [biːˈvəːr] *n* (ZOOL) ビーバー bība

became [bikeimˈ] *pt of* **become**

because [bikɔːzˈ] *conj* ...だから ...dá kàra, ...であるので ...de árù nodé
because of ...のため ...no tamé, ...のせいで ...no seí de

beck [bek] *n*: *to be at the beck and call of* ...の言いなりになっている ...no iínari ni nattè irú

beckon [bekˈən] *vt* (*also*: **beckon to**: person) ...に来いと合図する ...ni kóì to aízu suru

become [bikʌmˈ] (*pt* **became**, *pp* **become**) *vi* ...になる ...ni nárù
to become fat 太る futórù
to become thin やせる yasérù

becoming [bikʌmˈiŋ] *adj* (behavior) ふさわしい fusáwashiì; (clothes) 似合う niáù

bed [bed] *n* (piece of furniture) ベッド béddò; (of coal, clay) 層 sṓ; (bottom: of river, sea) 底 sokó; (of flowers) 花壇 kádàn *to go to bed* 寝る nerú

bed and breakfast *n* (place) 民宿 miñshuku; (terms) 朝食付き宿泊 chōshoku-tsuki shukùhaku

bedclothes [bed'klouz] *npl* シーツと毛布 shītsu to mōfu

bedding [bed'iŋ] *n* 寝具 shīngu

bedlam [bed'ləm] *n* 大騒ぎ ōsawàgi

bedraggled [bidræg'əld] *adj* (person, clothes, hair) びしょ濡れの bishōnure no

bedridden [bed'ridən] *adj* 寝たきりの netákiri no

bedroom [bed'ru:m] *n* 寝室 shiñshitsu

bedside [bed'said] *n: at someone's bedside* ...の枕元に ...no makúramòto ni

bedsit(ter) [bed'sit(ə:r)] (*BRIT*) *n* 寝室兼居間 shiñshitsu keñ imá

bedspread [bed'spred] *n* ベッドカバー beddókabà

bedtime [bed'taim] *n* 寝る時刻 nerú jíkòku

bee [bi:] *n* ミツバチ mitsúbàchi

beech [bi:tʃ] *n* (tree) ブナ búnà; (wood) ブナ材 bunázai

beef [bi:f] *n* 牛肉 gyūniku
roast beef ローストビーフ rōsutobīfu

beefburger [bi:f'bə:rgə:r] *n* ハンバーガー hañbāgà

Beefeater [bi:f'i:tə:r] *n* ロンドン塔の守衛 roñdontō nò shuéi

beehive [bi:'haiv] *n* ミツバチの巣箱 mitsúbàchi no súbàko

beeline [bi:'lain] *n: to make a beeline for* まっしぐらに...に向かう masshígùra ni ...ni mukáu

been [bin] *pp of* **be**

beer [bi:r] *n* ビール bīru

beet [bi:t] *n* (vegetable) サトウダイコン satódaìkon, ビート bīto; (*US: also: red beet*) ビーツ bītsu

beetle [bi:t'əl] *n* 甲虫 kốchū

beetroot [bi:t'ru:t] (*BRIT*) *n* ビーツ bītsu

before [bifɔ:r'] *prep* (of time, space) ...の前に〔で〕 ...no máè ni〔de〕
♦*conj* ...する前に ...surú maè ni
♦*adv* (time, space) 前に máè ni
before going 行く前に ikú maè ni

before she goes 彼女が行く前に kánòjo ga ikú maè ni

the week before (week past) 1週間前 isshūkan maè

I've never seen it before これまで私はそれを見た事はない koré madè watákushi wà soré wò mitá koto wà nái

beforehand [bifɔ:r'hænd] *adv* あらかじめ arákajime, 前もって maémottè

beg [beg] *vi* (as beggar) こじきをする kojíki wò suru
♦*vt* (*also: beg for*: food, money) こい求める koímotomerù; (: forgiveness, mercy etc) 願う negáù
to beg someone to do something ...に...してくれと頼む ...ni ...shité kurè to tanómù *see also* pardon

began [bigæn'] *pt of* **begin**

beggar [beg'ə:r] *n* こじき kojíki

begin [bigin'] (*pt* began, *pp* begun) *vt* 始める hajímeru
♦*vi* 始まる hajímaru
to begin doing/to do something ...し始める ...shihajímeru

beginner [bigin'ə:r] *n* 初心者 shoshíñsha

beginning [bigin'iŋ] *n* 始め hajíme

begun [bigʌn'] *pp of* **begin**

behalf [bihæf'] *n: on behalf of* (as representative of) ...を代表して ...wo daíhyō shitè; (for benefit of) ...のために ...no tamé ni
on my/his behalf 私〔彼〕のために watákukushi〔kárè〕nò tamé ni

behave [biheiv'] *vi* (person) 振舞う furúmaù; (well: *also: behave oneself*) 行儀良くする gyōgi yokù suru

behavior [biheiv'jə:r] (*BRIT* **behaviour**) *n* 行動 kốdō

behead [bihed'] *vt* ...の首を切る ...no kubí wò kírù

beheld [biheld'] *pt, pp of* **behold**

behind [bihaind'] *prep* (position: at the back of) ...の後ろに〔で〕 ...no ushíro ni〔de〕; (supporting) ...を支援して ...wo shién shite; (lower in rank, etc) ...に劣って ...ni otótte
♦*adv* (at/towards the back) 後ろに〔の方へ〕 ushíro ni〔no hỗ yokù e〕; (leave, stay) 後に

átò ni

♦*n* (buttocks) しり shirí

to be behind (schedule) 遅れている okúrete irù

behind the scenes (*fig*) 非公式に hikóshiki ni

behold [bihould'] (*pt*, *pp* **beheld**) *vt* 見る mírù

beige [beiʒ] *adj* ベージュ béju

Beijing [bei'dʒiŋ] *n* 北京 pékìn

being [bi:'iŋ] *n* (creature) 生き物 ikímonò; (existence) 存在 soñzai

Beirut [beiru:t'] *n* ベイルート beírùto

belated [bilei'tid] *adj* (thanks, welcome) 遅ればせの okúrebase no

belch [beltʃ] *vi* げっぷをする geppú wò suru

♦*vt* (*gen*: belch out: smoke etc) 噴出する fuñshutsu suru

belfry [bel'fri:] *n* 鐘楼 shốrō

Belgian [bel'dʒən] *adj* ベルギーの berúgì no

♦*n* ベルギー人 berúgìjin

Belgium [bel'dʒəm] *n* ベルギー berúgì

belie [bilai'] *vt* (contradict) 隠す kakúsù; (disprove) 反証する hañshō suru

belief [bili:f'] *n* (opinion) 信念 shíñnen; (trust, faith) 信仰 shíñkō

believe [bili:v'] *vt* 信じる shiñjirù

♦*vi* 信じる shiñjirù

to believe in (God, ghosts) ...の存在を信じる ...no soñzai wo shiñjirù; (method) ...が良いと考える ...ga yőì to kañgaerù

believer [bili:v'ə:r] *n* (in idea, activity) ...が良いと考える人 ...ga yőì to kañgaeru hito; (REL) 信者 shiñja

belittle [bilit'əl] *vt* 軽視する keíshi suru

bell [bel] *n* (of church) 鐘 kané; (small) 鈴 suzú; (on door, *also* electric) 呼び鈴 yobírin, ベル bérù

belligerent [bəlidʒ'ə:rənt] *adj* (person, attitude) けんか腰の keñkagoshi no

bellow [bel'ou] *vi* (bull) 大声で鳴く ốgoè de nakú; (person) どなる donárù

bellows [bel'ouz] *npl* (for fire) ふいご fuígo

belly [bel'i:] *n* (ANAT: of person, animal) 腹 hará

belong [bilɔ:ŋ'] *vi*: ***to belong to*** (person) ...の物である ...no monő de arù; (club etc) ...に所属している ...ni shozóku shite irù, ...の会員である ...no kaíiñ de arù

this book belongs here この本はここにしまうことになっている konő hoñ wa kokó ni shimaù kotó ni nattè irú

belongings [bilɔ:ŋ'iŋz] *npl* 持物 mochímòno

beloved [bilʌv'id] *adj* (person) 最愛の saíai no; (place) 大好きな dáisuki na; (thing) 愛用の aíyō no

below [bilou'] *prep* (beneath) ...の下に〔で〕 ...no shitá ni(de); (less than: level, rate) ...より低く ...yőrì hikúkù

♦*adv* (beneath) 下に shitá ni

see below (in letter etc) 下記参照 kakísañshō

belt [belt] *n* (of leather etc: *also* TECH) ベルト berúto; (*also*: **belt of land**) 地帯 chítài

♦*vt* (thrash) 殴る nagúrù

beltway [belt'wei] (*US*) *n* (AUT: ring road) 環状道路 kañjōdòro

bemused [bimju:zd'] *adj* (person, expression) ぼう然とした bőzen to shitá

bench [bentʃ] *n* (seat) ベンチ béñchi; (work bench) 作業台 sagyốdai; (*BRIT*: POL) 議員席 giíñseki

the Bench (LAW: judges) 裁判官 saíbañkan ◇総称 sốshō

bend [bend] (*pt*, *pp* **bent**) *vt* (leg, arm, pipe) 曲げる magéru

♦*vi* (person) かがむ kagámu

♦*n* (*BRIT*: in road) カーブ kâbu; (in pipe, river) 曲った所 magátta tokoro

bend down *vi* 身をかがめる mi wo kagámeru

bend over *vi* 身をかがめる mi wo kagámeru

beneath [bini:θ'] *prep* (position) ...の下に〔で〕 ...no shitá ni(de); (unworthy of) ...のこけんに関わる ...no kokén ni kakawarù

♦*adv* 下に shitá ni

benefactor [ben'əfæktə:r] *n* (to person, institution) 恩人 oñjin

beneficial [benəfiʃ'əl] *adj* (effect, influence) 有益な yū́eki na

beneficial (to) (...に) 有益な (...ni) yū́eki na

benefit [ben'əfit] n (advantage) 利益 ríeki; (money) 手当て teáte
♦vt ...の利益になる ...no ríeki ni narù
♦vi: **he'll benefit from it** それは彼のためになるだろう soré wà kárè no tamé ni narù darò

Benelux [ben'əlʌks] n ベネルクス benérukùsu

benevolent [bənev'ələnt] adj (person) 温和な oñwa na; (organization) 慈善の jizén no

benign [binain'] adj (person, smile) 優しい yasáshii; (MED) 良性の ryṓsei no

bent [bent] pt, pp of **bend**
♦n 才能 saínō
♦adj (inf: corrupt) 不正な fuséi na
to be bent on doing ...しようと心掛けている ...shíyō to kokórogakete irù

bequest [bikwest'] n (to person, charity) 遺贈 izṓ

bereaved [biri:vd'] n: **the bereaved** 喪中の人々 mochū́ no hitóbìto

beret [bərei'] n ベレー帽 bérēbō

Berlin [bə:rlin'] n ベルリン berúrin

berm [bə:rm] (US) n (AUT) 路肩 rokáta

Bermuda [bə:rmju:d'ə] n バーミューダ bámyùda

berry [be:r'i:] n ベリー berī́ ◇総称 sṓshō

berserk [bə:rsə:rk'] adj: **to go berserk** (madman, crowd) 暴れ出す abáredasù

berth [bə:rθ] n (on ship or train) 寝台 shíndai; (for ship) バース bā́su
♦vi (ship) 接岸する setsúgan suru

beseech [bisi:tʃ'] (pt, pp **besought**) vt (person, God) ...に嘆願する ...ni tañgan suru

beset [biset'] (pt, pp **beset**) vt (subj: fears, doubts, difficulties) 襲う osóu

beside [bisaid'] prep (next to) ...の横に〔で〕 ...no yokó ni(de)
to be beside oneself (with anger) 逆上している gyakújō shite irù
that's beside the point それは問題外です soré wà mońdaigài desu

besides [bisaidz'] adv (in addition) それ

に soré ni, その上 sonó ue; (in any case) とに角 toníkaku
♦prep (in addition to, as well as) ...の外に ...no hoká ni

besiege [bisi:dʒ'] vt (town) 包囲攻撃する hṍikōgeki suru; (fig: subj: journalists, fans) ...に押寄せる ...ni oshíyoserù

besought [bisɔ:t'] pt, pp of **beseech**

best [best] adj (quality, suitability, extent) 最も良い mottómò yoí
♦adv 最も良く mottómò yokù
the best part of (quantity) ...の大部分 ...no daíbubun
at best 良くても yókùte mo
to make the best of something ...を出来るだけ我慢する ...wo dekíru dake gamáñ suru
to do one's best 最善を尽す saízen wo tsukúsù, ベストを尽くす bésùto wo tsukúsù
to the best of my knowledge 私の知っている限りでは watákushi no shittè irú kagiri de wa
to the best of my ability 私に出来る限り watákushi ni dekírù kagíri

best man n 新郎付添い役 shiñrōtsukisoiyàku

bestow [bistou'] vt (honor, title: **to bestow something on someone** ...に...を授ける ...ni ...wo sazúkeru

bestseller [best'selə:r] n (book) ベストセラー besútoserà

bet [bet] n (wager) かけ kaké
♦vb (pt, pp **bet** or **betted**)
♦vt (wager): **to bet someone something** ...と...をかける ...to ...wo kakérù
♦vi (wager) かける kakérù
to bet money on something ...に金をかける ...ni kané wò kakérù

betray [bitrei'] vt (friends, country, trust, confidence) 裏切る urágirù

betrayal [bitrei'əl] n (action) 裏切り urágiri

better [bet'ə:r] adj (quality, skill, sensation) より良い yorí yoì; (health) 良くなった yókù nattá
♦adv より良く yorí yokù
♦vt (score) ...より高い得点をする ...yórì

takái tokúten wo suru; (record) 破る ya-búru

♦*n*: *to get the better of* ...に勝つ ...ni kátsù

you had better do it あなたはそうした方が良い anátà wa số shita hố ga yoî

he thought better of it 彼は考え直した kárè wa kañgaenaoshita

to get better (MED) 良くなる yốkù naru, 回復する kaîfuku suru

better off *adj* (wealthier) ...より金がある ...yórì kané ga arù; (more comfortable etc) ...の方が良い ...no hố ga yoî

betting [bet'iŋ] *n* (gambling, odds) かけ事 kakégòto, ギャンブル gyáñburu

betting shop (*BRIT*) *n* 私営馬券売り場 shiéibaken-urîba

between [bitwi:n'] *prep* (all senses) ...の間に［で］ ...no aîda ni[de]

♦*adv* 間に aîda ni

beverage [bev'ə:ridʒ] *n* 飲物 nomímòno, 飲料 iñryō

beware [biwe:r'] *vi*: *to beware (of)* (dog, fire) (...を) 用心する (...wo) yốjin suru

「*beware of the dog*」猛犬注意 mốkenchùi

bewildered [biwil'də:rd] *adj* (stunned, confused) 当惑した tốwaku shita

bewitching [biwitʃ'iŋ] *adj* (smile, person) うっとりさせる uttốrì saséru

beyond [bi:ɑ:nd'] *prep* (in space) ...より先に［で］ ...yórì sakí ni[de]; (past: understanding) ...を越えて ...wo koétè; (after: date) ...以降に ...îkồ ni; (above) ...以上に ...îjồ ni

♦*adv* (in space, time) 先に sakí ni

beyond doubt 疑いもなく utágai mo nakù

beyond repair 修理不可能で shûri fukánồ de

bias [bai'əs] *n* (prejudice) 偏見 heñken

bias(s)ed [bai'əst] *adj* (jury) 偏見を持った heñken wo mottá; (judgement, reporting) 偏見に基づいた heñken ni motózuîta

bib [bib] *n* (child's) よだれ掛け yodárekàke

Bible [bai'bəl] *n* (REL) 聖書 séîsho, バイブル báîburu

biblical [bib'likəl] *adj* 聖書の séîsho no

bibliography [bibli:ɑ:g'rəfi:] *n* (in text) 文献目録 buñkenmokùroku

bicarbonate of soda [baiɑkə:r'bənit-] *n* 重炭酸ソーダ jûtansansồda, 重曹 jûsồ

bicker [bik'ə:r] *vi* (squabble) 口論する kồron suru

bicycle [bai'sikəl] *n* 自転車 jitéñsha

bid [bid] *n* (at auction) 付値 tsukéné; (in tender) 入札 nyûsatsu; (attempt) 試み kokóromi

♦*vb* (*pt* **bade** *or* **bid**, *pp* **bidden** *or* **bid**)

♦*vi* (at auction) 競りに加わる serí ni kuwawarù

♦*vt* (offer) ...と値を付ける ...to né wồ tsukérù

to bid someone good day (hello) ...に今日はと言う ...ni konnichi wa to iu; (farewell) ...にさようならと言う ...ni sayốnara to iu

bidder [bid'ə:r] *n*: *the highest bidder* 最高入札者 saîkōnyūsatsùsha

bidding [bid'iŋ] *n* (at auction) 競り serí

bide [baid] *vt*: *to bide one's time* (for opportunity) 時期を待つ jíkì wo mátsù

bidet [bi:dei'] *n* ビデ bídè

bifocals [baifou'kəlz] *npl* 二重焦点眼鏡 nijûshōtenmegàne

big [big] *adj* (gen) 大きい ốkiî, 大きな ố-kina

big brother 兄 áni, 兄さん níisan

big sister 姉 ané, 姉さん nèsan

bigamy [big'əmi:] *n* 重婚 jûkon

big dipper [-dip'ə:r] (*BRIT*) *n* (at fair) ジェットコースター jettốkồsutā

bigheaded [big'hedid] *adj* うぬぼれた unúboreta

bigot [big'ət] *n* (on race, religion) 偏狭な人 heñkyō na hito

bigoted [big'ətid] *adj* (on race, religion) 偏狭な heñkyō na

bigotry [big'ətri:] *n* 偏狭さ heñkyōsầ

big top *n* (at circus) 大テント ốteñto

bike [baik] *n* (bicycle) 自転車 jitéñsha

bikini [biki:'ni:] *n* ビキニ bíkìni

bilateral [bailæt'ə:rəl] *adj* (agreement)

双務的な sṓmuteki na

bile [bail] *n* (BIO) 胆汁 tañjū

bilingual [bailiŋ'gwəl] *adj* (dictionary) 二か国語の nikákokugo no; (secretary) 二か国語を話せる nikákokugo wò hanáserù

bill [bil] *n* (account) 勘定書 kañjōgaki; (invoice) 請求書 seíkyūsho; (POL) 法案 hōan; (US: banknote) 紙幣 shíhèi; (of bird) くちばし kuchíbashi; (THEATER: of show: on the bill) 番組 bañgumi

「*post no bills*」張紙厳禁 harígamigenkin

to fit/fill the bill (*fig*) 丁度いい chṓdo iì

billboard [bil'bɔːrd] *n* 広告板 kṓkokuban

billet [bil'it] *n* (MIL) 軍人宿舎 guñjinshukùsha

billfold [bil'fould] (*US*) *n* 財布 saífu

billiards [bil'jəːrdz] *n* ビリヤード biríyàdo

billion [bil'jən] *n* (*BRIT*) 兆 chṓ; (*US*) 10億 jūoku

bin [bin] *n* (*BRIT*: for rubbish) ごみ入れ gomfíre; (container) 貯蔵箱 chōzōbako, 瓶 bín

binary [bai'nəːriː] *adj* (MATH) 二進法の nishíñhō no

bind [baind] (*pt*, *pp* **bound**) *vt* (tie, tie together) 縛る shibárù; (constrain) 束縛する sokúbaku suru; (book) 製本する seíhon suru

◆*n* (*inf*: nuisance) いやな事 iyá na koto

binding [bain'diŋ] *adj* (contract) 拘束力のある kṓsokuryòku no aru

binge [bindз] (*inf*) *n*: *to go on a binge* (drink a lot) 酒浸りになる sakébitari ni narù

bingo [biŋ'gou] *n* ビンゴ bíñgo

binoculars [bənɑːk'jələːrz] *npl* 双眼鏡 sōgankyō

biochemistry [baioukem'istriː] *n* 生化学 seíkagàku

biography [baiɑːg'rəfiː] *n* 伝記 deñki

biological [baiɑːlɑːdʒ'ikəl] *adj* (science, warfare) 生物学の seíbutsugàku no; (washing powder) 酵素洗剤 kṓsoseñzai

biology [baiɑːl'ədʒiː] *n* 生物学 seíbutsu-

gàku

birch [bəːrtʃ] *n* (tree) カバノキ kabá noki; (wood) カバ材 kabázài

bird [bəːrd] *n* (ZOOL) 鳥 torí; (*BRIT*: *inf*: girl) 女の子 oñna no ko

bird's-eye view [bəːrdzai-] *n* (aerial view) 全景 zeñkei; (overview) 概観 gaíkan

bird-watcher [bəːrd'wɑːtʃəːr] *n* バードウォッチャー bǎdowotchǎ

bird-watching [bəːrd'wɑːtʃiŋ] *n* バードウォッチング bǎdowotchìngu

Biro [bai'rou]® *n* ボールペン bṓrupen

birth [bəːrθ] *n* (of baby, animal, *also fig*) 誕生 tañjō

to give birth to (BIO: subj: woman, animal) ...を生む ...wo umú

birth certificate *n* 出生証明書 shusshō〔shusséi〕shṓmeisho

birth control *n* (policy) 産児制限 sañjiseìgen; (methods) 避妊 hinín

birthday [bəːrθ'dei] *n* 誕生日 tañjōbi

◆*cpd* (cake, card, present etc) 誕生日の tañjōbi no ¶ *see also* **happy**

birthplace [bəːrθ'pleis] *n* (country, town etc) 出生地 shusshōchì〔shusséichì〕, 生れ故郷 umárekokyò; (house etc) 生家 seíka

birth rate *n* 出生率 shusshṓritsu〔shussèiritsu〕

Biscay [bis'kei] *n*: *the Bay of Biscay* ビスケー湾 bisúkèwan

biscuit [bis'kit] (*BRIT*) *n* ビスケット bisúkettò

bisect [baisekt'] *vt* (angle etc) 二等分する nitṓbun suru

bishop [biʃ'əp] *n* (REL: Catholic etc) 司教 shíkyō; (: Protestant) 監督 kañtoku; (: Greek Orthodox) 主教 shúkyō; (CHESS) ビショップ bíshòppu

bit [bit] *pt of* **bite**

◆*n* (piece) 欠けら kakéra; (COMPUT) ビット bíttò; (of horse) はみ hámì

a bit of 少しの sukóshì no, ちょっとの chottó no

a bit mad ちょっと頭がおかしい chóttò atáma ga okáshiì

a bit dangerous ちょっと危ない chóttò abúnaì

bit by bit 少しずつ sukóshi zutsù

bitch [bitʃ] *n* (dog) 雌犬 mesúinu; (*inf!*: woman) あま ámà

bite [bait] (*pt* bit, *pp* bitten) *vt* (subj: person) かむ kámù; (: dog etc) ...にかみ付く ...ni kamítsuku; (: insect etc) 刺す sásù
♦*vi* (dog etc) かみ付く kamítsuku; (insect etc) 刺す sásù
♦*n* (insect bite) 虫刺され mushísasàre; (mouthful) 一口 hitókùchi

to bite one's nails つめをかむ tsumé wo kámù

let's have a bite (to eat) (*inf*) 何か食べよう nánì ka tabéyò

bitten [bit'ən] *pp of* bite

bitter [bit'ə:r] *adj* (person) 恨みを持った urámi wð mottá; (taste, experience, disappointment) 苦い nigáì; (wind) 冷たい tsumétaì; (struggle) 激しい hagéshiì; (criticism) 辛らつな shíñratsu na
♦*n* (*BRIT*: beer) ビター bitā ◇ホップの利いた苦いビール hoppú no kííta nigáî bíru

bitterness [bit'ə:rnis] *n* (anger) 恨み urámi; (bitter taste) 苦み nigámi

bizarre [bizɑ:r'] *adj* (conversation, contraption) 奇妙な kímyð na

blab [blæb] (*inf*) *vi* (to the press) しゃべる shabérù

black [blæk] *adj* (color) 黒い kuróì; (person) 黒人の kokújin no; (tea, coffee) ブラックの burákku no
♦*n* (color) 黒 kúrò; (person): *Black* 黒人 kokújin
♦*vt* (*BRIT*: INDUSTRY) ボイコットする boíkottð suru

black humor ブラックユーモア burákkuyùmoa

to give someone a black eye ...を殴って目にあざを作る ...wo nagúttè me ni azá wo tsukúrù

black and blue (bruised) あざだらけの azá daràke no

to be in the black (in credit) 黒字である kuróji de arù

blackberry [blæk'be:ri:] *n* ブラックベリー burákkuberì ◇キイチゴの一種 kiíchigo no isshù

blackbird [blæk'bə:rd] *n* (European bird) クロウタドリ kuróutadòri

blackboard [blæk'bɔ:rd] *n* 黒板 kokúban

black coffee *n* ブラックコーヒー burákku kōhī

blackcurrant [blækkʌr'ənt] *n* クロスグリ kurósugùri

blacken [blæk'ən] *vt* (*fig*: name, reputation) 汚す kegásù

black ice (*BRIT*) *n* (on road) 凍結路面 tóketsuromèn

blackleg [blæk'leg] (*BRIT*) *n* (INDUSTRY) スト破り sutóyabùri

blacklist [blæk'list] *n* ブラックリスト burákkurisùto

blackmail [blæk'meil] *n* ゆすり yusúri
♦*vt* ゆする yusúru

black market *n* やみ市 yamíichi

blackout [blæk'aut] *n* (MIL) 灯火管制 tókakañsei; (power cut) 停電 teíden; (TV, RADIO) 放送中止 hōsōchūshi; (faint) 一時的意識喪失 ichíjitekiishìkisō-shitsu, ブラックアウト burákkuaùto

Black Sea *n*: *the Black Sea* 黒海 kókkài

black sheep *n* (*fig*) 持て余し者 motéamashimono

blacksmith [blæk'smiθ] *n* 鍛冶屋 kajíya

black spot *n* (*BRIT*: AUT) 事故多発地点 jikótahátsuchitèn; (: for unemployment etc) ...が深刻になっている地域 ...ga shíñkoku ni nattè irú chíìki

bladder [blæd'ə:r] *n* (ANAT) ぼうこう bókō

blade [bleid] *n* (of knife, sword) 刃 hà; (of propeller) 羽根 hané

a blade of grass 草の葉 kusá no ha

blame [bleim] *n* (for error, crime) 責任 sekínin
♦*vt*: *to blame someone for something* ...を...のせいにする ...wo ...no seí ni suru

to be to blame 責任が...にある sekínin ga ...ni arù

blameless [bleim'lis] *adj* (person) 潔白な keppáku na

bland [blænd] *adj* (taste, food) 味気ない ajíke naì

blank [blæŋk] *adj* (paper etc) 空白の kúhaku no; (look) ぼう然とした bốzen to shitá

♦n (of memory) 空白 kúhaku; (on form) 空所 kúsho; (also: **blank cartridge**) 空包 kúhō

a blank sheet of paper 白紙 hakúshi

blank check n 金額未記入の小切手 kiñgakumi-kinyū no kogítte

blanket [blæŋ'kit] n (of cloth) 毛布 mốfu; (of snow, fog etc) 一面の... ichímen no ...

blare [ble:r] vi (brass band, horns, radio) 鳴り響く naríhibikù

blasé [blɑ:zei'] adj (reaction, tone) 無関心な mukáñshin na

blasphemy [blæs'fəmi:] n (REL) 冒とく bốtoku

blast [blæst] n (of wind) 突風 toppú; (of explosive) 爆発 bakúhatsu

♦vt (blow up) 爆破する bakúha suru

blast-off [blæst'ɔ:f] n (SPACE) 発射 hasshá

blatant [blei'tənt] adj (discrimination, bias) 露骨な rokótsu na

blaze [bleiz] n (fire) 火事 kájì; (fig: of color, glory) きらめき kirámeki; (: publicity) 大騒ぎ ốsawàgi

♦vi (fire) 燃え盛る moésakerù; (guns) 続け様に発砲する tsuzúkezama ni happố suru; (fig: eyes) 怒りで燃える ikári de moéru

♦vt: *to blaze a trail* (fig) 先べんを付ける señben wo tsúkeru

blazer [blei'zə:r] n (of school, team etc) ブレザー burēzā

bleach [bli:tʃ] n (also: **household bleach**) 漂白剤 hyốhakuzài

♦vt (fabric) 漂白する hyốhaku suru

bleached [bli:tʃt] adj (hair) 漂白した hyốhaku shitá

bleachers [bli:'tʃə:rz] (US) npl (SPORT) 外野席 gaíyasèki

bleak [bli:k] adj (countryside) もの寂しい monósabishiì; (weather) 悪い warúì; (prospect, situation) 暗い kurái; (smile) 悲しそうな kanáshisò na

bleary-eyed [bli:'ri:aid] adj 目がしょぼしょぼしている me ga shobòshobo shité

irù

bleat [bli:t] vi (goat, sheep) 鳴く nakú

bled [bled] pt, pp of **bleed**

bleed [bli:d] (pt, pp **bled**) vi (MED) 出血する shukkétsu suru

my nose is bleeding 鼻血が出ている hanáji ga dete irù

bleeper [bli:'pə:r] n (device) ポケットベル pokétto berù

blemish [blem'iʃ] n (on skin) 染み shimí; (on fruit) 傷 kizú; (on reputation) 汚点 otéń

blend [blend] n (of tea, whisky) 混合 koñgō, ブレンド buréndo

♦vt 混ぜ合せる mazéawaserù, 混合する koñgō suru

♦vi (colors etc: also: **blend in**) 溶け込む tokékomù

bless [bles] (pt, pp **blessed** or **blest**) vt (REL) 祝福する shukúfuku suru

bless you! (after sneeze) お大事に o-dáiji ni

blessing [bles'iŋ] n (approval) 承認 shốnin; (godsend) 恵み megúmi; (REL) 祝福 shukúfuku

blew [blu:] pt of **blow**

blight [blait] vt (hopes, life etc) 駄目にする damé ni suru

blimey [blai'mi:] (BRIT: inf) excl おやおや oyà

blind [blaind] adj (MED) 盲目の mốmoku no; (pej) めくらの mekúra no; (euphemistically) 目の不自由な me no fujíyū na; (fig): **blind (to)** (...を) 見る目がない (...wo) mirú mé ga naí

♦n (for window) ブラインド buráindo; (: also: **Venetian blind**) ベネシアンブラインド benéshian buraìndo

♦vt (MED) 失明させる shitsúmei sasérù; (dazzle) ...の目をくらます...no me wo kurámasù; (deceive) だます damásù

the blind (blind people) 盲人 mốjiñ ◇総称 sốshō

blind alley n (fig) 行き詰り yukízumari

blind corner (BRIT) n 見通しの悪い曲り角 mitốshi no waruì magárikadò

blindfold [blaind'fould] n 目隠し mekákùshi

♦adj 目隠しをした mekákùshi wo shitá
♦adv 目隠しをして mekákùshi wo shitè
♦vt 目隠しする mekákùshi suru

blindly [blaind'li:] adv (without seeing) よく見ないで yókù minàide; (without thinking) めくら滅法に mekúrameppò ni

blindness [blaind'nis] n (MED) 盲目 mô-moku; (euphemistically) 目の障害 me no shôgai

blind spot n (AUT) 死角 shikáku; (fig: weak spot) 盲点 môten

blink [bliŋk] vi (person, animal) 瞬く ma-bátakù; (light) 点滅する teñmetsu suru

blinkers [bliŋk'ə:rz] npl 馬の目隠し umá no mekákùshi

bliss [blis] n (complete happiness) 至福 shifúku

blister [blis'tə:r] n (on skin) 水膨れ mizú-bukùre; (in paint, rubber) 気胞 kihô
♦vi (paint) 気胞ができる kihô ga dekirù

blithely [blaið'li:] adv (proceed, assume) 軽率に keísotsu ni

blitz [blits] n (MIL) 空襲 kûshū

blizzard [bliz'ə:rd] n 吹雪 fubúki, ブリザード burízàdo

bloated [blou'tid] adj (face, stomach: swollen) はれた haréta; (person: full) たらふく食べた taráfùku tabèta

blob [blɑːb] n (of glue, paint) 滴 shizúku; (something indistinct) はっきり見えない もの hakkírì miénài monó

bloc [blɑːk] n (POL) 連合 reñgō, ブロック burókkù

block [blɑːk] n (of buildings) 街区 gáìku, ブロック burókkù; (of stone, wood) ブロック burókkù; (in pipes) 障害物 shôgaì-butsu
♦vt (entrance, road) 塞ぐ fuságu; (progress) 邪魔する jamá suru
block of flats (BRIT) マンション mañshon
mental block 精神的ブロック seíshinteki burokkù

blockade [blɑːkeid'] n 封鎖 fûsa

blockage [blɑːk'idʒ] n 閉そく heísoku

blockbuster [blɑːk'bʌstə:r] n (film, book) センセーション señsēshon

block letters npl 活字体 katsújitai

bloke [blouk] (BRIT: inf) n 男 otóko, 野郎 yárō

blond(e) [blɑːnd] adj (hair) 金髪の kiñpatsu no, ブロンドの buróndo no
♦n (woman) 金髪の女性 kiñpatsu no joséi, ブロンド buróndo

blood [blʌd] n (BIO) 血 chi, 血液 ketsúèki

blood donor n 献血者 keñketsùsha

blood group n 血液型 ketsúekigata

bloodhound [blʌd'haund] n ブラッドハウンド buráddohaùndo

blood poisoning [-poi'zəniŋ] n 敗血症 haíketsushō

blood pressure n 血圧 ketsúatsu

bloodshed [blʌd'ʃed] n 流血 ryúketsu

bloodshot [blʌd'ʃɑːt] adj (eyes) 充血した júketsu shitá

bloodstream [blʌd'striːm] n 血流 ketsúryū

blood test n 血液検査 ketsúekikeñsa

bloodthirsty [blʌd'θə:rsti:] adj (tyrant, regime) 血に飢えた chi ni úeta

blood vessel n 血管 kekkán

bloody [blʌd'i:] adj (battle) 血みどろの chimídoro no; (nose) 鼻血を出した hanáji wo dashìta; (BRIT: inf!): **this bloody ...** くそったれ... kusóttarè...
bloody strong/good (inf!) すごく強い〔良い〕sugókù tsuyóì〔yoì〕

bloody-minded [blʌd'i:main'did] (BRIT: inf) adj 意地悪な ijíwàru na

bloom [bluːm] n (BOT: flower) 花 haná
♦vi (tree) ...の花が咲く ...no haná ga sakú; (flower) 咲く sakú

blossom [blɑːs'əm] n (BOT) 花 haná
♦vi (BOT) 花が咲く haná ga sakú; (fig): **to blossom into** 成長して...になる seíchōshite ...ni narú

blot [blɑːt] n (on text) 染み shimí; (fig: on name etc) 傷 kizú
♦vt (with ink etc) 汚す yogósu

blotchy [blɑːtʃ'i:] adj (complexion) 染みだらけの shimídaràke no

blot out vt (view) 見えなくする miénàku suru; (memory) 消す kesú

blotting paper [blɑːt'iŋ-] n 吸取り紙 suítorigàmi

blow [blou] n (punch etc: also fig) 打撃 dagéki; (with sword) 一撃 ichígeki
♦vb (pt **blew**, pp **blown**)
♦vi (wind) 吹く fúkù; (person) 息を吹掛ける íki wo fukíkakerù
♦vt (subj: wind) 吹飛ばす fukítobasù; (instrument, whistle) 吹く fúkù; (fuse) 飛ばす tobásu
to blow one's nose 鼻をかむ haná wo kamú

blow away vt 吹飛ばす fukítobasù

blow down vt (tree) 吹倒す fukítaosù

blow-dry [blou'drai] n (hairstyle) ブロー仕上げ buróshiàge

blowlamp [blou'læmp] (BRIT) n = **blowtorch**

blow off vt (hat etc) 吹飛ばす fukítobasù

blow out vi (fire, flame) 吹消す fukíkesù

blow-out [blou'aut] n (of tire) パンク pañku

blow over vi (storm) 静まる shizúmarù; (crisis) 収まる osámarù

blowtorch [blou'tɔ:rtʃ] n ブローランプ buróraǹpu, トーチランプ tóchiraǹpu

blow up vi (storm) 起きる okírù; (crisis) 起る okórù
♦vt (bridge: destroy) 爆破する bakúha suru; (tire: inflate) 膨らます fukúramasu; (PHOT: enlarge) 引延ばす hikínobasù

blue [blu:] adj (color) 青い aóì, ブルーの burú no; (depressed) 憂うつな yúutsu na
blue film ポルノ映画 porúnoeìga
blue joke わいせつなジョーク waísetsu na jóku
out of the blue (fig) 青天のへきれきの様に seíten no hekirekí no yó ni

bluebell [blu:'bel] n ツルボ tsurúbò

bluebottle [blu:'bɑ:təl] n (insect) アオバエ aóbae

blueprint [blu:'print] n (fig): **a blueprint (for)** (...の) 計画 (...no) keíkaku, (...の) 青写真 (...no) aójashìn

blues [blu:z] n: **the blues** (MUS) ブルース búrùsu

bluff [blʌf] vi (pretend, threaten) はったりを掛ける hattári wo kakérù
♦n (pretense) はったり hattári
to call someone's bluff ...に挑戦する ...ni chōsen suru

blunder [blʌn'də:r] n (political) へま hémà
♦vi (bungle something) へまをする hémà wo suru

blunt [blʌnt] adj (pencil) 先が太い sakí ga futóì; (knife) 切れない kirénaì; (person, talk) 率直な sotchóku na

blur [blə:r] n (shape) かすんで見える物 kasúnde miérù monó
♦vt (vision) くらます kurámasu; (distinction) ぼかす bokásù

blurb [blə:rb] n (for book, concert etc) 宣伝文句 señdenmoǹku

blurt out [blə:rt-] vt 出し抜けに言い出す dashínuke ni iídasù

blush [blʌʃ] vi (with shame, embarrassment) 赤面する sekímen suru
♦n 赤面 sekímen

blustering [blʌs'tə:riŋ] adj (person) 威張り散らす ibárichirasù

blustery [blʌs'tə:ri:] adj (weather) 風の強い kazé no tsuyóì

boar [bɔ:r] n イノシシ inóshishì

board [bɔ:rd] n (cardboard) ボール紙 bórugami; (wooden) 板 ítà; (on wall: notice board) 掲示板 keíjiban; (for chess etc) ...盤 ...bañ; (committee) 委員会 iíñkai; (in firm) 役員会 yakúiñkai; (NAUT, AVIAT): **on board** ...に乗って ...ni notte
♦vt (ship, train) ...に乗る ...ni norú
full/half board (BRIT) 3食〔2食〕付き sañshoku(nishóku)tsukí
board and lodging 賄い付き下宿 makánaitsuki geshùku
to go by the board (fig) 捨てられる sutérareru

boarder [bɔ:r'də:r] n (SCOL) 寄宿生 kishúkuseì

boarding card [bɔ:r'diŋ-] n = **boarding pass**

boarding house n 下宿屋 geshúkuya

boarding pass n (AVIAT, NAUT) 搭乗券 tójōken

boarding school n 全寮制学校 zeñryōseigakkố

board room n 役員会議室 yakúinkaigi-shîtsu

board up vt (door, window) ...に板を張る ...ni ítà wo harú

boast [boust] vi: *to boast (about/of)* (...を) 自慢する (...wo) jimán suru

boat [bout] n (small) ボート bôto; (ship) 船 fúnè

boater [bou'tə:r] n (hat) かんかん帽 kań-kańbō

boatswain [bou'sən] n 甲板長 kốhańchō, ボースン bôsun

bob [ba:b] vi (boat, cork on water: *also*: **bob up and down**) 波に揺れる namí ni yuréru

bobby [ba:b'i:] (BRIT: *inf*) n (police-man) 警官 keîkan

bobsleigh [ba:b'slei] n ボブスレー bobûsurē

bob up vi (appear) 現れる aráwarerù

bode [boud] vi: *to bode well/ill (for)* (...にとって) 良い(悪い)前兆である (...ni tottè) yoî(warúî)zeńchō de arù

bodily [ba:d'əli:] adj (needs, functions) 身体の shiñtai no
♦adv (lift, carry) 体ごと karádagoto

body [ba:d'i:] n (ANAT: *gen*) 体 karáda, 身体 shíntai; (corpse) 死体 shitái; (object) 物体 buttái; (main part) 本体 hốntai; (of car) 車体 shatái, ボディー bôdì; (*fig*: group) 団体 dańtai; (: organization) 組織 sốshìki; (quantity: of facts) 量 ryô; (of wine) こく kokù

body-building [ba:d'i:bil'diŋ] n ボディービル bodíbirù

bodyguard [ba:d'i:ga:rd] n (of states-man, celebrity) 護衛 goéi, ボディーガード bodígàdo

bodywork [ba:d'i:wə:rk] n (AUT) 車体 shatái

bog [ba:g] n (GEO) 沼沢地 shốtakùchi
♦vt: *to get bogged down* (*fig*) 泥沼にはまり込む dorónuma ni hamárikomù

boggle [ba:g'əl] vi: *the mind boggles* 理解できない ríkài dekínai

bogus [bou'gəs] adj (claim, workman etc) 偽の nisé no

boil [bɔil] vt (water) 沸かす wakásu; (eggs, potatoes etc) ゆでる yudérù
♦vi (liquid) 沸く wakú; (*fig*: with anger) かんかんに怒る kańkan ni okórù; (: with heat) うだるような暑さになる udáru yô na atsùsa ni narú
♦n (MED) 出来物 dekímònð
to come to a (US)/the (BRIT) boil 沸き始める wakíhajimerù

boil down to vt *fus* (*fig*) 要するに...である yố surù ni ...de arù

boiled egg [bɔild-] n ゆで卵 yudétamàgo

boiled potatoes npl ゆでジャガイモ yudéjagaìmo

boiler [bɔi'lə:r] n (device) ボイラー bôîrā

boiler suit (BRIT) n つなぎの作業着 tsunági no sagyôgi

boiling point [bɔi'liŋ-] n (of liquid) 沸騰点 fúttōten

boil over vi (kettle, milk) 吹こぼれる fukíkoborerù

boisterous [bɔis'tə:rəs] adj (noisy, excit-able: person, crowd) 騒々しい sốzōshiî

bold [bould] adj (brave) 大胆な daîtañ na; (*pej*: cheeky) ずうずうしい zûzūshiî; (pattern) 際立った kiwádattà; (line) 太い futôî; (color) 派手な hadé na

Bolivia [bouliv'i:ə] n ボリビア boríbìa

bollard [ba:l'ə:rd] (BRIT) n (AUT) 標識柱 hyốshikichū ◇安全地帯などを示す ańzenchitái nadò wo shimésù

bolster [boul'stə:r] n (pillow) 長まくら nagámakùra

bolster up vt (case) 支持する shíjì suru

bolt [boult] n (lock) ラッチ rátchì; (with nut) ボルト borúto
♦adv: *bolt upright* 背筋を伸ばして sesúji wo nobàshite
♦vt (door) ...のラッチを掛ける ...no ratchì wo kakérù; (*also*: **bolt together**) ボルトで止める borúto de tomérù; (food) 丸のみする marúnomi suru
♦vi (run away: horse) 逃出す nigédasu

bomb [ba:m] n (device) 爆弾 bakúdan
♦vt 爆撃する bakúgeki suru

bombard [ba:m'ba:rd'] vt (MIL: with big guns etc) 砲撃する hốgeki suru; (: from planes) 爆撃する bakúgeki suru; (fig: with questions) ...に浴びせる ...ni abíseru

bombardment [bɑːmbɑːrd'mənt] n: *bombardment from guns* 砲撃 hógeki *bombardment from planes* 爆撃 bakúgeki

bombastic [bɑːmbæs'tik] adj (person, language) もったい振った mottáibuttà

bomb disposal n: *bomb disposal unit* 爆弾処理班 bakúdanshorihàn

bomber [bɑːm'əːr] n (AVIAT) 爆撃機 bakúgekikì

bombshell [bɑːm'ʃel] n (fig: revelation) 爆弾 bakúdan

bona fide [bou'nəfaid'] adj (traveler etc) 本物の honmono no

bond [bɑːnd] n (of affection, also gen: link) きずな kizúna; (binding promise) 約束 yakúsoku; (FINANCE) 証券 shóken; (COMM): *in bond* (of goods) 保税倉庫で hozéisòko de

bondage [bɑːn'didʒ] n (slavery) 奴隷の身分 doréi no mibùn

bone [boun] n (ANAT, gen) 骨 honé
♦vt (meat, fish) 骨を抜く honé wò nukú

bone idle adj ぐうたらの gútara no

bonfire [bɑːn'faiəːr] n たき火 takíbi

bonnet [bɑːn'it] n (hat: also BRIT: of car) ボンネット bofínettò

bonus [bou'nəs] n (payment) ボーナス bónasu; (fig: additional benefit) おまけ o-máke

bony [bou'niː] adj (MED: tissue) 骨のhoné no; (arm, face) 骨張った honébattà; (meat, fish) 骨の多い honé no ōi

boo [buː] excl (to surprise someone) わっ wát; (to show dislike) ぶー bū
♦vt 野次る yajírù

booby trap [buː'biː-] n (MIL) 仕掛爆弾 shikákebakùdan

book [buk] n (novel etc) 本 hóñ; (of stamps, tickets) 1つづり hitótsuzùri
♦vt (ticket, seat, room) 予約する yoyáku suru; (subj: traffic warden, policeman) ...に違反切符を書く ...ni ihánkippù wo kakù; (: referee) ...に勧告を与える ...ni kañkoku wò atáeru

bookcase [buk'keis] n 本棚 hóñdana

booking office [buk'iŋ-] (BRIT) n (RAIL, THEATER) 切符売り場 kippú urìba

book-keeping [bukkiː'piŋ] n 簿記 bókì

booklet [buk'lit] n 小冊子 shósasshì, パンフレット páñfurettò

bookmaker [buk'meikəːr] n 馬券屋 bakén-ya

books [buks] npl (COMM: accounts) 帳簿 chóbo

bookseller [buk'seləːr] n 本屋 hóñ-ya

bookshop [buk'ʃɑːp] n = **bookstore**

bookstore [buk'stɔːr] n 本屋 hóñ-ya, 書店 shotén

boom [buːm] n (noise) とどろき todóroki; (in prices, population etc) ブーム búmu
♦vi (guns, thunder) とどろく todórokù; (voice) とどろく様な声で言う todórokù yō na koè de iú; (business) 繁盛する hañjō suru

boomerang [buː'məræŋ] n ブーメラン búmeran

boon [buːn] n (blessing, benefit) 有難い物 arígataì monó

boost [buːst] n (to confidence, sales etc) 増す事 masú kotó
♦vt (confidence, sales etc) 増す masú; (economy) 促進する sokúshin suru

booster [buːs'təːr] n (MED) ブースター búsutā

boot [buːt] n (knee-length) 長靴 nagágutsu, ブーツ bútsu; (also: hiking/climbing boots) 登山靴 tozáñgutsu; (also: soccer boots) サッカーシューズ sakkáshùzu; (BRIT: of car) トランク toráñku
♦vt (COMPUT) 起動する kidő suru
... to boot (in addition) おまけに o-máke ni

booth [buːθ] n (at fair) 屋台 yátai; (telephone booth, voting booth) ボックス bokkùsu

booty [buː'tiː] n 戦利品 señrihin

booze [buːz] (inf) n 酒 saké

border [bɔːr'dəːr] n (of a country) 国境 kokkyő; (also: **flower border**) ボーダー花壇 bódākadàn; (band, edge: on cloth etc) へり herí
♦vt (road: subject: trees etc) ...に沿って

立っている ...ni sottě tattě irú; (another country: also: **border on**) ...に隣接する ...ni riňsetsu suru

borderline [boːrˈdəːrlain] n (fig): **on the borderline** 際どいところで kiwádoì tokóro de, ボーダーラインすれすれで bôˈdāraìn surésure de

borderline case n 決めにくいケース kiménikuì kēsu

border on vt fus (fig: insanity, brutality) ...に近い ...ni chikáì

Borders [boːrˈdəːrz] n: **the Borders** ボーダーズ州 bôdāzùshū ◇イングランドに隣接するスコットランド南部の1州 iňgurando ni riňsetsu surú sukóttòrando naňbu no isshū

bore [boːr] pt of **bear**
◆vt (hole) ...に穴を開ける ...ni anáwo akéru; (oil well, tunnel) 掘る hórù; (person) 退屈させる taíkutsu saséru
◆n (person) 退屈させない話で退屈させる人 tsumáranaì hanáshi de taíkutsu saséru hitô; (of gun) 口径 kôkei
to be bored 退屈する taíkutsu suru

boredom [boːrˈdəm] n (condition) 退屈 taíkutsu; (boring quality) 詰まらなさ tsumáranasà

boring [boːrˈiŋ] adj (tedious, unimaginative) 退屈な taíkutsu na

born [boːrn] adj: **to be born** 生れる umáreru
I was born in 1960 私は1960年に生れました watákushi wa séñkyúhyàkurokújūnen ni umáremashìta

borne [boːrn] pp of **bear**

borough [bəːrˈə] n (POL) 区 ku

borrow [baːrˈou] vt: **to borrow something** (from someone) ...を借りる ...wo karíru

bosom [buzˈəm] n (ANAT) 胸 munē

bosom friend n 親友 shiň-yū

boss [boːs] n (employer) 雇い主 yatóìnushi; (supervisor, superior) 上司 jôshi, 親方 oyákata, ボス bôsù
◆vt (also: **boss around**, **boss about**) こき使う kokítsukaù

bossy [boːsˈiː] adj (overbearing) 威張り散らす ibárichirasù

bosun [bouˈsən] n (NAUT) = **boatswain**

botany [baːtˈəniː] n 植物学 shokúbutsugàku

botch [baːtʃ] vt (bungle: also: **botch up**) 不手際で...をしくじる futégìwa de ...wo shikújirù

both [bouθ] adj 両方の ryôhô no
◆pron (things, people) 両方 ryôhô
◆adv: **both A and B** AもBもA mo B mo
both of us went, we both went 私たち2人共行きました watákushitàchi futáritomo ikímashìta

bother [baːðˈəːr] vt (worry) 心配させる shiňpai saséru; (disturb) ...に迷惑を掛ける ...ni mêìwaku wo kakérù
◆vi (also: **bother oneself**) ...に気付かう ...ni kizúkaù
◆n (trouble) 迷惑 mêìwaku; (nuisance) いやな事 iyá na kotô
to bother doing わざわざ...する wázàwaza...surú

bottle [baːtˈəl] n (container: for milk, wine, perfume etc) 瓶 bíñ; (of wine, whiskey etc) 瓶一杯 bíñ ippái; (amount contained) 瓶一杯 bíñ ippái; (baby's) ほ乳瓶 hó-nyūbin
◆vt (beer, wine) 瓶に詰める bíñ ni tsumérù

bottleneck [baːtˈəlnek] n (AUT: also fig: of supply) ネック nékkù

bottle-opener [baːtˈəloupənəːr] n 栓抜き seřnukì

bottle up vt (emotion) 抑える osáeru

bottom [baːtˈəm] n (of container, sea etc) 底 sokô; (buttocks) しり shirí; (of page, list) 一番下の所 ichíban shitá no tokôro; (of class) びり bírì
◆adj (lower: part) 下の方の shitá no hô no; (last: rung, position) 一番下の ichíban shitá no

bottomless [baːtˈəmlis] adj (funds, store) 際限のない saígeň no naì

bough [bau] n 枝 edá

bought [boːt] pt, pp of **buy**

boulder [boulˈdəːr] n 大きな丸石 ôkìna marúishi

bounce [bauns] vi (ball) 跳ね返る hanékaèru; (check) 不渡りになる fuwátàri ni narù

♦vt (ball) 跳ねさせる hanésaserù

♦n (rebound) 跳ね返る事 hanékaèru kotò

bouncer [baun'sə:r] (inf) n (at dance, club) 用心棒 yōjìnbō

bound [baund] pt, pp of **bind**

♦n (leap) 一飛び hitótòbi; (gen pl: limit) 限界 geńkai

♦vi (leap) 跳ぶ tobú

♦vt (border) ...の境界になる ...no kyōkai ni narù

♦adj: **bound by** (law, regulation) ...に拘束されている ...ni kōsoku sarête irù

to be bound to do something (obliged) やむを得ず...しなければならない yamú wo ezú ...shinákereba naranaì; (likely) 必ず...するだろう kanárazu ...surú darò

bound for (NAUT, AUT, RAIL) ...行きの ...yukí no

out of bounds (fig: place) 立入禁止で tachíirikinshi de

boundary [baun'də:ri:] n (border, limit) 境界 kyōkai

boundless [baund'lis] adj (energy etc) 果てし無い hatéshinaì

bouquet [bu:kei'] n (of flowers) 花束 hanátàba, ブーケ būke

bourgeois [bur'ʒwɑ:] adj ブルジョア根性の burújoakoǹjō no

bout [baut] n (of malaria etc) 発作 hossá; (of activity) 発作的にする事 hossáteki ni suru kotó; (BOXING etc) 試合 shiái

boutique [bu:ti:k'] n ブティック butíkku

bow[1] [bou] n (knot) チョウ結び chōmusùbi; (weapon, MUS) 弓 yumí

bow[2] [bau] n (of the head) 会釈 éshàku; (of the head and body) お辞儀 ojígi; (NAUT: also: **bows**) 船首 séñshu, へ先 hesáki

♦vi (with head) 会釈する éshàku suru; (with head and body) お辞儀する ojígi suru; (yield): **to bow to/before** (reason, pressure) ...に屈服する ...ni kuppúku suru

bowels [bau'əlz] npl (ANAT) 腸 chō; (of the earth etc) 深い所 fukáì tokóro

bowl [boul] n (container) 鉢 hachí, ボール bōru; (contents) ボール一杯 bōru ippái; (ball) 木球 mokkyū, ボール bōru

♦vi (CRICKET) 投球する tōkyū suru

bow-legged [bou'legid] adj がにまたの ganímata no

bowler [bou'lə:r] n (CRICKET) 投手 tōshu, ボウラー bōrā; (BRIT: also: **bowler hat**) 山高帽 yamátakabò

bowling [bou'liŋ] n (game) ボーリング bōringu

bowling alley n (building) ボーリング場 bōringujò; (track) レーン rēn

bowling green n ローンボーリング場 rōnbōringujō

bowls [boulz] n (game) ローンボーリング rōnbōringu

bow tie n チョウネクタイ chōnekùtai

box [bɑ:ks] n (gen) 箱 hakó; (also: **cardboard box**) 段ボール箱 dañbōrubàko; (THEATER) ボックス bókkùsu

♦vt (put in a box) 箱に詰める hakó ni tsumérù

♦vi (SPORT) ボクシングする bókùshingu suru

boxer [bɑ:k'sə:r] n (person) ボクシング選手 bokúshingu señshu, ボクサー bókùsā

boxing [bɑ:k'siŋ] n (SPORT) ボクシング bokúshingu

Boxing Day (BRIT) n ボクシングデー bokúshingudè

boxing gloves npl ボクシンググローブ bokúshinguguròbu

boxing ring n リング riñgu

box office n 切符売り場 kippú urība

boxroom [bɑ:ks'ru:m] (BRIT) n 納戸 nañdo

boy [bɔi] n (young) 少年 shōnen, 男の子 otóko no kò; (older) 青年 seínen; (son) 息子 musúko

boycott [bɔi'kɑ:t] n ボイコット boíkottò

♦vt (person, product, place etc) ボイコットする boíkottò suru

boyfriend [bɔi'frend] n 男友達 otōkotomòdachi, ボーイフレンド bōìfureǹdo

boyish [bɔi'iʃ] adj (man) 若々しい wakáwakashiì; (looks, smile, woman) 少年の様な shōnen no yò na

B.R. [biːɑːr] *n abbr* = **British Rail**

bra [brɑː] *n* ブラジャー burájà

brace [breis] *n* (on teeth) 固定器 kotêîki, ブレース burèsu; (tool) 曲り柄ドリル magáriedorîru
◆*vt* (knees, shoulders) ...に力を入れる ...ni chikára wo iréru
to brace oneself (for weight) 構えて待つ kamáete matsù; (for shock) 心を静めて待つ kokóro wo shizúmetè matsu

bracelet [breis'lit] *n* 腕輪 udéwa, ブレスレット burésuretto

braces [breiˈsiz] (*BRIT*) *npl* ズボンつり zubôntsuri, サスペンダー sasúpeñdā

bracing [breiˈsiŋ] *adj* (air, breeze) さわやかな sawáyàka na

bracken [bræk'ən] *n* ワラビ warábi

bracket [bræk'it] *n* (TECH) 腕金 udégane; (group) グループ gúrùpu; (range) 層 sò; (*also*: **brace bracket**) 中括弧 chūkakkò, ブレース búrèsu; (*also*: **round bracket**) 小括弧 shôkakkò, 丸括弧 marúkakkò, パーレン pàren; (*also*: **square bracket**) かぎ括弧 kagíkakkò
◆*vt* (word, phrase) ...に括弧を付ける ...ni kakkò wo tsúkerù

brag [bræg] *vi* 自慢する jimán suru

braid [breid] *n* (trimming) モール mòru; (of hair) お下げ o-ságe

Braille [breil] *n* 点字 teñji

brain [brein] *n* (ANAT) 脳 nò; (*fig*) 頭脳 zúnò

brainchild [brein'tʃaild] *n* (project) 発案 hatsúan; (invention) 発明 hatsúmei

brains [breinz] *npl* (CULIN) 脳みそ nômisò; (intelligence) 頭脳 zúnò

brainwash [brein'wɑːʃ] *vt* 洗脳する señnō suru

brainwave [brein'weiv] *n* 脳波 nòha

brainy [brei'niː] *adj* (child) 頭の良い atáma no yoî

braise [breiz] *vt* (CULIN) いためてから煮込む itámète kará nikómù

brake [breik] *n* (AUT) 制動装置 seídōsōchi, ブレーキ burèki; (*fig*) 歯止め hadóme
◆*vi* ブレーキを掛ける burèki wo kakérù

brake fluid *n* ブレーキ液 burékièki

brake light *n* ブレーキライト burékiraîto

bramble [bræm'bəl] *n* (bush) イバラ ibára

bran [bræn] *n* ふすま fusúma

branch [bræntʃ] *n* (of tree) 枝 edá; (COMM) 支店 shitén

branch out *vi* (*fig*): *to branch out into* ...に手を広げる ...ni te wo hirógeru

brand [brænd] *n* (trademark: *also*: **brand name**) 銘柄 meígara, ブランド burándo; (*fig*: type) 種類 shúrùi
◆*vt* (cattle) 焼印 yakíin

brandish [bræn'diʃ] *vt* (weapon) 振り回す furímawasù

brand-new [brænd'nuː'] *adj* 真新しい maátarashiî

brandy [bræn'diː] *n* ブランデー burándē

brash [bræʃ] *adj* (forward, cheeky) ずうずうしい zúzūshiî

brass [bræs] *n* (metal) 真ちゅう shiñchū
the brass (MUS) 金管楽器 kíñkangakkì

brass band *n* 吹奏楽団 suísōgakùdan, ブラスバンド burásubañdo

brassiere [brəziːr'] *n* ブラジャー burájà

brat [bræt] (*pej*) *n* (child) がき gakí

bravado [brəvɑː'dou] *n* 空威張り karáibàri

brave [breiv] *adj* (attempt, smile, action) 勇敢な yúkan na
◆*vt* (face up to) ...に立ち向う ...ni tachímukaù

bravery [brei'vəːriː] *n* 勇気 yûki

bravo [brɑː'vou] *excl* ブラボー burabò

brawl [brɔːl] *n* (in pub, street) けんか keñka

brawny [brɔː'niː] *adj* (arms etc) たくましい takúmashiî

bray [brei] *vi* (donkey) 鳴く nakú

brazen [brei'zən] *adj* (woman) ずうずうしい zúzūshiî; (lie, accusation) 厚かましい atsúkamashiî
◆*vt*: *to brazen it out* 最後までしらばくれる saígo madé shirábakurerù

brazier [brei'ʒəːr] *n* (on building site etc) 野外用簡易暖炉 yagáiyō kañ-i dañro

Brazil [brəzil'] *n* ブラジル burájiru

Brazilian [brəzil'iːən] *adj* ブラジルの bu-

rájiru no
♦n ブラジル人 burájirujìn

breach [briːtʃ] vt (defence, wall) 突破する toppá suru
♦n (gap) 突破口 toppákò; (breaking):
breach of contract 契約不履行 keíya-kufurikò
breach of the peace 治安妨害 chiánbògai

bread [bred] n (food) パン páǹ

bread and butter n バターを塗ったパン bátà wo nuttá páǹ; (fig: source of income) 金づる kanézuru

breadbox [bred'bɑːks] (BRIT **breadbin**) n パン入れ paǹ-irè

breadcrumbs [bred'krʌmz] npl (gen) パンくず paǹkuzù; (CULIN) パン粉 paǹko

breadline [bred'lain] n: **on the breadline** 貧しい mazúshiì

breadth [bredθ] n (of cloth etc) 幅 habá; (fig: of knowledge, subject) 広さ hírosa

breadwinner [bred'winər] n (in family) 稼ぎ手 kaségite

break [breik] (pt **broke**, pp **broken**) vt (cup, glass) 割る warú; (stick, leg, arm) 折る orù; (machine etc) 壊す kowásù; (promise, law, record) 破る yabúrù; (journey) 中断する chūdan suru
♦vi (crockery) 割れる waréru; (stick, arm, leg) 折れる orérù; (machine etc) 壊れる kowárerù; (storm) 起る okórù; (weather) 変る kawáru; (story, news) 報道される hōdō saréru; (dawn) dawn breaks 夜が明ける yo ga akéru
♦n (gap) 途切れた所 togíreta tokóro; (fracture: gen) 破損 hasón; (: of limb) 骨折 kossétsu; (pause for rest) 休憩 kyūkei; (at school) 休み時間 yasúmijikàn; (chance) チャンス cháǹsu
to break the news to someone ...に知らせる ...ni shiráseru
to break even (COMM) 収支がとんとんになる shūshi ga toǹton ni narú
to break free/loose (person, animal) 逃出す nigédasu
to break open (door etc) ...を壊して開ける ...wo kowáshite akéru

breakage [brei'kidʒ] n (act of breaking)

壊す事 kowásù kotó; (object broken) 損傷 sofshō

break down vt (figures, data) 分析する buǹseki suru
♦vi (machine, car) 故障する koshō suru; (person) 取乱す torímidasù; (talks) 物別れになる monówakàre ni narú

breakdown [breik'daun] n (AUT) 故障 koshō; (in communications) 中断 chūdan; (of marriage) 破たん hatán; (MED: also: **nervous breakdown**) 神経衰弱 shiňkeisuìjaku; (of statistics) 分析 buǹseki

breakdown van (BRIT) n レッカー車 rékkàsha

breaker [brei'kər] n (wave) 白波 shíránami

breakfast [brek'fəst] n 朝ご飯 asá gohàn, 朝食 chōshoku

break in vt (horse etc) 慣らす narásù
♦vi (burglar) 押入る oshírù; (interrupt) 割込む warfkomù

break-in [breik'in] n 押入り oshíiri

breaking and entering [breik'iŋ ænd en'tə:riŋ] n (LAW) 不法侵入 fuhō-shiǹ-nyū

break into vt fus (house) ...に押入る ...ni oshírù

break off vi (branch) 折れる orérù; (speaker) 話を中断する hanáshi wo chūdan suru

break out vi (begin: war) ぽっ発する boppátsu suru; (: fight) 始まる hajímaru; (escape: prisoner) 脱出する dasshútsu suru
to break out in spots/a rash にきび〔湿しん〕になる níkibi〔shisshín〕ni narú

breakthrough [breik'θruː] n (fig: in technology etc) 躍進 yakúshin

break up vi (ship) 分解する buǹkai suru; (crowd, meeting) 解散する kaísan suru; (marriage) 離婚に終る rikón ni owáru; (SCOL) 終る owáru
♦vt (rocks, biscuit etc) 割る warú; (fight etc) やめさせる yamésaseru

breakwater [breik'wɔ:tə:r] n 防波堤 bóhatei

breast [brest] n (of woman) 乳房 chíbùsa; (chest) 胸 muné; (of meat) 胸肉 munéníkù

breast-feed [brest'fi:d] (*pt, pp* **breast-fed**) *vt* ...に母乳を飲ませる ...ni bonyú wo nomáserù

♦*vi* 子供に母乳を飲ませる kodómo ni bonyú wo nomáserù

breaststroke [brest'strouk] *n* 平泳ぎ hiráoyôgi

breath [breθ] *n* 息 íkì

out of breath 息を切らせて íkì wo kirásete

Breathalyser [breθ'əlaizə:r] ® *n* 酒気検査器 shukíkensakì

breathe [bri:ð] *vt* 呼吸する kokyú suru

♦*vi* 呼吸する kokyú suru

breathe in *vt* 吸込む suíkomù

♦*vi* 息を吸込む íkì wo suíkomù

breathe out *vt* 吐出す hakídasu

♦*vi* 息を吐く íkì wo hakù

breather [bri:'ðə:r] *n* (break) 休憩 kyúkei

breathing [bri:'ðiŋ] *n* 呼吸 kokyú

breathless [breθ'lis] *adj* (from exertion) 息を切らせている íkì wo kirásète irú; (MED) 呼吸困難の kokyúkoñnan no

breathtaking [breθ'teikiŋ] *adj* (speed) 息が止る様な íkì ga tomáru yô na; (view) 息を飲むような íkì wo nomù yô na

bred [bred] *pt, pp of* **breed**

breed [bri:d] (*pt, pp* **bred**) *vt* (animals) 繁殖させる hañshoku saséru; (plants) 栽培する saíbai suru

♦*vi* (ZOOL) 繁殖する hañshoku suru

♦*n* (ZOOL) 品種 hiñshu; (type, class) 種類 shúrùi

breeding [bri:'diŋ] *n* (upbringing) 育ち sodáchi

breeze [bri:z] *n* そよ風 soyókàze

breezy [bri:'zi:] *adj* (manner, tone) 快活な kaíkatsu na; (weather) 風の多い kazé no òi

brevity [brev'iti:] *n* (shortness, conciseness) 簡潔さ kañketsusa

brew [bru:] *vt* (tea) 入れる iréru; (beer) 醸造する jôzô suru

♦*vi* (storm) 起ろうとしている okórò to shité irù; (*fig*: trouble, a crisis) 迫ってい

る semáttè irú

brewery [bru:'ə:ri:] *n* 醸造所 jôzôshò

bribe [braib] *n* 賄ろ waíro

♦*vt* (person, witness) 買収する baíshū suru

bribery [brai'bə:ri:] *n* (with money, favors) 贈賄 zôwai

bric-a-brac [brik'əbræk] *n* 置物類 okímonorùi

brick [brik] *n* (for building) れんが réñga

bricklayer [brik'leiə:r] *n* れんが職人 reñgashokùnin

bridal [braid'əl] *adj* (gown) 花嫁の hana-yôme no; (suite) 新婚者の shiñkoñsha no

bride [braid] *n* 花嫁 hanáyòme, 新婦 shiñpu

bridegroom [braid'gru:m] *n* 花婿 haná-mùko, 新郎 shiñrô

bridesmaid [braidz'meid] *n* 新婦付き添いの女性 shiñputsukísoi no joséi

bridge [bridʒ] *n* (TECH, ARCHIT) 橋 hashí; (NAUT) 船橋 señkyō, ブリッジ burijjì; (CARDS, DENTISTRY) ブリッジ buríjjì

♦*vt* (*fig*: gap, gulf) 乗越える noríkoerù

bridge of the nose 鼻柱 hanábashira

bridle [braid'əl] *n* くつわ kutsúwa

bridle path *n* 乗馬用の道 jôbayô no michí

brief [bri:f] *adj* (period of time, description, speech) 短い mijíkaì

♦*n* (LAW) 事件摘要書 jikéntekiyōsho; (*gen*: task) 任務 niñmu

♦*vt* (inform) ...に指示を与える ...ni shijí wo atáeru

briefcase [bri:f'keis] *n* かばん kabán, ブリーフケース burífukèsu

briefing [bri:'fiŋ] *n* (*gen*, PRESS) 説明 setsúmei

briefly [bri:f'li:] *adv* (smile, glance) ちらっと chiráttò; (explain, say) 短く mijíka-kù

briefs [bri:fs] *npl* (for men) パンツ pañtsu, ブリーフ burífu; (for women) パンティー pañtī, ショーツ shôtsu

brigade [brigeid'] *n* (MIL) 旅団 ryodán

brigadier [brigədi'ə:r] *n* (MIL) 准将 juñshō

bright [brait] *adj* (*gen*) 明るい akárui; (person, idea: clever) 利口な rikō na; (person: lively) 明朗な meírō na

brighten [brait'ən] (*also*: **brighten up**) *vt* (room) 明るくする akáruku suru; (event) 楽しくする tanóshiku suru ♦*vi* 明るくなる akáruku narù

brilliance [bril'jəns] *n* (of light) 明るさ akárusa; (of talent, skill) 素晴しさ subárashisà

brilliant [bril'jənt] *adj* (person, idea) 天才的な teñsaiteki na; (smile, career) 輝かしい kagáyakashiì; (sunshine, light) 輝く kagáyakù; (*BRIT*: *inf*: holiday etc) 素晴らしい subárashiì

brim [brim] *n* (of cup etc) 縁 fuchí; (of hat) つば tsubá

brine [brain] *n* (CULIN) 塩水 shiómìzu

bring [briŋ] (*pt*, *pp* **brought**) *vt* (thing) 持って来る motté kurù; (person) 連れて来る tsuréte kurù; (*fig*: satisfaction) もたらす motárasù; (trouble) 起す okósù

bring about *vt* (cause) 起こす okósù

bring back *vt* (restore: hanging etc) 復帰させる fukkí saséru; (return: thing/person) 持って〔連れて〕帰る mottê(tsu-rête)kaèrù

bring down *vt* (government) 倒す taósù; (MIL: plane) 撃墜する gekítsui suru; (price) 下げる sagérù

bring forward *vt* (meeting) 繰り上げる kuríagerù; (proposal) 提案する teían suru

bring off *vt* (task, plan) ...に成功する ...ni seíkō suru

bring out *vt* (gun) 取出す torídasu; (meaning) 明らかにする akíraka ni suru; (publish, produce: book) 出版する shuppán suru; (: album) 発表する happyô suru

bring round *vt* (unconscious person) 正気付かせる shôkizukaserù

bring up *vt* (carry up) 上に持って来る〔行く〕ué ni mottê kurù(ikù); (educate: person) 育てる sodáterù; (question, subject) 持出す mochídasù; (vomit: food) 吐く hakù

brink [briŋk] *n* (of disaster, war etc) 瀬戸際 setógiwa

brisk [brisk] *adj* (tone, person) きびきびした kíbìkibi shitá; (pace) 早い hayáì; (trade) 盛んな sakán na

bristle [bris'əl] *n* (animal hair, hair of beard) 剛毛 gômō; (of brush) 毛 ke ♦*vi* (in anger) 怒る okórù

Britain [brit'ən] *n* (*also*: **Great Britain**) 英国 eíkoku, イギリス igírisu ◇イングランド, スコットランド, ウェールズを含む iñguraňdo, sukóttoraňdo, uéruzu wo fukúmù

British [brit'iʃ] *adj* 英国の eíkoku no, イギリスの igírisu no ♦*npl*: **the British** 英国人 eíkokujìn, イギリス人 igírisujìn

British Isles *npl*: **the British Isles** イギリス諸島 igírisushotô

British Rail *n* 英国国有鉄道 eíkoku ko-kúyū tetsúdō

Briton [brit'ən] *n* 英国人 eíkokujìn, イギリス人 igírisujìn

brittle [brit'əl] *adj* (fragile: glass etc) 割れやすい waréyasuì; (: bones etc) もろい moróì

broach [broutʃ] *vt* (subject) 持出す mo-chídasu

broad [brɔːd] *adj* (street, shoulders, smile, range) 広い hiróì; (general: outlines, distinction etc) 大まかな ômakà na; (accent) 強い tsuyóì

in broad daylight 真っ昼間に mappí-rùma ni

broadcast [brɔːd'kæst] *n* (TV, RADIO) 放送 hôsō ♦*vb* (*pt*, *pp* **broadcast**) ♦*vt* (TV, RADIO) 放送する hôsō suru; (TV) 放映する hôei suru ♦*vi* (TV, RADIO) 放送する hôsō suru

broaden [brɔːd'ən] *vt* (scope, appeal) 広くする híròku suru, 広げる hirógeru ♦*vi* (river) 広くなる híròku narú, 広がる hírôgaru

to broaden one's mind 心を広くする kokôro wo hiròku suru

broadly [brɔːd'liː] *adv* (in general terms) 大まかに ômakà ni

broad-minded [brɔːd'main'did] *adj* 心の広い kokôro no hiroì

broccoli [brɑ'kɑli:] n (BOT, CULIN) ブロッコリー burókkòrī

brochure [brouʃuːr'] n (booklet) 小冊子 shósasshī, パンフレット pánfuretto

broil [brɔil] vt (CULIN) じか火で焼く jikábi de yakú

broke [brouk] pt of **break**
♦adj (inf: person, company) 無一文になった muíchimòn ni nattá

broken [brou'kən] pp of **break**
♦adj (window, cup etc) 割れた waréta; (machine: also: **broken down**) 壊れた kowárèta
a broken leg 脚の骨折 ashí no kossetsú
in broken English/Japanese 片言の英語〔日本語〕で katákoto no eígo〔nihóngo〕de

broken-hearted [brou'kənhɑːr'tid] adj 悲嘆に暮れた hitán ni kuréta

broker [brou'kəːr] n (COMM: in shares) 証券ブローカー shóken burókā; (: insurance broker) 保険代理人 hokén dairinin

brolly [brɑ'liː] n (BRIT: inf) n 傘 kásà

bronchitis [brɑŋkai'tis] n 気管支炎 kikánshien

bronze [brɑnz] n (metal) 青銅 seídō, ブロンズ burónzu; (sculpture) 銅像 dôzō

brooch [broutʃ] n ブローチ buróchi

brood [bruːd] n (of birds) 一腹のひな hitóhara no hinà
♦vi (person) くよくよする kuyókuyo suru

brook [bruk] n 小川 ogáwa

broom [bruːm] n (for cleaning) ほうき hôki; (BOT) エニシダ eníshida

broomstick [bruːm'stik] n ほうきの柄 hôki no e

Bros. abbr (= brothers) 兄弟 kyôdai

broth [brɔːθ] n (CULIN) スープ sûpu

brothel [brɑːθ'əl] n 売春宿 baíshun-yado

brother [brʌð'əːr] n (also: **older brother**) 兄 anī, 兄さん nîsan; (also: **younger brother**) 弟 otôtō; (REL) 修道士 shûdōshi

brother-in-law [brʌð'əːrinlɔ:] (pl **brothers-in-law**) n (older) 義理の兄 girí no anī; (younger) 義理の弟 girí no otôtō

brought [brɔːt] pt, pp of **bring**

brow [brau] n (forehead) 額 hitái; (rare: gen: eyebrow) まゆ mayù; (of hill) 頂上 chôjō

brown [braun] adj (color) 褐色の kasshóku no, 茶色の chaíro no; (tanned) 日焼けした hiyáke shitá
♦n (color) 褐色 kasshóku, 茶色 chaíro
♦vt (CULIN) ...に焼き目を付ける ...ni yakíme wo tsukérù

brown bread n 黒パン kurópan

brownie [brau'niː] n (Brownie guide) ブラウニー buráunī◇ガールスカウトの幼年団員 gārusukaùto no yônendañ in; (US: cake) チョコレートクッキーの一種 chokôrētokukkī no isshū

brown paper n クラフト紙 kuráfutoshī

brown sugar n 赤砂糖 akázatō

browse [brauz] vi (through book) 拾い読みする hiróiyomi suru; (in shop) 商品を見て回る shôhin wo mitè mawáru

bruise [bruːz] n (on face etc) 打撲傷 dabókushò, あざ azá
♦vt (person) ...に打撲傷を与える ...ni dabókushò wo atáeru

brunch [brʌntʃ] n ブランチ buráñchi

brunette [bruːnet'] n (woman) ブルネット burúnettò

brunt [brʌnt] n: *to bear the brunt of* (attack, criticism) ...の矢面に立つ ...no yaómòte ni tatsù

brush [brʌʃ] n (for cleaning, shaving etc) ブラシ buráshi; (for painting etc) 刷毛 hakè; (artist's) 筆 fudè, 絵筆 efùde; (quarrel) 小競り合い kozerìai
♦vt (sweep etc) ...にブラシを掛ける ...ni búràshi wo kakérù; (clean: teeth etc) 磨く migáku; (groom) ブラシでとかす búràshi de tokásù; (also: **brush against**: person, object) ...に触れる ...ni furéru

brush aside vt (emotion, criticism) 無視する mushí suru

brush up vt (subject, language) 復習する fukúshū suru

brushwood [brʌʃ'wud] n (sticks) しばshibá

brusque [brʌsk] adj (person, manner) 無愛想な buáìso na; (apology) ぶっきらぼうな bukkírabò na

Brussels [brʌs'əlz] n ブリュッセル buryūssèru

Brussels sprout n メキャベツ mekyábètsu

brutal [bru:'təl] adj (person, actions) 残忍な zańnin na; (honesty, frankness) 厳しい程の kibíshiì hodō no

brutality [bru:tæl'iti:] n 残忍さ zańnin-sa

brute [bru:t] n (person) 人でなし hitódenashi, けだもの kedámono; (animal) 獣 kemóno
♦adj: **by brute force** 暴力で bóryoku de

B.Sc. [bi:essi:'] abbr = **Bachelor of Science**

bubble [bʌb'əl] n (in liquid, soap) 泡 awá; (of soap etc) シャボン玉 shabóndama
♦vi (liquid) 沸く wakú; (: sparkle) 泡立つ awádatsù

bubble bath n 泡風呂 awáburo

bubble gum n 風船ガム fūsengamù

buck [bʌk] n (rabbit) 雄ウサギ osúsagi; (deer) 雄ジカ ojíka; (US: inf: dollar) ドル dorù
♦vi (horse) 乗手を振り落そうとする norímte wo furíotosò to surù
to pass the buck (to someone) (...に) 責任をなすり付ける (...ni) sekínin wo nasúritsukerù

bucket [bʌk'it] n (pail) バケツ bakétsu; (contents) バケツ一杯 bakétsu ippái

buckle [bʌk'əl] n (on shoe, belt) バックル bakkúru
♦vt (shoe, belt) ...のバックルを締める ...no bakkúru wo shimérù
♦vi (wheel) ゆがむ yugámu; (bridge, support) 崩れる kuzúrerù

buck up vi (cheer up) 元気を出す géñki wo dasù

bud [bʌd] n (of tree, plant, flower) 芽 me
♦vi 芽を出す me wo dasù

Buddhism [bu:'dizəm] n (REL) 仏教 bukkyò

budding [bʌd'iŋ] adj (actor, entrepreneur) 有望な yūbō na

buddy [bʌd'i:] n (US) (friend) 相棒 aíbō

budge [bʌdʒ] vt (object) ちょっと動かす chóttò ugókasù; (fig: person) 譲歩させる

jōho saséru
♦vi (object, person) ちょっと動く chóttò ugókù; (fig: person) 譲歩する jōho suru

budgerigar [bʌdʒ'ə:ri:gɑ:r] n セキセイインコ sekíseiiǹko

budget [bʌdʒ'it] n (person's, government's) 予算 yosán, 予算案 yosáñ-an
♦vi: **to budget for something** ...を予算案に入れる ...wo yosáñ-an ni iréru
I'm on a tight budget 台所が苦しい daídokoro ga kúrushiì

budgie [bʌdʒ'i:] n = **budgerigar**

buff [bʌf] adj (color: envelope) 薄茶色 usúchairo
♦n (inf: enthusiast) マニア máǹia

buffalo [bʌf'əlou] (pl **buffalo** or **buffaloes**) n (BRIT) スイギュウ suígyū; (US: bison) バイソン báìson

buffer [bʌf'ə:r] n (COMPUT) バッファ báffà; (RAIL) 緩衝機 kańshōki

buffet[1] [bufei'] (BRIT) n (in station) ビュッフェ byúffè; (food) 立食 risshóku

buffet[2] [bʌf'it] vt (subj: wind, sea) もみ揺さぶる momíyusaburù

buffet car (BRIT) n (RAIL) ビュッフェ車 byufféshà

bug [bʌg] n (esp US: insect) 虫 mushí; (COMPUT: of program) バグ bágù; (fig: germ) 風邪 kazé; (hidden microphone) 盗聴器 tōchōki
♦vt (inf: annoy) 怒らせる okóraserù; (room, telephone etc) ...に盗聴器を付ける ...ni tōchōki wo tsukérù

buggy [bʌg'i:] n (baby buggy) 乳母車 ubágurùma

bugle [bju:'gəl] n (MUS) らっぱ rappá

build [bild] n (of person) 体格 taíkaku
♦vb (pt, pp **built**)
♦vt (house etc) 建てる tatérù, 建築する keńchiku suru; (machine, cage etc) 作る tsukúrù

builder [bil'də:r] n (contractor) 建築業者 keńchikugyòsha

building [bil'diŋ] n (industry, construction) 建築業 keńchikugyò; (structure) 建物 tatémonò, ビル birù

building society (BRIT) n 住宅金融組合 júutakukin-yūkumìai

build up vt (forces, production) 増やす fuyásu; (morale) 高める takámerù; (stocks) 蓄積する chikúseki suru

built [bilt] pt, pp of **build**
♦adj: **built-in** (oven, wardrobes etc) 作り付けの tsukúritsuke no

built-up area [bilt'ʌp-] n 市街化区域 shigáikakuìki

bulb [bʌlb] n (BOT) 球根 kyúkon; (ELEC) 電球 deñkyuú

Bulgaria [bʌlgeːr'iːə] n ブルガリア burúgaria

Bulgarian [bʌlgeːr'iːən] adj ブルガリアの burúgaria no
♦n ブルガリア人 burúgariajìn

bulge [bʌldʒ] n (bump) 膨らみ fukúrami
♦vi (pocket, file, cheeks etc) 膨らむ fukúramu

bulk [bʌlk] n (mass: of thing) 巨大な姿 kyodái na sugàta; (: of person) 巨体 kyotái
in bulk (COMM) 大口で óguchi de
the bulk of (most of) …の大半 …no taíhan

bulky [bʌl'kiː] adj (parcel) かさばった kasábattà; (equipment) 大きくて扱いにくい ókikute atsúkainikuì

bull [bul] n (ZOOL) 雄牛 oúshi; (male elephant/whale) 雄 osú

bulldog [bul'dɔːg] n ブルドッグ burúdoggù

bulldozer [bul'douzəːr] n ブルドーザー burúdòzā

bullet [bul'it] n 弾丸 dañgan

bulletin [bul'itən] n (TV etc: news update) 速報 sokúhō; (journal) 会報 kaíhō, 紀要 kiyó

bulletproof [bul'itpruːf] adj (glass, vest, car) 防弾の bódan no

bullfight [bul'fait] n 闘牛 tógyū

bullfighter [bul'faitəːr] n 闘牛士 tógyùshi

bullfighting [bul'faitiŋ] n 闘牛 tógyū

bullhorn [bul'hɔːrn] (US) n ハンドマイク haňdomaìku

bullion [bul'jən] n (gold, silver) 地金 jigáne

bullock [bul'ək] n 去勢した雄牛 kyoséi

shitá oúshi

bullring [bul'riŋ] n 闘牛場 tógyūjō

bull's-eye [bulz'ai] n (on a target) 的の中心 mató no chúshin

bully [bul'iː] n 弱い者いじめ yowáimonoijìme
♦vt いじめる ijímeru

bum [bʌm] (inf) n (backside) しり shirí; (esp US: tramp) ルンペン ruñpen; (: good-for-nothing) ろくでなし rokúdenashi

bumblebee [bʌm'bəlbiː] n クマンバチ kumáñbachi

bump [bʌmp] n (in car: minor accident) 衝突 shótotsu; (jolt) 衝撃 shógeki; (swelling: on head) こぶ kobú; (on road) 段差 dañsa
♦vt (strike) …にぶつかる …ni butsúkaru

bumper [bʌm'pəːr] n (AUT) バンパー bañpā
♦adj: **bumper crop/harvest** 豊作 hósaku

bumper cars npl (in amusement park) バンパーカー bañpākā

bump into vt fus (strike: obstacle) …にぶつかる …ni butsúkaru; (inf: meet: person) …に出くわす …ni dekúwasù

bumptious [bʌmp'ʃəs] adj (person) うぬぼれた unúboreta

bumpy [bʌm'piː] adj (road) 凸凹な dekóboko na

bun [bʌn] n (CULIN) ロールパン rórupan, パン báñ; (of hair) まげ magé, シニヨン shíñyon

bunch [bʌntʃ] n (of flowers, keys) 束 tábà; (of bananas) 房 fusá; (of people) グループ gúrūpu

bunches [bʌntʃ'iz] npl (in hair) 左右のポニーテール sáyû no ponítèru

bundle [bʌn'dəl] n (parcel: of clothes, samples etc) 包み tsutsúmi; (of sticks, papers) 束 tabá
♦vt (also: **bundle up**) 厚着させる atsúgi saséru; (put): **to bundle something/someone into** …にほうり〔押〕込む …ni hóri(oshí)komù

bungalow [bʌŋ'gəlou] n バンガロー bañgarô

bungle [bʌŋˈgəl] vt (job, assassination) ...にしくじる ...ni shikújirù

bunion [bʌnˈjən] n (MED) けん膜りゅう kenmakuryū, バニオン bánìon

bunk [bʌŋk] n (bed) 作り付けベッド tsukūritsukebeddò

bunk beds npl 二段ベッド nidánbeddò

bunker [bʌŋˈkəːr] n (also: **coal bunker**) 石炭庫 sekítanko; (MIL) えんぺいごう efípeìgō; (GOLF) バンカー bañkā

bunny [bʌnˈiː] n (also: **bunny rabbit**) ウサちゃん usáchan

bunting [bʌnˈtiŋ] n (flags) 飾り小旗 kazárikobàta

buoy [buːˈiː] n (NAUT) ブイ buì

buoyant [bɔiˈənt] adj (ship) 浮力のある fúryòku no arù; (economy, market) 活気のある kakkí no arù; (fig: person, nature) 朗らかな hogáràka na

buoy up vt (fig) 元気づける geñkizukerù

burden [bəːrˈdən] n (responsibility, worry) 負担 fután; (load) 荷物 nímòtsu
♦vt (trouble): **to burden someone with** (oppress) ...を打明けて...に心配を掛ける ...wo uchſakete ...ni shiñpai wo kakérù

bureau [bjurˈou] (pl **bureaux** or **bureaus**) n (BRIT: writing desk) 書き物机 kakímonozukùe ◇ふたが書く面になる机を指す futá ga kakù meñ ni narù tsukúe wo sasù; (US: chest of drawers) 整理だんす seſridañsu; (office: government, travel, information) 局 kyòkù, 課 ka

bureaucracy [bjurɑːkˈrəsiː] n (POL, COMM) 官僚制 kaſryōsei

bureaucrat [bjurˈəkræt] n (administrator) 官僚 kaſryō; (pej: pen-pusher) 小役人 koyákùnin

bureaux [bjurˈouz] npl of **bureau**

burglar [bəːrˈgləːr] n 押込み強盗 oshíkomigòtō

burglar alarm n 盗難警報機 tónankeihòki

burglary [bəːrˈgləːriː] n (crime) 住居侵入罪 jūkyoshiſnyūzai

burial [beːrˈiːəl] n 埋葬 maísō

burly [bəːrˈliː] adj (figure, workman etc) ごつい gotsúi

Burma [bəːrmˈə] n ビルマ bírùma

burn [bəːrn] (pt, pp **burned** or **burnt**) vt (papers, fuel etc) 燃やす moyásu; (toast, food etc) 焦がす kogásù; (house etc: arson) ...に放火する ...ni hōka suru
♦vi (house, wood etc) 燃える moéru; (cakes etc) 焦げる kogérù; (sting) ひりひりする hírìhiri suru
♦n やけど yakédo

burn down vt 全焼させる zeñshō sasérù

burner [bəːrˈnəːr] n (on cooker, heater) 火口 hígùchi, バーナー bánā

burning [bəːrˈniŋ] adj (house etc) 燃えている moéte irù; (sand) 焼ける様に熱い yakéru yō ni atsuì; (desert) しゃく熱の shakúnetsu no; (ambition) 熱烈な netsúretsu na

burnt [bəːrnt] pt, pp of **burn**

burrow [bəːrˈou] n (of rabbit etc) 巣穴 suána
♦vi (dig) 掘る hórù; (rummage) あさる asáru

bursary [bəːrˈsəːriː] (BRIT) n (SCOL) 奨学金 shōgakukin

burst [bəːrst] (pt, pp **burst**) vt (bag, balloon, pipe etc) 破裂させる harétsu sasérù; (subj: river: banks etc) 決壊させる kekkái saserù
♦vi (pipe, tire) 破裂する harétsu suru
♦n (also: **burst pipe**) 破裂した水道管 harétsu shita suídōkan

a burst of energy/speed/enthusiasm 突発的なエネルギー〔スピード, 熱心さ〕 toppátsuteki na enérugī〔supído, nesshísa〕

a burst of gunfire 連射 reñsha

to burst into flames 急に燃え出す kyū ni moédasù

to burst into tears 急に泣き出す kyū ni nakídasù

to burst out laughing 急に笑い出す kyū ni waráidasù

to be bursting with (subj: room, container) はち切れんばかりに...で一杯になっている hachíkiréñbakari ni ...de ippái ni natté irù; (: person: emotion) ...で胸が一杯になっている ...de muné ga ippái ni natté irù

burst into vt fus (room etc) ...に飛び込む

bury [beː'riː] vt (gen) 埋める uméru; (at funeral) 埋葬する maísō suru

bus [bʌs] n (vehicle) バス básu

bush [buʃ] n (in garden) 低木 teíboku; (scrubland) 未開地 mikáĭchi, ブッシュ bússhu

　to beat about the bush 遠回しに言う tōmawáshi ni iú

bushy [buʃ'iː] adj (tail, hair, eyebrows) ふさふさした fúsafusa shitá

busily [biz'iliː] adv (actively) 忙しく isógashikù

business [biz'nis] n (matter, question) 問題 moñdai; (trading) 商売 shōbai; (firm) 会社 kaísha; (occupation) 仕事 shigóto

　to be away on business 出張して留守である shutchō shite rusù de arù

　it's my business to ... ...するのは私の務めです ...surú no wa watákushi no tsutóme desù

　it's none of my business 私の知った事じゃない watákushi no shittá kotó ja naí

　he means business 彼は本気らしい karè wa hoñki rashiì

businesslike [biz'nislaik] adj てきぱきした tekípaki shitá

businessman [biz'nismæn] (pl **businessmen**) n 実業家 jitsúgyōka

business trip n 出張 shutchō

businesswoman [biz'niswumən] (pl **businesswomen**) n 女性実業家 joséijitsugyōka

busker [bʌs'kəːr] (BRIT) n 大道芸人 daídōgeìnin

bus-stop [bʌs'staːp] n バス停留所 básutefryùjo

bust [bʌst] n (ANAT) 乳房 chíbusa, 胸 muné; (measurement) バスト básuto; (sculpture) 胸像 kyōzō

　♦adj (inf: broken) 壊れた kowáreta

　to go bust (company etc) つぶれる tsubúreru

bustle [bʌs'əl] n (activity) 雑踏 zattō

　♦vi (person) 忙しく飛回る isógashikù tobímawarù

bustling [bʌs'liŋ] adj (town, place) にぎ

やかな nígiyàka na

busy [biz'iː] adj (person) 忙しい isógashiì; (shop, street) にぎやかな nigíyàka na; (TEL: line) 話し中の hanáshichū no

　♦vt: **to busy oneself with** 忙しそうに...する isógashisō ni ...suru

busybody [biz'i:baːdiː] n でしゃばり屋 deshábariya

busy signal (US) n (TEL) 話中音 wáchūon

but [bʌt] conj 1 (yet) ...であるが ...de árù ga, ...であるけれども ...de árù keredomo, しかし shikáshì

　he's not very bright, but he's hard-working 彼はあまり頭は良くないが、よく働きます kárè wa amári àtama wà yókùnaì ga, yókù határakimasù

　I'm tired but Paul isn't 私は疲れていますが、ポールは疲れていません watákushi wa tsùkárète imasu ga, pórù wa tsukárète imásèn

　the trip was enjoyable but tiring 旅行は楽しかったけれども、疲れました ryokō wa tánoshikàtta keredomo, tsukáremashìta

2 (however) ...であるが ...de árù ga, ...であるけれども ...de árù keredomo, しかし shikáshì

　I'd love to come, but I'm busy 行きたいが、今忙しいんです ikítaì ga, ímà isógashiìn desu

　she wanted to go, but first she had to finish her homework 彼女は行きたかったけれども、先に宿題を済ます必要がありました kánojò wa ikítakàtta keredomo, sakí ni shùkúdai wo sùmásu hitsúyō ga àrimashìta

　I'm sorry, but I don't agree 済みませんが、私は同意できません sumímasèn ga, watákushi wa dōi dekimasèn

3 (showing disagreement, surprise etc) しかし shikáshì

　but that's far too expensive! しかしそれは高過ぎますよ shikáshì soré wa tàkásugimasù yo

　but that's fantastic! しかし素晴らし

いじゃありませんか shikáshì subárashiì ja arímasen ka

◆*prep* (apart from, except) ...を除いて ...wo nozóite, ...以外に ...ígai ni

he was nothing but trouble 彼は厄介な問題ばかり起していました kárè wa yákkài na móndai bakàri okóshìte imáshìta

we've had nothing but trouble 厄介な問題ばかり起っています yákkài na móndai bakàri okôttè imásù

no one but him can do it 彼を除けば出来る人はいません kárè wo nozôkèbà dekírù hito wo imásén

who but a lunatic would do such a thing? 気違いを除けばそんな事をする人はいないでしょう kichígai wo nozôkèbà sónna koto wò suru hitò wa inái deshō

but for you あなたがいなかったら anátà ga inákàttara

but for your help あなたが助けてくれなかったら anátà ga tasúketè kurénakàttara

I'll do anything but that それ以外なら何でもします soré igài nara nán de mo shimasù

◆*adv* (just, only) ただ tádà, ...だけ ...dàkê, ...しか...ない ...shika ...nâî

she's but a child 彼女はほんの子供です kánojò wa hón no kòdómo desù

had I but known 私がそれを知ってさえいたら watákushi ga sòrè wo shitte saè itárà

I can but try やってみるしかありません yátte mirù shika arímasèn

all but finished もう少しで出来上りです mô sukoshì de dekíagari desù

butcher [butʃ'ə:r] *n* (tradesman) 肉屋 nikúyà

◆*vt* (cattle etc for meat) と殺する tosátsu suru; (prisoners etc) 虐殺する gyakúsatsu suru

butcher's (shop) [butʃ'ə:rz-] *n* 精肉店 seínikutèn, 肉屋 nikúyà

butler [bʌt'lə:r] *n* 執事 shítsùji

butt [bʌt] *n* (large barrel) たる tarú; (of

pistol) 握り nigíri; (of rifle) 床尾 shòbi; (of cigarette) 吸い殻 suígara; (*fig*: target: of teasing, criticism etc) 的 mató

◆*vt* (subj: goat, person) 頭で突く atáma de tsukù

butter [bʌt'ə:r] *n* (CULIN) バター bátâ

◆*vt* (bread) ...にバターを塗る ...ni bátâ wo nurú

buttercup [bʌt'ə:rkʌp] *n* キンポウゲ kínpòge

butterfly [bʌt'ə:rflai] *n* (insect) チョウチョウ chôchō; (SWIMMING: *also*: **butterfly stroke**) バタフライ bátâfurai

butt in *vi* (interrupt) ...に割込む ...ni waríkomù

buttocks [bʌt'əks] *npl* (ANAT) しり shíri

button [bʌt'ən] *n* (on clothes) ボタン botán; (on machine) 押しボタン oshíbotàn; (US: badge) バッジ bájjì

◆*vt* (*also*: **button up**) ...のボタンをはめる ...no botán wo hamérù

◆*vi* ボタンで止まる botán de tomárù

buttress [bʌt'tris] *n* (ARCHIT) 控え壁 hikáekàbe

buxom [bʌk'səm] *adj* (woman) 胸の豊かな muné no yutàka na

buy [bai] (*pt, pp* **bought**) *vt* 買う kaú

◆*n* (purchase) 買物 kaímono

to buy someone something/something for someone ...に...を買って上げる ...ni ...wo katté agérù

to buy something from someone ...から...を買う ...kará ...wo kaú

to buy someone a drink ...に酒をおごる ...ni saké wo ogórù

buyer [bai'ə:r] *n* (purchaser) 買手 kaíte; (COMM) 仕入係 shiíregakàri, バイヤー báîya

buzz [bʌz] *n* (noise: of insect) ぶんぶんという音 buñbun to iú otò; (: of machine etc) うなり unári; (*inf*: phone call): *to give someone a buzz* ...に電話を掛ける ...ni deñwa wo kakérù

◆*vi* (insect) ぶんぶん羽音を立てる buñbun haôto wo taterù; (saw) うなる unárù

buzzer [bʌz'ə:r] *n* (ELEC) ブザー búzà

buzz word (*inf*) *n* 流行語 ryûkôgo

KEYWORD

---

by [bai] *prep* **1** (referring to cause, agent) ...に (よって) ...ni (yotte)

killed by lightning 雷に打たれて死んだ kamínari ni ùtárète shínda

surrounded by a fence 塀に囲まれた heí ni kakomareta

a painting by Picasso ピカソの絵画 pikásò no káĩga

it's by Shakespeare シェイクスピアの作品です sheíkusupìa no sakúhin desù

2 (referring to method, manner, means) ...で ...de

by bus/car/train バス〔車，列車〕で básù〔kurúma, réssha〕de

to pay by check 小切手で払う kogítte, de haráù

by moonlight/candlelight 月明り〔ろうそくの灯〕で tsukíakàri〔rósoku no a-kari〕de

by saving hard, he ... 一生懸命に金を貯めて彼は... isshókènmei ni kanè wo tamete karè wa...

3 (via, through) ...を 通って ...wo tóttè, ...経由で ...keíyu de

we came by Dover ドーバー経由で来ました dóbākeìyu de kimáshìta

he came in by the back door 彼は裏口から入りました kárè wa uráguchi kara hairimashìta

4 (close to) ...のそばに〔で〕...no sóbà ni 〔de〕, ...の近くに〔で〕...no chikákù ni 〔de〕

the house by the river 川のそばにある家 kawá no sobà ni árù ié

a holiday by the sea 海辺の休暇 umíbe no kyúka

she sat by his bed 彼女は彼のベッドのそばに座っていました kánòjo wa kárè no béddò no sobà ni suwátte imashìta

5 (past) ...を通り過ぎて ...wo tórisugìte

she rushed by me 彼女は足早に私の前を通り過ぎた kánòjo wa ashíbaya ni watákushi no maè wo tórisugìta

I go by the post office every day 私は毎日郵便局の前を通ります watákushi wa maínichi yúbìnkyoku no maè wo

tórimasù

6 (not later than) ...までに ...mádè ni

by 4 o'clock 4時までに yójì madè ni

by this time tomorrow 明日のこの時間までに myónichì no konó jikan madè ni

by the time I got here it was too late 私がここに着いたころにはもう手遅れでした watákushi ga kòkò ni tsuíta koro ni wá mò teókùre deshìta

7 (during): *by daylight* 日中に nitchú ni

8 (amount) ...単位で ...tàn-i de

by the kilo/meter キロ〔メーター〕単位で kirô〔mẽtā〕tàn-i de

paid by the hour 時給をもらって jikyú wo moratte

one by one (people) 1人ずつ hitórizutsù; (animals) 1匹 ずつ ippíkizutsù; (things) 1つずつ hitótsuzutsù

little by little 少しずつ sukóshizutsù

9 (MATH, measure): *to divide by 3* 3で割る sán de waru

to multiply by 3 3を掛ける sán wo kakerù

a room 3 meters by 4 3メーター掛ける4メーターの部屋 sánmẽtā kakérù yónmẽtā no heyá

it's broader by a meter 1メーターも広くなっている ichímẽtā mó hirôku náttè iru

10 (according to) ...に従って ...nì shitágatte

to play by the rules ルールを守る rúrù wo mamórù

it's all right by me 私は構いませんよ watákushi wa kàmáimasèn yó

11: *(all) by oneself etc* 一人だけで hitóri dakè de

he did it (all) by himself 彼は彼1人だけの力でやりました kárè wa karè hitóri dake nò chikára dè yarímashìta

he was standing (all) by himself in the corner 彼は1人ぼっちで隅に立っていました kárè wa hitóribotchì de súmì ni táttè imáshìta

12: *by the way* ところで tokóro dè

by the way, did you know Claire was back? ところでね，クレアが帰って来たのをご存知? tokóro dè ne, kùrea ga káètte kita no wo go-zònji?

this wasn't my idea by the way しか
しね、これを提案したのは私じゃないか
らね shikáshī né, koré wo teian shita nò
wa watákushi ja nài kara né

♦*adv* 1 *see* go; pass *etc*

2: *by and by* やがて yagáte

*by and by they came to a fork in the
road* やがて道路はY字路になりました
yagáte dòro ha wañjirò ni narímashìta

they'll come back by and by そのう
ち帰って来ますよ sonó uchi kaètte kimásù yo

by and large (on the whole) 大体におい
て dáitaì ni òite, 往々にして òō ni shite

*by and large I would agree with
you* 大体あなたと同じ意見です dáitaì a-
natà to onáji ikèn desu

*Britain has a poor image abroad, by
and large* 海外における英国のイメージ
は往々にして悪い kâígai ni okéru èíkoku no ìmèjì wa òō ni shite wàrùî

bye(-bye) [bai'(bai')] *n excl* じゃあね jà
ne, バイバイ bàíbai

by(e)-law [bai'lɔ:] *n* 条例 jòrei

by-election [bai'ilekʃən] (*BRIT*) *n* 補欠
選挙 hokétsuseñkyo

bygone [bai'gɔ:n] *adj* (age, days) 昔の
mukáshi no

♦*n*: *let bygones be bygones* 済んだ事を
水に流す súùda kotò wo mizú ni nagásù

bypass [bai'pæs] *n* (AUT) バイパス baípasu; (MED: operation) 冠状動脈バイパ
ス kañjòdōmyakubaìpasu

♦*vt* (town) ...にバイパスを設ける ...ni baípasu wo mòkerù

by-product [bai'prɑ:dəkt] *n* (of industrial process) 副産物 fukúsañbutsu; (of
situation) 二次的結果 nijítekikèkka

bystander [bai'stændər] *n* (at accident,
crime) 居合せた通行人 iáwasèta tsúkō-
nin

byte [bait] *n* (COMPUT) バイト báìto

byword [bai'wə:rd] *n*: *to be a byword
for* ...の代名詞である ...no daímeìshi de
arù

by-your-leave [baiju:rli:v'] *n*: *without*

so much as a by-your-leave 自分勝手
に jibúnkattè ni

C

C [si:] *n* (MUS: note) ハ音 há-òn; (: key) ハ
調 háchò

C. [si:] *abbr* = centigrade

C.A. [si:ei'] *abbr* = chartered accountant

cab [kæb] *n* (taxi) タクシー tákùshī; (of
truck, tractor etc) 運転台 uñtendai

cabaret [kæbærei'] *n* (nightclub) キャバ
レー kyábàrē; (floor show) フロアショー
furóashò

cabbage [kæb'idʒ] *n* キャベツ kyábètsu

cabin [kæb'in] *n* (on ship) キャビン kyá-
bìn; (on plane) 操縦室 sòjùshìtsu; (house)
小屋 koyá

cabin cruiser *n* 大型モーターボート ò-
gata mòtàbōto, クルーザー kúrùzā ◇居
室, 炊事場などのある物を指す kyóshìtsu, suíjiba nádò no árù monò wo sásù

cabinet [kæb'ənit] *n* (piece of furniture)
戸棚 todána, キャビネット kyabínettò;
(*also*: display cabinet) ガラス戸棚 garásu tòdàna; (POL) 内閣 náìkaku

cable [kei'bəl] *n* (strong rope) 綱 tsuná;
(ELEC, TEL, TV) ケーブル kèburu

♦*vt* (message, money) 電信で送る deñshin de okúru

cable-car [kei'bəlkɑ:r] *n* ケーブルカー
kèburukā

cable television *n* 有線テレビ yúsenterèbi

cache [kæʃ] *n*: *a cache of drugs* 隠匿さ
れた麻薬 iñtoku saretà mayáku

a weapons cache 隠匿武器 íñtokubùki

cackle [kæk'əl] *vi* (person, witch) 薄気味
悪い声で笑う usúkimiwaruî kôe de waráù; (hen) こここと鳴く kokoko to nákù

cacti [kæk'tai] *npl of* cactus

cactus [kæk'təs] (*pl* cacti) *n* サボテン
sabóten

caddie [kæd'i:] *n* (GOLF) キャディー
kyádì

caddy [kæd'i:] *n* = caddie

cadet [kədet'] *n* (MIL) 士官候補生 shikán-kōhosèi; (POLICE) 警察学校の生徒 keísatsugakkò no seíto

cadge [kædʒ] (*inf*) *vt* (lift, cigarette etc) ねだる nedáru

Caesarean [size:r'i:ən] (*BRIT*) = **Cesarean**

café [kæfei'] *n* (snack bar) 喫茶店 kíssaten

cafeteria [kæfiti:'ri:ə] *n* (in school, factory, station) 食堂 shokúdō

caffein(e) [kæ'fi:n] *n* カフェイン kaféin

cage [keidʒ] *n* (of animal) おり orí, ケージ kèji; (*also*: **bird cage**) 鳥かご toríkago, ケージ kèji; (of lift) ケージ kèji

cagey [kei'dʒi:] (*inf*) *adj* 用心深い yójinbukaì

cagoule [kəgu:l'] (*BRIT*) *n* カグール kágūru ◇薄手の雨ガッパ usúde no amágappa

Cairo [kai'rou] *n* カイロ kâiro

cajole [kədʒoul'] *vt* 丸め込む marúmekomù

cake [keik] *n* (CULIN: large) デコレーションケーキ dekóreshonkèki; (: small) 洋菓子 yōgàshi
a cake of soap 石けん1個 sekkén íkkò

caked [keikt] *adj*: **caked with** (blood, mud etc) ...の塊で覆われた ...no katámari de ōwareta

calamity [kəlæm'iti:] *n* (disaster) 災難 saínan

calcium [kæl'si:əm] *n* (in teeth, bones etc) カルシウム karúshiùmu

calculate [kæl'kjəleit] *vt* (work out: cost, distance, numbers etc) 計算する keísan suru; (: effect, risk, impact etc) 予測する yosóku suru

calculating [kæl'kjəleitiŋ] *adj* (scheming) ずる賢い zurúgashikoì

calculation [kælkjəlei'ʃən] *n* (MATH) 計算 keísan; (estimate) 予測 yosóku

calculator [kæl'kjəleitə:r] *n* 電卓 deñtaku

calculus [kæl'kjələs] *n* (MATH) 微積分学 bisékibungàku

calendar [kæl'əndə:r] *n* (of year) カレンダー káreñdā; (timetable, schedule) 予定表 yotéihyō

calendar month/year *n* 暦月〔年〕 rekígetsu〔nen〕

calf [kæf] (*pl* **calves**) *n* (of cow) 子ウシ koúshi; (of elephant, seal etc) ...の子 ...no ko; (*also*: **calfskin**) 子牛革 koúshigàwa, カーフスキン káfusukiñ; (ANAT) ふくらはぎ fukúrahàgi

caliber [kæl'əbə:r] (*BRIT* **calibre**) *n* (of person) 能力 nōryoku; (of skill) 程度 teído; (of gun) 口径 kōkei

call [kɔ:l] *vt* (christen, name) 名付ける nazúkerù; (label) ...を...と呼ぶ ...wo...to yobú; (TEL) ...に電話を掛ける ...ni defiwa wo kakérù; (summon: doctor etc) 呼ぶ yobú; (: witness etc) 召喚する shōkan suru; (arrange: meeting) 召集する shōshū suru

♦*vi* (shout) 大声で言う ōgoe de iú; (telephone) 電話を掛ける deñwa wo kakérù; (visit: *also*: **call in**, **call round**) 立寄る tachíyoru

♦*n* (shout) 呼声 yobígoè; (TEL) 電話 deñwa; (of bird) 鳴声 nakígoè
: to be called ...と呼ばれる ...to yobárerù, ...という ...to iú
on call (nurse, doctor etc) 待機して taíki shité

call back *vi* (return) また寄る matá yorú; (TEL) 電話を掛け直す deñwa wo kakénaosù

callbox [kɔ:l'bɑ:ks] (*BRIT*) *n* 電話ボックス deñwabokkùsu

caller [kɔ:l'ə:r] *n* (visitor) 訪問客 hōmoñkyaku; (TEL) 電話を掛けてくる人 deñwa wo kakète kurù hitò

call for *vt fus* (demand) 要求する yōkyū suru; (fetch) 迎えに行く mukáe ni ikú

call girl *n* (prostitute) コールガール kōrugāru

call-in [kɔ:l'in] (*US*) *n* (phone-in) ◇ 視聴者が電話で参加する番組 shíchōsha ga deñwa de sañka suru bangumi

calling [kɔ:l'iŋ] *n* (occupation) 職業 shokúgyð; (*also*: **religious calling**) 神のお召し kámî no o-méshi

calling card (*US*) *n* 名刺 meíshi

call off *vt* (cancel) 中止する chūshi suru

call on vt fus (visit) 訪ねる tazúnerù, 訪問する hőmon suru; (appeal to) ...に...を求める ...ni ...wo motómerù

callous [kæl'əs] adj (heartless) 冷淡な reítañ na

call out vt (name etc) 大声でいう őgoè de iù; (summon for help etc) 呼び出す yobidasu

♦vi (shout) 大声で言う őgoè de iú

call up vt (MIL) 召集する shőshū suru; (TEL) ...に電話をかける ...ni deñwa wo kakérù

calm [kɑːm] adj (unworried) 落着いている ochítsuite irú; (peaceful) 静かな shízuka na; (weather, sea) 穏やかな odáyàka na

♦n (quiet, peacefulness) 静けさ shizúkesà

♦vt (person, child) 落着かせる ochítsukasèru; (fears, grief etc) 鎮める shizúmerù

calm down vi (person) 落着く ochítsukù

♦vt (person) 落着かせる ochítsukasèru

Calor gas [kæ'lər-]® n ◇携帯用燃料ガスボンベの商品名 keítaiyō neñryō gasuboñbe no shőhìñmei

calorie [kæl'əːriː] n カロリー káròrī

calves [kævz] npl of **calf**

camber [kæm'bəːr] n (of road) 真ん中が高くなっている事 mañnaka ga takakù nattè irú kotő

Cambodia [kæmbou'diːə] n カンボジア kañbojìa

came [keim] pt of **come**

camel [kæm'əl] n (ZOOL) ラクダ rakúda

cameo [kæm'iːou] n (jewellery) カメオ kámèo

camera [kæm'əːrə] n (PHOT) 写真機 shashîñki, カメラ kámèra; (CINEMA) 映画カメラ eíga kámèra; (also: TV camera) テレビカメラ terébi kámèra

in camera (LAW) 非公開で híkòkai de

cameraman [kæm'əːrəmæn] (pl cameramen) n (CINEMA, TV) カメラマン kaméramàn

camouflage [kæm'əflɑːʒ] n (MIL) カムフラージュ kamúfuràju; (ZOOL) 隠ぺい的性態 iñpeitekigitài

♦vt (conceal: also MIL) 隠す kakúsù

camp [kæmp] n (encampment) キャンプ場 kyañpujō; (MIL: barracks) 基地 kíchì; (for prisoners) 収容所 shűyōjo; (faction) 陣営 jiñ-ei

♦vi (in tent) キャンプする kyañpu suru

♦adj (effeminate) 女々しい meméshìì

campaign [kæmpein'] n (MIL) 作戦 sakúsen; (POL etc) 運動 uñdō, キャンペーン kyañpèn

♦vi (objectors, pressure group etc) 運動をする uñdō wo suru

camp bed (BRIT) n 折畳みベッド orítatami beddò

camper [kæm'pəːr] n (person) キャンパー kyañpā; (vehicle) キャンピングカー kyañpingukà

camping [kæm'piŋ] n 野営 yaéi, キャンピング kyañpìngu

to go camping キャンピングに行く kyañpìngu ni iku

campsite [kæmp'sait] n キャンプ場 kyañpujō

campus [kæm'pəs] n (SCOL) キャンパス kyáñpasu

can¹ [kæn] n (container: for foods, drinks, oil etc) 缶 káñ

♦vt (foods) 缶詰にする kañzume ni suru

KEYWORD

can² [kæn] (negative **cannot, can't** conditional and pt **could**) aux vb 1 (be able to) 出来る dekírù

you can do it if you try 努力すればできますよ dóryòku suréba dekímasù yo

I'll help you all I can できるだけ力になりましょう dekíru dake chíkàra nì narímashő

she couldn't sleep that night その晩彼女は眠れませんでした sonő ban kanòjo wa nemúremasèn deshita

I can't go on any longer 私はもうこれ以上やっていけません watákushi wa mō koré ijő yatté ikemasèn

I can't see you あなたの姿が見えません anátā no súgàta ga miémasen

can you hear me? 私の声が聞えますか watákushi no koè ga kikőemasù ká

I can see you tomorrow, if you're

free 明日でよかったらお会いできますよ asú dè yōkàttara o-ái dekimasù yó

2 (know how to) ...の仕方が分かる ...no shikáta ga wakarù, ...ができる ...ga dekírù

I can swim/play tennis/drive 私は水泳〔テニス, 運転〕ができます watákushi wa suìei〔ténisù, únten〕ga dèkímasu

can you speak French? あなたはフランス語ができますか anátà wa furánsugo ga dèkímasù ká

3 (may) ...してもいいですか ...shítè mò íi desu ká

can I use your phone? 電話をお借りしてもいいですか dénwa wo ò-kári shite mò íi desu ká

could I have a word with you? ちょっと話しがあるんですが chóttò hanáshi gà árùn desu ga

you can smoke if you like タバコを吸いたければ遠慮なくどうぞ tabáko wo suitakèreba énryo nakù dōzò

can I help you with that? 手を貸しましょうか te wò kashímashò ka

4 (expressing disbelief, puzzlement): *it can't be true!* うそでしょう úsò deshô

what CAN he want? あいつは何をねらっているだろうね áitsu wa nánì wo nerátte iru dàrō nê

5 (expressing possibility, suggestion, etc) ...かも知れない ...ká mò shirenai

he could be in the library 彼は図書室にいるかも知れません kárè wa toshóshìtsu ni irú kà mo shiremasen

she could have been delayed 彼女は何かの原因で出発が遅れたかも知れません kánòjo no nánìka no gén-in de shùppátsu ga òkúreta kà mo shirémasèn

---

Canada [kǽnədə] *n* カナダ kánàda

Canadian [kənei'di:ən] *adj* カナダの kánàda no

♦*n* カナダ人 kanádajìn

canal [kənǽl'] *n* (for ships, barges, irrigation) 運河 úñga; (ANAT) 管 kàñ

canary [kəne:r'i:] *n* カナリヤ kanáriya

cancel [kǽn'səl] *vt* (meeting) 中止する chūshi suru; (appointment, reservation,

---

contract, order) 取消す toríkesu, キャンセルする kyáñseru suru; (cross out: words, figures) 線を引いて消す séñ wo hiíte kesú

the flight was canceled その便は欠航になった sonó bíñ wa kekkō ni nattá

the train was canceled その列車は運休になった sonó resshà wa uñkyū ni nattá

cancellation [kænsəlei'ʃən] *n* (of meeting) 中止 chūshi; (of appointment, reservation, contract, order) 取消し toríkeshi, キャンセル kyáñseru; (of flight) 欠航 kekkō; (of train) 運休 uñkyū

cancer [kæn'sə:r] *n* (MED) がん gáñ

Cancer (ASTROLOGY) かに座 kaníza

candid [kæn'did] *adj* (expression, comment) 率直な sotchóku na

candidate [kæn'dideit] *n* (for job) 候補者 kōhoshà; (in exam) 受験者 jukéñsha; (POL) 立候補者 rikkóhoshà

candle [kæn'dəl] *n* ろうそく rōsokù

candlelight [kæn'dəllait] *n*: *by candlelight* ろうそくの明りで rōsokù no akári de

candlestick [kæn'dəlstik] *n* (*also*: **candle holder**: plain) ろうそく立て rōsokutàte; (: bigger, ornate) しょく台 shokúdai

candor [kæn'də:r] (*BRIT* **candour**) *n* (frankness) 率直さ sotchókusà

candy [kæn'di:] *n* (*also*: **sugar-candy**) 氷砂糖 kōrizatò; (*US*: sweet) あめ amé

candy-floss [kæn'di:flɔ:s] (*BRIT*) *n* 綿あめ watá-ame, 綿菓子 watágashì

cane [kein] *n* (BOT) 茎 kukí ◊竹などの様に中が空洞になっている植物を指す také nadò no yō ni nakà ga kūdō ni nattè irú shokúbutsu wo sasù; (for furniture) 藤 tō; (stick) 棒 bō; (for walking) 杖 tsúè, ステッキ sutékkì

♦*vt* (*BRIT*: SCOL) むち打つ muchíutsù

canine [kei'nain] *adj* イヌの inú no

canister [kæn'istə:r] *n* (container: for tea, sugar etc) 容器 yōki ◊茶筒の様な物を指す chazútsu no yō na monò wo sasù; (pressurized container) スプレー缶 supúrēkañ; (of gas, chemicals etc) ボンベ bôñbe

cannabis [kæn'əbis] *n* マリファナ marífāna

canned [kænd] *adj* (fruit, vegetables etc) 缶詰の kańzume no

cannibal [kæn'ənəl] *n* (person) 人食い人間 hitókui nińgen; (animal) 共食いする動物 tomógui suru dóbutsu

cannon [kæn'ən] (*pl* **cannon** *or* **cannons**) *n* (artillery piece) 大砲 taíhō

cannot [kæn'ɑːt] = **can not**

canny [kæn'iː] *adj* (quick-witted) 抜け目ない nukémenai

canoe [kənuː'] *n* (boat) カヌー kánū

canon [kæn'ən] *n* (clergyman) 司教座聖堂参事会員 shikyózaseídō sańjikàiin; (rule, principle) 規準 kijún

canonize [kæn'ənaiz] *vt* (REL) 聖人の列に加える seíjin no retsù ni kuwáerù

can opener *n* 缶切 kańkiri

canopy [kæn'əpiː] *n* (above bed, throne etc) 天がい teńgai

can't [kænt] = **can not**

cantankerous [kæntæŋ'kərəs] *adj* (fault-finding, complaining) つむじ曲りの tsumújimagàri no

canteen [kæntiːn'] *n* (in workplace, school etc) 食堂 shokúdō; (*also*: **mobile canteen**) 移動食堂 idóshokùdō; (*BRIT*: of cutlery) 収納箱 shúnōbàko ◇ ナイフ、フォークなどを仕舞う箱 naífu, fóku nadò wo shimáu hakó

canter [kæn'təːr] *vi* (horse) キャンターで走る kyánta de hashírù

canvas [kæn'vəs] *n* (fabric) キャンバス kyáńbasu; (painting) 油絵 abúraè; (NAUT) 帆 hò ◇総称 sōshō

canvass [kæn'vəs] *vi* (POL): **to canvass for** ...のために選挙運動をする ...no tamè ni seńkyoundò wo suru
◆*vt* (investigate: opinions, views) 調査する chōsa surù

canyon [kæn'jən] *n* 峡谷 kyókoku

cap [kæp] *n* (hat) 帽子 bōshi ◇主につばのある物を指す ómò ni tsubà no arù monó wo sásù; (of pen) キャップ kyáppù; (of bottle) ふた futá; (contraceptive) ペッサリー péssàrī; (for toy gun) 紙雷管 kamíraìkan

◆*vt* (outdo) しのぐ shinógù

capability [keipəbil'əti:] *n* (competence) 能力 nóryoku

capable [kei'pəbəl] *adj* (person, object): **capable of doing** ...ができる ...ga dekírù; (able: person) 有能な yūnō na

capacity [kəpæs'iti:] *n* (of container, ship etc) 容積 yóseki; (of stadium etc) 収容力 shūyōryòku; (capability) 能力 nóryoku; (position, role) 資格 shikáku; (of factory) 生産能力 seísannòryòku

cape [keip] *n* (GEO) 岬 misáki; (short cloak) ケープ kèpu

caper [kei'pəːr] *n* (CULIN: *gen*: **capers**) ケーパー kèpā; (prank) いたずら itázura

capital [kæp'itəl] *n* (*also*: **capital city**) 首都 shútò; (money) 資本金 shihónkin; (*also*: **capital letter**) 大文字 ómoji

capital gains tax *n* 資本利得税 shihónritokùzei

capitalism [kæp'itəlizəm] *n* 資本主義 shihónshùgi

capitalist [kæp'itəlist] *adj* 資本主義の shihónshùgi no
◆*n* 資本主義者 shihónshugishà

capitalize [kæp'itəlaiz]: **capitalize on** *vt fus* (situation, fears etc) 利用する riyō suru

capital punishment *n* 死刑 shikéi

capitulate [kəpitʃ'uleit] *vi* (give in) 降参する kōsan suru

capricious [kəpriʃ'əs] *adj* (fickle: person) 気まぐれの kimágure no

Capricorn [kæp'rikɔːrn] *n* (ASTROLOGY) やぎ座 yagíza

capsize [kæp'saiz] *vt* (boat, ship) 転覆させる teńpuku saséru
◆*vi* (boat, ship) 転覆する teńpuku suru

capsule [kæp'səl] *n* (MED) カプセル kápùseru; (spacecraft) 宇宙カプセル uchűkapùseru

captain [kæp'tin] *n* (of ship) 船長 seńchō; (of plane) 機長 kichō; (of team) 主将 shushō; (in army) 大尉 taí-i; (in navy) 大佐 taísa; (*US*: in air force) 大尉 taí-i; (*BRIT*: SCOL) 主席の生徒 shusékì no seíto

caption [kæp'ʃən] *n* (to picture) 説明文

setsúmeìbun

captivate [kæp'təveit] *vt* (fascinate) 魅了する miryō suru

captive [kæp'tiv] *adj* (person) とりこの toríko no; (animal) 飼育下の shíikuka no
♦*n* (person) とりこ toríko; (animal) 飼育下の動物 shíikuka no dōbutsu

captivity [kæptiv'əti:] *n* 監禁状態 kañkinjōtai

capture [kæp't∫ər] *vt* (animal, person) 捕まえる tsukámaeru; (town, country) 占領する señryō suru; (attention) 捕える toráerù; (COMPUT) 収納する shūnō suru
♦*n* (seizure: of animal) 捕獲 hokáku; (: of person: by police) 逮捕 táiho; (: of town, country: by enemy) 占領 señryō; (COMPUT) 収納 shūnō

car [kɑːr] *n* (AUT) 自動車 jídōsha, 車 kurúma; (: US: carriage) 客車 kyakúsha; (RAIL: BRIT: dining car, buffet car) 特殊車両 tokúshusharyō

carafe [kəræf'] *n* 水差し mizúsashì

caramel [kær'əməl] *n* (CULIN: sweet) キャラメル kyarámeru; (: burnt sugar) カラメル karámeru

carat [kær'ət] *n* (of diamond, gold) カラット karáttò

caravan [kær'əvæn] *n* (BRIT: vehicle) キャンピングカー kyañpingukā; (in desert) 隊商 taíshō, キャラバン kyáràban

caravan site (BRIT) *n* オートキャンプ場 ōtokyanpujō

carbohydrate [kɑːrbouhai'dreit] *n* (CHEM, food) 炭水化物 tañsuikabùtsu

carbon [kɑːr'bən] *n* 炭素 táñso

carbon copy *n* カーボンコピー kāboñkopī

carbon dioxide [-daiɑːk'said] *n* 二酸化炭素 nisánkatanso

carbon monoxide [-mənɑːk'said] *n* 一酸化炭素 issánkatanso

carbon paper *n* カーボン紙 kāboñshi

carburetor [kɑːr'bəreitər] (BRIT **carburettor**) *n* (AUT) キャブレター kyábùretā

carcass [kɑːr'kəs] *n* (of animal) 死体 shitái

card [kɑːrd] *n* (cardboard) ボール紙 bōrugami; (greetings card, index card etc) カード kādo; (playing card) トランプのカード toráñpu no kādo; (visiting card) 名刺 meíshi

cardboard [kɑːrd'bɔːrd] *n* ボール紙 bōrugami

card game *n* トランプゲーム toráñpugēmu

cardiac [kɑːr'di:æk] *adj* (arrest, failure) 心臓の shiñzō no

cardigan [kɑːr'digən] *n* カーディガン kādigàn

cardinal [kɑːr'dənəl] *adj* (chief: principle) 重要な júyō na
♦*n* (REL) 枢機けい sūkikèi
of cardinal importance 極めて重要で kiwámète jūyō de

cardinal number 基数 kisū

card index *n* カード式索引 kādoshiki sakúin

care [ker] *n* (attention) 注意 chūi; (worry) 心配 shiñpai; (charge) 管理 káñri
♦*vi: to care about* (person, animal) ...を気に掛ける ...wo ki ni kakérù, ...を愛する ...wo aí surù; (thing, idea etc) ...に関心を持つ ...ni kañshin wo motsù
care of (on mail) ...方 ...gatá
in someone's care ...の管理に任せ（られ）て ...no kanri ni makáse(rarè)tè
to take care (to do) ...をするよう心掛ける ...wo suru yō kokórogakerù
to take care of (patient, child etc) ...の世話をする ...no sewá wo suru; (problem, situation) ...の始末を付ける ...no shimàtsu wo tsukerù
I don't care 私は構いません watákushi wa kamáimasèn
I couldn't care less 私はちっとも気にしない watákushi wa chittó mò ki ni shinaì

career [kəri:r'] *n* (job, profession) 職業 shokūgyō; (life: in school, work etc) キャリア kyarìa
♦*vi (also: career along*: car, horse) 猛スピードで走る mōsupído de hashirù

career woman (*pl* **career women**) *n* キャリアウーマン kyarìaūman

care for vt fus (look after) …の世話をする …no sewá wo suru; (like) …が好きである …ga sukí de árù, …を愛している …wo aí shité irú

carefree [keːrˈfriː] adj (person, attitude) 気苦労のない kigurō no naì

careful [keːrˈfəl] adj (cautious) 注意深い chūibukaì; (thorough) 徹底的な tettéiteki na

(be) careful! 気を付けてね ki wo tsukéte ne

carefully [keːrˈfəliː] adv (cautiously) 注意深く chūibukakù; (methodically) 念入りに nefi-iri ni

careless [keːrˈlis] adj (negligent) 不注意な fuchūi na; (heedless) 軽率な kefsotsu na

carelessness [keːrˈlisnis] n (negligence) 不注意 fuchūi; (lack of concern) 無とん着 mutofichaku

caress [kəresˈ] n (stroke) 愛ぶ aíbu
♦vt (person, animal) 愛ぶする aíbu suru

caretaker [keːrˈteikəːr] n (of flats etc) 管理人 kafirinin

car-ferry [kɑːrˈferiː] n カーフェリー kāferî

cargo [kɑːrˈgou] (pl **cargoes**) n (of ship, plane) 積荷 tsumíni, 貨物 kámotsu

car hire (BRIT) n レンタカーサービス refitakā sābisu

Caribbean [kærəbiːˈən] n: **the Caribbean (Sea)** カリブ海 karíbukaì

caricature [kærˈəkətʃəːr] n (drawing) 風刺漫画 fūshimañga, カリカチュア karíkachùa; (description) 風刺文 fūshibuñ; (exaggerated account) 真実のわい曲 shiñjitsu no waikyoku

caring [keːrˈiŋ] adj (person, society, behavior) 愛情深い aíjōbukaì; (organization) 健康管理の keñkōkañri no

carnage [kɑːrˈnidʒ] n (MIL) 虐殺 gyakúsatsu

carnal [kɑːrˈnəl] adj (desires, feelings) 肉体的な nikútaiteki na

carnation [kɑːrneiˈən] n カーネーション kánēshon

carnival [kɑːrˈnəvəl] n (festival) 謝肉祭 shanîkusài, カーニバル kánibaru; (US:

funfair) カーニバル kánibaru

carnivorous [kɑːrnivˈəːrəs] adj (animal, plant) 肉食の nikúshoku no

carol [kærˈəl] n: **(Christmas) carol** クリスマスキャロル kurísumasu kyaróru

carp [kɑːrp] n (fish) コイ koî

car park (BRIT) n 駐車場 chūshajō

carp at vt fus (criticize) とがめ立てする togámedate suru

carpenter [kɑːrˈpəntəːr] n 大工 daíku

carpentry [kɑːrˈpəntriː] n 大工仕事 daíkushigòto

carpet [kɑːrˈpit] n (in room etc) じゅうたん jútan, カーペット kápettò; (fig: of pine needles, snow etc) じゅうたんの様な… jútan no yō na…
♦vt (room, stairs etc) …にじゅうたんを敷く …ni jútan wo shikú

carpet slippers npl スリッパ súrìppa

carpet sweeper [-swiːˈpəːr] n じゅうたん掃除機 jútan sōjikì

carriage [kærˈidʒ] n (BRIT: RAIL) 客車 kyakúsha; (also: **horse-drawn carriage**) 馬車 bashá; (of goods) 運搬 ufipan; (transport costs) 運送料 uñsōryō

carriage return n (on typewriter etc) 復帰キー fukkî kî

carriageway [kærˈidʒwei] n (BRIT) (part of road) 車線 shaséñ ◇自動車道の上りまたは下り半分を指す jidōshadō no nobóri mata wá kudári hañbuñ wo sasù

carrier [kærˈiːəːr] n (transporter, transport company) 運送会社 uñsōgaìsha; (MED) 保菌者 hókìnsha, キャリア kyárìa

carrier bag (BRIT) n 買い物袋 kaímonobukùro, ショッピングバッグ shoppíngubaggù

carrot [kærˈət] n (BOT, CULIN) ニンジン nifijin

carry [kærˈiː] vt (take) 携帯する keítai suru; (transport) 運ぶ hakóbu; (involve: responsibilities etc) 伴う tomónaù; (MED: disease, virus) 保有する hoyū suru
♦vi (sound) 通る tōru

to get carried away (fig: by enthusiasm, idea) 夢中になる muchū ni narù

carrycot [kærˈiːkɑːt] (BRIT) n 携帯ベビ

一ベッド keítai bebíbeddò

carry on vi (continue) 続ける tsuzúkeru
♦vt (continue) 続ける tsuzúkeru

carry-on [kær'i:ɑːn] (inf) n (fuss) 大騒ぎ ōsawàgi

carry out vt (orders) 実行する jikkō suru; (investigation) 行う okónau

cart [kɑːrt] n (for grain, silage, hay etc) 荷車 nígùruma; (also: **horsedrawn cart**) 馬車 bâsha; (also: **handcart**) 手押し車 teóshigurùma
♦vt (inf: people) 否応なしに連れて行く iyáō nashi ni tsuréte ikú; (objects) 引きずる hikízuru

cartilage [kɑːr'təlidʒ] n (ANAT) 軟骨 nañkotsu

carton [kɑːr'tən] n (large box) ボール箱 bôrubako; (container: of yogurt, milk etc) 容器 yōki; (of cigarettes) カートン kâton

cartoon [kɑːrtuːn'] n (drawing) 漫画 mañga; (BRIT: comic strip) 漫画 mañga ◊四こま漫画などを指す yoňkoma manga nadò wo sasù; (CINEMA) アニメ映画 aníme-eîga

cartridge [kɑːr'tridʒ] n (for gun) 弾薬筒 dañ-yakutō, 実弾 jitsúdan; (of record-player) カートリッジ kâtorijjì; (of pen) インクカートリッジ íñku kâtorijjì

carve [kɑːrv] vt (meat) 切分ける kiríwakerù, スライスする suráisu surù; (wood, stone) 彫刻する chôkoku suru; (initials, design) 刻む kizámu

carve up vt (land, property) 切分ける kiríwakerù

carving [kɑːr'viŋ] n (object made from wood, stone etc) 彫刻 chôkoku; (in wood etc: design) 彫物 horímonò; (: art) 彫刻 chôkoku

carving knife n カービングナイフ kâbingunaîfu

car wash n 洗車場 señshajō, カーウォッシュ kâuosshù

cascade [kæskeid'] n (waterfall) 小さい滝 chiísaî takí
♦vi (water) 滝になって流れ落ちる takí ni nattè nagáreochirù; (hair, people, things) 滝の様に落ちる takí no yō ni o-

chirù

case [keis] n (situation, instance) 場合 baái; (MED) 症例 shōrei; (LAW) 事件 jíkèn; (container: for spectacles etc) ケース kêsu; (box: of whisky etc) 箱 hakó, ケース kêsu; (BRIT: also: **suitcase**) スーツケース sûtsukèsu

in case (of) (fire, emergency) ...の場合に ...no baái ni

in any case とにかく tonîkaku

just in case 万一に備えて mán-ichi ni sonáete

cash [kæʃ] n (money) 現金 geñkin
♦vt (check etc) 換金する kañkin suru

to pay (in) cash 現金で払う geñkin de haraù

cash on delivery 着払い chakúbarài

cash-book [kæʃ'buk] n 出納簿 suítòbo

cash card (BRIT) n (for cash dispenser) キャッシュカード kyasshúkàdo

cash desk (BRIT) n 勘定カウンター kañjōkauñtà

cash dispenser n 現金自動支払い機 geñkin jidōshiharaîki, カード機 kâdokì

cashew [kæʃ'uː] n (also: **cashew nut**) カシューナッツ kashúnattsù

cash flow n 資金繰り shikínguri

cashier [kæʃiˈɑːr] n (in bank) 出納係 suítōgakàri; (in shop, restaurant) レジ係 rejígakàri

cashmere [kæʒ'miːr] n (wool, jersey) カシミア kashímia

cash register n レジスター réjìsutà

casing [kei'siŋ] n (covering) 被覆 hífuku

casino [kəsi:'nou] n カジノ kájìno

cask [kæsk] n (of wine, beer) たる tarú

casket [kæs'kit] n (for jewelery) 宝石箱 hōsekibakò; (US: coffin) 棺 kâñ

casserole [kæs'əroul] n (of lamb, chicken etc) キャセロール kyasérðru; (pot, container) キャセロールなべ kyasérōrunabè

cassette [kəset'] n (tape) カセットテープ kasétto tépu

cassette player n カセットプレーヤー kasétto puréyà

cassette recorder n カセットレコーダー kasétto rekôdà

cast [kæst] (pt, pp cast) vt (throw: light, shadow) 映す utsúsù; (: object, net) 投げる nagérù; (: fishing-line) キャストする kyásùto surù; (: aspersions, doubts) 投掛ける nagékakerù; (glance, eyes) 向ける mukérù; (THEATER) ...に...の役を振当てる ...ni ...no yakú wo furíaterù; (: make: statue) 鋳込む ikómù

♦n (THEATER) キャスト kyásùto; (also: plaster cast) ギプス gípùsu

to cast a spell on (subject: witch etc) ...に魔法を掛ける ...ni mahō wo kakérù

to cast one's vote 投票する tōhyō suru

castaway [kæs'təwei] n 難破した人 nañpa shita hitó

caste [kæst] n (social class) カースト kásùto; (also: caste system) 階級制 kaíkyūsei, カースト制 kásutosei

caster [kæs'tə:r] n (wheel) キャスター kyásutā

caster sugar (BRIT) n 粉砂糖 konázatō

casting vote [kæs'tiŋ-] (BRIT) n 決定票 kettéihyō, キャスティングボート kyasútingubōto

cast iron [kæst'ai'ə:rn] n 鋳鉄 chūtetsu

castle [kæs'əl] n (building) 城 shiró; (CHESS) 城将 jōshō

cast off vi (NAUT) 綱を解く tsuná wo tokù; (KNITTING) 編み終える amíoerù

cast on vi (KNITTING) 編み始める amíhajimerù

castor [kæs'tə:r] (BRIT) n = caster

castor oil n ひまし油 himáshiyu

castrate [kæs'treit] vt (bull, man) 去勢する kyoséi suru

casual [kæʒ'u:əl] adj (by chance) 偶然の gűzen no; (irregular: work etc) 臨時の ríñji no; (unconcerned) さりげない sarígenaì; (informal: clothes) 普段用の fudán-yō no

casually [kæʒ'u:əli:] adv (in a relaxed way) さりげなく sarígenakù; (dress) 普段着で fudángi de

casualty [kæʒ'u:əlti:] n (of war, accident: someone injured) 負傷者 fushōsha; (: someone killed) 死者 shishá; (of situation, event: victim) 犠牲者 giséisha;

(MED: also: casualty department) 救急病棟 kyűkyūbyōtō

cat [kæt] n (pet) ネコ nekð; (wild animal) ネコ科の動物 nekóka no dóbutsu

catalogue [kæt'ələ:g] (US also: catalog) n (COMM: for mail order) カタログ katárogu; (of exhibition, library) 目録 mokúroku

♦vt (books, collection, events) ...の目録を作る ...no mokúroku wo tsukurù

catalyst [kæt'əlist] n (CHEM, fig) 触媒 shokúbai

catapult [kæt'əpʌlt] (BRIT) n (slingshot) ぱちんこ pachínko

cataract [kæt'ərækt] n (MED) 白内障 hakúnaìshō

catarrh [kətɑ:r'] n カタル kátàru

catastrophe [kətæs'trəfi:] n (disaster) 災害 saígai

catastrophic [kætəstrɑ:f'ik] adj (disastrous) 破局的な hakyőkuteki na

catch [kætʃ] (pt, pp caught) vt (animal) 捕る tórù, 捕まえる tsukámaeru; (fish: with net) 捕る tórù; (: with line) 釣る tsurú; (ball) 捕る tórù; (bus, train etc) ...に乗る ...ni norú; (: arrest: thief etc) 逮捕する taího suru; (surprise: person) びっくりさせる bikkúri saséru; (attract: attention) 引く hikú; (hear: comment, whisper etc) 聞く kikú; (MED: illness) ...に掛る ...ni kakarù; (person: also: catch up with/to) ...に追い付く ...ni oítsukù

♦vi (fire) 付く tsukù; (become trapped: in branches, door etc) 引っ掛る hikkákarù

♦n (of fish etc) 獲物 emóno; (of ball) 捕球 hokyū; (hidden problem) 落し穴 otóshiàna; (of lock) 留金 tomégane; (game) キャッチボール kyátchibōru

to catch one's breath (rest) 息をつく íkì wo tsukù, 一休みする hitoyásumi surù

to catch fire 燃え出す moédasù

to catch sight of 見付ける mitsúkeru

catching [kætʃ'iŋ] adj (infectious) 移る utsurù

catchment area [kætʃ'mənt-] (BRIT) n (of school) 学区 gákkù; (of hospital) 通院

圏 tsúiñken

catch on vi (understand) 分かる wakarù; (grow popular) 流行する ryūkō suru

catch phrase n キャッチフレーズ kyátchìfurèzu

catch up vi (fig: with person, on work) 追付く oítsukù

♦vt (person) ...に追い付く ...ni oítsukù

catchy [kætʃ'i:] adj (tune) 覚え易い obóeyasuî

catechism [kæt'əkizəm] n (REL) 公教要理 kōkyōyōri

categoric(al) [kætəgɔr'ik(əl)] adj (certain, absolute) 絶対的な zettáiteki na

category [kæt'əgɔ:ri:] n (set, class) 範ちゅう hañchū

cater [kei'tə:r] vi: **to cater for** (BRIT: person, group) ...向きである ...mukí de arù; (needs) ...を満たす ...wo mitasù; (COMM: weddings etc) ...の料理を仕出しする ...no ryōri wo shidáshi suru

caterer [kei'tə:rə:r] n 仕出し屋 shidáshiya

catering [kei'tə:riŋ] n (trade, business) 仕出し shidáshi

caterpillar [kæt'ə:rpilə:r] n (with hair) 毛虫 kemúshi; (without hair) 芋虫 imomùshi

caterpillar track n キャタピラ kyatápirà

cathedral [kəθi:'drəl] n 大聖堂 daíseidō

catholic [kæθ'əlik] adj (tastes, interests) 広い hiroî

Catholic [kæθ'əlik] adj (REL) カトリック教の katórikkukyō no

♦n (REL) カトリック教徒 katórikkukyòto

cat's-eye [kæts'ai'] (BRIT) n (AUT) 反射びょう hañshabyō ◇夜間の目印として道路の中央またはわきに埋込むガラスなどの反射器 yakán no mejírushi toshite dôro no chūō mata wà wakí ni umékomù garásu nadò no hañshakì

cattle [kæt'əl] npl ウシ ushî ◇総称 sôshō

catty [kæt'i:] adj (comment, woman) 意地悪な ijíwarù na

caucus [kɔ:'kəs] n (POL: group) 実力者会議 jitsúryokusha kaîgi; (: US) 党部会 tô-

bukài

caught [kɔ:t] pt, pp of **catch**

cauliflower [kɔ:'ləflauə:r] n カリフラワー karífurawà

cause [kɔ:z] n (of: outcome, effect) 原因 geñ-in; (reason) 理由 riyū; (aim, principle: also POL) 目的 mokúteki

♦vt (produce, lead to: outcome, effect) 引起こす hikíokosù

caustic [kɔ:s'tik] adj (CHEM) 腐食性の fushôkusei no; (fig: remark) 辛らつな shiñratsu na

caution [kɔ:'ʃən] n (prudence) 慎重さ shiñchōsa; (warning) 警告 keíkoku, 注意 chûi

♦vt (warn: also POLICE) 警告する keíkoku suru

cautious [kɔ:'ʃəs] adj (careful, wary) 注意深い chūibukaî

cautiously [kɔ:'ʃəsli:] adv 注意深く chūibukakù

cavalier [kævəliə:r'] adj (attitude, fashion) 威張り腐った ibárikusattà

cavalry [kæv'əlri:] n (MIL: mechanized) 装甲部隊 sôkōbutài; (: mounted) 騎兵隊 kihéitai

cave [keiv] n (in cliff, hill) 洞穴 horá-ana

cave in vi (roof etc) 陥没する kañbotsu suru, 崩れる kuzúrerù

caveman [keiv'mæn] (pl **cavemen**) n 穴居人 kêkkyojìn

cavern [kæv'ə:rn] n どうくつ dôkutsu

caviar(e) [kæv'i:ɑ:r] n キャビア kyàbia

cavity [kæv'iti:] n (in wall) 空どう kūdō; (ANAT) 腔 kō; (in tooth) 虫歯の穴 mushíba no aná

cavort [kəvɔ:rt'] vi (romp) はしゃぎ回る hashágimawarù

CB [si:'bi:'] n abbr (= Citizens' Band (Radio)) 市民バンド shimínbañdo, シチズンバンド shichízunbañdo

CBI [si:bi:ai'] n abbr (= Confederation of British Industry) 英国産業連盟 eíkokusañgyōreñmei

cc [si:si:'] abbr (= cubic centimeter(s)) 立方センチメートル rippósenchìmètoru, cc shíshì; = **carbon copy**

cease [si:s] vt (end, stop) 終える oéru

♦vi (end, stop) 終る owáru, 止る tomáru

ceasefire [si:s'faiər'] n (MIL) 停戦 teísen

ceaseless [si:s'lis] adj (chatter, traffic) 絶間ない taéma naî

cedar [si:'dər] n (tree) ヒマラヤスギ himárayasugî; (wood) シーダー材 shídazaì

cede [si:d] vt (land, rights etc) 譲る yuzúru

ceiling [si:'liŋ] n (in room) 天井 teñjō; (upper limit: on wages, prices etc) 天井 teñjō, 上限 jôgen

celebrate [sel'əbreit] vt (gen) 祝う iwáu; (REL: mass) 挙げる agéru
♦vi お祝いする o-íwai suru

celebrated [sel'əbreitid] adj (author, hero) 有名な yûmei na

celebration [seləbrei'ʃən] n (party, festival) お祝い o-íwai

celebrity [səleb'riti:] n (famous person) 有名人 yûmeîjin

celery [sel'ə:ri:] n セロリ sérðri

celestial [səles'tʃəl] adj (heavenly) 天上的な teñjōteki na

celibacy [sel'əbəsi:] n 禁欲生活 kiń-yoku seîkatsu

cell [sel] n (in prison: gen) 監房 kañbō; (: solitary) 独房 dokúbō; (in monastery) 個室 koshítsu; (BIO, also of revolutionaries) 細胞 saîbō; (ELEC) 電池 deńchi

cellar [sel'ə:r] n (basement) 地下室 chikáshītsu; (also: wine cellar) ワイン貯蔵室 waín chozōshītsu

cello [tʃel'ou] n (MUS) チェロ chérð

cellophane [sel'əfein] n セロハン sérðhan

cellular [sel'jələr] adj (BIO: structure, tissue) 細胞の saîbō no; (fabrics) 保温効果の高い hoônkôka no takaî, 防寒の bôkan no

cellulose [sel'jəlous] n (tissue) 繊維素 señisð

Celt [selt, kelt] n ケルト人 kerútðjin

Celtic [sel'tik, kel'tik] adj ケルト人の kerútðjin no; (language etc) ケルトの kêrùto no

cement [siment'] n (powder) セメント seménto; (concrete) コンクリート koñkuríto

cement mixer n セメントミキサー se-

cemetery [sem'ite:ri:] n 墓地 bôchî

cenotaph [sen'ətæf] n (monument) 戦没者記念碑 señbotsusha kineñhi

censor [sen'sə:r] n (POL, CINEMA etc) 検閲官 keñ-etsûkan
♦vt (book, play, news etc) 検閲する keñ-etsu suru

censorship [sen'sə:rʃip] n (of book, play, news etc) 検閲 keñ-etsu

censure [sen'ʃə:r] vt (reprove) とがめる togámerù

census [sen'səs] n (of population) 国勢調査 kokúzeichôsa

cent [sent] n (US: also: one-cent coin) 1 セント玉 isséntodamá ¶ see also **per**

centenary [senten'ə:ri:] n (of birth etc) 100周年 hyakúshùnen

center [sen'tə:r] (BRIT **centre**) n (of circle, room, line) 中心 chûshin; (of town) 中心部 chûshiñbu, 繁華街 hañkagâi; (of attention, interest) 的 matô; (heart: of action, belief etc) 核心 kakúshin; (building: health center, community center) センター séñtà; (POL) 中道 chûdō
♦vt (weight) ...の中心に置く ...no chûshin ni okú; (sights) ...にぴったり合わせる ...ni pittari awáserù; (SOCCER: ball) グランド中央へ飛ばす gurándo chûō e tobásu; (TYP: on page) 中央に合わせる chûō ni awáseru

center forward n (SPORT) センターフォワード señtáfowàdo

center half n (SPORT) センターハーフ señtāhàfu

centigrade [sen'tigreid] adj 摂氏 sesshî

centimeter [sen'təmi:tə:r] (BRIT **centimetre**) n センチメートル señchimêtoru

centipede [sen'təpi:d] n ムカデ mukáde

central [sen'trəl] adj (in the center) 中心点の chûshiñten no; (near the center) 中心の chûshin no; (committee, government) 中央の chûō no; (idea, figure) 中心の chûshin no

Central America n 中米 chûbei

central heating n セントラルヒーティング señtoraruhítiñgu

centralize [sen'trəlaiz] *vt* (decision-making, authority) 中央に集中させる chūō ni shūchū saséru

central reservation (*BRIT*) *n* (AUT: of road) 中央分離帯 chūōbunritai

centre [sen'tər] (*etc BRIT*) = **center etc**

century [sen'tʃəːriː] *n* 世紀 séíki
20th century 20世紀 nijússeíki

ceramic [səræm'ik] *adj* (art, tiles) セラミックの serámikku no

ceramics [səræm'iks] *npl* (objects) 焼物 yakímono

cereal [siːr'iːəl] *n* (plant, crop) 穀物 kókùmotsu; (food) シリアル shírìarù

cerebral [seːr'əbrəl] *adj* (MED: of the brain) 脳の nō no; (intellectual) 知的な chitéki na

ceremony [seːr'əmouniː] *n* (event) 式 shikí; (ritual) 儀式 gíshìki; (behavior) 形式 keíshìki
to stand on ceremony 礼儀にこだわる reígi ni kodáwarù

certain [səːr'tən] *adj* (sure: person) 確信している kakúshin shitě irú; (: fact) 確実な kakújitsu na; (person): *a certain Mr Smith* スミスと呼ばれる男 sumisù to yobareru otóko; (particular): *certain days/places* ある日〔場所〕árù hi 〔bashó〕; (some): *a certain coldness/pleasure* ある程度の冷たさ〔喜び〕árù teido no tsumétasa 〔yorókobi〕
for certain 確実に kakújitsu ni

certainly [səːr'tənliː] *adv* (undoubtedly) 間違いなく machígai nakù; (of course) もちろん mochíròn

certainty [səːr'təntiː] *n* (assurance) 確実性 kakújitsusei; (inevitability) 必然性 hitsúzensei

certificate [səːrtif'əkit] *n* (of birth, marriage etc) 証明書 shómeisho; (diploma) 資格証明書 shikákushōmeisho

certified mail [səːr'təfaid-] (*US*) *n* 配達証明付き書留郵便 haítatsushōmei tsukí kakítome yūbin

certified public accountant (*US*) *n* 公認会計士 kónin kaikèishi

certify [səːr'təfai] *vt* (fact) 証明する shó-

mei suru; (award a diploma to) ...に資格を与える ...ni shikáku wo atáeru; (declare insane) 精神異常と認定する seíshinijō to nínteí suru

cervical [səːr'vikəl] *adj* (smear, cancer) 子宮けい部の shikyúkeìbu no

cervix [səːr'viks] *n* (ANAT) 子宮けい部 shikyúkeìbu

Cesarean [sizeːr'iːən] (*BRIT* **Caesarean**) *adj*: *Cesarean (section)* 帝王切開 teíōsekkāi

cesspit [ses'pit] *n* (sewage tank) 汚水だめ osúidame

cf. *abbr* = **compare**

ch. *abbr* = **chapter**

chafe [tʃeif] *vt* (rub: skin) 擦る súrù

chagrin [ʃəgrin'] *n* (annoyance) 悔しさ kuyáshisa; (disappointment) 落胆 rakútan

chain [tʃein] *n* (for anchor, prisoner, dog etc) 鎖 kusári; (on bicycle) チェーン chén; (jewelery) 首飾り kubíkazàri; (of shops, hotels) チェーン chén; (of events, ideas) 連鎖 reñsa
♦*vt* (*also*: **chain up**: prisoner, dog) 鎖につなぐ kusári ni tsunágu
an island chain/a chain of islands 列島 rettō
a mountain chain/a chain of mountains 山脈 sañmyaku

chain reaction *n* 連鎖反応 reñsahañnō

chain-smoke [tʃein'smouk] *vi* 立続けにタバコを吸う tatétsuzuke ni tabáko wo súú

chain store *n* チェーンストア chéṅsutoà

chair [tʃeːr] *n* (seat) いす isú; (armchair) 安楽いす añrakuisù; (of university) 講座 kóza; (of meeting) 座長 zachō; (of committee) 委員長 iínchō
♦*vt* (meeting) 座長を務める zachō wo tsutómerù

chairlift [tʃeːr'lift] *n* リフト rífùto

chairman [tʃeːr'mən] (*pl* **chairmen**) *n* (of committee) 委員長 iínchō; (*BRIT*: of company) 社長 shachō

chalet [ʃælei'] *n* 山小屋 yamágoya

chalice [tʃæl'is] *n* (REL) 聖さん杯 seísaǹhai

chalk [tʃɔ:k] n (GEO) 白亜 hákùa; (for writing) 白墨 hakúboku, チョーク chöku

challenge [tʃǽl'indʒ] n (of new job, unknown, new venture etc) 挑戦 chösen; (to authority, received ideas etc) 反抗 hañkö; (dare) 挑戦 chösen

♦vt (SPORT) ...に試合を申込む ...ni shiái wo möshikomù; (rival, competitor) 挑戦する chösen suru; (authority, right, idea etc) ...に反抗する ...ni hañkö suru

to challenge someone to do something ...に...をやれるものならやってみろと挑戦する ...ni ...wo yaréru monó nara yatté miro to chösen suru

challenging [tʃǽl'indʒiŋ] adj (career, task) やりがいを感じさせる yarígai wo kañji saséru; (tone, look etc) 挑発的な chöhatsuteki na

chamber [tʃeim'bə:r] n (room) 部屋 heyá; (POL: house) 院 íñ; (BRIT: LAW: gen pl) 弁護士事務室 beñgoshi jimushìtsu; (: of judge) 判事室 hañjishìtsu

chamber of commerce 商工会議所 shökökaigisho

chambermaid [tʃeim'bə:rmeid] n (in hotel) メード mëdo

chamber music n 室内音楽 shitsúnai oñgaku

chamois [ʃæm'i:] n (ZOOL) シャモア shamòa; (cloth) セーム革 sëmugawa

champagne [ʃæmpein'] n シャンペン shañpeñ

champion [tʃæm'pi:ən] n (of league, contest, fight) 優勝者 yüshösha, チャンピオン chañpion; (of cause, principle, person) 擁護者 yögosha

championship [tʃæm'pi:ənʃip] n (contest) 選手権決定戦 señshuken kettéisen; (title) 選手権 señshuken

chance [tʃæns] n (likelihood, possibility) 可能性 kanösei; (opportunity) 機会 kikái, チャンス cháñsu; (risk) 危険 kikén, かけ kaké

♦vt (risk): *to chance it* 危険を冒すkikén wo okasù, 冒険をする böken wo suru

♦adj 偶然の gûzen no

to take a chance 危険を冒す kikén wo

okasù, 冒険をする böken wo suru

by chance 偶然に gûzen ni

chancellor [tʃæn'sələ:r] n (head of government) 首相 shushö

Chancellor of the Exchequer (BRIT) n 大蔵大臣 ökuradaìjin

chandelier [ʃændəli'ə:r] n シャンデリア shañderìa

change [tʃeindʒ] vt (alter, transform) 変える kaéru; (wheel, bulb etc) 取替える toríkaeru; (clothes) 着替える kigáerù; (job, address) 変える kaéru; (baby, diaper) 替える kaéru; (exchange: money) 両替する ryögae suru

♦vi (alter) 変る kawáru; (change one's clothes) 着替える kigáerù; (change trains, buses) 乗換える noríkaerù; (traffic lights) 変る kawáru; (be transformed): *to change into* ...に変る ...ni kawáru, ...になる ...ni narù

♦n (alteration) 変化 héñka; (difference) 違い chigái; (also: **change of clothes**) 着替え kigáe; (of government, climate, job) 変る事 kawáru kotó; (coins) 小銭 kozéni; (money returned) お釣 o-tsúri

to change one's mind 気が変る ki gá kawarù

for a change たまには tamá ni wa

changeable [tʃein'dʒəbəl] adj 変りやすい kawáriyasuì

change machine n 両替機 ryögaekì

changeover [tʃeindʒ'ouvə:r] n (to new system) 切替え kiríkae

changing [tʃein'dʒiŋ] adj (world, nature) 変る kawáru

changing room (BRIT) n 更衣室 köishìtsu

channel [tʃæn'əl] n (TV) チャンネル cháñneru; (in sea, river etc) 水路 sûro; (groove) 溝 mizó; (fig: means) 手続 tetsuzûki, ルート rûto

♦vt (money, resources) 流す nagásù

the (English) Channel イギリス海峡 igírisu kaìkyö

the Channel Islands チャネル諸島 chanéru shotö

chant [tʃænt] n (of crowd, fans etc) 掛声 kakégoè; (REL: song) 詠唱歌 eìshöka

◆*vt* (word, name, slogan) 唱える tonáerù

chaos [keiˈɑːs] *n* (disorder) 混乱 końran

chaotic [keiɑːtˈik] *adj* (mess, jumble) 混乱した końran shitá

chap [tʃæp] (*BRIT*: *inf*) *n* (man) やつ yátsù

chapel [tʃæpˈəl] *n* (in church) 礼拝堂 reíhaidō; (in hospital, prison, school etc) チャペル cháperù; (*BRIT*: non-conformist chapel) 教会堂 kyốkaidō

chaperone [ʃæpˈəroun] *n* (for woman) 付添い tsukísoi, シャペロン shapéroň

◆*vt* (woman, child) ...に付添う ...ni tsukísoù

chaplain [tʃæpˈlin] *n* (REL, MIL, SCOL) 付属牧師 fuzókubokùshi

chapped [tʃæpt] *adj* (skin, lips) あかぎれれした akágire shitá

chapter [tʃæpˈtəːr] *n* (of book) 章 shố; (of life, history) 時期 jíkì

char [tʃɑːr] *vt* (burn) 黒焦げにする kurókoge ni suru

◆*n* (*BRIT*) = **charwoman**

character [kærˈiktəːr] *n* (nature) 性質 seíshitsu; (moral strength) 気骨 kikótsu; (personality) 人格 jíňkaku; (in novel, film) 人物 jíňbutsu; (letter) 文字 mójì

characteristic [kæriktərisˈtik] *adj* (typical) 特徴的な tokúchōteki na

◆*n* (trait, feature) 特徴 tokúchō

characterize [kærˈiktəraiz] *vt* (typify) ...の特徴である ...no tokúchō de arú; (describe the character of) ...の特徴を描写する ...no tokúchō wo byốsha suru

charade [ʃəreidˈ] *n* (sham, pretence) 装い yosóoi

charcoal [tʃɑːrˈkoul] *n* (fuel) 炭 sumí, 木炭 mokútaň; (for drawing) 木炭 mokútaň

charge [tʃɑːrdʒ] *n* (fee) 料金 ryōkin; (LAW: accusation) 容疑 yốgi; (responsibility) 責任 sekínin

◆*vt* (for goods, services) ...の料金を取る ...no ryōkin wo torù; (LAW: accuse): **to charge someone (with)** 起訴する kisó suru; (battery) 充電する jứden suru; (MIL: enemy) ...に突撃する ...ni totsúgeki suru

◆*vi* (animal) 掛って来る〔行く〕kakáttè

kurù(ikú); (MIL) 突撃する totsúgeki suru

to take charge of (child) ...の面倒を見る ...no meńdō wo mirù; (company) ...の指揮を取る ...no shikí wo torú

to be in charge of (person, machine) ...の責任を持っている ...no sekínin wo motté irù; (business) ...の責任者である ...no sekíninshà de arù

how much do you charge? 料金はいくらですか ryōkin wa ikùra desù ka

to charge an expense (up) to someone's account ...の勘定に付ける ...no kańjō ni tsukerù

charge card *n* (for particular shop or organization) クレジットカード kuréjittokàdo ◇特定の店でしか使えない物を指す tokútei nò mise de shika tsukáenai monð wo sásù

charges [tʃɑːrˈdʒiz] *npl* (bank charges, telephone charges etc) 料金 ryōkin

to reverse the charges (TEL) 先方払いにする seńpōbarài ni surù

charisma [kərizˈmə] *n* カリスマ性 karísumasei

charitable [tʃærˈitəbəl] *adj* (organization) 慈善の jizén no

charity [tʃærˈiti:] *n* (organization) 慈善事業 jizénjigyò; (kindness) 親切さ shíńsetsusa; (generosity) 寛大さ kańdaisa; (money, gifts) 施し hodókoshi

charlady [tʃɑːrˈleidi:] (*BRIT*) *n* = **charwoman**

charlatan [ʃɑːrˈlətən] *n* 偽者 nisémono

charm [tʃɑːrm] *n* (attractiveness) 魅力 miryóku; (to bring good luck) お守 o-mámori; (on bracelet etc) 飾り kazári

◆*vt* (please, delight) うっとりさせる uttórì saséru

charming [tʃɑːrˈmiŋ] *adj* (person, place) 魅力的な miryókuteki na

chart [tʃɑːrt] *n* (graph) グラフ gúràfu; (diagram) 図 zu; (map) 海図 kaízu

◆*vt* (course) 地図に書く chízù ni kakù; (progress) 図に書く zù ni kakù

charter [tʃɑːrˈtəːr] *vt* (plane, ship etc) チャーターする chátā surù

◆*n* (document, constitution) 憲章 keńshō; (of university, company) 免許 mén̄kyo

chartered accountant [tʃɑːrˈtəːrd-] (*BRIT*) *n* 公認会計士 kônin kaikeíshi

charter flight *n* チャーターフライト chátāfuraíto

charts [tʃɑːrts] *npl* (hit parade): *the charts* ヒットチャート hittóchàto

charwoman [tʃɑːrˈwumən] (*pl* **charwomen**) *n* 掃除婦 sōjifu

chase [tʃeis] *vt* (pursue) 追掛ける oíkakerù; (*also*: **chase away**) 追払う oíharaù
♦*n* (pursuit) 追跡 tsuíseki

chasm [kæzˈəm] *n* (GEO) 深い割れ目 fúkài waréme

chassis [ʃæsˈiː] *n* (AUT) シャシ shashí

chastity [tʃæsˈtitiː] *n* (REL) 純潔 juńketsu

chat [tʃæt] *vi* (*also*: **have a chat**) おしゃべりする o-sháberì surù
♦*n* (conversation) おしゃべり o-sháberì

chat show (*BRIT*) *n* トーク番組 tôku bańgumi

chatter [tʃætˈəːr] *vi* (person) しゃべりまくる shabérimakurù; (animal) きゃっきゃっと鳴く kyákkyattó nakú; (teeth) がちがち鳴る gachígachi narú
♦*n* (of people) しゃべり声 shabérigoè; (of birds) さえずり saézuri; (of animals) きゃっきゃっという鳴き声 kyákkyattó iú nakígoè

chatterbox [tʃætˈəːrbɑːks] (*inf*) *n* おしゃべり好き o-sháberizuki

chatty [tʃætˈiː] *adj* (style, letter) 親しみやすい shitáshimiyasuì; (person) おしゃべりな o-sháberì na

chauffeur [ʃouˈfəːr] *n* お抱え運転手 okákae-unteńshu

chauvinist [ʃouˈvənist] *n* (male chauvinist) 男性優越主義者 dańseiyūetsushugishà; (nationalist) 熱狂的愛国主義者 nekkyōtekiaíkokushugishà

cheap [tʃiːp] *adj* (inexpensive) 安い yasuí; (poor quality) 安っぽい yasúppoì; (behavior, joke) 下劣な geŕētsu na
♦*adv*: *to buy/sell something cheap* 安く買う〔売る〕 yasúkù kaú〔urú〕

cheaper [tʃiːˈpəːr] *adj* (less expensive) も

cheaply [tʃiːpˈliː] *adv* (inexpensively) 安く yasúkù

cheat [tʃiːt] *vi* (in exam) カンニングする kańningu suru; (at cards) いかさまをする ikásama surú
♦*vt*: *to cheat someone (out of something)* ...から ...をだまし取る ...kara ...wo damáshitorù
♦*n* (person) いかさま師 ikásamashì

check [tʃek] *vt* (examine: bill, progress) 調べる shiráberù; (verify: facts) 確認する kakúnin suru; (halt: enemy, disease) 食止める kuítomerù; (restrain: impulse, person) 抑える osáerù
♦*n* (inspection) 検査 keńsa; (curb) 抑制 yokúsei; (*US*: bill) 勘定書 kańjōgaki; (BANKING) 小切手 kogittè; (pattern: *gen pl*) 市松模様 ichímatsumoyò
♦*adj* (pattern, cloth) 市松模様の ichímatsumoyò no

checkbook [tʃekˈbuk] (*US*) *n* 小切手帳 kogittéchò

checkerboard [tʃekˈəːrbɔːrd] *n* チェッカー盤 chekkában

checkered [tʃekˈəːrd] (*BRIT* **chequered**) *adj* (*fig*: career, history) 起伏の多い kifúku no ôì

checkers [tʃekˈəːrz] (*US*) *npl* (game) チェッカー chékkà

check in *vi* (at hotel, airport) チェックインする chekkúin surù
♦*vt* (luggage) 預ける azúkerù

check-in (desk) [tʃekˈin-] *n* フロント furônto

checking account [tʃekˈiŋ-] (*US*) *n* (current account) 当座預金 tôzayokìn

checkmate [tʃekˈmeit] *n* (CHESS) 王手 ôte

check out *vi* (of hotel) チェックアウトする chekkúauto surù

checkout [tʃekˈaut] *n* (in shop) 勘定カウンター kańjō kauńtà

checkpoint [tʃekˈpɔint] *n* (on border) 検問所 keńmonjo

checkroom [tʃekˈruːm] (*US*) *n* (left-luggage office) 手荷物一時預り所 teńmòtsu ichíjìazúkarijo

check up vi: **to check up on something/someone** ...を調べておく ...wo shirábetè okù

checkup [tʃek'ʌp] n (MED) 健康診断 keńkōshìndan

cheek [tʃi:k] n (ANAT) ほお hǒ; (impudence) ずうずうしさ zúzūshìsà; (nerve) 度胸 dokyǒ

cheekbone [tʃi:k'boun] n ほお骨 hǒbone

cheeky [tʃi:'ki:] adj (impudent) ずうずうしい zúzūshìì

cheep [tʃi:p] vi (bird) ぴよぴよ鳴く piyópiyo nakù

cheer [tʃi:r] vt (team, speaker) 声援する seíen suru; (gladden) 喜ばす yorókobasù
♦vi (shout) 声援する seíen suru
♦n (shout) 声援 seíen

cheerful [tʃi:r'fəl] adj (wave, smile, person) 朗らかな hogaràka na

cheerio [tʃi:ri:'ou] (BRIT) excl じゃあね já ne

cheers [tʃi:rz] npl (of crowd etc) 声援 seíen, かっさい kassái
cheers! (toast) 乾杯 kaṅpai

cheer up vi (person) 元気を出す geńki wo dasù
♦vt (person) 元気づける geńkizukerù

cheese [tʃi:z] n チーズ chīzu

cheeseboard [tʃi:z'bourd] n チーズボード chízubòdo ◊チーズを盛り合せる板または皿 chízu wo moríawaserù ità mata wa sará

cheetah [tʃi:'tə] n チーター chītā

chef [ʃef] n (in restaurant, hotel) コック kókkù

chemical [kem'ikəl] adj (fertilizer, warfare) 化学の kágàku no
♦n 化学薬品 kagákuyakùhin

chemist [kem'ist] n (BRIT: pharmacist) 薬剤師 yakúzaìshi; (scientist) 化学者 kagákùsha

chemistry [kem'istri:] n 化学 kágàku

chemist's (shop) [kem'ists-] (BRIT) n 薬局 yakkyókù

cheque [tʃek] (BRIT: BANKING) n = check

chequebook [tʃek'buk] (BRIT) n = checkbook

cheque card (BRIT) n (to guarantee cheque) 小切手カード kogítte kàdo

chequered [tʃek'ə:rd] (BRIT) adj = checkered

cherish [tʃe:r'iʃ] vt (person) 大事にする daíji ni suru; (memory, dream) 心に抱く kokórò ni idakù

cherry [tʃe:r'i:] n (fruit) サクランボウ sakúranbò; (also: **cherry tree**) サクラ sakúra

chess [tʃes] n チェス chésù

chessboard [tʃes'bo:rd] n チェス盤 chésuban

chest [tʃest] n (ANAT) 胸 muné; (box) ひつ hitsú
chest of drawers 整理だんす seíridaǹsu

chestnut [tʃes'nʌt] n クリ kurí; (also: **chestnut tree**) クリの木 kurí no ki

chew [tʃu:] vt (food) かむ kamù

chewing gum [tʃu:'iŋ-] n チューインガム chūìngamù

chic [ʃi:k] adj (dress, hat etc) スマートな súmàto na; (person, place) 粋な ikí na

chick [tʃik] n (bird) ひな hínà; (inf: girl) べっぴん beppín

chicken [tʃik'ən] n (bird) ニワトリ niwátori; (meat) 鶏肉 keíniku; (inf: coward) 弱虫 yowamùshi

chicken out (inf) vi おじ気付いて...から手を引く ojíkezuìte ...kara te wo hikú

chickenpox [tʃik'ənpɑ:ks] n 水ぼうそう mizúbòsō

chicory [tʃik'ə:ri:] n チコリ chíkòri

chief [tʃi:f] n (of tribe) しゅう長 shúchō; (of organization, department) ...長 ...chǒ
♦adj (principal) 主な ómò na

chief executive n 社長 shachǒ

chiefly [tʃi:f'li:] adv (principally) 主に ómò ni

chiffon [ʃifɑ:n'] n (fabric) シフォン shíffon

chilblain [tʃil'blein] n 霜焼け shimóyake

child [tʃaild] (pl **children**) n 子供 kodómo
do you have any children? お子さんは? o-kó-san wa?

childbirth [tʃaild'bə:rθ] n お産 osán

childhood [tʃaild'hud] n 子供時分 kodómojíbun

childish [tʃail'diʃ] adj (games, attitude, person) 子供っぽい kodómoppoî

childlike [tʃaild'laik] adj 無邪気な mújàki na

child minder (BRIT) n 保母 hóbò

children [tʃil'drən] npl of **child**

Chile [tʃil'i:] n チリ chírì

Chilean [tʃil'i:ən] adj チリの chírì no
♦n チリ人 chírijìn

chill [tʃil] n (coldness: in air, water etc) 冷え hié; (MED: illness) 風邪 kazé
♦vt (cool: food, drinks) 冷す hiyasù; (person: make cold): to be chilled 体が冷える karáda ga hierù

chilli [tʃil'i:] n チリ chirí

chilly [tʃil'i:] adj (weather) 肌寒い hadásamuî; (person) 寒気がする samúke ga suru; (response, look) 冷たい tsumétai

chime [tʃaim] n (of bell, clock) チャイム cháìmu
♦vi チャイムが鳴る chaîmu ga narú

chimney [tʃim'ni:] n (of house, factory) 煙突 eñtotsu

chimney sweep n 煙突掃除夫 eñtotsu sōjifù

chimpanzee [tʃimpænzi:'] n チンパンジー chiñpañjì

chin [tʃin] n あご agó

China [tʃai'nə] n 中国 chũgoku

china [tʃai'nə] n (clay) 陶土 tódo; (crockery) 瀬戸物 setómono

Chinese [tʃaini:z'] adj 中国の chũgoku no; (LING) 中国語の chũgokugo no
♦n inv (person) 中国人 chũgokujìn; (LING) 中国語 chũgokugo

chink [tʃiŋk] n (crack: in door, wall etc) 透き間 sukíma; (clink: of bottles etc) かちん kachín

chip [tʃip] n (BRIT: gen pl: CULIN) フライドポテト furáidopotèto; (US: also: **potato chip**) ポテトチップス potétochìppusu; (of wood, glass, stone) 欠けら kakéra; (COMPUT) チップ chippú
♦vt: to be chipped (cup, plate) 縁が欠けている fuchí ga kakéte irú

chip in (inf) vi (contribute) 寄付する kífù surù; (interrupt) 口を挟む kuchí wo

hasamù

chiropodist [kirəːp'ədist] (BRIT) n 足治療師 ashí chiryõshi

chirp [tʃəːrp] vi (bird) ちゅうちゅう鳴く chũchū nakú

chisel [tʃiz'əl] n (for wood) のみ nómì; (for stone) たがね tagáne

chit [tʃit] n (note) メモ mémò; (receipt) 領収書 ryõshūsho

chitchat [tʃit'tʃæt] n 世間話 sekénbanàshi

chivalrous [ʃiv'əlrəs] adj 親切な shíñsetsu na

chivalry [ʃiv'əlri:] n (behavior) 親切さ shíñsetsusa; (medieval system) 騎士道 kishídō

chives [tʃaivz] npl (herb) チャイブ cháìbu

chlorine [klɔːr'i:n] n (CHEM) 塩素 éñso

chock-a-block [tʃɑːk'əblɑːk'] adj 一杯で íppài de

chock-full [tʃɑːk'ful'] adj = **chock-a-block**

chocolate [tʃɔːk'əlit] n (bar, sweet, cake) チョコレート chokórèto; (drink) ココア kókòa

choice [tʃɔis] n (selection) 選んだ物 eránda monó; (option) 選択 señtaku; (preference) 好み konómi
♦adj (fine: cut of meat, fruit etc) 一級の ikkyũ no

choir [kwaiə:r] n (of singers) 聖歌隊 seíkatai; (area of church) 聖歌隊席 seíkataisèki

choirboy [kwaiə:r'bɔi] n 少年聖歌隊員 shõnen seikataiin

choke [tʃouk] vi (on food, drink etc) ...がのどに詰る ...ga nodó ni tsumarù; (with smoke, dust, anger etc) むせる musérù
♦vt (strangle) ...ののどを締める ...no nodò wo shimerù; (block): to be choked (with) (...で) 詰っている (...de) tsumattè irú
♦n (AUT) チョーク chõku

cholera [kɑːl'əːrə] n コレラ kórèra

cholesterol [kəles'tərɔːl] n (fat) コレステロール korésuteròru

choose [tʃuːz] (pt chose, pp chosen) vt 選

ぶ erábù
to choose to do...をする事に決める
...wo suru kotó ni kiméru
choosy [tʃúː'ziː] *adj* (difficult to please)
えり好みする erígonomi suru
chop [tʃɑːp] *vt* (wood) 割る warú;
(CULIN: *also*: **chop up**: vegetables, fruit,
meat) 刻む kizámu
♦*n* (CULIN) チョップ chóppù, チャップ
cháppu
chopper [tʃɑːp'əːr] *n* (helicopter) ヘリコ
プター heríkopùtā
choppy [tʃɑːp'iː] *adj* (sea) しけの shiké no
chops [tʃɑːps] *npl* (jaws) あご agó
chopsticks [tʃɑːp'stiks] *npl* はし háshì
choral [kɔːr'əl] *adj* (MUS) 合唱の gasshṓ
no
chord [kɔːrd] *n* (MUS) 和音 wáòn
chore [tʃɔːr] *n* (domestic task) 家事 kájì;
(routine task) 毎日の雑用 máìnichi no
zatsúyō
choreographer [kɔːriːɑːg'rəfəːr] *n* 振付
師 furítsukeshì
chortle [tʃɔːr'təl] *vi* 楽しそうに笑う tanóshisō ni waraù
chorus [kɔːr'əs] *n* (MUS: group) 合唱隊
gasshṓtai, コーラス kōrasu; (: song) 合唱
gasshṓ; (: refrain) リフレーン rifúrēn; (of
musical play) コーラス kōrasu
chose [tʃouz] *pt of* **choose**
chosen [tʃou'zən] *pp of* **choose**
Christ [kraist] *n* キリスト kirísuto
christen [kris'ən] *vt* (REL: baby) ...に洗
礼を施す ...ni señrei wo hodókosù; (nickname) ...を...と呼ぶ ...wo ...to yobú
Christian [kris'tʃən] *adj* キリスト教の
kirísutokyō no
♦*n* キリスト教徒 kirísutokyòto
Christianity [kristʃiːæn'itiː] *n* キリスト
教 kirísutokyō
Christian name *n* ファーストネーム fásutonèmu
Christmas [kris'məs] *n* (REL: festival)
クリスマス kurísumàsu; (period) クリス
マスの季節 kurísumàsu no kisetsù
Merry Christmas! メリークリスマス!
merī kurisumàsu!
Christmas card *n* クリスマスカード

kurísumasu kàdo
Christmas Day *n* クリスマス kurísumàsu
Christmas Eve *n* クリスマスイブ kurísumasu ibù
Christmas tree *n* クリスマスツリー kurísumasu tsurì
chrome [kroum] *n* クロームめっき kurṓ-
mumekkì
chromium [krou'miːəm] *n* = **chrome**
chromosome [krou'məsoum] *n* 染色体
señshokutai
chronic [krɑːn'ik] *adj* (continual: ill-
health, illness etc) 慢性の mañsei no;
(: drunkenness etc) 常習的な jṓshūteki
na; (severe: shortage, lack etc) ひどい
hídoì
chronicle [krɑːn'ikəl] *n* (of events) 記録
kiróku ◊年代順または日付順の記録を指
す neñdaijuñ mata wa hizúkejuñ no
kiróku wo sasù
chronological [krɑːnəlɑːdʒ'ikəl] *adj*
(order) 日付順の hizúkejuñ no
chrysanthemum [krisæn'θəməm] *n* キ
ク kikú
chubby [tʃʌb'iː] *adj* (cheeks, child) ぽっち
ゃりした potchárì shitá
chuck [tʃʌk] (*inf*) *vt* (throw: stone, ball
etc) 投げる nagerù; (BRIT: *also*: **chuck
up**) やめる yaméru
chuckle [tʃʌk'əl] *vi* くすくす笑う kúsùkusu waraù
chuck out *vt* (person) 追い出す oídasù;
(rubbish etc) 捨てる sutéru
chug [tʃʌg] *vi* (machine, car engine etc)
ぽっぽっと音を立てる póppòtto otó wo
taterù; (car, boat: *also*: **chug along**) ぽ
っぽっと音を立てて行く poppótto otó wo
tatète ikú
chum [tʃʌm] *n* (friend) 友達 tomódachi
chunk [tʃʌŋk] *n* (of stone, meat) 塊 katámari
church [tʃəːrtʃ] *n* (building) 教会 kyṓkai;
(denomination) 教派 kyōha, ...教 ...kyō
churchyard [tʃəːrtʃ'jɑːrd] *n* 教会墓地
kyṓkaibochì
churlish [tʃəːr'liʃ] *adj* (silence, behavior)
無礼な burèi na

churn [tʃəːrn] n (for butter) かく乳器 kakúnyùki; (BRIT: also: milk churn) 大型ミルク缶 ōgata mirukukan

churn out vt (mass-produce: objects, books etc) 大量に作る taíryō ni tsukurù

chute [ʃuːt] n (also: rubbish chute) ごみ捨て場 gomísuteba; (for coal, parcels etc) シュート shūto

chutney [tʃʌtni:] n チャツネ chátsùne

CIA [si:aiei'] (US) n abbr (= Central Intelligence Agency) 中央情報局 chūōjōhōkyoku

CID [si:aidi:'] (BRIT) n abbr (= Criminal Investigation Department) 刑事部 keíjibù

cider [sai'dəːr] n リンゴ酒 riñgoshù

cigar [sigɑːr'] n 葉巻 hamáki

cigarette [sigəret'] n (紙巻) タバコ (kamímaki) tàbako

cigarette case n シガレットケース shigárettokèsu

cigarette end n 吸殻 suígara

Cinderella [sindərel'ə] n シンデレラ shiñdererà

cinders [sin'dəːrz] npl (of fire) 燃え殻 moégara

cine-camera [sin'i:kæmə:rə] (BRIT) n 映画カメラ eíga kamèra

cine-film [sin'i:film] (BRIT) n 映画用フィルム eígayō firùmu

cinema [sin'əmə] n (THEATER) 映画館 eígakàn; (film-making) 映画界 eígakài

cinnamon [sin'əmən] n (CULIN) ニッケイ nikkéi, シナモン shinámoñ

cipher [sai'fəːr] n (code) 暗号 añgō

circle [səːr'kəl] n (shape) 円 éñ; (of friends) 仲間 nakáma; (in cinema, theater) 二階席 nikáiseki
◆vi (bird, plane) 旋回する señkai suru
◆vt (move round) 回る mawáru; (surround) 囲む kakómu

circuit [səːr'kit] n (ELEC) 回路 kaíro; (tour) 1周 isshū; (track) サーキット sākitto; (lap) 1周 isshū, ラップ ráppù

circuitous [səːrkju:'itəs] adj (route, journey) 遠回りの tōmawàri no

circular [səːr'kjələːr] adj (plate, pond etc) 丸い maríi

◆n (letter) 回状 kaíjō

circulate [səːr'kjəleit] vi (traffic) 流れる nagárerù; (blood) 循環する juñkan suru; (news, rumour, report) 出回る demáwaru; (person: at party etc) 動き回る ugókimawarù
◆vt (report) 回す mawásu

circulation [səːrkjəlei'tʃən] n (of report, book etc) 回される事 mawásareru kotó; (of traffic) 流れ nagáre; (of air, water, also MED: of blood) 循環 juñkan; (of newspaper) 発行部数 hakkōbusū

circumcise [səːr'kəmsaiz] vt (MED) ...の包皮を切除する ...no hōhi wo setsùjo surù; (REL) ...に割礼を行う ...ni katsúrei wo okónau

circumference [səːrkʌm'fəːrəns] n (edge) 周囲 shūi; (distance) 周囲の長さ shūi no nagàsa

circumflex [səːr'kəmfleks] n (also: circumflex accent) 曲折アクセント kyokúsetsu akùsento

circumspect [səːr'kəmspekt] adj (cautious, careful) 慎重な shiñchō na

circumstances [səːr'kəmstænsiz] npl (of accident, death) 状況 jōkyō; (conditions, state of affairs) 状態 jōtai; (also: financial circumstances) 経済状態 keízaijōtai

circumvent [səːrkəmvent'] vt (regulation) ...に触れない様にする ...ni furénai yō ni surù; (difficulty) 回避する kaíhi surù

circus [səːr'kəs] n (show) サーカス sàkasu; (performers) サーカス団 sàkasudañ

CIS [si:aies'] n abbr = Commonwealth of Independent States

cistern [sis'təːrn] n (water tank) 貯水タンク chosúitañku; (of toilet) 水槽 suísō

cite [sait] vt (quote: example, author etc) 引用する in-yō suru; (LAW) 召喚する shōkan suru

citizen [sit'əzən] n (gen) 住民 jūmin; (of a country) 国民 kokúmin, 市民 shímìn; (of a city) 市民 shímin, (of other political divisions) ...民 ...mìn

citizenship [sit'əzəñʃip] n (of a country) 市民権 shimíñken

citrus fruit [sit'rəs fru:t] n カンキツ類 kañkitsurùi

city [sit'i:] n 都市 toshì
the City (FINANCE) シティー shití ◇ ロンドンの金融業の中心地 rondon no kíñyūgyō no chūshíñchi

civic [siv'ik] adj (leader, duties, pride) 公民の kõmin no; (authorities) 自治体の jichítai no

civic centre (BRIT) n 自治体中心部 jichítaichūshiñbu

civil [siv'əl] adj (gen) 市民の shímin no, 公民の kõmin no; (authorities) 行政の gyõsei no; (polite) 礼儀正しい reígitadashìì

civil defense n 民間防衛 mińkañbōei

civil disobedience n 市民的不服従 shimíntekifufukujù

civil engineer n 土木技師 dobókugishì

civilian [sivil'jən] adj (attitudes, casualties, life) 民間の mińkan no
♦n 民間人 mińkanjin

civilization [sivələzei'ʃən] n (a society) 文明社会 buñmeishakài; (social organization) 文化 buñka

civilized [siv'əlaizd] adj (society) 文明的な buñmeiteki na; (person) 洗練された señren saréta

civil law n 民法 míñpō

civil rights npl 公民権 kõmiñken

civil servant n 公務員 kõmuìn

Civil Service n 文官職 buñkanshokù

civil war n 内乱 naíran

clad [klæd] adj: *clad (in)* ...を着た ...wo kitá

claim [kleim] vt (expenses) 請求する seíkyū suru; (inheritance) 要求する yõkyū suru; (rights) 主張する shuchõ suru; (assert): *to claim that/to be* ...である と主張する ...de arù to shuchõ suru
♦vi (for insurance) 請求する seíkyū suru
♦n (assertion) 主張 shuchõ; (for pension, wage rise, compensation) 請求 seíkyū; (to inheritance, land) 権利 kéñri
to claim responsibility (for) (...の) 犯行声明を出す (...no) hañkōseimèi wo dasù
to claim credit (for) (...が) 自分の業績

であると主張する (...ga) jibún no gyõseki de arù to shuchõ suru

claimant [klei'mənt] n (ADMIN) 要求者 yõkyūshà; (LAW) 原告 geñkoku

clairvoyant [kle:rvɔi'ənt] n (psychic) 霊媒 reíbai

clam [klæm] n (ZOOL, CULIN) ハマグリ hamagùri ◇英語では食用二枚貝の総称として使われる eígo de wa shokúyōnimaìgai no sõshō toshité tsukáwarerù

clamber [klæm'bə:r] vi (aboard vehicle) 乗る norú; (up hill etc) 登る nobóru ◇手足を使って物に乗ったり登ったりすると いう含みがある teáshi wo tsukátte monó ni nottári nobóttari suru to iú fukúmi ga arù

clammy [klæm'i:] adj (hands, face etc) 冷たくてべとべとしている tsumétakùte betòbeto shité irù

clamor [klæm'ə:r] (BRIT **clamour**) vi: *to clamor for* (change, war etc) ...をや かましく要求する ...wo yakámashikù yõkyū suru

clamp [klæmp] n (device) 留金 toméga-ne, クランプ kuráñpu
♦vt (two things together) クランプで留める kuráñpu de toméru; (put: one thing on another) 締付ける shimétsukerù

clamp down on vt fus (violence, speculation etc) 取り締まる toríshimarù

clan [klæn] n (family) 一族 ichízòku

clandestine [klændes'tin] adj (activity, broadcast) 秘密の himítsu no

clang [klæŋ] vi (bell, metal object) かん と鳴る kañ to narú

clap [klæp] vi (audience, spectators) 拍手する hákùshu suru

clapping [klæp'iŋ] n (applause) 拍手 hákùshu

claret [klær'it] n クラレット kuráret-tò ◇ボルドー産の赤ワイン bórudōsañ no aká waiñ

clarify [klær'əfai] vt (argument, point) はっきりさせる hakkíri saséru

clarinet [klærənet'] n (MUS: instrument) クラリネット kurárinettò

clarity [klær'iti:] n (of explanation, thought) 明りょうさ meíryōsa

clash [klæʃ] *n* (of opponents) 衝突 shōtotsu; (of beliefs, ideas, views) 衝突 shōtotsu, 対立 tairitsu; (of colors) 不調和 fuchōwa; (of styles) つり合わない事 tsuríawanai kotō; (of two events, appointments) かち合い kachíai; (noise) ぶつかる音 butsúkaru otó

♦*vi* (fight: rival gangs etc) 衝突する shōtotsu suru; (disagree: political opponents, personalities) 角突合いをする tsunótsukiaì wo surù; (beliefs, ideas, views) 相容れない aírènai; (colors, styles) 合わない awànai; (two events, appointments) かち合う kachíau; (make noise: weapons, cymbals etc) 音を立ててぶつかり合う otó wo tatéte butsúkariaù

clasp [klæsp] *n* (hold: with hands) 握る事 nigíru kotó, 握り nigíri; (: with arms) 抱締めること dakíshimerù kotó, 抱擁 hōyō; (of necklace, bag) 留金 tomégane, クラスプ kurásupù

♦*vt* (hold) 握る nigíru; (embrace) 抱締める dakíshimerù

class [klæs] *n* (SCOL: pupils) 学級 gakkyū, クラス kùrasu; (: lesson) 授業 jugyō; (of society) 階級 kaíkyū; (type, group) 種類 shuruì

♦*vt* (categorize) 分類する buńrui suru

classic [klæsik] *adj* (example, illustration) 典型的な teńkeiteki na; (film, work etc) 傑作の kessáku no; (style, dress) 古典的な kotenteki na

♦*n* (film, novel etc) 傑作 kessáku

classical [klæsikəl] *adj* (traditional) 伝統的な deńtōteki na; (MUS) クラシックの kuráshikkù no; (Greek, Roman) 古代の kódài no

classification [klæsəfəkeiʃən] *n* (process) 分類する事 buńrui suru kotó; (category, system) 分類 buńrui

classified [klæsəfaid] *adj* (information) 秘密の himítsu no

classified advertisement *n* 分類広告 buńruikōkoku

classify [klæsəfai] *vt* (books, fossils etc) 分類する buńrui suru

classmate [klæsmeit] *n* 同級生 dōkyūsei, クラスメート kurásumēto

classroom [klæsruːm] *n* 教室 kyōshitsu

clatter [klætər] *n* (of dishes, pots etc) がちゃがちゃ gáchàgacha; (of hooves) かたかた kátàkata

♦*vi* (dishes, pots etc) がちゃがちゃいう gachàgacha iú; (hooves) かたかた鳴る kátàkata narú

clause [klɔːz] *n* (LAW) 条項 jōkō; (LING) 文節 buńsetsu

claustrophobia [klɔːstrəfouˈbiːə] *n* (PSYCH) 閉所恐怖症 heíshokyōfushō

claw [klɔː] *n* (of animal, bird) つめ tsumé; (of lobster) はさみ hasámi

claw at *vt fus* (curtains, door etc) 引っかく hikkáku

clay [klei] *n* 粘土 néndo

clean [kliːn] *adj* (person, animal) きれい好きな kiréizuki na; (place, surface, clothes etc) 清潔な seíketsu na; (fight) 反則のない hańsoku no naì; (record, reputation) 無傷の múkīzu no; (joke, story) 下品でない gehìn de naì; (MED: fracture) 単純な tańjun na

♦*vt* (car, hands, face etc) 洗う aráu; (room, house) 掃除する sōji suru

clean-cut [kliːnˈkʌt] *adj* (person) 品の良い hìn no yoì

cleaner [kliːˈnər] *n* (person) 掃除係 sōjigakàri; (substance) 洗剤 señzai

cleaner's [kliːˈnərz] *n* (*also:* **dry cleaner's**) クリーニング店 kurīningùten

cleaning [kliːˈniŋ] *n* (of room, house) 掃除 sōji

cleanliness [klenˈliːnis] *n* 清潔 seíketsu

clean out *vt* (cupboard, drawer) 中身を出してきれいにする nakámì wo dashíte kiréi ni suru

cleanse [klenz] *vt* (purify) 清める kiyómerù; (face, cut) 洗う aráu

cleanser [klenˈzər] *n* (for face) 洗顔料 señgañryo

clean-shaven [kliːnˈʃeiˈvən] *adj* ひげのない higé no naì

cleansing department [klenˈziŋ-] (*BRIT*) *n* 清掃局 seísōkyoku

clean up *vt* (mess) 片付ける katázukerù; (child) 身ぎれいにする migírei ni surù

clear [kliːˈər] *adj* (easy to understand:

report, argument) 分かりやすい wakáriyasuì; (easy to see, hear) はっきりした hakkírì shitá; (obvious: choice, commitment) 明らかな akíràka na; (glass, plastic) 透明な tōmei na; (water, eyes) 澄んだ súnda; (road, way, floor etc) 障害のない shōgai no naì; (conscience) やましい所のない yamashiì tokóro no naì; (skin) 健康そうな keńkòsō na; (sky) 晴れた haréta

♦vt (space, room) 開ける akéru; (LAW: suspect) 容疑を晴らす yógi wo harasù; (fence, wall) 飛越える tobíkoerù; (check) 払う haraù

♦vi (weather, sky) 晴れる harerù; (fog, smoke) 消える kierù

♦adv: clear of (trouble) ...を避けて ...wo sakéte; (ground) ...から離れて ...kara hanárete

to clear the table 食卓を片付ける shokútaku wo katázukerù

clearance [klí:'rəns] n (removal: of trees, slums) 取払う事 toríharaù kotó; (permission) 許可 kyóka

clear-cut [kli:'ə:rkʌt'] adj (decision, issue) 明白な meíhaku na

clearing [kli:'riŋ] n (in woods) 開けた所 hiráketà tokórò

clearing bank (BRIT) n 手形交換組合銀行 tegátakōkankumiaigìnkō ◇ロンドンの中央手形交換所を通じて他の銀行との取引を行う銀行 róndon no chūō tegata kōkaǹjo wo tsūjitè tá no giǹkō to no toríhiki wò okónaù giǹkō

clearly [kli:'ə:rli:] adv (distinctly, coherently) はっきりと hakkírì to; (evidently) 明らかに akíràka ni

clear up vt (room, mess) 片付ける katázukerù; (mystery, problem) 解決する kaíketsu suru

clearway [kli:r'wei] (BRIT) n 駐停車禁止道路 chūteíshakinshidòro

cleaver [kli:'və:r] n 骨切り包丁 honéwaribōchō ◇なたに似た物で，肉のブロックをたたき切ったり骨を割ったりするのに使う natá ni nitá monó de, nikú no burokkù wo tatákikittarì honé wo wattárì surù no ni tsukaù

clef [klef] n (MUS) 音部記号 oñbukigō

cleft [kleft] n (in rock) 割れ目 waréme

clemency [klem'ənsi:] n 恩情 oñjō

clench [klentʃ] vt (fist) 握り締める nigírishimerù; (teeth) 食いしばる kuíshibarù

clergy [klə:r'dʒi:] n 聖職者 seíshokùsha ◇総称 sōshō

clergyman [klə:r'dʒi:mən] (pl clergymen) n (Protestant) 牧師 bókùshi; (Catholic) 神父 shíñpu

clerical [kle:r'ikəl] adj (worker, job) 事務の jímù no; (REL) 聖職者の seíshokùsha no

clerk [klə:rk] n (BRIT: office worker) 事務員 jimúìn; (US: sales person) 店員 teñin

clever [klev'ə:r] adj (intelligent) 利口な rikō na; (deft, crafty) こうかつな kōkatsu na; (device, arrangement) 良く工夫した yókù kufū shitá

cliché [kli:ʃei'] n 決り文句 kimárimoñku

click [klik] vt (tongue) 鳴らす narásu; (heels) 打鳴らす uchínarasu

♦vi (device, switch etc) かちっと鳴る kachíttò narú

client [klai'ənt] n (of bank, company) 客 kyakú; (of lawyer) 依頼人 iráiniñ

cliff [klif] n (GEO) 断崖 dañgai

climate [klai'mit] n (weather) 気候 kikō; (of opinion etc) 雰囲気 fuñ-ìki

climax [klai'mæks] n (of battle, career) 頂点 chōteń; (of film, book) クライマックス kuráimakkùsu; (sexual) オルガズム orúgazùmu

climb [klaim] vi (sun, plant) 上がる agáru; (plant) は い 上 が る haíagarù; (plane) 上昇する jōshō suru; (prices, shares) 上昇する jōshō suru; (move with effort): to climb over a wall 塀を乗り越える heí wo noríkoerù

♦vt (stairs, ladder) 上 が る agáru; (登る noboru; (hill) 登る noboru; (tree) ...に登る ...ni noborù

♦n (of hill, cliff etc) 登る事 noboru kotó; (of prices etc) 上昇 jōshō

to climb into a car 車に乗り込む kurúma ni noríkomù

climb-down [klaim'daun] n (retraction)

撤回 tekkái

climber [klai'mə:r] *n* (mountaineer) 登山者 tozańsha; (plant) つる性植物 tsurúseishokubútsu

climbing [klai'miŋ] *n* (mountaineering) 山登り yamánobòri, 登山 tózan

clinch [klintʃ] *vt* (deal) まとめる matómeru; (argument) ...に決着を付ける ...ni ketcháku wo tsukerù

cling [kliŋ] (*pt, pp* **clung**) *vi*: **to cling to** (mother, support) ...にしがみつく ...ni shigámitsukù; (idea, belief) 固執する koshū surù; (subj: clothes, dress) ...にぴったりくっつく ...ni pittári kuttsùku

clinic [klin'ik] *n* (MED: center) 診療所 shińryōjo

clinical [klin'ikəl] *adj* (MED: tests) 臨床の rińshō no; (: teaching) 臨床の rińshō no; (*fig*: thinking, attitude) 冷淡な reítan na; (: building, room) 潤いのない uruòi no naì

clink [kliŋk] *vi* (glasses, cutlery) ちんと鳴る chíñ to narú

clip [klip] *n* (*also*: **paper clip**) クリップ kurippù; (*also*: **hair clip**) 髪留 kamídome; (TV, CINEMA) 断片 dańpen
♦*vt* (fasten) 留める toméru; (cut) はさみで切る hasámi de kiru

clippers [klip'ə:rz] *npl* (for gardening) せん定ばさみ seńteibasàmi; (*also*: **nail clippers**) つめ切り tsumékiri

clipping [klip'iŋ] *n* (from newspaper) 切抜き kirínuki

clique [kli:k] *n* 徒党 totó

cloak [klouk] *n* (cape) マント mańto
♦*vt* (*fig*: in mist, secrecy) 隠す kakúsù

cloakroom [klouk'ru:m] *n* (for coats etc) クローク kuròku; (*BRIT*: WC) お手洗 o-téarai

clock [klɑ:k] *n* 時計 tokéi

clock in *vi* (for work) 出勤する shukkín suru

clock off *vi* (from work) 退社する taísha suru

clock on *vi* = **clock in**

clock out *vi* = **clock off**

clockwise [klɑ:k'waiz] *adv* 時計回りに tokéimawàri ni

clockwork [klɑ:k'wə:rk] *n* 時計仕掛 tokéijikàke
♦*adj* (model, toy) 時計仕掛の tokéijikàke no

clog [klɑ:g] *n* (leather) 木底の靴 kizóko no kutsú; (*also*: **wooden clog**) 木靴 kígùtsu
♦*vt* (drain, nose) ふさぐ fuságu
♦*vi* (*also*: **clog up**: sink) 詰る tsumarù

cloister [klɔis'tə:r] *n* 回廊 kaírō

clone [kloun] *n* (of animal, plant) クローン kúrōn

close[1] [klous] *adj* (near) 近くの chikáku no; (friend) 親しい shitáshiì; (relative) 近縁の kiń-en no; (contact) 密な mítsù na; (link, ties) 密接な missétsu na; (examination, watch) 注意深い chūibukaì; (contest) 互角の gokáku no; (weather) 重苦しい omókurushiì
♦*adv* (near) 近くに chikáku ni
close to ...の近くに ...no chikàku ni
close at hand, close by *adj* 近くの chikáku no
♦*adv* 近くに chikáku ni
to have a close shave (*fig*) 間一髪で助かる kań-ippátsu de tasukaru

close[2] [klouz] *vt* (shut: door, window) しめる shimérù; (finalize: sale) 取決める toríkimerù; (end: case, speech) 終える oéru
♦*vi* (shop etc) 閉店する heíten suru; (door, lid) 閉る shimarù; (end) 終る owáru

closed [klouzd] *adj* (door, window, shop etc) 閉っている shimattè irù

close down *vi* (factory) 廃業する haígyō suru; (magazine) 廃刊する haíkan suru

closed shop *n* (*fig*) クローズドショップ kurózudo shoppù ◇特定の労働組合員だけしか雇わない事業所 tokútei no ròdōkumiaîn dake shika yatówanaì jigyósho

close-knit [klous'nit'] *adj* (family, community) 堅く結ばれた katáku musúbareta

closely [klous'li:] *adv* (examine, watch) 注意深く chūibukakù; (connected) 密接に missétsu ni; (related) 近縁になって kiń-en ni natté; (resemble) そっくり sokkúrì

closet [klɑːz'it] n (cupboard) たんす tañsu

close-up [klous'ʌp] n (PHOT) クローズアップ kurôzuappù

closure [klou'ʒəːr] n (of factory) 閉鎖 heísa; (of magazine) 廃刊 haíkan

clot [klɑːt] n (gen: blood clot) 血の塊 chi no katámari; (inf: idiot) ばか bákà
♦vi (blood) 固まる katámaru, 凝固する győko suru

cloth [klɔːθ] n (material) 布 nunó; (rag) ふきん fukíñ

clothe [klouð] vt (dress) ...に服を着せる ...ni fukú wo kiséru

clothes [klouz] npl 服 fukú

clothes brush n 洋服ブラシ yőfukuburàshi

clothes line n 物干綱 monóhoshizùna

clothes pin (BRIT **clothes peg**) n 洗濯ばさみ señtakubasàmi

clothing [klou'ðiŋ] n = **clothes**

cloud [klaud] n (in sky) 雲 kúmò
a cloud of smoke/dust もうもうとした煙〔ほこり〕mőmő to shita kemúri (hokori)

cloudburst [klaud'bəːrst] n 集中豪雨 shűchūgồu

cloudy [klau'diː] adj (sky) 曇った kumottà; (liquid) 濁った nigottà

clout [klaut] vt (hit, strike) 殴る nagurù

clove [klouv] n (spice) チョウジ chőji, クローブ kurőbu
clove of garlic ニンニクの一粒 nińniku no hitőtsubu

clover [klou'vəːr] n クローバー kurőbà

clown [klaun] n (in circus) ピエロ píèro
♦vi (also: **clown about**, **clown around**) おどける odőkeru

cloying [klɔi'iŋ] adj (taste, smell) むかつかせる mukátsukaseru

club [klʌb] n (society, place) クラブ kúràbu; (weapon) こん棒 końbō; (also: **golf club**) クラブ kúràbu
♦vt (hit) 殴る nagurù
♦vi: *to club together* (BRIT: for gift, card) 金を出し合う kanê wo dashiaù

club car (US) n (RAIL) ラウンジカー raúnjikà ◊休憩用客車 kyűkeiyō kyakùsha

clubhouse [klʌb'haus] n (of sports club) クラブハウス kurábuhaùsu ◊スポーツクラブのメンバーが集まる部屋, 建物など supótsukuràbu no meñba ga atsúmarù heyá, tatémono nadò

clubs [klʌbz] npl (CARDS) クラブ kúràbu

cluck [klʌk] vi (hen) こっこっと鳴く kőkkòtto nakú

clue [kluː] n (pointer, lead) 手掛かり tégàkari; (in crossword) かぎ kagí
I haven't a clue さっぱり分らない sáppàri wakáranaì

clump [klʌmp] n (gen) 塊 katámari; (of buildings etc) 一連 ichíren
a clump of trees 木立 kódàchi

clumsy [klʌm'ziː] adj (person, movement) 不器用な búkìyō na; (object) 扱いにくい atsúkainikuì; (effort, attempt) 下手な hetá na

clung [klʌŋ] pt, pp of **cling**

cluster [klʌs'təːr] n (of people, stars, flowers etc) 塊 katámari
♦vi 固まる katámaru, 群がる murágarù

clutch [klʌtʃ] n (grip, grasp) つかむ事 tsukamù kotő; (AUT) クラッチ kurátchi
♦vt (purse, hand, stick) しっかり持つ shíkkàri motsù

clutter [klʌt'əːr] vt (room, table) 散らかす chirákasu

cm abbr = **centimeter**

CND [siːendiː'] n abbr (= *Campaign for Nuclear Disarmament*) 核廃絶運動 kakúhaizetsu uñdő

Co. abbr = **county**; **company**

c/o abbr = **care** of

coach [koutʃ] n (bus) バス básù; (also: **horse-drawn coach**) 馬車 báshà; (of train) 客車 kyakúsha; (SPORT: trainer) コーチ kőchi; (tutor) 個人教師 kojínkyồshi
♦vt (sportsman/woman) コーチする kőchi suru; (student) ...に個人指導をする ...ni kojínshidồ wo surù

coach trip n バス旅行 basúryokồ

coagulate [kouæg'jəleit] vi (blood, paint etc) 凝固する győko surù

coal [koul] n (substance) 石炭 sekítañ;

(also: lump of coal) 石炭1個 sekítaň ikkŏ

coal face n 石炭切り場 sekítankiriba

coalfield [koul'fi:ld] n 炭田 tandeň

coalition [kouəlíʃ'ən] n (POL: also: coalition government) 連合政権 reňgóseikeň; (of pressure groups etc) 連盟 reňmei

coalman [koul'mən] (pl coalmen) n 石炭屋 sekítaňya

coal merchant n = coalman

coalmine [koul'main] n 炭坑 taňkŏ

coarse [kɔ:rs] adj (texture: rough) 荒い aráì; (person: vulgar) 下品な gehiň na

coast [koust] n 海岸 kaígaň
◆vi (car, bicycle etc) 惰力走行する daryókusokŏ suru

coastal [kous'təl] adj (cities, waters) 海岸沿いの kaíganzòi no

coastguard [koust'gɑ:rd] n (officer) 沿岸警備隊員 eňgankeibitáiin; (service) 沿岸警備隊 eňgankeibitái

coastline [koust'lain] n 海岸線 kaígansen

coat [kout] n (overcoat) コート kŏto; (of animal) 毛 ke; (of paint) 塗り nurí
◆vt: coated with ...で覆われた ...de ōwaréta

coat hanger n ハンガー háňgā

coating [kou'tiŋ] n (of dust, mud etc) 覆う物 ōù monŏ; (of chocolate, plastic etc) 被覆 hifúku

coat of arms n 紋 móň

coax [kouks] vt (person: persuade) 説得する settóku suru

cob [kɑ:b] n see corn

cobbler [kɑ:b'lə:r] n (maker/repairer of shoes) 靴屋 kutsúyà

cobbles [kɑ:b'əlz] npl 敷石 shikíishi

cobblestones [kɑ:b'əlstounz] npl = cobbles

cobweb [kɑ:b'web] n クモの巣 kúmò no su

cocaine [koukein'] n コカイン kókàin

cock [kɑ:k] n (rooster) おん鳥 oňdori; (male bird) 鳥の雄 torí no osú
◆vt (gun) ...の撃鉄を起す ...no gekítetsu wo okosù

cockerel [kɑ:k'ə:rəl] n 雄のひな鳥 osú no hinàdori

cock-eyed [kɑ:k'aid] adj (fig: idea, method) ばかな bákà na

cockle [kɑ:k'əl] n ホタテガイ hotátègai

cockney [kɑ:k'ni:] n ◇ロンドンのEast End地区生れの人 roňdon no Eást End chíkù umáre no hitó

cockpit [kɑ:k'pit] n (in aircraft) 操縦室 sójūshitsu, コックピット kokkúpittò; (in racing car) 運転席 uňteňseki, コックピット kokkúpittò

cockroach [kɑ:k'routʃ] n ゴキブリ gokíburi

cocktail [kɑ:k'teil] n (drink) カクテル kákùteru; (mixture: fruit cocktail, prawn cocktail etc) ...カクテル ...kakúteru

cocktail cabinet n ホームバー hŏmubà

cocktail party n カクテルパーティ kakúterupāti

cocoa [kou'kou] n (powder, drink) ココア kókòa

coconut [kou'kənʌt] n (fruit) ヤシの実 yáshì no mi; (flesh) ココナッツ kokónattsu

cocoon [kəku:n'] n (of butterfly) 繭 máyù

cod [kɑ:d] n タラ tárà

C.O.D. [si:oudi:'] abbr (= cash or also (US) collect on delivery) 着払い chakúbarài

code [koud] n (of practice, behavior) 規定 kitéi; (cipher) 暗号 aňgŏ; (dialling code, post code) 番号 baňgŏ

cod-liver oil [kɑ:d'livə:r-] n 肝油 kaň-yu

coercion [kouə:r'ʃən] n (pressure) 強制 kyósei

coffee [kɔ:f'i:] n (drink, powder) コーヒー kŏhī; (cup of coffee) コーヒー一杯 kŏhī ippài

coffee bar (BRIT) n 喫茶店 kíssàten

coffee bean n コーヒー豆 kŏhīmamè

coffee break n コーヒーブレーク kŏhīburèku

coffeepot [kɔ:f'i:pɑ:t] n コーヒーポット kŏhīpottò

coffee table n コーヒーテーブル kŏhītēburu

coffin [kɔ:f'in] n ひつぎ hitsúgi

cog [kɑ:g] n (TECH: wheel) 歯車 hágùruma; (: tooth) 歯車の歯 hágùruma no há

cogent [kou'dʒənt] adj (argument etc) 説得力ある settőkuryőku arù

cognac [koun'jæk] n コニャック kő-nyàkku

coherent [kouhi:'rənt] adj (answer, theory, speech) 筋の通った sujî no tôtta; (person) 筋の通った事を言う sujî no tôtta kotő wo iú

cohesion [kouhi:'ʒən] n (political, ideological etc) 団結 dańketsu

coil [kɔil] n (of rope, wire) 一巻 hitőmaki; (ELEC) コイル kőiru; (contraceptive) 避妊リング hinínrińgu
♦vt (rope) 巻く makú

coin [kɔin] n (money) 硬貨 kőka, コイン kőin
♦vt (word, slogan) 造る tsukúru

coinage [kɔi'nidʒ] n 貨幣制度 kahéiseìdo

coin-box [kɔin'bɑ:ks] n (BRIT) コイン電話 koíndeñwa ◇公衆電話でカードだけしか使えない物に対比して言う kőshūdeñwa de kắdo dakè shiká tsukáenai monő ni taíhi shité iú

coincide [kouinsaid'] vi (events) 同時に起る dōji ni okőru; (ideas, views) 一致する itchî suru

coincidence [kouin'sidəns] n 偶然の一致 gűzen no itchî

Coke [kouk]® n (drink) コカコーラ ko-kákőra

coke [kouk] n (coal) コークス kőkusu

colander [kɑ:l'əndə:r] n 水切り mizúkiri ◇ボール型で穴の比較的大きい物を指す bőrugata de aná no hikákuteki őkiì monő wo sasú

cold [kould] adj (water, food) 冷たい tsu-métai; (weather, room) 寒い samúi; (person, attitude: unemotional) 冷たい tsu-métai, 冷淡な reítań na
♦n (weather) 寒さ samùsa; (MED) 風邪 kazé

it's cold 寒い samui

to be cold (person, object) 冷たい tsu-métai

to catch (a) cold 風邪を引く kazé wo hikú

in cold blood (kill etc) 冷酷に reíkoku ni

coldly [kould'li:] adv (speak, behave) 冷たく tsumétaku, 冷淡に reítań ni

cold-shoulder [kould'[ouldə:r] vt 冷たくあしらう tsumétaku ashíraù

cold sore n 口角炎 kőkakuèn

coleslaw [koul'slɔ:] n コールスロー kő-rusurō

colic [kɑ:l'ik] n (MED) 腹痛 fukútsū

collaborate [kəlæb'əreit] vi (on book, research) 協同する kyődō suru; (with enemy) 協力する kyőryoku suru

collaboration [kəlæbərei'[ən] n 協力 kyőryoku

collage [kəla:ʒ'] n コラージュ kőrầju

collapse [kəlæps'] vi (building, system, resistance) 崩れる kuzúrerù, 崩壊する hőkai suru; (government) 倒れる taőrerù; (MED: person) 倒れる taőrerù; (table) 壊れる kowárerù, つぶれる tsubúrerù; (company) つぶれる tsubúrerù, 破産する hasán suru
♦n (of building, system, government, resistance) 崩壊 hőkai; (MED: of person) 倒れる事 taőreru kotő; (of table) 壊れる〔つぶれる〕事 kowáreru(tsubureru)kotő; (of company) 破産 hasán

collapsible [kəlæps'əbəl] adj (seat, bed, bicycle) 折畳みの orítatami no

collar [kɑ:l'ə:r] n (of coat, shirt) 襟 erí, カラー kárầ; (of dog, cat) 首輪 kubíwa, カラー karằ

collarbone [kɑ:l'ə:rboun] n (ANAT) 鎖骨 sakőtsu

collateral [kəlæt'ə:rəl] n (COMM) 担保 tấnpo

colleague [kɑ:l'i:g] n 同僚 dőryō

collect [kəlekt'] vt (gather: wood, litter etc) 集める atsúmerù; (as a hobby) 収集する shūshū suru; (BRIT: call and pick up: person) 迎えに行く mukáe ni ikú; (: object) 取りに行く torí ni ikú; (for charity, in church) 募金する bokín suru; (debts, taxes etc) 集金する shūkin suru; (mail) 収集する shushū suru

♦*vi* (crowd) 集る atsúmarù
to call collect (US: TEL) コレクトコールする korékutokòru suru

collection [kəlek'ʃən] *n* (of art, stamps etc) コレクション kórèkushon; (of poems, stories etc) ...集 ...shū; (from place, person) 受取る事 ukétoru kotó; (for charity) 募金 bokín; (of mail) 取集 shushū

collective [kəlek'tiv] *adj* (farm, decision) 共同の kyódō no

collector [kəlek'tə:r] *n* (of art, stamps etc) 収集家 shūshūka; (of taxes etc) 集金人 shūkínnin

college [kɑːl'idʒ] *n* (SCOL: of university) 学寮 gakúryō; (: of agriculture, technology) 大学 daígaku

collide [kəlaid'] *vi* (cars, people) ぶつかる butsúkaru, 衝突する shótotsu suru

collie [kɑːl'iː] *n* コリー犬 koríken

colliery [kɑːl'jə:riː] (*BRIT*) *n* 炭坑 tańkō

collision [kəliʒ'ən] *n* (of vehicles) 衝突 shótotsu

colloquial [kəlou'kwiːəl] *adj* (LING: informal) 口語の kōgo no

collusion [kəluː'ʒən] *n* (collaboration) 結託 kettáku

colon [kou'lən] *n* (punctuation mark) コロン kóròn; (ANAT) 大腸 dáìchō

colonel [kə:r'nəl] *n* 大佐 taísa

colonial [kəlou'niːəl] *adj* 植民地の shokúmiñchi no

colonize [kɑːl'ənaiz] *vt* (country, territory) 植民地にする shokúmiñchi ni surù

colony [kɑːl'əniː] *n* (subject territory) 植民地 shokúmiñchi; (of people) ...人街 ...jíñgai; (of animals) 個体群 kotáigùn

color [kʌl'ə:r] (*BRIT* **colour**) *n* (gen) 色 iro
♦*vt* (paint) ...に色を塗る ...ni irő wo nurú; (dye) 染める soméru; (*fig*: account) ...に色を付ける ...ni irő wo tsukerù; (judgment) ゆがめる yugámerù
♦*vi* (blush) 赤面する sekímen suru
in color 天然色で teñneñshoku de, カラーで kárā de

color bar *n* 人種差別 jiñshusabètsu ◇有色人種, 特に黒人に対する差別を指す

yūshokujiñshu, tokù ni kokújin ni taí suru sabétsu wo sasù

color-blind [kʌl'ə:rblaind] *adj* 色盲の shikímō no

colored [kʌl'ə:rd] *adj* (person) 有色の yúshoku no; (illustration etc) カラーの kárā no

color film *n* カラーフィルム karáfirùmu

colorful [kʌl'ə:rfəl] *adj* (cloth) 色鮮やかな irő azáyaka na; (account, story) 華やかな hanáyaka na; (personality) 華々しい hanábanashiì

color in *vt* (drawing) ...に色を塗る ...ni irő wo nurú

coloring [kʌl'ə:riŋ] *n* (complexion) 肌の色合い hadà no iróai; (*also*: **food coloring**) 着色料 chakúshokùryō

colors [kʌl'ə:rz] *npl* (of party, club etc) 色 irő

color scheme *n* 配色計画 haíshokukeìkaku

color television *n* カラーテレビ karáterèbi

colossal [kəlɑːs'əl] *adj* 巨大な kyodái na

colour [kʌl'ə:r] *etc* (*BRIT*) *n* = **color** *etc*

colt [koult] *n* 子ウマ koúma

column [kɑːl'əm] *n* (ARCHIT) 円柱 eñchū; (of smoke) 柱 hashíra; (of people) 縦隊 jútai; (gossip column, sports column) コラム kóràmu

columnist [kɑːl'əmist] *n* コラムニスト korámunisùto

coma [kou'mə] *n* (MED) こん睡状態 koñsuijòtai

comb [koum] *n* くし kushí
♦*vt* (hair) くしでとかす kushí de tokasù; (*fig*: area) 捜索する sōsaku suru

combat [*n* kɑːm'bæt *vb* kəmbæt'] *n* (MIL: fighting) 戦闘 señtō; (fight, battle) 戦い tatákai
♦*vt* (oppose) 反抗する hañkō suru

combination [kɑːmbənei'ʃən] *n* (mixture) 組合せ kumíawase; (for lock, safe etc) 組合せ番号 kumíawasebañgō

combine [*vb* kəmbain' *n* kɑːm'bain] *vt*:
to combine something with something ...を...と組合せる ...wo ...to kumía-

waserù; (qualities) 兼 備 え る kanésonae-
rù; (two activities) 兼任する kefinin suru
♦*vi* (people, groups) 合併する gappéi suru
♦*n* (ECON) 連合 reñgō
combine (harvester) [kɑːmˈbain(hɑːrˈ-
vestəːr)] *n* コンバイン kofibaìn
combustion [kəmbʌsˈtʃən] *n* (act, process) 燃焼 neñshō

KEYWORD

---

come [kʌm] (*pt* **came**, *pp* **come**) *vi* **1**
(movement towards) 来る kúrù
come here! ここにおいで kokó ni oide
I've only come for an hour 1時間しか
いられません ichíjikàn shika iráremasèn
come with me ついて来て下さい tsúìte
kite kudasai
are you coming to my party? 私のパ
ーティに来てくれますね watákushi no
pātì ni kité kùrèmasu né
to come running 走って来る hashíttè
kúrù
2 (arrive) 着く tsúkù, 到着する tốchaku
suru, 来る kúrù
he's just come from Aberdeen 彼はア
バーディーンから来たばかりです kárè
wa abádìn kara kitá bakàri desu
he's come here to work 彼はここには
働きに来ました kárè wa kokó ni wà
határaki ni kimashìta
they came to a river 彼らは川に着きま
した kárèra wa kawá nì tsukímashìta
to come home 家に戻って来る ié nì
modóttè kuru
3 (reach): *to come to* ...に届く ...ni todókù, ...になる ...ni nárù
the bill came to £40 勘定は計40ポン
ドだった kánjō wa kếĩ yónjuppòndo datta
her hair came to her waist 彼女の髪
の毛は腰まで届いていた kánojò no kamí
no kè wa koshí madè todóìte ita
to come to power 政権を握る seíken
wo nigiru
to come to a decision 結論に達する
ketsúron ni tassuru
4 (occur): *an idea came to me* いい考え

が浮かびました íi kángaè ga ukábima-
shìta
5 (be, become) なる nárù
to come loose/undone etc 外れる hazúreru
I've come to like him 彼が好きになり
ました kárè ga sukí nì narímashìta

come about *vi* 起る okórù
come across *vt fus* (person, thing) ...に
出会う ...ni deáù
come away *vi* (leave) 帰 る kaéru, 出て
来 る détè kure; (become detached) 外れ
る hazúreru
come back *vi* (return) 帰って来る káètte kuru
comeback [kʌmˈbæk] *n* (of film star
etc) 返り咲き kaérizaki, カムバック ka-
múbakkù
come by *vt fus* (acquire) 手に入れる tế
nì iréru
comedian [kəmiːˈdiːən] *n* (THEATER,
TV) コメディアン kốmèdian
comedienne [kəmiːdiːenˈ] *n* 女性コメデ
ィアン joséi kòmèdian
come down *vi* (price) 下がる sagárù;
(tree) 倒れる taórerù; (building) 崩れ落ち
る kuzúreochirù
comedy [kɑːmˈidiː] *n* (play, film) 喜劇 kígèki, コメディー kômèdī; (humor) 喜劇
性 kigékisei, ユーモア yùmoa
come forward *vi* (volunteer) 進んで...す
る susúnde ...sùrù
come from *vt fus* (place, source etc)
...から来る ...kara kúrù
come in *vi* (visitor) 入る háìru; (on deal
etc) 加わる kuwáwarù; (be involved) 関
係する kánkei suru
come in for *vt fus* (criticism etc) 受け
る ukérù
come into *vt fus* (money) 相続する sôzoku suru; (be involved) ...に関係する
...ni kánkei suru
to come into fashion 流行する ryúkō
suru
come off *vi* (button) 外れる hazúreru;
(attempt) 成功する sefkō suru
come on *vi* (pupil, work, project) 進歩す

る shínpo suru; (lights, electricity) つく tsúkú

come on! さあさあ sāsā

come out vi (fact) 発覚する hakkáku suru; (book) 出版される shúppan sareru; (stain) 取れる torérù, 落ちる ochírù; (sun) 出る dérù

come round vi (after faint, operation) 正気に返る shóki ni kaèru, 目が覚める mé gà samérù, 気が付く ki gá tsukù

comet [kɑːmˈit] n すい星 suísei

come to vi (regain consciousness) 正気に戻る shóki ni modorù, 目が覚める mé gà samérù

come up vi (sun) 出る dérù; (problem) 起おこる, 出る dérù; (event) 起る okórù; (in conversation) 出る dérù

come up against vt fus (resistance, difficulties) ぶつかる butsúkaru

come upon vt fus (find) 見付ける mitsúkeru

comeuppance [kʌmˈʌpˈəns] n: **to get one's comeuppance** 当然の罰を受ける tózen no batsù wo ukerù

come up with vt fus (idea) 持出す mochídasù; (money) 出す dásù

comfort [kʌmˈfəːrt] n (well-being: physical, material) 安楽 ánraku; (relief) 慰め nagúsame

♦vt (console) 慰める nagúsamerù

comfortable [kʌmˈfəːrtəbəl] adj (person: physically) 楽な rákù na; (: financially) 暮しに困らない kuráshi ni kómaranài; (furniture) 座り心地の良い suwárigokochi no yoì; (room) 居心地のよい igókochi nò yoì; (patient) 苦痛のない kutsú no naì; (easy: walk, climb etc) 楽な rákù na

comfortably [kʌmˈfəːrtəbliː] adv (sit, live etc) 楽に rákù ni

comforts [kʌmˈfəːrts] npl (of home etc) 生活を楽にするもの seíkatsu wo rakú ni suru monò

comfort station (US) n お手洗 o-téaraì

comic [kɑːmˈik] adj (also: **comical**) こっけいな kokkéi na

♦n (comedian) コメディアン kómèdian; (BRIT: magazine) 漫画(雑誌) mañ-ga(zasshì)

comic strip n 連続漫画 reñzokumañga

coming [kʌmˈiŋ] n (arrival) 到着 tóchaku

♦adj (event, attraction) 次の tsugí no, これからの koré kara no

coming(s) and going(s) n(pl) 行き来 yukíki, 往来 ốrai

comma [kɑːmˈə] n コンマ kôñma

command [kəmændˈ] n (order) 命令 meírei; (control, charge) 指揮 shikí; (MIL: authority) 司令部 shírèibu; (mastery: of subject) マスターしていること masùté shité irù kotó

♦vt (give orders to): **to command someone to do something** ...に...をする 様に命令する ...ni ...wo suru yố ni meírei suru; (troops) ...の司令官である ...no shiréìkan de arù

commandeer [kɑːməndiːrˈ] vt (requisition) 徴発する chốhatsu suru; (fig) 勝手 に取って使う katté ni tottế tsukáù

commander [kəmændˈəːr] n (MIL) 司令 官 shírèikan

commandment [kəmændˈmənt] n (REL) 戒律 kaíritsu

commando [kəmændˈou] n (group) コマ ンド部隊 komándobùtai; (soldier) コマン ド隊員 komándotaìin

commemorate [kəmemˈəːreit] vt (with statue, monument, celebration, holiday) 記念する kinén suru

commence [kəmensˈ] vt (begin, start) 始 める hajímeru

♦vi 始まる hajímaru

commend [kəmendˈ] vt (praise) ほめる homérù; (recommend) ゆだねる yudánerù

commensurate [kəmenˈsərit] adj: **commensurate with** ...に相応した ...ni sốō shitá

comment [kɑːmˈent] n (remark: written or spoken) コメント kométo

♦vi: **to comment (on)** (...について) コ メントする (...ni tsuité) kométo surù

no comment ノーコメント nốkomento

commentary [kɑːmˈənteːriː] n (TV, RADIO) 実況放送 jikkyốhōsō; (book, article) 注解 chúkai

commentator [kɑ:m'ənteitə:r] *n* (TV, RADIO) 解説者 kaísetsùsha

commerce [kɑm'ə:rs] *n* 商業 shōgyō

commercial [kəmər'ʃəl] *adj* (organization, activity) 商業の shōgyō no; (success, failure) 商業上の shōgyōjō no
♦*n* (TV, RADIO: advertisement) コマーシャル kōmāsharu, CM shīemu

commercialized [kəmər'ʃəlaizd] (*pej*) *adj* (place, event etc) 営利本意の efrihoñi no

commercial radio/television *n* 民間ラジオ〔テレビ〕放送 mifkan rajio〔terebi〕hōsō, 民放 mifpō

commiserate [kəmiz'əreit] *vi*: *to commiserate with* ...をいたわる ...wo itáwarù

commission [kəmiʃ'ən] *n* (order for work: esp of artist) 依頼 irái; (COMM) 歩合 buái, コミッション kōmìsshon; (committee) 委員会 iñkai
♦*vt* (work of art) 依頼する irái suru
out of commission (not working) 故障して koshō shité

commissionaire [kəmiʃəne:r'] (*BRIT*) *n* ドアマン dōaman

commissioner [kəmiʃ'ənə:r] *n* (POLICE) 長官 chōkan

commit [kəmit'] *vt* (crime, murder etc) 犯す okásu; (money, resources) 充当する jūtō suru; (to someone's care) 任せる makáserù
to commit oneself (to do) (...する事を) 約束する (...surú kotó wo) yakúsoku suru
to commit suicide 自殺する jisátsu suru

commitment [kəmit'mənt] *n* (to ideology, system) 献身 keñshin; (obligation) 責任 sekínin; (undertaking) 約束 yakúsoku

committee [kəmit'i:] *n* (of organization, club etc) 委員会 iñkai

commodity [kəmɑːd'iti:] *n* (saleable item) 商品 shōhin

common [kɑ:m'ən] *adj* (shared by all: knowledge, property, good) 共同の kyō-

dō no; (usual, ordinary: event, object, experience etc) 普通の futsū no; (vulgar: person, manners) 下品な gehín na
♦*n* (area) 共有地 kyōyūchi
in common 共通で kyōtsū de

commoner [kɑ:m'ənə:r] *n* 庶民 shomín

common law *n* コモン・ロー komón rō ◊成文化されてない慣習に基づく英米の一般法を指す seíbunka saréte naí kañshū ni motózukù eíbei no ippánhō wo sasù

commonly [kɑ:m'ənli:] *adv* (usually) 通常 tsūjō

Common Market *n* ヨーロッパ共同市場 yōroppa kyōdōshijō

commonplace [kɑ:m'ənpleis] *adj* 平凡な heíbon na

common room *n* (SCOL) 談話室 dañwashìtsu

Commons [kɑ:m'ənz] (*BRIT*) *npl*: *the Commons* 下院 ká-ìn

common sense *n* 常識 jōshiki, コモンセンス komónseñsu

Commonwealth [kɑ:m'ənwelθ] *n* (British Commonwealth): *the Commonwealth* イギリス連邦 igírisureñpō
the Commonwealth of Independent States 独立国家共同体 dokúritsu kòkka kyōdōtai

commotion [kəmou'ʃən] *n* (uproar) 騒ぎ sáwàgi

communal [kəmju:'nəl] *adj* (shared) 共同の kyōdō no

commune [*n* kɑ:m'ju:n *vb* kəmju:n'] *n* (group) コミューン komyūn
♦*vi*: *to commune with* (nature, God) ...に親しむ ...ni shitáshimù

communicate [kəmju:'nikeit] *vt* (idea, decision, feeling) 伝える tsutáerù
♦*vi*: *to communicate (with)* ...と通信する ...to tsūshin suru

communication [kəmju:nikei'ʃən] *n* (process) 通信 tsūshin; (letter, call) 連絡 refraku

communication cord (*BRIT*) *n* (on train) 非常通報装置 hijōtsūhōsōchi

communion [kəmju:n'jən] *n* (*also*: **Holy Communion**) 聖体拝領 seítaihaìryō

communiqué [kəmjuːˈnikeiʔ] *n* (POL, PRESS) コミュニケ kṓmyùnike

communism [kaːˈmjənizəm] *n* 共産主義 kyṓsanshùgi

communist [kaːˈmjənist] *adj* 共産主義の kyṓsanshùgi no
♦*n* 共産主義者 kyṓsanshugishà

community [kəmjuːˈniːtiː] *n* (group of people) 共同体 kyṓdōtai; (within larger group) 社会 shákài

community center *n* 公民館 kṓmìnkan

community chest (*US*) *n* 共同募金 kyṓdōbòkin

community home (*BRIT*) *n* 養育施設 yṓikushisètsu

commutation ticket [kaːmjəteiˈʃən-] (*US*) *n* 定期券 teíkìken

commute [kəmjuːˈt] *vi* (to work) 通う kayóu
♦*vt* (LAW: sentence) 減刑する geńkei suru

commuter [kəmjuːˈtəːr] *n* 通勤者 tsúkìnsha

compact [kaːˈmpækt] *adj* (taking up little space) 小型の kogáta no
♦*n* (*also*: **powder compact**) コンパクト kṓnpakuto

compact disk *n* コンパクトディスク kónpakuto disùku

companion [kəmpænˈjən] *n* 相手 aíte

companionship [kəmpænˈjənʃip] *n* つきあい tsukíai

company [kʌmˈpəni:] *n* (COMM) 会社 kaísha; (THEATER) 劇団 gekídan; (companionship) 付合い tsukíai
to keep someone company ...の相手になる ...no aíte ni narù

company secretary (*BRIT*) *n* 総務部長 sṓmubùchō

comparable [kaːˈmpəːrəbəl] *adj* (size, style, extent) 匹敵する hittékì suru

comparative [kəmpærˈətiv] *adj* (peace, stranger, safety) 比較的 hikákuteki; (study) 比較の hikáku no

comparatively [kəmpærˈətivliː] *adv* (relatively) 比較的に hikákuteki ni

compare [kəmpeːˈr] *vt*: *to compare someone/something with/to* (set side by side) ...を...と比較する ...wo ...to hikáku suru; (liken) ...を...に例える ...wo ...ni tatóerù
♦*vi*: *to compare (with)* (...に) 匹敵する (...ni) hittékì suru

comparison [kəmpærˈisən] *n* (setting side by side) 比較 hikáku; (likening) 例え tatóe
in comparison (with) ...と比較して ...to hikáku shité

compartment [kəmpaːrˈtmənt] *n* (RAIL) 客室 kyakúshitsu, コンパートメント koñpātomènto; (section: of wallet, fridge etc) 区画 kukáku

compass [kʌmˈpəs] *n* (instrument: NAUT, GEO) 羅針盤 rashínban, コンパス kóñpasu

compasses [kʌmˈpəsiz] *npl* (MATH) コンパス koñpasu

compassion [kəmpæʃˈən] *n* (pity, sympathy) 同情 dṓjō

compassionate [kəmpæʃˈənit] *adj* (person, look) 情け深い nasákebukaì

compatible [kəmpætˈəbəl] *adj* (people) 気が合う ki ga aù; (ideas etc) 両立できる ryṓritsu dekírù; (COMPUT) 互換性のある gokáñsei no arù

compel [kəmpel] *vt* (force) 強制する kyṓsei suru

compelling [kəmpelˈiŋ] *adj* (fig: argument, reason) 止むに止まれぬ yamú ni yamárenù

compensate [kaːˈmpənseit] *vt* (employee, victim) ...に補償する ...ni hoshṓ suru
♦*vi*: *to compensate for* (loss, disappointment, change etc) ...を埋め合せる ...wo uméawaserù

compensation [kaːmpənseiˈʃən] *n* (to employee, victim) 補償 hoshṓ; (for loss, disappointment, change etc) 埋め合せ uméawase

compère [kaːˈmpeːr] (*BRIT*) *n* (TV, RADIO) 司会者 shíkàisha

compete [kəmpiːˈt] *vi* (companies, rivals): *to compete (with)* (...と) 競り合う (...to) seríaù; (in contest, game) 参加する sañka suru

competence [kaːˈmpitəns] *n* (of worker

etc) 能力 nóryoku

competent [ka:m'pitənt] *adj* 有 能 な yúnō na

competition [ka:mpiti'ʃən] *n* (between firms, rivals) 競 争 kyōsō; (contest) コンクール koñkúru; (ECON) ライバル商品 raíbaru shōhin

competitive [kəmpet'ətiv] *adj* (industry, society) 競争の激しい kyōsō no hageshiì; (person) 競争心の強い kyōsōshin no tsuyói; (price, product) 競争できる kyōsō dekírù

competitive sports 競技 kyṓgi

competitor [kəmpet'itə:r] *n* (rival) 競争相手 kyōsōaìte; (participant) 参加者 sañkashà

compile [kəmpail'] *vt* (book, film, report) 編集する heñshū suru

complacency [kəmplei'sənsi:] *n* (smugness) 自己満足 jikómañzoku

complacent [kəmplei'sənt] *adj* (smug) 自己満足にふける jikómañzoku ni fukérù

complain [kəmplein'] *vi* (grumble) 不 平不満を言う fuhéifùman wo iú; (protest: to authorities, shop etc) 訴える uttáerù

to complain of (pain) ...を訴える ...wo uttáerù

complaint [kəmpleint'] *n* (objection) 訴え uttáe; (criticism) 非 難 hínàn; (MED: illness) 病気 byṓki

complement [*n* ka:m'pləmənt *vb* ka:m'pləment] *n* (supplement) 補う物 ogínaù monó; (esp ship's crew) 人員 jiñ-in

♦*vt* (enhance) 引立たせる hikítataserù

complementary [ka:mpləmen'tə:ri:] *adj* (mutually supportive) 補足し合う hosóku shiaù

complete [kəmpli:t'] *adj* (total, whole) 完全な kañzen na; (finished: building, task) 完成した kañsei shitá

♦*vt* (finish: building, task) 完成する kañsei suru; (: set, group etc) そろえる soróerù; (fill in: a form) ...に記入する ...ni kinyū suru

completely [kəmpli:t'li:] *adv* (totally) 全く mattáku, 完全に kañzen ni

completion [kəmpli:'ʃən] *n* (of building)

完成 kañsei; (of contract) 履行 rikṓ

complex [*adj* kəmpleks' *n* ka:m'pleks] *adj* (structure, problem, decision) 複雑な fukúzatsu na

♦*n* (group: of buildings) 団 地 dañchi; (PSYCH) コンプレックス koñpurekkùsu

complexion [kəmplek'ʃən] *n* (of face) 顔の肌 kaó no hadà

complexity [kəmplek'siti:] *n* (of problem, law) 複雑さ fukúzatsuùsa

compliance [kəmplai'əns] *n* (submission) 服従 fukújù; (agreement) 同意 dói

in compliance with ...に従って ...ni shitágatte

complicate [ka:m'pləkeit] *vt* (matters, situation) 複雑にする fukúzatsu ni suru

complicated [ka:m'pləkeitid] *adj* (explanation, system) 複雑な fukúzatsu na

complication [ka:mpləkei'ʃən] *n* (problem) 問題 moñdai; (MED) 合併症 gappéishō

complicity [kəmplis'əti:] *n* (in crime) 共犯 kyṓhan

compliment [*n* ka:m'pləmənt *vb* ka:m'pləment] *n* (expression of admiration) ほめ言葉 homékotòba

♦*vt* (express admiration for) ほめる homérù

to pay someone a compliment ...をほめる ...wo homéru

complimentary [ka:mpləmen'tə:ri:] *adj* (remark) 賛辞の sañji no; (ticket, copy of book etc) 無料の muryō no

compliments [ka:m'pləmənts] *npl* (regards) 挨拶 aísatsu

comply [kəmplai'] *vi*: *to comply with* (law, ruling) ...に従う ...ni shitágaù

component [kəmpou'nənt] *adj* (parts, elements) 構成している kōsei shité irù

♦*n* (part) 部分 búbùn

compose [kəmpouz'] *vt* (form): *to be composed of* ...から出来ている ...kará dekíteì irú; (write: music, poem, letter) 書く kákù

to compose oneself 心を落着かせる kokórò wo ochítsukaserù

composed [kəmpouzd'] *adj* (calm) 落 着いている ochítsuite irù

composer [kəmpou'zə:r] *n* (MUS) 作曲家 sakkyókuka

composition [kɑ:mpəzi'ʃən] *n* (of substance, group etc) 構成 kōsei; (essay) 作文 sakúbun; (MUS) 作曲 sakkyóku

compost [kɑ:m'poust] *n* たい肥 taíhi

composure [kəmpou'ʒə:r] *n* (of person) 落着き ochítsuki

compound [kɑ:m'paund] *n* (CHEM) 化合物 kágōbutsu; (enclosure) 囲い地 kakóichi; (LING) 複合語 fukúgōgo

♦*adj* (fracture) 複雑な fukúzatsu na

compound interest 複利 fúkùri

comprehend [kɑ:mprihend'] *vt* (understand) 理解する rikái suru

comprehension [kɑ:mprihen'ʃən] *n* (understanding) 理解 ríkài

comprehensive [kɑ:mprihen'siv] *adj* (description, review, list) 包括的な hōkatsuteki na; (INSURANCE) 総合的な sōgōteki na

comprehensive (school) (*BRIT*) *n* 総合中等学校 sōgōchūtōgakkō ◇あらゆる能力の子供に適した課程のある中等学校 aráyurù nőryoku no kodómo ni tekí shita katéi no arù chūtōgakkō

compress [*vb* kɑ:mpres' *n* kɑ:m'pres] *vt* (air, cotton, paper etc) 圧縮する asshúku suru; (text, information) 要約する yőyaku suru

♦*n* (MED) 湿布 shippú

comprise [kəmpraiz'] *vt* (*also*: **be comprised of**) ...からなる ...kárá narù; (constitute) 構成する kősei suru

compromise [kɑ:m'prəmaiz] *n* 妥協 dakyő

♦*vt* (beliefs, principles) 傷つける kizú tsukerù

♦*vi* (make concessions) 妥協する dakyő suru

compulsion [kəmpʌl'ʃən] *n* (desire, impulse) 強迫観念 kyőhakukaǹnen; (force) 強制 kyősei

compulsive [kəmpʌl'siv] *adj* (liar, gambler etc) 病的な byőteki na; (viewing, reading) 止められない yamérarenài

compulsory [kəmpʌl'sə:ri:] *adj* (attendance, retirement) 強制的な kyőseiteki na

computer [kəmpju:'tə:r] *n* コンピュータ koñpyūta

computerize [kəmpju:'təraiz] *vt* (system, filing, accounts etc) コンピュータ化する koñpyūtáka surù; (information) コンピュータに覚えさせる koñpyūta ni obóesaserù

computer programmer *n* プログラマー puróguràmā

computer programming *n* プログラミング puróguramiǹgu

computer science *n* コンピュータ科学 koñpyūta kágàku

computing [kəmpju:'tiŋ] *n* (activity, science) コンピュータ利用 koñpyūta riyő

comrade [kɑ:m'ræd] *n* (POL, MIL) 同志 dōshi; (friend) 友人 yűjin

comradeship [kɑ:m'rədʃip] *n* 友情 yűjō

con [kɑ:n] *vt* (deceive) だます damásù; (cheat) ぺてんに掛ける petén ni kakérù

♦*n* (trick) いかさま ikásama

concave [kɑ:nkeiv'] *adj* 凹面の őmen no

conceal [kənsi:l'] *vt* (hide: weapon, entrance) 隠す kakúsù; (keep back: information) 秘密にする himítsu ni surù

concede [kənsi:d'] *vt* (admit: error, point, defeat) 認める mitómeru

conceit [kənsi:t'] *n* (arrogance) うぬぼれ unúbore

conceited [kənsi:'tid] *adj* (vain) うぬぼれた unúboreta

conceivable [kənsi:'vəbəl] *adj* (reason, possibility) 考えられる kañgaerarerù

conceive [kənsi:v'] *vt* (child) はらむ harámù; (plan, policy) 考え出す kañgaedasù

♦*vi* (BIO) 妊娠する nińshin suru

concentrate [kɑ:n'səntreit] *vi* (on problem, activity etc) 専念する seńnen suru; (in one area, space) 集中する shúchū suru

♦*vt* (energies, attention) 集中させる shúchū saséru

concentration [kɑ:nsəntrei'ʃən] *n* (on problem, activity etc) 専念 seńnen; (in one area, space) 集中 shúchū; (attention) 注意 chűi; (CHEM) 濃縮 nőshuku

concentration camp *n* 強制収容所 kyōseishūyōjo

concept [ka:n'sept] *n* (idea, principle) 概念 gáinen

conception [kənsep'ʃən] *n* (idea) 概念 gáinen; (of child) 妊娠 nínshin

concern [kənsə:rn'] *n* (affair) 責任 sekínin; (anxiety, worry) 心配 shínpai; (COMM: firm) 企業 kígyò
♦*vt* (worry) 心配させる shínpai saséru; (involve, relate to) ...に関係がある ...ni kańkè ga arù
to be concerned (about) (person, situation etc) (...について) 心配する (...ni tsuitè) shínpai suru

concerning [kənsə:r'niŋ] *prep* (regarding) ...について ...ni tsuìte

concert [ka:n'sə:rt] *n* (MUS) 演奏会 eńsòkai, コンサート końsàto

concerted [kənsə:r'tid] *adj* (effort etc) 共同の kyōdō no

concert hall *n* コンサートホール końsātohòru

concertina [ka:nsə:rti:'nə] *n* (MUS: instrument) コンサーティーナ końsātìna ◇六角形の小型アコーディオン rokkákkèi no kogáta akòdion

concerto [kəntʃe:r'tou] *n* 協奏曲 kyōsōkyoku, コンチェルト kóńcheruto

concession [kənseʃ'ən] *n* (compromise) 譲歩 jòho; (COMM: right) 特権 tokkén
tax concession 減税 geńzei

conciliatory [kənsil'i:ətɔ:ri:] *adj* (gesture, tone) 懐柔的な kaíjūteki na

concise [kənsais'] *adj* (description, text) 簡潔な kańketsu na

conclude [kənklu:d'] *vt* (finish: speech, chapter) 終える oéru; (treaty) 締結する teíketsu suru; (deal etc) まとめる matómeru; (decide) (...だと) 結論する (...da to) ketsúron suru

conclusion [kənklu:'ʒən] *n* (of speech, chapter) 終り owári; (of treaty) 締結 teíketsu; (of deal etc) まとめる事 matómeru kotò; (decision) 結論 ketsúron

conclusive [kənklu:'siv] *adj* (evidence, defeat) 決定的な kettéiteki na

concoct [kənka:kt'] *vt* (excuse) でっち上げる detchíagerù; (plot) 企てる kuwádaterù; (meal, sauce) 工夫して作る kufū shitè tsukúrù

concoction [kənka:k'ʃən] *n* (mixture) 調合物 chōgōbutsu

concourse [ka:n'kɔ:rs] *n* (hall) 中央ホール chūōhòru, コンコース końkòsu

concrete [ka:n'kri:t] *n* コンクリート końkurìto
♦*adj* (block, floor) コンクリートの końkurìto no; (proposal, idea) 具体的な gútáiteki na

concur [kənkə:r'] *vi* 同意する dōi suru

concurrently [kənkə:r'əntli:] *adv* (happen, run) 同時に dōji ni

concussion [kənkʌʃ'ən] *n* (MED) 脳震とう nōshintō

condemn [kəndem'] *vt* (denounce: action, report etc) 非難する hínan suru; (sentence: prisoner) ...に...刑を宣告する ...ni...keí wo seńkoku suru; (declare unsafe: building) 使用に耐えない物と決定する shiyō ni taénài monó to kettéi suru

condemnation [ka:ndemnei'ʃən] *n* (criticism) 非難 hínan

condensation [ka:ndensei'ʃən] *n* (on walls, windows) 結露 kétsuro

condense [kəndens'] *vi* (vapor) 液化する ekíka suru
♦*vt* (report, book) 要約する yōyaku suru

condensed milk [kəndenst'-] *n* 練乳 reńnyū

condescending [ka:ndisen'diŋ] *adj* (reply, attitude) 恩着せがましい ońkisegamashìi

condition [kəndiʃ'ən] *n* (state: *gen*) 状態 jōtai; (MED: of illness) 病状 byōjō; (requirement) 条件 jōken; (MED: illness) 病気 byṓki
♦*vt* (person) 慣れさせる narésaserù
on condition that ...という条件で ...to iú jōken de

conditional [kəndiʃ'ənəl] *adj* 条件付きの jōkentsuki no

conditioner [kəndiʃ'ənə:r] *n* (*also*: **hair conditioner**) ヘアコンディショナー heákondishōnā; (for fabrics) 柔軟剤 jūnańzai

conditions [kəndiʃ'ənz] *npl* (circumstances) 状況 jŏkyō

condolences [kəndou'lənsiz] *npl* お悔み o-kúyami

condom [kɑːn'dəm] *n* コンドーム koñdōmu, スキン sukín

condominium [kɑːndəmin'iːəm] (*US*) *n* 分譲マンション buñjōmañshon

condone [kəndoun'] *vt* (misbehavior, crime) 容認する yŏnin suru

conducive [kənduː'siv] *adj*: **conducive to** (rest, study) ...を助ける ...wo tasúkerù

conduct [*n* kɑːn'dʌkt *vb* kəndʌkt'] *n* (of person) 振舞 furúmai

♦*vt* (survey, research etc) 行う okónaù; (orchestra, choir etc) 指揮する shikí suru; (heat, electricity) 伝導する deñdō suru

to conduct oneself (behave) 振舞う furúmaù

conducted tour [kəndʌk'tid-] *n* ガイド付き見物 gaídotsuki keñbutsu

conductor [kəndʌk'təːr] *n* (of orchestra) 指揮者 shikíshà; (*BRIT*: on bus, *US*: on train) 車掌 shashŏ; (ELEC) 伝導体 deñdōtai

conductress [kəndʌk'tris] *n* (on bus) 女性車掌 joséishashō, バスガール basúgārù

cone [koun] *n* (shape) 円すい形 eñsuikei; (on road) カラーコーン karákōn, セーフティコーン sēfutikōn; (BOT) 松かさ matsúkasà; (ice cream cornet) コーン kŏn

confectioner [kənfek'ʃənəːr] *n* (person) 菓子職人 kashíshokunìn

confectioner's (shop) [kənfek'ʃənəːrz-] *n* (sweet shop) 菓子屋 kashíyà

confectionery [kənfek'ʃəneːriː] *n* (sweets, candies) 菓子類 kashírui

confederation [kənfedəreiʃ'ən] *n* (POL, COMM) 連合 reñgō

confer [kənfəːr'] *vt*: **to confer something (on someone)** (honor, degree, advantage) (...に) ...を与える (...ni) ...wo atáerù

♦*vi* (panel, team) 協議する kyŏgi suru

conference [kɑːn'fəːrəns] *n* (meeting) 会議 kaígi

confess [kənfes'] *vt* (sin, guilt, crime) 白

状する hákùjō suru; (weakness, ignorance) 認める mitómeru

♦*vi* (admit) 認める mitómeru

confession [kənfeʃ'ən] *n* (admission) 白状 hákùjō; (REL) ざんげ záñge

confetti [kənfet'iː] *n* コンフェティ kôñfeti ◇紙吹雪き用に細かく切った色紙 kamífubuki yō ni komákaku kittá irógami

confide [kənfaid'] *vi*: **to confide in** ...に打明ける ...ni uchífakerù

confidence [kɑːn'fidəns] *n* (faith) 信用 shiñ-yō; (also: **self-confidence**) 自信 jishín; (secret) 秘密 himítsu

in confidence (speak, write) 内緒で naísho de

confidence trick *n* いかさま ikásama

confident [kɑːn'fidənt] *adj* (self-assured) 自信のある jishín no arù; (positive) 確信している kakúshin shité irù

confidential [kɑːnfiden'ʃəl] *adj* (report, information) 秘密の himítsu no; (tone) 親しげな shitáshige na

confine [kənfain'] *vt* (limit) 限定する geñtei suru; (shut up) 閉じ込める tojíkomerù

confined [kənfaind'] *adj* (space) 限られた kagírareta

confinement [kənfain'mənt] *n* (imprisonment) 監禁 kañkin

confines [kɑːn'fainz] *npl* (of area) 境 sakái

confirm [kənfəːrm'] *vt* (belief, statement) 裏付ける urázukerù; (appointment, date) 確認する kakúnin suru

confirmation [kɑːnfəːrmeiʃ'ən] *n* (of belief, statement) 裏付け urázuke; (of appointment, date) 確認 kakúnin; (REL) 堅信礼 keñshiñrei

confirmed [kənfəːrmd'] *adj* (bachelor, teetotaller) 常習的な jŏshūteki na

confiscate [kɑːn'fiskeit] *vt* (impound, seize) 没収する bosshū suru

conflict [*n* kɑːn'flikt *vb* kənflikt'] *n* (disagreement) 論争 roñsō; (difference: of interests, loyalties etc) 対立 taíritsu; (fighting) 戦闘 señtō

♦*vi* (opinions) 対立する taíritsu suru; (research etc) 矛盾する mujún suru

conflicting [kənflik'tiŋ] *adj* (reports) 矛盾する mujún suru; (interests etc) 対立する taíritsu suru

conform [kənfɔːrm'] *vi* (comply) 従う shitágaù
to conform to (law, wish, ideal) ...に従う ...ni shitágaù

confound [kənfaund'] *vt* (confuse) 当惑させる tówaku saséru

confront [kənfrʌnt'] *vt* (problems, task) ...と取組む ...to toríkumù; (enemy, danger) ...に立向かう ...ni tachímukaù

confrontation [kɑːnfrəntei'ʃən] *n* (dispute, conflict) 衝突 shótotsu

confuse [kənfjuːz'] *vt* (perplex: person) 当惑させる tówaku saséru; (mix up: two things, people etc) 混同する konídō suru; (complicate: situation, plans) 混乱させる konran saséru

confused [kənfjuːzd'] *adj* (bewildered) 当惑した tówaku shitá; (disordered) 混乱した konran shitá

confusing [kənfjuː'ziŋ] *adj* (plot, instructions) 分かりにくい wakárinikuì

confusion [kənfjuː'ʒən] *n* (perplexity) 当惑 tówaku; (mix-up) 混同 konídō; (disorder) 混乱 konran

congeal [kəndʒiːl'] *vi* (blood, sauce) 凝結する gyóketsu suru

congenial [kəndʒiːn'jəl] *adj* (person) 気の合った ki no attá; (atmosphere etc) 楽しい tanóshiì

congenital [kəndʒen'itəl] *adj* (MED: defect, illness) 先天性の señtensei no

congested [kəndʒes'tid] *adj* (MED: with blood) うっ血した ukkétsu shitá; (: with mucus: nose) 詰まった tsumátta; (road) 渋滞した jūtai shitá; (area) 人口密集の jínkōmisshū no

congestion [kəndʒes'tʃən] *n* (MED: with blood) うっ血 ukkétsu; (: with mucus) 鼻詰まり hanázumàri; (of road) 渋滞 jūtai; (of area) 人口密集 jínkōmisshū

conglomerate [kəngla:m'ə:rit] *n* (COMM) 複合企業 fukúgōkigyò, コングロマリット kofiguromarítto

conglomeration [kəngla:mərei'ʃən] *n* (group, gathering) 寄せ集め yoséatsume

congratulate [kəngrætʃ'uleit] *vt* (parents, bridegroom etc) ...にお祝いを言う ...ni o-íwai wo iú

congratulations [kəngrætʃulei'ʃənz] *npl* 祝詞 shukúji
congratulations! おめでとうございます omédetō gozáimasù

congregate [ka:ŋ'grəgeit] *vi* (people) 集まる atsúmaru; (animals) 群がる murágarù

congregation [ka:ŋgrəgei'ʃən] *n* (of a church) 会衆 kaíshū

congress [ka:ŋ'gris] *n* (conference) 大会 taíkai; *(US)*: *Congress* 議会 gikái

congressman [ka:ŋ'grismən] *(US: pl* **congressmen**) *n* 下院議員 ka-íngiîn

conical [ka:n'ikəl] *adj* (shape) 円すい形の efisuikei no

conifer [kou'nifə:r] *n* 針葉樹 shiń-yōju

conjecture [kəndʒek'tʃə:r] *n* (speculation) 憶測 okúsoku

conjugal [ka:n'dʒəgəl] *adj* 夫婦間の fúfùkàn no

conjugate [ka:n'dʒəgeit] *vt* (LING) ...の活用形を挙げる ...no katsúyōkei wo agérù

conjunction [kəndʒʌŋk'ʃən] *n* (LING) 接続詞 setsúzokushì

conjunctivitis [kəndʒʌŋktəvai'tis] *n* (MED) 結膜炎 ketsúmakuèn

conjure [ka:n'dʒə:r] *vi* (magician) 奇術をする kijútsu wo suru

conjurer [ka:n'dʒə:r] *n* (magician) 奇術師 kijútsushì, マジシャン majíshan

conjure up *vt* (ghost, spirit) 呼出す yobídasù; (memories) 思い起す omóiokosù

conk out [ka:ŋk-] *(inf) vi* (machine, engine) 故障する koshō suru

con man [ka:n'mən] *(pl* **con men**) *n* ペてん師 petéñshi

connect [kənekt'] *vt* (join, *also* TEL) つなぐ tsunágù; (ELEC) 接続する setsúzoku suru; *(fig*: associate) 関係付ける kañkeizùkeru
♦*vi*: *to connect with* (train, plane etc) ...に連絡する ...ni refíraku suru
to be connected with (associated) 関係付ける kafíkeizùkeru

connection [kənek'ʃən] n (joint, link) つなぎ tsunági; (ELEC, TEL) 接続 setsúzoku; (train, plane etc) 連絡 reńraku; (fig: association) 関係 kańkei

connive [kənaiv'] vi: **to connive at** (misbehavior) ...を容認する ...wo yóⁿin suru

connoisseur [kɑːnisəːr'] n (of food, wine, art etc) 通 tsū

connotation [kɑːnətei'ʃən] n (implication) 含み fukúmi

conquer [kɑːŋ'kəːr] vt (MIL: country, enemy) 征服する seífuku suru; (fear, feelings) 克服する kokúfuku suru

conqueror [kɑːŋ'kəːrəːr] n (MIL) 征服者 seífukushà

conquest [kɑːn'kwest] n (MIL) 征服 seífuku; (prize) 勝得た物 kachíeta monó; (mastery: of space etc) 征服 seífuku

cons [kɑːnz] npl see **convenience**; **pro**

conscience [kɑːn'ʃəns] n (sense of right and wrong) 良心 ryóshin

conscientious [kɑːnʃiːen'ʃəs] adj (worker) 良心的な ryóshinteki na

conscious [kɑːn'ʃəs] adj (aware): **conscious (of)** (...に) 気が付いている (...ni) ki ga tsuíte irù; (deliberate) 意識的な ishíkiteki na; (awake) 目が覚めている me ga samête irù

consciousness [kɑːn'ʃəsnis] n (awareness, mentality: also MED) 意識 ishíki

conscript [kɑːn'skript] n (MIL) 徴集兵 chōshūhei

conscription [kənskrip'ʃən] n (MIL) 徴兵 chōhei

consecrate [kɑːn'səkreit] vt (building, place) 奉献する hōken suru

consecutive [kənsek'jətiv] adj (days, wins) 連続の reńzoku no

consensus [kənsen'səs] n 合意 gōi

consent [kənsent'] n (permission) 許可 kyóka
♦vi: **to consent to** ...に同意する ...ni dōi suru

consequence [kɑːn'səkwens] n (result) 結果 kekká; (significance) 重要さ jūyōsa

consequently [kɑːn'səkwentliː] adv (as a result, so) 従って shitágattè

conservation [kɑːnsəːrvei'ʃən] n (of the environment) 保護 hogò, 保全 hozéⁿ; (of energy) 節約 setsúyaku; (of paintings, books) 保全 hozéⁿ

conservative [kənsəːr'vətiv] adj (traditional, conventional: person, attitudes) 保守的な hoshúteki na; (cautious: estimate etc) 控え目な hikáeme no; (BRIT: POL): **Conservative** 保守党の hoshútō no
♦n (BRIT: POL): **Conservative** 保守党員 hoshútōìn

conservatory [kənsəːr'vətɔːriː] n (greenhouse) 温室 ońshitsu; (MUS) 音楽学校 ońgaku gakkō

conserve [vb kənsəːrv' n kɑːn'səːrv] vt (preserve) 保護する hogò suru; (supplies, energy) 節約する setsúyaku suru
♦n (jam) ジャム jámù

consider [kənsid'əːr] vt (believe) ...だと思う ...da to omóù; (study) 熟考する jukkô suru; (take into account) 考慮に入れる kōryo ni irérù
to consider doing something ...しようかと考える ...shiyō ka to kángaerù

considerable [kənsid'əːrəbəl] adj (amount, expense, difference etc) かなりの kanári no

considerably [kənsid'əːrəbliː] adv (improve, deteriorate) かなり kanári

considerate [kənsid'əːrit] adj (person) 思いやりのある omóiyari no arù

consideration [kənsidərei'ʃən] n (deliberation) 熟考 jukkô; (factor) 考慮すべき点 kōryo subeki téⁿ; (thoughtfulness) 思いやり omóiyarì

considering [kənsid'əːriŋ] prep (bearing in mind) ...を考慮すると ...wo kōryo suru to

consign [kənsain'] vt (something unwanted): **to consign to** (place) ...にしまっておく ...ni shimátte okù; (person): **to consign to** (someone's care etc) ...に委ねる ...ni yudánerù; (poverty etc) ...に追込む ...ni ofkomù

consignment [kənsain'mənt] n (COMM) 輸送貨物 yusókamòtsu

consist [kənsist'] vi: **to consist of** (comprise) ...から成る ...kará narù

consistency [kənsis'tənsi:] n (of actions, policies etc) 一貫性 ikkánsei; (of yoghurt, cream etc) 固さ katása

consistent [kənsis'tənt] adj (person) 変らない kawáranaì; (argument, idea) 一貫性のある ikkánsei no arù

consolation [kɑːnsəlei'ʃən] n (comfort) 慰め nagúsame

console [vb kənsoul' n kɑːn'soul] vt (comfort) 慰める nagúsamerù
♦ n (panel) コンソール końsòru

consolidate [kənsɑːl'ideit] vt (position, power) 強化する kyóka suru

consommé [kɑːnsəmei'] n (CULIN) コンソメ końsome

consonant [kɑːn'sənənt] n (LING) 子音 shíìn

consortium [kənsɔːr'ʃiːəm] n (COMM) 協会 kyókai

conspicuous [kənspik'juːəs] adj (noticeable: person, feature) 目立つ medátsu

conspiracy [kənspir'əsi:] n (plot) 陰謀 iñbō

conspire [kənspai'əːr] vi (criminals, revolutionaries etc) 共謀する kyóbō suru; (events) 相重なる aíkasanarù

constable [kɑːn'stəbəl] (BRIT) n 巡査 juńsa
chief constable (BRIT) 警察本部長 keísatsu hoñbuchō

constabulary [kənstæb'jələːriː] (BRIT) n 警察 keísatsu ◇一地区の警察隊を指す ichíchiku no keísatsutai wo sasù

constant [kɑːn'stənt] adj (continuous: criticism, pain) 絶えない taénaì; (fixed: temperature, level) 一定の ittéi no

constantly [kɑːn'stəntliː] adv (continually) 絶間なく taémanàku

constellation [kɑːnstəlei'ʃən] n (ASTRONOMY) 星座 seíza

consternation [kɑːnstəːrnei'ʃən] n (dismay) ろうばい róbai

constipated [kɑːn'stəpeitid] adj (MED) 便秘している beñpi shité irù

constipation [kɑːnstəpei'ʃən] n (MED) 便秘 beñpi

constituency [kənstitʃ'uːənsiː] n (POL:

area) 選挙区 seńkyokù; (: electors) 選挙民 seńkyomìn

constituent [kənstitʃ'uːənt] n (POL) 有権者 yūkeñsha; (component) 部分 búbùn

constitute [kɑːn'stitut] vt (represent: challenge, emergency) ...である ...de arù; (make up: whole) 構成する kōsei suru

constitution [kɑːnstitu'ʃən] n (of country) 憲法 keńpō; (of club etc) 会則 kaísoku; (health) 体質 taíshitsu; (make-up: of committee etc) 構成 kōsei

constitutional [kɑːnstitu'ʃənəl] adj (government, reform etc) 憲法の keńpō no

constraint [kənstreint'] n (restriction) 制限 seígen; (compulsion) 強制 kyósei

construct [kən'strʌkt] vt (building) 建てる tatérù; (bridge, road etc) 建設する keńsetsu suru; (machine) 作る tsukúrù

construction [kənstrʌk'ʃən] n (of building etc) 建築 keńchiku; (of bridge, road etc) 建設 keńsetsu; (of machine) 製作 seísaku; (structure) 構造物 kózōbùtsu

constructive [kənstrʌk'tiv] adj (remark, criticism) 建設的な keńsetsuteki na

construe [kənstru'] vt (statement, event) 解釈する kaíshaku suru

consul [kɑːn'səl] n 領事 ryóji

consulate [kɑːn'səlit] n 領事館 ryójikàn

consult [kənsʌlt'] vt (doctor, lawyer, friend) ...に相談する ...ni sódan suru; (reference book) 調べる shiráberù

consultant [kənsʌl'tənt] n (MED) 顧問医 komón-i; (other specialist) 顧問 kómòn, コンサルタント końsarùtanto

consultation [kɑːnsəltei'ʃən] n (MED) 診察 shiñsatsu; (discussion) 協議 kyógi

consulting room [kənsʌl'tiŋ-] (BRIT) n 診察室 shiñsatsushìtsu

consume [kənsuːm'] vt (food) 食べる tabérù; (drink) 飲む nómù; (fuel, energy, time etc) 消費する shóhi suru

consumer [kənsuː'məːr] n (COMM) 消費者 shóhishà

consumer goods npl 消費財 shóhizài

consumerism [kənsuː'məːrizəm] n 消費者運動 shóhishauńdō

consumer society n 消費社会 shṓhishakāi

consummate [kɑːnˈsəmeit] vt (ambition etc) 全うする mattṓ suru

to consummate a marriage 床入りする tokó-iri suru

consumption [kənsʌmpˈʃən] n (of food) 食べる事 tabérù kotó; (of drink) 飲む事 nómù kotó; (of fuel, energy, time etc) 消費 shōhi; (amount consumed) 消費量 shṓhiryṓ; (buying) 消費 shōhi

cont. abbr (= continued) 続く tsuzúku

contact [kɑːnˈtækt] n (communication) 連絡 reńraku; (touch) 接触 sesshóku; (person) 連絡相手 reńrakuaīte

♦vt (by phone, letter) ...に連絡する ...ni reńraku suru

contact lenses npl コンタクトレンズ koñtakutoreñzu

contagious [kənˈteidʒəs] adj (MED: disease) 伝染性の deńsensei no; (fig: laughter, enthusiasm) 移りやすい utsúriyasuī

contain [kəntein'] vt (hold: objects) ...に...が入っている ...ni ...ga haítte irù; (have: component, ingredient etc) ...に...が含まれている ...ni ...ga fukúmarète irù; (subj: piece of writing, report etc) ...に...が書いてある ...ni ...ga kaíte arù; (curb: growth, spread, feeling) 抑える osáerù

to contain oneself 自制する jiséi suru

container [kənteiˈnəːr] n (box, jar etc) 入れ物 irémono; (COMM: for shipping etc) コンテナー kóñtenā

contaminate [kəntæməˈneit] vt (water, food, soil etc) 汚染する osén suru

contamination [kəntæməneiˈʃən] n (of water, food, soil etc) 汚染 osén

cont'd abbr (= continued) 続く tsuzuku

contemplate [kɑːnˈtəmpleit] vt (idea, subject, course of action) じっくり考える jikkúrī kañgaerù; (person, painting etc) 眺める nagámerù

contemporary [kəntemˈpəːriː] adj (present-day) 現代の geńdai no; (belonging to same time) 同時代の dṓjidài no

♦n (person) 同時代の人 dṓjidai no hitó

contempt [kəntempt'] n (scorn) 軽べつ keíbetsu

contempt of court (LAW) 法廷侮辱罪 hṓteibujokuzaì

contemptible [kəntempˈtəbəl] adj (conduct) 卑劣な hirétsu na

contemptuous [kəntempˈtʃuːəs] adj (attitude) 軽べつ的な keíbetsuteki na

contend [kəntend'] vt (assert): **to contend that** ...だと主張する ...da to shuchṓ suru

♦vi (struggle): **to contend with** (problem, difficulty) ...と戦う ...to tatákaù; (compete): **to contend for** (power etc) ...を争う ...wo arásoù

contender [kəntenˈdəːr] n (in competition) 競争者 kyṓsōshà; (POL) 候補者 kṓhoshà; (SPORT) 選手 señshu

content [adj, vb kəntent' n kɑːnˈtent] adj (happy and satisfied) 満足して mañzoku shitế

♦vt (satisfy) 満足させる mañzoku saséru

♦n (of speech, novel) 内容 naíyō; (fat content, moisture content etc) 含有量 gañ-yūryṓ

contented [kəntenˈtid] adj (happy and satisfied) 満足して mañzoku shitế

contention [kəntenˈʃən] n (assertion) 主張 shuchṓ; (disagreement, argument) 論争 roñsō

contentment [kəntentˈmənt] n (happiness, satisfaction) 満足 mañzoku

contents [kɑːnˈtents] npl (of bottle, packet) 中身 nakámî; (of book) 内容 naíyō

(table of) contents 目次 mokúji

contest [n kɑːnˈtest vb kəntest'] n (competition) コンテスト kóñtesuto, コンクール kóñkūru; (struggle: for control, power etc) 争い arásoì

♦vt (election, competition) ...で競う ...de kisôù; (statement, decision: also LAW) ...に対して異義を申立てる ...ni taíshite igí wo mōshítaterù

contestant [kəntesˈtənt] n (in quiz, competition) 参加者 sańkashà; (in fight) 競争者 kyṓsōshà

context [kɑːnˈtekst] n (circumstances: of events, ideas etc) 背景 haíkei; (of word, phrase) 文脈 buñmyaku

continent [kɑːn'tənənt] *n* (land mass) 大陸 taîriku

the Continent (BRIT) ヨーロッパ大陸 yôroppa tairìku

continental [kɑːntənen'təl] *adj* 大陸の taîriku no

continental quilt (BRIT) *n* 掛布団 kakêbuton

contingency [kəntin'dʒənsiː] *n* 有事 yûji

contingent [kəntin'dʒənt] *n* (group of people: *also* MIL) 一団 ichîdan

continual [kəntin'juːəl] *adj* (movement, process, rain etc) 絶間ない taêmanai

continually [kəntin'juːəliː] *adv* 絶間なく taêmanàku

continuation [kəntinjuːei'ʃən] *n* 継続 keîzoku

continue [kəntin'juː] *vi* 続く tsuzúkù
♦*vt* 続ける tsuzúkerù

continuity [kɑːntənuː'itiː] *n* (in policy, management etc) 連続性 reñzokusei; (TV, CINEMA) 撮影台本 satsúeidaìhon, コンテ kôñte

continuous [kəntin'juːəs] *adj* (process, growth etc) 絶間ない taêmanai; (line) 途切れのない togîre no naî; (LING) 進行形の shiñkôkei no

continuous stationery *n* 連続用紙 reñzokuyôshi

contort [kəntɔːrt'] *vt* (body) ねじる nejírù; (face) しかめる shikámerù

contortion [kəntɔːr'ʃən] *n* (of body) ねじれ nejíre; (of face) こわばり kowábari

contour [kɑːn'tuːr] *n* (on map: *also*: **contour line**) 等高線 tôkôsen; (shape, outline: *gen pl*) 輪郭 riñkaku

contraband [kɑːn'trəbænd] *n* 密輸品 mitsúyuhìn

contraception [kɑːntrəsep'ʃən] *n* 避妊 hinín

contraceptive [kɑːntrəsep'tiv] *adj* (method, technique) 避妊の hinín no
♦*n* (device) 避妊用具 hinín yôgu; (pill etc) 避妊薬 hínín-yaku

contract [*n* kɑːn'trækt *vb* kəntrækt'] *n* (LAW, COMM) 契約 keîyaku
♦*vi* (become smaller) 収縮する shúshuku suru; (COMM): *to contract to do*

something ...をする契約をする ...wo suru keîyaku wo suru
♦*vt* (illness) ...に掛かる ...ni kakárù

contraction [kəntræk'ʃən] *n* (of metal, muscle) 収縮 shúshuku; (of word, phrase) 短縮形 tañshukukei

contractor [kɑːn'træktəːr] *n* (COMM) 請負人 ukéoinìn

contradict [kɑːntrədikt'] *vt* (person) ...の言う事を否定する ...no iú kotó wo hitéi suru; (statement etc) 否定する hitéi suru

contradiction [kɑːntrədik'ʃən] *n* (inconsistency) 矛盾 mujún

contradictory [kɑːntrədik'təːriː] *adj* (ideas, statements) 矛盾する mujún suru

contraption [kəntræp'ʃən] *n* (*pej*) (device, machine) 珍妙な機械 chiñmyô na kikáì

contrary[1] [kɑːn'treːriː] *adj* (opposite, different) 反対の hañtai no
♦*n* (opposite) 反対 hañtai

on the contrary それどころか soredokoro ka

unless you hear to the contrary そうではないと聞かされない限り sô de wa nái to kikásarenài kagíri

contrary[2] [kəntreːr'iː] *adj* (perverse) つむじ曲りな tsumújimagàri na, へそ曲りな hesómagari na

contrast [*n* kɑːn'træst *vb* kəntræst'] *n* (difference) 相違 sôi, コントラスト koñtorasùto
♦*vt* (techniques, texts etc) 対照する taîshô suru

in contrast to ...と違って ...to chigátte

contrasting [kəntræs'tiŋ] *adj* (colors, attitudes) 対照的な taîshôteki na

contravene [kɑːntrəviːn'] *vt* (law) ...に違反する ...ni ihán suru

contribute [kəntrib'juːt] *vi* (give) 寄付する kifú suru
♦*vt*: *to contribute an article to* (commissioned) ...に記事を寄稿する ...ni kíjì wo kikô suru; (unsolicited) ...に記事を投稿する ...ni kíjì wo tôkô suru: *to contribute $10* 10ドルを寄付する jûdòru wo kifú suru

to contribute to (charity) ...に寄付する ...ni kifú suru; (newspaper: commissioned) ...に寄稿する ...ni kikó suru; (unsolicited) ...に投稿する ...ni tókó suru; (discussion) 意見を言う ikén wo iú; (problem etc) ...を悪くする ...wo warúkù surù

contribution [kɑːntrəbjuːˈʃən] n (donation) 寄付 kifú; (BRIT: for social security) 掛金 kakékìn; (to debate, campaign) 貢献 kóken; (to journal: commissioned) 寄稿 kikó; (: unsolicited) 投稿 tókó

contributor [kəntribˈjətəːr] n (to appeal) 寄付者 kifushà; (to newspaper) 投稿者〔寄稿者〕tókóshà〔kikóshà〕

contrive [kəntraivˈ] vi: **to contrive to do** 努力して...に成功する doryòku shite ...ni seíkó suru

control [kəntroulˈ] vt (country, organization) 支配する shiháí suru; (machinery, process) 制御する seígyo suru; (wages, prices) 規制する kiséi suru; (temper) 自制する jiséi suru; (disease) 抑制する yokúsei suru

◆n (of country, organization) 支配 shiháì; (of oneself, emotions) 自制心 jiséishin

to be in control of (situation) ...を掌握している ...wo shóaku shité irù; (car etc) ...を思いのままに動かしている ...wo omôi no mamá ni ugókashite irù

under control (crowd) 指示に従って shijí ni shitágatte; (situation) 収拾が付いて shúshū ga tsuíte; (dog) 言う事を聞いて iú kotó wo kííte

out of control (crowd) 制止が利かなくなって seíshi ga kikánakù natté; (situation) 手に負えなくなって te ni oénakù natté; (dog) 言う事を聞かなくなって iú kotó wo kikánakù natté

control panel n 制御盤 seígyoban

control room n 制御室 seígyoshitsu

controls [kəntroulzˈ] npl (of vehicle) ハンドル hándoru ◇ブレーキ, クラッチなど全ての運転制御装置を含む burèki, kurátchì nado súbete no uñtenseigyosóchi wo fukúmù; (on radio, television etc) コントロール盤 koñtorórùban ◇全てのス

イッチ, 調節用つまみ, ボタンなどを含む súbete no suítchì, chósetsu yó tsumami, botán nadò wo fukúmù; (governmental) 規制 kiséi

control tower n (AVIAT) 管制塔 kańséitó

controversial [kɑːntrəvəːrˈʃəl] adj (topic, person) 論争の的になっている roñsó no mató ni natté irù

controversy [kɑːnˈtrəvəːrsiː] n 論争 roñsó

conurbation [kɑːnəːrbeiˈʃən] n 大都市圏 daítoshiken

convalesce [kɑːnvəlesˈ] vi (MED) 回復する kaífuku suru

convalescence [kɑːnvəlesˈəns] n (MED) 回復期 kaífukukì

convector [kənvekˈtəːr] n (heater) 対流式暖房器 taíryūshikidanbōkì, コンベクター koñbekùtā

convene [kənviːnˈ] vt (meeting, conference) 召集する shóshū suru

◆vi (parliament, inquiry) 開会する kaíkai suru

convenience [kənviːnˈjəns] n (easiness: of using something, doing something) 便利 béñri; (suitability: of date, meeting, house etc) 好都合 kótsugó; (advantage, help) 便宜 béñgi

at your convenience ご都合の良い時に go-tsúgó no yoì tokí ni

all modern conveniences, (BRIT) **all mod cons** 近代設備完備 kiñdaisetsubikañbi ◇不動産の広告などに使われる語句 fudósan no kókoku nadò ni tsukáwarerù gokù

convenient [kənviːnˈjənt] adj (handy) 便利な béñri na; (suitable) 都合の良い tsugó no yoì

convent [kɑːnˈvent] n (REL) 女子修道院 joshíshūdóin

convention [kənvenˈʃən] n (custom) 慣例 kañrei; (conference) 大会 taíkai; (agreement) 協定 kyótei

conventional [kənvenˈʃənəl] adj (person) 型にはまった katá ni hamátta; (method) 伝統的な deñtóteki na

converge [kənvəːrdʒˈ] vi (roads) 合流す

る gốryū suru; (people): **to converge on** (place, person) ...に集まる ...ni atsúmarù

conversant [kənvəːr'sənt] *adj*: **to be conversant with** (problem, requirements) ...に通じている ...ni tsûjite irù

conversation [kɑːnvəːrsei'ʃən] *n* (talk) 会話 kaíwa

conversational [kɑːnvəːrsei'ʃənəl] *adj* (tone, language, skills) 会話的な kaíwateki na

converse [*n* kɑːn'vəːrs *vb* kənvəːrs'] *n* (of statement) 逆 gyakú
♦*vi* (talk): **to converse (with someone)** (...と) 話をする (...to) hanáshi wo suru

conversely [kənvəːrs'liː] *adv* 逆に gyakú ni

conversion [kənvəːr'ʒən] *n* (of weights, substances etc) 変換 heńkan; (REL) 改宗 kaíshū

convert [*vb* kənvəːrt' *n* kɑːn'vəːrt] *vt* (change): **to convert something into/to** ...を...に変換する ...wo ...ni heńkan suru; (person: REL) 改宗させる kaíshū saséru; (: POL) 党籍を変えさせる tốseki wo kaésaserù
♦*n* (REL) 改宗者 kaíshùsha; (POL) 党籍を変える人 tốseki wo kaéru hitõ

convertible [kənvəːr'təbəl] *n* (AUT) コンバーチブル koñbáchibùru ◊畳込み式屋根を持つ乗用車 tatámikomishiki yané wo motsû jốyồsha

convex [kɑːnveks'] *adj* 凸面の totsúmen no

convey [kənvei'] *vt* (information, idea, thanks) 伝える tsutáerù; (cargo, traveler) 運ぶ hakóbu

conveyor belt [kənvei'əːr-] *n* ベルトコンベヤー berútokonbeyà

convict [*vb* kənvikt' *n* kɑːn'vikt] *vt* (of a crime) ...に有罪の判決を下す ...ni yûzai no hañketsu wo kudásù
♦*n* (person) 囚人 shūjin

conviction [kənvik'ʃən] *n* (belief) 信念 shíñnen; (certainty) 確信 kakúshin; (LAW) 有罪判決 yûzaihañketsu

convince [kənvins'] *vt* (assure) 分からせる wakáraserù; (persuade) 納得させる

nattôku saséru

convinced [kənvinst'] *adj*: **convinced of/that** ...を〔だと〕確信している ...wo 〔dátò〕 kakúshin shité irù

convincing [kənvin'siŋ] *adj* (case, argument) 納得のいく nattôku no ikú

convoluted [kɑːn'vəluːtid] *adj* (statement, argument) 込入った komíittà

convoy [kɑːn'vɔi] *n* (of trucks) 護衛付き輸送車隊 goéitsuki yusôshatai; (of ships) 護衛付き輸送船団 goéitsukiyusôseñdan

convulse [kənvʌls'] *vt*: **to be convulsed with laughter** 笑いこける waráikokerù

to be convulsed with pain もだえる modáerù

convulsion [kənvʌl'ʃən] *n* (MED) けいれん keíren

coo [kuː] *vi* (dove, pigeon) くーくー鳴く kûkū nakú; (person) 優しい声で言う yasáshii koè de iú

cook [kuk] *vt* (food, meal) 料理する ryôri suru
♦*vi* (person) 料理する ryôri suru; (meat, pie etc) 焼ける yakéru
♦*n* 料理人 ryôrinìn, コック kokkù

cookbook [kuk'buk] *n* 料理の本 ryôri no hoñ

cooker [kuk'əːr] *n* (stove) レンジ rénji

cookery [kuk'əːriː] *n* 料理する事 ryôri suru kotô

cookery book (*BRIT*) *n* = **cookbook**

cookie [kuk'iː] (*US*) *n* ビスケット bisúkettò, クッキー kúkkì

cooking [kuk'iŋ] *n* (activity) 料理すること ryôri suru kotô; (food) 料理 ryôri

cool [kuːl] *adj* (temperature, clothes) 涼しい suzúshiì; (drink) 冷たい tsumétai; (person: calm) 落着いている ochítsuite irù; (: unfriendly) そっけない sokkénaì
♦*vt* (make colder: tea) 冷ます samásù; (: room) 冷す hiyásù
♦*vi* (become colder: water) 冷たくなる tsumétaku narù; (: air) 涼しくなる suzúshiku narù

coolness [kuːl'nis] *n* (of temperature, clothing) 涼しさ suzúshisà; (of drink) 冷たさ tsumétasà; (calm) 落着き ochítsuki;

(unfriendliness) そっけなさ sokkénasà

coop [kuːp] n (also: **rabbit coop**) ウサギ小屋 uságigoya; (also: **hen coop**) ニワトリ小屋 niwátorigoya

♦vt: **to coop up** (fig: imprison) 閉込める tojíkomerù

cooperate [kouə:p'əreit] vi (collaborate) 協同する kyōdō suru; (assist) 協力する kyōryoku suru

cooperation [kouə:pərei'ʃən] n (collaboration) 協同 kyōdō; (assistance) 協力 kyōryoku

cooperative [kouə:p'rətiv] adj (farm, business) 協同組合の kyōdōkùmiai no; (person) 協力的な kyōryokuteki na

♦n (factory, business) 協同組合 kyōdōkùmiai

coordinate [vb kouə:r'dəneit n kouə:r'dənit] vt (activity, attack) 指揮する shikí suru; (movements) 調整する chōsei suru

♦n (MATH) 座標 zahyō

coordinates [kouə:r'dənits] npl (clothes) コーディネートされた服 kōdinēto saréta fukú

coordination [kouə:rdənei'ʃən] n (of services) 指揮 shikí; (of one's movements) 調整 chōsei

co-ownership [kouou'nə:rʃip] n 協同所有 kyōdōshoyū

cop [kɑːp] (inf) n (policeman/woman) 警官 keíkan

cope [koup] vi: **to cope with** (problem, situation etc) ...に対応する ...ni taíō suru

copious [kou'piːəs] adj (helpings) たっぷりの táppùri no

copious amounts of 多量の taryō no

copper [kɑːp'əːr] n (metal) 銅 dō; (inf: policeman/woman) 警官 keíkan

coppers [kɑːp'əːrz] npl (small change, coins) 小銭 kozéni

coppice [kɑːp'is] n 木立ち kodáchi

copse [kɑːps] n = **coppice**

copulate [kɑːp'jəleit] vi (people) 性交する seíkō suru; (animals) 交尾する kōbi suru

copy [kɑːp'iː] n (duplicate) 複写 fukúsha, コピー kópì; (of book) 1冊 issátsu; (of record) 1枚 ichímaì; (of newspaper) 1部 ichíbù

♦vt (person, idea etc) まねる manérù; (something written) 複写する fukúsha suru, コピーする kópì suru

copyright [kɑːp'iːrait] n 著作権 chosákukèn

coral [kɔːr'əl] n (substance) さんご sango

coral reef n さんご礁 sañgoshō

cord [kɔːrd] n (string) ひも himó; (ELEC) コード kōdo; (fabric) コールテン kōruten

cordial [kɔːr'dʒəl] adj (person, welcome) 暖かい atátakaì; (relationship) 親密な shiñmitsu na

♦n (BRIT: drink) フルーツシロップ furūtsu shiròppu

cordon [kɔːr'dən] n (MIL, POLICE) 非常線 hijōsen

cordon off vt 非常線を張って...への立入りを禁止する hijōsen wo hatté ...e no tachíiri wo kiñshi suru

corduroy [kɔːr'dərɔi] n コールテン kōruten

core [kɔːr] n (of fruit) しん shiñ; (of organization, system, building) 中心部 chūshiñbu; (heart: of problem) 核心 kakúshin

♦vt (an apple, pear etc) ...のしんをくりぬく ...no shiñ wo kurínukù

coriander [kɔːriːæn'dəːr] n (spice) コリアンダー koríañdà

cork [kɔːrk] n (stopper) 栓 señ; (bark) コルク kórùku

corkscrew [kɔːrk'skruː] n 栓抜き señnuki

corn [kɔːrn] n (US: maize) トウモロコシ tōmoròkoshi; (BRIT: cereal crop) 穀物 kokúmotsu; (on foot) 魚の目 uó no me

corn on the cob 軸付きトウモロコシ jikútsuki tōmoròkoshi

cornea [kɔːr'niːə] n (of eye) 角膜 kakúmaku

corned beef [kɔːrnd-] n コーンビーフ kōnbīfu

corner [kɔːr'nəːr] n (outside) 角 kádò; (inside) 隅 súmì; (in road) 角 kádò; (SOCCER) コーナーキック kōnākikkù; (BOXING) コーナー kōnā

♦vt (trap) 追詰める oítsumerù, 袋のネズ

ミにする fukúro no nezumi ni suru;
(COMM: market) 独占する dokúsen suru

♦vi (in car) コーナリングする kónariñgu
surù

cornerstone [kɔːrˈnəːrstoun] n (fig) 土台
dodái

cornet [kɔːrnetˈ] n (MUS) コルネット
korúnettò; (BRIT: of ice-cream) アイス
クリームコーン afsukurīmukòn

cornflakes [kɔːrnˈfleiks] npl コーンフレ
ーク kónfurēku

cornflour [kɔːrnˈflauəːr] (BRIT) n =
cornstarch

cornstarch [kɔːrnˈstɑːrtʃ] (US) n コーン
スターチ kónsutāchi

Cornwall [kournˈwɔːl] n コーンウォール
kón-uòru

corny [kɔːrˈniː] (inf) adj (joke) さえない
saénai

corollary [kɔːrˈələːriː] n (of fact, idea) 当
然の結果 tōzen no kekká

coronary [kɔːrˈoneːriː] n (also: **coronary
thrombosis**) 肝動脈血栓症 kañdómyaku-
kesséñshō

coronation [kɔːrəneiˈʃən] n たい冠式 taíkañshiki

coroner [kɔːrˈənəːr] n (LAW) 検死官 keñ-
shikàn

coronet [kɔːrˈənit] n コロネット koró-
nettò ◇貴族などがかぶる小さな冠 kizó-
ku nadò ga kabúrù chíisana kañmuri

corporal [kɔːrˈpəːrəl] n (MIL) ご長 gó-
chō

♦adj: **corporal punishment** 体罰 taíbat-
su

corporate [kɔːrˈpəːrit] adj (action,
effort, ownership) 共同の kyódō no;
(finance, image) 企業の kigyó no

corporation [kɔːrpəreiˈʃən] n (COMM)
企業 kigyó; (of town) 行政部 gyóseibù

corps [kɔːr pl kɔːrz] (pl **corps**) n (MIL)
兵団 heídan; (of diplomats, journalists)
...団 ...dàn

corpse [kɔːrps] n 遺体 itái

corpuscle [kɔːrˈpəsəl] n (BIO) 血球 kek-
kyū

corral [kərælˈ] n (for cattle, horses) 囲い

kakói

correct [kərektˈ] adj (right) 正しい tadáshiì; (proper) 礼儀正しい reígitadashiì

♦vt (mistake, fault) 直す naósù; (exam)
採点する saíten suru

correction [kərekˈʃən] n (act of correcting) 直す事 naósù kotó; (instance) 直し
naóshi

correlation [kɔːrəleiˈʃən] n (link) 相互関
係 sōgokañkei

correspond [kɔːrəspɑːndˈ] vi (write): **to
correspond (with)** (...と) 手紙のやり
取りをする (...to) tegámi no yarítòri
wo surù; (be equivalent): **to correspond
(to)** (...に) 相当する (...ni) sōtō suru;
(be in accordance): **to correspond
(with)** (...と) 一致する (...to) itchí
suru

correspondence [kɔːrəspɑːnˈdəns] n
(letters) 手紙 tegámi; (communication
by letters) 文通 buñtsū; (relationship) 一
致 itchí

correspondence course n (SCOL) 通
信講座 tsūshinkōza

correspondent [kɔːrəspɑːnˈdənt] n
(journalist) 特派員 tokúhaìn

corridor [kɔːrˈidəːr] n (in house, building
etc) 廊下 rōka; (in train) 通路 tsūro

corroborate [kərɑːbˈəreit] vt (facts,
story) 裏付ける urázukerù

corrode [kəroudˈ] vt (metal) 浸食する
shiñshoku suru

♦vi (metal) 腐食する fushóku suru

corrosion [kərouˈʒən] n 腐食 fushóku

corrugated [kɔːrˈəgeitid] adj (roof,
cardboard) 波型の namígata no

corrugated iron n なまこ板 namákoi-
tà

corrupt [kərʌptˈ] adj (person) 腐敗した
fuhái shitá; (COMPUT: data) 化けた ba-
kétà, 壊れた kowáreta

♦vt (person) 買収する baíshū suru;
(COMPUT: data) 化けさせる bakésase-
rù

corruption [kərʌpˈʃən] n (of person) 汚
職 oshóku; (COMPUT: of data) 化ける事
bakérù kotó

corset [kɔːrˈsit] n (undergarment: also

MED) コルセット kórùsetto

Corsica [kɔːrˈsikə] *n* コルシカ島 korú-shikatō

cosh [kɑːʃ] (*BRIT*) *n* (cudgel) こん棒 koñbō

cosmetic [kɑːzmetˈik] *n* (beauty product) 化粧品 keshốhin
♦*adj* (*fig*: measure, improvement) 表面的な hyṓmenteki na

cosmic [kɑːzˈmik] *adj* 宇宙の uchū no

cosmonaut [kɑːzˈmənɔːt] *n* 宇宙飛行士 uchūhikṓshi

cosmopolitan [kɑːzməpəːˈlitən] *adj* (place, person) 国際的な kokúsaiteki na

cosmos [kɑːzˈməs] *n* 宇宙 uchū

cosset [kɑːsˈit] *vt* (person) 甘やかす amáyakasū

cost [kɔːst] *n* (price) 値段 nedán; (expenditure) 費用 híyō
♦*vt* (*pt*, *pp* **cost**) (be priced at) ...の値段である ...no nedán de arū; (find out cost of: project, purchase etc: *pt*, *pp* **costed**) ...の費用を見積る ...no hiyō wo mitsúmorù

how much does it cost? いくらですか ikùra desu ká

to cost someone time/effort ...に時間〔労力〕を要する ...ni jikán〔rṓryoku〕wo yṓ surù

it cost him his life そのために彼は命をなくした sono tamé ni kárè wa ínòchi wo nákù shitá

at all costs 何があっても nanì ga atté mò

co-star [kouˈstɑːr] *n* (TV, CINEMA) 共演者 kyṓeñsha

cost-effective [kɔːstifekˈtiv] *adj* 費用効果比の高い hiyṓkōkahi no takáì

costly [kɔːstˈliː] *adj* (high-priced) 値段の高い nedán no takáì; (involving much expenditure) 費用の掛かる hiyṓ no kakárù

cost-of-living [kɔːstəvliːvˈiŋ] *adj* (allowance, index) 生計費の seíkeihi no

cost price (*BRIT*) *n* 原価 géñka

costs [kɔːsts] *npl* (COMM: overheads) 経費 keíhi; (LAW) 訴訟費用 soshṓhiyō

costume [kɑːsˈtuːm] *n* (outfit, style of dress) 衣装 íshō; (*BRIT*: *also*: **swimming costume**) 水着 mizúgi

costume jewelry *n* 模造宝石類 mozṓhōsekìrùi

cosy [kouˈziː] (*BRIT*) *adj* = **cozy**

cot [kɑːt] *n* (*BRIT*: child's) ベビーベッド bebíbeddò; (*US*: campbed) キャンプベッド kyañpubeddò

cottage [kɑːtˈidʒ] *n* (house) 小さな家 chíisa na ie, コッテージ kottḗji

cottage cheese *n* カッテージチーズ kattḗji chīzù

cotton [kɑːtˈən] *n* (fabric) 木綿 momén, コットン kóttòn; (*BRIT*: thread) 縫い糸 nuí-itò

cotton batting [-bætˈiŋ] *n* (*US*) 脱脂綿 dasshímèn

cotton candy (*US*) *n* (candy floss) 綿菓子 watágashì, 綿あめ watá-ame

cotton on to (*inf*) *vt fus* ...に気が付く ...ni kì ga tsúkù

cotton wool (*BRIT*) *n* = **cotton batting**

couch [kautʃ] *n* (sofa) ソファー sófà; (doctor's) 診察台 shiñsatsudai

couchette [kuːʃetˈ] *n* (on train, boat) 寝台 shindai ◇昼間壁に畳み掛けるか普通の座席に使う物を指す hirúma kabé ni tatámikakerù ka futsū no zaséki ni tsukáù monó wo sasù

cough [kɔːf] *vi* (person) せきをする sekí wo surù
♦*n* (noise) せき sekí; (illness) せきの多い病気 sekí no ōì byōki

cough drop *n* せき止めドロップ sekídome doróppu

could [kud] *pt of* **can**

couldn't [kudˈənt] = **could not**

council [kaunˈsəl] *n* (committee, board) 評議会 hyṓgìkài

city/town council 市〔町〕議会 shi〔chō〕gíkài

council estate (*BRIT*) *n* 公営住宅団地 kṓeijūtakudañchi

council house (*BRIT*) *n* 公営住宅 kṓeijūtaku

councillor [kaunˈsələːr] *n* 議員 gíìn

counsel [kaunˈsəl] *n* (advice) 助言 jogén;

(lawyer) 弁護人 beñgonin

♦*vt* (advise) ...に助言する ...ni jogén suru

counsel(l)or [kaun'sələr] *n* (advisor) カウンセラー káunserā; (*US*: lawyer) 弁護人 beñgonin

count [kaunt] *vt* (add up: numbers, money, things, people) 数える kazóerù; (include) 入れる iréru, 含む fukúmù

♦*vi* (enumerate) 数える kazóerù; (be considered) ...と見なされる ...to minasareru; (be valid) 効果をもつ kōka wo mótsu

♦*n* (of things, people, votes) 数 kazù; (level: of pollen, alcohol etc) 値 atái, 数値 súchi; (nobleman) 伯爵 hakúshaku

countdown [kaunt'daun] *n* (to launch) 秒読み byōyomi

countenance [kaun'tənəns] *n* (face) 顔 kaó

♦*vt* (tolerate) 容認する yónin suru

counter [kaun'tər] *n* (in shop, café, bank etc) カウンター káuntā; (in game) こま komá

♦*vt* (oppose) ...に対抗する ...ni taikō suru

♦*adv*: **counter to** ...に反して ...ni hañ shite

counteract [kauntəːrækt'] *vt* (effect, tendency) 打消す uchíkesu

counter-espionage [kauntəːres'pi:ənɑːʒ] *n* 対抗的スパイ活動 taíkōteki supáikatsudō

counterfeit [kaun'təːrfit] *n* (forgery) 偽物 nisémono

♦*vt* (forge) 偽造する gizō suru

♦*adj* (coin) 偽物の nisémono no

counterfoil [kaun'təːrfoil] *n* (of check, money order) 控え hikáe

countermand [kauntəːrmænd'] *vt* (order) 取消す toríkesu

counterpart [kaun'təːrpɑːrt] *n*: **counterpart of** (person) ...に相当する人 ...ni sōtō suru hitó; (thing) ...に相当するもの ...ni sōtō suru mono

counterproductive [kauntəːrprədʌk'-tiv] *adj* (measure, policy etc) 逆効果的な gyakúkōkateki na

countersign [kaun'təːrsain] *vt* (document) ...に副署する ...ni fukúsho surù

countess [kaun'tis] *n* 伯爵夫人 hakúshakufùjin

countless [kaunt'lis] *adj* (innumerable) 無数の músū no

count on *vt fus* (expect) ...の積りでいる ...no tsumóri de irù; (depend on) ...を頼りにする ...wo táyòri ni suru

country [kʌn'tri:] *n* (state, nation) 国 kuní; (native land) 母国 bókòku; (rural area) 田舎 ináka; (region) 地域 chíīki

country dancing (*BRIT*) *n* 英国郷土舞踊 eíkokukyōdòbuyō

country house *n* 田舎の大邸宅 ináka no daíteitàku

countryman [kʌn'triːmən] (*pl* **countrymen**) *n* (compatriot) 同国人 dōkokujìn; (country dweller) 田舎者 inákamòno

countryside [kʌn'triːsaid] *n* 田舎 ináka

county [kaun'ti:] *n* (POL, ADMIN) 郡 gúñ

coup [ku:] (*pl* **coups**) *n* (MIL, POL: *also*: **coup d'état**) クーデター kūdetà; (achievement) 大成功 daíseikō

coupé [ku:pei'] *n* (AUT) クーペ kūpe

couple [kʌp'əl] *n* (*also*: **married couple**) 夫婦 fūfu; (cohabiting etc) カップル káppùru; (of things) 一対 ittsúi

a couple of (two people) 2人の futári no; (two things) 2つの futátsu no; (a few people) 数人の súnin no; (a few things) 幾つかの ikútsuka no

coupon [ku:'pɑːn] *n* (voucher) クーポン券 kúpoñken; (detachable form) クーポン kúpon

courage [kəːr'idʒ] *n* (bravery) 勇気 yúki

courageous [kərei'dʒəs] *adj* (person, attempt) 勇敢な yūkan na

courgette [kurʒet'] (*BRIT*) *n* ズッキーニ zúkkìni

courier [kəːr'iːər] *n* (messenger) メッセンジャー méssènjā; (for tourists) 添乗員 teñjoìn

course [kɔːrs] *n* (SCOL) 課程 katéi; (process: of life, events, time etc) 過程 katéi; (of treatment) クール kūru; (direction: of argument, action) 方針 hōshin; (: of ship) 針路 shíñro; (part of meal) 一品 ippín, コース kōsu; (for golf) コース kōsu *the course of a river* 川筋 kawásuji

of course (naturally) もちろん mochíròn, 当然 tṓzen; (certainly) いいとも fi to mo

court [kɔːrt] *n* (royal) 宮殿 kyúden; (LAW) 法廷 hṓtei; (for tennis, badminton etc) コート kṓto

♦*vt* (woman) 妻にしようとして…と交際する tsumā ni shiyṓ to shité …to kṓsai suru

to take someone to court (LAW) …を相手取って訴訟を起す …wo aítedottè soshṓ wo okósù

courteous [kə́ːrʼtiːəs] *adj* (person, conduct) 丁寧な teínei na

courtesan [kɔːrʼtizən] *n* 宮廷しょう婦 kyúteishōfu

courtesy [kə́ːrʼtisiː] *n* (politeness) 礼儀正しさ reígitadashīsa

(by) courtesy of (thanks to) …のお陰で …no okáge de

court-house [kɔːrʼthaus] (*US*) *n* 裁判所 saíbansho

courtier [kɔ́ːrtiːər] *n* 廷臣 teíshin

court-martial [kɔːrtʼmɑːrʼʃəl] (*pl courts-martial*) *vt* (MIL) 軍法会議 guńpōkaìgi

courtroom [kɔːrtʼruːm] *n* 法廷 hṓtei

courtyard [kɔːrtʼjɑːrd] *n* (of castle, house) 中庭 nakániwa

cousin [kʌ́zʼin] *n* (relative) 親せき shińseki

first cousin いとこ itókò

second cousin はとこ hatókò, またいとこ mata-ítoko

cove [kouv] *n* (bay) 入江 irîe

covenant [kʌ́vʼənənt] *n* (promise) 契約 keíyaku

cover [kʌ́vʼəːr] *vt* (hide: face, surface, ground): *to cover (with)* …で覆う …de ṓù; (hide: feelings, mistake): *to cover (with)* …で隠す …de kakúsù; (shield: book, table etc): *to cover (with)* …に (…を) 掛ける …ni (…wo) kakérù; (with lid): *to cover (with)* …にふたをする …ni futá wo suru; (travel: distance) 行く ikú; (protect: *also* INSURANCE) カバーする kábà suru; (discuss: topic, subject: *also* PRESS) 取上げる toríagerù; (include) 含

む fukúmù

♦*n* (for furniture) 覆い ṓi; (lid) ふた futá; (on bed) 上掛 uwágake; (of book, magazine) 表紙 hyṓshi; (shelter: for hiding) 隠れ場所 kakúrebasho; (: from rain) 雨宿りの場所 amáyadòri no bashó; (INSURANCE) 保険 hokén; (of spy) 架空の身分 kakú no míbùn

to take cover (shelter: from rain) 雨宿りをする amáyadòri wo suru; (: from gunfire etc) 隠れる kakúrerù

under cover (indoors) 屋根の下で〔に〕 yané no shitá de 〔ni〕

under cover of darkness やみに紛れて yamí ni magíretè

under separate cover (COMM) 別便で betsúbin de

coverage [kʌ́vʼəːridʒ] *n* (TV, PRESS) 報道 hṓdō

cover charge *n* (in restaurant) サービス料 sábisuryò

covering [kʌ́vʼəːriŋ] *n* (layer) 覆い ṓi; (of snow, dust etc) 覆う物 ṓu monò

covering letter (*US also*: cover letter) *n* 添状 soéjō

cover note (*BRIT*) *n* (INSURANCE) 仮保険証 karíhokeñshō

covert [kouʼvəːrt] *adj* (glance, threat) 隠れた kakúretà

cover up *vi*: *to cover up for someone* …をかばう …wo kabáù

cover-up [kʌ́vʼəːrʌp] *n* もみ消し momíkeshi

covet [kʌ́vʼit] *vt* (desire) 欲しがる hoshígarù

cow [kau] *n* (animal) 雌ウシ meúshi; (*inf!*: woman) あま amá

♦*vt* (oppress): *to be cowed* おびえる obíerù

coward [kauʼəːrd] *n* おく病者 okúbyōmono

cowardice [kauʼəːrdis] *n* おく病 okúbyō

cowardly [kauʼəːrdliː] *adj* おく病な okúbyō na

cowboy [kauʼbɔi] *n* (in US) カウボーイ kaúbòi

cower [kauʼəːr] *vi* い縮する ishúku suru

coxswain [kɑːkʼsin] *n* (ROWING: abbr:

cox) コックス kókkùsu

coy [kɔi] *adj* (demure, shy) はにかんでみせる haníkaǹde misérù

coyote [kaiout'i:] *n* コヨーテ kóyòte

cozy [kou'zi:] (*BRIT* **cosy**) *adj* (room, house) こじんまりした kojiǹmarì shita; (person) 心地よい kokóchi yoí

CPA [si:pi:ei'] (*US*) *abbr* = **certified public accountant**

crab [kræb] *n* カニ kaní

crab apple *n* ヒメリンゴ himériǹgo

crack [kræk] *n* (noise: of gun) パン páǹ; (: of thunder) ばりばり bárìbari; (: of twig) ぽっきり pokkíri; (: of whip) パン baǹ; (gap) 割れ目 waréme; (in bone, dish, glass, wall) ひび hibí

♦*vt* (whip, twig) 鳴らす narásù; (bone, dish, glass, wall) ひびを入れる hibí wo irérù; (nut) 割る warú; (solve: problem) 解決する kaíketsu suru; (: code) 解く tókù; (joke) 飛ばす tobásu

♦*adj* (expert) 優秀な yúshù na

crack down on *vt fus* (crime, expenditure etc) 取り締まる toríshimarù

cracker [kræk'əːr] *n* (biscuit, Christmas cracker) クラッカー kurákkà

crackle [kræk'əl] *vi* (fire) ぱちぱちと音を立てる páchìpachi to otó wo tatérù; (twig) ぽきぽきと音を立てる pókìpoki to otó wo tatérù

crack up *vi* (PSYCH) 頭がおかしくなる atáma ga okáshikù nárù

cradle [krei'dəl] *n* (baby's) 揺りかご yuríkago

craft [kræft] *n* (skill) 芸術 geíjutsu; (trade) 職業 shokúgyò; (boat: *pl inv*) 船 fúnè; (plane: *pl inv*) 飛行機 hikóki

craftsman [kræfts'mən] (*pl* **craftsmen**) *n* (artisan) 職人 shokúnin

craftsmanship [kræfts'mənʃip] *n* (quality) 芸術 geíjutsu

crafty [kræf'ti:] *adj* (sneaky) 腹黒い haráguroì, こうかつな kókatsu na

crag [kræg] *n* 険しい岩山 kewáshiì iwáyama

cram [kræm] *vt* (fill): **to cram something with** ...を...で一杯にする ...wo ...de ippái ni surù; (put): **to cram something into** ...を...に詰込む ...wo ...ni tsumékomù

♦*vi*: **to cram for exams** 一夜漬の試験勉強をする ichíyazuke no shikénbenkyò wo suru

cramp [kræmp] *n* (MED) けいれん keíren

cramped [kræmpt] *adj* (accommodation) 窮屈な kyúkutsu na

crampon [kræm'pɑːn] *n* (CLIMBING) アイゼン áìzen

cranberry [kræn'beːri:] *n* (berry) コケモモ kokémòmo, クランベリー kuránberì

crane [krein] *n* (machine) クレーン kúrèn; (bird) ツル tsúrù

crank [kræŋk] *n* (person) 変人 heńjin; (handle) クランク kuráǹku

crankshaft [kræŋk'ʃæft] *n* (AUT) クランクシャフト kuráǹkushafùto

cranny [kræn'i:] *n see* **nook**

crash [kræʃ] *n* (noise) 大音響 daíoǹkyo ◇物が落ちる, ぶつかるなどの大きな音を指す monó ga ochírù, butsúkarù nádò no ókìna otó wo sásù; (of car, train etc) 衝突 shótotsu; (of plane) 墜落 tsuíraku; (COMM: of stock-market) 暴落 bóraku; (COMM: of business etc) 倒産 tósan

♦*vt* (car etc) 衝突させる shótotsu saséru; (plane) 墜落させる tsuíraku saséru

♦*vi* (car) 衝突する shótotsu suru; (plane) 墜落する tsuíraku suru; (COMM: market) 暴落する bóraku suru; (COMM: firm) 倒産する tósan suru

crash course *n* 速成コース sokúseikòsu

crash helmet *n* ヘルメット herúmettò

crash landing *n* (AVIAT) 不時着陸 fujíchakùriku

crass [kræs] *adj* (behavior, comment, person) 露骨な rokótsu na

crate [kreit] *n* (box) 箱 hakó; (for bottles) ケース kèsu

crater [krei'təːr] *n* (of volcano) 噴火口 funkakò; (on moon etc) クレーター kurétā

bomb crater 爆弾孔 bakúdankò

cravat [krəvæt'] *n* アスコットタイ asúkottotaì

crave [kreiv] *vt*, *vi*: **to crave for** ...を強く欲しがる ...wo tsuyókù hoshígarù

crawl [krɔːl] vi (person) 四つんばいには う yotsúnbai ni háú; (vehicle) のろのろと進む nórðnoro ni susúmù
♦n (SWIMMING) クロール kúrðru

crayfish [krei'fiʃ] n inv (freshwater) ザリガニ zarígani; (saltwater) エビガニ ebígani

crayon [krei'ɑːn] n クレヨン kuréyon

craze [kreiz] n (fashion) 大流行 daíryūkõ

crazy [krei'zi:] adj (insane) 正気でない shõki de náí; (inf: keen): **crazy about someone/something** ...が大好きである ...ga daísuki de arù

crazy paving (BRIT) n 不ぞろい舗装 fuzóroi hosõ ◊不ぞろいの敷石からなる舗装 fuzóroi no shikíishi kara narù hosõ

creak [kri:k] vi (floorboard, door etc) きしむ kishímù

cream [kri:m] n (of milk) (生)クリーム (namá)kúrīmu; (also: **artificial cream**) 人造クリーム jinfzōkurīmu; (cosmetic) 化粧クリーム keshõkurīmu; (élite) 名士たち meíshi tachì
♦adj (color) クリーム色の kúrīmuírð no

cream cake n クリームケーキ kurīmukēki

cream cheese n クリームチーズ kurīmuchīzu

creamy [kri:'mi:] adj (color) クリーム色の kurīmuírð no; (taste) 生クリームたっぷりの namákurīmu táppúri no

crease [kri:s] n (fold) 折目 orīme; (wrinkle) しわ shiwá; (in trousers) 折目 orīme
♦vt (wrinkle) しわくちゃにする shiwákucha ni suru
♦vi (wrinkle up) しわくちゃになる shiwakucha ni naru

create [kri:eit'] vt (cause to happen, exist) 引起こす hikíokosù; (produce, design) 作る tsukúrù

creation [kri:ei'ʃən] n (causing to happen, exist) 引起こす事 hikíokosù kotõ; (production, design) 作る事 tsukúrù kotõ; (REL) 天地創造 teñchisōzõ

creative [kri:ei'tiv] adj (artistic) 芸術的な geíjutsuteki na; (inventive) 創造性のある sõzosei no árù

creator [kri:ei'tər] n (maker, inventor) 作る人 tsukúrù hitõ

creature [kri:'tʃər] n (living animal) 動物 dõbutsu; (person) 人 hitõ

crèche [kreʃ] n 託児所 takújisho

credence [kri:d'əns] n: **to lend credence to** (prove) ...を信じさせる ...wo shiñji sasérù
to give credence to (prove) ...を信じさせる ...wo shiñji sasérù; (believe) 信じる shiñjirù

credentials [kriden'ʃəlz] npl (references) 資格 shikáku; (identity papers) 身分証明証 mibúnshōmeishō

credibility [kredəbil'əti:] n (of person, fact) 信頼性 shiñraisei

credible [kred'əbəl] adj (believable) 信じられる shiñjirarerù; (trustworthy) 信用できる shiñ-yō dekírù

credit [kred'it] n (COMM: loan) 信用 shiñ-yō; (recognition) 名誉 mēlyo
♦vt (COMM) ...の入金にする ...no nyúkin ni suru; (believe: also: **give credit to**) 信じる shiñjirù
to be in credit (person, bank account) 黒字になっている kuróji ni natté irù
to credit someone with (fig) ...に...の美徳があると思う ...ni...no bitóku ga arù to omõû

credit card n クレジットカード kuréjittokādo

creditor [kred'itər] n (COMM) 債権者 saíkeñsha

credits [kred'its] npl (CINEMA) クレジット kuréjitto

creed [kri:d] n (REL) 信条 shíñjō

creek [kri:k] n (US: stream) 小川 ogáwa; (BRIT: inlet) 入江 irīe

creep [kri:p] (pt, pp **crept**) vi (person, animal) 忍び足で歩く shinóbiàshi de arúkù

creeper [kri:'pər] n (plant) つる tsurú

creepy [kri:'pi:] adj (frightening: story, experience) 薄気味悪い usúkimiwaruì

cremate [kri:'meit] vt (corpse) 火葬にする kasõ ni surù

cremation [krimei'ʃən] n 火葬 kasõ

crematoria [kri:mətɔːr'iːə] npl of crematorium

crematorium [krɪ:mətɔ:r'i:əm] (*pl* **crematoria**) *n* 火葬場 kasôba

crêpe [kreip] *n* (fabric) クレープ kúrēpu; (rubber) クレープゴム kurépugomù ◊靴底に使う表面がしわ状のゴム kutsúzoko ni tsukáù hyômen ga shiwájō no gómù

crêpe bandage (*BRIT*) *n* 伸縮性包帯 shiñshukuseihōtai

crept [krept] *pt, pp of* **creep**

crescent [kres'ənt] *n* (shape) 三日月形 mikázukigata; (street) ...通り ...dôri ◊特にカーブになっている通りの名前に使う tôkù ni kâbu ni natté irù tôri no namáe ni tsukáù

cress [kres] *n* (BOT, CULIN) クレソン kurésoñ

crest [krest] *n* (of hill) 頂上 chôjō; (of bird) とさか tosáka; (coat of arms) 紋 môñ

crestfallen [krest'fɔ:lən] *adj* しょんぼりした shoñborí shitá

Crete [kri:t] *n* クレタ kurétà

crevice [krev'is] *n* (gap, crack) 割れ目 waréme

crew [kru:] *n* (NAUT) 乗組員 noríkumiìn; (AVIAT) 乗員 jôin; (TV, CINEMA) カメラ班 kamérahàn ◊3つの意味とも総称として使う mittsú no imî to mo sôshō toshite tsukáù

crew-cut [kru:'kʌt] *n* 角刈り kakúgari

crew-neck [kru:'nek] *n* (of jersey) 丸首 marúkubi

crib [krib] *n* (cot) ベビーベッド bebíbeddò

♦*vt* (*inf*: copy: during exam etc) カンニングする kañníñgu suru; (: from writings etc of others) 盗用する tôyō suru

crick [krik] *n*: **to have a crick in one's neck** 首が痛い kubí ga itái

cricket [krik'it] *n* (game) クリケット kuríkettò; (insect) コオロギ kôrogi

crime [kraim] *n* (no pl: illegal activities) 犯罪 hañzai; (illegal action) 犯罪(行為) hañzai(kôi); (*fig*) 罪 tsumí

criminal [krim'ənəl] *n* 犯罪者 hañzaìsha
♦*adj* (illegal) 違法の ihô no; (morally wrong) 罪悪の zaíaku no

crimson [krim'zən] *adj* 紅色の beníiro no

cringe [krindʒ] *vi* (in fear, embarrassment) 縮こまる chijíkomarù

crinkle [kriŋ'kəl] *vt* (crease, fold) しわくちゃにする shiwákucha ni suru

cripple [krip'əl] *n* (MED) 身障者 shiñshôsha
♦*vt* (person) 不具にする fúgù ni suru

crises [krai'si:z] *npl of* **crisis**

crisis [krai'sis] (*pl* **crises**) *n* 危機 kikî

crisp [krisp] *adj* (vegetables) ぱりぱりした párìpari shitá; (bacon) かりかりした kárìkari shitá; (weather) からっとした karáttò shitá; (manner, tone, reply) 無愛想な buáìsō na

crisps [krisps] (*BRIT*) *npl* ポテトチップ potétochippù

criss-cross [kris'krɔ:s] *adj* (pattern, design) 十字模様の jûjimoyô no

criteria [kraiti:'ri:ə] *npl of* **criterion**

criterion [kraiti:r'i:ən] (*pl* **criteria**) *n* (standard) 規準 kijún

critic [krit'ik] *n* (of system, policy etc) 反対者 hañtaìsha; (reviewer) 評論家 hyôronka

critical [krit'ikəl] *adj* (time, situation) 重大な jûdai na; (opinion, analysis) 批評的な hihyôteki na; (person: fault-finding) 粗捜し好きな arásagashizùki na; (illness) 危険な kikén na

critically [krit'ikli:] *adv* (speak, look etc) 批判的に hihánteki ni
critically ill 重症で jôshō de

criticism [krit'isizəm] *n* (disapproval, complaint) 非難 hínan; (of book, play etc) 批評 hihyô

criticize [krit'əsaiz] *vt* (find fault with) 非難する hínan suru

croak [krouk] *vi* (frog) げろげろ鳴く gérògero nakú; (bird etc) かーかー鳴く kâkā nakú; (person) がらがら声で言う garágaragoe de iu

crochet [krouʃei'] *n* かぎ針編み kagíbariami

crockery [krɑ:k'ə:ri:] *n* (dishes) 皿類 saráruì

crocodile [krɑ:k'ədail] *n* ワニ wánì

crocus [krou'kəs] n クロッカス kurókkàsu

croft [krɔːft] (BRIT) n (small farm) 小農場 shōnōjō

crony [krou'niː] (inf: pej) n 仲間 nakáma

crook [kruk] n (criminal) 悪党 akútō; (also: shepherd's crook) 羊飼のつえ hitsújikai no tsúe ◇片端の曲った物を指す katáhashi no magátta monó wo sásù

crooked [kruk'id] adj (bent, twisted) 曲った magátta; (dishonest) 不正の fuséi no

crop [krɑːp] n (of fruit, cereals, vegetables) 作物 sakúmòtsu; (harvest) 収穫 shúkaku; (riding crop) むち múchí ◇乗馬用の物を指す jōbayō no monó wo sásù
◆vt (hair) 刈込む karíkomù

crop up vi (problem, topic) 持ち上る mochíagarù

croquet [kroukei'] n クロッケー kurókkē ◇複雑なゲートボールに似た球技 fukúzatsu na gétobòru ni nitá kyūgi

croquette [krouket'] n (CULIN) コロッケ kórðkke

cross [krɔːs] n (shape) 十字 jūji; (REL) 十字架 jūjika; (mark) ばつ(印) bátsù(jírùshi); (hybrid) 合の子 aínoko
◆vt (street, room etc) 横断する ōdan suru; (arms, legs) 組む kúmù; (animal, plant) 交雑する kōzatsu suru
◆adj (angry) 不機嫌な fukígen na

to cross a check 線引小切手にする seńbiki kogíttè ni suru

crossbar [krɔːs'bɑːr] n (SPORT) ゴールの横棒 gōru no yokóbō

cross country (race) n クロスカントリーレース kurósukantorīrèsu

cross-examine [krɔːs'igzæm'in] vt (LAW) 反対尋問する hańtaijìnmon suru

cross-eyed [krɔːs'aid] adj 寄り目の yoríme no

crossfire [krɔːs'faiə·r] n 十字射撃 jūjishagèki

crossing [krɔːs'iŋ] n (sea passage) 船旅 funátabi; (also: pedestrian crossing) 横断歩道 ōdanhodō

crossing guard (US) n 交通指導員 kōtsūshidòin ◇交通事故を防ぐために横断

歩道に立って学童などの横断を助ける係員 kōtsūjikò wo fuségù tamé ni ōdanhodō ni tatté gakúdō nádò no ōdan wo tasúkerù kakáriìn

cross out vt (delete) 線を引いて消す séñ wo hiíte kesú

cross over vi (move across) 横断する ōdan suru

cross-purposes [krɔːs'pəːr'pəsiz] npl: to be at cross-purposes 話が食違っている hanáshi ga kuíchigatte irù

cross-reference [krɔːs'ref'əːrəns] n 相互参照 sōgosañshō

crossroads [krɔːs'roudz] n 交差点 kōsatèn

cross section n (of an object) 断面 dañmeñ; (sketch) 断面図 dañmeñzu
cross section of the population 国民を代表する人々 kokumin wo daíhyō suru hitóbìto

crosswalk [krɔːs'wɔːk] (US) n 横断歩道 ōdanhodō

crosswind [krɔːs'wind] n 横風 yokókaze

crossword [krɔːs'wəːrd] n クロスワードパズル kurósuwādopazùru

crotch [krɑːtʃ] n (ANAT, of garment) また matá

crotchet [krɑːtʃ'it] n (MUS) 四分音符 shibúoñpu

crotchety [krɑːtʃ'ətiː] adj (person) 気難しい kimúzukashiì

crouch [krautʃ] vi (person, animal) うずくまる uzúkumarù

croupier [kruːp'iːəːr] n (in casino) とばく台の元締 tobákudai no motójime, ディーラー dīrā

crow [krou] n (bird) カラス káràsu; (of cock) 鳴き声 nakígoè
◆vi (cock) 鳴く nakú

crowbar [krou'bɑːr] n バール bāru

crowd [kraud] n: crowd of people 群衆 guńshū
◆vt (fill: room, stadium etc) ...にぎっしり入る ...ni gisshírì haírù
◆vi (gather): to crowd round ...の回りに群がる ...no mawári ni murágarù; (cram): to crowd in ...の中へ詰めかける ...no nákà e tsumékakerù

a crowd of fans 大勢のファン ōzei nò fáñ

crowded [krau'did] *adj* (full) 込み入った komfitta; (densely populated) 人口密度の高い jíñkōmitsùdo no takaî

crown [kraun] *n* (*gen*) 冠 kañmuri; (of monarch) 王冠 ōkan; (monarchy): *the Crown* 国王 kokuō; (of head, hill) てっぺん téppeñ; (of tooth) 歯冠 shikáñ
♦*vt* (monarch) 王位に就かせる ōi ni tsukáserù; (*fig*: career, evening) ...に有終の美を飾る ...ni yūshū no bí wo kazárù

crown jewels *npl* 王位の象徴 ōi no shóchō ◇王冠, しゃくなど国家的儀式で王または女王が王位の象徴として用いる物を指す ōkan, shákù nádò kokkáteki gishíki de ō matá wa jóō ga ōi no shóchō toshité mochíirù monó wo sásù

crown prince *n* 皇太子 kōtaìshi

crow's feet *npl* 目じりの小じわ méjìri no kojíwa, カラスの足跡 káràsu no ashíatò

crucial [kru:'ʃəl] *adj* (decision, vote) 重大な jūdai na

crucifix [kru:'səfiks] *n* (REL) 十字架像 jūjikazō

crucifixion [kru:səfik'ʃən] *n* (REL) キリストのはりつけ kirísuto no harítsuke

crude [kru:d] *adj* (materials) 原...géñ...; (*fig*: basic) 原始的な geñshiteki na; (: vulgar) 露骨な rokótsu na

crude (oil) *n* 原油 geñ-yu

cruel [kru:'əl] *adj* (person, action) 残酷な zañkoku na; (situation) 悲惨な hisán na

cruelty [kru:'əlti:] *n* (of person, action) 残酷さ zañkokusa; (of situation) 悲惨さ hisánsa

cruise [kru:z] *n* (on ship) 船旅 funátabi
♦*vi* (ship) 巡航する juñkō suru; (car) 楽に走行する ráků ni sōkō suru

cruiser [kru:'zə:r] *n* (motorboat) 大型モーターボート ōgata mōtābòto, クルーザー kurūzà; (warship) 巡洋艦 juñ-yōkan

crumb [krʌm] *n* (of bread, cake) くず kúzù

crumble [krʌm'bəl] *vt* (bread, biscuit etc) 崩す kuzúsù
♦*vi* 崩れる kuzúrerù

crumbly [krʌm'bli:] *adj* (bread, biscuits etc) 崩れやすい kuzúreyasùi, ぼろぼろした pórðporo shitá

crumpet [krʌm'pit] *n* クランペット kuránpettð ◇マフィンの一種 mafíñ no isshū

crumple [krʌm'pəl] *vt* (paper, clothes) しわくちゃにする shiwákucha ni suru

crunch [krʌntʃ] *vt* (food etc) かみ砕く kamíkudakù; (underfoot) 踏み砕く fumíkudakù
♦*n* (*fig*: moment of truth) いざという時 izá to iú tokì

crunchy [krʌn'tʃi:] *adj* (food) ぱりぱりした parípari shitá

crusade [kru:seid'] *n* (campaign) 運動 uñdō

crush [krʌʃ] *n* (crowd) 人込み hitógomi; (love): *to have a crush on someone* ...にのぼせる ...ni noboseru; (drink): *lemon crush* レモンスカッシュ remóñsukasshù
♦*vt* (press, squeeze) 押しつぶす oshítsubusù; (crumple: paper, clothes) しわくちゃにする shiwákucha ni suru; (defeat: army, opposition) 圧倒する attō suru; (devastate: hopes) 台無しにする daínashi ni suru; (: person) 落胆させる rakútan saséru

crust [krʌst] *n* (of bread, pastry) 皮 kawá; (of snow, ice) アイスバーン aísubàn; (of the earth) 地殻 chikáku

crutch [krʌtʃ] *n* (support, stick) 松葉づえ matsúbazùe

crux [krʌks] *n* (of problem, matter) 核心 kakúshin

cry [krai] *vi* (weep) 泣く nakú; (shout: *also*: **cry out**) 叫ぶ sakébù
♦*n* (shriek) 悲鳴 himéi; (shout) 叫び声 sakébigoè; (of bird, animal) 鳴き声 nakígoè

cry off *vi* (change one's mind, cancel) 手を引く te wo hikú

crypt [kript] *n* 地下室 chikáshìtsu ◇特に納骨堂などに使われる教会の地下室を指す tókù ni nōkotsudō nadò ni tsukáwarerù kyōkai no chikáshìtsu wo sásù

cryptic [krip'tik] *adj* (remark, clue) なぞめいた nazómeità

crystal [kris'təl] n (mineral) 結晶 kesshō; (in jewelery) 水晶 suíshō; (glass) クリスタル kurísùtaru

crystal-clear [kris'təlkli:'ə:r] adj (transparent) よく澄んだ yókù súnda; (fig: easy to understand) 明白な meíhaku na

crystallize [kris'təlaiz] vt (opinion, thoughts) まとめる matómeru
♦vi (sugar etc) 結晶する kesshō suru

cub [kʌb] n (of lion, wolf etc) …の子 …no ko; (also: **cub scout**) カブスカウト kabúsukàuto

Cuba [kju:'bə] n キューバ kyūba

Cuban [kju:'bən] adj キューバの kyūba no
♦n キューバ人 kyūbajìn

cubbyhole [kʌb'i:houl] n 小さな納戸 chíìsa na nàndo

cube [kju:b] n (shape) 立方体 rippótai; (MATH: of number) …の3乗 …no sañjō
♦vt (MATH) 3乗する sañjō suru

cube root n (MATH) 立方根 rippókon

cubic [kju:'bik] adj (volume) 立方の rippó no

cubic capacity n 体積 taíseki

cubicle [kju:'bikəl] n (at pool) 更衣室 kóishîtsu ◇小さい個室について言う chíìsaí koshîtsu ni tsuíte iú; (in hospital) カーテンで仕切った1病床分のスペース kâten de shikítta ichíbyōshòbun no supêsu

cuckoo [ku:'ku:] n カッコウ kákkô

cuckoo clock n はと時計 hatódokèi

cucumber [kju:'kʌmbə:r] n キューリ kyūri

cuddle [kʌd'əl] vt (baby, person) 抱締める dakíshimerù
♦vi (lovers) 抱合う dakíaù

cue [kju:] n (snooker cue) キュー kyū; (THEATER etc) 合図 aízu, キュー kyū
off the cuff (impromptu) 即座に〔の〕 sókùza ni 〔no〕

cufflinks [kʌf'liŋks] npl カフスボタン kafúsubotàn

cuisine [kwizi:n'] n (of country, region) 料理 ryōri

cul-de-sac [kʌl'dəsæk'] n (road) 行き止り yukídomari

culinary [kju:'lənə:ri:] adj 料理の ryōri no

cull [kʌl] vt (story, idea) えり抜く erínukù
♦n (of animals) 間引き mabíki

culminate [kʌl'məneit] vi: **to culminate in** (gen) 遂に…となる tsuí ni …to narù; (unpleasant outcome) 挙句の果てに…となってしまう agéku no hàté ni …to natté shimáù

culmination [kʌlmənei'ʃən] n (of career, process etc) 頂点 chōten

culottes [kju:lots'] npl キュロット kyúròtto

culpable [kʌl'pəbəl] adj (blameworthy) とがむべき togámùbeki

culprit [kʌl'prit] n (of crime) 犯人 hañnin

cult [kʌlt] n (REL: worship) 崇拝 súhai; (: sect, group) 宗派 shūha; (fashion) 流行 ryūkō

cultivate [kʌl'təveit] vt (land) 耕す tagáyasù; (crop) 栽培する saíbai suru; (person) 近付きになろうとする chikázuki ni nárò to suru

cultivation [kʌltəvei'ʃən] n (AGR) 耕作 kōsaku

cultural [kʌl'tʃə:rəl] adj (traditions etc) 文化文明の buñkabunmei no; (activities etc) 芸術の geíjutsu no

culture [kʌl'tʃə:r] n (of a country, civilization) 文明 buñmei, 文化 buñka; (the arts) 芸術 geíjutsu; (BIO) 培養 baíyō

cultured [kʌl'tʃə:rd] adj (individual) 教養のある kyōyō no arù

cumbersome [kʌm'bə:rsəm] adj (object) 扱いにくい atsúkainikui ◇かさ張る物, 重い物, 大きくて不格好な物などについて言う kasábarù monó, omói monó, ốkikûte bukákkô na monó nadð ni tsuíte iú; (process) 面倒な meñdð na

cumulative [kju:m'jələtiv] adj (effect, result) 累積する ruíseki suru

cunning [kʌn'iŋ] n (craftiness) こうかつさ kókatsusa
♦adj (crafty) こうかつな kókatsu na

cup [kʌp] n (for drinking) カップ káppù;

(as prize) 賞杯 shōhai, カップ káppù; (of bra) カップ káppù

cupboard [kʌb'ə:rd] n 戸棚 todána

Cupid [kju:'pid] n キューピッド kyūpiddo

cup-tie [kʌp'tai] (BRIT) n (SOCCER) トーナメント tōnamento

curate [kju:'rit] n 助任牧師 joninbokùshi

curator [kjurei'tə:r] n (of museum, gallery) キューレーター kyūrētā ◊学芸員の管理職に相当する人を指す gakúgeìn no kañrishòku ni sōtō suru hitó wo sásù

curb [kə:rb] vt (powers, expenditure) 制限する seígen suru; (person) 抑える osáerù
♦n (restraint) 抑制 yokúsei; (US: kerb) 縁石 fuchíishi

curdle [kə:r'dəl] vi (milk) 凝結する gyōketsu suru

cure [kju:r] vt (illness, patient) 治す naósù; (CULIN) 保存食にする hozónshoku ni suru
♦n (MED) 治療法 chiryōhō; (solution) 解決 kaíketsu

curfew [kə:r'fju:] n (MIL, POL) 夜間外出禁止令 yakán gaíshutsu kiñshirei

curio [kju:'ri:ou] n 骨とう品 kottōhin

curiosity [kju:ri:ɑ:s'əti:] n (of person) 好奇心 kōkishīn; (object) 珍しい物 mezúrashiì monó

curious [kju:'ri:əs] adj (person: interested) 好奇心がある kōkishīn ga arù; (: nosy) せん索好きな seńsakuzùki na; (thing: strange, unusual) 変った kawátta

curl [kə:rl] n (of hair) カール kāru
♦vt (hair) カールする kāru suru
♦vi (hair) カールになっている kāru ni natté irù

curler [kə:r'lə:r] n (for hair) カーラー kārā

curl up vi (person, animal) 縮こまる chijíkomarù

curly [kə:r'li:] adj 巻毛の makíge no

currant [kə:r'ənt] n (dried fruit) レーズン rēzun ◊小型の種無しブドウから作った物を指す kogáta no tanénashibùdo kara tsukúttà monó wo sásù; (bush, fruit: blackcurrant, redcurrant) スグリ súgùri

currency [kə:r'ənsi:] n (system) 通貨 tsūka; (money) 貨幣 káhèi
to gain currency (fig) 通用する様になる tsūyō suru yō ni nárù

current [kə:r'ənt] n (of air, water) 流れ nagáre; (ELEC) 電流 dénryū
♦adj (present) 現在の geñzai no; (accepted) 通用している tsūyō shité irù

current account (BRIT) n 当座預金 tōzayokìn

current affairs npl 時事 jiji

currently [kə:r'əntli:] adv 現在は geñzai wa

curricula [kərik'jələ] npl of **curriculum**

curriculum [kərik'jələm] (pl **curriculums** or **curricula**) n (SCOL) 指導要領 shidōyōryō

curriculum vitae [-vi:'tai] n 履歴書 rirékisho

curry [kə:r'i:] n (dish) カレー karé
♦vt: *to curry favor with* ...にへつらう ...ni hetsurau

curry powder n カレー粉 karéko

curse [kə:rs] vi (swear) 悪態をつく akútai wo tsukú
♦vt (swear at) ののしる nonóshirù; (bemoan) のろう norou
♦n (spell) 呪い noríi; (swearword) 悪態 akútai; (problem, scourge) 災の元 wazáwai no motó

cursor [kə:r'sə:r] n (COMPUT) カーソル kāsoru

cursory [kə:r'sə:ri:] adj (glance, examination) 何気ない nanígenài

curt [kə:rt] adj (reply, tone) 無愛想な buáisō na

curtail [kə:rteil'] vt (freedom, rights) 制限する seígen suru; (visit etc) 短くする mijíkaku suru; (expenses etc) 減らす herásu

curtain [kə:r'tən] n (at window) カーテン kāten; (THEATER) 幕 makú

curts(e)y [kə:rt'si:] vi (woman, girl) ひざを曲げて御辞儀をする hizá wo magéte ojígi wo suru

curve [kə:rv] n (bend: in line etc) 曲線 kyokúsen; (: in road) カーブ kābu

♦*vi* 曲る magáru

cushion [kuʃ'ən] *n* (on sofa, chair) クッション kusshòn, 座布団 zabúton; (*also*: **air cushion**) エアクッション eákusshòn ◇ホバークラフトなどを支える空気の事 hobákurafùto nádò wo sasáeru kūki no kotó

♦*vt* (collision, fall) ...の衝撃を和らげる ...no shōgeki wo yawáragerù; (shock, effect) 和らげる yawáragerù

custard [kʌs'tə:rd] *n* カスタード kasútādo

custodian [kʌstou'di:ən] *n* (of building, collection) 管理人 kañrinìn

custody [kʌs'tədi:] *n* (LAW: of child) 親権 shiñken

to take into custody (suspect) 逮捕する taího suru

custom [kʌs'təm] *n* (tradition) 伝統 deñtō; (convention) 慣習 kañshū; (habit) 習慣 shūkan; (COMM) ひいき hiíki

customary [kʌs'təme:ri:] *adj* (behavior, method, time) いつもの itsúmo no, 相変らずの aíkawarazu no

customer [kʌs'təmə:r] *n* (of shop, business etc) 客 kyakú

customized [kʌs'təmaizd] *adj* (car etc) 改造した kaízō shità

custom-made [kʌs'təmmeid'] *adj* (shirt, car etc) あつらえの atsúraè no, オーダーメードの ōdāmèdo no

customs [kʌs'təmz] *npl* (at border, airport etc) 税関 zeíkan

customs duty *n* 関税 kañzei

customs officer *n* 税関史 zeíkanri

cut [kʌt] (*pt, pp* **cut**) *vt* (bread, meat, hand etc) 切る kirú; (shorten: grass, hair) 刈る karú; (: text, program) 短くする mijíkakù suru; (reduce: prices, spending, supply) 減らす herásù

♦*vi* (knife, scissors) 切れる kirérù

♦*n* (in skin) 切り傷 kiríkîzu; (in salary) 減給 geñkyū; (in spending etc) 削減 sakúgen; (of meat) ブロック burókkù; (of garment) カット káttò

to cut a tooth 歯が生える há ga haérù

cutback [kʌt'bæk] *n* 削減 sakúgen

cut down *vt* (tree) 切り倒す kirítaosù;

(consumption) 減らす herásu

cute [kju:t] *adj* (*US*: pretty) かわいい kawáii; (sweet) 陳腐な chîṅpu na

cuticle [kju:'tikəl] *n* (of nail) 甘皮 amákawa

cutlery [kʌt'lə:ri:] *n* ナイフとフォークとスプーン naífu to fōku to súpūn ◇総称 sōshō

cutlet [kʌt'lit] *n* (piece of meat) カツ（レツ) katsú(retsu); (vegetable cutlet, nut cutlet) コロッケ kórokke

cut off *vt* (limb) 切断する setsúdan suru; (piece) 切る kírù; (person, village) 孤立させる korítsu saséru; (supply) 遮断する shadán suru; (TEL) 切る kírù

cut out *vt* (shape, article from newspaper) 切抜く kirínukù; (stop: an activity etc) やめる yaméru; (remove) 切除する setsújo suru

cutout [kʌt'aut] *n* (switch) 非常遮断装置 hijōshadansōchi, 安全器 añzeñki; (shape) 切抜き kirínuki

cut-rate [kʌt'reit] (*BRIT* **cut-price**) *adj* 安売りの yasúuri no

cutthroat [kʌt'θrout] *n* (murderer) 人殺し hitógoroshi

♦*adj* (business, competition) 殺人的な satsújinteki na

cutting [kʌt'iŋ] *adj* (remark) 辛らつな shiñratsu na

♦*n* (from newspaper) 切抜き kirínuki; (from plant) 穂木 hogí, さし穂 sashího

cut up *vt* (paper, meat) 刻む kizámu

CV [si:vi:'] *n abbr* = **curriculum vitae**

cwt *abbr* = **hundredweight(s)**

cyanide [sai'ənaid] *n* 青酸化物 seísankabùtsu

cyclamen [sik'ləmən] *n* シクラメン shikúramèn

cycle [sai'kəl] *n* (bicycle) 自転車 jitéñsha; (series: of events, seasons etc) 周期 shūki; (: TECH) サイクル saíkuru; (: of songs etc) 一連 ichíren

♦*vi* (on bicycle) 自転車で行く jitéñsha de ikú

cycling [saik'liŋ] *n* サイクリング saíkuringu

cyclist [saik'list] *n* サイクリスト saîkuri-suto

cyclone [saik'loun] *n* (storm) サイクロン saîkuron

cygnet [sig'nit] *n* 若いハクチョウ wakâî hakúchô

cylinder [sil'ində:r] *n* (shape) 円柱 eñchū; (of gas) ボンベ bôñbe; (in engine,machine etc) 気筒 kitô, シリンダー shírîndâ

cylinder-head gasket [sil'ində:rhed-] *n* (AUT) シリンダーヘッドのパッキング shirîndâheddô no pakkìngu

cymbals [sim'bəlz] *npl* (MUS) シンバル shîñbaru

cynic [sin'ik] *n* 皮肉屋 hinîkuya, シニック shínîkku

cynical [sin'ikəl] *adj* (attitude, view) 皮肉な hinîku na, シニカルな shínîkaru na

cynicism [sin'əsizəm] *n* シニカルな態度 shínîkaru na tâîdo

cypress [sai'pris] *n* (tree) イトスギ itôsùgi

Cypriot [sip'ri:ət] *adj* キプロスの kípûrosu no
♦*n* キプロス人 kipúrosujin

Cyprus [saip'rəs] *n* キプロス kípûrosu

cyst [sist] *n* (MED) のうしゅ nôshu

cystitis [sistai'tis] *n* (MED) ぼうこう炎 bôkōen

czar [zɑ:r] *n* = **tsar**

Czech [tʃek] *adj* チェコスロバキアの chékôsurôbakìa no
♦*n* (person) チェコスロバキア人 chékôsurôbakîajìn; (language) チェコスロバキア語 chékôsurôbakiago

Czechoslovak [tʃekəslou'væk] *adj, n* = **Czechoslovakian**

Czechoslovakia [tʃekəsləvɑ:k'i:ə] *n* チェコスロバキア chékôsurôbakìa

Czechoslovakian [tʃekəsləvɑ:k'i:ən] *adj* チェコスロバキアの chékôsurôbakìa no
♦*n* (person) チェコスロバキア人 chékôsurôbakîajìn

D

D [di:] *n* (MUS: note) ニ音 nîon; (: key) ニ

dab [dæb] *vt* (eyes, wound) 軽くふく karúku fùkú; (paint, cream) 軽く塗る karúku nurú

dabble [dæb'əl] *vi*: **to dabble in** (politics, antiques etc) 趣味でやる shúmî de yarú

dad [dæd] (*inf*) *n* 父ちゃん tôchan

daddy [dæd'i:] (*inf*) *n* = **dad**

daffodil [dæf'ədil] *n* スイセン suísen

daft [dæft] *adj* (silly) ばかな bákà na

dagger [dæg'ə:r] *n* 短刀 tántō

daily [dei'li:] *adj* (dose, wages, routine etc) 毎日の maînichi no
♦*n* (also: **daily paper**) 日刊新聞 nikkan-shîñbùn
♦*adv* (pay, see) 毎日 maînichi

dainty [dein'ti:] *adj* (petite) 繊細な sénsai na

dairy [de:r'i:] *n* (BRIT: shop) 牛乳店 gyű-nyüten; (on farm) 牛乳小屋 gyúnyügo-ya ◊酪農場で牛乳を置いたり加工したりする小屋 rakúnōjō dè gyúnyū wò oítarì kakô shitarî suru koyá

dairy farm *n* 酪農場 rakúnōjō

dairy products *npl* 乳製品 nyűseîhin

dairy store (US) *n* 牛乳店 gyűnyüten

dais [dei'is] *n* 演壇 éndan

daisy [dei'zi:] *n* デイジー deîjī

daisy wheel *n* (on printer) デイジーホイール deîjīhoîrù

dale [deil] *n* (valley) 谷 taní

dam [dæm] *n* (on river) ダム dámù
♦*vt* (river, stream) ...にダムを造る ...ni dámù wo tsukúrù

damage [dæm'idʒ] *n* (harm: also fig) 害 gaî; (dents etc) 損傷 soñshō
♦*vt* (harm: reputation etc) 傷付ける kizutsukérù; (spoil, break: toy, machine etc) 壊す kowásù

damages [dæm'idʒiz] *npl* (LAW) 損害賠償 sóngaibaîshō

damn [dæm] *vt* (curse at) ...に悪態を浴びせる ...ni akútai wo àbíseru; (condemn) 非難する hínàn suru
♦*n* (inf): **I don't give a damn** おれの知った事じゃない oré no shìttá koto jà náî

◆*adj* (*inf*: also: **damned**) くそったれの kusóttare no, 畜生の chikúshṓ no
damn (it)! 畜生 chikúshṓ

damning [dæm'iŋ] *adj* (evidence) 動かぬ ugókanù

damp [dæmp] *adj* (building, wall) 湿っぽい shiméppoì; (cloth) 湿った shimétta
◆*n* (in air, in walls) 湿り気 shimérike
◆*vt* (also: **dampen**: cloth, rag) 湿らす shimérasu; (: enthusiasm etc) ...に水を差す ...ni mizú wo sasù

damson [dæm'zən] *n* (fruit) ダムソンスモモ damúsonsumòmo

dance [dæns] *n* (movements, MUS, dancing) 踊り odóri, ダンス dànsu; (social event) 舞踏会 butṓkai, ダンスパーティ dánsupàti
◆*vi* (person) 踊る odóru

dance hall *n* ダンスホール dánsuhòru

dancer [dæn'sə:r] *n* (for pleasure) 踊る人 odóru hito; (professional) ダンサー dànsā

dancing [dæn'siŋ] *n* (skill, performance) 踊り odóri, ダンス dànsu

dandelion [dæn'dəlaiən] *n* タンポポ tànpopo

dandruff [dæn'drəf] *n* ふけ fuké

Dane [dein] *n* デンマーク人 dénmākujìn

danger [dein'dʒə:r] *n* (hazard, risk) 危険 kikén; (possibility): *there is a danger of ...* ...の危険がある ...no kikén ga arù
「*danger!*」 (on sign) 危険 kikén
in danger 危険にさらされて kikén ni sàrásareté
to be in danger of (risk, be close to) ...される危険がある ...saréru kikén ga arù

dangerous [dein'dʒə:rəs] *adj* 危険な kikén na

dangle [dæŋ'gəl] *vt* (keys, toy) ぶら下げる burásageru; (arms, legs) ぶらぶらさせる burábura saséru
◆*vi* (earrings, keys) ぶら下がる burásagaru

Danish [dei'niʃ] *adj* デンマークの dénmāku no; (LING) デンマーク語の dénmākugo no
◆*n* (LING) デンマーク語 dénmākugo

dapper [dæp'ə:r] *adj* (man, appearance) きびきびした kíbìkibi shitá

dare [de:r] *vt*: *to dare someone to do* 出来るものならしてみろと...にけし掛ける dekírù monó nàrá shité mirð to ...ni keshíkakerù
◆*vi*: *to dare (to) do something* 敢えて...する áète ...surú
I dare say (I suppose) 多分 tábùn

daredevil [de:r'devəl] *n* 無謀な人 mubṓ na hito

daring [de:r'iŋ] *adj* (escape, person, dress, film, raid, speech) 大胆な daítàn na
◆*n* 大胆さ daítànsa

dark [dɑ:rk] *adj* (room, night) 暗い kurái; (hair) 黒っぽい kuróppoì; (complexion) 浅黒い aságuroì; (color: blue, green etc) 濃い kôì
◆*n*: *in the dark* やみの中で〔に〕yamí no nakà de〔ni〕
to be in the dark about (*fig*) ...について何も知らない ...ni tsúìte naní mo shìránai
after dark 暗くなってから kuráku nattè kará

darken [dɑ:r'kən] *vt* (color) 濃くする kṓkù suru
◆*vi* (sky, room) 暗くなる kuráku narù

dark glasses *npl* サングラス sángùrasu

darkness [dɑ:rk'nis] *n* (of room, night) 暗やみ kuráyami

darkroom [dɑ:rk'ru:m] *n* (PHOT) 暗室 ánshitsu

darling [dɑ:r'liŋ] *adj* (child, spouse) 愛する aí surù
◆*n* (dear) あなた anáta; (favorite) ひいきの人 hiíki no hitð

darn [dɑ:rn] *vt* (sock, jersey) 繕う tsukúroù

dart [dɑ:rt] *n* (in game) 投げ矢 nagéya, ダート dāto; (in sewing) ダーツ dātsu
◆*vi* 素早く走る subáyakù hashírù
to dart away/along 素早く走っていく subáyakù hashíttè ikú

dartboard [dɑ:rt'bɔ:rd] *n* ダーツの的 dātsu no matð

darts [dɑ:rts] *n* (game) ダーツ dàtsu

dash [dæʃ] n (small quantity) 少々 shǒ-shǒ; (sign) ダッシュ dásshù
♦vt (throw) 投付ける nagétsukerù; (hopes) くじく kujíkù
♦vi 素早く行く subáyakù ikú

dash away vi 走って行く hashíttè ikú

dashboard [dæʃ'bɔːrd] n (AUT) ダッシュボード dasshúbòdò

dashing [dæʃ'iŋ] adj さっそうとした sàssǒ to shita

dash off vi = **dash away**

data [dei'tə] npl (ADMIN, COMPUT) 情報 jōhō, データ dèta

database [dei'təbeis] n データベース dětabèsu

data processing n 情報処理 jōhōshòrì

date [deit] n (day) 日にち hiníchi; (with boy/girlfriend) デート dèto; (fruit) ナツメヤシの実 natsúmeyashì no mí
♦vt (event) ...の年代を決める ...no néndai wo kìméru; (letter) ...に日付を書く ...ni hizúke wo kakù; (person) ...とデートをする ...to dèto wo suru

date of birth 生年月日 seínengàppi

to date (until now) 今まで imá madè

dated [dei'tid] adj (expression, style) 時代遅れの jidáiokùre no

daub [dɔːb] vt (mud, paint) 塗付ける nurítsukerù

daughter [dɔːt'əːr] n 娘 musúme

daughter-in-law [dɔːt'təːrinlɔː] (p l **daughters-in-law**) n 嫁 yome

daunting [dɔːn'tiŋ] adj (task, prospect) しりごみさせる様な shirígomì saséru yǒ na, ひるませる hirúmaserù yǒ nà

dawdle [dɔːd'əl] vi (go slow) ぐずぐずする gúzùguzu suru

dawn [dɔːn] n (of day) 夜明け yoáke; (of period, situation) 始まり hajímari
♦vi (day) 夜が明ける yǒ gà akéru; (fig): **it dawned on him that ...** 彼は...だと気が付いた kárè wa ...da tò ki gá tsuíta

day [dei] n (period) 日 hi, 1日 ichínichi; (daylight) 昼間 hirúma; (heyday) 全盛期 zensêiki

the day before 前の日 maé no hi, 前日 zénjitsu

the day after 翌日 yokújitsu

the day after tomorrow 明後日 asáttè

the day before yesterday 一昨日 otótoi

the following day 次の日 tsugí nò hi, 翌日 yokújitsu

by day 昼間に hirúma nì

daybreak [dei'breik] n 明け方 akégata, 夜明け yoáke

daydream [dei'driːm] vi 空想にふける kūsō ni fùkérù

daylight [dei'lait] n (sunlight) 日光 níkkō; (daytime) 昼間 hirúma, 日中 nítchū

day return (BRIT) n (ticket) 往復券 ōfukukèn

daytime [dei'taim] n 昼間 hirúma

day-to-day [dei'tədei'] adj (life, organization) 日常の nichíjō no

daze [deiz] vt (stun) ぼう然とさせる bōzen to sàséru
♦n: **in a daze** (confused, upset) ぼう然として bōzen to shite

dazzle [dæz'əl] vt (bewitch) 感嘆させる kántan sàséru; (blind) ...の目をくらます ...no mé wò kurámasu

DC [diːsiː'] abbr (= direct current) 直流 chokúryū

D-day [di:'dei] n 予定日 yotêibi

dead [ded] adj (not alive: person, animal) 死んだ shínda; (flowers) 枯れた karéta; (numb) しびれた shibíreta; (telephone) 通じない tsūjinai; (battery) 上がった agátta
♦adv (completely) 全く máttaku; (directly, exactly) 丁度 chódo
♦npl: **the dead** 死者 shíshà

to shoot someone dead 射殺す uchíkorosù

dead tired へとへとに疲れた hetóheto ni tsùkárèta

to stop dead 突然止る totsúzen tòmáru

deaden [ded'ən] vt (blow, pain) 和らげる yawáragerù; (sound) 鈍くする nibúkù suru

dead end n (street) 行き止り ikídomari

dead heat n (SPORT) 同着 dóchaku

deadline [ded'lain] n (PRESS etc) 締切り shimékiri

deadlock [ded'lɑːk] n (POL, MIL) 行き詰

り ikízumari

dead loss (inf) n: **to be a dead loss** (person) 役立たず yakútatàzu

deadly [ded'li:] adj (lethal: poison) 致命的な chiméiteki na; (devastating: accuracy) 恐ろしい osóroshiì; (: insult) 痛烈な tsúretsu na

deadpan [ded'pæn] adj (look, tone) 無表情の muhyójò no

Dead Sea n: **the Dead Sea** 死海 shikái

deaf [def] adj (totally) 耳の聞えない mimí no kíkòenai

deafen [def'ən] vt ...の耳を聞えなくする ...no mimí wò kikóenaku sùrú

deafness [def'nis] n 難聴 nánchō

deal [di:l] n (agreement) 取引 toríhikì
♦vt (pt, pp **dealt**) (card) 配る kubárù
a great deal (of) 沢山 (の) takúsan (nò)

dealer [di:'lə:r] n (COMM) 販売業者 hánbaigyòsha, ディーラー dírā

deal in vt fus (COMM) 取扱う toríatsukau

dealings [di:'liŋz] npl (business) 取引 toríhikì; (relations) 関係 kánkei

dealt [delt] pt, pp of **deal**

deal with vt fus (person) ...と取引をする ...to toríhikì wo suru; (problem) 処理する shórì suru; (subject) 取扱う toríatsukau

dean [di:n] n (REL) 主任司祭 shunínshisài; (SCOL) 学部長 gakúbuchò

dear [di:r] adj (person) 愛しい itóshiì; (expensive) 高価な kókà na
♦n: **my dear** あなた anátà, お前 omáe
♦excl: **dear me!** おや oyá ◊驚きを表す odóroki wo àráwasù
Dear Sir/Madam (in letter) 拝啓 hàíkei
Dear Mr/Mrs X 親愛なる...さん shín-ai narù ...sàn

dearly [di:r'li:] adv (love) 深く fukákù
to pay dearly for one's carelessness 自らの不注意が高く付く mízùkara no fuchúi gà tákàku tsukú

death [deθ] n (BIO) 死 shí, 死亡 shibó; (fig) 死 shí

death certificate n 死亡証明書 shibó-shōmeisho

deathly [deθ'li:] adj (color) 死人の様な shinín no yò na; (silence) 不気味な bukími na

death penalty n 死刑 shikéi

death rate n 死亡率 shibóritsu

death toll n 死者の数 shíshà no kázù

debacle [dəba:k'əl] n 大失敗 daíshippài

debar [diba:r'] vt: **to debar someone from doing** ...が...をするのを禁止する ...gà ...wo sùrú nò wo kínshi suru

debase [dibeis'] vt (value, quality) 下げる sagérù

debatable [dibei'təbəl] adj (decision, assertion) 疑問のある gimón no arù

debate [dibeit'] n (discussion, also POL) 討論 tórðn
♦vt 討議する tógì suru

debauchery [dəbɔː'tʃə:ri:] n (drunkenness, promiscuity) 放とう hótō

debilitating [dibil'əteitiŋ] adj (illness etc) 衰弱させる suíjaku sàséru

debit [deb'it] n (COMM) 支払額 shihárai-gàku
♦vt: **to debit a sum to someone/to someone's account** ...の口座から落す ...no kóza kara òtósù ¶ see direct

debris [dəbri:'] n (rubble) がれき garéki

debt [det] n 借金 shákkín
to be in debt 借金がある shàkkín gà árù

debtor [det'ə:r] n 負債者 fusáìsha

debunk [dibʌŋk'] vt (myths, ideas) ...の正体をあばく ...no shótaî wo abákù

début [deibju:'] n (THEATER, SPORT) デビュー débyū

decade [dek'eid] n 10年間 júnènkan

decadence [dek'ədəns] n (moral, spiritual) 堕落 daráku

decaffeinated [di:kæf'əneitid] adj カフェインを取除いた kaféìn wo torínozòìta

decanter [dikæn'tə:r] n (for wine, whiskey) デカンター dekántā

decay [dikei'] n (of meat, fish etc) 腐敗 fuhái; (of building) 老朽 rókyū; (of tooth) カリエス kárìesu
♦vi (rot: body, leaves etc) 腐敗する fuhái suru; (teeth) 虫歯になる mushíba ni narù

deceased [disi:st'] n: **the deceased** 故人

kójìn

deceit [disi:t'] *n* (duplicity) 偽り itsúwari

deceitful [disi:t'fəl] *adj* 不正な fuséi na

deceive [disi:v'] *vt* (fool) だます damásù

December [disem'bə:r] *n* 12月 jûnigatsu

decency [di:'sənsi:] *n* (propriety) 上品さ jóhìnsa; (kindness) 親切さ shínsetsusa

decent [di:'sənt] *adj* (proper) 上品な jóhìn na; (kind) 親切な shínsetsu na

deception [disep'ʃən] *n* ごまかし gomákashi

deceptive [disep'tiv] *adj* (appearance) 見掛けによらない mikáke ni yòranai

decibel [des'əbəl] *n* デシベル déshìberu

decide [disaid'] *vt* (person: persuade) 納得させる nattóku sàséru; (question, argument: settle) 解決する káìketsu su ru

♦*vi* 決める kiméru

to decide to do/that ...する〔...だ〕と決める ...sùrú 〔...da〕to kìméru

to decide on something (choose something) ...を選ぶ ...wo erábù

decided [disai'did] *adj* (resolute) 決意の固い kétsùi no katái; (clear, definite) はっきりした hakkírì shita

decidedly [disai'didli:] *adv* (distinctly) はっきりと hakkírì to; (emphatically: act, reply) き然と kizén to

deciduous [disidʒ'u:əs] *adj* (tree, bush) 落葉の rakúyō no

decimal [des'əməl] *adj* (system, currency) 十進法 jisshínhō

♦*n* (fraction) 小数 shósù

decimal point *n* 小数点 shósùten

decimate [des'əmeit] *vt* (population) 多数の...を死なせる tasú nò ...wo shináseru

decipher [disai'fə:r] *vt* (message, writing) 解読する kaídoku sùrú

decision [disiʒ'ən] *n* (choice) 決定した事 kettéi shita koto; (act of choosing) 決定 kettéi; (decisiveness) 決断力 ketsudànryoku

decisive [disai'siv] *adj* (action, intervention) 決定的な kettéiteki na; (person) 決断力のある ketsudànryoku no árù

deck [dek] *n* (NAUT) 甲板 kánpàn, デッキ dekkí; (of bus) 階 kái; (record deck)

デッキ dékkì; (of cards) 一組 hitókùmi

deckchair [dek'tʃe:r] *n* デッキチェア dekkíchèa

declaration [deklərei'ʃən] *n* (statement) 断言 dangèn; (public announcement) 布告 fukóku

declare [diklei:r'] *vt* (truth, intention, result) 発表する happyō suru; (reveal: income, goods at customs etc) 申告する shínkoku suru

decline [diklain'] *n*: *decline in/of* (drop, lowering) ...の下落 ...no gèraku; (lessening) ...の減少 ...no génshō

♦*vt* (turn down: invitation) 辞退する jítai suru

♦*vi* (strength, old person) 弱る yowárù; (business) 不振になる fushín ni narù

decode [di:koud'] *vt* (message) 解読する kaídoku suru

decompose [di:kəmpouz'] *vi* (organic matter, corpse) 腐敗する fùhái suru

décor [deikour'] *n* (of house, room) 装飾 shóshoku; (THEATER) 舞台装置 butáisōchi

decorate [dek'ə:reit] *vt* (adorn): *to decorate (with)* (...で) 飾る (...de) kazáru; (paint and paper) ...の室内を改装する ...no shitsúnài wo kaísō suru

decoration [dekərei'ʃən] *n* (on tree, dress etc) 飾り kazári; (act) 飾る事 kazáru koto; (medal) 勲章 kúnshō

decorative [dek'ə:rətiv] *adj* 装飾の sóshoku no

decorator [dek'ə:reitə:r] *n* (BRIT: painter) ペンキ屋 pénkiya

decorum [dikɔ:r'əm] *n* (propriety) 上品さ jóhìnsa

decoy [di:'kɔi] *n* (person, object) おとり otóri

decrease [*n* di:'kri:s *vb* dikri:s'] *n* (reduction, drop): *decrease (in)* 減少 génshō

♦*vt* (reduce, lessen) 減らす herásu

♦*vi* (drop, fall) 減る herú

decree [dikri:'] *n* (ADMIN, LAW) 命令 meírei

decree nisi [-nai'sai] *n* 離婚の仮判決 rikón no kàríhànketsu

decrepit [dikrep'it] *adj* (run-down: shack) おんぼろの ónboro no; (person) よぼよぼの yòboyobo no

dedicate [ded'ikeit] *vt* (time, effort etc): *to dedicate to* ...につぎ込む ...ni tsugí-komù; (oneself): *to dedicate to* ...に専念する ...ni sénnen suru; (book, record): *to dedicate to* ...に捧げる ...ni saságeru

dedication [dedikei'ʃən] *n* (devotion) 献身 kénshin; (in book, on radio) 献辞 kénji

deduce [didu:s'] *vt* 推測する suísoku suru

deduct [didʌkt'] *vt* (subtract) 差引く sashíhikù

deduction [didʌk'ʃən] *n* (act of deducing) 推測 suísoku; (act of deducting) 差引 sashíhiki; (amount) 差引く分 sashíhikù bùn

deed [di:d] *n* (feat) 行為 kóì; (LAW: document) 証書 shósho

deem [di:m] *vt* (judge, consider) ...だと判断する ...dá tò hándàn suru

deep [di:p] *adj* (hole, water) 深い fukáì; (in measurements) 奥行の okúyuki no; (voice) 太い futóì; (color) 濃い kóì

◆*adv: the spectators stood 20 deep* 観衆は20列に並んで立っていた kánshū wa nijûretsu ni naránde tàtte ita

a deep breath 深呼吸 shínkokyù

to be 4 meters deep 深さは4メータである fukásà wa yón mèta de árù

deepen [di:'pən] *vt* (hole, canal etc) 深くする fukákù suru

◆*vi* (crisis, mystery) 深まる fukámarù

deep-freeze [di:p'fri:z'] *n* 冷凍庫 réitōkò, フリーザー furízā

deep-fry [di:p'frai'] *vt* 揚げる agéru

deeply [di:p'li:] *adv* (breathe) 深く fukákù; (interested, moved, grateful) 非常に hijô ni

deep-sea diving [di:p'si:'-] *n* 深海ダイビング shínkaidàibingu

deep-seated [di:p'si:'tid] *adj* (beliefs, fears, dislike etc) 根の深い né nò fukáì

deer [di:r] *n inv* (ZOOL) シカ shiká

deerskin [di:r'skin] *n* シカ皮 shikágawa

deface [difeis'] *vt* (wall, notice) 汚す yogósu

defamation [defəmei'ʃən] *n* (LAW) 名誉毀損 méïyokisón

default [difo:lt'] *n* (COMPUT) デフォルト値 défórutone

by default (win) 不戦勝で fusénshō de

defeat [difi:t'] *n* (of enemy) 敗北 háiboku; (failure) 失敗 shippái

◆*vt* (enemy, opposition) 破る yabúrù

defeatist [difi:'tist] *adj* 敗北主義の háibokushugî no

◆*n* 敗北主義者 háibokushùgísha

defect [*n* di:'fekt *vb* difekt'] *n* (flaw, imperfection: in machine etc) 欠陥 kekkán; (: in person, character etc) 欠点 kettén

◆*vi: to defect to the enemy* 敵側に亡命する tekígawa ni bōmei suru

defective [difek'tiv] *adj* (goods) 欠陥のある kekkán no arù

defence [difens'] (*BRIT*) *n* = **defense**

defend [difend'] *vt* (protect, champion) 守る mamórù; (justify) 釈明する shàkúmei suru; (LAW) 弁護する bèngo suru; (SPORT: goal) 守る mamórù; (: record, title) 防衛する bôei suru

defendant [difen'dənt] *n* (LAW: in criminal case) 被告人 hìkôkunin; (: in civil case) 被告 hìkóku

defender [difen'də:r] *n* (*also fig*, SPORT) 防衛者 bôeishà

defense [difens'] (*BRIT* **defence**) *n* (protection, assistance) 防衛 bôei; (justification) 釈明 shàkúmei

defenseless [difens'lis] *adj* (helpless) 無防備の mùbôbi no

defensive [difen'siv] *adj* (weapons, measures) 防衛の bôei no; (behavior, manner) 釈明的な shàkúmeiteki na

◆*n: on the defensive* 守勢に立って shuséi ni tàtté

defer [difə:r'] *vt* (postpone) 延期する énki suru

deference [def'ə:rəns] *n* (consideration) 丁重さ tèîchòsa

defiance [difai'əns] *n* (challenge, rebellion) 反抗 hánkó

in defiance of (despite: the rules, someone's orders etc) ...を無視して ...wo múshî shite

defiant [difai'ənt] *adj* (challenging,

rebellious: tone, reply, person) 反抗的な hánkōteki na

deficiency [difiʃ'ənsi:] n (lack) 欠如 kétsùjo; (defect) 欠点 kettén

deficient [difiʃ'ənt] adj (inadequate): **deficient in** ...が不足している ...ga fùsóku shìté iru; (defective) 欠点の多い kettén no ối

deficit [def'isit] n (COMM) 赤字 akáji

defile [difail'] vt (memory, statue etc) 汚す kegásu

define [difain'] vt (limits, boundaries) 明らかにする akíraka ni suru; (expression, word) 定義する téigi suru

definite [def'ənit] adj (fixed) 決まった kimátta; (clear, obvious) 明白な mếîhaku na; (certain) 確実な kàkújitsu na **he was definite about it** 彼はその事をはっきり言った kárè wa sonố koto wò hakkírì ittá

definitely [def'ənitli:] adv (positively, certainly) 確実に kàkújitsu ni

definition [defəniʃ'ən] n (of word) 定義 téigi; (clearness of photograph etc) 鮮明さ sènmeisa

definitive [difin'ətiv] adj (account, version) 決定的な kèttéiteki na

deflate [difleit'] vt (tire, balloon) ...の空気を抜く ...no kūkî wo nukú

deflect [diflekt'] vt (fend off: attention, criticism) 回避する káîhi suru; (divert: shot, light) 横へそらす yokó e sòrásù

deform [difɔːrm'] vt (distort) 変形させる hénkei sàséru

deformed [difɔːrmd'] adj 変形した hénkei shita

deformity [difɔːr'miti:] n 奇形 kîkéi

defraud [difrɔːd'] vt: **to defraud someone (of something)** ...から (...を) だまし取る ...kàrá (...wo) dàmáshitorù

defrost [difrɔːst'] vt (fridge, windshield) ...の霜取りをする ...no shimótori wò suru; (food) 解凍する kàitō suru

defroster [difrɔːs'tər] (US) n 霜取り装置 shimótorisòchi

deft [deft] adj (movement, hands) 器用な kíyố na

defunct [difʌŋkt'] adj (industry, organi-

zation) 現存しない génzon shìnáì

defuse [di:fjuːz'] vt (bomb) ...の信管を外す ...no shínkan wo hàzúsu; (fig: crisis, tension) 緩和する kánwa suru

defy [difai'] vt (resist) ...に抵抗する ...ni téîkō suru; (challenge) 挑発する chốhatsu suru; (fig: description, explanation) ...の仕様がない ...no shìyố ga naî

degenerate
[vb didʒen'ə:reit adj didʒen'ə:rit]   vi (condition, health) 悪化する àkká suru ◆adj (depraved) 堕落した dárāku shita

degrading [digrei'diŋ] adj (conduct, activity) 恥ずべき hàzúbekî; (task etc) 誇りを傷つけられる様な hokóri wo kìzútsukerârérù yố na

degree [digri:'] n (extent) 度合 doái; (of temperature, angle, latitude) 度 do; (SCOL) 学位 gákùi **a degree in science** 科学の学位 súgaku no gákùi **by degrees** (gradually) 徐々に jójô ni **to some degree** ある程度 arú teîdo

dehydrated [di:hai'dreitid] adj (MED) 脱水状態の dassúijòtai no; (milk) エバミルク ebámirùku

de-ice [di:ais'] vt (windshield) ...の霜取りをする ...no shimótorî wo suru

deign [dein] vi: **to deign to do** ...をしてくれてやる ...wo shìté kurete yaru

deity [di:'iti:] n 神 kámî

dejected [didʒek'tid] adj (depressed) がっかりした gakkárî shita

delay [dilei'] vt 遅らせる okúraseru ◆vi (linger) 待つ mátsù; (hesitate) ためらう tàméraù ◆n (waiting period) 待つべき期間 mátsùbeki kikàn; (postponement) 延期 énki **to be delayed** (person, flight, departure etc) 遅れる ókúreru **without delay** 直ちに tádàchi ni

delectable [dilek'təbəl] adj (person) 美しい ùtsúkushiî; (food) おいしい òíshiî

delegate [n del'əgit vb del'əgeit] n 代表 dàíhyố ◆vt (person) 任命する nínmei suru; (task) 任せる màkáserù

delegation [deləgei'ʃən] n (group) 代表団

dáìhyŏdan; (by manager, leader) 任命 nínmei

delete [dili:t'] vt (cross out, also COMPUT) 消す kèsú, 削除する sákùjo suru

deliberate [adj dilib'ə:rit vb dilib'ə:reit] adj (intentional) 故意の kóì no; (slow) 落着いた òchítsuita
◆vi (consider) 熟考する jukkŏ suru

deliberately [dilib'ə:ritli:] adv (on purpose) 故意に kóì ni, わざと wázà to

delicacy [del'əkəsi:] n (of movement) しとやかさ shìtóyakasà; (of material) 繊細さ sénsaisa; (of problem etc) 微妙さ bìmyŏsa; (choice food) 珍味 chìnmi

delicate [del'əkit] adj (movement) しとやかな shìtóyakà na; (taste, smell, color) 淡い awáì; (material) 繊細な sénsai na; (approach, problem) 微妙な bimyŏ na; (health) 弱い yowáì

delicatessen [deləkətes'ən] n 総菜屋 sŏzaiya, デリカテッセン dèríkatessèn

delicious [dilíʃəs] adj (food) おいしい òíshìì; (smell) おいしそうな òíshisò na; (feeling) 心地好い kòkóchiyoì; (person) 魅力的な mìryókuteki na

delight [dilait'] n 喜び yòròkobi
◆vt (please) 喜ばす yòròkobasu
to take (a) delight in ...するのが大好きである ...surú nò ga dáìsuki de aru

delighted [dilai'tid] adj: **delighted (at/with)** (...で)喜んでいる (...de) yòròkònde iru
delighted to do 喜んで...する yòròkònde ...suru

delightful [dilait'fəl] adj (evening, house, person etc) 楽しい tànóshiì

delinquency [diliŋ'kwənsi:] n 非行 hikŏ

delinquent [diliŋ'kwint] adj (boy/girl) 非行の hikŏ no
◆n (youth) 非行少年〔少女〕hikŏshōnen〔shŏjo〕

delirious [dilir'i:əs] adj: **to be delirious** (with fever) うわ言を言う ùwágoto wo iu; (with excitement) 夢中になっている mùchū ni nattè irú

deliver [diliv'ə:r] vt (distribute) 配達する hàítatsu suru; (hand over) 引渡す hìkíwatasù; (message) 届ける tòdókerù; (MED: baby) ...の出産を助ける ...no shùssán wo tàsukerù
to deliver a speech 演説をする ènzetsu wo sùrú

delivery [diliv'ə:ri:] n (distribution) 配達 hàítatsu; (of speaker) 演説振り ènzetsuburi; (MED) 出産 shùssán
to take delivery of ...を受取る ...wo ùkétorù

delta [del'tə] n (of river) デルタ地帯 dèrútachitài

delude [dilu:d'] vt (deceive) だます damásù

deluge [del'ju:dʒ] n (also: **deluge of rain**) 大雨 ōamè; (fig: of petitions, requests) 殺到 sàttŏ

delusion [dilu:'ʒən] n (false belief) 錯覚 sàkkáku

de luxe [dilʌks'] adj (car, holiday) 豪華な gŏkà na

delve [delv] vi: **to delve into** (subject) ...を探求する ...wo tánkyū suru; (cupboard, handbag) ...の中を捜す ...no nákà wo sagásù

demand [dimænd'] vt 要求する yŏkyū suru
◆n 要求 yŏkyū; (ECON) 需要 juyŏ
to be in demand ...の需要がある ...no jùyŏ ga arú
on demand (available, payable) 請求次第 sèíkyūshidài

demanding [dimænd'iŋ] adj (boss, child) 気難しい kìmúzukashiì; (work) きつい kìtsuì

demarcation [di:mɑ:rkei'ʃən] n (of areas) 境 sàkáì; (of tasks) 区分 kúbùn

demean [dimi:n'] vt: **to demean oneself** 軽べつを招く事をする kèíbetsu wo mànékù kotó wo suru

demeanor [dimi:'nɔ:r] (BRIT **demeanour**) n 振舞 fùrúmai

demented [dimen'tid] adj 気の狂った kì nò kurúttà

demise [dimaiz'] n (end) 消滅 shŏmetsu; (death) 死亡 shibŏ

demister [dimis'tə:r] (BRIT) n (AUT) 霜取り装置 shimótorisŏchi

demo [dem'ou] (*BRIT: inf*) *n abbr* = **demonstration**

democracy [dimɑ:k'rəsi:] *n* (POL: system) 民主主義 mínshushugì; (country) 民主主義国 mínshushùgíkòku

democrat [dem'əkræt] *n* (*gen*) 民主主義者 mínshushugishà; (*US*) 民主党員 mínshutòin

democratic [deməkræt'ik] *adj* (*gen*) 民主的な mínshuteki na; (*US*) 民主党の mínshutō no

demolish [dimɑ:l'iʃ] *vt* (building) 取壊す toríkowasù; (*fig*: argument) 論破する rónpà suru

demolition [deməliʃ'ən] *n* (of building) 取壊し toríkowashi; (of argument) 論破 rònpa

demon [di:'mən] *n* (evil spirit) 悪魔 ákùma

demonstrate [dem'ənstreit] *vt* (prove: theory) 立証する rìsshó suru; (show: skill, appliance) 見せる misérù
♦*vi* (POL) デモをする démò wo suru

demonstration [demənstrei'ʃən] *n* (POL) デモ démò; (proof) 立証 risshó; (exhibition) 実演 jitsúen

demonstrator [dem'ənstreitə:r] *n* (POL) デモの参加者 démò no sánkashà; (COMM) 実演をする店員 jitsúen wo sùrú tén-in

demoralize [dimɔ:r'əlaiz] *vt* (dishearten) がっかりさせる gàkkárì saséru

demote [dimout'] *vt* (*also* MIL) 降格する kôkaku sùrú

demure [dimjur'] *adj* (smile, dress, little girl) しとやかな shitóyàka ná

den [den] *n* (of animal) 巣穴 sùána; (of thieves) 隠れ家 kàkúregà, アジト ájito; (room) 書斎 shòsái

denatured alcohol [di:nei'tʃə:rd-] (*US*) *n* 変性アルコール hénseiàrúkòoru

denial [dinai'əl] *n* (refutation) 否定 hītéi; (refusal) 拒否 kyóhì

denim [den'əm] *n* (fabric) デニム dénìmu

denims [den'əmz] *npl* ジーパン jípan, ジーンズ jínzù

Denmark [den'mɑ:rk] *n* デンマーク dénmākù

denomination [dinɑ:mənei'ʃən] *n* (of money) 額面 gakúmen; (REL) 宗派 shúhà

denominator [dinɑ:m'əneitə:r] *n* (MATH) 分母 búnbò

denote [dinout'] *vt* (indicate, represent) 示す shimésù

denounce [dinauns'] *vt* (person, action) 非難する hínàn suru

dense [dens] *adj* (crowd) 密集した mìsshú shita; (smoke, fog etc) 濃い kôì; (foliage) 密生した mìsséi shita; (*inf*: person) 鈍い nibúì

densely [dens'li:] *adv*: **densely populated** 人口密度の高い jínkōmitsùdo no takáì

density [den'siti:] *n* (of population: *also* PHYSICS) 密度 mítsùdo
single / double-density disk (COMPUT) 単(倍)密度ディスク tán(bái)mitsùdo disuku ◊日本語では廃語 nihón go de wà haígo

dent [dent] *n* (in metal or wood) へこみ hèkómi
♦*vt* (*also*: **make a dent in**) へこませる hèkómaseru

dental [den'təl] *adj* (treatment, hygiene etc) 歯科の shíká no

dental surgeon *n* 歯医者 haísha

dentist [den'tist] *n* 歯医者 haísha

dentistry [den'tistri:] *n* 歯科医学 shíkáigàku

dentures [den'tʃə:rz] *npl* 入れ歯 iréba

denunciation [dinʌnsi:ei'ʃən] *n* (condemnation) 非難 hínàn

deny [dinai'] *vt* (charge, allegation, involvement) 否定する hitéi suru; (refuse: permission, chance) 拒否する kyóhì suru

deodorant [di:ou'də:rənt] *n* 防臭剤 bôshùzai

depart [dipɑ:rt'] *vi* (visitor) 帰る káèru; (plane) 出発する shùppátsu suru; (bus, train) 発車する hàsshá suru
to depart from (*fig*: stray from) ...を離れる ...wo hànárerù

department [dipɑ:rt'mənt] *n* (COMM) 部 bú; (SCOL) 講座 kôza; (POL) 省 shô

department store n (COMM) デパート depātō

departure [dipɑːr'tʃəːr] n (of visitor) 帰る事 káeru koto; (of plane) 出発 shuppátsu; (of bus, train) 発車 hàsshá; (of employee, colleague) 退職 tàíshoku

a new departure (in or from policy etc) 新方針 shínhōshin

departure lounge n (at airport) 出発ロビー shuppátsurobī

depend [dipend'] vi: *to depend on* (be supported by) ...に頼っている ...ni tàyóttè irú; (rely on, trust) 信用する shínyō suru

it depends 時と場合によりけりだ tòkí tò baái ni yòríkeri dá

depending on the result ... 結果次第で... kèkkà shidài dé

dependable [dipen'dəbəl] adj (person) 頼りになる táyòri ni nárù; (watch, car etc) 信頼性の高い shínraisei no tàkáî

dependant [dipen'dənt] n 扶養家族 fuyōkazòku

dependence [dipen'dəns] n (on drugs, systems, partner) 依存 izón

dependent [dipen'dənt] adj: *to be dependent on* (person, decision) ...に頼っている ...ni tàyóttè iru

♦n = **dependant**

depict [dipikt'] vt (in picture) 描く egákù; (describe) 描写する byósha suru

depleted [dipliːt'id] adj (stocks, reserves) 減少した génshō shita

deplorable [diplɔːr'əbəl] adj (conditions) 悲惨な hísàn na; (lack of concern) 嘆かわしい nàgékawashiì

deplore [diplɔːr'] vt (condemn) 非難する hínàn suru

deploy [diplɔi'] vt (troops, resources) 配置する haíchi suru

depopulation [dipɑːpjəlei'ʃən] n 人口減少 jínkōgénshō

deport [dipɔːrt'] vt (criminal, illegal immigrant) 強制送還する kyósēisōkan suru

deportment [dipɔːrt'mənt] n (behavior, way of walking etc) 態度 tàído

depose [dipouz'] vt (ruler) 退位させる táiî

sàséru

deposit [dipɑːz'it] n (money: in account) 預金 yòkín; (: down payment) 手付金 tètsúkekin; (on bottle etc) 保証金 hòshōkín; (CHEM) 沈殿物 chíndènbutsu; (of ore) 鉱床 kóshō; (of oil) 石油埋蔵量 sèkíyumaízōryō

♦vt (money) 預金する yòkín suru; (case, bag) 預ける azúkerù

deposit account n 普通預金口座 fùtsúyokinkózà

depot [diː'pou] n (storehouse) 倉庫 sókò; (for vehicles) 車庫 shákò; (US: station) 駅 ékí

depraved [dipreivd'] adj (conduct, person) 邪悪な jàáku na

depreciate [dipriː'ʃieit] vi (currency, property, value etc) 値下がりする nèságari suru

depreciation [dipriːʃiːei'ʃən] n 値下がり nèságari

depress [dipres'] vt (PSYCH) 憂うつにさせる yúutsu ni sàséru; (price, wages) 下落させる gèráku saseru; (press down: switch, button etc) 押える osáerù; (: accelerator) 踏む fùmú

depressed [dsiprest'] adj (person) 憂うつな yúutsu na; (price, industry) 下落した gèráku shita

depressing [dipres'iŋ] adj (outlook, time) 憂うつな yúutsu na

depression [dipreʃ'ən] n (PSYCH) 憂うつ yúutsu; (ECON) 不況 fùkyó; (of weather) 低気圧 tèíkiatsù; (hollow) くぼみ kùbómi

deprivation [deprəvei'ʃən] n (poverty) 貧乏 bínbō

deprive [dipraiv'] vt: *to deprive someone of* (liberty, life) ...から奪う ...kárá ubáu

deprived [dipraivd'] adj 貧しい màzúshiî

depth [depθ] n (of hole, water) 深さ fùkásà; (of cupboard etc) 奥行 ókúyuki; (of emotion, feeling) 深さ tsúyòsa; (of knowledge) 豊富さ hófusa

in the depths of despair 絶望のどん底に zètsúbō no dònzoko ní

out of one's depth (in water) 背が立た

ない sé gà tatánài; (fig)力が及ばない chīkára gà òyóbanai

deputation [depjətei'ʃən] n (delegation) 代表団 dàihyōdàn

deputize [dep'jətaiz] vi: **to deputize for someone** (stand in) ...の代りに...する ...no kàwári ni ...sùrú

deputy [dep'jəti:] adj: **deputy head** (BRIT: SCOL: primary/secondary) 副校長 fùkúkōchō
♦n (assistant) 代理 dàiri; (POL) (下院) 議員 (kàin)gíin; (: also: **deputy sheriff**) 保安官代理 hồánkàndàiri

derail [direil'] vt: **to be derailed** 脱線する dàssén suru

derailment [direil'mənt] n 脱線 dàssén

deranged [direindʒd'] adj (person) 精神病の sēíshinbyō no

derby [də:r'bi:] (US) n (bowler hat) 山高帽 yàmátakabō

derelict [der'əlikt] adj (building) 廃虚になった hāīkyo ni nàttà

deride [diraid'] vt (mock, ridicule) ばかにする bàká ni suru

derisory [dirai'sə:ri:] adj (sum) 笑うべき wàráubekì; (laughter, person) ばかにする bàká ni suru

derivative [diriv'ətiv] n (CHEM) 派生物 hàséìbutsú; (LING) 派生語 hàséígo

derive [diraiv'] vt (pleasure, benefit) 受ける ùkérù
♦vi: **to derive from** (originate in) ...に由来する ...ni yùrái suru

dermatitis [də:rmətai'tis] n 皮膚炎 hīfúèn

derogatory [dirɑːg'ətɔːri:] adj (remark) 中傷的な chūshōteki na

derv [də:rv] (BRIT) n 軽油 kēíyu

descend [disend'] vt (stairs, hill) 降りる òrírù
♦vi (go down) 降りる òrírù
to descend from ...から降りる ...kárà orírù
to descend to (lying, begging etc) ...するまでに成り下がる ...surú madè ni narísagarù

descendant [disen'dənt] n 子孫 shísòn

descent [disent'] n (of stairs, hill, by person etc) 降りる事 òrírù koto; (AVIAT) 降下 kồkà; (origin) 家系 kàkéi

describe [diskraib'] vt (event, place, person, shape) 描写する byồsha suru

description [diskrip'ʃən] n (account) 描写 byồsha; (sort) 種類 shúrùi

descriptive [diskrip'tiv] adj (writing, painting) 写実的な shàjítsuteki na

desecrate [des'əkreit] vt (altar, cemetery) 汚す kègásu

desert [n dez'ə:rt vb dizə:rt'] n (GEO) 砂漠 sàbáku; (fig: wilderness) 殺風景な所 sàppūkei na tokóro
♦vt (place, post) 放置して逃亡する hồchi shite tồbō sùrú; (partner, family) 見捨てる mìsúteru
♦vi (MIL) 脱走する dàssố suru

deserter [dizə:r'tə:r] n (MIL) 脱走兵 dassốhei

desertion [dizə:r'ʃən] n (MIL) 脱走 dassố; (LAW) 遺棄 íkì

desert island n 熱帯の無人島 nèttái no mùjíntō

deserts [dizə:rts'] npl: **to get one's just deserts** 天罰を受ける tènbatsu wo ukérù

deserve [dizə:rv'] vt (merit, warrant) ...に値する ...ni àtái suru

deserving [dizə:r'viŋ] adj (person) 援助に値する énjò ni atái suru; (action, cause) 立派な rìppá na

design [dizain'] n (art, process) 意匠 ishố; (sketch) スケッチ sùkétchì; (layout, shape) デザイン dèzáīn; (pattern) 模様 mòyố; (intention) 意図 ítò
♦vt (house, kitchen, product etc) 設計する sèkkéi suru; (test etc) ...の案を作る ...no àn wo tsùkúrù

designate [vb dez'igneit adj dez'ignit] vt (nominate) 任命する nínmei suru
♦adj (chairman etc) 任命された nínmei sàréta

designer [dizai'nə:r] n (ART) デザイナー dèzáinā; (TECH) 設計者 sèkkéishà; (also: **fashion designer**) ファッションデザイナー fàsshóndezàinā

desirable [dizai'ə:rəbəl] adj (proper) 望ましい nòzómashiì; (attractive) 魅力的な

mĭryőkuteki na

desire [dizai'əːr'] *n* (urge) 望み nŏzŏmi; (*also*: **sexual desire**) 性欲 sĕiyoku
♦*vt* (want) 欲しがる hŏshîgarù; (lust after) ...とセックスをしたがる ...to sékkùsu wo shîtágarù

desk [desk] *n* (in office, for pupil) 机 tsŭkŭe, デスク dĕsùku; (in hotel) フロント fŭrőnto; (at airport) カウンター kâùntā; (*BRIT*: in shop, restaurant) 勘定カウンター kánjôkâuntā

desolate [des'əlit] *adj* (place) 物寂しい mònŏsabishîì; (person) 惨めな mĭjîme na

desolation [desəlei'ʃən] *n* (of place) 物寂しさ mònŏsabishìsà; (of person) 惨めさ mĭjîmesà

despair [dispe:r'] *n* (hopelessness) 絶望 zĕtsûbő
♦*vi*: **to despair of** (give up on) ...をあきらめる ...wo ákìramerù

despatch [dispæt'] *n, vt* = **dispatch**

desperate [des'pərit] *adj* (scream, shout) 恐怖の kyőfù no; (situation, shortage) 絶望的な zĕtsûbőteki na; (fugitive) 必死の hìsshî no
to be desperate for something/to do 必死の思いで...を欲しがって〔したがって〕いる hìsshî no ŏmŏî dé ...wó hŏshîgattè 〔shîtágattè〕irú

desperately [des'pəːritli:] *adv* (in despair, frantically: struggle, shout etc) 必死になって hìsshî ni nattè; (very) とても tŏtèmo

desperation [despərei'ʃən] *n* (recklessness) 必死の思い hìsshí no ŏmŏî
in (sheer) desperation 必死の思いで hìsshí no ŏmŏî dé, 死に物狂いで shînímonogurùi dé

despicable [des'pikəbəl] *adj* (action, person) 卑劣な hìrètsu na

despise [dispaiz'] *vt* 軽べつする kĕîbetsu suru

despite [dispait'] *prep* (in spite of) ...にもかかわらず ...nî mŏ kakáwarazu

despondent [dispɑːn'dənt] *adj* (downcast) 意気消沈している îkîshốchin shîté iru

despot [des'pət] *n* 暴君 bőkùn

dessert [dizəːrt'] *n* (CULIN) デザート dĕzátő

dessertspoon [dizəːrt'spuːn] *n* (object) 小さじ kŏsáji; (quantity) 小さじ一杯 kŏsáji íppai

destination [destənei'ʃən] *n* (of traveler) 目的地 mŏkútekîchi; (of mail) 宛先 átésaki

destined [des'tind] *adj*: **to be destined to do/for** ...する〔される〕事になっている ...sùrú 〔sareru〕koto nî náttě iru

destiny [des'təni:] *n* (fate) 運命 ùnmĕî

destitute [des'tituːt] *adj* (person) 一文無しの ìchímôn nàshi nő

destroy [distrɔi'] *vt* (demolish, wreck, *also fig*) 破壊する hàkái suru; (animal) 安楽死させる ánrakùshi sàseru

destroyer [distrɔi'əːr] *n* (NAUT) 駆逐艦 kùchîkukan

destruction [distrʌk'ʃən] *n* (act, state) 破壊 hàkái

destructive [distrʌk'tiv] *adj* (capacity, force) 破壊的な hàkáiteki na; (child) 暴れん坊の àbárembô no; (not constructive: criticism etc) 建設的でない kénsetsuteki de náî

detach [ditætʃ'] *vt* (remove, unclip, unstick) 外す hàzúsu

detachable [ditætʃ'əbəl] *adj* (removable) 外せる hàzúseru

detached [ditætʃt'] *adj* (attitude, person) 無とん着な mútŏnchaku na
a detached house 一軒家 ìkkén-yà

detachment [ditætʃ'mənt] *n* (aloofness) 無関心な mùkánshìn; (MIL: detail) 分遣隊 bùnkèntaî

detail [diteil'] *n* (fact, feature) 詳細 shősai; (no pl: in picture, one's work etc) 細かい事 kòmákaì kotő; (trifle) ささいな事 sásăi na kòmákaî
♦*vt* (list) 詳しく話す kùwáshìku hanásù
in detail 細かく kòmákakù

detailed [diteild'] *adj* (account, description) 細かい kòmákaî

detain [ditein'] *vt* (keep, delay) 引留める hîkítomerù; (in captivity) 監禁する kánkin sùrú; (in hospital) 入院させる nyűin saserù

detect [ditekt'] *vt* (sense) ...に感付く ...ni kánzukù; (MED) 発見する hàkkén suru; (MIL, POLICE, RADAR, TECH) 関知する kánchi suru

detection [ditek'ʃən] *n* (discovery) 発見 hàkkén

detective [ditek'tiv] *n* (POLICE) 刑事 kéîji

private detective 私立探偵 shìrítsutàntèî

detective story *n* 探偵小説 tànteishósetsù

detector [ditek'tə:r] *n* (TECH) 探知機 tánchikì

détente [deita:nt'] *n* (POL) 緊張緩和 kínchōkànwa, デタント dètánto

detention [diten'tʃən] *n* (arrest) 監禁 kánkin; (SCOL) 居残り inókori

deter [ditə:r'] *vt* (discourage, dissuade) 阻止する sóshì suru

detergent [ditə:r'dʒənt] *n* 洗剤 sénzai

deteriorate [diti:'ri:əreit] *vi* (health, sight, weather) 悪くなる wárùku nárù; (situation) 悪化する àkká suru

deterioration [diti:ri:ərei'ʃən] *n* 悪化 àkká

determination [ditə:rmənei'ʃən] *n* (resolve) 決意 kétsùi; (establishment) 決定 kèttéi

determine [ditə:r'min] *vt* (facts) 確認する kàkúnin suru; (limits etc) 決める kìméru

determined [ditə:r'mind] *adj* (person) 意志の強い íshì no tsùyóì

determined to do どうしても...すると決心している dōshitemo ...sùrú tò késshìn shité iru

deterrent [ditə:r'ənt] *n* (MIL, LAW) 抑止する物 yókùshi suru mònó

detest [ditest'] *vt* 嫌う kìráu

detonate [det'əneit] *vi* 爆発する bàkúhatsu suru

♦*vt* 爆発させる bàkúhatsu sàséru

detour [di:'tu:r] *n* (from route) 回り道 màwárimìchí; (US: AUT: diversion) う回路 ùkáîro

detract [ditrækt'] *vi*: *to detract from* (effect, achievement) ...を損なう ...wo sò-

kónaù

detriment [det'rəmənt] *n*: *to the detriment of* ...に損害を与えて ...ni sóngai wo àtáete

detrimental [detrəmen'təl] *adj*: *detrimental to* 損害になる sóngai ni nárù

devaluation [di:vælju:ei'ʃən] *n* (ECON) 平価切下げ hèîkakirîsage

devalue [di:væl'ju:] *vt* (work, person) 見くびる mìkúbirù; (currency) ...の平価を切り下げる ...no hèîka wo kìrísagerù

devastate [dev'əsteit] *vt* (destroy) さんざん荒らす sánzan àrásu; (*fig*: shock): *to be devastated by* ...に大きなショックを受ける ...ni ókìna shókkù wo ùkérù

devastating [dev'əsteitiŋ] *adj* (weapon, storm etc) 破壊力の大きい hàkáîryoku no ókìì; (announcement, news, effect) 衝撃的な shógekiteki na, ショッキングな shókkìngu ná

develop [divel'əp] *vt* (business, land, idea, resource) 開発する kàîhatsu sùrú; (PHOT) 現像する génzō sùrú; (disease) ...にかかる ...ni kàkárù; (fault, engine trouble) ...が発生する ...ga hàsséi suru

♦*vi* (advance) 発展する hàttén sùrú; (evolve: situation, disease) 発生する hàsséi sùrú; (appear: facts, symptoms) 現れる àráwarerù

developer [divel'əpə:r] *n* (*also*: **property developer**) 開発業者 kàîhatsugyósha

developing country [divel'əpiŋ-] *n* 発展途上国 hàtténtojōkokù

development [divel'əpmənt] *n* (advance) 発展 hàttén; (of affair, case) 新事実 shínjijitsù; (of land) 開発 kàîhatsu

deviate [di:'vi:eit] *vi*: *to deviate (from)* (...から) それる (...kára) sòrérù

deviation [di:vi:ei'ʃən] *n* 脱線 dàssén

device [divais'] *n* (apparatus) 仕掛け shìkáke

devil [dev'əl] *n* (REL, *fig*) 悪魔 ákùma

devilish [dev'əliʃ] *adj* (idea, action) 悪魔的な àkúmateki na

devious [di:'vi:əs] *adj* (person) 腹黒い hàrágurò

devise [divaiz'] *vt* (plan, scheme, machine) 発案する hàtsúan sùrú

devoid [dɪvɔɪd'] *adj*: **devoid of** (lacking) ...が全くない ...ga mầttaku naî

devolution [devəluː'ʃən] *n* (POL) 権限委譲 kéngenìjồ

devote [dɪvout'] *vt*: **to devote something to** (dedicate) ...に...をつぎ込む ...ni ...wo tsugíkomů

devoted [dɪvout'id] *adj* (loyal: service, friendship) 忠実な chūjitsu na; (: admirer, partner) 熱心な nésshin na
to be devoted to someone ...を熱愛している ...wo nètsúai shitè iru
the book is devoted to politics その本は政治の専門書である sonó hòn wa sèìji no sénmonsho dè árù

devotee [devoutiː'] *n* (fan) ファン fàn; (REL) 信徒 shíntò

devotion [dɪvou'ʃən] *n* (affection) 愛情 àijō; (dedication: to duty etc) 忠誠 chūsei; (REL) 信心 shínjìn

devour [dɪvauː'ər] *vt* (meal, animal) むさぼり食う mùsáborikúù

devout [dɪvaut'] *adj* (REL) 信心深い shínjinbùkâî

dew [duː] *n* (on grass) 露 tsúyù

dexterity [dekste:r'iti:] *n* (manual, mental) 器用さ kìyồsà

diabetes [daiəbiː'tis] *n* 糖尿病 tốnyōbyồ

diabetic [daiəbet'ik] *adj* 糖尿病の tốnyōbyō no
♦*n* 糖尿病患者 tốnyōbyōkànja

diabolical [daiəbɑːl'ikəl] *adj* (behavior) 悪魔的な àkúmateki na; (weather) ひどい hídôî

diagnose [daiəgnous'] *vt* (illness, problem) 診断する shíndan sùrú

diagnoses [daiəgnou'siːz] *npl of* **diagnosis**

diagnosis [daiəgnou'sis] (*pl* **diagnoses**) *n* 診断 shíndan

diagonal [daiæg'ənəl] *adj* (line) 斜めの nánamê nố
♦*n* (MATH) 対角線 tàīkakùsèn

diagram [dai'əgræm] *n* 図 zu

dial [dail] *n* (of phone, radio etc) ダイヤル dàîyaru; (on instrument, clock etc) 文字盤 mòjíban
♦*vt* (number) ダイヤルする dàíyaru sùrú

dial code (*BRIT* **dialling code**) *n* 市外番号 shígáibàngō

dialect [dai'əlekt] *n* 方言 hốgèn

dialogue [dai'ɔlɔːg] (*US also*: **dialog**) *n* (communication) 対話 tàīwa; (conversation) 会話 kàīwa

dial tone (*BRIT* **dialling tone**) *n* 発信音 hàsshín-òn, ダイヤルトーン dàīyarutồn

diameter [daiæm'itəːr] *n* 直径 chòkkeî

diamond [dai'mənd] *n* (gem) ダイヤモンド dàîyamòndo, ダイヤ dàîya; (shape) ひし形 híshígata

diamonds [dai'məndz] *npl* (CARDS) ダイヤ dàîya

diaper [dai'pəːr] (*US*) *n* おむつ ômútsù

diaphragm [dai'əfræm] *n* (ANAT) 横隔膜 ốkakumàkú; (contraceptive) ペッサリー péssarî

diarrhea [daiəri:'ə] (*BRIT* **diarrhoea**) *n* げり gèrí

diary [dai'əːri:] *n* (engagements book) 手帳 tèchồ; (daily account) 日記 nìkkî

dice [dais] *n inv* (in game) さいころ sàîkorô
♦*vt* (CULIN) 角切りにする kàkúgiri ni sùrú

dichotomy [daikɑːt'əmi:] *n* 二分化 nìbúnkà

Dictaphone [dik'təfoun] ® *n* ディクタフォーン dìkútafồn ◇一種の録音機の商品名 ísshù no ròkúonkì no shốhinmeì

dictate [dik'teit] *vt* (letter) 書取らせる kàkítorasèrú; (conditions) 指図する sáshizu sùrú

dictation [diktei'ʃən] *n* (of letter: *also* SCOL) 書取り kàkítori; (of orders) 指図 sáshizu

dictator [dik'teitəːr] *n* (POL, MIL, *fig*) 独裁者 dòkúsaìsha

dictatorship [dikteit'əːrʃip] *n* 独裁政権 dòkúsaisèîken

diction [dik'ʃən] *n* (in speech, song) 発音 hàtsúon

dictionary [dik'ʃəneːri:] *n* (monolingual, bilingual etc) 辞書 jíshò, 字引 jíbíki

did [did] *pt of* **do**

didactic [daidæk'tik] *adj* (teaching, purpose, film) 教育的な kyốikuteki na

didn't [did'ənt] = **did not**

die [dai] *vi* (person, animal) 死 ぬ shinú; (plant) 枯れる karéru; (*fig*: cease) やむ yámù; (: fade) 次第に消える shídai ni kiéru

to be dying for something/to do something 死ぬ程...が欲しい〔...をしたい〕 shinú hodo ...ga hoshíì〔...wo shitáì〕

die away *vi* (sound, light) 次第に消える shídai ni kiéru

die down *vi* (wind) 弱まる yowámarù; (fire) 小さくなる chíìsaku nárù; (excitement, noise) 静まる shízúmarù

diehard [dai'hɑːrd] *n* 頑固な保守派 gànko na hoshúha

die out *vi* (activity) 消えてなくなる kiéte nàkú narù; (animal, bird) 絶滅する zétsúmetsu sùrú

diesel [diːzəl] *n* (vehicle) ディーゼル車 dízerushà; (*also*: **diesel oil**) 軽油 kéìyu

diesel engine *n* ディーゼルエンジン dízeruènjin

diet [dai'ət] *n* (food intake) 食べ物 tabémònò; (restricted food: MED, when slimming) 減食 génshoku, ダイエット dáìetto

♦*vi* (*also*: **be on a diet**) 減食する génshoku sùrú, ダイエットする dáìetto sùrú

differ [dif'əːr] *vi* (be different): *to differ (from)* (...と) 違う (...to) chigáu; (disagree): *to differ (about)* (...について) 意見が違う (...ni tsuíte) íkèn ga chigáu

difference [dif'əːrəns] *n* (dissimilarity) 違い chigái; (disagreement) 意見の相違 íkèn no sóì

different [dif'əːrənt] *adj* 別の bétsu no

differentiate [difərən'tʃiːeit] *vi*: *to differentiate (between)* (...を) 区別する (...wo) kúbètsu sùrú

differently [dif'əːrəntliː] *adv* 違う風に chigáu fū ni

difficult [dif'əkʌlt] *adj* (task, problem) 難しい mùzúkashiī; (person) 気難しい kímúzúkashiī

difficulty [dif'əkʌltiː] *n* 困難 kònnàn; (problem) 問題 móndai

diffident [dif'idənt] *adj* (hesitant, self-effacing) 気の小さい kì nó chíìsaì

diffuse [*adj* difjuːs' *vb* difjuːz'] *adj* (idea, sense) 不鮮明な fùsénmèi na

♦*vt* (information) 広める hirómerù

diffuse light 反射光 hánshakō

dig [dig] (*pt, pp* **dug**) *vt* (hole, garden) 掘る hórù

♦*n* (prod) 小突く事 kozúkù kotó; (archeological) 発掘現場 hàkkútsugèn-ba; (remark) 当てこすり àtékosuri

digest [dai'dʒest] *vt* (food: *also fig*: facts) 消化する shōka suru

♦*n* (book) 要約 yōyaku, ダイジェスト版 dáìjesutoban

digestion [didʒes'tʃən] *n* (process) 消化 shōka; (system) 消化器系 shōkakikei

digestive [didʒes'tiv] *adj* (juices, system) 消化の shōka no

dig into *vt* (savings) 掘り出す hōrídasù

to dig one's nails into 引っかく hìkkákù

digit [didʒ'it] *n* (number) 数字 sūji; (finger) 指 yūbí

digital [didʒ'itəl] *adj* (clock, watch) デジタルの déjìtaru nó

digital computer *n* デジタルコンピュータ dèjítarukònpyūtá

dignified [dig'nəfaid] *adj* (person, manner) 品のある hín no arù

dignity [dig'nitiː] *n* (poise, self-esteem) 気品 kíhìn

digress [digres'] *vi*: *to digress (from)* (topic, subject) (...から) それる (...kárà) sórérù

digs [digz] (*BRIT*: *inf*) *npl* 下宿 geshúku

dig up *vt* (plant) 掘り起す hòríokosù; (information) 探り出す sàgúridasù

dike [daik] *n* = **dyke**

dilapidated [dilæp'ədeitid] *adj* (building) 老朽した rōkyū shitá

dilate [daileit'] *vi* (eyes) 見張る míháru

dilemma [dilem'ə] *n* (political, moral) 板挟み itábasàmì, ジレンマ jírēhma

diligent [dil'idʒənt] *adj* (worker, research) 勤勉な kínben na

dilute [diluːt'] *vt* (liquid) 薄める usúmeru, 希釈する kisháku sùrú

dim [dim] *adj* (light, room) 薄暗い ùsúguraì; (outline, figure) ぼんやりした bónyarì shitá; (*inf*: person) 頭の悪い àtáma no no wàrúî

♦vt (light) 暗くする kùráku sùrú; (AUT: headlights) 下向きにする shìtámuki ni sùrú

dime [daim] (US) n 10セント玉 jùssénto-dámà

dimension [dimen'tʃən] n (aspect) 面 mèn; (measurement) 寸法 súnpō; (also pl: scale, size) 大きさ ōkisa

diminish [dimin'iʃ] vi (size, effect) 小さくなる chíisakù nárù

diminutive [dimin'jətiv] adj (tiny) 小型の kògáta no
♦n (LING) 指小辞 shìshōjì

dimmers [dim'ə:rz] (US) npl (AUT: dipped headlights) 下向きのヘッドライト shìtámuki no hèddóraìto; (: parking lights) 車幅灯 shàfúkutō

dimple [dim'pəl] n (on cheek, chin) えくぼ ékùbo

din [din] n (row, racket) 騒音 sóon

dine [dain] vi 食事する shokúji suru

diner [dain'ə:r] n (person) レストランの客 résùtoran no kyakú; (US: restaurant) 簡易食堂 kań-ishokúdō

dinghy [diŋ'i:] n ボート bōto
rubber dinghy ゴムボート gomúbòto

dingy [din'dʒi:] adj (streets, room) 薄暗い usúgurài; (clothes, curtains etc) 薄汚い usúgitanaì

dining car [dain'iŋ-] n (RAIL) 食堂車 shokúdōsha

dining room [dain'iŋ-] n (in house, hotel) 食堂 shokúdō

dinner [din'ə:r] n (evening meal) 夕食 yūshoku; (lunch) 昼食 chūshoku; (banquet) 宴会 eńkai

dinner jacket n タキシード takíshìdo

dinner party n 宴会 eńkai

dinner time n (midday) 昼食時 chūshokudòki; (evening) 夕食時 yūshokudòki

dinosaur [dai'nəsɔ:r] n 恐竜 kyóryū

dint [dint] n: **by dint of** ...によって ...ni yottè

diocese [dai'əsis] n 司教区 shikyókù

dip [dip] n (slope) 下り坂 kudárizaka; (in sea) 一泳ぎ hitóòyòg; (CULIN) ディップ díppù

♦vt (in water etc) ...に浸す ...ni hitásù; (ladle etc) 入れる irérù; (BRIT: AUT: lights) 下向きにする shitámuki nī suru
♦vi (ground, road) 下り坂になる kudárizaka ni narù

diphthong [dif'θɔ:ŋ] n 二重母音 nijūboìn

diploma [diplou'mə] n 卒業証書 sotsúgyōshòsho

diplomacy [diplou'məsi:] n (POL) 外交 gaíkō; (gen) 如才なさ josáinasà

diplomat [dip'ləmæt] n (POL) 外交官 gaíkōkan

diplomatic [dipləmæt'ik] adj (mission, corps) 外交の gaíkō no; (person, answer, behavior) 如才ない josáinaì

dipstick [dip'stik] n (AUT) 油量計 yuryōkèi, オイルゲージ oírugèji

dipswitch [dip'switʃ] (BRIT) n (AUT) ヘッドライト切替えスイッチ heddóraìto kiríkaesuìtchi

dire [dai'ə:r] adj (consequences, effects) 恐ろしい osóroshiî

direct [direkt'] adj (route) 直行の chokkō no; (sunlight, light) 直射の chokúsha no; (control, payment) 直接の chokúsetsu no; (challenge) あからさまな akárasàma na; (person) 率直な sotchóku na
♦vt (address: letter) 宛てる atérù; (aim: attention, remark) 向ける mukérù; (manage: company, project etc) 管理する kánri suru; (play, film, programme) 監督する kańtoku suru; (order): **to direct someone to do something** ...に ...する様に命令する ...ni ...surú yō ni meírei suru
♦adv (go, write) 直接 chokúsetsu
can you direct me to ...? ...に行くにはどう行けばいいんですか ...ni ikú nī wa dō ikébà iîñ desu kà

direct debit (BRIT) n 自動振替 jidófùrikae

direction [direk'ʃən] n (way) 方向 hókō; (TV, RADIO, CINEMA) 演出 eńshutsu
sense of direction 方向感覚 hókōkañkaku

directions [direk'ʃənz] npl (instructions) 指示 shíjì
directions for use 取扱い説明 toríatsu-

kaisetsùmei

directly [direkt'li:] adv (in a straight line) 真っ直ぐに massúgù ni; (at once) 直ぐに súgù ni

director [direk'tər] n (COMM) 取締役 toríshimariyàku; (of project) 責任者 sekínìnsha; (TV, RADIO, CINEMA) 監督 kañtoku

directory [direk'tə:ri:] n (TEL) 電話帳 deñwachō; (COMPUT) ディレクトリー dirékutòrī; (COMM) 名簿 meíbo

dirt [də:rt] n (stains, dust) 汚れ yogóre; (earth) 土 tsuchí

dirt-cheap [də:rt'tʃi:p'] adj べら安の beráyàsu no

dirty [də:r'ti:] adj (clothes, face) 汚い kitánai, 汚れた yogóretà; (joke) わいせつ な waísetsu na
♦vt (clothes, face) 汚す yogósù

dirty trick n: **to play a dirty trick on someone** ...に卑劣なまねをする ...ni hirétsu na manè wo suru

disability [disəbil'əti:] n (also: **physical disability**) 身体障害 shíntaishōgai; (also: **mental disability**) 精神障害 seíshinshōgai

disabled [disei'bəld] adj (physically) 身体 障害のある shíntaishōgai no aru; (mentally) 精神障害のある seíshinshōgai no árù
♦npl: **the disabled** 身体傷害者 shíntaishōgaishà ◇総称 sōshō

disadvantage [disədvæn'tidʒ] n (drawback) 不利な点 fúrì na teñ; (detriment) 不利な立場 fúrì na tachíba

disaffection [disəfek'ʃən] n (with leadership etc) 不満 fumán

disagree [disəgri:'] vi (differ) 一致しない itchí shinaì; (be against, think otherwise): **to disagree (with)** (...と) 意見が合わない (...to) íkèn ga awánaì

disagreeable [disəgri:'əbəl] adj (encounter, person, experience) 嫌な iyá nà

disagreement [disəgri:'mənt] n (lack of consensus) 不一致 fuítchì; (argument) けんか keñka

disallow [disəlau'] vt (LAW: appeal) 却下する kyákkà suru

disappear [disəpiər'] vi (person, object, vehicle: from sight) 見えなくなる miénaku narù; (: deliberately) 姿を消す súgàta wo kesú; (custom etc) 消えてなくなる kiéte naku narù

disappearance [disəpiər'əns] n (from sight) 消える事 kiéru kotò; (deliberate) 失そう shissō; (of custom etc) なくなる事 nakú naru kotò

disappoint [disəpoint'] vt (person) がっかりさせる gakkárì sasérù

disappointed [disəpoin'tid] adj がっかりしている gakkárì shitě irù

disappointing [disəpoin'tiŋ] adj (outcome, result, book etc) 期待外れの kitáihazùre no

disappointment [disəpoint'mənt] n (emotion) 落胆 rakútan; (cause) 期待外れ kitáihazùre

disapproval [disəpru:'vəl] n 非難 hínàn

disapprove [disəpru:v'] vi: **to disapprove (of)** (person, thing) (...を) 非難の目で見る (...wo) hínàn no mé dè mírù

disarm [disɑ:rm'] vt (MIL) 武装解除する busōkaìjo suru

disarmament [disɑ:r'məmənt] n (MIL, POL) 軍備縮小 guñbishukushō

disarming [disɑ:rm'iŋ] adj (smile, friendliness) 心を和ませるような kokórò wo nagómaseru yō na

disarray [disərei'] n: **in disarray** (army, organization) 混乱して koñran shitè; (hair, clothes) 乱れて midáretè

disaster [dizæs'tər] n (also: **natural disaster**) 天災 teñsai; (AVIAT etc) 災害 saígai; (fig: mess) 大失敗 daíshippài

disastrous [dizæs'trəs] adj (mistake, effect, results) 悲惨な hisán na

disband [disbænd'] vt (regiment, group) 解散する kaísan suru
♦vi (regiment, group) 解散する kaísan suru

disbelief [disbili:f'] n 信じられない事 shiñjirarenai kotò

disc [disk] n (ANAT) つい間板 tsuíkanbañ; (record) レコード rekōdò; (COMPUT) = **disk**

discard [diskɑːrd'] *vt* (old things: *also fig*) 捨てる sutérù

discern [disəːrn'] *vt* (see) 見分ける miwákerù; (identify) 理解する ríkài suru

discerning [disəːr'niŋ] *adj* (judgement, look, listeners etc) 理解のある ríkài no árù

discharge [*vb* distʃɑːrdʒ' *n* dis'tʃɑːdʒ] *vt* (duties) 履行する rikő suru; (waste) 放出する hőshutsu suru; (patient) 退院させる taíin saserù; (employee) 解雇する káiko suru; (soldier) 除隊にする jotái ni surù; (defendant) 釈放する shakúhő suru
◆*n* (CHEM, ELEC) 放電 hőden; (MED) 排出 haíshutsu; (of employee) 解雇 káiko; (of soldier) 除隊 jotái; (of defendant) 釈放 shakúhő

disciple [disai'pəl] *n* (REL: *also fig*: follower) 弟子 deshí

discipline [dis'əplin] *n* (control) 規律 kirítsu; (self-control) 自制心 jiséishìn; (branch of knowledge) 分野 búñ-ya
◆*vt* (train) 訓練する kúñren suru; (punish) 罰する bassúrù

disc jockey [disk'-] *n* ディスクジョッキー disúkujokkì

disclaim [diskleim'] *vt* (knowledge, responsibility) 否定する hitéi suru

disclose [disklouz'] *vt* (interest, involvement) 打明ける uchíakerù

disclosure [disklou'ʒəːr] *n* (revelation) 打明け話 uchíakebanàshi

disco [dis'kou] *n abbr* (event) ディスコダンス disúkodañsu; (place) = **discotheque**

discolored [diskʌl'əːrd] (*BRIT* **discoloured**) *adj* (teeth, pots) 変色した heñshoku shitắ

discomfort [diskʌm'fəːrt] *n* (unease) 不安 fuấn; (physical) 不便 fúbèn

disconcert [diskənsəːrt'] *vt* どぎまぎさせる dőgìmagi saserù

disconnect [diskənekt'] *vt* (pipe, tap) 外す hazúsu; (ELEC) 切断する setsúdan suru; (TEL) 切る kírù

discontent [diskəntent'] *n* 不満 fumán

discontented [diskəntent'id] *adj* 不満の fumán no

discontinue [diskəntin'juː] *vt* (visits) やめる yamérù; (payments) 止める tomérù
discontinued (COMM) 生産中止 seísanchùshi

discord [dis'kɔːrd] *n* (quarrelling) 不和 fúwà; (MUS) 不協和音 fukyőwaòn

discordant [diskɔːr'dənt] *adj* (*fig*) 不協和音の fukyőwaòn no

discotheque [dis'koutek] *n* (place) ディスコ dísùko

discount [*n* dis'kaunt *vb* diskaunt'] *n* (for students, employees etc) 割引 waríbiki
◆*vt* (COMM) 割引く waríbikù; (idea, fact) 無視する múshì suru

discourage [diskəːr'idʒ] *vt* (dishearten) 落胆させる rakútan saserù; (advise against): *to discourage something* ...を阻止する ...wo sőshì suru
to discourage someone from doing ...するのを...に断念させようとする ...surú no wő ...ni dañnen saseyő to suru

discouraging [diskəːr'idʒiŋ] *adj* (remark, response) がっかりさせる様な gakkárì saséru na

discourteous [diskəːr'tiːəs] *adj* 失礼な shitsúrei na

discover [diskʌv'əːr] *vt* 発見する hakkén suru
to discover that (find out) ...だと発見する ...dá tò hakkén suru

discovery [diskʌv'əːriː] *n* 発見 hakkén

discredit [diskred'it] *vt* (person, group) ...の信用を傷付ける ...no shiñyő wő kizútsukerù; (claim, idea) ...に疑問を投げ掛ける ...ni gimőn wő nagékakerù

discreet [diskriːt'] *adj* (tactful, careful) 慎重な shiñchő na; (unremarkable) 目立たない medátanaì

discrepancy [diskrep'ənsiː] *n* (difference) 不一致 fuítchì

discretion [diskreʃ'ən] *n* (tact) 慎重さ shiñchősa
at the discretion of ...の判断次第で ...no hañdan shidài de

discriminate [diskrim'əneit] *vi*: *to discriminate between* ...と...を区別する ...to ...wo kúbètsu suru *to discriminate against* ...を差別する ...wo sábètsu suru

discriminating [diskrim'əneitiŋ] *adj* (public, audience) 理解のある ríkài no árù

discrimination [diskrimənei'ʃən] *n* (bias) 差別 sábètsu; (discernment) 理解 ríkài

discuss [diskʌs'] *vt* (talk over) 話し合う hanáshiàu; (analyze) 取上げる toríagerù

discussion [diskʌʃ'ən] *n* (talk) 話し合い hanáshiai; (debate) 討論 tôròn

disdain [disdein'] *n* 軽べつ keíbetsu

disease [diziːz'] *n* (MED, *fig*) 病気 byôki

disembark [disembɑːrk'] *vt* (goods) 陸揚げする rikúagè suru; (passengers: from boat) 上陸させる jôriku saserù; (: from plane, bus) 降ろす orósù
♦*vi* (passengers: from boat) 上陸する jôriku suru; (: from plane, bus) 降りる orí-rù

disenchanted [disentʃæn'tid] *adj*: *disenchanted (with)* (...の) 魅力を感じなくなった (...no) miryóku wò kañjinaku nattá

disengage [disengeidʒ'] *vt* (AUT: clutch) 切る kírù

disentangle [disentæŋ'gəl] *vt* ほどく hodókù

disfigure [disfig'jəːr] *vt* (person) ...の美ぼうを損なう ...no bibô wò sokónaù; (object, place) 汚す yogósù

disgrace [disgreis'] *n* (shame, dishonor) 恥 hají; (cause of shame, scandal) 恥ずべき事 hazúbeki kotò
♦*vt* (one's family, country) ...の恥になる ...no hají ni narù; (one's name) 汚す kegásù

disgraceful [disgreis'fəl] *adj* (behavior, condition, state) 恥ずべき hazúbeki

disgruntled [disgrʌn'təld] *adj* (supporter, voter) 不満の fumán no

disguise [disgaiz'] *n* (make-up, costume) 変装の道具 heñsô no dôgu; (art) 変装 heñsô
♦*vt* (person, object): *to disguise (as)* (...に) 見せ掛ける (...ni) misékakerù
in disguise 変装して heñsô shitè

disgust [disgʌst'] *n* (aversion, distaste) 嫌悪 kéñ-o
♦*vt* うんざりさせる uñzari saserù

disgusting [disgʌs'tiŋ] *adj* (revolting: food etc) むかつかせる mukátsukaserù; (unacceptable: behavior etc) いやな iyá nà

dish [diʃ] *n* (piece of crockery) 皿 sará; (food) 料理 ryôri
to do/wash the dishes 皿洗いをする saráarai wo suru

dishcloth [diʃ'klɔːθ] *n* (for washing) 皿洗いのふきん saráarai no fukíñ

dishearten [dishɑːr'tən] *vt* がっかりさせる gakkárì saserù

disheveled [diʃev'əld] (*BRIT* **dishevelled**) *adj* (hair, clothes) 乱れた midáretà

dishonest [disɑːn'ist] *adj* (person, means) 不正な fuséi na

dishonesty [disɑːn'isti:] *n* 不正 fuséi

dishonor [disɑːn'əːr] (*BRIT* **dishonour**) *n* 不名誉 fuméîyo

dishonorable [disɑːn'əːrəbəl] *adj* 不名誉な fuméîyo na

dish out *vt* (distribute) 配る kubárù

dishtowel [diʃ'tauəl] *n* 皿ぶきん sarábukiñ

dish up *vt* (food) 皿に盛る sará ni morù

dishwasher [diʃ'wɑːʃəːr] *n* (machine) 皿洗い機 saráaraikì

disillusion [disilu:'ʒən] *vt* ...の迷いを覚ます ...no mayóî wo samásù

disincentive [disinsen'tiv] *n* (to work, investment) 阻害要因 sogáiyòin

disinfect [disinfekt'] *vt* 消毒する shôdoku suru

disinfectant [disinfek'tənt] *n* 消毒剤 shôdokuzài

disintegrate [disin'təgreit] *vi* (object) 分解する buñkai suru

disinterested [disin'tristid] *adj* (impartial: advice, help) 私欲のない shiyóku no naî

disjointed [disdʒɔint'id] *adj* (thoughts, words) まとまりのない matómari no naî

disk [disk] *n* (COMPUT) ディスク dísùku

disk drive *n* ディスクドライブ disúkudoraíbu

diskette [disket'] *n* = **disk**

dislike [dislaik'] *n* (feeling) 嫌悪 kéñ·o; (*gen pl*: object of dislike) 嫌いな物 kirái na monò
♦*vt* 嫌う kiráù

dislocate [dis'loukeit] *vt* (joint) 脱きゅうさせる dakkyū saserù

dislodge [dislɑːdʒ'] *vt* (boulder etc) 取除く torínozokù

disloyal [disloi'əl] *adj* (to country, family) 裏切り者の urágirimono no

dismal [diz'məl] *adj* (depressing: weather, song, person, mood) 陰気な íñki na; (very bad: prospects, failure) 最低の saítei no

dismantle [dismæn'təl] *vt* (machine) 分解する buñkai suru

dismay [dismei'] *n* 困惑 koñwaku
♦*vt* 困惑させる koñwaku saserù

dismiss [dismis'] *vt* (worker) 解雇する káīko suru; (pupils, soldiers) 解散させる kaísan saseru; (LAW: case) 却下する kyákkà suru; (possibility, idea) 考えない様にする kañgaenai yō ni suru

dismissal [dismis'əl] *n* (sacking) 解雇 káīko

dismount [dismaunt'] *vi* (from horse, bicycle) 降りる orírù

disobedience [disəbi:'di:əns] *n* 不服従 fufúkujù

disobedient [disəbi:'di:ənt] *adj* (child, dog) 言う事を聞かない iú koto wò kikánaì

disobey [disəbei'] *vt* (person, order) 違反する ihán suru

disorder [disɔːr'dəːr] *n* (untidiness) 乱雑さ rañzatsu; (rioting) 騒動 sōdō; (MED) 障害 shōgai

disorderly [disɔːr'dəːli:] *adj* (untidy: room etc) 整理されていない seíri sarete inaì; (meeting) 混乱の koñran no; (behavior) 治安を乱す chián wò midásù

disorganized [disɔːr'gənaizd] *adj* (person, event) 支離滅裂な shírìmetsúretsu na

disorientated [disɔː'ri:inteitid] *adj* (person: after journey, deep sleep) 頭が混乱

している atáma gà koñran shite irù

disown [disoun'] *vt* (action) ...との関係を否定する ...tó nò kañkei wò hitéi suru; (child) 勘当する kañdō suru

disparaging [dispær'idʒiŋ] *adj* (remarks) 中傷的な chūshōteki na

disparate [dis'pəːrit] *adj* (levels, groups) 異なった kotónattà

disparity [dispæːr'iti:] *n* 差異 sáì

dispassionate [dispæʃ'ənit] *adj* (approach, reaction) 客観的な kyakkánteki na

dispatch [dispætʃ'] *vt* (send: message, goods, mail) 送る okúrù; (: messenger) 派遣する hakén suru
♦*n* (sending) 送付 sōfu; (PRESS, MIL) 派遣 hakén

dispel [dispel'] *vt* (myths, fears) 払いのける haráinokerù

dispense [dispens'] *vt* (medicines) 調剤する chōzai suru

dispenser [dispen'səːr] *n* (machine) 自動販売機 jidōhanbaikī

dispense with *vt fus* (do without) ...なしで済ませる ...náshì de sumáserù

dispensing chemist [dispens'iŋ-] (*BRIT*) *n* (shop) 薬屋 kusúriya

dispersal [dispəːr'səl] *n* (of objects, group, crowd) 分散 buñsan

disperse [dispəːrs'] *vt* (objects, crowd etc) 散らす chirásù
♦*vi* (crowd) 散って行く chitté ikù

dispirited [dispir'itid] *adj* 意気消沈した íkìshōchin shita

displace [displeis'] *vt* (shift) 押し出す o-shídasù

displaced person [displeist'-] *n* (POL) 難民 nañmin

display [displei'] *n* (in shop) 陳列 chiñretsu; (exhibition) 展示 teñji; (of feeling) 表現 hyōgen; (COMPUT, TECH) ディスプレー disúpurè, モニター mónìtā
♦*vt* (show) 展示する teñji suru; (ostentatiously) 見せびらかす misébirakasù

displease [displiːz'] *vt* (offend, annoy) 怒らせる okóraserù

displeased [displiːzd'] *adj*: *displeased with* (unhappy, disappointed) ...にがっか

りしている ...ni gakkárì shité irù

displeasure [displɛʒ'ər] n 怒り ikári

disposable [dispou'zəbəl] adj (lighter, bottle) 使い捨ての tsukáisute no; (income) 自由に使える jiyú nì tsukáerù

disposable nappy (BRIT) n 紙おむつ kamfòmutsù

disposal [dispou'zəl] n (of goods for sale) 陳列 chíñretsu; (of property) 売却 baíkyaku; (of rubbish) 処分 shóbun
at one's disposal ...の自由になる ...no jiyú ni narù

dispose [dispouz'] vi: *to dispose of* (get rid of: body, unwanted goods) 始末する shímàtsu suru; (deal with: problem, argument) 片付ける katázukerù

disposed [dispouzd'] adj: *disposed to do* (inclined, willing) ...する気がある ...surú ki gà árù
to be well disposed towards someone ...に好意を寄せている ...ni kóì wo yoséte irù

disposition [dispəziʃ'ən] n (nature) 性質 seíshitsu; (inclination) 傾向 keíkō

disproportionate [disprəpɔ:r'ʃənit] adj (amount, effect) 過剰な kajṓ na

disprove [dispru:v'] vt (belief, assertion) 反証する haríshō suru

dispute [dispju:t'] n (domestic) けんか keñka; (also: **industrial dispute**) 争議 sṓgi; (POL) 論議 róñgi
♦vt (fact, statement) 反ばくする hañbaku suru; (ownership etc) 争う arásòu
territorial dispute 領土紛争 ryṓdofuñsō
border dispute 国境紛争 kokkyṓfuñsō

disqualify [diskwa:l'əfai] vt (SPORT) ...の資格を取り上げる ...no shikáku wò toríagerù
to disqualify someone for something/from doing something ...から ...の〔...する〕資格を取上げる ...kárà ...no 〔...surú〕shikáku wò toríagerù

disquiet [diskwai'it] n (anxiety) 不安 fuán

disregard [disrigɑ:rd'] vt (ignore, pay no attention to) 無視する múshì suru

disrepair [disripe:r'] n: *to fall into*

disrepair (machine, building) ひどく痛んでしまう hídòku itáñde shimaù

disreputable [disrep'jətəbəl] adj (person, behavior) いかがわしい ikágawashiì

disrespectful [disrispekt'fəl] adj (person, conduct) 無礼な búrèi na

disrupt [disrʌpt'] vt (plans) 邪魔する jamá suru; (conversation, proceedings) 妨害する bṓgai suru

disruption [disrʌp'ʃən] n (interruption) 中断 chúdan; (disturbance) 妨害 bṓgai

dissatisfaction [dissætisfæk'ʃən] n 不満 fumán

dissatisfied [dissæt'isfaid] adj 不満な fumán na

dissect [disekt'] vt (dead person, animal) 解剖する kaíbō suru

disseminate [disem'əneit] vt 普及させる fukyṓ saserù

dissent [disent'] n (disagreement, protest) 反対 hañtai

dissertation [disə:rtei'ʃən] n (also SCOL) 論文 roñbun

disservice [dissə:r'vis] n: *to do someone a disservice* (person: harm) ...に迷惑を掛ける ...ni meíwaku wo kakérù

dissident [dis'idənt] adj (faction, voice) 反対の hañtai no
♦n (POL, REL) 反対分子 hañtaibuñshi

dissimilar [disim'ilə:r] adj 異なる kotónarù

dissipate [dis'əpeit] vt (heat) 放散する hṓsan suru; (clouds) 散らす chirásù; (money, effort) 使い果す tsukáihatasù

dissociate [disou'ʃi:eit] vt ...との関係を否定する ...tó nò kañkei wò hitéi suru
to dissociate oneself from ...との関係を否定する ...tó nò kañkei wò hitéi suru

dissolute [dis'əlu:t] adj (individual, behavior) 道楽ざんまいの dṓrakuzañmai no

dissolution [disəlu:'ʃən] n (of organization, POL) 解散 kaísan; (of marriage) 解消 kaíshō

dissolve [diza:lv'] vt (in liquid) 溶かす tokásù; (organization, POL) 解散させる kaísan saserù; (marriage) 解消する kaíshō suru

◆*vi* (material) 溶ける tokérù

to dissolve in(to) tears 泣崩れる nakíkuzurerù

dissuade [disweid'] *vt*: *to dissuade someone (from)* (...を) 思い止まる様 ...を説得する (...wo) omóitodomaru yố ...wo settóku suru

distance [dis'təns] *n* (gap: in space) 距離 kyórì; (: in time) 隔たり hedátarì

in the distance ずっと向うに zúttò mukố nì

distant [dis'tənt] *adj* (place, time, relative) 遠い tối; (manner) よそよそしい yosóyososhiì

distaste [disteist'] *n* (dislike) 嫌悪 kén̄o

distasteful [disteist'fəl] *adj* (offensive) いやな iyá nà

distended [distend'id] *adj* (stomach) 膨らんだ fukúraǹda

distill [distil'] (*BRIT* **distil**) *vt* (water, whiskey) 蒸留する jőryū suru

distillery [distil'ə:ri:] *n* 醸造所 jőzōjò

distinct [distiŋkt'] *adj* (different) 別個の békkò no; (clear) はっきりした hakkírì shita; (unmistakable) 明白な meíhaku na

as distinct from (in contrast to) ...ではなくて ...dé wà nákùte

distinction [distiŋk'ʃən] *n* (difference) 区別 kúbètsu; (honor) 名誉 meíyo; (in exam) 優等の成績 yútō no seisèki

distinctive [distiŋk'tiv] *adj* 独特な dokútoku na

distinguish [distiŋ'gwiʃ] *vt* (differentiate) 区別する kúbètsu suru; (identify: details etc: by sight) 見分ける miwákerù; (: by sound) 聞分ける kikíwakerù

to distinguish oneself (in battle etc) 見事な活躍をする mígòto na katsúyaku wo surù

distinguished [distiŋ'gwiʃt] *adj* (eminent) 有名な yúmei na; (in appearance) 気品のある kihín no arù

distinguishing [distiŋ'gwiʃiŋ] *adj* (feature) 特徴的な tokúchōteki na

distort [distɔ:rt'] *vt* (argument) 曲げる magérù; (sound) ひずませる hizúmaserù; (shape, image) ゆがめる yugámerù

distortion [distɔ:r'ʃən] *n* (of argument

etc) わい曲 waíkyoku; (of sound, image, shape etc) ひずみ hizúmi

distract [distrækt'] *vt* (sb's attention) 散らす chirásù; (person) ...の気を散らす ...no ki wo chirásù

distracted [distræk'tid] *adj* (dreaming) ぼんやりした boñ-yarì shita; (anxious) 気が動転している ki ga dốten shite irù

distraction [distræk'ʃən] *n* (inattention) 気を散らす事[物] ki wo chirásù kotó [monő]; (confusion) 困惑 koñwaku; (amusement) 気晴らし kibárashi

distraught [distrɔ:t'] *adj* (with pain, worry) 気が動転している ki ga dốten shite irù

distress [distres'] *n* (anguish) 苦痛 kutsū
◆*vt* (cause anguish) 苦しめる kurúshimerù

distressing [distres'iŋ] *adj* (experience, time) 苦しい kurúshiì

distress signal *n* (AVIAT, NAUT) 遭難信号 sốnanshiǹgō

distribute [distrib'jut] *vt* (hand out: leaflets, prizes etc) 配る kubárù; (share out: profits etc) 分ける wakérù; (spread out: weight) 分布する búñpu suru

distribution [distrəbju:'ʃən] *n* (of goods) 流通 ryūtsū; (of profits etc) 分配 buñpai

distributor [distrib'jətə:r] *n* (COMM) 流通業者 ryūtsūgyòsha; (AUT, TECH) ディストリビュータ disútoribyùta

district [dis'trikt] *n* (of country) 地方 chihố; (of town, ADMIN) 地区 chíkù

district attorney (*US*) *n* 地方検事 chihốkeǹji

district nurse (*BRIT*) *n* 保健婦 hokéñfu

distrust [distrʌst'] *n* 不信感 fushíñkan
◆*vt* 信用しない shiñ-yō shinaì

disturb [distə:rb'] *vt* (interrupt) 邪魔する jamá suru; (upset) 心配させる shiñpai serù; (disorganize) 乱す midásù

disturbance [distə:r'bəns] *n* (upheaval) 邪魔 jamá; (political etc) 騒動 sốdō; (violent event) 動乱 dốran; (of mind) 心配 shiñpai

disturbed [distə:rbd'] *adj* (person: worried, upset) 不安な fuán na; (childhood)

乱れた midáretà
emotionally disturbed 情緒障害の jó-choshōgai no

disturbing [distə:rb'iŋ] *adj* (experience, moment) 動転させる dōten saserù

disuse [disju:s'] *n*: **to fall into disuse** (be abandoned: methods, laws etc) 廃れる sutárerù

disused [disju:zd'] *adj* (building, airfield) 使われていない tsukáwarete inaì

ditch [ditʃ] *n* (at roadside) どぶ dobú; (also: **irrigation ditch**) 用水路 yōsuirò
♦*vt* (inf: person) ...と縁を切る ...to én wo kírù; (: plan, car etc) 捨てる sutérù

dither [ðið'ə:r] (pej) *vi* (hesitate) ためらう tamérau

ditto [dit'ou] *adv* 同じく onájìku

divan [divæn'] *n* (also: **divan bed**) ソファベッド sofábeddò

dive [daiv] (*pt* **dived** *also US* **dove**, *pp* **dived**) *n* (from board) 飛込み tobíkomi; (underwater) 潜水 sensui, ダイビング dáìbingu; (of submarine) 潜水 sensui
♦*vi* (swimmer: into water) 飛込む tobíkomù; (under water) 潜水する sensui suru, ダイビングする dáibingu suru; (fish) 潜る mogúrù; (bird) 急降下する kyúkòka suru; (submarine) 潜水する sensui suru
to dive into (bag, drawer etc) ...に手を突っ込む ...ni té wò tsukkómù; (shop, car etc) ...に飛込む ...ni tobíkomù

diver [dai'və:r] *n* (person) ダイバー dáìbā

diverge [divə:rdʒ'] *vi* (paths, interests) 分かれる wakárerù

diverse [divə:rs'] *adj* 様々な samázàma na

diversify [divə:r'səfai] *vi* (COMM) 多様化する tayōka suru

diversion [divə:r'ʒən] *n* (BRIT: AUT) う回路 ukáirò; (distraction) 気分転換 kibúnteñkan; (of funds) 流用 ryūyō

diversity [divə:r'siti:] *n* (range, variety) 多様性 tayōsei

divert [divə:rt'] *vt* (funds) 流用する ryūyō suru; (someone's attention) 反らす sorásù; (re-route) う回させる ukái saserù

divide [divaid'] *vt* (separate) 分ける wakérù; (MATH) 割る warú; (share out) 分

ける wakérù, 分配する buñpai suru
♦*vi* (cells etc) 分裂する buñretsu suru; (road) 分岐する búnki suru; (people, groups) 分裂する buñretsu suru
8 divided by 4 is 2 8割る4は2 hachí warù yón wa ní

divided highway [divaid'id-] (US) *n* 中央分離帯のある道路 chūōbuñritai no árù dōrò

dividend [div'idend] *n* (COMM) 配当金 haftōkiñ; (fig): **to pay dividends** 利益になる ríeki ni nárù

divine [divain'] *adj* (REL) 神の kámì no; (fig: person, thing) 素晴らしい subárashiì

diving [daiv'iŋ] *n* (underwater) 飛込み tobíkomi; (SPORT) 潜水 sensui, ダイビング dáibingu

diving board *n* 飛込み台 tobíkomidài

divinity [divin'əti:] *n* (nature) 神性 shiñsei; (god) 神 kámì; (subject) 神学 shiñgàku

division [diviʒ'ən] *n* (of cells etc) 分裂 buñretsu; (MATH) 割算 warízan; (sharing out) 分配 buñpai; (disagreement) 分裂 buñretsu; (COMM) 部門 búmòn; (MIL) 師団 shídàn; (especially SOCCER) 部 bú

divorce [divɔ:rs'] *n* 離婚 ríkòn
♦*vt* (spouse) ...と離婚する ...to ríkòn suru; (dissociate) 別々に扱う betsúbetsu nì atsúkaù

divorcé [divɔ:rsi:'] *n* 離婚男性 rikóndañsei

divorced [divɔ:rst'] *adj* 離婚した ríkòn-shita

divorcée [divɔ:rsi:'] *n* 離婚女性 rikónjòsei

divulge [divʌldʒ'] *vt* (information, secret) 漏らす morásù

D.I.Y. [di:aiwai'] (BRIT) *n abbr* = **do-it-yourself**

dizzy [diz'i:] *adj*: **a dizzy spell/turn** めまい memáì
to feel dizzy めまいがする memáî ga suru

DJ [di:'dʒei] *n abbr* (= *disk jockey*) ディスクジョッキー disúkujokkì

KEYWORD

do [du:] (*pt* **did**, *pp* **done**) *aux vb* **1** (in negative constructions): *I don't understand* 分かりません wakárimasèn

she doesn't want it 彼女はそれを欲しがっていません kánojo wa soré wo hoshígattè imásèn

he didn't seem to care 彼はどうでもいい様でした kárè wa dó de mo iî yō deshita

2 (to form questions): *didn't you know?* 知りませんでしたか shirímasèn deshita ká

why didn't you come? どうして来てくれなかったのですか dóshìte kité kùrénakàtta no desu ká

what do you think? どう思いますか dô omóimasù ká

3 (for emphasis, in polite expressions): *people do make mistakes sometimes* だれだって間違いをしますよ dáre datte machígaì wo shimásù yo

she does seem rather late そう言えば彼女は本当に遅い様ですね só iebà kánojo wa hôntō ni òsói yô desu nê

do sit down/help yourself どうぞお掛け〔お召し上がり〕下さい dôzo o-káke 〔o-méshiagari〕kudasái

do take care! くれぐれもお気をつけて kurégurè mo o-kí wo tsuketè

oh do shut up! いい加減に黙ってくれませんか iíkagen ni dámáttè kurémasèn ká

4 (used to avoid repeating vb): *she swims better than I do* 彼女は私より泳ぎがうまい kánojo wa watákushi yorí oyógi gà umáì

do you agree? - yes, I do/no, I don't 賛成しますか - はい，します〔いいえ，しません〕sánsei shimasù ká · háì, shimásù〔iíe, shimásèn〕

she lives in Glasgow - so do I 彼女はグラスゴーに住んでいます - 私もそうです kánojo wa gurásugò ni súndè imásù · watákushi mo sō dèsu

he didn't like it and neither did we 彼はそれを気に入らなかったし，私たち

もそうでした kárè wa soré wo kì ní iranakàtta shi, watákushitàchi mó sō dèshita

who made this mess? - I did だれだ，ここを汚したのは - 私です dárè da, kokó wo yògóshita nò wa - watákushi desù

he asked me to help him and I did 助けてくれと彼に頼まれたのでそうしました tasúketè kure to kárè ni tanómaretà no de só shimashìta

5 (in question tags): *you like him, don't you?* あなたは彼を好きでしょう？ anáta wa kárè wo sukí dèshô?

he laughed, didn't he? 彼は笑ったでしょう？ kárè wa waráttà dèshô?

I don't know him, do I? 私の知らない人でしょう？ watákushi no shìránai hito dèshô?

♦*vt* **1** (*gen*: carry out, perform etc) する surú, やる yarú

what are you doing tonight? 今夜のご予定は? kòn-ya no gò-yótei wá?

have you done your homework? 宿題をしましたか shùkúdai wo shìmáshìta ká

I've got nothing to do 何もする事がありません nàní mo surú koto gà arímasèn

what can I do for you? どんなご用でしょうか dònna go-yô dèshô ka

to do the cooking/washing-up 料理〔皿洗い〕をする ryóri〔saráàrai〕wo surú

to do one's teeth/hair/nails 歯を磨く〔髪をとかす，つめにマニキュアをする〕 há wò migáku〔kàmí wò tokásù, tsùmé ni mànîkyua wo surú〕

we're doing "Othello" at school (studying it) 学校で今オセロを勉強しています gàkkô de ímà ósèro wo bénkyō shite imasù; (performing it) 学校で今オセロを上演しています gàkkô de ímà ósèro wo jōen shite imasù

2 (AUT etc) 走る hashírù

the car was doing 100 車は時速100マイルを出していた kurúma wa jisóku hyakúmaìru wo dáshìte ita

we've done 200 km already 私tachiはもう200キロメーター走ってきました watákushitàchi wa mô nihyákukiromètā hashíttè kimáshìta

he can do 100 mph in that car あの車で彼は時速100マイル出せます anó kuruma de karè wa jisóku hyàkúmàiru dasémasù

♦*vi* 1 (act, behave) する sùrú

do as I do 私のする通りにしなさい watákushi no sùrú tōrì ni shinásaì

do as I tell you 私の言う通りにしなさい watákushi no iu tōrì ni shinásaì

you did well to come so quickly すぐに来てくれて良かったよ súgù ni kité kùrete yókàtta yó

2 (get on, fare): *he's doing well/badly at school* 彼は学校の成績がいい〔良くない〕kárè wa gakkố no seiseki ga ìi 〔yokùnáì〕

the firm is doing well 会社は繁盛しています kaísha wa hànjō shité imasù

how do you do? 初めまして hajímemashìte

3 (suit) 適当である tekítō de arù

will it do? 役に立ちますか yakú nì tachímasù ká

will this dress do for the party? パーティにはこのドレスでいいかしら paấtì ni wa konó dorèsu de íi kashira

4 (be sufficient) 間に合う júbùn de árù

will £10 do? 10ポンドで間に合いますか júppòndo de ma ní aimasù ká

that'll do 十分です júbùn desu

that'll do! (in annoyance) いい加減にしなさい íìkagen ni shinásaì

to make do (with) (...で) 間に合せる (...dé) mà ní awaserú

you'll have to make do with $15 15ドルで間に合せなさい júgòdòru de ma ní awasenasài

♦*n* (*inf*: party etc) パーティ pấtì

we're having a little do on Saturday 土曜日にちょっとしたパーティをしようと思っています doyóbì ni chótto shita pấtì wo shiyố tò omốttè imásù

it was rather a do なかなかいいパーティだった nakánaka ìi pấtì datta

do away with *vt fus* (kill) 殺す korósu; (abolish: law etc) なくす nakúsu

docile [dɑ:'səl] *adj* (person) 素直な súnào na; (beast) 大人しい otónashiì

dock [dɑ:k] *n* (NAUT) 岸壁 gañpeki; (LAW) 被告席 hikókusèki

♦*vi* (NAUT) 接岸する setsúgan suru; (SPACE) ドッキングする dokkíngu suru

docker [dɑ:k'ər] *n* 港湾労働者 kốwanrōdòsha

docks [dɑ:ks] *npl* (NAUT) 係船きょ keísenkyo

dockyard [dɑ:k'jɑ:rd] *n* 造船所 zốsenjo

doctor [dɑ:k'tər] *n* (MED) 医者 ishá; (PhD etc) 博士 hákàse

♦*vt* (drink etc) ...に薬物をこっそり混ぜる ...ni yakúbùtsu wo kossórì mazérù

Doctor of Philosophy *n* 博士号 hakásegồ

doctrine [dɑ:k'trin] *n* (REL) 教義 kyốgi; (POL) 信条 shiñjō

document [dɑ:k'jəmənt] *n* 書類 shorúi

documentary [dɑ:kjəmen'tə:ri:] *adj* (evidence) 書類による shorúi ni yorù

♦*n* (TV, CINEMA) ドキュメンタリー dokyúmeñtarī

documentation [dɑ:kjəməntei'ʃən] *n* (papers) 書類 shorúi

dodge [dɑ:dʒ] *n* (trick) 策略 sakúryaku

♦*vt* (question) はぐらかす hagúrakasù; (tax) ごまかす gomákasù; (blow, ball) 身を交して避ける mi wố kawàshite sakérù

dodgems [dɑ:dʒ'əmz] (*BRIT*) *npl* ドジェム dojémù ◇遊園地の乗り物の一種：相手にぶっつかったりして遊ぶ小型電気自動車 yúeñchi no norímono no isshù: aíte nì buttsúketàri shité asobù kogáta denki jidōsha

doe [dou] *n* (deer) 雌 ジカ mesújikà; (rabbit) 雌ウサギ mesúusàgi

does [dʌz] *vb see* **do**

doesn't [dʌz'nt] = **does not**

dog [dɔ:g] *n* (ZOOL) イヌ inú

♦*vt* (subj: person) ...の後を付ける ...no átồ wo tsukérù; (: bad luck) ...に付きまとう ...ni tsukímatoù

dog collar *n* (of dog) 首輪 kubiwa, カラー kárà; (REL) ローマンカラー rốmankarā

dog-eared [dɔ:g'i:rd] *adj* (book, paper)

手擦れした tezúre shitá

dogged [dɔ:ˈgid] adj (determination, spirit) 根気強い konkizuyoí

dogma [dɔ:ˈgmə] n (REL) 教理 kyóri; (POL) 信条 shiñjō

dogmatic [dɔ:gmætˈik] adj (attitude, assertion) 独断的な dokúdanteki na

dogsbody [dɔ:gzˈbɑːdiː] (BRIT: inf) n 下っ端 shitáppa

doings [duːˈiŋz] npl (activities) 行動 kódō

do-it-yourself [duːˈitjurselfˈ] n 日曜大工 nichíyōdaíku

doldrums [doulˈdrəmz] npl: **to be in the doldrums** (person) ふさぎ込んでいる fuságikonde irù; (business) 沈滞している chintai shite irù

dole [doul] (BRIT) n (payment) 失業手当 shitsúgyōteàte

on the dole 失業手当を受けて shitsúgyōteàte wo úkete

doleful [doulˈfəl] adj (voice, expression) 悲しげな kanáshige na

dole out vt (food, money) 配る kubárù

doll [dɑːl] n (toy) 人形 niñgyō; (US: inf: woman) 美人 bijín

dollar [dɑːlˈər] (US etc) n ドル dórù

dolled up [dɑːldʌpˈ] (inf) adj おめかしした o-mékàshi shita

dolphin [dɑːlˈfin] n イルカ irúka

domain [doumeinˈ] n (sphere) 分野 búñya; (empire) 縄張 nawábari

dome [doum] n (ARCHIT) 円がい eñgai, ドーム dómu

domestic [dəmesˈtik] adj (of country: trade, situation) 国内の kokúnai no; (of home: tasks, appliances) 家庭の katéi no

domestic animal 家畜 kachíku

domesticated [dəmesˈtikeitid] adj (animal) 家畜化の kachíkuka no; (husband) 家庭的な katéiteki na

dominant [dɑːmˈənənt] adj (share, part, role) 主な ómò na; (partner) 支配的な shiháiteki na

dominate [dɑːmˈəneit] vt (discussion) …の主な話題になる …no ómò na wadái ni narù; (people) 支配する shíhai suru; (place) …の上にそびえ立つ …no ué nì so-

bíetatsù

domineering [dɑːmənirˈiŋ] adj (overbearing) 横暴な óbō na

dominion [dəminˈjən] n (authority) 支配権 shiháiken; (territory) 領土 ryódò

domino [dɑːmˈənou] (pl **dominoes**) n (block) ドミノ dómìno

dominoes [dɑːmˈənouz] n (game) ドミノ遊び domínoasòbi

don [dɑːn] (BRIT) n (SCOL) 大学教官 daígakukyōkan

donate [douˈneit] vt 寄付する kifú suru

donation [douˈneiʃən] n 寄付 kifú

done [dʌn] pp of **do**

donkey [dɑːŋˈkiː] n (ZOOL) ロバ róba

donor [douˈnər] n (MED: of blood, heart etc) 提供者 teíkyōsha; (to charity) 寄贈者 kizóshà

don't [dount] = **do not**

doodle [duːdˈəl] vi 落書する rakúgaki suru

doom [duːm] n (fate) 悲運 híùn

♦vt: **to be doomed to failure** 失敗するに決っている shippái suru nì kimátte irù

doomsday [duːmzˈdei] n 世の終り yó nò owári

door [dɔːr] n 戸 to, 扉 tobíra, ドア dóa

doorbell [dɔːrˈbel] n 呼び鈴 yobírin

door handle n (gen) 取っ手 tottè; (of car) ドアハンドル doáhandoru

doorman [dɔːrˈmæn] (pl **doormen**) n (in hotel) ドアマン doámàn

doormat [dɔːrˈmæt] n (mat) 靴ふき kutsúfuki, マット máttò

doorstep [dɔːrˈstep] n 玄関階段 geñkan-kaídan

door-to-door [dɔːrˈtədɔːrˈ] adj (selling, salesman) 訪問販売の hómonhañbai no

doorway [dɔːrˈwei] n 戸口 tógùchi

dope [doup] n (inf: illegal drug) 麻薬 mayáku; (: person) ばか bákà

♦vt (horse, person) …に麻薬を与える …ni mayáku wò atáerù

dopey [douˈpiː] (inf) adj (groggy) ふらふらになっている furáfura nì natté irù; (stupid) ばかな bákà na

dormant [dɔːrˈmənt] adj (plant) 休眠中の kyúminchū no

a dormant volcano 休火山 kyūkazàn

dormice [dɔːr'mais] npl of **dormouse**

dormitory [dɔːr'mitɔːri:] n (room) 共同寝室 kyōdōshìnshitsu; (US: building) 寮 ryō

dormouse [dɔːr'maus] (pl **dormice**) n ヤマネ yamáne

DOS [dous] n abbr (COMPUT) (= disk operating system) ディスク・オペレーティング・システム dísuku operētingu shisutèmu

dosage [dou'sidʒ] n 投薬量 tōyakuryō

dose [dous] n (of medicine) 一回量 ikkái-ryō

doss house [dɑːs-] (BRIT) n 安宿 yasú-yado, どや doyá

dossier [dɑːs'i:ei] n (POLICE etc) 調書一式 chōsho isshìki

dot [dɑːt] n (small round mark) 点 teń; (speck, spot) 染み shimí
♦vt: **dotted with** ...が点々とある ...ga teñten tò árù

on the dot (punctually) きっかり kikká-rì

dote [dout]: **to dote on** vt fus (child, pet, lover) でき愛する dekíai suru

dot-matrix printer [dɑːtmeit'riks-] n (COMPUT) ドットプリンタ dottópurìñta

dotted line [dɑːt'id-] n 点線 teñseñ

double [dʌb'əl] adj (share, size) 倍の baí no; (chin etc) 二重の nijū no; (yolk) 二つある futátsu arù
♦adv (twice): **to cost double** 費用は二倍掛かる hiyō wa nibái kakarù
♦n (twin) そっくりな人 sokkúrì na hitó
♦vt (offer) 二倍にする nibái ni surù; (fold in two: paper, blanket) 二つに折る futátsu nì órù
♦vi (population, size) 二倍になる nibái ni narù

on the double, (BRIT) **at the double** 駆け足で kakéàshi de

double bass n コントラバス koñtorabasù

double bed n ダブルベッド dabúrubeddò

double bend (BRIT) n S-カーブ esúkā-

bu

double-breasted [dʌb'əlbres'tid] adj (jacket, coat) ダブルの dábùru no

doublecross [dʌb'əlkrɔːs'] vt (trick, betray) 裏切る urágirù

doubledecker [dʌbəldek'əːr] n (also: **doubledecker bus**) 二階建てバス nikái-datebasù

double glazing [-gleiz'iŋ] (BRIT) n 二重ガラス nijūgarāsu

double room n ダブル部屋 dabúrubeya

doubles [dʌb'əlz] n (TENNIS) ダブルス dábùrusu

doubly [dʌb'li:] adv (especially) 更に sárā ni

doubt [daut] n (uncertainty) 疑問 gimóñ
♦vt (disbelieve) 信じない shiñjinaì; (mistrust, suspect) 信用しない shiñ-yō shinaì

to doubt that ... ...だとは思わない ...dá tò wa omówanaì

doubtful [daut'fəl] adj (fact, provenance) 疑わしい utágawashiì; (person) 疑っている utágatte irù

doubtless [daut'lis] adv (probably, almost certainly) きっと ...だろう kíttò ...darō

dough [dou] n (CULIN) 生地 kíjì

doughnut [dou'nʌt] n ドーナッツ dōnat-tsu

do up vt (laces) 結ぶ musúbu; (buttons) かける kakérù; (dress) しめる shimérù; (renovate: room, house) 改装する kaísō suru

douse [daus] vt (drench) ...に水を掛ける ...ni mizú wò kakérù; (extinguish) 消す kesú

dove [dʌv] n (bird) ハト hátò

Dover [dou'vəːr] n ドーバー dōbā

dovetail [dʌv'teil] vi (fig) 合う áù

dowdy [dau'di:] adj (clothes, person) 野暮な yábò na

do with vt fus (need) いる irù; (want) 欲しい hòshíì; (be connected) ...と関係がある ...to kánkei ga arù

I could do with a drink 一杯飲みたい ìppai nomítaì

I could do with some help だれかに手伝ってもらいたい darèka ni tetsúdatte moráitaì

what has it got to do with you? あなたとはどういう関係ですか anátà to wa dô īu kánkeì desù ká

I won't have anything to do with it その件にはかかわりたくない sonó kèn ni wa kakáwaritakùnâì

it has to do with money 金銭関係の事です kínsen kànkeì no kotó desù

do without *vi* なしで済ます náshì de sumásù

♦*vt fus* …なしで間に合せる …náshì de ma nî awaserù

if you're late for lunch then you'll do without 昼食の時間に遅れたら何もなしだからね chúshoku no jikan ni ôkúretarà naní mo nashî da kara nê

I can do without a car 私には車はいりません watákushi ni wà kurúma wa írímasèn

we'll have to do without a holiday this year 私たちは今年休暇を取るのは無理な様です watákushitàchi wa kotóshi kyûka wo torù no wa múrì na yô desù

down [daun] *n* (feathers) 羽毛 úmò

♦*adv* (downwards) 下へ shitá e; (on the ground) 下に shitá ni

♦*prep* (towards lower level) …の下へ …no shitá e; (movement along) …に沿って …ni sôtté

♦*vt* (*inf*: drink) 飲む nómù

down with X! 打倒X! datô X!

down-and-out [daun'anaut] *n* 浮浪者 furôshà, ルンペン rúñpen

down-at-heel [daunæthi:l'] *adj* (shoes etc) 使い古した tsukáifurushità; (appearance, person) 見すぼらしい misúborashiì

downcast [daun'kæst] *adj* がっかりした gakkárì shita

downfall [daun'fɔ:l] *n* 失脚 shikkyáku

downhearted [daun'hɑ:r'tid] *adj* 落胆した rakútan shita

downhill [daun'hil'] *adv*: *to go downhill* (road, person, car) 坂を下る saká wò kudárù; (*fig*: person, business) 下り坂になる kudárizaka ni narù

down payment *n* (first payment of series) 頭金 atámakin; (deposit) 手付金 tetsúkekin

downpour [daun'pɔ:r] *n* 土砂降 dosháburi

downright [daun'rait] *adj* (lie, liar etc) 全くの mattáku no; (refusal) きっぱりした kippárì shita

a downright lie 真っ赤なうそ makká nà úsò

downstairs [daun'ste:rz'] *adv* (below) 下の階に〔de〕 shitá nò kâî ni〔de〕; (downwards: go, run etc) 下の階へ shitá nò kâî e

downstream [daun'stri:m'] *adv* (be) 川下に kawáshimo ni; (go) 川下へ kawáshimo e

down-to-earth [dauntuə:rθ'] *adj* (person, solution) 現実的な geñjitsuteki na

downtown [daun'taun'] *adv* 繁華街に〔で, へ〕 hañkagai ni〔de, e〕

down under *adv* (Australia etc) オーストラリア〔ニュージーランド〕に〔で〕 ôsutoraríà〔nyûjîrañdo〕ni〔de〕

downward [daun'wə:rd] *adv* 下へ shitá e

♦*adj* 下への shitá e nô

downwards [daun'wə:rdz] *adv* 下へ shitá e

dowry [dau'ri:] *n* (bride's) 持参金 jisáñkin

doz. abbr = **dozen**

doze [douz] *vi* 居眠りする inémurî suru

dozen [dʌz'ən] *n* 1ダース ichî dâsu

a dozen books 本12冊 hôñ jûni sàtsu

dozens of 幾つもの íkutsu mo no

doze off *vi* (nod off) まどろむ madóromù

Dr. abbr = **doctor** (in street names) = **drive**

drab [dræb] *adj* (weather, building, clothes) 陰気な íñki nà

draft [dræft] *n* (first version) 草案 sôan; (POL: of bill) 原案 geñ-an; (*also*: **bank draft**) 小切手 kogítte; (*US*: call-up) 徴兵 chôhei; (of air: *BRIT*: **draught**) すきま風 sukímakaze; (NAUT: *BRIT*: **draught**) 喫水 kissuì

♦*vt* (plan) 立案する ritsúan suru; (write roughly) …の下書きをする …no shitágaki wo surù

draft beer 生ビール namábîru

draftsman [dræfts'mən] (*pl* **drafts-men**: *BRIT* **draughtsman**) *n* 製図工 seízukō

drag [dræg] *vt* (bundle, person) 引きずる hikízurù; (river) さらう saráù

♦*vi* (time, a concert etc) 長く感じられる nágàku kaňjirarerù

♦*n* (*inf*: bore) 退屈な人 taíkutsu na hitò; (women's clothing): *in drag* 女装して josō shite

drag on *vi* (case, concert etc) だらだらと長引く dáràdara to nagábikù

dragon [dræg'ən] *n* 竜 ryū

dragonfly [dræg'ənflai] *n* トンボ tôňbo

drain [drein] *n* (in street) 排水口 haísuìkō; (on resources, source of loss) 負担 fután

♦*vt* (land, marshes, pond) 干拓する kaňtaku suru; (vegetables) ...の水切りをする ...no mizúkiri wò suru

♦*vi* (liquid) 流れる nagárerù

drainage [drei'nidʒ] *n* (system) 排水 haísui; (process) 水はけ mizúhake

drainboard [drein'bɔːrd] (*BRIT* **drain-ing board**) *n* 水切り板 mizúkiribàn

drainpipe [drein'paip] *n* 排水管 haísuìkan

drama [drɑːm'ə] *n* (art) 劇文学 gekíbuňgaku; (play) 劇 gékì, ドラマ dôrama; (excitement) ドラマ dôrama

dramatic [drəmæt'ik] *adj* (marked, sudden) 劇的な gekíteki na; (theatrical) 演劇の eňgeki no

dramatist [dræm'ətist] *n* 劇作家 gekísakka

dramatize [dræm'ətaiz] *vt* (events) 劇的に描写する gekíteki nì byôsha suru; (adapt: for TV, cinema) 脚色する kyakúshoku suru

drank [dræŋk] *pt of* **drink**

drape [dreip] *vt* (cloth, flag) 掛ける kakérù

drapes [dreips] (*US*) *npl* (curtains) カーテン kâten

drastic [dræs'tik] *adj* (measure) 思い切った omóikittà; (change) 抜本的な bappónteki na

draught [dræft] (*BRIT*) = **draft**

draughtboard [dræft'bɔːrd] (*BRIT*) = **checkerboard**

draughts [dræfts] (*BRIT*) = **checkers**

draughtsman [dræfts'mən] (*BRIT*) = **draftsman**

draw [drɔː] (*pt* **drew**, *pp* **drawn**) *vt* (ART, TECH) 描く kákù; (pull: cart) 引く hikú; (: curtain) 引く hikú, 閉じる tojírù, 閉める shimérù; (take out: gun, tooth) 抜く nukú; (attract: admiration, attention) 引く hikú, 引付ける hikítsukerù; (money) 引出す hikídasù; (wages) もらう moráù

♦*vi* (SPORT) 引分けになる hikíwake ni narù

♦*n* (SPORT) 引分け hikíwake; (lottery) 抽選 chûsen

to draw near (approach: person, event) 近付く chikázukù

drawback [drɔː'bæk] *n* 欠点 kettén

drawbridge [drɔː'bridʒ] *n* 跳ね橋 hanébàshi

drawer [drɔː'əːr] *n* (of desk etc) 引出し hikídashi

drawing [drɔː'iŋ] *n* (picture) 図 zu, スケッチ sukétchi; (skill, discipline) 製図 seízu

drawing board *n* 製図板 seízuban

drawing pin (*BRIT*) *n* 画びょう gábyò

drawing room *n* 居間 imá

drawl [drɔːl] *n* のろい話振り norôi hanáshibùri

drawn [drɔːn] *pp of* **draw**

draw out *vi* (lengthen) 引延ばす hikínobasù

♦*vt* (money: from bank) 引出す hikídasù, 下ろす orósù

draw up *vi* (stop) 止まる tomárù

♦*vt* (document) 作成する sakúsei suru; (chair etc) 引寄せる hikíyoserù

dread [dred] *n* (great fear, anxiety) 恐怖 kyōfu

♦*vt* (fear) 恐れる osórerù

dreadful [dred'fəl] *adj* (weather, day, person etc) いやな iyá nà

dream [driːm] *n* (PSYCH, fantasy, ambition) 夢 yumé

♦*vb* (*pt*, *pp* **dreamed** *or* **dreamt**)

♦*vt* 夢に見る yumé ni mirù

♦*vi* 夢を見る yumé wo mirù

dreamer [dri:'mər] *n* 夢を見る人 yumé wo miru hitò; (*fig*) 非現実的な人 higeñjitsuteki na hitò

dreamt [dremt] *pt, pp of* **dream**

dreamy [dri:'mi:] *adj* (expression, person) うっとりした uttórì shita; (music) 静かな shízùka na

dreary [dri:'ri:] *adj* (weather, talk, time) 陰気な iñki na

dredge [dredʒ] *vt* (river, harbor) しゅんせつする shuñsetsu suru

dregs [dregz] *npl* (of drink) かす kásù, おり orí; (of humanity) くず kúzù

drench [drentʃ] *vt* (soak) びしょ濡れにする bishōnùre ni suru

dress [dres] *n* (frock) ドレス dórèsu; (no pl: clothing) 服装 fukúsō

♦*vt* (child) ...に服を着せる ...ni fukú wò kisérù; (wound) ...の手当をする ...no téàte wo suru

♦*vi* 服を着る fukú wò kirú

to get dressed 服を着る fukú wò kirú

dress circle (*BRIT*) *n* (THEATER) 2階席 nikáisèki

dresser [dres'ər] *n* (*BRIT*: cupboard) 食器戸棚 shokkítodàna; (*US*: chest of drawers) 整理だんす sefrídañsu

dressing [dres'iŋ] *n* (MED) 包帯 hótai; (CULIN: for salad) ドレッシング dorésshiñgu

dressing gown (*BRIT*) *n* ガウン gáùn

dressing room *n* (THEATER) 楽屋 gakúya; (SPORT) 更衣室 kőishìtsu

dressing table *n* 鏡台 kyődai

dressmaker [dres'meikər] *n* 洋裁師 yősaishì, ドレスメーカー dorésumèkā

dress rehearsal *n* (THEATER) ドレスリハーサル dorésurihàsaru ◇衣装を着けて本番並に行う舞台げいこ íshō wo tsukétè hoñbannami nì okónaù butáigeìko

dress up *vi* (wear best clothes) 盛装する seíshō suru; (in costume) 仮装する kasō suru

dressy [dres'i:] (*inf*) *adj* (smart: clothes) スマートな sumátò na

drew [dru:] *pt of* **draw**

dribble [drib'əl] *vi* (baby) よだれを垂らす yodáre wò tarásu

♦*vt* (ball) ドリブルする doríbùru suru

dried [draid] *adj* (fruit) 干した hóshìta, 干し... hoshí...; (eggs, milk) 粉末の fuñmatsu no

drier [drai'ər] *n* = **dryer**

drift [drift] *n* (of current etc) 方向 hőkō; (of snow) 吹きだまり fukídamarì; (meaning) 言わんとする事 iwán tò suru kotð, 意味 ímì

♦*vi* (boat) 漂流する hyőryū suru; (sand, snow) 吹寄せられる fukíyoserarerù

driftwood [drift'wud] *n* 流木 ryūbòku

drill [dril] *n* (*also*: **drill bit**) ドリル先 dorírusakì, ドリル dóriru; (machine: for DIY, dentistry, mining etc) ドリル dóriru; (MIL) 教練 kyőren

♦*vt* (troops) 練兵する kyőren suru

♦*vi* (for oil) ボーリングする bőriñgu suru

to drill a hole in something ドリルで...に穴を開ける dóriru de ...ni aná wò akérù

drink [driŋk] *n* (*gen*) 飲物 nomímono, ドリンク doríñku; (alcoholic drink) 酒 saké; (sip) 一口 hitókùchi

♦*vb* (*pt* **drank**, *pp* **drunk**)

♦*vt* 飲む nómù

♦*vi* 飲む nómù

to have a drink 1杯飲む íppaì nómù

a drink of water 水1杯 mizú íppaì

drinker [driŋ'kər] *n* (of alcohol) 酒飲み sakénomì

drinking water [driŋ'kiŋ-] *n* 飲料水 iñryōsui

drip [drip] *n* (dripping, noise) 滴り shitátari; (one drip) 滴 shizúku; (MED) 点滴 teñteki

♦*vi* (water, rain) 滴る shitátarù; (tap) ...から水が垂れる ...kara mizú gà tarérù

drip-dry [drip'drai] *adj* (shirt) ドリップドライの doríppudorài no

dripping [drip'iŋ] *n* (CULIN) 肉汁 nikújū

drive [draiv] *n* (journey) ドライブ dorátbu; (*also*: **driveway**) 車道 shadő ◇私有地内を通って公道と家などをつなぐ私道を

指す shiyúchinaì wo tótte kódō tò ié nadò wo tsunágù shidō wo sásu; (energy) 精力 seíryoku; (campaign) 運動 uńdō; (COMPUT: also: **disk drive**) ディスクドライブ disúkudoraìbu

♦*vb* (*pt* **drove**, *pp* **driven**)

♦*vt* (car) 運転する uńten suru; (push: *also* TECH: motor etc) 動かす ugókasu; (nail): *to drive something into* ...を...に打込む ...wo ...ni uchíkomù

♦*vi* (AUT: at controls) 運転する uńten suru; (travel) 車で行く kurúma de ikù

left-/right-hand drive 左(右)ハンドル hidári(migí)haǹdoru

to drive someone mad ...をいらいらさせる ...wo íraìra saséru

drivel [driv'əl] (*inf*) *n* 与太話 yotábanàshi

driven [driv'ən] *pp of* **drive**

driver [drai'vər] *n* (of own car) 運転者 uńteǹsha, ドライバー doráìba; (chauffeur) お抱え運転手 o-kákae uńteǹshu; (of taxi, bus) 運転手 uńteǹshu; (RAIL) 運転士 uńteǹshi

driver's license (*US*) *n* 運転免許証 uńtenmenkyoshō

driveway [draiv'wei] *n* 車道 shadō ◇ 私有地内を通って公道と家などをつなぐ私道を指す shiyúchinaì wo tótte kódō tò ié nadò wo tsunágù shidō wò sásù

driving [drai'viŋ] *n* 運転 uńten

driving instructor *n* 運転指導者 uńtenshidōsha

driving lesson *n* 運転教習 uńtenkyōshū

driving licence (*BRIT*) *n* 運転免許証 uńtenmenkyoshō

driving mirror *n* バックミラー bakkúmirà

driving school *n* 自動車教習所 jidōshakyōshūjo

driving test *n* 運転免許試験 uńtenmenkyoshikèn

drizzle [driz'əl] *n* 霧雨 kirísame

drone [droun] *n* (noise) ぶーんという音 bún to iú otò; (male bee) 雄バチ osúbachi

drool [dru:l] *vi* (dog etc) よだれを垂らす yodáre wò tarásù

droop [dru:p] *vi* (flower) しおれる shióre-

rù; (of person: shoulders) 肩を落す kátà wo otósù; (: head) うつむく utsúmukù

drop [drɑ:p] *n* (of water) 滴 shizúku; (lessening) 減少 geńshō; (fall) 落差 rákùsa

♦*vt* (allow to fall: object) 落す otósù; (voice) 潜める hisómerù; (eyes) 落す otósù; (reduce: price) 下げる sagérù; (set down from car) 降ろす orósù; (omit: name from list etc) 削除する sakújo suru

♦*vi* (object) 落ちる ochírù; (wind) 弱まる yowámarù

drop off *vi* (go to sleep) 眠る nemúrù

♦*vt* (passenger) 降ろす orósù

drop out *vi* (withdraw) 脱退する dattái suru

drop-out [drɑ:p'aut] *n* (from society) 社会からの脱落者 shákài kara no datsúrakushà; (SCOL) 学校からの中退者 gakkō kara nò chútaishà

dropper [drɑ:p'ə:r] *n* スポイト supóìto

droppings [drɑ:p'iŋz] *npl* (of bird, mouse) ふん fúǹ

drops [drɑ:ps] *npl* (MED: for eyes) 点眼剤 teńgaǹzai; (: for ears) 点耳薬 teńjiyàku

drought [draut] *n* かんばつ kańbatsu

drove [drouv] *pt of* **drive**

drown [draun] *vt* (kill: person, animal) 水死させる suíshi saserù; (*fig*: voice, noise) 聞えなくする kikóenakù suru, 消す kesú

♦*vi* (person, animal) おぼれ死ぬ obóreshinù

drowsy [drau'zi:] *adj* (sleepy) 眠い nemúì

drudgery [drʌdʒ'əːriː] *n* (uninteresting work) 骨折り仕事 honéorishigòto

drug [drʌg] *n* (MED) 薬剤 yakúzai, 薬 kusúri; (narcotic) 麻薬 mayáku

♦*vt* (sedate: person, animal) 薬で眠らせる kusúri dè nemúraserù

to be on drugs 麻薬を打って〔飲んで〕いる mayáku wò útte〔nóǹde〕irù

hard/soft drugs 中毒性の強い〔弱い〕麻薬 chúdokusei nò tsuyóì〔yowáì〕mayáku

drug addict *n* 麻薬常習者 mayákujōshūsha

druggist [drʌg'ist] (*US*) *n* (person) 薬剤師 yakúzaìshi; (store) 薬屋 kusúriya

drugstore [drʌg'stɔ:r] (*US*) *n* ドラッグストア dorággusutòa

drum [drʌm] *n* (MUS) 太鼓 taíko, ドラム dóramu; (for oil, petrol) ドラム缶 dorámukaǹ

drummer [drʌm'ə:r] *n* ドラマー dorámà

drums [drʌmz] *npl* ドラム dóramu

drunk [drʌŋk] *pp of* **drink**
♦*adj* (with alcohol) 酔っ払った yoppárattà
♦*n* (*also*: **drunkard**) 酔っ払い yoppárai

drunken [drʌŋ'kən] *adj* (laughter, party) 酔っ払いの yoppárai no; (person) 酔っ払った yoppárattà

dry [drai] *adj* (ground, climate, weather, skin) 乾いた kawáìta, 乾燥した kaǹsō shita; (day) 雨の降らない ámè no furánaì; (lake, riverbed) 干上がった hiágattà; (humor) 皮肉っぽい hiníkuppòi; (wine) 辛口の karákuchi no
♦*vt* (ground, clothes etc) 乾かす kawákasù; (tears) ふく fukú
♦*vi* (paint etc) 乾く kawákù

dry-cleaner's [drai'kli:'nə:rz] *n* ドライクリーニング屋 doráikurìninguya

dry-cleaning [drai'kli:'niŋ] *n* ドライクリーニング doráikurìniǹgu

dryer [drai'ə:r] *n* (*also*: **hair dryer**) ヘアドライヤー heádoraìyā; (for laundry) 乾燥機 kaǹsōki; (*US*: spin-drier) 脱水機 dassúìki

dryness [drai'nis] *n* (of ground, climate, weather, skin) 乾燥 kaǹsō

dry rot *n* 乾腐病 kaǹpubyò

dry up *vi* (river, well) 干上がる hiágarù

DSS [di:eses'] (*BRIT*) *n abbr* (= *Department of Social Security*) 社会保障省 shakáihoshōshò

dual [du:'əl] *adj* 二重の nijū no

dual carriageway (*BRIT*) *n* 中央分離帯のある道路 chūōbuǹritai no árù dórò

dual nationality *n* 二重国籍 nijūkokuseki

dual-purpose [du:'əlpə:r'pəs] *adj* 二重目的の nijūmokutèki no

dubbed [dʌbd] *adj* (CINEMA) 吹き替えの fukíkae nò

dubious [du:'bi:əs] *adj* (claim, reputation, company) いかがわしい ikágawashi ̀; (person) 疑っている utágatte irù

Dublin [dʌb'lin] *n* ダブリン dábùrin

duchess [dʌtʃ'is] *n* 公爵夫人 kōshakufujiǹ

duck [dʌk] *n* (ZOOL, CULIN: domestic bird) アヒル ahíru; (wild bird) カモ kámò
♦*vi* (*also*: **duck down**) かがむ kagámù

duckling [dʌk'liŋ] *n* (ZOOL, CULIN: domestic bird) アヒルの子 ahíru no kò; (: wild bird) カモの子 kámò no ko

duct [dʌkt] *n* (ELEC, TECH) ダクト dákùto; (ANAT) 管 káñ

dud [dʌd] *n* (bomb, shell etc) 不発弾 fuhátsudàn; (object, tool etc) 欠陥品 kekkáñhin
♦*adj*: **dud cheque** (*BRIT*) 不渡り小切手 fuwátarikogittè

due [du:] *adj* (expected: meeting, publication, arrival) 予定した yotéi shita; (owed: money) 払われるべき haráwarerubeki; (proper: attention, consideration) 当然の tōzen no
♦*n*: **to give someone his (or her) due** ...に当然の物を与える ...ni tōzen no monò wo atáerù
♦*adv*: **due north** 真北に ma-kíta ni

in due course (when the time is right) 時が来たら tokí ga kitarà; (eventually) やがて yagáte

due to (owing to) ...が原因で ...ga geñ-in de

to be due to do ...する事になっている ...surú kotò ni natté irù

duel [du:'əl] *n* (*also fig*) 決闘 kettő

dues [du:z] *npl* (for club, union) 会費 kaíhi; (in harbor) 使用料 shiyőryò

duet [du:et'] *n* (MUS) 二重唱 nijūshō, デュエット dúètto

duffel bag [dʌf'əl-] *n* 合切袋 gassáibukùro

duffel coat [dʌf'əl-] *n* ダッフルコート daffúrukòto ◇丈夫なフード付き防寒コート jōbu nà fúdotsuki bōkan kòto

dug [dʌg] *pt, pp of* **dig**

duke [du:k] *n* 公爵 kōshaku

dull [dʌl] *adj* (weak: light) 暗い kuráì;

(intelligence, wit) 鈍い nibúi; (boring: event) 退屈な taíkutsu na; (sound, pain) 鈍い nibúi; (gloomy: weather, day) 陰気な íńki na

♦vt (pain, grief) 和らげる yawáragerù; (mind, senses) 鈍くする níbùku suru

duly [du:'li:] adv (properly) 正当に seítō ni; (on time) 予定通りに yotéidòri ni

dumb [dʌm] adj (mute, silent) 話せない hanásenaì; (pej: stupid) ばかな bákà na

dumbfounded [dʌmfaund'id] adj あ然とした azéń tò shita

dummy [dʌm'i:] n (tailor's model) 人台 jińdai; (TECH, COMM: mock-up) 模型 mokéi; (BRIT: for baby) おしゃぶり o-shábùri

♦adj (bullet) 模擬の mógì no; (firm) ダミーの dámì no

dump [dʌmp] n (also: **rubbish dump**) ごみ捨て場 gomísuteba; (inf: place) いやな場所 iyá na bashò

♦vt (put down) 落す otósù; (get rid of) 捨てる sutérù; (COMPUT: data) 打ち出す uchídasù, ダンプする dáńpu suru

dumpling [dʌmp'liŋ] n (CULIN: with meat etc) 団子 dańgo

dumpy [dʌmp'i:] adj (person) ずんぐりした zuńgurī shita

dunce [dʌns] n (SCOL) 劣等生 rettósei

dune [du:n] n (in desert, on beach) 砂丘 sakyū

dung [dʌŋ] n (AGR, ZOOL) ふん fúń

dungarees [dʌŋgəri:z'] npl オーバーオール ōbāòru

dungeon [dʌn'dʒən] n 地下ろう chikárō

duo [du:'ou] n (gen, MUS) ペア péà

dupe [du:p] n (victim) かも kámò

♦vt (trick) だます damásù

duplex [du:p'leks] (US) n (house) 2世帯用住宅 nisétaiyōjūtaku; (apartment) 複層式アパート fukúsōushikiapàto

duplicate [n du:'plikit vb du:'plikeit] n (of document, key etc) 複製 fukúsei

♦vt (copy) 複製する fukúsei suru; (photocopy) ...のコピーを取る ...no kópì wo toru, ...をコピーする ...wo kópì suru; (repeat) 再現する saígen suru

in duplicate 2部で nibù de

duplicity [du:plis'əti:] n (deceit) いかさま ikásama

durable [du:r'əbəl] adj (goods, materials) 丈夫な jōbu na

duration [durei'ʃən] n (of process, event) 継続期間 keízokukikañ

duress [dures'] n: *under duress* (moral, physical) 強迫 kyōhaku

during [du:r'iŋ] prep ...の間に ...no aída ni

dusk [dʌsk] n 夕暮 yūgure

dust [dʌst] n ほこり hokóri

♦vt (furniture) ...のほこりを拭く ...no hokóri wò fukú; (cake etc): *to dust with* ...に...を振掛ける ...ni ...wo furíkakerù

dustbin [dʌst'bin] (BRIT) n ごみ箱 gomíbàko

duster [dʌs'tə:r] n (cloth) 雑きん zōkin

dustman [dʌst'mæn] (BRIT pl **dustmen**) n ごみ収集人 gomíshūshūnin

dusty [dʌs'ti:] adj (road) ほこりっぽい hokórippoì; (furniture) ほこりだらけの hokóridaràke no

Dutch [dʌtʃ] adj オランダの oráñda no; (LING) オランダ語の orándagò no

♦vt (LING) オランダ語 orándagò

♦npl: *the Dutch* オランダ人 orándajìn

to go Dutch (inf) 割勘にする waríkan ni surù

Dutchman/woman [dʌtʃ'mən/wumən] (pl **Dutchmen/Dutchwomen**) n オランダ人男性〔女性〕orándajin dańsei〔joséi〕

dutiful [du:'tifəl] adj (son, daughter) 従順な jújun na

duty [du:'ti:] n (responsibility) 義務 gímù; (tax) 税金 zefkin

on/off duty (policeman, nurse) 当番〔非番〕で tōban〔híbàn〕de

duty-free [du:'ti:fri:'] adj (drink, cigarettes) 免税の meńzei no

duvet [du:'vei] (BRIT) n 掛布団 kakébutòn

dwarf [dwɔ:rf] (pl **dwarves**) n (person) 小人 kobíto; (animal, plant) わい小種 waíshōshù

♦vt 小さく見せる chíisaku misérù

dwarves [dwɔ:rvz] npl of **dwarf**

dwell [dwel] (pt, pp **dwelt**) vi (reside,

stay) 住む súmù

dwelling [dwel'iŋ] *n* (house) 住居 júkyò

dwell on *vt fus* (brood on) 長々と考える nagánaga tò kañgaerù

dwelt [dwelt] *pt, pp of* **dwell**

dwindle [dwin'dəl] *vi* (interest, attendance) 減る hérù

dye [dai] *n* (for hair, cloth) 染料 señryō
♦*vt* 染める somérù

dying [dai'iŋ] *adj* (person, animal) 死に掛っている shiñíkakatte irù

dyke [daik] (*BRIT*) *n* (wall) 堤防 teíbō

dynamic [dainæm'ik] *adj* (leader, force) 力強い chikárazuyoì

dynamite [dai'nəmait] *n* ダイナマイト daínamaìto

dynamo [dai'nəmou] *n* (ELEC) 発電機 hatsúdeñki, ダイナモ daínamo

dynasty [dai'nəsti:] *n* (family, period) 王朝 ōchō

dyslexia [dislek'si:ə] *n* 読書障害 dokúshoshōgai

E

E [i:] *n* (MUS: note) ホ音 hó-oñ; (: key) ホ調 hóchō

each [i:tʃ] *adj* (thing, person, idea etc) それぞれの soréz̀òre no
♦*pron* (each one) それぞれ soréz̀òre

each other 互いを[に] tagái wò [nì]

they hate each other 彼らは互いに憎み合っている kárèra wa tagái nì nikúmiatte irù

they have 2 books each 彼らはそれぞれ2冊の本を持っている kárèra wa soréz̀òre nísatsu no hóñ wo mottè irù

eager [i:'gə:r] *adj* (keen) 熱心な nesshín na

to be eager to do something 一生懸命に...をしたがっている isshókeñmei ni ... wo shitágatte irú

to be eager for とても...をほしがっている totémo ...wo hoshígatte irú

eagle [i:'gəl] *n* ワシ washí

ear [i:r] *n* (ANAT) 耳 mimí; (of corn) 穂 hó

earache [i:r'eik] *n* 耳の痛み mimí nò itámi

eardrum [i:r'drʌm] *n* 鼓膜 komáku

earl [ə:rl] (*BRIT*) *n* 伯爵 hakúshaku

earlier [ə:r'li:ə:r] *adj* (date, time, edition etc) 前の máè no
♦*adv* (leave, go etc) もっと早く móttò háyàku

early [ə:r'li:] *adv* (in day, month etc) 早く háyàku; (ahead of time) 早めに hayáme ni
♦*adj* (near the beginning: work, hours) 早朝の sóchō no; (Christians, settlers) 初期の shókì no; (sooner than expected: departure) 早めの hayáme no; (quick: reply) 早期の sókì no

an early death 早死に hayájinì

to have an early night 早めに寝る hayáme nì nérù

in the early/early in the spring 春先に harúsaki ni

in the early/early in the 19th century 19世紀の初めに júkyūseìki no hajíme ni

early retirement *n* 早めの引退 hayáme nò iñtai

earmark [i:r'mɑrk] *vt*: *to earmark (for)* (...に)当てる (...ni) atérù

earn [ə:rn] *vt* (salary) 稼ぐ kaségù; (COMM: interest) 生む umú; (praise) 受ける ukérù

earnest [ə:r'nist] *adj* (wish, desire) 心からの kokórò kara no; (person, manner) 真剣な shiñken na

in earnest 真剣に shiñken ni

earnings [ə:r'niŋz] *npl* (personal) 収入 shűnyū; (of company etc) 収益 shőeki

earphones [i:r'founz] *npl* イヤホーン iyáhòn

earring [i:r'riŋ] *n* イヤリング íyàringu

earshot [i:r'ʃɑt] *n*: *within earshot* 聞える範囲に kikőerù háñ-i ni

earth [ə:rθ] *n* (planet) 地球 chikyú; (land surface) 地面 jímèn; (soil) 土 tsuchí; (*BRIT*: ELEC) アース ásu
♦*vt* (*BRIT*: ELEC) アースに落す ásu ni otósù

earthenware [ə:r'θənwe:r] *n* 土器 dőki

earthquake [ə:rθ'kweik'] *n* 地震 jishín

earthy [ə:r'θi:] *adj* (*fig*: humor: vulgar) 下品な gehín na

ease [i:z] *n* (easiness) 容易さ yóisà; (comfort) 楽 rakú
♦*vt* (lessen: problem, pain) 和らげる yawáragerù; (: tension) 緩和する kañwa suru

to ease something in/out ゆっくりと ...を入れる〔出す〕yukkúrì to ...wo irérù〔dásù〕

at ease! (MIL) 休め! yasúmè!

easel [i:'zəl] *n* 画架 gákà, イーゼル ízèru

ease off *vi* (lessen: wind) 弱まる yowámarù; (: rain) 小降りになる kobúri ni narù; (slow down) スピードを落す supídò wo otósù

ease up *vi* = **ease off**

easily [i:'zili:] *adv* (with ease) 容易に yóì ni; (in comfort) 楽に rakú ni

east [i:st] *n* (direction) 東 higáshi; (of country, town) 東部 tôbù
♦*adj* (region) 東の higáshi no; (wind) 東からの higáshi karà no
♦*adv* 東に〔へ〕higáshi ni〔e〕
the East (Orient) 東洋 tôyô; (POL) 東欧 tôô, 東ヨーロッパ higáshi yôroppa

Easter [i:s'tə:r] *n* 復活祭 fukkátsusài, イースター ísutā

Easter egg *n* イースターエッグ ísutāeggù◇復活祭の飾り，プレゼントなどに使う色や模様を塗ったゆで卵 fukkátsusài no kazári, purézènto nádò ni tsukáu irô ya moyô wo nuttà yudétamàgo

easterly [i:s'tə:rli:] *adj* (to the east: direction, point) 東への higáshi e nò; (from the east: wind) 東からの higáshi kara nò

eastern [i:s'tə:rn] *adj* (GEO) 東の higáshi no; (oriental) 東洋の tôyô no; (communist) 東欧の tôô no, 東ヨーロッパの higáshi yôroppa no

East Germany *n* 東ドイツ higáshi doìtsu

eastward(s) [i:st'wə:rd(z)] *adv* 東へ higáshi e

easy [i:'zi:] *adj* (simple) 簡単な kañtan na; (relaxed) 寛いだ kutsúroìda; (com-

fortable) 楽な rakú na; (victim) だまされやすい damásareyasuì; (prey) 捕まりやすい tsukámariyasuì
♦*adv*: *to take it/things easy* (go slowly) 気楽にやる kiráku ni yarù; (not worry) 心配しない shifpai shinaì; (rest) 休む yasúmù

easy chair *n* 安楽いす añrakuisù

easy-going [i:'zi:gou'iŋ] *adj* 穏やかな odáyàka na

eat [i:t] (*pt* **ate**, *pp* **eaten**) *vt* (breakfast, lunch, food etc) 食べる tabérù
♦*vi* 食べる tabérù

eat away *vt fus* = **eat into**

eat into *vt fus* (metal) 腐食する fushóku suru; (savings) ...に食込む ...ni kuíkomù

eau de Cologne [ou' də kəloun'] *n* オーデコロン ôdekoròn

eaves [i:vz] *npl* (of house) 軒 nokí

eavesdrop [i:vz'drɑ:p] *vi*: *to eavesdrop (on)* (person, conversation) (...を) 盗み聞きする (...wo) nusúmigiki suru

ebb [eb] *n* (of sea, tide) 引く事 hikú kotò
♦*vi* (tide, sea) 引く hikú; (*fig*: *also*: **ebb away**: strength, feeling) 段々なくなる dañdan nakùnaru

ebony [eb'əni:] *n* (wood) 黒たん kokútan

EC [i:'si:'] *n abbr* (= *European Community*) 欧州共同体 ôshûkyôdôtai

eccentric [iksen'trik] *adj* (choice, views) 風変りな fûgawàri na
♦*n* (person) 変り者 kawárimono

ecclesiastical [ikli:zi:æs'tikəl] *adj* 教会の kyôkai no

echo [ek'ou] (*pl* **echoes**) *n* (of noise) こだま kodáma, 反響 hañkyô
♦*vt* (repeat) 繰返す kuríkaesù
♦*vi* (sound) 反響する hañkyô suru; (place) ...で鳴り響く ...de naríhibiku

echoes [ek'ouz] *npl* of **echo**

éclair [ikler'] *n* (cake) エクレア ekúrea

eclipse [iklips'] *n* (*also*: **eclipse of the sun**) 日食 nisshóku; (*also*: **eclipse of the moon**) 月食 gesshóku

ecology [ikɑ:l'ədʒi:] *n* (environment) 環境 kañkyô, エコロジー ekórojì; (SCOL) 生態学 seítaigaku

economic [i:kənɑ:m'ik] *adj* (system, history) 経済の keízai no; (*BRIT*: profitable: business etc) もうかる mōkarù

economical [i:kənə'mɪkəl] *adj* (system, car, machine) 経済的な keízaiteki na; (person) 倹約な keñ-yaku na

economics [i:kənɑ:'mɪks] *n* (SCOL) 経済学 keízaigàku
♦*npl* (of project, situation) 経済問題 keízaimoñdai

economist [ikɑ:n'əmist] *n* 経済学者 keízaigakùsha

economize [ikɑ:n'əmaiz] *vi* (make savings) 節約する setsúyaku suru

economy [ikɑ:n'əmi:] *n* (of country) 経済 keízai; (financial prudence) 節約 setsúyaku

economy class *n* (AVIAT) エコノミークラス ekónomikuràsu

economy size *n* (COMM) お買い得サイズ o-káidoku saìzu

ecstasy [ek'stəsi:] *n* (rapture) 狂喜 kyōki, エクスタシー ekúsutashī

ecstatic [ekstæt'ik] *adj* (welcome, reaction) 熱烈な netsúretsu na; (person) 無我夢中になった múgàmuchū ni nattà

ecumenical [ekju:men'ikəl] *adj* 超宗派の chōshūha no

eczema [ek'səmə] *n* (MED) 湿しん shisshín

edge [edʒ] *n* (border: of lake, table, chair etc) 縁 fuchí; (of knife etc) 刃 há
♦*vt* (trim) 縁取りする fuchídori suru
on edge (*fig*) = **edgy**
to edge away from じりじり...から離れる jírìjiri ...kara hanárerù

edgeways [edʒ'weiz] *adv*: **he couldn't get a word in edgeways** 何一つ発言出来なかった nanihitōtsu hatsúgen dekinakattà

edgy [edʒ'i:] *adj* (nervous, agitated) いらいらした íràira shita

edible [ed'əbəl] *adj* (mushroom, plant) 食用の shokúyō no

edict [i:'dikt] *n* (order) 政令 seírei

edifice [ed'əfis] *n* (building, structure) 大建造物 daíkenzōbùtsu

Edinburgh [ed'ənbə:rə] *n* エジンバラ ejínbara

edit [ed'it] *vt* (text, report) 校正する kōsei suru; (book, film, newspaper etc) 編集する heñshū suru

edition [idiʃ'ən] *n* (of book) 版 hán; (of newspaper, magazine) 号 gō; (TV, RADIO) 回 kái

editor [ed'itər] *n* (of newspaper) 編集局長 heñshūkyokuchō, デスク désùku; (of magazine) 編集長 heñshūchō; (of column: foreign/political editor) 編集主任 heñshūshuniñ; (of book) 編集者 heñshūsha

editorial [editɔːr'i:əl] *adj* (staff, policy, control) 編集の heñshū no
♦*n* (of newspaper) 社説 shasétsu

educate [edʒ'u:keit] *vt* (teach) 教育する kyōiku suru; (instruct) ...に教える ...ni oshíerù

education [edʒu:kei'ʃən] *n* (schooling, teaching) 教育 kyōiku; (knowledge, culture) 教養 kyōyō

educational [edʒu:kei'ʃənəl] *adj* (institution, policy etc) 教育の kyōiku no; (experience, toy) 教育的な kyōikuteki na

EEC [i:i:si:'] *n abbr* (= *European Economic Community*) 欧州経済共同体 ōshūkeizaikyōdōtai

eel [i:l] *n* ウナギ unági

eerie [i:'ri:] *adj* (strange, mysterious) 不気味な bukími na

effect [ifekt'] *n* (result, consequence) 結果 kekká; (impression: of speech, picture etc) 効果 kōka
♦*vt* (repairs) 行う okónau; (savings etc) ...に成功する ...ni seíkō suru
to take effect (law) 実施される jisshí sarerù; (drug) 効き始める kikíhajimerù
in effect 要するに yō surù ni

effective [ifek'tiv] *adj* (successful) 効果的な kōkateki na; (actual: leader, command) 実際の jissái no

effectively [ifek'tivli:] *adv* (successfully) 効果的に kōkateki ni; (in reality) 実際には jissái ni wa

effectiveness [ifek'tivnis] *n* (success) 有効性 yūkōsei

effeminate [ifem'ənit] *adj* (boy, man) 女々しい memēshiī

effervescent [efə:rves'ənt] *adj* (drink) 炭酸ガス入りの taṅsangasuirí no

efficacy [ef'ikəsi:] *n* (effectiveness) 有効性 yū́kōsei

efficiency [ifiʃ'ənsi:] *n* (of person, organization) 能率 nṓritsu; (of machine) 効率 kṓritsu

efficient [ifiʃ'ənt] *adj* (person, organization) 能率的な nṓritsuteki na; (machine) 効率の良い kṓritsu no yoì

effigy [ef'idʒi:] *n* (image) 像 zṓ

effort [ef'ə:rt] *n* (endeavor) 努力 dóryòku; (determined attempt) 試み kokóromì, 企て kuwádate; (physical/mental exertion) 苦労 kúrṓ

effortless [ef'ə:rtlis] *adj* (achievement) 楽な rakú nà; (style) ごく自然な gókù shizén na

effrontery [ifrʌn'tə:ri:] *n* (cheek, nerve) ずうずうしさ zúzūshisà

effusive [ifju:'siv] *adj* (handshake, welcome) 熱烈な netsúretsu na

e.g. [i:dʒi:'] *adv abbr* (= *exempli gratia*) 例えば tatóèba

egg [eg] *n* 卵 tamágò
  hard-boiled/soft-boiled egg 堅ゆで〔半熟〕卵 katáyude〔haṅjuku〕tamàgo

eggcup [eg'kʌp] *n* エッグカップ eggúkappù

egg on *vt* (in fight etc) そそのかす sosónokasù

eggplant [eg'plænt] (*esp US*) *n* (aubergine) ナス násù

eggshell [eg'ʃel] *n* 卵の殻 tamágò no kará

ego [i:'gou] *n* (self-esteem) 自尊心 jisóñshin

egotism [i:'gətizəm] *n* 利己主義 rikóshugì

egotist [i:'gətist] *n* 利己主義者 rikóshugishà, エゴイスト egóisùto

Egypt [i:'dʒipt] *n* エジプト ejíputo

Egyptian [idʒip'ʃən] *adj* エジプトの ejíputo no
  ◆*n* エジプト人 ejíputojìn

eiderdown [ai'də:rdaun] *n* (quilt) 羽布団 haṅébutòn

eight [eit] *num* 八 (の) hachí(no), 八つ

(の) yattsú no

eighteen [ei'ti:n'] *num* 十八 (の) júhachi (no)

eighth [eitθ] *num* 第八の dáihachi no

eighty [ei'ti:] *num* 八十 (の) hachíjū(no)

Eire [e:r'ə] *n* アイルランド aíruraṅdo

either [i:'ðə:r] *adj* (one or other) どちらかの dóchìraka no; (both, each) 両方の ryōhò no
  ◆*pron*: *either (of them)* どちらも...ない dóchìra mo ...nai
  ◆*adv* ...も...ない ...mo ...naì
  ◆*conj*: *either yes or no* はいかいいえか hái ka iíe kà
  on either side 両側に ryógawa ni
  I don't like either どちらも好きじゃない dóchìra mo sukí ja naì
  no, I don't either いいえ, 私もしない iíe, watákushi mò shinaì

eject [idʒekt'] *vt* (object) 放出する hōshutsu suru; (tenant) 立ちのかせる tachínokaserù; (gatecrasher etc) 追出す oídasù

eke [i:k]: *to eke out* *vt* (make last) 間に合せる ma ni awaserù

elaborate [*n* ilæb'ə:rit *vb* ilæb'ə:reit] *adj* (complex: network, plan, ritual) 複雑な fukúzatsu na
  ◆*vt* (expand) 拡張する kakúchō suru; (refine) 洗練する señren suru
  ◆*vi*: *to elaborate (on)* (idea, plan etc) (...を) 詳しく説明する (...wo) kuwáshikù setsúmei suru

elapse [ilæps'] *vi* (time) 過ぎる sugírù

elastic [ilæs'tik] *n* (material) ゴムひも gomúhimo
  ◆*adj* (stretchy) 弾力性のある dañryokusei no arù; (adaptable) 融通の利く yúzū no kikù

elastic band (*BRIT*) *n* 輪ゴム wagómu

elated [ilei'tid] *adj*: *to be elated* 大喜びになっている ōyorðkobi ni natté irù

elation [ilei'ʃən] *n* (happiness, excitement) 大喜び ōyorðkobi

elbow [el'bou] *n* (ANAT: *also* of sleeve) ひじ hijí

elder [el'də:r] *adj* (brother, sister etc) 年上の toshúe no

♦*n* (tree) ニワトコ niwátoko; (older person: *gen pl*) 年上の人々 toshíue no hitóbìto

elderly [el'də:rli:] *adj* (old) 年寄の toshíyorì no
♦*npl*: *the elderly* 老人 rójin

eldest [el'dist] *adj* 最年長の saíneňchò no
♦*n* 最年長の人 saíneňchò no hitó
the eldest child/son/daughter 長子〔長男，長女〕chóshì〔chónàn, chójò〕

elect [ilekt'] *vt* (government, representative, spokesman etc) 選出する seňshutsu suru
♦*adj*: *the president elect* 次期大統領 jíkìdaítòryò ◊当選したものの，まだ就任していない人について言う tôsen shita mono nò, mádà shûnin shite inaî hitó nì tsuîte iú
to elect to do (choose) ...する事にする ...surú kotò ni suru

election [ilek'∫ən] *n* (voting) 選挙 séňkyo; (installation) 当選 tôsen

electioneering [ilek∫əni:'riŋ] *n* (campaigning) 選挙運動 seňkyouňdō

elector [ilek'tə:r] *n* (voter) 有権者 yúkeňsha

electoral [ilek'tə:rəl] *adj* (register, roll) 有権者の yúkeňsha no

electorate [ilek'tə:rit] *n* (of constituency, country) 有権者 yúkeňsha no ◊ 総称 sóshō

electric [ilek'trik] *adj* (machine, current, power) 電気の déňki no

electrical [ilek'trikəl] *adj* (appliance, system, energy) 電気の déňki no

electric blanket *n* 電気毛布 deňkimôfu

electric chair (*US*) *n* 電気いす deňkiîsu

electric fire *n* 電気ヒーター deňkihîtā

electrician [ilektri∫'ən] *n* 電気屋 deňkiyà

electricity [ilektris'əti:] *n* 電気 déňki

electrify [ilek'trəfai] *vt* (fence) 帯電させる taíden saserù; (rail network) 電化する deňka suru; (audience) ぎょっとさせる gyóttò saserù

electrocute [ilek'trəkju:t] *vt* 感電死させる kaňdeňshi sasérù

electrode [ilek'troud] *n* 電極 deňkyoku

electron [ilek'tra:n] *n* (PHYSICS) 電子 denshi

electronic [ilektra:n'ik] *adj* (device, equipment) 電子の déňshi no

electronic mail *n* 電子郵便 deňshiyûbin

electronics [ilektra:n'iks] *n* (industry, technology) 電子工学 deňshikôgaku

elegance [el'əgəns] *n* (of person, building) 優雅さ yûgàsa, エレガンス érègansu; (of idea, plan) 見事さ migótosà

elegant [el'əgənt] *adj* (person, building) 優雅な yûga na; (idea, plan) 洗練された seňren saretá

element [el'əmənt] *n* (part: of whole, job, process) 要素 yôso; (CHEM) 元素 geňso; (of heater, kettle etc) ヒーター素子 hîtāsoshi

elementary [elimen'tə:ri:] *adj* (basic) 基本的な kihônteki na; (primitive) 原始的な geňshiteki na; (school, education) 初等の shotô no

elephant [el'əfənt] *n* ゾウ zô

elevation [eləvei'∫ən] *n* (raising, promotion) 向上 kôjō; (height) 海抜 kâíbatsu

elevator [el'əveitə:r] *n* (*US*: lift) エレベーター erébètā

eleven [ilev'ən] *num* 十一 (の) jûichi no

elevenses [ilev'ənziz] (*BRIT*) *npl* (coffeebreak) 午前のおやつ gózèn no o-yátsu

eleventh [ilev'ənθ] *num* 第十一の dáîjûichi no

elf [elf] (*pl* **elves**) *n* 小妖精 shóyōsei

elicit [ilis'it] *vt*: *to elicit (from)* (information, response, reaction) (...から)...を引出す (...karà) ...wò hikîdasù

eligible [el'idʒəbəl] *adj* (qualified, suitable) 資格のある shikáku no arù; (man, woman) 好ましい結婚相手である konómashiî kekkón aîte de arù
to be eligible for something (qualified, suitable) ...する資格がある ...suru shikáku ga arù

eliminate [əlim'əneit] *vt* (eradicate: poverty, smoking) 無くす nakúsù; (candidate, team, contestant) 除外する jogái suru

elimination [əlimənei'∫ən] *n* (eradication) 根絶 koňzetsu; (of candidate, team etc) 除外 jogái

élite [ili:t'] n エリート erítð

elm [elm] n (tree) ニレ niré; (wood) ニレ材 nirézài

elocution [eləkju:'ʃən] n 話術 wájùtsu

elongated [ilɔ:ŋ'geitid] adj (body, shadow) 細長い hosónagaì

elope [iloup'] vi 駆落ちする kakéochi suru

elopement [iloup'mənt] n 駆落ち kakéochi

eloquence [el'əkwəns] n (of person, description, speech) 雄弁 yúben

eloquent [el'əkwənt] adj (person, description, speech) 雄弁な yúben na

else [els] adv (other) 外に hoká ni

something else 外の物 hoká no monð

somewhere else 外の場所 hoká no bashò

everywhere else 外はどこも hoká wà dókò mo

where else? 外にどこ? hoká nì dókò?

there was little else to do 外にする事はなかった hoká nì suru kotð wa nákàtta

nobody else spoke 外にだれもしゃべらなかった hoká nì daré mò shabéranakàttà

elsewhere [els'we:r] adv (be) 外の所にhoká no tokorð ni; (go) 外の所へ hoká no tokorð e

elucidate [ilu:'sideit] vt (argument, point) 解明する kaímei suru

elude [ilu:d'] vt (subj: fact, idea: not realized) 気付かれない kizúkarenaì; (: : not remembered) 思い出せない omóidasenaì; (: : not understood) 理解されない ríkai sarénaì; (captor) ...から逃げる ...kara nigérù; (capture) 免れる manúgarerù

elusive [ilu:'siv] adj (person, animal) 見付けにくい mitsúkenikuì; (quality) 分かりにくい wakárinikuì

elves [elvz] npl of elf

emaciated [imei'ʃi:eitid] adj (person, animal) 衰弱した suíjaku shita

emanate [em'əneit] vi: *to emanate from* (idea, feeling) ...から放たれる ...ka-

ra hanatárerù; (sound) ...から聞こえる ...kara kikóerù; (light) ...から放射される ...kara hósha sarerù

emancipate [imæn'səpeit] vt (poor, slave, women) 解放する kaíhō suru

emancipation [imænsəpei'ʃən] n (of poor, slaves, women) 解放 kaíhō

embankment [embæŋk'mənt] n (of road, railway) 土手 dotè; (of river) 堤防teíbō

embargo [emba:r'gou] (pl **embargoes**) n (POL, COMM) 通商停止 tsúshōteíshi

embark [emba:rk'] vi (NAUT): *to embark (on)* (...に)乗船する (...ni) jósen suru

♦vt (passengers, cargo) 乗せる nosérù

to embark on (journey) ...に出発する ...ni shuppátsu surù; (task, course of action) ...に乗出す ...ni norídasù

embarkation [emba:rkei'ʃən] n (of people) 乗船 jósen; (of cargo) 船積み funázumi

embarrass [embær'əs] vt (emotionally) 恥をかかせる hají wò kakáserù; (politician, government) 困らせる komáraserù

embarrassed [embær'əst] adj (laugh, silence) 極り悪そうな kimáriwarusò na

embarrassing [embær'əsiŋ] adj (statement, situation, moment) 恥ずかしい hazúkashiì

embarrassment [embær'əsmənt] n (shame) 恥 hají; (embarrassing problem) 厄介な問題 yákkài na mońdai

embassy [em'bəsi:] n (diplomats) 使節団 shisétsudàn; (building) 大使館 taíshikàn

embedded [embed'id] adj (object) 埋め込まれた umékomareta

embellish [embel'iʃ] vt (place, dress) 飾る kazáru; (account) 潤色する juńshoku suru

embers [em'bə:rz] npl: *the embers (of the fire)* 残り火 nokóribì

embezzle [embez'əl] vt (LAW) 横領する ôryð suru

embezzlement [embez'əlmənt] n 横領 ôryð

embitter [embit'ə:r] vt (fig: sour) 世の中を憎ませる yo nð nàka wo nikúmaserù

emblem [em'bləm] n (design) 標章 hyóshō、マーク mǎku; (symbol) 象徴 shóchō

embody [əmbə:d'i:] vt (idea, principle) 現す aráwasù; (features: include, contain) 含む fukúmù

embossed [embɔ:st'] adj (design, word) 浮き出しの ukídashi no

embrace [embreis'] vt (hug) 抱く dakú; (include) 含む fukúmù
♦vi (hug) 抱合う dakíaù
♦n (hug) 抱擁 hōyō

embroider [embrɔi'də:r] vt (cloth) 刺しゅうする shishū suru

embroidery [embrɔi'də:ri:] n 刺しゅう shishū

embryo [em'bri:ou] n (BIO) はい haí

emerald [em'ə:rəld] n エメラルド émárùdo

emerge [imə:rdʒ'] vi: **to emerge (from)** (...から) 出て来る (...kara) détè kuru; (fact: from discussion etc) (...で) 明らかになる (...de) akíraka ni nárù; (new idea, industry, society) 現れる aráwarerù
to emerge from sleep 目が覚める mé gà samérù
to emerge from prison 釈放される shakúhō sarerù

emergency [imə:r'dʒənsi:] n (crisis) 非常時 hijójì
in an emergency 緊急の場合 kiñkyū no baái
state of emergency 緊急事態 kiñkyūjitài

emergency cord (US) n 非常の際に引くコード hijó no saí ni hikú kōdo

emergency exit n 非常口 hijóguchi

emergency landing n (AVIAT) 不時着陸 fujíchakùriku

emergency services npl (fire, police, ambulance) 非常時のサービス機関 hijójì no sábisukikàn

emergent [imə:r'dʒənt] adj (nation) 最近独立した saíkin dokùritsu shitá; (group) 最近創立された saíkin sōritsu saretá

emery board [em'ə:ri:-] n つめやすり tsuméyasùri ◇ボール紙製の物を指す bōrugamisei no monò wo sásù

emigrant [em'əgrənt] n (from native country) 移住者 ijūshà

emigrate [em'əgreit] vi (from native country) 移住する ijū suru

emigration [eməgrei'ʃən] n 移住 ijū

eminent [em'ənənt] adj (scientist, writer) 著名な chomei na

emission [imiʃ'ən] n (of gas) 放出 hōshutsu; (of radiation) 放射 hōsha

emit [imit'] vt (smoke, smell, sound) 出す dásù; (light, heat) 放射する hōsha suru

emotion [imou'ʃən] n 感情 kañjō

emotional [imou'ʃənəl] adj (needs, exhaustion, person, issue etc) 感情的な kañjōteki na; (scene etc) 感動的な kañdōteki na

emotive [imou'tiv] adj (subject, language) 感情に訴える kañjō nì uttáerù

emperor [em'pə:rə:r] n (gen) 皇帝 kōtei; (of Japan) 天皇 tefinō

emphases [em'fəsi:z] npl of emphasis

emphasis [em'fəsis] (pl **emphases**) n (importance) 重点 jūten; (stress) 強調 kyōchō

emphasize [em'fəsaiz] vt (word, point) 強調する kyōchō suru; (feature) 浮彫にする ukíbori ni surù

emphatic [əmfæt'ik] adj (statement, denial, manner, person) 断固とした dáñko to shita

emphatically [əmfæt'ikli:] adv (forcefully) 断固として dáñko to shitē; (certainly) 絶対に zéttái ni

empire [em'paiə:r] n (also fig) 帝国 teíkoku

empirical [empir'ikəl] adj (knowledge, study) 経験的な keíkenteki na

employ [emplɔi'] vt (workforce, person) 雇う yatóù; (tool, weapon) 使用する shiyō suru

employee [emplɔi'i:] n 雇用人 koyóñìn

employer [emplɔi'ə:r] n 雇い主 yatóinùshi

employment [emplɔi'mənt] n (work) 就職 shūshoku

employment agency n 就職あっ旋会社 shūshokuassengaìsha

empower [empau'ə:r] vt: **to empower**

someone to do something (LAW, ADMIN) ...に...する権限を与える ...ni ...suru keñgen wò atáerù

empress [em'pris] *n* (woman emperor) 女帝 jotéi; (wife of emperor) 皇后 kốgō

emptiness [emp'ti:nis] *n* (of area, region etc) 何もない事 nání mo naì kotò; (of life etc) むなしさ munáshìsa

empty [emp'ti:] *adj* (container) 空の kará no, 空っぽの karáppò no; (place, street) だれもいない darè mò inaî; (house, room, space) 空きの akí no
♦*vt* 空にする kará ni suru
♦*vi* (house, container) 空になる kará nì nárù; (liquid) 注ぐ sosógù

an empty threat こけおどし kokéodòshi

an empty promise 空約束 karáyakùsoku

empty-handed [empti:hæn'did] *adj* 手ぶらの tebúra no

emulate [em'jəleit] *vt* (hero, idol) まねる manérù

emulsion [imʌl'ʃən] *n* (liquid) 乳剤 nyúzai; (*also:* **emulsion paint**) 水溶ペンキ suíyōpeñki

enable [enei'bəl] *vt:* *to enable someone to do* (permit, allow) ...が...する事を許可する ...ga ...surú kotò wo kyókà suru; (make possible) ...が...する事を可能にする ...ga ...surú kotò wo kanố ni surù

enact [enækt'] *vt* (law) 制定する seítei suru; (play, role) 上演する jốen suru

enamel [inæm'əl] *n* (for decoration) エナメル enámerù; (*also:* **enamel paint**) エナメルペイント enámerupeíñto; (of tooth) エナメル質 enámerushìtsu

enamored [enæm'ə:rd] *adj:* *to be enamored of* (person, pastime, idea, belief) ...に惚れる ...ni horérù

encased [enkeist'] *adj:* *encased in* (plaster, shell) ...に覆われた ...ni ốwaretà

enchant [entʃænt'] *vt* (delight) 魅了する miryố suru

enchanted [entʃæn'tid] *adj* (castle, island) 魔法の mahố no

enchanting [entʃæn'tiŋ] *adj* (appearance, behavior, person) 魅力的な miryố-

kuteki na

encircle [ensə:r'kəl] *vt* (place, prisoner) 囲む kakómù

encl. *abbr* (= *enclosed*) 同封の dốfū no

enclave [en'kleiv] *n* 飛び地 tobíchi

enclose [enklouz'] *vt* (land, space) 囲む kakómù; (object) 閉じ込める tojíkomerù; (letter etc): *to enclose (with)* (...に) 同封する (...ni) dốfū suru

please find enclosed ...を同封します ...wo dốfū shimasù

enclosure [enklou'ʒə:r] *n* (area of land) 囲い kakói

encompass [enkʌm'pəs] *vt* (include: subject, measure) 含む fukúmù

encore [ɑ:ŋ'kɔːr] *excl* アンコール añkồru
♦*n* (THEATER) アンコール añkồru

encounter [enkaun'tə:r] *n* (with person etc) 出会い deaî; (with problem etc) 直面 chokúmen
♦*vt* (person) ...に出会う ...ni deaû; (new experience, problem) 直面する chokúmen suru

encourage [enkə:r'idʒ] *vt* (person): *to encourage someone (to do something)* (...する事を) ...に勧める (...surú kotò wo) ...ni susúmerù; (activity, attitude) 激励する gekírei suru; (growth, industry) 刺激する shigéki suru

encouragement [enkə:r'idʒmənt] *n* (to do something) 勧め susúme; (of activity, attitude) 激励 gekírei; (of growth, industry) 刺激 shigéki

encroach [enkroutʃ'] *vi:* *to encroach (up)on* (rights) ...を侵す ...wo okásù; (property) ...に侵入する ...ni shiñnyū suru; (time) ...の邪魔をする ...no jamá wo surù

encrusted [enkrʌs'tid] *adj:* *encrusted with* (gems) ...をちりばめられた ...wo chiríbamereretà; (snow, dirt) ...に覆われた ...ni ốwaretà

encumber [enkʌm'bə:r] *vt:* *to be encumbered with* (suitcase, baggage etc) ...が邪魔になっている ...ga jamá nì natté irù; (debts) ...を背負っている ...wo seôtte irù

encyclop(a)edia [ensaikləpi:'di:ə] *n* 百

科辞典 hyakkájíten

end [end] *n* (of period, event, book etc)
終り owári; (of table, street, line, rope)
端 hashí; (of town) 外れ hazúre; (of
pointed object) 先 sakí; (aim) 目的 mokúteki

♦*vt* (finish) 終える oérù; (stop: activity,
protest etc)

JPNや止める yamérù

♦*vi* (situation, activity, period etc) 終る
owárù

in the end 仕舞いには shimái ni wà
on end (object) 縦になって táte ni natté
to stand on end (hair) よだつ yodátsù
for hours on end ぶっ続けて何時間も
buttsúzuke dè nañjikàn mo

endanger [endein'dʒəːr] *vt* (lives, prospects) 危険にさらす kikén nì sarásù

endearing [endiːr'iŋ] *adj* (personality,
conduct) 愛敬のある aíkyo no arù

endeavor [endev'əːr] (*BRIT* **endeavour**)
n (attempt) 試み kokóromi; (effort) 努力
dóryòku

♦*vi*: *to endeavor to do* (attempt) ...しよ
うとする ...shiyó tò surù; (strive) ...しよ
うと努力する ...shiyó tò dóryòku suru

endemic [endem'ik] *adj* (poverty, disease) 地方特有の chihótokuyù no

ending [en'diŋ] *n* (of book, film, play
etc) 結末 ketsúmatsu; (LING) 語尾 góbì

endive [en'daiv] *n* (curly) エンダイブ eñ-
daìbu; (smooth: chicory) チコリ chikórì

endless [end'lis] *adj* (argument, search)
果てし無い hatéshinaì; (forest, beach)
延々と続く eñ-en tò tsuzúkù

endorse [endɔːrs'] *vt* (check) ...に裏書き
する ...ni urágaki suru; (approve: proposal, plan, candidate) 推薦する suísen
suru

endorsement [endɔːrs'mənt] *n* (approval) 推薦 suísen; (*BRIT*: on driving
licence) 違反記録 ihánkiròku

endow [endau'] *vt* (provide with money)
...に金を寄付する ...ni kané wò kifú suru
to be endowed with (talent, quality)
...の持主である ...no mochínùshi de árù

end up *vi*: *to end up in* (place) ...に行っ
てしまう ...ni itté shimaù; (condition)
...になってしまう ...ni natté shimaù

endurance [enduːr'əns] *n* (stamina) 耐久
力 taíkyuryòku; (patience) 忍耐強さ niñ-
taizuyòsa

endure [enduːr'] *vt* (bear: pain, suffering)
耐える taérù

♦*vi* (last: friendship, love etc) 長続きす
る nagátsuzùki suru
an enduring work of art 不朽の名作
fukyū no meísaku

enemy [en'əmiː] *adj* (forces, strategy) 敵
の tekí no

♦*n* 敵 tekí

energetic [enəːrdʒet'ik] *adj* (person,
activity) 精力的な seíryokuteki na

energy [en'əːrdʒiː] *n* (strength, drive) 精
力 seíryoku; (power: nuclear energy etc)
エネルギー enérùgī

enforce [enfɔːrs'] *vt* (LAW) 実施する jisshí suru

engage [engeidʒ'] *vt* (attention, interest)
引く hikú; (employ: consultant, lawyer)
雇う yatóù; (AUT: clutch) つなぐ tsunágù

♦*vi* (TECH) 掛る kakárù
to engage in (commerce, study,
research etc) ...に従事する ...ni jūji suru
to engage someone in conversation
...に話し掛ける ...ni hanáshikakerù

engaged [engeidʒd'] *adj* (betrothed) 婚約
している koñ-yaku shite irù; (*BRIT*:
busy, in use) 使用中の shiyóchū
to get engaged 婚約する koñ-yaku suru

engaged tone (*BRIT*) *n* (TEL) 話し中
の信号音 hanáshichù no shiñgōon

engagement [engeidʒ'mənt] *n* (appointment) 約束 yakúsoku; (booking: for
musician, comedian etc) 仕事 shigóto;
(to marry) 婚約 koñ-yaku

engagement ring *n* 婚約指輪 koñ-yaku yubìwa, エンゲージリング eñgējiriñ-
gu

engaging [engei'dʒiŋ] *adj* (personality,
trait) 愛敬のある aíkyo no arù

engender [endʒen'dəːr] *vt* (feeling,
sense) 生む umú

engine [en'dʒən] *n* (AUT) エンジン éñjin;
(RAIL) 機関車 kikáñsha

engine driver n (RAIL) 運転手 uńteñshu

engineer [endʒəni:r'] n (designer) 技師 gíshì; (BRIT: for repairs) 修理工 shúrikō; (US: RAIL) 運転手 uńteñshu; (on ship) 機関士 kikáńshi

engineering [endʒəni:r'iŋ] n (science) 工学 kṓgaku; (design, construction: of roads, bridges) 建設 keńsetsu; (: of cars, ships, machines) 製造 seízō

England [iŋ'glənd] n イングランド íŋgurando

English [iŋ'gliʃ] adj イングランドの íŋgurando no; (LING) 英語の eígo no
♦n (LING) 英語 eígo
♦npl: **the English** イングランド人 iŋgurandojìn ◇総称 sṓshō

English Channel n: **the English Channel** イギリス海峡 igírisukaíkyō

Englishman/woman [iŋ'gliʃmən/wumən] (pl **Englishmen/women**) n イングランド人男性[女性] iŋgurandojin dañsei(jòsei)

engraving [engrei'viŋ] n (picture, print) 版画 hañga

engrossed [engroust'] adj: **engrossed in** (book, program) ...に夢中になった ...ni muchū ni nattà

engulf [engʌlf'] vt (subj: fire) 巻込む makíkomù; (water) 飲込む nomíkomù; (: panic, fear) 襲う osóù

enhance [enhæns'] vt (enjoyment, reputation) 高める takámerù; (beauty) 増す masú

enigma [enig'mə] n (mystery) なぞ nazó

enigmatic [enigmæt'ik] adj (smile) なぞめいた nazómeìta; (person) 得体の知れない etái no shirenaì

enjoy [endʒɔi'] vt (like) ...が好きである ...ga sukí de arù; (take pleasure in) 楽しむ tanóshimù; (have benefit of: health, fortune, success) ...に恵まれる ...ni megúmarerù
to enjoy oneself 楽しむ tanóshimù

enjoyable [endʒɔi'əbəl] adj (pleasant) 楽しい tanóshiì

enjoyment [endʒɔi'mənt] n (feeling of pleasure) 楽しさ tanóshìsa; (activity) 楽

しみ tanóshimì

enlarge [enla:rdʒ'] vt (size, scope) 拡大する kakúdai suru; (PHOT) 引伸ばす hikínobasù
♦vi: **to enlarge on** (subject) 詳しく話す kuwáshikù hanásù

enlargement [enla:rdʒ'mənt] n (PHOT) 引伸ばし hikínobashi

enlighten [enlait'ən] vt (inform) ...に教える ...ni oshíerù

enlightened [enlait'ənd] adj (person, policy, system) 聡明な sōmei na

enlightenment [enlait'ənmənt] n: **the Enlightenment** (HISTORY) 啓もう運動 keímōuñdō

enlist [enlist'] vt (soldier) 入隊させる nyútai saserù; (person) ...の助けを借りる ...no tasúke wò karírù; (support, help) 頼む tanómù
♦vi: **to enlist in** (army, navy etc) ...に入隊する ...ni nyútai suru

enmity [en'miti:] n (hostility) 恨み urámi

enormity [inɔ:r'miti:] n (of problem, danger) 物すごさ monósugòsa

enormous [inɔ:r'məs] adj (size, amount) 巨大な kyodái na; (delight, pleasure, success etc) 大きな ṓkìna

enough [inʌf'] adj (time, books, people etc) 十分な jūbuñ na
♦pron 十分 jūbuñ
♦adv: **big enough** 十分に大きい júbuñ ni ṓkìì
he has not worked enough 彼の努力が足りない kárè no dóryòku ga tarínaì
have you got enough? 足りましたか tarímashìta ka
enough to eat 食べ物が足りる tabémonò ga tarírù
enough! もういい! mố iì!
that's enough, thanks もう沢山です。有難う。mố takusañ desu. arígàtō.
I've had enough of him 彼にはもううんざりだ kárè ni wa mố uñzari dá
... which, funnily/oddly enough ... おかしいけれども、それは... okáshiì kerédomo, soré wà ...

enquire [enkwai'ə:r] vt, vi = **inquire**

enrage [enreidʒ'] vt (anger, madden) 激

怒させる gékìdo saseru

enrich [enritʃ'] vt (morally, spiritually) 豊かにする yútàka ni suru; (financially) 金持ちにする kanémochi ni surù

enroll [enroul'] (BRIT: **enrol**) vt (at school, university) 入学させる nyúgaku saserù; (on course) 登録する tōroku suru; (in club etc) 入会させる nyúkai saserù

♦vi (at school, university) 入学する nyúgaku suru; (on course) 参加手続きをする sañkatetsuzúki wo suru; (in club etc) 入会する nyúkai suru

enrollment [enroul'mənt] (BRIT: **enrolment**) n (registration) 登録 tōroku

en route [ɔːn ruːt'] adv (on the way) 途中で tochú de

ensue [ensuː'] vi (follow) ...の結果として起る ...no kekká toshitè okōrù

ensure [enʃuːr'] vt (result, safety) 確実にする kakújitsu ni surù

entail [enteil'] vt (involve) 要する yō surù

entangled [entæŋ'gəld] adj: **to become entangled (in)** (in net, rope etc) ...に絡まる ...ni karámarù

enter [en'təːr] vt (room, club) ...に入る ...ni háirù; (race, competition) ...に参加する ...ni sañkà suru, ...に出場する ...ni shutsújo suru; (someone for a competition) ...に...の参加を申込む ...ni ...no sañka wò mōshikomù; (write down) 記入する kinyū suru; (COMPUT: data) 入力する nyúryòku suru

♦vi (come or go in) 入る háiru

enter for vt fus (race, competition, examination) ...に参加を申込む ...ni sañka wò mōshikomù

enter into vt fus (discussion, correspondence, negotiations) 始める hajímerù; (agreement) 結ぶ musúbù

enterprise [en'təːrpraiz] n (company, business) 企業 kigyō; (undertaking) 企画 kikáku; (initiative) 進取の気 shíñshu no ki

free enterprise 自由企業 jiyúkigyò

private enterprise (private company) 民間企業 miñkankigyō, 私企業 shikígyò

enterprising [en'təːrpraiziŋ] adj (adventurous) 進取の気に富んだ shíñshu no ki ni tóñda

entertain [entəːrtein'] vt (amuse) 楽しませる tanóshimaserù; (invite: guest) 接待する séttài suru; (idea, plan) 考える kañgaerù

entertainer [entəːrtein'əːr] n (TV etc) 芸能人 geínōjìn

entertaining [entəːrtei'niŋ] adj 面白い omóshiroì

entertainment [entəːrtein'mənt] n (amusement) 娯楽 goráku; (show) 余興 yokyō

enthralled [enθrɔːld'] adj (engrossed, captivated) 魅せられた miséraretà

enthusiasm [enθuː'ziːæzəm] n (eagerness) 熱心さ nesshíñsa

enthusiast [enθuː'ziːæst] n (fan) マニア máñia

enthusiastic [enθuːziːæs'tik] adj (excited, eager) 熱心な nesshíñ na

to be enthusiastic about ...に夢中になっている ...ni muchū nì natté irù

entice [entais'] vt (lure, tempt) 誘惑する yūwaku suru

entire [entai'əːr] adj (whole) 全体の zeñtai no

entirely [entaiə'r'li:] adv (completely) 全く mattákù

entirety [entai'ə'rti:] n: **in its entirety** 全体に zeñtai ni

entitle [entait'əl] vt: **to entitle someone to something** ...に...に対する権利を与える ...ni ...ni taísuru keñri wò atáerù

entitled [entait'əld] adj (book, film etc) ...という題の ...to iú dai no

to be entitled to do (be allowed) ...する権利がある ...suru keñri ga árù

entity [en'titi:] n 物 monó

entourage [ɑːnturɑːʒ'] n (of celebrity, politician) 取巻き連 torímakireñ

entrails [en'treilz] npl (ANAT, ZOOL) 内臓 naízò

entrance [n en'trəns vb entræns'] n (way in) 入口 irígùchi; (arrival) 登場 tōjō

♦vt (enchant) 魅惑する miwáku suru

to gain entrance to (university, profession etc) ...に入る ...ni hâîru

entrance examination n 入学試験 nyûgakushikeñ, 入試 nyûshi

entrance fee n 入場料 nyûjōryō

entrance ramp (US) n (AUT) 入口ランプ iríguchiranpu

entrant [en'trənt] n (in race, competition etc) 参加者 sañkashà; (BRIT: in exam) 受験者 jukéñsha

entreat [entri:t'] vt (implore) 嘆願する tañgan suru

entrenched [entrentʃt'] adj (position, power) 固められた katámeraretà; (ideas) 定着した teíchakushità

entrepreneur [ɑ:ntrəprənər'] n (COMM) 企業家 kigyōka

entrust [entrʌst'] vt: **to entrust something to someone** ...を...に預ける ...wo ...ni azúkerù

entry [en'tri:] n (way in) 入口 iríguchi; (in competition) 参加者 sañkashà; (in register, account book) 記入 kinyû; (in reference book) 記事 kíjì; (arrival) 登場 tōjō; (to country) 入国 nyûkoku
「**no entry**」(to room etc) 立入禁止 tachíirikiñshi; (AUT) 進入禁止 shíñnyūkiñshi

entry form n (for club etc) 入会申込書 nyûkaimōshikomìsho; (for competition etc) 参加申込書 sañkamōshikomìsho

entry phone n 玄関のインターホン géñkan no iñtāhon

enumerate [inu:'mə:reit] vt (list) 列挙する rékkyo suru

enunciate [inʌn'si:eit] vt (word) はっきりと発音する hakkírì to hatsúon suru; (principle, plan etc) 明確に説明する meíkaku nì setsúmei suru

envelop [envel'əp] vt (cover, enclose) 覆い包む ôitsutsumù

envelope [en'vəloup] n 封筒 fûtō

envious [en'vi:əs] adj (person, look) うらやましい uráyamashiì

environment [envai'rənmənt] n (surroundings) 環境 kañkyō; (natural world):
the environment 環境 kañkyō

environmental [envairənmen'təl] adj 環境の kañkyō no

envisage [enviz'idʒ] vt (foresee) 予想する yosō suru

envoy [en'vɔi] n (diplomat) 特使 tôkùshi

envy [en'vi:] n (jealousy) せん望 señbō
♦vt うらやましく思う uráyamashìku omóù
to envy someone something ...の...をうらやましく思う ...no ...wo uráyamashìku omóù

enzyme [en'zaim] n (BIO, MED) 酵素 kôso

ephemeral [ifem'ə:rəl] adj (fashion, fame) つかの間の tsuká no mà no

epic [ep'ik] n (poem) 叙事詩 jojíshì; (book, film) 大作 taisaku
♦adj (journey) 歴史的な rekíshiteki na

epidemic [epidem'ik] n (of disease) 流行病 ryúkōbyō

epilepsy [ep'əlepsi:] n (MED) てんかん teñkan

epileptic [epəlep'tik] adj てんかんの teñkan no
♦n てんかん患者 teñkankañja

episode [ep'isoud] n (period, event) 事件 jíkèn; (TV, RADIO: installment) 1回 ikkái

epistle [ipis'əl] n (letter: also REL) 書簡 shokán

epitaph [ep'itæf] n 墓碑銘 bohímei

epithet [ep'əθet] n 形容語句 keíyōgokù

epitome [ipit'əmi:] n (model, archetype) 典型 teñkei

epitomize [ipit'əmaiz] vt (characterize, typify) ...の典型である ...no teñkei dè árù

epoch [ep'ək] n (age, era) 時代 jidái

equable [ek'wəbəl] adj (climate) 安定した añteishità; (temper, reply) 落着いた ochítsuità

equal [i:'kwəl] adj (size, number, amount) 等しい hitóshiì; (intensity, quality) 同様の dôyo na; (treatment, rights, opportunities) 平等な byôdo na
♦n (peer) 同輩 dôhai
♦vt (number) イコール ikôrù; (quality) ...と同様である ...to dôyo dè árù
to be equal to (task) ...を十分出来る ...wo jûbuñ dekírù

equality [ikwɑ:l'iti:] n 平等 byôdō

equalize [i:'kwəlaiz] vi (SPORT) 同点に

する dṓten ni surù

equally [iːkwəliː] adv (share, divide etc) 平等 に byṓdō ni; (good, brilliant, bad etc) 同様 に dṓyō ni

equanimity [iːkwənimˈitiː] n (calm) 平静 さ heíseisà

equate [ikweitˈ] vt: *to equate something with* ...を...と同等視する ...wo ...to dṓtōshī surù

equation [ikweiˈʒən] n (MATH) 方程式 hōteishiki

equator [ikweiˈtər] n 赤道 sekídō

equestrian [ikwesˈtriːən] adj 乗馬 の jṓba no

equilibrium [iːkwəlibˈriːəm] n (balance) 均衡 kíñkō; (composure) 平静 さ heíseisà

equinox [iːˈkwənɑːks] n: *spring/autumn equinox* 春〔秋〕分 の 日 shuñ〔shū〕bun no hí

equip [ikwipˈ] vt (person, army, car etc) ...に...を装備させる ...ni ...wo sōbi saserù; (room) ...に...を備え付ける ...ni ...wo sonáetsukerù

to be well equipped 装備が十分である sōbi gà jūbuñ de árù

to be equipped with ...を装備している ...wo sōbi shite irù

equipment [ikwipˈmənt] n (tools, machinery) 設備 sétsùbi

equitable [ekˈwitəbəl] adj (settlement, agreement) 公正な kōsei na

equities [ekˈwitiːz] (*BRIT*) npl (COMM) 普通株 futsúkabu

equivalent [ikwivˈələnt] adj: *equivalent (to)* (...に)相当する (...ni) sōtō suru
♦n (equal) 相当の物 sōtō no monò

equivocal [ikwivˈəkəl] adj (ambiguous) あいまいな aímai na; (open to suspicion) いかがわしい ikágawashiì

era [iːˈrə] n (age, period) 時代 jidái

eradicate [irædˈikeit] vt (disease, problem) 根絶する koñzetsu suru

erase [ireisˈ] vt (tape, writing) 消す kesú

eraser [ireiˈsəːr] n (for pencil etc) 消しゴム keshígomu; (*US*: for blackboard etc) 黒板消し kokúbañkeshi

erect [irektˈ] adj (posture) 直立の chokúritsu no; (tail, ears) ぴんと立てた piñ tō tatétā
♦vt (build) 建てる tatérù; (assemble) 組立てる kumítaterù

erection [irekˈʃən] n (of building) 建築 keñchiku; (of statue) 建立 koñryū; (of tent) 張る事 harú kotò; (of machinery etc) 組立て kumítate; (PHYSIOL) ぼっ起 bokkí

ermine [əːrˈmin] n (fur) アーミン ámìn

erode [iroudˈ] vt (soil, rock) 侵食する shiñshoku suru; (metal) 腐食する fushóku suru; (confidence, power) 揺るがす yurúgasù

erosion [irouˈʒən] n (of soil, rock) 侵食 shiñshoku; (of metal) 腐食 fushóku; (of confidence, power) 揺るがされる事 yurúgasarerù kotò

erotic [irɑːtˈik] adj (activities) 性的なseíteki na; (dreams, books, films) 扇情的な señjōteki na, エロチックな erōchikkù na

eroticism [irɑːtˈisizəm] n 好色 kṓshoku, エロチシズム erōchishizùmu

err [əːr] vi (formal: make a mistake) 過ちを犯す ayámachi wò okásù

errand [eːrˈənd] n お使い o-tsúkai

erratic [irætˈik] adj (behavior) 突飛な toppí na; (attempts, noise) 不規則な fukísoku na

erroneous [irouˈniːəs] adj (belief, opinion) 間違った machígattà

error [eːrˈəːr] n (mistake) 間違い machígaì, エラー érā

erudite [eːrˈjudait] adj (person) 博学な hakúgaku na

erupt [irʌptˈ] vi (volcano) 噴火する fuñka suru; (war, crisis) ぼっ発する boppátsu suru

eruption [irʌpˈʃən] n (of volcano) 噴火 fuñka; (of fighting) ぼっ発 boppátsu

escalate [esˈkəleit] vi (conflict, crisis) 拡大する kakúdai suru, エスカレートする esúkarēto suru

escalator [esˈkəleitəːr] n エスカレータ ー esúkarētā

escapade [esˈkəpeid] n (adventure) 冒険 bṓken

escape [eskeipˈ] n (from prison) 脱走 dassṓ; (from person) 逃げる事 nigéru kotò; (of gas) 漏れる事 moréru kotò

♦vi (get away) 逃げる nigérù; (from jail) 脱走する dassō suru; (leak) 漏れる moréru

♦vt (consequences, responsibility etc) 回避する kaíhi suru; (elude): *his name escapes me* 彼の名前を思い出せない kárè no namáe wò omóidasenaì

to escape from (place) ...から脱出する ...kara dasshútsu suru; (person) ...から逃げる ...kara nigérù

escapism [eskei'pizəm] *n* 現実逃避 geñjitsutòhi

escort [*n* es'kɔːrt *vb* eskɔːrt'] *n* (MIL, POLICE) 護衛 goéi; (companion) 同伴者 dōhañsha

♦vt (person) ...に同伴する ...ni dōhan suru

Eskimo [es'kəmou] *n* エスキモー人 esúkimòjin

esoteric [esəte:r'ik] *adj* 難解な nañkai na

especially [espeʃ'əli:] *adv* (above all, particularly) 特に tókù ni

espionage [es'pi:ənɑːʒ] *n* (POL, MIL, COMM) スパイ行為 supáikòi

esplanade [espləneid'] *n* (by sea) 海岸の遊歩道 kaígan nò yūhodō

espouse [espauz'] *vt* (policy) 採用する saíyō suru; (idea) 信奉する shiñpō suru

Esq. *n abbr* = **Esquire**

Esquire [es'kwaiəːr] *n*: *J. Brown, Esquire* J.ブラウン様 jē buráun samá

essay [es'ei] *n* (SCOL) 小論文 shōroñbun; (LITERATURE) 随筆 zuíhitsu, エッセーéssè

essence [es'əns] *n* (soul, spirit) 本質 hoñshitsu; (CULIN) エキス ékìsu, エッセンス éssènsu

essential [əsen't∫əl] *adj* (necessary, vital) 不可欠な fukáketsu na; (basic) 根本的な koñponteki na

♦n (necessity) 不可欠な事柄 fukáketsu nà kotógarà

essentially [əsen't∫əli:] *adv* (basically) 根本的に koñponteki ni

establish [əstæb'liʃ] *vt* (organization, firm) 創立する sōritsu suru; (facts,

proof) 確認する kakúnin suru; (relations, contact) 樹立する jurítsu suru; (reputation) 作り上げる tsukúriagerù

established [əstæb'liʃt] *adj* (business) 定評のある teíhyō no arù; (custom, practice) 定着した teíchaku shità

establishment [əstæb'liʃmənt] *n* (of organization etc) 創立 sōritsu; (of facts etc) 確認 kakúnin; (of relations etc) 樹立 jurítsu; (of reputation) 作り上げる事 tsukúriageru kotò; (shop etc) 店 misé; (business, firm) 会社 kaísha; (institution) 施設 shísètsu

the Establishment 体制 taísei

estate [əsteit'] *n* (land) 屋敷 yashíki; (BRIT: also: **housing estate**) 住宅団地 jūtakudañchi; (LAW) 財産 zaísan

estate agent (BRIT) *n* 不動産屋 fudōsan-yà

estate car (BRIT) *n* ステーションワゴン sutéshonwagòn

esteem [əsti:m'] *n*: *to hold someone in high esteem* (admire, respect) ...を尊敬する ...wo soñkei suru

esthetic [esθet'ik] (US) *adj* = **aesthetic**

estimate [*n* es'təmit *vb* es'təmeit] *n* (calculation) 概算 gaísan; (assessment) 推定 suítei; (COMM: builder's etc) 見積 mitsúmori

♦vt (reckon, calculate) 推定する suítei suru

estimation [estəmei'∫ən] *n* (opinion) 意見 íkèn; (calculation) 推定 suítei

estranged [əstreindʒd'] *adj* (from spouse) ...と別居している ...to bekkyó shite irù; (from family, friends) ...と仲たがいしている ...to nakátagai shite irù

estuary [es't∫uːeri:] *n* 河口 kakō

etc *abbr* (= *et cetera*) など nádò

etching [etʃ'iŋ] *n* 版画 hañga, エッチング etchíngu

eternal [itəːr'nəl] *adj* (everlasting, unceasing) 永遠の eíen no; (unchanging: truth, value) 不変的な fuhénteki na

eternity [itəːr'niti:] *n* (REL) 永遠 eíen

ether [i:'θəːr] *n* (CHEM) エーテル ēteru

ethical [eθ'ikəl] *adj* (question, problem) 道徳的な dōtokuteki na

ethics [eθ'iks] n (science) 倫理学 riṅrigàku
♦npl (morality) 道徳 dótoku

Ethiopia [i:θi:ou'pi:ə] n エチオピア echíopìa

ethnic [eθ'nik] adj (population, music, culture etc) 民族の miṅzoku no

ethos [i:'θɑ:s] n 気風 kifū

etiquette [et'əkit] n (manners, conduct) 礼儀作法 reígisahò, エチケット échìketto

eucalyptus [ju:kəlip'təs] n (tree) ユーカリ yūkari

euphemism [ju:'fəmizəm] n えん曲表現 eṅkyokuhyōgen

euphoria [ju:fɔ:r'i:ə] n (elation) 幸福感 kōfukukaṅ

Eurocheque [ju:'routʃek] n ユーロチェック yūrochekkù ◊ ヨーロッパ諸国で通用する小切手 yōroppa shokòku de tsūyō surù kogíttè

Europe [ju:'rəp] n 欧州 ṓshù, ヨーロッパ yōroppà

European [ju:rəpi:'ən] adj 欧州の ṓshù no, ヨーロッパの yōroppà no
♦n ヨーロッパ人 yōroppajìn

euthanasia [ju:θənei'ʒə] n 安楽死 aṅrakushì

evacuate [ivæk'ju:eit] vt (people) 避難させる hínàn sasérù; (place) ...から避難させる ...kara hínàn sasérù

evacuation [ivækju:ei'ʃən] n 避難 hínàn

evade [iveid'] vt (tax, duty) 脱税する datsúzei suru; (question) 言逃れる iínogarerù; (responsibility) 回避する kaíhi suru; (person) 避ける sakérù

evaluate [ivæl'ju:eit] vt (importance, achievement, situation etc) 評価する hyṓka suru

evaporate [ivæp'əreit] vi (liquid) 蒸発する jṓhatsu suru; (feeling, attitude) 消えてなくなる kiéte nakunarù

evaporated milk [ivæp'əreitid-] n エバミルク ebámiruku

evasion [ivei'ʒən] n (of responsibility, situation etc) 回避 kaíhi
tax evasion 脱税 datsúzei

evasive [ivei'siv] adj (reply, action) 回避的な kaíhiteki na

eve [i:v] n: **on the eve of** ...の前夜に ...no zeṅ-ya ni

even [i:'vən] adj (level) 平らな taíra na; (smooth) 滑らかな naméràka na; (equal) 五分五分の gobúgobu no
♦adv (showing surprise) ...さえ ...sáè; (introducing a comparison) 更に sárà ni
an even number 偶数 gūsū
even if 例え...だとしても tatóe ...dá tò shité mò
even though 例え...だとしても tatóe ...dá tò shité mò
even more なおさら naósara
even so それにしても soré ni shite mò
not even ...さえも...ない ...sáè mo ...náì
even he was there 彼さえもいた kárè sáè mo itá
even on Sundays 日曜日にも nichíyòbi ni mo
to get even with someone ...に復しゅうする ...ni fukúshū suru

evening [i:v'niŋ] n (early) 夕方 yūgata; (late) 夜 yórù; (whole period, event) ...の夕べ ...no yūbe
in the evening 夕方に yūgata ni

evening class n 夜間学級 yakángakkyù

evening dress n (no pl: formal clothes) 夜会服 yakáifùku; (woman's) イブニングドレス ibúningu dorèsu

even out vi (ground) 平らになる taíra ni narù; (prices etc) 安定する aṅtei suru

event [ivent'] n (occurrence) 事件 jíkèn; (SPORT) イベント ibéṅto
in the event of ...の場合... ...no baái

eventful [ivent'fəl] adj (day) 忙しい isógashiì; (life, game) 波乱の多い háràn no ōì

eventual [iven'tʃu:əl] adj (outcome, goal) ゆくゆくの yukúyuku no

eventuality [ventʃu:æl'iti:] n (possibility) 可能性 kanṓsei

eventually [iven'tʃu:əli:] adv (finally) 結局 kekkyōku; (in time) やがて yagáte

ever [ev'ə:r] adv (always) 常に tsúnè ni; (at any time) いつか ítsù ka; (in question): **why ever not?** どうしてまたしないのか dṓshite matá shinaì no ká *the best ever* 絶対に一番良い物 zettái nī ichíban yoî monó

have you ever seen it? それを見た事がありますか soré wò míta kotó gà arímasù ká

better than ever なお一層良くなった náò issō yokù nátta

ever since それ以来 soré iraî

♦*conj* ...して以来 ...shité iraî

evergreen [ev'ə:rgri:n] *n* (tree, bush) 常緑樹 jóryokujù

everlasting [evə:rlæs'tiŋ] *adj* (love, life etc) 永遠の eîen no

KEYWORD

every [ev'ri:] *adj* 1 (each) すべての subète no, 皆の miná nò

every one of them (persons) 彼らは〔を〕皆 karèra wa 〔wo〕miná; (objects) それらは〔を〕皆 sorérà wa〔wo〕miná

I interviewed every applicant 私は応募者全員に面接しました watákushi wa ôboshà zén-in ni ménsetsu shimashìta

every shop in the town was closed 町中の店が閉っていました machíjū no misè gà shímáttè imáshita

2 (all possible) 可能な限りすべての kanô na kagìri subète no

I gave you every assistance 私は可能な限りあなたを助けました watákushi wa kanô na kagìri anátà wo tasúkemashìta

I have every confidence in him 私は完全に彼を信用しています watákushi wa kánzen ni karè wo shín-yōshite imasù

we wish you every success ご成功を祈ります go-séikō wo inórimasù

he's every bit as clever as his brother 才能に関しては彼は彼の兄に少しも引けを取りません saínō ni kàn shite wa kárè wa kárè no ánì ni sukóshi mo hike wo tòrimasèn

3 (showing recurrence) 毎... maî...

every day/week 毎日〔週〕máinichi〔shū〕

every Sunday 毎日曜日 máinichiyōbî

every other car (had been broken

into) 車は2台に1台ドアが壊されていた kurúma wa nidài ni ichídai doa ga kowásaretè ita

she visits me every other/third day 彼女は1日〔2日〕置きに面会に来てくれます kánòjo wa ichínichi〔futsúka〕oki nī ménkai ni kite kùrémasù

every now and then 時々 tokídoki

everybody [ev'ri:ba:di:] *pron* (*gen*) だれも dáre mo; (form of address) 皆さん mínásàn

everyday [ev'ri:dei] *adj* (daily) 毎日の maînichi no; (usual, common) 平凡な heîbon na

everyone [ev'ri:wʌn] *pron* = **everybody**

everything [ev'ri:θiŋ] *pron* 何もかも nánî mo ká mò

everywhere [ev'ri:hwe:r] *adv* (all over) いたる所に itárù tokorò ni; (wherever) どこにでも dókò ni de mo

evict [ivikt'] *vt* (squatter, tenant) 立ちのかせる tachínokaserù

eviction [ivik'ʃən] *n* (from house, land) 立ちのかせる事 tachínokaseru kotò

evidence [ev'idəns] *n* (proof) 証拠 shôko; (of witness) 証言 shôgen; (sign, indication) 印 shirúshi

to give evidence 証言する shôgen suru

evident [ev'idənt] *adj* (obvious) 明らかな akíràka na

evidently [ev'idəntli:] *adv* (obviously) 明らかに akíràka ni; (apparently) ...らしい ...rashiî

evil [i:'vəl] *adj* (person, system, influence) 悪い warûî

♦*n* (wickedness, sin) 罪 悪 zaíaku; (unpleasant situation or activity) 悪 ákù

evocative [iva:k'ətiv] *adj* (description, music) 想像を刺激する sôzō wò shigéki suru

evoke [ivouk'] *vt* (feeling, memory, response) 呼び起す yobíokosù

evolution [evəlu:'ʃən] *n* (BIO: process) 進化 shînka; (*also*: **theory of evolution**) 進化論 shínkarôn; (development) 発展 hattén

evolve [iva:lv'] *vt* (scheme, style) 練上げ

る neríagerù

♦vi (animal, plant etc) 進化する shínka suru; (plan, idea, style etc) 展開する teñkai suru

ewe [ju:] n 雌ヒツジ mesúhitsùji

ex- [eks] prefix 元... mótò...

exacerbate [igzæs'əːrbeit] vt (crisis, problem) 悪化させる akká saserù

exact [igzækt'] adj (correct: time, amount, word etc) 正確な seîkaku na; (person, worker) き帳面な kichốmen na

♦vt: to exact something (from) (obedience, payment etc) (...に) ...を強要する (...ni) ...wo kyốyō suru

exacting [igzæk'tiŋ] adj (task, conditions) 難しい muzúkashiì; (person, master etc) 厳しい kibíshiì

exactly [igzækt'li:] adv (precisely) 正確に seîkaku ni, 丁度 chôdo; (indicating emphasis) 正に másà ni; (indicating agreement) その通り sonố tồri

exaggerate [igzædʒə'reit] vt (difference, situation, story etc) 大げさに言う ốgesa nì iú

♦vi 大げさな事を言う ốgesa na kotð wo iú

exaggeration [igzædʒərei'ʃən] n 大げさ ốgesa

exalted [igzɔ:l'tid] adj (prominent) 著名な chomêi na

exam [igzæm'] n abbr (SCOL) = examination

examination [igzæmənei'ʃən] n (of object, accounts etc) 検査 kéñsa; (of idea, plan etc) 検討 keñtő; (SCOL) 試験 shikeñ; (MED) 診察 shiñsatsu

examine [igzæm'in] vt (inspect: object, idea, plan, accounts etc) 調べる shiráberù; (SCOL: candidate) 試験する shikeñ suru; (MED: patient) 診察する shiñsatsu suru

examiner [igzæm'inəːr] n (SCOL) 試験 官 shikéñkan

example [igzæm'pəl] n (typical illustration) 例 reî; (model: of good behavior etc) 手本 tehôñ

for example 例えば tatőeba

exasperate [igzæs'pəreit] vt (annoy,

frustrate) 怒らせる okốraserù

exasperating [igzæs'pəreitiŋ] adj いら いらさせる íraira saserù

exasperation [igzæspərei'ʃən] n いらだ ち irádachi

excavate [eks'kəveit] vt (site) 発掘する hakkútsu suru

excavation [eks'kəvei'ʃən] n (act) 発掘 hakkútsu; (site) 発掘現場 hakkútsugeñba

exceed [iksi:d'] vt (number, amount, budget) 越える koérù; (speed limit etc) 越す kosú; (powers, hopes) 上回る uwámawarù

exceedingly [iksi:'diŋli:] adv (enormously) 極めて kiwámète

excel [iksel'] vi: to excel (in/at) (sports, business etc) (...に) 優れる (...ni) sugúrerù

excellence [ek'sələns] n 優れる事 sugúreru kotð

Excellency [ek'selənsi:] n: His Excellency 閣下 kákkà

excellent [ek'sələnt] adj (idea, work etc) 優秀な yűshū na

except [iksept'] prep (apart from: also: except for, excepting) ...を除いて ...wo nozðite

♦vt: to except someone (from) (attack, criticism etc) (...から) ...を除く (...kara) ...wo nozðku

except if/when ...する場合を除いて ...suru baái wð nozðite

except that がしかし... ga shikáshì...

exception [iksep'ʃən] n (special case) 例外 reígai

to take exception to ...が気に食わない ...ga ki ní kuwanaì

exceptional [iksep'ʃənəl] adj (person, talent) 優れた sugúretà; (circumstances) 例外的な reígaiteki na

excerpt [ek'səːrpt] n (from text, film) 抜粋 bassúi

excess [ek'ses] n (surfeit) 過剰 kajố

excess baggage n 超過手荷物 chôkatenimòtsu

excesses [ekses'iz] npl (of cruelty, stupidity etc) 極端な行為 kyokútan na kôi

excess fare (*BRIT*) *n* (RAIL) 乗越し運賃 noríkoshi uńchin

excessive [ikses'iv] *adj* (amount, extent) 過剰の kajó no

exchange [ikstʃeindʒ'] *n* (of presents, prisoners etc) 交換 kókan; (conversation) 口論 kóron; (*also*: **telephone exchange**) 電話局 deńwakyòku

♦*vt*: **to exchange (for)** (goods etc) (…と) 交換する (…to) kókan suru

exchange rate *n* 為替相場 kawásesòba

Exchequer [eks'tʃekə:r] (*BRIT*) *n*: **the Exchequer** 大蔵省 ókurashò

excise [ek'saiz] *n* (tax) 消費税 shóhizèi

excite [iksait'] *vt* (stimulate) 興奮させる kófun saserù; (arouse) 性的に刺激する seíteki nì shigéki suru

to get excited 興奮する kófun suru

excitement [iksait'mənt] *n* (agitation) 興奮 kófun; (exhilaration) 喜び yorókobì

exciting [iksai'tiŋ] *adj* (time, event, place) 興奮の kófun no, エキサイティングな ekísaitìngu na

exclaim [ikskleim'] *vi* (cry out) 叫ぶ sakébù

exclamation [eksklǝmei'ʃǝn] *n* (cry) 叫び sakébì

exclamation mark *n* 感嘆符 kańtaǹfu

exclude [iksklu:d'] *vt* (fact, possibility, person) 除外する jogái suru

exclusion [iksklu:'ʒǝn] *n* 除外 jogái

exclusive [iksklu:'sivli:] *adj* (club, district) 高級な kókyū na; (use, story, interview) 独占の dokúsen no

exclusive of tax 税別の zeíbetsu no

exclusively [iksklu:'sivli:] *adv* (only, entirely) 独占的に dokúsenteki ni

excommunicate [ekskǝmju:'nǝkeit] *vt* (REL) 破門する hamón suru

excrement [eks'krǝmǝnt] *n* ふん fuń

excruciating [ikskru:'ʃi:eitiŋ] *adj* (pain, agony, embarrassment etc) 極度の kyókùdo no, 耐えがたい taégataì; (noise) 耳をつんざくような mimí wò tsuńzaku yò na

excursion [ikskǝ:r'ʒǝn] *n* (tourist excursion, shopping excursion) ツアー tsúà

excuse [*n* ekskju:s' *vb* eksku:z'] *n* (justification) 言訳 iíwake

♦*vt* (justify: personal fault, mistake) …の言訳をする …no iíwake wo suru; (forgive: someone else's mistake) 許す yurúsù

to excuse someone from doing something …する義務を…に免除する …suru gímù wo …ni méǹjo suru

excuse me! (attracting attention) 済みません(が)… sumímaseǹ (ga)…; (as apology) 済みません sumímaseǹ

if you will excuse me … ちょっと失礼します chóttò shitsúrei shimasù

ex-directory [eksdirek'tǝ:ri:] (*BRIT*) *adj* 電話帳に載っていない deńwachò ni notté inaì

execute [ek'sǝkju:t] *vt* (person) 死刑にする shikéi ni surù; (plan, order) 実行する jikkó suru; (maneuver, movement) する surú

execution [eksǝkju:'ʃǝn] *n* (of person) 死刑 shikéì; (of plan, order, maneuver etc) 実行 jikkó

executioner [eksǝkju:'ʃǝnǝ:r] *n* 死刑執行人 shikéishikkònìn

executive [igzek'jǝtiv] *n* (person: of company) 重役 júyaku; (committee: of organization, political party etc) 執行委員会 shikkóiìnkai

♦*adj* (board, role) 幹部の káǹbu no

executor [igzek'jǝtǝ:r] *n* (LAW) 執行人 shikkóniǹ

exemplary [igzem'plǝ:ri:] *adj* (conduct) 模範的な mohánteki na; (punishment) 見せしめの misésime no

exemplify [igzem'plǝfai] *vt* (typify) …の典型である …no teńkei dè árù; (illustrate) …の例を挙げる …no reí wò agérù

exempt [igzempt'] *adj*: **exempt from** (duty, obligation) …を免除された …wo méǹjo saréta

♦*vt*: **to exempt someone from** (duty, obligation) …の…を免除する …no …wo méǹjo suru

exemption [igzemp'ʃǝn] *n* 免除 méǹjo

exercise [ek'sǝ:rsaiz] *n* (no pl: keep-fit) 運動 uńdò; (energetic movement) 体操 taísò; (SCOL) 練習問題 reńshūmoǹdai;

(MUS) 練習曲 reńshūkyoku; (MIL) 軍事演習 guńjieńshū; (of authority etc) 行使 kốshì
♦vt (right) 行使する kốshì suru; (dog) ...に運動をさせる ...ni uńdō wò saséru; (mind) 働かせる határakaseru
♦vi (also: to take exercise) 運動する uńdō suru
to exercise patience 我慢する gámàn suru

exercise book n (SCOL) ノート nòto

exert [igzə:rt'] vt (influence) 及ぼす oyóbosù; (authority) 行使する kốshì suru
to exert oneself 努力する dốryòku suru

exertion [igzə:r'ʃən] n 努力 dốryòku

exhale [ekshei'l'] vt (air, smoke) 吐き出す hakídasù
♦vi (breathe out) 息を吐く íkì wo hákù

exhaust [igzɔ:st'] n (AUT: also: exhaust pipe) 排気管 haíkikàn; (: fumes) 排気ガス haíkigasù
♦vt (person) へとへとに疲れさせる hetóhetð ni tsukáresaserù; (money, resources etc) 使い果す tsukáihatasù; (topic) ...について語り尽す ...ni tsúìte katáritsukusù

exhausted [igzɔ:s'tid] adj (person) へとへとに疲れた hetóhetð ni tsukáretà

exhaustion [igzɔ:s'tʃən] n (tiredness) 極度の疲労 kyókùdo no hiró
nervous exhaustion 神経衰弱 shińkeisuijàku

exhaustive [igzɔ:s'tiv] adj (search, study) 徹底的な tettéiteki na

exhibit [eksəbij't] n (ART) 展示品 teńjihìn; (LAW) 証拠品 shốkohìn
♦vt (quality, ability, emotion) 見せる misérù; (paintings) 展示する teńji suru

exhibition [eksəbij'ən] n (of paintings etc) 展示会 teńjikai; (of ill-temper etc) 極端な態度 kyokútàn na taído; (of talent etc) 素晴らしい例 subárashiì reí

exhibitionist [eksəbij'ənist] n (show-off) 気取り屋 kidóriya

exhilarating [igzil'əreitiŋ] adj (experience, news) 喜ばしい yorókobashiì

exhort [igzɔ:rt'] vt 訓戒する kuńkai suru

exile [eg'zail] n (condition, state) 亡命 bốmei; (person) 亡命者 bốmeisha
♦vt 追放する tsuíhō suru

exist [igzist'] vi (be present) 存在する sońzai suru; (live) 生活する seíkatsu suru

existence [igzis'təns] n (reality) 存在 sońzai; (life) 生活 seíkatsu

existing [igzis'tiŋ] adj (present) 現存の geńzon no, geńson no

exit [eg'zit] n (from room, building, motorway etc) 出口 dégùchi; (departure) 出ていく事 détè ikú kotð
♦vi (THEATER) 退場する taíjō suru; (COMPUT) プログラムを終了する purógurāmu wo shúryō suru

exit ramp (US) n (AUT) 出口ランプ dégùchiràňpu

exodus [ek'sədəs] n 大脱出 daídasshùtsu

exonerate [igzɑ:n'əreit] vt: to exonerate someone from something (blame, guilt etc) ...について...の容疑を晴らす ...ni tsúìte ...no yốgi wð harásù

exorbitant [igzɔ:r'bətənt] adj (prices, rents) 法外な hốgai na

exorcize [ek'sɔ:rsaiz] vt (spirit) 追い払う oíharaù; (person, place) ...から悪魔を追い払う ...kara ákùma wo oíharaù

exotic [igzɑ:t'ik] adj (food, place) 異国的な ikókuteki na, エキゾチックな ekízochikkù na

expand [ikspænd'] vt (business etc) 拡張する kakúchō suru; (staff, numbers etc) 増やす fuyásù
♦vi (population etc) 増える fuérù; (business etc) 大きくなる ốkìku nárù; (gas, metal) 膨張する bốchō suru

expanse [ikspæns'] n (of sea, sky etc) 広がり hirógarì

expansion [ikspæn'tʃən] n (of business, population, economy etc) 増大 zốdai

expatriate [ekspei'tri:it] n 国外在住者 kokúgai zaijùsha

expect [ikspekt'] vt (anticipate) 予想する yosó suru; (await) 待つ mátsù; (require) 要求する yốkyū suru; (suppose) ...だと思う ...dá tò omóù
♦vi: to be expecting (be pregnant) 妊娠している nińshin shite irù

expectancy [ikspek'tənsi:] *n* (anticipation) 期待 kitái

life expectancy 寿命 jumyő

expectant mother [ikspek'tənt-] *n* 妊婦 nífipu

expectation [ekspektei'ʃən] *n* (hope, belief) 期待 kitái

expedience [ikspi:'di:əns] *n* (convenience) 便宜 bengí, 都合 tsugő

expediency [ikspi:'di:ənsi:] *n* = **expedience**

expedient [ikspi:'di:ənt] *adj* (useful, convenient) 都合の良い tsugő no yoì

♦*n* (measure) 便法 benpő

expedition [ekspədiʃ'ən] *n* (for exploration) 探検旅行 tañkenryokő; (for shopping etc) ツアー tsuā

expel [ikspel'] *vt* (person: from school) 退学させる taígaku saserù; (: from organization, place) 追出す oídasù; (gas, liquid) 排出する haíshutsu suru

expend [ikspend'] *vt* (money, time, energy) 費やす tsuíyasù

expendable [ikspen'dəbəl] *adj* (person, thing) 消耗品的な shőmōhinteki na

expenditure [ikspen'ditʃər] *n* (of money, energy, time) 消費 shőhi

expense [ikspens'] *n* (cost) 費用 híyő; (expenditure) 出費 shuppí

at the expense of ...を犠牲にして ...wo giséi ni shitè

expense account *n* 交際費 kősaìhi

expenses [ikspen'siz] *npl* (traveling expenses, hotel expenses etc) 経費 kefhi

expensive [ikspen'siv] *adj* (article) 高価な kőka na; (mistake, tastes) 高く付く tákàku tsukú

experience [ikspi:r'i:əns] *n* 経験 keíken

♦*vt* (situation, feeling etc) 経験する keíken suru

experienced [ikspi:r'i:ənst] *adj* (in job) 熟練した jukúren shità

experiment [ikspe:r'əmənt] *n* (trial: *also* SCIENCE) 実験 jikkén

♦*vi*: *to experiment (with/on)* (...を使って) 実験する (...wo tsukátte) jikkén suru

experimental [ikspe:rəmen'təl] *adj* 実験

的な jikkénteki na

expert [ek'spə:rt] *adj* (opinion, help) 専門家な seímonka no; (driver etc) 熟練した jukúren shità

♦*n* (specialist) 専門家 seímonka, エキスパート ekísupāto

expertise [ekspərti:z'] *n* (know-how) 技術 gíjutsu, ノーハウ nőhaù

expire [ikspai'ər] *vi* (passport, licence etc) 切れる kirérù

expiry [ikspaiər'i:] *n* (of passport, lease etc) 満期 máñki

explain [iksplein'] *vt* 説明する setsúmei suru

explanation [eksplənei'ʃən] *n* 説明 setsúmei

explanatory [iksplæn'ətɔːriː] *adj* (statement, comment) 説明の setsúmei no

explicit [ikspli'sit] *adj* (clear) 明白な meíhaku na; (frank) 隠し立てしない kakúshidate shinaì

explode [iksploud'] *vi* (bomb) 爆発する bakúhatsu suru; (population) 爆発的に増える bakúhatsuteki nì fuérù; (person: with rage etc) 激怒する gékìdo suru

exploit [*n* eks'plɔit *vb* iksplɔit'] *n* (deed, feat) 手柄 tegára

♦*vt* (workers) 搾取する sákùshu suru; (person, idea) 私利私欲に利用する shírìshiyòku ni riyő suru; (opportunity, resources) 利用する riyő suru

exploitation [eksplɔitei'ʃən] *n* (of workers) 搾取 sákùshu; (of person, idea, resources, opportunity etc) 利用 riyő

exploration [eksplərei'ʃən] *n* (of place, space) 探検 tañken; (with hands etc) 探る事 sagúru kotő; (of idea, suggestion) 検討 keñtō

exploratory [ikspləːr'ətɔːriː] *adj* (expedition) 探検の tañken no; (talks, operation) 予備的な yobíteki na

explore [ikspləːr'] *vt* (place, space) 探検する tañken suru; (with hands etc) 探る sagúrù; (idea, suggestion) 検討する keñtō suru

explorer [ikspləːr'əːr] *n* (of place, country etc) 探検家 tañkenka

explosion [iksplou'ʒən] *n* (of bomb) 爆発

explosive [iksplou'siv] adj (device, effect) 爆発の bakúhatsu no; (situation, temper) 爆発的な bakúhatsuteki na
♦n (substance) 爆薬 bakúyaku; (device) 爆弾 bakúdan

exponent [ekspou'nent] n (of idea, theory) 擁護者 yógoshà; (of skill, activity) 達人 tatsújin

export [vb ekspɔːrt' n eks'pɔːrt] vt (goods) 輸出する yushútsu suru
♦n (process) 輸出 yushútsu; (product) 輸出品 yushútsuhiǹ
♦cpd (duty, permit) 輸出... yushútsu...

exporter [ekspɔːr'tər] n 輸出業者 yushútsugyōsha

expose [ikspouz'] vt (reveal: object) むき出しにする mukídashi ni surù; (unmask: person) ...の悪事を暴く ...no ákùji wo abákù

exposed [ikspouzd'] adj (house, place etc) 雨風にさらされた ámèkaze ni sarásaretà

exposure [ikspou'ʒər] n (to heat, cold, radiation) さらされる事 sarásareru kotò; (publicity) 報道 hódð; (of person) 暴露 bákùro; (PHOT) 露出 roshútsu
to die from exposure (MED) 低体温症で死ぬ teítaiońshō de shinú

exposure meter n (PHOT) 露出計 roshútsukei

expound [ikspaund'] vt (theory, opinion) 説明する setsúmei suru

express [ikspres'] adj (clear: command, intention) 明白な meíhaku na; (BRIT: letter etc) 速達の sokútatsu no
♦n (train, bus, coach) 急行 kyúkō
♦vt (idea, view) 言表す iíarawasù; (emotion, quantity) 表現する hyôgen suru

expression [ikspreʃ'ən] n (word, phrase) 言方 iíkata; (of idea, emotion) 表現 hyôgen; (on face) 表情 hyôjō; (of actor, singer etc: feeling) 表現力 hyôgeńryoku

expressive [ikspres'iv] adj (glance) 意味ありげな ímìarige na; (ability) 表現の hyôgen no

expressly [ikspres'li] adv (clearly, intentionally) はっきりと hakkírì to

expressway [ikspres'wei] (US) n (urban motorway) 高速道路 kôsokudōro

expulsion [ikspʌl'ʃən] n (SCOL) 退学処分 taígakushobùn; (from organization etc) 追放 tsuíhō; (of gas, liquid etc) 排出 haíshutsu

expurgate [eks'pərgeit] vt (text, recording) 検閲する keń-etsu suru

exquisite [ekskwiz'it] adj (perfect: face, lace, workmanship, taste) 見事な mígòto na

extend [ikstend'] vt (visit) 延ばす nobásù; (street) 延長する eńchō suru; (building) 増築する zôchiku suru; (arm, hand) 伸ばす nobásù
♦vi (land) 広がる hirógarù; (road) 延びる nobírù; (period) 続く tsuzúkù
to extend an offer of help 援助を申出る eńjo wo môshiderù
to extend an invitation to ...を招待する ...wo shôtai suru

extension [iksten'tʃən] n (of building) 増築 zôchiku; (of time) 延長 eńchō; (of campaign, rights) 拡大 kakúdai; (ELEC) 延長コード eńchōkōdo; (TEL: in private house, office) 内線 naísen

extensive [iksten'siv] adj (area) 広い hirôi; (effect, damage) 甚大な jińdai na; (coverage, discussion) 広範囲の kôhań-i no

extensively [iksten'sivli] adv: **he's traveled extensively** 彼は広く旅行している kárè wa hírðku ryokô shite irù

extent [ikstent'] n (size: of area, land etc) 広さ hírðsa; (: of problem etc) 大きさ ôkìsa
to some extent ある程度 árù teído
to the extent of ......までも ...mádè mo
to such an extent that ......という程 ...to iú hodð
to what extent? どのぐらい? donó guraí?

extenuating [iksten'juːeitiŋ] adj: **extenuating circumstances** 酌量すべき情状 shakúryō subèki jôjō

exterior [iksti:r'i:ər] adj (external) 外部の gáibu no
♦n (outside) 外部 gáibu; (appearance) 外見 gaíken

exterminate [ikstə:r'məneit] vt (animals) 撲滅する bokúmetsu suru; (people) 根絶する końzetsu suru

external [ikstə:r'nəl] adj (walls etc) 外部の gáibu no; (examiner, auditor) 部外の búgài no
external evidence 外的証拠 gaítekishòko
「*for external use*」外用薬 gaíyòyaku

extinct [ikstiŋkt'] adj (animal, plant) 絶滅した zetsúmetsu shitá
an extinct volcano 死火山 shikázàn

extinction [ikstiŋk'ʃən] n (of species) 絶滅 zetsúmetsu

extinguish [ikstiŋ'gwiʃ] vt (fire, light) 消す kesú

extinguisher [ikstiŋ'gwiʃə:r] n 消火器 shòkakì

extort [ikstɔ:rt'] vt (money) ゆすり取る yusúritorù; (confession) 強要する kyóyò suru

extortion [ikstɔ:r'ʃən] n (of money etc) ゆすり yusúri; (confession) 強要 kyóyò

extortionate [ikstɔ:r'ʃənit] adj (price, demands) 法外な hògai na

extra [eks'trə] adj (thing, person, amount) 余分の yobún no
♦adv (in addition) 特別に tokúbetsu ni
♦n (luxury) 特別の物 tokúbetsu no monò, 余分の物 yobún no monò; (surcharge) 追加料金 tsuíkaryòkin; (CINEMA, THEATER) エキストラ ekísutòra

extra-... [eks'trə] prefix 特別に ... tokúbetsu ni ...

extract [vt ikstrækt' n eks'trækt] vt (take out: object) 取出す torídasù; (: tooth) 抜く nukú, 抜歯する basshí suru; (mineral: from ground) 採掘する saíkutsu suru, 抽出する chùshutsu suru; (money) 強要して取る kyóyò shitè tórù; (promise) 無理強いする muríjii suru
♦n (of novel, recording) 抜粋 bassúi; (malt extract, vanilla extract etc) エキス ékìsu, エッセンス éssènsu

extracurricular [ekstrəkərik'jələ:r] adj (activities) 課外の kagái no

extradite [eks'trədait] vt (from country) 引渡す hikíwatasù; (to country) ...の引渡しを受ける ...no hikíwatashi wò ukérù

extradition [ekstrədiʃ'ən] n 外国への犯人引渡し gaíkoku e nò hánnin hikíwatashi

extramarital [ekstrəmær'itəl] adj (affair, relationship) 婚外の kongai no, 不倫の furín no

extramural [ekstrəmju:r'əl] adj (lectures, activities) 学外の gakúgai no

extraordinary [ikstrɔ:r'dəne:ri:] adj (person) 抜きん出た nukíndetà; (conduct, situation) 異常な ijó na; (meeting) 臨時の rínji no

extravagance [ikstræv'əgəns] n (no pl: spending) 浪費 ròhi; (example of spending) ぜいたく zeítaku

extravagant [ikstræv'əgənt] adj (lavish: person) 気前の良い kimáe no yoì; (: gift) ぜいたくな zeítaku na; (wasteful: person) 金遣いの荒い kanézukài no arai; (: machine) 不経済な fukéizai na

extreme [ikstri:m'] adj (cold, poverty etc) 非常な hijó na; (opinions, methods etc) 極端な kyokútan na; (point, edge) 末端の mattán no
♦n (of behavior) 極端 kyokútan

extremely [ikstri:m'li:] adv 非常に hijó ni

extremity [ikstrem'iti:] n (edge, end) 端 hashí; (of situation) 極端 kyokútan

extricate [ek'strikeit] vt: *to extricate someone/something (from)* (trap, situation) (...から) ...を救い出す (...kara) ...wo sukúidasù

extrovert [ek'strouvə:rt] n 外向的な人 gaíkòteki na hitò

exuberant [igzu:'bə:rənt] adj (person etc) 元気一杯の geñkiippài no; (imagination etc) 豊かな yútàka na

exude [igzu:d'] vt (liquid) にじみ出させる nijímidasaserù; (smell) 放つ hanátsu
to exude confidence 自信満々である jishín mañman dè árù
to exude enthusiasm 意気込む ikígo-

mù

exult [igzʌlt'] *vi* (rejoice) 喜び勇む yorókobiisamù

eye [ai] *n* (ANAT) 目 mé
♦*vt* (look at, watch) 見詰める mitsúmerù
the eye of a needle 針の目 hárì no mé
to keep an eye on ...を見張る ...wo mihárù

eyeball [ai'bɔːl] *n* 眼球 gañkyū

eyebath [ai'bæθ] *n* 洗眼カップ señgankappù

eyebrow [ai'brau] *n* 眉毛 máyùge

eyebrow pencil *n* アイブローペンシル aíburōpeñshiru

eyedrops [ai'drɑːps] *npl* 点眼薬 teñgañyaku

eyelash [ai'læʃ] *n* まつげ mátsùge

eyelid [ai'lid] *n* まぶた mábùta

eyeliner [ai'lainəːr] *n* アイライナー aíraínā

eye-opener [ai'oupənəːr] *n* (revelation) 驚くべき新事実 odórokubèki shiñjijîtsu

eyeshadow [ai'ʃædou] *n* アイシャドー aíshadõ

eyesight [ai'sait] *n* 視力 shíryòku

eyesore [ai'sɔːr] *n* (building) 目障り mezáwàri

eye witness *n* (to crime, accident) 目撃者 mokúgekishà

F

F [ef] *n* (MUS: note) ヘ音 hé-òn; (: key) ヘ調 héchõ

F. *abbr* (= *Fahrenheit*) 華氏 káshì

fable [fei'bəl] *n* (story) ぐう話 gǘwa

fabric [fæb'rik] *n* (cloth) 生地 kíjì

fabrication [fæbrikei'ʃən] *n* (lie) うそ úsò; (making) 製造 seízō

fabulous [fæb'jələs] *adj* (inf: super) 素晴らしい subárashì; (extraordinary) 途方もない tohő mo nài; (mythical) 伝説的な deñsetsuteki na

facade [fəsɑːd'] *n* (of building) 正面 shőmen; (fig: pretence) 見せ掛け misékake

face [feis] *n* (ANAT) 顔 kaó; (expression) 表情 hyójō; (of clock) 文字盤 mojí-

ban; (of cliff) 面 méñ; (of building) 正面 shőmen
♦*vt* (particular direction) ...に向かう ...ni mukáù; (facts, unpleasant situation) 直視する chókushi suru

face down (person) 下向きになって shitámuki ni nattè; (card) 伏せてあって fuséte attè

to lose face 面目を失う meñboku wo ushínaù

to make/pull a face 顔をしかめる kaó wo shikámerù

in the face of (difficulties etc) ...にめげず ...ni megézù

on the face of it (superficially) 表面は hyőmen wa

face to face (with person, problem) 面と向かって meñ to mukáttè

face cloth (*BRIT*) *n* フェースタオル fésutaòru

face cream *n* フェースクリーム fésukurīmu

face lift *n* (of person) 顔のしわ取り手術 kaó no shiwátori shujútsu; (of building etc) 改造 kaízō

face powder *n* フェースパウダー fésupaùdā

face-saving [feis'seiviŋ] *adj* (compromise, gesture) 面子を立てる méñtsu wo tatérù

facet [fæs'it] *n* (of question, personality) 側面 sokúmen; (of gem) 切子面 kiríkomèn

facetious [fəsiː'ʃəs] *adj* (comment, remark) ふざけた fuzáketà

face up to *vt fus* (obligations, difficulty) ...に立ち向かう ...ni tachímukaù

face value *n* (of coin, stamp) 額面 gakúmen

to take something at face value (*fig*) そのまま信用する sonő mama shiñ-yō suru

facial [fei'ʃəl] *adj* (hair, expression) 顔の kaó no

facile [fæs'əl] *adj* (comment, reaction) 軽々しい karúgarushiì

facilitate [fəsil'əteit] *vt* 助ける tasúkerù

facilities [fəsil'ətiːz] *npl* (buildings,

equipment) 設備 setsúbi

credit facilities 分割払い取扱いbuñkatsubarài toríatsukai

facing [fei'siŋ] *prep* (opposite) ...の向い側の ...no mukáigawa no

facsimile [fæksim'əli:] *n* (exact replica) 複製 fukúsei; (*also*: **facsimile machine**) ファックス fákkùsu; (transmitted document) ファックス fákkùsu

fact [fækt] *n* (true piece of information) 事実 jijítsu; (truth) 真実 shiñjitsu

in fact 事実は jijítsu wa

faction [fæk'ʃən] *n* (group: *also* REL, POL) 派 há

factor [fæk'tə:r] *n* (of problem, decision etc) 要素 yōso

factory [fæk'tə:ri:] *n* (building) 工場 kōjō

factual [fæk'tʃu:əl] *adj* (analysis, information) 事実の jijítsu no

faculty [fæk'əlti:] *n* (sense, ability) 能力 nōryoku; (of university) 学部 gakúbu; (*US*: teaching staff) 教職員 kyōshokuin ◇総称 sōshō

fad [fæd] *n* (craze) 一時的流行 ichíjiteki-ryūkō

fade [feid] *vi* (color) あせる asérù; (light, sound) 次第に消える shidái ni kiérù; (flower) しぼむ shibómù; (hope, memory, smile) 消える kiérù

fag [fæg] (*BRIT*: *inf*) *n* (cigarette) もくmokú

fail [feil] *vt* (exam) 落第する rakúdai surù; (candidate) 落第させる rakúdai saserù; (subj: leader) ...の期待を裏切る ...no kitái wo urágirù; (: courage, memory) なくなる nakúnarù

◆*vi* (candidate, attempt etc) 失敗する shippái surù; (brakes) 故障する koshō surù; (eyesight, health) 衰える otóroerù; (light) 暗くなる kuráku narù

to fail to do something (be unable) ...する事が出来ない ...surú koto gà dekínài; (neglect) ...する事を怠る ...surú koto wò okótarù

without fail 必ず kanárazu

failing [fei'liŋ] *n* (weakness) 欠点 kettéñ

◆*prep* ...がなければ ...ga nakéreba

failure [feil'jə:r] *n* (lack of success) 失敗 shippái; (person) 駄目人間 daméniñgen; (mechanical etc) 故障 koshō

faint [feint] *adj* かすかな kásùka na

◆*n* (MED) 気絶 kizétsu

◆*vi* 気絶する kizétsu suru

to feel faint 目まいがする memái ga suru

fair [fe:r] *adj* (reasonable, right) 公平な kōhei na; (quite large) かなりな kánàri na; (quite good) 悪くない warúkunài; (skin) 白い shiróì; (hair) 金色の kiń-iro no; (weather) 晴れの haré no

◆*adv* (play) 正々堂々と seíseidōdō to

◆*n* (*also*: **trade fair**) トレードフェアー torédofeà; (*BRIT*: funfair) 移動遊園地 idōyūeñchi

fairly [fe:r'li:] *adv* (justly) 公平に kōhei ni; (quite) かなり kánàri

fairness [fe:r'nis] *n* (justice, impartiality) 公平さ kōheisa

fair play *n* 公平さ kōheisa

fairy [fe:r'i:] *n* (sprite) 妖精 yōsei

fairy tale *n* おとぎ話 otógibanàshi

faith [feiθ] *n* (trust) 信用 shiń-yō; (religion) 宗教 shūkyō; (religious belief) 信仰 shiñkō

faithful [feiθ'fəl] *adj* 忠実な chūjitsu na

faithfully [feiθ'fəli:] *adv* 忠実に chūjitsu ni

yours faithfully (*BRIT*: in letters) 敬具 kēīgu

fake [feik] *n* (painting etc) 偽物 nisémono; (person) ぺてん師 petéñshi

◆*adj* (phoney) いんちきの íñchiki no

◆*vt* (painting etc) 偽造する gizō suru; (illness, emotion) ...だと見せ掛ける ...da to misékakerù

falcon [fæl'kən] *n* ハヤブサ hayábusa

fall [fɔ:l] *n* (of person, object: from height) 転落 teñraku; (of person, horse: from standing position) 転倒 teñtō; (of price, temperature, dollar) 下がる事 sagáru kotò; (of government, leader, country) 倒れる事 taóreru kotò; (*US*: autumn) 秋 ákì

◆*vi* (*pt* **fell**, *pp* **fallen**) (person, object: from height) 落ちる ochírù; (person, horse: from standing position) 転ぶ koróbù; (snow, rain) 降る fúrù; (price, temperature, dollar) 下がる sagárù; (government, leader, country) 倒れる taórerù; (night, darkness) (...に) なる (...ni) nárù

snowfall 降雪 kōsetsu

rainfall 降雨 kŏu

the fall of darkness 暗くなる事 kuráku naru kotŏ

the fall of night 夜になる事 yórù ni náru kotŏ

to fall flat (on one's face) うつぶせに倒れる utsúbuse ni taórerù; (plan) 失敗する shippái suru; (joke) 受けない ukénaì

fallacy [fæl'əsi:] n (misconception) 誤信 goshín

fall back vt fus (retreat) 後ずさりする atózusàri suru; (MIL) 後退する kōtaisuru

fall back on vt fus (remedy etc) ...に頼る ...ni tayórù

fall behind vi 遅れる okúrerù

fall down vi (person) 転ぶ koróbù; (building) 崩壊する hōkai suru

fallen [fɔ:l'ən] pp of **fall**

fall for vt fus (trick) ...にだまされる ...ni damásarerù; (person) ...にほれる ...ni horérù

fallible [fæl'əbəl] adj (person, memory) 間違いをしがちな machígaì wo shigáchi na

fall in vi (roof) 落込む ochíkomù; (MIL) 整列する seíretsu suru

fall off vi (person, object) 落ちる ochírù; (takings, attendance) 減る herú

fall out vi (hair, teeth) 抜ける nukérù; (friends etc) けんかする keñka suru

fallout [fɔ:l'aut] n (radiation) 放射性落下物 hōshaseìràkkabutsu, 死の灰 shí nò hai

fallout shelter n 放射性落下物待避所 hōshaseìràkkabutsu taíhijò

fallow [fæl'ou] adj (land, field) 休閑中の kyūkañchū no

falls [fɔ:lz] npl (waterfall) 滝 takí

fall through vi (plan, project) 失敗に終る shippái ni owarù

false [fɔ:ls] adj (untrue: statement, accusation) うその usó no; (wrong: impres-

sion, imprisonment) 間違った machígattà; (insincere: person, smile) 不誠実な fuséijitsu na

false alarm n 誤った警報 ayámattà keíhō

false pretenses npl: **under false pretenses** うその申立てで usó nò mŏshitate de

false teeth npl 入れ歯 irēba

falter [fɔ:l'tə:r] vi (engine) 止りそうになる tomárisò ni nárù; (person: hesitate) ためらう tamēraù; (: stagger) よろめく yorōmekù

fame [feim] n 名声 meísei

familiar [fəmil'jə:r] adj (well-known: face, voice) おなじみの onájimi no; (intimate: behavior, tone) 親しい shitáshiì

to be familiar with (subject) よく知っている yókù shittē iru

familiarize [fəmil'jəraiz] vt: **to familiarize oneself with** ...になじむ ...ni najímù

family [fæm'li:] n (relations) 家族 kázòku; (children) 子供 kodómo ◇総称 sōshō

family business n 家族経営の商売 kazòkukeíei no shōbai

family doctor n 町医者 machí-ìsha

famine [fæm'in] n 飢餓 kígà

famished [fæm'iʃt] adj (hungry) 腹がぺこぺこの hará gà pekópeko no

famous [fei'məs] adj 有名な yūmei na

famously [fei'məsli:] adv (get on) 素晴らしく subárashikù

fan [fæn] n (person) ファン fáñ; (folding) 扇子 séñsu; (ELEC) 扇風機 señpūki
♦vt (face, person) あおぐ aógù; (fire, quarrel) あおる aórù

fanatic [fənæt'ik] n (extremist) 熱狂者 nekkyōshà; (enthusiast) マニア máni̥a

fan belt n (AUT) ファンベルト fañberùto

fanciful [fæn'sifəl] adj (notion, idea) 非現実的な hígeñjitsuteki na; (design, name) 凝った kóttà

fancy [fæn'si:] n (whim) 気まぐれ kimágurè; (imagination) 想像 sŏzō; (fantasy) 夢 yumé
♦adj (clothes, hat, food) 凝った kóttà;

(hotel etc) 高級の kốkyū no
♦vt (feel like, want) 欲しいなと思う hoshíí na to omốù; (imagine) 想像する sốzō suru; (think) ...だと思う ...da to omốù
to take a fancy to ...を気に入る ...wo kí ni irù
he fancies her (inf) 彼は彼女が好きだ kárè wa kanójò ga sukí dà

fancy dress n 仮装の衣裳 kasố no ishố

fancy-dress ball n 仮装舞踏会 kasốbutōkai

fanfare [fæn'fe:r] n ファンファーレ fanfáre

fang [fæŋ] n (tooth) きば kibá

fan out vi 扇形に広がる ốgigata nì hirốgarù

fantastic [fæntæs'tik] adj (enormous) 途方もない tohốmonàì; (strange, incredible) 信じられない shíñjirarenàì; (wonderful) 素晴らしい subá rashìî

fantasy [fæn'tǝsi:] n (dream) 夢 yumế; (unreality, imagination) 空想 kūsố

far [fɑːr] adj (distant) 遠い tối
♦adv (a long way) 遠く tốku; (much) はるかに hárùka ni
far away/off 遠く tốku
far better ...の方がはるかにいい ...no hố ga hárùka ni ii
far from 決して...でない kesshíte ...denáî ◇強い否定を現す tsuyối hitéi wo aráwasù
by far はるかに hárùka ni
go as far as the farm 農場まで行って下さい nốjō madè itté kudasaî
as far as I know 私の知る限り watákushi nò shirú kagirî
how far? (distance) どれぐらいの距離 doré gurai no kyòri; (referring to activity, situation) どれ程 doré hodò

faraway [fɑːr'ǝwei] adj (place) 遠くの tốku no; (look) 夢見る様な yumémiru yố na; (thought) 現実離れの geñjitsubanare no

farce [fɑːrs] n (THEATER) 笑劇 shốgeki, ファース fásù; (fig) 茶番劇 chabáñgeki

farcical [fɑːr'sikǝl] adj (situation) ばかげた bakágèta

fare [fe:r] n (on trains, buses) 料金 ryốkin; (also: **taxi fare**) タクシー代 takúshìdai; (food) 食べ物 tabémòno
half/full fare 半〔全〕額 hañ〔zeñ〕gàku

Far East n: *the Far East* 極東 kyokútō

farewell [fe:r'wel'] excl さようなら sayốnarà
♦n 別れ wakáre

farm [fɑːrm] n 農場 nốjō
♦vt (land) 耕す tagáyasù

farmer [fɑːr'mǝr] n 農場主 nốjōshù

farmhand [fɑːrm'hænd] n 作男 sakúotòko

farmhouse [fɑːrm'haus] n 農家 nốka

farming [fɑːr'miŋ] n (agriculture) 農業 nốgyō; (of crops) 耕作 kốsaku; (of animals) 飼育 shíîku

farmland [fɑːrm'lænd] n 農地 nốchi

farm worker n = **farmhand**

farmyard [fɑːrm'jɑːrd] n 農家の庭 nốka no niwà

far-reaching [fɑːr'ri:'tʃiŋ] adj (reform, effect) 広範囲の kốhañ-i no

fart [fɑːrt] (inf!) vi おならをする onára wo surù

farther [fɑːr'ðǝr] compar of **far**

farthest [fɑːr'ðist] superl of **far**

fascinate [fæs'ǝneit] vt (intrigue, interest) うっとりさせる uttốri saserù

fascinating [fæs'ǝneitiŋ] adj (story, person) 魅惑的な miwákuteki na

fascination [fæsǝnei'ʃǝn] n 魅惑 miwáku

fascism [fæʃ'izǝm] n (POL) ファシズム fashízùmu

fashion [fæʃ'ǝn] n (trend: in clothes, thought, custom etc) 流行 ryūkố, ファッション fásshon; (also: **fashion industry**) ファッション業界 fasshòn gyốkai; (manner) やり方 yaríkata
♦vt (make) 作る tsukúrù
in fashion 流行して ryūkố shite
out of fashion 廃れて sutárete

fashionable [fæʃ'ǝnǝbǝl] adj (clothes, club, subject) 流行の ryūkố no

fashion show n ファッションショー fasshòn shố

fast [fæst] *adj* (runner, car, progress) 速い hayáì; (clock): *to be fast* 進んでいる susúnde irù; (dye, color) あせない asénài
♦*adv* (run, act, think) 速く hayákù; (stuck, held) 固く katáku
♦*n* (REL etc) 断食 dańjiki
♦*vi* (REL etc) 断食する dańjiki suru
fast asleep ぐっすり眠っている gussúrì nemútte irù

fasten [fæs'ən] *vt* (tie, join) 縛る shibárù; (buttons, belt etc) 締める shimérù
♦*vi* 締まる shimárù

fastener [fæs'ənər] *n* (button, clasp, pin etc) ファスナー fásùnā

fastening [fæs'əniŋ] *n* = **fastener**

fast food *n* (hamburger etc) ファーストフード fásùtofūdo

fastidious [fæstid'i:əs] *adj* (fussy) やかましい yakámashiì

fat [fæt] *adj* (person, animal) 太った futótttà; (book, profit) 厚い atsúì; (wallet) 金がたんまり入った kanế gà tańmarì haítttà; (profit) 大きな ỗkina
♦*n* (on person, animal: *also* CHEM) 脂肪 shibỗ; (on meat) 脂身 abúramì; (for cooking) ラード rãdo

fatal [feit'əl] *adj* (mistake) 重大な júdai na; (injury, illness) 致命的な chiméiteki na

fatalistic [feitəlis'tik] *adj* (person, attitude) 宿命論的な shukúmeirontekí na

fatality [feitæl'iti:] *n* (road death etc) 死亡事故 shibỗjikò

fatally [feit'əli:] *adv* (mistaken) 重大に júdai ni; (injured etc) 致命的に chiméiteki ni

fate [feit] *n* (destiny) 運命 úńmei; (of person) 安否 áńpi

fateful [feit'fəl] *adj* (moment, decision) 決定的な kettéiteki na

father [fɑː'ðər] *n* 父 chichí, 父親 chichíoya, お父さん o-tỗsàn

father-in-law [fɑː'ðəːrinlɔː] *n* しゅうと shúto

fatherly [fɑː'ðəːli:] *adj* (advice, help) 父親の様な chichíoya no yỗ na

fathom [fæð'əm] *n* (NAUT) 尋 hírò ◊水深の単位、約1.83メーター suíshin no táń-i,

yáku 1.83métầ
♦*vt* (understand: mystery, reason) 理解する rikái suru

fatigue [fəti:g'] *n* (tiredness) 疲労 hirỗ
metal fatigue 金属疲労 kińzokuhirỗ

fatten [fæt'ən] *vt* (animal) 太らせる futóraserù
♦*vi* 太る futórù

fatty [fæt'i:] *adj* (food) 脂肪の多い shibỗ no ỗi
♦*n* (*inf*: person) でぶ débù

fatuous [fætʃ'u:əs] *adj* (idea, remark) ばかな bákà na

faucet [fɔː'sit] (*US*) *n* (tap) 蛇口 jagúchi

fault [fɔːlt] *n* (blame) 責任 sekínin; (defect: in person) 欠点 kettén; (: in machine) 欠陥 kekkán; (: GEO) 断層 dańsỗ; (TENNIS) フォールト fỗruto
♦*vt* (criticize) 非難する hínàn suru
it's my fault 私が悪かった watákushi gà warúkattà
to find fault with ...を非難する ...wo hínàn suru
at fault ...のせいで ...no seí de

faulty [fɔːl'ti:] *adj* (machine) 欠陥のある kekkán no arù

fauna [fɔː'nə] *n* 動物相 dỗbutsusỗ

faux pas [fou pɑː'] *n inv* 非礼 hiréi

favor [fei'vər] (*BRIT* **favour**) *n* (approval) 賛成 sańsei; (help) 助け tasúke
♦*vt* (prefer: solution etc) ...の方に賛成する ...no hỗ ní sańsei surù; (: pupil etc) ひいきする hiíki suru; (assist: team, horse) ...に味方する ...ni mikáta suru
to do someone a favor ...の頼みを聞く ...no tánòmi wo kíkù
to find favor with ...の気に入る ...no kí ní irù
in favor of ...に賛成して ...ni sańsei shite

favorable [fei'vərəbəl] *adj* (*gen*) 有利な yúri na; (reaction) 好意的な kỗiteki na; (impression) 良い yỗi; (comparison) 賞賛的な shỗsanteki na; (conditions) 好適な kỗteki na

favorite [fei'vərit] *adj* (child, author etc) 一番好きな ichíban suki na
♦*n* (of teacher, parent) お気に入り o-kí-

niiri; (in race) 本命 honmei

favoritism [fei'vəːritizəm] *n* えこひいき ekóhiîki

favour [fei'vəːr] *etc* = **favor** *etc*

fawn [fɔːn] *n* (young deer) 子ジカ kojíka
♦*adj* (*also*: **fawn-colored**) 薄茶色 usúcha-iro
♦*vi*: *to fawn* (*up*)*on* ...にへつらう ...ni hetsúraù

fax [fæks] *n* (machine, document) ファックス fákkùsu
♦*vt* (transmit document) ファックスで送る fákkùsu de okúrù

FBI [efbiːai'] (*US*) *n abbr* (= *Federal Bureau of Investigation*) 連邦捜査局 reñpōsōsakyòku

fear [fiːr] *n* (being scared) 恐怖 kyōfu; (worry) 心配 shiñpai
♦*vt* (be scared of) 恐れる osórerù; (be worried about) 心配する shiñpai suru
for fear of (in case) ...を恐れて ...wo osóretè

fearful [fiːr'fəl] *adj* (person) 怖がっている kowágatte irù; (risk, noise) 恐ろしい osóroshiì

fearless [fiːr'lis] *adj* (unafraid) 勇敢な yúkan na

feasible [fiː'zəbəl] *adj* (proposal, idea) 可能な kanō na

feast [fiːst] *n* (banquet) 宴会 eñkai; (delicious meal) ごちそう gochísō; (REL: *also*: **feast day**) 祝日 shukújitsu
♦*vi* (take part in a feast) ごちそうを食べる gochísō wò tabérù

feat [fiːt] *n* (of daring, skill) 目覚しい行為 mezámashiì kōi

feather [feð'əːr] *n* (of bird) 羽根 hanè

feature [fiː'tʃəːr] *n* (characteristic) 特徴 tokúchō; (of landscape) 目立つ点 medátsu tèn; (PRESS) 特別記事 tokúbetsukijî; (TV) 特別番組 tokúbetsu bañgumi
♦*vt* (subj: film) 主役とする shuyáku to surù
♦*vi*: *to feature in* (situation, film etc) ...で主演する ...de shuén suru

feature film *n* 長編映画 chōhen eìga

features [fiː'tʃəːrz] *npl* (of face) 顔立ち kaódachi

February [feb'jəweːriː] *n* 2月 nigátsu

fed [fed] *pt*, *pp* of **feed**

federal [fed'əːrəl] *adj* (system, powers) 連邦の reñpō no

federation [fedəreiˈʃən] *n* (association) 連盟 reñmei

fed up [fed ʌp'] *adj*: *to be fed up* うんざりしている uñzarì shite iru

fee [fiː] *n* (payment) 料金 ryōkin; (of doctor, lawyer) 報酬 hōshū; (for examination, registration) 手数料 tesūryō
school fees 授業料 jugyōryō

feeble [fiː'bəl] *adj* (weak) 弱い yowáì; (ineffectual: attempt, joke) 効果的でない kōkateki dè naì

feed [fiːd] *n* (of baby) ベビーフード bebífūdo; (of animal) えさ esá; (on printer) 給紙装置 kyūshisōchi
♦*vt* (*pt*, *pp* **fed**) (person) ...に食べさせる ...ni tabésaserù; (baby) ...に授乳する ...ni junyū suru; (horse etc) ...にえさをやる ...ni esá wò yárù; (machine) ...に供給する ...ni kyōkyū suru; (data, information): *to feed into* ...に入力する ...ni nyūryoku suru

feedback [fiːd'bæk] *n* (response) フィードバック fídobàkku

feeding bottle [fiː'diŋ-] (*BRIT*) *n* ほ乳瓶 honyūbin

feed on *vt fus* (*gen*) ...を食べる ...wo tabérù, ...を常食とする ...wo jōshoku to suru; (*fig*) ...にはぐくまれる ...ni hagúkumarerù

feel [fiːl] *n* (sensation, touch) 感触 kañshoku; (impression) 印象 iñshō
♦*vt* (*pt*, *pp* **felt**) (touch) ...に触る ...ni sawárù; (experience: desire, anger) 覚える obóerù; (: cold, pain) 感じる kañjirù; (think, believe) ...だと思う ...da to omóù
to feel hungry おなかがすく onáka gà sukú
to feel cold 寒がる samúgarù
to feel lonely 寂しがる sabíshigarù
to feel better 気分がよくなる kíbùn ga yóku narù
I don't feel well 気分が悪い kíbùn ga warúì
it feels soft 柔らかい感じだ yawárakai

kañji da

to feel like (want) ...が欲しい ...ga ho-shíi

feel about/around vi ...を手探りで捜す ...wo teságuri de sagásù

feeler [fiːˈləːr] n (of insect) 触角 shokkáku

to put out a feeler/feelers (fig) 打診する dashín suru

feeling [fiːˈliŋ] n (emotion) 感情 kañjō; (physical sensation) 感触 kañshoku; (impression) 印象 iñshō

feet [fiːt] npl of **foot**

feign [fein] vt (injury, interest) 見せ掛ける misékakerù

feline [fiːˈlain] adj (cat-like) ネコの様な nékò no yō na

fell [fel] pt of **fall**

♦vt (tree) 倒す taósù

fellow [felˈou] n (man) 男 otóko; (comrade) 仲間 nakáma; (of learned society) 会員 kaíìn

fellow citizen n 同郷の市民 dōkyō nò shímìn

fellow countryman (pl **countrymen**) n 同国人 dōkokujìn

fellow men npl 外の人間 hoká no niñgen

fellowship [felˈouʃip] n (comradeship) 友情 yūjō; (society) 会 kái; (SCOL) 大学特別研究員 daígaku tokubetsu kenkyūin

felony [felˈəniː] n 重罪 jūzai

felt [felt] pt, pp of **feel**

♦n (fabric) フェルト férùto

felt-tip pen [feltˈtipˈ-] n サインペン saínpen

female [fiːˈmeil] n (ZOOL) 雌 mesú; (pej: woman) 女 ofina

♦adj (BIO) 雌の mesú no; (sex, character, child) 女の ofina no, 女性の joséi no; (vote etc) 女性たちの joséitachi no

feminine [femˈənin] adj (clothes, behavior) 女性らしい joséi rashìi; (LING) 女性の joséi no

feminist [femˈənist] n 男女同権論者 dañjodōkenroñsha, フェミニスト féminisùto

fence [fens] n (barrier) 塀 heí

♦vt (also: **fence in**: land) 塀で囲む heí de kakómù

♦vi (SPORT) フェンシングをする féñshingu wo suru

fencing [fenˈsiŋ] n (SPORT) フェンシング féñshingu

fend [fend] vi: **to fend for oneself** 自力でやっていく jíriku dè yatté ikù

fender [fenˈdəːr] n (of fireplace) 火格子 higőshi; (on boat) 防げん物 bőgenbùtsu; (US: of car) フェンダー feñdā

fend off vt (attack etc) 受流す ukénagasù

ferment [vb fəːrmentˈ n fəːrˈment] vi (beer, dough etc) 発酵する hakkő suru

♦n (fig: unrest) 動乱 dőran

fern [fəːrn] n シダ shídà

ferocious [fərouˈʃəs] adj (animal, behavior) どう猛な dőmo na; (competition) 激しい hagéshìì

ferocity [fərɑːsˈitiː] n (of animal, behavior) どう猛さ dőmòsa; (of competition) 激しさ hagéshisà

ferret [ferˈit] n フェレット férètto

ferret out vt (information) 捜し出す sagáshidasù

ferry [ferˈiː] n (also: **ferry boat**) フェリー férì, フェリーボート feríbòto

♦vt (transport: by sea, air, road) 輸送する yusô suru

fertile [fəːrˈtəl] adj (land, soil) 肥よくな hiyóku na; (imagination) 豊かな yútàka na; (woman) 妊娠可能な niñshinkanō na

fertility [fəːrtilˈətiː] n (of land) 肥よくさ hiyőkusa; (of imagination) 独創性 dokúsōsei; (of woman) 繁殖力 hañshokuryòku

fertilize [fəːrˈtəlaiz] vt (land) ...に肥料をやる ...ni hiryő wò yárù; (BIO) 受精させる juséi saserù

fertilizer [fəːrˈtəlaizəːr] n (for plants, land) 肥料 hiryő

fervent [fəːrˈvənt] adj (admirer, belief) 熱心な nesshín na

fervor [fəːrˈvəːr] n 熱心さ nesshíñsa

fester [fesˈtəːr] vi (wound) 化のうする kanő suru

festival [fesˈtəvəl] n (REL) 祝日 shukújitsu; (ART, MUS) フェスティバル fésùtibaru

festive [fes'tiv] adj (mood, atmosphere) お祭気分の o-mátsurikibùn no
the festive season (BRIT: Christmas) クリスマスの季節 kurísumasu no kisétsu

festivities [festiv'iti:z] npl (celebrations) お祝い o-íwai

festoon [festu:n'] vt: *to festoon with* ...で飾る ...de kazárù

fetch [fetʃ] vt (bring) 持って来る notté kurù; (sell for) ...の値で売れる ...no ne de urérù

fetching [fetʃ'iŋ] adj (woman, dress) 魅惑的な miwákuteki na

fête [feit] n (at church, school) バザー bazá

fetish [fet'iʃ] n (obsession) 強迫観念 kyóhakukañnen

fetus [fi:'təs] (BRIT **foetus**) n (BIO) 胎児 táiji

feud [fju:d] n (quarrel) 争い arásoì

feudal [fju:d'əl] adj (system, society) 封建的な hókenteki na

fever [fi:'və:r] n (MED) 熱 netsú

feverish [fi:'və:riʃ] adj (MED) 熱がある netsú ga arù; (emotion) 激しい hagéshiì; (activity) 慌ただしい awátadashiì

few [fju:] adj (not many) 少数の shósū no; (some): *a few* 幾つかの íkùtsuka no
♦pron (not many) 少数 shósū; (some): *a few* 幾つかの íkùtsuka

fewer [fju:'ə:r] adj compar of **few**

fewest [fju:'ist] adj superl of **few**

fiancé [fi:ɑ:nsei'] n 婚約者 koń-yakushà, フィアンセ fiáñse ◇男性 dañsei

fiancée [fi:ɑ:nsei'] n 婚約者 koń-yakushà, フィアンセ fiáñse ◇女性 joséi

fiasco [fi:æs'kou] n (disaster) 失敗 shippái

fib [fib] n (lie) うそ úsò

fiber [fai'bə:r] (BRIT **fibre**) n (thread, roughage) 繊維 sén-i; (cloth) 生地 kíji; (ANAT: tissue) 神経繊維 shiñkeiseñ-i

fiber-glass [fai'bə:rglæs] n ファイバーグラス faíbāguràsu

fickle [fik'əl] adj (person) 移り気な utsúrigi na; (weather) 変りやすい kawáriyasuì

fiction [fik'ʃən] n (LITERATURE) フィクション fíkùshon; (invention) 作り事 tsukúrigoto; (lie) うそ úsò

fictional [fik'ʃənəl] adj (character, event) 架空の kakū no

fictitious [fiktiʃ'əs] adj (false, invented) 架空の kakū no

fiddle [fid'əl] n (MUS) バイオリン baíorin; (inf: fraud, swindle) 詐欺 ságì
♦vt (BRIT: accounts) ごまかす gomákasù

fiddle with vt fus (glasses etc) いじくる ijíkurù

fidelity [fidel'iti:] n (faithfulness) 忠誠 chúsei

fidget [fidʒ'it] vi (nervously) そわそわする sówàsowa suru; (in boredom) もぞもぞする mózòmozo suru

field [fi:ld] n (on farm) 畑 hatáke; (SPORT: ground) グランド guráñdo; (fig: subject, area of interest) 分野 búñya; (range: of vision) 視野 shíyà; (: of magnet: also ELEC) 磁場 jíbà

field marshal n (MIL) 元帥 geñsui

fieldwork [fi:ld'wə:rk] n (research) 現地調査 géñchichòsa, 実地調査 jitchíchòsa, フィールドワーク fírudowàku

fiend [fi:nd] n (monster) 怪物 kaíbutsu

fiendish [fi:n'diʃ] adj (person, problem) 怪物の様な kaíbutsu no yồ na; (problem) ものすごく難しい monósugokù muzúkashiì

fierce [fi:rs] adj (animal, person) どう猛な dồmō na; (fighting) 激しい hagéshiì; (loyalty) 揺るぎない yurúginaì; (wind) 猛烈な móretsu na; (heat) うだる様な udáru yồ na

fiery [fai'ə:ri:] adj (burning) 燃え盛る moésakarù; (temperament) 激しい hagéshiì

fifteen [fif'ti:n'] num 十五 (の) júgo (no)

fifth [fifθ] num 第五(の) dáigo (no)

fifty [fif'ti:] num 五十 (の) gojū (no)

fifty-fifty [fif'ti:fif'ti:] adj (deal, split) 五分五分の gobúgobu no
♦adv 五分五分に gobúgobu ni

fig [fig] n (fruit) イチジク ichíjiku

fight [fait] n 戦い tatákai
♦vb (pt, pp **fought**)
♦vt (person, enemy, cancer etc: also MIL)...と戦う ...to tatákaù; (election)...に出馬する ...ni shutsúba suru; (emotion) 抑える osáerù
♦vi (people: also MIL) 戦う tatákaù

fighter [fai'tə:r] n (combatant) 戦う人 tatákaù hitò; (plane) 戦闘機 seńtōki

fighting [fai'tiŋ] n (battle) 戦い tatákai; (brawl) けんか kéñka

figment [fig'mənt] n: **a figment of the imagination** 気のせい kí nò séi

figurative [fig'jə:rətiv] adj (expression, style) 比ゆ的な hiyúteki na

figure [fig'jə:r] n (DRAWING, GEOM) 図 zu; (number, statistic etc) 数字 sújì; (body, shape, outline) 形 katáchi; (person, personality) 人 hitò
♦vt (think: esp US) (...だと) 思う (...da to) omóù
♦vi (appear) 見える miérù

figurehead [fig'jə:rhed] n (NAUT) 船首像 seńshuzō; (pej: leader) 名ばかりのリーダー na bákarī no rīdā

figure of speech n 比ゆ hiyù

figure out vt (work out) 理解する rikái suru

filament [fil'əmənt] n (ELEC) フィラメント fírâmento

filch [filtʃ] (inf) vt (steal) くすねる kusúnerù

file [fail] n (dossier) 資料 shiryō; (folder) 書類ばさみ shorúibàsami; (COMPUT) ファイル fáiru; (row) 列 rétsù; (tool) やすり yasúrì
♦vt (papers) 保管する hokán suru; (LAW: claim) 提出する teíshutsu suru; (wood, metal, fingernails)...にやすりを掛ける ...ni yasúri wo kakérù

file in/out vi 1列で入る〔出る〕 ichíretsu dè haíru〔dérù〕

filing cabinet [fai'liŋ-] n ファイルキャビネット faíru kyabinètto

fill [fil] vt (container, space): **to fill (with)** (...で) 一杯にする (...de) ippái ni surù; (vacancy) 補充する hojū suru; (need) 満たす mitásù

♦n: **to eat one's fill** たらふく食べる taráfuku taberù

fillet [filei'] n (of meat, fish) ヒレ hire

fillet steak n ヒレステーキ hiresutèki

fill in vt (hole) うめる umérù; (time) つぶす tsubúsù; (form)...に書入れる ...ni ka-kíirerù

filling [fil'iŋ] n (for tooth) 充てん jūten; (CULIN) 中身 nakámi

filling station (AUT) ガソリンスタンド gasórinsutañdo

fill up vt (container, space) 一杯にする ippái ni surù
♦vi (AUT) 満タンにする mañtan ni surù

film [film] n (CINEMA, TV) 映画 eíga; (PHOT) フィルム fírùmu; (of powder, liquid etc) 膜 makú
♦vt (scene) 撮影する satsúei suru
♦vi 撮影する satsúei suru

film star n 映画スター eígasutā

film strip n (slide) フィルムスライド firúmusuraìdo

filter [fil'tə:r] n (device) ろ過装置 rokásōchi, フィルター fírùtā; (PHOT) フィルター fírùtā
♦vt (liquid) ろ過する rokā suru

filter lane (BRIT) n (AUT) 右〔左〕折車線 u(sa)sétsu shaseñ

filter-tipped [fil'tə:rtipt] adj フィルター付きの fírùtātsuki no

filth [filθ] n (dirt) 汚物 obútsu

filthy [fil'θi:] adj (object, person) 不潔な fukétsu na; (language) みだらな mídàra na

fin [fin] n (of fish) ひれ hire

final [fai'nəl] adj (last) 最後の saígo no; (ultimate) 究極の kyúkyoku no; (definitive: answer, decision) 最終的な saíshūteki na
♦n (SPORT) 決勝戦 kesshósen

finale [finæl'i:] n フィナーレ fínàre

finalist [fai'nəlist] n (SPORT) 決勝戦出場選手 kesshósen shutsujō señshu

finalize [fai'nəlaiz] vt (arrangements, plans) 最終的に決定する saíshūteki nì kettéi surù

finally [fai'nəli:] adv (eventually) ようやく yōyaku; (lastly) 最後に saígo ni

finals [fai'nəlz] *npl* (SCOL) 卒業試験 so-tsúgyōshikèn

finance [*n* fai'næns *vb* finæns'] *n* (money, backing) 融資 yūshi; (money management) 財政 zaísei
♦*vt* (back, fund) 融資する yūshi suru

finances [finæn'siz] *npl* (personal finances) 財政 zaísei

financial [finæn'tʃəl] *adj* (difficulties, year, venture) 経済的な keízaiteki na

financial year *n* 会計年度 kaíkeinèndo

financier [finænsi:r'] *n* (backer, funder) 出資者 shusshíshà

find [faind] (*pt, pp* **found**) *vt* (person, object, answer) 見付ける mitsúkeru; (discover) 発見する hakkén suru; (think) ...だと思う ...da to omóu
♦*n* (discovery) 発見 hakkén

to find someone guilty (LAW) ...に有罪判決を下す ...ni yūzaihañketsu wo kudásù

findings [fain'diŋz] *npl* (LAW, of report) 調査の結果 chōsa no kekkà

find out *vt* (fact, truth) 知る shírù; (person) ...の悪事を知る ...no ákùji wo shírù

to find out about (subject) 調べる shiráberù; (by chance) 知る shírù

fine [fain] *adj* (excellent: quality, performance etc) 見事な mígòto na; (thin: hair, thread) 細い hosóì; (not coarse: sand, powder etc) 細かい komákaì; (subtle: detail, adjustment etc) 細かい komákaì
♦*adv* (well) うまく úmàku
♦*n* (LAW) 罰金 bakkín
♦*vt* (LAW) ...に罰金を払わせる ...ni bakkín wò haráwaserù

to be fine (person) 元気である géñki de árù; (weather) 良い天気である yóì tếñki de árù

fine arts *npl* 美術 bíjutsu

finery [fai'nə:ri:] *n* (dress) 晴着 harégi; (jewelery) 取って置きの装身具 tottéoki nò sōshiñgu

finesse [fines'] *n* 手腕 shúwàn

finger [fiŋ'gə:r] *n* (ANAT) 指 yubí
♦*vt* (touch) ...に指で触る ...ni yubí dè sawárù

little/index finger 小〔人指し〕指 ko

(hitósashi)yúbi

fingernail [fiŋ'gə:rneil] *n* つめ tsumé

fingerprint [fiŋ'gə:rprint] *n* (mark) 指紋 shimón

fingertip [fiŋ'gə:rtip] *n* 指先 yubísaki

finicky [fin'iki:] *adj* (fussy) 気難しい kimúzukashiì

finish [fin'iʃ] *n* (end) 終り owári; (SPORT) ゴール gṓru; (polish etc) 仕上り shiágari
♦*vt* (work, eating, book etc) 終える oérù
♦*vi* (person, course, event) 終る owárù

to finish doing something ...し終える ...shi oérù

to finish third (in race etc) 3着になる sañchaku ni naru

finishing line [fin'iʃiŋ-] *n* ゴールライン gōrurain

finishing school [fin'iʃiŋ-] *n* 花嫁学校 hanáyomegàkkō

finish off *vt* (complete) 仕上げる shiágerù; (kill) 止めを刺す todóme wo sasù

finish up *vt* (food, drink) 平らげる taíragerù
♦*vi* (end up) 最後に...に行ってしまう saígo ni ...ni itté shimaù

finite [fai'nait] *adj* (time, space) 一定の ittéi no; (verb) 定形の teíkei no

Finland [fin'lənd] *n* フィンランド fíñrando

Finn [fin] *n* フィンランド人 fiñrandojìn

Finnish [fin'iʃ] *adj* フィンランドの fíñrando no; (LING) フィンランド語の fíñrando-dogo no
♦*n* (LING) フィンランド語 fíñrandogo

fiord [fjourd] = **fjord**

fir [fə:r] *n* モミ mómì

fire [fai'ə:r] *n* (flames) 火 hí; (in hearth) たき火 takíbi; (accidental) 火事 kají; (gas fire, electric fire) ヒーター hītā
♦*vt* (shoot: gun etc) うつ útsù; (: arrow) 射る írù; (stimulate: imagination, enthusiasm) 刺激する shigéki suru; (*inf*: dismiss: employee) 首にする kubí ni surù
♦*vi* (shoot) 発砲する happṓ suru

on fire 燃えて moéte

fire alarm *n* 火災警報装置 kasáikeihō-sòchi

firearm [faiə:r'ɑ:rm] *n* 銃砲 jūhō ◇ 特に

ピストルを指す tŏkù ni pisútoru wŏ sásù

fire brigade n 消防隊 shŏbŏtai

fire department (US) n = **fire brigade**

fire engine n 消防自動車 shŏbŏjidŏsha

fire escape n 非常階段 hijŏkaîdan

fire extinguisher n 消化器 shŏkakî

fireman [faiə:r'mən] (pl **firemen**) n 消防士 shŏbŏshi

fireplace [faiə:r'pleis] n 暖炉 dánro

fireside [faiə:r'said] n 暖炉のそば dánro no sŏbà

fire station n 消防署 shŏbŏsho

firewood [faiə:r'wud] n まき makî

fireworks [faiə:r'wə:rks] npl 花火 hánàbi

firing squad [faiə:r'iŋ-] n 銃殺隊 júsatsutai

firm [fə:rm] adj (mattress, ground) 固い katái; (grasp, push, tug) 強い tsuyôî; (decision) 断固とした dánko to shita; (faith) 固い katái; (measures) 強固な kyŏko na; (look, voice) しっかりした shikkárì shita

◆n (company) 会社 kaísha

firmly [fə:rm'li:] adv (grasp, pull, tug) 強く tsúyòku; (decide) 断固として dánko to shite; (look, speak) しっかりと shikkárì to

first [fə:rst] adj (before all others) 第一の dáìchi no, 最初の saîsho no

◆adv (before all others) 一番に ichîban ni, 一番最初に ichîban saîsho ni; (when listing reasons etc) 第一に dáìchi ni

◆n (person: in race) 1着 itcháku; (AUT) ローギヤ rŏgiya; (BRIT SCOL: degree) 1級優等卒業学位 îkkyū yūtŏ sotsugyŏ gakùì ◇英国では優等卒業学位は成績の高い順に1級、2級、3級に分けられる eîkoku de wà yūtŏ sotsugyŏ gakùì wa seísèki no takái jùn ni ikkyû, nikyû, sankyû nî wakérarerù

at first 最初は saîsho wa

first of all まず第一に mázù dáìchi ni

first aid n 応急手当 ŏkyūteàte

first-aid kit n 救急箱 kyúkyùbako

first-class [fə:rst'klæs'] adj (excellent: mind, worker) 優れた sugúretà; (car-

riage, ticket, post) 1等の ittŏ no

first-hand [fə:rst'hænd'] adj (account, story) 直接の chokúsetsu no

first lady (US) n 大統領夫人 daítŏryŏfujìn

firstly [fə:rst'li:] adv 第一に daîchi ni

first name n 名 na, ファーストネーム fásutonèmu

first-rate [fə:rst'reit'] adj (player, actor etc) 優れた sugúretà

fiscal [fis'kəl] adj (year) 会計の kaíkei no; (policies) 財政の zaísei no

fish [fiʃ] n inv 魚 sakána

◆vt (river, area) ...で釣りをする ...de tsurí wo surù

◆vi (commercially) 漁をする ryŏ wo surù; (as sport, hobby) 釣をする tsurí wo surù

to go fishing 釣に行く tsurí ni ikù

fisherman [fiʃ'ə:rmən] (pl **fishermen**) n 漁師 ryŏshi

fish farm n 養魚場 yŏgyojŏ

fish fingers (BRIT) npl = **fish sticks**

fishing boat [fiʃ'iŋ-] n 漁船 gyosén

fishing line n 釣糸 tsurîitò

fishing rod n 釣ざお tsurîzao

fishmonger's (shop) [fiʃ'mʌŋgə:rz-] n 魚屋 sakánaya

fish sticks (US) npl フィッシュスティック fisshúsutikkù ◇細長く切った魚にパン粉をまぶして揚げた物 hosónagaku kittà sakána ni pánko wo mabúshite agéta monò

fishy [fiʃ'i:] (inf) adj (tale, story) 怪しい ayáshiì

fission [fiʃ'ən] n 分裂 buńretsu

fissure [fiʃ'ə:r] n 亀裂 kirétsu

fist [fist] n こぶし kóbùshi, げんこつ geńkotsu

fit [fit] adj (suitable) 適当な tekítŏ na; (healthy) 健康な keńkŏ na

◆vt (subj: clothes, shoes) ...にぴったり合う ...ni pittárì au; (put in) ...に入れる ...ni iréru; (attach, equip) ...に取り付ける ...ni torítsukeru; (suit) ...に合う ...ni áù

◆vi (clothes) ぴったり合う pittárì áù; (parts) 合う áù; (in space, gap) ぴったりはいる pittárì haîrù

♦*n* (MED) 発作 hossá; (of coughing, giggles) 発作的に...する事 hossáteki ni ...suru kotó

fit to (ready) ...出来る状態にある ...dekirù jōtai ni arù

fit for (suitable for) ...に適当である ...ni tekítō de arù

a fit of anger かんしゃく kańshaku

this dress is a good fit このドレスはぴったり体に合う konó doresu wa pittárì karáda ni aù

by fits and starts 動いたり止ったりして ugóitarì tomáttarì shité

fitful [fit'fəl] *adj* (sleep) 途切れ途切れの togíretogìre no

fit in *vi* (person) 溶込む tokékomù

fitment [fit'mənt] *n* (in room, cabin) 取付け家具 torítsukekagù ◊つり戸棚など壁などに固定した家具を指す tsurítodàna nádò kabé nadò ni kotéi shita kagù wo sásù

fitness [fit'nis] *n* (MED) 健康 keńkō

fitted carpet [fit'id-] *n* 敷込みじゅうたん shikfkomijũtan

fitted kitchen [fit'id-] *n* システムキッチン shisútemu kitchiñ

fitter [fit'ər] *n* (of machinery, equipment) 整備工 seíbikō

fitting [fit'iŋ] *adj* (compliment, thanks) 適切な tekísetsu na

♦*n* (of dress) 試着 shicháku; (of piece of equipment) 取付け torítsuke

fitting room *n* (in shop) 試着室 shichákushìtsu

fittings [fit'iŋz] *npl* (in building) 設備 sétsubi

five [faiv] *num* 五 (の) gó (no), 五つ (の) itsútsù (no)

fiver [fai'və:r] *n* (*inf*: *BRIT*: 5 pounds) 5 ポンド札 gópondo satsù; (*US*: 5 dollars) 5 ドル札 gódoru satsù

fix [fiks] *vt* (attach) 取付ける torítsukerù; (sort out, arrange) 手配する tehái suru; (mend) 直す naósù; (prepare: meal, drink) 作る tsukúrù

♦*n*: *to be in a fix* 困っている komátte irù

fixation [fiksei'ʃən] *n* 固着 kocháku

fixed [fikst] *adj* (price, amount etc) 一定の ittéi no

a fixed idea 固定観念 kotéikañnen

a fixed smile 作り笑い tsukúriwarài

fixture [fiks'tʃər] *n* (bath, sink, cupboard etc) 設備 sétsubi; (SPORT) 試合の予定 shiái no yotèi

fix up *vt* (meeting) 手配する tehái suru

to fix someone up with something ...のために...を手に入れる ...no tamé ni ...wo té ni irerù

fizzle out [fiz'əl-] *vi* (event) しりすぼみに終ってしまう shirísùbomi ni owátte shimaù; (interest) 次第に消えてしまう shidái ni kiète shimaù

fizzy [fiz'i:] *adj* (drink) 炭酸入りの tañsan-iri no

fjord [fjourd] *n* フィヨルド fíyòrudo

flabbergasted [flæb'ə:rgæstid] *adj* (dumbfounded, surprised) あっけにとられた akké ni torareta

flabby [flæb'i:] *adj* (fat) 締まりのない shimárì no nàl

flag [flæg] *n* (of country, organization) 旗 hatá; (for signalling) 手旗 tebáta; (*also*: **flagstone**) 敷石 shikfishi

♦*vi* (person, spirits) 弱る yowárù

to flag someone down (taxi, car etc) ...を振って...を止める té wo futté ...wo tomérù

flagpole [flæg'poul] *n* 旗ざお hatázao

flagrant [fleig'rənt] *adj* (violation, injustice) 甚だしい hanáhadashìi

flagship [flæg'ʃip] *n* (of fleet) 旗艦 kikáñ; (*fig*) 看板施設 kañbanshisètsu

flair [fle:r] *n* (talent) 才能 saínō; (style) 粋なセンス ikí na señsu

flak [flæk] *n* (MIL) 対空砲火 taíkūhòka; (*inf*: criticism) 非難 hínan

flake [fleik] *n* (of rust, paint) はげ落ちた欠けら hagéochita kakéra; (of snow, soap powder) 一片 ippéñ

♦*vi* (*also*: **flake off**: paint, enamel) はげ落ちる hagéochirù

flamboyant [flæmboi'ənt] *adj* (dress, design) けばけばしい kebákebashìi; (person) 派手な hadé na

flame [fleim] *n* (of fire) 炎 honó-ò

flamingo [fləmiŋ'gou] n フラミンゴ furámiṅgo

flammable [flæm'əbəl] adj (gas, fabric) 燃えやすい moéyasuî

flan [flæn] n フラン fúràn ◇菓子の一種 kashî no isshù

flank [flæŋk] n (of animal) わき腹 wakíbàra; (of army) 側面 sokúmèn
♦vt ...のわきにある〔いる〕 ...no wakí ni arû (iru)

flannel [flæn'əl] n (fabric) フランネル furánneru; (BRIT: also: face flannel) フェースタオル fésutaòru

flannels [flæn'əlz] npl フランネルズボン furánneruzubòn

flap [flæp] n (of pocket, envelope, jacket) ふた futá
♦vt (arms, wings) ばたばたさせる bátàbata saserù
♦vi (sail, flag) はためく hátamekù; (inf: also: be in a flap) 興奮している kôfun shite irû

flare [fle:r] n (signal) 発煙筒 hatsúentò; (in skirt etc) フレア furéa

flare up vi (fire) 燃え上る moéagarù; (fig: person) 怒る okórù; (: fighting) ぼっ発する boppátsu suru

flash [flæʃ] n (of light) 閃光 seṅkō; (also: news flash) ニュースフラッシュ nyūsufurasshù; (PHOT) フラッシュ furásshù
♦vt (light, headlights) 点滅させる teṅmetsu saserù; (send: news, message) 速報する sokúhō suru; (: look, smile) 見せる misérù
♦vi (lightning, light) 光る hikárù; (light on ambulance etc) 点滅する teṅmetsu suru

in a flash 一瞬にして isshún nî shite

to flash by/past (person) 走って通り過ぎる hashítte tôrisugirù

flashback [flæʃ'bæk] n (CINEMA) フラッシュバック furásshubakkù

flashbulb [flæʃ'bʌlb] n フラッシュバルブ furásshubarùbu

flashcube [flæʃ'kju:b] n フラッシュキューブ furásshukyùbu

flashlight [flæʃ'lait] n 懐中電灯 kaíchūdeñtō

flashy [flæʃ'i:] (pej) adj 派手な hadé na

flask [flæsk] n (bottle) 瓶 bíñ; (also: vacuum flask) 魔法瓶 máhòbin, ポット póttò

flat [flæt] adj (ground, surface) 平な taíra na; (tire) パンクした pánku shita; (battery) 上がった agátta; (beer) 気が抜けた ki gá nùketa; (refusal, denial) きっぱりした kippárî shita; (MUS: note) フラットの furáttò no; (: voice) そっけない sokkénài; (rate, fee) 均一の kiń-itsu no
♦n (BRIT: apartment) アパート ápàto; (AUT) パンク pánku; (MUS) フラット furáttò

to work flat out 力一杯働く chikára ippài hataraku

flatly [flæt'li:] adv (refuse, deny) きっぱりと kippárî to

flatten [flæt'ən] vt (also: flatten out) 平にする taíra ni surù; (building, city) 取壊す toríkowasù

flatter [flæt'ə:r] vt (praise, compliment) ...にお世辞を言う ...ni oséji wò iú

flattering [flæt'ə:riŋ] adj (comment) うれしい uréshiî; (dress) よく似合う yókù niáù

flattery [flæt'ə:ri:] n お世辞 oséji

flaunt [flɔ:nt] vt (wealth, possessions) 見せびらかす misébirakasù

flavor [flei'və:r] (BRIT **flavour**) n (of food, drink) 味 ajî; (of ice-cream etc) 種類 shúrùi
♦vt ...に味を付ける ...ni ajî wo tsukerù
strawberry-flavored イチゴ味の ichígoajî no

flavoring [flei'və:riŋ] n 調味料 chốmiryò

flaw [flɔ:] n (in argument, policy) 不備な点 fúbî na teñ; (in character) 欠点 kettén; (in cloth, glass) 傷 kizú

flawless [flɔ:'lis] adj 完璧な kañpeki na

flax [flæks] n 亜麻 amá

flaxen [flæk'sən] adj (hair) ブロンドの buróñdo no

flea [fli:] n (human, animal) ノミ nomí

fleck [flek] n (mark) 細かいはん点 komákaî hañten

fled [fled] pt, pp of **flee**

flee [fli:] (*pt, pp* **fled**) *vt* (danger, famine, country) 逃れる nogárerù, ...から逃げる ...kara nigérù
♦*vi* (refugees, escapees) 逃げる nigérù

fleece [fli:s] *n* (sheep's wool) 羊毛一頭分 yőmőitőbun; (sheep's coat) ヒツジの毛 hitsúji no kè
♦*vt* (*inf*: cheat) ...から大金をだまし取る ...kara taíkin wò damáshitorù

fleet [fli:t] *n* (of ships: for war) 艦隊 kańtai; (: for fishing etc) 船団 señdan; (of trucks, cars) 車両団 sharyódan

fleeting [fli:'tiŋ] *adj* (glimpse) ちらっと 見える chiráttò miérù; (visit) 短い mijíkaì; (happiness) つかの間の tsuká no mà no

Flemish [flem'iʃ] *adj* フランダースの furándàsu no; (LING) フランダース語の furándàsugo no
♦*n* (LING) フランダース語 furándàsugo

flesh [fleʃ] *n* (ANAT) 肉 nikú; (skin) 肌 hadá; (of fruit) 果肉 kaníku

flesh wound *n* 軽傷 keíshō

flew [flu:] *pt of* **fly**

flex [fleks] *n* (of appliance) コード kồdo
♦*vt* (leg, muscles) 曲げたり伸したりする magétarì nobáshitarì suru

flexibility [fleksəbil'əti:] *n* (of material) しなやかさ shináyakasà; (of response, policy) 柔軟性 jūnañsei

flexible [flek'səbəl] *adj* (material) 曲げ やすい magéyasuì; (response, policy) 柔 軟な jūnan na

flick [flik] *n* (of hand, whip etc) 一振り hitófùri
♦*vt* (with finger, hand) はじき飛ばす hajíkitobasù; (towel, whip) ぴしっと振る pishíttò furú; (switch: on) 入れる iréru; (: off) 切る kírù

flicker [flik'əːr] *vi* (light) ちらちらする chíràchira suru; (flame) ゆらゆらする yúràyura suru; (eyelids) まばたく mabátakù

flick through *vt fus* (book) ぱらぱらと ...のページをめくる páràpara to ...no pèji wo mekúru

flier [flai'əːr] *n* (pilot) パイロット paírottò

flight [flait] *n* (action: of birds, plane) 飛 行 hikṓ; (AVIAT: journey) 飛行機旅行 hikṓkiryokṓ; (escape) 逃避 tṓhi; (*also*: **flight of steps/stairs**) 階段 kaídan

flight attendant (*US*) *n* 乗客係 jṓkyakugakàri

flight deck *n* (AVIAT) 操縦室 sṓjūshìtsu; (NAUT) 空母の飛行甲板 kúbo no hikṓkañban

flimsy [flim'zi:] *adj* (shoes) こわれやすい kowáreyasuì; (clothes) 薄い usuí; (building) もろい moróì; (excuse) 見え透いた miésuità

flinch [flintʃ] *vi* (in pain, shock) 身震いす る mibúrùi suru
to flinch from (crime, unpleasant duty) ...するのをしり込みする ...surú no wò shirígomi surù

fling [fliŋ] (*pt, pp* **flung**) *vt* (throw) 投げ る nagérù

flint [flint] *n* (stone) 火打石 hiúchiishì; (in lighter) 石 ishí

flip [flip] *vt* (switch) はじく hajíkù; (coin) トスする tósù suru

flippant [flip'ənt] *adj* (attitude, answer) 軽率な keísotsu na

flipper [flip'əːr] *n* (of seal etc) ひれ足 hiréashì; (for swimming) フリッパー furíppā̀

flirt [fləːrt] *vi* (with person) いちゃつく ichátsuku
♦*n* 浮気者 uwákimono

flit [flit] *vi* (birds, insects) ひょいと飛ぶ hyoí tò tobú

float [flout] *n* (for swimming, fishing) 浮 き ukí; (vehicle in parade) 山車 dashí; (money) つり用の小銭 tsuríyō nò kozéni
♦*vi* 浮く ukú

flock [flɑ:k] *n* 群れ muré; (REL) 会衆 kaíshū
♦*vi*: **to flock to** (place, event) ぞくぞく 集まる zókùzoku atsúmarù

flog [flɑ:g] *vt* (whip) むち打つ múchìutsu

flood [flʌd] *n* (of water) 洪水 kṓzui; (of letters, imports etc) 大量 taíryō
♦*vt* (subj: water) 水浸しにする mizúbitàshi ni suru; (: people) ...に殺到する ...ni sattṓ suru

◆*vi* (place) 水浸しになる mizúbitàshi ni nárù; (people): **to flood into** ...に殺到する ...ni sattő suru

flooding [flʌ'dɪŋ] *n* 洪水 kőzui

floodlight [flʌd'lait] *n* 照明灯 shőmeitő

floor [flɔːr] *n* (of room) 床 yuká; (storey) 階 kái; (of sea, valley) 底 sókò
◆*vt* (subj: blow) 打ちのめす uchínomesù; (: question) 慌てさせる győten saserù
ground floor 1階 ikkái
first floor (*US*) 1階 ikkai (*BRIT*) 2階 nikái

floorboard [flɔːr'bɔːrd] *n* 床板 yuká-ita

floor show *n* フロアショー furőashō

flop [flɑːp] *n* (failure) 失敗 shippái
◆*vi* (fail) 失敗する shippái suru; (fall: into chair, onto floor etc) どたっと座り込む dotáttò suwárikomù

floppy [flɑːp'i:] *adj* ふにゃふにゃした fúnyàfunya shita

floppy (disk) *n* (COMPUT) フロッピー（ディスク）furőppī(disùku)

flora [flɔːr'ə] *n* 植物相 shokúbutsuső

floral [flɔːr'əl] *adj* (dress, wallpaper) 花柄の hanágara no

florid [flɔːr'id] *adj* (style) ごてごてした gótègote shitá; (complexion) 赤らんだ akárañda

florist [flɔːr'ist] *n* 花屋 hanáyà

florist's (shop) *n* 花屋 hanáyà

flounce [flauns] *n* (frill) 縁飾り fuchíkazarì

flounce out *vi* 怒って飛び出す okóttè tobídasù

flounder [flaun'dəːr] *vi* (swimmer) もがく mogákù; (fig: speaker) まごつく magótsukù; (economy) 停滞する teítai suru
◆*n* (ZOOL) ヒラメ hiráme

flour [flau'əːr] *n* (gen) 粉 koná; (also: **wheat flour**) 小麦粉 komúgiko

flourish [fləːr'iʃ] *vi* (business) 繁栄する haň-ei suru; (plant) 生い茂る oíshigerù
◆*n* (bold gesture): **with a flourish** 大げさな身振りで őgesa na mibúri de

flourishing [fləːr'iʃiŋ] *adj* (company) 繁栄する haň-ei suru; (trade) 盛んな sakán na

flout [flaut] *vt* (law, rules) 犯す okásù

flow [flou] *n* 流れ nagáre
◆*vi* 流れる nagárerù

flow chart *n* 流れ図 nagárezù, フローチャート furőchāto

flower [flau'əːr] *n* 花 haná
◆*vi* (plant, tree) 咲く sakú

flower bed *n* 花壇 kádàn

flowerpot [flau'əːrpɑːt] *n* 植木鉢 uékibàchi

flowery [flau'əːri:] *adj* (perfume) 花の様な haná no yő na; (pattern) 花柄の hanágara no; (speech) 仰々しい győgyōshiì

flown [floun] *pp of* **fly**

flu [flu:] *n* (MED) 流感 ryűkan

fluctuate [flʌk'tʃueit] *vi* (price, rate, temperature) 変動する heńdō suru

fluctuation [flʌktʃuei'ʃən] *n*: **fluctuation (in)** (...の) 変動 (...no) heńdō

fluent [flu:'ənt] *adj* (linguist) 語学たん能な gogákutañnő na; (speech, writing etc) 滑らかな namáràka na
he speaks fluent French, he's fluent in French 彼はフランス語が堪能だ kárè wa furánsugo gà tañnő da

fluently [flu:'əntli:] *adv* (speak, read, write) 流ちょうに ryűchō ni

fluff [flʌf] *n* (on jacket, carpet) 毛羽 kebá; (fur: of kitten etc) 綿毛 watáge

fluffy [flʌf'i:] *adj* (jacket, toy etc) ふわふわした fúwàfuwa shitá

fluid [flu:'id] *adj* (movement) しなやかな shináyàka na; (situation, arrangement) 流動的な ryűdōteki na
◆*n* (liquid) 液 ékì

fluke [flu:k] (*inf*) *n* まぐれ magúrè

flung [flʌŋ] *pt, pp of* **fling**

fluorescent [flu:əres'ənt] *adj* (dial, paint, light etc) 蛍光の keíkō no

fluoride [flu:'əraid] *n* フッ化物 fukkábutsu

flurry [fləːr'i:] *n*: **a snow flurry** にわか雪 niwákayùki
flurry of activity 慌ただしい動き a-wátadashiì ugóki

flush [flʌʃ] *n* (on face) ほてり hotéri; (fig: of youth, beauty etc) 輝かしさ kagáyakashisà
◆*vt* (drains, pipe) 水を流して洗う mizú

wǒ nagáshite araù

♦*vi* (become red) 赤くなる akáku narù

♦*adj*: **flush with** (level) ...と同じ高さの ...to onáji takasà no

to flush the toilet トイレの水を流す tòire no mizú wo nagasù

flushed [flʌʃt] *adj* 赤らめた akáraметà

flush out *vt* (game, birds) 茂みから追出す shigémi kàra oídasù

flustered [flʌs'tə:rd] *adj* (nervous, confused) まごついた magótsuità

flute [flu:t] *n* フルート fúrùto

flutter [flʌt'ə:r] *n* (of wings) 羽ばたき habátaki; (of panic, excitement, nerves) うろたえ urótae

♦*vi* (bird) 羽ばたきする habátaki suru

flux [flʌks] *n*: **in a state of flux** 流動的状態で ryūdōtekijòtai de

fly [flai] *n* (insect) ハエ haé; (on trousers: also: **flies**) ズボンの前 zubóń no máè

♦*vb* (*pt* **flew**, *pp* **flown**)

♦*vt* (plane) 操縦する sōjū suru; (passengers, cargo) 空輸する kūyu suru; (distances) 飛ぶ tobú

♦*vi* (bird, insect, plane) 飛ぶ tobú; (passengers) 飛行機で行く hikōki de ikú; (escape) 逃げる nigérù; (flag) 掲げられる kakágerarerù

fly away *vi* (bird, insect) 飛んで行く tofíde ikù

flying [flai'iŋ] *n* (activity) 飛行機旅行 hikōkiryokò; (action) 飛行 hikō

♦*adj*: **a flying visit** ほんの短い訪問 hofíno mijíkaì hōmon

with flying colors 大成功で daíseikō de

flying saucer *n* 空飛ぶ円盤 sórà tobú efíban

flying start *n*: **to get off to a flying start** 好調な滑りだしをする kōchō na suberidàshi wo suru

fly off *vi* = **fly away**

flyover [flai'ouvə:r] (*BRIT*) *n* (overpass) 陸橋 rikkyò

flysheet [flai'ʃi:t] *n* (for tent) 入口の垂れ布 iríguchi nò tarénuno

foal [foul] *n* 子ウマ koúma

foam [foum] *n* (of surf, water, beer) 泡 awá; (also: **foam rubber**) フォームラバー fōmurabā

♦*vi* (liquid) 泡立つ awádatsu

to foam at the mouth (person, animal) 泡をふく awá wo fukù

fob [fɑ:b] *vt*: **to fob someone off** ...をだます ...wo damásù

focal point [fou'kəl-] *n* (of room, activity etc) 中心 chūshin

focus [fou'kəs] (*pl* **focuses**) *n* (PHOT) 焦点 shōten; (of attention, storm etc) 中心 chūshin

♦*vt* (field glasses etc) ...の焦点を合せる ...no shōten wò awáserù

♦*vi*: **to focus (on)** (with camera) (...に) カメラを合せる (...ni) kámèra wò awáserù; (person) (...に) 注意を向ける (...ni) chūi wo mukérù

in/out of focus 焦点が合っている〔いない〕 shōten ga attè irú 〔ináì〕

fodder [fɑ:d'ə:r] *n* (food) 飼葉 kaíba

foe [fou] *n* (rival, enemy) 敵 tekí

foetus [fi:'təs] *n* (*BRIT*) = **fetus**

fog [fɔ:g] *n* 霧 kirí

foggy [fɔ:g'i:] *adj*: **it's foggy** 霧が出ている kirí ga detè irú

fog light (*BRIT* **fog lamp**) *n* (AUT) フォッグライト fōggùraito

foil [fɔil] *vt* (attack, plan) くじく kujíkù

♦*n* (metal foil, kitchen foil) ホイル hoíru; (complement) 引立てる物 hikítaterù monò; (FENCING) フルーレ furúrè

fold [fould] *n* (bend, crease) 折目 oríme; (of skin etc) しわ shiwá; (in cloth, curtain etc) ひだ hidá; (AGR) ヒツジの囲い hitsúji nò kakòi; (*fig*) 仲間 nakáma

♦*vt* (clothes, paper) 畳む tatámu; (arms) 組む kúmù

folder [foul'də:r] *n* (for papers) 書類挟み shorúibasàmi

folding [foul'diŋ] *adj* (chair, bed) 折畳み式の orítatamishiki no

fold up *vi* (map, bed, table) 折畳める orítatamerù; (business) つぶれる tsubúrerù

♦*vt* (map, clothes etc) 畳む tatámu

foliage [fou'li:idʒ] *n* (leaves) 葉 ha ◇総称 sōshō

folk [fouk] *npl* (people) 人々 hitobito

♦adj (art, music) 民族の mínzoku no

folks (parents) 両親 ryōshin

folklore [fouk'lɔːr] n 民間伝承 mińkandeńshō

folk song n 民謡 miń-yō

follow [fɑːl'ou] vt (person) ...について行く ...ni tsúíte ikú; (suspect) 尾行する bikō suru; (event) ...に注目する ...ni chūmoku suru; (story) 注意して聞く chūí shite kikú; (leader, example, advice, instructions) ...に従う ...ni shitágaù; (route, path) たどる tadórù

♦vi (person, period of time) 後に来る(いく) átò ni kúru(ikú); (result) ...という結果になる ...to iú kekka ni nárù

to follow suit (fig) (...と) 同じ事をする (...to) onáji kotò wo suru

follower [fɑːl'ouər] n (of person) 支持者 shijíshà; (of belief) 信奉者 shińpōsha

following [fɑːl'ouiŋ] adj 次の tsugí no

♦n (of party, religion, group etc) 支持者 shijíshà ◇総称 sōshō

follow up vt (letter, offer) ...に答える ...ni kotáerù; (case) 追及する tsuíkyū suru

folly [fɑːl'iː] n (foolishness) ばかな事 bákà na kotó

fond [fɑːnd] adj (memory) 楽しい tanóshiī; (smile, look) 愛情に満ちた aíjō ni michita; (hopes, dreams) 愚かな óròka na

to be fond of ...が好きである ...ga sukí de arù

fondle [fɑːn'dəl] vt 愛ぶする aíbù suru

font [fɑːnt] n (in church) 洗礼盤 seńreíban; (TYP) フォント fóñto

food [fuːd] n 食べ物 tabémonò

food mixer n ミキサー míkìsā

food poisoning [-pɔi'zəniŋ] n 食中毒 shokúchūdoku

food processor [-prɑːs'esəːr] n ミキサー míkìsā ◇食べ物を混ぜたりひいたりおろしたりするための家庭電気製品 tabemono wo mazetari hiitari oroshitari suru tame no katei denki seihin

foodstuffs [fuːd'stʌfs] npl 食料 shokúryō

fool [fuːl] n (idiot) ばか bákà; (CULIN)

フール fūrù ◇果物入りムースの一種 kudámono-iri mūsu no ísshù

♦vt (deceive) だます damásù

♦vi (also: fool around: be silly) ふざける fuzákerù

foolhardy [fuːl'hɑːrdiː] adj (conduct) 無謀な mubō na

foolish [fuːl'iʃ] adj (stupid) ばかな bákà na; (rash) 無茶な muchá na

foolproof [fuːl'pruːf] adj (plan etc) 絶対確実な zettáikakújitsu na

foot [fut] (pl feet) n (of person, animal) 足 ashí; (of bed, cliff) ふもと fumóto; (measure) フィート fíto

♦vt (bill) 支払う shiháraù

on foot 徒歩で tóhò de

footage [fut'idʒ] n (CINEMA) 場面 bámèn

football [fut'bɔːl] n (ball: round) サッカーボール sakkábòru; (: oval) フットボール futtóbòru; (sport: BRIT) サッカー sakká; (: US) フットボール futtóbòru

football player n (BRIT: also: footballer) サッカー選手 sakká seńshu; (US) フットボール選手 futtóbòru seńshu

footbrake [fut'breik] n 足ブレーキ ashíburèki

footbridge [fut'bridʒ] n 橋 hashí ◇歩行者しか渡れない狭い物を指す hokóshà shika watárenài semáî monó wo sasù

foothills [fut'hilz] npl 山ろくの丘陵地帯 sańroku nò kyūryōchitai

foothold [fut'hould] n 足場 ashíba

footing [fut'iŋ] n (fig: position) 立場 tachíba

to lose one's footing 足を踏み外す ashí wo fumihazusù

footlights [fut'laits] npl (THEATER) フットライト futtóraìto

footman [fut'mən] (pl footmen) n (servant) 下男 genán

footnote [fut'nout] n 脚注 kyakúchū

footpath [fut'pæθ] n 遊歩道 yūhodō

footprint [fut'print] n (of person, animal) 足跡 ashíato

footstep [fut'step] n (sound) 足音 ashíoto; (footprint) 足跡 ashíato

footwear [fut'weər] n (shoes, sandals

etc) 履物 hakímono

KEYWORD

for [fɔːr] *prep* **1** (indicating destination, intention) ...行きの ...yuki no, ...に向かって ...ni mùkátte, ...のために〔の〕 ...notaméní(no)

the train for London ロンドン行きの電車 róndonyuki no densha

he left for Rome 彼はローマへ出発しました kárè wa rómà e shúppatsu shimashìta

he went for the paper 彼は新聞を取りに行きました kárè wa shínbun wo torì ni ikímashìta

is this for me? これは私に? koré wa wàtákushi nî?

there's a letter for you あなた宛の手紙が来ています ànáta ate no tegami ga kíté ìmasu

it's time for lunch 昼食の時間です chúshoku no jikan desù

2 (indicating purpose) ...のために〔の〕 ...no tamé nì (no)

what's it for? それは何のためですか soré wa nàn no tamé dèsu ká

give it to me - what for? それをよこせ-何で? soré wo yòkósè - nàndé?

clothes for children 子供服 kodómofùku

to pray for peace 平和を祈る héiwa wo inorú

3 (on behalf of, representing) ...の代理として ...no daírì toshite

the MP for Hove ホーブ選出の議員 hōbùshénshutsu no giîn

he works for the government/a local firm 彼は政府〔地元の会社〕に雇われています kárè wa séifu(jimóto no kaisha)ni yatówarète imasù

I'll ask him for you あなたに代って私が彼に聞きましょう anátà ni kawátte wàtákushi ga karè ni kikímashò

G for George GはジョージのG G wà jójì no G

4 (because of) ...の理由で ...no riyú de, ...のために ...no tamé nì

for this reason このため kònó tame

for fear of being criticized 批判を恐れて hìhán wo ósórète

the town is famous for its canals 町は運河で有名です machí wà úngà de yúmei desù

5 (with regard to) ...にしては ...ni shité wà

it's cold for July 7月にしては寒い shichígatsu nì shité wà samúi

he's mature for his age 彼はませている kárè wa másète iru

a gift for languages 語学の才能 gógàku no saínō

for everyone who voted yes, 50 voted no 賛成1に対して反対50だった sánsei ìchí nì tái shite hántaihyò gojú dàtta

6 (in exchange for) ...と交換して ...to kókàn shite

I sold it for $5 5ドルでそれを売りました gódòru de soré wo ùrímashìta

to pay $2.50 for a ticket 切符を2ドル50セントで買う kìppú wo nídòru gojússeñto de kaú

7 (in favor of) ...に賛成して ...ni sánsei shite

are you for or against us? あなたは我々に賛成なのか反対なのかはっきり言いなさい anátà wa waréware ni sánsei na nò ka hántai na nò ka hakkírì íinasaí

I'm all for it 私は無条件で賛成です watákushi wa mùjókèn de sánsei desù

vote for X Xに投票する ékkùsu ni tóhyō suru

8 (referring to distance): *there are roadworks for 5 km* 5キロの区間が工事中です gókìro mo no kúkàn ga kójichū desù

we walked for miles 何マイルも歩きました nánmaìru mo arúkimashìta

9 (referring to time) ...の間 ...no aída

he was away for 2 years 彼は2年間家を離れていました kárè wa ninéñkan ié wò hanárete imashìta

she will be away for a month 彼女は1か月間出掛ける事になっています kánòjo wa ikkágetsukàn dekákeru kotò ni natté imasù *it hasn't rained for 3 weeks* 雨は3週間も降っていません ámè wa sañshūkan mo futté imaseñ

I have known her for years 何年も前から彼女とは知り合いです nánnen mo máè kara kánôjo to wa shiríai desù

can you do it for tomorrow? 明日までに出来ますか asú madè ni dekímasù ká

10 (with infinitive clause): *it is not for me to decide* 私が決める事ではありません watákushi gà kiméru kotò de wa arímaseñ

it would be best for you to leave あなたは帰った方がいい anátà wa káètta hō ga íi

there is still time for you to do it あなたはまだまだそれをする時間があります anátà wa mádàmada soré wò suru jikañ ga arímasù

for this to be possible ... これが可能になるのには... koré gà kanó ni narù no ni wa...

11 (in spite of) ...にもかかわらず ...ní mò kakáwarazù

for all his complaints, he is very fond of her 彼は色々と文句を言うが、結局彼女を愛しています kárè wa iróiro tò móñku wo iú gà, kekkyóku kanôjo wo áí shite imásù

for all he said he would write, in the end he didn't 手紙を書く書くと言っていましたけれども、結局書いてくれませんでした tegámi wò kákù kákù to itté imashìtà keredomo, kekkyóku kaitè kurémasen deshìta

♦*conj* (since, as: rather formal) なぜならば...だから názènaraba ...dá kàra

she was very angry, for he was late again 彼女はかんかんになっていました、というのは彼はまたも遅刻したからです kánôjo wa kañkañ ni nattè imashìta, to iú no wà kárè wa matá mò chikóku shita kara desù

forage [fɔːrˈidʒ] *vi* (search: for food, interesting objects etc) ...をあさる ...wo asárù

foray [fɔːrˈei] *n* (raid) 侵略 shiñryaku

forbad(e) [fəːrˈbædˈ] *pt of* **forbid**

forbid [fəːrˈbidˈ] (*pt* **forbad(e)**, *pp* **forbidden**) *vt* (sale, marriage, event etc) 禁ずる kiñzurù

to forbid someone to do something ...に...するのを禁ずる ...ni ...surú no wò kiñzurù

forbidden [fəːrˈbidˈən] *pp of* **forbid**

forbidding [fəːrˈbidˈiŋ] *adj* (look, prospect) 怖い kowái

force [fɔːrs] *n* (violence) 暴力 bóryoku; (PHYSICS, *also* strength) 力 chikára

♦*vt* (compel) 強制する kyósei suru; (push) 強く押す tsúyòku osú; (break open: lock, door) こじ開ける kojíakerù

in force (in large numbers) 大勢で ózei de; (LAW) 有効で yúkō de

to force oneself to do 無理して...する múrì shite ...suru

forced [fɔːrst] *adj* (labor) 強制的な kyóseiteki na; (smile) 作りの tsukúri no

forced landing (AVIAT) 不時着 fujíchaku

force-feed [fɔːrsˈfiːd] *vt* (animal, prisoner) ...に強制給餌をする ...ni kyóseikyū̀ji wo suru

forceful [fɔːrsˈfəl] *adj* (person) 力強い chikárazuyoì; (attack) 強烈な kyóretsu na; (point) 説得力のある settókuryoku no arù

forceps [fɔːrˈsəps] *npl* ピンセット piñsettò

forces [fɔːrˈsiz] (*BRIT*) *npl*: *the Forces* (MIL) 軍隊 guñtai

forcibly [fɔːrˈsəbliː] *adv* (remove) 力ずくで chikárazukù de; (express) 力強く chikárazuyokù

ford [fɔːrd] *n* (in river) 浅瀬 asáse ◊船を使わないで川を渡れる場所を指す fúnè wo tsukáwanaìde kawá wò watáreru bashò wo sásù

fore [fɔːr] *n*: *to come to the fore* 前面に出て来る zeñmen ni dete kurù

forearm [fɔːrˈɑːrm] *n* 前腕 maéude

foreboding [fɔːrbouˈdiŋ] *n* (of disaster) 不吉な予感 fukítsu na yokañ

forecast [fɔːrˈkæst] *n* (of profits, prices,

weather) 予報 yohô
♦vt (pt, pp **forecast**) (predict) 予報する yohô suru

forecourt [fɔːr'kɔːrt] n (of garage) 前庭 maéniwa

forefathers [fɔːr'fɑːðəːrz] npl (ancestors) 先祖 senzo

forefinger [fɔːr'fiŋgəːr] n 人差指 hitósashiyùbi

forefront [fɔːr'frʌnt] n: **in the forefront of** (industry, movement) ...の最前線で ...no saízeñsen de

forego [fɔːrgou'] (pt **forewent** pp **foregone**) vt (give up) やめる yamérù; (go without) ...なしで我慢する ...náshì de gámàn suru

foregone [fɔːrgɔːn'] adj: **it's a foregone conclusion** 結果は決まっている kekká wa kimattè irú

foreground [fɔːr'graund] n (of painting) 前景 zeñkei

forehead [fɔːr'hed] n 額 hitái

foreign [fɔːr'in] adj (country) 外国の gaíkoku no; (trade) 対外の taígai no; (object, matter) 異質の ishítsu no

foreigner [fɔːr'ənəːr] n 外国人 gaíkokujìn

foreign exchange n 外国為替 gaíkokukawàse; (currency) 外貨 gaíka

Foreign Office (BRIT) n 外務省 gaímushō

Foreign Secretary (BRIT) n 外務大臣 gaímudaìjin

foreleg [fɔːr'leg] n (of animal) 前足 maéashi

foreman [fɔːr'mən] (pl **foremen**) n (in factory, on building site etc) 現場監督 geñbakañtoku

foremost [fɔːr'moust] adj (most important) 最も大事な mottómò dáìji na
♦adv: **first and foremost** 先ず第一に mázù dáìichi ni

forensic [fərən'sik] adj (medicine, test) 法医学的な hōígàkuteki na

forerunner [fɔːr'rʌnəːr] n 先駆者 señkushà

foresee [fɔːrsiː'] (pt **foresaw** pp **foreseen**) vt (problem, development) 予想する yosô suru

foreseeable [fɔːrsiː'əbəl] adj (problem, development) 予想出来る yosô dekirù

foreshadow [fɔːrʃæd'ou] vt (event) ...の前兆となる ...no zeñchō ni narù

foresight [fɔːr'sait] n 先見の明 señken nò meî

forest [fɔːr'ist] n 森 môrì

forestall [fɔːrstɔːl'] vt (person) 出し抜く dashínuku; (discussion) 防ぐ fuségù

forestry [fɔːr'istriː] n 林業 riñgyō

foretaste [fɔːr'teist] n 前兆 zeñchō

foretell [fɔːrtel'] (pt, pp **foretold**) vt (predict) 予言する yogén suru

forever [fɔːrev'əːr] adv (for good) 永遠に eîen ni; (continually) いつも ítsumo

forewent [fɔːrwent'] pt of **forego**

foreword [fɔːr'wəːrd] n (in book) 前書 maégaki

forfeit [fɔːr'fit] vt (lose: right, friendship etc) 失う ushínaù

forgave [fərgeiv'] pt of **forgive**

forge [fɔːrdʒ] n (smithy) 鍛冶屋 kajíyà
♦vt (signature, money) 偽造する gizô suru; (wrought iron) 鍛えて作る kitáetè tsukúrù

forge ahead vi (country, person) 前進する zeñshin suru

forger [fɔːr'dʒəːr] n 偽造者 gizôshà

forgery [fɔːr'dʒəːriː] n (crime) 偽造 gizô; (object) 偽物 nisémono

forget [fərget'] (pt **forgot**, pp **forgotten**) vt (fact, face, skill, appointment) 忘れる wasúrerù; (leave behind: object) 置き忘れる okíwasurerù; (put out of mind: quarrel, person) 考えない事にする kañgaenài kotó ni surù
♦vi (fail to remember) 忘れる wasúrerù

forgetful [fərget'fəl] adj (person) 忘れっぽい wasúreppoì

forget-me-not [fərget'miːnɑːt] n ワスレナグサ wasúrenagùsa

forgive [fərgiv'] (pt **forgave**, pp **forgiven**) vt (pardon) 許す yurúsù
to forgive someone for something (excuse) ...の...を許す ...no...wo yurúsù

forgiveness [fərgiv'nis] n 許し yurúshi

forgo [fɔːrgou'] vt = **forego**

forgot [fəˈrgɑːt'] *pt of* **forget**

forgotten [fəˈrgɑːt'ən] *pp of* **forget**

fork [fɔːrk] *n* (for eating) フォーク fóku; (for gardening) ホーク hóku; (in road, river, railway) 分岐点 buńkitèn

♦*vi* (road) 分岐する buńki suru

fork-lift truck [fɔːrk'lift-] *n* フォークリフト fókurifùto

fork out (*inf*) *vt* (pay) 払う haráu

forlorn [fɔːrlɔːrn'] *adj* (person, place) わびしい wabíshiì; (attempt) 絶望的な zetsúbōteki na; (hope) 空しい munáshiì

form [fɔːrm] *n* (type) 種類 shúrùi; (shape) 形 katáchi; (SCOL) 学年 gakúnen; (questionnaire) 用紙 yóshi

♦*vt* (make: shape, queue, object, habit) 作る tsukúrù; (make up: organization, group) 構成する kōsei suru; (idea) まとめる matómerù

in top form 調子が最高で chōshi gà saíkō de

formal [fɔːr'məl] *adj* (offer, statement, occasion) 正式な seíshiki na; (person, behavior) 堅苦しい katágurushiì; (clothes) 正装の seísō no; (garden) 伝統的な deńtōteki na ◊極めて幾何学的な配置の庭園について言う kiwámetè kikágakuteki na haíchi nò teien ni tsuitè iú; (education) 正規の seíki no

formalities [fɔːrmæl'iti:z] *npl* (procedures) 手続き tetsúzùki

formality [fɔːrmæl'iti:] *n* (procedure) 形式 keíshiki

formally [fɔːr'məli:] *adv* (make offer etc) 正式に seíshiki ni; (act) 堅苦しく katágurushikù; (dress): *to dress formally* 正装する seísō suru

format [fɔːr'mæt] *n* (form, style) 形式 keíshiki

♦*vt* (COMPUT: disk) 初期化する shōkìka suru, フォーマットする fómatto suru

formation [fɔːrmeiˈʃən] *n* (creation: of organization, business) 創立 sōritsu; (: of theory) 考案 kōan; (pattern) 編隊 heńtai; (of rocks, clouds) 構造 kōzō

formative [fɔːr'mətiv] *adj* (years, influence) 形成的な keíseiteki na

former [fɔːr'mər] *adj* (one-time) かつて

の katsùte no; (earlier) 前の máè no

the former ... the latter ... 前者...後者... zeńsha... kōsha...

formerly [fɔːr'məːrli:] *adv* (previously) 前は máè wa

formidable [fɔːr'midəbəl] *adj* (task, opponent) 手ごわい tegówaì

formula [fɔːr'mjələ] (*pl* **formulae** *or* **formulas**) *n* (MATH, CHEM) 公式 kōshiki; (plan) 方式 hōshiki

formulate [fɔːr'mjəleit] *vt* (plan, strategy) 練る nérù; (opinion) 表現する hyōgen suru

forsake [fɔːrseik'] (*pt* **forsook**, *pp* **forsaken**) *vt* (abandon: person) 見捨てる misúterù; (: belief) 捨てる sutérù

forsook [fɔːrsuk'] *pt of* **forsake**

fort [fɔːrt] *n* (MIL) とりで toríde

forte [fɔːr'tei] *n* (strength) 得意 tokúì

forth [fɔːrθ] *adv* (out) 外へ sótò e

back and forth 行ったり来たりして ittárì kitárì shité

and so forth など nádò

forthcoming [fɔːrθ'kʌm'iŋ] *adj* (event) 今度の końdo no; (help, evidence) 手に入る té ni hairù; (person) 率直な sotchóku na

forthright [fɔːrθ'rait] *adj* (condemnation, opposition) はっきりとした hakkírì to shitá

forthwith [fɔːrθwiθ'] *adv* 直ちに tádàchi ni

fortify [fɔːr'təfai] *vt* (city) ...の防備を固める ...no bóbi wo katámerù; (person) 力付ける chikárazukerù

fortitude [fɔːr'tətuːd] *n* 堅忍 keńnin

fortnight [fɔːrt'nait] *n* (two weeks) 2週間 nishūkan

fortnightly [fɔːrt'naitli:] *adj* (payment, visit, magazine) 2週間置きの nishūkanoki no

♦*adv* (pay, meet, appear) 2週間置きに nishūkan-oki ni

fortress [fɔːr'tris] *n* 要塞 yōsai

fortuitous [fɔːrtuː'itəs] *adj* (discovery, result) 偶然の gūzen no

fortunate [fɔːr'tʃənit] *adj* (person) 運のいい úñ no íi; (event) 幸運な kōun na *it is fortunate that ...* 幸いに... saíwai ni ...

fortunately [fɔːrˈtʃənitliː] adv (happily, luckily) 幸いに saíwai ni

fortune [fɔːrˈtʃən] n (luck) 運 úñ; (wealth) 財産 zaísan

fortune-teller [fɔːrˈtʃəntelər] n 易者 ekísha

forty [fɔːrˈtiː] num 40 (の) yóñjū (no)

forum [fɔːrˈəm] n フォーラム fóramu

forward [fɔːrˈwərd] adj (in position) 前方の zeñpō no; (in movement) 前方への zeñpō e no; (in time) 将来のための shórai nò tame no; (not shy) 出過ぎた desúgità
♦n (SPORT) フォワード fowádo
♦vt (letter, parcel, goods) 転送する teñsō suru; (career, plans) 前進させる zeñshin saserù

to move forward (progress) 進歩する shíñpo suru

forward(s) [fɔːrˈwərd(z)] adv 前へ máè e

fossil [fɑːsˈəl] n 化石 kaséki

foster [fɔːsˈtəːr] vt (child) 里親として育てる satóoya toshitè sodáterù; (idea, activity) 助成する joséi suru

foster child n 里子 satógo

fought [fɔːt] pt, pp of **fight**

foul [faul] adj (state, taste, smell, weather) 悪い warúî; (language) 汚い kitánaî; (temper) ひどい hidóî
♦n (SPORT) 反則 hañsoku, ファウル fáùru
♦vt (dirty) 汚す yogósù

foul play n (LAW) 殺人 satsújin

found [faund] pt, pp of **find**
♦vt (establish: business, theater) 設立する setsúritsu suru

foundation [faundeiˈʃən] n (act) 設立 setsúritsu; (base) 土台 dodái; (organization) 財団 zaídan; (also: **foundation cream**) ファンデーション fañdēshon

foundations [faundeiˈʃənz] npl (of building) 土台 dodái

founder [faunˈdəːr] n (of firm, college) 設立者 setsúritsushà
♦vi (ship) 沈没する chíñbotsu suru

foundry [faunˈdriː] n 鋳造工場 chūzōkō-

jō

fountain [faunˈtin] n 噴水 fuñsui

fountain pen n 万年筆 mañneñhitsu

four [fɔːr] num 4 (の) yóñ (no), 四つ (の) yotsu (no)

on all fours 四つんばいになって yotsúñbai ni nattè

four-poster [fɔːrˈpousˈtəːr] n (also: **four-poster bed**) 天がい付きベット teñgaitsukibetto

foursome [fɔːrˈsəm] n 4人組 yoníñgumi

fourteen [fɔːrˈtiːn] num 14 (の) júyon (no)

fourth [fɔːrθ] num 第4(の) daíyon (no)

fowl [faul] n 家きん kakíñ

fox [fɑːks] n キツネ kitsúne
♦vt (baffle) 困らす komárasu

foyer [fɔiˈəːr] n (of hotel, theater) ロビー róbī

fraction [frækˈʃən] n (portion) 一部 ichíbù; (MATH) 分数 buñsū

fracture [frækˈtʃəːr] n (of bone) 骨折 kossétsu
♦vt (bone) 折る órù

fragile [frædʒˈəl] adj (breakable) 壊れやすい kowáreyasuî

fragment [frægˈmənt] n (small piece) 破片 hahéñ

fragrance [freigˈrəns] n (scent) 香り kaóri

fragrant [freigˈrənt] adj 香り高い kaóritakaî

frail [freil] adj (person, invalid) か弱い kayówaî; (structure) 壊れやすい kowáreyasuî

frame [freim] n (of building, structure) 骨組 honégumi; (of human, animal) 体格 taíkaku; (of door, window) 枠 wakú; (of picture) 額縁 gakúbuchi; (of spectacles: also: **frames**) フレーム fúrēmu
♦vt (picture) 額縁に入れる gakúbuchi ni irerù

frame of mind n 気分 kibúñ

framework [freimˈwəːrk] n (structure) 骨組 honégumi

France [fræns] n フランス furánsu

franchise [frænˈtʃaiz] n (POL) 参政権 sañseikèn; (COMM) フランチャイズ fu-

furánchaîzu

frank [fræŋk] *adj* (discussion, look) 率直
な sotchóku na, フランクな furáñku na
◆*vt* (letter) ...に料金別納の判を押す ...ni
ryókinbetsunó no háñ wo osú

frankly [fræŋk'li:] *adv* (honestly) 正直に
shójiki ni; (candidly) 率直に sotchóku ni

frankness [fræŋk'nis] *n* (honesty) 正 直
さ shójikisà; (candidness) 率直さ sotchókusa

frantic [fræn'tik] *adj* (distraught) 狂 乱
した kyóran shita; (hectic) てんてこ舞い
の teñtekomâi no

fraternal [frətə:r'nəl] *adj* (greetings,
relations) 兄弟の様な kyódai no yó na

fraternity [frətə:r'niti:] *n* (feeling) 友 愛
yúai; (group of people) 仲間 nakáma

fraternize [fræt'ə:rnaiz] *vi* 付 き 合 う
tsukâu

fraud [frɔ:d] *n* (crime) 詐欺 sagí; (person)
ぺてん師 peteñshi

fraudulent [frɔ:'dʒələnt] *adj* (scheme,
claim) 不正な fuséi na

fraught [frɔ:t] *adj*: *fraught with* (danger, problems) ...をはらんだ ...wo haráñ-
da

fray [frei] *n* (battle, fight) 戦い tatákai
◆*vi* (cloth, rope) 擦切れる surîkirerù;
(rope end) ほつれる hotsúrerù
tempers were frayed 皆短気になって
いた miná táñki ni nátte itá

freak [fri:k] *n* (person: in attitude,
behavior) 変人 heñjin; (: in appearance)
奇形 kikéi
◆*adj* (event, accident) まぐれの mágùre
no

freckle [frek'əl] *n* そばかす sobákasù

free [fri:] *adj* (person, press, movement)
自由な jíyù na; (not occupied: time) 暇な
hímà na; (: seat) 空いている afte irù;
(costing nothing: meal, pen etc) 無料の
muryó no
◆*vt* (prisoner etc) 解放する kaího suru;
(jammed object) 動ける様にする ugóke-
ru yó ni suru
free (of charge) 無料で muryó de
for free = *free of charge*

freedom [fri:'dəm] *n* (liberty) 自由 jíyù

free-for-all [fri:'fə:rɔ:l'] *n* 乱闘 rañtō

free gift *n* 景品 kefhin

freehold [fri:'hould] *n* (of property) 自由
保有権 jiyúhoyúkeñ

free kick *n* (SPORT) フリーキック furî-
kikkù

freelance [fri:'læns] *adj* (journalist, photographer, work) フリーランサーの furî-
rañsā no

freely [fri:'li:] *adv* (without restriction,
limits) 自由に jíyù ni; (liberally) 気ままに
kimáma ni

Freemason [fri:'meisən] *n* フリーメーソ
ン furîmēson

Freepost [fri:'poust] (® *BRIT*) *n* (postal
service) 料金受取人払い ryókin uketori-
ninbarái

free-range [fri:'reindʒ] *adj* 放し飼いの
hanáshigai no ◇特にニワトリやその卵に
ついて言う tókù ni niwátori yà sonó
tamagó ni tsúîte iú

free trade *n* 自由貿易 jiyúbōeki

freeway [fri:'wei] (*US*) *n* 高速道路 kóso-
kudóro

free will *n* 自由意志 jiyúishì
of one's own free will 自発的に jihátsuteki ni

freeze [fri:z] (*pt* **froze**, *pp* **frozen**) *vi*
(weather) 氷点下になる hyóteñka ni ná-
rù; (liquid, pipe) 凍る kórù; (person: with
cold) 冷える hiérù; (: stop moving) 立ち
すくむ tachísukumù
◆*vt* (water, lake) 凍らせる kóraserù;
(food) 冷凍にする reítō ni surù; (prices,
salaries) 凍結する tóketsu suru
◆*n* (weather) 氷点下の天気 hyóteñka no
téñki; (on arms, wages) 凍結 tóketsu

freeze-dried [fri:z'draid'] *adj* 凍結乾燥
の tóketsukañsō no

freezer [fri:'zə:r] *n* フリーザー fúrîza

freezing [fri:'ziŋ] *adj* (wind, weather,
water) 凍る様な kóru yó na
3 degrees below freezing 氷点下3度
hyóteñka sándo

freezing point *n* 氷点 hyóteñ

freight [freit] *n* (goods) 貨 物 kámòtsu;
(money charged) 運送料 uñsōryó

freight train (*US*) *n* (goods train) 貨物

列車 kamótsuresshà

French [frentʃ] *adj* フランス の furánsu no; (LING) フランス語の furánsugo no
♦*n* (LING) フランス語 furánsugo
♦*npl*: **the French** (people) フランス人 furánsujin

French bean *n* サヤインゲン sayá-iñgen

French fried potatoes *npl* フレンチフライ（ポテト) furénchifurài(pótèto)

French fries [-fraiz] (*US*) *npl* = **French fried potatoes**

Frenchman/woman [fren'tʃmən/wumən] (*pl* **Frenchmen/women**) *n* フランス人男性〔女性〕furánsujin dañsei (jòsei)

French window *n* フランス窓 furánsu madò

frenetic [frənet'ik] *adj* (activity, behavior) 熱狂的な nekkyōteki na

frenzy [fren'zi:] *n* (of violence) 逆上 gyakújō; (of joy, excitement) 狂乱 kyōran

frequency [fri:'kwənsi:] *n* (of event) 頻度 híndo; (RADIO) 周波数 shūhasū

frequent [*adj* fri:'kwint *vb* frikwent'] *adj* (intervals, visitors) 頻繁な hińpan na
♦*vt* (pub, restaurant) ...によく行く ...ni yókù iku

frequently [fri:'kwintli:] *adv* (often) しばしば shíbàshiba

fresco [fres'kou] *n* フレスコ画 furésukoga

fresh [freʃ] *adj* (food, vegetables, bread, air etc) 新鮮な shíñsen na; (memories, footprint) 最近の saíkin no; (instructions) 新たな áràta na; (paint) 塗立ての nurítate no; (new: approach, start) 新しい atárashiî; (cheeky: person) 生意気な namáîki na

freshen [freʃ'ən] *vi* (wind) 強くなる tsuyókù narù; (air) 涼しくなる suzúshiku narù

freshen up *vi* (person) 化粧直しをする keshōnaòshi wo suru

fresher [freʃ'ə:r] (*BRIT*: *inf*) *n* = **freshman**

freshly [freʃ'li:] *adv* (made, cooked, painted) ...されたばかりで ...saréta bakàri de

freshman [freʃ'mən] (*pl* **freshmen**) *n* (*US*: SCOL) 1年生 ichínensei ◊大学生や高校生について言う daígakùsei ya kōkōsei ni tsuitè iú

freshness [freʃ'nis] *n* 新鮮さ shíñsensà

freshwater [freʃ'wɔ:tə:r] *adj* (lake, fish) 淡水の tañsui no

fret [fret] *vi* (worry) 心配する shíñpai suru

friar [frai'ə:r] *n* (REL) 修道士 shūdōshì

friction [frik'ʃən] *n* (resistance, rubbing) 摩擦 masátsu; (between people) 不仲 fúnàka

Friday [frai'dei] *n* 金曜日 kiń-yòbi

fridge [fridʒ] (*BRIT*) *n* 冷蔵庫 reízòko

fried [fraid] *adj* (steak, eggs, fish etc) 焼いた yaíta; (chopped onions etc) いためた itámetà; (in deep fat) 揚げた agétà, フライした furái shita

friend [frend] *n* 友達 tomódachi

friendly [frend'li:] *adj* (person, smile) 愛想のいい aísò nò ií; (government) 友好的な yūkōteki na; (place, restaurant) 居心地の良い igókochi no yoî; (game, match) 親善の shínzen no

friendship [frend'ʃip] *n* 友情 yūjō

frieze [fri:z] *n* フリーズ fúrīzu ◊壁の一番高い所に付ける細長い飾り、彫刻などを指す kabé no ichíban takaî tokórò ni tsukérù hosónagaî kazárî, chōkoku nadò wo sásù

frigate [frig'it] *n* フリゲート艦 furígètokan

fright [frait] *n* (terror) 恐怖 kyōfu; (scare) 驚き odóroki
　to take fright 驚く odórokù

frighten [frait'ən] *vt* 驚かす odórokasù

frightened [frait'ənd] *adj* (afraid) 怖がった kowágattà; (worried, nervous) 不安に駆られた fúàn ni karáreta

frightening [frait'niŋ] *adj* (experience, prospect) 恐ろしい osóroshiî

frightful [frait'fəl] *adj* (dreadful) 恐ろしい osóroshiî

frightfully [frait'fəli:] *adv* 恐ろしく osóroshikù

frigid [fridʒ'id] *adj* (woman) 不感症の fukánshō no

frill [fril] *n* (of dress, shirt) フリル fúrìru

fringe [frindʒ] *n* (*BRIT*: of hair) 前髪 maégami; (decoration: on shawl, lampshade etc) 縁飾り fuchíkazàri; (edge: of forest etc) へり herí

fringe benefits *npl* 付加給付 fukákyūfu

frisk [frisk] *vt* (suspect) ボディーチェックする bodíchekkù suru

frisky [fris'ki:] *adj* (animal, youngster) はつらつとした hatsúratsu to shità

fritter [frit'ə:r] *n* (CULIN) フリッター furíttā

fritter away *vt* (time, money) 浪費する róhi suru

frivolous [friv'ələs] *adj* (conduct, person) 軽率な keísotsu na; (object, activity) 下らない kudáranaì

frizzy [friz'i:] *adj* (hair) 縮れた chijíretà

fro [frou] *see* **to**

frock [frɑːk] *n* (dress) ドレス dórèsu

frog [frɔːg] *n* カエル kaérù

frogman [frɔːg'mæn] (*pl* **frogmen**) *n* ダイバー dáibā

frolic [frɑːl'ik] *vi* (animals, children) 遊び回る asóbimawarù

KEYWORD

from [frʌm] *prep* **1** (indicating starting place) ...から ...kárà

where do you come from?, where are you from? (asking place of birth) ご出身はどちらですか go-shússhìn wa dóchìra désù ká

from London to Glasgow ロンドンからグラスゴーへ róndon kara gurásugò e

to escape from something/someone ...から逃げる ...kárà nigérù

2 (indicating origin etc) ...から ...kárà

a letter/telephone call from my sister 妹からの手紙〔電話〕imóto kàrà no tegámi〔deñwa〕

tell him from me that ... 私からの伝言で彼に...と言って下さい watákushi karà no deñgon dè kárè ni ...to itté kudasaì

a quotation from Dickens ディケンズからの引用 díkènzu kara no iñyō

to drink from the bottle 瓶から飲む bíñ kara nómù

3 (indicating time) ...から ...kárà

from one o'clock to/until/till two 1時から2時まで ichíji karà nìji madè

from January (on) 1月から(先) ichígatsu karà (sakí)

4 (indicating distance) ...から ...kárà

the hotel is 1 km from the beach ホテルは浜辺から1キロ離れています hôteru wa hamabé kàrà ichíkiro hanaréte imásù

we're still a long way from home まだまだ家まで遠い mádamada ié madè tôi

5 (indicating price, number etc) ...から ...kárà, ...ないし... ...naíshi ...

prices range from $10 to $50 値段は10ドルないし50ドルです nedán wà jûdòru naíshi gojûdòru désù

there were from 20 to 30 people there 20ないし30人いました nìju naíshi sañjūnìn imáshìta

the interest rate was increased from 9% to 10% 公定歩合は9パーセントから10パーセントに引き上げられました kôteibùai wa kyûpāseñto kara juppáseñto ni hikíageraremashìta

6 (indicating difference) ...と ...tò

he can't tell red from green 彼は赤と緑の区別ができません kárè wa ákà to mídòri no kúbètsu ga dekímaseñ

to be different from someone/something ...と違っている ...tò chigátte irù

7 (because of, on the basis of) ...から ...kárà, ...によって ...ni yottè

from what he says 彼の言う事によると kárè no iú kotò ni yorú to

from what I understand 私が理解したところでは watákushi gà ríkai shita tokóro de wà

to act from conviction 確信に基づいて行動する kakúshin ni motozuíte kôdò suru

weak from hunger 飢えでぐったりになって ué dè guttárì ni náttè

---

front [frʌnt] *n* (of house, dress) 前面 zeñmeñ; (of coach, train, car) 最前部 saízeñbu; (promenade: *also*: **sea front**) 海岸沿いの遊歩道 kaíganzoi no yúhodō; (MIL) 戦線 señsen; (METEOROLOGY) 前線 zeñsen; (*fig*: appearances) 外見 gaíken

♦*adj* (*gen*) 前の máe no, 一番前の ichíbanmae no; (gate) 正面の shōmeñ no

in front (of) (...の) 前に (...no) máe ni

front tooth 前歯 máeba

frontage [frʌn'tidʒ] *n* (of building) 正面 shōmen

frontal [frʌn'təl] *adj* 真っ向からの makkō kara no

front door *n* 正面玄関 shōmengeñkan

frontier [frʌntiːr'] *n* (between countries) 国境 kokkyō

front page *n* (of newspaper) 第一面 daíichimen

front room (*BRIT*) *n* 居間 imá

front-wheel drive [frʌnt'wi:l-] *n* (AUT) 前輪駆動 zeńrinkúdō

frost [frɔːst] *n* (weather) 霜が降りる事 shimó ga orírù koto; (*also*: **hoarfrost**) 霜 shimó

frostbite [frɔːst'bait] *n* 霜焼け shimóyake

frosted [frɔːs'tid] *adj* (glass) 曇のkumóri no

frosty [frɔːs'tiː] *adj* (weather, night) 寒い samúi ◊気温が氷点下であるが雪が降っていない状態について言う kíon ga hyótenka de arù ga yukí ga futte inái jōtai ni tsuíte iú; (welcome, look) 冷たい tsumétaì

froth [frɔːθ] *n* (on liquid) 泡 awá

frown [fraun] *vi* 顔をしかめる káo wo shikámerù

froze [frouz] *pt of* **freeze**

frozen [frou'zən] *pp of* **freeze**

frugal [fruː'gəl] *adj* (person) 倹約的なkeñ-yakuteki na; (meal) つましい tsumáshiì

fruit [fruːt] *n inv* (AGR, BOT) 果物 kudámono; (*fig*: results) 成果 seíka

fruiterer [fruːt'əːrəːr] (*BRIT*) *n* 果物屋 kudámonoyà

fruiterer's (shop) [fruːt'əːrəːrz-] (*BRIT*) *n* 果物屋 kudámonoyà

fruitful [fruːt'fəl] *adj* (meeting, discussion) 有益な yūeki na

fruition [fruːiʃ'ən] *n*: *to come to fruition* 実る minórù

fruit juice *n* 果汁 kajū́, フルーツジュース furū́tsujùsu

fruit machine (*BRIT*) *n* スロットマシン suróttomashiñ

fruit salad *n* フルーツサラダ furū́tsusaràda

frustrate [frʌs'treit] *vt* (upset) ...に欲求不満を起させる ...ni yokkyū́fumàn wo okósaserù; (block) ざ折させる zasétsu saserù

frustration [frʌstrei'ʃən] *n* (irritation) 欲求不満 yokkyū́fumàn; (disappointment) がっかり gakkárì

fry [frai] (*pt, pp* **fried**) *vt* (CULIN: steak, eggs etc) 焼く yákù; (: chopped onions etc) いためる itámerù; (: in deep fat) 揚げる agérù ¶ *see also* **small fry**

frying pan [frai'iŋ-] *n* フライパン furáipan

ft. *abbr* = **foot; feet**

fuddy-duddy [fʌd'iːdʌdiː] (*pej*) *n* 古臭い人 furúkusaì hitó

fudge [fʌdʒ] *n* (CULIN) ファッジ fájjì

fuel [fjuː'əl] *n* 燃料 neñryō

fuel oil *n* 重油 jū́yu

fuel tank *n* 燃料タンク neñryōtañku

fugitive [fjuː'dʒətiv] *n* (runaway, escapee) 逃亡者 tōbōsha

fulfil [fulfil'] *vt* (function) 果す hatásù; (condition) 満たす mitásù; (request, wish, desire) かなえる kanáerù; (order) 実行する jikkō suru

fulfilment [fulfil'mənt] *n* (satisfaction) 満足 mañzoku; (of promise, desire) 実現 jitsúgen

full [ful] *adj* (container, cup, car, cinema) 一杯の ippái no; (maximum: use, volume) 最大限の saídaìgen no; (complete: details, information) 全ての súbète no; (price) 割引なしの warÉbikinashì no; (skirt) ゆったりした yuttárì shitá

♦*adv*: *to know full well that* ...という事を重々承知している ...to iú kotò wo jū́jū shōchi shite irù

I'm full (up) 満腹だ manpuku da

a full two hours 2時間も nijíkàn mo

at full speed 全速力で zeńsokuryòku de

in full (reproduce, quote, pay) 完全に kańzen ni

full employment *n* 100パーセントの就業率 hyakú pāsènto no shúgyōrìtsu

full-length [ful'leŋkθ'] *adj* (film, novel etc) 長編の chóhen no; (coat) 長い nágài; (portrait) 全身の zeńshin no

full moon *n* 満月 mángetsu

full-scale [ful'skeil'] *adj* (attack, war) 全面的な zeńmenteki na; (model) 実物大の jitsúbutsudai no

full stop *n* 終止符 shúshifù, ピリオド pírìodo

full-time [ful'taim] *adj* (work, study) 全時間制の zeńjikànsei no

♦*adv* 全時間で zeńjikàn de

fully [ful'i:] *adv* (completely) 完全に kańzen ni; (at least): *fully as big as* 少なくとも…と同じぐらいの大きさの sukúnàkutomo …to onaji gurai no ōkisa no

fully-fledged [ful'i:fledʒd'] *adj* (teacher, barrister) 一人前の ichíninmaè no

fulsome [ful'səm] (*pej*) *adj* (praise, compliments) 大げさな ōgesa na

fumble [fʌm'bəl] *vi*: *to fumble with* (key, catch) …でもたもたする …de mótàmota suru

fume [fju:m] *vi* (rage) かんかんに怒る kánkan ni okórù

fumes (of fire, fuel, car) ガス gásù

fun [fʌn] *n* (amusement) 楽しみ tanóshimi

to have fun 楽しむ tanóshimù

for fun 冗談として jódan toshité

to make fun of (ridicule, mock) ばかにする bákà ni suru

function [fʌŋk'ʃən] *n* (role) 役割 yakúwari, 機能 kinó; (product) …による物 …ni yórù monó; (social occasion) 行事 gyóji

♦*vi* (operate) 作動する sadó suru

functional [fʌŋk'ʃənəl] *adj* (operational) 作動できる sadó dekirù; (practical) 機能的な kinóteki na

fund [fʌnd] *n* (of money) 基金 kikín;

(source, store) 貯蓄 chochíku

fundamental [fʌndəmen'təl] *adj* (principle, change, mistake) 基本的な kihónteki na

fundamentalist [fʌndəmen'təlist] *n* 原理主義者 geńrishugishà

funds [fʌndz] *npl* (money) 資金 shikín

funeral [fju:'nə:rəl] *n* 葬式 sōshiki

funeral parlor *n* 葬儀屋 sōgiya

funeral service *n* 葬式 sōshiki

funfair [fʌn'fe:r] (*BRIT*) *n* 移動遊園地 idōyūenchi

fungi [fʌn'dʒai] *npl of* **fungus**

fungus [fʌŋ'gəs] (*pl* **fungi**) *n* (plant) キノコ kínòko; (mold) かび kabí

funnel [fʌn'əl] *n* (for pouring) じょうご jōgo; (of ship) 煙突 eńtotsu

funny [fʌn'i:] *adj* (amusing) こっけいな kokkéi na; (strange) 変な hén na

fur [fə:r] *n* (on animal) 毛 ke; (animal skin for clothing etc) 毛皮 kegáwa; (*BRIT*: in kettle etc) 湯あか yuáka

fur coat *n* 毛皮コート kegáwakòto

furious [fju:r'i:əs] *adj* (person) 猛烈な mōretsu na

furlong [fə:r'lɔ:ŋ] *n* (HORSE-RACING) ハロン hárõn ◇距離の単位で、約201メーター kyórì no tấñ-i de, yakú 201 mềta

furlough [fə:r'lou] *n* (MIL: leave) 休暇 kyūka

furnace [fə:r'nis] *n* (in foundry) 炉 ro; (in power plant) ボイラー bóīrā

furnish [fə:r'niʃ] *vt* (room, building) …に家具調度を備える …ni kagúchōdo wo sonáerù; (supply) …に供給する …ni kyókyū suru

furnishings [fə:r'niʃiŋz] *npl* 家具と設備 kágù to sétsùbi

furniture [fə:r'nitʃə:r] *n* 家具 kágù

piece of furniture 家具一点 kágù ittén

furrow [fə:r'ou] *n* (in field) 溝 mizó; (in skin) しわ shiwá

furry [fə:r'i:] *adj* 毛で覆われた ke de ōwareta

further [fə:r'ðə:r] *adj* (additional) その上の sonó ue no, 追加の tsuíka no

♦*adv* (farther) もっと遠くに móttò tőku ni; (more) それ以上 soré ijõ; (moreover) 更に sárà ni, なお nảò

◆*vt* (career, project) 促進する sokúshin suru

further education (*BRIT*) *n* 成人教育 seíjin kyóiku

furthermore [fəːrˈðəːrmɔːr] *adv* (more-over) 更に sárà ni, なお nao

furthest [fəːrˈðist] *superl of* **far**

furtive [fəːrˈtiv] *adj* (glance, movement) こっそりとする kossórì to surù

fury [fjuːˈriː] *n* (anger, rage) 憤慨 fuñgai

fuse [fjuːz] *n* (ELEC: in plug, circuit) ヒューズ hyúzu; (for bomb etc) 導火線 dókasèn

◆*vt* (metal) 融合させる yúgō saserù; (*fig*: ideas, systems) 混合する koñgō suru

◆*vi* (metal: *also fig*) 融合する yúgō suru

  to fuse the lights (*BRIT*: ELEC) ヒューズを飛ばす hyúzu wo tobásu

fuse box *n* (ELEC) ヒューズ箱 hyúzubàko

fuselage [fjuːˈsəlɑːʒ] *n* (AVIAT) 胴体 dótai

fusion [fjuːˈʒən] *n* (of ideas, qualities) 混合 koñgō; (*also*: **nuclear fusion**) 核融合 kakúyūgō

fuss [fʌs] *n* (anxiety, excitement) 大騒ぎ ósawàgi; (complaining, trouble) 不平 fuhéi

  to make a fuss 大騒ぎをする ósawàgi wo suru

  to make a fuss of someone ...をちやほやする ...wo chíyàhoya suru

fussy [fʌsˈiː] *adj* (person) 小うるさい koúrusaì; (clothes, room etc) 凝った kóttà

futile [fjuːˈtəl] *adj* (attempt, comment, existence) 無駄な mudá na

future [fjuːˈtʃər] *adj* (date, generations) 未来の mírài no; (president, spouse) 将来の shốrai no

◆*n* (time to come) 未来 mírài; (prospects) 将来 shốrai; (LING) 未来形 mírái-kei

  in future 将来に shốrai ni

fuze [fjuːz] (*US*) = **fuse**

fuzzy [fʌzˈiː] *adj* (PHOT) ぼやけた boyáketa; (hair) 縮れた chijíretà

G

G [dʒiː] *n* (MUS: note) ト音 to-óñ; (: key) ト調 tóchò

g. *abbr* = **gram(s)**

gabble [gæbˈəl] *vi* ぺちゃくちゃしゃべる péchàkucha shábèru

gable [geiˈbəl] *n* (of building) 切妻 kirízùma

gadget [gædʒˈit] *n* 装置 sóchi

Gaelic [geiˈlik] *adj* ゲール語の gérugo no

◆*n* (LING) ゲール語 gérugo

gaffe [gæf] *n* (in words) 失言 shitsúgen; (in actions) 失態 shittái

gag [gæg] *n* (on mouth) 猿ぐつわ sarúgutsùwa; (joke) ギャグ gyágù

◆*vt* (prisoner) ...に猿ぐつわをはめる ...ni sarúgutsùwa wo hamérù

gaiety [geiˈəti:] *n* お祭り騒ぎ o-mátsuri sawàgi

gaily [geiˈli:] *adv* (talk, dance, laugh) 楽しそうに tanóshisò ni; (colored) 華やかに hanáyàka ni

gain [gein] *n* (increase) 増加 zóka; (improvement) 進歩 shíñpo; (profit) 利益 ríèki

◆*vt* (speed, weight, confidence) 増す masú

◆*vi* (benefit): *to gain from something* ...から利益を得る ...kara ríèki wo érù; (clock, watch) 進む susúmù

  to gain on someone ...に迫る ...ni semárù

  to gain 3lbs (in weight) (体重が) 3ポンド増える (taíjū ga) sañpoñdo fuérù

gait [geit] *n* 歩調 hochó

gal. *abbr* = **gallon**

gala [geiˈlə] *n* (festival) 祝祭 shukúsai

galaxy [gælˈəksi:] *n* (SPACE) 星雲 seíun

gale [geil] *n* (wind) 強風 kyófū

gallant [gælˈənt] *adj* (brave) 勇敢な yúkan na; (polite) 紳士的な shíñshiteki na

gallantry [gælˈəntri:] *n* (bravery) 勇気 yúki; (politeness) 礼儀正しさ reígitadashìsa

gall bladder [gɔːl-] *n* 胆のう tañnō

gallery [gǽlə:ri:] n (also: **art gallery**: public) 美術博物館 bijútsu hakubutsukàn; (: private) 画廊 garó; (in hall, church, theater) 二階席 nikáiseki

galley [gǽli:] n (ship's kitchen) 調理室 chórishìtsu

gallon [gǽlən] n (= 8 pints; BRIT = 4.5 l; US = 3.8 l) ガロン gárðn

gallop [gǽləp] n ギャロップ gyárðppu
♦vi (horse) ギャロップで走る gyárðppu de hashírù

gallows [gǽlouz] n 絞首台 kőshudai

gallstone [gɔ:lstoun] n (MED) 胆石 tañseki

galore [gəlɔ:r] adv どっさり dossárì

galvanize [gǽlvənaiz] vt (audience) ぎょっとさせる győttò saséru; (support) 求める motómeru

gambit [gǽmbit] n (fig): **(opening) gambit** 皮切り kawákiri

gamble [gǽmbəl] n (risk) かけ kaké
♦vt (money) かける kakéru
♦vi (take a risk) 冒険をする bőken wo suru; (bet) ばくちをする bakúchi wo suru, ギャンブルをする gyáñburu wo suru
to gamble on something (horses, race, success etc) ...にかける ...ni kakéru

gambler [gǽmblə:r] n (punter) ばくち打ち bakúchiuchi

gambling [gǽmbliŋ] n (betting) ばくち bakúchi, ギャンブル gyáñburu

game [geim] n (activity, sport) 遊び asóbi; (match) 試合 shiái; (part of match: esp TENNIS: also: **board game**) ゲーム gēmu; (strategy, scheme) 策略 sakúryaku; (HUNTING) 猟鳥獣 ryőchōjū; (CULIN) 猟鳥獣の肉 ryőchōjū no nikú
♦adj (willing): **game (for)** (...をする) 気がある (...wo suru) kí ga arù
big game 大型猟獣 őgataryòjū

gamekeeper [geimˈki:pə:r] n 猟番 ryőban

gammon [gǽmən] n (bacon) ベーコン bēkon; (ham) スモークハム sumőkuhamù

gamut [gǽmət] n (range) 範囲 háñ-i

gang [gǽŋ] n (of criminals, hooligans) 一味 ichímī; (of friends, colleagues) 仲間 nakama; (of workmen) 班 háñ

gangrene [gǽŋgri:n] n (MED) えそ ésð

gangster [gǽŋstə:r] n (criminal) 暴力団員 bőryokudañ-in, ギャング gyáñgu

gang up vi: **to gang up on someone** 寄ってたかって...をやっつける yotté takattè ...wo yattsukeru

gangway [gǽŋwei] n (from ship) タラップ taráppù; (BRIT: in cinema, bus, plane etc) 通路 tsūro

gaol [dʒeil] (BRIT) n, vt = **jail**

gap [gǽp] n (space) すき間 sukíma, ギャップ gyappu; (: in time) 空白 kűhaku; (difference): **gap (between)** (...の) 断絶 (...no) dañzetsu

gape [geip] vi (person) ぽかんと口を開けて見詰める pokáñ to kuchí wo aketè mitsúmerù; (shirt, hole) 大きく開いている őkiku aíte irù

gaping [geiˈpiŋ] adj (shirt, hole) 大きく開いた őkiku aítà

garage [gərɑ:ʒ] n (of private house) 車庫 shákð; (for car repairs) 自動車修理工場 jidőshashūrikōjō

garbage [gɑ:rbidʒ] n (US: rubbish) ごみ gomí; (inf: nonsense) でたらめ detárame

garbage can (US) n ごみ容器 gomíyòki

garbled [gɑ:rbəld] adj (account, message) 間違った machígattà

garden [gɑ:rdən] n (private) 庭 niwá

gardener [gɑ:rdˈnə:r] n 庭師 niwáshì

gardening [gɑ:rdˈniŋ] n 園芸 eñgei

gardens [gɑ:rdənz] npl (public park) 公園 kően

gargle [gɑ:rgəl] vi うがいする ugái suru

garish [ge:rˈiʃ] adj けばけばしい kebákebashìi

garland [gɑ:rlənd] n (also: **garland of flowers**) 花輪 hanáwa

garlic [gɑ:rlik] n (BOT, CULIN) ニンニク niñniku

garment [gɑ:rmənt] n (dress) 衣服 ífùku

garnish [gɑ:rniʃ] vt (food) 飾る kazárù

garrison [gǽrisən] n (MIL) 守備隊 shubítai

garrulous [gǽrələs] adj (talkative) 口数の多い kuchíkazu no ōi

garter [gɑ:rˈtə:r] n (for sock etc) 靴下止

め kutsúshitadome, ガーター gǎtā; (US: suspender) ガーターベルト gǎtāberùto

gas [gæs] n (CHEM) 気体 kítài; (fuel) ガス gásù; (US: gasoline) ガソリン gasórin
♦vt (kill) ガスで殺す gásù de korósù

gas cooker (BRIT) n ガスレンジ gasúrenji

gas cylinder n ガスボンベ gasúboñbe

gas fire (BRIT) n ガスストーブ gasúsutōbu

gash [gæʃ] n (wound) 切り傷 kiríkìzu; (tear) 裂け目 sakéme
♦vt (wound) 傷を負わせる kizú wò owáserù

gasket [gæs'kit] n (AUT) ガスケット gasúkettò

gas mask n ガスマスク gasúmasùku

gas meter n ガスメーター gasúmētā

gasoline [gæsəli:n'] (US) n ガソリン gasórin

gasp [gæsp] n (breath) 息切れ ikígire; (of shock, horror) はっとする事 háttò suru kotó
♦vi (pant) あえぐ aégù

gasp out vt (say) あえぎながら言う aéginagàra iú

gas station (US) n ガソリンスタンド gasórinsutañdo

gassy [gæs'i:] adj (beer etc) 炭酸ガスの入った tañsangasù no haítta

gastric [gæs'trik] adj 胃の í no

gastroenteritis [gæstrouentərai'tis] n 胃腸炎 ichôen

gate [geit] n (of garden, field, grounds) 門 môn; (at airport) ゲート gêto

gatecrash [geit'kræʃ] (BRIT) vt ...に押し掛ける ...ni oshíkakerù

gateway [geit'wei] n (entrance: also fig) 入口 iríguchi

gather [gæð'əːr] vt (flowers, fruit) 摘む tsúmù; (pick up) 拾う hiróù; (assemble, collect: objects, information) 集める atsúmerù; (understand) 推測する suísoku suru; (SEWING) ...にギャザーを寄せる ...ni gyázā wo yosérù
♦vi (assemble) 集まる atsúmerù
to gather speed スピードを上げる supído wo agerù

gathering [gæð'əːriŋ] n 集まり atsúmarì

gauche [gouʃ] adj (adolescent, youth) ぎこちない gigóchinài

gaudy [gɔːd'i:] adj 派手な hadé na

gauge [geidʒ] n (instrument) 計器 keíki
♦vt (amount, quantity) 計る hakárù; (fig: feelings, character etc) 判断する hañdan suru

gaunt [gɔːnt] adj (haggard) やせこけた yasékoketà; (bare, stark) 荒涼とした kôryō to shita

gauntlet [gɔːnt'lit] n (glove) 長手袋 nagátebukùro; (fig): **to run the gauntlet** 方々から やられる hôbō kara yarárerù
to throw down the gauntlet 挑戦する chôsen suru

gauze [gɔːz] n (fabric: also MED) ガーゼ gâze

gave [geiv] pt of **give**

gay [gei] adj (homosexual) 同性愛の dôseìai no, ホモの hómò no; (cheerful) 陽気な yôki na; (color, music, dress etc) 華やかな hanáyàka na

gaze [geiz] n (look, stare) 視線 shisén
♦vi: **to gaze at something** ...をじっと見る ...wo jíttò mírù

gazelle [gəzel'] n ガゼル gázèru

gazetteer [gæziti:r'] n (index) 地名辞典 chiméijitèn

gazumping [gəzʌm'piŋ] (BRIT) n (of house buyer) 詐欺 ságì

GB [dʒi:bi:'] abbr = **Great Britain**

GCE [dʒi:si:i:'] (BRIT) n abbr (= General Certificate of Education) 普通教育証書 futsūkyōikushōsho ◇16才の時に受けるOレベルと大学入学前に受けるAレベルの2種類がある jūrokusài no tokí nì ukérù O rébèru to daígaku nyūgaku máè ni ukérù A rébèru no nishúrui ga arù

GCSE [dʒi:si:esi:'] (BRIT) n abbr (= General Certificate of Secondary Education) ◇1988年から GCE のOレベルは GCSEに置換えられた señkyūhyakuhachijūhachi nèn ni GCE no O rébèru wa GCSE ni okíkaeraretà

gear [gi:r] n (equipment) 道具 dôgu; (TECH) 歯車 hagúruma; (AUT) ギヤ gíyà

◆vt (fig: adapt): to gear something to ...に...を適応させる ...ni ...wo tekíō sasérù

high (US) or top (BRIT) / low gear ハイ［ロー］ギヤ haí[rō]giyà

in gear ギヤを入れて gíyà wo iréte

gear box n ギヤボックス giyábokkùsu

gear shift (BRIT gear lever) n シフトレバー shífùtorebā

geese [gi:s] npl of goose

gel [dʒel] n (for hair) ジェル jérù; (CHEM) ゲル gérù

gelatin(e) [dʒel'ətin] n (CULIN) ゼラチン zeráchìn

gelignite [dʒel'ignait] n (explosive) ゼリグナイト zerígunaìto

gem [dʒem] n (stone) 宝石 hóseki

Gemini [dʒem'ənai] n (ASTROLOGY) 双子座 futágoza

gender [dʒen'dəːr] n (sex: also LING) 性 seí

gene [dʒiːn] n (BIO) 遺伝子 idéñshi

general [dʒen'əːrəl] n (MIL) 大将 taíshō

◆adj (overall, non-specific, miscellaneous) 一般の ippán no, 一般的な ippánteki na; (widespread: movement, interest) 全面的な zeñmenteki na

in general 一般に ippán ni

general delivery (US) n (poste restante) 局留 kyokúdome

general election n 総選挙 sōseñkyo

generalization [dʒenəːrələzeiʃ'ən] n 一般化 ippáñka

generally [dʒen'əːrəli:] adv (in general) 一般に ippán ni; (usually) 普通は futsū wa

general practitioner n 一般開業医 ippán kaigyòi

generate [dʒen'əːreit] vt (power, energy) 発生させる hasséi saserù; (jobs, profits) 生み出す umídasù

to generate electricity 発電する hatsúden suru

generation [dʒenəːrei'ʃən] n (period of time) 世代 sedái; (of people, family) 同じ世代の人々 onáji sedài no hitobito; (of heat, steam, gas etc) 発生 hasséi; (of electricity) 発電 hatsúden

generator [dʒen'əːreitəːr] n (ELEC) 発電機 hatsúdeñki

generosity [dʒenərɑ:s'əti:] n 寛大さ kañdaisa

generous [dʒen'əːrəs] adj (person, measure, remuneration etc) 寛大な kañdai na

genetics [dʒənet'iks] n (science) 遺伝学 idéñgaku

Geneva [dʒəni:'və] n ジュネーブ júnēbu

genial [dʒi:'ni:əl] adj (host, smile) 愛想の良い aíso no yoì

genitals [dʒen'itəlz] npl (ANAT) 性器 seíki

genius [dʒi:n'jəs] n (ability, skill, person) 天才 teñsai

genocide [dʒen'əsaid] n 民族虐殺 miñzoku-gyakusàtsu, ジェノサイド jénòsaido

gent [dʒent] n abbr = gentleman

genteel [dʒenti:l'] adj (person, family) 家柄の良い iégara no yoì

gentle [dʒen'təl] adj (person) 優しい yasáshiì; (animal) 大人しい otónashiì; (movement, shake) 穏やかな odáyàka na, 静かな shizúkà na; (slope, curve) 緩やかな yurúyàka na

a gentle breeze そよ風 soyókàze

gentleman [dʒen'təlmən] (pl gentlemen) n (man) 男の方 otóko no katà; (referring to social position: also wellmannered man) 紳士 shíñshi, ジェントルマン jéñtoruman

gentleness [dʒen'təlnis] n (of person) 優しさ yasáshisà; (of animal) 大人しさ otónashisà; (of movement, breeze, shake) 穏やかさ odáyàkasa, 静かさ shizúkàsa; (of slope, curve) 緩やかさ yurúyàkasa

gently [dʒen'tli:] adv (subj: person) 優しく yasáshikù; (: animal) 大人しく otónashikù; (: breeze etc) 静かに shizúkàni; (: slope, curve) 緩やかに yurúyàka ni

gentry [dʒen'tri:] n 紳士階級 shíñshikaìkyū

gents [dʒents] (BRIT) n (men's toilet) 男性トイレ dañseitoirè

genuine [dʒen'ju:in] adj (real) 本物の hoñmonò no; (person) 誠実な seíjitsu na

geographic(al) [dʒiːəgræf'ik(əl)] *adj* 地理の chírī no

geography [dʒiːɑ:g'rəfiː] *n* (of town, country etc: *also* SCOL) 地理 chírī

geological [dʒiːələdʒ'ikəl] *adj* 地質学の chishítsugàku no

geologist [dʒiːɑːl'ədʒist] *n* 地質学者 chishítsugakushà

geology [dʒiːɑːl'ədʒiː] *n* (of area, rock etc) 地質 chíshìtsu; (SCOL) 地質学 chishítsugàku

geometric(al) [dʒiːəmet'rik(əl)] *adj* (problem, design) 幾何学的な kikágakuteki na

geometry [dʒiːɑːm'ətriː] *n* (MATH) 幾何学 kikágaku

geranium [dʒərei'niːəm] *n* ゼラニウム zeránìumu

geriatric [dʒeːriːæt'rik] *adj* (of old people) 老人の rójin no

germ [dʒəːrm] *n* ばい菌 baíkin

German [dʒəːr'mən] *adj* (of Germany) ドイツの dóītsu no; (LING) ドイツ語の doítsugo no
♦*n* ドイツ人 doítsujin; (LING) ドイツ語 doítsugo

German measles *n* (rubella) 風しん fúshin

Germany [dʒəːr'məni:] *n* ドイツ dóītsu

germination [dʒəːrmənei'ʃən] *n* (of seed) 発芽 hatsúga

gesticulate [dʒestik'jəleit] *vi* (with arms, hands) 手振りをする tébùri wo suru

gesture [dʒes'tʃəːr] *n* (movement) 手振り tébùri, ジェスチャー jésùchà; (symbol, token) ジェスチャー jésùchà

|KEYWORD|

get [get] (*pt, pp* got, (*US*) *pp* gotten) *vi* 1 (become, be) ...になる ...ni nárù
to get old (thing) 古くなる fúrùku naru; (person) 年を取る toshí wò toru
to get cold 寒くなる sámùku naru
to get annoyed/bored/tired 怒る〔退屈する, 疲れる〕okórù(taíkutsu surù, tsukárerù)
to get drunk 酔っ払う yoppárau

to get dirty 汚れる yogórerù
to get killed 殺される korósarerù
to get married 結婚する kekkón surù
when do I get paid? 金はいつ払ってくれますか kané wà ítsu harátte kuremasù ká
it's getting late 遅くなってきました osóku nattè kimáshìta

2 (go): *to get to/from* ...へ〔から〕行く ...é(karà)ikù
to get home 家に帰る ié ni kaerù
how did you get here? あなたはどうやってここへ来ましたか anátà wa dó yattè kokó è kimáshita ká

3 (begin): *to get to know someone* ...と親しくなる ...tò shitáshikù naru
I'm getting to like him 彼を好きになってきました kárè wo sukí ni nattè kimáshìta
let's get going/started さあ, 行きましょう sâ, ikímashõ

♦*modal aux vb*: *you've got to do it* あなたはどうしてもそれをしなければなりません anátà wa dóshite mò sorè wò shinákereba narimaseñ
I've got to tell the police 警察に知らせなければなりません keísatsu nì shirásenakereba narimaseñ

♦*vt* 1: *to get something done* (do) ...を済ます ...wò sumásù; (have done) ...をしてもらう ...wò shité moraù
to get the washing/dishes done 洗濯〔皿洗い〕を済ます señtaku(saráarài)wo sumásù
to get one's hair cut 散髪してもらう sañpatsu shite moraù
to get the car going/to go 車のエンジンをかける kurúma no eñjin wo kakérù
to get someone to do something ...に...をさせる ...ní ...wò sasérù
to get something ready ...を用意する ...wò yõī suru
to get someone ready ...に用意をさせる ...nì yõī wo sasérù
to get someone drunk/into trouble ...を酔っ払わせる〔困らせる〕...wò yoppárawaserù(komáraserù)

2 (obtain: money) 手に入れる té ni irerù;

(: permission, results) 得る érù; (find: job, flat) 見付ける mitsúkerù; (fetch: person, doctor) 呼んで来る yóñde kurù; (: object) 持って来る motté kurù

to get something for someone ...のために...を持って来る ...no tamé nì ...wò motté kurù

he got a job in London 彼はロンドンに仕事を見付けました kárè wa róñdon ni shigóto wò mitsúkemashìta

get me Mr Jones, please (TEL) ジョーンズさんをお願いしたいんですが jóñzu san wo o-négai shitaiñ desù ga

I think you should get the doctor 医者を呼んだ方がいいと思います ishá wò yoñda hô ga íi to omóimasù

can I get you a drink? 何か飲みませんか nánika nomímasèn ka

3 (receive: present, letter) 受ける ukérù; (acquire: reputation, prize) 得る érù, 獲得する kakútoku suru

what did you get for your birthday? お誕生日に何をもらいましたか o-táñjòbi ni nánì wo moráimashìta ká

he got a prize for French 彼はフランス語の成績で賞をもらいました kárè wa furáñsugò no seíseki dè shô wò moráimashìta

how much did you get for the painting? 絵画はいくらで売れましたか kaíga wa íkùra de urémashìta ká

4 (catch) つかむ tsukámù; (hit: target etc) ...に当る ...ni atárù

to get someone by the arm/throat ...の腕〔のど〕をつかむ ...no udé〔nódò〕wò tsukámù

get him! やつを捕まえろ yátsù no tsukámaerò

the bullet got him in the leg 弾丸は彼の脚に当った dañgan wà kárè no ashí ni atattà

5 (take, move) 連れて〔持って〕いく tsuréte〔motté〕ikù, 移動する idő suru

to get something to someone ...に...を持って行く ...ní ...wò motté ikù

do you think we'll get it through the door? それは戸口から入ると思いますか soré wà tógùchi kara háìru to omő-

imasù ká

I'll get you there somehow 何とかしてあなたを連れて行きます náñ to ka shite anátà wo tsuréte ikimasù

we must get him to (US the) hospital どうしても彼を病院に連れて行かなくちゃ dőshìte mo kárè wo byóìn ni tsuréte ikanakùcha

6 (catch, take: plane, bus etc) 乗る norú

where do I get the train - Birmingham? 電車はどこで乗ればいいんですか-バーミンガムですか deñsha wà dőkò de noréba íi desù ka - bámíñgamu desu ká

7 (understand) 理解する ríkài suru; (hear) 聞き取る kikítorù

I've got it 分かった wakáttà

I don't get your meaning あなたが言おうとしている事が分かりません anátà ga iő to shite iru kotò ga wakárimasèn

I'm sorry, I didn't get your name 済みませんが、お名前を聞き取れませんでした sumímasèn ga, o-námae wò kikítoremasen deshìta

8 (have, possess): **to have got** 持つ mótsù

how many have you got? いくつ持っていますか íkùtsu motté imasù ká

get about vi 動き回る ugókimawarù; (news) 広まる hirómarù

get along vi (agree) 仲良くする nákàyoku suru; (depart) 帰る káèru; (manage) = **get by**

get at vt fus (attack, criticize) 批判する hihán suru; (reach) ...に手が届く ...ni té gà todókù

get away vi (leave) 帰る káèru; (escape) 逃げる nigérù

get away with vt fus ...をうまくやりおおせる ...wò úmàku yaríōseru

get back vi (return) 帰る káèru
♦vt 返す káèsu

get by vi (pass) 通る tőrù; (manage) やって行く yatté ikù

get down vi 降りる orírù
♦vt fus 降りる orírù
♦vt 降ろす orósù; (depress: person) がっかりさせる gakkárì saseru

get down to vt fus (work) ...に取り掛る ...ni toríkakarù

get in vi 入る háiru; (train) 乗る norú; (arrive home) 帰って来る kaétte kurù

get into vt fus ...に入る ...ni háiru; (vehicle) ...に乗る ...ni norú; (clothes) 着る kirú

to get into bed ベッドに入る béddò ni háiru

to get into a rage かんかんに怒る kaíkan nì okórù

get off vi (from train etc) 降りる orírù; (depart: person, car) 出発する shuppátsu suru; (escape punishment etc) 逃れる nogárerù

♦vt (remove: clothes) 脱ぐ núgù; (: stain) 消す kesú, 落す otósù; (send off) 送る okúrù

♦vt fus (train, bus) 降りる orírù

get on vi (at exam etc): how are you getting on? 万事うまく行っていますかbáñji úmaku ittè imasù ká; (agree): to get on (with) (...と) 気が合う (...tò) ki gá aù

♦vt fus ...に乗る ...ni norú

get out vi 出る dérù; (of vehicle) 降りる orírù

♦vt 取り出す torídasù

get out of vt fus ...から出る ...kara dérù; (vehicle) ...から降りる ...kara orírù; (bed) ...から起きる ...kara okírù; (duty etc) 避ける sakérù, 逃れる nogárerù

get over vt fus (illness) ...が直る ...ga naórù

get round vt fus (problem, difficulty) 避ける sakérù; (law, rule) ...に触れないようにする ...ni furénai yô ni suru; (fig: person) 言いくるめる iíkurumerù

get through vi (TEL) 電話が通じる deńwa gà tsújiru

get through to vt fus (TEL) ...に電話が通じる ...ni deńwa gà tsújiru

get together vi (people) 集まる atsúmarù

♦vt 集める atsúmerù

get up vi (rise) 起きる okírù

♦vt fus 起す okósù

get up to vt fus (reach) ...に着く ...ni

tsukú; (BRIT: prank etc) 仕出かす shidékasù

geyser [gai'zə:r] n (GEO) 間欠温泉 kaíketsu oñsen; (BRIT: water heater) 湯沸かし器 yuwákashikì

Ghana [gɑːn'ə] n ガーナ gâna

ghastly [gæst'li:] adj (horrible: person, behavior, situation) いやな íyà na, ひどい hídòi; (: building, appearance) 薄気味悪い usúkimiwaruì; (pale: complexion) 青白い aójiroì

gherkin [gəːr'kin] n キュウリのピクルス kyűri no píkùrusu

ghetto [get'ou] n (ethnic area) ゲットー géttò

ghost [goust] n (spirit) 幽霊 yűrei, お化け o-bákè

giant [dʒai'ənt] n (in myths, children's stories) 巨人 kyojín, ジャイアント jáìanto; (fig: large company) 大企業 daíkigyō

♦adj (enormous) 巨大な kyodái na

gibberish [dʒib'əːriʃ] n (nonsense) でたらめ detárame

gibe [dʒaib] n = **jibe**

giblets [dʒib'lits] npl 鳥の内臓 torí nò naízò

Gibraltar [dʒibrɔːl'təːr] n ジブラルタル jíbùrarutaru

giddy [gid'i:] adj (dizzy) めまいがする memái ga suru

gift [gift] n (present) 贈り物 okúrimonò, プレゼント purézènto, ギフト gífùto; (ability) 才能 saínō

gifted [gif'tid] adj (actor, sportsman, child) 才能ある saínō arù

gift token n ギフト券 gifútokèn

gift voucher n = **gift token**

gigantic [dʒaigæn'tik] adj 巨大な kyodái na

giggle [gig'əl] vi くすくす笑う kusúkùsu waráù

gill [dʒil] n (= 0.25 pints; BRIT = 0.15 l; US = 0.12 l) ギル gírù

gills [gilz] npl (of fish) えら erá

gilt [gilt] adj (frame, jewelery) 金めっきした kiñmekkî shita

♦n 金めっき kiñmekkî

gilt-edged [gilt'edʒd] adj (stocks, securities) 優良な yūryō na

gimmick [gím'ik] n (sales, electoral) 仕掛け shikáke

gin [dʒin] n ジン jíñ

ginger [dʒin'dʒəːr] n (spice) ショウガ shóga

ginger ale n ジンジャーエール jíñjāèru

ginger beer n ジンジャービール jíñjābīru

gingerbread [dʒin'dʒəːrbred] n (cake) ジンジャーブレッドケーキ jíñjābureddokēki; (biscuit) ジンジャーブレッドクッキー jíñjābureddokukkī

gingerly [dʒin'dʒəːrliː] adv (tentatively) 慎重に shiñchō ni

gipsy [dʒip'siː] n = **gypsy**

giraffe [dʒəræf'] n キリン kirín

girder [gəːr'dəːr] n 鉄骨 tekkótsu

girdle [gəːr'dəl] n (corset) ガードル gádoru

girl [gəːrl] n (child) 女の子 ofína nò ko, 少女 shōjo; (young unmarried woman) 若い女性 wakáî joséi, ガール gắru; (daughter) 娘 musúme

an English girl 若いイングランド人女性 wakáî íngurandojîn joséi

girlfriend [gəːrl'frend] n (of girl) 女友達 ofína tomodàchi; (of boy) ガールフレンド gắrufureñdo

girlish [gəːr'liʃ] adj 少女の様な shōjo nò yō na

giro [dʒai'rou] n (also: **bank giro**) 銀行振替 ginkôfurikaekawàse; (also: **post office giro**) 郵便振替 yūbinfurikaekawàse; (BRIT: welfare check) 生活保護の小切手 seíkatsuhogò no kogítte

girth [gəːrθ] n (circumference) 周囲 shūi; (of horse) 腹帯 haráobi

gist [dʒist] n (of speech, program) 骨子 kósshi

| KEYWORD |

give [giv] (pt **gave**, pp **given**) vt **1** (hand over): **to give someone something, give something to someone** ...に...を与える ...nî ...wò atáerù, ...に...を渡す ...nî ...wò watásu

I gave David the book, I gave the book to David 私は本をデービッドに渡しました watákushi wà hóñ wò débiddo ni watáshimashìta

give him your key あなたのかぎを彼に渡しなさい anátá no kagí wò kárè ni watáshinasaì

he gave her a present 彼は彼女にプレゼントをあげた kárè wa kánòjo ni purézeñto wo agéta

give it to him, give him it それを彼に渡しなさい soré wò kárè ni watáshi nasaì

I'll give you £5 for it それを5ポンドで私に売ってくれませんか soré wò gopóñdo de watákushi nî utté kuremaseñ ká

2 (used with noun to replace a verb): **to give a sigh** ため息をつく taméikì wo tsuku

to give a cry/shout 叫ぶ sakébù

to give a push 押す osú

to give a groan うめく umékù

to give a shrug 肩をすくめる kátà wo sukúmerù

to give a speech/a lecture 演説〔講演〕をする eñzetsu〔kóeñ〕wo surù

to give three cheers 万歳三唱をする bañzaisañshō wo suru

3 (tell, deliver: news, advice, message etc) 伝える tsutáerù, 言う iú, 与える atáerù

did you give him the message/the news? 彼にメッセージ〔ニュース〕を伝えましたか kárè ni mésseji〔nyúsù〕wo tsutáemashìta ká

let me give you some advice ちょっと忠告をあげよう chóttò chűkoku wo ageyō

he gave me his new address over the phone 彼は電話で新しい住所を教えてくれました kárè wa deñwa dè atárashii jūsho wo oshíete kuremashìta

to give the right/wrong answer 正しい〔間違った〕答を言う tadáshii〔machígatta〕kotàe wo iú

4 (supply, provide: opportunity, surprise, job etc) 与える atáerù, 提供する teíkyō suru; (bestow: title) 授与する júyò suru;

(: honor, right) 与える atáerù

I gave him the chance to deny it そ
れを否定するチャンスを彼に与えました
soré wò hitéi suru chañsu wo kárè ni
atáemashìta

the sun gives warmth and light 太陽
は熱と光を我々に与えてくれる tályō wa
netsú tò hikári wò waréware nì atáete
kurerù

what gives you the right to do that?
何の権利でそんな事をするのか nán no
keñri de soñna kotò wo suru nò ka

that's given me an idea あれでいい事
を思い付いたんですが aré de ii kotò wo
omóitsuitan desù ga

5 (dedicate: time) 当てる atérù; (: one's
life) 捧げる saságerù; (: attention) 払う
haráù

you'll need to give me more time も
っと時間を下さい móttò jikan wo kudasaì

she gave it all her attention 彼女は
それに専念した kánòjo wa soré nì señnen
shità

6 (organize): *to give a party/dinner
etc* パーティ〔晩さん会〕を開催する pátì
〔bañsañkai〕wo kaísai suru

♦*vi* **1** (*also:* **give way**: break, collapse) 崩
れる kuzúrerù

his legs gave beneath him 彼は突然立
てなくなった kárè wa totsúzen taténa-
ku nattà

*the roof/floor gave as I stepped on
it* 私が踏んだとたん屋根〔床〕が抜け落ち
た watákushi ga funda totañ yáné〔yu-
ká〕ga nukéochità

2 (stretch: fabric) 伸びる nobírù

give away *vt* (money) 人にやる hitó nì
yarú; (opportunity) 失う ushínaù; (secret,
information) 漏らす morásù; (bride) 新郎
に渡す shifuró nì watásu

give back *vt* 返す káèsu

give in *vi* (yield) 降参する kósan suru

♦*vt* (essay etc) 提出する teíshutsu suru

give off *vt* (heat) 放つ hanátsù; (smoke)
出す dásù

give out *vt* (distribute: prizes, books,

drinks etc) 配る kubárù; (make known:
news etc) 知らせる shiráserù

give up *vi* (surrender) 降参する kósan
suru

♦*vt* (renounce: job, habit) やめる yamérù; (boyfriend) …との交際をやめる …to
no kósai wò yamérù; (abandon: idea,
hope) 捨てる sutérù

to give up smoking タバコをやめる tabáko wò yamérù

to give oneself up 自首する jishú suru

give way *vi* (yield) 譲る yuzúru; (break,
collapse: floor, ladder etc) 崩れる kuzúrerù, 壊れる kowárerù; (: rope) 切れる
kirérù; (*BRIT*: AUT) 道を譲る michí wò
yuzúru

glacier [glei'{ʃə:r] *n* 氷河 hyōga

glad [glæd] *adj* (happy, pleased) うれしい
uréshiì

gladly [glæd'li:] *adv* (willingly) 喜んで
yorókoñde

glamorous [glæm'ə:rəs] *adj* 魅惑的な
miwákuteki na

glamour [glæm'ə:r] *n* 魅惑 miwáku

glance [glæns] *n* (look) ちらっと見る事
chiráttò mírù koto

♦*vi*: *to glance at* …をちらっと見る
…wo chiráttò mírù

glance off *vt fus* …に当って跳ね返る
…ni attáte hanékaerù

glancing [glæn'siŋ] *adj* (blow) かすめる
kasúmerù

gland [glænd] *n* せん señ

glare [gle:r] *n* (of anger) にらみ nirámi;
(of light) まぶしさ mabúshisà; (of publicity) 脚光 kyakkō

♦*vi* (light) まぶしく光る mabúshikù hikárù

to glare at (glower) …をにらみ付ける
…wo nirámitsukerù

glaring [gle:r'iŋ] *adj* (mistake) 明白な
meíhaku na

glass [glæs] *n* (substance) ガラス garásu;
(container) コップ koppù, グラス gúràsu;
(contents) コップ一杯 koppú ippài

glasses [glæs'iz] *npl* 眼鏡 mégàne

glasshouse [glæs'haus] *n* 温室 oñshitsu

glassware [glæs'we:r] *n* グラス類 gurásurui

glassy [glæs'i:] *adj* (eyes) うつろな utsúro na

glaze [gleiz] *vt* (door, window) ...にガラスをはめる ...ni garásu wò hamérù; (pottery) ...にうわぐすりを掛ける ...ni uwágusùri wo kakérù
♦*n* (on pottery) うわぐすり uwágusùri

glazed [gleizd] *adj* (eyes) うつろな utsúro na; (pottery, tiles) うわぐすりを掛けた uwágusùri wo kakéta

glazier [glei'ʒəːr] *n* ガラス屋 garásuyà

gleam [gli:m] *vi* (shine: light, eyes, polished surface) 光る hikárù

glean [gli:n] *vt* (information) かき集める kakíatsumerù

glee [gli:] *n* (joy) 喜び yorókobi

glen [glen] *n* 谷間 taníaí

glib [glib] *adj* (person) 口達者な kuchídasshà na; (promise, response) 上辺だけの uwábe dake no

glide [glaid] *vi* (snake, dancer, boat etc) 滑る様に動く subéru yò ni ugókù; (AVIAT, birds) 滑空する kakkū́ suru

glider [glai'dəːr] *n* (AVIAT) グライダー guraídà

gliding [glai'diŋ] *n* (AVIAT) 滑空 kakkū́

glimmer [glim'əːr] *n*: *a glimmer of light* かすかな光 kásùka na hikári
a glimmer of interest かすかな表情 kásùka na hyójò
a glimmer of hope かすかな希望 kásùka na kibó

glimpse [glimps] *n* (of person, place, object) ...がちらっと見える事 ...ga chiráttò miérù koto
♦*vt* ...がちらっと見える ...ga chiráttò miérù

glint [glint] *vi* (flash: light, eyes, shiny surface) ぴかっと光る pikáttò hikárù

glisten [glis'ən] *vi* (with sweat, rain etc) ぎらぎらする gíràgira suru

glitter [glit'əːr] *vi* (sparkle: light, eyes, shiny surface) 輝く kagáyakù

gloat [glout] *vi*: *to gloat (over)* (exult) ...にほくそえむ ...ni hokúsoemu

global [glou'bəl] *adj* (worldwide) 世界的な sekáiteki na

globe [gloub] *n* (world) 地球 chikyū́; (model) 地球儀 chikyū́gì; (shape) 球 kyū́

gloom [glu:m] *n* (dark) 暗やみ kuráyami; (sadness) 失望 shitsúbō

gloomy [glu:'mi:] *adj* (dark) 薄暗い usúgurai; (sad) 失望した shitsúbō shita

glorious [glɔːr'i:əs] *adj* (sunshine, flowers, weather) 素晴らしい subárashiï; (victory, future) 栄光の eíkō no

glory [glɔːr'i:] *n* (prestige) 栄光 eíkō; (splendor) 華々しさ hanábanashisà

gloss [glɔːs] *n* (shine) つや tsuyá; (*also:* **gloss paint**) つや出しペイント tsuyádashipeíntò

glossary [glɑːs'əːri:] *n* 用語集 yógoshū̀

gloss over *vt fus* (error) 言繕う iítsukuroù; (problem) 言いくるめる iíkurumerù

glossy [glɔːs'i:] *adj* (hair) つやつやした tsuyátsùya shitá; (photograph) つや出しの tsuyádashi no; (magazine) アート紙の átoshi no

glove [glʌv] *n* (gen) 手袋 tebúkuro; (in baseball) グローブ gúròbu, グラブ gúràbu

glove compartment *n* (AUT) グローブボックス gurôbubokkùsu

glow [glou] *vi* (embers) 赤く燃える akákù moérù; (stars) 光る hikárù; (face, eyes) 輝く kagáyakù

glower [glau'əːr] *vi*: *to glower at* ...をにらみ付ける ...wo nirámitsukerù

glucose [glu:'kous] *n* ブドウ糖 budótō, グルコース gurúkòsu

glue [glu:] *n* (adhesive) 接着剤 setcháku-zài
♦*vt* 接着する setchákù suru

glum [glʌm] *adj* (miserable) ふさぎ込んだ fuságikoñda

glut [glʌt] *n* (of oil, goods etc) 生産過剰 seísankajō

glutton [glʌt'ən] *n* 大食らい ōgurai
a glutton for work 仕事の鬼 shigóto nò oní

gluttony [glʌt'əni:] *n* 暴食 bóshoku

glycerin(e) [glis'əːrin] *n* グリセリン gu-ríserìn

gnarled [nɑːrld] *adj* (tree, hand) 節くれだった fushíkuredattà

gnat [næt] *n* ブヨ búyò
gnaw [nɔː] *vt* (bone) かじる kajírù
gnome [noum] *n* 地の小鬼 chi no koóni

KEYWORD
---

go [gou] (*pt* **went**, *pp* **gone**) *vi* **1** (travel, move) 行く ikú
she went into the kitchen 彼女は台所に行った kánòjo wa daídokoro ni ittá
shall we go by car or train? 車で行きましょうか、それとも電車で行きましょうか kuruma dè ikímashò ka, soréto-mò deñsha dè ikímashò ka
a car went by 車が通り過ぎた kuruma gà tòri sugità
to go round the back 裏へ回る urá e mawàru
to go by the shop 店の前を通る misé no maè wo tòrù
he has gone to Aberdeen 彼はアバーディーンへ行きました kárè wa abádìn e ikímashìta
2 (depart) 出発する shuppátsu suru, たつ tátsù, 帰る káèru, 行ってしまう itté shimaù
"I must go," she said 「帰ります」と彼女は言った "kaérimasù" to kánòjo wa ittá
our plane went at 6 pm 我々の飛行機は夕方6時に出発しました wáreware no hikòki wa yūgata rokují ni shuppátsu shimashìta
they came at 8 and went at 9 彼らは8時に来て9時に帰った kárèra wa ha-chíji ni kitè kújì ni kaérimashìta
3 (attend) 通う kayóu
she went to university in Aberdeen 彼女はアバーディーンの大学に通った kánòjo wa abádìn no daígaku nì kayóttà
she goes to her dancing class on Tuesdays 彼女がダンス教室に通うのは火曜日です kánòjo ga dañsukyòshitsu ni kayóu no wà kayóbì desu
he goes to the local church 彼は地元の教会に通っています kárè wa jimoto no kyòkai ni kayótte imasù
4 (take part in an activity) ...に行く ...ni ikú, ...する ...surù

to go for a walk 散歩に行く sañpo ni ikù, 散歩する sanpo suru
to go dancing ダンスに行く dáñsu ni iku
5 (work) 作動する sadò suru
the clock stopped going 時計が止りました tokéi gà tomárimashìta
is your watch going? あなたの時計は動いていますか anátà no tokéi wà ugóite imasù ká
the bell went just then 丁度その時ベルが鳴りました chòdo sono tokì bérù ga narímashìta
the tape recorder was still going テープレコーダーはまだ回っていました tè-purekòdà wa mádà mawátte imashìta
6 (become) ...になる ...ni nárù
to go pale 青白くなる aójiroku narù
to go moldy かびる kabíru
7 (be sold): *to go for $10* 10ドルで売れる jùdòru de urérù
8 (fit, suit) 合う áù
to go with ...に合う ...ni áù
that tie doesn't go with that shirt そのネクタイはシャツと合いません sonò nekùtai wa shátsù to aímaseñ
9 (be about to, intend to): *he's going to do it* 彼は今それをやる所です kárè wa ímà sorè wò yarú tokorò desu
we're going to leave in an hour 1時間したら出発します ichíjikan shitarà shup-pátsu shimasù
are you going to come? あなたも一緒に来ますか anátà mo isshò nì kimásù ká
10 (time) 経つ tátsù
time went very slowly/quickly 時間が経つのがとても遅く〔早く〕感じられました jikan ga tatsù no ga totémò osòku 〔háyàku〕 kanjiraremashìta
11 (event, activity) 行く ikú
how did it go? うまく行きましたか úmàku ikímashìta ká
12 (be given) 与えられる atáerarerù
the job is to go to someone else そのポストは他の人のところへいきました sonò posùto wa hokà no hito no tokorò e ikímashìta
13 (break etc: glass etc) 割れる warérù;

(: stick, leg, pencil etc) 折れる orérù;
(: thread, rope, chain etc) 切れる kirérù
the fuse went ヒューズが切れた〔飛んだ〕hyúzù ga kiréta(tóñda)
the leg of the chair went いすの脚が折れた isú no ashí ga órèta
14 (be placed) ...にしまう事になっている ...ni shimáu kotò ni nátte irù
where does this cup go? このカップはどこにしまうのですか konó kappù wa dókò ni shimáu no desu ká
the milk goes in the fridge ミルクは冷蔵庫にしまう事になっています mírùku wa reízòko ni shimáu kotò ni nátte imasù
◆*n* (*pl* **goes**) **1** (try): ***to have a go (at)*** (...を) やってみる (...wo) yatté mirù
2 (turn) 番 báñ
whose go is it? だれの番ですか dáre no báñ desu ká
3 (move): ***to be on the go*** 忙しくする isógashiku surù

go about *vi* (*also*: **go around**: rumor) 流れる nagárerù
◆*vt fus*: ***how do I go about this?*** どういう風にやればいいんですか dó iu fù ni yareba íiñ desu ká
goad [goud] *vt* (fig) 刺激する shigéki suru
go ahead *vi* (make progress) 進歩する shíñpo suru; (get going) 取り掛かる toríkakarù
go-ahead [gou'əhed] *adj* (person, firm) 進取の気に富んだ shíñshu no ki ni tóñda
◆*n* (for project) 許可 kyókà, ゴーサイン gósaìn
goal [goul] *n* (SPORT) ゴール góru; (aim) 目標 mokúhyō
goalkeeper [goul'ki:pə:r] *n* ゴールキーパー górukìpā
go along *vi* ついて行く tsúite ikú
◆*vt fus* ...を行く ...wò ikú
to go along with (agree with: plan, idea, policy) ...に賛成する ...ni sañsei surù
goalpost [goul'poust] *n* ゴールポスト górupòsùto
goat [gout] *n* ヤギ yágì

go away *vi* (leave) どこかへ行く dókò ka e ikú
go back *vi* (return) 帰る káèru; (go again) また行く matá ikú
go back on *vt fus* (promise) 破る yabúrù
gobble [gɑːbʹəl] *vt* (*also*: **gobble down**, **gobble up**) むさぼり食う musáborikuù
go-between [gouʹbitwiːn] *n* 仲介者 chúkaishà
go by *vi* (years, time) 経つ tátsù
◆*vt fus* (book, rule) ...に従う ...ni shitágaù
God [gɑːd] *n* (REL) 神 kámì
god [gɑːd] *n* (MYTHOLOGY, *fig*) 神 kámì
godchild [gɑːdʹtʃaild] *n* 名付け子 nazúkegò
goddaughter [gɑːdʹdɔːtəːr] *n* 名付け娘 nazúkemusùme
goddess [gɑːdʹis] *n* (MYTHOLOGY, REL, *fig*) 女神 mégàmi
godfather [gɑːdʹfɑːðəːr] *n* 名付け親 nazúkeòya, 代父 daífù, 教父 kyófù
godforsaken [gɑːdʹfəːrseiʹkən] *adj* (place, spot) 荒れ果てた aréhatetà
godmother [gɑːdʹmʌðəːr] *n* 名付け親 nazúkeòya, 代母 daíbò, 教母 kyóbò
go down *vi* (descend) 降りる orírù; (ship) 沈む shizúmu, 沈没する chíñbotsu suru; (sun) 沈む shizúmu
◆*vt fus* (stairs, ladder) ...を降りる ...wo orírù
godsend [gɑːdʹsend] *n* (blessing) 天の恵み teñ nò megúmì
godson [gɑːdʹsʌn] *n* 名付け息子 nazúkemusùko
go for *vt fus* (fetch) 取りに行く tórì ni ikú; (like) 気に入る ki ní irù; (attack) ...に襲い掛る ...ni osóikakarù
goggles [gɑːgʹəlz] *npl* (for skiing, motorcycling) ゴーグル góguru
go in *vi* (enter) 入る háìru
go in for *vt fus* (competition) ...に参加する ...ni sañka suru; (like) ...が好きである ...ga sukí de arù, ...を気に入る ...wò ki ní irù
going [gouʹiŋ] *n* (conditions) 状況 jókyō

♦*adj: the going rate* 相場 sóba

go into *vt fus* (enter) ...に入る ...ni háìru; (investigate) 調べる shiráberù; (embark on) ...に従事する ...ni júji suru

gold [gould] *n* (metal) 金 kíñ

♦*adj* (jewelery, watch, tooth etc) 金の kíñ no

gold reserves 金の正貨準備 kíñ no séìka juñbi

golden [goul'dən] *adj* (made of gold) 金の kíñ no; (gold in color) 金色の kiñ-iro no

goldfish [gould'fiʃ] *n* 金魚 kíñgyo

goldmine [gould'main] *n* 金山 kíñzan; (*fig*) ドル箱 dorúbako

gold-plated [gouldplei'tid] *adj* 金めっきの kíñmekkì no

goldsmith [gould'smiθ] *n* 金細工師 kíñzaikushì

golf [gɑ:lf] *n* ゴルフ górùfu

golf ball *n* (for game) ゴルフボール gorúfubòru; (on typewriter) 電動タイプライターのボール deñdōtaipuraìta no bòru

golf club *n* (organization, stick) ゴルフクラブ gorúfukuràbu

golf course *n* ゴルフコース gorúfukòsu

golfer [gɑ:l'fəːr] *n* ゴルファー górùfā

gondola [gɑ:n'dələ] *n* (boat) ゴンドラ góñdora

gone [gɔ:n] *pp of* go

gong [gɔ:ŋ] *n* どら dorá, ゴング góñgu

good [gud] *adj* (pleasant, satisfactory etc) 良い yoì; (high quality) 高級な kôkyù na; (tasty) おいしい oíshiì; (kind) 親切な shiñsetsu na; (well-behaved: child) 行儀の良い gyôgi no yoì; (morally correct) 正当な seítō na

♦*n* (virtue, morality) 善 zéñ; (benefit) 利益 rîeki

good! よろしい! yoróshiì!

to be good at ...が上手である ...ga jôzu dè árù

to be good for (useful) ...に使える ...ni tsukáerù

it's good for you あなたのためにいい anáta no tamè ni íì

would you be good enough to ...? 済みませんが...して下さいませんか sumí-

masèn ga ...shite kudásaimasèn ká

a good deal (of) 沢山 (の) takúsan (no)

a good many 沢山の takúsan no

to make good (damage, loss) 弁償する beñshō suru

it's no good complaining 不平を言ってもしようがない fuhéi wo ittè mo shiyô ga nài

for good (forever) 永久に eíkyù ni

good morning! お早うございます o-háyō gozaimasù

good afternoon! 今日は koñnichi wa

good evening! 今晩は koñban wa

good night! お休みなさい o-yásumi na-saì

goodbye [gudbai'] *excl* さようなら sayônarà

to say goodbye 別れる wakárerù

Good Friday *n* (REL) 聖金曜日 seíkinyòbi

good-looking [gud'luk'iŋ] *adj* (woman) 美人の bijíñ no; (man) ハンサムな háñsamu na

good-natured [gud'nei'tʃəːrd] *adj* (person, pet) 気立ての良い kidáte no yoì

goodness [gud'nis] *n* (of person) 優しさ yasáshisà

for goodness sake! 後生だから goshô da kara

goodness gracious! あらまあ! ará mâ

goods [gudz] *npl* (COMM) 商品 shôhin

goods train (*BRIT*) *n* 貨物列車 kamótsuressha

goodwill [gud'wil'] *n* (of person) 善意 zéñ-i

go off *vi* (leave) どこかへ行く dókò ka é ikù; (food) 悪くなる warúku naru; (bomb) 爆発する bakúhatsu suru; (gun) 暴発する bôhatsu suru; (event): *to go off well* うまくいく úmàku iku

♦*vt fus* (person, place, food etc) 嫌いになる kirái ni narù

go on *vi* (continue) 続く tsuzúku; (happen) 起る okórù

to go on doing something ...をし続ける ...wò shitsúzukerù

goose [gu:s] (*pl* geese) *n* ガチョウ gachô

gooseberry [gu:s'be:ri:] *n* (tree, fruit) ス

グリ súguri

to play gooseberry (BRIT) アベックの
邪魔をする abékku no jamá wo surù

gooseflesh [gu:s'fleʃ] n 鳥肌 torîhada

goose pimples npl = **gooseflesh**

go out vi (leave: room, building) 出る dérù; (for entertainment): **are you going
out tonight?** 今夜どこかへ出掛けます
か kôń-ya dókòka e dekákemasù ká;
(couple): **they went out for 3 years** 彼
らは3年交際した kárèra wa sańnen kō-
sai shita; (fire, light) 消える kiérù

go over vi (ship) 転覆する teńpuku suru
♦vt fus (check) 調べる shirábabrù

gore [gɔːr] vt (subj: bull, buffalo) 角で刺
す tsunó dè sásù
♦n (blood) 血のり chinóri

gorge [gɔːrdʒ] n (valley) 峡谷 kyōkoku
♦vt: **to gorge oneself (on)** (...を) た
らふく食う (...wo) taráfùku kúù

gorgeous [gɔːr'dʒəs] adj (necklace, dress
etc) 豪華な gōka na; (weather) 素晴らし
い subárashiì; (person) 美しい utsúkushiì

gorilla [gəril'ə] n ゴリラ górìra

gorse [gɔːrs] n ハリエニシダ haríenishì-
da

gory [gɔːr'iː] adj (details, situation) 血み
どろの chimîdoro no

go-slow [gou'slou'] (BRIT) n 遵法闘争
juńpōtōsō

gospel [gɑːs'pəl] n (REL) 福音 fukúìn

gossip [gɑːs'əp] n (rumors) うわさ話 u-
wásabanashi, ゴシップ goshíppù; (chat)
雑談 zatsúdan; (person) おしゃべり o-
sháberi, ゴシップ屋 goshíppuyà
♦vi (chat) 雑談する zatsúdan suru

got [gɑːt] pt, pp of **get**

go through vt fus (town etc) ...を通る
...wò tôrù; (search through: files, papers)
...を一つ一つ調べる ...wò hitótsu hitótsù
shirábberù; (examine: list, book, story) 調
べる shirábberù

gotten [gɑːt'ən] (US) pp of **get**

go up vi (ascend) 登る nobóru; (price,
level) 上がる agáru

gout [gaut] n 通風 tsūfū

govern [gʌv'əːrn] vt (country) 統治する
tôchi suru; (event, conduct) 支配する shi-

hái suru

governess [gʌv'əːrnis] n (children's) 女
性家庭教師 joséikateikyōshī

government [gʌv'əːrnmənt] n (act of
governing) 政治 seíji; (governing body)
政府 seffu; (BRIT: ministers) 内閣 naíkaku

governor [gʌv'əːrnəːr] n (of state) 知事
chíjî; (of colony) 総督 sōtoku; (of bank,
school, hospital) 理事 rîjî; (BRIT: of
prison) 所長 shochō

go without vt fus (food, treats) ...無し
で済ます ...náshì de sumásù

gown [gaun] n (dress: also of teacher) ガ
ウン gáùn; (BRIT: of judge) 法服 hōfuku

GP [dʒiːpiː'] n abbr = **general practitioner**

grab [græb] vt (seize) つかむ tsukámù
♦vi: **to grab at** ...をつかもうとする
...wo tsukámô to suru

grace [greis] n (REL) 恩恵 ońkei;
(gracefulness) しとやかさ shitóyakasà
♦vt (honor) ...に栄誉を与える ...ni éìyo
wo atáerù; (adorn) 飾る kazárù

5 days' grace 5日間の猶予 itsúkakań
no yúyo

graceful [greis'fəl] adj (animal, athlete)
しなやかな shináyàka na; (style, shape)
優雅な yūga na

gracious [grei'ʃəs] adj (person) 親切な
shińsetsu na

grade [greid] n (COMM: quality) 品質 hiń-
shitsu; (in hierarchy) 階級 kaíkyū;
(SCOL: mark) 成績 seíseki; (US: school
class) 学年 gakúnen
♦vt (rank, class) 格付けする kakúzuke
suru; (exam papers etc) 採点する saíten
suru

grade crossing (US) n 踏切 fumîkiri

grade school (US) n 小学校 shōgakkō

gradient [grei'diːənt] n (of road, slope)
こう配 kōbai

gradual [grædʒ'uːəl] adj (change, evolution) 少しずつの sukóshizutsu no

gradually [grædʒ'uːəliː] adv 徐々に jójò
ni

graduate [n grædʒ'uːit vb grædʒ'uːeit]
n (also: **university graduate**) 大学の卒

業生 daígaku nò sotsúgyòsei; (US: also: **high school graduate**) 高校の卒業生 kôkō nò sotsúgyòsei

♦vi 卒業する sotsúgyō suru

graduation [grædʒuːeiˈʃən] n (also: **graduation ceremony**) 卒業式 sotsúgyòshiki

graffiti [grəfiːˈtiː] npl 落書き rakúgaki

graft [græft] n (AGR) 接木 tsugíki; (MED) 移植 ishóku; (BRIT: inf: hard work) 苦労 kúrò; (bribery) 汚職 oshóku

♦vt (AGR) 接木する tsugíki suru; (MED) 移植する ishóku suru

grain [grein] n (of rice, wheat, sand, salt) 粒 tsúbù; (no pl: cereals) 穀物 kokúmòtsu; (of wood) 木目 mokúme

gram [græm] n グラム gúràmu

grammar [græmˈəːr] n (LING) 文法 buńpō; (book) 文法書 buńpòsho

grammar school (BRIT) n 公立高等学校 kôritsukōtôgakkò ◇大学進学教育をする公立高校 daígakushingakukyôiku wo suru kôritsukôkò; (US) 小学校 shôgakkò

grammatical [grəmætˈikəl] adj (LING) 文法の buńpō no

gramme [græm] n = **gram**

gramophone [græmˈəfoun] n 蓄音機 chikúoñki

grand [grænd] adj (splendid, impressive) 壮大な sôdai na; (inf: wonderful) 素晴らしい subárashiì; (also humorous: gesture etc) 大げさな ôgesa na

grandchildren [grænˈtʃilˌdrən] npl 孫 mágò

granddad [grænˈdæd] n (inf) おじいちゃん ojíichan

granddaughter [grænˈdɔːtəːr] n 孫娘 magómusùme

grandeur [grænˈdʒəːr] n (of scenery etc) 壮大さ sôdaisa

grandfather [grænˈfɑːðəːr] n 祖父 sófù

grandiose [grænˈdiːous] adj (scheme, building) 壮大な sôdai na; (pej) 大げさな ôgesa na

grandma [græmˈə] n (inf) おばあちゃん obáàchan

grandmother [grænˈmʌðəːr] n 祖母 só-

bò

grandpa [grænˈpə] n (inf) = **granddad**

grandparents [grænˈpeːrənts] npl 祖父母 sófùbo

grand piano n グランドピアノ gurándopiàno

grandson [grænˈsʌn] n 孫息子 magómusùko

grandstand [grænˈstænd] n (SPORT) 観覧席 kañrañseki, スタンド sutáñdo

granite [grænˈit] n 御影石 mikágeìshi

granny [grænˈiː] n (inf) おばあちゃん obáàchan

grant [grænt] vt (money) 与える atáerù; (request etc) かなえる kanáerù; (visa) 交付する kôfu suru; (admit) 認める mitômerù

♦n (SCOL) 助成金 joséikin; (ADMIN: subsidy) 交付金 kôfùkin

to take someone/something for granted ...を軽く見る ...wo karúkù mírù

granulated sugar [grænˈjəleitid-] n グラニュー糖 gurányùtō

granule [grænˈjuːl] n (of coffee, salt) 粒 tsúbù

grape [greip] n ブドウ budó

grapefruit [greipˈfruːt] (pl **grapefruit** or **grapefruits**) n グレープフルーツ gurépufurùtsu

graph [græf] n (diagram) グラフ gúràfu

graphic [græfˈik] adj (account, description) 写実的な shajítsuteki na; (art, design) グラフィックの guráfikkù no

graphics [græfˈiks] n (art, process) グラフィックス guráfikkùsu

♦npl (drawings) グラフィックス guráfikkùsu

grapple [græpˈəl] vi: **to grapple with someone** ...ともみ合う ...to momíaù

to grapple with something (problem etc) ...と取組む ...to toríkumù

grasp [græsp] vt (hold, seize) 握る nigírù; (understand) 理解する rikái suru

♦n (grip) 握り nigírì; (understanding) 理解 rikái

grasping [græsˈpiŋ] adj (money-grabbing) 欲深い yokúfukaì

grass [græs] n (BOT) 草 kusá; (lawn) 芝生 shibáfu

grasshopper [græs'hɑːpər] n バッタ battá

grass-roots [græs'ruːts] adj (level, opinion) 一般人の ippánjìn no

grate [greit] n (for fire) 火格子 higóshi
♦vi (metal, chalk): **to grate (on)** (...に すれて) きしる (...ni suréte) kishírù
♦vt (CULIN) すりおろす surîorosù

grateful [greit'fəl] adj (thanks) 感謝の kánsha no; (person) 有難く思っている a-rígatakù omótte irù

grater [grei'tər] n (CULIN) 卸し金 oróshigàne

gratifying [græt'əfaiiŋ] adj (pleasing, satisfying) 満足な mánzoku na

grating [grei'tiŋ] n (iron bars) 鉄格子 tetsúgòshi
♦adj (noise) きしる kishírù

gratitude [græt'ətuːd] n 感謝 kánsha

gratuity [grətu'iti:] n (tip) 心付け kokórozùke, チップ chíppù

grave [greiv] n (tomb) 墓 haká
♦adj (decision, mistake) 重大な júdai na; (expression, person) 重々しい omóomoshiì

gravel [græv'əl] n 砂利 jarí

gravestone [greiv'stoun] n 墓石 hakáishi

graveyard [greiv'jɑːrd] n 墓場 hakába, 墓地 bóchi

gravity [græv'iti:] n (PHYSICS) 引力 ínryoku; (seriousness) 重大さ júdaisa

gravy [grei'vi:] n (juice of meat) 肉汁 nikújū; (sauce) グレービーソース gurébīsòsu

gray [grei] adj = **grey**

graze [greiz] vi (animal) 草を食う kusá wo kuù
♦vt (touch lightly) かすめる kasúmerù; (scrape) こする kosúrù
♦n (MED) かすり傷 kasúrikìzu

grease [griːs] n (lubricant) グリース gurísù; (fat) 脂肪 shibó
♦vt ...にグリースを差す ...ni gurísù wo sásù

greaseproof paper [griːs'pruːf-] (BRIT) n パラフィン紙 paráfiñshi

greasy [griː'siː] adj (food) 脂っこい abúrakkoì; (tools) 油で汚れた abúra dè yogóretà; (skin, hair) 脂ぎった abúragittà

great [greit] adj (large: area, amount) 大きい ókii; (intense: heat, pain) 強い tsuyóì; (important, famous: city, man) 有名な yúmei na; (inf: terrific) 素晴らしい subárashiì

Great Britain n 英国 eíkoku, イギリス igírisu

great-grandfather [greit'græn'faːðər] n そう祖父 sósofù

great-grandmother [greit'græn'mʌðər] n そう祖母 sósobò

greatly [greit'li:] adv とても totémo

greatness [greit'nis] n (importance) 偉大さ idáisa

Greece [griːs] n ギリシア gírîshia

greed [griːd] n (also: **greediness**) どん欲 dóñ-yoku

greedy [griː'diː] adj どん欲な dóñ-yoku na

Greek [griːk] adj ギリシアの gírîshia no; (LING) ギリシア語の girîshiago no
♦n (person) ギリシア人 giríshiajìn; (LING) ギリシア語 giríshiago

green [griːn] adj (color) 緑（色）の mídòri(iro) no; (inexperienced) 未熟な mijúku na; (POL) 環境保護の kañkyóhogò no
♦n (color) 緑（色）mídòri(iro); (stretch of grass) 芝生 shibáfu; (on golf course) グリーン gurín

green belt n (round town) 緑地帯 ryokúchitài, グリーンベルト gurínberùto

green card n (BRIT: AUT) グリーンカード gurínkàdo ◇海外自動車保険証 kaígai jidōsha hokeñshō; (US: ADMIN) グリーンカード gurínkàdo ◇外国人入国就労許可書 gaíkokujìn nyūkoku shūrō kyokasho

greenery [griː'nəːriː] n 緑 mídòri ◇主に人為的に植えた樹木などを指す ómò ni jiñ-iteki ni ueta júmòku nádà wo sásù

greengrocer [griːn'grousər] (BRIT) n 八百屋 yaóya

greenhouse [griːn'haus] n 温室 oñshitsu

greenish [griː'niʃ] adj 緑がかった midórigakattā

Greenland [gri:n'lənd] n グリーンランド gurínraǹdo

greens [gri:nz] npl (vegetables) 葉物 hamóno, 葉菜 yōsai

greet [gri:t] vt (welcome: person) ...にあいさつする ...ni áisatsu suru, 歓迎する kaṅgei suru; (receive: news) 受けとめる ukétomerú

greeting [gri:'tiṅ] n (welcome) あいさつ áisatsu, 歓迎 kaṅgei

greeting(s) card n グリーティングカード gurítiṅgukādo

gregarious [grige:r'i:əs] adj (person) 社交的な shakōteki na

grenade [grineid'] n (also: **hand grenade**) 手りゅう弾 teryūdan, shuryūdan

grew [gru:] pt of **grow**

grey [grei] adj (color) 灰色 haíiro; (dismal) 暗い kuráì

grey-haired [grei'he:rd] adj 白髪頭の shirágaatāma no, 白髪の hakúhatsu no

greyhound [grei'haund] n グレーハウンド gurḗhauṅdo

grid [grid] n (pattern) 碁盤の目 góbàn no me; (ELEC: network) 送電網 sōdenmō

grief [gri:f] n (distress, sorrow) 悲しみ kanáshimì

grievance [gri:'vəns] n (complaint) 苦情 kujō

grieve [gri:v] vi (feel sad) 悲しむ kanáshimù

♦vt (cause sadness or distress to) 悲しませる kanáshimaserù

to grieve for (dead spouse etc) ...を嘆く ...wo nagékù

grievous [gri:'vəs] adj: **grievous bodily harm** (LAW) 重傷 jūshō

grill [gril] n (on cooker) グリル gúrìru; (grilled food: also: **mixed grill**) グリル料理 gurírùryðri

♦vt (BRIT: food) グリルで焼く gúrìru de yákù; (inf: question) 尋問する jiǹmon suru

grille [gril] n (screen: on window, counter etc) 鉄格子 tetsúgðshi; (AUT) ラジエーターグリル rajíētāgùriru

grim [grim] adj (unpleasant: situation)

厳しい kibíshiì; (unattractive: place) 陰気な íǹki na; (serious, stern) 険しい kewáshiì

grimace [grim'əs] n (ugly expression) しかめっ面 shikámettsura

♦vi しかめっ面をする shikámetsura wo surù

grime [graim] n (dirt) あか aká

grin [grin] n (smile) にやにや笑い níyàniyawarai

♦vi にやにやと笑う níyàniya to waráù

grind [graind] (pt, pp **ground**) vt (crush) もみつぶす momítsubusù; (coffee, pepper etc: also US: meat) 挽く hikú; (make sharp: knife) 研ぐ tógù

♦n (work) 骨折れ仕事 honéoreshigòto

grip [grip] n (hold) 握り nigíri; (control, grasp) 支配 shiháì; (of tire, shoe) グリップ guríppù; (handle) 取っ手 tottế; (holdall) 旅行かばん ryokōkabàn

♦vt (object) つかむ tsukámù, 握る nigírù; (audience, attention) 引付ける hikítsukerù

to come to grips with (problem, difficulty) ...と取組む ...to toríkumù

gripping [grip'iṅ] adj (story, film) 引付ける hikítsukerù

grisly [griz'li:] adj (death, murder) ひどい hidóì

gristle [gris'əl] n (on meat) 軟骨 náǹkotsu

grit [grit] n (sand, stone) 砂利 jarí; (determination, courage) 根性 koǹjō

♦vt (road) ...に砂利を敷く ...ni jarí wð shíkù

to grit one's teeth 歯を食いしばる há wð kuíshibarù

groan [groun] n (of person) うめき声 umékigoè

♦vi うめく umékù

grocer [grou'sə:r] n 食料品商 shokúryō-hiǹshō

groceries [grou'sə:ri:z] npl (provisions) 食料品 shokúryðhin

grocer's (shop) [grou'sə:rz-] n 食料品店 shokúryðhiǹten

groggy [gra:g'i:] adj ふらふらする fúràfura suru, グロッキーの gurókkì no

groin [grɔin] n そけい部 sokeību

groom [gruːm] n (for horse) 馬丁 batéi; (also: **bridegroom**) 花婿 hanámukð
♦vt (horse) ...の手入れをする ...no teíre wð suru; (fig: **to groom someone for** (job) 仕込む shikómù

well-groomed (person) 身だしなみのいい midáshinami no íi

groove [gruːv] n 溝 mizó

grope [group] vi (fumble): **to grope for** 手探りで探す teságuri de sagásù

gross [grous] adj (flagrant: neglect, injustice) 甚だしい hanáhadashiī; (vulgar: behavior, building) 下品な gehín na; (COMM: income, weight) 全体の zeńtai no

grossly [grous'liː] adv (greatly) 甚だしく hanáhadashikù

grotesque [groutesk'] adj (exaggerated, ugly) 醜悪な shūaku na, グロテスクな gurótesùku na

grotto [grɑt'ou] n (cave) 小さな洞穴 chíisana horáana

grotty [grɑt'iː] (BRIT inf) adj (dreadful) ひどい hídði

ground [graund] pt, pp of **grind**
♦n (earth, soil) 土 tsuchí; (land) 地面 jímèn; (SPORT) グランド guráňdo; (US: also: **ground wire**) アース線 ásùsen; (reason: gen pl) 根拠 koñkyo
♦vt (plane) 飛べない様にする tobénai yǒ ni suru; (US: ELEC) ...のアースを取付ける ...no ásu wò torítsukerù

on the ground 地面に〔で〕 jímèn ni 〔de〕

to the ground 地面へ jímèn e

to gain/lose ground 前進〔後退〕する zeńshin〔kǒtai〕surù

ground cloth (US) n = **groundsheet**

grounding [graun'diŋ] n (in education) 基礎 kisó

groundless [graund'lis] adj (fears, suspicions) 根拠のない koñkyo no nài

grounds [graundz] npl (of coffee etc) かす kásù; (gardens etc) 敷地 shikíchi

groundsheet [graund'ʃiːt] n グラウンドシート guráundoshìto

ground staff n (AVIAT) 整備員 seíbiìn

◇総称 sǒshō

ground swell n (of opinion) 盛り上がり moríagari

groundwork [graund'wəːrk] n (preparation) 準備 júnbi

group [gruːp] n (of people) 集団 shūdan, グループ gúrùpu; (of trees etc) 一群れ hitómùre; (of cars etc) 一団 ichídan; (also: **pop group**) グループ gúrùpu; (COMM) グループ gúrùpu
♦vt (also: **group together**: people, things etc) 一緒にする ísshð ni suru, グループにする gúrùpu ni suru
♦vi (also: **group together**) 群がる murágarù, グループになる gúrùpu ni nárù

grouse [graus] n inv (bird) ライチョウ raíchō
♦vi (complain) 不平を言う fuhéi wð iú

grove [grouv] n 木立 kodáchì

grovel [grʌv'əl] vi (fig): **to grovel (before)** (boss etc) (...に) ぺこぺこする (..ni) pékðpeko suru

grow [grou] (pt **grew**, pp **grown**) vi (plant, tree) 生える haérù; (person, animal) 成長する seíchō suru; (increase) 増える fuérù; (become) なる nárù;(develop): **to grow (out of/from)** (...から) 発生する (...kara) hasséi suru
♦vt (roses, vegetables) 栽培する saíbai suru; (beard) 生やす hayásù

grower [grou'əːr] n (BOT, AGR) 栽培者 saíbaishà

growing [grou'iŋ] adj (fear, awareness, number) 増大する zǒdai suru

growl [graul] vi (dog, person) うなる unárù

grown [groun] pp of **grow**

grown-up [groun'ʌp'] n (adult) 大人 otóna

growth [grouθ] n (development, increase: of economy, industry) 成長 seíchō; (what has grown: of weeds, beard etc) 生えた物 haéta monð; (growing: of child, animal etc) 発育 hatsúiku; (MED) しゅよう shuyó

grow up vi (child) 育つ sodátsù

grub [grʌb] n (larva) 幼虫 yǒchū; (inf: food) 飯 meshí

grubby [grʌb'i:] *adj* (dirty) 汚い kitánaí

grudge [grʌdʒ] *n* (grievance) 恨み urámí

♦*vt*: *to grudge someone something* (be unwilling to give) ...に...を出し惜しみする ...ni ...wo dashíoshimi suru; (envy) ...の...をねたむ ...no ...wo netámú
to bear someone a grudge ...に恨みがある ...ni urámi ga arù

gruelling [gru:'əliŋ] *adj* (trip, journey, encounter) きつい kitsúi

gruesome [gru:'səm] *adj* (tale, scene) むごたらしい mugótarashií

gruff [grʌf] *adj* (voice, manner) ぶっきらぼうな bukkírabō na

grumble [grʌm'bəl] *vi* (complain) 不平を言う fuhéi wò iú

grumpy [grʌm'pi:] *adj* (bad-tempered) 機嫌が悪い kigéñ ga warúi

grunt [grʌnt] *vi* (pig) ぶーぶー言う būbū iú; (person) うなる unáru

G-string [dʒi:'striŋ] *n* (garment) バタフライ bátáfurai

guarantee [gærənti:'] *n* (assurance) 保証 hoshō; (COMM: warranty) 保証書 hoshō-shó

♦*vt* 保証する hoshō suru

guard [gɑ:rd] *n* (one person) 警備員 keíbiñ, ガードマン gādoman; (squad) 護衛隊 goéitai; (BRIT: RAIL) 車掌 shashō; (on machine) 安全カバー añzenkabā; (also: **fireguard**) 安全格子 añzenkōshi

♦*vt* (protect: place, person, secret etc):
to guard (against) (...から) 守る (...kara) mamórù; (prisoner) 見張る mihárù
to be on one's guard 警戒する keíkai suru

guard against *vt fus* (prevent: disease, damage etc) 防ぐ fuségù

guarded [gɑ:r'did] *adj* (statement, reply) 慎重な shiñchō na

guardian [gɑ:r'di:ən] *n* (LAW: of minor) 保護者 hógòsha; (defender) 監視人 kañshiñin

guard's van (BRIT) *n* (RAIL) 乗務員車 jōmuiñsha

guerrilla [gəril'ə] *n* ゲリラ gérìra

guess [ges] *vt, vi* (estimate: number, distance etc) 推定する suítei suru; (correct answer) 当ててみる atétè mírù; (US: think) ...だと思う ...da to omóù

♦*n* (attempt at correct answer) 推定 suítei
to take/have a guess 推定する suítei suru, 当ててみる atétè mírù

guesswork [ges'wə:rk] *n* (speculation) 当て推量 atézuiryō

guest [gest] *n* (visitor) 客 kyákù; (in hotel) 泊り客 tomárikyàku

guest-house [gest'haus] *n* 民宿 míñshuku

guest room *n* 客間 kyakúma

guffaw [gʌfɔ:'] *vi* ばか笑い bakáwaraì

guidance [gaid'əns] *n* (advice) 指導 shidō

guide [gaid] *n* (person: museum guide, tour guide, mountain guide) 案内人 annáinñin, ガイド gáido; (book) ガイドブック gaídobukkù; (BRIT: also: **girl guide**) ガールスカウト gārusukaùto

♦*vt* (round city, museum etc) 案内する annái suru; (lead) 導く michíbikù; (direct) ...に道を教える ...ni michí wò o-shíerù

guidebook [gaid'buk] *n* ガイドブック gaídobukkù

guide dog *n* 盲導犬 mōdōkèn

guidelines [gaid'lainz] *npl* (advice) 指針 shishñi, ガイドライン gaídoraìn

guild [gild] *n* (association) 組合 kumíaì, 協会 kyōkai

guile [gail] *n* (cunning) 悪意 akúi

guillotine [gil'əti:n] *n* (for execution) 断頭台 dañtōdai, ギロチン giróchin; (for paper) 裁断機 saídañki

guilt [gilt] *n* (remorse) 罪の意識 tsumí nò ishíki; (culpability) 有罪 yūzai

guilty [gil'ti:] *adj* (person) 有罪の yūzai no; (expression) 後ろめたそうな ushíro-metasō na; (secret) やましい yamáshiì

guinea [gin'i:] (BRIT) *n* (old money) ギニー gínī

guinea pig *n* (animal) モルモット morúmottò; (fig: person) 実験台 jikkéñdai

guise [gaiz] *n*: *in/under the guise of* ...の装いで ...no yosóoì de

guitar [gitɑ:'r] *n* ギター gítà

gulf [gʌlf] *n* (GEO) 湾 wáñ; (abyss: *also fig*: difference) 隔たり hedátarì

gull [gʌl] *n* カモメ kamóme

gullet [gʌl'it] *n* 食道 shokúdō

gullible [gʌl'əbəl] *adj* (naive, trusting) だまされやすい damásareyásuì

gully [gʌl'i:] *n* (ravine) 峡谷 kyōkoku

gulp [gʌlp] *vi* (swallow) 息を飲み込む íkì wo nomíkomù
♦*vt* (*also*: **gulp down**: drink) がぶがぶ飲み込む gábùgabu nomíkomù; (: food) 急いで食べる isóide tabérù

gum [gʌm] *n* (ANAT) 歯茎 hágùki; (glue) アラビア糊 arábia nòri; (sweet: *also*: **gumdrop**) ガムドロップ gamúdoroppù; (*also*: **chewing-gum**) チューインガム chúingugàmu, ガム gámù
♦*vt* (stick): **to gum (together)** 張り合わせる haríawaserù

gumboots [gʌm'bu:ts] (BRIT) *npl* ゴム靴 gomúgùtsu

gumption [gʌmp'ʃən] *n* (sense, wit) 度胸 dokyō

gun [gʌn] *n* (small: revolver, pistol) けん銃 keñjū, ピストル písùtoru, ガン gáñ; (medium-sized: rifle) 銃 jū, ライフル raífùru; (: *also*: **airgun**) 空気銃 kūkijū; (large: cannon) 大砲 taíhō

gunboat [gʌn'bout] *n* 砲艦 hōkan

gunfire [gʌn'faiə:r] *n* 銃撃 jūgeki

gunman [gʌn'mən] (*pl* **gunmen**) *n* (criminal) ガンマン gáñman

gunpoint [gʌn'pɔint] *n*: **at gunpoint** (pointing a gun) ピストルを突付けて písùtoru wo tsukítsuketè; (threatened with a gun) ピストルを突付けられて písùtoru wo tsukítsukerarète

gunpowder [gʌn'paudə:r] *n* 火薬 kayákù

gunshot [gʌn'ʃɑt] *n* (act) 発砲 happō; (sound) 銃声 jūsei

gurgle [gə:r'gəl] *vi* (baby) のどを鳴らす nodó wò narásù; (water) ごぼごぼ流れる góbògobo nagárerù

guru [gu:'ru:] *n* (REL: *also fig*) 教師 kyōshi

gush [gʌʃ] *vi* (blood, tears, oil) どっと流れ出る dóttò nagárederù; (person) 大げさに言う ōgesa ni iu

gusset [gʌs'it] *n* (SEWING) まち máchì

gust [gʌst] *n* (*also*: **gust of wind**) 突風 toppū; (of smoke) 渦巻 uzúmàki

gusto [gʌs'tou] *n* (enthusiasm) 楽しみ tanóshimì

gut [gʌt] *n* (ANAT: intestine) 腸 chō

guts [gʌts] *npl* (ANAT: of person, animal) 内臓 naízō; (*inf*: courage) 勇気 yūki, ガッツ gáttsù

gutter [gʌt'ə:r] *n* (in street) どぶ dobu; (of roof) 雨どい amádoì

guttural [gʌt'ə:rəl] *adj* (accent, sound) のどに絡まった様な nódò ni karámatta yō na

guy [gai] *n* (*inf*: man) 野郎 yarō, やつ yátsù; (*also*: **guyrope**) 支線 shisèn; (figure) ガイフォークスの人形 gaífōkusu no niñgyō

guzzle [gʌz'əl] *vt* (drink) がぶがぶ飲む gábùgabu nómù; (food) がつがつ食う gátsùgatsu kúù

gym [dʒim] *n* (building, room: *also*: **gymnasium**) 体育館 taíikukàn; (activity: *also*: **gymnastics**) 体操 taísō

gymnast [dʒim'næst] *n* 体操選手 taísōseñshu

gymnastics [dʒimnæs'tiks] *n* 体操 taísō

gym shoes *npl* 運動靴 uñdōgùtsu, スニーカー súnīkā

gym slip (BRIT) *n* (tunic) スモック sumókkù ◇そで無しの上っ張りでかつて女子学童の制服として使われた物. sodénashi no uwápparì de katsutè joshí gakudō no seífuku toshite tsukáwaretà monó.

gynecologist [gainəkɑl'ədʒist] (BRIT **gynaecologist**) *n* 婦人科医 fujíñka-i

gypsy [dʒip'si:] *n* ジプシー jípùshī

gyrate [dʒai'reit] *vi* (revolve) 回転する kaíten suru

H

haberdashery [hæb'ə:rdæʃə:ri:] *n* (US) 紳士服店 shiñshifukutèn; (BRIT) 小間物店 komámonotèn

habit [hæb'it] n (custom, practice) 習慣 shūkan; (addiction) 中毒 chūdoku; (REL: costume) 修道服 shūdōfuku

habitable [hæb'itəbəl] adj 住める suméru

habitat [hæb'itæt] n 生息地 seísokuchì

habitual [həbitʃ'u:əl] adj (action) 習慣的な shūkanteki na; (drinker, liar) 常習的な jōshūteki na

hack [hæk] vt (cut, slice) ぶった切る buttágirù
◆n (pej: writer) 三文文士 sanmonbunshi

hacker [hæk'əːr] n (COMPUT) コンピュータ破り confpyūtayaburì, ハッカー hákkā

hackneyed [hæk'ni:d] adj 陳腐な chínpu na

had [hæd] pt, pp of **have**

haddock [hæd'ək] (pl **haddock** or **haddocks**) n タラ tárà

hadn't [hæd'ənt] = **had not**

haemorrhage [hem'ə:ridʒ] (BRIT) n = **hemorrhage**

haemorrhoids [hem'ə:rɔidz] (BRIT) npl = **hemorrhoids**

haggard [hæg'ə:rd] adj (face, look) やつれた yatsúretà

haggle [hæg'əl] vi (bargain) 値切る negírù

Hague [heig] n: **The Hague** ハーグ hāgù

hail [heil] n (frozen rain) ひょう hyō; (of objects, criticism etc) 降り注ぐ物 furísosogù monó
◆vt (call: person) 呼ぶ yobú; (flag down: taxi) 呼止める yobítomerù; (acclaim: person, event etc) ほめる homérù
◆vi (weather) ひょうが降る hyō ga fúrù

hailstone [heil'stoun] n ひょうの粒 hyō no tsubú

hair [he:r] n (of animal: also gen) 毛 ke; (of person's head) 髪の毛 kamí no kè
to do one's hair 髪をとかす kamí wò tokásu

hairbrush [he:r'brʌʃ] n ヘアブラシ heáburashì

haircut [he:r'kʌt] n (action) 散髪 sanpatsu; (style) 髪型 kamígata, ヘアスタイル heásutaîru

hairdo [he:r'du:] n 髪型 kamígata, ヘアスタイル heásutaîru

hairdresser [he:r'dresəːr] n 美容師 biyōshì

hairdresser's [he:r'dresə:rz] n (shop) 美容院 biyōîn

hair dryer n ヘアドライヤー heádoraîyā

hairgrip [he:r'grip] n 髪止め kamídome

hairnet [he:r'net] n ヘアネット heánettò

hairpin [he:r'pin] n ヘアピン heápiǹ

hairpin curve (BRIT **hairpin bend**) n ヘアピンカーブ heápinkābu

hair-raising [he:r'reiziŋ] adj (experience, tale) ぞっとする様な zóttò suru yō na

hair remover [-rimu:'və:r] n (cream) 脱毛クリーム datsúmōkurīmù

hair spray n ヘアスプレー heásupurè

hairstyle [he:r'stail] n 髪型 kamígata, ヘアスタイル heásutaîru

hairy [he:r'i:] adj (person, animal) 毛深い kebúkaì; (inf: situation) 恐ろしい osóroshiì

hake [heik] (pl inv or **hakes**) n タラ tárà

half [hæf] (pl **halves**) n (of amount, object) 半分 hanbuǹ; (of beer etc) 半パイント hanpaìnto; (RAIL, bus) 半額 hangaku
◆adj (bottle, fare, pay etc) 半分の hanbuǹ no
◆adv (empty, closed, open, asleep) 半ば nakábà
two and a half 2と2分の1 ní tò nibún no ichi
two and a half years/kilos/hours 2年〔キロ, 時間〕半 ninén〔kíro, jíkan〕hàn
half a dozen 半ダース handāsu
half a pound 半ポンド hanpòndo
to cut something in half ...を半分に切る ...wo hanbuǹ ni kírù

half-baked [hæf'beikt] adj (idea, scheme) ばかげた bakágetà

half-caste [hæf'kæst] n 混血児 konketsujî, ハーフ hâfu

half-hearted [hæf'hɑːr'tid] adj (attempt) いい加減な ífkagen na

half-hour [hæf'au'ər] n 半時間 hañjikàn

half-mast [hæf'mæst']: *a flag at half-mast* 半旗 háñki

halfpenny [hei'pəni:] (BRIT) n 半ペニー hañpeni

half-price [hæf'prais'] adj 半額の hañgaku no
◆adv 半額で hañgaku de

half term (BRIT) n (SCOL) 中間休暇 chūkankyūka

half-time [hæf'taim'] n (SPORT) ハーフタイム háfutaimù

halfway [hæf'wei'] adv (between two points in space, time) 中途で chūto de

halibut [hæl'əbət] n inv オヒョウ ohyó

hall [hɔːl] n (entrance way) 玄関ホール geñkanhồru; (for concerts, meetings etc) 講堂 kồdō, ホール hồru

hall of residence (BRIT) n 学生寮 gakúseiryồ

hallmark [hɔːl'mɑːrk] n (on metal) 太鼓判 taíkoban; (of writer, artist etc) 特徴 tokúchō

hallo [həlou'] excl = hello

Hallowe'en [hæləwiːn'] n ハロウイーン haróuìn

hallucination [həluːsənei'ʃən] n 幻覚 geñkaku

hallway [hɔːl'wei] n (entrance hall) 玄関ホール geñkanhồru

halo [hei'lou] n (of saint) 後光 gokố

halt [hɔːlt] n (stop) 止る事 tomáru kotồ
◆vt (progress, activity, growth etc) 止める tomérù
◆vi (stop) 止る tomárù

halve [hæv] vt (reduce) 半分に減らす hañbuñ ni herásù; (divide) 半分に切る hañbuñ ni kírù

halves [hævz] pl of **half**

ham [hæm] n (meat) ハム hámù

hamburger [hæm'bəːrgəːr] n ハンバーガー hañbāgà

hamlet [hæm'lit] n (village) 小さな村 chíisana murá

hammer [hæm'əːr] n (tool) 金づち kanázuchì, とんかち toñkàchi
◆vt (nail) たたく tatákù
◆vi (on door, table etc) たたく tatákù

to hammer an idea into someone ...にある考え方をたたき込む ...ni árù kañgaèkata wo tátakikomù

to hammer a message across ある考えを繰返し強調する aru kañgaè wo kuríkaeshì kyồchō suru

hammock [hæm'ək] n (on ship, in garden) ハンモック hañmokkù

hamper [hæm'pəːr] vt (person, movement, effort) 邪魔する jamá suru
◆n (basket) ふた付きバスケット futátsukibasukettồ

hamster [hæm'stəːr] n ハムスター hámùsutā

hand [hænd] n (ANAT) 手 tế; (of clock) 針 hárì; (handwriting) 筆跡 hisséki; (worker) 使用人 shíyònin; (of cards) 持札 mochífùda
◆vt (pass, give) 渡す watásù

to give/lend someone a hand ...の手伝いをする ...no tetsúdaì wo suru

at hand 手元に temóto nì

in hand (time) 空いていて aíte itè; (job, situation) 当面の tồmen no

on hand (person, services etc) 利用できる ríyō dekirù

to hand (information etc) 手元に temóto nì

on the one hand ..., on the other hand ... 一方では...他方では... ippố de wa ..., tahố de wa ...

handbag [hænd'bæg] n ハンドバッグ hañdobaggù

handbook [hænd'buk] n (manual) ハンドブック hañdobukkù

handbrake [hænd'breik] n (AUT) サイドブレーキ saídoburèki

handcuffs [hænd'kʌfs] npl (POLICE) 手錠 tejố

handful [hænd'ful] n (of soil, stones) 一握り hitónigìri

a handful of people 数人 sùnin

handicap [hæn'di:kæp] n (disability) 障害 shồgai; (disadvantage) 不利 fúrì; (SPORT) ハンデ háñde
◆vt (hamper) 不利にする fúrì ni suru

mentally/physically handicapped 精神的〔身体〕障害のある seíshinteki 〔shiñtai) shōgai no árù

handicraft [hæn'di:kræft] n (activity) 手芸 shúgèi; (object) 手芸品 shugéihìn

hand in vt (essay, work) 提出する teíshutsu suru

handiwork [hæn'di:wə:rk] n やった事 yattá kotò

handkerchief [hæŋ'kə:rtʃif] n ハンカチ hañkachi

handle [hæn'dəl] n (of door, window, drawer etc) 取っ手 tottê; (of cup, knife, brush etc) 柄 e; (for winding) ハンドル hañdôru

♦vt (touch: object, ornament etc) いじる ijírù; (deal with: problem, responsibility etc) 処理する shórì suru; (treat: people) 扱う atsúkaù

「**handle with care**」取扱い注意 toríatsukai chūì

to fly off the handle 怒る okórù

handlebar(s) [hæn'dəlba:r(z)] n(pl) ハンドル hañdôru

hand luggage n 手荷物 tenímòtsu

handmade [hænd'meid'] adj (clothes, jewellery, pottery etc) 手作りの tezúkùri no

hand out vt (object, information) 配る kubárù; (punishment) 与える atáerù

handout [hænd'aut] n (money, clothing, food) 施し物 hodókoshimono; (publicity leaflet) パンフレット páñfuretto; (summary: of lecture) 講演の要約 kōen nò yōyaku

hand over vt (thing) 引渡す hikíwatasù; (responsibility) 譲る yuzúrù

handrail [hænd'reil] n (on stair, ledge) 手すり tesúri

handshake [hænd'ʃeik] n 握手 ákùshu

handsome [hæn'səm] adj (man) 男前の otōkomaè no, ハンサムな háñsamu na; (woman) きりっとした kiríttò shita; (building) 立派な rippá na; (fig: profit, return) 相当な sōtō na

handwriting [hænd'raitiŋ] n (style) 筆跡 hisséki

handy [hæn'di:] adj (useful) 便利な bêñri na; (skilful) 手先の器用な tesáki nò kíyò na; (close at hand) 手元にある temótò nì

árù

handyman [hæn'di:mæn] (pl **handymen**) n (at home) 手先の器用な人 tesáki nò kíyò na hitŏ; (in hotel etc) 用務員 yōmuin

hang [hæŋ] (pt, pp **hung**) vt (painting, coat etc) 掛ける kakérù; (criminal: pt, pp hanged) 絞首刑にする kōshukei ni surù

♦vi (painting, coat, drapery etc) 掛っている kakátte irù; (hair etc) 垂れ下がる tarésagarù

to get the hang of something (inf) ...のこつが分かる ...no kótsù ga wakárù

hang about vi (loiter) ぶらつく burátsukù

hangar [hæŋ'ə:r] n (AVIAT) 格納庫 kakúnôko

hang around vi = hang about

hanger [hæŋ'ə:r] n (for clothes) 洋服掛け yōfukukàke, ハンガー hâñgā

hanger-on [hæŋ'ə:ra:n'] n (parasite) 取巻き torímaki

hang-gliding [hæŋ'glaidiŋ] n (SPORT) ハンググライダー hañguguraìdā

hang on vi (wait) 待つ mátsù

hangover [hæŋ'ouvə:r] n (after drinking) 二日酔い futsúkayoì

hang up vi (TEL) 電話を切る deñwa wò kírù

♦vt (coat, painting etc) 掛ける kakérù

hang-up [hæŋ'ʌp] n (inhibition) ノイローゼ noírōze

hanker [hæŋ'kə:r] vi: **to hanker after** (desire, long for) 渇望する katsúbō suru

hankie [hæŋ'ki:] n abbr = **handkerchief**

hanky [hæŋ'ki:] n abbr = **handkerchief**

haphazard [hæp'hæz'ə:rd] adj (system, arrangement) いい加減な iíkagen na

happen [hæp'ən] vi (event etc: occur) 起る okórù; (chance): **to happen to do something** 偶然に...する gūzen ni ...surù

as it happens 実は jitsú wà

happening [hæp'əniŋ] n (incident) 出来事 dekígòto

happily [hæp'ili:] adv (luckily) 幸い saíwai; (cheerfully) 楽しそうに tanóshisō ni

happiness [hæp'i:nis] *n* (contentment) 幸せ shiáwase

happy [hæp'i:] *adj* (pleased) うれしい uréshiĩ; (cheerful) 楽しい tanóshiĩ

to be happy (with) (content) (...に) 満足する (...ni) mañzoku suru

to be happy to do (willing) 喜んで...する yorókoñde ...surù

happy birthday! 誕生日おめでとう! tañjōbi omédetò!

happy-go-lucky [hæp'i:goulʌk'i:] *adj* (person) のんきな nóñki na

harangue [həræŋ'] *vt* (audience, class) ...に向かって熱弁を振るう ...ni mukáttè netsúben wò furúù

harass [həræs'] *vt* (annoy, pester) ...にいやがらせをする ...ni iyágarase wo surù

harassment [həræs'mənt] *n* (hounding) 嫌がらせ iyágarase

harbor [hɑːr'bər] (*BRIT* **harbour**) *n* (NAUT) 港 mináto

♦*vt* (hope, fear etc) 心に抱く kokórò ni idákù; (criminal, fugitive) かくまう kakúmaù

hard [hɑːrd] *adj* (surface, object) 堅い katái; (question, problem) 難しい muzúkashiĩ; (work) 骨の折れる honé no orérù; (life) 苦しい kurúshiĩ; (person) 非情な hijō na; (facts, evidence) 確実な kakújitsu na

♦*adv* (work, think, try) 一生懸命に isshōkeñmei ni

to look hard at ...を見詰める ...wo mitsúmerù

no hard feelings! 悪く思わないから warúkù omówanài kará

to be hard of hearing 耳が遠い mimí ga tôi

to be hard done by 不当な扱いを受けた futố na atsukái wo ukétà

hardback [hɑːrd'bæk] *n* (book) ハードカバー hádokabā

hard cash *n* 現金 geñkin

hard disk *n* (COMPUT) ハードディスク hádodisùku

harden [hɑːr'dən] *vt* (wax, glue, steel) 固める katámerù; (attitude, person) かたくなにする katákùna ni suru

♦*vi* (wax, glue, steel) 固まる katámarù; (attitude, person) かたくなになる katákùna ni nárù

hard-headed [hɑːrd'hed'id] *adj* (businessman) 現実的な geñjitsuteki na

hard labor *n* (punishment) 懲役 chôeki

hardly [hɑːrd'li:] *adv* (scarcely) ほとんど...ない hotóñdo ...náĩ; (no sooner) ...するや否や ...surú ya inà ya

hardly ever ほとんど...しない hotóñdo ...shinảĩ

hardship [hɑːrd'ʃip] *n* (difficulty) 困難 koñnañ

hard up (*inf*) *adj* (broke) 金がない kané ga naĩ, 懐が寂しい futôkoro ga sabishiĩ

hardware [hɑːrd'we:r] *n* (ironmongery) 金物 kanámono; (COMPUT) ハードウェア hádoueà; (MIL) 兵器 héîki

hardware shop *n* 金物屋 kanámonoya

hard-wearing [hɑːrd'we:r'iŋ] *adj* (clothes, shoes) 丈夫な jôbu na

hard-working [hɑːrd'wəːr'kiŋ] *adj* (employee, student) 勤勉な kiñben na

hardy [hɑːr'di:] *adj* (plants, animals, people) 丈夫な jôbu na

hare [he:r] *n* ノウサギ noúsàgi

hare-brained [he:r'breind] *adj* (scheme, idea) バカげた bakágetà

harem [he:r'əm] *n* (of wives) ハーレム hāremu

harm [hɑːrm] *n* (injury) 害 gáĩ; (damage) 損害 soñgai, ダメージ damēji

♦*vt* (person) ...に危害を加える ...ni kígai wo kuwáerù; (thing) 損傷する soñshō suru

out of harm's way 安全な場所に añzen na bashò ni

harmful [hɑːrm'fəl] *adj* (effect, toxin, influence etc) 有害な yūgai na

harmless [hɑːrm'lis] *adj* (animal, person) 無害な mugái na; (joke, pleasure, activity) たわいのない tawai no nai

harmonica [hɑːrmɑːn'ikə] *n* ハーモニカ hāmonika

harmonious [hɑːrmou'niːəs] *adj* (discussion, relationship) 友好的な yūkōteki na; (layout, pattern) 調和の取れた chôwa no torétà; (sound, tune) 調子の良い chôshi no yoĩ

harmonize [haːrmənaiz] *vi* (MUS) ハーモニーを付ける hāmonī wo tsukérù; (colors, ideas): *to harmonize (with)* (...と)調和する (...to) chōwa suru

harmony [haːrməniː] *n* (accord) 調和 chōwa; (MUS) ハーモニー hāmonī

harness [haːrnis] *n* (for horse) 馬具 bágù; (for child, dog) 胴輪 dōwa, ハーネス hānesù; (safety harness) 安全ハーネス ańzenhānesu

♦*vt* (resources, energy etc) 利用する riyō suru; (horse) ...に馬具をつける ...ni bágù wo tsukérù; (dog) ...にハーネスを付ける ...ni hānesù wo tsukérù

harp [haːrp] *n* (MUS) たて琴 tatégòto, ハープ hāpu

♦*vi*: *to harp on about* (*pej*) ...の事をくどくどと話し続ける ...no kotó wò kúdòkudo to hanáshitsuzukerù

harpoon [hɑːrpuːn] *n* もり mórĩ

harrowing [hærʾouiŋ] *adj* (experience, film) 戦りつの seńritsu no

harsh [haːrʃ] *adj* (sound) 耳障りな mimízawàri na; (light) どぎつい dogítsui; (judge, criticism) か酷な kakóku na; (life, winter) 厳しい kibíshiĩ

harvest [haːrvist] *n* (harvest time) 収穫期 shūkakukì; (of barley, fruit etc) 収穫 shūkaku

♦*vt* (barley, fruit etc) 収穫する shūkaku suru

has [hæz] *vb see* **have**

hash [hæʃ] *n* (CULIN) ハッシュ hásshù; (*fig*: mess) めちゃめちゃな有様 mechámecha na arisama

hashish [hæʃʾiːʃ] *n* ハシシ háshìshi

hasn't [hæzʾənt] = **has not**

hassle [hæsʾəl] (*inf*) *n* (bother) 面倒 meńdō

haste [heist] *n* (hurry) 急ぎ isógi

hasten [heiʾsən] *vt* (decision, downfall) 早める hayámerù

♦*vi* (hurry): *to hasten to do something* 急いで...する isóide ...surù

hastily [heisʾtiliː] *adv* (hurriedly) 慌ただしく awátadashikù; (rashly) 軽はずみに karúhazùmi ni

hasty [heisʾtiː] *adj* (hurried) 慌ただしい awátadashiĩ; (rash) 軽はずみの karúhazùmi no

hat [hæt] *n* (headgear) 帽子 bōshi

hatch [hætʃ] *n* (NAUT: *also*: **hatchway**) 倉口 sōkō, ハッチ hátchì; (*also*: **service hatch**) サービス口 sābisugùchi, ハッチ hátchì

♦*vi* (bird) 卵からかえる tamágò kara kaérù; (egg) かえる kaérù, ふ化する fuká suru

hatchback [hætʃʾbæk] *n* (AUT) ハッチバック hatchíbakkù

hatchet [hætʃʾit] *n* (axe) おの ónò

hate [heit] *vt* (wish ill to: person) 憎む nikúmù; (dislike strongly: person, thing, situation) 嫌う kiráu

♦*n* (illwill) 増悪 zōo; (strong dislike) 嫌悪 kéñ-o

hateful [heitʾfəl] *adj* ひどい hidóĩ

hatred [heiʾtrid] *n* (illwill) 増悪 zōo; (strong dislike) 嫌悪 kéñ-o

haughty [hɔːʾtiː] *adj* (air, attitude) 尊大な sońdai na

haul [hɔːl] *vt* (pull) 引っ張る hippáru

♦*n* (of stolen goods etc) 獲物 emóno; (*also*: **a haul of fish**) 漁獲 gyokáku

haulage [hɔːʾlidʒ] *n* (business, costs) 運送 uñsō

hauler [hɔːʾləːr] (*BRIT* **haulier**) *n* 運送屋 uñsōya

haunch [hɔːntʃ] *n* (ANAT) 腰 koshí; (of meat) 腰肉 koshíniku

haunt [hɔːnt] *vt* (subj: ghost) (place) ...に出る ...ni dérù; (person) ...に付きまとう ...ni tsukimatou; (: problem, memory etc) 悩ます nayámasù

♦*n* (of crooks, childhood etc) 行き付けの場所 ikítsuke nò bashò

haunted house お化け屋敷 obákeyashĩki

KEYWORD

have [hæv] (*pt, pp* **had**) *aux vb* **1** (*gen*)

to have arrived/gone/eaten/slept 着いた〔行った, 食べた, 眠った〕tsúĩta〔ittá, tábèta, nemútta〕

he has been kind/promoted 彼は親切

だった〔昇格した〕kárè wa shíñsetsu dát-
ta〔shōkaku shita〕
has he told you? 彼はあなたにそれを
話しましたか kárè wa anátà ni soré wò
hanáshimashìta ká
*having finished/when he had fin-
ished, he left* 仕事が済むと彼は帰った
shigóto ga sumù to kárè wa kâetta
2 (in tag questions): *you've done it,
haven't you?* あなたはその仕事をやっ
たんでしょう anátà wa sonó shigòto wo
yattáñ deshō
he hasn't done it, has he? 彼は仕事
をやらなかったんでしょう kárè wa shi-
góto wò yaránakattàñ deshō
3 (in short answers and questions): *you'
ve made a mistake - no I haven't/so
I have* あなたは間違いをしました‐違い
ますよ〔そうですね〕anátà wa machígaì
wo shimáshìta - chigáimasù yó〔sō desu
né〕
we haven't paid - yes we have! 私た
ちはまだ金を払っていません‐払いました
よ watákushitàchi wa mádà kané wo
haráttè imaseñ - haráimashìta yó
I've been there before, have you? 私
は前にあそこへ行った事がありますが,
あなたは？ watákushi wà máè ni asóko
è ittá kotò ga arímasù ga, anátà wá?
◆*modal aux vb* (be obliged): *to have
(got) to do something* ...をしなければ
ならない ...wò shinákereba naranaì
she has (got) to do it 彼女はどうして
もそれをしなければなりません kánòjo
wa dōshitè mo soré wò shinákereba
narimaseñ
I have (got) to finish this work 私は
この仕事を済まさなければなりません
watákushi wà konó shigòto wo sumása-
nakereba narimaseñ
you haven't got to tell her 彼女に言わな
くてもいい〔言ってはならない〕kánòjo
ni iwánakute mò íi〔itté wa naránaì〕
*I haven't got/I don't have to wear
glasses* 私は眼鏡を掛けなくてもいい
watákushi wà mégàne wò kakénakute
mò íi
this has to be a mistake これは何かの

間違いに違いない koré wa náníka no
machígaì ni chigái naì
◆*vt* **1** (possess) 持っている móttè iru,
...がある ...gá arù
he has (got) blue eyes/dark hair 彼
は目が青い〔髪が黒い〕kárè wa mé wa
aóì〔kamí gà kuróì〕
*do you have/have you got a car/
phone?* あなたは車〔電話〕を持っていま
すか anátà wa kurúma〔deñwa〕wò móttè imasu ká
I have (got) an idea いい考えがありま
す íi kañgaè ga arímasù
have you any more money? もっとお
金がありませんか móttò o-káne gà arímaseñ ká
2 (take: food) 食べる tabérù; (: drink) 飲
む nómù
to have breakfast/lunch/dinner 朝食
〔昼食, 夕食〕を食べる chōshoku〔chū-
shoku, yūshoku〕wò tabérù
to have a drink 何かを飲む nánìka wo
nómù
to have a cigarette タバコを吸う tabáko wo suù
3 (receive, obtain etc) 受ける ukérù, 手
に入れる té ni irérù
may I have your address? ご住所を
教えて頂けますか go-jūsho wò oshíete
itadakemasù ká
you can have it for $5 5ドルでそれを
譲ります gódòru de soré wò yuzúrimasù
I must have it by tomorrow どうして
も明日までにそれをもらいたいのです
dōshite mò ashíta made nì soré wò
moráitai no desù
to have a baby 子供を産む kodómo wo
umù
4 (maintain, allow) 主張する shuchō suru, 許す yurúsù
he will have it that he is right 彼は
自分が正しいと主張している kárè wa ji-
búñ gà tadáshiì to shuchō shite irù
I won't have it/this nonsense! それ
〔こんなばかげた事〕は許せません soré
〔koñna bakageta kotò〕wà yurúsemaseñ
we can't have that そんな事は許せま
せん soñna kotò wa yurúsemaseñ

5: *to have something done* ...をさせる ...wò sasérù, ...をしてもらう ...wò shité mòraù

to have one's hair cut 散髪をしてもらう sañpatsu wò shité moraù

to have a house built 家を建てる ié wò tatérù

to have someone do something ...に ...をさせる ...ní ...wò sasérù

he soon had them all laughing/working まもなく彼は皆を笑わせて〔働かせて〕いた ma mó nàku kárè wa miná wò waráwasete〔határakasete〕ità

6 (experience, suffer) 経験する keíken suru

to have a cold 風邪を引いている kazé wò hiíte irù

to have (the) flu 感冒にかかっている kañbō nì kakátte irù

she had her bag stolen/her arm broken 彼女はハンドバッグを盗まれた〔腕を折った〕 kánòjo wa hañdobaggù wo nusúmaretà〔udé wo ottà〕

to have an operation 手術を受ける shújùtsu wo ukérù

7 (+ noun: take, hold etc) ...する ... suru

to have a swim/walk/bath/rest 泳ぐ〔散歩する, 風呂に入る, ひと休みする〕 oyógù〔sañpo suru, fúrò ni háîru, hitóyàsumi suru〕

let's have a look 見てみましょう mítè mimashō

to have a meeting/party 会議〔パーティ〕を開く káîgi〔pâtî〕wo hirákù

let me have a try 私に試させて下さい watákushi nì tamésasete kudasaì

8 (*inf*: dupe) だます damásu

he's been had 彼はだまされた kárè wa damásaretà

haven [hei'vən] *n* (harbor) 港 mináto; (safe place) 避難所 hináñjo

haven't [hæv'ənt] = **have not**

have out *vt*: *to have it out with someone* (settle a problem etc) ...と決着をつける ...tò ketcháku wò tsukérù

haversack [hæv'ə:ræk] *n* (of hiker, soldier) リュックサック ryukkúsakkù

havoc [hæv'ək] *n* (chaos) 混乱 koñran

Hawaii [həwai'ji:] *n* ハワイ háwài

hawk [hɔ:k] *n* タカ taká

hay [hei] *n* 干草 hoshíkusa

hay fever *n* 花粉症 kafúñshō

haystack [hei'stæk] *n* 干草の山 hoshíkusa no yama

haywire [hei'waiə:re] (*inf*) *adj*: *to go haywire* (machine etc) 故障する koshő suru; (plans etc) とんざする tóñza suru

hazard [hæz'ə:rd] *n* (danger) 危険 kikén
♦*vt* (risk: guess, bet etc) やってみる yatté mirù

hazardous [hæz'ə:rdəs] *adj* (dangerous) 危険な kikén na

hazard (warning) lights *npl* (AUT) 非常点滅灯 hijőtenmetsutő

haze [heiz] *n* (of heat, smoke, dust) かすみ kasúmi

hazelnut [hei'zəlnʌt] *n* ヘーゼルナッツ hēzerunattsù

hazy [hei'zi:] *adj* (sky, view) かすんだ kasúnda; (idea, memory) ぼんやりとした boñ·yarî to shita

he [hi:] *pron* (が) kárè wa 〔ga〕

he who ... ...する人は ...surú hitò wa

head [hed] *n* (ANAT, mind) 頭 atáma; (of table) 上席 jốseki; (of queue) 先頭 señtō; (of company, organization) 最高責任者 saíkōsekininsha; (of school) 校長 kőchō
♦*vt* (list, queue) ...の先頭にある〔いる〕 ...no señtō ni arù〔irù〕; (group, company) 取仕切る toríshikirù

heads (or tails) 表か〔裏か〕 omôte kà〔urá kà〕

head first (fall) 真っ逆様に massákàsama ni; (rush) 向こう見ずに mukő mîzu ni

head over heels (in love) ぞっこん zokkőn

to head a ball ボールをヘディングで飛ばす bőru wo hedíñgu de tobásu

headache [hed'eik] *n* 頭痛 zutsű

headdress [hed'dres] (*BRIT*) *n* (of bride) ヘッドドレス heddődoresù

head for *vt fus* (place) ...に向かう ...ni mukáù; (disaster) ...を招く ...wo manékù

heading [hed'iŋ] *n* (of chapter, article)

表題 hyódai, タイトル táitoru

headlamp [hed'læmp] (*BRIT*) *n* = **headlight**

headland [hed'lænd] *n* 岬 misáki

headlight [hed'lait] *n* ヘッドライト heddóraìto

headline [hed'lain] *n* (PRESS, TV) 見出し midáshi

headlong [hed'lɔ:ŋ] *adv* (fall) 真っ逆様に massákàsama ni; (rush) 向こう見ずに mukó mízu ni

headmaster [hed'mæs'tə:r] *n* 校長 kóchō ◇男性の場合 dańsei nò baái

headmistress [hed'mis'tris] *n* 校長 kóchō ◇女性の場合 joséi nò baái

head office *n* (of company etc) 本社 hóñsha

head-on [hed'ɑ:n'] *adj* (collision, confrontation) 正面の shómen no

headphones [hed'founz] *npl* ヘッドホン heddóhòn

headquarters [hed'kwɔ:rtə:rz] *npl* (of company, organization) 本部 hóñbu; (MIL) 司令部 shiréìbu

headrest [hed'rest] *n* (AUT) ヘッドレスト heddórèsuto

headroom [hed'ru:m] *n* (in car) 天井の高さ teñjō no takàsa; (under bridge) 通行可能な高さ tsúkōkanò na takàsa

headscarf [hed'skɑ:rf] *n* スカーフ sukáfù

headstrong [hed'strɔ:ŋ] *adj* (determined) 強情な gójō na

head waiter *n* (in restaurant) 給仕頭 kyújigashira

headway [hed'wei] *n*: **to make headway** 進歩する shíñpo suru

headwind [hed'wind] *n* 向かい風 mukáikaze

heady [hed'i:] *adj* (experience, time) 陶酔の tósui no; (drink, atmosphere) 酔わせる yowáserù

heal [hi:l] *vt* (injury, patient) 治す naósù
◆*vi* (injury, damage) 治る naórù

health [helθ] *n* (condition: *also* MED) 健康状態 keńkōjòtai; (good health) 健康 keńkō

health food *n* 健康食品 keńkōshokùhin

Health Service (*BRIT*) *n*: **the Health Service** 公共衛生機構 kókyōeiseikikō

healthy [hel'θi:] *adj* (person, appetite etc) 健康な keńkō na; (air, walk) 健康に良い keńkō ni yoì; (economy) 健全な keńzen na; (profit etc) 大いなる ói naru

heap [hi:p] *n* (pile: of clothes, papers, sand etc) 山 yamá
◆*vt* (stones, sand etc): **to heap (up)** 積み上げる tsumíagerù

to heap something with (plate) ...に...を山盛りする ...ni ...wo yamámori suru; (sink, table etc) ...に...を山積みする ...ni ...wo yamázumi suru

to heap something on (food) ...を...に山盛りする ...wo ...ni yamámori suru; (books etc) ...を...に山積みする ...wo ...ni yamázumi suru

heaps of (*inf*: time, money, work etc) 一杯の ippái no

hear [hi:r] (*pt, pp* **heard**) *vt* (sound, voice etc) ...を聞く ...wo kikú, ...が聞える ...ga kikóeru; (news, information) ...を聞く ...wo kikú, ...で聞いて知る ...de kiíte shirú; (LAW: case) 審理する shíñri suru

to hear about (event, person) ...の事を聞く ...no kotó wo kikú

to hear from someone ...から連絡を受ける ...kara reńraku wo ukérù

heard [hə:rd] *pt, pp of* **hear**

hearing [hi:'riŋ] *n* (sense) 聴覚 chókaku; (of facts, witnesses etc) 聴聞会 chómoñkai

hearing aid *n* 補聴器 hochóki

hearsay [hi:r'sei] *n* (rumor) うわさ uwása

hearse [hə:rs] *n* 霊きゅう車 reíkyūsha

heart [hɑ:rt] *n* (ANAT) 心臓 shiñzō; (*fig*: emotions, character) 心 kokórò; (of problem) 核心 kakúshin; (of city) 中心部 chúshiñbu; (of lettuce) しん shíñ; (shape) ハート形 hátogata

to lose heart (courage) 落胆する rakútan suru

to take heart (courage) 勇気を出す yúki wò dásù

at heart (basically) 根は... né wà ...

by heart (learn, know) 暗記で ańki de

heart attack n (MED) 心臓発作 shiñzō-hossà

heartbeat [haːrtˈbiːt] n 心拍 shiñpaku

heartbreaking [haːrtˈbreikiŋ] adj (news, story) 悲痛な hitsū na

heartbroken [haːrtˈbroukən] adj: **to be heartbroken** 悲嘆に暮れている hitán ni kurete irù

heartburn [haːrtˈbəːrn] n (indigestion) 胸焼け muñéyake

heart failure n (MED) 心不全 shiñfûzen

heartfelt [haːrtˈfelt] adj (prayer, wish) 心からの kokórò kara no

hearth [haːrθ] n (fireplace) 炉床 roshō

heartland [haːrtˈlænd] n (of country, region) 中心地 chūshiñchi

heartless [haːrtˈlis] adj (person, attitude) 非情な hijố na

hearts [haːrts] npl (CARDS) ハート hấto

hearty [haːrˈtiː] adj (person) 明朗な meíröß na; (laugh) 大きな őkina; (appetite) お盛なő sei na; (welcome) 熱烈な netsúretsu na; (dislike) 絶対的な zettáiteki na; (support) 心からの kokórò kara no

heat [hiːt] n (warmth) 暑さ atsùsa; (temperature) 温度 óñdo; (excitement) 熱気 nekkî; (SPORT: also: **qualifying heat**) 予選 yosén

♦vt (water) 沸かす wákasù; (food) ...に火を通す ...ni hǐ wò tốsu; (room, house) 暖める atátamerù

heated [hiːtid] adj (pool) 温水の oñsui no; (room etc) 暖房した dañbō shita; (argument) 激しい hagéshiˀ

heater [hiːtəːr] n ヒーター hǐtā

heath [hiːθ] (BRIT) n 荒野 aréno

heathen [hiːˈðən] n (REL) 異教徒 ikyốto

heather [heˈðəːr] n エリカ érìka, ヒース hǐsù

heating [hiːtiŋ] n (system, equipment) 暖房 dáñbō

heatstroke [hiːtˈstrouk] n (MED) 熱射病 nesshábyō

heat up vi (water, room) 暖まる atátamarù

♦vt (food, water, room) 暖める atátamerù

heatwave [hiːtˈweiv] n 熱波 néppà

heave [hiːv] vt (pull) 強く引く tsúyoku hikú; (push) 強く押す tsúyoku osú; (lift) ぐいと持上げる guí to mochíagerù

♦vi (vomit) 吐く hákù; (feel sick) むかつく mukátsukù

♦n (of chest) あえぎ aégi; (of stomach) むかつき mukátsuki

to heave a sigh ため息をつく taméikî wo tsukú

his chest was heaving 彼はあえいでいた kárè wa aéide itá

heaven [hevˈən] n (REL: also fig) 天国 téñgoku

heavenly [hevˈənliː] adj (REL) 天からの téñ kara no; (fig: day, place) 素晴らしい subárashiˀ

heavily [hevˈiliː] adv (land, fall) どしんと dóshin to; (drink, smoke) 大量に tairyő ni; (sleep) ぐっすりと gussúrî to; (sigh) 深く fukákù; (depend, rely) すっかり sukkárî

heavy [hevˈiː] adj (person, load, responsibility) 重い omóì; (clothes) 厚い atsúi; (rain, snow) 激しい hagéshiˀ; (of person: build, frame) がっしりした gasshírî shita; (blow) 強い tsúyoì; (breathing) 荒い aráì; (sleep) 深い fukáì; (schedule, week) 過密な kamîtsu na; (work) きつい kitsúi; (weather) 蒸し暑い mushíatsuˀ; (food, meal) もたれる motárerù

a heavy drinker 飲兵衛 nốñbē

a heavy smoker ヘビースモーカー hebísumôkā

heavy goods vehicle (BRIT) n 大型トラック őgatatoràkku

heavyweight [hevˈiːweit] n (SPORT) ヘビー級選手 hebíkyūseñshu

Hebrew [hiːˈbruː] adj ヘブライの hebúrài no; (LING) ヘブライ語の hebúraigo no

♦n (LING) ヘブライ語 hebúraigo

Hebrides [hebˈridiːz] npl: **the Hebrides** ヘブリディーズ諸島 hebúridizushotồ

heckle [hekˈəl] vt (speaker, performer) 野次る yajírù

hectic [hekˈtik] adj (event, week) やたらに忙しい yatára ni isogashiˀ

he'd [hiːd] = **he would**; **he had**

hedge [hedʒ] n (in garden, on roadside)

生け垣 ikégàki
♦vi (stall) あいまいな態度を取る aímai nà táido wo tórù
to hedge one's bets (fig) 失敗に備える shippái nì sonáerù

hedgehog [hedʒ'hɑːg] n ハリネズミ harínezùmi

heed [hiːd] vt (also: **take heed of**: advice, warning) 聞き入れる kikíirerù

heedless [hiːd'lis] adj: **heedless (of)** (...を) 無視して (...wo) múshì shité

heel [hiːl] n (of foot, shoe) かかと kakáto
♦vt: **to heel shoes** 靴のかかとを修理する kutsú nò kakáto wò shúri suru

hefty [hef'tiː] adj (person) がっしりした gasshírì shita; (parcel etc) 大きくて重い ōkikute omóì; (profit) 相当な sótō na

heifer [hef'əːr] n 若い雌ウシ wakáì méùshi ◇まだ子を生んだ事のない物を指す mádà ko wo uñda kotò no náì monó wo sásù

height [hait] n (of tree, building, mountain) 高さ takása; (of person) 身長 shíñchō; (of plane) 高度 kốdo; (high ground) 高地 kōchì; (fig: of powers) 絶頂期 zetchốki; (: of season) 真っ最中 massáìchū; (: of luxury, stupidity) 極み kiwámi

heighten [hait'ən] vt (fears, uncertainty) 高める takámerù

heir [eːr] n (to throne) 継承者 keíshōshà; (to fortune) 相続人 sốzokuniñ

heiress [eːr'is] n 大遺産の相続人 daísan no sốzokuniñ ◇女性について言う joséi ni tsuité iú

heirloom [eːr'luːm] n 家宝 kahố

held [held] pt, pp of **hold**

helicopter [hel'əkɑːptəːr] n (AVIAT) ヘリコプター heríkopùtā

heliport [hel'əpɔːrt] n (AVIAT) ヘリポート herípòto

helium [hiː'liːəm] n ヘリウム heríùmu

he'll [hiːl] = **he will, he shall**

hell [hel] n (life, situation: also REL) 地獄 jigóku
hell! (inf) 畜生！ chikúshò!, くそ！ kusó!

hellish [hel'iʃ] (inf) adj (traffic, weather, life etc) 地獄の様な jigóku no yố na

hello [helou'] excl (as greeting) や あ yá, 今日 は koñnichi wa; (to attract attention) おい ối; (on telephone) もしもし mōshìmoshi; (expressing surprise) お や oyá

helm [helm] n (NAUT: stick) かじ棒 kajíbồ, チラー chirá; (: wheel) だ輪 daríñ

helmet [hel'mit] n (gen) ヘルメット herúmettò

help [help] n (assistance, aid) 助け tasúke, 手伝い tetsúdaì; (charwoman) お手伝いさん o-tétsùdaisan
♦vt (person) 助ける tasúkerù, 手伝う tétsùdau; (situation) ...に役に立つ ...ni yakú ni tatsù
help! 助けてくれ！ tasúketè kuré!
help yourself (to) (...を) 自由に取って下さい (...wo) jiyú ni tottè kudásai
he can't help it 彼はそうせざるを得ない kárè wa số sezarù wo énài

helper [hel'pəːr] n (assistant) 助手 joshú, アシスタント ashísùtanto

helpful [help'fəl] adj (person, advice, suggestion etc) 役に立つ yakú ni tatsù

helping [hel'piŋ] n (of food) 一盛り hitómori
a second helping お代り o-káwarì

helpless [help'lis] adj (incapable) 何 も できない naní mo dekínaì; (defenceless) 無防備の mubóbi no

hem [hem] n (of skirt, dress) すそ susó
♦vt (skirt, dress etc) ...のすそ縫いをする ...no susónui wo suru

hem in vt 取囲む toríkakomù

hemisphere [hem'isfiːr] n 半球 hañkyū

hemorrhage [hem'əːridʒ] (BRIT **haemorrhage**) n 出血 shukkétsu

hemorrhoids [hem'əːroidz] (BRIT **haemorrhoids**) npl じ ji

hen [hen] n (female chicken) メンドリ meñdori; (female bird) 雌の鳥 mesú no torí

hence [hens] adv (therefore) 従 っ て shitágattè
2 years hence 今から2年先 ímà kara níneñ saki

henceforth [hens'fɔːrθ] adv (from now on) 今後 kốñgo; (from that time on) その

後 sonó go

henchman [hentʃ'mən] (*pej*: *pl* **henchmen**) *n* (of gangster, tyrant) 手下 teshíta, 子分 kóbūn

henpecked [hen'pekt] *adj* (husband) 妻のしりに敷かれた tsúmā no shirí ni shikaretà

hepatitis [hepətai'tis] *n* (MED) 肝炎 kánen

her [həːr] *pron* (direct) 彼女を kánòjo wo; (indirect) 彼女に kánòjo ni
♦*adj* 彼女の kánòjo no ¶ *see also* **me; my**

herald [heːr'əld] *n* (forerunner) 兆し kizáshi
♦*vt* (event, action) 予告する yokóku suru

heraldry [heːr'əldriː] *n* (study) 紋章学 mońshōgàku; (coat of arms) 紋章 mońshō ◊総称 sōshō

herb [əːrb] *n* (*gen*) ハーブ hābu; (BOT, MED) 薬草 yakúsō; (CULIN) 香草 kōsō

herd [həːrd] *n* (of cattle, goats, zebra etc) 群れ murē

here [hiːr] *adv* (this place): *she left here yesterday* 彼女は昨日ここを出ました kanòjo wa kínō kokó wò demáshìta; (beside me): *I have it here* ここに持っています kokó ni mottè imásū; (at this point): *here he stopped reading ...* その時彼は読むのをやめて... sonó tokì kárè wa yómù no wo yaméte ...
here! (I'm present) はい！ háî!; (take this) はいどうぞ háî dōzo
here is/are はい、...です háî, ...désù
here she is! 彼女はここにいました！ kanòjo wa kokó ni imáshìta!

hereafter [hiːræf'təːr] *adv* (in the future) 今後 kóngo

hereby [hiːrbai'] *adv* (in letter) これをもって korē wo mottè

hereditary [həred'iteːriː] *adj* (disease) 先天的な seńtenteki na; (title) 世襲の seshū no

heredity [həred'itiː] *n* (BIO) 遺伝 idén

heresy [heːr'isiː] *n* (opposing belief: *also* REL) 異端 itán

heretic [heːr'itik] *n* 異端者 itánsha

heritage [heːr'itidʒ] *n* (of country, nation) 遺産 isán

hermetically [həːrmet'ikliː] *adv*: *hermetically sealed* 密閉した mippéi shita

hermit [həːr'mit] *n* 隠とん者 iñtoñsha

hernia [həːr'niːə] *n* (MED) 脱腸 datchō

hero [hiː'rou] (*pl* **heroes**) *n* (in book, film) 主人公 shujíñkō, ヒーロー hīrō ◊男性を指す dansei wo sasu; (of battle, struggle) 英雄 eíyū; (idol) アイドル áídoru

heroic [hirou'ik] *adj* (struggle, sacrifice, person) 英雄的な eíyūteki na

heroin [heːr'ouin] *n* ヘロイン heróìn

heroine [heːr'ouin] *n* (in book, film) 女主人公 ofnashujìñkō, ヒロイン hiróìn; (of battle, struggle) 英雄的女性 eíyūtekijosei; (idol) アイドル áídoru

heroism [heːr'ouizəm] *n* (bravery, courage) 勇敢さ yúkansa

heron [heːr'ən] *n* アオサギ aósagi

herring [heːr'iŋ] *n* (fish) ニシン níshìn

hers [həːrz] *pron* 彼女の物 kanòjo no monò ¶ *see also* **mine**

herself [həːrself'] *pron* 彼女自身 kanòjojishìn ¶ *see also* **oneself**

he's [hiːz] = **he is; he has**

hesitant [hez'ətənt] *adj* (smile, reaction) ためらいがちな taméraigachi na

hesitate [hez'əteit] *vi* (pause) ためらう taméraù; (be unwilling) 後込みする shirígomì suru

hesitation [hezətei'ʃən] *n* (pause) ためらい tamérai; (unwillingness) 後込み shirígomì

heterosexual [hetəːrəsek'ʃuːəl] *adj* (person, relationship) 異性愛の iséiai no

hew [hjuː] *vt* (stone, wood) 刻む kizámu

hexagonal [heksæg'ənəl] *adj* (shape, object) 六角形の rokkákukèi no

heyday [hei'dei] *n*: *the heyday of* ...の全盛時代 ...no zeńseijidài

HGV [eitʃgiːviː'] (*BRIT*) *n abbr* = **heavy goods vehicle**

hi [hai] *excl* (as greeting) やあ yā, 今日は kofnichi wa; (to attract attention) おい óî

hiatus [haiei'təs] *n* (gap: in manuscript etc) 脱落個所 datsúrakukashò; (pause)

中断 chūdan

hibernate [hai'bərneit] vi (animal) 冬眠
する tōmin suru

hiccough [hik'ʌp] vi しゃっくりする
shákkùri suru

hiccoughs [hik'ʌps] npl しゃっくり
shákkùri

hiccup [hik'ʌp] vi = hiccough

hiccups [hik'ʌps] npl = hiccoughs

hid [hid] pt of hide

hidden [hid'ən] pp of hide

hide [haid] n (skin) 皮 kawá

♦vb (pt hid, pp hidden)

♦vt (person, object, feeling, information)
隠す kakúsù; (obscure: sun, view) 覆い隠
す ōikakusù

♦vi: to hide (from someone) (...に見
つからない様に) 隠れる (...ni mitsúkara-
nai yō ni) kakúrerù

hide-and-seek [haid'ənsi:k'] n (game)
隠れん坊 kakúreñbō

hideaway [haid'əwei] n (retreat) 隠れ家
kakúregà

hideous [hid'i:əs] adj (painting, face) 醜
い miníkuì

hiding [hai'diŋ] n (beating) むち打ち muchíuchi

to be in hiding (concealed) 隠れている
kakúrete irú

hierarchy [hai'ə:rɑ:rki:] n (system of
ranks) 階級制 kaíkyūsei; (people in
power) 幹部 kánbu ◇総称 sōshō

hi-fi [hai'fai'] n ステレオ sutéreo

♦adj (equipment, system) ステレオの sutéreo no

high [hai] adj (gen) 高い takáì; (speed) 速
い hayáì; (wind) 強い tsuyóì; (quality) 上
等な jōtō na; (principles) 崇高な sūkō na

♦adv (climb, aim etc) 高く tákàku

it is 20 m high その高さは20メーター
です sonó takàsa wa nijū mētā desu

high in the air 空高く sórátakaku

highbrow [hai'brau] adj (intellectual) 知
的な chitéki na

highchair [hai'tʃe:r] n (for baby) ベビー
チェア bebíchèa

higher education [hai'ə:r-] n 高等教育
kōtōkyōìku

high-handed [hai'hæn'did] adj (decision, rejection) 横暴な ōbō na

high-heeled [hai'hi:ld] adj (shoe) ハイヒ
ールの haíhīru no

high jump n (SPORT) 走り高飛び ha-
shíritakátobi

highlands [hai'ləndz] npl: the Highlands スコットランド高地地方 sukótto-
rañdo kōchichihō

highlight [hai'lait] n (fig: of event) 山場
yamába, ハイライト haíraìto; (of news
etc) 要点 yōten, ハイライト haíraìto; (in
hair) 光る部分 hikárù búbùn, ハイライト
haíraìto

♦vt (problem, need) ...に焦点を合せる
...ni shōten wò awáserù

highly [hai'li:] adv (critical, confidential)
非常に hijō ni; (a lot): to speak highly
of ...をほめる ...wo homérù

to think highly of ...を高く評価する
...wo tákàku hyōka suru

highly paid 高給取りの kōkyūtòri no

highly strung (BRIT) adj = high-
strung

highness [hai'nis] n: Her (or His)
Highness 陛下 héìka

high-pitched [hai'pitʃt'] adj (voice,
tone, whine) 調子の高い chōshi no tákaì

high-rise block [hai'raiz'-] n 摩天楼
matéñrō

high school n (US: for 14-18 year-olds)
高等学校 kōtōgakkō, ハイスクール haí-
sùkūru; (BRIT: for 11-18 year-olds) 総合
中等学校 sōgōchūtōgakkō

high season (BRIT) n 最盛期 saiseiki,
シーズン shīzun

high street (BRIT) n 本通り hoñdōri

high-strung [hai'strʌŋ'] (US) adj 神経
質な shiñkeishitsu na

highway [hai'wei] n 幹線道路 kañsendōro, ハイウエー haíwē

Highway Code (BRIT) n 道路交通法
dōrokōtsūhō

hijack [hai'dʒæk] vt (plane, bus) 乗っ取
る nottórù, ハイジャックする haíjakkù
suru

hijacker [hai'dʒækə:r] n 乗っ取り犯 not-
tórihañ

hike [haik] *vi* (go walking) ハイキングする haíkingu suru
♦*n* (walk) ハイキング háikingu

hiker [hai'kəːr] *n* ハイカー haíkā

hilarious [hileːr'iːəs] *adj* (account, adventure) こっけいな kokkéi na

hill [hil] *n* (small) 丘 okā; (fairly high) 山 yamá; (slope) 坂 saká

hillside [hil'said] *n* 丘の斜面 okā no shamén

hilly [hil'iː] *adj* 丘の多い okā no ōi
a hilly area 丘陵地帯 kyúryōchitái

hilt [hilt] *n* (of sword, knife) 柄 e
to the hilt (fig: support) とことんまで tokóton made

him [him] *pron* (direct) 彼を kárè wo; (indirect) 彼に kárè ni ¶ *see also* **me**

himself [himself'] *pron* 彼自身 kárèjishin ¶ *see also* **oneself**

hind [haind] *adj* (legs, quarters) 後ろの ushíro no

hinder [hin'dəːr] *vt* (progress, movement) 妨げる samátagerù

hindrance [hin'drəns] *n* 邪魔 jamá

hindsight [haind'sait] *n*: *with hindsight* 後になってみると átò ni nátte mirú to

Hindu [hin'duː] *adj* ヒンズーの hiñzū no

hinge [hindʒ] *n* (on door) ちょうつがい chótsugai
♦*vi* (fig): *to hinge on* ...による ...ni yorú

hint [hint] *n* (suggestion) 暗示 añji, ヒント híñto; (advice) 勧め susúme, 提言 teígen; (sign, glimmer) 兆し kizáshi
♦*vt*: *to hint that* (suggest) ...だとほのめかす ...da to honómekasù
♦*vi*: *to hint at* (suggest) ほのめかす honómekasù

hip [hip] *n* (ANAT) 腰 koshí, ヒップ híppù

hippopotamus [hipəpɑt'əməs] (*pl* **hippopotamuses** *or* **hippopotami**) *n* カバ kábà

hire [haiəːr] *vt* (BRIT: car, equipment, hall) 賃借りする chíñgari suru; (worker) 雇う yatóù
♦*n* (BRIT: of car, hall etc) 賃借り chíñgari

for hire (taxi, boat) 賃貸し用の chíñga-shiyō no

hire purchase (BRIT) *n* 分割払い購入 buñkatsubaraikōnyù

his [hiz] *pron* 彼の物 kárè no monó
♦*adj* 彼の kárè no ¶ *see also* **my; mine**

hiss [his] *vi* (snake, gas, roasting meat) しゅーっと言う shūttò iú; (person, audience) しーっと野次る shíttò yajírù

historian [histɔːr'iːən] *n* 歴史学者 rekíshigakushā

historic(al) [histɔːr'ik(əl)] *adj* (event, person) 歴史上の rekíshijō no, 歴史的な rekíshiteki na; (novel, film) 歴史に基づく rekíshi ni motózukù

history [his'təːriː] *n* (of town, country, person: *also* SCOL) 歴史 rekíshi

hit [hit] (*pt*, *pp* **hit**) *vt* (strike: person, thing) 打つ utsú, たたく tatáku; (reach: target) ...に当る ...ni atárù; (collide with: car) ...にぶつかる ...ni butsúkarù; (affect: person, services, event etc) ...に打撃を与える ...ni dagéki wò atáerù
♦*n* (knock) 打撃 dagéki; (success: play, film, song) 大当り ōatári, ヒット híttò
to hit it off with someone ...と意気投合する ...to ríkitōgō suru

hit-and-run driver [hit'ənrʌn'-] *n* ひき逃げ運転者 hikínige unteñsha

hitch [hitʃ] *vt* (fasten) つなぐ tsunágù; (*also*: **hitch up**: trousers, skirt) 引上げる hikíagerù
♦*n* (difficulty) 問題 mofídai
to hitch a lift ヒッチハイクをする hitchíhaiku wo suru

hitch-hike [hitʃ'haik] *vi* ヒッチハイクをする hitchíhaiku wo suru

hitch-hiker [hitʃ'haikəːr] *n* ヒッチハイクをする人 hitchíhaiku wo suru hitó

hi-tech [hai'tek'] *adj* ハイテクの haíteku no
♦*n* ハイテク haíteku

hitherto [hið'əːrtuː] *adv* (until now) 今まで imá madè

hive [haiv] *n* (of bees) ミツバチの巣箱 mitsúbàchi no súbàko

hive off (*inf*) *vt* (company) ...の一部を切放す ...no ichíbu wo kiríhanasù

HMS [eitʃemes'] *abbr* (= *Her/His Majesty's Ship*) 軍艦...号 guñkan ...gō ◇英国海軍の軍艦の名前の前に付ける eîkoku-kaigùn no guñkan no namáe no máe ni tsukérù

hoard [hɔːrd] *n* (of food etc) 買いだめ kaídame; (of money, treasure) 蓄え takúwaè

♦*vt* (food etc) 買いだめする kaídamesuru

hoarding [hɔːr'diŋ] (*BRIT*) *n* (for posters) 掲示板 keíjiban

hoarfrost [hɔːr'frɑːst] *n* (on ground) 霜 shimó

hoarse [hɔːrs] *adj* (voice) しわがれた shiwágaretà

hoax [houks] *n* (trick) いんちき îñchiki, いかさま ikásama

hob [hɑːb] *n* (of cooker, stove) レンジの上部 reñji no jòbu

hobble [hɑːb'əl] *vi* (limp) びっこを引く bíkkò wo hikú

hobby [hɑːb'iː] *n* (pastime) 趣味 shúmì

hobby-horse [hɑːb'iːhɔːrs] *n* (*fig*: favorite topic) 十八番の話題 oháko nò wadái

hobo [hou'bou] (*US*) *n* (tramp) ルンペン rúñpen

hockey [hɑːk'iː] *n* (game) ホッケー hőkkè

hoe [hou] *n* (tool) くわ kuwá, ホー hồ

hog [hɔːg] *n* (pig) ブタ butá ◇去勢した雄ブタを指す kyoséi shita osubùta wo sasu

♦*vt* (*fig*: road, telephone etc) 独り占めにする hitórijime nì suru

to go the whole hog とことんまでやる tokóton made yarú

hoist [hɔist] *n* (apparatus) 起重機 kijūkì, クレーン kurén

♦*vt* (heavy object) 引上げる hikíagerù; (flag) 掲げる kakágerù; (sail) 張る harú

hold [hould] (*pt, pp* **held**) *vt* (bag, umbrella, someone's hand etc) 持つ mótsù; (contain: subj: room, box etc) ...に ...が入っている ...ni ...ga haîtte iru; (have: power, qualification, opinion) ...を持っている ...wo mótte iru, ...がある ...ga árù; (meeting) 開く hirákù; (detain: prisoner,

hostage) 監禁する kañkin suru; (consider): *to hold someone responsible/liable etc* ...の責任と見なす ...no sekínin tò minásù; (keep in certain position): *to hold one's head up* 頭を上げる atáma wò agérù

♦*vi* (withstand pressure) 持ちこたえる mochíkotaeru; (be valid) 当てはまる atéhamarù

♦*n* (grasp) 握り nígìri; (of ship) 船倉 señsō; (of plane) 貨物室 kamótsushitsu; (control): *to have a hold over* ...の急所を握っている ...no kyūsho wò nigītte irú

to hold a conversation with ...と話し合う ...to hanáshiaù

hold the line! (TEL) 少々お待ち下さい shōshō o-máchi kudasai

hold on! ちょっと待って chótto mátte

to hold one's own (*fig*) 引けを取らない hiké wò toránaì, 負けない makénaì

to catch/get (a) hold of ...に捕まる ...ni tsukámarù

holdall [hould'ɔːl] (*BRIT*) *n* 合切袋 gas-sáibukùro

hold back *vt* (person, thing) 制止する seíshi suru; (thing, emotion) 押さえる osáerù; (secret, information) 隠す kakúsù

hold down *vt* (person) 押さえつける o-sáetsukerù; (job) ...についている ...ni tsú-īte iru

holder [hould'əːr] *n* (container) 入れ物 i-rémono, ケース kḕsu, ホールダー hőrudā; (of ticket, record, title) 保持者 hojísha; (of office) 在職者 zaíshokusha

holding [hould'diŋ] *n* (share) 持株 mochíkabu; (small farm) 小作農地 kosákunōchi

hold off *vt* (enemy) ...に持ちこたえる ...ni mochítkotaerù

hold on *vi* (hang on) 捕まる tsukámarù; (wait) 待つ mátsù

hold on to *vt fus* (for support) ...に捕まる ...ni tsukámarù; (keep) 預かる azúkarù

hold out *vt* (hand) 差伸べる sashínoberù; (hope, prospect) 持たせる motáserù

♦*vi* (resist) 抵抗する teíkō suru

hold up *vt* (raise) 上げる agérù; (support) 支える sasáerù; (delay) 遅らせる o-kúraserù; (rob: person, bank) 武器を突付けて...から金を奪う búkì wo tsukítsuke-tè ...kara kané wò ubáù

hold-up [hould'ʌp] *n* (robbery) 強盗 gṓtō; (delay) 遅れ okúre; (*BRIT*: in traffic) 渋滞 jútai

hole [houl] *n* 穴 aná
♦*vt* (ship, building etc) ...に穴を開ける ...ni aná wò akérù

holiday [ha:l'idei] *n* (*BRIT*: vacation) 休暇 kyúka; (day off) 休暇の日 kyúka no hi; (public holiday) 祝日 shukújitsu
on holiday 休暇中 kyúkachū

holiday camp (*BRIT*) *n* (*also:* **holiday centre**) 休暇村 kyúkamùra

holiday-maker [ha:l'ideimeikə:r] *n* (*BRIT*) 行楽客 kṓrakukyàku

holiday resort *n* 行楽地 kṓrakuchì, リゾート rizṓtò

holiness [hou'li:nis] *n* (of shrine, person) 神聖さ shifiseisa

Holland [ha:l'ənd] *n* オランダ oráñda

hollow [ha:l'ou] *adj* (container) 空っぽの karáppo no; (log, tree) うろのある urō no arù; (cheeks, eyes) くぼんだ kubóñda; (laugh) わざとらしい wazátorashiì; (claim) 根拠のない kofikyo no naì; (sound) うつろな utsúro na
♦*n* (in ground) くぼみ kubómi
♦*vt*: *to hollow out* (excavate) がらんどうにする garándō ni surù

holly [ha:l'i:] *n* (tree, leaves) ヒイラギ hiíragi

holocaust [ha:l'əkɔ:st] *n* 大虐殺 daígyakùsatsu

hologram [hou'ləgræm] *n* ホログラム horógurāmu

holster [houl'stə:r] *n* (for pistol) ホルスター horúsutā

holy [hou'li:] *adj* (picture, place, person) 神聖な shifisei na
holy water 聖水 seísui

homage [ha:m'idʒ] *n* (honor, respect) 敬意 kéìi
to pay homage to (hero, idol) ...に敬意を表す ...ni kéìi wo aráwasù

home [houm] *n* (house) 家 ié, 住い sumáì;

(area, country) 故郷 kokyṓ; (institution) 収容施設 shūyōshisètsu
♦*cpd* (domestic) 家庭の katéi no; (ECON, POL) 国内の kokúnài no; (SPORT: team, game) 地元の jimóto no
♦*adv* (go, come, travel etc) 家に ié ni
at home (in house) 家に〔で〕ié ni 〔de〕; (in country) 本国に〔で〕hóñgoku ni 〔de〕; (in situation) ...に通じて ...ni tsújite
make yourself at home どうぞお楽にdṓzo o-ráku ni
to drive something home (nail etc) ...を打込む ...wo uchíkomù; (*fig*: point etc) ...を強調する ...wo kyṓchō suru

home address *n* 自宅の住所 jitáku no jùsho

home computer *n* パーソナルコンピュータ pásonarukonpyùta, パソコン pasókon

homeland [houm'lænd] *n* 母国 bókòku

homeless [houm'lis] *adj* (family, refugee) 家のない ié no naì

homely [houm'li:] *adj* (simple, plain) 素朴な sobóku na; (*US*: not attractive: person) 不器量な bukíryō na

home-made [houm'meid'] *adj* (bread, bomb) 手製の teséi no, 自家製の jikásei no

Home Office (*BRIT*) *n* 内務省 naímushō

homeopathy [houmi:a:p'əθi:] (*BRIT* **homœopathy**) *n* (MED) ホメオパシー homéopashī

home rule *n* (POL) 自治権 jichíkèn

Home Secretary (*BRIT*) *n* 内務大臣 naímudaìjin

homesick [houm'sik] *adj* ホームシックの hōmushikkù no

hometown [houmtaun'] *n* 故郷 kokyṓ

homeward [houm'wə:rd] *adj* (journey) 家に帰る ié ni kaerù

homework [houm'wə:rk] *n* (SCOL) 宿題 shukúdai

homicide [ha:m'isaid] (*US*) *n* 殺人 satsújin

homoeopathy [houmi:a:p'əθi:] (*BRIT*) *n* = **homeopathy**

homogeneous [houmədʒi:'ni:əs] *adj*

(group, class) 均質の kínshitsu no

homosexual [houməsek'ʃuəl] *adj* (person, relationship: *gen*) 同性愛の dóseiai no; (man) ホモの hómò no; (woman) レズの rézù no
◆*n* (man) 同性愛者 dóseiaishà, ホモ hómò; (woman) 同姓愛者 dóseiaishà, レズ rézù

honest [ɑ:n'ist] *adj* (truthful, trustworthy) 正直な shōjiki na; (sincere) 率直な sotchoku na

honestly [ɑ:n'istli:] *adv* (truthfully) 正直に shōjiki ni; (sincerely, frankly) 率直に sotchóku ni

honesty [ɑ:n'isti:] *n* (truthfulness) 正直 shōjiki; (sincerity) 率直さ sotchókusa

honey [hʌn'i:] *n* (food) はちみつ hachímitsu

honeycomb [hʌn'i:koum] *n* (of bees) ミツバチの巣 mitsúbàchi no su

honeymoon [hʌn'i:mu:n] *n* (holiday, trip) 新婚旅行 shiñkonryokò, ハネムーン hanémùn

honeysuckle [hʌn'i:sʌkəl] *n* (BOT) スイカズラ suíkazùra

honk [hɑ:ŋk] *vi* (AUT: horn) 鳴らす narásu

honorary [ɑ:n'ə:re:ri:] *adj* (unpaid: job, secretary) 無給の mukyū no; (title, degree) 名誉の meíyo no

honor [ɑ:n'ə:r] (*BRIT* **honour**) *vt* (hero, author) ほめたたえる hométataerù; (commitment, promise) 守る mamórù
◆*n* (pride, self-respect) 名誉 meíyo; (tribute, distinction) 光栄 kóei

honorable [ɑ:n'ə:rəbəl] *adj* (person, action, defeat) 名誉ある meíyo aru

honors degree [ɑ:n'ə:rz-] *n* (SCOL) 専門学士号 señmongakushigō

hood [hud] *n* (of coat, cooker etc) フード fùdo; (*US*: AUT: engine cover) ボンネット boñnettò; (*BRIT*: AUT: folding roof) 折畳み式トップ orítatamishiki toppù

hoodlum [hu:d'ləm] *n* (thug) ごろつき gorótsuki, 暴力団員 bóryokudan-ìn

hoodwink [hud'wiŋk] *vt* (con, fool) だます damásù

hoof [huf] (*pl* **hooves**) *n* ひずめ hizúme

hook [huk] *n* (for coats, curtains etc) かぎ kagí, フック fúkkù; (on dress) ホック hókkù; (*also*: **fishing hook**) 釣針 tsuríbàri
◆*vt* (fasten) 留める tomérù; (fish) 釣る tsurú

hooligan [hu:'ligən] *n* ちんぴら chíñpira

hoop [hu:p] *n* (ring) 輪 wá

hooray [hərei'] *excl* = **hurrah, hurray**

hoot [hu:t] *vi* (AUT: horn) クラクションを鳴らす kurákùshon wo narásù; (siren) 鳴る narú; (owl) ほーほーと鳴く hōhō nakú

hooter [hu:'tər] *n* (*BRIT*: AUT) クラクション kurákùshon, ホーン hòn; (NAUT, factory) 警報機 keíhōkì

hoover [hu:'və:r] ® (*BRIT*) *n* (vacuum cleaner) (真空) 掃除機 (shiñkū)sōjikì
◆*vt* (carpet) ...に掃除機を掛ける ...ni sōjikì wo kakérù

hooves [huvz] *npl* of **hoof**

hop [hɑ:p] *vi* (on one foot) 片足で跳ぶ katáashi de tobù; (bird) ぴょんぴょん跳ぶ pyóñpyon tobú

hope [houp] *vt*: **to hope that/to do** ...だと〔する事を〕望む ...da to 〔surú kotò wo〕nozómù
◆*vi* 希望する kibō suru
◆*n* (desire) 望み nozómi; (expectation) 期待 kitái; (aspiration) 希望 kibō
I hope so/not そうだ〔でない〕といいが sō dà 〔de naì〕to í ga

hopeful [houp'fəl] *adj* (person) 楽観的な rakkánteki na; (situation) 見込みのある mikómi no arù

hopefully [houp'fəli:] *adv* (expectantly) 期待して kitái shite; (one hopes) うまくいけば úmàku ikébà

hopeless [houp'lis] *adj* (grief, situation, future) 絶望的な zetsúbōteki na; (person: useless) 無能な munóna

hops [hɑ:ps] *npl* (BOT) ホップ hóppù

horde [hɔ:rd] *n* (of critics, people) 大群 taígun

horizon [hərai'zən] *n* (skyline) 水平線 suíheìsen

horizontal [hɔ:rizɑ:n'təl] *adj* 水平の suíhei no

hormone [hɔːr'moun] n (BIO) ホルモン hórùmon

horn [hɔːrn] n (of animal) 角 tsunó; (material) 角質 kakúshitsu; (MUS: also: **French horn**) ホルン hórùn; (AUT) クラクション kurákùshon, ホーン hőn

hornet [hɔːr'nit] n (insect) スズメバチ suzúmebàchi

horny [hɔːr'niː] (inf) adj (aroused) セックスをしたがっている sékkùsu wo shitágatte irú

horoscope [hɔːr'əskoup] n (ASTROLOGY) 星占い hoshíurànai

horrendous [hɔːren'dəs] adj (crime) 恐ろしい osóroshiì; (error) ショッキングな shókkìngu na

horrible [hɔːr'əbəl] adj (unpleasant: color, food, mess) ひどい hidőì; (terrifying: scream, dream) 恐ろしい osóroshiì

horrid [hɔːr'id] adj (person, place, thing) いやな iyá na

horrify [hɔːr'əfai] vt (appall) ぞっとさせる zóttð saserù

horror [hɔːr'əːr] n (alarm) 恐怖 kyőfù; (abhorrence) 憎悪 zőo; (of battle, warfare) むごたらしさ mugótarashisà

horror film n ホラー映画 horáeìga

hors d'oeuvre [ɔːr dəːrv'] n (CULIN: gen) 前菜 zeńsai; (: Western food) オードブル ődobùru

horse [hɔːrs] n 馬 umá

horseback [hɔːrs'bæk]: **on horseback** adj 乗馬の jőba no
♦adv 馬に乗って umá ni nottè

horse chestnut n (tree) トチノキ tochí no kī; (nut) とちの実 tochí no mì

horseman/woman [hɔːrs'mən/wumən] (pl **horsemen/women**) n (rider) 馬の乗り手 umá nð norìte

horsepower [hɔːrs'pauəːr] n (of engine, car etc) 馬力 barīki

horse-racing [hɔːrs'reisiŋ] n (SPORT) 競馬 keíba

horseradish [hɔːrs'rædiʃ] n (BOT, CULIN) ワサビダイコン wasábidaìkon, セイヨウワサビ seíyōwasàbi

horseshoe [hɔːrs'ʃuː] n てい鉄 teítetsu

horticulture [hɔːr'təkʌltʃəːr] n 園芸 eńgei

hose [houz] n ホース hősu

hosiery [hou'ʒəːriː] n (in shop) 靴下類 kutsúshitarùi

hospice [hɑːs'pis] n (for the dying) ホスピス hósùpisu

hospitable [hɑːspit'əbəl] adj (person) 持て成しの良い moténashi no yoì; (behavior) 手厚い teátsuì

hospital [hɑːs'pitəl] n 病院 byőin

hospitality [hɑːspətæl'itiː] n (of host, welcome) 親切な持て成し shińsetsu nà moténashi

host [houst] n (at party, dinner etc) 主人 shújìn, ホスト hósùto; (TV, RADIO) 司会者 shikáishà; (REL) 御聖体 go-séitai; (large number): **a host of** 多数の tasű no

hostage [hɑːs'tidʒ] n (prisoner) 人質 hitójichi

hostel [hɑːs'təl] n (for homeless etc) 収容所 shúyōjo; (also: **youth hostel**) ユースホステル yúsuhosùteru

hostess [hous'tis] n (at party, dinner etc) 女主人 ofinashujìn, ホステス hősùtesu; (BRIT: air hostess) スチュワーデス suchúwàdesu; (TV, RADIO) （女性）司会者 (joséi)shikáisha

hostile [hɑːs'təl] adj (person, attitude: aggressive) 敵対する tekítai suru, 敵意のある tékì-i no árù; (: unwelcoming): **hostile to** ...に対して排他的な ...ni táishite haítateki na; (conditions, environment) か酷な kakőku na

hostilities [hɑːstil'ətiːz] npl (fighting) 戦闘 sentō

hostility [hɑːstil'ətiː] n (antagonism) 敵対 tekítai, 敵意 tékì-i; (lack of welcome) 排他的態度 haítatekitaìdo; (of conditions, environment) か酷さ kakőkusa

hot [hɑːt] adj (moderately hot) 暖かい atátakaì; (very hot) 熱い atsúi; (weather, room etc) 暑い atsúi; (spicy: food) 辛い karáì; (fierce: temper, contest, argument etc) 激しい hagéshiì

it is hot (weather) 暑い atsúi; (object) 熱い atsúi

I am hot (person) 私は暑い watákushi wà atsúì

he is hot 彼は暑がっている kárè wa atsúgatte irù

hotbed [haːt'bed] *n* (*fig*) 温床 onshō

hot dog *n* (snack) ホットドッグ hottódoggù

hotel [houtel'] *n* ホテル hóteru

hotelier [ɔːteljeiʔ] *n* (owner) ホテルの経営者 hóteru no keíeìsha; (manager) ホテルの支配人 hóteru no shihǎinin

hotheaded [haːt'hedid] *adj* (impetuous) 気の早い kí no hayáì

hothouse [haːt'haus] *n* (BOT) 温室 onshitsu

hot line *n* (POL) ホットライン hottórain

hotly [haːt'liː] *adv* (speak, contest, deny) 激しく hageshikù

hotplate [haːt'pleit] *n* (on cooker) ホットプレート hottópurèto

hot-water bottle [haːtwɔːt'əːr-] *n* 湯たんぽ yutánpo

hound [haund] *vt* (harass, persecute) 迫害する hakúgai suru
♦*n* (dog) 猟犬 ryóken, ハウンド haúndo

hour [auʔəːr] *n* (sixty minutes) 1時間 ichí jikàn; (time) 時間 jíkàn

hourly [auəːr'liː] *adj* (service, rate) 1時間当りの ichí jikan atàri no

house [*n* haus *vb* hauz] *n* (home) 家 ié, うち uchí; (household) 家族 kázòku; (company) 会社 kaísha; (POL) 議院 gíin; (THEATER) 客席 kyakúseki; (dynasty) ...家 ...ké
♦*vt* (person) ...に住宅を与える ...ni jútaku wò atáerù; (collection) 収容する shúyō suru

on the house (*fig*) サービスで sǎbisu de

house arrest *n* (POL, MIL) 軟禁 nańkin

houseboat [haus'bout] *n* 屋形船 yakátabune, ハウスボート haúsubòto ◊住宅用の船を指す jútakuyō no funè wo sásù

housebound [haus'baund] *adj* (invalid) 家から出られない ié kara derárenaì

housebreaking [haus'breikiŋ] *n* 家宅侵入 kátakushinnyū

housecoat [haus'kout] *n* 部屋着 heyági

household [haus'hould] *n* (inhabitants)

家族 kázòku; (home) 家 ié

housekeeper [haus'kiːpəːr] *n* (servant) 家政婦 kaséifù

housekeeping [haus'kiːpiŋ] *n* (work) 家事 kájì; (money) 家計費 kakéîhi

house-warming party [haus'wɔːrmiŋ-] *n* 新居祝いのパーティ shiñkyo-iwaì no pǎti

housewife [haus'waif] (*pl* **housewives**) *n* 主婦 shúfu

housework [haus'wəːrk] *n* (chores) 家事 kájì

housing [hau'ziŋ] *n* (houses) 住宅 jútaku; (provision) 住宅供給 jútakukyòkyū

housing development *n* 住宅団地 jútakudañchi

housing estate (*BRIT*) *n* 住宅団地 jútakudañchi

hovel [hʌv'əl] *n* (shack) あばら屋 abár
ya

hover [hʌv'əːr] *vi* (bird, insect) 空中に止まる kúchū ni tomarù

hovercraft [hʌv'əːrkræft] *n* (vehicle) ホバークラフト hobǎkurafùto

KEYWORD

how [hau] *adv* **1** (in what way) どう dǒ, どの様に donó yò ni, どうやって dǒ yattè
how did you do it? どうやってそれができたんですか dǒ yattè soré gà dekítan desù ká

I know how you did it あなたがどの様にしてそれができたか私には分かっています anátà ga donó yò ni shite soré gà dekíta kà watákushi ni wà wakátte imasù

to know how to do something ...の仕方を知っている ...no shikáta wò shitté irù

how is school? 学校はどうですか gakkō wa dǒ desu ká

how was the film? 映画はどうでしたか eíga wa dǒ deshita ká

how are you? お元気ですか o-génki desu ká

2 (to what degree) どのくらい donó kurai

how much milk? どのくらいのミルク

donő kurai nò mírüku

how many people? 何人の人々 nâñnin no hitőbito

how much does it cost? 値段はいくらですか nedán wà íkùra desu ká

how long have you been here? いつからここにいますか ítsù kara kokő nì imásù ká

how old are you? お幾つですか o-íkùtsu desu ká

how tall is he? 彼の身長はどれくらいですか kárè no shiñchő wà doré gùrai desu ká

how lovely/awful! なんて美しい〔ひどい〕 nâñte utsúkushiì〔hidőì〕

howl [haul] *vi* (animal) 遠ぼえする tőboe suru; (baby, person) 大声で泣く őgoè de nakú; (wind) うなる unárù

H.P. [eitʃpi:'] *abbr* = **hire purchase**

h.p. *abbr* = **horsepower**

HQ [eitʃkju:'] *abbr* = **headquarters**

hub [hʌb] *n* (of wheel) ハブ hábù; (*fig:* centre) 中心 chúshin

hubbub [hʌb'ʌb] *n* (din, commotion) どよめき doyőmeki

hubcap [hʌb'kæp] *n* (AUT) ホイールキャップ hoírukyappù

huddle [hʌd'əl] *vi*: *to huddle together* (for heat, comfort) 体を寄合う karáda wò yoséaù

hue [hju:] *n* (color) 色 iró; (shade of color) 色合い iróaì

hue and cry *n* (outcry) 騒ぎ sáwàgi

huff [hʌf] *n*: *in a huff* (offended) 怒っておこて okőttè

hug [hʌg] *vt* (person, thing) 抱締める dakíshimerù

huge [hju:dʒ] *adj* (enormous) ばく大な bakúdai na

hulk [hʌlk] *n* (ship) 廃船 haísen; (person) 図体ばかり大きい人 zútai bakari őkìi hitő, うどの大木 udo no taiboku; (building etc) ばかでかい物 bakádekai monő

hull [hʌl] *n* (of ship) 船体 señtai, ハル hárù

hullo [həlou'] *excl* = **hello**

hum [hʌm] *vt* (tune, song) ハミングで歌う hamingu de utau

♦*vi* (person) ハミングする hámïngu suru; (machine) ぶーんと鳴る búñ to narú; (insect) ぶんぶんいう búñbun iu

human [hju:'mən] *adj* (existence, body) 人の hitő no, 人間の niñgen no; (weakness, emotion) 人間的な niñgenteki na

♦*n* (person) 人 hitő, 人間 niñgen

humane [hju:mein'] *adj* (treatment, slaughter) 苦痛を与えない kutsű wò atáenai

humanitarian [hju:mænite:r'i:ən] *adj* (aid, principles) 人道的な jiñdőteki na

humanity [hju:mæn'iti:] *n* (mankind) 人類 jíñrui, 人間 niñgen; (human nature) 人間性 niñgensei; (humaneness, kindness) 思いやり omőiyari

humble [hʌm'bəl] *adj* (modest) 謙虚な kéñkyo na; (lowly: background) 身分の低い míbùn no hikűî

♦*vt* (humiliate, crush) ...の高慢な鼻を折る ...no kőman na haná wò őrù

humbug [hʌm'bʌg] *n* (of statement, writing) でたらめ detárame; (BRIT: sweet) はっかあめ hakká-ame

humdrum [hʌm'drʌm] *adj* (dull, boring) 退屈な taíkutsu na

humid [hju:'mid] *adj* (atmosphere, climate) 湿度の高い shitsűdő no takáî

humidity [hju:mid'əti:] *n* 湿度 shitsűdő

humiliate [hju:mil'i:eit] *vt* (rival, person) ...の高慢な鼻を折る ...no kőman na haná wò őrù

humiliation [hju:mili:ei'ʃən] *n* (embarrassment) 恥 hají; (situation, experience) 恥辱 chijóku

humility [hju:mil'əti:] *n* (modesty) 謙そん keñson

humor [hju:'mər] (BRIT **humour**) *n* (comedy, mood) ユーモア yůmoa

♦*vt* (child, person) ...の機嫌を取る ...no kigén wo tőrù

humorous [hju:'mərəs] *adj* (remark, book) おどけた odőketa; (person) ユーモアのある yůmoa no árù

hump [hʌmp] *n* (in ground) 小山 koyáma; (of camel: *also* deformity) こぶ kobú

humpbacked [hʌmp'bækt] *adj*: *hump-*

backed bridge 反り橋 soríhàshi

hunch [hʌntʃ] *n* (premonition) 直感 chokkán

hunchback [hʌntʃˈbæk] *n* せむしの人 semúshi nò hitó ◇べっ称 besshō

hunched [hʌntʃt] *adj* (bent, stooped: shoulders) 曲げた magéta; (: person) 肩を落した kátà wo otóshità

hundred [hʌnˈdrid] *num* 百 (の) hyakú (no); (before *n*): **a/one hundred books** 100冊の本 hyakúsatsu nò hôn; **a/one hundred people** 100人の人 hyakúnin nò hitó; **a/one hundred dollars** 100ドル hyakú doru

hundreds of 何百もの nañbyaku mo no

hundredweight [hʌnˈdridweit] *n* (*US = 45.3 kg, 100 lb; BRIT = 50.8 kg, 112 lb*)

hung [hʌŋ] *pt, pp of* **hang**

Hungarian [hʌŋgeˈriːən] *adj* ハンガリーの hañgarī no; (LING) ハンガリー語の hañgarìgo no

♦*n* (person) ハンガリー人 hañgarījìn; (LING) ハンガリー語 hañgarìgo

Hungary [hʌŋˈgəriː] *n* ハンガリー hañgarī

hunger [hʌŋˈgəːr] *n* (lack of food) 空腹 kúfuku; (starvation) 飢餓 kígà

♦*vi*: **to hunger for** (desire) ...に飢える ...ni uérù

hunger strike *n* ハンガーストライキ hañgāsutoraìki, ハンスト hañsuto

hungry [hʌŋˈgriː] *adj* (person, animal) 空腹な kúfuku na; (keen, avid): **hungry for** ...に飢えた ...ni uéta

to be hungry おなかがすいた onáka ga suità

hunk [hʌŋk] *n* (of bread etc) 塊 katámari

hunt [hʌnt] *vt* (for food: subj: animal) 捜し求める sagáshimotomerù, あさる asárù; (SPORT) 狩る kárù, ...の狩りをする ...no kárì wo suru; (criminal, fugitive) 捜す sagásu, 捜索する sōsaku suru

♦*vi* (search): **to hunt (for)** (...を) 捜す (...wo) sagású; (SPORT) (...の) 狩りをする (...no) kárì wo suru

♦*n* (for food: *also* SPORT) 狩り kárì; (search) 捜す事 sagásu kotò; (for criminal) 捜索 sōsaku

hunter [hʌnˈtəːr] *n* (sportsman) ハンター háñtā

hunting [hʌnˈtiŋ] *n* (for food: *also* SPORT) 狩り kárì

hurdle [həːrˈdəl] *n* (difficulty) 障害 shōgai; (SPORT) ハードル hādoru

hurl [həːrl] *vt* (object) 投げる nagérù; (insult, abuse) 浴びせ掛ける abísekakerù

hurrah [həruːˈ] *n* (as cheer) 歓声 kañsei

hurray [həreiˈ] *n* = **hurrah**

hurricane [həːrˈəkein] *n* (storm) ハリケーン haríkèn

hurried [həːrˈiːd] *adj* (hasty, rushed) 大急ぎの ōisògi no

hurriedly [həːrˈiːdliː] *adv* 大急ぎで ōisògi de

hurry [həːrˈiː] *n* (haste, rush) 急ぎ isógi

♦*vi* (*also*: **hurry up**: hasten, rush) 急ぐ isógù

♦*vt* (*also*: **hurry up**: person) 急がせる isógaserù; (: work) 急いでする isóide surù

to be in a hurry 急いでいる isóide irù

hurt [həːrt] (*pt, pp* **hurt**) *vt* (cause pain to) 痛める itámerù; (injure, *fig*) 傷付ける kizútsukerù

♦*vi* (be painful) 痛む itámù

it hurts! 痛い！itái!

hurtful [həːrtˈfəl] *adj* (remark) 傷付ける様な kizútsukeru yō na

hurtle [həːrˈtəl] *vi*: **to hurtle past** (train, car) 猛スピードで通り過ぎる mōsupído de tōrisugirù

to hurtle down (fall) 落ちる ochírù

husband [hʌzˈbənd] *n* 夫 ottó

hush [hʌʃ] *n* (silence) 沈黙 chiñmoku; (stillness) 静けさ shizúkesà

♦*vt* (silence) 黙らせる damáraserù

hush! 静かに shízùka ni

hush up *vt* (scandal etc) もみ消す momíkesù

husk [hʌsk] *n* (of wheat, rice) 殻 kará; (of maize) 皮 kawá

husky [hʌsˈkiː] *adj* (voice) しわがれた shiwágaretà, ハスキーな hásùkī na

♦*n* (dog) ハスキー hásùkī

hustle [hʌsˈəl] *vt* (hurry) 急がせる isógaserù

♦*n: hustle and bustle* 雑踏 zattő

hut [hʌt] *n* (house) 小屋 koyá; (shed) 物置 monő-oki

hutch [hʌtʃ] *n* (*also*: **rabbit hutch**) ウサ ギ小屋 uságigoya

hyacinth [hai'əsinθ] *n* ヒヤシンス hiyá-shiñsu

hybrid [hai'brid] *n* (plant, animal) 交雑 種 kőzatsushù, ハイブリッド haíbι riddò; (mixture) 混成物 koñseibùtsu

hydrant [hai'drənt] *n* (*also*: **fire hydrant**) 消火栓 shőkasen

hydraulic [haidrɔ:'lik] *adj* (pressure, system) 油圧の yuátsu no

hydroelectric [haidrouilek'trik] *adj* (energy, complex) 水力発電の suíryoku-hatsùden no

hydrofoil [hai'drəfɔil] *n* (boat) 水中翼船 suíchūyokùsen

hydrogen [hai'drədʒən] *n* (CHEM) 水 素 suíso

hyena [haii:'nə] *n* ハイエナ haíena

hygiene [hai'dʒi:n] *n* (cleanliness) 衛生 eísei

hygienic [haidʒi:en'ik] *adj* 衛生的な eíseiteki na

hymn [him] *n* 賛美歌 sañbika

hype [haip] (*inf*) *n* 売込み口上 uríkomi-kōjő

hypermarket [hai'pə:rma:rkit] (*BRIT*) *n* 大型スーパー őgatasūpā

hyphen [hai'fən] *n* (dash) ハイフン haífun

hypnosis [hipnou'sis] *n* 催眠 saímin

hypnotic [hipnɑ:t'ik] *adj* (trance) 催眠術 の saímiñjutsu no; (rhythms) 催眠 的 な saímiñteki na

hypnotism [hip'nətizəm] *n* 催眠術 saímiñ-jutsu

hypnotist [hip'nətist] *n* (person) 催 眠 術 師 saíminjutsushì

hypnotize [hip'nətaiz] *vt* (MED etc) ...に 催眠術を掛ける ...ni saímiñjutsu wo ka-kérù; (*fig*: mesmerise) 魅惑する miwáku suru

hypochondriac [haipəkɑ:n'dri:æk] *n* 心 気症患者 shiñkishōkañja

hypocrisy [hipɑ:k'rəsi:] *n* (falseness, in-

sincerity) 偽善 gizén

hypocrite [hip'əkrit] *n* (phoney) 偽 善 者 gizéñsha

hypocritical [hipəkrit'ikəl] *adj* (person) 偽善の gizén no; (behavior) 偽善者的 な gizéñshateki na

hypothermia [haipəθə:r'mi:ə] *n* (MED) 低体温症 teítaioñshō

hypothesis [haipɑ:θ'əsis] (*pl* **hypotheses**) *n* (theory) 仮説 kasétsu

hypothetic(al) [haipəθet'ik(əl)] *adj* (question, situation) 仮定の katéi no

hysteria [histi:'ri:ə] *n* (panic: *also* MED) ヒステリー hisúterì

hysterical [histe:r'ikəl] *adj* (person, rage) ヒステリックな hisúterikkù na; (situation: funny) 笑いが止らない様な warái gà tomáranai yő na

hysterical laughter ばか笑い bakáwa-ràì

hysterics [histe:r'iks] *npl* (anger, panic) ヒステリー hisúterì; (laughter) 大笑い ő-warài

I

I [ai] *pron* 私は〔が〕 watákushi wa〔ga〕

ice [ais] *n* (frozen water) 氷 kőri, (*also*: **ice cream**) アイスクリーム aísukurìmu

♦*vt* (cake) ...にアイシングを掛ける ...ni áishingu wo kakérù

♦*vi* (*also*: **ice over, ice up**: road, window etc) 氷に覆われる kőri nì ŏwarerù

iceberg [ais'bə:rg] *n* 氷山 hyőzan

icebox [ais'ba:ks] *n* (*US*: fridge) 冷蔵庫 reízőko; (*BRIT*: compartment) 冷凍室 reítőshitsu; (insulated box) クーラー kū-rā

ice cream *n* アイスクリーム aísukurìmu

ice cube *n* 角氷 kakúgőri

iced [aist] *adj* (cake) アイシングを掛けた áishingu wo kákèta; (beer) 冷した hiyá-shìta

iced tea アイスティー aísutì

ice hockey *n* (SPORT) アイスホッケー aísuhokkē

Iceland [ais'lənd] *n* アイスランド **aísurañ-**

do

ice lolly [-lɑːˈliː] (*BRIT*) *n* アイスキャンディー aísukyàndī

ice rink *n* スケートリンク sukḗtoriǹku

ice-skating [aisˈskeitiŋ] *n* アイススケート aísusukḗto

icicle [aiˈsikəl] *n* (on gutter, ledge etc) つらら tsurára

icing [aiˈsiŋ] *n* (CULIN) 砂糖衣 satôgorōmo, アイシング áishingu

icing sugar (*BRIT*) *n* 粉砂糖 konázatô

icon [aiˈkɑːn] *n* (REL) 聖像画 seízôga, イコン íkòn

icy [aiˈsiː] *adj* (air, water, temperature) 冷たい tsumétai; (road) 氷に覆われた kôri ni ôwareta

I'd [aid] = **I would; I had**

idea [aiˈdiːˈə] *n* (scheme, notion) 考え kañgaè; (opinion) 意見 íkèn; (objective) つもり tsumôri

ideal [aiˈdiːˈəl] *n* (principle) 理想 risô; (epitome) 模範 mohán

♦*adj* (perfect) 理想的な risôteki na

idealist [aiˈdiːˈəlist] *n* 理想主義者 risôshugishà

identical [aiˈdenˈtikəl] *adj* 同一の dôitsu no

identification [aidentəfəkeiˈʃən] *n* (process) 識別 shikíbetsu; (of person, dead body) 身元の確認 mimóto nò kakúnin

(means of) identification 身分証明書 mibúnshōmeìsho

identify [aiˈdenˈtəfai] *vt* (recognize) 見分ける miwákerù; (distinguish) 識別する shikíbetsu suru; (associate: *to identify someone/something (with)*) ...を (...と) 関連付ける ...wo (...to) kañrenzukerù

Identikit [aiˈdenˈtakit] ® *n*: *Identikit (picture)* モンタージュ写真 moñtājushashìn

identity [aiˈdenˈtiti] *n* (of person, suspect etc) 身元 mimóto, 正体 shôtai; (of group, culture, nation etc) 特性 tokúsei

identity card *n* 身分証明書 mibúnshōmeìsho

ideology [aidiːˈɑːˈədʒi] *n* (beliefs) 思想

shisô, イデオロギー idéorðgī

idiom [idˈiːˈəm] *n* (style) 作風 sakúfū; (phrase) 熟語 jukúgo, イディオム ídìomu

idiomatic [idiːˈəmætˈik] *adj* 熟語的な jukúgoteki na

idiosyncrasy [idiːˈəsiŋˈkrəsiː] *n* (foible) 特異性 tokúisei

idiot [idˈiːət] *n* (fool) ばか bákà

idiotic [idiːˈɑːtˈik] *adj* (stupid) ばかな bákà na

idle [aiˈdəl] *adj* (inactive) 暇な himá na; (lazy) 怠惰な taída na; (unemployed) 失業中の shitsúgyōchū no; (machinery) 動いていない ugôîte inâî; (factory) 休業中の kyúgyōchū no; (question, conversation) 無意味な muími na; (pleasure) むなしい munáshiî

♦*vi* (machine, engine) 空回りする káramawàri suru, アイドリングする aídoriǹgu suru

idle away *vt*: *to idle away the time* のらくらする nórakura suru

idol [aiˈdəl] *n* (hero) アイドル áîdoru; (REL) 偶像 gûzô

idolize [aiˈdəlaiz] *vt* ...に心酔する ...ni shíñsui suru

idyllic [aidilˈik] *adj* のどかな nódòka na

i.e. [aiiːˈ] *abbr* (= *id est: that is*) 即ち súnawàchi

KEYWORD

---

if [if] *conj* **1** (conditional use: given that, providing that etc) (もし) ...すれば (mōshi) ...surébà (súrú narába)

I'll go if you come with me あなたが一緒に来れば、私は行ってもいいです anátà ga isshô ni kurêba watákushi wà itté mò íi desu

I'd be pleased if you could do it あなたがそれをやって下されば私は助かりますが anátà gà sore wò yatté kudasarèba watákushi wà tasúkarimasù ga

if anyone comes in だれかが入って来れば dárèka ga háitte kurêba

if necessary 必要であれば hitsúyō de arèba

if I were you 私があなただったら watákushi gà anátà dáttara

2 (whenever) ...の時 ...no tŏkî
if we are in Scotland, we always go to see her スコットランドにいる時私たちは必ず彼女に会いに行きます sukóttorañdo ni irú tokî watákushitáchi wa kanárazù kánòjo ni áî ni ikímasù
3 (although): *(even) if* たとえ...でも tatôè ...dé mò
I am determined to finish it, (even) if it takes all week たとえ今週いっぱいかかっても私はこの仕事を片付けたい tatôè koñshū ippài kakátte mò watákushi wà konó shigoto wò katázuketaî
I like it, (even) if you don't あなたがいやでも、私はこれが好きです anátà ga iyá de mò, watákushi wà koré gà sukî desù
4 (whether) ...かどうか ...ka dŏ ka
I don't know if he is here 彼がここにいるかどうか私には分かりません kárè ga kokó nî irú ka dŏka watákushi ni wà wakárimaseñ
ask him if he can come 来られるかどうか彼に聞いて下さい koráreru ka dŏka kárè ni kiîte kudasaî
5: *if so/not* そうであれば〔なければ〕 sŏ de arèba〔nakerèba〕
if only ...であったらなあ ...dé àttara nâ
if only I could 私にそれができたらなあ watákushi nî soré gà dékîtara nâ
¶ *see also* **as**

igloo [ig'lu:] *n* イグルー ígùrū
ignite [ignait'] *vt* (set fire to) ...に火をつける ...ni hî wò tsukérù
♦*vi* 燃え出す moédasù
ignition [igni'ʃən] *n* (AUT: process) 点火 teñka; (: mechanism) 点火装置 teñkasŏchi
to switch on/off the ignition エンジンスイッチを入れる〔切る〕 eñjinsuîtchi wo irérù〔kîrù〕
ignition key *n* (AUT) カーキー kâkî
ignorance [ig'nə:rəns] *n* (lack of knowledge) 無知 múchì
ignorant [ig'nə:rənt] *adj* (uninformed, unaware) 無学な múgàku na, 無知な múchî na

to be ignorant of (subject, events) ...を知らない ...wo shiránaî
ignore [ignɔ:r'] *vt* (person, advice, event, fact) 無視する mushî suru
I'll [ail] = **I will; I shall**
ill [il] *adj* (sick) 病気の byŏki no; (harmful: effects) 悪い warûî
♦*n* (evil) 悪 ákù; (trouble) 凶兆 kyŏchō
♦*adv*: *to speak ill of someone* ...の悪口を言う ...no warúgùchi wo iú
to think ill (of someone) (...を) 悪く思う (...wo) warúkù omóù
to be taken ill 病気になる byŏki ni narù, 倒れる taórerù
ill-advised [il'ædvaizd'] *adj* (decision) 軽率な keîsotsu na; (person) 無分別な mufúñbetsu na
ill-at-ease [il'əti:z'] *adj* (awkward, uncomfortable) 落着かない ochîtsukanaî
illegal [ili:'gəl] *adj* (not legal: activity, organization, immigrant etc) 不法の fuhŏ no
illegible [iledʒ'əbəl] *adj* (writing) 読めない yoménaî
illegitimate [ilidʒit'əmit] *adj*: *an illegitimate child* 私生児 shiséiji
ill-fated [il'fei'tid] *adj* (doomed) 不運な fûñn na
ill feeling *n* (animosity, bitterness) 恨み urámi
illicit [ilis'it] *adj* (unlawful: sale, association, substance) 不法の fuhŏ no
illiterate [ilit'ə:rit] *adj* (person) 文盲の mofímo no; (letter) 無学な múgàku na
ill-mannered [il'mæn'ə:rd] *adj* (rude: child etc) 行儀の悪い gyŏgi no warûì
illness [il'nis] *n* 病気 byŏki
illogical [ilɑ:dʒ'ikəl] *adj* (fear, reaction, argument) 不合理な fugŏri na
ill-treat [il'tri:t'] *vt* (child, pet, prisoner) 虐待する gyakútai suru
illuminate [ilu:'məneit] *vt* (light up: room, street) 明るくする akárukù suru; (decorate with lights: building, monument etc) ライトアップする raîtoappù suru; (shine light on) 照らす terásù
illumination [ilu:mənei'ʃən] *n* (lighting) 照明 shŏmei

illuminations [ilu:mənei'ʃənz] *npl* (decorative lights) 電飾 denshoku, イルミネーション irúmineshon

illusion [ilu:'ʒən] *n* (false idea, belief) 錯覚 sakkáku; (trick) いんちき inchiki, トリック torīkku

illusory [ilu:'sə:ri:] *adj* (hopes, prospects) 錯覚の sakkáku no

illustrate [il'əstreit] *vt* (point) 例を挙げて説明する rei wò agéte setsúmei suru; (book) ...に挿絵を入れる ...ni sashíe wo iréru; (talk) ...にスライド（など）を使う ...ni suráido (nádò) wo tsukáu

illustration [iləstrei'ʃən] *n* (act of illustrating) 図解 zukái; (example) 例 reí; (in book) 挿絵 sashíe

illustrious [ilʌs'tri:əs] *adj* (career) 輝かしい kagáyakashiî; (predecessor) 著名な choméi na

ill will *n* (hostility) 恨み urámi

I'm [aim] = **I am**

image [im'idʒ] *n* (picture) 像 zố; (public face) イメージ ímēji; (reflection) 姿 sugáta

imagery [im'idʒri:] *n* (in writing, painting etc) 比ゆ híyu

imaginary [imædʒ'əne:ri:] *adj* (being, danger) 想像上の sổzōjō no

imagination [imædʒənei'ʃən] *n* (part of the mind) 想像 sốzō; (inventiveness) 想像力 sôzôryoku

imaginative [imædʒ'ənətiv] *adj* (person) 想像力に富んだ sôzôryoku ni tońdà; (solution) 奇抜な kibátsu na

imagine [imædʒ'in] *vt* (visualise) 想像する sôzō suru; (dream) ...だと錯覚する ...da to sakkáku suru; (suppose) ...だと思う ...da to omóu

imbalance [imbæl'əns] *n* (inequality) 不均等 fukíntō, アンバランス ańbaransu

imbecile [im'bəsil] *n* (idiot) ばか bákà

imbue [imbju:'] *vt*: **to imbue someone/something with** ...に ...を吹き込む ...ni ...wo fukíkomù

imitate [im'əteit] *vt* (copy) まねる manérù; (mimic) ...の物まねをする ...no monómane wò suru

imitation [imətei'ʃən] *n* (act of copying) まね mané; (act of mimicking) 物まね monómane; (copy) 偽物 nisémono

immaculate [imæk'jəlit] *adj* (room) 汚れ一つない yogóre hitotsù náî; (appearance) 清潔な seíketsu na; (piece of work) 完璧な kańpeki na; (REL) 原罪のない geñzai nò náî

immaterial [iməti:'ri:əl] *adj* (unimportant) どうでもいい dố dè mo íi

immature [imətu:r'] *adj* (fruit, cheese) 熟していない jukú shite inái; (organism) 未成熟の miséijuku no; (person) 未熟な mijúku na

immediate [imi:'di:it] *adj* (reaction, answer) 即時の sokúji no; (pressing: need) 緊迫した kiñpaku shita; (nearest: neighborhood, family) 最も近い mottô-mò chikáî

immediately [imi:'di:itli:] *adv* (at once) 直ぐに súgù ni, 直ちに tádàchi ni; (directly) 真っ直ぐに massúgù ni

immediately next to ...の直ぐ隣に ...no súgù tonárî ni

immense [imens'] *adj* (huge: size) 巨大な kyodái na; (: progress, importance) 大変な taíhen na

immerse [imə:rs'] *vt* (submerge) 浸す hitásù

to be immersed in (*fig*: work, study etc) ...に熱中している ...ni netchú shite irú

to be immersed in thought 考え込んでいる kańgaekoñde irú

immersion heater [imə:r'ʒən-] (*BRIT*) *n* 投入式湯沸かし器 tốnyūshiki yuwakashikî

immigrant [im'əgrənt] *n* 移民 imín

immigration [iməgrei'ʃən] *n* (process) 移住 ijú; (control: at airport etc) 入国管理局 nyúkoku kańrikyoku

imminent [im'ənənt] *adj* (arrival, departure) 差迫った sashísematta

immobile [imou'bəl] *adj* (motionless) 動かない ugókanaî

immobilize [imou'bəlaiz] *vt* (person, machine) 動けなくする ugókenakù suru

immoral [imɔ:r'əl] *adj* (person, behavior, idea etc) 不道徳な fudôtoku na

immorality [iməræl'iti:] *n* 不道徳 fudōtoku

immortal [imɔːr'təl] *adj* (living for ever: god) 永遠に生きる eíen nì ikírù; (unforgettable: poetry, fame) 不滅の fumétsu no

immortalize [imɔːr'təlaiz] *vt* (hero, event) ...に不朽の名声を与える ...ni fukyū no meísei wo atáerù

immune [imjuːn'] *adj*: **immune (to)** (disease) (...に) 免疫がある (...ni) meñ-eki ga arù; (flattery) (...が) ...に通じない (...ga) ...ni tsūjinài; (criticism, attack) ...に (...の) しようがない ...ni (...no) shíyō ga nai

immunity [imjuː'niti:] *n* (to disease etc) 免疫 meñ-eki; (from prosecution, taxation etc) 免除 méñjo

diplomatic immunity 外交特権 gaíkoutokkèn

immunize [im'jənaiz] *vt* (MED: *gen*) ...に免疫性を与える ...ni meñ-ekisei wò atáerù; (with injection) ...に予防注射をする ...ni yobōchùsha wo suru

imp [imp] *n* (small devil) 小鬼 ko-óni; (child) いたずらっ子 itázurakkò

impact [im'pækt] *n* (of bullet, crash) 衝撃 shōgeki, インパクト íñpakuto; (of law, measure) 影響 eíkyō

impair [impeːr'] *vt* (vision, judgement) 損なう sokónaù

impale [impeil'] *vt* くし刺しにする kushízashi ni suru

impart [impɑːrt'] *vt* (make known: information) 与える atáerù; (bestow: flavor) 添える soérù

impartial [impɑːr'ʃəl] *adj* (judge, observer) 公平な kōhei na

impassable [impæs'əbəl] *adj* (river) 渡れない watárenaì; (road, route etc) 通行不可能な tsūkōfukanō na

impasse [im'pæs] *n* (in war, negotiations) 行き詰り ikízumari

impassive [impæs'iv] *adj* (face, expression) 無表情な muhyōjō na

impatience [impei'ʃəns] *n* (annoyance due to waiting) じれったさ jiréttasà; (irritation) 短気 táñki; (eagerness) 意欲 fyòku

impatient [impei'ʃənt] *adj* (annoyed by waiting) じれったい jiréttaì; (irritable) 短気な táñki na; (eager, in a hurry): **impatient to ...** ...従っている ...shitágatte irù

to get/grow impatient もどかしがる modókashigarù

impeccable [impek'əbəl] *adj* (perfect: manners, dress) 申分のない mōshibùn no nái

impede [impiːd'] *vt* (progress, development etc) 妨げる samátagerù

impediment [impe'dəmənt] *n* (to growth, movement) 障害 shōgai; (*also*: **speech impediment**) 言語障害 geñgoshōgai

impending [impen'diŋ] *adj* (arrival, catastrophe) 差迫る sashísemarù

impenetrable [impen'itrəbəl] *adj* (wall, jungle) 通れない tōrenaì; (*fig*: law, text) 難解な nañkai na

imperative [impeːr'ətiv] *adj* (need) 緊急の kíñkyū no; (tone) 命令的な meíreiteki na

♦*n* (LING) 命令形 meíreikei

imperceptible [impəːrsep'təbəl] *adj* (change, movement) 気付かれない kizúkarenaì

imperfect [impəːr'fikt] *adj* (goods, system etc) 不完全な fukánzen na

♦*n* (LING: *also*: **imperfect tense**) 過去進行形 kakóshinkōkei

imperfection [impəːrfek'ʃən] *n* (failing, blemish) 欠点 kettéñ

imperial [impiːr'iːəl] *adj* (history, power) 帝国の teíkoku no; (*BRIT*: measure) ヤードポンド法の yādopondohō no

imperialism [impiːr'iːəlizəm] *n* 帝国主義 teíkokushùgi

impersonal [impəːr'sənəl] *adj* (place, organization) 人間味のない niñgeñmi no nái

impersonate [impəːr'səneit] *vt* (another person, police officer etc) ...の名をかたる ...no ná wò katárù, ...に成り済ます ...ni narísumasù; (THEATER) ...にふんする ...ni fuñ surù

impertinent [impəːr'tənənt] *adj* (pupil, question) 生意気な namáiki na

impervious [impəːr'viːəs] *adj* (*fig*): **impervious to** (criticism etc) ...に影響されない ...ni eíkyō sarenái

impetuous [impetʃ'uːəs] *adj* (impulsive) 無鉄砲な mutéppō na

impetus [im'pitəs] *n* (momentum: of flight, runner) 惰性 daséi; (*fig*: driving force) 原動力 gefidōryoku

impinge [impindʒ']: **to impinge on** *vt fus* (person) ...の行動を制限する ...no kōdō wò seígen suru; (rights) 侵害する shiñgai suru

implacable [implæk'əbəl] *adj* (hatred, anger etc) なだめがたい nadámegàtai; (opposition) 執念深い shūnenbùkai

implement
[*n* im'pləmənt *vb* im'pləment] *n* (tool: for farming, gardening, cooking etc) 道具 dōgu
♦*vt* (plan, regulation) 実行する jikkō suru

implicate [im'plikeit] *vt* (in crime, error) ...のかかわり合いを立証する ...no kakáwariaì wo risshō suru

implication [implikei'ʃən] *n* (inference) 含み fukúmi; (involvement) 係り合い kakáwariai

implicit [implis'it] *adj* (inferred: threat, meaning etc) 暗黙の afimoku no; (unquestioning: belief, trust) 盲目的な mōmokuteki na

implore [implɔːr'] *vt* (beg) ...に嘆願する ...ni tañgan suru

imply [implai'] *vt* (hint) ...の意味を含む ...no imí wo fukúmù; (mean) ...を意味する ...wo imí suru

impolite [impəlait'] *adj* (rude, offensive) 失礼な shitsúrei na

import [*vb* impɔːrt' *n* im'pɔːrt] *vt* (goods etc) 輸入する yunyū suru
♦*n* (COMM: article) 輸入品 yunyūhin; (: importation) 輸入 yunyū

importance [impɔːr'təns] *n* (significance) 重大さ jūdaisa; (of person) 有力 yūryoku

important [impɔːr'tənt] *adj* (significant: decision, difference etc) 重要な jūyō na, 重大な jūdai na; (influential: person) 偉い erái
it's not important 大した事じゃない taíshita kotò ja naí

importer [impɔːr'tər] *n* (COMM) 輸入業者 yunyūgyōsha

impose [impouz'] *vt* (sanctions, restrictions, discipline etc) 負わせる owáserù
♦*vi*: **to impose on someone** ...に付込む ...ni tsukékomù, ...に迷惑を掛ける ...ni méîwaku wo kakérù

imposing [impou'ziŋ] *adj* (building, person, manner) 貫ろくある kañroku arù

imposition [impəziʃ'ən] *n* (of tax etc) 賦課 fuká
to be an imposition on (person) ...に付込む ...ni tsukékomù, ...に迷惑を掛ける ...ni méîwaku wo kakérù

impossible [impɑs'əbəl] *adj* (task, demand etc) 不可能な fukánō na; (situation) 厄介な yakkáî na; (person) どうしようもない dō shiyō mo nai

impostor [impɑs'tər] *n* 偽者 nisémono

impotence [im'pətəns] *n* (lack of power) 無力 múryòku; (MED) 性交不能 seíkōfù-nō, インポテンツ íñpotentsu

impotent [im'pətənt] *adj* (powerless) 無力な múryòku na; (MED) 性交不能の seíkōfùnō no

impound [impaund'] *vt* (belongings, passports) 没収する bosshū suru

impoverished [impɑv'əriʃt] *adj* (country, person etc) 貧しくなった mazúshiku nattà

impracticable [impræk'tikəbəl] *adj* (idea, solution) 実行不可能な jikkōfukanō na

impractical [impræk'tikəl] *adj* (plan) 実用的でない jitsúyōteki de naî; (person) 不器用な bukíyō na

imprecise [imprisais'] *adj* (inexact) 不正確な fuséîkaku na

impregnable [impreg'nəbəl] *adj* (castle, fortress) 難攻不落の nañkōfuràku no

impregnate [impreg'neit] *vt* (saturate) ...に染込ませる ...ni shimíkomaserù

impresario [impresɑː'riːou] *n* (THEA-

TER) 興業師 kōgyōshǐ

impress [impres'] *vt* (person) ...に印象を与える ...ni ínshō wò atáerù; (mark) ...に押付ける ...ni oshítsukerù

to impress something on someone ...に...を強く言い聞かす ...ni ...wo tsuyókù ifkikasù

impression [impreʃ'ən] *n* (of place, situation, person) 印象 ínshō; (of stamp, seal) 判 hán, 刻印 kokúin; (idea) 思い込み omóikomi; (effect) 効果 kōka; (mark) 跡 átò; (imitation) 物まね monómane

to be under the impression that ...だと思い込んでいる ...da to omóikonde irú

impressionable [impreʃ'ənəbəl] *adj* (child, person) 感じやすい kañjiyasui

impressionist [impreʃ'ənist] *n* (entertainer) 物真似芸人 monómanegeìnin; (ART): *Impressionist* 印象派画家 ínshōhagaka

impressive [impres'iv] *adj* (reputation, collection) 印象的な ínshōteki na

imprint [im'print] *n* (outline: of hand etc) 跡 ato; (PUBLISHING) 奥付 okúzuke

imprison [impriz'ən] *vt* (criminal) 拘置する kōchi suru, 刑務所に入れる keímushò ni irérù

imprisonment [impriz'ənmənt] *n* 拘置 kōchi

improbable [imprɑːb'əbəl] *adj* (unlikely: outcome) ありそうもない arísō mò náì; (: explanation, story) 本当らしくない hoñtōrashikù náì

impromptu [imprɑːmp'tuː] *adj* (celebration, party) 即席の sokúseki no

improper [imprɑːp'əːr] *adj* (unsuitable: conduct, procedure) 不適切な futékisetsu na; (dishonest: activities) 不正な fuséi na

improve [impruːv'] *vt* (make better: character, housing, result) 改善する kaízen suru

◆*vi* (get better: weather, pupil, patient, health etc) 良くなる yókù naru

improvement [impruːv'mənt] *n* (making better) 改善 kaízen; (getting better) 良くなる事 yókù naru kotó; **improve-**

ment (in) (making better) (...を) 改善する事 (...wo) kaízen surù kotó; (getting better) (...が) 良くなる事 (...ga) yókù naru kotó

improvise [im'prəvaiz] *vt* (meal, bed etc) 有り合せの物で作る aríawase no mono dè tsukúrù

◆*vi* (THEATER, MUS) 即興的にしゃべる〔演奏する〕 sokkyóteki nì shaberù〔eñsō suru〕, アドリブする adóribu suru

imprudent [impruːd'ənt] *adj* (unwise) 賢明でない keñmei de naí

impudent [im'pjədənt] *adj* (child, comment, remark) 生意気な namáiki na

impulse [im'pʌls] *n* (urge: *gen*) 衝動 shōdō; (: to do wrong) 出来心 dekígokòro; (ELEC) 衝撃 shōgeki, インパルス íñparusu

to act on impulse 衝動的に行動する shōdōteki ni kōdō suru

impulsive [impʌl'siv] *adj* (purchase, gesture, person) 衝動的な shōdōteki na

impunity [impjuː 'niti:] *n*: *with impunity* 罰せられずに bassérarezù ni

impure [impjuːr'] *adj* (adulterated) 不純な fujún na; (sinful) みだらな mídàra na

impurity [impjuːr'iti:] *n* (foreign substance) 不純物 fujúnbutsu

---

KEYWORD

in [in] *prep* 1 (indicating place, position) ...に〔で〕 ...ni〔dè〕

in the house/garden 家〔庭〕に〔で〕 ié〔niwà〕nì〔dè〕

in the box/fridge/drawer 箱〔冷蔵庫, 引き出し〕に〔で〕hakó〔reízòko, hikídashi〕nì〔dè〕

I have it in my hand 手に持っています té nì móttè imasu

to spend a day in town/the country 町〔田舎〕で1日を過ごす machí〔ináka〕dè ichínichi wò sugósù

in school 学校に〔で〕 gakkō nì〔dè〕

in here/there ここ〔あそこ〕に〔で〕 kokó〔asóko〕nì〔dè〕

2 (with place names: of town, region, country) ...に〔で〕... nì〔dè〕

in London ロンドンに〔で〕 róñdon ni

〔de〕

in England/Japan/Canada/the United States 英国〔日本，カナダ，アメリカ〕に〔で〕efkoku(nippón, kánada, amérĭka〕nǐ〔dè〕

in Burgundy バーガンディーに〔で〕bágandì ni(de)

3 (indicating time: during) ...に ...nǐ

in spring/summer 春〔夏〕に hárù(natsú)nì

in 1998 1998年 に señkyūhyakukyū́jū-hachi néñ ni

in May 5月に gógàtsu ni

I'll see you in July 7月に会いましょう shichígàtsu ni aímashṓ

in the afternoon 午後に gógò ni

at 4 o'clock in the afternoon 午後4時に gógò yójì ni

4 (indicating time: in the space of) ...で ...dè

I did it in 3 hours/days 3時間〔3日〕でやりました sañjikàn〔mikká〕de yarímashìta

I'll see you in 2 weeks/in 2 weeks' time 2週間したらまた会いましょう nishū́kan shitara matá aimashṓ

5 (indicating manner etc) ...で ...dè

in a loud/soft voice 大きな〔小さな〕声で ốkìna(chíisana)kồe de

in pencil/ink 鉛筆〔インク〕で eñpitsu 〔íñku〕dè

in English/French 英語〔フランス語〕で eígo(furánsugo)dè

the boy in the blue shirt 青いシャツの少年 aóì shátsu no shṓnen

6 (indicating circumstances): *in the sun* 直射日光に当って chokúshanikkṓ ni a-táttè, 日なたに hináta ni

in the rain 雨の中 áme no nákà

in the shade 日陰で hikáge de

a change in policy 政策の変更 seísaku nò heñkō

a rise in prices 物価の上昇 búkkà no jồshō

7 (indicating mood, state): *in tears* 泣いて naîte

in anger 怒って okóttè

in despair 失望して shitsúbō shitè

in good condition 無事に bují nì

to live in luxury ぜいたくに暮す zeítaku ni kurásu

8 (with ratios, numbers): *1 in 10 households has a second car, 1 household in 10 has a second car* 10世帯中1世帯は車を2台持っている jussétaichū issétai wà kurúma wò nídài mótte irù

6 months in the year 1年の内6か月 ichínen no uchì rokkágetsu

they lined up in twos 彼らは2人ずつ並んだ kárèra wa futárizùtsu naránda

9 (referring to people, works): *the disease is common in children* この病気は子供によく見られる konó byồki wa kodómo nì yókù mirárerù

in (the works of) Dickens ディケンズの作品の中に díkènzu no sakúhin no nakà ni

she has it in her to succeed 彼女には成功する素質がある kánòjo ni wa seíkō suru soshitsù ga árù

they have a good leader in him 彼らにとって彼は素晴らしいリーダーです kárèra ni tóttè kárè wa subárashiî rídà desu

10 (indicating profession etc): *to be in teaching* 教員である kyốin de árù

to be in publishing 出版関係の仕事をしている shuppánkañkei no shigóto wò shité irù

to be in the army 軍人である guñjìn de árù

11 (after superlative): *the best pupil in the class* クラスで最優秀の生徒 kúràsu de saíyūshū no seíto

the biggest/smallest in Europe ヨーロッパ中で最も大きな〔小さな〕物 yốroppajū de mottómò ốkìna(chíisana)monó

12 (with present participle): *in saying this* こう言って kṓ ittè

in doing things the way she did, she alienated everyone 彼女のやり方は皆の反感を買った kánòjo no yaríkata wà miná nò hañkan wo kattá

◆*adv*: *to be in* (person: at home) 在宅である zaítaku de árù; (: at work) 出社して

いる shushsá shite irù; (train, plane) 到着
している tóchaku shite irù; (ship) 入港し
ている nyūkō shite irù; (in fashion) 流行
している ryūkō shite irù

he'll be in later today 2-3時間したら
出社すると思います nisánjikàn shitárà
shusshá suru tò omóimasù

miniskirts are in again this year 今
年ミニスカートが再び流行しています
kotóshi mínisukàto ga futátabì ryūkō
shite imasù

to ask someone in ...を家に上がらせる
...wò ié nì agáraserù

to run/limp etc in 走って〔びっこを引
いて〕入って来る hashíttè〔bíkkò wo hií-
tè〕háitte kuru

♦*n: the ins and outs* (of proposal,
situation etc) 詳細 shōsai

*he explained all the ins and outs of
the deal to me* 彼は私に取引の詳細を
説明してくれました kárè wa watákushi
nì toríhiki no shōsai wo setsúmei shite
kuremashìta

---

in. *abbr* = **inch**

inability [inəbil'əti:] *n* (incapacity): *inability (to do)* (...する事が) できない
事 (...surú kotò ga) dekínaî kotó

inaccessible [inækses'əbəl] *adj* (place)
入りにくい haírinikùi, 近付きにくい chi-
kázukinikùi; (*fig*: text, music) 難解な naíi-
kai na

inaccurate [inæk'jə:rit] *adj* (account,
answer, person) 不正確な fuséikaku na

inactivity [inæktivi'ti:] *n* (idleness) 活動
しない事 katsúdōshinài kotó

inadequate [inæd'əkwit] *adj* (income,
amount, reply) 不十分な fujūbùn na;
(person) 無能な munō na

inadvertently [inədvə:r'təntli:] *adv* (unintentionally) うっかり ukkárì

inadvisable [inədvai'zəbəl] *adj* 得策でな
い tokúsaku de naî

inane [inein'] *adj* (smile, remark) 愚かな
órōka na

inanimate [inæn'əmit] *adj* 生命のない
seímei no naî

inappropriate [inəprou'pri:it] *adj* (un-

suitable) 不適切な futékisetsu na; (improper: word, expression) 非難すべき hinánsubeki

inarticulate [inɑ:rtik'jəlit] *adj* (person)
口下手な kuchíbeta na; (speech) 分かり
にくい wakárinikuî

inasmuch as [inəzmʌt∫'-] *adv* (in that)
...という点で ...to iú teñ de; (insofar as)
できる限り dekíru kagíri

inaudible [inɔ:'dəbəl] *adj* (voice, aside)
聞取れない kikítorenaî

inaugural [inɔ:'gjə:rəl] *adj* (speech) 就任
の shúnin no; (meeting) 発会の hakkái
no

inaugurate [inɔ:'gjə:reit] *vt* (president,
official) ...の就任式を行う ...no shúniñshiki wo okonau; (system, measure) 始
める hajímeru; (organization) 発足させ
る hossóku saserù

inauguration [inɔ:gjərei'∫ən] *n* (of president, official) 就任式 shúniñshiki; (of
system, measure) 開始 kaíshi; (of organization) 発足 hossóku

in-between [in'bitwi:n] *adj* (intermediate) 中間的な chūkanteki na

inborn [in'bɔ:rn] *adj* (quality) 生れ付きの
umáretsuki no

inbred [in'bred] *adj* (quality) 生まれつき
の umáretsuki no; (family) 近親交配の
kiñshinkōhai no

Inc. *abbr* = **incorporated**

incalculable [inkæl'kjələbəl] *adj* (effect,
loss) 途方もない tohō mo naî

incapable [inkei'pəbəl] *adj* (helpless) 無
能な munō na; (unable to): *to be incapable of something/doing something* ...が〔する事が〕できない ...ga〔surú
kotò ga〕dekínaî

incapacitate [inkəpæs'əteit] *vt* 不具に
する fúgù ni suru

incapacity [inkəpæs'iti:] *n* (weakness)
弱さ yówàsa; (inability) 不能 funō

incarcerate [inkɑ:r'sə:rit] *vt* 拘置する
kōchi suru, 刑務所に入れる keímushò ni
irérù

incarnation [inkɑ:rnei'∫ən] *n* (of beauty)
化身 késhìn; (of evil) 権化 góñge; (REL)
神が人間の姿を取る事 kámî ga niñgen

no sugatá wo tórù kotó

incendiary [insen'di:e:ri:] *adj* (device) 放火の hōka no

an incendiary bomb 焼い弾 shōídàn

incense [*n* in'sens *vb* insens'] *n* (perfume: *also* REL) 香 kō
♦*vt* (anger) 怒らせる okóraserù

incentive [insen'tiv] *n* (inducement) 動機 dōki, 刺激 shigéki

incessant [inses'ent] *adj* (bickering, criticism) 引っ切り無しの hikkíri nashí no

incessantly [inses'entli:] *adv* 引っ切り無しに hikkíri nashí ni

incest [in'sest] *n* 近親相かん kiñshinsōkan

inch [intʃ] *n* (measurement) インチ ínchi

to be within an inch of doing 危うく ...するところである ayáuku ...surú tokóro de árù

he didn't give an inch (*fig*: back down, yield) 一寸も譲ろうとしなかった issúñ mo yuzúrṓ to shinákatta

inch forward *vi* 一寸刻みに進む issúñkizami ni susúmù

incidence [in'sidens] *n* (of crime, disease) 発生率 hasséiritsu

incident [in'sident] *n* (event) 事件 jíkèn

incidental [insiden'tel] *adj* (additional, supplementary) 付随的な fuzúiteki na

incidental to ...に対して二次的な ...ni táishite nijíteki na

incidentally [insiden'teli:] *adv* (by the way) ところで tokóro dè

incinerator [insin'e:reito:r] *n* (for waste, refuse) 焼却炉 shōkyakurò

incipient [insip'i:ent] *adj* (baldness, madness) 初期の shōkí no

incision [insiʒ'en] *n* (cut: *also* MED) 切開 sékkài

incisive [insai'siv] *adj* (comment, criticism) 痛烈な tsúretsu na

incite [insait'] *vt* (rioters, violence) 扇動する señdō suru; (hatred) あおりたてる aóritatèru

inclination [inklenei'ʃen] *n* (tendency) 傾向 keíkō; (disposition, desire) 望み nozómi

incline [in'klain] *n* (slope) 坂 saká

♦*vt* (bend: head) 下げる sagérù
♦*vi* (surface) 傾斜する keísha suru

to be inclined to (tend) ...する傾向がある ...suru keíkō ga arù

include [inkluːd'] *vt* (incorporate: in plan, team etc) 入れる irérù; (: in price) 含む fukúmù

including [inkluːd'iŋ] *prep* ...を含めて ...wo fukúmète

inclusion [inkluː'ʒen] *n* (incorporation: in plan etc) 入れる事 irérù kotó; (: in price) 含む事 fukúmù kotó

inclusive [inkluː'siv] *adj* (price, terms) 含んでいる fukúnde iru

inclusive of ...を含めて ...wo fukúmète

incognito [inkɑːgniː'tou] *adv* (travel) 御忍びで o-shínobi de

incoherent [inkouhiː'rent] *adj* (argument, speech, person) 分かりにくい wakárinikuì

income [in'kʌm] *n* 収入 shúnyū

income tax *n* 所得税 shotókuzèi

incoming [in'kʌmiŋ] *adj* (flight, passenger) 到着の tōchaku no; (call, mail) 着信の chakúshin no; (government, official) 新任の shíñnin no; (wave) 寄せて来る yoséte kurù

the incoming tide 上げ潮 agéshio

incomparable [inkɑːm'pe:rebel] *adj* (genius, efficiency etc) 類のない rúì no náì

incompatible [inkəmpæt'ebel] *adj* (lifestyles, systems, aims) 相容れない aíirénai

incompetence [inkɑːm'pitens] *n* 無能 munō

incompetent [inkɑːm'pitent] *adj* (person) 無能な munō na; (job) 下手な hetá na

incomplete [inkəmpliːt'] *adj* (unfinished: book, painting etc) 未完成の mikánsei no; (partial: success, achievement) 部分的な bubúnteki na

incomprehensible [inkɑːmprihen'səbəl] *adj* (conduct) 不可解な fukákai na; (language) 分からない wakáranaì

inconceivable [inkənsiː'vəbəl] *adj* (unthinkable) 考えられない kañgaerarenaì

incongruous [inkɑːŋ'gruːəs] *adj* (strange: situation, figure) 変った kawátta; (inappropriate: remark, act) 不適当な futékitō na

inconsiderate [inkənsid'əːrit] *adj* (person, action) 心ない kokőronaī

inconsistency [inkənsis'tənsiː] *n* (of behavior, person etc) 一貫しない事ikkán shinai koto; (in work) むら murá; (in statement, action) 矛盾 mujūn

inconsistent [inkənsis'tənt] *adj* (behavior, person) 変りやすい kawáriyasuī; (work) むらの多い murá no ōi; (statement, action) 矛盾した mujūn shita
inconsistent with (beliefs, values) ...と矛盾する ...to mujún suru

inconspicuous [inkənspik'juːəs] *adj* (person, color, building etc) 目立たない medátanaī

incontinent [inkɑːn'tənənt] *adj* (MED) 失禁の shikkín no

inconvenience [inkənviː'njəns] *n* (problem) 問題 mońdai; (trouble) 迷惑 meíwaku
♦*vt* ...に迷惑を掛ける ...ni meíwaku wò kakérù

inconvenient [inkənviː'njənt] *adj* (time, place, house) 不便な fubén na; (visitor, incident etc) 厄介な yakkái na

incorporate [inkɔːr'pəːrit] *vt* (make part of) 取入れる toríirerù; (contain) 含む fukúmù

incorporated company [inkɔːr'pəːreitid-] (*US*) *n* (*abbr* **Inc.**) 会社 kaísha

incorrect [inkərekt'] *adj* (information, answer, attitude etc) 間違った machígattà

incorrigible [inkɔːr'idʒəbəl] *adj* (liar, crook) 救い様のない sukúiyō no náī

incorruptible [inkərʌp'təbəl] *adj* (not open to bribes) 買収のできない baíshū no dekinaī

increase [*n* in'kriːs *vb* inkriːs'] *n* (rise): *increase (in/of)* (...の) 増加 (...no) zōka
♦*vi* (: price, level, productivity etc) 増す masú
♦*vt* (make greater: price, knowledge

etc) 増す masú

increasing [inkriːs'iŋ] *adj* (number, use) 増加する zōka suru

increasingly [inkriːs'iŋliː] *adv* (more intensely, more often) ますます masúmàsu

incredible [inkred'əbəl] *adj* (unbelievable) 信じられない shiñjirarenaī; (enormous) ばく大な bakúdai na

incredulous [inkredʒ'ələs] *adj* (tone, expression) 半信半疑の hańshiñhangi no

increment [in'krəmənt] *n* (in salary) 定期昇給 teíkishōkyū

incriminate [inkrim'əneit] *vt* (LAW) ...の罪を立証する ...no tsúmì wo risshő suru

incubation [inkjəbei'ʃən] *n* (of eggs) ふ卵 furán; (of illness) 潜伏期間 seńpukukikàn

incubator [in'kjəbeitəːr] *n* (for babies) 保育器 hoíkukĭ

incumbent [inkʌm'bənt] *n* (official: POL, REL) 現役 gén-eki
♦*adj*: *it is incumbent on him to ...* ...するのが彼の義務である ...surú no gà kárè no gímù de árù

incur [inkəːr'] *vt* (expenses) ...が掛る ...ga kakárù; (loss) 受ける ukérù; (debt) こしらえる koshíraerù; (disapproval, anger) 被る kőmurù

incurable [inkjuːr'əbəl] *adj* (disease) 不治の fújĭ no

incursion [inkəːr'ʒən] *n* (MIL: invasion) 侵入 shińnyū

indebted [indet'id] *adj*: *to be indebted to someone* (grateful) ...に感謝している ...ni káñsha shitё irū

indecent [indiː'sənt] *adj* (film, book) みだらな mídàra na

indecent assault (*BRIT*) *n* 強制わいせつ罪 kyősei waisetsuzaì

indecent exposure *n* 公然わいせつ罪 kőzen waisetsuzaì

indecisive [indisai'siv] *adj* (person) 決断力のない ketsúdanryoku no naī

indeed [indiːd'] *adv* (certainly) 確かに táshĭka ni, 本当に hoñtő ni; (in fact) 実は jitsú wà; (furthermore) なお náò *yes indeed!* 確かにそうだ! táshĭka ni só dà!

indefinite [indef'ənit] *adj* (answer, view) 不明確な fuméikaku na; (period, number) 不定の futéi no

indefinitely [indef'ənitli:] *adv* (continue, wait) いつまでも ítsŭ made mo

indelible [indel'əbəl] *adj* (mark, stain, ink) 消せない kesénaĭ
indelible pen 油性フェルトペン yuséi ferútopen

indemnity [indem'niti:] *n* (insurance) 賠償保険 baíshōhokèn; (compensation) 賠償 baíshō

independence [indipen'dəns] *n* (of country, person etc) 独立 dokúritsu; (of thinking etc) 自主性 jishúsei

independent [indipen'dənt] *adj* (country, business etc) 独立した dokúritsu shita; (person, thought) 自主的な jishúteki na; (school) 私立の shírĭtsu no; (broadcasting company) 民間の miñkan no; (inquiry) 独自の dokúji no

indestructible [indistrʌk'təbəl] *adj* 破壊できない hakái dekinaĭ

indeterminate [inditə:r'mənit] *adj* (number, nature) 不明の fuméi no

index [in'deks] (*pl* indexes) *n* (in book) 索引 sakúin, インデックス íñdekkùsu; (in library etc) 蔵書目録 zóshomokùroku; (*pl*: indices: ratio) 率 rítsŭ, 指数 shísŭ; (: sign) 印 shírushi

index card *n* インデックスカード íñdekkusukàdo

indexed [in'dekst] (*BRIT* index-linked) *adj* (income, payment) スライド制のsuráidosei no

index finger *n* 人差指 hitósashiyùbi

India [in'di:ə] *n* インド íñdo

Indian [in'di:ən] *adj* インドの íñdo no
Red Indian アメリカインディアン amérika iñdian

Indian Ocean *n*: *the Indian Ocean* インド洋 íñdoyŏ

indicate [in'dikeit] *vt* (show) 示す shimésù; (point to) 指す sásù; (mention) 示唆する shisá suru

indication [indikei'ʃən] *n* (sign) しるし

shirúshi

indicative [indik'ətiv] *adj*: *indicative of* ...のしるしである ...no shirúshi de aru
♦*n* (LING) 直接法 chokúsetsuhŏ

indicator [in'dikeitər] *n* (marker, signal) しるし shirúshi; (AUT) 方向指示器 hŏkōshijĭki, ウインカー uíñkā

indices [in'disi:z] *npl of* index

indictment [indait'mənt] *n* (denunciation) 避難 hínàn; (charge) 起訴 kisó

indifference [indif'ə:rəns] *n* (lack of interest) 無関心 mukánshin

indifferent [indif'ə:rənt] *adj* (uninterested: attitude) 無関心な mukánshin na; (mediocre: quality) 平凡な heíbon na

indigenous [indidʒ'ənəs] *adj* (wildlife) 固有の koyú no
the indigenous population 原住民 geñjūmin

indigestion [indidʒes'tʃən] *n* 消化不良 shŏkafuryŏ

indignant [indig'nənt] *adj*: *to be indignant at something/with someone* (angry) ...に怒っている ...ni okótte irù

indignation [indignei'ʃən] *n* (outrage, resentment) 立腹 rippúku

indignity [indig'niti:] *n* (humiliation) 侮辱 bujóku

indigo [in'dəgou] *n* (color) あい áĭ

indirect [indirekt'] *adj* (way, route) 遠回しの tŏmawashĭ no; (answer, effect) 間接的な kañsetsuteki na

indirectly [indirekt'li:] *adv* (responsible) 間接的に kañsetsuteki ni

indiscreet [indiskri:t'] *adj* (person, behavior, comment) 軽率な keísotsu na

indiscriminate [indiskrim'ənit] *adj* (bombing) 無差別の musábetsu no; (taste) はっきりしない hakkírĭ shináĭ

indispensable [indispen'səbəl] *adj* (tool, worker) 掛替えのない kakégae no naĭ

indisposed [indispouzd'] *adj* (unwell) 体調の悪い taíchō no warúĭ

indisputable [indispju:'təbəl] *adj* (undeniable) 否めない inámenaĭ

indistinct [indistiŋkt'] *adj* (image, memory) ぼんやりした boñ-yarĭ shita; (noise) かすかな kásŭka na

individual [indəvidʒ'u:əl] *n* (person: different from all others) 個人 kójìn; (: with *adj*) 人 hitő, 人物 jinbutsu

♦*adj* (personal) 個人個人の kojínkòjin no; (single) それぞれの soréezòre no; (particular: characteristic) 独特な dokútoku na

individualist [indəvidʒ'u:əlist] *n* 個人主義者 kojínshugishà

individually [indəvidʒ'u:əli:] *adv* (singly: persons) 一人一人で hitórihitorí de; (: things) 一つ一つで hitótsuhitotsù de

indivisible [indəviz'əbəl] *adj* (matter, power) 分割できない buńkatsu dekinái

indoctrinate [indα:k'trəneit] *vt* ...に ...を教え込む ...ni ...wo oshíekomù, 洗脳する sefínō suru

indoctrination [indα:ktrənei'ʃən] *n* 教え込む事 oshíekomù kotő, 洗脳 sefínō

indolent [in'dələnt] *adj* (lazy) 怠惰な tái-da na

Indonesia [indəni:'ʒə] *n* インドネシア ifídoneshìa

indoor [in'dɔ:r] *adj* 屋内の okúnai no

indoors [indɔ:rz'] *adv* (inside) 屋内で o-kúnai de

induce [indu:s'] *vt* (bring about) 引起こす hikíokosù; (persuade) 説得する settőku suru; (MED: birth) 誘発する yúhatsu suru

inducement [indu:s'mənt] *n* (incentive) 動機 dőki, 刺激 shigéki; (*pej*: bribe) 賄ろ wáìro

indulge [indʌldʒ'] *vt* (desire, whim) 満たす mitásù; (person, child) 気ままにさせる kimáma ni saserù

♦*vi*: **to indulge in** (vice, hobby) ...にふける ...ni fukérù

indulgence [indʌl'dʒəns] *n* (pleasure) 楽しみ tanőshimi; (leniency) 寛大さ kańdaisa

indulgent [indʌl'dʒənt] *adj* (parent, smile) 甘やかす amáyakasù

industrial [indʌs'tri:əl] *adj* 産業の sańgyō no, 工業の kőgyō no

industrial action (*BRIT*) *n* 争議行為 sőgikòi

industrial estate (*BRIT*) *n* = **industrial park**

industrialist [indʌs'tri:əlist] *n* 実業家 jitsúgyōka

industrialize [indʌs'tri:əlaiz] *vt* (country, society) 工業化する kőgyōka suru

industrial park (*US*) *n* 工業団地 kő-gyōdañchi

industrious [indʌs'tri:əs] *adj* (student, worker) 勤勉な kiñben na

industry [in'dəstri:] *n* (manufacturing) 産業 sańgyō, 工業 kőgyō; (oil industry, textile industry etc) ...業界 ...győkai; (diligence) 勤勉さ kiñbensa

inebriated [ini:b'ri:eitid] *adj* (drunk) 酔っ払った yoppáratta

inedible [ined'əbəl] *adj* (disgusting) 食べられない tabérarenaì; (poisonous) 食用に適さない shokúyō nì tekísanaì

ineffective [inifek'tiv] *adj* (policy, government) 効果のない kőka no naì

ineffectual [inifek'tʃu:əl] *adj* = **ineffective**

inefficiency [inifiʃ'ənsi:] *n* 非能率 hinő-ritsu

inefficient [inifiʃ'ənt] *adj* (person, machine, system) 能率の悪い nőritsu no waruì

inept [inept'] *adj* (politician, management) 無能な munő na

inequality [inikwa:l'iti:] *n* (of system) 不平等 fubyődō; (of amount, share) 不等 futő

inert [inə:rt'] *adj* (immobile) 動かない u-gőkanaì; (gas) 不活性の fukássei no

inertia [inə:r'ʃə] *n* (apathy) 物臭 monőgusa; (PHYSICS) 惰性 daséi

inescapable [inəskei'pəbəl] *adj* (conclusion, impression) 避けられない sakérarenaì

inevitable [inev'itəbəl] *adj* (outcome, result) 避けられない sakérarenaì, 必然的な hitsúzenteki na

inevitably [inev'itəbli:] *adv* 必然的に hitsúzenteki ni

inexcusable [inikskju:'zəbəl] *adj* (behavior, error) 許されない yurúsarenaì

inexhaustible [inigzɔ:s'təbəl] *adj* (wealth, resources) 無尽蔵の mujíñzō no

inexorable [inek'sə:rəbəl] *adj* (progress, decline) 止め様のない toméyō no naí

inexpensive [inikspen'siv] *adj* (cheap) 安い yasúi

inexperience [inikspi:r'i:əns] *n* (of person) 不慣れ fúnàre

inexperienced [inikspi:r'i:ənst] *adj* (swimmer, worker) 不慣れの fúnàre no

inexplicable [ineks'plikəbəl] *adj* (decision, mistake) 不可解な fukákài na

inextricably [ineks'trikəbli:] *adv* (entangled, linked) 分けられない程 wakérarenái hodo

infallible [infæl'əbəl] *adj* (person, guide) 間違いのない machígaì no náì

infamous [in'fəməs] *adj* (crime, murderer) 悪名高い akúmeidakaì

infamy [in'fəmi:] *n* (notoriety) 悪評 akúhyō

infancy [in'fənsi:] *n* (of person) 幼年時代 yōnenjidài

infant [in'fənt] *n* (baby) 赤ちゃん ákàchan; (young child) 幼児 yōjì

infantile [in'fəntail] *adj* (disease) 幼児の yōjì no; (foolish) 幼稚な yōchì na

infantry [in'fəntri:] *n* (MIL) 歩兵隊 hohéitai

infant school (*BRIT*) *n* 幼稚園 yōchien

infatuated [infætʃ'u:eitid] *adj*: **to be infatuated with** ...にのぼせている ...ni nobósete irù

infatuation [infætʃu:ei'ʃən] *n* (passion) ...にのぼせる事 ...ni nobóseru koto

infect [infekt'] *vt* (person, animal) ...に感染させる ...ni kañsen saserù; (food) 汚染する osén suru

infection [infek'ʃən] *n* (MED: disease) 感染 kañsen; (contagion) 伝染 defisen

infectious [infek'ʃəs] *adj* (person, animal) 伝染病にかかった defisenbyō ni kakáttà; (disease) 伝染性の defisensei no; (*fig*: enthusiasm, laughter) 移りやすい utsúriyasuì

infer [infər'] *vt* (deduce) 推定する suítei suru; (imply) ...の意味を含む ...no ímì wo fukúmù

inference [in'fə:rəns] *n* (deduction) 推定 suítei; (implication) 含み fukúmi

inferior [infi:'ri:ə:r] *adj* (in rank) 下級の kakyū no; (in quality, quantity) 劣った otóttà

♦*n* (subordinate) 下の者 shitá no monò; (junior) 年下の者 toshíshita no monò

inferiority [infi:ri:ɔ:r'iti:] *n* (in rank) 下級である事 kakyū de arù kotò; (in quality) 品質の悪さ hiñshitsu nò wárùsa

inferiority complex *n* (PSYCH) 劣等感 rettōkan

infernal [infə:r'nəl] *adj* (racket, temper) ひどい hidóì

inferno [infə:r'nou] *n* (blaze) 大火事 ōkajì

infertile [infə:r'təl] *adj* (soil) 不毛の fumō no; (person, animal) 不妊の funín no

infertility [infə:rtil'əti:] *n* (of soil) 不毛 fumō; (of person, animal) 不妊症 funínshō

infested [infes'tid] *adj*: **infested with** (vermin, pests) ...がうじゃうじゃいる ...ga újàuja irú

infidelity [infidel'iti:] *n* (unfaithfulness) 浮気 uwáki

in-fighting [in'faitiŋ] *n* 内紛 naífun, 内ゲバ uchígeba

infiltrate [infil'treit] *vt* ...に潜入する ...ni sefinyū suru

infinite [in'fənit] *adj* (very great: variety, patience) ばく大な bakúdai na; (without limits: universe) 無限の mugén no

infinitive [infin'ətiv] *n* (LING) 不定詞 futéishi

infinity [infin'əti:] *n* (infinite number) 無限大 mugéndai; (infinite point) 無限 mugén

infirm [infə:rm'] *adj* (weak) 虚弱な kyojáku na; (ill) 病弱な byójaku na

infirmary [infə:r'mə:ri:] *n* (hospital) 病院 byóin

infirmity [infə:r'miti:] *n* (weakness) 虚弱さ kyojákusa; (being ill) 病弱さ byójakusa; (specific illness) 病気 byóki

inflamed [infleimd'] *adj* (tongue, appendix) 炎症を起した efishō wò okóshità

inflammable [inflæm'əbəl] *adj* (fabric, chemical) 可燃性の kanénsei no, 燃えや

すい moéyasuì

inflammation [infləmei'ʃən] *n* (of throat, appendix etc) 炎症 eñshō

inflatable [inflei'təbəl] *adj* (life jacket, dinghy, doll) 膨らます事のできる fukúramasu kotō no dekírù

inflate [infleit'] *vt* (tire, balloon) 膨らます fukúramasù; (price) つり上げる tsuríagerù

inflation [inflei'ʃən] *n* (ECON) インフレ iñfure

inflationary [inflei'ʃəneːri:] *adj* (spiral) インフレの iñfure no; (demand) インフレを引起こす iñfure wo hikíokosù

inflexible [inflek'səbəl] *adj* (rule, timetable) 融通が利かない yūzū ga kikánai; (person) 譲らない yuzúranaì

inflict [inflikt'] *vt*: **to inflict something on someone** (damage, suffering) ...に...を加える ...ni ...wo kuwáerù

influence [in'flu:əns] *n* (power) 実力 jitsúryoku; (effect) 影響 eíkyō

◆*vt* (person, situation, choice etc) 左右する sáyū suru

under the influence of alcohol 酒に酔って saké ni yottè

influential [influen'tʃəl] *adj* (politician, critic) 有力な yūryoku na

influenza [influen'zə] *n* (MED) 流感 ryūkan

influx [in'flʌks] *n* (of refugees, funds) 流入 ryūnyū

inform [infoːrm'] *vt*: **to inform someone of something** (tell) ...に...を知らせる ...ni ...wo shiráserù

◆*vi*: **to inform on someone** (to police, authorities) ...を密告する ...wo mikkóku suru

informal [infoːr'məl] *adj* (manner, discussion, party) 寛いだ kutsúroidà; (clothes) 普段の fúdan no; (unofficial: visit, meeting) 非公式の hikóshiki no

informality [infoːrmæl'iti:] *n* (of manner, party etc) 寛いだ雰囲気 kutsúroida fuñ-iki

informant [infoːr'mənt] *n* (source) 情報提供者 jōhōteikyōsha, インフォーマント iñfōmànto

information [infəːrmei'ʃən] *n* 情報 jōhō

a piece of information 1つの情報 hitótsu no jōhō

information office *n* 案内所 añnaijo

informative [infoːr'mətiv] *adj* (report, comment) 有益な yūeki na

informer [infoːr'məːr] *n* (*also*: **police informer**) 密告者 mikkókushà, スパイ supáì

infra-red [in'frəred] *adj* (rays, light) 赤外線の sekígaisen no

infrastructure [in'frəstrʌk'tʃəːr] *n* (of system etc) 下部構造 kabúkōzō, インフラストラクチャー iñfurasutorakùchā

infrequent [infri:'kwint] *adj* (visits) 間遠な madō na; (buses) 本数の少ない hoñsū nò sukúnaì

infringe [infrindʒ'] *vt* (law) 破る yabúrù

◆*vi*: **to infringe on** (rights) ...を侵す ...wo okásù

infringement [infrindʒ'mənt] *n* (of law) 違反 ihán; (of rights) 侵害 shiñgai

infuriating [infjur'i:eitiŋ] *adj* (habit, noise) いらいらさせる íraira saséru

ingenious [indʒi:n'jəs] *adj* (idea, solution) 巧妙な kōmyō na

ingenuity [indʒənu:'iti:] *n* (cleverness, skill) 才能 saínō

ingenuous [indʒen'ju:əs] *adj* (innocent, trusting) 無邪気な mújàki na

ingot [iŋ'gət] *n* (of gold, platinum) 延べ棒 nobébō, インゴット iñgòtto

ingrained [ingreind'] *adj* (habit, belief) 根深い nebúkaì

ingratiate [ingrei'ʃi:eit] *vt*: **to ingratiate oneself with** ...に取入る ...ni toríiru

ingratitude [ingræt'ətu:d] *n* (of beneficiary, heir) 恩知らず oñshirázu

ingredient [ingri:'di:ənt] *n* (of cake) 材料 zaíryō; (of situation) 要素 yṓso

inhabit [inhæb'it] *vt* (town, country) ...に住む ...ni súmù

inhabitant [inhæb'ətənt] *n* (of town, street, house, country) 住民 jūmin

inhale [inheil'] *vt* (breathe in: smoke, gas etc) 吸込む suíkomù

◆*vi* (breathe in) 息を吸う íkì wo suu; (when smoking) 煙を吸込む kemúri wò suíkomù

inherent [inhe:r'ent] *adj*: **inherent in** ...に固有の ...ni koyû no

inherit [inhe:r'it] *vt* (property, money) 相続する sôzoku suru; (characteristic) 遺伝で受継ぐ idén de ukétsugù

inheritance [inhe:r'itəns] *n* (property, money etc) 相続財産 sôzoku zaisàn; (characteristics etc) 遺伝 idén

inhibit [inhib'it] *vt* (growth: *also* PSYCH) 抑制する yokúsei suru

inhibited [inhib'itid] *adj* (PSYCH) 抑制の多い yokúsei no ôi

inhibition [inibi∫'ən] *n* 抑制 yokúsei

inhospitable [inhɑ:spit'əbəl] *adj* (person) もてなしの悪い moténashi nò warui; (place, climate) 住みにくい sumínikuì

inhuman [inhju:'mən] *adj* (behavior) 残忍な zafínin na; (appearance) 非人間的な hiníngenteki na

inimitable [inim'itəbəl] *adj* (tone, style) まねのできない mané no dekinài

iniquity [inik'witi:] *n* (wickedness) 悪akù; (injustice) 不正 fuséi

initial [ini∫'əl] *adj* (stage, reaction) 最初の saísho no
♦*n* (letter) 頭文字 kashíramojì
♦*vt* (document) ...に頭文字で署名する ...ni kashíramojì de shoméi surù

initials [ini∫'əlz] *npl* (of name) 頭文字 kashíramojì; (as signature) 頭文字の署名 kashíramojì no shoméi

initially [ini∫'əli:] *adv* (at first) 最初は saísho wa; (first) まず最初に mázù saísho ni

initiate [ini∫'i:it] *vt* (begin: talks, process) 始める hajímerù; (new member) 入会させる nyúkai saséru
to initiate someone into a secret ...に秘密を教える ...ni himítsu wò oshíerù
to initiate proceedings against someone (LAW) ...を起訴する ...wo kisó suru

initiation [ini∫i:ei∫'ən] *n* (beginning) 開始 kaíshi; (into organization etc) 入会式 nyúkaìshiki; (into secret etc) 伝授 défiju

initiative [ini∫'i:ətiv] *n* (move) 企画 kikáku; (enterprise) 進取の気 shífishu no kí
to take the initiative 先手を打つ sefíte

wò útsù

inject [ind3ekt'] *vt* (drugs, poison) 注射する chúsha suru; (patient): *to inject someone with something* ...に...を注射する ...ni ...wo chúsha suru; (funds) つぎ込む tsugíkomù

injection [ind3ek'∫ən] *n* (of drugs, medicine) 注射 chúsha; (of funds) つぎ込む事 tsugíkomù kotó

injunction [ind3ʌŋk'∫ən] *n* (LAW) 差止め命令 sashítomemeîrei

injure [in'd3ə:r] *vt* (hurt: person, leg etc) 傷付ける kizútsukerù; (: feelings, reputation) 害する gaî surù

injured [in'd3ə:rd] *adj* (person, arm) 傷付いた kizútsuità; (feelings) 害された gaî saretà; (tone) 感情を害された kafíjō wò gaî saretà

injury [in'd3ə:ri:] *n* (wound) 傷 kizú, けが kegá

injury time *n* (SPORT) 延長時間 efíchōjikàn ◇傷の手当てなどに使った分の延長時間 kizú no teàte nádò ni tsukátta buñ no efíchōjikàn

injustice [ind3ʌs'tis] *n* (unfairness) 不公平 fukôhei

ink [iŋk] *n* (in pen, printing) インク ífiku

inkling [iŋk'liŋ] *n* (idea, clue) 薄々と気付く事 usúusu tò kizúku kotó

inlaid [in'leid] *adj* (with gems, wood etc) ...をちりばめた ...wo chirîbametà

inland [in'lænd] *adj* (port, sea, waterway) 内陸の naíriku no
♦*adv* (travel) 内陸へ naíriku e

Inland Revenue (*BRIT*) *n* 国税庁 kokúzeichō

in-laws [in'lɔ:z] *npl* 義理の親せき girí nò shifíseki, 姻せき ifíseki

inlet [in'let] *n* (GEO) 入江 irîe

inmate [in'meit] *n* (in prison) 受刑者 jukêîsha; (in asylum) 入院患者 nyúinkañja

inn [in] *n* 旅館 ryokáń

innate [ineit'] *adj* (skill, quality, characteristic) 生来の seírai no

inner [in'ə:r] *adj* (office, courtyard) 内側の uchígawa no; (calm, feelings) 内心の naíshin no

inner city *n* インナーシティー ifínàshīti◇スラム化した都心部を指す súramuka shita toshínbu wo sásù

inner tube n (of tire) チューブ chùbu

inning [in'iŋ] n (BASEBALL) イニング íniŋgu

innings [in'iŋz] n (CRICKET) イニング íniŋgu

innocence [in'əsəns] n (LAW) 無罪 múzài; (naivety: of child, person) 純真さ juńshinsa

innocent [in'əsənt] adj (not guilty of crime etc) 無罪の múzài no, 潔白な keppáku na; (naive: child, person) 純真な juńshin na; (not involved: victim) 罪のない tsúmì no nái; (remark, question) 無邪気な mújàki na

innocuous [inɑ:k'ju:əs] adj (harmless) 無害の múgài no

innovation [inəvei'ʃən] n (change) 刷新 sasshín

innuendo [inju:en'dou] (pl innuendoes) n (insinuation) 当てこすり atékosuri

innumerable [inu:'mə:rəbəl] adj (countless) 無数の musú no

inoculation [inɑ:kjəlei'ʃən] n (MED) 接種 sesshú

inopportune [inɑ:pə:rtu:n'] adj (event, moment) 都合の悪い tsugó no warùi

inordinately [inɔ:r'dənitli:] adv (proud, long, large etc) 極度に kyokúdò ni

in-patient [in'peiʃənt] n (in hospital) 入院患者 nyūinkañja

input [in'put] n (information) 情報 jóhò; (resources etc) つぎ込む事 tsugíkomù kotó; (COMPUT) 入力 nyúryoku, インプット ínputtò

inquest [in'kwest] n (on someone's death) 検死訊問 keńshishimòn

inquire [inkwaiə:r'] vi (ask) 尋ねる tazúnerù, 聞く kíkù

♦vt (ask) ...に尋ねる ...ni tazúnerù, ...に聞く ...ni kíkù

to inquire about (person, fact) ...について問い合せる ...ni tsúìte toíawase surù

inquire into vt fus (death, circumstances) 調べる shiráberù

inquiry [inkwaiə:r'i:] n (question) 質問 shitsúmon; (investigation) 調査 chósa

inquiry office (BRIT) n 案内所 afinaijò

inquisitive [inkwiz'ətiv] adj (curious) せん索好きな seńsakuzuki na

inroads [in'roudz] npl: **to make inroads into** (savings, supplies) ...を消費する ...wo shóhi suru

ins abbr = **inches**

insane [insein'] adj (foolish, crazy) 気違い染みた kichígaijimità; (MED) 狂気の kyóki no

insanity [insæn'iti:] n (foolishness) 狂気のさた kyóki nò satá; (MED) 狂気 kyóki

insatiable [insei'ʃəbəl] adj (greed, appetite) 飽く事のない akú kotò no nái

inscription [inskrip'ʃən] n (on gravestone, memorial etc) 碑文 hibún; (in book) 献呈の言葉 keñtei no kotòba

inscrutable [inskru:'təbəl] adj (comment, expression) 不可解な fukákài na

insect [in'sekt] n 虫 mushi, 昆虫 końchū

insecticide [insek'tisaid] n 殺虫剤 satchúzài

insecure [insikju:r'] adj (structure, lock, door: weak) 弱い yówài; (: unsafe) 安全でない añzen de naì; (person) 自信のない jishín no naì

insecurity [insikju:r'iti:] n (of structure, lock etc: weakness) 弱さ yówàsa; (: lack of safety) 安全でない añzen de naì kotó; (of person) 自信欠如 jishínketsujò

insemination [inseminei'ʃən] n: **artificial insemination** (AGR, MED) 人工授精 jiñkōjùsei

insensible [insen'səbəl] adj (unconscious) 意識を失った íshìki wo ushínattà

insensitive [insen'sətiv] adj (uncaring, indifferent) 思いやりのない omóiyarì no nái

inseparable [insep'ə:rəbəl] adj (ideas, elements) 分離できない buñri dekinài; (friends) いつも一緒な ítsùmo isshó no

insert [insə:rt'] vt (between two things) ...の間に入れる ...no aídà ni irérù; (into something) 差込む sashíkomù, 挿入する sónyū suru

insertion [insə:r'ʃən] n (of needle, comment, peg etc) 差込む事 sashíkomù kotó, 挿入 sónyū

in-service [in'sər'vis] *adj* (training, course) 現職の geñshoku no

inshore [in'ʃɔːr] *adj* (fishing, waters) 近海の kiñkai no
♦*adv* (be) 岸の近くに kishí no chikakù ni; (move) 岸の近くへ kishí no chikakù e

inside [in'saɪd] *n* (interior) 中 nákà, 内側 uchígawa
♦*adj* (interior) 中〔内側〕 nákà〔uchígawa〕no
♦*adv* (go) 中〔内側〕へ nákà〔uchígawa〕e; (be) 中〔内側〕に nákà〔uchígawa〕ni
♦*prep* (of location) …の中へ〔に〕…no nákà e〔ni〕; (of time): *inside 10 minutes* 10分以内に juppún inâi ni

inside forward *n* (SPORT) インサイドフォワード íñsaidofowâdo

inside information *n* 内部情報 naíbujōhō

inside lane *n* (AUT) 内側車線 uchígawashaseñ

inside out *adv* (be, turn) 裏返しで urágaeshi de; (know) すっかり sukkárī

insides [in'saɪdz] *npl* (inf: stomach) おなか onáka

insidious [insid'i:əs] *adj* (effect, power) 潜行的な señkōteki na

insight [in'saɪt] *n* (into situation, problem) 洞察 dōsatsu

insignia [insig'ni:ə] *npl* 記章 kishō

insignificant [insignif'ikənt] *adj* (extent, importance) ささいな sasái na

insincere [insinsi:r'] *adj* (smile, welcome) 偽りの itsúwarī no

insinuate [insin'ju:eit] *vt* (imply) 当てこする atékosurù

insipid [insip'id] *adj* (person, activity, color) 面白くない omóshirokunāi; (food, drink) 風味のない fûmi no nâi

insist [insist'] *vi* (maintain) 主張する shuchō suru, 言い張る iíharù
to insist on (demand) …を要求する …wo yōkyū suru
to insist that (demand) …する様要求する …surú yō yōkyū suru; (claim) …だと言い張る …da to iíharù

insistence [insis'təns] *n* (determination) 強要 kyōyō

insistent [insis'tənt] *adj* (determined: person) しつこい shitsúkoī; (continual: noise, action) 絶間ない taémanaī

insole [in'soul] *n* (of shoe) 敷皮 shikíkawa

insolence [in'sələns] *n* (rudeness) 横柄さ ōheisa

insolent [in'sələnt] *adj* (attitude, remark) 横柄な ōhei na

insoluble [insɑːl'jəbəl] *adj* (problem) 解決のできない kaíketsu nò dekínaī

insolvent [insɑːl'vənt] *adj* (bankrupt) 破産した hasán shita

insomnia [insɑːm'ni:ə] *n* 不眠症 fumíñshō

inspect [inspekt'] *vt* (examine: gen) 調べる shiráberù; (premises) 捜査する sōsa suru; (equipment) 点検する teñken suru; (troops) 査閲する saétsu suru; (BRIT: ticket) 改札する kaísatsu suru

inspection [inspek'ʃən] *n* (examination: gen) 検査 keñsa; (of premises) 捜査 sōsa, (of equipment) 点検 teñken; (of troops) 査閲 saétsu; (BRIT: of ticket) 改札 kaísatsu

inspector [inspek'tər] *n* (ADMIN) 検査官 keñsakàn; (BRIT: on buses, trains) 車掌 shashō; (: POLICE) 警部 keibu

inspiration [inspərei'ʃən] *n* (encouragement) 発憤 happún; (influence, source) 発憤させる物 happún saserù mono; (idea) 霊感 reíkan, インスピレーション íñsupirēshon

inspire [inspaiər'] *vt* (workers, troops) 奮い立たせる furúitataserù; (confidence, hope etc) 持たせる motáserù

instability [instəbil'əti:] *n* (of place, person, situation) 不安定 fuáñtei

install [instɔːl'] *vt* (machine) 取付ける torítsukerù; (official) 就任させる shūnin saserù

installation [instəlei'ʃən] *n* (of machine, equipment) 取付け torítsuke, 設置 sétchì; (plant: INDUSTRY) 工場施設 kōjōshisètsu, プラント puráñto; (: MIL) 基地 kichí

installment [instɔːl'mənt] (BRIT **instalment**) *n* (of payment, story, TV serial etc) 1回分 ikkáíbun

in installments (pay, receive) 分割払いで buñkatsubarài de

instance [in'stəns] *n* (example) 例 rêi

for instance 例えば tatôeba

in the first instance まず最初に mázù saísho ni

instant [in'stənt] *n* (moment) 瞬間 shuñkan

♦*adj* (reaction, success) 瞬間的な shuñkanteki na; (coffee, food) 即席の sokúseki no, インスタントの fñsutanto no

instantaneous [instəntei'ni:əs] *adj* (immediate) 即時の sokúji no

instantly [in'stəntli:] *adv* (immediately) 即時に sokúji ni

instead [insted'] *adv* (in place of) (その) 代りに (sonô) kawári ni

instead of ...の代りに ...no kawári ni

instep [in'step] *n* (of foot) 足の甲 ashí no kô; (of shoe) 靴の甲 kutsú no kô

instigate [in'stəgeit] *vt* (rebellion etc) 起させる okósaserù; (talks etc) 始めさせる hajímesaserù

instil(l) [instil'] *vt*: *to instil something into* (confidence, fear etc) ...を...に吹込む ...wo ...ni fukíkomù

instinct [in'stiŋkt] *n* 本能 hoñnō

instinctive [instiŋk'tiv] *adj* (reaction, feeling) 本能的な hoñnōteki na

institute [in'stitu:t] *n* (for research, teaching) 施設 shisétsu; (professional body: of architects, planners etc) 協会 kyôkai

♦*vt* (system, rule, course of action) 設ける mōkerù; (proceedings, inquiry) 始める hajímerù

institution [institu:'ʃən] *n* (of system etc) 開設 kaísetsu; (custom, tradition) 伝統 deñtō; (organization: financial, religious, educational) 協会 kyôkai; (hospital, mental home) 施設 shisétsu

instruct [instrʌkt'] *vt*: *to instruct someone in something* (teach) ...に...を教える ...ni ...wo oshíerù

to instruct someone to do something (order) ...する様に...に命令する ...surú yồ ...ni meírei suru

instruction [instrʌk'ʃən] *n* (teaching) 教育 kyôiku

instructions [instrʌk'ʃənz] *npl* (orders) 命令 meírei

instructions (for use) 取扱い説明 torítsukai setsúmei

instructive [instrʌk'tiv] *adj* (lesson, response) 有益な yûeki na

instructor [instrʌk'tə:r] *n* (teacher) 先生 señsei; (for skiing, driving etc) 指導者 shidôshà

instrument [in'strəmənt] *n* (tool) 道具 dôgu; (measuring device etc) 計器 keíki; (MUS) 楽器 gakkí

instrumental [instrəmen'təl] *adj* (MUS) 器楽の kígàku no

to be instrumental in ...に大きな役割を果す ...ni ồkina yakúwari wo hatasù

instrument panel *n* 計器盤 keíkiban

insubordination [insəbɔ:rdənei'ʃən] *n* (disobedience) 不服従 fufúkujù

insufferable [insʌf'ə:rəbəl] *adj* (arrogance, laziness) 耐えがたい taégataì; (person) 我慢のならない gámàn no naránaì

insufficient [insəfiʃ'ənt] *adj* (funds, data, research) 不十分な fujûbun na

insular [in'sələ:r] *adj* (outlook, person) 狭量な kyôryō na

insulate [in'səleit] *vt* (protect: person, group) 孤立させる korítsu saserù; (against cold: house, body) 断熱する dañnetsu suru; (against sound) 防音にする bôon ni suru; (against electricity) 絶縁する zetsúen suru

insulating tape [in'səleitiŋ-] *n* (ELEC) 絶縁テープ zetsúentēpu

insulation [insəlei'ʃən] *n* (of person, group) 孤立させる事 korítsu saserù kotó; (against cold) 断熱材 dañnetsuzài; (against sound) 防音材 bôonzai; (against electricity) 絶縁材 zetsúenzài

insulin [in'səlin] *n* (MED) インシュリン iñshurin

insult [*n* in'sʌlt *vb* insʌlt'] *n* (offence) 侮辱 bujóku

♦*vt* (offend) 侮辱する bujóku suru

insulting [insʌl'tiŋ] *adj* (attitude, language) 侮辱的な bujôkuteki na

insuperable [insu:'pə:rəbəl] *adj* (obstacle, problem) 乗越えられない noríkoerarenaî

insurance [inʃɔ:r'əns] *n* (on property, car, life etc) 保険 hokén

fire/life insurance 火災〔生命〕保険 kasái〔seímei〕hokèn

insurance agent *n* 保険代理店 hokéndairitèn

insurance policy *n* 保険証書 hokénshôsho

insure [inʃuːr'] *vt* (life, property): *to insure (against)* ...に (...の) 保険を掛ける ...ni (...no) hokén wò kakérù

to insure (oneself) against (disappointment, disaster) ...に備える ...ni sonáerù

insurrection [insərek'ʃən] *n* (uprising) 反乱 hańran

intact [intækt'] *adj* (whole) 元のままの mótō no mamá no; (unharmed) 無傷の múkîzu no

intake [in'teik] *n* (gen) 取込み toríkomi; (of food etc) 摂取 sésshù; (of air) 吸入 kyū́nyū; (*BRIT*: *SCOL*): *an intake of 200 a year* 毎年の新入生は200人 maítoshi nò shińnyûsei wa nihyákunîn

intangible [intæn'dʒəbəl] *adj* (quality, idea, benefit) ばく然とした bakúzen to shita

integral [in'təgrəl] *adj* (feature, element) 不可欠な fukákètsu na

integrate [in'təgreit] *vt* (newcomer) 溶け込ませる tokékomaserù; (ideas, systems) 取入れる torîirerû

♦*vi* (groups, individuals) 溶け込む tokékomù

integrity [integ'riti:] *n* (morality: of person) 誠実さ seíjitsusa

intellect [in'təlekt] *n* (intelligence) 知性 chiséi; (cleverness) 知能 chinô

intellectual [intəlek'tʃuːəl] *adj* (activity, interest, pursuit) 知的な chitéki na

♦*n* (intelligent person) 知識人 chishíkijìn, インテリ ińteri

intelligence [intel'idʒəns] *n* (cleverness, thinking power) 知能 chinô; (MIL etc) 情報 jôhō

intelligence service *n* 情報部 jôhōbu

intelligent [intel'idʒənt] *adj* (person) 知能の高い chinô no takaî; (decision) 利口な rikô na; (machine) インテリジェントの ińterijeńto no

intelligentsia [intelidʒen'tsi:ə] *n* 知識階級 chishíkikaìkyū, インテリ階級 ińterikaîkyū

intelligible [intel'idʒəbəl] *adj* (clear, comprehensible) 分かりやすい wakáriyasuî

intend [intend'] *vt* (gift etc): *to intend something for* ...を...に上げようと思っている ...wo ...ni agéyô to omótte irù

to intend to do something (mean) ...する決心でいる ...suru kesshíñ de irú; (plan) ...するつもりである ...suru tsumóri de arû

intended [inten'did] *adj* (effect, insult) 意図した îtô shita; (journey) 計画した keíkaku shita; (victim) ねらった nerátta

intense [intens'] *adj* (heat, effort, anger, joy) 猛烈な môretsu na; (person) 情熱的な jônetsuteki na

intensely [intens'li:] *adv* (extremely) 激しく hagéshikù

intensify [inten'səfai] *vt* (efforts, pressure) 増す másu

intensity [inten'siti:] *n* (of heat, anger, effort) 激しさ hagéshisa

intensive [inten'siv] *adj* (concentrated) 集中的な shúchūteki na

intensive care unit *n* (MED) 集中治療室 shúchūchiryôshitsu, ICU aishíyū

intent [intent'] *n* (intention) 意図 îtô; (LAW) 犯意 háñ-i

♦*adj* (absorbed): *intent (on)* (...しようとして) 余念がない (...shíyô to shite) yonéñ ga naî; (attentive) 夢中な muchû na

to all intents and purposes 事実上 jijítsujô

to be intent on doing something (determined) ...しようとして余念がない ...shíyô to shite yonéñ ga naî

intention [inten'tʃən] *n* (purpose) 目的 mokúteki; (plan) 意図 îtô

intentional [inten't∫ənəl] *adj* (deliberate) 意図的な ítðteki na

intentionally [inten't∫ənəli:] *adv* (deliberately) 意図的に ítðteki ni, わざと wázà to

intently [intent'li:] *adv* (listen, watch) 熱心に nesshín ni

inter [intər'] *vt* (bury) 埋葬する maísō suru

interact [intə:rækt'] *vi*: **to interact (with)** (people, things, ideas) (...と) 相互に反応し合う (...to) sōgo ni hañnō shiaù

interaction [intə:ræk'∫ən] *n* 相互反応 sōgohañnō

intercede [intə:rsi:d'] *vi*: **to intercede (with)** (...に) 取りなしをする (...ni) torínashi wo surù

intercept [in'tə:rsept] *vt* (person, car) 途中で捕まえる tochū de tsukamaerù; (message) 傍受する bốju suru

interchange [in'tə:rt∫eindʒ] *n* (exchange) 交換 kốkan; (on motorway) インターチェンジ íntachieñji

interchangeable [intə:rt∫ein'dʒəbəl] *adj* (terms, ideas, things) 置換えられる okíkaerarerù

intercom [in'tə:rkɑ:m] *n* (in office etc) インターホーン íntahōn

intercourse [in'tə:rkɔ:rs] *n* (*also*: **sexual intercourse**) 性交 seíkō

interest [in'trist] *n* (in subject, idea, person etc) 興味 kyốmi; (pastime, hobby) 趣味 shúmi; (advantage, profit) 利益 rīeki; (COMM: in company) 株 kábù; (: sum of money) 利息 risóku

♦*vt* (subj: work, subject, idea etc) ...の興味をそそる ...no kyốmī wo sosórù

to be interested in ...に興味がある ...ni kyốmī ga árù

interesting [in'tristiŋ] *adj* (idea, place, person) 面白い omóshiroì

interest rate *n* 利率 rirítsu

interface [in'tə:rfeis] *n* (COMPUT) インターフェース íntāfēsu

interfere [intə:rfi:r'] *vi*: **to interfere in** (quarrel, other people's business) ...に干渉する ...ni kañshō suru

to interfere with (object) ...をいじる

...wo ijírù; (plans, career, duty, decision) ...を邪魔する ...wo jamá suru

interference [intə:rfi:r'əns] *n* (in someone's affairs etc) 干渉 kañshō; (RADIO, TV) 混信 koñshin

interim [in'tə:rim] *adj* (agreement, government) 暫定的な zañteiteki na

♦*n*: **in the interim** (meanwhile) その間 sonó aidà

interior [inti:'ri:ər] *n* (of building, car, box etc) 内部 naíbu; (of country) 内陸 naíriku

♦*adj* (door, window, room etc) 内部の naíbu no; (minister, department) 内務の naímu no

interior designer *n* インテリアデザイナー iñteriadezaìnā

interjection [intə:rdʒek'∫ən] *n* (interruption) 野次 yájì; (LING) 感嘆詞 kañtañshi

interlock [in'tə:rlɑ:k] *vi* かみ合う kamíaù

interloper [intə:rlou'pə:r] *n* (in town, meeting etc) ちん入者 chíñnyūsha

interlude [in'tə:rlu:d] *n* (break) 休憩 kyúkei; (THEATER) 休憩時間 kyúkeijikàn

intermarry [intə:rmær'i:] *vi* 交婚する kốkon suru

intermediary [intə:rmi:'di:e:ri:] *n* 仲介者 chúkaìsha

intermediate [intə:rmi:'di:it] *adj* (stage, student) 中間の chúkan no

interminable [intə:r'mənəbəl] *adj* (process, delay) 果てし無い hatéshinaì

intermission [intə:rmi∫'ən] *n* (pause) 休止 kyúshi; (THEATER, CINEMA) 休憩時間 kyúkeijikàn

intermittent [intə:rmit'ənt] *adj* (noise, publication etc) 断続的な dañzokuteki na

intern [in'tə:rn] *vt* (imprison) 拘置する kốchi suru

♦*n* (*US*: houseman) 研修医 keñshūī

internal [intə:r'nəl] *adj* (layout, structure, memo etc) 内部の naíbu no; (pipes etc) 埋め込みの umékomi no; (bleeding, injury) 体内の taínai no; (security, politics) 国内の kokúnài no

internally [intə:r'nəli:] *adv* 「*not to be taken internally*」内服外用薬 naífuku-gaiyõyaku

Internal Revenue Service (*US*) *n* 国税庁 kokúzeichõ

international [intə:rnæʃ'ənəl] *adj* (trade, agreement etc) 国際的な kokúsa-iteki na, 国際... kokúsai...

♦*n* (*BRIT*: SPORT: match) 国際試合 ko-kúsaijiài

interplay [in'tə:rplei] *n*: *interplay (of/ between)* (...の) 相互反応 (...no) sõgo-hañnõ

interpret [intə:r'prit] *vt* (explain, understand) 解釈する kaíshaku suru; (translate) 通訳する tsűyaku suru

♦*vi* (translate) 通訳する tsűyaku suru

interpretation [intə:rpritei'ʃən] *n* (explanation) 解釈 kaíshaku; (translation) 通訳 tsűyaku

interpreter [intə:r'pritər] *n* (translator) 通訳 (者) tsűyaku(sha)

interrelated [intə:rilei'tid] *adj* (causes, factors etc) 相互関係のある sõgokankèi no aru

interrogate [inte:r'əgeit] *vt* (question: witness, prisoner, suspect) 尋問する jiñmon suru

interrogation [inte:rəgei'ʃən] *n* (of witness, prisoner etc) 尋問 jiñmon

interrogative [intərɑg'ətiv] *adj* (LING) 疑問の gímòn no

interrupt [intər'ʌpt] *vt* (speaker) ...の話に割込む ...no hanáshi nì waríkomù; (activity) 邪魔する jamá suru

♦*vi* (during someone's conversation etc) 話に割込む hanáshi ni waríkomù; (during activity) 邪魔する jamá suru

interruption [intər'ʌpʃən] *n* (act) 邪魔する事 jamá suru kotò; (instance) 邪魔jamá

intersect [intə:r'sekt] *vi* (roads) 交差する kõsa suru

intersection [intə:rsek'ʃən] *n* (of roads) 交差点 kõsatèn

intersperse [intə:rspə:rs'] *vt*: *to intersperse with* ...を所々に入れる ...wo to-kõrodokòro ni irérù

intertwine [intə:rtwain'] *vi* 絡み合う ka-rámiaù

interval [in'tə:rvəl] *n* (break, pause) 間隔 kañkaku; (*BRIT*: SCOL: *also* THEATER, SPORT) 休憩時間 kyűkeijikàn

at intervals (periodically) 時々 tokído-ki

intervene [intə:rvi:n'] *vi* (person: in situation: interfere) 介入する kaínyu suru; (: : to help) 仲裁に入る chűsai ni hairù; (: in speech) 割込む waríkomù; (event) 間に起る aída ni okorù; (time) 経つ tátsù

intervention [intə:rven'tʃən] *n* (of person: interference) 介入 kaínyu; (help) 仲裁 chűsai

interview [in'tə:rvju:] *n* (for job etc) 面接 meñsetsu; (RADIO, TV etc) インタビュー íñtabyū

♦*vt* (for job etc) ...と面接する ...to meñse-tsu suru; (RADIO, TV etc) ...にインタビューする ...ni íñtabyū suru

interviewer [in'tə:rvju:ər] *n* (of candidate, job applicant) 面接者 meñsetsushà; (RADIO, TV etc) インタビューア íñta-byūa

intestine [intes'tin] *n* 腸 chõ

intimacy [in'təməsi:] *n* (closeness) 親しみ shitáshimi

intimate [*adj* in'təmit *vb* in'təmeit] *adj* (friendship, relationship) 親しい shitá-shiì; (detail) 知られざる shirárezarù; (restaurant, dinner, atmosphere) こじんまりした kojínmarì shita; (knowledge) 詳しい kuwáshiì

♦*vt* (announce) ほのめかす honómekasù

intimidate [intim'ideit] *vt* (frighten) 脅す odósu

intimidation [intimidei'ʃən] *n* 脅し odó-shi

KEYWORD

---

into [in'tu:] *prep* **1** (indicating motion or direction) ...の中に〔へ〕...no nákà ni(e)

come into the house/garden 家〔庭〕に入って来て下さい ié(niwá)nì hâitte kitê kudasaí

go into town 町に出掛ける machí ni dekakerù

he got into the car 彼は車に乗った kárè wa kurúma ni nottà

throw it into the fire 火の中へ捨てて下さい hí no nakà e sutéte kudasaì

research into cancer がんの研究 gáñ no keñkyū

he worked late into the night 彼は夜遅くまで働いた kárè wa yórù osóku madè határaìta

the car bumped into the wall 車は塀にぶつかった kurúma wà heí nì butsúkattà

she poured tea into the cup 彼女は紅茶をカップについだ kánòjo wa kốcha wò káppù ni tsuídà

2 (indicating change of condition, result): *she burst into tears* 彼女は急に泣き出した kánòjo wa kyū̄ nì nakídashìta

he was shocked into silence 彼はショックで物も言えなかった kárè wa shókkù de monó mò iénakattà

it broke into pieces ばらばらに割れた barábara nì warétá

she translated into French 彼女はフランス語に訳した kánòjo wa furánsugo nì yakúshìta

they got into trouble 彼らは問題を起こした kárèra wa moñdai wò okóshità

---

intolerable [intɑ:lʼəːrəbəl] *adj* (extent, quality) 我慢できない gámàn dekínaì

intolerance [intɑ:lʼəːrəns] *n* (bigotry, prejudice) 偏狭さ heñkyōsa

intolerant [intɑ:lʼəːrənt] *adj*: *intolerant (of)* (...に対して) 偏狭な (...ni táìshite) heñkyō na

intonation [intounei'ʼən] *n* (of voice, speech) 抑揚 yokúyō, イントネーション íñtoneshon

intoxicated [intɑ:kʼsikeitid] *adj* (drunk) 酔っ払った yoppárattà

intoxication [intɑ:ksikei'ʼən] *n* 泥酔 deísui

intractable [intrækʼtəbəl] *adj* (child, problem) 手に負えない té ni oenài

intransigent [intrænʼsidʒənt] *adj* (attitude) 頑固な gañko na

intransitive [intrænʼsətiv] *adj* (LING): *intransitive verb* 自動詞 jidóshì

intravenous [intrəviːʼnəs] *adj* (injection, drip) 静脈内の jőmyakunàì no

in-tray [inʼtrei] *n* (in office) 着信のトレー chakúshin no torế

intrepid [intrepʼid] *adj* (adventurer, explorer) 勇敢な yūkan na

intricate [inʼtrəkit] *adj* (pattern, design) 複雑な fukúzatsu na

intrigue [intriːgʼ] *n* (plotting) 策略 sakúryàku

◆*vt* (fascinate) ...の好奇心をそそる ...no kókìrshin wò sosórù

intriguing [intriˈgiŋ] *adj* (fascinating) 面白い omóshiroì

intrinsic [intrinʼsik] *adj* (quality, nature) 本質的な hoñshitsuteki na

introduce [intrədusʼ] *vt* (new idea, measure etc) 導入する dốnyū suru; (speaker, TV show etc) 紹介する shốkai suru

to introduce someone (to someone) (...に) ...を紹介する (...ni) ...wo shốkai suru

to introduce someone to (pastime, technique) ...に...を初めて経験させる ...ni ...wo hajímète keíken saserù

introduction [intrədʌkʼʼən] *n* (of new idea, measure etc) 導入 dốnyū; (of person) 紹介 shốkai; (to new experience) 初めて経験させる事 hajímète keíken saserù kotő; (to book) 前書 maếgaki

introductory [intrədʌkʼtəːriː] *adj* (lesson) 導入の dốnyū no; (offer) 初回の shokái no

introspective [intrəspekʼtiv] *adj* (person, mood) 内省的な naíseiteki na

introvert [inʼtrəvəːrt] *n* 内向性の人 naíkōsei no hitő

◆*adj* (*also*: **introverted**: behavior, child etc) 内向性の naíkōsei no

intrude [intruːdʼ] *vi* (person) 邪魔する jamá suru

to intrude on (conversation, grief, party etc) ...のところを邪魔する ...no tokőro wò jamá suru

intruder [intruːʼdəːr] *n* (into home, camp) 侵入者 shiñnyūshà

intrusion [intruː'ʒən] n (of person, outside influences) 邪魔 jamá

intuition [intuː'iʃən] n (feeling, hunch) 直感 chokkán

intuitive [intuː'ətiv] adj (instinctive) 直感的な chokkánteki na

inundate [in'ʌndeit] vt: to inundate with (calls, letters etc) ...が殺到する ...ga sattō surú

invade [inveid'] vt (MIL) ...を侵略する ...wo shiñryaku suru

invalid [n in'vəlid adj invæ'lid] n (MED: disabled person) 身障者 shiñshōsha; (: sick and weak person) 病弱な人 byōjaku na hitò
♦adj (not valid) 無効の mukō no

invaluable [invæl'juːəbəl] adj (person, thing) 貴重な kichō na

invariable [inveːr'iːəbəl] adj 変らない kawáranaì, 不変の fuhén no

invariably [inveːr'iːəbliː] adv 必ず kanárazù

invasion [invei'ʒən] n (MIL) 侵略 shiñryaku

invent [invent'] vt (machine, game, phrase etc) 発明する hatsúmei suru; (fabricate: lie, excuse) でっち上げる detchíagerù

invention [inven'tʃən] n (machine, system) 発明品 hatsúmeihin; (untrue story) 作り話 tsukúribanàshi; (act of inventing: machine, system) 発明 hatsúmei

inventor [inven'təːr] n (of machines, systems) 発明家 hatsúmeika

inventory [in'vəntɔːriː] n (of house, ship etc) 物品目録 buppíñmokùroku

inverse [inveːrs'] n (relationship) 逆の gyakú no

invert [inveːrt'] vt (turn upside down) 逆さにする sakása ni surù

invertebrate [inveːr'təbrit] n 無せきつい動物 musékitsuidòbutsu

inverted commas [inveːr'tid-] (BRIT) npl 引用符 iñyōfù

invest [invest'] vt (money) 投資する tōshi suru; (fig: time, energy) つぎ込む tsugíkomù
♦vi: invest in (COMM) ...に投資する ...ni tōshi suru; (fig: something useful) 購入する kōnyū suru

investigate [inves'təgeit] vt (accident, crime, person) 取調べる toríshiraberù, 捜査する sōsa suru

investigation [investəgei'ʃən] n 取調べ toríshirabe, 捜査 sōsa

investigator [inves'təgeitəːr] n (of events, situations, people) 捜査官 sōsakàn

investiture [inves'titʃəːr] n (of chancellor) 就任式 shūniñshiki; (of prince) たい冠式 taíkañshiki

investment [invest'mənt] n (activity) 投資 tōshi; (amount of money) 投資額 tōshigàku

investor [inves'təːr] n (COMM) 投資者 tōshishà

inveterate [invet'əːrit] adj (liar, cheat etc) 常習的な jōshūteki na

invidious [invid'iːəs] adj (task, job: unpleasant) 憎まれ役の nikúmareyàku no; (comparison, decision: unfair) 不公平な fukōhei na

invigilator [invidʒ'əleitəːr] (BRIT) n (in exam) 試験監督 shikéñkañtoku

invigorating [invig'əːreitiŋ] adj (air, breeze etc) さわやかな sawáyàka na; (experience etc) 元気が出る様な geñki ga deru yō na

invincible [invin'səbəl] adj (army, team: unbeatable) 無敵の mútèki no

invisible [inviz'əbəl] adj 目に見えない mé ni mienài

invitation [invitei'ʃən] n (to party, meal, meeting etc) 招待 shōtai; (written card, paper) 招待状 shōtaijō

invite [in'vait] vt (to party, meal, meeting etc) 招く manékù, 招待する shōtai suru; (encourage: discussion, criticism) 求める motómerù
to invite someone to do ...に...するよう求める ...ni ...surú yō motómerù

inviting [invai'tiŋ] adj (attractive, desirable) 魅力的な miryókuteki na

invoice [in'vɔis] n (COMM) 請求書 sefkyūsho
♦vt ...に請求書を送る ...ni sefkyūsho wo

okúrù

invoke [invouk'] *vt* (law, principle) ...に
訴える ...ni uttáerù

involuntary [invɑːl'ənteːriː] *adj* (action,
reflex etc) 反射的な hańshateki na

involve [invɑːlv'] *vt* (person, thing:
include, use) 伴う tomónaù, 必要とする
hitsúyō to surù; (: concern, affect) ...に関
係する ...ni kańkei suru
　to involve someone (in something)
(...に) ...を巻込む (...ni) ...wo makíkomù

involved [invɑːlvd'] *adj* (complicated) 複
雑な fukúzatsu na
　to be involved in (take part: in activity
etc) ...にかかわる ...ni kakáwarù; (be engrossed) ...に夢中になっている ...ni muchū ni nattě irú

involvement [invɑːlv'mənt] *n* (participation) 参加 sańka; (concern, enthusi-
asm) 感情的かかわり合い kańjōteki nà
kakáwariaì

inward [in'wəːrd] *adj* (thought, feeling)
内心の naíshin no; (movement) 中の方へ
の nákà no hổ e no

inward(s) [in'wəːrd(z)] *adv* (move, face)
中の方へ nákà no hổ e

I/O [ai'ou'] *abbr* (COMPUT: = *input/*
output) 入出力 nyūshutsuryòku

iodine [ai'ədain] *n* (chemical element) ヨ
ウ素 yōso, ヨード yòdo; (disinfectant) ヨ
ードチンキ yòdochiñki

ion [ai'ɑːn] *n* イオン iòn

iota [aiou'tə] *n*: *not one/an iota* 少しも
...ない sukóshì mo ...nâì

IOU [aiouju:'] *n abbr* (= *I owe you*) 借用
証 shakúyōshò

IQ [aikju:'] *n abbr* (= *intelligence quo-*
tient) 知能指数 chinôshisū, IQ aikyū

IRA [aiɑːrei'] *n abbr* (= *Irish Republi-*
can Army) アイルランド共和国軍 aírú-
rando kyōwakakugùn

Iran [iræn'] *n* イラン íràn

Iranian [irei'ni:ən] *adj* イランの íràn no
　♦*n* イラン人 iráñjin

Iraq [iræk'] *n* イラク íràku

Iraqi [irɑːk'i:] *adj* イラクの íràku no
　♦*n* イラク人 iràkujìn

irascible [iræs'əbəl] *adj* 怒りっぽい okó-

rippoì

irate [aireit'] *adj* 怒っている okótte irù

Ireland [aiə:r'lənd] *n* アイルランド aíru-
rando

iris [ai'ris] (*pl* **irises**) *n* (ANAT) こう彩
kōsai; (BOT) アヤメ ayáme, アイリス áì-
risu

Irish [ai'riʃ] *adj* アイルランドの aírurà-
ndo no
　♦*npl*: *the Irish* アイルランド人 aíruran-
dojìn ◇総称 sōshō

Irishman/woman [ai'riʃmən/wumən]
(*pl* **Irishmen/women**) *n* アイルランド
男性〔女性〕aírurandojìn dañsei〔joséi〕

Irish Sea *n*: *the Irish Sea* アイリッシ
ュ海 aírisshukài

irksome [əːrk'səm] *adj* いらいらさせるí-
ràira saséru

iron [ai'əːrn] *n* (metal) 鉄 tetsú; (for
clothes) アイロン aíron
　♦*cpd* (bar, railings) 鉄の tetsú no; (will,
discipline etc) 鉄の様な tetsú no yồ na
　♦*vt* (clothes) ...にアイロンを掛ける ...ni
aíron wò kakérù

Iron Curtain *n*: *the Iron Curtain* 鉄
のカーテン tetsú no kâten

ironic(al) [airɑːn'ik(əl)] *adj* (remark,
gesture, situation) 皮肉な híníku na

ironing [ai'əːrniŋ] *n* (activity) アイロン
掛け aíronkake; (clothes) アイロンを掛
けるべき衣類 aíron wò kakérubeki irùi

ironing board *n* アイロン台 aírondai

ironmonger [ai'əːrnmʌŋgəːr] (*BRIT*) *n*
金物屋 kanámonoya ◇人を指す hitô wồ
sásù

ironmonger's (shop)
[ai'əːrnmʌŋgəːrz-] *n* 金物屋 kanámonoya ◇店を指す misê wồ sásù

iron out *vt* (*fig*: problems) 打開する da-
kái suru

irony [ai'rəni:] *n* 皮肉 híníku

irrational [iræʃ'ənəl] *adj* (feelings,
behavior) 不合理な fugóri na

irreconcilable [irek'ənsailəbəl] *adj*
(ideas, views) 両立しない ryóritsu shina-
ì; (disagreement) 調和不可能な chōwafu-
kanô na

irrefutable [irifju:'təbəl] *adj* (fact) 否

られない inámerarenaì; (argument) 反ば
くてきない hańbaku dekinaì

irregular [ireg'jələ:r] *adj* (surface) 凸 凹
の dekóboko no; (pattern, action, event
etc) 不規則な fukísoku na; (not acceptable: behavior) 良くない yókunaì; (verb,
noun, adjective) 不規則変化の fukísoku-
heńka no

irregularity [iregjəlær'iti:] *n* (of surface) 凸凹 dekóboko; (of pattern, action
etc) 不規則 fukísoku; (instance of behavior) 良くない行為 yókunai kói

irrelevant [irel'əvənt] *adj* (fact, information) 関係のない kańkei no naì

irreparable [irep'ə:rəbəl] *adj* (harm,
damage etc) 取返しの付かない toríkae-
shi no tsukanaì

irreplaceable [iriplei'səbəl] *adj* 掛替え
のない kakégae no naì

irrepressible [iripres'əbəl] *adj* 陽 気 な
yóki na

irresistible [irizis'təbəl] *adj* (force) 抵抗
できない teíkō dekinaì; (urge, desire) 抑
えきれない osáekirenaì; (person, thing)
とても魅惑的な totémo miwákuteki na

irresolute [irez'əlu:t] *adj* 決断力のない
ketsúdanryòku no naì

irrespective [irispek'tiv]: **irrespective
of** *prep* ...と関係なく ...to kańkei nakù

irresponsible [irispɑ:n'səbəl] *adj* (person, action) 無責任な musékinin na

irreverent [irev'ə:rənt] *adj* 不敬な fukéi
na

irrevocable [irev'əkəbəl] *adj* (action,
decision) 変更できない heńkō dekinaì

irrigate [ir'igeit] *vt* (AGR) かんがいする
kańgai suru

irrigation [irigei'ʃən] *n* (AGR) か ん が い
kańgai

irritable [ir'itəbəl] *adj* 怒りっぽい okórippoì

irritate [ir'əteit] *vt* (annoy) い ら い ら さ
せる íraira saséru; (MED) 刺激する shi-
géki suru

irritating [ir'əteitiŋ] *adj* (person, sound
etc) いらいらさせる íraira saséru

irritation [iritei'ʃən] *n* (feeling of annoyance) いら立ち irádachi; (MED) 刺激 shi-

géki; (annoying thing) いら立ちの元 irádachi no motð

IRS [aiɑ:res'] (*US*) *n abbr* = **Internal
Revenue Service**

is [iz] *vb see* **be**

Islam [iz'lɑ:m] *n* イスラム教 isúramukyō

Islamic [izlɑ:m'ic] *adj* イスラム教 の isúramukyō no

island [ai'lənd] *n* (GEO) 島 shimá

islander [ai'ləndə:r] *n* 島の住民 shimá no
júmin

isle [ail] *n* (GEO) 島 shimá

isn't [iz'ənt] = **is not**

isolate [ai'səleit] *vt* (physically, socially:
set apart) 孤立させる korítsu saserú;
(substance) 分離する buńri suru; (sick
person, animal) 隔離する kakúri suru

isolated [ai'səleitid] *adj* (place) へんぴな
heńpi na; (person) 孤立した korítsu shita; (incident) 単独の tańdoku no

isolation [aisəlei'ʃən] *n* 孤立 korítsu

isotope [ai'sətoup] *n* (PHYSICS) 同位体
dóitai, アイソトープ aísotōpu

Israel [iz'reiəl] *n* イスラエル isúraèru

Israeli [izrei'li:] *adj* イスラエルの isúraèru no
♦*n* イスラエル人 isúraerujìn

issue [iʃ'u:] *n* (problem, subject, most
important part) 問題 mońdai; (of newspaper, magazine etc) 号 gó; (of book) 版
háñ; (of stamp) 発行部数 hakkóbùsū
♦*vt* (statement) 発表する happyó suru;
(rations, equipment, documents) 配給す
る kaíkyū suru
at issue 問題は(の) mońdai wa(no)
to take issue with someone (over)
(...について) ...と争う (...ni tsuíte) ...to
arásoù

isthmus [is'məs] *n* (GEO) 半島 hańtō

KEYWORD

it [it] *pron* **1** (specific: subject) そ れ は
〔が〕 soré wà〔gà〕; (: direct object) それ
を soré wò; (: indirect object) それにそ/re
nì ◊通常日本語では表現しない tsújō ni-
hongo de wa hyōgen shínài
where's my book? - it's on the table
私の本はどこですか-テーブルにあります

watákushi no hoǹ wa dókò desu ká -
tébùru ni arímasù
I can't find it 見当りません miátari-
maseǹ
give it to me それを私に渡して下さい
soré wò watákushi nǐ watáshite kudasaí
about/from/in/of/to it それについて
〔から、の中に、の、の方へ〕soré ni tsu-
íte〔kárà, no nákà ni, nó, no hò ê〕
I spoke to him about it その件につい
て私は彼に話しました sonó keǹ ni tsúte
watákushi wà kárè ni hanáshimashìta
what did you learn from it? その事
からあなたは何を学びましたか sonó ko-
tò kara anátà wa nánì wo manábimashì-
ta ká
what role did you play in it? その件
に関してあなたはどんな役割をしました
か sonó keǹ ni káǹ shite anátà wa doǹna
yakùwari wo shimáshìta ká
I'm proud of it それを誇りに思ってい
ます soré wò hokóri nì omótte imasù
did you go to it? (party, concert etc)
行きましたか ikímashìta ká
2 (impersonal): *it's raining* 雨が降って
いる ámè ga futté irù
it's cold today 今日は寒い kyô wà samúî
it's Friday tomorrow 明日は金曜日で
す asú wà kiǹ-yôbi desu
it's 6 o'clock/the 10th of August 6
時〔8月10日〕です rokúji〔hachígatsu tô-
kà〕desu
*how far is it? - it's 10 miles/2
hours on the train* そこまでどのぐらい
ありますか-10マイルあるいは〔列車で2時
間です〕sokó madè donó gurai arimasù
ká - júmaîru arímasù〔ressha dè nijíkàn
desu〕
who is it? - it's me どなたですか-私で
す dónàta desu ká - watákushi desù

Italian [itæl'jən] *adj* イタリアの itária
no; (LING) イタリア語の itáriago
♦*n* (person) イタリア人 itáriajìn; (LING)
イタリア語 itáriago
italics [itæl'iks] *npl* (TYP) 斜体文字 sha-
táimòji, イタリック体 itárikkutai

Italy [it'əli:] *n* イタリア itária
itch [itʃ] *n* (irritation) かゆみ kayúmi
♦*vi* (person) かゆがる kayúgarù; (part of
body) かゆい kayúî
to itch to do something ...をしたくて
むずむずしている ...wo shitákutè múzù-
muzu shité irù
itchy [itʃ'i:] *adj* (person) かゆがっている
kayúgatte irù; (skin etc) かゆい kayúî
it'd [it'əd] = **it would; it had**
item [ai'təm] *n* (one thing: of list, collection) 品目 hifìmoku; (on agenda) 項目 kô-
moku; (*also*: **news item**) 記事 kíjì
itemize [ai'təmaiz] *vt* (list) 明細に書く
meísai ni kakù, リストアップする risúto-
appù suru
itinerant [aitin'ə:rənt] *adj* (laborer,
salesman, priest etc) 巡回する juǹkai suru
itinerary [aitin'ərE:ri:] *n* 旅程 ryotéi
it'll [it'əl] = **it will; it shall**
its [its] *adj* それ〔あれ〕の soré〔arê〕no
it's [its] = **it is; it has**
itself [itself'] *pron* それ〔あれ〕自身 soré
〔arê〕jishiǹ
ITV [ait:vi:'] *n abbr* (*BRIT*: = *Independent Television*) 民間テレビ放送 miǹkan
terebi hôsô
IUD [aiju:di:'] *n abbr* (= *intra-uterine
device*) 子宮内避妊具 shikyúnaihiniǹgu,
IUD aiyúdī
I've [aiv] = **I have**
ivory [ai'və:ri:] *n* (substance) 象げ zôge;
(color) アイボリー áiborī
ivory tower *n* (*fig*) 象げの塔 zôge no tô
ivy [ai'vi:] *n* (BOT) キヅタ kízùta, アイビ
ー áibī

J

jab [dʒæb] *vt* (poke: with elbow, stick) 突
く tsukú
♦*n* (*inf*: injection) 注射 chúsha
to jab something into something ...を
...に突っ込む ...wo...ni tsukkómù
jabber [dʒæb'ə:r] *vi* (*also*: **jabber away**)
ぺちゃくぺちゃしゃべる péchàkucha

shabéru

jack [dʒæk] n (AUT) ジャッキ jákkî; (CARDS) ジャック jákkù

jackal [dʒæk'əl] n ジャッカル jákkàru

jackdaw [dʒæk'dɔ:] n コクマルガラス kokúmarugarāsu

jacket [dʒæk'it] n (garment) ジャケット jákètto; (of book) ジャケット jákètto, カバー kábā
potatoes in their jackets 皮ごと料理したジャガイモ kawágòto ryóri shita jagáimo

jack-knife [dʒæk'naif] vi (trailer truck) ジャックナイフ現象を起す jakkúnaifu genshō wo okósù ◊鋭角に折り曲って動けなくなる eíkaku ni orímagatte ugokenáku nárù

jack plug n (ELEC: for headphones etc) プラグ purágù

jackpot [dʒæk'pɑ:t] n 大賞金 daíshokin
to hit the jackpot 大賞金を当てる daíshokin wo atérù, 大当りする óatàri suru

jack up vt (AUT) ジャッキで持上げる jákkî de mochíagerù

jade [dʒeid] n (stone) ひすい hisúi

jaded [dʒei'did] adj (tired) 疲れ切った tsukárekittà; (fed-up) うんざりした uñzarishita

jagged [dʒæg'id] adj (outline, edge) ぎざぎざの gízàgiza no

jail [dʒeil] n 刑務所 keímusho
◊vt 刑務所に入れる keímusho ni irérù

jam [dʒæm] n (food) ジャム jámù; (also: *traffic jam*) 交通渋滞 kótsùjūtai; (inf: difficulty): *to be in a jam* 困っている komátte irù
◊vt (passage etc) ふさぐ fuságù; (mechanism, drawer etc) 動けなくする ugókenáku suru; (RADIO) 妨害する bógai suru
◊vi (mechanism, drawer etc) 動けなくなる ugókenáku nárù
to jam something into something (cram, stuff) ...に...を押込む ...ni...wo oshíkomù

Jamaica [dʒəmei'kə] n ジャマイカ jámaìka

jangle [dʒæŋ'gəl] vi (keys, bracelets etc) じゃらじゃら鳴る járàjara narú

janitor [dʒæn'itər] n (caretaker: of building) 管理人 kañrinin

January [dʒæn'ju:we:ri:] n 1月 ichígatsu

Japan [dʒəpæn'] n 日本 nihóñ〔nippóñ〕

Japanese [dʒæpəni:z'] adj 日本の nihóñ〔nippóñ〕no; (LING) 日本語の nihóngo no
◊n inv (person) 日本人 nihóñ〔nippóñ〕jin; (LING) 日本語 nihóngo

jar [dʒɑ:r] n (container: glass with wide mouth) 瓶 bíñ; (: stone, earthenware) つぼ tsubó, かめ kamé
◊vi (sound) 耳ざわりである mimízawàri de aru, きしる kishírù; (colors) 釣合わない tsuríawanài

jargon [dʒɑ:r'gən] n 専門用語 señmonyōgo, 隠語 íñgo

jasmine [dʒæz'min] n ジャスミン jásùmin

jaundice [dʒɔ:n'dis] n (MED) 黄だん ódan

jaundiced [dʒɔ:n'dist] adj *to view with a jaundiced eye* 白い目で見る shiróî me de mírù

jaunt [dʒɔ:nt] n (trip, excursion) 遠足 eñsoku

jaunty [dʒɔ:n'ti:] adj (attitude, tone) 陽気な yóki na; (step) 軽やかな karóyàka na

javelin [dʒæv'lin] n (SPORT) やり投げ yarínage

jaw [dʒɔ:] n (ANAT) あご agó

jay [dʒei] n カケス kakésu

jaywalker [dʒei'wɔ:kər] n ◊交通規則を無視して道路を横断する人 kótsùkisòku wo mushí shite dóro wo ódan surù hitó

jazz [dʒæz] n (MUS) ジャズ jázù

jazz up vt (liven up: party) 活気付ける kakkízukeru; (: taste) ぴりっとさせる pirítto saseru; (: image) 派手にする hadé ni surù

jazzy [dʒæz'i:] adj (shirt, pattern) 派手な hadé na

jealous [dʒel'əs] adj (suspicious: husband etc) 嫉妬深い shittóbukai; (envious: person) うらやましい uráyamashiî, うらやましっている uráyamashigàtte irú; (look etc) うらやましそうな uráyamashisōna

jealousy [dʒel'əsi:] n (resentment) ねた

み netámi; (envy) うらやむ事 uráyamù kotó

jeans [dʒiːnz] *npl* (trousers) ジーパン jíːpaǹ

jeep [dʒiːp] *n* (AUT, MIL) ジープ jíːpù

jeer [dʒiːr] *vi* (mock, scoff): **to jeer (at)** 野次る yajírù

jelly [dʒelˈiː] *n* (CULIN) ゼリー zéríː

jellyfish [dʒelˈiːfiʃ] *n* クラゲ kuráge

jeopardize [dʒepˈəːrdaiz] *vt* 危険にさらす kikén ni sarásù

jeopardy [dʒepˈəːrdi:] *n*: **to be in jeopardy** 危険にさらされる kikén ni sarásarerù

jerk [dʒəːrk] *n* (jolt, wrench)◇急な動き kyū na ugokí; (*inf*: idiot) 間抜け manúke
♦*vt* (pull) ぐいと引っ張る guí to hippárù
♦*vi* (vehicle, person, muscle) 急に動く kyū ni ugókù

jerkin [dʒəːrˈkin] *n* チョッキ chokkí

jersey [dʒəːrˈziː] *n* (pullover) セーター sētā; (fabric) ジャージー jàjí

jest [dʒest] *n* 冗談 jódaǹ

Jesus [dʒiːˈsəs] *n* イエス iésù

jet [dʒet] *n* (of gas, liquid) 噴射 fuńsha, ジェット jéttò; (AVIAT) ジェット機 jéttokì

jet-black [dʒetˈblækˈ] *adj* 真っ黒な makkúrò na

jet engine *n* ジェットエンジン jétto eǹjin

jet lag *n* 時差ぼけ jisáːbòke

jettison [dʒetˈəsən] *vt* (fuel, cargo) 捨てる sutéru

jetty [dʒetˈiː] *n* 波止場 hatóba

Jew [dʒuː] *n* ユダヤ人 yudáyajìn

jewel [dʒuːˈəl] *n* (*also fig*) 宝石 hóseki; (in watch) 石 ishí

jeweler [dʒuːˈəːr] (*BRIT* **jeweller**) *n* (dealer in jewelery) 宝石商 hósekishò; (dealer in watches) 時計屋 tokéiya

jeweler's (shop) [dʒuːˈələːrz-] *n* (jewelery shop) 宝石店 hósekiteǹ; (watch shop) 時計店 tokéiteǹ

jewelry [dʒuːˈəlriː] (*BRIT* **jewellery**) *n* 装身具 sōshiǹgu

Jewess [dʒuːˈis] *n* ユダヤ人女性 yudáyajìn jòsei

Jewish [dʒuːˈiʃ] *adj* ユダヤ人の yudáyajiǹ no

jibe [dʒaib] *n* 野次 yájì

jiffy [dʒifˈiː] (*inf*) *n*: **in a jiffy** 直ぐ súgù

jig [dʒig] *n* (dance) ジグ jígù ◇動きの早い活発なダンス ugóki nò hayáì kappátsu na dáǹsu

jigsaw [dʒigˈsɔː] *n* (*also*: **jigsaw puzzle**) ジグソーパズル jígùsō-pazuru

jilt [dʒilt] *vt* (lover etc) 振る furú

jingle [dʒiŋˈgəl] *n* (for advert) コマーシャルソング komáshāru soǹgu
♦*vi* (bells, bracelets) ちりんちりんと鳴る chíríǹchirin to narú

jinx [dʒiŋks] *n* ジンクス jíǹkusu

jitters [dʒitˈəːrz] (*inf*) *npl*: **to get the jitters** びびる bibírù

job [dʒɑːb] *n* (chore, task) 仕事 shigóto; (post, employment) 職 shokú
it's not my job (duty, function) それは私の仕事ではない soré wà watákushi nò shigóto de wa naì
it's a good job that ... (*BRIT*) ...して良かったね ...shite yókàtta né
just the job! (*BRIT*: *inf*) おあつらえ向きだ o-átsurae muki da, 丁度いい chódo iì

job centre (*BRIT*) *n* 公共職業安定所 kōkyōshokugyō anteishò

jobless [dʒɑːbˈlis] *adj* (ECON) 失業の shitsúgyō no

jockey [dʒɑːkˈiː] *n* (SPORT) 騎手 kíshù
♦*vi*: **to jockey for position** (rivals, competitors) 画策する kakúsaku suru

jocular [dʒɑːkˈjələːr] *adj* (person, remark) ひょうきんな hyókiǹ na

jog [dʒɑːg] *vt* (bump) 小突く kozúkù
♦*vi* (run) ジョギングする jógiǹgu suru
to jog someone's memory ...に...を思い起させる ...ni ...wo omói okosaserù

jog along *vi* (person, vehicle) のんびりと進む noǹbirì to susúmù

jogging [dʒɑːgˈiŋ] *n* ジョギング jógiǹgu

join [dʒɔin] *vt* (queue) ...に加わる ...ni kuwáwarù; (party) ...に参加する ...ni saǹka suru; (club etc) ...に入会する ...ni nyúːkai suru; (put together: things, places) つなぐ tsunágu; (meet: group of people) 一緒

になる isshō ni narú
♦vi (roads, rivers) 合流する gōryū suru
♦n つなぎ目 tsunágimè

joiner [dʒɔi'nəːr] (BRIT) n 建具屋 tatéguya

joinery [dʒɔi'nəːriː] n 建具職 tatégushòku

join in vi 参加する sañka suru
♦vt fus (work, discussion etc) …に参加する …ni sañka suru

joint [dʒɔint] n (TECH: in woodwork, pipe) 継目 tsugíme; (ANAT) 関節 kañsetsu; (of meat) ブロック肉 búròkku niku; (inf: nightclub, pub, cheap restaurant etc) 店 mìsé; (: of cannabis) マリファナタバコ marífàna tabakò
♦adj (common) 共通の kyōtsū no; (combined) 共同の kyōdō no

joint account n (at bank etc) 共同預金口座 kyōdō yokin kòza

join up vi (meet) 一緒になる isshō ni narù; (MIL) 入隊する nyūtai suru

joist [dʒɔist] n はり harí

joke [dʒouk] n (gag) 冗談 jōdan; (also: practical joke) いたずら itázura
♦vi 冗談を言う jōdan wo iú
to play a joke on …をからかう …wo karákaù

joker [dʒou'kəːr] n (inf) 冗談を言う人 jōdan wo iu hitó; (pej: person) 野郎 yárò; (cards) ジョーカー jōkà

jolly [dʒɑː'liː] adj (merry) 陽気な yōki na; (enjoyable) 楽しい tanóshiì
♦adv (BRIT: inf) とても totémo

jolt [dʒoult] n (physical) 衝撃 shōgeki; (emotional) ショック shókkù
♦vt (physically) …に衝撃を与える …ni shōgeki wò atáerù; (emotionally) ショックを与える shókkù wo atáerù

Jordan [dʒɔːr'dʌn] n ヨルダン yórùdan

jostle [dʒɑːs'əl] vt: *to be jostled by the crowd* 人込みにもまれる hitógomi ni momárerù

jot [dʒɑt] n: *not one jot* 少しも…ない sukóshì mo …nái

jot down vt (telephone number etc) 書留める kakítomerù

jotter [dʒɑːt'əːr] (BRIT) n (notebook,

pad) ノート（ブック）nōto(búkkù), メモ帳 memóchō

journal [dʒəːr'nəl] n (magazine, periodical) 雑誌 zasshí; (diary) 日記 nikkí

journalese [dʒəːrnəliːz'] n (pej) 大衆新聞調 taíshūshinbunchō

journalism [dʒəːr'nəlizəm] n ジャーナリズム jánarizùmu

journalist [dʒəːr'nəlist] n ジャーナリスト jánarisùto

journey [dʒəːr'niː] n (trip, route) 旅行 ryokō; (distance covered) 道のり michínori

jovial [dʒou'viːəl] adj (person, air) 陽気な yōki na

joy [dʒɔi] n (happiness, pleasure) 喜び yorókobi

joyful [dʒɔi'fəl] adj (news, event) うれしい uréshiì; (look) うれしそうな uréshisōna

joyride [dʒɔi'raid] n (AUT: US) 無謀運転のドライブ mubōuñten no doráibù; (: BRIT) 盗難車でのドライブ tōnanshà de no doráibù

joystick [dʒɔi'stik] n (AVIAT) 操縦かん sōjūkan; (COMPUT) 操縦レバー sōjū rebā, ジョイスティック joísùtikku

JP [dʒeipiː'] n abbr = Justice of the Peace

Jr abbr = junior

jubilant [dʒuː'bələnt] adj 大喜びの ōyorokobi no

jubilee [dʒuː'bəliː] n (anniversary) …周年記念日 …shūnen kineñbi

judge [dʒʌdʒ] n (LAW) 裁判官 saíbankan; (in competition) 審査員 shiñsa-in; (fig: expert) 通 tsū
♦vt (LAW) 裁く sabákù; (competition) 審査する shiñsa suru; (person, book etc) 評価する hyōka suru; (consider, estimate) 推定する suítei suru

judg(e)ment [dʒʌdʒ'mənt] n (LAW) 判決 hañketsu; (REL) 審判 shiñpan; (view, opinion) 意見 ikén; (discernment) 判断力 hañdanryoku

judicial [dʒuːdiʃ'əl] adj (LAW) 司法の shihō no

judiciary [dʒuːdiʃ'iːeːriː] n 司法部 shihō

bù

judicious [dʒu:ˈdiʃˈəs] *adj* (action, decision) 分別のある funbetsu no árù

judo [dʒu:ˈdou] *n* 柔道 júdò

jug [dʒʌɡ] *n* 水差し mizúsashi

juggernaut [dʒʌɡˈəːrnɔ:t] (*BRIT*) *n* (huge truck) 大型トラック ōgata torakkù

juggle [dʒʌɡˈəl] *vi* 品玉をする shinádama wo surù ◊幾つもの玉などを投上げて受止める曲芸 íkutsu mo no tamá nadò wo nagéagete ukétomerù kyokúgei

juggler [dʒʌɡˈləːr] *n* 品玉をする曲芸師 shinádama wo suru kyokúgeishì

Jugoslav [ju:ˈɡouslɑːv] *etc* = **Yugoslav** *etc*

juice [dʒu:s] *n* (of fruit, plant, meat) 汁 shírù; (beverage) ジュース jùsu

juicy [dʒu:ˈsi:] *adj* (food) 汁の多い shírù no ōi; (*inf*: story, details) エッチな étchì na

jukebox [dʒu:kˈbɑ:ks] *n* ジュークボックス júkùbokkusu

July [dʒʌlaiˈ] *n* 7月 shichí gatsu

jumble [dʒʌmˈbəl] *n* (muddle) ごたまぜ gotámaze
◆*vt* (*also*: **jumble up**) ごたまぜにする gotámaze ni surù

jumble sale (*BRIT*) *n* 慈善バザー jizén bazá

jumbo (jet) [dʒʌmˈbou] *n* ジャンボジェット機 jánbo jettókì

jump [dʒʌmp] *vi* (into air) 飛び上る tobíagarù; (with fear, surprise) ぎくっとする gíkùtto suru; (increase: price etc) 急上昇する kyújóshò suru; (: population etc) 急増する kyúzò suru
◆*vt* (fence) 飛び越える tobíkoeru
◆*n* (into air etc) 飛び上る事 tobíagarù kotó; (increase: in price etc) 急上昇 kyúijóshò; (: in population etc) 急増 kyúzò
to jump the queue (*BRIT*) 列に割込む rétsu ni waríkomù

jumper [dʒʌmˈpəːr] *n* (*BRIT*: pullover) セーター sétà; (*US*: dress) ジャンパースカート jañpásukàto

jumper cables *npl* (*US*) ブースターケーブル búsutākèburu ◊外のバッテリーから

電気を得るために用いるコード hoká nò báttèri kara dénki wo érù tamé nì mochírù kōdo

jump leads (*BRIT*) [-li:dz] *npl* = **jumper cables**

jumpy [dʒʌmˈpi:] *adj* (nervous) びくびくしている bíkùbiku shité írù

Jun. *abbr* = **junior**

junction [dʒʌŋkˈʃən] *n* (*BRIT*: of roads) 交差点 kōsaten; (RAIL) 連絡駅 refiraku-eki

juncture [dʒʌŋkˈtʃəːr] *n*: *at this juncture* この時 konó tokí

June [dʒu:n] *n* 6月 rokúgatsu

jungle [dʒʌŋˈɡəl] *n* ジャングル jánguru; (*fig*) 弱肉強食の世界 jakúniku kyóshoku nò sékài

junior [dʒu:nˈjəːr] *adj* (younger) 年下の toshíshita no; (subordinate) 下位の káì no; (SPORT) ジュニアの jùnia no
◆*n* (office junior) 後輩 kóhai; (young person) 若者 wakámono
he's my junior by 2 years 彼は私より2才年下です kárè wa watákushi yorí nísaì toshíshita desu

junior school (*BRIT*) *n* 小学校 shógakkò

junk [dʒʌŋk] *n* (rubbish, cheap goods) がらくた garákuta; (ship) ジャンク船 jánku sen

junk food *n* ジャンクフード jáñku fúdo ◊ポテトチップス，ファーストフードなど高カロリーだが低栄養のスナック食品 potétochippùsu, fásuto fúdo nádò kókarorī da ga teíeiyó no sunákku shokùhin

junkie [dʒʌŋkˈi:] (*inf*) *n* ペイ中 peichū

junk shop *n* 古物商 kobútsushò

Junr. *abbr* = **junior**

jurisdiction [dʒu:risdikˈʃən] *n* (LAW) 司法権 shihókèn; (ADMIN) 支配権 shihái-kèn

juror [dʒu:ˈrəːr] *n* (person on jury) 陪審員 baíshiñ-in

jury [dʒu:ˈri:] *n* (group of jurors) 陪審員 baíshiñ-in

just [dʒʌst] *adj* (fair: decision) 公正な kōsei na; (: punishment) 適切な tekísetsu na

◆*adv* (exactly) 丁度 chōdo; (only) ただ tádà; (barely) ようやく yōyaku

he's just done it ついさっきそれをやったばかりだ tsuí sakkí sore wo yatta bákàri da

he's just left ついさっき出た〔帰った〕ばかりだ tsuí sakkí détà〔kaéttà〕bákàri da

just right 丁度いい chōdo iì

just two o'clock 丁度2時 chōdo nīji

she's just as clever as you 彼女はあなたに負けないぐらい頭がいい kánòjo wa anátà ni makénai gùrài atáma ga iì

just as well that ... ...して良かった ...shítè yokátta

just as he was leaving 丁度出掛けるところに chōdo dekákerù tokóro ni

just before 丁度前に chōdo máè ni

just enough 辛うじて間に合って kárōjite ma ní attè

just here ぴったりここに pittárì kokó ni

he just missed わずかの差で外れた wázùka no sá dè hazúreta

just listen ちょっと聞いて chottó kiite

justice [dʒʌs'tis] *n* (LAW: system) 司法 shihō; (rightness: of cause, complaint) 正当さ seítōsa; (fairness) 公正さ kōseisa; (US: judge) 裁判官 saíbankan

to do justice to (*fig*: task) ...をやりこなす ...wo yaríkonasù; (: meal) ...を平らげる ...wo taíragerù; (: person) ...を正当に扱う ...wo seítō ni atsúkaù

Justice of the Peace *n* 治安判事 chián hañji

justifiable [dʒʌs'tifaiəbəl] *adj* (claim, statement etc) もっともな móttòmo na

justification [dʒʌstəfəkei'ʃən] *n* (reason) 正当とする理由 seítō to suru riyú

justify [dʒʌs'təfai] *vt* (action, decision) 正当である事を証明する seítō de arù kotó wo shōmei suru; (text) 行の長さをそろえる gyō no nágàsa wo soróerù

justly [dʒʌst'li:] *adv* (with reason) 正当に seítō ni; (deservedly) 当然 tōzen

jut [dʒʌt] *vi* (*also*: **jut out**: protrude) 突出る tsukíderù

juvenile [dʒu:'vənəl] *adj* (court) 未成年の

miséìnen no; (books) 少年少女向きの shōnen shōjo mukí no; (humor, mentality) 子供っぽい kodómoppoì

◆*n* (LAW, ADMIN) 未成年者 miséìneñsha

juxtapose [dʒʌkstəpouz'] *vt* (things, ideas) 並べておく narábete okù

K

K [kei] *abbr* (= *one thousand*) 1000 sén = **kilobyte**

kaleidoscope [kəlai'dəskoup] *n* 万華鏡 mañgekyō

Kampuchea [kæmpu:tʃi:'ə] *n* カンプチア káñpuchia

kangaroo [kæŋgəru:'] *n* カンガルー kañgarū

karate [kərɑ:'ti:] *n* 空手 karáte

kebab [kəbɑ:b'] *n* くし刺の焼肉 kushísashi nò yakíniku, シシカバブ shishikababu

keel [ki:l] *n* 竜骨 ryūkotsu

on an even keel (*fig*) 安定して añtei shite

keen [ki:n] *adj* (eager) やりたがっている yarítagattè írù; (intense: interest, desire) 熱心な nesshíñ na; (acute: eye, intelligence) 鋭い surúdoì; (fierce: competition) 激しい hagéshiì; (sharp: edge) 鋭い surúdoì

to be keen to do/on doing something (eager, anxious) ...をやりたがっている ...wo yarítagattè írù

to be keen on something/someone ...に熱を上げている ...ni netsú wò agéte irù

keep [ki:p] (*pt*, *pp* **kept**) *vt* (retain: receipt etc) 保管する hōkan suru; (: money etc) 自分の物にする jíbun no monó ni surù; (: job etc) なくさない様にする nakúsanai yō ni suru, 守る mamórù; (preserve, store) 貯蔵する chozō suru; (maintain: house, garden etc) 管理する káñri suru; (detain) 引留める hikítomerù; (run: shop etc) 経営する keíei suru; (chickens, bees etc) 飼育する shíìku suru; (accounts, diary etc) ...を付ける ...wo tsukérù; (support: family etc) 養う yashínaù; (fulfill: promise) 守る mamórù; (prevent): **to keep someone from doing something** ...が...をできない様に阻止する ...ga ...wo dekínai yō ni soshí surù

♦vi (remain: in a certain state) ...でいる [ある] ...de irú (árù); (: in a certain place) ずっと ...にいる zuttó ...ni irú; (last: food) 保存がきく hozón ga kikù

♦n (cost of food etc) 生活費 seíkatsuhì; (of castle) 本丸 hoímaru

to keep doing something ...をし続ける ...wo shitsúzukerù

to keep someone happy ...の期限をとる ...no kígèn wo torú

to keep a place tidy ある場所をきちんとさせておく árù bashó wo kichín to saséte okù

to keep something to oneself ...について黙っている ...ni tsúite damátte irù

to keep something (back) from someone ...の事を...に隠す ...no kotó wo ...ni kakúsù

to keep time (clock) 時間を正確に計る jíkàn wo seíkaku ni hakárù

for keeps (inf) 永久に eíkyū ni

keeper [ki:'pər] n (in zoo, park) 飼育係 shí-ikugakàri, キーパー kípā

keep-fit [ki:p'fit'] n (BRIT) 健康体操 keñkōtaísō

keeping [ki:'piŋ] n (care) 保管 hokán
in keeping with ...に合って ...ni áttè, ...に従って ...ni shitagatte

keep on vi (continue): **to keep on doing** ...し続ける ...shitsúzukerù
to keep on (about something) (...を話題に) うるさくしゃべる (...wo wadái ni) urúsakù shaberù

keep out vt (intruder etc) 締出す shimédasù
「**keep out**」立入禁止 tachíiri kinshi

keepsake [ki:p'seik'] n 形見 katámi

keep up vt (maintain: payments etc) 続ける tsuzúkerù; (: standards etc) 保持する hojí suru
♦vi: **to keep up (with)** (match: pace)

(...と) 速度を合せる (...to) sókùdo wo awáserù; (: level) (...に) 遅れない様にする (...ni) okúrenai yō ni suru

keg [keg] n たる tarú

kennel [ken'əl] n イヌ小屋 inúgoya
kennels [ken'əlz] npl (establishment) イヌ屋 inúyà

Kenya [ken'jə] n ケニア kénìa
Kenyan [ken'jən] adj ケニアの kénìa no
♦n ケニア人 keníajìn

kept [kept] pt, pp of **keep**

kerb [kə:rb] (BRIT) n = **curb**

kernel [kə:r'nəl] n (BOT: of nut) 実 mi; (fig: of idea) 核 kákù

kerosene [ke:r'əsi:n] n 灯油 tóyu

ketchup [ketʃ'əp] n ケチャップ kecháppù

kettle [ket'əl] n やかん yakán
kettle drum n ティンパニ tíñpani

key [ki:] n (for lock etc) かぎ kagí; (MUS: scale) 調 chó; (of piano, computer, typewriter) キー kī
♦adj (issue etc) 重要な júyō na
♦vt (also: **key in**: into computer etc) 打込む uchíkomù, 入力する nyúryoku suru

keyboard [ki:'bɔ:rd] n (of computer, typewriter) キーボード kíbòdo; (of piano) けん盤 keñban, キーボード kíbòdo

keyed up [ki:d-] adj (person) 興奮している kófun shite irù

keyhole [ki:'houl] n 鍵穴 kagíana

keynote [ki:'nout] n (MUS) 主音 shúòn; (of speech) 基調 kichó

key ring n キーホルダー kíhorùdā

kg abbr = **kilogram**

khaki [kæk'i:] n (color) カーキ色 kákì iro; (also: **khaki cloth**) カーキ色服地 kákì iro fukùji

kibbutz [kibuts'] n キブツ kíbùtsu ◊イスラエルの農業共同体 ísùraeru no nógyō kyódōtai

kick [kik] vt (person, table, ball) ける kérù; (inf: habit, addiction) やめる yamérù
♦vi ける kérù
♦n (from person, animal) けり kéri; (to ball) キック kíkkù; (thrill): **he does it for kicks** 彼はそんな事をやるのはスリ

ルのためだ kárè wa soñna kotó wo yárù no wa surírù no tamé dà

kick off vi (FOOTBALL, SOCCER) 試合を開始する shiái wò kaíshi suru

kick-off [kik'ɔːf] n (FOOTBALL, SOCCER) 試合開始 shiái kaishi, キックオフ kíkkùofu

kid [kid] n (inf: child) がき gakí, じゃり jarí; (animal) 子ヤギ koyágì; (also: **kid leather**) キッド革 kíddðgawa

♦vi (inf) 冗談を言う jốdan wo iú

kidnap [kid'næp] vt 誘拐する yúkai suru

kidnapper [kid'næpər] n 誘拐犯人 yúkai hañnin

kidnapping [kid'næpiŋ] n 誘拐事件 yúkai jikèn

kidney [kid'niː] n (ANAT) じん臓 jiñzō; (CULIN) キドニー kídðnī

kill [kil] vt (person, animal) 殺す korósù; (plant) 枯らす karásù; (murder) 殺す korosu, 殺害する satsúgai suru

♦n 殺し koróshi

to kill time 時間をつぶす jíkàn wo tsubúsù

killer [kil'əːr] n 殺し屋 koróshiya

killing [kil'iŋ] n (action) 殺す事 korósu kotò; (instance) 殺人事件 satsújin jikèn

to make a killing (inf) 大もうけする ốmòke suru

killjoy [kil'dʒɔi] n 白けさせる人 shirákesaserù hitó

kiln [kiln] n 窯 kamá

kilo [kiː'lou] n キロ kíró

kilobyte [kil'əbait] n (COMPUT) キロバイト kiróbaìto

kilogram(me) [kil'əgræm] n キログラム kiróguràmu

kilometer [kil'əmiːtəːr] (BRIT **kilometre**) n キロメーター kirómètā

kilowatt [kil'əwɑːt] n キロワット kiрówattð

kilt [kilt] n キルト kirúto

kimono [kimou'nou] n 着物 kimóno, 和服 wafúku

kin [kin] n see **kith**; **next-of-kin**

kind [kaind] adj 親切な shíñsetsu na

♦n (type, sort) 種類 shúrùi; (species) 種 shú

to pay in kind 現物で支払う geñbutsu de shiháraù

a kind of ...の一種 ...no ísshù

to be two of a kind 似たり寄ったりする nitári yottárì suru, 似た者同志である nitá mono dôshi de árù

kindergarten [kin'dəːrgɑːrtən] n 幼稚園 yốchièn

kind-hearted [kaind'hɑːr'tid] adj 心の優しい kokóro no yasáshiì

kindle [kin'dəl] vt (light: fire) たく takú, つける tsukeru; (arouse: emotion) 起す okósù, そそる sosórù

kindly [kaind'liː] adj 親切な shíñsetsu na

♦adv (smile) 優しく yasáshikù; (behave) 親切に shíñsetsu ni

will you kindly ... ...して下さいませんか ...shîté kudásaìmasen ká

kindness [kaind'nis] n (personal quality) 親切 shíñsetsu; (helpful act) 親切な行為 shíñsetsu na kồì

kindred [kin'drid] adj: **kindred spirit** 自分と気の合った人 jíbùn to kí no attà hitó

kinetic [kinet'ik] adj 動的な dồteki na

king [kiŋ] n (monarch) 国王 kokúố; (CARDS, CHESS) キング kíñgu

kingdom [kiŋ'dəm] n 王国 ốkoku

kingfisher [kiŋ'fíʃəːr] n カワセミ kawásemi

king-size [kiŋ'saiz] adj 特大の tokúdai no

kinky [kiŋ'kiː] (pej) adj (person, behavior) へんてこな heñteko na, 妙な myố na; (sexually) 変態気味の heñtaigimi no

kiosk [kiːɑːsk'] n (shop) キオスク kiósùku; (BRIT: TEL) 電話ボックス deñwa bokkùsu

kipper [kip'əːr] n 薫製ニシン kuñsei nishìn

kiss [kis] n キス kísù

♦vt ...にキスする ...ni kísù suru

to kiss (each other) キスする kísù suru

kiss of life n 口移しの人工呼吸 kuchíutsushi no jiñkōkokyữ

kit [kit] n (clothes: sports kit etc) 運動服一式 uñdōfuku isshíki; (equipment, set of tools: also MIL) 道具一式 dốgu isshîki; (for assembly) キット kíttò

kitchen [kitʃ'ən] n 台所 daídokoro, キッチン kítchìn

kitchen sink n 台所 の 流し daídokoro no nagáshi

kite [kait] n (toy) たこ takó

kith [kiθ] n: **kith and kin** 親せき知人 shińsekichijin

kitten [kit'ən] n 子ネコ konékò

kitty [kit'i:] n (pool of money) お金の蓄え o-káne no takúwae; (CARDS) 総掛金 sõkakekìn

kleptomaniac [kleptəmei'ni:æk] n 盗 癖 のある人 tõheki no árù hitó

km abbr = **kilometer**

knack [næk] n: **to have the knack of doing something** ...をするのが上手である ...wo suru nò ga jõzu de árù

knapsack [næp'sæk] n ナップサック nappúsakkù

knead [ni:d] vt (dough, clay) 練る nérù

knee [ni:] n ひざ hizá

kneecap [ni:'kæp] n ひざ頭 hizágashìra, ひざ小僧 hizákozõ

kneel [ni:l] (pt, pp **knelt**) vi (also: **kneel down**) ひざまずく hizámazukù

knelt [nelt] pt, pp of **kneel**

knew [nu:] pt of **know**

knickers [nik'ə:rz] (BRIT) npl パンティー pántì

knife [naif] (pl **knives**) n ナイフ náìfu
♦vt ナイフで刺す náìfu de sásù

knight [nait] n (HISTORY) 騎士 kishí; (BRIT) ナイト náìto; (CHESS) ナイト náìto

knighthood [nait'hud] (BRIT) n (title): **to get a knighthood** ナイト爵位を与えられる náìto shakùi wo atáerarerù

knit [nit] vt (garment) 編む ámù
♦vi (with wool) 編物をする amímòno wo suru; (broken bones) 治る naórù
to knit one's brows まゆをひそめる máyù wo hisómerù

knitting [nit'iŋ] n 編物 amímòno

knitting machine n 編機 amíkì

knitting needle n 編棒 amíbõ

knitwear [nit'we:r] n ニット・ウェアー nittó ueà

knives [naivz] npl of **knife**

knob [na:b] n (handle: of door) 取っ手 tottè, つまみ tsumámi; (: of stick) 握り nigíri; (on radio, TV etc) つまみ tsumámi

knock [na:k] vt (strike) たたく tatákù; (inf: criticize) 批判する hihán suru
♦vi (at door etc): **to knock at/on** ...にノックする ...ni nókku surù
♦n (blow, bump) 打撃 dagéki; (on door) ノック nókkù

knock down vt (subj: person) 殴り倒す nagúritaosù; (: car) ひき倒す hikítaosù

knocker [na:k'ə:r] n (on door) ノッカー nokkã

knock-kneed [na:k'ni:d] adj X脚の ekúsukyaku no

knock off vi (inf: finish) やめる yamérù, 終りにする owári ni surù
♦vt (from price) 値引する nebíki suru; (inf: steal) くすねる kusúnerù

knock out vt (subj: drug etc) 気絶させる kizétsu saserù, 眠らせる nemúraserù; (BOXING etc, also fig) ノックアウトする nokkúauto surù; (defeat: in game, competition) ...に勝つ ...ni kátsù, 敗退させる haítai saséru

knockout [na:k'aut] n (BOXING) ノックアウト nokkúautò
♦cpd (competition etc) 決定的な kettéiteki na

knock over vt (person, object) 倒す taósù

knot [na:t] n (in rope) 結び目 musúbime; (in wood) 節目 fushíme; (NAUT) ノット nóttõ
♦vt 結ぶ musúbù

knotty [na:t'i:] adj (fig: problem) 厄介な yakkái na

know [nou] (pt **knew**, pp **known**) vt (facts, dates etc) 知っている shitté irù; (language) できる dekírù; (be acquainted with: person, place, subject) 知っている shitté irù; (recognize: by sight) 見て分かる mítè wakárù; (: by sound) 聞いて分かる kiite wakaru
to know how to swim 泳げる oyógerù
to know about/of something/some-

one ...の事を知っている ...no kotó wo shitté irú

know-all [nou'ɔːl] *n* 知ったか振りの人 shittákaburi no hitó

know-how [nou'hau] *n* 技術知識 gijútsu-chishíki, ノウハウ nóuháú

knowing [nou'iŋ] *adj* (look: of complicity) 意味ありげな imírarige na

knowingly [nou'iŋliː] *adv* (purposely) 故意に kói ni; (smile, look) 意味ありげに ímírarige ni

knowledge [nɑːl'idʒ] *n* (understanding, awareness) 認識 nínshiki; (learning, things learnt) 知識 chíshiki

knowledgeable [nɑːl'idʒəbəl] *adj* 知識の ある chíshiki no árù

known [noun] *pp of* **know**

knuckle [nak'əl] *n* 指関節 yubí kañsetsu ◇特に指の付根の関節を指す tókù ni yubí no tsukéne no kañsetsu wò sásù

KO [kei'ou'] *n abbr* = **knockout**

Koran [kɔːrɑːn'] *n* コーラン kóran

Korea [kɔːriː'ə] *n* 韓国 káñkoku, 朝鮮 chósen

Korean [kɔːriː'ən] *adj* 韓国の káñkoku no, 朝鮮の chósen no; (LING) 韓国語の kañkokugo no, 朝鮮語の chósengo no
◆*n* (person) 韓国人 kañkokujîn, 朝鮮人 chósenjìn; (LING) 韓国語 kañkokugo, 朝鮮語 chósengo

kosher [kou'ʃər] *adj* 適法の tekíhō no ◇ユダヤ教の戒律に合った食物などについて言う yudáyakyō no kaíritsu ni attá shokúmòtsu nádò ni tsuíte iú

L

L (*BRIT*) *abbr* = **learner driver**

l. *abbr* = **liter**

lab [læb] *n abbr* = **laboratory**

label [lei'bəl] *n* (on suitcase, merchandise etc) ラベル rábèru
◆*vt* (thing) ...にラベルを付ける ...ni rábèru wo tsukérù

labor [lei'bəːr] (*BRIT* **labour**) *n* (hard work) 労働 rōdō; (work force) 労働者 rōdōsha ◇総称 sōshō; (work done by work force) 労働 rōdō; (MED): *to be in labor* 陣痛が始まっている jiñtsū ga hajímatte irù
◆*vi*: *to labor (at something)* (...に) 苦心する (...ni) kushín suru
◆*vt*: *to labor a point* ある事を余計に強調する árù kotó wo yokéi ni kyóchō suru

laboratory [læb'rətɔːriː] *n* (scientific: building, institution) 研究所 keñkyūjo; (: room) 実験室 jikkéñshitsu; (school) 理科教室 rikákyōshitsu

labored [lei'bəːrd] *adj* (breathing: one's own) 苦しい kurúshiî; (: someone else's) 苦しそうな kurúshisō na

laborer [lei'bəːrəːr] *n* (industrial) 労働者 rōdōsha
farm laborer 農場労務者 nójōrōmùsha

laborious [ləbɔːr'iːəs] *adj* 骨の折れる honé no orérù

labour [lei'bəːr] *etc n* = **labor** *etc*
Labour, the Labour Party (*BRIT*) 労働党 rōdōtō

labyrinth [læb'ə:rinθ] *n* 迷路 méîro

lace [leis] *n* (fabric) レース rḗsu; (of shoe etc) ひも himó
◆*vt* (shoe etc: *also*: **lace up**) ...のひもを結ぶ ...no himó wo musúbù

lack [læk] *n* (absence) 欠如 kétsùjo
◆*vt* (money, confidence) ...が無い ...ga naî; (intelligence etc) 欠いている kaíte irù
through/for lack of ...が無いために ...ga naî tamé ni
to be lacking ...がない ...ga naî
to be lacking in (intelligence, generosity etc) ...を欠いている ...wo kaíte iru

lackadaisical [lækədei'zikəl] *adj* (lacking interest, enthusiasm) 気乗りしない kinóri shinaî

laconic [ləkɑːn'ik] *adj* 言葉数の少ない kotóbakazù no sukúnaî

lacquer [læk'əːr] *n* (paint) ラッカー rákkầ; (*also*: **hair lacquer**) ヘアスプレー heásupurḕ

lad [læd] *n* (boy) 少年 shṓnen; (young man) 若者 wakámonô

ladder [læd'əːr] *n* (metal, wood, rope) は

しご子 hashígo; (*BRIT*: in tights) 伝線 deńseń

laden [lei'dən] *adj*: **laden (with)** (ship, truck etc) (...を) たっぷり積んだ (...wo) tappúrì tsuńda; (person) (...を) 沢山抱えている (...wo) takúsań kakáete irù

laden with fruit (tree) 実をたわわに付けている mi wo tawáwa ni tsukéte irù

ladle [lei'dəl] *n* 玉じゃくし tamájakùshi

lady [lei'di:] *n* (woman) 女性 joséi; (: dignified, graceful etc) 淑女 shukújò, レディー rédì; (in address): **ladies and gentlemen ...** 紳士淑女の皆様 shińshishukujò no minásàma

young lady 若い女性 wakáì josèi

the ladies' (room) 女性用トイレ joséiyòtoìre

ladybird [lei'di:bə:rd] *n* テントウムシ teńtòmushi

ladybug [lei'debʌg] (*US*) *n* = **ladybird**

ladylike [lei'di:laik] *adj* (behavior) レディーらしい rédìrashii

ladyship [lei'di:ʃip] *n*: **your ladyship** 奥様 ókùsama

lag [læg] *n* (period of time) 遅れ okúre
♦*vi* (*also*: **lag behind**: person, thing) ...に遅れる ...ni okúrerù; (: trade, investment etc) ...の勢いが衰える ...no íkíoì ga otóroerù
♦*vt* (pipes etc) ...に断熱材を巻く ...ni dańnetsuzài wo makú

lager [lɑ:'gər] *n* ラガービール ragábìru

lagoon [ləgu:n'] *n* 潟 katá, ラグーン rágūn

laid [leid] *pt, pp of* **lay**³

laid back (*inf*) *adj* のんびりした nońbiri shitá

laid up *adj*: **to be laid up (with)** (...で) 寝込んでいる (...de) nekónde irù

lain [lein] *pp of* **lie**

lair [le:r] *n* (ZOOL) 巣穴 suána

lake [leik] *n* 湖 mizú-umì

lamb [læm] *n* (animal) 子ヒツジ kohítsujì; (meat) ラム rámù

lamb chop *n* ラムチャップ ramúchappù, ラムチョップ ramúchoppù

lambswool [læmz'wul] *n* ラムウール ramúùru

lame [leim] *adj* (person, animal) びっこの bíkkò no; (excuse, argument, answer) 下手な hetá na

lament [ləment'] *n* 嘆き nagéki
♦*vt* 嘆く nagékù

laminated [læm'əneitid] *adj* (metal, wood, glass) 合板の góhan no; (covering, surface) プラスチック張りの purásuchikkubari no

lamp [læmp] *n* (electric, gas, oil) 明り akári, ランプ ráñpu

lamppost [læmp'poust] *n* 街灯 gaítō

lampshade [læmp'ʃeid] *n* ランプの傘 ráñpu no kasá, シェード shèdo

lance [læns] *n* やり yarí
♦*vt* (MED) 切開する sekkái suru

land [lænd] *n* (area of open ground) 土地 tochí; (property, estate) 土地 tochí, 所有地 shoyúchì; (as opposed to sea) 陸 rikú; (country, nation) 国 kuní
♦*vi* (from ship) 上陸する jóriku suru; (AVIAT) 着陸する chakúriku suru; (*fig*: fall) 落ちる ochírù
♦*vt* (passengers, goods) 降ろす orósù

to land someone with something (*inf*) ...に...を押付ける ...ni ...wo oshítsukerù

landing [læn'diŋ] *n* (of house) 踊り場 odóriba; (AVIAT) 着陸 chakúriku

landing gear *n* (AVIAT) 着陸装置 chakúrikusòchi

landing strip *n* 滑走路 kassórò

landlady [lænd'leidi:] *n* (of rented house, flat, room) 女大家 oñnaòya; (of pub) 女主人 oñnashujìn, おかみ okámi

landlocked [lænd'lɑːkt] *adj* 陸地に囲まれた rikúchi ni kakómareta

landlord [lænd'lɔːrd] *n* (of rented house, flat, room) 大家 ōya; (of pub) 主人 shujìn

landmark [lænd'mɑːrk] *n* (building, hill etc) 目標 mokúhyō; (*fig*) 歴史的な事件 rekíshiteki na jíkèn

landowner [lænd'ounər] *n* 地主 jinúshi

landscape [lænd'skeip] *n* (view over land, buildings etc) 景色 késhìki; (ART) 風景画 fúkeiga

landscape gardener *n* 造園家 zóenka

landslide [lænd'slaid] *n* (GEO) 地滑り jisúberi; (*fig*: electoral) 圧勝 asshō

land up *vi*: *to land up in/at* 結局...に行くはめになる kekkyókù ...ni ikú hame ni narù

lane [lein] *n* (in country) 小道 komíchi; (AUT: of carriageway) 車線 shasén; (of race course, swimming pool) コース kôsu

language [læŋ'gwidʒ] *n* (national tongue) 国語 kokúgo; (ability to communicate verbally) 言語 géñgo; (specialized terminology) 用語 yôgo; (style: of written piece, speech etc) 言葉遣 kotóbazukài; (SCOL) 語学 gógàku

bad language 下品な言葉 gehíñ na kotóba

he is studying languages 彼は外国語を勉強している kare wa gaikokugo wo benkyō shite iru

language laboratory *n* ランゲージラボラトリー rañgējiraboratòrī, エルエル éruèru

languid [læŋ'gwid] *adj* (person, movement) 元気のない géñki no nâî

languish [læŋ'gwiʃ] *vi* 惨めに生きる míjìme ni ikírù

lank [læŋk] *adj* (hair) 長くて手入れしない nagákutè teíre shinai

lanky [læŋ'ki:] *adj* ひょろっとした hyorottð shita

lantern [læn'tə:rn] *n* カンテラ kañtera

lap [læp] *n* (of person) ひざの上 hizá nð ué; (in race) 1周 ísshū, ラップ ráppù

♦*vt* (*also*: *lap up*: drink) ぴちゃぴちゃ飲む pichápìcha nómu

♦*vi* (water) ひたひたと打寄せる hitáhìta to uchíyoserù

lapel [ləpel'] *n* 折えり oríeri, ラペル rápèru

Lapland [læp'lənd] *n* ラップランド ráppùrando

lapse [læps] *n* (bad behavior) 過失 kashítsu; (of memory) 喪失 sóshitsu; (of time) 経過 keíka

♦*vi* (law) 無効になる mukó ni narù; (contract, membership, passport) 切れる kirérù

a lapse of concentration 不注意 fu-

chūì

to lapse into bad habits (of behavior) 堕落する daráku suru

lap up *vt* (*fig*: flattery etc) 真に受ける ma ni ukérù

larceny [lɑːr'səni:] *n* (LAW) 窃盗罪 settōzai

larch [lɑːrtʃ] *n* (tree) カラマツ karámàtsu

lard [lɑːrd] *n* ラード râdo

larder [lɑːr'də:r] *n* 食料貯蔵室 shokúryōchozòshitsu

large [lɑːrdʒ] *adj* (big: house, person, amount) 大きい ōkii

at large (as a whole) 一般に ippán ni; (at liberty) 捕まらないで tsukámaranaîde ¶ *see also* **by**

largely [lɑːrdʒ'liː] *adv* (mostly) 大体 daítai; (mainly: introducing reason) 主に ô-mò ni

large-scale [lɑːrdʒ'skeil'] *adj* (action, event) 大規模の daíkibò no; (map, diagram) 大縮尺の daíshukùshaku no

largesse [lɑːrdʒes'] *n* (generosity) 気前良さ kimáeyosà; (money etc) 贈り物 okúrimonò

lark [lɑːrk] *n* (bird) ヒバリ hibári; (joke) 冗談 jôdañ

lark about *vi* ふざけ回る fuzákemawaru

larva [lɑːr'və] (*pl* **larvae**) *n* 幼虫 yôchū

larvae [lɑːr'viː] *npl of* **larva**

laryngitis [lærəndʒai'tis] *n* こうとう炎 kôtōèn

larynx [lær'iŋks] *n* (ANAT) こうとう kôtō

lascivious [ləsiv'iːəs] *adj* (person, conduct) みだらな midára na

laser [lei'zəːr] *n* レーザー rêzā

laser printer *n* レーザープリンター rêzāpurìñtā

lash [læʃ] *n* (eyelash) まつげ mátsùge; (blow of whip) むち打ち muchíuchi

♦*vt* (whip) むち打つ muchíutsù; (subj: rain) 激しくたたく hagéshiku tatákù; (: wind) 激しく揺さぶる hagéshiku yusáburù; (tie): *to lash to/together* ...を...に [...と一緒に] 縛る ...wo ...ni(...to isshó ni]

shibárù

lash out *vi*: *to lash out (at someone)* (hit) (...に) 打ち掛る (...ni) uchíkakarù
to lash out against someone (criticize) ...を激しく非難する ...wo hagéshikù hínàn suru

lass [læs] *n* (girl) 少女 shójo; (young woman) 若い女性 wakáì joséi

lasso [læs'ou] *n* 投縄 nagénawa

last [læst] *adj* (latest: period of time, event, thing) 前の máè no; (final: bus, hope etc) 最後の saígo no; (end: of series, row) 一番後の ichíban atò no; (remaining: traces, scraps etc) 残りの nokórì no.
♦*adv* (most recently) 最近 saíkin; (finally) 最後に saígo ni
♦*vi* (continue) 続く tsuzúkù; (: in good condition) もつ mótsù; (money, commodity) ...に足りる ...ni tarírù
last week 先週 senshū
last night 昨晩 sakúbàn, 昨夜 sakúyà
at last (finally) とうとう tótò
last but one 最後から2番目 saígo kara nibánme

last-ditch [læst'ditʃ'] *adj* (attempt) 絶体絶命の zettáizetsumei no

lasting [læs'tiŋ] *adj* (friendship, solution) 永続的な eízokuteki na

lastly [læst'li:] *adv* 最後に saígo ni

last-minute [læst'min'it] *adj* (decision, appeal etc) 土壇場の dotánba no

latch [lætʃ] *n* (on door, gate) 掛け金 kakégàne, ラッチ rátchi

late [leit] *adj* (far on in time, process, work etc) 遅い osóì; (not on time) 遅れた okúreta; (former) 前の máè no, 前...zén...
♦*adv* (far on in time, process, work etc) 遅く osóku; (behind time, schedule) 遅れて okúrete
of late (recently) 最近 saíkin
in late May 5月の終り頃 gógàtsu no owári gorò
the late Mr X (deceased) 故Xさん ko ékusu san

latecomer [leit'kʌmə:r] *n* 遅れて来る人 okúrete kurù hitó

lately [leit'li:] *adv* 最近 saíkin

latent [leit'tənt] *adj* (energy, skill, ability) 表に出ない omóte nì dénài

later [lei'tə:r] *adj* (time, date, meeting etc) もっと後の móttò átò no; (version etc) もっと新しい móttò atárashiì
♦*adv* 後で átò de
later on 後で átò de

lateral [læt'ə:rəl] *adj* (position) 横の yokô no; (direction) 横への yokô e no

latest [lei'tist] *adj* (train, flight etc) 最後の saígo no; (novel, film, news etc) 最新の saíshin no
at the latest 遅くとも osókùtomo

lathe [leið] *n* (for wood, metal) 旋盤 señban

lather [læð'ə:r] *n* 石けんの泡 sekkén nò awá
♦*vt* ...に石けんの泡を塗る ...ni sekkén nò awá wò nurú

Latin [læt'in] *n* (LING) ラテン語 raténgo
♦*adj* ラテン語の raténgo no

Latin America *n* ラテンアメリカ raténamèrika

Latin American *adj* ラテンアメリカの ratén-amèrika no
♦*n* ラテンアメリカ人 ratén-amerikajìn

latitude [læt'ətu:d] *n* (GEO) 緯度 ídò; (*fig*: freedom) 余裕 yoyū

latrine [lətri:n'] *n* 便所 beñjo

latter [læt'ə:r] *adj* (of two) 後者の kôsha no; (recent) 最近の saíkin no; (later) 後の方の átò no hô no
♦*n*: *the latter* (of two people, things, groups) 後者 kôsha

latterly [læt'ə:rli:] *adv* 最近 saíkin

lattice [læt'is] *n* (pattern, structure) 格子 kôshi

laudable [lɔ:'dəbəl] *adj* (conduct, motives etc) 感心な kañshin na

laugh [læf] *n* 笑い waráí
♦*vi* 笑う waráù
(to do something) for a laugh 冗談として (...をする) jódañ toshité (...wo suru)

laugh at *vt fus* ...をばかにする ...wo ba-ká ni surù

laughable [læf'əbəl] *adj* (attempt, quality etc) ばかげた bakágeta

laughing stock [læf'ɪŋ-] n: *to be the laughing stock of* ...の笑い者になる ...no waráimono ni narú

laugh off vt (criticism, problem) 無視する mushí suru

laughter [læf'tə:r] n 笑い声 waráigoè

launch [lɔːntʃ] n (of rocket, missile) 発射 hasshá; (of satellite) 打上げ uchíage; (COMM) 新発売 shínhatsubai; (motorboat) ランチ ráñchi
♦vt (ship) 進水させる shíñsui saséru; (rocket, missile) 発射する hasshá suru; (satellite) 打上げる uchíagerù; (fig: start) 開始する kaíshi suru; (COMM) 発売する hatsúbai suru

launch into vt fus (speech, activity) 始める hajímerù

launch(ing) pad [lɔːn'tʃ(ɪŋ)-] n (for missile, rocket) 発射台 hasshádai

launder [lɔːn'də:r] vt (clothes) 洗濯する señtaku suru

launderette [lɔːndəret'] (BRIT) n コインランドリー koíñrañdorī

Laundromat [lɔːn'drəmæt] (® US) n コインランドリー koíñrañdorī

laundry [lɔːn'dri:] n (dirty, clean) 洗濯物 señtakumono; (business) 洗濯屋 señtakuya ◊ドライクリーニングはしない doráikurīningu wa shináì; (room) 洗濯場 señtakuba

laureate [lɔː'ri:it] adj see **poet laureate**

laurel [lɔːr'əl] n (tree) ゲッケイジュ gekkéìju

lava [læv'ə] n 溶岩 yógan

lavatory [læv'ətɔː:ri:] n お手洗い otéaraì

lavender [læv'əndə:r] n (BOT) ラベンダー rabéñdā

lavish [læv'iʃ] adj (amount) たっぷりの tappúrì no, 多量の taryó no; (person): *lavish with* ...を気前良く与える ...wo kimáeyokù atáerù
♦vt: *to lavish something on someone* ...に...を気前よく与える ...ni ...wo kimáeyokù atáerù

law [lɔː] n (system of rules: of society, government) 法 hó; (a rule) 法律 hóritsu; (of nature, science) 法則 hósoku; (lawyers) 弁護士の職 beñgoshì no shokú;

(police) 警察 keísatsu; (SCOL) 法学 hógaku

law-abiding [lɔː'əbaidiŋ] adj 法律を遵守する hóritsu wò júñshu suru

law and order n 治安 chíañ

law court n 法廷 hótei

lawful [lɔː'fəl] adj 合法の góhō no

lawless [lɔː'lis] adj (action) 不法の fuhó no

lawn [lɔːn] n 芝生 shibáfu

lawnmower [lɔːn'mouə:r] n 芝刈機 shibákarikì

lawn tennis n ローンテニス róñtenisu

law school (US) n (SCOL) 法学部 hógakùbu

lawsuit [lɔː'suːt] n 訴訟 soshó

lawyer [lɔː'jə:r] n (gen) 弁護士 beñgoshì; (solicitor) 事務弁護士 jimúbeñgoshi; (barrister) 法廷弁護士 hóteibeñgoshi

lax [læks] adj (behavior, standards) いい加減な iíkagen na

laxative [læk'sətiv] n 下剤 gezái

lay[1] [lei] pt of **lie**

lay[2] [lei] adj (REL) 俗人の zokújin no; (not expert) 素人の shíròto no

lay[3] [lei] (pt, pp laid) vt (place) 置く okú; (table) ...に食器を並べる ...ni shokkî wo náraberù; (carpet etc) 敷く shíkù; (cable, pipes etc) 埋設する maísetsu suru; (ZOOL: egg) 産む úmù

layabout [lei'əbaut] (BRIT: inf) n のらくら者 norákuramono

lay aside vt (put down) わきに置く wakí ni okù; (money) 貯蓄する chochíku suru; (belief, prejudice) 捨てる sutérù

lay by vt = **lay aside**

lay-by [lei'bai] (BRIT) n 待避所 taíhijo

lay down vt (object) 置く okú; (rules, laws etc) 設ける mókerù
to lay down the law (pej) 威張り散らす ibárichirasu
to lay down one's life (in war etc) 命を捨てる inóchi wo sutérù

layer [lei'ə:r] n 層 só

layman [lei'mən] (pl laymen) n (nonexpert) 素人 shíròto

lay off vt (workers) 一時解雇にする ichíjikaìko ni suru, レイオフにする refofù ni suru

lay on *vt* (meal, entertainment etc) 提供する teíkyō suru

lay out *vt* (spread out: things) 並べて置く narábete okù

layout [leiˈaut] *n* (arrangement: of garden, building) 配置 haíchi; (: of piece of writing etc) レイアウト reíaùto

laze [leiz] *vi* (*also*: **laze about**) ぶらぶらする búràbura suru

laziness [leiˈziːnis] *n* 怠惰 táida

lazy [leiˈziː] *adj* (person) 怠惰な táida na; (movement, action) のろい noróì

lb *abbr* = **pound (weight)**

lead[1] [liːd] *n* (front position: SPORT, *fig*) 先頭 seńtō; (piece of information) 手掛かり tegákàri; (in play, film) 主演 shuén; (for dog) 引綱 hikízùna, ひも himó; (ELEC) リード線 rídosen

♦*vb* (*pt, pp* **led**)

♦*vt* (walk etc in front) 先導する señdō suru; (guide): **to lead someone somewhere** ...を...に案内する ...wo ...ni afinaí suru; (group of people, organization) ...のリーダーになる ...no rídà ni nárù; (start, guide: activity) ...の指揮を取る ...no shikí wo torù

♦*vi* (road, pipe, wire etc) ...に通じる ...ni tsújiru; (SPORT) 先頭に立つ señtō ni tatsù

in the lead (SPORT, *fig*) 先頭に立って seńtō ni tatte

to lead the way (*also fig*) 先導する señdō suru

lead[2] [led] *n* (metal) 鉛 namári; (in pencil) しん shíñ

lead away *vt* 連れ去る tsurésarù

lead back *vt* 連れ戻す tsurémodosù

leaden [ledˈən] *adj* (sky, sea) 鉛色のnamáriiro no

leader [liːˈdəːr] *n* (of group, organization) 指導者 shidóshà, リーダー rídà; (SPORT) 先頭を走る選手 seńtō wo hashírù señshù

leadership [liːˈdəːrʃip] *n* (group, individual) 指導権 shidókèn; (position, quality) リーダーシップ rídāshìppu

lead-free [ledfriːˈ] *adj* (petrol) 無鉛の

muén no

leading [liːˈdiŋ] *adj* (most important: person, thing) 主要な shuyô na; (role) 主演の shuén no; (first, front) 先頭の señtō no

leading lady *n* (THEATER) 主演女優 shuénjoyù

leading light *n* (person) 主要人物 shuyôjinbùtsu

leading man (*pl* **leading men**) *n* (THEATER) 主演男優 shuéndañ-yū

lead on *vt* (tease) からかう karákaù

lead singer *n* (in pop group) リードシンガー rídoshiñgà, リードボーカリスト rídobōkarìsuto

lead to *vt fus* ...の原因になる ...no geń-in ni narù

lead up to *vt fus* (events) ...の原因になる ...no geń-in ni narù; (in conversation) 話題を...に向ける wadái wo ...ni mukérù

leaf [liːf] (*pl* **leaves**) *n* (of tree, plant) 葉ha

♦*vi*: **to leaf through** (book, magazine) ...にさっと目を通す ...ni sátto me wo tôsù

to turn over a new leaf 心を入れ換える kokórò wo irékaerù

leaflet [liːfˈlit] *n* ビラ birá, 散らし chiráshi

league [liːg] *n* (group of people, clubs, countries) 連盟 reńmei, リーグ rígu

to be in league with someone ...と手を組んでいる ...to te wo kuñdè irú

leak [liːk] *n* (of liquid, gas) 漏れ moré; (hole: in roof, pipe etc) 穴 aná; (piece of information) 漏えい rôei

♦*vi* (shoes, ship, pipe, roof) ...から...が漏れる ...kara ...ga moreru; (liquid, gas) 漏れる morérù

♦*vt* (information) 漏らす môrasù

the news leaked out そのニュースが漏れた sonó nyùsu ga moréta

lean [liːn] *adj* (person) やせた yaséta; (meat) 赤身の akámi no

♦*vb* (*pt, pp* **leaned** *or* **leant**)

♦*vt*: **to lean something on something** ...を...にもたせかける ...wo ...ni motásekakerù

♦*vi* (slope) 傾く katámukù

to lean against ...にもたれる ...ni motárerù

to lean on ...に寄り掛る ...ni yoríkakerù

lean back *vi* 後ろへもたれる ushíro e motárerù

lean forward *vi* 前にかがむ máe ni kagámù

leaning [liːniŋ] *n*: *leaning (towards)* (tendency, bent) (...する) 傾向 (...surú) keíkō

lean out *vi* ...から体を乗出す ...kara karáda wò norídasù

lean over *vi* ...の上にかがむ ...no ué nì kagámù

leant [lent] *pt, pp of* **lean**

leap [liːp] *n* (jump) 跳躍 chóyaku; (in price, number etc) 急上昇 kyújōshō

♦*vi* (*pt, pp* **leaped** *or* **leapt**) (jump: high) 跳ね上がる hanéagarù; (: far) 跳躍する chóyaku suru; (price, number etc) 急上昇する kyújōshō suru

leapfrog [liːpʼfrɑːg] *n* 馬跳び umátobi

leapt [lept] *pt, pp of* **leap**

leap year *n* うるう年 urúùdoshi

learn [ləːrn] (*pt, pp* **learned** *or* **learnt**) *vt* (facts, skill) 学ぶ manábù; (study, repeat: poem, play etc) 覚える obóerù, 暗記する añki suru

♦*vi* 習う naráù

to learn about something (hear, read) ...を知る ...wo shírù

to learn to do something ...の仕方を覚える ...no shikáta wò obóerù

learned [ləːrnid] *adj* (person) 学識のある gakúshiki no arù; (book, paper) 学術の gakújutsu no

learner [ləːrnəːr] (*BRIT*) *n* (*also*: **learner driver**) 仮免許運転者 karímenkyo unteñsha

learning [ləːrniŋ] *n* (knowledge) 学識 gakúshiki

learnt [ləːrnt] *pt, pp of* **learn**

lease [liːs] *n* (legal agreement, contract: to borrow something) 賃借契約 chiñshakukukeíyaku, リース rīsu; (: to lend something) 賃貸契約 chiñtaikeíyaku, リース rīsu

♦*vt* (borrow) 賃借する chiñshaku suru; (lend) 賃貸する chiñtai suru

leash [liːʃ] *n* (for dog) ひも himó

least [liːst] *adj*: *the least* (+noun: smallest) 最も小さい móttòmo chíísaì; (: smallest amount of) 最も少ない móttòmo sukúnaì

♦*adv* (+verb) 最も...しない móttòmo ...shináì; (+adjective): *the least* 最も...でない móttòmo ...de náì

the least possible effort 最小限の努力 saíshōgen no dóryòku

at least 少なくとも sukúnakùtomo

you could at least have written 少なくとも手紙をくれたら良かったのに sukúnakùtomo tegámi wò kurétara yokattá no ni

not in the least ちっとも...でない chíttò mo ...de náì

leather [leðəːr] *n* なめし革 naméshigàwa, 革 kawá

leave [liːv] (*pt, pp* **left**) *vt* (place: go away from) 行ってしまう itté shimaù, 帰る kaérù; (place, institution: permanently) 去る sárù, 辞める yamérù; (leave behind: person) 置去りにする okízari ni surù, 見捨てる misúterù; (: thing: accidentally) 置忘れる okíwasurerù; (: deliberately) 置いて行く oíte ikù; (husband, wife) ...と別れる ...to wakárerù; (allow to remain: food, space, time etc) 残す nokósù

♦*vi* (go away) 去る sárù, 行ってしまう itté shimaù; (: permanently) 辞める yamérù; (bus, train) 出発する shuppátsu suru, 出る dérù

♦*n* 休暇 kyúka

to leave something to someone (money, property etc) ...に...を残して死ぬ ...ni ...wo nokóshite shinù; (responsibility etc) ...に...を任せる ...ni ...wo makáserù

to be left 残る nokórù

there's some milk left over ミルクは少し残っている mírùku wa sukóshì nokótte irù

on leave 休暇中で kyúkachū de

leave behind *vt* (person, object) 置いて

行く oíte ikù; (object: accidentally) 置忘れる okíwasurerù

leave of absence n 休暇 kyúka, 暇 hímá

leave out vt 抜かす nukásù

leaves [li:vz] npl of leaf

Lebanon [leb'ənən] n レバノン rebánòn

lecherous [letʃ'ə:rəs] (pej) adj 助平 な sukêbè na

lecture [lek'tʃə:r] n (talk) 講演 kôen; (SCOL) 講義 kôgi
♦vi (talk) 講演する kôen suru; (SCOL) 講義する kôgi sùru
♦vt (scold): to lecture someone on/about something ...の事で...をしかる ...no kotó de ...wo shikárù
to give a lecture on ...について講演する ...ni tsúite kôen suru

lecturer [lek'tʃə:rə:r] (BRIT) n (at university) 講師 kôshi

led [led] pt, pp of lead[1]

ledge [ledʒ] n (of mountain) 岩棚 iwádana; (of window) 桟 sáñ; (on wall) 棚 tanâ

ledger [ledʒ'ə:r] n (COMM) 台帳 dáichō

lee [li:] n 風下 kazáshimo

leech [li:tʃ] n ヒル hírù

leek [li:k] n リーキ ríki, リーク ríku

leer [li:r] vi: to leer at someone ..をいん乱な目で見る ...wo ifran na me de mirù

leeway [li:'wei] n (fig): to have some leeway 余裕がある yoyū ga arù

left [left] pt, pp of leave
♦adj (direction, position) 左の hídari no
♦n (direction, side, position) 左 hídari
♦adv (turn, look etc) 左に〔へ〕hídari ni 〔e〕
on the left 左に〔で〕hídari ni〔de〕
to the left 左に〔へ〕hídari ni〔e〕
the Left (POL) 左翼 sáyòku

left-handed [left'hæn'did] adj 左利きの hídarikiki no, ぎっちょの gítchò no

left-hand side [left'hænd'-] n 左側 hídarigawa

left-luggage (office) [leftlʌg'idʒ-] (BRIT) n 手荷物預かり所 tenímotsu azukarishò

leftovers [left'ouvə:rz] npl (of meal) 残り物 nokórimono

left-wing [left'wiŋ] adj (POL) 左翼の sáyòku no

leg [leg] n (gen) 脚 ashí; (CULIN: of lamb, pork, chicken) もも mômò; (part: of journey etc) 区切り kugfri

legacy [leg'əsi:] n (of will: also fig) 遺産 isán

legal [li:'gəl] adj (of law) 法律の hôritsu no; (action, situation) 法的な hôteki na

legal holiday (US) n 法定休日 hôteikyūjitsu

legality [li:gæl'iti:] n 合法性 gôhosei

legalize [li:'gəlaiz] vt 合法化する gôhoka suru

legally [li:'gəli:] adv (by law) 法的に hôteki ni

legal tender n (currency) 法定通貨 hôteitsùka, 法貨 hôka

legend [ledʒ'ənd] n (story) 伝説 deñsetsu; (fig: person) 伝説的人物 deñsetsutekijinbutsu

legendary [ledʒ'əndeːriː] adj (of legend) 伝説の deñsetsu no; (very famous) 伝説的な deñsetsuteki na

legible [ledʒ'əbəl] adj 読める yomérù

legion [li:'dʒən] n (MIL) 軍隊 guñtai

legislation [ledʒislei'ʃən] n 法律 hôritsu

legislative [ledʒ'isleitiv] adj 立法の rippô no

legislature [ledʒ'isleitʃə:r] n (POL) 議会 gíkài

legitimate [lidʒit'əmit] adj (reasonable) 正当な seítō na; (legal) 合法な gôhō na

leg-room [leg'ru:m] n (in car, plane etc) 脚を伸ばせる空間 ashí wo nobáserù kûkan

leisure [li:'ʒə:r] n (period of time) 余暇 yoká, レジャー rejā
at leisure ゆっくり yukkúrì

leisure centre (BRIT) n レジャーセンター rejásentà ◇スポーツ施設, 図書室, 会議室, 喫茶店などを含んだ文化施設 supôtsushisetsù, toshôshìtsu, kaígishìtsu, kissáteñ nádò wo fukúnda buñkashisetsù

leisurely [li:'ʒə:rli:] adj (pace, walk) ゆっくりした yukkúrì shitá

lemon [lem'ən] n (fruit) レモン rémòn

lemonade [leməneid'] n (BRIT: fizzy drink) ラムネ rámùne; (with lemon juice) レモネード remónèdo

lemon tea n レモンティー remóntī

lend [lend] (pt, pp **lent**) vt: **to lend something to someone** (money, thing) ...に...を貸す ...ni ...wo kásù

lending library [len'diŋ-] n 貸出し図書館 kashídashitoshokàn

length [leŋkθ] n (measurement) 長さ nagása; (distance): **the length of** ...の端から端まで ...no hashí kara hashi madè; (of swimming pool) プールの長さ pūru no nagása; (piece: of wood, string, cloth etc) 1本 ippón; (amount of time) 時間 jikán

at length (at last) とうとう tōtō; (for a long time) 長い間 nagái aída

lengthen [leŋk'θən] vt 長くする nágàku suru

♦vi 長くなる nágàku naru

lengthways [leŋkθ'weiz] adv (slice, fold, lay) 縦に táte ni

lengthy [leŋk'θi:] adj (meeting, explanation, text) 長い nagái

lenient [li:'ni:ənt] adj (person, attitude) 寛大な kańdai na

lens [lenz] n (of spectacles, camera) レンズ rénzu; (telescope) 望遠鏡 bőenkyō

Lent [lent] n 四旬節 shijúnsetsu

lent [lent] pt, pp of **lend**

lentil [len'təl] n ヒラマメ hirámame

Leo [li:'ou] n (ASTROLOGY) しし座 shishíza

leopard [lep'ə:rd] n (ZOOL) ヒョウ hyő

leotard [li:'əta:rd] n レオタード reőtàdo

leprosy [lep'rəsi:] n らい病 raíbyō, ハンセン病 hańsenbyō

lesbian [lez'bi:ən] n 女性同性愛者 joséidōseiaishà, レスビアン resúbiàn

less [les] adj (in size, degree) ...より小さい ...yórì chíìsai; (in amount, quality) ...より少ない ...yórì sukúnaì

♦pron ...より少ないもの ...yórì sukúnaì monő

♦adv ...より少なく ...yórì sukúnakù

♦prep: **less tax / 10% discount** ...から税金〔1割り〕を引いて ...kara zeíkin(ichíwàri〕wo hiíte

less than half 半分以下 hańbun íkà

less than ever 更に少なく sárà ni sukúnàku

less and less ますます少なく masúmàsu sukúnàku

the less he talks the better ... 彼はできるだけしゃべらない方がいい kárè wa dekíru dake shabéranai hỗ ga íi

lessen [les'ən] vi 少なくなる sukúnaku narù

♦vt 少なくする sukúnàku suru

lesser [les'ə:r] adj (smaller: in degree, importance, amount) 小さい〔少ない〕方の chíìsai〔sukúnaì〕hỗ no

to a lesser extent それ程ではないが ...mo soré hodỗ de wa naî ga ...mo

lesson [les'ən] n (class: history etc) 授業 jugyỗ; (: ballet etc) けいこ kéìko, レッスン réssùn; (example, warning) 見せしめ miséshime

to teach someone a lesson (fig) ...に思い知らせてやる ...ni omóishirasete yarù

lest [lest] conj ...しない様に ...shináì yỗ ni

let [let] (pt, pp **let**) vt (allow) 許す yurúsù; (BRIT: lease) 賃貸する chíntai suru

to let someone do something ...に...をするのを許す ...ni ...surú no wò yurúsù

to let someone know something ...に...を知らせる ...ni ...wo shiráserù

let's go 行きましょう ikímashō

let him come (permit) 彼が来るのを邪魔しないで下さい kárè ga kúrù no wo jamá shinàide kudásaì

「to let」貸し家 kashíyà

let down vt (tire etc) ...の空気を抜く ...no kűki wo nuku; (person) がっかりさせる gakkárì saséru

let go vi (stop holding: thing, person) 手を放すte wo hanásù

♦vt (release: person, animal) 放す hanásu

lethal [li:'θəl] adj (chemical, dose etc) 致命的な chiméiteki na

a lethal weapon 凶器 kyỗki

lethargic [ləθɑ:r'dʒik] adj 無気力の mukíryòku no

let in vt (water, air) ...が漏れる ...ga morérù; (person) 入らせる haíraserù

let off *vt* (culprit) 許す yurúsù; (firework, bomb) 爆発させる bakúhatsu saserù; (gun) 撃つ útsù

let on *vi* 漏らす morásù

let out *vt* (person, dog) 外に出す sótò ni dásù; (breath) 吐く hákù; (water, air) 抜く n'úkù; (sound) 出す dásù

letter [let'ə:r] *n* (correspondence) 手紙 tegámi; (of alphabet) 文字 mójì

letter bomb *n* 手紙爆弾 tegámibakùdan

letterbox [let'ə:rba:ks] (*BRIT*) *n* (for receiving mail) 郵便受け yúbin-uke; (for sending mail) 郵便ポスト yúbinposùto, ポスト pósùto

lettering [let'ə:riŋ] *n* 文字 mójì

lettuce [let'is] *n* レタス rétàsu

let up *vi* (cease) やむ yámù; (diminish) 緩む yurúmù

let-up [let'ʌp] *n* (of violence, noise etc) 減少 geñshò

leukemia [lu:ki:'mi:ə] (*BRIT* **leukaemia**) *n* 白血病 hakkétsubyð

level [lev'əl] *adj* (flat) 平らな taíra na

♦*adv*: to be level with (person, vehicle) ...に追い付く ...ni oítsukù

♦*n* (point on scale, height etc) 高さ tákàsa, レベル rébèru; (of lake, river) 水位 súìi

♦*vt* (land: make flat) 平らにする taíra ni suru; (building, forest etc: destroy) 破壊する hakái suru

to be level with ...と同じぐらいである ...to onáji guraì de árù

"A" levels (*BRIT*) 学科の上級試験 gakkà no jókyù shikèn ◊大学入学資格を得るための試験 daígakunyùgaku shikakù wo érù tamé nò shikén

"O" levels (*BRIT*) 学科の普通級試験 gakkà no futsúkyù shikèn ◊中等教育を5年受けた後に受ける試験 chūtōkyōiku wò gonén ukéta nochi ni ukérù shikén

on the level (*fig*: honest) 正直で shójiki de

level crossing (*BRIT*) *n* 踏切 fumíkiri

level-headed [lev'əlhed'id] *adj* (calm) 分別のある fúñbetsu no árù

level off *vi* (prices etc) 横ばい状態にな

る yokóbaijòtai ni nárù

level out *vi* = **level off**

lever [lev'ə:r] *n* (to operate machine) レバー rébà; (bar) バール bárù; (fig) 人を動かす手段 hitó wò ugókasù shúdàn, てこ tékò

leverage [lev'ə:ridʒ] *n* (using bar, lever) てこの作用 tékò no sáyò; (fig: influence) 影響力 eíkyōryòku

levity [lev'iti:] *n* (frivolity) 不真面目さ fumájimesa

levy [lev'i:] *n* (tax, charge) 税金 zeíkin

♦*vt* 課する ka súru

lewd [lu:d] *adj* (look, remark etc) わいせつな waísetsu na

liabilities [laiəbil'əti:z] *npl* (COMM) 債務 saímu

liability [laiəbil'əti:] *n* (person, thing) 負担 fután; (LAW: responsibility) 責任 sekínin

liable [lai'əbəl] *adj* (subject): **liable to** ...の罰則が適用される ...no bassóku ga tekíyō sarerù; (responsible): **liable for** ...の責任を負うべきである ...no sekínin wò oúbeki de arù; (likely): **liable to do** ...しがちである ...shigáchi de arù

liaise [li:eiz'] *vi*: **to liaise (with)** (...と) 連携する (...to) reñkei suru

liaison [li:ei'za:n] *n* (cooperation, coordination) 連携 reñkei; (sexual relationship) 密通 mittsú

liar [lai'ə:r] *n* うそつき usótsùki

libel [lai'bəl] *n* 名誉毀損 meíyokisòn

♦*vt* 中傷する chúshò suru

liberal [lib'ə:rəl] *adj* (tolerant) 開放的な kaíhoteki na; (large: offer, amount etc) 寛大な kaídai na

liberate [lib'ə:reit] *vt* 解放する kaíhō suru

liberation [libərei'ʃən] *n* 解放 kaíhō

liberty [lib'ə:rti:] *n* (gen) 自由 jiyú; (criminal): **to be at liberty** 捕まらないでいる tsukámaranàide írù, 逃走中である tósōchū de arù

to be at liberty to do 自由に...できる jiyú ni ...dekírù

to take the liberty of doing something 勝手に...する katté ni ...surú

Libra [li:'brə] *n* (ASTROLOGY) 天びん座 teñbinza

librarian [laibre:r'i:ən] *n* (worker) 図書館員 toshōkán-in; (qualified) 司書 shíshò

library [lai'bre:ri:] *n* (institution, SCOL: building) 図書館 toshōkàn; (: room) 図書室 toshóshìtsu; (private collection) 蔵書 zōsho

libretto [libret'ou] *n* (OPERA) 脚本 kyakúhon

Libya [lib'i:ə] *n* リビア ríbìa

Libyan [lib'i:ən] *adj* リビアの ríbìa no
♦*n* リビア人 ribíajìn

lice [lais] *npl of* **louse**

licence [lai'səns] (*US also*: **license**) *n* (official document) 免許 méñkyo; (AUT) 運転免許証 uñtenmenkyoshō

license [lai'səns] *n* (*US*) = **licence**
♦*vt* (person, organization, activity) 認可する níñka suru

licensed [lai'sənst] *adj* (driver, pilot etc) 免許を持った méñkyo wo mottá; (for alcohol) 酒類販売許可を持った sakéruihanbaikyòka wo mottá

license plate (*US*) *n* ナンバープレート nañbāpurèto

licentious [laisen't∫əs] *adj* いん乱な iñranna

lichen [lai'kən] *n* 地衣 chíi

lick [lik] *vt* (stamp, fingers etc) なめる namérù; (*inf*: defeat) ...に楽勝する ...ni rakúshō suru
to lick one's lips (*also fig*) 舌なめずりする shitánamèzuri suru

licorice [lik'ə:ris] (*US*) *n* カンゾウあめ kañzōame

lid [lid] *n* (of box, case, pan) ふた futá; (eyelid) まぶた mábùta

lie [lai] (*pt* **lay**, *pp* **lain**) *vi* (person) 横になる yokó ni narù; (be situated: place, object: *also fig*) ...にある ...ni árù; (be placed: in race, league etc) 第...位である dái ...í de arù; (tell lies: *pt*, *pp* **lied**) うそをつく usó wo tsúkù
♦*n* (untrue statement) うそ usó
to lie low (*fig*) 人目を避ける hitóme wo sakéru

lie about/around *vi* (things) 散らばっ

ている chirábatte irú; (people) ごろりと寝ている gorórì to neté iru

lie-down [lai'daun] (*BRIT*) *n*: *to have a lie-down* 昼寝する hirúne suru

lie-in [lai'in] (*BRIT*) *n*: *to have a lie-in* 寝坊する nebō suru

lieu [lu:]: *in lieu of prep* ...の代りに ...no kawári ni

lieutenant [lu:ten'ənt] *n* (MIL) (*also*: **first lieutenant**) 中尉 chūi; (*also*: **second lieutenant**) 小尉 shōi

life [laif] (*pl* **lives**) *n* (quality of being alive) 生命 seímeì; (live things) 生物 seíbùtsu; (state of being alive) 命 ínòchi; (lifespan) 一生 isshō; (events, experience, activities) 生活 seíkatsu
to come to life (*fig*: person, party etc) 活気付く kakkízukù

life assurance (*BRIT*) *n* = **life insurance**

lifebelt [laif'belt] *n* 救命具 kyúmeìgu

lifeboat [laif'bout] *n* (rescue launch) 巡視艇 juñshitèi; (on ship) 救命ボート kyúmeibòto

lifeguard [laif'gɑ:rd] *n* (at beach, swimming pool) 看視員 kañshiìn

life imprisonment *n* 無期懲役 mukíchòeki

life insurance *n* 生命保険 seímeihokèn

life jacket *n* 救命胴衣 kyúmeidòi

lifeless [laif'lis] *adj* (dead: person, animal) 死んだ shíñda; (*fig*: person) 元気のない géñki no náì; (: party etc) 活気のない kakkí no náì

lifelike [laif'laik] *adj* (model, dummy, robot etc) 生きている様な íkìte irú yòna; (realistic: painting, performance) 写実的な shajítsuteki na

lifeline [laif'lain] *n* (means of surviving) 命綱 ínòchizùna

lifelong [laif'lɔ:ŋ] *adj* (friend, ambition etc) 一生の isshō no

life preserver (*US*) *n* = **lifebelt**; **life jacket**

life sentence *n* 無期懲役 mukíchòeki

life-size(d) [laif'saiz(d)] *adj* (painting, model etc) 実物大の jitsúbutsudaì no

life-span [laif'spæn] *n* (of person, animal, plant: *also fig*) 寿命 jumyố

life style *n* 生き方 ikíkata, ライフスタイル raífusutaìru

life support system *n* (MED) 生命維持装置 seímeiijisòchi

lifetime [laif'taim] *n* (of person) 生涯 shōgai; (of thing) 寿命 jumyố

lift [lift] *vt* (raise: thing, part of body) 上げる agéru; (end: ban, rule) 撤廃する teppái suru

♦*vi* (fog) 晴れる harérù

♦*n* (*BRIT*: machine) エレベーター erébētā

to give someone a lift (AUT) ...を車に乗せて上げる ...wo kurúma ni noséte agerù

lift-off [lift'ɔːf] *n* (of rocket) 離昇 rishố

ligament [lig'əmənt] *n* じん帯 jíntai

light [lait] *n* (brightness: from sun, moon, lamp, fire) 光 hikári; (ELEC) 電気 deñki; (AUT) ライト raîto; (for cigarette etc): *have you got a light?* 火をお持ちですか hí wò o-móchì desu ká

♦*vt* (*pt, pp* **lit**) (fire) たく takú; (candle, cigarette) ...に火を付ける ...ni hí wo tsukérù; (room): *to be lit by* ...で照明されている ...de shốmei saréte irù

♦*adj* (pale) 淡い awáì; (not heavy: object) 軽い karúì; (: rain) 細かい komákaì; (: traffic) 少ない sukúnaì; (not strenuous: work) 軽い karúì; (bright: building, room) 明るい akárui; (graceful, gentle: movement, action) 軽やかな karóyaka na; (not serious: book, play, film, music) 肩の凝らない katá no koránaì

to come to light 明るみに出る akárumi ni derù

in the light of (discussions, new evidence etc) ...を考慮して ...wo kốryo shite

light bulb *n* 電球 deñkyū

lighten [lai'tən] *vt* (make less heavy) 軽くする karúku surù

lighter [lai'tə:r] *n* (*also:* **cigarette lighter**) ライター ráìtā

light-headed [lait'hed'id] *adj* (dizzy) 頭がふらふらする atáma ga fúrafura suru; (excited) 浮わついた uwátsuita

light-hearted [lait'hɑːr'tid] *adj* (person)

陽気な yốki na; (question, remark etc) 気楽な kiráku na

lighthouse [lait'haus] *n* 燈台 tốdai

lighting [lai'tiŋ] *n* (system) 照明 shốmei

lightly [lait'liː] *adv* 軽く karúku; (thoughtlessly) 軽率に keísotsu ni; (slightly) 少し sukóshì

to get off lightly 軽い罰だけで逃れる karúi bátsù dàke de nogárerù

lightness [lait'nis] *n* (in weight) 軽さ karúsa

lightning [lait'niŋ] *n* (in sky) 稲妻 inázùma

lightning conductor (*BRIT*) *n* = **lightning rod**

lightning rod (*US*) *n* 避雷針 hiráìshin

light pen *n* ライトペン raítopeǹ

lights [laits] *npl* (AUT: traffic lights) (交通)信号 (kōtsū)shiñgō

light up *vi* (face) 輝く kagáyakù

♦*vt* (illuminate) 明るくする akáruku suru

lightweight [lait'weit] *adj* (suit) 薄いusúi

♦*n* (BOXING) ライト級のボクサー raítokyū no bókùsā

light year *n* (PHYSICS) 光年 kốnen

like [laik] *vt* (find pleasing, attractive, acceptable: person, thing) ...が好きである ...ga sukí de arù

♦*prep* (similar to) ...の様な ...no yố na; (in comparisons) ...の様に ...no yố ni; (such as) 例えば...の様な〔に〕tatóèba ...nádò no yố na(ni)

♦*adj* 似た nitá

♦*n: and the like* など nádò

his likes and dislikes 彼の好きな物と嫌いな物 kárè no sukí na monò to kiráì na monò

I would like, I'd like ...が欲しいのですが ...ga hoshíì no desu gà

would you like a coffee? コーヒーはいかがですか kốhī wa ikágà desu ká

to be/look like someone/something ...に似ている ...ni nité irù

what does it look/taste/sound like? どんな格好〔味, 音〕ですか dôǹna kákkò〔ají, otó〕dèsu ká

that's just like him 彼らしいね karé
rashíi né

do it like this やり方はこうです yarikata wa kô desu

it is nothing like ... ...とは全く違いま
す ...to wa mattáku chigaimasu

likeable [lai'kəbəl] *adj* (person) 人好きの
する hitózuki no suru

likelihood [laik'li:hud] *n* 可能性 kanôsei

likely [laik'li:] *adj* (probable) ありそうな
arísô na

to be likely to do ...しそうである ...shi-
sô de arù

not likely! 何があっても...しない nání
ga atté mo ...shínài, とんでもない tondé-
monài

likeness [laik'nis] *n* (similarity) 似ている
事 nité irù kotó

that's a good likeness (photo, portrait) 実物そっくりだ jitsúbùtsu sokkúrí
da

likewise [laik'waiz] *adv* (similarly) 同じ
く onájìku

to do likewise 同じ様にする onáji yô ni
suru

liking [lai'kiŋ] *n:* *to have a liking for*
(person, thing) ...が好きである ...ga sukí
de arù

to be to someone's liking ...の気に入っ
ている ...no kí ni itte irù

lilac [lai'lək] *n* (BOT: tree, flower) ライ
ラック raírakkù, リラ rírà

lily [lil'i:] *n* (plant, flower) ユリ yurí

lily of the valley *n* スズラン suzúran

limb [lim] *n* (ANAT) 手足 téàshi, 肢 shí

limber up [lim'bə:r-] *vi* (SPORT) 準備運
動をする juńbiundô wo suru, ウオーミン
グアップする uôminguappù suru

limbo [lim'bou] *n:* *to be in limbo* (fig) 忘
れ去られている wasúresararete irù

lime [laim] *n* (fruit) ライム ráimu; (also:
lime tree) ライムの木 ráimu no ki; (also:
lime juice) ライムジュース raímujùsu;
(for soil) 石灰 sékkài; (rock) 石灰岩 sek-
káĩgan

limelight [laim'lait] *n:* *to be in the
limelight* 注目を浴びている chúmoku
wò abíte irù

limerick [lim'ə:rik] *n* 五行わい歌 gogyô-
waìka

limestone [laim'stoun] *n* 石灰岩 sekkáĩ-
gan

limit [lim'it] *n* (greatest amount, extent,
degree) 限界 geńkai; (restriction: of
time, money etc) 制限 seígen; (of area)
境界 kyôkai

♦*vt* (production, expense etc) 制限する
seígen suru

limitation [limitei'ʃən] *n* (control,
restriction) 制限 seígen; (of person,
thing) 限界 geńkai

limited [lim'itid] *adj* (small: choice,
resources etc) 限られた kagírarèta

to be limited to ...に限られる ...ni kagí-
rarerù

limited (liability) company (BRIT)
有限会社 yúgengaìsha

limousine [lim'əzi:n] *n* リムジン rímùjin

limp [limp] *n:* *to have a limp* びっこを
引く bíkkò wo hikú

♦*vi* (person, animal) びっこを引く bíkkò
wo hikú

♦*adj* (person) ぐにゃぐにゃの gúnyàgu-
nya no

limpet [lim'pit] *n* カサガイ kaságai

line [lain] *n* (long thin mark) 線 séñ;
(wrinkle: on face) しわ shiwá; (row: of
people, things) 列 rétsu; (of writing,
song) 行 gyô; (rope) 綱 tsuná, ロープ rô-
pu; (also: **fishing line**) 釣糸 tsurííto;
(also: **power line**) 送電線 sôdensen; (also:
telephone line) 電話線 deńwasen; (TEL)
回線 kaísen; (railway track) 線路 séñro;
(bus, coach, train route) ...線 ...sén; (fig:
attitude, policy) 方針 hôshin; (: business,
work) 分野 búñ-ya; (COMM: of
product(s)) シリーズ shírìzu

♦*vt* (road, room) ...に並ぶ ...ni narábù;
(subj: person: container) ...の内側に...を
張る ...no uchigawa ni ...wo hárù; (: clothing) ...に裏地を付ける ...ni uráji wo tsukerù

to line something with ...に...の裏を付
ける ...ni ...no urá wo tsukérù

to line the streets 道路の両側に並ぶ
dôro no ryôgawa ni narábù

in line (in a row) 1列に ichíretsu ni

in line with (according to) ...に従って ...ni shitágatte

linear [lin'i:ər] *adj* (process, sequence) 一直線の itchókusen no; (shape, form) 線形の seńkei no

lined [laind] *adj* (face) しわのある shiwá no arù; (paper) 線を引いた séń wo hiíta

linen [lin'ən] *n* (cloth) リンネル ríńneru, リネン rínèn; (tablecloths, sheets etc) リネン rínèn

liner [lai'nə:r] *n* (ship) 豪華客船 gókakyakùsen; (for bin) ごみ袋 gomíbukuro

linesman [lainz'mən] (*pl* **linesmen**) *n* (SPORT) 線審 seńshin, ラインズマン raíńzuman

line up *vi* 列を作る rétsù wo tsukúrù

♦*vt* (people) 1列に並ばせる ichíretsu ni naráhaserù; (prepare: event, celebration) 手配する tehái suru

line-up [lain'ʌp] *n* (*US*: queue) 行列 gyóretsu; (SPORT) ラインアップ raín-appù

linger [liŋ'gə:r] *vi* (smell, tradition etc) 残る nokórù; (person) ぐずぐずする gúzùguzu suru

lingerie [lɑ:n'dʒərei] *n* 女性下着類 joséishitagirùi, ランジェリー ráñjerī

lingo [liŋ'gou] (*pl* **lingoes**: *inf*) *n* (language) 言葉 kotóba

linguist [liŋ'gwist] *n* (person who speaks several languages) 数カ国語を話せる人 súkakokùgo wo hanáserù hitő

linguistic [liŋgwis'tik] *adj* (studies, developments, ideas etc) 語学の gógaku no

linguistics [liŋgwis'tiks] *n* 語学 gógaku

lining [lai'niŋ] *n* (cloth) 裏地 uráji; (ANAT) 粘膜 neñmaku

link [liŋk] *n* (relationship) 関係 kańkei; (of a chain) 輪 wá

♦*vt* (join) つなぐ tsunágu; (associate): *to link with/to* ...と関連付ける ...to kańrenzukerù

links [liŋks] *npl* (GOLF) ゴルフ場 gorúfujò

link up *vt* (machines, systems) つなぐ tsunágu

♦*vi* 合流する góryū suru

lino [lai'nou] *n* = **linoleum**

linoleum [linou'li:əm] *n* リノリウム rínóriumu

lion [lai'ən] *n* (ZOOL) ライオン raíon

lioness [lai'ənis] *n* 雌ライオン mesúràion

lip [lip] *n* (ANAT) 唇 kuchíbiru

lip-read [lip'ri:d] *vi* 読唇する dokúshin suru

lip salve *n* 唇の荒れ止め kuchíbiru no arédome

lip service *n*: *to pay lip service to something* (*pej*) 上辺だけ...に賛成する uwábe dake ...ni sańsei suru

lipstick [lip'stik] *n* 口紅 kuchíbeni

liqueur [likə:r'] *n* リキュール ríkyùru

liquid [lik'wid] *adj* 液体の ekítai no

♦*n* 液 ékì, 液体 ekítai

liquidate [lik'wideit] *vt* (opponents, rivals) 消す késù, 殺す korósù; (company) つぶす tsubúsù

liquidize [lik'widaiz] *vt* (CULIN) ミキサーに掛ける míkìsā ni kakérù

liquidizer [lik'widaizə:r] (*BRIT*) *n* ミキサー míkìsā

liquor [lik'ə:r] *n* 酒 saké

liquorice [lik'ə:ris] (*BRIT*) *n* = **licorice**

liquor store (*US*) *n* 酒屋 sákayà

Lisbon [liz'bən] *n* リスボン rísùbon

lisp [lisp] *n* 舌足らずの発音 shitátaràzu no hatsúòn

♦*vi* 舌足らずに発音する shitátaràzu ni hatsúòn suru

list [list] *n* (catalog: of things) 目録 mokúroku, リスト rísùto; (: of people) 名簿 meíbo, リスト rísùto

♦*vt* (mention) 並べてあげる nárábete agerù; (put on list) ...のリストを作る ...no rísùto wo tsukúrù

listed building [lis'tid-] (*BRIT*) *n* 指定建造物 shitéikenzòbutsu

listen [lis'ən] *vi* 聞く kikú

to listen to someone/something ...を〔...の言う事を〕聞く ...wo〔...no iú kotò wo〕kikú

listener [lis'ənə:r] *n* (person listening to speaker) 聞いている人 kiíte irù hitő; (RADIO) 聴取者 chőshushà

listless [list'lis] *adj* 物憂い monóuì

lit [lit] *pt, pp of* **light**

liter [li:'tə:r] (*US*) *n* (unit of volume) リットル rīttōru

literacy [lit'ə:rəsi:] *n* 識字 shikíji

literal [lit'ə:rəl] *adj* (exact: sense, meaning) 厳密な geñmitsu na; (word for word: translation) 逐語的な chikúgoteki na

literally [lit'ə:rəli:] *adv* (in fact) 本当に hoñtō ni; (really) 文字通りに mojídōri ni

literary [lit'əre:ri:] *adj* 文学の buñgaku no

literate [lit'ə:rit] *adj* (able to read etc) 読み書きできる yomíkaki dekírù; (educated) 教養のある kyōyō no arù

literature [lit'ə:rətʃə:r] *n* (novels, plays, poetry) 文学 buñgaku; (printed information: scholarly) 文献 buñken; (: brochures etc) 印刷物 iñsatsubùtsu, カタログ katárogu

lithe [laið] *adj* (person, animal) しなやかな shináyàka na

litigation [litəgei'ʃən] *n* 訴訟 soshō

litre [li:'tə:r] (*BRIT*) *n* = **liter**

litter [lit'ə:r] *n* (rubbish) 散らばっているごみ chirábatte irù gomi; (young animals) 一腹 hitóhara

litter bin (*BRIT*) *n* ごみ入れ gomíire

littered [lit'ə:rd] *adj*: **littered with** (scattered) ...を散らかされた ...wo chirákasareta

little [lit'əl] *adj* (small: thing, person) 小さい chiísai; (young: child) 幼い osánài; (short: distance) 近い chikáì; (time, event) 短い mijíkaì
 ♦*adv* 少ししか...ない sukóshì shika ...náì
 a little (amount) 少し(の) sukóshì (no)
 a little bit 少し sukóshì
 little brother/sister 弟〔妹〕otóto〔imóto〕
 little by little 少しずつ sukóshizùtsu

little finger *n* 小指 koyúbi

live [*vb* liv *adj* laiv] *vi* (reside: in house, town, country) 住む súmù; (lead one's life) 暮す kurásù; (be alive) 生きている ikíte irù
 ♦*adj* (animal, plant) 生きている ikíte irù; (TV, RADIO) 生の namá no, ライブの ráibu no; (performance) 実演の jitsúen

no; (ELEC) 電流が通じている deñryū ga tsūjite irù; 生きている ikíte irù; (bullet, bomb, missile) 使用可能状態の shiyôkanôjōtai no, 実の jitsú no
 to live with someone (cohabit) ...と同せいする ...to dōsei suru

live down *vt* (defeat, error, failure): *I'll never live it down* 一生の恥だ isshô no hájì da

livelihood [laiv'li:hud] *n* (income source) 生計 seíkei

lively [laiv'li:] *adj* (person) 活発な kappátsu na; (interesting: place etc) 活気に満ちた kakkí ni michità; (: event) にぎやかな nigíyaka na; (: book) 面白い omóshiroì; (enthusiastic: interest, admiration etc) 熱心な nesshín na

liven up [laiv'ən-] *vt* (person) ...に元気を付ける ...ni geñki wo tsukérù; (discussion, evening etc) 面白くする omóshirokù suru
 ♦*vi* (person) 元気になる geñki ni nárù; (discussion, evening etc) 面白くなる omóshirokù nárù

live on *vt fus* (food) ...を食べて暮す ...wo tábète kurásu

liver [liv'ə:r] *n* (ANAT) 肝臓 kañzō; (CULIN) レバー rēbà

livery [liv'ə:ri:] *n* (of servant) お仕着せ o-shíkise

lives [laivz] *npl of* **life**

livestock [laiv'sta:k] *n* (AGR) 家畜 kachíku

live together *vi* (cohabit) 同せいする dōsei suru

live up to *vt fus* (fulfil) 守る mamórù

livid [liv'id] *adj* (color: of bruise) 青黒い aóguroì; (: of angry face) どす黒い dosúguroì; (: of sky) 鉛色の namáiiro no; (furious: person) 激怒した gekído shità

living [liv'iŋ] *adj* (alive: person, animal) 生きている ikíte iru
 ♦*n*: *to earn/make a living* 生計を立てる seíkei wo tatérù

living conditions *npl* 暮しの状況 kuráshi no jōkyō

living room *n* 居間 imá

living standards *npl* 生活水準 seíkatsusuijùn

living wage n 生活賃金 seíkatsuchiñgin

lizard [liz'əːrd] n トカゲ tokáge

load [loud] n (thing carried: of person) 荷物 nímòtsu; (: of animal) 荷 ní; (: of vehicle) 積荷 tsumíni; (weight) 負担 fután

♦vt (also: **load up**: vehicle, ship etc): **to load (with)** (...を) ...に積む (...wo) ...ni tsúmù; (COMPUT: program) メモリーに読込む mémòri ni yomíkomù, ロードする rōdo suru; (gun) ...に弾丸を込める ...ni dañgan wo komérù; (camera) ...にフィルムを入れる ...ni fírùmu wo iréru; (tape recorder) ...にテープを入れる ...ni tḗpu wo iréru

a load of rubbish (inf) でたらめ detárame

loads of/a load of (fig) 沢山の takúsañ no

loaded [lou'did] adj (vehicle): **to be loaded with** ...を積んでいる ... wo tsuñde iru; (question) 誘導的な yūdōteki na; (inf: rich) 金持の kanémochi no

loaf [louf] (pl **loaves**) n 一かたまりのパン hitókàtamari no pan

loan [loun] n (sum of money) 貸付金 kashítsukekin, ローン rōn

♦vt (money, thing) 貸す kasú

on loan (borrowed) 借りている karíte irù

loath [louθ] adj: **to be loath to do something** ...をしたくない ...wo shitáku naì

loathe [louð] vt (person, activity) ...が大嫌いである ...ga daíkiraì de árù

loaves [louvz] npl of **loaf**

lobby [lɑːb'iː] n (of building) ロビー robī; (POL: pressure group) 圧力団体 atsúryokudañtai

♦vt (POL) ...に圧力を掛ける ...ni atsúryoku wò kakérù

lobe [loub] n (also: **earlobe**) 耳たぶ mimítabù

lobster [lɑːb'stəːr] n ロブスター róbùsutā

local [lou'kəl] adj (council, paper, police station) 地元の jimóto no

♦n (BRIT: pub) 地元のパブ jimóto no pábù

local anesthetic n (MED) 局部麻酔 kyokúbumasùi

local authority n 地方自治体 chihójichitài

local call n (TEL) 市内通話 shináitsūwa

local government n 地方自治体 chihójichitài

locality [loukæl'itiː] n 場所 basho

locally [lou'kəliː] adv 地元で jimóto de

locals [lou'kəlz] npl: **the locals** (local inhabitants) 地元の住民 jimóto no jūmiñ

locate [lou'keit] vt (find: person, thing) 見付ける mitsúkeru; (situate): **to be located in** ...にある〔いる〕 ...ni árù〔irú〕

location [loukei'ʃən] n (particular place) 場所 basho

on location (CINEMA) ロケで roké de

loch [lɑːk] n 湖 mizúumì

lock [lɑːk] n (of door, drawer, suitcase) 錠 jō; (on canal) こう門 kōmon; (also: **lock of hair**) 髪の一房 kamí no hitófùsa

♦vt (door, drawer, suitcase: with key) ...のかぎを掛ける ...no kagí wo kakérù

♦vi (door etc) かぎが掛る kagí ga kakárù; (wheels) 回らなくなる mawáranaku narù

locker [lɑːk'əːr] n (in school, railway station etc) ロッカー rókkà

locket [lɑːk'it] n ロケット rokéttò

lock in vt 閉じ込める tojíkomerù

lock out vt (person) 閉出す shimédasu

locksmith [lɑːk'smiθ] n 錠前師 jōmaeshi

lock up vt (criminal) 刑務所に入れる keímushò ni iréru; (mental patient) 施設に預ける shisétsu ni azúkerù; (house) ...のかぎを掛ける ...no kagí wo kakérù

♦vi ...のかぎが掛ける ...no kagí wo kakérù

lockup [lɑːk'ʌp] n (jail) 刑務所 keímushò

locomotive [loukəmou'tiv] n 機関車 kikáñsha

locum tenens [lou'kəm tiː'nenz] (BRIT **locum**) n (MED) 代診 daíshin

locust [lou'kəst] n イナゴ inágo

lodge [lɑːdʒ] n (small house) 守衛室 shuéishìtsu; (hunting lodge) 山小屋 yamágoya

♦vi (person): **to lodge (with)** (...の家に) 下宿する (...no íe ni) geshúku suru; (bullet, bone etc) ...に支える ...ni tsukáerù

♦vt (complaint, protest etc) 提出する teíshutsu suru

lodger [lɑːdʒˈəːr] n 下宿人 geshúkunin

lodgings [lɑːdʒˈiŋz] npl 下宿 geshúku

loft [lɔːft] n (attic) 屋根裏部屋 yanéurabèya

lofty [lɔːfˈtiː] adj (noble: ideal, aim) 高尚な kôshō na; (self-important: manner) 横柄な ōhei na

log [lɔːg] n (piece of wood) 丸太 marúta; (written account) 日誌 nisshí

♦vt (event, fact) 記録する kiróku suru

logarithm [lɔːgˈəriðəm] n (MATH) 対数 taísū

logbook [lɔːgˈbuk] n (NAUT) 航海日誌 kôkainisshī; (AVIAT) 航空日誌 kôkūnisshi; (BRIT: of car) 登録帳 tôrokuchō

loggerheads [lɔːgˈəːrhedz] npl: **to be at loggerheads** 対立している taíritsu shite iru

logic [lɑːdʒˈik] n (method of reasoning) 論理学 roñrigàku; (process of reasoning) 論理 rônri

logical [lɑːdʒˈikəl] adj (argument, analysis) 論理的な roñriteki na; (conclusion, result) 当然な tôzen na; (course of action) 合理的な gôriteki na

logistics [loudʒisˈtiks] n (planning and organization) 仕事の計画と実行 shigóto nò kefkaku tò jikkô

logo [louˈgou] n (of firm, organization) シンボルマーク shíñborumàku, ロゴ rôgò

loin [lɔin] n (of meat) 腰肉 koshíniku

loiter [lɔiˈtəːr] vi (linger) ぶらつく burátsuku

loll [lɑːl] vi (person: also: **loll about**) ごろ寝する goróne suru

lollipop [lɑːlˈiːpɑːp] n 棒あめ bôame

lollipop lady (BRIT) n 緑のおばさん midóri no obasàn ◇学童道路横断監視員 gakúdō dōroōdan kañshiin

lollipop man (BRIT: pl **lollipop men**) n ◇緑のおばさんの仕事をする男性 midó-

ri no obasàn no shigóto wò suru dañsei

London [lʌnˈdən] n ロンドン rôñdon

Londoner [lʌnˈdənəːr] n ロンドンっ子 rôñdonkko

lone [loun] adj (person) たったひとりの tattá hitóri no; (thing) たったひとつの tattá hitótsu no

loneliness [lounˈliːnis] n 孤独 kodóku

lonely [lounˈliː] adj (person) 寂しい sabíshiî; (situation) 孤独な kodóku na; (place) 人気のない hitóke no naî

long [lɔːŋ] adj 長い nagaî

♦adv 長く nagáku

♦vi: **to long for something** ...を恋しがる ...wo koíshigarù

so/as long as ...さえすれば ...sáè suréba

don't be long! 早く帰って来て下さいね háyàku kaétte kite kudásai né

how long is the street? この道の端から端までどのぐらいありますか konó michí no hashí kara hashí madè donó guraî arímasù ká

how long is the lesson? レッスンの時間はどのぐらいですか réssùn no jíkàn wa donó guraî desu ká

6 meters long 長さは6メーター nágàsa wa rokú mētā

6 months long 期間は6か月 kíkàn wa rokkágetsu

all night long ひと晩中 hitóbanjū

he no longer comes 彼はもう来ない kárè wa mô kônai

long before ずっと前に zuttó máè ni

before long (+future, +past) まもなく mamónàku

at long last やっと yattó

long-distance [lɔːŋˈdisˈtəns] adj (travel, phone call) 長距離の chôkyori no

longevity [lɑːndʒevˈitiː] n 長生き nagáiki

long-haired [lɔːŋˈheːrd] adj (person) 長髪の chôhatsu no

longhand [lɔːŋˈhænd] n 普通の書き方 futsū no kakíkata

longing [lɔːŋˈiŋ] n あこがれ akógare

longitude [lɑːndʒətuːd] n 経度 keído

long jump n 走り幅跳び hashírihabàtobi

long-life [lɔːŋ'laif] *adj* (batteries etc) 寿命の長い jumyő no nagáì; (milk) ロングライフの rongur, aìfu no

long-lost [lɔːŋ'lɔːst] *adj* (relative, friend) 長年会わなかった nagánen awánakattá

long-playing record [lɔːŋ'plei'iŋ-] *n* L Pレコード erúpírekòdo

long-range [lɔːŋ'reindʒ] *adj* (plan, forecast) 長期の chőki no; (missile, plane etc) 長距離の chőkyori no

long-sighted [lɔːŋ'saitid] *adj* (MED) 遠視の eñshi no

long-standing [lɔːŋ'stæn'diŋ] *adj* 長年にわたる nagánen ni watárù

long-suffering [lɔːŋ'sʌf'əːriŋ] *adj* (person) 忍耐強い niñtaizuyoì

long-term [lɔːŋ'təːrm] *adj* (project, solution etc) 長期の chőki no

long wave *n* (RADIO) 長波 chőha

long-winded [lɔːŋ'win'did] *adj* (speech, text) 長たらしい nagátarashiì

loo [luː] (*BRIT*: *inf*) *n* トイレ tôìre

look [luk] *vi* (see) 見る mírù; (seem, appear) ...に見える ...ni miérù; (building etc) to look south/(out) onto the sea 南〔海〕に面している minámi〔úmì〕ni mêñ shite irú

♦*n* (*gen*): **to have a look** 見る mírù; (glance: expressing disapproval etc) 目付き métsùki; (appearance, expression) 様子 yősu

look (here)! (expressing annoyance etc) おい ôi

look! (expressing surprise: male language) 見てくれ mítè kuré; (: female language) 見て mítè

look after *vt fus* (care for) ...の面倒を見る ...no meñdō wo mírù; (deal with) 取扱う toríatsukaù

look at *vt fus* (see) ...を見る ...wo mírù; (read quickly) ...にさっと目を通す ...ni sattő me wo tősù; (study: problem, subject etc) 調べる shiráberù

look back *vi* (remember) 振返ってみる furíkaette mirù

look down on *vt fus* (*fig*) 軽べつする keíbetsu suru

look for *vt fus* (person, thing) 捜す sa-gásu

look forward to *vt fus* ...を楽しみにする ...wo tanóshimi ni suru; (in letters): *we look forward to hearing from you* ご返事をお待ちしております go-héñji wo o-máchi shité orímasù

look into *vt* (investigate) ...を調べる ...wo shiráberù

look on *vi* (watch) 傍観する bőkan suru

look out *vi* (beware): *to look out (for)* (...に) 注意する (...ni) chűì suru

lookout [luk'aut] *n* (tower etc) 看視所 kañshijò; (person) 見張り人 miháriniñ *to be on the lookout for something* ...を警戒する ...wo keíkai suru

look out for *vt fus* (seek) 捜す sagásu

look round *vi* 見回す mimáwasù

looks [luks] *npl* (good looks) 容ぼう yő-bō

look through *vt fus* (examine) ...を調べる ...wo shiráberù

look to *vt fus* (rely on) ...を頼りにする ...wo tayóri ni surù

look up *vi* (with eyes) 見上げる miágerù; (situation) ...の見通しがよくなる ...no mitőshi ga yokú naru

♦*vt* (piece of information) 調べる shiráberù

look up to *vt fus* (hero, idol) ...を尊敬する ...wo soñkei suru

loom [luːm] *vi* (*also*: **loom up**: object, shape) ぼんやりと姿を現す boñ-yarì to sugáta wò aráwasù; (: event: approach) 迫っている semátte irù

♦*n* (for weaving) 機織機 hatáorikì

loony [luː'niː] (*inf*) *adj* 狂っている kurútte irù

♦*n* 気違い kichígaì

loop [luːp] *n* (in string, ribbon etc) 輪 wá

♦*vt*: *to loop something round something* ...に...を巻付ける ...ni ...wo makítsukerù

loophole [luː'phoul] *n* (*fig*) 抜け穴 nukéàna

loose [luːs] *adj* (not firmly fixed) 緩い yurúì; (not close fitting: clothes etc) ゆったりした yuttárì shita; (not tied back: long hair) 縛ってない shibátte naì; (promiscuous: life, morals) ふしだらな fushídàra na

♦*n*: *to be on the loose* (prisoner, maniac) 逃亡中である tôbōchū de arù

loose change *n* 小銭 kozéni

loose chippings [-tʃíp'iŋz] *npl* (on road) 砂利 jarí

loose end *n*: *to be at loose ènds (US) or a loose end (BRIT)* 暇を持て余している himá wo motéamashite irù

loosely [luːsˈliː] *adv* 緩く yúrùku

loosen [luːˈsən] *vt* 緩める yurúmerù

loot [luːt] *n* (*inf*) 分捕り品 buñdorihìn

♦*vt* (steal from: shops, homes) 略奪する ryakúdatsu suru

lop off [lɑːp-] *vt* (branches etc) 切り落す kirŕotosù

lopsided [lɑːpˈsaiˈdid] *adj* (crooked) 偏った katáyottà

lord [lɔːrd] *n* (*BRIT*: peer) 貴族 kízoku

Lord Smith スミス卿 sumísukyð

the Lord (REL) 主 shú

my lord (to bishop, noble, judge) 閣下 kákka

good Lord! えっ ét

the (House of) Lords (*BRIT*) 上院 jóin

lordship [lɔːrdˈʃip] *n*: *your Lordship* 閣下 kákka

lore [lɔːr] *n* (of particular culture) 伝承 deńshō

lorry [lɔːrˈiː] *n* (*BRIT*) トラック torákkù

lorry driver (*BRIT*) *n* トラック運転手 torákku unteñshu

lose [luːz] (*pt, pp* **lost**) *vt* (object) 紛失する fuñshitsu suru, なくす nakúsù; (job) 失う ushínaù; (weight) 減らす herásù; (friend, relative through death) 失う ushínaù, なくす nakusu; (waste: time) 無駄にする mudá ni surù; (: opportunity) 逃す nogásù; (money) 損する sóñ suru

♦*vi* (competition, argument) ...に負ける ...ni makérù

to lose time (clock) 遅れる okúrerù

loser [luːˈzəːr] *n* (in game, contest) 敗者 háisha; (*inf*: failure: person, thing) 出来損ない dekísokonai

loss [lɔːs] *n* (act of losing something) 紛失 fuñshitsu; (occasion of losing some-

thing) 喪失 sôshitsu; (death) 死亡 shibô; (COMM): *to make a loss* 損する sóñ suru

heavy losses (MIL) 大きな損害 ōkina soñgai

to be at a loss 途方に暮れる tohô ni kurèru

lost [lɔːst] *pt, pp* of **lose**

♦*adj* (person, animal: in unknown place) 道に迷った michí ni mayótta; (: missing) 行方不明の yukúe fumèi no; (object) なくした nakúshita

lost and found (*US*) *n* 遺失物 ishítsubùtsu

lost property (*BRIT*) *n* = **lost and found**

lot [lɑːt] *n* (set, group: of things) ひと組 hitókùmi; (at auctions) ロット róttò

the lot (everything) 全部 zéñbu

a lot (large number, amount) 沢山 takusan

a lot of 沢山の takusan no

lots of (things, people) 沢山の takúsañ no

I read a lot 私は沢山の本を読みます watákushi wa takúsañ no hoñ wò yomímasù

to draw lots (for something) (...のために) くじを引く (...no tamé nì) kújì wo híkù

lotion [louˈʃən] *n* (for skin, hair) ローション rôshon

lottery [lɑːtˈəːriː] *n* (game) 宝くじ takárakùji

loud [laud] *adj* (noise, voice, laugh) 大きい ōkii; (support, condemnation) 強い tsuyôi; (clothes) 派手な hadé na

♦*adv* (speak etc) 大きな声で ōkina kôe de

out loud (read, laugh, pray etc) 声を出して kôe wo dáshìte

loudhailer [laudˈheiləːr] (*BRIT*) *n* = **bullhorn**

loudly [laudˈliː] *adv* 大きな声で ōkina kôè de

loudspeaker [laudˈspiːkəːr] *n* 拡声器 kakúseìki, スピーカー súpīkā

lounge [laundʒ] *n* (*BRIT*: in house) 居間

imá; (in hotel, at airport, station) ロビー róbī; (BRIT: also: **lounge bar**) ラウンジバー raúnjibā

◆vi ぐったりもたれる guttárī motárerù

lounge about vi ぶらぶらする búràbura suru

lounge around vi = **lounge about**

lounge suit (BRIT) n 背広 sebíro, スーツ sū́tsu

louse [laus] (pl **lice**) n (insect) シラミ shirámi

lousy [lau'zi:] adj (inf: bad quality: show, meal etc) 最低の saítei no; (: ill) 気持が悪い kimóchi gà warúī

lout [laut] n ちんぴら chiñpira

lovable [lʌv'əbəl] adj 愛らしい aírashiì

love [lʌv] n (gen) 愛 aí, 愛情 aíjō; (romantic) 恋愛 reñ-ai; (sexual) 性愛 seíai; (strong liking: for music, football, animals etc) 愛着 aíchaku, 好み konómi

◆vt (gen) 愛する aí surù; (thing, activity etc) ...が大好きである ...ga daísuki de arù

love (from) Anne (on letter) 愛を込めて、アン（より）aí wo komête, áñ (yórī)

to love to do ...するのが大好きである ...surú nò ga daísuki de arù

to be in love with ...にほれている ...ni horéte irù, ...が好きである ...ga sukí de arù

to fall in love with ...と恋に落ちる ...to kóì ni ochírù, ...が好きになる ...ga sukí ni narù

to make love (have sex) 性交する seíkō suru, セックスする sékkùsu suru

15 love (TENNIS) 15対0 jū́go táì zérò, フィフティーンラブ fífùtīn rabu

I love chocolate 私はチョコレートが大好きです watákushi wà chokórèto ga daísuki desù

love affair n 情事 jōji

love letter n ラブレター rábùretā

love life n 性生活 seíseikatsu

lovely [lʌv'li:] adj (beautiful) 美しい utsúkushiì; (delightful) 楽しい tanóshiì

lover [lʌv'əːr] n (sexual partner) 愛人 aíjin; (person in love) 恋人 koíbito

a lover of art/music 美術〔音楽〕の愛

好者 bíjùtsu〔óñgaku〕no áikōsha

loving [lʌv'iŋ] adj (person) 愛情深い aíjōbukaì; (actions) 愛情のこもった aíjō no komótta

low [lou] adj (gen) 低い hikuī; (income, price etc) 安い yasúī; (quality) 粗悪な soáku na; (sound: deep) 深い fukáī; (: quiet) 低い hikuī

◆adv (sing) 低音で teíon de; (fly) 低く hikúkù

◆n (METEOROLOGY) 低気圧 teíkìatsu

to be low on (supplies etc) ...が少なくなっている ...ga sukúnàku natté irù

to feel low (depressed) 元気がない géñki ga naí

low-alcohol [lou'æl'kəhɔːl] adj (wine, beer) 度の低い低の低い hikúī

low-cut [lou'kʌt] adj (dress) 襟ぐりの深いeríguri no fukáī, ローカットの rōkatto no

lower [lou'əːr] adj (bottom, less important) 下の shitá no

◆vt (object, price etc) 下げる sagérù; (voice) 低くする hikúkù suru; (eyes) 下に向ける shitá ni mukérù

low-fat [lou'fæt] adj 低脂肪の teíshibō no, ローファットの rōfattò no

lowlands [lou'ləndz] npl (GEO) 低地 teíchi

lowly [lou'li:] adj (position, origin) 卑しい iyáshiì

loyal [lɔi'əl] adj (friend, support etc) 忠実な chújitsu na

loyalty [lɔi'əlti:] n 忠誠 chúsei

lozenge [lɑːz'indʒ] n (MED) ドロップ dóròppu

LP [el'pi:'] n abbr = **long-playing record**

L-plates [el'pleits] (BRIT) npl 仮免許運転中の表示プレート karímenkyo untenchū no hyójipurēto

Ltd abbr (COMM) = **limited (liability) company**

lubricate [lu:b'rikeit] vt (part of machine, chain etc) ...に油を差す ...ni abúra wo sásù

lucid [lu:'sid] adj (writing, speech) 分かりやすい wakáriyasuì; (able to think clearly) 正気な shōki na

luck [lʌk] *n* (*also*: **good luck**) 運 úñ
  bad luck 悪運 akúuñ
  good luck! 成功を祈るよ seíkō wò inórù yo
  bad/hard/tough luck! 残念だね zañneñ da né

luckily [lʌk'ili:] *adv* 幸いに saíwai ni

lucky [lʌk'i:] *adj* (person: fortunate) 運の良い úñ no yóì; (: at cards etc) ...に強い ...ní tsuyóì; (situation, event) まぐれの magúrè no; (object) 好運をもたらす kóuñ wo motárasù

lucrative [lu:'krətiv] *adj* もうかる mókarù

ludicrous [lu:'dəkrəs] *adj* (feeling, situation, price etc) ばかばかしい bakábakashii

lug [lʌg] (*inf*) *vt* (heavy object, suitcase etc) 引きずる hikízuru

luggage [lʌg'idʒ] *n* 手荷物 tenímòtsu

luggage rack *n* (on car) ルーフラック rúfurakku; (in train) 網棚 amidana

lukewarm [lu:k'wɔːrm'] *adj* (liquid) ぬるい nurúì; (person, reaction etc) 気乗りしない kinóri shinai

lull [lʌl] *n* (break: in conversation, fighting etc) 途切れる事 togíreru kotó
  ♦*vt*: *to lull someone to sleep* ゆすって...を寝付かせる yusútte ...wo netsúkaserù
  to be lulled into a false sense of security 油断する yudán suru

lullaby [lʌl'əbai] *n* 子守歌 komóriùta

lumbago [lʌmbei'gou] *n* (MED) 腰痛 yótsu

lumber [lʌm'bəːr] *n* (wood) 材木 zaímoku; (*BRIT*: junk) 粗大ごみ sodáigomi

lumberjack [lʌm'bəːrdʒæk] *n* きこり kikóri

lumber with *vt*: *to be lumbered with something* ...を押付けられる ...wo oshítsukerarerù

luminous [lu:'minəs] *adj* (fabric, color, dial, instrument etc) 蛍光の keíkō no

lump [lʌmp] *n* (of clay, butter etc) 塊 katámari; (on body) しこり shikóri; (on head) こぶ kobú; (*also*: **sugar lump**) 角砂

糖 kakúzatō
  ♦*vt*: *to lump together* 一緒くたに扱う isshókuta ni atsúkaù
  a lump sum 一時払い金額 ichíjibaraikiñgaku

lumpy [lʌm'pi:] *adj* (sauce) 塊だらけの katámaridàrake no; (bed) ごつごつの gotsúgotsuno

lunar [lu:'nəːr] *adj* (landscape, module, landing etc) 月の tsukí no

lunatic [lu:'nətik] *adj* (behavior) 気違い染みた kichígaijimità

lunch [lʌntʃ] *n* 昼食 chúshoku

luncheon [lʌn'tʃən] *n* (formal meal) 昼食会 chúshokukài

luncheon meat *n* ランチョンミート rañchonmìto

luncheon voucher (*BRIT*) *n* 昼食券 chúshokukèn

lunch time *n* 昼食時 chúshokudoki

lung [lʌŋ] *n* (ANAT) 肺 haí

lunge [lʌndʒ] *vi* (*also*: **lunge forward**) 突進する tosshín suru
  to lunge at ...を目掛けて突っ掛る ...wo megákete tsukkákarù

lurch [ləːrtʃ] *vi* (person) よろめく yorómekù; (vehicle) 揺れる yurérù
  ♦*n* (movement: of person) よろめき yorómeki; (: of vehicle) 揺れる事 yurérù kotó
  to leave someone in the lurch 見捨てる misúterù

lure [lu:r] *n* (attraction) 魅惑 miwáku
  ♦*vt* (entice, tempt) 魅惑する miwáku suru

lurid [lu:'rid] *adj* (violent, sexually graphic: story etc) どぎつい dogítsuì; (*pej*: brightly colored: dress etc) けばけばしい kebákebashiì

lurk [ləːrk] *vi* (animal, person) 待ち伏せする machíbuse surù

luscious [lʌʃ'əs] *adj* (attractive: person, thing) 魅力的な miryókuteki na; (food) おいしそうな oíshisō na

lush [lʌʃ] *adj* (fields, gardens) 生茂った oíshigettà

lust [lʌst] (*pej*) *n* (sexual desire) 性欲 seíyoku; (desire for money, power etc) 欲望

yokúbō

lust after vt fus (desire: strongly) ...の欲に駆られる ...no yokú ni karárerù; (: sexually) ...とセックスをしたがる ...to sekkúsù wo shitágarù

luster [lʌs'tər] (BRIT **lustre**) n (shining: of metal, polished wood etc) つや tsuyá

lust for vt fus = **lust after**

lusty [lʌs'ti:] adj (healthy, energetic) 元気一杯の geñkiippaì no

Luxembourg [lʌk'səmbə:rg] n ルクセンブルク rukúseñburuku

luxuriant [lʌgʒu:r'i:ənt] adj (plants, trees) 生茂った oíshigettà; (gardens) 植込みの生茂った uékomi no oíshigettà; (hair) 豊富な hőfu na

luxurious [lʌgʒu:r'i:əs] adj (hotel, surroundings etc) 豪華な gőka na

luxury [lʌk'ʃə:ri:] n (great comfort) ぜいたく zeítaku; (expensive extra) ぜいたく品 zeítakuhìn; (infrequent pleasure) 得難い楽しみ egátaì tanóshimì
♦cpd (hotel, car etc) 豪華... gőka...

lying [lai'iŋ] n うそをつく事 usó wo tsúkù kotó
♦adj うそつきの usótsuki no

lynch [lintʃ] vt (prisoner, suspect) 勝手に絞り首にする katté ni shibárikùbi ni suru

lyrical [lir'ikəl] adj (poem) 叙情の jojő no; (fig: praise, comment) 叙情的な jojő-teki na

lyrics [lir'iks] npl (of song) 歌詞 káshì

M

m. abbr = **meter; mile; million**

M.A. [emei'] abbr = **Master of Arts**

mac [mæk] (BRIT) n = **mackintosh**

macabre [məka:'brə] adj 背筋の凍る様なsesúji no kőru yő na

macaroni [mækərou'ni:] n マカロニ makároni

machine [məʃi:n'] n (piece of equipment) 機械 kikái; (fig: party machine, war machine etc) 組織 sőshìki
♦vt (TECH) 機械で作る kikái de tsukú-

rù; (dress etc) ミシンで作る míshìn de tsukúrù

machine gun n 機関銃 kikáñjū

machine language n (COMPUT) 機械語 kikáigo

machinery [məʃi:'nə:ri:] n (equipment) 機械類 kikáirùi; (fig: of government) 組織 sőshìki

macho [ma:'tʃ'ou] adj (man, attitude) 男っぽい otőkoppoi

mackerel [mæk'ə:rəl] n inv サバ sabá

mackintosh [mæk'inta:ʃ] (BRIT) n レーンコート réñkoto

mad [mæd] adj (insane) 気の狂った ki no kurúttà; (foolish) ばかげた bakágetà; (angry) 怒っている okótte irù; (keen): **to be mad about** (person, football etc) ...に夢中になっている ...ni muchū ni nátte iru

madam [mæd'əm] n (form of address) 奥様 őkùsama

madden [mæd'ən] vt 怒らせる okóraserù

made [meid] pt, pp of **make**

Madeira [mədei'rə] n (GEO) マデイラ madéira; (wine) マデイラ madéira

made-to-measure [meid'təmeʒ'ə:r] (BRIT) adj = **made-to-order**

made-to-order [meid'tu:ɔ:r'də:r] (US) adj オーダーメードの ődămèdo no

madly [mæd'li:] adv (frantically) 死物狂いで shiñímonogurùi de
madly in love ぞっこんほれ込んで zokkón horékoǹde

madman [mæd'mæn] (pl **madmen**) n 気違い kichígaì

madness [mæd'nis] n (insanity) 狂気 kyőki; (foolishness) 気違い沙汰 kichígaizata

Madrid [mədrid'] n マドリード madőrĭdo

Mafia [ma:f'i:ə] n マフィア máfìa

magazine [mægəzi:n'] n (PRESS) 雑誌 zasshí; (RADIO, TV) 放送ジャーナル hősō jānarù

maggot [mæg'ət] n ウジムシ ujímùshi

magic [mædʒ'ik] n (supernatural power) 魔法 mahő; (conjuring) 手品 téjìna, マジック májìkku

◆*adj* (powers, ritual) 魔法の mahṓ no

magical [mædʒˈikəl] *adj* (powers, ritual) 魔法の mahṓ no; (experience, evening) 夢の様な yumé no yṓ na

magician [mədʒˈiʃˈən] *n* (wizard) 魔法使い mahṓtsukaì; (conjurer) マジシャン májìshan

magistrate [mædʒˈistreit] *n* 軽犯罪判事 keíhanzai hanji

magnanimous [mægnænˈəməs] *adj* (person, gesture) 寛大な kañdai na

magnate [mægˈneit] *n* 大立者 ōdatemṓno, ...王 ...ō

magnesium [mægniːˈziːəm] *n* マグネシウム magúneshiùmu

magnet [mægˈnit] *n* 磁石 jíshàku

magnetic [mægnetˈik] *adj* (PHYSICS) 磁石の jíshàku no; (personality) 魅力的な miryṓkuteki na

magnetic tape *n* 磁気テープ jikí tèpu

magnetism [mægnˈitizəm] *n* 磁気 jíkì

magnificent [mægnifˈəsənt] *adj* 素晴らしい subárashiì

magnify [mægˈnəfai] *vt* (enlarge: object) 拡大する kakúdai suru; (increase: sound) 大きくする ōkiku suru

magnifying glass [mægˈnəfaiiŋ-] *n* 拡大鏡 kakúdaikyō

magnitude [mægˈnətuːd] *n* (size) 大きさ ōkisa; (importance) 重要性 jūyṓsei

magnolia [mægnoulˈjə] *n* マグノリア magúnorìa ◇モクレン, コブシ, タイサンボクを含む植物の類 mókùren, kóbùshi, taísañboku wo fukúmù shokúbùtsu no ruí

magpie [mægˈpai] *n* カササギ kasásagi

mahogany [məhɑːgˈəniː] *n* マホガニー mahṓgànī

maid [meid] *n* (servant) メイド meídð

old maid (*pej*: spinster) ハイミス haímìsu

maiden [meidˈən] *n* (literary: girl) 少女 shōjo ◆*adj* (aunt etc) 未婚の mikón no; (speech, voyage) 処女... shṓjo ...

maiden name *n* 旧姓 kyūsei ◇既婚女性について使う kikónjòsei ni tsuíte tsukáù

mail [meil] *n* (postal service) 郵便 yūbin;

(letters etc) 郵便物 yūbiñbutsu ◆*vt* (post) 投かんする tókan suru

mailbox [meilˈbɑːks] (*US*) *n* ポスト pósùto

mailing list [meilˈiŋ-] *n* 郵送先名簿 yūsōsaki meìbo

mail-order [meilˈɔːrdər] *n* (system) 通信販売 tsūshinhañbai

maim [meim] *vt* 重傷を負わせる júshō wo owáserù ◇その結果不具になる場合について言う sonó kekká fúgù ni nárù baái ni tsuíte iú

main [mein] *adj* 主な ómò na, 主要の shuyṓ na, メーンの mēn no ◆*n* (pipe) 本管 hoñkan

in the main (in general) 概して gái shite

mainframe [meinˈfreim] *n* (COMPUT) メインフレーム meínfurèmu

mainland [meinˈlənd] *n* 本土 hóndo

mainly [meinˈliː] *adv* 主に ómò ni

main road *n* 幹線道路 kañsendṓro

mains [meinz] *npl*: *the mains* (gas, water) 本管 hoñkan; (ELEC) 本線 hoñsen

mainstay [meinˈstei] *n* (*fig*: prop) 大黒柱 daíkokubàshira

mainstream [meinˈstriːm] *n* (*fig*) 主流 shuryū

maintain [meinteinˈ] *vt* (preserve: contact, friendship, system) 続ける tsuzúkeru, 保持する hojí suru; (keep up: momentum, output) 維持する ijí suru; (provide for: dependant) 養う yashínaù; (look after: building) 管理する káñri suru; (affirm: belief, opinion) 主張する shuchṓ suru

maintenance [meinˈtənəns] *n* (of contact, friendship, system) 保持 hojí; (of momentum, output) 維持 ijí; (provision for dependent) 扶養 fuyṓ; (looking after building) 管理 káñri; (affirmation: of belief, opinion) 主張する事 shuchṓ suru koto; (*BRIT*: LAW: alimony) 離婚手当 rikónteate

maize [meiz] *n* トウモロコシ toúmorðkoshi

majestic [mədʒesˈtik] *adj* (splendid: scenery etc) 壮大な sodái na; (dignified)

堂々とした dōdō to shitá

majesty [mædʒ'isti:] *n* (title): *Your Majesty* 陛下 héîka; (sovereignty) 王位 ối; (splendor) 威厳 igén

major [mei'dʒəːr] *n* (MIL) 少佐 shốsa
♦*adj* (important, significant): event, factor) 重要な júyō na; (MUS: key) 長調の chốchō no

Majorca [məjɔːr'kə] *n* マジョルカ majốrūka

majority [mədʒɔːr'iti:] *n* (larger group: of people, things) 過半数 kahánsū; (margin: of votes) 得票差 tokūhyốsa

make [meik] (*pt, pp* **made**) *vt* (produce, form: object, clothes, cake) 作る tsukúrù; (: noise) 立てる tatérù; (: speech, mistake) する surú; (: remark) 言う iú; (manufacture: goods) 作る tsukúrù, 製造する seízō surú; (cause to be): *to make someone sad* ...を悲しくさせる ...wo kanáshikù saséru; (force): *to make someone do something* ...に...をさせる ...ni ...wo saseru; (earn: money) もうける mốkerù; (equal): *2 and 2 make 4* 2足す2は4 2 tásù 2 wà 4
♦*n* (brand): *it's a Japanese make* 日本製です nihốnsei desu

to make the bed ベッドを整える béddò wo totónoerù

to make a fool of someone ...をばかにする ...wo bákà ni suru

to make a profit 利益を得る ríèki wò érù

to make a loss 損をする sóñ wo suru

to make it (arrive on time) 間に合う ma ní aù; (achieve something) 成功する seíkō suru

what time do you make it? 今何時ですか imá náñji desu ká

to make do with ...で間に合せる ...de ma ní awaserù

make-believe [meik'bili:v] *n* (pretense) 見せ掛け misékake

make for *vt fus* (place) ...に向かう ...ni mukáù

make out *vt* (decipher) 解読する kaídoku suru; (understand) 分かる wakárù; (see) 見る mírù; (write: cheque) 書く kákù

maker [mei'kəːr] *n* (of program, film etc) 制作者 seísakushà; (manufacturer) 製造者 seízōshà, メーカー mēkā

makeshift [meik'ʃift] *adj* (temporary) 間に合せの ma ní awase no

make up *vt* (constitute) 構成する kốsei suru; (invent) でっち上げる detchíagerù; (prepare: bed) 用意する yối suru; (: parcel) 包む tsutsúmù
♦*vi* (after quarrel) 仲直りする nakánaori suru; (with cosmetics) 化粧する keshố suru

make-up [meik'ʌp] *n* (cosmetics) メーキャップ mếkyappù

make up for *vt fus* (loss, disappointment) ...の埋め合せをする ...no uméawase wò suru

make-up remover *n* 化粧落し keshố otồshi

making [mei'kiŋ] *n* (*fig*): *a doctor etc in the making* 医者の卵 ishá no tamágo

to have the makings of ...の素質がある ...no soshítsu ga arù

malaise [mæleiz'] *n* 倦怠 keńtai

malaria [mələːr'i:ə] *n* マラリア marária

Malaya [məlei'jə] *n* マラヤ máràya

Malaysia [məlei'ʒə] *n* マレーシア marếshìa

male [meil] *n* (BIOL: not female) 雄 osú
♦*adj* (animal) 雄の osú no; (human) 男の otốko no, 男性の dańsei no; (attitude etc) 男性的な dańseiteki na

malevolent [məlev'ələnt] *adj* (evil, harmful: person, intention) 悪魔の様な ákùma no yṓ na

malfunction [mælfʌŋk'ʃən] *n* (of computer, machine) 故障 koshố

malice [mæl'is] *n* (ill will) 悪意 ákùi; (rancor) 恨み urámi

malicious [məliʃ'əs] *adj* (spiteful: person, gossip) 悪意に満ちた ákùi ni michíta

malign [məlain'] *vt* (slander) 中傷する chūshō suru

malignant [məlig'nənt] *adj* (MED: tumor, growth) 悪性の akúsei no

mall [mɔːl] *n* (*also*: **shopping mall**) ショ

ッピング・モール shoppíngu mòru

mallet [mæl'it] *n* 木づち kízùchi

malnutrition [mælnu:trìʃ'ən] *n* 栄養失調 eíyōshìtchō

malpractice [mælpræk'tis] *n* (MED) 医療過誤 iryōkagò; (LAW) 不正行為 fuséikòi

malt [mɔːlt] *n* (grain) もやし moyáshi, モルト mōrùto; (*also*: **malt whisky**) モルトウイスキー morúto uisùkī

Malta [mɔːl'tə] *n* マルタ márùta

Maltese [mɔːltiːz'] *adj* マルタの márùta no
♦*n inv* マルタ人 marútajìn

maltreat [mæltriːt'] *vt* (treat badly, violently: child, animal) 虐待する gyakútai suru

mammal [mæm'əl] *n* ほ乳類 honyūrùi

mammoth [mæm'əθ] *n* (animal) マンモス mánmosu
♦*adj* (colossal, enormous: task) ばく大な bakúdai na

man [mæn] (*pl* **men**) *n* (adult male) 男 otóko, 男性 dañsei; (mankind) 人類 jínrui
♦*vt* (NAUT: ship) 乗組ませる noríkumaserù; (MIL: gun, post) 配置につく haíchi ni tsúkù; (operate: machine) 操作する sṓsa suru

an old man 老人 rōjìn

man and wife 夫婦 fūfu

manage [mæn'idʒ] *vi* (succeed) うまくなんとかする úmàku nántoka suru; (get by financially) なんとかして暮す nántoka shite kurásù
♦*vt* (be in charge of: business, shop, organization) 管理する káñri suru; (control: ship) 操縦する sṓjū suru; (: person) うまくあしらう úmàku ashíraù

manageable [mæn'idʒəbəl] *adj* (task, number) 扱いやすい atsúkaiyasuì

management [mæn'idʒmənt] *n* (of business etc: control, organization) 管理 káñri; (: persons) 管理職 kañrishòku

manager [mæn'idʒəːr] *n* (of business etc) 支配人 shiháirìn; (of pop star) マネージャー manéjà; (SPORT) 監督 kañtoku

manageress [mæn'idʒəːris] *n* (of business etc) 女性支配人 joséishihaìnin; (of pop star) 女性マネージャー joséi manèjà; (SPORT) 女性監督 joséi kañtoku

managerial [mænidʒi:'ri:əl] *adj* (role, skills) 管理職の kañrishòku no

managing director [mæn'idʒiŋ-] *n* 専務取締役 sêñmutorìshimariyàku

mandarin [mæn'dərin] *n* (*also*: **mandarin orange**) みかん míkàn; (high-ranking bureaucrat) 高級官僚 kōkyū kañryō

mandate [mæn'deit] *n* (authority) 権限 keñgen; (task) 任務 nínmu

mandatory [mæn'dətɔːri:] *adj* (obligatory) 義務的な gimūteki na

mane [mein] *n* (of horse, lion) たてがみ tatégami

maneuver [mənu:'vəːr] (*US*) *vt* (move: car, bulky, object) 巧みに動かす tákùmi ni ugókasù; (manipulate: person, situation) 操る ayátsuru
♦*vi* (move: car, plane) 巧みに動く tákùmi ni ugókù; (MIL) 軍事演習を行う guñjieñshū wo okonau
♦*n* 巧みな動き tákùmi na ugóki

manfully [mæn'fəli:] *adv* (valiantly) 勇ましく isámashikù

mangle [mæŋ'gəl] *vt* (crush, twist) めちゃくちゃにする mechákucha ni suru

mango [mæŋ'gou] (*pl* **mangoes**) *n* マンゴー máñgō

mangy [mein'dʒi:] *adj* (animal) 汚らしい kitánarashiì

manhandle [mæn'hændəl] *vt* (mistreat) 手荒に扱う teára ni atsúkaù

manhole [mæn'houl] *n* マンホール mañhōru

manhood [mæn'hud] *n* (age) 成人時代 seíjin jidài; (state) 成人である事 seíjin de arù kotó ◇男性のみについて言う dañsei nomì ni tsùīte iú

man-hour [mæn'auəːr] *n* (time) 人時 nínji

manhunt [mæn'hʌnt] *n* (POLICE) 人間狩り nińgeñgari

mania [mei'ni:ə] *n* (craze) ...狂 ...kyō; (illness) そう病 sōbyō

maniac [mei'ni:æk] *n* (lunatic) 狂人 kyōjin; (*fig*) 無謀な人 mubō na hitò

manic [mǽn'ik] *adj* (behavior, activity) 猛烈な mṓretsu na

manic-depressive [mǽn'ikdipres'iv] *n* そううつ病患者 sṓutsubyō kaǹja

manicure [mǽn'əkjur] *n* マニキュア maníkyùa

manicure set *n* マニキュア・セット maníkyua settō

manifest [mǽn'əfest] *vt* (show, display) 表す aráwasù
♦*adj* (evident, obvious) 明白な meíhaku na

manifestation [mǽnəfestei'ʃən] *n* 現れ aráware

manifesto [mǽnəfes'tou] *n* 声明書 seímeisho

manipulate [mənip'jəleit] *vt* (people) 操る ayátsurù; (system, situation) 操作する sṓsa suru

mankind [mǽn'kaind'] *n* (human beings) 人類 jíǹrui

manly [mǽn'li:] *adj* (masculine) 男らしい otókorashiǐ

man-made [mǽn'meid] *adj* (environment, satellite etc) 人工の jiǹkō no; (fiber, lake etc) 人造の jiǹzō no

manner [mǽn'əːr] *n* (way) やり方 yaríkata; (behavior) 態度 taído; (type, sort): *all manner of things* あらゆる物 aráyuru monò

mannerism [mǽn'əːrizəm] *n* 癖 kusé

manners [mǽn'əːrz] *npl* (conduct) 行儀 gyógi, マナー mánā
bad manners 行儀の悪い事 gyógi no warúǐ kotó

manoeuvre [mənuː'vəːr] (*BRIT*) = maneuver

manor [mǽn'əːr] *n* (*also:* **manor house**) 屋敷 yashíki

manpower [mǽn'pauəːr] *n* (workers) 人手 hitóde

mansion [mǽn'tʃən] *n* 豪邸 gótei

manslaughter [mǽn'slɔːtəːr] *n* (LAW) 殺意なき殺人 satsúinaki satsújin

mantelpiece [mǽn'təlpiːs] *n* マントルピース maǹtorupīsu

manual [mǽn'juːəl] *adj* (work, worker) 肉体の nikútai no; (controls) 手動の shudṓ no
♦*n* (book) マニュアル mányùaru

manufacture [mǽnjəfæk'tʃəːr] *vt* (make, produce: goods) 製造する seízō suru
♦*n* (making) 製造 seízō

manufacturer [mǽnjəfæk'tʃəːrəːr] *n* 製造業者 seízōgyòsha, メーカー mḗkā

manure [mənuːr'] *n* 肥やし koyáshi

manuscript [mǽn'jəskript] *n* (of book, report) 原稿 geńkō; (old document) 写本 shahóǹ

many [men'i:] *adj* (a lot of: people, things, ideas) 沢山の takúsaǹ no
♦*pron* (several) 多数 tasú
a great many 非常に沢山の hijṓ ni takúsaǹ no
many a time 何回も nańkai mo

map [mǽp] *n* (of town, country) 地図 chízù

maple [mei'pəl] *n* (tree) カエデ kaéde; (wood) カエデ材 kaédezài

map out *vt* (plan, task) 計画する keíkaku suru

mar [mɑːr] *vt* (spoil: appearance) 損なう sokónaù; (: day, event) ぶち壊す buchíkowasù

marathon [mǽr'əθɑːn] *n* (race) マラソン marásoǹ

marauder [mərɔːd'əːr] *n* (robber, killer) ◇殺人, 略奪などを繰返しながら荒し回る無法者 satsújin, ryakúdatsu nado wo kuríkaeshinagara arashimawarù muhōmòno

marble [mɑːr'bəl] *n* (stone) 大理石 daírisèki; (toy) ビー玉 bídama

March [mɑːrtʃ] *n* 3月 saǹgatsu

march [mɑːrtʃ] *vi* (MIL: soldiers) 行進する kóshin suru; (*fig*: protesters) デモ行進をする demó kṓshin wo suru; (walk briskly) 足音も高く歩く ashíoto mo takákù arúkù
♦*n* (MIL) 行進 kṓshin; (demonstration) デモ行進 demó kṓshin

mare [meːr] *n* 牝ウマ mesú uma

margarine [mɑːr'dʒəːrin] *n* マーガリン mágarin

margin [mɑːr'dʒin] *n* (difference: of

votes) 差 sa; (extra amount) 余裕 yoyū; (COMM: profit) 利ざや rizáya, マージン májin; (space: on page) 余白 yoháku; (edge: of area, group) 外れ hazúre

marginal [mɑːrˈdʒinəl] *adj* (unimportant) 二次的な nijíteki na

marginal (seat) *n* (POL) 不安定な議席 fuántei na giséki ◊わずかな票の差で得たので, 次の選挙で失う可能性のある議席 tsugí nò seńkyo de ushínaù kańōsei no arù giséki

marigold [mærˈəgould] *n* マリーゴールド marígoōrudo

marijuana [mærəwɑːˈnə] *n* マリファナ maríſàna

marina [məriːˈnə] *n* (harbor) マリーナ marína

marinate [mærˈəneit] *vt* (CULIN) マリネにする márīne ni suru

marine [məriːnˈ] *adj* (life, plant, biology) 海の umí no; (engineer, engineering) 船舶の señpaku no
♦*n* (US: sailor) 海兵隊員 kaíheitaìin; (BRIT: soldier) 海兵隊員 kaíheitaìin

marital [mærˈitəl] *adj* (problem, relations) 夫婦の fúfu no
marital status ◊未婚, 既婚, 離婚を尋ねる時に使う言葉 mikón, kikón, ríkon wo tazúnerù tokí ni tsukaù kotóba

maritime [mærˈitaim] *adj* 海事の káiji no

marjoram [mɑːrˈdʒərəm] *n* マヨラナ mayónàra, マージョラム májòramu

mark [mɑːrk] *n* (symbol: cross, tick etc) 印 shirúshi; (stain) 染み shimí; (of shoes, fingers, tires: in snow, mud etc) 跡 átò; (sign: of friendship, respect etc) 印 shirúshi; (SCOL) 成績 seíseki; (level, point):
the halfway mark 中間点の目印 chúkanteñ no mejírùshi; (currency) マルク márùku
♦*vt* (make a mark on: with pen etc) 印を書く shirúshi wo kákù; (: with shoes, tires etc) 跡を残す átò wo nokósù; (damage: furniture etc) 傷を付ける kizú wo tsukérù; (stain: clothes, carpet etc) 染みを付ける shimí wo tsukérù; (indicate:

place, time, price) 示す shimésù; (commemorate: event) 記念する kinén suru; (BRIT: SCOL) 成績をつける seíseki wò tsukérù

to mark time (MIL, *fig*) 足踏みする ashíbumi suru

marked [mɑːrkt] *adj* (obvious) 著しい ichíjirushiì

marker [mɑːrˈkəːr] *n* (sign) 目印 mejírùshi; (bookmark) しおり shiórì
marker pen サインペン saínpen

market [mɑːrˈkit] *n* (for fish, cattle, vegetables etc, 市場 íchìba; (in proper names) 市場 íchìba, 市場 shijó; (COMM: business and trading activity) 市場 shijó; (: demand) 需要 juyō
♦*vt* (COMM: sell) 市場に出す shijó ni dásù

market garden (BRIT) *n* 野菜農園 yasáinōen ◊主に市場向けの野菜や果物を栽培する小規模農場 ómò ni shijómuke nò yasái ya kudámono wò saíbai surù shókibo nōjō

marketing [mɑːrˈkitiŋ] *n* (COMM) 販売 hańbai

marketplace [mɑːrˈkitpleis] *n* (area, site: *also* COMM) 市場 íchìba

market research *n* 市場調査 shijóchōsa

marksman [mɑːrksˈmən] (*pl* **marksmen**) *n* 射撃の名手 shagéki no meíshù

marmalade [mɑːrˈməleid] *n* マーマレード mámarēdo

maroon [məruːnˈ] *vt*: *to be marooned* (shipwrecked) 遭難で置去りになる sónan dè okízari ni narù; (*fig*: abandoned) 置去りにされる okízari ni sarèru
♦*adj* (color) クリ色 kuríiro

marquee [mɑːrkiːˈ] *n* (tent) テント téñto ◊運動会, 野外パーティーなどで使う物を指す uńdōkai, yagái pàti nádò de tsukáù monó wo sásù

marquess [mɑːrˈkwis] *n* 侯爵 kōshaku

marquis [mɑːrˈkwis] *n* = **marquess**

marriage [mærˈidʒ] *n* (relationship, institution) 結婚 kekkón; (wedding) 結婚式 kekkónshiki

marriage bureau *n* 結婚相談所 kekkónsōdanjo

marriage certificate n 結婚証明書 kekkónshōmeishŏ

married [mær'i:d] *adj* (man, woman) 既婚の kikón no; (life, love) 結婚の kekkón no

marrow [mær'ou] n (vegetable) セイヨウカボチャ seíyōkabòcha; (*also*: **bone marrow**) 骨髄 kotsúzui

marry [mær'i:] *vt* (man, woman) ...と結婚する ...to kekkón surù; (subj: father, priest etc) ...の結婚式を行う ...no kekkónshiki wo okónaù

♦*vi* (*also*: **get married**) 結婚する kekkón suru

Mars [ma:rz] n (planet) 火星 kaséi

marsh [ma:rʃ] n (bog) 沼沢地 shótakùchi; (*also*: **salt marsh**) 塩性沼沢地 eñsei shótakuchi

marshal [ma:r'ʃəl] n (MIL: *also*: **field marshal**) 陸軍元帥 rikúgun geñsui; (official: at sports meeting etc) 役員 yakúìn; (*US*: of police, fire department) 長官 chōkan

♦*vt* (organize: thoughts) 整理する seíri suru; (: support) 集める atsúmerù; (: soldiers) 整列させる seíretsu saserù

marshy [ma:r'ʃi:] *adj* 沼沢の多い shótaku nŏ ŏi

martial [ma:r'ʃəl] *adj* (military) 軍の gún no

martial arts *npl* 武術 bújùtsu

martial law n 戒厳令 kaígeñrei

martyr [ma:r'tər] n (for beliefs) 殉教者 juñkyŏsha

martyrdom [ma:r'tərdəm] n 殉教 juñkyō

marvel [ma:r'vəl] n (wonder) 驚異 kyŏi

♦*vi*: **to marvel (at)** 驚嘆する kyótan suru

marvelous [ma:r'vələs] (*BRIT* **marvellous**) *adj* 素晴らしい subárashiì

Marxism [ma:rk'sizəm] n マルクス主義 marúkusushùgi

Marxist [ma:r'ksist] *adj* マルクス主義の marúkusushùgi no

♦n マルクス主義者 marúkusushùgisha

marzipan [ma:r'zəpæn] n マジパン majípan

mascara [mæskæ:r'ə] n マスカラ masúkara

mascot [mæs'ka:t] n マスコット masúkŏtto

masculine [mæs'kjəlin] *adj* (male: characteristics, pride) 男性の dañsei no; (: atmosphere) 男性的な dañseiteki na; (woman) 男の様な otóko no yŏ na; (LING: noun, pronoun etc) 男性の dañsei no

mash [mæʃ] *vt* つぶす tsubúsu

mashed potatoes [mæʃt-] *npl* マッシュポテト masshú potèto

mask [mæsk] n (disguise) 覆面 fukúmen; (shield: gas mask, face mask) マスク másùku

♦*vt* (cover: face) 覆い隠す óikakùsu; (hide: feelings) 隠す kakúsù

masochist [mæs'əkist] n マゾヒスト mazóhisùto

mason [mei'sən] n (*also*: **stone mason**) 石屋 ishíya; (*also*: **freemason**) フリーメーソン furímēson

masonic [məsa:n'ik] *adj* (lodge, dinner) フリーメーソンの furímēson no

masonry [mei'sənri:] n (stonework) 石造部 sekízòbu ◇建物の石やれんがなどで造られた部分 tatémòno no ishí yà reñga nadò de tsukúrarèta búbùn

masquerade [mæskəreid'] *vi*: **to masquerade as** ...を装う ...wo yosóoù

mass [mæs] n (large number: of papers, people etc) 多数 tasŭ; (large amount: of detail, hair etc) 大量 taíryō; (amount: of air, liquid, land) 集団 shúdan; (PHYSICS) 物量 butsúryŏ; (REL) ミサ聖祭 misá seisài

♦*cpd* (communication, unemployment etc) 大量の taíryō no

♦*vi* (troops, protesters) 集合する shŭgo suru

massacre [mæs'əkər] n 大虐殺 daígyakùsatsu

massage [məsa:ʒ'] n マッサージ massájì

♦*vt* (rub) マッサージする massájì suru

masses [mæs'iz] *npl*: **the masses** (ordinary people) 大衆 taíshū *masses of* (*inf*: food, money, people) 一杯の ippái no

masseur [mæsə:r'] *n* マッサージ師 massájishì

masseuse [məsu:s'] *n* マッサージ嬢 massájijò

massive [mæs'iv] *adj* (large and heavy: furniture, door, person) どっしりした dosshírì shita; (huge: support, changes, increase) 膨大な bódai na

mass media [-mi:'di:ə] *npl* マスメディア masúmèdia

mass production (*BRIT* **mass-production**) *n* 大量生産 taíryoseisan, マスプロ masúpuro

mast [mæst] *n* (NAUT) マスト másùto; (RADIO etc) 放送アンテナ hōsō aǹtena

master [mæs'tə:r] *n* (of servant, slave) 主人 shujín; (in secondary school) 先生 seǹseì; (title for boys): *Master X* X君 ékusu kùn

◆*vt* (control: situation) 掌握する shōaku suru; (: one's feelings etc) 抑える osáerù; (learn: skills, language) 修得する shútoku suru, マスターする masútā suru

to be master of the situation (*fig*) 事態を掌握している jítài wo shōaku shite irù

master key *n* マスターキー masútā kī

masterly [mæs'tə:rli:] *adj* あっぱれな appárè na

mastermind [mæs'tə:rmaind] *n* (of crime etc) 首謀者 shubóshà, 黒幕 kurómaku

◆*vt* 計画を練って実行させる keíkaku wò netté jikkō saserù

Master of Arts/Science *n* (person) 文学〔理学〕修士 buǹgaku (rígaku) shūshi; (qualification) 文学〔理学〕修士号 buǹgaku (rígaku) shūshigō

masterpiece [mæs'tə:rpi:s] *n* 傑作 kessáku

mastery [mæs'tə:ri:] *n* (of skill, language) 修得 shútoku

masturbate [mæs'tə:rbeit] *vi* マスターベーション〔オナニー〕をする masútābèshon〔onánī〕wo suru

masturbation [mæstə:rbei'ʃən] *n* マスタ

ーベーション masútābèshon, オナニー onánī

mat [mæt] *n* (on floor) マット máttò; (at door: *also*: **doormat**) ドアマット doámattò; (on table: *also*: **table mat**) テーブルマット téburumattò

◆*adj* = **matt**

match [mætʃ] *n* (game: of football, tennis etc) 試合 shiái, マッチ mátchì; (for lighting fire, cigarette) マッチ mátchì; (equal) 力が同等な人 chíkara ga dōtō na hitò

◆*vt* (go well with: subj: colors, clothes) ...に合う ...ni áù; (equal) ...と同等である ...to dōtō de arù; (correspond to) ...に合う ...ni áù; (pair: *also*: **match up**) ...と合せる ...to awáserù, ...と組ませる ...to kumáserù

◆*vi* (colors, materials) 合う áù

to be a good match (colors etc) よく合う yokù áù; (couple) 似合いの...である niái no ...de árù

matchbox [mætʃ'bɑ:ks] *n* マッチ箱 matchíbakò

matching [mætʃ'iŋ] *adj* (clothes etc) そろいの soróì no

mate [meit] *n* (workmate) 仲間 nakáma; (*inf*: friend) 友達 tomódachi; (animal) 相手 aíte; (in merchant navy: first, second) ...等航海士 ...tō kōkaishì

◆*vi* (animals) 交尾する kōbi suru

material [məti:'ri:əl] *n* (substance) 物質 busshítsu; (cloth) 生地 kijí; (information, data) 情報 jóhō

◆*adj* (possessions, existence) 物質的な busshítsuteki na

materialistic [məti:ri:əlis'tik] *adj* 唯物主義的な yuíbutsushugiteki na

materialize [məti:r'i:əlaiz] *vi* (happen) 起る okórù; (appear) 現れる aráwarerù

materials [məti:'ri:əlz] *npl* (equipment) 材料 zaíryō

maternal [mətə:r'nəl] *adj* (feelings, role) 母性の boséi no

maternity [mətə:r'niti:] *n* 母性 boséi

maternity dress *n* マタニティドレス matánitidorèsu

maternity hospital *n* 産院 sań-in

math [mæθ] (BRIT **maths**) n 数学 sū́gaku

mathematical [mæθəmǽtʼikəl] adj (formula) 数学の sū́gaku no; (mind) 数学的な sū́gakuteki na

mathematician [mæθəmətiʃʼən] n 数学者 sū́gakushà

mathematics [mæθəmǽtʼiks] n 数学 sū́gaku

maths [mæθs] (BRIT) n = **math**

matinée [mætənei] n マチネー machíne

mating call [mei'tiŋ-] n (of animals) 求愛の声 kyū́ai no kóè

matrices [meit'risi:z] npl of **matrix**

matriculation [mətrikjəlei'ʃən] n (enrollment) 大学入学 daígakunyū̀gaku

matrimonial [mætrəmou'ni:əl] adj 結婚の kekkón no

matrimony [mæt'rəmouni:] n (marriage) 結婚 kekkón

matrix [mei'triks] n (pl **matrices**) (context, environment) 環境 kankyō

matron [mei'trən] n (in hospital) 婦長 fuchṓ; (in school) 養護員 yṓgoiǹ

mat(t) [mæt] adj つや消しの tsuyákeshi no

matted [mæt'id] adj もつれた motsúretà

matter [mæt'əːr] n (event) 事件 jíkèn; (situation) 事情 jijṓ; (problem) 問題 mońdai; (PHYSICS) 物質 busshítsu; (substance, material) 素材 sozái; (written material: reading matter etc) 印刷物 insatsubùtsu, 本 hón; (MED: pus) うみ umí
♦vi (be important: family, job etc) 大切である taísetsu de arù

it doesn't matter 構わない kamáwanài

what's the matter? どうしましたか dṓ shimashita ká

no matter what (whatever happens) 何があっても nánì ga atté mo

as a matter of course (automatically) 当然ながら tṓzen nagara

as a matter of fact 実は jitsú wa

matter-of-fact [mæt'əːrʌvfækt'] adj 無味乾燥な mumíkañsō na

matters [mæt'əːrz] npl (affairs) 物事 monógòto; (situation) 状況 jṓkyo

mattress [mæt'ris] n マットレス mattórèsu

mature [mətuːr'] adj (person) 成熟した seíjuku shita; (cheese, wine etc) 熟成した jukúsei shita
♦vi (develop: child, style) 成長する seíchō suru; (grow up: person) 成熟する seíjuku suru; (ripen, age: cheese, wine etc) 熟成する jukúsei suru

maturity [mətuː'riti:] n (adulthood) 成熟 seíjuku; (wisdom) 分別 fúñbetsu

maul [mɔːl] vt ...に大けがをさせる ...ni ṓkega wò saséru

mausoleum [mɔːsəli:'əm] n 納骨堂 nṓkotsudò

mauve [mouv] adj フジ色の fujíro no

maverick [mæv'əːrik] n 一匹オオカミ ippíki ōkami

maxim [mæk'sim] n 格言 kakúgen

maximum [mæk'səməm] (pl **maxima**) adj (efficiency, speed, dose) 最大の saídai no
♦n 最大限 saídaìgen

May [mei] n 5月 gógatsu

may [mei] (conditional: **might**) vi (indicating possibility): _he may come_ 彼は来るかも知れない kárè wa kurú ka mo shirénài; (be allowed to): _may I smoke?_ タバコをすってもいいですか tabáko wo sutté mò íi desu ká; (wishes): _may God bless you!_ 神の祝福をあなたに！kamí nò shukúfuku wò anáta ni _you may as well go_ 行ってもいいかも知れない itté mò íi ka mo shirenai; (dismissive) 行った方がいいかも知れない itta hō ga íi ka mo shirénài

maybe [mei'bi:] adv 事によると kotó ni yorù to

May Day n メーデー mḕdē

mayhem [mei'hem] n 混乱 koñran

mayonnaise [meiəneiz'] n マヨネーズ mayónèzu

mayor [mei'əːr] n (of city, town) 市(町，村)長 shi (chō, son) chō

mayoress [mei'əːris] n (partner) 市(町，村)長夫人 shi (chō, son) chō fujìn

maze [meiz] n (labyrinth, puzzle) 迷路 mḕro

M.D. [emdi:'] *abbr* = **Doctor of Medicine**

KEYWORD

me [mi:] *pron* **1** (direct) 私 を watákushi wo

can you hear me? 私の声が聞えますか watákushi no koè ga kikóemasù ká

he heard me 彼は私の声を聞いた kárè wa watákushi no koè wo kiítà

he heard ME! (not anyone else) 彼が聞いたのは私の声だった kárè ga kiítà no wa watákushi no koè dáttà

it's me 私です watákushi desù

2 (indirect) 私に watákushi nì

he gave me the money, he gave the money to me 彼は私に金を渡した kárè wa watákushi nì kané wò watáshità

give them to me それらを私に下さい sorérà wo watákushi nì kudásaì

3 (after prep): *the letter's for me* 手紙は私宛てです tegámi wà watákushi ate dèsu

with me 私と一緒に watákushi tò isshó nì

without me 私抜きで watákushi nukì de

meadow [med'ou] *n* 草原 kusáhara

meager [mi:'gə:r] (*BRIT* **meagre**) *adj* 乏しい tobóshiì

meal [mi:l] *n* (occasion, food) 食事 shokúji; (flour) 粉 koná

mealtime [mi:l'taim] *n* 食事時 shokúji-dòki

mean [mi:n] *adj* (with money) けちな kechí na; (unkind: person, trick) 意地悪な ijíwarù na; (shabby: street, lodgings) 見すぼらしい misúborashiì; (average: height, weight) 中位の chúgurai no

◆*vt* (*pt, pp* **meant**) (signify): *I thought you meant her* あなたは彼女の事を言っていると私は思った anátà wa kanójo no kotó wò itté irú to watákushi wà omótta; (intend): *to mean to do something* …をするつもりでいる …wo suru tsumórí de irú

◆*n* (average) 平均 heíkin

do you mean it? 本当ですか hofitō desù ká

what do you mean? それはどういう事ですか soré wa dō iú kotò desu ká

to be meant for someone/something …に当てた物である …ni atéta monò de árù

meander [mi:æn'də:r] *vi* (river) 曲がりくねって流れる magárikunettè nagárerù

meaning [mi:'niŋ] *n* (of word, gesture, book) 意味 ímì; (purpose, value) 意義 ígì

meaningful [mi:'niŋfəl] *adj* (result) 意味のある ímì no árù; (explanation) 納得できる nattóku dekirù; (glance, remark) 意味ありげな imíarige na; (relationship, occasion) 意味深い imíbùkai

meaningless [mi:'niŋlis] *adj* 無意味な muími na

meanness [mi:n'nis] *n* (with money) けちkechí; (unkindness) 意地悪 ijíwàru; (shabbiness) 見すぼらしさ misúborashi-sà

means [mi:nz] *npl* (way) 方法 hóhō; (money) 財産 zaísan

by means of …を使って …wo tsukátte

by all means! ぜひどうぞ zéhì dózò

meant [ment] *pt, pp of* **mean**

meantime [mi:n'taim] *adv* (*also:* **in the meantime**) その間に sonó aìda ni

meanwhile [mi:n'wail] *adv* (meantime) その間に sonó aìda ni

measles [mi:'zəlz] *n* はしか hashíka

measly [mi:'zli:] (*inf*) *adj* ちっぽけな chippókè na

measure [meʒ'ə:r] *vt* (size, weight, distance) 計る hakárù

◆*vi* (room, person) …だけの寸法がある …dakê nò sufipō ga arù

◆*n* (amount: of protection etc) ある程度 árù teídò; (: of whisky etc) 定量 teíryō; (ruler, *also:* **tape measure**) 巻尺 makíjaku, メジャー mejá; (action) 処置 shochí

measured [meʒ'ə:rd] *adj* 慎重な shifichō na

measurements [meʒ'ə:rmənts] *npl* (size) 寸法 sufipō

meat [mi:t] *n* 肉 nikú

cold meat コールドミート kőrudomĭto

meatball [miːˈbɔːl] *n* ミートボール mĭtobŏru

meat pie *n* ミートパイ mĭtopầi

Mecca [mekˈə] *n* (city) メッカ mékkà; (*fig*) あこがれの地 akőgare nò chí

mechanic [məkænˈik] *n* 自動車整備士 jidŏsha seĩbishi

mechanical [məkænˈikəl] *adj* 機械仕掛の kikáijikakè no

mechanics [məkænˈiks] *n* (PHYSICS) 力学 rikĩgaku
♦*npl* (of reading, government etc) 機構 kikŏ

mechanism [mekˈənizəm] *n* (device) 装置 sŏchi; (procedure) 方法 hŏhō; (automatic reaction) 反応 hannŏ

mechanization [mekənizeiˈʃən] *n* 機械化 kikáika

medal [medˈəl] *n* (award) メダル médàru

medallion [mədælˈjən] *n* メダリオン medárìon

medalist [medˈlist] (*BRIT* **medallist**) *n* (SPORT) メダリスト medárìsùto

meddle [medˈəl] *vi*: *to meddle in* ...にちょっかいを出す ...ni chokkái wo dásù
to meddle with something ...をいじる ...wo ijírù

media [miːˈdiə] *npl* マスメディア masúmedìa

mediaeval [miːdiːˈiːˈvəl] *adj* = **medieval**

median [miːˈdiən] (*US*: *also*: **median strip**) 中央分離帯 chŭō buṅritai

mediate [miːˈdiːit] *vi* (arbitrate) 仲裁する chŭsai suru

mediator [miːˈdiːeitər] *n* 仲裁者 chŭsaishà

Medicaid [medˈəkeid] (*US*) *n* メディケイド medíkeĩdo ◊低所得者への医療扶助 teíshotŏkusha e no iryŏfujo

medical [medˈikəl] *adj* (treatment, care) 医学的な igákuteki na
♦*n* (*BRIT*: examination) 健康診断 keṅkŏshindan

Medicare [medˈəkeːr] (*US*) *n* メディケア medíkeầ ◊高齢者への医療扶助 kŏreishầ e no iryŏfujo

medicated [medˈikeitid] *adj* 薬用の yakúyō no

medication [medikeiˈʃən] *n* (drugs etc) 薬 kusúri

medicinal [mədisˈənəl] *adj* 薬効のある yakkŏ no arù

medicine [medˈisin] *n* (science) 医学 ĩgàku; (drug) 薬 kusúri

medieval [miːdiːiˈvəl] *adj* 中世の chŭsei no

mediocre [miːˈdiːoukəːr] *adj* (play, artist) 粗末な sŏmatsu na

mediocrity [miːdiːɑːkˈriti:] *n* (poor quality) 粗末さ sŏmatsusà

meditate [medˈəteit] *vi* (think carefully) 熟考する jukkŏ suru; (REL) めい想する meĩsō suru

meditation [mediteiˈʃən] *n* (thinking) 熟考 jukkŏ; (REL) めい想 meĩsō

Mediterranean [meditəreiˈniːən] *adj* 地中海の chichŭkai no
the Mediterranean (Sea) 地中海 chichŭkai

medium [miːˈdiːəm] *adj* (average: size, color) 中位の chŭgurai no
♦*n* (*pl* **media**: means) 手段 shúdàn; (*pl* **mediums**: people) 霊媒 reĩbai

medium wave *n* 中波 chŭha

medley [medˈliː] *n* (mixture) ごったまぜ gottámaze; (MUS) メドレー medŏrē

meek [miːk] *adj* 穏和な oṅwa na

meet [miːt] (*pt, pp* **met**) *vt* (friend: accidentally) ...に出会う ...ni deáù; (: by arrangement) ...に会う ...ni áù; (stranger: for the first time) ...と知合いになる ...to shíriai ni naru; (go and fetch: at station, airport) 出迎える demúkaerù; (opponent) ...と試合をする ...to shiái wo surù; (obligations) 果す hatásù; (problem, need) 解決する kaĩketsu suru
♦*vi* (friends: accidentally) 出会う deáù; (: by arrangement) 会う áù; (strangers: for the first time) 知合いになる shiríai ni narù; (for talks, discussion) 会合する kaĩgō suru; (join: lines, roads) 合流する gŏryū suru

meeting [miːˈtiŋ] *n* (assembly: of club, committee etc) 会合 kaĩgō; (: of people) 集会 shŭkai; (encounter: with friend) 出

会い deaî; (COMM) 会議 káigi; (POL) 集会 shūkai

meet with vt fus (encounter: difficulty) 合う áu

to meet with success 成功する seíkō suru

megabyte [meg'əbait] n (COMPUT) メガバイト megábaîto

megaphone [meg'əfoun] n メガホン megáhòn

melancholy [mel'ənkɑ:li:] n (sadness) 憂うつ yūutsu, メランコリー meránkorī

♦adj (sad) 憂鬱な yūutsu na

mellow [mel'ou] adj (sound, light, color) 柔らかい yawárakaî; (wine) 芳じゅんな hôjun na

♦vi (person) 角が取れる kádò ga torérù

melodrama [mel'ədræmə] n メロドラマ meródòrama

melody [mel'ədi:] n 旋律 seńritsu, メロディー méròdī

melon [mel'ən] n メロン méròn

melt [melt] vi (metal, snow) 溶ける tokérù

♦vt (metal, snow, butter) 溶かす tokásù

melt down vt (metal) 溶かす tokásù

meltdown [melt'daun] n (in nuclear reactor) メルトダウン merútodàun

melting pot [melt'iŋ-] n (fig: mixture) るつぼ rútsùbo

member [mem'bəːr] n (of group, family) 一員 ichî-in; (of club) 会員 kaíin, メンバー mémbā; (ANAT) 体の一部 karáda no íchìbu

Member of Parliament (BRIT) 国会議員 kokkái giîn

Member of the European Parliament (BRIT) 欧州議会議員 ôshūgikai giîn

membership [mem'bəːrʃip] n (members) 会員一同 kaíin ichidô; (state) 会員である事 kaíin de arù kotó

membership card n 会員証 kaíinshō

membrane [mem'brein] n 膜 makú

memento [məmen'tou] n 記念品 kinéñhin

memo [mem'ou] n 覚書 obôegaki, メモ mémò

memoirs [mem'wɑːrz] npl 回顧録 kaíko-roku

memorable [mem'əːrəbəl] adj 記念すべき kinéńsubeki

memorandum [meməræn'dəm] (pl **memoranda**) n (official note) 覚書 obôegaki; (order to employees etc) 社内通達 shanái tsūtatsu

memorial [məmɔːr'riːəl] n (statue, monument) 記念碑 kinéñhi

♦adj (service) 追悼の tsuítō no; (prize) 記念の kinén no

memorize [mem'əːraiz] vt (learn) 暗記する ańki suru

memory [mem'əːriː] n (ability to remember) 記憶 kíòku; (things one remembers) 思い出 omôide; (instance) 思い出 omôide; (of dead person): *in memory of* ...を記念して ...wo kinén shìte; (COMPUT) 記憶装置 kíòkusòchi, メモリー mémòrī

men [men] pl of **man**

menace [men'is] n (threat) 脅威 kyôi; (nuisance) 困り者 komárimono

♦vt (threaten) 脅かす odôkasu; (endanger) 危険にさらす kikén ni sarásu

menacing [men'isiŋ] adj (person, gesture) 脅迫的な kyôhakuteki na

mend [mend] vt (repair) 修理する shúri suru; (darn: socks etc) 繕う tsukúroù, 修繕する shūzen suru

♦n: *to be on the mend* 回復に向かっている kaífuku nì mukátte irù

to mend one's ways 心を入替える kokôrò wo irékaerù

mending [mend'iŋ] n (repairing) 修繕 shūzen; (clothes) 繕い物 tsukúroimòno

menial [mi:'niːəl] adj (lowly: often pej) 卑しい iyáshiî

meningitis [menindʒai'tis] n 脳膜炎 nô-makuèn

menopause [men'əpɔːz] n 更年期 kôneñki

menstruation [menstruːei'ʃən] n 月経 gekkéi, 生理 sefri, メンス méñsu

mental [men'təl] adj (ability, effort) 精神的な seíshinteki na; (illness, health) 精神の seíshin no

mental arithmetic/calculation 暗算 ańzan

mentality [mentæl'iti:] n (attitude) 考え方 kañgaekáta

menthol [men'θɔ:l] n メントール meñtōru

mention [men'tʃən] n (reference) 言及 geñkyū
♦vt (speak of) ...に言及する ...ni geñkyū suru
don't mention it! どういたしまして dō itáshimashitè

mentor [men'tɔːr] n 良き指導者 yokí shidōsha

menu [men'ju:] n (set menu) 献立 koñdate; (printed) 献立表 koñdatehyō, メニュー ményū; (COMPUT) メニュー ményū

MEP [emi:pi:'] (BRIT) n abbr = **Member of the European Parliament**

mercenary [mɔːr'sɔneri:] adj 金銭ずくの kiñsenzuku no
♦n (soldier) よう兵 yốhei

merchandise [mɔːr'tʃɔndais] n 商品 shốhin

merchant [mɔːr'tʃɔnt] n (trader) 貿易商 bốekishō

merchant bank (BRIT) n マーチャントバンク māchantobañku

merchant marine (BRIT **merchant navy**) n 商船 shōsen ◇一国の全商船を集合的に指す ikkóku no zeñshōsen wò shūgōteki ni sasù

merciful [mɔːr'sifəl] adj (kind, forgiving) 情け深い nasákebukaì; (fortunate): *merciful release* 苦しみからの解放 kurúshimì kara no kaíhō ◇重病人などの死亡について言う jūbyōnin nado no shibō ni tsuitè iú

merciless [mɔːr'silis] adj (person, regime) 冷酷な reíkoku na

mercury [mɔːr'kjɔːri:] n 水銀 suígin

mercy [mɔːr'si:] n (clemency: also REL) 情け nasáke, 慈悲 jihí
at the mercy of ...のなすがままになって ...no nasù ga mamá ni nattè

mere [mir] adj (emphasizing insignificance: child, trifle, amount) ほんの hoñ no; (emphasizing significance): *his mere presence irritates her* 彼がそこにいるだけで彼女は頭に来る kárè ga sokó ni

irù dake de kánòjo wa atáma ni kurù

merely [mir'li:] adv ただ...だけ tádà ...daké

merge [mɔːrdʒ] vt (combine: companies, institutions etc) 合併させる gappéi saserù
♦vi (COMM) 合併する gappéi suru; (colors, sounds, shapes) 次第に溶合う shidái ni tokéaù; (roads) 合流する gốryū suru

merger [mɔːr'dʒɔːr] n (COMM) 合併 gappéi

meringue [mɔræŋ'] n メレンゲ meréñge

merit [me'rit] n (worth, value) 価値 kachí; (advantage) 長所 chốsho, 利点 ritén
♦vt ...に値する ...ni atái suru

mermaid [mɔːr'meid] n 人魚 níñgyo

merry [me'ri:] adj (happy: laugh, person) 陽気な yốki na; (cheerful: music) 活気ある kakkí arù
Merry Christmas! メリークリスマス merí kurisùmasu

merry-go-round [me'ri:gouraund] n 回転木馬 kaíteñmokuba

mesh [meʃ] n (net) メッシュ mésshù

mesmerize [mez'mɔːraiz] vt 魅惑する miwáku suru

mess [mes] n (muddle: in room) 散らかしっ放し chirákashippanashi, めちゃくちゃ mechákucha; (: of situation) 混乱 koñran; (dirt) 汚れ yogóre; (MIL) 食堂 shokúdō

mess about/around (inf) vi (fool around) ぶらぶらする búràbura suru

mess about/around with vt fus (play around with) いじる ijírù

message [mes'idʒ] n (piece of information) 伝言 deñgon, メッセージ mésséji; (meaning: of play, book etc) 教訓 kyốkun

messenger [mes'indʒɔːr] n 使者 shíshà, メッセンジャー mésséñjā

Messrs. [mes'ɔːrz] abbr (on letters) ◇Mr. の複数形 Mr. no fukúsūkei

mess up vt (spoil) 台無しにする daínashi ni suru; (dirty) 汚す yogósù

messy [mes'i:] adj (dirty) 汚れた yogóreta; (untidy) 散らかした chirákashita

met [met] pt, pp of **meet**

metabolism [mətæb'əlizəm] *n* 新陳代謝 shińchintaísha

metal [met'əl] *n* 金属 kińzoku

metallic [mitæl'ik] *adj* (made of metal) 金属の kińzoku no; (sound, color) 金属的な kińzokuteki na

metallurgy [met'ələ:rdʒi:] *n* や金学 yakíngaku

metamorphosis [metəmɔ:r'fəsis] (*pl* **metamorphoses**) *n* 変態 heńtai

metaphor [met'əfɔ:r] *n* 隠ゆ iń-yu, メタファー metáfā

mete [mi:t] *vt*: **to mete out** (punishment, justice) 与える atáerù, 加える kuwáerù

meteor [mi:'ti:our] *n* 流れ星 nagárebòshi

meteorite [mi:'ti:ərait] *n* いん石 íńseki

meteorology [mi:ti:ərɑ:l'ədʒi:] *n* 気象学 kishốgàku

meter [mi:'tə:r] *n* (instrument: gas meter, electricity meter) ...計 ...kéi, メーター mḗtā; (*also*: **parking meter**) パーキングメーター pákingumètā; (*US*: unit) メートル mḗtoru

method [meθ'əd] *n* (way) 方法 hốhō

methodical [məθɑ:d'ikəl] *adj* (careful, thorough) 慎重な shińchō na

Methodist [meθ'ədist] *n* メソジスト教徒 mesójisuto kyòto

methodology [meθədɑ:l'ədʒi:] *n* 方法論 hốhōrðn

meths [meθs] (*BRIT*) *n* = **methylated spirit**

methylated spirit [meθ'əleitid-] (*BRIT*) *n* 変性アルコール heńsei arukðru

meticulous [mətik'jələs] *adj* 厳密な geńmitsu na

metre [mi:'tə:r] (*BRIT*) *n* (unit) = **meter**

metric [met'rik] *adj* メートル法の mḗtoruhð no

metropolis [mitrɑ:p'əlis] *n* 大都会 daítokai

metropolitan [metrəpɑ:l'itən] *adj* 大都会の daítokai no

Metropolitan Police (*BRIT*) *n*: **the Metropolitan Police** ロンドン市警察 roñdon shikeísatsu

mettle [met'əl] *n* (spirit, courage): **to be on one's mettle** 張切っている haríkitte irù

mew [mju:] *vi* (cat) にゃあと鳴く nyấ tò nakú

mews [mju:z] *n* (*BRIT*): **mews flat** アパート apǎto ◇昔の馬屋をアパートに改造した物を指す mukáshi nò umǎya wò apǎto ni kaízō shita monò wo sásù

Mexican [mek'səkən] *adj* メキシコの mekíshiko no

◆*n* メキシコ人 mekíshikojìn

Mexico [mek'səkou] *n* メキシコ mekíshiko

Mexico City *n* メキシコ市 mekíshikoshi

miaow [miau'] *vi* (cat) にゃあと鳴く nyấ tò nakú

mice [mais] *pl of* **mouse**

micro- [mai'krou] *prefix* 微小... bishố ...

microbe [mai'kroub] *n* 細菌 saíkin

microchip [mai'krətʃip] *n* マイクロチップ maíkurochippù

micro(computer) [maikrou(kəmpju:'tə:r)] *n* マイクロコンピュータ maíkurokompyùta, パソコン pasókòn

microcosm [mai'krəkə:zəm] *n* 小宇宙 shốuchū, ミクロコスモス mikúrokosumòsu

microfilm [mai'krəfilm] *n* マイクロフィルム maíkurofirùmu

microphone [mai'krəfoun] *n* マイクロホン maíkurohðn

microprocessor [maikrouprɑ:s'esə:r] *n* マイクロプロセッサー maíkuropurosessã

microscope [mai'krəskoup] *n* 顕微鏡 keńbikyò

microscopic [mai'krəskɑ:p'ik] *adj* 微小の bishố no

microwave [mai'krouweiv] *n* (*also*: **microwave oven**) 電子レンジ deńshi reñji

mid [mid] *adj*: **in mid May** 5月半ばに gogátsu nakàba ni

in mid afternoon 昼下がりに hirúsagari ni

in mid air 空中に kűchū ni

midday [mid'dei] *n* 正午 shốgo

middle [mid'əl] *n* (center) 真ん中 mańnaka, 中央 chūō; (half-way point) 中間 chúkan; (waist) ウエスト uésùto

♦adj (of place, position) 真ん中の mañnaka no; (average: quantity, size) 中位の chūgurai no

in the middle of the night 真夜中に mayónaka ni

middle-aged [mid'əleidʒd'] adj 中年の chūnen no

Middle Ages npl: **the Middle Ages** 中世 chūseī

middle-class [mid'əlklæs] adj 中流の chūryū no

middle class(es) [mid'əlklæs(iz)] n(pl): **the middle class(es)** 中流階級 chūryū-kaīkyū

Middle East n: **the Middle East** 中東 chūtō

middleman [mid'əlmæn] (pl **middlemen**) n 仲買人 nakágainin

middle name n ミドルネーム midórunēmu

middle-of-the-road [mid'əlʌvðəɔroud'] adj (politician, music) 中道の chūdō no

middleweight [mid'əlweit] n (BOXING) ミドル級の midórukyū no

middling [mid'liŋ] adj 中位の chūgurai no

midge [midʒ] n ブヨ búyò ◇ブヨの様な小さい虫の総称 búyò no yō na chiísaì mushí no sōshō

midget [midʒ'it] n 小人 kobíto

Midlands [mid'ləndz] (BRIT) npl: **the Midlands** イングランド中部地方 iñgurando chūbu chihō

midnight [mid'nait] n 真夜中 mayónaka

midriff [mid'rif] n おなか onáka ◇ウエストから胸までの部分を指す uésùto kara muné madè no búbùn wo sásù

midst [midst] n: **in the midst of** (crowd, group) ...の中に〔で〕...no nákà ni (de); (situation, event) ...のさなかに ...no sanákà ni; (action) ...をしている所 ...wo shité irù tokoró

midsummer [mid'sʌm'ə:r] n 真夏 manátsu

midway [mid'wei] adj: **midway (between/through)** ...の途中で ...no to-

chū de

♦adv: **midway (between/through)** ...の途中に〔で〕...no tochū ni (de)

midweek [mid'wi:k] adv 週半ば shū nakabà

midwife [mid'waif] (pl **midwives**) n 助産婦 josáñpu

midwinter [mid'win'tə:r] n: **in midwinter** 真冬に mafúyu ni

might[1] [mait] see **may**

might[2] [mait] n (power) 力 chikára

mighty [mai'ti:] adj 強力な kyőryoku na

migraine [mai'grein] n 偏頭痛 heñzutsū

migrant [mai'grənt] adj: **migrant bird** 渡り鳥 watáridòri

migrant worker 渡り季節労働者 watári kisetsurōdōshà

migrate [mai'greit] vi (bird etc) 移動する idō suru; (person) 移住する ijū suru

migration [maigrei'ʃən] n (bird etc) 移動 idō; (person) 移住 ijū

mike [maik] n abbr = **microphone**

Milan [milæn'] n ミラノ miránò

mild [maild] adj (gentle: character) 大人しい otónashiì; (climate) 穏やかな odáyàka na; (slight: infection, illness) 軽い karúi; (: interest) 少しの sukóshì no; (taste) 甘口の amákuchi no

mildew [mil'du:] n かび kabí

mildly [maild'li:] adv (gently) 優しく yasáshiku; (somewhat) 少し sukóshì

to put it mildly 控え目に言って hikáeme ni ittè

mile [mail] n (unit) マイル maírù

mileage [mai'lidʒ] n (number of miles) マイル数 maírùsū

mileometer [mailɑ:m'itə:r] (BRIT) n = **odometer**

milestone [mail'stoun] n (marker) 一里塚 ichírìzùka; (fig: important event) 画期的な出来事 kakkíteki na dekígòto

milieu [mi:lju:'] n 環境 kañkyō

militant [mil'ətənt] adj 戦闘的な señtōteki na

military [mil'ite:ri:] adj 軍隊の gúntai no

militate [mil'əteit] vi: **to militate against** (prevent) 邪魔する jamá suru

militia [miliʃ'ə] n 民兵 miñpei

milk [milk] *n* (of any mammal) 乳 chichí; (of cow) 牛乳 gyǔnyū, ミルク mírùku

♦*vt* (cow, goat) ...の乳を搾る ...no chichí wò shibórù; (*fig*: situation, person) 食い物にする kuímonò ni suru

milk chocolate *n* ミルクチョコレート mirúkuchokorḕto

milkman [milk'mæn] (*pl* **milkmen**) *n* 牛乳配達人 gyǔnyūhaitatsunin

milkshake [milk'ʃeik] *n* ミルクセーキ mirúkusḕki

milky [mil'ki:] *adj* (color) 乳白色の nyǔhakùshoku no; (drink) ミルク入りの mirúku iri no

Milky Way *n* 銀河 gíñga

mill [mil] *n* (windmill etc: for grain) 製粉機 seífuñki; (*also*: **coffee mill**) コーヒーひき kṓhīhikì; (factory: steel mill, saw mill) 製...工場 seí...kòjō

♦*vt* (grind: grain, flour) ひく híkù

♦*vi* (*also*: **mill about**: people, crowd) 右往左往する uósaò suru

woolen mill 織物工場 orímonokòjo

miller [mil'ər] *n* 製粉業者 seífuñgyōsha

milligram(me) [mil'əgræm] *n* ミリグラム mirígurāmu

millimeter [mil'əmi:tər] (*BRIT* **millimetre**) *n* ミリメートル mirímḕtoru

millinery [mil'əne:ri:] *n* 婦人帽子店 fujínbōshiten

million [mil'jən] *n* 100万 hyakúmañ

a million times 何回も nañkai mo

millionaire [miljəne:r'] *n* 大富豪 daífugṑ

milometer [mai'loumi:tər] *n* = **mileometer**

mime [maim] *n* (action) パントマイム pañtomaìmu; (actor) パントマイム役者 pañtomaimu yakùsha

♦*vt* (act) 身振り手振りでまねる mibúritebùri de manérù

♦*vi* (act out) パントマイムを演ずる pañtomaìmu wo eñzurù

mimic [mim'ik] *n* 物まね師 monómaneshì

♦*vt* (imitate) ...のまねをする ...no mané wo surù

min. *abbr* minute(s); minimum

minaret [minəret'] *n* ミナレット miná-

rètto ◊モスクのせん塔 mósùku no señtō

mince [mins] *vt* (meat) ひく híkù

♦*vi* (in walking) 気取って歩く kidótte arukù

♦*n* (*BRIT*: CULIN) ひき肉 hikíniku

mincemeat [mins'mi:t] *n* (fruit) ミンスミート mínsumìto ◊ドライフルーツなどの細切り doráifurùtsu nádò no komágiri; (*US*: meat) ひき肉 hikíniku

mincemeat pie (*US*) *n* (sweet) ミンスミートパイ mínsumìtopaì

mince pie (*BRIT*) *n* (sweet) = **mincemeat pie**

mincer [min'sər] *n* 肉ひき器 nikúhikikì

mind [maind] *n* (thoughts) 考え kañgaè; (intellect) 頭脳 zunṓ; (opinion): *to my mind* 私の意見では watákushi no ikén de wa; (sanity): *to be out of one's mind* 気が狂っている ki ga kurútte irù

♦*vt* (attend to, look after: shop, home etc) ...の番をする ...no báñ wo suru; (: children, pets etc) ...の面倒を見る ...no meñdō wò mírù; (be careful of) ...に注意する ...ni chūi suru; (object to): *I don't mind the noise* その音を気にしません sonó otó wo kì ni shimáseñ

it is on my mind 気に掛っている kì ni kakátte irù

to keep/bear something in mind ...を気にする ...wo kì ni suru

to make up one's mind 決心する kesshíñ suru

I don't mind 構いませんよ kamáimasèn yó

mind you, ... でもこれだけ言っておく ... de mo koré dakè itté okù ...

never mind! (it makes no odds) 気にしないで下さい kì ni shináìde kudásaì; (don't worry) ほうっておきなさい hṓtte oki nasái, 心配しないで下さい shiñpai shinaìde kudásaì

「*mind the step*」階段に注意 kaídan ni chūi

minder [maind'ər] *n* (childminder) ベビーシッター bebíshittà; (*BRIT inf*: bodyguard) ボディーガード bodígàdo

mindful [maind'fəl] *adj*: *mindful of* ...を気に掛ける ...wo kì ni kakérù

mindless [maind'lis] *adj* (violence) 愚かな ôroka na, 愚劣な gurêtsu na; (boring: job) 退屈な taíkutsu na

KEYWORD

mine[1] [main] *pron* 私の物 watákushi no monð

that book is mine その本は私のです sonð hoñ wa watákushi no dèsu

these cases are mine それらのケースは私のです sorérà no kèsù wa watákushi no dèsu

this is mine これは私の物です korè wà watákushi no monð desu

yours is red, mine is green あなたのは赤いが，私のは緑色です anátà no wa akáì ga, watákushi no wà midóri irð desu

a friend of mine 私のある友達 watákushi nð árù tomódàchi

mine[2] [main] *n* (*gen*) 鉱山 kôzan; (*also*: **land mine**) 地雷 jirái; (bomb in water) 機雷 kirái

♦*vt* (coal) 採掘する saíkutsu suru; (beach) 地雷を敷設する jirái wo fusétsu suru; (harbor) 機雷を敷設する kirái wo fusétsu suru

coal mine 炭坑 tañkō

gold mine 金坑 kiñkō

minefield [main'fi:ld] *n* (area: land) 地雷原 jiráigeñ; (: water) 機雷敷設水域 kiráifusetsu suíìki; (*fig*: situation) 危険をはらんだ事態 kikén wð haráñda jítai

miner [main'ə:r] *n* 鉱山労働者 kôzanrōdòshà

mineral [min'ə:rəl] *adj* (deposit, resources) 鉱物の kôbutsu no

♦*n* (in earth) 鉱物 kôbutsu; (in food) ミネラル minérarù

minerals [min'ə:rəlz] (*BRIT*) *npl* (soft drinks) 炭酸飲料水 tañsan-inryōsui

mineral water *n* ミネラルウォーター minéraru uðtà

mingle [miŋ'gəl] *vi*: **to mingle with** ...と交わる ...to majíwaru ◇特にパーティなどで多くの人に声を掛けて回るなどの意味で使う tókù ni pàti nádò de ôkù no

hitô ni kôè wo kakétè mawárù nádò no ímî de tsukáù

miniature [min'i:ətʃə:r] *adj* (small, tiny) ミニチュアの miníchùa no

♦*n* ミニチュア miníchùa

minibus [min'i:bʌs] *n* マイクロバス maíkurobàsu

minim [min'əm] *n* (MUS) 二分音符 níbun oñpu

minimal [min'əməl] *adj* 最小限(度)の saíshōgen(do) no

minimize [min'əmaiz] *vt* (reduce: risks, disease) 最小限(度)に抑える saíshōgen (do) ni osáerù; (play down: role) 見くびる mikúbirù; (: weakness) 問題にしない moñdai ni shinái, 避けて通る sakéte tòru

minimum [min'əməm] (*pl* **minima**) *n* 最小限(度) saíshōgeñ(do)

♦*adj* 最小限(度)の saíshōgeñ(do) no

mining [mai'niŋ] *n* 鉱業 kôgyō

miniskirt [min'i:skə:rt] *n* ミニスカート minísukàto

minister [min'istə:r] *n* (POL) 大臣 dáìjin; (REL) 牧師 bôkùshi

♦*vi*: **to minister to** (people, needs) ...に仕える ...ni tsukáerù

ministerial [ministi:r'i:əl] (*BRIT*) *adj* (POL) 大臣の dáìjin no

ministry [min'istri:] *n* (POL) ...省 ...shð; (REL) 聖職 seíshoku

mink [miŋk] *n* (fur) ミンクの毛皮 míñku no kegàwa; (animal) ミンク míñku

mink coat *n* ミンクのコート míñku no kòto

minnow [min'ou] *n* 小魚 kozákàna

minor [mai'nə:r] *adj* (unimportant: repairs) ちょっとした chottð shità; (: injuries) 軽い karúì; (: poet) 二流の niryũ no; (MUS) 短調の tanchō no

♦*n* (LAW) 未成年者 misênen

minority [minə:r'iti:] *n* (less than half: of group, society) 少数派 shôsùha

mint [mint] *n* (plant) ハッカ hakkâ; (sweet) ハッカあめ hakkâ amè

♦*vt* (coins) 鋳造する chũzō suru

the (US) Mint (US), the (Royal) Mint (BRIT) 造幣局 zôheìkyoku

in mint condition 新品同様で shiñpindōyō de

minus [mai'nəs] *n* (*also*: **minus sign**) マ
イナス記号 maínasu kigō
♦*prep*: *12 minus 6 equals 6* 12引く6は
6 jūni hikú rokú wà rokú; (*temperature*):
minus 24 零下24度 reíka nijūyoñ do

minuscule [min'əskju:l] *adj* 微々たる bí-
bītaru

minute [min'it] *n* (*unit*) 分 fuñ; (*fig*: *short
time*) ちょっと chottó
♦*adj* (*search, detail*) 細かい komákaì
at the last minute 土壇場に dotáñba
ni

minutes [min'its] *npl* (*of meeting*) 会議
録 kaígirðku

miracle [mir'əkəl] *n* (REL, *fig*) 奇跡 ki-
séki

miraculous [miræk'jələs] *adj* 奇跡的な
kisékiteki na

mirage [mirɑ:ʒ'] *n* しん気楼 shiñkirō

mirror [mir'ər] *n* (*in bedroom, bathroom*) 鏡 kagámi, ミラー mírā; (*in car*)
バックミラー bakkúmirā

mirth [mə:rθ] *n* (*laughter*) 笑い waráì

misadventure [misədven'tʃər] *n* 災難
saínañ

misapprehension [misæprihen'tʃən] *n*
誤解 gokái

misappropriate [misəprou'pri:eit] *vt*
(*funds, money*) 横領する ōryō suru

misbehave [misbiheiv'] *vi* 行儀悪くする
gyōgiwarukù suru

miscalculate [miskæl'kjəleit] *vt* 見込み
違いする mikómichigaì suru

miscarriage [miskær'idʒ] *n* (MED) 流産
ryūzan; (*failure*): *miscarriage of justice* 誤審 goshín

miscellaneous [misəlei'ni:əs] *adj* (*collection, group: of tools, people*) 雑多な zattá na; (*subjects, items*) 種々の shujú no

mischance [mistʃæns'] *n* (*misfortune*) 不
運 fúuñ

mischief [mis'tʃif] *n* (*naughtiness: of
child*) いたずら itázura; (*playfulness,
fun*) いたずら itázura; (*maliciousness*) 悪
さ wárùsa

mischievous [mis'tʃəvəs] *adj* (*naughty,
playful*) いたずらな itázura na

misconception [miskənsep'ʃən] *n* 誤解
gokái

misconduct [miskɑ:n'dʌkt] *n* (*behavior*)
非行 hikō
professional misconduct 背任 haínin,
職権乱用 shokkéñ rañyō

misdemeanor [misdimi:'nə:r] (*BRIT*
misdemeanour) *n* 軽犯罪 keíhañzai

miser [mai'zə:r] *n* けちん坊 kéchìnbō, 守
銭奴 shuséñdo

miserable [miz'ə:rəbəl] *adj* (*unhappy:
person, expression*) 惨めな míjìme na, 不
幸な fukō na; (*wretched: conditions*) 哀
れな áwàre na; (*unpleasant: weather,
person*) いやな iyá na; (*contemptible:
offer, donation*) ちっぽけな chippókè na;
(: *failure*) 情けない nasákenaì

miserly [mai'zə:rli:] *adj* けちな kechí na

misery [miz'ə:ri:] *n* (*unhappiness*) 惨めさ
mijímesà, 不幸せ fushiawase; (*wretched-
ness*) 哀れな状態 áwàre na jōtai

misfire [misfair'] *vi* (*plan etc*) 失敗する
shippái suru

misfit [mis'fit] *n* (*person*) 適応不能者 te-
kíōfunōsha

misfortune [misfɔ:r'tʃən] *n* (*bad luck*) 不
運 fúuñ

misgiving [misgiv'iŋ] *n* (*apprehension*)
心もとなさ kokóromotonasà, 疑念 ginéñ
to have misgivings about something
...を疑問に思う ...wo gimóñ nì omóù

misguided [misgai'did] *adj* (*opinion,
view*) 心得違いの kokóroechigaì no

mishandle [mishæn'dəl] *vt* (*mismanage:
problem, situation*) ...の処置を誤る ...no
shóchì wo ayámarù

mishap [mis'hæp] *n* 事故 jíkò

misinform [misinfɔ:rm'] *vt* ...にうそを伝
える ...ni úsò wo tsutáerù

misinterpret [misintə:r'prit] *vt* 誤解す
る gokái suru

misjudge [misdʒʌdʒ'] *vt* ...の判断を誤る
...no hañdañ wo ayámarù

mislay [mislei'] (*pt, pp* **mislaid**) *vt* (*lose*)
なくす nakúsù, 置忘れる okíwasurerù

mislead [misli:d'] (*pt, pp* **misled**) *vt* うそ
を信じ込ませる úsò wo shiñjikomaserù

misleading [misli:'diŋ] *adj* (*information*)

誤解させる gokái saserù

mismanage [mismæn'idʒ] *vt* (manage badly: business, institution) 下手な管理をする hetá na kánri wo suru; (: problem, situation) ...の処置を誤る ...no shóchi wo ayámarù

misnomer [misnou'mər] *n* (term) 誤った名称 ayámattà meíshō

misogynist [misɑːdʒ'ənist] *n* 女嫌い onnágirai

misplace [mispleis'] *vt* (lose) なくす nakúsù, 置忘れる okíwasurerù

misprint [mis'print] *n* 誤植 goshóku

Miss [mis] *n* ...さん ...sán ◇未婚の女性に対する敬称 míkòn no joséi ni taí surù keíshō

miss [mis] *vt* (train, bus etc) ...に乗遅れる ...ni noríokurerù; (fail to hit: target) ...に当て損なう ...ni atésokonaù; (fail to see): *you can't miss it* 見落しっこない miótoshikkonài; (regret the absence of) ...が恋しい ...ga koíshiì, ...が懐かしい ...ga natsúkashiì; (chance, opportunity) 逃す nigásù, のがす nogásù; (class, meeting) ...に欠席する ...ni kesséki suru

◆*vi* (fail to hit) 当り損なう atárisokonaù, それる sorérù

◆*n* (failure to hit) 当て損ない atésokonaì, ミス mísù

misshapen [misʃei'pən] *adj* 不格好な bukákkō na

missile [mis'əl] *n* (weapon: MIL) ミサイル misáìru; (: object thrown) 飛ぶ道具 tobídōgu

missing [mis'iŋ] *adj* (lost: person, pupil) 行方不明の yukúefumèi no; (: object) なくなっている nakúnatte irù; (removed: tooth) 抜かれた nukáretà; (: wheel) 外された hazúsaretà; (MIL) 行方不明の yukúefumèi no

to be missing 行方不明である yukúefumèi de aru

mission [miʃ'ən] *n* (task) 任務 nínmu; (official representatives) 代表団 daíhyōdan; (MIL) 出撃 shutsúgeki ◇特に爆撃機について言う tókù ni bakúgekikì ni tsuíte iú; (REL: activity) 伝道 deńdō; (: building) 伝道所 deńdōjò

missionary [miʃ'əneri:] *n* 伝道師 deńdōshi

miss out (*BRIT*) *vt* (leave out) 落す otósù

misspent [misspent'] *adj*: *his misspent youth* 浪費した彼の青春 rōhi shitá kárè no seíshun

mist [mist] *n* (light) もや móyà; (heavy) 濃霧 nòmu

◆*vi* (also: **mist over**; **mist up**) (eyes) 涙ぐむ namídagùmu; (windows) 曇る kumórù

mistake [misteik'] *n* (error) 間違い machígaì

◆*vt* (*pt* **mistook**, *pp* **mistaken**) (be wrong about) 間違える machígaerù

by mistake 間違って machígattè

to make a mistake 間違いをする machígaì wo suru

to mistake A for B AをBと間違える A wo B to machígaerù

mistaken [mistei'kən] (*pp* of **mistake**) *adj* (idea, belief etc) 間違った machígattà

to be mistaken 間違っている machígattè irú

mister [mis'tər] (*inf*) *n* ◇男性への呼び掛け dańsei e no yobíkake ¶ *see* **Mr.**

mistletoe [mis'əltou] *n* ヤドリギ yadórigì

mistook [mistuk'] *pt* of **mistake**

mistress [mis'tris] *n* (lover) 愛人 aíjin; (of house, servant) 女主人 ońna shùjin; (in primary, secondary schools) 先生 seńsei

to be mistress of the situation (*fig*) 事態を掌握している jítài wo shóaku shite irù

mistrust [mistrʌst'] *vt* 信用しない shiń-yō shinái

misty [mis'ti:] *adj* (day etc) もやった moyáttà; (glasses, windows) 曇った kumóttà

misunderstand [misʌndə:rstænd'] (*irreg*) *vt* (fail to understand: person, book) 誤解する gokái suru

◆*vi* (fail to understand) 誤解する gokái suru

misunderstanding [misʌndə:rstæn'diŋ]

n (failure to understand) 誤解 gokái; (disagreement) 口げんか kuchígeñka

misuse [misju:s'] *n* (of power) 乱用 rañyō; (of funds) 悪用 akúyō

♦*vt* (power) 乱用する rañ-yō suru; (funds) 悪用する akúyō suru

mitigate [mit'əgeit] *vt* 和らげる yawáragerù

mitt(en) [mit'(ən)] *n* ミトン mítòn

mix [miks] *vt* (combine: liquids, ingredients, colors) 混ぜる mazérù; (cake, cement) こねる konérù; (drink, sauce) 作る tsukúrù

♦*vi* (people): **to mix (with)** …と交わる …to majíwarù ◊特にパーティなどで多くの人に声を掛けて回るなどの意味で使う tókù ni pâti nádò de ŏku no hitó nì kóè wo kakétè máwarù nádò no ímì de tsukáù

♦*n* (combination) 混合物 koñgōbùtsu; (powder) ミックス mikkùsu

mixed [mikst] *adj* (salad) コンビネーションの koñbinéshon no; (grill) 盛り合せの moríawase no; (feelings, reactions) 複雑な fukúzatsu na; (school, education etc) 共学の kyógaku no

a mixed marriage (religion) 異なった宗教の信徒間の結婚 kotónàtta shúkyō no shinto kan no kekkon; (race) 異なった人種間の結婚 kotónàtta jiñshu kan no kekkon

mixed-up [mikst'ʌp] *adj* (confused) 混乱している koñran shite irù

mixer [mik'sə:r] *n* (for food) ミキサー míkìsā; (person): *to be a good mixer* 付合い上手である tsukíaijôzu de aru

mixture [miks'tʃə:r] *n* (combination) 混合物 koñgōbùtsu; (MED: for cough etc) 飲薬 nomígusùri

mix up *vt* (confuse: people, things) 混同する koñdō suru

mix-up [miks'ʌp] *n* (confusion) 混乱 koñran

mm *abbr* = **millimeter**

moan [moun] *n* (cry) うめき umèki

♦*vi* (*inf*: complain): *to moan (about)* (…について) 愚痴を言う (…ni tsuíte) guchí wo iù

moat [mout] *n* 堀 horí

mob [mɑːb] *n* (crowd) 群衆 guñshū

♦*vt* (person) …の回りにわっと押し寄せる …no mawárì ni wáttò oshíyoserù

mobile [mou'bəl] *adj* (able to move) 移動式の idóshiki no

♦*n* (decoration) モビール móbìru

mobile home *n* モビールハウス móbìruhaùsu

mobility [moubil'əti:] *n* 移動性 idósei

mobilize [mou'bəlaiz] *vt* (friends, work force) 動員する dóin suru; (MIL: country, army) 戦時態勢を取らせる señji taísei wo toráserù

moccasin [mɑːk'əsin] *n* モカシン mokáshìn

mock [mɑːk] *vt* (ridicule) ばかにする bákà ni suru; (laugh at) あざ笑う azáwaraù

♦*adj* (fake) 見せ掛けの misékake no; (exam, battle) 模擬の mógì no

mockery [mɑːk'ə:ri:] *n* (derision) あざけり azákeri

to make a mockery of …をばかにする …wo bákà ni suru

mock-up [mɑːk'ʌp] *n* (model) 模型 mokéi

mod [mɑːd kɑːnz] *adj see* **convenience**

mode [moud] *n* (form: of life) 様式 yóshiki; (: of transportation) 手段 shùdan

model [mɑːd'əl] *n* (representation: of boat, building etc) 模型 mokéi; (fashion model, artist's model) モデル módèru; (example) 手本 téhòn

♦*adj* (excellent) 模範的な mohánteki na

♦*vt* (clothes) …のモデルをする …no módèru wo suru; (with clay etc) …の模型を作る …no mokéi wo tsukúrù; (copy): *to model oneself on* …の模範に習う …no móhàn ni naráù

♦*vi* (for designer, photographer etc) モデルをする módèru wo suru

model railway *n* 模型鉄道 mokéi tetsudò

modem [mou'dem] *n* (COMPUT) モデム módèmu

moderate [*adj* mɑːd'ə:rit *vb* mɑːd'ə:reit] *adj* (views, opinion) 穏健な oñken na; (amount) 中位の chúgurai no; (change)

ある程度の arú teĩdo no
♦*vi* (storm, wind etc) 弱まる yawámarù
♦*vt* (tone, demands) 和らげる yawáragerù

moderation [mɑ:dərei'ʃən] *n* 中庸 chǘyō

modern [mɑ:d'ə:rn] *adj* 現代的な geńdaiteki na, 近代的な kíńdaiteki na, モダン
な modáñ na

modernize [mɑ:d'ə:rnaiz] *vt* 現代的にす
る geńdaiteki ni suru

modest [mɑ:d'ist] *adj* (small: house,
budget) 質素な shíssð na; (unassuming:
person) 謙虚な keńkyo na

modesty [mɑ:d'isti:] *n* 慎み tsutsúshimi

modicum [mɑ:d'əkəm] *n*: *a modicum
of* ちょっとだけの... chóttð dake no ...

modification [mɑ:dəfəkei'ʃən] *n* (alteration: of law) 改正 kaĩsei; (: of building)
改修 kaĩshū; (: of car, engine etc) 改造
kaĩzō

modify [mɑ:d'əfai] *vt* (law) 改正する kaĩsei suru; (building, car, engine) 改造する
kaĩzō suru

module [mɑ:dʒ'u:l] *n* (unit, component,
SPACE) モジュール mojúrù

mogul [mou'gəl] *n* (fig) 大立者 ðdatemð-
no

mohair [mou'he:r] *n* モヘア móheà

moist [mɔist] *adj* (slightly wet: earth,
eyes, lips) 湿った shiméttà

moisten [mɔis'ən] *vt* (lips, sponge) 湿ら
す shimérasù

moisture [mɔis'tʃə:r] *n* 湿り気 shimérike

moisturizer [mɔis'tʃə:raizə:r] *n* (cream)
モイスチュアクリーム moĩsuchua kurĩ-
mu; (lotion) モイスチュアローション moĩsuchua rðshon

molar [mou'lə:r] *n* きゅう歯 kyǘshi

mold [mould] (*BRIT* **mould**) *n* (cast: for
jelly, metal) 型 katá; (mildew) かび kabí
♦*vt* (shape: plastic, clay etc) ...で...の形を
作る ...de ...no katáchi wð tsukúrù; (fig:
influence: public opinion, character) 作
り上げる tsukúriagerù

moldy [moul'di:] (*BRIT* **mouldy**) *adj*
(bread, cheese) かびた kabíta; (smell) か
び臭い kabíkusaì

mole [moul] *n* (spot) ほくろ hokúro; (ani-

mal) モグラ mogúra; (fig: spy) 秘密工作
員 himĩtsukōsakuìn

molecule [mɑ:l'əkju:l] *n* 分子 búńshi

molest [məlest'] *vt* (assault sexually)
...にいたずらをする ...ni itázura wo surù;
(harass) いじめる ijímerù

mollycoddle [mɑ:l'i:kɑ:dəl] *vt* (pamper)
甘やかす amáyakasù

molt [moult] (*BRIT* **moult**) *vi* (animal,
bird) 換毛する kańmō suru

molten [moul'tən] *adj* (metal, rock) 溶解
の yðkai no

mom [mɑ:m] (*US: inf*) *n* かあちゃん kà-
chan, ママ mámà

moment [mou'mənt] *n* (period of time):
for a moment ちょっと chóttð; (point
in time): *at that moment* 丁度その時
chódð sonð tokì

at the moment 今の所 imá no tokòro

momentary [mou'mənte:ri:] *adj* (brief:
pause, glimpse) 瞬間的な shuńkanteki
na

momentous [moumen'təs] *adj* (occasion, decision) 重大な júdai na

momentum [moumen'təm] *n*
(PHYSICS) 運動量 uńdōryð; (fig: of
events, movement, change) 勢い ikĩði, 惰
性 daséi

to gather momentum (*lit, fig*) 勢いが付
く ikĩði ga tsúkù

mommy [mɑ:m'i:] (*US*) *n* ママ mámà ◇幼
児用語 yōjiyðgo

Monaco [mɑ:n'əkou] *n* モナコ mónàko

monarch [mɑ:n'ə:rk] *n* 君主 kúńshu

monarchy [mɑ:n'ə:rki:] *n* (system) 王制
ðsei; (royal family) 王室 ðshitsu, 王族 ð-
zoku

monastery [mɑ:n'əste:ri:] *n* 修道院 shǘ-
dðin

Monday [mʌn'dei] *n* 月曜日 getsúyðbi

monetary [mɑ:n'ite:ri:] *adj* (system, policy, control) 金融の kiń-yū no

money [mʌn'i:] *n* (coins and notes) 金 kané; (currency) 通貨 tsǘka

to make money (earn) 金をもうける kané wo mðkerù

money order *n* 郵便為替 yúbinkawàse

money-spinner [mʌn'i:spinə:r] (*BRIT*:

inf) *n* (person, idea, business) ドル箱 dorúbako

mongol [mɑːŋ'gəl] *adj* モンゴルの móngoru no

♦*n* (MED) ダウン症候群患者 daúnshōkōgun kañja

mongrel [mʌŋ'grəl] *n* (dog) 雑種 zasshú

monitor [mɑːn'itəːr] *n* (machine) モニター装置 monítāsōchi; (screen: *also*: **television monitor**) ブラウン管 buráuñkan; (of computer) モニター móñitā

♦*vt* (broadcasts) 傍受する bōju suru; (heartbeat, pulse) モニターする móñitā suru; (progress) 監視する kañshi suru

monk [mʌŋk] *n* 修道師 shúdōshi

monkey [mʌŋ'ki:] *n* (animal) サル sarú

monkey nut (*BRIT*) *n* ピーナッツ pínattsu

monkey wrench *n* モンキーレンチ moñkíreñchi

mono [mɑːn'ou] *adj* (recording) モノラルの móñoraru no

monochrome [mɑːn'əkroum] *adj* (film, photograph) 白黒の shírōkuro no, モノクロの monókuro no

monogram [mɑːn'əgræm] *n* モノグラム monógūramu

monologue [mɑːn'əlɔːg] *n* 会話の独占 kaíwa no dokúsen; (THEATER) 独白 dokúhaku, モノローグ monórōgu

monopolize [mənɑːp'əlaiz] *vt* 独占する dokúsen suru

monopoly [mənɑːp'əli:] *n* (domination) 独占 dokúsen; (COMM) 専売 señbai, モノポリー monópōrī

monosyllable [mɑːn'əsiləbəl] *n* 単音節語 tañ-onsetsugó

monotone [mɑːn'ətoun] *n*: **to speak in a monotone** 単調な声で話す tañchō na kóe de hanásu

monotonous [mənɑːt'ənəs] *adj* (life, job etc) 退屈な taíkutsu na; (voice, tune) 単調な tañchō na

monotony [mənɑːt'əni:] *n* 退屈 taíkutsu

monsoon [mɑːnsuːn'] *n* モンスーン móñsūn

monster [mɑːn'stəːr] *n* (animal, plant: misshapen) 奇形 kikéi; (: enormous) 怪物

kaíbutsu, お化け obákè; (imaginary creature) 怪物 kaíbutsu; (person: cruel, evil) 怪物 kaíbutsu

monstrosity [mɑːnstrɑːs'əti:] *n* (hideous object, building) 見るに堪えない代物 mírù ni taénai shirómòno

monstrous [mɑːn'strəs] *adj* (huge) 巨大な kyodái na; (ugly) 見るに堪えない mírù ni taénai; (atrocious) 極悪な gokúaku na

month [mʌnθ] *n* 月 tsukí

monthly [mʌnθ'li:] *adj* (ticket etc) 一カ月の ikkágetsu no; (magazine) 月刊の gekkán no; (payment etc) 毎月の maítsuki no; (meeting) 月例の getsúrei no

♦*adv* 毎月 maítsuki

monument [mɑːn'jəmənt] *n* (memorial) 記念碑 kinéñhi; (historical building) 史的記念物 shitékikineñbutsu

monumental [mɑːnjəmen'təl] *adj* (large and important: building, statue) 歴史的な rekíshiteki na; (important: book, piece of work) 画期的な kakkíteki na; (terrific: storm, row) すごい sugóì, すさまじい susámajiì

moo [mu:] *vi* (cow) もーと鳴く mố tò nakú

mood [mu:d] *n* (humor: of person) 機嫌 kigén; (: of crowd, group) 雰囲気 fuñ-ikì, ムード mūdo

to be in a good/bad mood (temper) 機嫌がいい〔悪い〕 kigén gà íi(warúi)

moody [mu:'di:] *adj* (variable) むら気な muráki na; (sullen) 不機嫌な fukígèn na

moon [mu:n] *n* 月 tsukí

moonlight [mu:n'lait] *n* 月光 gekkố

moonlighting [mu:n'laitiŋ] *n* (work) アルバイト arúbaito ◇本職の外にする仕事で，特に規定，規則違反の仕事を指す hoñshòku no hoká ni suru shigóto dè, tókù ni kitéi, kisóku ihàn no shigóto wò sásù

moonlit [mu:n'lit] *adj*: **a moonlit night** 月夜 tsukíyo

moor [mu:r] *n* (heath) 荒れ野 aréno

♦*vt* (ship) つなぐ tsunágù

♦*vi* 停泊する teíhaku suru

moorland [mu:r'lænd] *n* 荒れ野 aréno

moose [mu:s] n inv アメリカヘラジカ a-mérikaherajìka

mop [mɑ:p] n (for floor) モップ moppú; (for dishes) スポンジたわし supónjitawàshi ◇短い柄の付いた皿洗い用を指す mijíkaì e no tsúta saráarai yò wo sásù

◆vt (floor) モップでふく moppú de fukú; (eyes, face) ふく fukú, ぬぐう nugúù

a mop of hair もじゃもじゃ頭 mojámoja atáma

mope [moup] vi ふさぎ込む fuságikomù

moped [mou'ped] n モペット mopéttò ◇ペダルで動かす事も出来る小型オートバイ pedárù de ugókasù kotó mo dekirù kogáta ōtóbai

mop up vt (liquid) ふく fukú

moral [mɔːr'əl] adj 倫理的な ríñriteki na

◆n (of story etc) 教訓 kyōkun

moral support (encouragement) 精神的支え seíshinteki sasàe

morale [məræl'] n (of army, staff) 士気 shikí

morality [məræl'iti:] n (good behavior) 品行 hínkō; (system of morals: also correctness, acceptability) 倫理 ríñri

morals [mɔːr'əlz] npl (principles, values) 倫理 ríñri

morass [məræs'] n (lit, fig) 泥沼 dorónuma

morbid [mɔːr'bid] adj (imagination, ideas) 陰気な íñki na

KEYWORD

more [mɔːr] adj 1 (greater in number etc) より多くの yorí ðku no

more people/work/letters than we expected 私たちが予定していたより多くの人々〔仕事, 手紙〕watákushitàchi ga yotéi shite ita yorí ðkù no hitóbito (shigóto, tegámi)

I have more books/money than you 私はあなたより沢山の本〔金〕を持っています watákushi wà anátà yori takúsan nð hóñ(kanè)wo mótte imasù

this store has more wine than beer この店はビールよりワインが沢山あります konó mise wà bírù yori wáin ga takúsan arimasù

2 (additional) もっと móttò

do you want (some) more tea? もっと紅茶をいかがですか móttò kôcha wð ikága desù ká

is there any more wine? ワインはまだありますか mádà arímasù ká

I have no/I don't have any more money お金はもうありません o-káne wa mð arímaseñ

it'll take a few more weeks あと数週間掛けります átò sūshúkàn kakárimasù

◆pron 1 (greater amount) もっと沢山 móttò takúsan

more than 10 10以上 júijò ◇この成句の英語には「10」が含まれないが, 日本語の場合「10」も含まれる konó seîku no éigo ni wà "jú" gà fukúmarenaì ga, nihóngo no baài "jú" mð fukúmarerù. (Note: the English phrase indicates a quantity of 11 and above, but the Japanese indicates 10 and above.)

it cost more than we expected 予想以上に金が掛けました yosó ijð ni kané gà kakárimashìta

2 (further or additional amount) もっと沢山 móttò takúsan

is there any more? まだありますか mádà arímasù ká

there's no more もうありません mð arímaseñ

a little more もう少し mð sukoshì

many/much more ...よりずっと沢山 ...yorí zuttò takúsan

◆adv ...よりもっと... ...yorí mòttò...

more dangerous/difficult etc (than) ...より危ない〔難しい〕...yorí abúnai(muzúkashiì)

more easily/economically/quickly (than) ...よりたやすく〔経済的に, 早く〕...yorí tayasukù(keizaiteki ni, hayáku)

more and more ますます masúmasu

more and more excited/friendly/expensive ますます興奮して〔親しくなって, 高くなって〕masúmasu kôfun shitè (shitáshiku nattè, tákàku nattè)

he grew to like her more and more 彼はますます彼女が好きになった kárè wa masúmasu kánòjo ga sukí ni nattà *more or less* 大体 daítai, 大よそ őyoso

the job's more or less finished 仕事は大体できています shigóto wà daítai dékîte imasu

it should cost £500, more or less 大よそ500ポンド掛りそうです őyoso gohyákupoñdo kakárisō desu

more than ever ますます masúmàsu, より一層 yorí isső

more beautiful than ever ますます美しい masúmàsu utsúkushiî

more quickly than ever ますます早く masúmàsu háyàku

he loved her more than ever 彼はより一層彼女を愛する様になった kárè wa yorí isső kánòjo wo aí suru yō nì náttà

moreover [mɔːrouˈvəːr] *adv* なお nâő

morgue [mɔːrg] *n* 死体保管所 shitáihokaňjo, モルグ morúgù

moribund [mɔːrˈəbʌnd] *adj* (organization, industry) 斜陽の shayő no

Mormon [mɔːrˈmən] *n* モルモン教徒 morúmon kyőto

morning [mɔːrˈniŋ] *n* (period after daybreak) 朝 asá; (from midnight to noon) 午前 gózeñ

in the morning 朝に asá ni, 午前中に gozéñchū ni

7 o'clock in the morning 午前7時 gózeñ shichíji

morning paper 朝刊 chőkan

morning sun 朝日 ásàhi

morning walk 朝の散歩 ásà no sañpo

morning sickness *n* つわり tsuwári

Morocco [mərəˈkou] *n* モロッコ morókkð

moron [mɔːrˈɑːn] *(inf)* *n* ばか bákà

morose [mərousˈ] *adj* (miserable) 陰気な îñki na

morphine [mɔːrˈfiːn] *n* モルヒネ morúhine

Morse [mɔːrs] *n* (*also*: **Morse code**) モールス信号 mőrusu shiñgő

morsel [mɔːrˈsəl] *n* (of food) 一口 hitőkùchi

mortal [mɔːrˈtəl] *adj* (man) いつか死ぬ ítsùka shinú; (wound) 致命的な chiméíte-

ki na; (danger) 命にかかわる ínòchi ni kakáwarù

♦*n* (human being) 人間 niñgen

mortal combat 死闘 shitő

mortal enemy 宿敵 shukúteki

mortal remains 遺骨 ikótsu

mortal sin 大罪 taízai

mortality [mɔːrtælˈitiː] *n* いつか死ぬ事 ítsùka shinú kotő; (number of deaths) 死亡率 shibőrîtsu

mortar [mɔːrˈtəːr] *n* (cannon) 迫撃砲 hakúgekihő; (CONSTR) モルタル mórùtaru; (bowl) 乳鉢 nyūbachi

mortgage [mɔːrˈgidʒ] *n* 住宅ローン jútakurőn

♦*vt* (house, property) 抵当に入れて金を借りる teftő ni irète kané wo karfrù

mortify [mɔːrˈtəfai] *vt*: *to be mortified* 恥を感じる hajf wo kañjirù

mortuary [mɔːrˈtʃuːeriː] *n* 霊安室 reíañshitsu

mosaic [mouzeiˈik] *n* モザイク mozáîku

Moscow [mɑːsˈkau] *n* モスクワ mosúkuwa

Moslem [mɑːzˈləm] *adj*, *n* = **Muslim**

mosque [mɑːsk] *n* イスラム教寺院 isúramukyō jîñ, モスク mósùku

mosquito [məskiːˈtou] (*pl* **mosquitoes**) *n* 蚊 ká

moss [mɔːs] *n* (plant) コケ koké

KEYWORD

most [moust] *adj* 1 (almost all: people, things etc) ほとんどの hotóñdo no

most people ほとんどの人 hotóñdo no hitő

most men/dogs behave like that ほとんどの男性〔イヌ〕はそういう振舞をする hotóñdo no dañsei〔inú〕wà ső iú furúmai wo surù

most houses here are privately owned ここのほとんどの家は個人所有の物です kokő nð hotóñdo no iế wà kojíñshoyū nð monő desù

2 (largest, greatest: interest, money etc) 最も沢山の mottőmð takúsañ no

who has (the) most money? 最も多くの金を持っているのは誰でしょう mottőmò ōku no kane wo motte iru no wa dare deshò

he derived the most pleasure from her visit 最も彼を喜ばせたのは彼女の訪問だった mottómò kárè wo yorókobaseta no wà kánòjo no hômon dattà

♦*pron* (greatest quantity, number) ほとんど hotóndo

most of it/them それ〔それら〕のほとんど soré〔sorérà〕no hotóndo

most of the money/her friends 金〔彼女の友達〕のほとんど kanê〔kánòjo no tomódàchi〕nò hotóndo

most of the time ほとんどの場合 hotóndo no baái

do the most you can できるだけの事をして下さい dekíru dakè no kotó wò shité kudasaì

I saw the most 私が一番沢山見ました watákushi gà ichíban takùsan mimáshìta

to make the most of something …を最大限に利用する …wò saídaìgen ni riyô surù

at the (very) most 最大に見積っても saídai nì mitsúmotte mò

♦*adv* (+ verb: spend, eat, work etc) 最も多く mottómò ôkù;(+ adjective): *the most intelligent/expensive* etc 最も利口〔高価〕な mottómò rikô〔kôka〕nà;(+ adverb: carefully, easily etc) 最も注意深く〔たやすく〕 mottómò chûibukakù〔tayásukù〕;(very: polite, interesting etc) とても totémo

a most interesting book とても面白い本 totémo omoshiroì hóñ

mostly [moust'li:] *adv* (chiefly) 主に ómò ni;(usually) 普段は fúdàn wa, 普通は futsû wa

MOT [emouti:'] *n abbr* = **Ministry of Transport**: *the MOT (test)* (BRIT) 車検 shakéñ

motel [moutel'] *n* モーテル mòteru

moth [mɔ:θ] *n* (insect) ガ gá;(clothes moth) イガ igá

mothball [mɔ:θ'bɔ:l] *n* 防虫剤 bôchūzai

mother [mʌð'ə:r] *n* 母 háhà, 母親 haháo-

ya, お母さん o-káasan

♦*adj*: *mother country* 母国 bôkoku

♦*vt* (act as mother to) 母親として育てる haháoya toshitè sodáterù;(pamper, protect) 甘やかす amáyakasù

mother company 親会社 oyágaìsha

motherhood [mʌð'ə:rhud] *n* 母親である事 hahâoya de arù kotó

mother-in-law [mʌð'ə:rinlɔ:] (*pl* **mothers-in-law**) *n* しゅうとめ shúto

motherly [mʌð'ə:rli:] *adj* 母の様な háhà no yô na

mother-of-pearl [mʌð'ə:rəvpə:rl'] *n* 真珠母 shiñjùbo

mother-to-be [mʌð'ə:rtəbi:'] (*pl* **mothers-to-be**) *n* 妊婦 níñpu

mother tongue *n* 母国語 bokókugò

motif [mouti:f'] *n* (design) 模様 moyô

motion [mou'ʃən] *n* (movement) 動き ugòki;(gesture) 合図 aízu;(at meeting) 動議 dôgi

♦*vt*: *to motion (to) someone to do something* …する様に…に合図をする …surú yô ni …ni aízu wo suru

motionless [mou'ʃənlis] *adj* 動かない ugókanaì

motion picture *n* (film) 映画 eîga

motivated [mou'təveitid] *adj* (enthusiastic) 張切っている haríkitte irù;(impelled): *motivated by* (envy, desire) …の動機で …no dôki de

motivation [moutəvei'ʃən] *n* (drive) 動機 dôki

motive [mou'tiv] *n* (aim, purpose) 目標 mokúhyo

motley [mɑ:t'li:] *adj* 雑多で奇妙な zattá dè kimyô na

motor [mou'tə:r] *n* (of machine) 原動機 geñdôki, モーター mòta;(of vehicle) エンジン éñjin;(BRIT: inf: vehicle) 車 kurúma

♦*cpd* (industry, trade) 自動車の jídòsha no

motorbike [mou'tə:rbaik] *n* オートバイ ôtòbai

motorboat [mou'tə:rbout] *n* モーターボート môtàbòto

motorcar [mou'tə:rkɑ:r] (BRIT) *n* 自動

車 jídōsha

motorcycle [mou'tə:rsai'kəl] n オートバイ ōtōbai

motorcycle racing n オートバイレーシング ōtōbairēshiṅgu

motorcyclist [mou'tə:rsaiklist] n オートバイのライダー ōtōbai no raídā

motoring [mou'tə:riŋ] (BRIT) n 自動車運転 jidōsha uṅten

motorist [mou'tə:rist] n 運転者 uṅteṅsha

motor racing (BRIT) n カーレース kārēsu

motor vehicle n 自動車 jídōsha

motorway [mou'tə:rwei] (BRIT) n ハイウェー haíuē

mottled [mɑːt'əld] adj ぶちの buchí no

motto [mɑːt'ou] (pl mottoes) n 標語 hyōgo, モットー mottō

mould [mould] (BRIT) n, vt = mold

mouldy [moul'di:] (BRIT) adj = moldy

moult [moult] (BRIT) vi = molt

mound [maund] n (heap: of blankets, leaves, earth etc) 一山 hitóyàma

mount [maunt] n (mountain in proper names): *Mount Carmel* カルメル山 karúmeruzàn

♦vt (horse) ...に乗る ...ni norú; (exhibition, display) 開催する kaísai suru; (fix: jewel) 台座にはめる daíza ni hamérù; (: picture) 掛ける kakérù; (staircase) 昇る nobórù

♦vi (increase: inflation) 上昇する jōshō suru; (: tension) つのる tsunoru; (: problems) 増える fuérù

mountain [maun'tən] n (GEO) 山 yamá

♦cpd (road, stream) 山の yamá no

mountaineer [mauntəni:r'] n 登山家 tozáñka

mountaineering [mauntəni:'riŋ] n 登山 tózàn

mountainous [maun'tənəs] adj (country, area) 山の多い yamá no ōi

mountain rescue team n 山岳救助隊 sañgaku kyūjotai

mountainside [maun'tənsaid] n 山腹 sañpuku

mount up vi (bills, costs, savings) たま

る tamárù

mourn [mɔːrn] vt (death) 悲しむ kanáshimù

♦vi: *to mourn for* (someone) ...の死を悲しむ ...no shí wo kanáshimù

mourner [mɔːr'nəːr] n 会葬者 kaísōsha

mournful [mɔːrn'fəl] adj (sad) 悲しそうな kanáshisō na

mourning [mɔːr'niŋ] n 喪 mo
in mourning 喪中で mochū de

mouse [maus] (pl mice) n (animal) ハツカネズミ hatsúkanezùmi; (COMPUT) マウス máùsu

mousetrap [maus'træp] n ネズミ取り nezúmitòri

mousse [muːs] n (CULIN) ムース mūsu; (also: hair mousse) ヘアムース heámùsu

moustache [məstæʃ'] (BRIT) n = mustache

mousy [mau'si:] adj (hair) 薄汚い茶色の usugitanai cha-íro no

mouth [mauθ] (pl mouths) n (ANAT) 口 kuchí; (of cave, hole) 入口 iríguchi; (of river) 河口 kakō

mouthful [mauθ'ful] n (amount) 口一杯 kuchí ippaí

mouth organ n ハーモニカ hámonika

mouthpiece [mauθ'piːs] n (of musical instrument) 吹口 fukígùchi; (spokesman) スポークスマン supōkusumàn

mouthwash [mauθ'wɔːʃ] n マウスウォッシュ máùsu uósshū ◇口臭防止洗口液 kōshūbōshi senkòeki

mouth-watering [mauθ'wɔːtəriŋ] adj おいしそうな oíshisō na

movable [muː'vəbəl] adj 可動な kadó na

move [muːv] n (movement) 動き ugóki; (in game: change of position) 手 tē; (: turn to play) 番 báñ; (change: of house) 引っ越し hikkóshi; (: of job) 転職 teñshoku

♦vt (change position of: furniture, car, curtains etc) 動かす ugókasù; (chessmen etc: in game) 動かす ugókasù; (emotionally) 感動させる kañdō saserù; (POL: resolution etc) 提議する teígi suru

♦vi (person, animal) 動く ugókù; (traffic) 流れる nagárerù; (also: **move house**)

引っ越す hikkósù; (develop: situation, events) 進展する shiñten suru

to get a move on 急ぐ isógù

to move someone to do something ...に ...をする気を起させる ...ni ...wo suru ki wò okósaserù

moveable [muːˈvəbəl] *adj* = **movable**

move about/around *vi* (change position) そわそわする sówàsowa suru; (travel) 頻繁に旅行する hiñpan ni ryokó suru; (change: residence) 頻繁に引っ越す hiñpan ni hikkósù; (: job) 頻繁に転職する hiñpan ni teñshoku suru

move along *vi* 立ち去る tachísarù

move along! 立ち止るな tachídomarù ná

move away *vi* (leave: town, area) よそへ引っ越す yosó e hikkósù

move back *vi* (return) 元の所へ引っ越す mótò no tokórò e hikkósù

move forward *vi* (advance) 前進する zeñshin suru

move in *vi* (to a house) 入居する nyúkyo suru; (police, soldiers) 攻撃を加える kógeki wò kuwáerù

movement [muːˈvmənt] *n* (action: of person, animal) 動き ugóki, 動作 dósà; (: of traffic) 流れ nagáre; (gesture) 合図 aízù; (transportation: of goods etc) 運輸 úñ-yu; (shift: in attitude, policy) 変化 heñka; (group of people: esp REL, POL) 運動 uñdō; (MUS) 楽章 gakúshō

move on *vi* 立ち去る tachísarù

move on! 立ち止るな tachídomarù ná

move out *vi* (of house) 引っ越す hikkósù

move over *vi* (to make room) 横へどいて場所を空ける yokó è dóite bashó wò akérù

move up *vi* (employee, deputy) 昇進する shóshin suru; (pupil) 進級する shiñkyū suru

movie [muːˈviː] *n* 映画 eígà

to go to the movies 映画を見に行く eígà wo mí ni ikú

movie camera *n* 映画カメラ eígà kaméra

moving [muːˈviŋ] *adj* (emotional) 感動的

に感動的 ni kañdōteki ni; (that moves) 動く ugó-kù

mow [mou] (*pt* **mowed**, *pp* **mowed** *or* **mown**) *vt* (grass, corn) 刈る karú

mow down *vt* (kill) なぎ払う様に殺す nagíharaù yṓ nì korósù

mower [mouˈəːr] *n* (*also*: **lawnmower**) 芝刈機 shibákarikì

MP [empiːˈ] (*BRIT*) *n abbr* = **Member of Parliament**

m.p.h. [empieit́ʃ] *abbr* (= *miles per hour*) 時速...マイル jísòku ...máìru

Mr, Mr. [misˈtəːr] *n*: *Mr. Smith* スミスさん sumisu sán ◇男性の敬称 dañsei no keíshō

Mrs, Mrs. [misˈiz] *n*: *Mrs Smith* スミスさん sumisu sán ◇既婚女性の敬称 kíkònjoséi no keíshō

Ms, Ms. [miz] *n*: *Ms. Smith* スミスさん sumisu sán ◇既婚・未婚を問わず女性の敬称 kíkòn, míkòn wo towázù joséi no keíshō

M.Sc. [emessiː́] *abbr* = **Master of Science**

KEYWORD
---

much [mʌtʃ] *adj* (time, money, effort) 沢山の takúsañ no, 多くの ókù no

we haven't got much time/money あまり多くの時間〔金〕はありません amári ókù no jikán〔kané〕wà arímaseñ

much effort was expended on the project その企画に多くの努力を費やした sonó kikáku ni ókù no dóryòku wo tsuíyashìta

how much money/time do you need? お金〔時間〕はどのぐらい必要ですか o-káne〔jikán〕wà dónò gurai hitsúyō desù ká

he's done so much work for the charity その慈善事業のために彼は様々な仕事をしてくれました sonó jizéñjigyō no tamé nì kárè wa samázàma na shigó-to wò shité kuremashìta

it's too much あんまりだ añmarì da

it's not much 大した事じゃない táìshita kotó jà nai

to have too much money/free time 金

〔暇〕が有り余る kané〔himá〕gà aríamarù
as much as ...と同じぐらい ...to onáji
gùrài
*I have as much money/intelligence
as you* 私はあなたと同じぐらいの金〔知
識〕を持っています watákushi wà anáta
to onáji gùrài no kané〔chíshìkì〕wò
móttè imasu

◆*pron* 沢山の物 takúsan no monò
there isn't much to do あまりする事は
ありません amári suru kotò wa arímaseñ
*much has been gained from our
discussions* 我々の話し合いは多くの成
果を産みました warêwarè no hanáshiai
wà ôkù no seíka wò umímashìta
how much does it cost? - too much
値段はいくらですか−べらぼうな nedán
wà íkura desu ká - berábō sà
how much is it? いくらですか íkura
desu ká

◆*adv* **1** (greatly, a great deal) とても totémo
thank you very much 大変有難うござ
います taíhen arígatò gozáimasù
much bigger (than) (...より) はるか
に大きい (...yori) haruka ni ōkii
*we are very much looking forward
to your visit* あなたが来られるのを首
を長くして待っております anáta ga ko-
rárerù no wo kubí wò nágàku shite
mattê orimasù
*he is very much the gentleman/poli-
tician* 彼はれっきとした紳士〔政治家〕で
す kárè wa rekkí tò shita shíñshi〔seíji-
ka〕desu
however much he tries 彼はどんなに努
力しても kárè wa dóñna ni doryòku
shite mò
as much as ...と同じぐらい沢山 ...tò o-
náji gùrài takúsañ
I read as much as ever 私はいつもと
同じぐらい沢山の本を読んでいます wa-
tákushi wà ítsùmo to onáji gùrài takúsañ no hóñ wo yóñde imásù
I read as much as possible/as I can
私はできるだけ沢山の本を読む事にして
います watákushi wà dekíru dakè takúsañ no hóñ wo yómù koto ni shitê imasù

*he is as much a part of the commu-
nity as you* 彼はあなたと同様ここの社
会の一員です kárè wa anáta to dôyō
kokó no shakài no ichíin desù
2 (by far) ずっと zúttò
I'm much better now 私はずっと元気
になっています watákushi wà zúttò géñki ni nattê imasù
much reduced in price ずっと安くなっ
て zuttô yasúku natte
*it's much the biggest publishing
company in Europe* あれは断然ヨーロ
ッパ最大の出版社です arê wà dañzen
yôroppasaídài no shuppáñsha desu
3 (almost) ほとんど hotóñdo
*the view is much as it was 10 years
ago* 景色は10年前とほとんど変っていま
せん késhìki wa jûnen maè to hotóñdo
kawátte imaseñ
the 2 books are much the same その
2冊の本はどちらも同じ様な物です sonô
nisàtsu no hóñ wa dôchìra mo onáji yô
na monô desù
*how are you feeling? - much the
same* ご気分はいかがですか−大して変り
ません go-kíbùn wa ikága dèsu ká -
taíshite kawárimaseñ

muck [mʌk] *n* (dirt) 泥 doró; (excrement)
くそ kusó
muck about/around *vi* (*inf*: fool a-
bout) ぶらぶらする búràbura suru
muck up *vt* (*inf*: ruin) 台無しにする daínashi ni suru
mucus [mjuːˈkəs] *n* 粘液 néñ-eki
mud [mʌd] *n* 泥 doró
muddle [mʌdˈəl] *n* (mess, mix-up) めちゃ
くちゃ mechákucha, 混乱 koñran
◆*vt* (*also*: **muddle up**) (confuse: person,
things) 混乱させる koñran saserù;
(: story, names) ごちゃごちゃにする go-
chágocha ni suru
muddle through *vi* (get by) どうにかし
て切抜ける dô ni ka shite kirínukerù
muddy [mʌdˈiː] *adj* (floor, field) どろどろ
の doródoro no
mudguard [mʌdˈgɑːrd] *n* フェンダー féñ-
dā

muesli [mjuːzˈliː] n ムースリ mùsuri ◇朝食用のナッツ、ドライフルーツ、穀物の混合 chōshoku yō no náttsù, doráifurùtsu, kokúmotsu no koñgō

muffin [mʌfˈin] n (US) マドレーヌ madórènu; (BRIT) マフィン máfiñ

muffle [mʌfˈəl] vt (sound) 弱める yowámerù; (against cold) ...に防寒具を付ける ...ni bōkàngu wo tsukérù

muffled [mʌfˈəld] adj (sound) 弱い yowáì

muffler [mʌfˈləːr] (US) n (AUT) マフラー máfūrā

mug [mʌg] n (cup) マグ mágù; (for beer) ジョッキ jókkì; (inf: face) 面 tsurá; (: BRIT: fool) ばか bákà
♦vt (assault) 襲う osóù ◇特に強盗行為について言う tókù ni gōtōkòi ni tsúìte iú

mugging [mʌgˈiŋ] n 強盗事件 gōtōjikèn

muggy [mʌgˈiː] adj (weather, day) 蒸暑い mushíatsuì

mule [mjuːl] n ラバ rábà

mull [mʌl] vt: **to mull over** ...について考え込む ...ni tsúìte kañgaekomù

multi... [mʌlˈtiː] prefix 複数の ... fukúsū no ...

multicolored [mʌlˈtikʌləːrd] (BRIT **multicoloured**) adj 多色の tashóku no

multilateral [mʌltilætˈəːrəl] adj (disarmament, talks) 多国間の takókukan no

multi-level [mʌltiːlevˈəl] (US) adj = **multistory**

multinational [mʌltənæʃˈənəl] adj (company, business) 多国籍の takókuseki no

multiple [mʌlˈtəpəl] adj (collision) 玉突きの tamátsuki no; (interests) 複数の fukúsū no
♦n (MATH) 倍数 baísū

multiple sclerosis [-sklirouˈsis] n 多発性硬化症 tahátsusei kōkashō

multiplication [mʌltəpləkeiˈʃən] n (MATH) 掛算 kakézàn; (increase) 増加 zōka

multiply [mʌlˈtəplai] vt (MATH): **4 multiplied by 2 is 8** 4掛ける2は8 yóñ kakérù ní wa hachí
♦vi (increase) 増える fuérù

multistory [mʌltiːstɔːrˈiː] (BRIT **multistorey**) adj (building etc) 高層の kōsō no

multitude [mʌlˈtətuːd] n (crowd) 群衆 guñshū; (large number): **a multitude of** (reasons, ideas) 沢山の takúsañ no

mum [mʌm] (BRIT: inf) n = **mom**
♦adj: **to keep mum** 黙っている damátte irù

mumble [mʌmˈbəl] vt (speak indistinctly) もぐもぐ言う mógùmogu iú
♦vi ぶつぶつ言う bútsùbutsu iú

mummy [mʌmˈiː] n (embalmed) ミイラ míira; (BRIT: mother) = **mommy**

mumps [mʌmps] n おたふく風邪 otáfukukàze

munch [mʌntʃ] vt (chew) かむ kámù
♦vi かむ kámù

mundane [mʌndeinˈ] adj (task, life) 平凡な heíbon na

municipal [mjuːnisˈəpəl] adj 市の shí no

munitions [mjuːniʃˈənz] npl 兵器弾薬 heíkidañ-yaku

mural [mjuːrˈəl] n 壁画 hekíga

murder [məːrˈdəːr] n (killing) 殺人 satsújin
♦vt (kill) 殺す korósù

murderer [məːrˈdəːrəːr] n 人殺し hitógoroshi

murderous [məːrˈdəːrəs] adj (person) 殺人も辞さない satsújin mo jisanài; (attack) 殺しを目的とする koróshi wò mokúteki to surù

murky [məːrˈkiː] adj (street, night) 暗い kurái; (water) 濁った nigótta

murmur [məːrˈməːr] n: **a murmur of voices** かすかな人声 kásùkana hitógòe; (of wind, waves) さざめき sazámeki
♦vt (speak quietly) 声をひそめて言う kóè wo hisómetè iú
♦vi 声をひそめて話す kóè wo hisómetè hanásù

muscle [mʌsˈəl] n (ANAT) 筋肉 kiñniku; (fig: strength) 力 chikára

muscle in vi 割込む warîkomù

muscular [mʌsˈkjələːr] adj (pain) 筋肉の kiñniku no; (build) たくましい takúmashiì; (person) 強そうな tsuyósō na

muse [mju:z] *vi* (think) 考え込む kañgae-komù
♦*n* (MYTHOLOGY) ミューズ myūzu ◇人間の知的活動をつかさどるという女神 niñgen no chitékikatsudō wo tsukásadorù to iú mégami

museum [mju:zi:'əm] *n* 博物館 hakúbùtsukan

mushroom [mʌʃ'ru:m] *n* (fungus: edible, poisonous) キノコ kínòko
♦*vi* (*fig*: town, organization) 急速に成長する kyúsoku ni seíchō suru

music [mju:'zik] *n* (sound, art) 音楽 óñgaku; (written music, score) 楽譜 gakúfu

musical [mju:'zikəl] *adj* (career, skills, person) 音楽の óñgaku no; (sound, tune) 音楽的な oñgákuteki na
♦*n* (show, film) ミュージカル myūjikaru

musical instrument *n* 楽器 gakkí

music hall *n* (place) ボードビル劇場 bōdobiru gekijō

musician [mju:ziʃ'ən] *n* ミュージシャン myūjishàn

musk [mʌsk] *n* じゃ香 jakó

Muslim [mʌz'lim] *adj* イスラム教の isúramukyō no
♦*n* イスラム教徒 isúramukyòto

muslin [mʌz'lin] *n* モスリン mósùrin

mussel [mʌs'əl] *n* ムールガイ mūrugai

must [mʌst] *aux vb* (necessity, obligation): *I must do it* 私はそれをしなければならない watákushi wa soré wo shinákereba naranài; (probability): *he must be there by now* もう彼はあそこに着いているでしょう mō kárè wa asōko ni tsuíte frù deshō; (suggestion, invitation): *you must come and see me soon* そのうち是非遊びに来て下さい sonó uchi zéhì asóbi ni kìte kudasaì; (indicating something unwelcome): *why must he behave so badly?* どうしてまたあの子はそんなに行儀悪くするのだろう dōshite mata áñō kò wa soñna ni gyógiwarukù suru no darō
♦*n* (necessity): *it's a must* 必needs品だ hitsújuhin da

mustache [məstæʃ'] (*US*) *n* 鼻ひげ hanáhige

mustard [mʌs'tə:rd] *n* (Japanese) 辛子 karáshi, 和辛子 wagárashi; (Western) 辛子 karáshi, 洋辛子 yōgarashi, マスタード masútādo

muster [mʌs'tə:r] *vt* (support) 求める motómerù; (energy, strength) 奮い起す furúiokosù; (MIL) 召集する shōshū suru

mustn't [mʌs'ənt] = **must not**

musty [mʌs'ti:] *adj* かび臭い kabíkusaì

mutation [mju:tei'ʃən] *n* (alteration) 変化 heñka

mute [mju:t] *adj* (silent) 無言の mugón no

muted [mju:'tid] *adj* (color) 地味な jimí na; (reaction) ひそめた hisómeta

mutilate [mju:'təleit] *vt* (person, thing) 傷付ける kizútsukerù ◇特に体の部分を切断する場合に使う tókù ni karáda no búbùn wo setsúdan suru baáì ni tsukáù

mutiny [mju:'təni:] *n* (rebellion: of soldiers, sailors) 反乱 hañran
♦*vi* 反乱を起す hañran wò okósù

mutter [mʌt'ə:r] *vt* (speak quietly) つぶやく tsubúyakù
♦*vi* ぶつぶつ不平を言う bútsùbutsu fuhéi wò iú

mutton [mʌt'ən] *n* (meat) マトン mátòn

mutual [mju:'tʃuːəl] *adj* (shared: benefit, interest) 共通の kyótsū no; (reciprocal: feeling, attraction) 相互の sōgo no

mutually [mju:'tʃuːəli:] *adv* 相互に sōgo ni

muzzle [mʌz'əl] *n* (mouth: of dog) ふんfún, 鼻づら hanázura; (: of gun) 銃口 jūkō; (guard: for dog) 口輪 kuchíwa
♦*vt* (dog) ...に口輪をはめる ...ni kuchíwa wo hamérù

KEYWORD

my [mai] *adj* 私の watákushi nò
this is my house/car/brother これは私の家〔車, 兄〕です koré wà watákushi nò ie〔kurúma, áni〕desu
I've washed my hair/cut my finger 私は髪を洗いました〔指を切りました〕 watákushi wà kamí wò aráimashìta 〔yubí wò kirímashìta〕
is this my pen or yours? これは私の

ペンですか，それともあなたのですか koré wà watákushi nò pén desu ká, sorétomò anátà no desu ká

Myanmar [mai'ænmɑːr] n ミャンマー myáñmā

myopic [maiɑːp'ik] adj 近眼の kíñgan no

myriad [mir'iːəd] n (of people, things) 無数 musú

myself [maiself'] pron 私自身 watákushi-jishìn ¶ see also **oneself**

mysterious [mistiː'riːəs] adj (strange) なぞの nazó no

mystery [mis'təriː] n (puzzle) なぞ nazó
shrouded in mystery (place) なぞに包まれた nazó nì tsutsúmareta

mystic [mis'tik] n (person) 神秘主義者 shíñpishùgisha

mystic(al) [mis'tik(əl)] adj 神秘的な shíñpiteki na

mystify [mis'təfai] vt (perplex) ...の理解を越える ...no rikái wò koérù

mystique [mistiːk'] n 神秘 shíñpi

myth [miθ] n (legend, story) 神話 shíñwa; (fallacy) 俗信 zokúshin

mythology [miθɑːl'ədʒiː] n 神話集 shíñwáshū

N

n/a abbr (= not applicable) ◇申請用紙などで空欄にしておく場合に書く shiñsei yōshi nádò de kúran ni shite oku baài ni kákù

nag [næg] vt (scold) がみがみ言う gámìgami iú

nagging [næg'iŋ] adj (doubt) 晴れない harénaì; (pain) しつこい shitsúkoì

nail [neil] n (on fingers, toes) つめ tsumé; (metal) くぎ kugí
◆vt: *to nail something to something* ...を...にくぎで留める ...wo ...ni kugí de toméru
to nail someone down to doing something 強制的に...に...をさせる kyőseiteki ni ...ni ...wò sasérù

nailbrush [neil'brʌʃ] n つめブラシ tsuméburàshi

nailfile [neil'fail] n つめやすり tsuméya-sùri

nail polish n マニキュア maníkyùa

nail polish remover n 除光液 jokőèki, マニキュア落し maníkyua otóshi

nail scissors npl つめ切りばさみ tsumékiribasàmi

nail varnish (BRIT) n = **nail polish**

naive [naiiːv'] adj (person, ideas) 無邪気な mújàki na, ナイーブな naíbù na

naked [nei'kid] adj 裸の hadáka no

name [neim] n (of person, animal, place) 名前 namáe; (surname) 名字 myőjì, 姓 séi; (reputation) 評判 hyőban
◆vt (child) ...に名前を付ける ...ni namáe wò tsukérù; (identify: accomplice, criminal) 名指す nazásù; (specify: price, date etc) 指定する shitéi suru
what's your name? お名前は何とおっしゃいますか o-námae wà náñto ósshái-masù ká
by name 名指しで nazáshi dè
in the name of (fig) ...の名において ...no ná ni oìte
to give one's name and address (to police etc) 名前と住所を知らせる namáe tò jûshò wo shiráserù

nameless [neim'lis] adj (unknown) 無名の muméi no; (anonymous: witness, contributor) 匿名の tokúmei no

namely [neim'liː] adv 即ち sunáwachi

namesake [neim'seik] n 同姓同名の人 dőseidőmei no hitó

nanny [næn'iː] n 養育係 yőikugakàri

nap [næp] n (sleep) 昼寝 hirúne
to be caught napping (fig) 不意を突かれる fuí wò tsukárerù

napalm [nei'pɑːm] n ナパーム napámù

nape [neip] n: *nape of the neck* えり首 eríkùbi

napkin [næp'kin] n (also: **table napkin**) ナプキン nápùkin

nappy [næp'iː] (BRIT) n おむつ o-mútsù

nappy rash (BRIT) n おむつかぶれ o-mútsukabùre

narcissus [nɑːrsis'əs] (pl **narcissi**) n (BOT) スイセン suísen

narcotic [nɑːrkɑːtˈik] *adj* 麻酔性の masúisei no
♦*n* 麻薬 mayáku

narrative [nærˈətiv] *n* 物語 monógatàri

narrator [nærˈeitər] *n* (in book) 語り手 katárite; (in film etc) ナレーター narḗtā

narrow [nærˈou] *adj* (space, road etc) 狭い semáì; (*fig*: majority, advantage) ぎりぎりの girígìri no; (: ideas, attitude) 狭量な kyṓryō na
♦*vi* (road) 狭くなる sémàku naru; (gap, difference: diminish) 小さくなる chíisàku naru

to have a narrow escape 間一髪で逃れる kán-ippatsu dè nogárerù

to narrow something down to (choice, possibility) …を…に絞る …wo …ni shibórù

narrowly [nærˈouli] *adv* (miss) 辛うじて karṓjìte, 間一髪で kán-ippatsu dè

narrow-minded [nærˈoumainˈdid] *adj* 狭量な kyṓryō na

nasal [neiˈzəl] *adj* (of the nose) 鼻の haná no; (voice, sound) 鼻にかかった haná ni kakattà

nasty [næsˈtiː] *adj* (unpleasant: remark, person) いやな iyá nà; (malicious) 腹黒い haráguroì; (rude) 無礼な búrèi na; (revolting: taste, smell) むかつかせる mukátsukaserù; (wound, disease etc) ひどい hidóì

nation [neiˈʃən] *n* (country) 国 kuní, 国家 kókkà; (people) 国民 kokúmin

national [næsˈʃənəl] *adj* 国の kuní no
♦*n*: *a foreign national* 外国人 gaíkokujìn

national dress *n* 民族衣装 mińzokuishṑ

National Health Service (*BRIT*) *n* 国民医療制度 kokúmin iryōseìdo

National Insurance (*BRIT*) *n* 国民保険 kokúminhokèn

nationalism [næsˈʃənəlizəm] *n* 国家主義 kokkáshugì, 民族主義 mínzokushugì

nationalist [næsˈʃənəlist] *adj* 国家主義の kokkáshugì no, 民族主義の mínzokushugì no
♦*n* 国家主義者 kokkáshugishà, 民族主義者 mińzokushugishà

nationality [næʃənælˈəti:] *n* 国籍 kokúseki

nationalization [næʃnəlizeiˈʃən] *n* 国有化 kokúyùka, 国営化 kokúeika

nationalize [næsˈʃnəlaiz] *vt* 国営にする kokúei ni sùrū

nationally [næsˈʃnəli:] *adv* (nationwide) 全国的に zeńkokuteki ni; (as a nation) 国として kuní toshite

nationwide [neiˈʃənwaidˈ] *adj* (problem, campaign) 全国的な zeńkokuteki na
♦*adv* (campaign, search) 全国的に zeńkokuteki ni

native [neiˈtiv] *n* (local inhabitant) 地元の人 jimóto no hitò; (of tribe etc) 原住民 geñjūmin
♦*adj* (indigenous) 地元の jimóto no, 地元生れの jimóto umàre no; (of one's birth) 生れの umáre no; (innate) 生れつきの umáretsuki no

a native of Russia ロシア生れの人 roshía umare no hitò

a native speaker of French フランス語を母国語とする人 furánsugo wò bokókugo to surù hitò

native language *n* 母国語 bokókugo

Nativity [nətivˈəti:] *n*: *the Nativity* キリストの降誕 kirísuto nò kṓtan

NATO [neiˈtou] *n abbr* (= *North Atlantic Treaty Organization*) 北大西洋条約機構 kitátaiseiyō jōyaku kikō

natural [næᵗʃˈəːrəl] *adj* (gen) 自然の shizén no; (innate) 生れつきの umáretsuki no

natural gas *n* 天然ガス teńnengasù

naturalist [næᵗʃˈəːrəlist] *n* 博物学者 hakúbutsugakushà

naturalize [næᵗʃˈəːrəlaiz] *vt*: *to become naturalized* (person, plant) 帰化する kiká suru

naturally [næᵗʃˈəːrəli:] *adv* (gen) 自然に shizén ni; (of course) もちろん mochíròn, 当然 tṓzen

nature [neiˈtʃər] *n* (*also*: **Nature**) 自然 shizén, 大自然 daíshizèn; (character) 性質 seíshitsu; (type, sort) 種類 shúrùi

by nature 生れつき umáretsuki

naught [nɔːt] *n* 零 réì, ゼロ zérò

naughty [nɔːtˈiː] adj (child) 行儀の悪い gyōgi no warúì

nausea [nɔːˈziːə] n 吐気 hakíke

nauseate [nɔːˈziːeit] vt むかつかせる mukátsukaserù, 吐気を起させる hakíke wò okósaserù; (fig) いやな感じを与える iyá na kañji wo atáerù

nautical [nɔːˈtikəl] adj (uniform) 船員の señ-in no; (people) 海洋の kaíyō no
  a nautical mile 海里 kaíri

naval [neiˈvəl] adj (uniform, academy) 海軍の kaígun no
  a naval battle 海戦 kaísen
  naval forces 海軍力 kaígunryòku

naval officer n 海軍将校 kaígunshōkò

nave [neiv] n 外陣 gaíjin

navel [neiˈvəl] n へそ hesó

navigate [nævˈəgeit] vi (NAUT, AVIAT) 航行する kōkō suru; (AUT) 道案内する michíannai suru

navigation [nævəgeiˈʃən] n (action) 航行 kōkō; (science) 航海術 kōkaijùtsu

navigator [nævˈəgeitər] n (NAUT) 航海長 kōkaichō; (AVIAT) 航空士 kōkùshi; (AUT) 道案内をする人 michíannai wo suru hitò

navvy [nævˈiː] (BRIT) n 労働者 rōdōsha

navy [neiˈviː] n 海軍 kaígun

navy(-blue) adj 濃紺の nōkon no

Nazi [nɑːtˈsiː] n ナチ náchì

NB [enbiˈ] abbr (= nota bene) 注 chū ◇脚注などに使う略語 kyakúchū nadò ni tsukáù ryakúgo

near [niːr] adj (place, time, relation) 近い chikáì
  ♦adv 近く chikákù
  ♦prep (also: near to: space, time) ...の近くに ...no chikákù ni
  ♦vt (place, event) ...に近づく ...ni chikázukù

nearby [niːrˈbai] adj 近くの chikákù no
  ♦adv 近くに chikákù ni

nearly [niːrˈliː] adv (not totally) ほとんど hotóñdo; (on the point of) 危うく ayáukù
  I nearly fell 危うく転ぶところだった ayáukù koróbu tokoro dattà

near miss n (narrow escape) ニアミス niámisù; (of planes) 異常接近 ijōsekkìn,

ニアミス niámisù; (of cars etc): *that was a near miss!* 危ないところだった abúnai tokoro dattà

nearside [niːrˈsaid] n (AUT: in Britain, Japan) 左側 hidárigawa; (: in US, Europe etc) 右側 migígawa

near-sighted [niːrˈsaitid] adj 近眼の kiñgan no, 近視の kiñshi no

neat [niːt] adj (place, person) きちんとした kichíñ to shita; (skillful: work, plan) 上手な jōzu na; (spirits) ストレートの sutőrēto no

neatly [niːtˈliː] adv (tidily) きちんと kichíñ to; (skillfully) 上手に jōzu nì

necessarily [nesəserˈiliː] adv (inevitably) 必然的に hitsúzenteki ni
  not necessarily (not automatically) 必ずしも...でない kanárazushìmo ...de náì

necessary [nesˈiseːriː] adj (required: skill, quality, measure) 必要な hitsúyō na; (inevitable: result, effect) 必然の hitsúzen no
  it is necessary to/that ...する必要がある ...suru hitsúyō ga arù

necessitate [nəsesˈəteit] vt 必要とする hitsúyō to surù

necessities [nəsesˈitiːz] npl (essentials) 必需品 hitsújuhin

necessity [nəsesˈitiː] n (thing needed) 必需品 hitsújuhin; (compelling circumstances) 必然 hitsúzen

neck [nek] n (of person, animal, garment, bottle) 首 kubí
  ♦vi (inf) ペッティングする pettíñgu suru
  neck and neck 接戦して sessén shite

necklace [nekˈlis] n ネックレス nékkùresu

neckline [nekˈlain] n ネックライン nekkúraìn

necktie [nekˈtai] (US) n ネクタイ nékùtai

née [nei] adj: *née Scott* 旧姓スコット kyūsei sukóttò

need [niːd] n (lack) 欠乏 ketsúbō; (necessity) 必要 hitsúyō; (thing needed) 必需品 hitsújuhin
  ♦vt (require) ...を必要とする ...wo hitsú-

yō to surù

I need to do it 私はそれをしなければ ならない watákushi wà soré wò shinákereba naranaî, 私はそれをする必要があ る watákushi wà soré wò suru hitsúyō ga arù

you don't need to go 行かなくてもい い ikánakute mo iî

needle [ni:'dəl] *n* (*gen*) 針 hárî; (for knitting) 編棒 amîbồ

♦*vt* (*fig*: *inf*) からかう karákaù

needless [ni:d'lis] *adj* (criticism, risk) 不 必要な fuhítsuyō na

needless to say 言うまでもなく iú made mo nakù

needlework [ni:d'əlwə:rk] *n* (item(s) of needlework) 縫い物 nuímonò; (activity) 針仕事 harîshigòto

needn't [ni:d'ənt] = **need not**

needy [ni:'di:] *adj* 貧しい mazúshiî

negation [nigei'ʃən] *n* 否定 hitéi

negative [neg'ətiv] *adj* (answer) 否定の hitéi no; (attitude) 否定的な hitéiteki na; (reaction) 消極的な shốkyokuteki na; (ELEC) 陰極の iñkyoku no, マイナスの maínasu no

♦*n* (LING) 否定形 hitéikei; (PHOT) 陰画 íñga, ネガ négà

neglect [niglekt'] *vt* (child) 放任する hốnin suru, ほったらかす hottárakasù; (one's duty) 怠る okótarù

♦*n* (of child) 放任 hốnin; (of area, house, garden) ほったらかす hottárakasu kotồ; (of duty) 怠る事 okótaru kotồ

negligee [neg'ləʒei] *n* (dressing gown) ネ グリジェ negúrijè

negligence [neg'lidʒəns] *n* (carelessness) 不注意 fuchū́i

negligible [neg'lidʒəbəl] *adj* (cost, difference) わずかな wázùka na

negotiable [nigou'ʃəbəl] *adj* (check) 譲渡 できる jồto dekirù

negotiate [nigou'ʃi:eit] *vi*: *to negotiate (with)* (...と) 交渉する (...to) kốshō suru

♦*vt* (treaty, transaction) 協議して決める kyốgi shite kimerù; (obstacle) 乗越える norîkoerù; (bend in road) 注意して通る

chū́i shite tồrù

negotiation [nigouʃi:ei'ʃən] *n* 交渉 kốshō

negotiator [nigou'ʃi:eitə:r] *n* 交渉する人 kốshō suru hitồ

Negress [ni:g'ris] *n* 黒人女性 kokújinjosèi

Negro [ni:g'rou] *adj* 黒人の kokújin no

♦*n* 黒人 kokújin

neigh [nei] *vi* いななく inánakù

neighbor [nei'bə:r] (*BRIT* **neighbour**) *n* (next door) 隣の人 tonári no hitồ; (in vicinity) 近くの人 kíñjo no hitồ

neighborhood [nei'bə:rhud] *n* (place) 近 所 kíñjo, 界隈 káīwai; (people) 近所の 人々 kíñjo no hitồbito

neighboring [nei'bə:riŋ] *adj* (town, state) 隣の tonári no

neighborly [nei'bə:rli:] *adj* (person, attitude) 親切な shíñsetsu na

neighbour [nei'bə:r] *etc* (*BRIT*) *n* = **neighbor** *etc*

neither [ni:'ðə:r] *adj* どちらの...も...でな い dóchìra no ...mo ...de naî

neither story is true どちらの話も本当 ではない dóchìra no hanáshi mồ hoñtồ de wa naî

♦*conj*: *I didn't move and neither did John* 私も動かなかったしジョンも動か なかった watákushi mồ ugốkanakattà shi, jóñ mo ugốkanakattà

♦*pron* どちらも...でない dóchìra mo ...de naî

neither is true どちらも本当でない dóchìra mo hoñtồ de naî

♦*adv*: *neither good nor bad* よくも悪 くもない yókù mo warúkù mo naî

neon [ni:'ɑːn] *n* ネオン néồn; (*also*: **neon sign**) ネオンサイン neồnsaìn

neon light *n* ネオン灯 neốntồ

nephew [nef'ju:] *n* おい oî

nerve [nə:rv] *n* (ANAT) 神経 shíñkei; (courage) 勇気 yū́kì; (impudence) 厚かま しさ atsúkamashisà, 図々しさ zúzūshisà

to have a fit of nerves 神経質になる shiñkeishitsu ni narù

nerve-racking [nə:rv'rækiŋ] *adj* いらい らさせる íraira saserù

nervous [nəːr'vəs] *adj* (ANAT) 神経の shíñkei no; (anxious) 神経質な shíñkeishitsu na; (timid: person) 気の小さい ki no chíisai; (: animal) おく病な okúbyō na

nervous breakdown *n* 神経衰弱 shíñkeisuijaku

nest [nest] *n* 巣 sú
◆*vi* 巣を作る sú wò tsukúrù

nest egg *n* (*fig*) へそくり hesókuri

nestle [nes'əl] *vi*: **to nestle in a valley/the mountains** (village etc) 谷間 〔山あい〕に横たわる taníma 〔yamá-ai〕ni yokótawarù

net [net] *n* (*gen*) 網 amí; (fabric) レース rḗsù; (TENNIS, VOLLEYBALL etc) ネット néttò; (*fig*) わな wánà
◆*adj* 正味の shṓmi no
◆*vt* (fish, game) 網で取る amí dè tórù; (profit) 得る érù

netball [net'bɔːl] *n* ネットボール nettóbōru ◇英国で行われるバスケットボールに似た球技 eíkoku de okonawarerù basúkettobōru ni nítà kyúgì

net curtains *npl* レースのカーテン rḗsù no kāten

Netherlands [neð'əːrləndz] *npl*: **the Netherlands** オランダ oránda

nett [net] (*BRIT*) *adj* = **net**

netting [net'iŋ] *n* 網 amí

nettle [net'əl] *n* イラクサ irákusa

network [net'wəːrk] *n* (of roads, veins, shops) ネットワーク nettówàku; (TV, RADIO) 放送網 hṓsōmō, ネットワーク nettówàku

neurotic [nurɑːt'ik] *adj* 神経過敏な shíñkeikabìn na, ノイローゼの noírōze no
◆*n* ノイローゼの人 noírōze no hitó

neuter [nu:'təːr] *adj* (LING) 中性の chúsei no
◆*vt* (cat etc) 去勢する kyoséi suru

neutral [nu:'trəl] *adj* (person) 中立の chúritsu no; (color etc) 中間色の chúkañshoku no; (ELEC) 中性の chúsei no
◆*n* (AUT) ニュートラル nyútoraru

neutrality [nu:træl'iti:] *n* 中立 chúritsu

neutralize [nu:'trəlaiz] *vt* (acid, poison etc) 中和する chúwa suru; (campaign, goodwill) 台無しにする daínashi ni surù

never [nev'əːr] *adv* どんな時でも…ない dóñna toki de mo …naî
I never went 行かなかった ikánakattà
never in my life …したことがない …shitá kotò ga naî ¶ *see also* **mind**

never-ending [nev'əːren'diŋ] *adj* 終りのない owári no naî, 果てしない hatéshinaî

nevertheless [nevəːrðəles'] *adv* それにもかかわらず soré ni mð kakáwarazù, それでもやはり soré de mo yahárî

new [nu:] *adj* (brand new) 新しい atárashiî; (recent) 最近の saíkin no; (different) 今までになかった imá madè ni nákàtta; (inexperienced) 新入りの shiñ-iri no

newborn [nu:'bɔːrn] *adj* 生れたばかりの umáreta bakàri no

newcomer [nu:'kʌməːr] *n* 新顔 shíñgao, 新入り shíñ-iri

new-fangled [nu:'fæŋ'gəld] (*pej*) *adj* 超モダンな chṓmodàn na

new-found [nu:'faund] *adj* (enthusiasm, confidence) 新たに沸いた árata ni waíta; (friend) 新しくできた atárashikù dékìta

newly [nu:'li:] *adv* 新しく atárashikù

newly-weds [nu:'li:wedz] *npl* 新婚者 shíñkoñsha

new moon *n* 新月 shíñgetsu

news [nu:z] *n* ニュース nyúsu
a piece of news ニュース項目 nyúsukōmoku, ニュース nyúsu
the news (RADIO, TV) ニュース nyúsu

news agency *n* 通信社 tsúshiñsha

newsagent [nu:z'eidʒənt] (*BRIT*) *n* = **newsdealer**

newscaster [nu:z'kæstəːr] *n* ニュースキャスター nyúsukyasùtā

newsdealer [nu:z'di:ləːr] (*US*) *n* (shop) 新聞販売店 shiñbunhanbaitèn; (person) 新聞販売業者 shiñbunhanbaigyōsha

newsflash [nu:z'flæʃ] *n* ニュース速報 nyúsusokuhò

newsletter [nu:z'letəːr] *n* ニュースレター nyúsuretà

newspaper [nu:z'peipəːr] *n* 新聞 shíñbun

newsprint [nu:z'print] *n* 新聞印刷用紙 shiñbun insatsuyōshi

newsreader [nu:z'ri:dəːr] *n* = **newscaster**

newsreel [nu:z'ri:l] *n* ニュース映画 nyúsueìga

newsstand [nu:z'stænd] *n* (in station etc) 新聞スタンド shíñbun sutañdo

newt [nu:t] *n* イモリ imórì

New Year *n* 新年 shíñnen

New Year's Day *n* 元旦 gañtan, 元日 gañjitsu

New Year's Eve *n* 大みそ日 ómisòka

New York [-jɔ:rk] *n* ニューヨーク nyúyòku

New Zealand [-zi:'lənd] *n* ニュージーランド nyújìrando

New Zealander [-zi:'ləndə:r] *n* ニュージーランド人 nyújìrandojìn

next [nekst] *adj* (in space) 隣の tonári no; (in time) 次の tsugí no
♦*adv* (place) 隣に tonári ni; (time) 次に tsugí ni, 今度 kóñdo

the next day 次の日 tsugí no hì, 翌日 yokújitsu

next time 次回に jíkài ni, 今度 kóñdo

next year 来年 raínen

next to ...の隣に ...no tonári ni

to cost next to nothing ただ同然である tádà dózen de arù

to do next to nothing ほとんど何もしない hotóñdo naní mo shìnaì

next please! (at doctor's etc) 次の方 tsugí no katà

next door *adv* 隣の家に tonári nò ié nì
♦*adj* (neighbor, flat) 隣の tonári no

next-of-kin [nekst'əvkin'] *n* 最も近い親せき mottómo chikaì shíñseki

NHS [eneitʃes] *n abbr* = **National Health Service**

nib [nib] *n* ペン先 peñsakì

nibble [nib'əl] *vt* 少しずつかじる sukóshizutsù kajírù, ちびちび食べる chíbìchibi tabérù

Nicaragua [nikərɑ:g'wə] *n* ニカラグア nikáragua

nice [nais] *adj* (likeable) 感じのよい kañji no yoî; (kind) 親切な shíñsetsu na; (pleasant) 天気のよい téñki no yoî; (attractive) 魅力的な miryókuteki na

nicely [nais'li:] *adv* (pleasantly) 気持よく kimóchi yokù; (kindly) 親切に shíñsetsu

ni; (attractively) 魅力的に miryókuteki ni

niceties [nai'sətiːz] *npl* 細かい点 komákaì teñ

nick [nik] *n* (wound) 切傷 kiríkìzu; (cut, indentation) 刃の跡 há no atò
♦*vt* (BRIT inf: steal) かっ払う kappáraù

in the nick of time 際どい時に kiwádoî tókì ni, 危ういところで ayáui tokoro dè

nickel [nik'əl] *n* (metal) ニッケル nikkéru; (US) 5セント玉 5 señto dama

nickname [nik'neim] *n* あだ名 adána, 愛称 aíshō, ニックネーム nikkúnēmu
♦*vt* ...に...のあだ名をつける ...ni ...no adána wò tsukérù

nicotine [nik'əti:n] *n* ニコチン nikóchin

niece [ni:s] *n* めい meí

Nigeria [naidʒi:'ri:ə] *n* ナイジェリア naíjeria

Nigerian [naidʒi:'ri:ən] *adj* ナイジェリアの naíjeria no
♦*n* ナイジェリア人 naíjeriajìn

nigger [nig'ə:r] (*inf*) *n* (highly offensive) 黒人坊 kuróñbō

niggling [nig'liŋ] *adj* (trifling) つまらない tsumáranaì; (annoying) いらいらさせる fráira sasérù

night [nait] *n* (period of darkness) 夜 yórù; (evening) 夕方 yúgata

the night before last おとといの夜 otótoì no yórù

at night 夜（に）yórù (ni)

by night 夜に yórù ni

nightcap [nait'kæp] *n* (drink) 寝酒 nezáke, ナイトキャップ naítokyappù

nightclub [nait'klʌb] *n* ナイトクラブ naítokuràbu

nightdress [nait'dres] *n* 寝巻 nemáki ◇女性用のを指す joséiyō no wò sásù

nightfall [nait'fɔ:l] *n* 夕暮 yúgure

nightgown [nait'gaun] *n* = **nightdress**

nightie [nai'ti:] *n* = **nightdress**

nightingale [nai'təngeil] *n* ヨナキウグイス yonákiugùisu, サヨナキドリ sayónakidòri, ナイチンゲール naíchingèru

nightlife [nait'laif] *n* 夜の生活 yórù no seíkatsu

nightly [nait'li:] *adj* 毎晩の máîban no
♦*adv* 毎晩 máîban

nightmare [nait'me:r] *n* 悪夢 ákùmu

night porter *n* 夜間のフロント係 yákàn no furôntogakàri

night school *n* 夜間学校 yakángakkô

night shift *n* 夜間勤務 yakánkìnmu

night-time [nait'taim] *n* 夜 yórù

night watchman *n* 夜警 yakéi

nil [nil] *n* ゼロ zérð; (BRIT: SPORT) 零点 reîten, ゼロ zérð

Nile [nail] *n*: *the Nile* ナイル川 naírugà-wa

nimble [nim'bəl] *adj* (agile) 素早い subáyaì, 軽快な keîkai na; (skillful) 器用な kíyô na

nine [nain] *num* 9 (の) kyû (no), 九 (の) kokônôtsu (no)

nineteen [nain'ti:n'] *num* 19 (の) jûku (no)

ninety [nain'ti:] *num* 90 (の) kyûjû (no)

ninth [nainθ] *adj* 第9 (の) dáîku (no)

nip [nip] *vt* (pinch) つねる tsunérù; (bite) かむ kámù

nipple [nip'əl] *n* (ANAT) 乳首 chikúbì

nitrogen [nai'trədʒən] *n* 窒素 chíssò

KEYWORD

no [nou] (*pl* **noes**) *adv* (opposite of "yes") いいえ iíe

are you coming? - no (I'm not) 一緒に来ませんか-いいえ (行きません) isshô ni kimaseñ ká - iíe (ikímaseñ)

would you like some? - no thank you いりませんか-いいえ, 結構です irímaseñ ká - iíe, kékkô desu

♦*adj* (not any) 何も...ない naní mò ...naî

I have no money/time/books 私には金 (時間, 本) がありません watákushi ni wà kané (jikán, hóñ) ga arimaseñ

no other man would have done it 他の人ならだれもそれをしてくれなかったでしょう hoká no hitð nara daré mð soré wð shité kurenakatta deshð

「*no entry*」立入禁止 tachíirikìñshi

「*no smoking*」禁煙 kiñ-en

♦*n* 反対意見 hañtai ikèn, 反対票 hañtai-

hyð

there were 20 noes and one "don't know" 反対意見20に対し、「分からない」は1つだった hañtai ikèn níjû ni tai shi, "wakáranaì" wa hitótsu dattà

---

nobility [noubil'əti:] *n* (dignity) 気高さ kedákasà; (social class) 貴族 kízòku

noble [nou'bəl] *adj* (person, character: worthy) 気高い kedákaî; (title, family: of high social class) 貴族の kízòku no

nobody [nou'bɑ:di:] *pron* だれも...ない daré mò ...naî

nocturnal [nɑ:ktə:r'nəl] *adj* (tour, visit) 夜の yórù no, 夜間の yákàn no; (animal) 夜行性の yakôsei no

nod [nɑ:d] *vi* (gesture) 頭で合図する atáma dè áîzu suru; (*also*: **nod in agreement**) うなずく unázukù; (doze) うとうとする útðuto suru
♦*vt*: *to nod one's head* うなずく unázukù
♦*n* うなずき unazuki

nod off *vi* 居眠りする inémuri suru

noise [nɔiz] *n* (sound) 音 otð; (din) 騒音 sôon

noisy [nɔi'zi:] *adj* (audience, child, machine) うるさい urúsaî

nomad [nou'mæd] *n* 遊牧民 yúbokumìn

nominal [nɑ:m'ənəl] *adj* (leader) 名目上の meîmokujð no; (rent, price) わずかな wázùka na

nominate [nɑ:m'əneit] *vt* (propose) 推薦する suísen suru; (appoint) 任命する níñmei suru

nomination [nɑ:mənei'ʃən] *n* (proposal) 推薦 suísen; (appointment) 任命 níñmei

nominee [nɑ:məni:'] *n* (proposed person) 推薦された人 suísen sareta hitð; (appointed person) 任命された人 níñmei sareta hitð

non... [nɑ:n] *prefix* 非... hí..., 無... mú..., 不... fú...

non-alcoholic [nɑ:nælkəhɔ:l'ik] *adj* アルコールを含まない arúkòru wð fukúmanaî

non-aligned [nɑ:nəlaind'] *adj* 非同盟の hidðmei no

nonchalant [nɑːnʃələːnt'] *adj* 平然とした heízen to shitá

noncommittal [nɑːnkəmit'əl] *adj* (person, answer) どっちつかずの dotchí tsukazù no

nondescript [nɑːn'diskript] *adj* (person, clothes, color) 特徴のない tokúchò no naí

none [nʌn] *pron* (person) だれも ...ない daré mò ...naĩ; (thing) どれも...ない dórè mo ...naĩ

none of you あなたたちの1人も...ない anátatàchi no hitóri mò ...naĩ

I've none left 何も残っていません naní mò nokótte imaseñ

he's none the worse for it それでも彼は大丈夫です soré de mò kare wa dafjōbu desu

nonentity [nɑːnen'titi:] *n* 取るに足らない人 tórù ni taránai hitò

nonetheless [nʌn'ðəles'] *adv* それにもかかわらず soré ni mò kakáwarazù, それでもやはり soré de mò yahárì

non-existent [nɑːnigzis'tənt] *adj* 存在しない soñzai shinaĩ

non-fiction [nɑːnfik'ʃən] *n* ノンフィクション nofifikùshon

nonplussed [nɑːnplʌst'] *adj* 困惑した koñwaku shita, 困った komáttà

nonsense [nɑːn'sens] *n* でたらめ detárame, ナンセンス náñsensu

nonsense! そんな事はない sofína koto wà naĩ, ナンセンス náñsensu

non-smoker [nɑːnsmou'kər] *n* タバコを吸わない人 tabáko wò suwánai hitò, 非喫煙者 híkitsueñsha

non-stick [nɑːnstik'] *adj* (pan, surface) こげつかない kogétsukanaĩ

non-stop [nɑːn'stɑːp'] *adj* (conversation) 止らない tomáranaĩ; (flight, train) 直行の chokkô no, ノンストップの noñsutoppù no

◆*adv* 止らずに tomárazu ni

noodles [nuː'dəlz] *npl* ヌードル nū́doru

noon [nuːn] *n* 正午 shốgò

no one (*BRIT* no-one) *pron* = **nobody**

noose [nuːs] *n* (loop) 引結び hikímusùbi

hangman's noose 絞首刑用の縄 kốshukeiyō no nawà

nor [nɔːr] *conj* = **neither**

◆*adv see* **neither**

norm [nɔːrm] *n* (convention) 慣習 kañshū; (rule, requirement) ノルマ nórùma

normal [nɔːr'məl] *adj* (usual, ordinary: life, behavior, result) 普通の futsū́ no; (child: not abnormal) 異常のない ijố no naí, ノーマルな nố̄màru na

normally [nɔːr'məli:] *adv* 普通は futsū́ wa, 普通に futsū́ ni

north [nɔːrθ] *n* 北 kitá

◆*adj* 北の kitá no

◆*adv* 北へ kitá e

North America *n* 北米 hokúbei

north-east [nɔːrθi:st'] *n* 北東 hokútō

northerly [nɔːr'ðərli:] *adj* (point) 北方の hoppố no; (direction) 北方への hoppố e nò

a northerly wind 北からの風 kitá kara nò kazé

northern [nɔːr'ðərn] *adj* 北の kitá no

the northern hemisphere 北半球 kitáhañkyū

Northern Ireland *n* 北アイルランド kitá airurañdo

North Pole *n* 北極 hokkyóku

North Sea *n* 北海 hokkái

northward(s) [nɔːrθ'wərd(z)] *adv* 北へ kitá e

north-west [nɔːrθwest'] *n* 北西 hokúsei

Norway [nɔːr'wei] *n* ノルウェー norúuề

Norwegian [nɔːrwi:'dʒən] *adj* ノルウェーの norúuề no; (LING) ノルウェー語の norúuềgo no

◆*n* (person) ノルウェー人 norúuềjìn; (LING) ノルウェー語 norúuềgo

nose [nouz] *n* (ANAT, ZOOL) 鼻 haná; (sense of smell) きゅう覚 kyū́kaku

◆*vi*: *nose about* せん索する señsaku suru

nosebleed [nouz'bli:d] *n* 鼻血 hanáji

nose-dive [nouz'daiv] *n* (of plane) 急降下 kyū́kōka

nosey [nou'zi:] (*inf*) *adj* = **nosy**

nostalgia [nəstæl'dʒə] *n* 郷愁 kyốshū, ノ

スタルジア nosutarùjia

nostalgic [nɑstælˈdʒik] *adj* (person, book, film) 懐かしい natsúkashiĩ

nostril [nɑ́ːstrəl] *n* (of person, animal) 鼻のあな haná no anà, 鼻孔 bikó

nosy [nou´zi:] (*inf*) *adj* せん索好きな señsakuzùki na

KEYWORD

not [nɑːt] *adv* ...でない ...de naî

he is not/isn't here 彼はいません kárè wa imáseñ

you must not/you mustn't do that それをしてはいけません soré wò shité wà ikémaseñ

it's too late, isn't it? 遅過ぎますよね osósugimasù yo né, 遅過ぎるでしょう osósugirù deshō

he asked me not to do it それをしないで下さいと彼に頼まれました soré wò shináide kudasaĩ to kárè ni tanómaremashìta

not that I don't like him/he isn't interesting 彼を嫌い〔面白くない〕というのではないが kárè wo kiráì〔omóshirokùnai〕tò iú no de wa naĩ gá

not yet まだ mádà

not now では駄目 ímà wa damé ¶ *see also* all; only

---

notably [nou´təbli:] *adv* (particularly) 特に tókù ni; (markedly) 著しく ichíjirushikù

notary [nou´tə:ri:] *n* 公証人 kōshōnin

notch [nɑːtʃ] *n* (in wood, blade, saw) 刻み目 kizámime, ノッチ notchí

note [nout] *n* (record) 覚書 obóegaki, ノート nōto, メモ mémò; (letter) 短い手紙 mijíkaì tegámi; (banknote) 紙幣 shíhèi, 札 satsú; (MUS) 音符 oñpu; (tone) 音 otó
♦*vt* (observe) ...に気が付く ...ni ki gá tsukù; (write down) 書留める kakítomerù

notebook [nout´buk] *n* 帳面 chōmen, ノート nōto

noted [nou´tid] *adj* (famous) 有名な yūmei na

notepad [nout´pæd] *n* メモ用紙 memóyòshi ◇糊などでつづった物を指す norí

nadð de tsuzútta mono wò sásù

notepaper [nout´peipə:r] *n* 便せん biñsen

nothing [nʌθ´iŋ] *n* (not anything) 何も...ない naní mò ...naĩ; (zero) ゼロ zérò

he does nothing 彼は何もしない kárè wa naní mò shinaĩ

nothing new/much/special 目新しい〔大した，特別な〕ことはない meátarashiĩ〔táishita, tokúbetsu nâ〕kotó wa naĩ

for nothing (free) 無料で muryō de, ただで tádà de; (in vain) 無駄に mudá ni

notice [nou´tis] *n* (announcement) 通知 tsǔchi; (warning) 通告 tsǔkoku; (dismissal) 解雇通知 kaíkotsùchi; (resignation) 辞表 jihyō; (period of time) 予告 yokóku
♦*vt* (observe) ...に気が付く ...ni ki gá tsukù

to bring something to someone's notice (attention) ...を...に知らせる ...wo ...ni shiráserù

to take notice of ...に気が付く ...ni ki gá tsukù

at short notice 急に kyǔ ni

until further notice 追って通知があるまで otté tsǔchi ga aru madè

to hand in one's notice 辞表を出す jihyō wò dásù

noticeable [nou´tisəbəl] *adj* (mark, effect) はっきりした hakkírì shita

noticeboard [nou´tisbɔːrd] (*BRIT*) *n* 掲示板 keíjiban

notify [nou´təfai] *vt*: *to notify someone (of something)* (...を) ...に知らせる (...wo) ...ni shiráserù

notion [nou´ʃən] *n* (idea) 考え kañgaè, 概念 gáĩnen; (opinion) 意見 íkèn

notorious [noutɔːr´iːəs] *adj* (criminal, liar, place) 悪名高い akúmeitakaĩ

notwithstanding [nɑːtwiθstæn´diŋ] *adv* ...にもかかわらず ...níˀ mò kakáwarazù
♦*prep* ...にもかかわらず ...níˀ mò kakáwarazù

nougat [nuː´gət] *n* ヌガー núgầ ◇クルミなどの入ったキャラメル風のお菓子 kurúmi nadð no haĩttà kyarámerufū no okáshî

nought [nɔːt] *n* = **naught**

noun [naun] *n* 名詞 meíshi

nourish [nəːˈriʃ] *vt* (feed) 養う yashínaù; (*fig*: foster) 心中にはぐくむ shíńchū ni hagúkumù

nourishing [nəːˈriʃiŋ] *adj* (food) 栄養のある eíyō no arù

nourishment [nəːˈriʃmənt] *n* (food) 栄養 eíyō

novel [nɑːˈvəl] *n* 小説 shōsetsu
◆*adj* (new, fresh: idea, approach) 目新しい meátarashiĩ, 新鮮な shińsen na

novelist [nɑːˈvəlist] *n* 小説家 shōsetsuka

novelty [nɑːˈvəlti:] *n* (newness) 新鮮さ shíńsensa; (object) 変ったもの kawátta monð

November [nouvemˈbəːr] *n* 11月 júichigatsu

novice [nɑːˈvis] *n* (beginner) 初心者 shoshíńsha; (REL) 修練者 shū́reńsha

now [nau] *adv* 今 ímà
◆*conj: now (that)* ...であるから ...de árù kara
right now (immediately) 今すぐ ímà súgù; (at the moment) 今の所 ímà no tokoro
by now 今ごろはもう imágoro wà mố
just now 今の所 ímà no tokoro
now and then, now and again 時々 tokídoki
from now on 今後 kốňgo

nowadays [nauˈədeiz] *adv* このごろ (は) konőgoro (wa)

nowhere [nouˈweːr] *adv* (be, go) どこにも...ない dốkð ni mo ...náĩ

nozzle [nɑːzˈəl] *n* (of hose, fire extinguisher) ノズル nốzùru; (of vacuum cleaner) 吸口 suíkuchi

nuance [nuːˈɑːns] *n* ニュアンス nyúáñsu

nubile [nuːˈbail] *adj* (woman) セクシーな sékùshī na

nuclear [nuːˈkliːəːr] *adj* (fission, weapons) 核... kákù...
the nuclear industry 原子力産業界 geńshiryoku sangyṓkai
nuclear physics 原子物理学 geńshibutsurigầku, 核物理学 kakúbutsurigầku
nuclear power 原子力 geńshiryðku

nucleus [nuːˈkliːəs] (*pl* **nuclei**) *n* (of atom, cell) 核 kákù; (of group) 中心 chū́shin

nude [nuːd] *adj* 裸の hadáka no
◆*n* ヌード nūdo
in the nude (naked) 裸で hadáka de

nudge [nʌdʒ] *vt* (person) 小突く kozúkù

nudist [nuːˈdist] *n* 裸体主義者 ratáishugishà, ヌーディスト nūdisùto

nudity [nuːˈditi:] *n* 裸 hadáka

nuisance [nuːˈsəns] *n* (state of affairs) 厄介な事情 yákkài na jijṓ; (thing) 厄介な物 yákkài na monð; (person: irritating) 迷惑な人 meíwaku na hitð
what a nuisance! 困ったもんだ komátta moň da

null [nʌl] *adj: null and void* (contract, agreement) 無効な mukṓ na

numb [nʌm] *adj: numb (with)* (with cold etc) ...でしびれた ...de shibíretà; (*fig*: with fear etc) ...で気が動転した ...de ki ga dṓten shità

number [nʌmˈbəːr] *n* (MATH) 数字 súji; (quantity) 数 kázù; (of house, bank account etc) 番号 bańgṓ
◆*vt* (pages etc) ...に番号を付ける ...ni bańgṓ wo tsukérù; (amount to) 総数は...である sṓsū wa ...de árù
to be numbered among ...の1人である ...no hitórĩ de árù
a number of (several) 数...の sū̀... no
they were ten in number (people) 彼らは10人だった kárèra wa jū́nĩn datta; (things) 10個あった júkkð atta

number plate (*BRIT*) *n* (AUT) ナンバープレート nańbāpurèto

numeral [nuːˈməːrəl] *n* 数詞 sū́shi

numerate [nuːˈməːreit] *adj* 数学ができる sū́gaku gà dekírù

numerical [nuːmeːˈrikəl] *adj* (value) 数字で表した sū́ji dè aráwashità; (order) 数字の sū́ji no

numerous [nuːˈməːrəs] *adj* (many, countless) 多くの ốkù no, 多数の tasū́ no

nun [nʌn] *n* (Christian) 修道女 shū́dðjo; (Buddhist) 尼 ámà

nurse [nəːrs] *n* (in hospital) 看護婦 kańgofù; (*also*: **nursemaid**) 保母 hóbð

♦*vt* (patient) 看護する kángo suru; (baby) ...に乳を飲ませる ...ni chichí wǒ nomáserù

nursery [nəːr'səːriː] *n* (institution) 保育園 hoíkuèn; (room) 育児室 ikújishìtsu; (for plants: commercial establishment) 種苗園 shubyṓen

nursery rhyme *n* 童謡 dóyō

nursery school *n* 保育園 hoíkuèn

nursery slope (*BRIT*) *n* (SKI) 初心者用ゲレンデ shoshínshayō gerénde

nursing [nəːrs'iŋ] *n* (profession) 看護職 kaṅgoshòku; (care) 看病 kaṅbyò

nursing home *n* (*gen*) 療養所 ryṓyōjo; (for old people) 老人ホーム rōjinhòmu

nursing mother *n* 授乳している母親 junyū shite irù haháoya

nurture [nəːr'tʃəːr] *vt* (child, plant) 育てる sodáterù

nut [nʌt] *n* (TECH) ナット náttò; (BOT) 木ノ実 kínòmi(kónòmi), ナッツ náttsù

nutcracker [nʌt'krækəːr] *npl* クルミ割り kurúmiwarì

nutmeg [nʌt'meg] *n* ニクズク nikúzùku, ナツメッグ natsúmeggù ◊香辛料の一種 kōshinryō no ísshù

nutrient [nuː'triːənt] *n* 養分 yṓbùn

nutrition [nuːtriʃ'ən] *n* (diet, nourishment) 栄養 eíyō; (proteins, vitamins etc) 養分 yṓbùn

nutritious [nuːtriʃ'əs] *adj* (food) 栄養価の高い eíyōka no takáî

nuts [nʌts] (*inf*) *adj* 頭がおかしい atáma gà okáshîì

nutshell [nʌt'ʃel] *n* クルミの殻 kurúmi no karà

in a nutshell (*fig*) 簡単に言えば kańtan nì iébà

nylon [nai'lɑːn] *n* ナイロン náîron
♦*adj* ナイロンの náîron no

O

oak [ouk] *n* オーク ōkù
♦*adj* (table) オークの ōkù no

O.A.P. [oueipiː'] (*BRIT*) *n abbr* = **old-age pensioner**

oar [ɔːr] *n* かい kaî, オール ōrú

oasis [ouei'sis] (*pl* **oases**) *n* (in desert) オアシス oáshîsu

oath [ouθ] *n* (promise) 誓い chikáì; (swear word) 悪態 akútaî

under or on (BRIT) oath 宣誓して seńsei shite

oatmeal [out'miːl] *n* オートミール ōtómìru

oats [outs] *n* カラスムギ karásumugî

obedience [oubiːd'iːəns] *n* 服従 fukújū

obedient [oubiːd'iːənt] *adj* (child, dog etc) 素直な sunào na, よく言う事を聞く yokù iú koto wo kikù

obesity [oubiː'sitiː] *n* 肥満 himán

obey [oubei'] *vt* (instructions, person) ...に従う ...ni shitágau; (regulations) 守る mamóru

obituary [oubitʃ'uːeːriː] *n* 死亡記事 shibṓkijì

object [*n* ɑːb'dʒikt *vt* əbdʒekt'] *n* (thing) 物 monó; (aim, purpose) 目的 mokuteki; (of affection, desires) 対象 taishō; (LING) 目的語 mokútekigo
♦*vi*: *to object to* ...に反対する ...ni hańtai suru

to object that ...だと言って反対する ...da to itté hańtai suru

expense is no object 費用にはこだわらない hiyō ni wa kodáwaranaî

I object! 反対です hańtai dèsu

objection [əbdʒek'ʃən] *n* 異議 igî

I have no objection to ... ...に異議はありません ...ni igî wa arímasèn

objectionable [ədʒek'ʃənəbəl] *adj* (person, language, conduct) いやな iyá na

objective [əbdʒek'tiv] *adj* (impartial: person, information) 客観的な kyakúkanteki na
♦*n* (aim, purpose) 目的 mokúteki

obligation [ɑːbləgei'ʃən] *n* (duty, commitment) 義務 gimù

without obligation (COMM) 買う義務なしで kaú gimù nashi de

obligatory [əblig'ətɔːriː] *adj* 強制的な kyōseiteki na

oblige [əblaidʒ'] *vt* (force): *to oblige someone to do something* 強制的に

...に..をさせる kyṓseiteki ni ...ni ...wo saserù; (do a favor for) ...の頼みを聞く ...no tanõmi wo kikú
to be obliged to someone for something (grateful) ...の事で...に感謝している ...no kotṓ de ...ni kañsha shité irù

obliging [əblai'dʒiŋ] *adj* (helpful) 親切な shínsetsu na

oblique [əbli:k'] *adj* (line) 斜めの nanáme no; (comment, reference) 間接的な kañsetsuteki na

obliterate [əblit'əreit] *vt* 跡形もなくする atókata mo nakúsuru

oblivion [əbliv'i:ən] *n* (unawareness) 無意識 muíshìki; (being forgotten) 忘却 bṓkyaku

oblivious [əbliv'i:əs] *adj*: *oblivious of/to* ...を意識していない ...wo ishíki shité inai

oblong [ɑ:b'lɔ:ŋ] *adj* 長方形の chṓhōkei no
♦*n* 長方形 chṓhōkei

obnoxious [əbnɑ:k'ʃəs] *adj* (unpleasant: behavior, person) 不愉快な fuyúkài na; (: smell) いやな iyá na

oboe [ou'bou] *n* オーボエ ōbòe

obscene [əbsi:n'] *adj* (gesture, remark, behavior) わいせつな waísetsu na

obscenity [əbsen'iti:] *n* (of book, behavior etc) わいせつ waísetsu; (offensive word) 卑語 hígò

obscure [əbskju:r'] *adj* (little known: place, author etc) 無名の muméi no; (difficult to understand) 難解な nañkai na
♦*vt* (obstruct: view, sun etc) 覆い隠す ōíkakusù; (conceal: truth, meaning etc) 隠す kakúsù

obsequious [əbsi:'kwi:əs] *adj* ぺこぺこする pekòpeko suru

observance [əbzə:r'vəns] *n* (of law) 遵守 juñshu; (of custom) 守る事 mamórù koto

observant [əbzə:r'vənt] *adj* (person) 観察力の優れた kañsatsuryòku no sugureta; (remark) 鋭い surúdoì

observation [ɑ:bzə:rvei'ʃən] *n* (remark) 意見 ikèn; (act of observing) 観察 kañsatsu; (MED) 監視 kañshi

observatory [əbzə:r'vətɔ:ri:] *n* 観測所 kañsokujo

observe [əbzə:r'v] *vt* (watch) 観察する kañsatsu suru; (comment) 意見を述べる ikèn wo nobérù; (abide by: rule) 守る mamórù, 遵守する juñshu suru

observer [əbzə:r'və:r] *n* 観察者 kañsatsushā

obsess [əbses'] *vt* ...に取付く ...ni torítsuku

obsession [əbseʃ'ən] *n* 強迫観念 kyṓhakukannen

obsessive [əbses'iv] *adj* (person, tendency, behavior) 妄想に取付かれた様な mōsō ni torítsukareta yō na

obsolescence [ɑ:bsəles'əns] *n* 旧式化 kyūshikika

obsolete [ɑ:bsəli:t'] *adj* (out of use: word etc) 廃れた sutáreta; (: machine etc) 旧式の kyūshiki no

obstacle [ɑ:b'stəkəl] *n* (obstruction) 障害物 shōgaibutsù; (*fig*: problem, difficulty) 障害 shōgai

obstacle race *n* 障害物競走 shōgaibutsukyōsō

obstetrics [əbstet'riks] *n* 産科 sañka

obstinate [ɑ:b'stənit] *adj* (determined: person, resistance) 頑固な gañko na

obstruct [əbstrʌkt'] *vt* (block) ふさぐ fuságu; (*fig*: hinder) 妨害する bṓgai suru

obstruction [əbstrʌk'ʃən] *n* (action) 妨害 bṓgai; (object) 障害物 shōgaibutsu

obtain [əbtein'] *vt* (get) 手に入れる te ní iréru, 獲得する kakútoku suru; (achieve) 達成する tasséi suru

obtainable [əbtein'əbəl] *adj* (object) 入手できる nyúshu dekírù

obvious [ɑ:b'vi:əs] *adj* (clear) 明かな akíraka na; (self-evident) 分かり切った wakárikitta

obviously [ɑ:b'vi:əsli:] *adv* 明らかに akíraka ni
obviously not 明らかに...でない akíraka ni ...de nai

occasion [əkei'ʒən] *n* (point in time) 時 tokí, 時点 jitén; (event, celebration etc) 行事 gyōji, イベント ibénto; (opportunity) 機会 kikái, チャンス chañsu

occasional [əkei'ʒənəl] *adj* (infrequent)

時々の tokídokì no

occasionally [əkeiˈʒənəli:] adv 時々 tokídokì

occult [əkʌlt'] n: the occult 超自然 chốshizen, オカルト okáruto

occupant [ɑ:k'jəpənt] n (long-term: of house etc) 居住者 kyojūshà; (of office etc) テナント tenánto; (temporary: of car, room etc) 中にいる人 nakà ni iru hitó

occupation [ɑ:kjəpei'ʃən] n (job) 職業 shokúgyò; (pastime) 趣味 shumì; (of building, country etc) 占領 señryo

occupational hazard [ɑ:kjəpei'ʃənəl-] n 職業上の危険 shokúgyōjō no kikén

occupier [ɑ:k'jəpaiə:r] n 居住者 kyojūshà

occupy [ɑ:k'jəpai] vt (inhabit: house) ...に住む ...ni sumù; (take: seat, place etc) ...に居る ...ni irú; (take over: building, country etc) 占領する señryo suru; (take up: time) ...が掛る ...ga kakárù; (: attention) 奪う ubáù; (: space) 取る torù

to occupy oneself in doing (to be busy with) ...に専念する ...ni señnen suru

occur [əkə:r'] vi (event: take place) 起る okórù; (phenomenon: exist) 存在する sofizai suru

to occur to someone ...の頭に浮ぶ ...no atáma ni ukábu

occurrence [əkə:r'əns] n (event) 出来事 dekigoto; (existence) 存在 soñzai

ocean [ou'ʃən] n 海 umì

Indian Ocean インド洋 iñdoyò ¶ see also Atlantic; Pacific

ocean-going [ou'ʃəngouiŋ] adj 外洋の gaíyo no

ocher [ou'kə:r] (BRIT: ochre) adj (color) 黄土色の ōdóiro no, オークルの ōkùru no

o'clock [əklɑ:k'] adv: it is 5 o'clock 5時です gojì desu

OCR [ousi:ɑ:r'] n abbr (COMPUT: = optical character recognition) 光学読取り kốgakuyomitorì (: = optical character reader) 光学読取り装置 kốgakuyomisōchì

octagonal [ɑ:ktæg'ənəl] adj 八角形の hákkakukeì no

octave [ɑ:k'tiv] n (MUS) オクターブ okútābù

October [ɑ:ktou'bə:r] n 10月 júgatsu

octopus [ɑ:k'təpəs] n タコ takò

odd [ɑ:d] adj (strange: person, behavior, expression) 変な heñ na, 妙な myồ na; (uneven: number) 奇数の kísū no; (not paired: sock, glove, shoe etc) 片方の kátàhō no

60-odd 60幾つ rokújū ikutsu

at odd times 時々 tokídokì

to be the odd one out 例外である reígai de aru

oddity [ɑ:d'iti:] n (person) 変り者 kawarimono; (thing) 変った物 kawatta mono

odd-job man [ɑ:dʒɑ:b'-] n 便利屋 beñriya

odd jobs npl 雑用 zatsúyō

oddly [ɑ:d'li:] adv (strangely: behave, dress) 変な風に heñ na fū ni ¶ see also enough

oddments [ɑ:d'mənts] npl (COMM) 残り物 nokórimono

odds [ɑ:dz] npl (in betting) かけ率 kakéritsu, オッズ ozzù

it makes no odds 構いません kamáimasen

at odds 仲たがいして nakátagaìshite

odds and ends npl 半端物 hañpamono

ode [oud] n しょう歌 shōkà, オード ōdò

odious [ou'di:əs] adj 不快な fukái na

odometer [oudɑ:m'itə:r] n 走行距離計 sōkōkyorikeì

odor [ou'də:r] (BRIT odour) n (smell) におい nióì; (: unpleasant) 悪臭 akúshū

KEYWORD

of [ʌv] prep 1 (gen) ...の ...nò

the history of France フランスの歴史 furánsu nò rekíshi

a friend of ours 私たちのある友達 watákushitàchi no árù tomódachi

a boy of 10 10才の少年 jússai no shốnen

that was kind of you ご親切にどうも go-shíñsetsu ni dồmo

a man of great ability 才能抜群の人 saínō batsugùn no hitó

the city of New York ニューヨーク市 nyúyōkushì

south of Glasgow グラスゴーの南 gurásugō no mínámi

2 (expressing quantity, amount, dates etc): *a kilo of flour* 小麦粉1キロ komúgiko ichíkiro

how much of this do you need? これはどのぐらい要りますか koré wa donó gurai irimasù ká

there were 3 of them (people) 3人いました sáñniñ imáshìta; (objects) 3個ありました sáñko arímashìta

3 of us went 私たちの内から3人行きました watákushitàchi no uchí kàrà sáñnin ikímashìta

the number of road accidents is increasing 交通事故の数が増えています kótsújikò no kázù ga fúète imásù

a cup of tea お茶1杯 o-chá ippài

a vase of flowers 花瓶に生けた花 kabín nì íkèta haná

the 5th of July 7月5日 shichígàtsu itsúkà

the winter of 1987 1987年の冬 señkyúhyakuhachíjùnanáneñ no fuyú

3 (from, out of): *a bracelet of solid gold* 純金の腕輪 juñkín nò udéwa

a statue of marble 大理石の彫像 dáírisèki no chốzō

made of wood 木製の mokúsei no

KEYWORD

---

off [ɔ:f] *adv* 1 (referring to distance, time) 離れて hanárète

it's a long way off あれは遠い arè wa tối

the game is 3 days off 試合は3日先です shiái wà mikká saki desù

2 (departure) 出掛けて dekáketè

to go off to Paris/Italy パリ〔イタリア〕へ出掛ける párì〔itária〕e dekákerù

I must be off そろそろ出掛けます soròsoro dekákemasù

3 (removal) 外して hazúshitè

to take off one's hat/coat/clothes 帽子〔コート，服〕を脱ぐ bốshi〔kòto, fu-

kú〕wo núgù

the button came off ボタンが取れた botán gà tórèta

10% off (COMM) 10パーセント引き juppásentobiki

4 (not at work: on holiday) 休暇中で kyúkachū dè; (: due to sickness) 欠勤して kekkín shitè

I'm off on Fridays 私の休みは金曜日です watákushi nò yasúmi wa kiñ-yồbi desu

he was off on Friday (on holiday) 金曜日には彼は休みでした kiñ-yồbi ni wa kárè wa yasúmi deshìta; (sick etc) 金曜日には彼は欠勤しました kiñ-yồbi ni wa kárè wa kékkin shimashìta

to have a day off (from work) 1日の休みを取る ichínichi nò yasúmi wò tórù

to be off sick 病欠する byóketsu suru

♦*adj* 1 (not turned on: machine, engine, water, gas etc) 止めてある tométe arù; (: tap) 締めてある shiméte arù; (: light) 消してある keshíte arù

2 (cancelled: meeting, match, agreement) 取消された toríkesàreta

3 (BRIT: not fresh: milk, cheese, meat etc) 悪くなった wáròku natta

4: *on the off chance* (just in case) …の場合に備えて …no baái ni sonaete

to have an off day (not as good as usual) 厄日である yakúbi de árù

♦*prep* 1 (indicating motion, removal etc) …から …kárà

to fall off a cliff 崖から落ちる gakè kara ochírù

the button came off my coat コートのボタンが取れた kōtò no botán gà tórèta

to take a picture off the wall 壁に掛けてある絵を降ろす kabé nì kákète aru é wò orósù

2 (distant from) …から離れて …kárà hanárète

it's just off the M1 国道M1を降りて直ぐの所にあります kokúdō emúwañ wo őrìte súgu no tokórò ni arímasù

it's 5 km off the main road 幹線道路から5キロの所にあります kañsendòro

kara gókìro no tokórò ni arímasù

an island off the coast 沖合の島 okí-ai nò shimá

to be off meat (no longer eat it) 肉をやめている nikú wò yaméte irù; (no longer like it) 肉が嫌いになっている nikú gà kirái nì natté irù

offal [ɔːfˈəl] *n* (CULIN) もつ motsù

off-color [ɔːfˈkʌlˈəːr] (*BRIT* **off-colour**) *adj* (ill) 病気の byóki no

offend [əfendˈ] *vt* (upset: person) 怒らせる okóraserù

offender [əfendəːr] *n* (criminal) 犯罪者 hanzáìsha, 犯人 hannìn, ...犯 ...haǹ

offense [əfensˈ] (*BRIT* **offence**) *n* (crime) 犯罪 hanzáì

to take offense at ...に怒る ...ni okórù

offensive [əfenˈsiv] *adj* (remark, gesture, behavior) 侮辱的な bujókuteki na; (smell etc) いやな iyá na; (weapon) 攻撃用の kógekiyó no

♦*n* (MIL) 攻撃 kógeki

offer [ɔːfˈəːr] *n* (proposal: to help etc) 申出 móshide; (: to buy) 申込み móshikomi

♦*vt* (advice, help, information) ...すると申出る ...surú to mófshideru; (opportunity, service, product) 提供する tefkyō suru

on offer (*BRIT*: COMM) 値下げ品で neságehin de

offering [ɔːfˈəːrin] *n* (of a company: product) 売物 urímono; (REL) 供物 sonáemono

off-hand [ɔːfˈhænd] *adj* (behavior etc) いい加減な iíkagen na

♦*adv* 即座に sokúza ni

office [ɔːfˈis] *n* (place) 事務所 jimúshò, オフィス ofisu; (room) 事務室 jimúshìtsu; (position) 職 shokú

doctor's office (US) 医院 iìn

to take office 職に就く shokú ni tsuku

office automation *n* オフィスオートメーション ofisu ōtómèshon

office building (*BRIT* **office block**) *n* オフィスビル ofísubiru

office hours *npl* (COMM) 業務時間 gyómujikan; (*US*: MED) 診察時間 shiǹ-

satsujikan

officer [ɔːfˈisəːr] *n* (MIL etc) 将校 shókō; (*also*: **police officer**) 警官 keíkan; (of organization) 役員 yakûìn

office worker *n* 事務員 jimúìn

official [əfiʃˈəl] *adj* (authorized) 公認の kónin no; (visit, invitation, letter etc) 公式の kóshiki no

♦*n* (in government) 役人 yakúnin; (in trade union etc) 役員 yakúin

official residence 官邸 kaǹtei

officialdom [əfiʃˈəldəm] (*pej*) *n* 官僚の世界 kaǹryō no sekài

officiate [əfiʃˈiːeit] *vi* 司会する shikái suru

officious [əfiʃˈəs] *adj* (person, behavior) 差出がましい sashídegamashiì

offing [ɔːfˈin] *n*: *in the offing* (*fig*: imminent) 差迫って sashísematte

off-licence [ɔːfˈlaisəns] *BRIT n* (shop selling alcohol) 酒屋 sakáya

off-line [ɔːfˈlain] *adj* (COMPUT) オフラインの ofúrain no

♦*adv* オフラインで ofúrain de

off-peak [ɔːfˈpiːk] *adj* (heating) オフピークの ofúpīku no; (train, ticket) 混んでいない時の koǹde inai tokî no

off-putting [ɔːfˈputˈin] (*BRIT*) *adj* (person, remark etc) 気を悪くさせる kî wo warûku saseru

off-season [ɔːfˈsiːzən] *adj* (holiday, ticket) オフシーズンの ofúshizun no

♦*adv* (travel, book etc) オフシーズンに ofúshizun ni

offset [ɔːfset] (*pt, pp* **offset**) *vt* (counteract) 補う oginaù

offshoot [ɔːfˈʃuːt] *n* (*fig*) 副産物 fukúsaǹbutsu

offshore [ɔːfˈʃɔːr] *adj* (breeze) 陸からの rikú kara no; (oilrig, fishing) 沖合の okí-ai no

offside [ɔːfˈsaid] *adj* (SPORT) オフサイドの ofúsaido no; (AUT: with right-hand drive) 右の migî no; (: with left-hand drive) 左の hidári no

offspring [ɔːfˈsprin] *n inv* 子孫 shisòn

offstage [ɔːfˈsteidʒ] *adv* 舞台裏に[で] butáiura ni[de]

off-the-rack [ɔːˈðəræk'] (BRIT **off-the-peg**) adj (clothing) 出来合いの dekíai no, 既製の kiséi no

off-white [ɔːˈfwait] adj (grayish white) 灰色がかった白の haíirogakatta shiró no; (yellowish white) 黄色がかった白の kiírogakatta shiró no

often [ɔːf'ən] adv (frequently) よく yokù, しょっちゅう shotchū, 度々 tabítabi
how often do you go? どのぐらい行きますか donó gurai ikímasu ká

ogle [ou'gəl] vt 色目で見る irómè de mirù

oh [ou] excl あっ át

oil [ɔil] n (gen) 油 abúra, オイル oírù; (CULIN) サラダ油 sarádayu; (petroleum) 石油 sekíyu; (crude) 原油 geńyu; (for heating) 石油 sekíyu, 灯油 tōyu
♦vt (lubricate: engine, gun, machine) ...に油を差す ...ni abúra wo sasù

oilcan [ɔil'kæn] n 油差し abúrasashi

oilfield [ɔil'fiːld] n 油田 yudén

oil filter n (AUT) オイルフィルター oírufirutā

oil painting n 油絵 abúrae

oil refinery [-riːfain'əːriː] n 精油所 seíyujo

oil rig n 石油掘削装置 sekíyu kússaku-sōchi

oilskins [ɔil'skinz] npl 防水服 bōsuifuku

oil tanker n (ship) オイルタンカー oíru-tankā; (truck) タンクローリー tańkurōrī

oil well n 油井 yuséi

oily [ɔi'liː] adj (rag) 油染みた abúrajimità; (substance) 油の様な abúra no yō na; (food) 脂っこい abúrakkoi

ointment [ɔint'mənt] n 軟こう nańkō

O.K., okay [oukei'] (inf) excl (agreement: alright) よろしい yoróshii, オーケー ōkē; (: don't fuss) 分かったよ wakáttá yo
♦adj (average: film, book, meal etc) まあまあの mā̀ma no
♦vt (approve) 承認する shōnin suru

old [ould] adj (aged: person) 年寄の toshíyori no; (: thing) 古い furúi; (former: school, home etc) 元の motò no, 前の maè no

how old are you? お幾つですか o-íkutsu desu ká

he's 10 years old 彼は10才です karè wa jussái desu

older brother (one's own) 兄 ani; (of person spoken to) お兄さん o-níisan; (of third party) 兄さん níisan

old age n 老齢 rōrei

old-age pensioner [ould'eidʒ-] (BRIT) n 年金で生活する老人 neńkin dè seíkatsu surù rōjin, 年金暮しの人 neńkingurà-shi no hitò

old-fashioned [ould'fæʃ'ənd] adj (style, design) 時代遅れの jidáiokùre no, 古くさい furúkusai; (person, values) 保守的な hoshúteki na

olive [ɑːl'iv] n (fruit) オリーブ oríbù; (also: **olive tree**) オリーブの木 oríbù no ki
♦adj (also: **olive-green**) オリーブ色の oríbùiro no

olive oil n オリーブ油 oríbùyu

Olympic [oulim'pik] adj 五輪の gorín no, オリンピックの orínpikkù no

Olympic Games npl: the Olympic Games 五輪 gorín, オリンピック orínpikkù
the Olympics 五輪 gorín, オリンピック orínpikkù

omelet(te) [ɑːm'lit] n オムレツ omúretsu

omen [ou'mən] n (sign) 兆し kizáshi, 前触れ maébure

ominous [ɑːm'ənəs] adj (worrying) 不気味な bukìmi na

omission [oumiʃ'ən] n 省略 shōryaku

omit [oumit'] vt (deliberately) 省略する shōryaku suru; (by mistake) うっかりして抜かす ukkárì shite nukásu

---

KEYWORD

---

on [ɑːn] prep 1 (indicating position) ...(の上)に〔で〕...(no ué) ni(de)
on the wall 壁に kabé ni
it's on the table テーブル(の上)にあります tēburu (no ué) nì arímasù
on the left 左に hidári nì
the house is on the main road 家は幹線道路に面しています ié wà kańsendōro

ni mén shite imásù

2 (indicating means, method, condition etc) ...で ...dè

on foot (go, be) 歩いて arúïte

on the train/plane (go) 電車〔飛行機〕で dénsha〔hikőkì〕de; (be) (be) 電車〔飛行機〕に乗って dénsha〔hikőkì〕ni notté

on the telephone/radio/television 電話〔ラジオ，テレビ〕で dénwa〔rájì, térèbi〕de

she's on the telephone 彼女は電話に出ています〔電話中です〕kánòjo wa dénwa ni détè imasu〔deñwachū desù〕

I heard it on the radio/saw him on television 私はラジオで聞きました〔テレビで彼を見ました〕watákushi wà rájì-o de kikímashìta〔térèbi de kárè wo mimáshìta〕

to be on drugs 麻薬をやっている mayáku wò yatté irù

to be on holiday 休暇中である kyúkachū de arù

to be away on business 商用で出掛けている shóyō dè dekákete irù

3 (referring to time) ...に ...ni

on Friday 金曜日に kiń-yőbì ni

on Fridays 金曜日に kiń-yőbi ni, 毎週金曜日に maíshū kiń-yőbi ni, 金曜日毎に kiń-yőbi gőtò ni

on June 20th 6月20日に rokúgatsu hatsúka ni

on Friday, June 20th 6月20日金曜日に rokúgatsu hatsúka kiń-yőbi ni

a week on Friday 来週の金曜日に raíshū nò kiń-yőbi ni

on arrival he went straight to his hotel 到着すると彼は真っ直ぐにホテルへ行きました tőchaku suru tò kárè wa massúgù ni hőtèru e ikímashìta

on seeing this これを見ると koré wò mírù to

4 (about, concerning) ...について ...ni tsúïte, ...に関して ...ni káñ shite

information on train services 列車に関する情報 resshá nì kań surù jőhō

a book on physics 物理の本 bútsuri no hőñ

♦*adv* **1** (referring to dress) 身につけて

mi ní tsukète

to have one's coat on コートを着ている kőto wo kité irù

what's she got on? 彼女は何を着ていますか kánòjo wa nánì wo kité imasù ká

she put her boots/gloves/hat on 彼女はブーツを履いた〔手袋をはめた，帽子をかぶった〕kánòjo wa bútsu wo haíta〔tebúkuro wò haméta, bőshì wo kabútta〕

2 (referring to covering): ***screw the lid on tightly*** ふたをしっかり締めて下さい futá wò shikkárï shímète kudásaï

3 (further, continuously) 続けて tsuzúkete

to walk/drive/go on 歩き〔車で走り，行き〕続ける arúkì〔kurúma dè hashíri, ikí〕tsuzukèru

to read on 読み続ける yomítsuzukèru

♦*adj* **1** (functioning, in operation: machine) 動いている ugóite irù; (: radio, TV, light) ついている tsúïte iru; (: faucet) 水が出ている mizú gà deté irù; (: brakes) かかっている kakátte irù; (: meeting) 始まっている tsuzúite irù

is the meeting still on? (in progress) まだ会議中ですか mádà kaígichū desù ká; (not cancelled) 会議は予定通りにやるんですか káïgi wa yoteí dòri ni yarún desù ká

there's a good film on at the cinema 映画館で今いい映画をやっています eígakàn de ímà iî eíga wò yatté imasu

2: ***that's not on!*** (*inf*: of behavior) それはいけません soré wà ikémaseñ

---

once [wʌns] *adv* (on one occasion) 一度 ichído, 一回 ikkái; (formerly) 前 は maè wa, かつて katsúte

♦*conj* (immediately afterwards) ...した後 ...shitá ato, ...してから ...shité kara

once he had left/it was done 彼が出て〔事が済んで〕から karè ga deté〔kotó ga suñde〕kara

at once (immediately) 直ちに tadáchi ni, 直ぐに sugú ni; (simultaneously) 同時に dőjì ni

once a week 週一回 shū ikkái

once more もう一度 mố ichído
once and for all 断然 dańzen
once upon a time 昔々 mukáshi muka-shi

oncoming [ɑːnˈkʌmiŋ] *adj* (approaching: traffic etc) 向ってくる mukátte kurù

KEYWORD
---

one [wʌn] *num* 一（の）ichí (no), 1つ（の）hitótsù (no)

one hundred and fifty 150 hyakúgojù
I asked for two coffees, not one 注文したのは1つじゃなくて2つのコーヒーです chúmon shita no wà hitótsu jànakute futátsu nò kôhî desu

one day there was a sudden knock at the door ある日突然だれかがドアをノックした árù hi totsúzen dáreka ga dôa wo nôkkù shita

one by one 1つずつ hitótsu zùtsu

♦*adj* 1 (sole) ただ一つの tádà hitótsù no, 唯一の yúîtsu no

it's the one book which interests me 私が興味を感じる唯一の本です watákushi gà kyômi wo kañjiru yúîtsu no hôñ desu

that is my one worry 私が心配しているのはそれだけです watákushi gà shiñpai shite iru nò wa soré dake dèsu

the one man who ... ...する唯一の人 ...suru yúîtsu no hitó

2 (same) 同じ onáji

they came in the one car 彼らは皆同じ車で来ました kárèra wa mínà onáji kurùma de kimáshìta

they all belong to the one family 彼らは皆身内です kárèra wa mínà miúchi desù

♦*pron* 1 物 monó

this one これ koré

that one それ soré, あれ aré

I've already got one/a red one 私は既に1つ[赤いのを]持っています watákushi wà súdè ni hitótsù[akái nò wo] móttè imasu

2: *one another* お互いに o-tágai nì

do you two ever see one another? お二人は付合っていますか o-fútàri wa tsu-

kíattè imasu ká

the boys didn't dare look at one another 少年たちはあえて顔を合せる事ができなかった shốnentàchi wa áète ka-ó wò awáseru kotò ga dekínakattà

3 (impersonal): *one never knows* どうなるか分かりませんね dố naru ka waká-rimaseñ né

to cut one's finger 指を切る yubí wò kírù

one needs to eat 人は食べる必要がある hitó wà tabérù hitsúyò ga arù

---

one-day excursion [wʌn'dei-] (*US*) *n* (day return) 日帰り往復券 higáeri ôfuku-ken

one-man [wʌn'mæn] *adj* (business) 1人だけの hitóri dake no, ワンマンの wañman no

one-man band *n* ワンマンバンド wañ-manbando

one-off [wʌn'ɔːf] (*BRIT: inf*) *n* 一つだけの物 hitótsu dake no mono

---
KEYWORD
---

oneself [wʌnselfˈ] *pron* (reflexive) 自分自身を jibúnjishìn wo; (after prep) 自分自身に jibúnjishìn ni; (alone: often after prep) 自分一人で jibún hitòri de; (emphatic) 自分で jibún dè

to hurt oneself けがする kegá surù

to keep something for oneself 自分のために...を取って置く jibún no tamè ni ...wò tôttè oku

to talk to oneself 独り言を言う hitóri-gotò wo iú

---

one-sided [wʌnˈsaidid] *adj* (argument) 一方的な ippôteki na

one-to-one [wʌnˈtəwʌn] *adj* (relation-ship) 一対一の ittáiichi no

one-upmanship [wʌnʌpˈmənʃip] *n* 自分の方が一枚上だと見せ付ける事 jibún no hô ga ichímai uè da to misétsukerù koto

one-way [wʌnˈwei] *adj* (street, traffic) 一方通行の ippôtsùkō no

ongoing [ɑːnˈgouiŋ] *adj* (project, situa-tion etc) 進行中の shiñkôchù no

onion [ʌn'jən] n タマネギ tamánegì

on-line [ɑːn'lain] adj (COMPUT) オンラインの oírraìn no
♦adv (COMPUT) オンラインで oírraìn de

onlooker [ɑːn'lukəːr] n 見物人 keñbutsu-nìn

only [oun'liː] adv ...だけ ...dake
♦adj (sole, single) ただ一つ〔一人〕の tadá hitótsù[hitórì] no
♦conj (but) しかし shikáshì
  an only child 一人っ子 hitórikkð
  not only ... but also ... ...ばかりでなく...も ...bakàri de naku ...mo

onset [ɑːn'set] n (beginning: of war, winter, illness) 始まり hajímari, 始め hajíme

onshore [ɑːn'jɔːr] adj (wind) 海からの umì kara no

onslaught [ɑːn'slɔːt] n 攻撃 kðgeki

onto [ɑːn'tuː] prep = **on to**

onus [ou'nəs] n 責任 sekínin

onward(s) [ɑːn'wəːrd(z)] adv (forward: move, progress) 先へ sakí e
  from that time onward(s) それ以後 soré igo

onyx [ɑːn'iks] n オニキス onîkisu

ooze [uːz] vi (mud, water, slime) にじみでる nijímideru

opal [ou'pəl] n オパール opáru

opaque [oupeik'] adj (substance) 不透明な futðmèi na

OPEC [ou'pek] n abbr (= Organization of Petroleum-Exporting Countries) 石油輸出国機構 sekíyu yushutsukoku kikð

open [ou'pən] adj (not shut: window, door, mouth etc) 開いた aíta; (: shop, museum etc) 営業中の eígyōchū no, 開いている aíte iru; (unobstructed: road) 開通している kaítsū shite iru; (: view) 開けた hiŕaketa; (not enclosed: land) 囲いのない kakói no nai; (fig: frank: person, manner, face) 率直な sótchoku na; (unrestricted: meeting, debate, championship) 公開の kõkai no
♦vt 開ける akéru, 開く hiŕaku
♦vi (flower, eyes, door, shop) 開く akú, 開く hiŕaku; (book, debate etc: commence) 始まる hajímaru

in the open (air) 野外に yagái ni
an open car オープンカー ðpùnkā

opening [ou'pəniŋ] adj (commencing: speech, remarks etc) 開会の kaíkai no, 冒頭の bõtð no
♦n (gap, hole) 穴 aná; (start: of play, book etc) 始め hajíme, 冒頭 bõtð; (opportunity) 機会 kikái, チャンス chañsu

openly [ou'pənliː] adv (speak, act) 公然と kõzen to; (cry) 人目をはばからず hitóme wo habákarazu

open-minded [ou'pənmain'did] adj 偏見のない heñken no nai

open-necked [ou'pənnekt'] adj (shirt) 開きんの kaíkin no

open on to vt fus (subj: room, door) ...に面している ...ni mén shite iru

open-plan [ou'pənplæn'] adj 間仕切のない majíkiri no nai

open up vt (building, room: unlock) 開ける akéru; (blocked road) ...の障害物を取除く ...no shðgaíbutsu wo torínozoku
♦vi (COMM: shop, business) 開く akú

opera [ɑːp'rə] n 歌劇 kagèki, オペラ opèra

opera singer n オペラ歌手 opèrakashu

operate [ɑːp'əːreit] vt (machine) 操作する sõsa suru; (vehicle) 運転する uñten suru
♦vi (machine) 動く ugðkù; (vehicle) 走る hashiru, 動く ugðkù; (company, organization) 営業する eígyō suru
to operate on someone (for) (MED) ...に (...の) 手術をする ...ni (...no) shujùtsu wo suru

operatic [ɑːpəræt'ik] adj 歌劇の kagèki no, オペラの opèra no

operating [ɑːp'əːreitiŋ] adj: *operating table* 手術台 shujùtsudai
operating theater 手術室 shujùtsushitsu

operation [ɑːpəreiʃən] n (of machine etc) 操作 sõsa; (of vehicle) 運転 uñten; (MIL, COMM etc) 作戦 sakúsen; (MED) 手術 shujútsu
to be in operation (law, regulation) 実施されている jisshí sarete iru
to have an operation (MED) 手術を受

ける shujútsu wo ukérù

operational [ɑːpəreiˈʃənəl] *adj* (working: machine, vehicle etc) 使用可能な shíyōkanō na

operative [ɑːpˈrətiv] *adj* (law, measure, system) 実施されている jisshí saretè iru

operator [ɑːpˈəːreitər] *n* (TEL) 交換手 kōkanshu, オペレーター opérētā; (of machine) 技師 gishí

ophthalmic [ɑːfˈælˈmik] *adj* 眼科の gañka no

opinion [əpinˈjən] *n* (point of view, belief) 意見 ikén

in my opinion 私の意見では watákushi no ikèn de wa

opinionated [əpinˈjəneitid] *(pej) adj* 独善的な dokúzenteki na

opinion poll *n* 世論調査 yorónchōsa

opium [ouˈpiːəm] *n* あへん ahén

opponent [əpouˈnənt] *n* (person not in favor) 反対者 hañtaisha; (MIL) 敵 tekí; (SPORT) 相手 aíte

opportunism [ɑːpəːrtuːˈnizəm] *(pej) n* 日和見主義 hiyórimishugì

opportunist [ɑːpəːrtuːˈnist] *(pej) n* 日和見主義者 hiyórimishugishà

opportunity [ɑːpəːrtjuːˈnitiː] *n* 機会 kikái, チャンス chañsu

to take the opportunity of doing 折角の機会を利用して...する sekkáku no kikái wo riyō shite ...suru

oppose [əpouzˈ] *vt* (object to: wish, opinion, plan) ...に反対する ...ni hañtai suru

to be opposed to something ...に反対である ...ni hañtai de aru

as opposed to ...ではなくて ...de wa nakutè

opposing [əpouzˈiŋ] *adj* (side, ideas) 反対の hañtai no; (team) 相手の aíte no

opposite [ɑːpˈəzit] *adj* (house) 向かい側の mukáigawa no; (end, direction, side) 反対の hañtai no; (point of view, effect) 逆の gyakú no

♦*adv* (live, stand, work, sit) 向い側に〔で〕mukáigawa ni〔de〕

♦*prep* (in front of) ...の向い側に〔で〕...no mukáigawa ni〔de〕

♦*n*: *the opposite* (say, think, do etc) 反対 hañtai

the opposite sex 異性 iséi

opposition [ɑːpəziʃˈən] *n* (resistance) 反対 hañtai; (those against) 反対勢力 hañtaiseiryokù; (POL) 野党 yatố

oppress [əpresˈ] *vt* 抑圧する yokúatsu suru

oppression [əpreʃˈən] *n* 抑圧 yokúatsu

oppressive [əpresˈiv] *adj* (political regime) 抑圧的な yokúatsuteki na; (weather, heat) 蒸し暑い mushíatsuì

opt [ɑːpt] *vi*: *to opt for* ...を選ぶ ...wo erábù

to opt to do ...する事にする ...surú koto ni suru

optical [ɑːpˈtikəl] *adj* (instrument, device etc) 光学の kōgaku no

optical illusion *n* 目の錯覚 mé no sakkáku

optician [ɑːptiʃˈən] *n* 眼鏡屋 megáneya

optimism [ɑːpˈtəmizəm] *n* 楽観 rakkán, 楽天主義 rakútenshugì

optimist [ɑːpˈtəmist] *n* 楽天家 rakútenka

optimistic [ɑːptəmisˈtik] *adj* 楽観的な rakkánteki na

optimum [ɑːpˈtəməm] *adj* (conditions, number, size) 最良の saíryō no, 最善の saízen no

option [ɑːpˈʃən] *n* (choice) 選択 sefitaku, オプション opúshon

optional [ɑːpˈʃənəl] *adj* (not obligatory) 自由選択の jiyúsentakuno

opt out *vi*: *to opt out of* ...から手を引く ...kara te wò hiku

opulent [ɑːpˈjələnt] *adj* (very wealthy: person, society etc) 大金持の ốganemochi no

or [ɔːr] *conj* (linking alternatives: up or down, in or out etc) それとも sorétomo, または matá wa; (otherwise) でないと de naí to, さもないと sa mò nai to; (with negative): *he hasn't seen or heard anything* 彼は何一つ見ても聞いてもいない karè wa nanì hitótsu mitè mo kiíte mo inai

or else (otherwise) でないと de naí to

oracle [ɔːrˈəkəl] *n* 予言者 yogénsha

oral [ɔːˈrəl] *adj* (spoken: test, report) 口頭の kốtō no; (MED: vaccine, medicine) 経口の keíkō no
♦*n* (spoken examination) 口頭試問 kốtō shimon

orange [ɔːrˈindʒ] *n* (fruit) オレンジ orènji
♦*adj* (color) だいだい色の daídaiiro no, オレンジ色の orènjiiro no

orator [ɔːrˈətəːr] *n* 雄弁家 yúbenka

orbit [ɔːrˈbit] *n* (SPACE) 軌道 kidố
♦*vt* (circle: earth, moon etc) ...の周囲を軌道を描いて回る ...no shūi wo kidố wo egaite mawaru

orchard [ɔːrˈtʃəːrd] *n* 果樹園 kajúen

orchestra [ɔːrˈkistrə] *n* (MUS) 楽団 gakúdan, オーケストラ ốkesùtora; (US: THEATER: seating) 舞台前の特等席 butáimae no tokútōseki

orchestrate [ɔːrˈkistreit] *vt* (stage-manage) 指揮する shikí suru

orchid [ɔːrˈkid] *n* ラン rañ

ordain [ɔːrˈdein] *vt* (REL) 聖職に任命する seíshoku ni nímmei suru

ordeal [ɔːrˈdiːl] *n* 試練 shíren

order [ɔːrˈdəːr] *n* (command) 命令 meírei; (COMM: from shop, company etc: *also* in restaurant) 注文 chúmon; (sequence) 順序 juñjo; (good order) 秩序 chitsújò; (law and order) 治安 chiàn
♦*vt* (command) 命ずる mèizuru; (COMM: from shop, company etc: *also* in restaurant) 注文する chúmon suru; (*also*: **put in order**) 整理する seíri suru

in order (gen) 整理されて seíri sarete; (of document) 規定通りで kitéidōri de

in (working) order 整備されて seíbi sarete

in order to do/that ...するために ...surú tame ni

on order (COMM) 発注してあって hatchú shite atte

out of order (not in correct order) 順番が乱れて juñban ga midárete; (not working) 故障して koshố shite

to order someone to do something ...に...する様に命令する ...ni ...suru yō ni meírei suru

order form *n* 注文用紙 chúmon yōshi

orderly [ɔːrˈdəːrli] *n* (MIL) 当番兵 tōbànhei; (MED) 雑役夫 zatsúekifù
♦*adj* (well-organized: room) 整とんされた seíton sareta; (: person, system etc) 規則正しい kisókutadashii

ordinary [ɔːrˈdəneːriː] *adj* (everyday, usual) 普通の futsú no; (*pej*: mediocre) 平凡な heíbon na

out of the ordinary (exceptional) 変った kawátta

Ordnance Survey [ɔːrˈdnəns-] (*BRIT*) *n* 英国政府陸地測量局 eíkokuseifù rikúchi sokuryókyoku

ore [ɔːr] *n* 鉱石 kốseki

organ [ɔːrˈgən] *n* (ANAT: kidney, liver etc) 臓器 zōki; (MUS) オルガン orúgan

organic [ɔːrˈgænˈik] *adj* (food, farming etc) 有機の yúki no

organism [ɔːrˈgənizəm] *n* 有機体 yúkìtai, 生物 seíbutsu

organist [ɔːrˈgənist] *n* オルガン奏者 orúgansōsha, オルガニスト orúganisuto

organization [ɔːrgənaizˈeiʃən] *n* (business, club, society) 組織 soshìki, 機構 kikố, オーガニゼーション ốganizēshon

organize [ɔːrˈgənaiz] *vt* (arrange: activity, event) 企画する kikáku suru

organizer [ɔːrˈgənaizəːr] *n* (of conference, party etc) 主催者 shusáisha

orgasm [ɔːrˈgæzəm] *n* オルガズム orúgazumù

orgy [ɔːrˈdʒiː] *n* 乱交パーティ rañkōpāti

Orient [ɔːrˈiːənt] *n*: *the Orient* 東洋 tốyō

oriental [ɔːriːenˈtəl] *adj* 東洋の tōyō no

orientate [ɔːriːˈenteit] *vt*: *to orientate oneself* (in place) 自分の居場所を確認する jibún no ibásho wo kakúnin suru; (in situation) 環境になれる kañkyō ni narérù

origin [ɔːrˈidʒin] *n* (beginning, source) 起源 kigèn; (of person) 生れ umare

original [əridʒˈənəl] *adj* (first: idea, occupation) 最初の saísho no; (genuine: work of art, document etc) 本物の hoñmono no; (*fig*: imaginative: thinker, writer, artist) 独創的な dokúsōteki na

♦*n* (genuine work of art, document) 本物 hofmono

originality [əridʒənæl'iti:] *n* (imagination: of artist, writer etc) 独創性 dokúsōsei

originally [əridʒ'ənəli:] *adv* (at first) 最初は saísho wa, 当初 tôsho

originate [əridʒ'əneit] *vi*: **to originate from** (person, idea, custom etc) ...から始まる ...karà hajímaru

to originate in ...で始まる ...dè hajímaru

Orkneys [ɔːrk'niːz] *npl*: **the Orkneys** (*also*: **the Orkney Islands**) オークニー諸島 ōkúnīshotō

ornament [ɔːr'nəmənt] *n* (*gen*) 飾り kazári, 装飾 sōshoku; (to be worn) 装身具 sōshiñgu

ornamental [ɔːrnəmen'təl] *adj* (decorative: garden, pond) 装飾的な sōshokuteki na

ornate [ɔːrneit'] *adj* (highly decorative: design, style) 凝った kottà

ornithology [ɔːrnəθɑːl'ədʒiː] *n* 鳥類学 chōruigaku

orphan [ɔːr'fən] *n* 孤児 kojî

orphanage [ɔːr'fənidʒ] *n* 孤児院 kojîin

orthodox [ɔːr'θədɑːks] *adj* (REL: *also fig*) 正統派の seítōha no

orthodoxy [ɔːr'θədɑːksiː] *n* (traditional beliefs) 正統思想 seítōshisō

orthopedic [ɔːrθəpiː'dik] (*BRIT* **orthopaedic**) *adj* 整形外科の seíkeigeka no

oscillate [ɑːsəleit] *vi* (ELEC) 発振する hasshín suru; (PHYSICS) 振動する shiñdō suru; (*fig*: mood, person, ideas) 頻繁に変る hiñpan ni kawáru

ostensibly [ɑːsten'səbliː] *adv* 表面上 hyőmeñjō

ostentatious [ɑːstentei'ʃəs] *adj* (showy: building, car etc) 派手な hadé na; (: person) 万事に派手な bañji ni hadé na

osteopath [ɑːs'tiːəpæθ] *n* 整骨療法医 seíkotsuryōhōī

ostracize [ɑːs'trəsaiz] *vt* のけ者にする nokémono ni suru

ostrich [ɔːs'tritʃ] *n* ダチョウ dachő

other [ʌð'əːr] *adj* (that which has not

been mentioned: person, thing) 外の hoká no; (second of 2 things) もう一つの mő hitotsu no

♦*pron*: **the other (one)** 外の物 hoká no mono

♦*adv*: **other than** ...を除いて ...wo nozóite

others (other people) 他人 tanín

the other day (recently) 先日 señjitsu, この間 konó aida

otherwise [ʌð'əːrwaiz] *adv* (in a different way) 違ったやり方で chígatta yaríkata de; (apart from that) それを除けば sorê wo nozókeba

♦*conj* (if not) そうでないと sō dè nai to

otter [ɑːt'əːr] *n* カワウソ kawáuso

ouch [autʃ] *excl* 痛い itáī

ought [ɔːt] (*pt* **ought**) *aux vb*: **she ought to do it** 彼女はそれをやるべきです kanòjo wa sorê wo yarubeki desu

this ought to have been corrected これは直すべきだった korê wa naósubeki datta

he ought to win (probability) 彼は勝つはずです karè wa katsù hazu desu

ounce [auns] *n* (unit of weight) オンス oñsu

our [au'əːr] *adj* 私たちの watákushitachi no ¶ *see also* **my**

ours [au'əːrz] *pron* 私たちの物 watákushitachi no mono ¶ *see also* **mine**

ourselves [auəːrselvz'] *pron* 私たち自身 watákushitachi jishìn ¶ *see also* **oneself**

oust [aust] *vt* (forcibly remove: government, MP etc) 追放する tsuíhō suru

┌─────────────┐
│ **KEYWORD** │
└─────────────┘

out [aut] *adv* **1** (not in) 外に〔で，へ〕sótò ni〔de, e〕

they're out in the garden 彼らは庭にいます kárèra wa niwá ni imasù

(to stand) out in the rain/snow 雨〔雪〕の降る中に立っている ámè〔yukî〕no fúrù nákà ni tátte irù

it's cold out here/out in the desert 外〔砂漠〕は寒い sótò〔sabáku〕wa samúî

out here/there ここ〔あそこ〕だ-外の方に kokó〔asóko〕dà - sótò no hő nì *to go/come etc out* 出て行く〔来る〕déte iku(kuru)

(to speak) out loud 大きな声で言う ốkina koè de iú

2 (not at home, absent) 不在で fuzái de, 留守で rúsù de

Mr Green is out at the moment グリーンさんはただ今留守ですが gurín san wa tadáima rúsù desu ga

to have a day/night out 1日〔晩〕外出して遊ぶ ichínichi(hitóbàn)gaíshutsu shitè asóbù

3 (indicating distance): *the boat was 10 km out* 船は10キロ沖にあった fúnè wa jukkírò okí ni attà

3 days out from Plymouth プリマスを出港して3日の所 purímàsu wo shukkố shitè mikká no tokorò

4 (SPORT) アウトで áùto de

the ball is/has gone out ボールはアウトだ〔出た〕bốru wa áùto da(détà)

out! (TENNIS etc) アウト áùto

♦*adj* **1**: *to be out* (person: unconscious) 気絶〔失神〕している kizétsu(shisshín) shite irù; (: SPORT) アウトである áùto de árù; (out of fashion: style) 流行遅れである ryúkōòkùre de árù, 廃れている sutáreru irù; (: singer) 人気がなくなった nínki gà nakúnatta

2 (have appeared: flowers): *to be out* 咲いている saíte irù; (: news) 報道されている hốdō sarete irù; (: secret) ばれた báretà, 発覚した hakkáku shità

3 (extinguished: fire, light, gas) 消えた kiétà

before the week was out (finished) その週が終らない内に sonó shū ga owáranai uchi nì

4: *to be out to do something* (intend) ...しようとしている ...shiyố to shité irù

to be out in one's calculations (wrong) 計算が間違っている keísan gà machígatte irù

out-and-out [aut'əndaut'] *adj* (liar, thief etc) 全くの mattáku no, 根っからの nekkára no

outback [aut'bæk] *n* (in Australia) 奥地

okúchi

outboard [aut'bɔːrd] *adj*: *outboard motor* アウトボードエンジン aùtobōdoenjin

outbreak [aut'breik] *n* (of war, disease, violence etc) ぼっ発 boppátsu

outburst [aut'bəːrst] *n* (sudden expression of anger etc) 爆発 bakúhatsu

outcast [aut'kæst] *n* のけ者 nokémono

outcome [aut'kʌm] *n* (result) 結果 kekká

outcrop [aut'krɑːp] *n* (of rock) 露頭 rotố

outcry [aut'krai'] *n* 反発 hañpatsu

outdated [autdei'tid] *adj* (old-fashioned) 時代遅れの jidáiokùre no

outdo [autduː'] (*pt* **outdid** *pp* **outdone**) *vt* しのぐ shinôgu

outdoor [aut'dɔːr] *adj* (open-air: activities, games etc) 野外の yagái no, 屋外の okúgai no; (clothes) 野外用の yagáiyō no

outdoors [aut'dɔːrz'] *adv* (play, stay, sleep: in the open air) 野外に〔で〕yagái ni〔de〕

outer [aut'əːr] *adj* (exterior: door, wrapping, wall etc) 外側の sotốgawa no

outer space *n* 宇宙空間 uchúkūkan

outfit [aut'fit] *n* (set of clothes) 衣装 ishố

outgoing [aut'gouiŋ] *adj* (extrovert) 外向性の gaíkōsei no; (retiring: president, mayor etc) 退陣する taíjin suru

outgoings [aut'gouiŋz] (*BRIT*) *npl* 出費 shuppí

outgrow [autgrou'] (*pt* **outgrew** *pp* **outgrown**) *vt* (one's clothes) 大きくなって...が着られなくなる ốkiku natte ...ga kiráreruku naru

outhouse [aut'haus] *n* 納屋 nayà; (*US*) 屋外便所 okúgaibenjo

outing [au'tiŋ] *n* (excursion: family outing, school outing) 遠足 eñsoku

outlandish [autlæn'diʃ] *adj* (strange: looks, behavior, clothes) 奇妙な kimyố na

outlaw [aut'lɔː] *n* 無法者 muhốmono
♦*vt* (person, activity, organization) 禁止する kiñshi suru

outlay [aut'lei] *n* (expenditure) 出費

shuppí

outlet [aut'let] *n* (hole, pipe) 排水口 haísuìkō; (*US*: ELEC) コンセント kóńseńto; (COMM: *also*: **retail outlet**) 販売店 hańbaìten

outline [aut'lain] *n* (shape: of object, person etc) 輪郭 rińkaku, アウトライン aúttoraìn; (brief explanation: of plan) あらまし arámashi, アウトライン aútoraìn; (rough sketch) 略図 ryakúzu

♦*vt* (*fig*: theory, plan etc) ...のあらましを説明する ...no arámashi wo setsúmei suru

outlive [autliv'] *vt* (survive: person) ...より長生きする ...yorí naga-ikí suru; (: war, era) 生き延びる ikínobiru

outlook [aut'luk] *n* (view, attitude) 見方 mikáta; (*fig*: prospects) 見通し mitóshi; (: for weather) 予報 yohō

outlying [aut'laiiŋ] *adj* (away from main cities: area, town etc) 中心部を離れた chūshinbu wo hanáreta

outmoded [autmou'did] *adj* (old-fashioned: custom, theory) 時代遅れの jidáiokùre no

outnumber [autnʌm'bəːr] *vt* ...より多い ...yorí ōi

KEYWORD

out of *prep* **1** (outside, beyond) ...の外へ〔に, で〕...no sótò e〔ni, de〕

to go out of the house 家から外へ出る ié kara sótò e dérù

to look out of the window 窓から外を見る mádò kara sótò wo mírù

to be out of danger (safe) 危険がなくなった kikén gà nakúnattà

2 (cause, motive) ...に駆られて ...ni karáretè

out of curiosity/fear/greed 好奇心〔恐怖, どん欲〕に駆られて kókishìn〔kyófu, dóń-yoku〕ni karáretè

3 (origin) ...から ...kara

to drink something out of a cup カップから...を飲む káppù kara ...wo nomù

to copy something out of a book 本から...を写す hóń kara ...wò utsúsù

4 (from among) ...の中から ...no nákà

kara, ...の内 ...no uchì

1 out of every 3 smokers 喫煙者3人に1人 kitsúeńsha sańnin nì hitórì

out of 100 cars sold, only one had any faults 売れた100台の車の内、1台だけに欠陥があった uréta hyakúdài no kurúma no uchi, íchidai dake ni kekkán ga atta

5 (without) ...が切れて ...ga kírète, ...がなくなって ...ga nakúnattè

to be out of milk/sugar/gas (US)/petrol (BRIT) etc ミルク〔砂糖, ガソリン〕が切れている mírùku〔satő, gasórin〕ga kírète iru

---

out-of-date [autəvdeit'] *adj* (passport) 期限の切れた kigén no kírèta; (clothes etc) 時代遅れの jidáiokùre no

out-of-the-way [autəvðəwei'] *adj* (place) へんぴな heńpi na

outpatient [aut'peiʃənt] *n* (MED) 外来患者 gaírakanja

outpost [aut'poust] *n* (MIL, COMM) 前しょう zeńshō; (COMM) 前進基地 zeńshinkichi

output [aut'put] *n* (production: of factory, mine etc) 生産高 seísańdaka; (: of writer) 作品数 sakúhinsū; (COMPUT) 出力 shutsúryoku, アウトプット aútoputtu

outrage [aut'reidʒ] *n* (action: scandalous) 不法行為 fuhókòi; (: violent) 暴力行為 bóryokukòi; (anger) 激怒 gekído

♦*vt* (shock, anger) 激怒させる gekído saseru

outrageous [autrei'dʒəs] *adj* 非難すべき hinánsubeki

outright [adv autrait' adj aut'rait] *adv* (absolutely: win) 圧倒的に attőteki ni; (at once: kill) 即座に sokúza ni; (openly: ask, deny, refuse) はっきりと hakkíri to

♦*adj* (absolute: winner, victory) 圧倒的な attőteki na; (open: refusal, denial, hostility) 明白な meíhaku na

outset [aut'set] *n* (start) 始め hajíme

outside [aut'said'] *n* (exterior: of container, building) 外側 sotógawa

♦*adj* (exterior) 外側の sotógawa no

♦*adv* (away from the inside: to be, go,

wait) 外に〔で〕sotó ni〔de〕

♦*prep* (not inside) ...の外に〔で〕...no sotó ni〔de〕; (not included in) ...の外に ...no hoká ni〔de〕; (beyond) ...を越えて ...wo koéte

at the outside (fig) せいぜい seízei

outside lane *n* (AUT) 追越し車線 oíkoshishaseñ

outside line *n* (TEL) 外線 gaísen

outsider [autsaɪ'dər] *n* (stranger) 部外者 bugáisha

outside-left/-right [aut'saidleft'/rait] *n* (SOCCER) レフト〔ライト〕ウイング refúto〔raíto〕uíñgu

outsize [aut'saiz] *adj* (clothes) キングサイズの kíñgusaìzu no

outskirts [aut'skərts] *npl* (of city, town) 外れ hazúre

outspoken [aut'spou'kən] *adj* (statement, opponent, reply) 遠慮のない eñryo no nai

outstanding [autstæn'diŋ] *adj* (exceptional) 並外れた namíhazureta, 優れた sugúretà; (remaining: debt, work etc) 残っている nokótte iru

outstay [austei'] *vt*: *to outstay one's welcome* 長居して嫌われる nagái shite kiráwareru

outstretched [austretʃt'] *adj* (hand) 伸ばした nobáshìta; (arms) 広げた hirógetà

outstrip [austrip'] *vt* (competitors, demand) 追抜く oínuku

out-tray [aut'trei] *n* 送信のトレー sóshin no torē

outward [aut'wərd] *adj* (sign, appearances) 外部の gaíbu no; (journey) 行きの ikí no

outwardly [aut'wərdli:] *adv* 外部的に gaíbuteki ni

outweigh [autwei'] *vt* ...より重要である ...yorí jūyō de aru

outwit [autwit'] *vt* ...の裏をかく ...no urá wo kaku

oval [ou'vəl] *adj* (table, mirror, face) だ円形の daéñkei no
♦*n* だ円形 daéñkei

ovary [ou'vəri:] *n* 卵巣 rañsō

ovation [ouvei'ʃən] *n* 大喝さい daíkassai

oven [ʌv'ən] *n* (CULIN) 天火 teñpi, オーブン ōbùn; (TECH) 炉 ro

ovenproof [ʌv'ənpru:f] *adj* (dish etc) オーブン用の ōbùn yō no

KEYWORD

over [ou'vər] *adv* **1** (across: walk, jump, fly etc) ...を越えて ...wò koétè

to cross over to the other side of the road 道路を横断する dōro wo ōdan suru

over here/there ここ〔あそこ〕に〔で〕kokó〔asóko〕nì〔dè〕

to ask someone over (to one's house) ...を家に招く ...wò ié nì manékù

2 (indicating movement from upright: fall, knock, turn, bend etc) 下へ shitá è, 地面へ jímen e

3 (excessively: clever, rich, fat etc) 余り amári, 過度に kádò ni

she's not over intelligent, is she? 彼女はあまり頭が良くないね kánòjo wa amári atáma gà yókùnai né

4 (remaining: money, food etc) 余って amátte, 残って nokótte

there are 3 over 3個が残っている sáñko ga nokótte irù

is there any cake (left) over? ケーキが残っていませんか kèki ga nokótte imaseñ ká

5: *all over* (everywhere) 至る所に〔で〕itárù tokoro ni〔de〕, どこもかしこも dókò mo káshikò mo

over and over (again) (repeatedly) 何度〔何回、何返〕も náñdo〔náñkai, náñben〕mo

♦*adj* (finished): *to be over* (game, life, relationship etc) 終りである owári de arù

♦*prep* **1** (on top of) ...の上に〔で〕...no ué nì〔de〕; (above) ...の上方に〔で〕...no jōhō nì〔de〕

to spread a sheet over something ...の上にシーツを掛ける ...no ué nì shítsu wo kakérù

there's a canopy over the bed ベッドの上に天がいがある béddò no ué nì teñgai ga arù

2 (on the other side of) ...の向こう側に

〔で〕...no mukṓgawa nǐ(dè)

the pub over the road 道路の向こう側
にあるパブ dṓrò no mukṓgawa ni arù
pábù

he jumped over the wall 彼は塀を飛
越えた kárè wa heí wò tobíkoèta

3 (more than) 以上 ijō

over 200 people came 200人以上の人
が来ました nihyákunìn íjō no hitṓ gà
kimáshìta

over and above ...の外に ...no hōkà ni,
...に加えて ...ni kuwáetè

*this order is over and above what
we have already ordered* この注文は
これまでの注文への追加です konṓ chū-
mon wa korḗ madè no chūmon e no
tsuíka desù

4 (during) ...の間 ...no aída

over the last few years 過去数年の間
kákò sūnèn no aída

over the winter 冬の間 fuyú nò aída

let's discuss it over dinner 夕食をし
ながら話し合いましょう yūshoku wò
shinágàra hanáshiaimashō

---

overall [*adj, n* ou've:ro:l *adv* ouve:ro:l']
adj (length, cost etc) 全体の zentai no;
(general: study, survey) 全面的な zenmen-
teki na

♦*adv* (view, survey etc) 全面的に zenmen-
teki ni; (measure, paint) 全体に zentai ni

♦*n* (BRIT: woman's, child's, painter's)
上っ張り uwáppari

overalls [ou've:ro:lz] *npl* オーバーオール
ōbāōrù

overawe [ouve:ro:'] *vt* 威圧する iátsu suru

overbalance [ouve:rbæl'əns] *vi* バラン
スを失う baránsu wo ushínau

overbearing [ouve:rber'iŋ] *adj* (person,
behavior, manner) 横暴な ōbō na

overboard [ou've:rbo:rd] *adv* (NAUT):
to fall overboard 船から水に落ちる fu-
nè kara mizú ni ochírù

overbook [ou've:rbuk] *vt* 予約を取り過
ぎる yoyáku wo torísugiru

overcast [ou've:rkæst] *adj* (day, sky) 曇
った kumóttà

overcharge [ou've:rtʃɑ:rdʒ] *vt* ...に不当
な金額を請求する ...ni futō na kingaku
wo seíkyū suru

overcoat [ou've:rkout] *n* オーバーコー
ト ōbākōto, オーバー ōbā

overcome [ouve:rkʌm'] (*pt* **overcame** *pp*
overcome) *vt* (defeat: opponent, enemy)
...に勝つ ...ni katsù; (*fig*: difficulty, problem) 克服する kokúfuku suru

overcrowded [ouve:rkrau'did] *adj*
(room, prison) 超満員の chōman-in no;
(city) 過密な kamítsu na

overdo [ouve:rdu:'] (*pt* **overdid** *pp* **over-
done**) *vt* (exaggerate: concern, interest)
誇張する kochō suru; (overcook) 焼き過
ぎる yakísugiru

to overdo it (work etc) やり過ぎる yarí-
sugirù

overdose [ou've:rdous] *n* (MED: dangerous dose) 危険量 kikénryō; (: fatal dose)
致死量 chíshìryō

overdraft [ou've:rdræft] *n* 当座借越 tō-
zakarikoshi

overdrawn [ouve:rdrɔ:n'] *adj* (account)
借越した karíkoshi shita

overdue [ouve:rdu:'] *adj* (late: person,
bus, train) 遅れている okúrete iru;
(change, reform etc) 待望の taíbō no

overestimate [ouve:res'təmeit] *vt* (cost,
importance, time) 高く見積りすぎる ta-
kàku mitsúmorisugirù; (person's ability,
skill etc) 買いかぶる kaíkaburu

overexcited [ouve:riksai'tid] *adj* 過度に
興奮した kadò ni kōfun shita

overflow [*vb* ouve:rflou' *n* ou've:rflou]
vi (river) はん濫する hanran suru; (sink,
vase etc) あふれる afúreru

♦*n* (also: **overflow pipe**) 放出パイプ hō-
shutsupaipu

overgrown [ouve:rgroun'] *adj* (garden)
草がぼうぼうと生えた kusa ga bṓbō to
haèta

overhaul [*vb* ouve:rhɔ:l' *n* ou've:rhɔ:l]
vt (engine, equipment etc) 分解検査する
bunkaikensa suru, オーバーホールする
ōbāhōru suru

♦*n* オーバーホール ōbāhōru

overhead [*adv* ouve:rhed' *adj, n*

ou'və:rhed] adv (above) 頭上に〔で〕zujő ni(de); (in the sky) 上空に〔で〕jőkű ni 〔de〕
♦adj (lighting) 上からの ué kara no; (cables, railway) 高架の kőkà no
♦n (US) = **overheads**

overheads [ou'və:rhedz] npl (expenses) 経費 keíhi

overhear [ouvə:rhiə:r'] (pt, pp **overheard**) vt 耳にする mimí ni suru

overheat [ouvə:rhi:t'] vi (engine) 過熱する kanétsu suru, オーバーヒートする ő-bàhíto suru

overjoyed [ouvə:rdʒɔid'] adj 大喜びした őyőrokobi shita

overkill [ou'və:rkil] n やり過ぎ yarísugi

overland [ou'və:rlænd] adj (journey) 陸路の rikúro no
♦adv (travel) 陸路で rikúro de

overlap [ouvə:rlæp'] vi (edges) 部分的に重なる bubúnteki ni kasánaru, オーバーラップする őbàrappu suru; (fig: ideas, activities etc) 部分的に重複する bubúnteki ni chőfuku suru, オーバーラップする őbàrappu suru

overleaf [ou'və:rli:f] adv ページの裏に péji no urá ni

overload [ou'və:rloud] vt (vehicle) ...に積み過ぎる ...ni tsumísugiru; (ELEC) ...に負荷を掛け過ぎる ...ni fuká wo kakésugiru; (fig: with work, problems etc) ...に負担を掛け過ぎる ...ni fután wo kakésugiru

overlook [ou'və:rluk] vt (have view over) 見下ろす míorosu; (miss: by mistake) 見落とす miőtosu; (excuse, forgive) 見逃す minőgasu

overnight [adv ouvə:rnait' adj ou'və:rnait] adv (during the whole night) 一晩中 hitóbànjū; (fig: suddenly) いつの間にか itsú no ma ni ka
♦adj (bag, clothes) 1泊用の ippákuyō no
to stay overnight 一泊する ippáku suru

overpass [ou'və:rpæs] n 陸橋 ríkkyō

overpower [ouvə:rpau'ə:r] vt (person) 腕力で抑え込む wañryoku de osáekomù; (subj: emotion, anger etc) 圧倒する attő

overpowering [ouvə:rpau'ə:riŋ] adj (heat, stench) 圧倒する様な attő suru yő na

overrate [ouvə:rreit'] vt (person, film, book) 高く評価し過ぎる takáku hyőka shisúgiru

override [ouvə:rraid'] (pt **overrode** pp **overridden**) vt (order) 無効にする mukő ni suru; (objection) 無視する mushí suru

overriding [ouvə:rraid'iŋ] adj (importance) 最大の saídai no; (factor, consideration) 優先的な yűsénteki na

overrule [ouvə:rru:l'] vt (decision, claim, person) 無効にする mukő ni suru; (person) ...の提案を退ける ...no teían wo shirízokerù

overrun [ou'və:rʌn] (pt **overran** pp **overrun**) vt (country) 侵略する shifiryaku suru; (time limit) 越える koéru

overseas [adv ouvə:rsi:z' adj ou'və:rsi:z] adv (live, travel, work: abroad) 海外に〔で〕kaígai ni(de)
♦adj (market, trade) 海外の kaígai no; (student, visitor) 外国人の gaíkokujìn no

overshadow [ouvə:rʃæd'ou] vt (throw shadow over: place, building etc) ...の上に覆える ...no ué ni sobíerù; (fig) ...の影を薄くさせる ...no kagé wo usúku saseru

overshoot [ouvə:rʃu:t'] (pt, pp **overshot**) vt (subj: plane, train, car etc) ...に行き過ぎる ...ni tomárazu ni ikísugirù

oversight [ou'və:rsait] n 手落ち teőchi

oversleep [ouvə:rsli:p'] (pt, pp **overslept**) vi 寝過ごす nesúgosu, 寝坊する nebő suru

overstate [ouvə:rsteit'] vt (exaggerate: case, problem, importance) 誇張する kochő suru

overstep [ouvə:rstep'] vt: **to overstep the mark** (go too far) 行き過ぎをやる ikísugi wo yaru

overt [ouvə:rt'] adj あからさまな akárasama na

overtake [ouvə:rteik'] (pt **overtook** pp **overtaken**) vt (AUT) 追越す oíkosu

overthrow [ouvə:rθrou'] vt (government, leader) 倒す taósù

overtime [ou'vəːrtaim] *n* 残業 zañgyō

overtone [ou'vəːrtoun] *n* (fig) 含み fukúmì

overture [ou'vəːrtʃəːr] *n* (MUS) 序曲 jokyōku; (fig) 申出 mōshide

overturn [ouvəːrtəːrn'] *vt* (car, chair) 引っ繰り返す hikkúrikaèsu; (fig: decision, plan, ruling) 翻す hirúgaèsu; (: government, system) 倒す taósù
♦*vi* (car, train, boat etc) 転覆する teñpuku suru

overweight [ouvəːrweit'] *adj* (person) 太り過ぎの futórìsugi no

overwhelm [ouvəːrwelm'] *vt* 圧倒する attō suru

overwhelming [ouvəːrwel'miŋ] *adj* (victory, heat, feeling) 圧倒的な attōteki na

overwork [ouvəːrwəːrk'] *n* 働き過ぎ határakisugì, 過労 karō

overwrought [ou'vərɔːt'] *adj* 神経が高ぶった shiñkei ga tákabuttà

owe [ou] *vt*: *to owe someone something, to owe something to someone* (money) ...に...を借りている ...ni ...wo karíte iru, ...に...を払う義務がある ...ni ...wo haráù gimù ga aru; (fig: gratitude, respect, loyalty) ...に...しなければならない ...ni ...shinákereba naranaì; (: life, talent, good looks etc) ...は...のおかげである ...wa ...no o-káge de aru

owing to [ou'iŋ tuː] *prep* (because of) ...のために ...no tamé nì

owl [aul] *n* フクロウ fukúrō, ミミズク mimízuku

own [oun] *vt* (possess: house, land, car etc) 所有する shoyū suru, 保有する hoyū suru
♦*adj* (house, work, style etc) 自分の jibún no, 自分自身の jubúnjishìn no
a room of my own 自分の部屋 jibún no heyá
to get one's own back (take revenge) 復しゅうする fukushū suru
on one's own (alone) 自分で jibun de, 自分の力で jibún no chikára de

owner [ou'nəːr] *n* (gen) 所有者 shoyūsha, 持主 móchìnushi, オーナー ōnā; (of shop)

主人 shujìn, 経営者 kéieìsha; (of pet) 飼主 kaínushi

ownership [ou'nəːrʃip] *n* (possession) 所有 shoyū

own up *vi* (admit: guilt, error) ...を認める ...wo mitómeru

ox [ɑːks] (*pl* **oxen**) *n* ウシ ushí ◇通常去勢した牡ウシを指す tsūjō kyoséi shita oùshi wo sasu

oxtail [ɑːks'teil] *n*: *oxtail soup* オックステールスープ okkùsutērusūpu

oxygen [ɑːk'sidʒən] *n* 酸素 sañso

oxygen mask/tent *n* 酸素マスク〔テント〕sañsomasuku(tento)

oyster [ɔis'təːr] *n* カキ kaki

oz. *abbr* = **ounce(s)**

ozone [ou'zoun] *n* オゾン ozòn

ozone layer *n* オゾン層 ozònsō

P

p [piː] *abbr* = **penny; pence**

P.A. [piːei'] *n abbr* = **personal assistant; public address system**

p.a. *abbr* = **per annum**

pa [pɑː] (*inf*) *n* 父ちゃん tōchan, パパ pápà

pace [peis] *n* (step) 1歩 íppò; (distance) 歩幅 hohába; (speed) 早さ háyàsa, 速度 sókùdo, ペース pḕsu
♦*vi*: *to pace up and down* (walk around angrily or impatiently) うろうろする úròuro suru
to keep pace with (person) ...と足並をそろえる ...to ashínami wò soróerù

pacemaker [peis'meikəːr] *n* (MED) ペースメーカー pḕsumēkà; (SPORT: *also*: **pacesetter**) ペースメーカー pḕsumēkā

Pacific [pəsif'ik] *n*: *the Pacific (Ocean)* 太平洋 taíheìyō

pacifist [pæs'əfist] *n* 平和主義者 heíwashugìsha

pacify [pæs'əfai] *vt* (soothe: person) なだめる nadámerù; (: fears) 鎮める shizúmerù

pack [pæk] *n* (packet) 包み tsutsúmi; (US: of **cigarettes**) 1箱 hitóhàko; (group:

of hounds) 群れ muré; (: of people) グループ gúrūpu; (back pack) リュックサック ryukkúsakkù; (of cards) 1組 hitókùmi

♦vt (fill: box, container, suitcase etc) ...に詰込む ...ni tsumékomù; (cram: people, objects): *to pack into* ...を...に詰込む ...wo ...ni tsumékomù

to pack (one's bags) 荷造りをする nizúkùri wo suru

to pack someone off ...を追出す ...wo oídasù

pack it in! (*inf*: stop it!) やめなさい! yaménasaì!

package [pæk'idʒ] n (parcel) 小包 kozútsumi; (*also*: **package deal**) 一括取引 ikkátsutorihìki

package holiday n = **package tour**

package tour n パッケージツアー pakkéjitsuà, パックツアー pakkútsuà

packed lunch [pækt-] n 弁当 beńtō

packet [pæk'it] n (box) 1箱 hitóhàko; (bag) 1袋 hitófùkuro

packing [pæk'iŋ] n (act) 詰込み事 tsumékomù kotó; (external: paper, plastic etc) 包装 hósō

packing case n 木箱 kíbàko

pact [pækt] n 協定 kyótei

pad [pæd] n (block of paper) 一つづり hitótsuzuri; (to prevent friction, damage) こん包材 końpōzài; (in shoulders of dress, jacket etc) パッド páddò; (*inf*: home) 住い súmài

♦vt (SEWING: cushion, soft toy etc) ...に詰物をする ...ni tsumémòno wo suru

padding [pæd'iŋ] n (material) 詰物 tsumémòno

paddle [pæd'əl] n (oar) かい kaí, パドル páddòru; (US: for table tennis) ラケット rakéttò

♦vt (boat, canoe etc) こぐ kógù

♦vi (with feet) 水の中を歩く mizú no nakà wo arúkù

paddle steamer n (on river) 外輪船 gaírinsen

paddling pool [pæd'liŋ-] (BRIT) n (children's) 子供用プール kodómoyō pùru

paddock [pæd'ək] n (for horse: small field) 放牧場 hóbokujò; (: at race course)

パドック pádòkku

paddy field [pæd'i:-] n 水田 suíden, 田んぼ tañbo

padlock [pæd'lɑ:k] n (on door, bicycle etc) 錠 (前) jó(mae)

paediatrics [pi:di:æt'riks] (BRIT) n = **pediatrics**

pagan [pei'gən] adj (gods, festival, worship) 異教の ikyó no ◊キリスト教, ユダヤ教, イスラム教以外の宗教をさげすんで言う語 kirísutokyō, yudáyakyō, isúramukyō igai no shúkyò wo sagésuñde iú go

♦n (worshipper of pagan gods) 異教徒 ikyóto

page [peidʒ] n (of book, magazine, newspaper) ページ péji; (*also*: **page boy**) 花嫁付添いの少年 hanáyòmetsukisoi no shónen

♦vt (in hotel etc) ボーイ bôi

pageant [pædʒ'ənt] n (historical procession, show) ページェント péjento

pageantry [pædʒ'əntri:] n 見世物 misémono

paid [peid] pt, pp of **pay**

♦adj (work) 有料の yúryō no; (staff, official) 有給の yúkyū no; (gunman, killer) 雇われた yatówaretà

a paid holiday 有給休暇 yúkyūkyūka

to put paid to (BRIT: end, destroy) ...を台無しにする ...wo daínashi ni surù

pail [peil] n (for milk, water etc) バケツ bakétsu

pain [pein] n (unpleasant physical sensation) 痛み itámi, 苦痛 kutsú; (*fig*: unhappiness) 苦しみ kurúshimi, 心痛 shińtsū

to be in pain (person, animal) 苦痛を感じている kutsú wò kañjite irù, 苦しんでいる kurúshinde irù

to take pains to do something (make an effort) 苦心して...する kushín shite ...surù

pained [peind] adj (expression) 怒った okóttà

painful [pein'fəl] adj (back, wound, fracture etc) 痛い itái, 痛む itámù; (upsetting, unpleasant: sight etc) 痛々しい itáitashii; (memory) 不快な fukái na; (decision) 苦しい kurúshiî; (laborious: task, progress etc) 骨の折れる honé no orerù

painfully [pein'fəli] *adv* (*fig*: very) 痛い程 itáihodo

painkiller [pein'kilər] *n* (aspirin, paracetamol etc) 鎮痛剤 chíntsūzai

painless [pein'lis] *adj* (operation, childbirth) 無痛の mutsū no

painstaking [peinz'teikiŋ] *adj* (work) 骨折れの honёore no; (person) 勤勉な kínben na

paint [peint] *n* (decorator's: for walls, doors etc) 塗料 toryō, ペンキ peńki, ペイント peńto; (artist's: oil paint, watercolor paint etc) 絵の具 e nó gu

♦*vt* (wall, door, house etc) ...にペンキを塗る ...ni peńki wo nurù; (picture, portrait) 描く kákù

to paint the door blue ドアに水色のペンキを塗る dóa ni mizúiro nò peńki wò nurù

paintbrush [peint'brʌʃ] *n* (decorator's) 刷毛 haké, ブラシ búrashi; (artist's) 絵筆 éfùde

painter [pein'tər] *n* (artist) 画家 gaká; (decorator) ペンキ屋 peńkiya

painting [pein'tiŋ] *n* (activity: decorating) ペンキ塗り peńkinùri; (: art) 絵描き ekáki; (picture) 絵画 kãĩga

an oil painting 油絵 abúraè

paintwork [peint'wəːrk] *n* (painted parts) 塗装の部分 tosō no bubùn

pair [peːr] *n* (of shoes, gloves etc) 対 tsuí

a pair of scissors はさみ hasámi

a pair of trousers ズボン zubón

pajamas [pədʒɑːm'əz] (*US*) *npl* パジャマ pájàma

Pakistan [pæk'istæn] *n* パキスタン pakísùtan

Pakistani [pæk'əstæni:] *adj* パキスタンの pakísùtan no

♦*n* パキスタン人 pakísutanjìn

pal [pæl] (*inf*) *n* (friend) 友達 tomódachi

palace [pæl'is] *n* (residence: of monarch) 宮殿 kyúden; (: of president etc) 官邸 kań tei; (: of Japanese emperor) 皇居 kõkyo, 御所 gósho

palatable [pæl'ətəbəl] *adj* (food, drink)

おいしい oíshiî

palate [pæl'it] *n* 口がい kõgai

palatial [pəlei'ʃəl] *adj* (surroundings, residence) 豪華な gõka na

palaver [pəlæv'əːr] *n* (*US*) 話し合い hanáshiai; (*BRIT*: *inf*: fuss) 大騒ぎ ōsawàgi

pale [peil] *adj* (whitish: color) 白っぽい shiróppoî; (: face) 青白い aőjiroî, 青ざめた aőzametà; (: light) 薄暗い usúguraî

♦*n: beyond the pale* (unacceptable) 容認できない yőnin dekinài

Palestine [pæl'istain] *n* パレスチナ parésùchina

Palestinian [pælistin'i:ən] *adj* パレスチナの parésùchina no

♦*n* パレスチナ人 parésuchinajìn

palette [pæl'it] *n* (ART: paint mixing board) パレット parёttð

palings [pei'liŋz] *npl* (fence) さく sakú

pall [pɔːl] *n: a pall of smoke* 一面の煙 ichímen no kemuri

♦*vi* ...が詰まらなくなる ...ga tsumáranakù naru, ...に飽きる ...ni akírù

pallet [pæl'it] *n* (for goods) パレット parёttð

pallid [pæl'id] *adj* (person, complexion) 青白い aőjiroî

pallor [pæl'əːr] *n* そう白 sõhaku

palm [pɑːm] *n* (*also*: **palm tree**) ヤシ yáshî; (of hand) 手のひら tenőhìra

♦*vt: to palm something off on someone* (*inf*) ...に...をつかませる ...ni ...wo tsukámaserù

Palm Sunday *n* 枝の主日 edá nð shujítsu

palpable [pæl'pəbəl] *adj* (obvious: lie, difference etc) 明白な meíhaku na

palpitations [pælpitei'ʃənz] *npl* (MED) 動き iki

paltry [pɔːl'tri:] *adj* (amount: tiny, insignificant) ささいな sásài na

pamper [pæm'pəːr] *vt* (cosset: person, animal) 甘やかす amáyakasù

pamphlet [pæm'flit] *n* (political, literary etc) 小冊子 shōsasshì, パンフレット páñfuretto

pan [pæn] *n* (CULIN: *also*: **saucepan**) 片

手なべ katátenabè; (: also: **frying pan**) フライパン furáipan

panacea [pænəsiː'ə] n 万能薬 bañnōyàku

panache [pənæʃ'] n 気取り kidóri

Panama [pæn'əmɑː] n パナマ pánama

Panama Canal n: the Panama Canal パナマ運河 panáma uñga

pancake [pæn'keik] n パンケーキ pañkèki, ホットケーキ hottókèki

pancreas [pæn'kriːəs] n すい臓 suízō

panda [pæn'də] n (ZOOL) ジャイアントパンダ jaíantopañda

panda car (BRIT) n (police car) パトカー patókā

pandemonium [pændəmou'niːəm] n (noisy confusion) 大混乱 daíkoñran

pander [pæn'dəːr] vi: **to pander to** (person, whim, desire etc) ...に迎合する ...ni geígō suru

pane [pein] n (of glass) 窓ガラス madógarāsu

panel [pæn'əl] n (oblong piece: of wood, metal, glass etc) 羽目板 haméita, パネル páneru; (group of judges, experts etc) ...の一団 ...no ichídan, パネル páneru

paneling [pæn'əliŋ] (BRIT **panelling**) n 羽目板 haméita ◇総称 sōshō

pang [pæŋ] n: a **pang of regret** 悔恨の情 kaíkon nò jō

hunger pangs (physical pain) 激しい空腹感 hagéshiī kūfukukan

panic [pæn'ik] n (uncontrollable terror, anxiety) パニック pánìkku

◆vi (person) うろたえる urótaerù; (crowd) パニック状態になる paníkkujōtai ni nárù

panicky [pæn'ikiː] adj (person) うろたえる urótaerù

panic-stricken [pæn'ikstrikən] adj (person, face) パニックに陥った pánìkku ni ochíttà

panorama [pænəræm'ə] n (view) 全景 zeñkei, パノラマ panórama

pansy [pæn'ziː] n (BOT) サンシキスミレ sañshikisumìre, パンジー páñjī; (inf: pej) 弱虫 yowámùshi

pant [pænt] vi (gasp: person, animal) あえぐ aégù

panther [pæn'θəːr] n ヒョウ hyō

panties [pæn'tiːz] npl パンティー páñtī

pantomime [pæn'təmaim] (BRIT) n クリスマスミュージカル kurísumasu myūjikaru

pantry [pæn'triː] n 食料室 shokúryōshìtsu, パントリー páñtorī

pants [pænts] n (BRIT: underwear: woman's) パンティー páñtī; (: man's) パンツ páñtsu; (US: trousers) ズボン zubón

panty hose n パンティーストッキング pañtīsutokkìñgu

papal [pei'pəl] adj ローマ法王の rōmahō̄ō no

paper [pei'pəːr] n (gen) 紙 kamí; (also: **newspaper**) 新聞 shiñbun; (exam) 試験 shikén; (academic essay) 論文 roñbun, ペーパー pēpā; (also: **wallpaper**) 壁紙 kabégami

◆adj (made from paper: hat, plane etc) 紙の kamí no

◆vt (room: with wallpaper) ...に壁紙を張る ...ni kabégami wò hárù

paperback [pei'pəːrbæk] n ペーパーバック pépābakku

paper bag n 紙袋 kamíbukùro

paper clip n クリップ kuríppù

paper hankie n ティッシュ tísshù

papers [pei'pəːrz] npl (documents) 書類 shórùi; (also: **identity papers**) 身分証明書 mibúnshōmeishò

paperweight [pei'pəːrweit] n 文鎮 buñchin

paperwork [pei'pəːrwəːrk] n (in office: dealing with letters, reports etc) 机上の事務 kijō no jìmu, ペーパーワーク pēpāwāku

papier-mâché [pei'pəːrməʃei'] n 張り子 haríko

paprika [pɑːpriː'kə] n パプリカ papúrìka

par [pɑːr] n (equality of value) 同等 dōtō; (GOLF) 基準打数 kijúndasù, パー pā

to be on a par with (be equal with) ...と同等である ...to dōtō de arù

parable [pær'əbəl] n たとえ話 tatóebanàshi

parachute [pær'əʃuːt] n 落下傘 rakkásàn, パラシュート paráshūto

parade [pəreid'] n (public procession) パ
レード parêdò

♦vt (show off: wealth, knowledge etc) 見
せびらかす misébirakasù

♦vi (MIL) 行進する kốshin suru

paradise [pær'ədais] n (REL: heaven,
nirvana etc: also fig) 天国 têṅgoku, 極楽
gokúraku

paradox [pær'ədɑ:ks] n (thing, statement) 逆説 gyakúsetsu

paradoxically [pærədɑ:k'sikli:] adv 逆
説的に言えば gyakúsetsuteki nì iébà

paraffin [pær'əfin] (BRIT) n (also: paraffin oil) 灯油 tốyu

paragon [pær'əgɑ:n] n (of honesty, virtue etc) 模範 móhan, かがみ kagámi

paragraph [pær'əgræf] n 段落 dañraku,
パラグラフ parágùrafu

Paraguay [pær'əgwei] n パラグアイ pa-
rágùai

parallel [pær'əlel] adj (lines, walls,
streets etc) 平行の heíkō no; (fig: similar) 似た nitá

♦n (line) 平行線 heíkōsen; (surface) 平行
面 heíkōmen; (GEO) 緯度線 ídòsèn; (fig:
similarity) 似た所 nitá tokoro

paralysis [pəræl'isis] n (MED) 麻ひ máhì

paralyze [pær'əlaiz] vt (MED) 麻ひさせ
る máhì saséru; (fig: organization, production etc) 麻ひ状態にする mahíjōtai ni
suru

parameters [pəræm'itə:rz] npl (fig) 限
定要素 geñteiyóso

paramilitary [pærəmil'ite:ri:] adj (organization, operations) 準軍事的な juñguñ-
jiteki na

paramount [pær'əmaunt] adj: of paramount importance 極めて重要な kiwámète júyō na

paranoia [pærənɔi'ə] n 被害妄想 higái-
mồsò

paranoid [pær'ənɔid] adj (person, feeling) 被害妄想の higáimồsồ no

parapet [pær'əpit] n 欄干 rañkan

paraphernalia [pærəfəːrneil'jə] n (gear)
道具 dồgu

paraphrase [pær'əfreiz] vt (poem, arti-

cle etc) やさしく言替える yasáshikù iíkaerù

paraplegic [pærəpli:'dʒik] n 下半身麻ひ
患者 kahánshinmahi kañja

parasite [pær'əsait] n (insect: also fig:
person) 寄生虫 kiséichū; (plant) 寄生植物
kiséishokùbutsu

parasol [pær'əsɔ:l] n 日傘 higasa, パラソ
ル páràsoru

paratrooper [pær'ətru:pə:r] n (MIL) 落
下傘兵 rakkásanhei

parcel [pɑ:r'səl] n (package) 小包 kozútsumi

♦vt (object, purchases: also: parcel up)
小包にする kozútsùmi ni suru

parch [pɑ:rtʃ] vt (land) 干上がらす hiága-
rasu; (crops) からからに枯らす karákara
ni karasù

parched [pɑ:rtʃt] adj (person) のどがから
からの nódò ga karákara no

parchment [pɑ:rtʃ'mənt] n (animal skin)
羊皮紙 yốhishì; (thick paper) 硫酸紙 ryū-
sanshì

pardon [pɑ:r'dən] n (LAW) 赦免 shamén

♦vt (forgive: person, sin, error etc) 許す
yurúsù

pardon me!, I beg your pardon! (I'm
sorry) 済みません sumímasen, 失礼しま
した shitsúreì shimashita, ご免なさい
gomén nasaì

(I beg your) pardon?, pardon me?
(what did you say?) もう一度言って下さ
い mố ichido ittè kudásaì

parent [pe:r'ənt] n (mother or father) 親
oyá; (mother) 母親 haháoya; (father) 父
親 chichíoya

parental [pəren'təl] adj (love, control,
guidance etc) 親の oyá no

parenthesis [pəren'θəsis] (pl parentheses) n 括弧 kákkò

parents [pe:r'ənts] npl (mother and
father) 両親 ryốshin

Paris [pær'is] n パリ párì

parish [pær'iʃ] n (REL) 教区 kyốkù;
(BRIT: civil) 行政教区 gyốseikyòku

Parisian [pəriʒ'ən] adj パリの párì no

♦n パリっ子 paríkkò

parity [pær'iti:] n (equality: of pay, conditions etc) 平等 byōdō

park [pɑːrk] n (public) 公園 kōen
♦vt (AUT) 駐車させる chūsha saséru
♦vi (AUT) 駐車する chūsha suru

parka [pɑːrˈkə] n パーカ pákà, アノラック anórakkū

parking [pɑːrˈkiŋ] n 駐車 chūsha
「**no parking**」駐車禁止 chūshakinshi

parking lot (US) n 駐車場 chūshajō

parking meter n パーキングメーター pákingumētā

parking ticket n (fine) 駐車違反切符 chūshaihan kippū

parlance [pɑːrˈləns] n 用語 yṓgo

parliament [pɑːrˈləmənt] (BRIT) n (institution) 議会 gíkai

parliamentary [pɑːrləmənˈtɑːriː] adj (business, behavior etc) 議会の gíkai no

parlor [pɑːrˈlər] (BRIT **parlour**) n (in house) 居間 imá, 応接間 ōsetsuma

parochial [pərouˈkiːəl] (pej) adj (person, attitude) 偏狭な heńkyō na

parody [pærˈədiː] n (THEATER, LITERATURE, MUS) パロディー páròdī

parole [pəroulˈ] n: **on parole** (LAW) 仮釈放で karíshakuhō de

paroxysm [pærˈəksizəm] n (of rage, jealousy, laughter) 爆発 bakúhatsu

parquet [pɑːrkeiˈ] n: **parquet floor(ing)** 寄せ木張りの床 yoségibari nò yuká

parrot [pærˈət] n オウム ṓmu

parry [pærˈiː] vt (blow) かわす kawásu

parsimonious [pɑːrsəmouˈniːəs] adj けちな kechí na

parsley [pɑːrzˈliː] n パセリ pásèri

parsnip [pɑːrsˈnip] n 白にんじん shironinjin, パースニップ pāsunippū

parson [pɑːrˈsən] n (REL) 牧師 bókùshi

part [pɑːrt] n (section, division) 部分 búbun; (of machine, vehicle) 部品 buhín; (THEATER, CINEMA etc: role) 役 yakú; (PRESS, RADIO, TV: of serial) 第...回 dái...bù; (US: in hair) 分け目 wakéme
♦adv = **partly**
♦vt (separate: people, objects, hair) 分ける wakérù

♦vi (people: leave each other) 別れる wákarerù; (crowd) 道を開ける michí wo akerù
to take part in (participate in) ...に参加する ...ni sańka suru
to take something in good part ...を怒らない ...wo okóranaì
to take someone's part (support) ...の肩を持つ ...no kátà wo mótsù
for my part 私としては watákushi toshite wà
for the most part (usually, generally) ほとんど hotóndo wa

part exchange n: **in part exchange** (BRIT: COMM) 下取りで shitádòri de

partial [pɑːrˈʃəl] adj (not complete: victory, support, solution) 部分的な bubúnteki na
to be partial to (like: person, food, drink etc) ...が大好きである ...ga daísuki de arù

participant [pɑːrtisˈəpənt] n (in competition, debate, campaign etc) 参加者 sańkashà

participate [pɑːrtisˈəpeit] vi: **to participate in** (competition, debate, campaign etc) ...に参加する ...ni sańka suru

participation [pɑːrtisəpeiˈʃən] n (in competition, debate, campaign etc) 参加 sańka

participle [pɑːrˈtisipəl] n (LING) 分詞 búnshi

particle [pɑːrˈtikəl] n (tiny piece: gen) 粒子 ryūshi; (: of dust) 一片 ippéñ; (of metal) 砕片 saíhen; (of food) 粒 tsúbù

particular [pərtikˈjələr] adj (distinct from others: person, time, place etc) 特定の tokútei no; (special) 特別な tokúbetsu na; (fussy, demanding) やかましい yakámashiì
in particular 特に tókù ni

particularly [pərtikˈjələːrliː] adv 特に tókù ni

particulars [pərtikˈjələːrz] npl (facts) 詳細 shōsai; (personal details) 経歴 keíreki

parting [pɑːrˈtiŋ] n (action) 分ける事 wakérù kotó; (farewell) 別れ wakáre;

(BRIT: hair) 分け目 wakéme

♦adj (words, gift etc) 別れの wakáre no

partisan [pɑːr'tizən] adj (politics, views) 党派心の tōhashìn no

♦n (supporter) 支援者 shiéñsha; (fighter) パルチザン parúchizañ

partition [pɑːrtiʃ'ən] n (wall, screen) 間仕切 majíkìri; (POL: of country) 分割 buñkatsu

partly [pɑːrt'liː] adv (to some extent) 幾分か ikúbun ka

partner [pɑːrt'nəːr] n (wife, husband) 配偶者 haígùsha; (girlfriend, boyfriend) 交際の相手 kōsai nò aíte; (COMM) 共同経営者 kyōdōkeieìsha; (SPORT) パートナー pātònā; (at dance) 相手 aíte

partnership [pɑːrt'nəːrʃip] n (COMM) 共同経営事業 kyōdōkeieijigyō; (POL etc) 協力 kyōryoku

partridge [pɑːr'tridʒ] n ウズラ uzúra

part-time [pɑːrt'taim] adj (work, staff) 非常勤の hijōkin no, パートタイムの pátotaìmu no

♦adv (work, study) パートタイムで pátotaìmu de

part with vt fus (money, possessions) ...を手放す ...wo tebánasù

party [pɑːr'tiː] n (POL) 政党 seítō; (celebration, social event) パーティ pàti; (group of people) 一行 ikkō, パーティ pàti; (LAW) 当事者 tōjishà; (individual) 人 hitó

♦cpd (POL) 党の tō no

party dress n パーティドレス pátidòresu

party line n (TEL) 共同線 kyōdōsen

pass [pæs] vt (spend: time) 過ごす sugósù; (hand over: salt, glass, newspaper etc) 渡す watásù; (go past: place) 通り過ぎる tōrisugírù; (overtake: car, person etc) 追越す oíkosù; (exam) ...に合格する ...ni gōkaku suru; (approve: law, proposal) 可決する kakétsu suru

♦vi (go past) 通る tōrù; (in exam) 合格する gōkaku suru, パスする pásù suru

♦n (permit) 許可証 kyokáshō; (membership card) 会員証 kaíinshō; (in mountains) 峠 tōge; (SPORT) パス pásù;

(SCOL: also: pass mark): to get a pass in ...に及第する ...de kyūdai suru, ...でパスする ...de pásù suru

to pass something through something ...を...に通す ...wo ...ni tōsu

to make a pass at someone (inf) ...にモーションを掛ける ...ni mōshon wo kakérù

passable [pæs'əbəl] adj (road) 通行できる tsūkō dekirù; (acceptable: work) まずまずの mázùmazu no

passage [pæs'idʒ] n (also: **passageway**: indoors) 廊下 rōka; (: outdoors) 通路 tsūro; (in book) 一節 issétsu; (ANAT): the nasal passages 鼻こう bikō; (act of passing) 通過 tsūka; (journey: on boat) 船旅 funátabi

pass away vi (die) 死ぬ shinú

passbook [pæs'buk] n 銀行通帳 giñkōtsūchō

pass by vi (go past) ...のそばを通る ...no sóbà wo tōrù

♦vt (ignore) 無視する múshì suru

passenger [pæs'indʒəːr] n (in car, boat, plane etc) 乗客 jōkyaku

passer-by [pæsəːrbai'] n 通行人 tsūkōnin

pass for vt fus ...で通る ...de tōrù

passing [pæs'iŋ] adj (fleeting: moment, glimpse, thought etc) 束の間の tsúká no ma no

in passing (incidentally) ついでに tsuíde ni

passing place n (AUT) 待避所 taíhijò

passion [pæʃ'ən] n (love: for person) 情欲 jōyoku; (fig: for cars, football, politics etc) 熱狂 nekkyō, マニア mánìa

passionate [pæʃ'ənit] adj (affair, embrace, person etc) 情熱的な jōnetsuteki na

passive [pæs'iv] adj (person, resistance) 消極的な shōkyokuteki na; (LING) 受動態の judōtai no, 受け身の ukémi no

pass on vt (news, object) 伝える tsutáerù; (illness) 移す utsúsù

pass out vi (faint) 気絶する kizétsu suru

Passover [pæs'ouvəːr] n 過越し祭 sugíkòshisai

passport [pæs'pɔːrt] n (official document) 旅券 ryokén, パスポート pasúpòto

passport control n 出入国管理所 shutsúnyūkoku kaǹrijo

pass up vt (opportunity) 逃す nogásù

password [pæs'wə:rd] n (secret word, phrase) 合言葉 aíkotòba, パスワード pasúwàdo

past [pæst] prep (drive, walk, run: in front of) ...を通り過ぎて ...wo tórisugite; (: beyond: also in time: later than) ...を過ぎて ...wo sugíte

♦adj (previous: government, monarch etc) 過去の kákò no; (: week, month etc) この前の konó maè no, 先...seń...

♦n (period and events prior to the present: also of person) 過去 kákò

he's past forty (older than) 彼は40才を過ぎている kárè wa yońjussaì wo sugíte irù

ten/quarter past eight 8時10分〔15分〕過ぎ hachíji juppùn〔jūgofun〕sugí

for the past few/3 days この数日〔3日〕の間 konó sūjitsu〔mikkà〕no aída

pasta [pɑ:s'tə] n パスタ pásùta

paste [peist] n (wet mixture) 練り物 nerímòno; (glue) のり norí; (CULIN: fish, meat, tomato etc paste) ペースト pèsuto

♦vt (stick: paper, label, poster etc) 張る harú

pastel [pæstel'] adj (color) パステルの pásùteru no

pasteurized [pæs'tʃə:raizd] adj (milk, cream) 低温殺菌された teíonsakkìn sareta

pastille [pæsti:l'] n (sweet) ドロップ dóròppu

pastime [pæs'taim] n (hobby) 趣味 shúmì

pastoral [pæs'tə:rəl] adj (REL: duties, activities) 牧師としての bókùshi toshite no

pastry [peis'tri:] n (dough) 生地 kíjì; (cake) 洋菓子 yōgashi, ケーキ kèki

pasture [pæs'tʃə:r] n (grassland) 牧場 bokújō

pasty [n pæs'ti: adj peis'ti:] n (meat and vegetable pie) ミートパイ mítopài

♦adj (complexion, face) 青ざめた aóza-

metà

pat [pæt] vt (with hand: dog, someone's back etc) 軽くたたく karúkù tatákù

patch [pætʃ] n (piece of material) 継ぎ tsugí; (also: **eye patch**) 眼帯 gaǹtai; (area: damp, bald, black etc) 一部 ichíbù; (repair: on tire etc) 継ぎはぎ tsugíhagi

♦vt (clothes) ...に継ぎを当てる ...ni tsugí wo aterú

to go through a bad patch 不運の時期に合う fúuǹ no jíkì ni áù

patch up vt (mend temporarily) 応急的に直す ōkyūteki ni naosù; (quarrel) ...をやめて仲直りする ...wo yamétè nakánaori surù

patchwork [pætʃ'wə:rk] n (SEWING) パッチワーク patchíwàku

patchy [pætʃ'i:] adj (uneven: color) むらの多い murá no òi; (incomplete: information, knowledge etc) 不完全な fukáǹzen na

pâté [pɑ:tei'] n パテ páte ◇肉, 魚などを香辛料とすり合せて蒸焼きにして冷ました物 nikú, sakana nadò wo kōshìnryō to suríawasetè mushíyaki ni shitè samáshita monò

patent [pæt'ənt] n (COMM) 特許 tókkyo

♦vt (COMM) ...の特許を取る ...no tókkyò wo tórù

♦adj (obvious) 明白な meíhaku na

patent leather n: **patent leather shoes** エナメル靴 enámerugùtsu

paternal [pətə:r'nəl] adj (love, duty) 父親の chichíoya no; (grandmother etc) 父方の chichígata no

paternity [pətə:r'niti:] n 父親である事 chichíoya de arù kotó

path [pæθ] n (trail, track) 小道 kómìchi; (concrete path, gravel path etc) 道 michí; (of planet, missile) 軌道 kidō

pathetic [pəθet'ik] adj (pitiful: sight, cries) 哀れな áware na; (very bad) 哀れな程悪い áware na hódò warui

pathological [pæθəlɑ:dʒ'ikəl] adj (liar, hatred) 病的な byóteki na; (of pathology: work) 病理の byóri no

pathology [pəθɑ:l'ədʒi:] n (medical field) 病理学 byórigàku

pathos [peɪˈθɑːs] *n* 悲哀 hiái

pathway [pæθˈweɪ] *n* (path) 歩道 hodō

patience [peɪˈʃəns] *n* (personal quality) 忍耐 níntai; (*BRIT*: CARDS) 一人トランプ hitóritoraṅpu

patient [peɪˈʃənt] *n* (MED) 患者 kañja
♦*adj* (person) 忍耐強い níntaizuyoì

patio [pætˈiːou] *n* テラス térasu

patriot [peɪˈtriːət] *n* 愛国者 aíkokushà

patriotic [peɪtriːɑːtˈik] *adj* (person) 愛国心の強い aíkokushìn no tsuyóì; (song, speech etc) 愛国の aíkoku no

patriotism [peɪˈtriːətizəm] *n* 愛国心 aíkokushìn

patrol [pətroulˈ] *n* (MIL, POLICE) 巡回 juṅkai, パトロール patórōru
♦*vt* (MIL, POLICE: city, streets etc) 巡回する juṅkai suru, パトロールする patórōru suru

patrol car *n* (POLICE) パトカー patókā

patrolman [pətroulˈmən] (*pl* **patrolmen**: *US*) *n* (POLICE) 巡査 júnsa

patron [peɪˈtrən] *n* (customer, client) 客 kyakú; (benefactor: of charity) 後援者 kóeñsha
patron of the arts 芸術のパトロン geíjutsu no pátoron

patronage [peɪˈtrənidʒ] *n* (of artist, charity etc) 後援 kóen

patronize [peɪˈtrənaiz] *vt* (*pej*: look down on) 尊大にあしらう sofidai nì ashíraù; (artist, writer, musician) 後援する kóen suru; (shop, club, firm) ひいきにする hiíki ni surù

patron saint *n* (REL) 守護聖人 shugóseijìn

patter [pætˈəːr] *n* (sound: of feet) ぱたぱたという音 pátàpata to iú oto; (of rain) パラパラという音 páràpara to iú otò; (sales talk) 売込み口上 uríkomikōjò
♦*vi* (footsteps) ぱたぱたと歩く pátàpata to arúkù; (rain) ぱらぱらと降る páràpara to fúrù

pattern [pætˈəːrn] *n* (design) 模様 moyó; (SEWING) 型紙 katágami, パターン patáñ

paunch [pɔːntʃ] *n* 太鼓腹 taíkobara

pauper [pɔːˈpəːr] *n* 貧乏人 bíñbōnin

pause [pɔːz] *n* (temporary halt) 休止 kyúshi, ポーズ pózu
♦*vi* (stop temporarily) 休止する kyúshi suru; (: while speaking) 間を置く má wò okú

pave [peiv] *vt* (street, yard etc) 舗装する hosō suru
to pave the way for (*fig*) ...を可能にする ...wo kanō ni suru

pavement [peivˈmənt] *n* (*US*) 路面 romén; (*BRIT*) 歩道 hodō

pavilion [pavilˈjən] *n* (*BRIT*: SPORT) 選手更衣所 seńshukōijò

paving [peivˈiŋ] *n* (material) 舗装材 hosōzài

paving stone *n* 敷石 shikíishi

paw [pɔː] *n* (of animal) 足 ashí

pawn [pɔːn] *n* (CHESS) ポーン póñ; (*fig*) 操り人形 ayátsuriniñgyo
♦*vt* 質に入れる shichí ni irerù

pawnbroker [pɔːnˈbroukəːr] *n* 質屋 shichíyà

pawnshop [pɔːnˈʃɑːp] *n* 質屋 shichíyà

pay [pei] *n* (wage, salary etc) 給料 kyúryo
♦*vb* (*pt*, *pp* **paid**)
♦*vt* (sum of money, debt, bill, wage) 払う haraú
♦*vi* (be profitable) 利益になる ríeki ni nárù
to pay attention (to) (...に) 注意する (...ni) chūi suru
to pay someone a visit ...を訪問する ...wo hómon suru
to pay one's respects to someone ...にあいさつをする ...ni aísatsu wo suru

payable [peiˈəbəl] *adj* (sum of money) 支払うべき shiháraubeki
payable to bearer (check) 持参人払いの jisánninbaraì no

pay back *vt* (money) 返す kaésù; (person) ...に仕返しをする ...ni shikáeshi wò suru

payday [peiˈdei] *n* 給料日 kyúryōbi

payee [peiiːˈ] *n* (of check, postal order) 受取人 ukétorinìn

pay envelope (*US*) *n* 給料袋 kyúryōbukùro

pay for vt fus (purchases) ...の代金を払う ...no daíkin wò haraú; (fig) 償う tsugunaù

pay in vt (money, check etc) 預け入れる azúkeirerù, 入金する nyúkin suru

payment [pei'mənt] n (act) 支払い shiháraì; (amount of money) 支払い金額 shiháraikingaku

a monthly payment 月賦 géppù

pay off vt (debt) 返済する heñsai suru; (person: with bribe etc) 買収する baíshū suru

♦vi (scheme, decision) 成功する seíkō suru

pay packet (BRIT) n = **pay envelope**

pay phone n 公衆電話 kōshūdeñwa

payroll [pei'roul] n 従業員名簿 júgyōinmeibo

pay slip n 給料明細書 kyúryōmeisaishò

pay up vt 払う haraú

PC [pi:si:'] n abbr = **personal computer**; (BRIT: = **police constable**) 巡査 júnsa

p.c. abbr = **per cent**

pea [pi:] n エンドウマメ eñdōmame

peace [pi:s] n (not war) 平和 heíwa; (calm: of place, surroundings) 静けさ shizúkesà; (: personal) 心の平和 kokórò no heíwa

peaceful [pi:s'fəl] adj (calm: place, time) 静寂な seíjaku na; (: person) 穏和な owa na

peach [pi:tʃ] n モモ momó

peacock [pi:'kɑːk] n クジャク kujáku

peak [pi:k] n (of mountain: top) 頂上 chójò; (of cap) つば tsúbà; (fig: physical, intellectual etc) 頂点 chóten, ピーク píku

peak hours npl ピーク時 píkuji

peak period n ピーク時 píkuji

peal [pi:l] n (of bells) 響き hibíki

peal of laughter 大きな笑い声 ōkina waráigoè

peanut [pi:'nʌt] n 落花生 rakkáseì, ピーナッツ pínattsù

peanut butter n ピーナッツバター pínattsubatā

pear [pe:r] n セイヨウナシ seíyōnashì

pearl [pəːrl] n 真珠 shiñju, パール pàru

peasant [pez'ənt] n 百姓 hyakúshò, 農夫 nòfu

peat [pi:t] n 泥炭 deítan

pebble [peb'əl] n 小石 koíshi

peck [pek] vt (also: **peck at**: subj: bird) つつく tsutsúkù

♦n (of bird) つつく事 tsutsúkù kotò; (kiss) 軽いキス karúi kísù

pecking order [pek'iŋ-] n (fig: hierarchy) 序列 jorétsu

peckish [pek'iʃ] (BRIT: inf) adj (hungry): *to be peckish* おなかがすいた onáka ga suità

peculiar [pikju:l'jəːr] adj (strange: person, taste, shape etc) 変った kawátta; (belonging exclusively): *peculiar to* 独特な dokútoku na

peculiarity [pikju:li:ær'iti:] n (strange habit, characteristic) 癖 kusè; (distinctive feature: of person, place etc) 特徴 tokúchō

pedal [ped'əl] n (on bicycle, car, machine) ペダル pédaru

♦vi (on bicycle) こぐ kógù

pedantic [pədæn'tik] adj げん学的な geñgakuteki na

peddler [ped'ləːr] n (also: **drug peddler**) 麻薬の売人 mayáku nò baínin

pedestal [ped'istəl] n 台座 daíza

pedestrian [pədes'tri:ən] n 歩行者 hokóshà

♦adj 歩行者の hokóshà no

pedestrian crossing (BRIT) n 横断歩道 ōdanhodō

pediatrics [pi:di:æt'riks] (BRIT **paediatrics**) n (hospital department) 小児科 shōnika; (study) 小児科学 shōnikagàku

pedigree [ped'əgri:] n (of animal) 血統 kettō; (fig: background) 経歴 keíreki

♦cpd (animal) 純血の juñketsu no

pee [pi:] (inf) vi おしっこする o-shíkkò suru

peek [pi:k] vi のぞく nozóku

peel [pi:l] n (of orange, apple, potato) 皮 kawá

♦vt (vegetables, fruit) ...の皮をむく ...no kawá wo mukú

♦vi (paint, wallpaper) はげる hagérù; (skin) むける mukérù

peep [pi:p] n (look) のぞき見 nozókimi; (sound) 鳴き声 nakígoè
♦vi (look) のぞく nozóku

peephole [pi:p'houl] n のぞき穴 nozókiàna

peep out vi (be visible) のぞく nozóku

peer [pi:r] vi: **to peer at** ...をじっと見る ...wo jíttò mírù
♦n (noble) 貴族 kízòku; (equal) 同等の人 dótò nò hitó; (contemporary) 同輩 dóhai

peerage [pi:'ridʒ] n (rank) 貴族の地位 kízòku no chíì

peeved [pi:vd] adj (annoyed) 怒った okóttà

peevish [pi:'viʃ] adj (bad-tempered) 機嫌の悪い kigén nò warúì

peg [peg] n (hook, knob: for coat etc) フック fúkkù; (BRIT: also: **clothes peg**) 洗濯ばさみ seftakubasámi

pejorative [pidʒɔ:r'ətiv] adj (word, expression) 軽べつ的な keíbetsuteki na

Peking [pi:kiŋ'] n 北京 pékìn

Peking(g)ese [pi:kəni:z'] n (dog) ペキニーズ pekínìzu

pelican [pel'ikən] n (ZOOL) ペリカン períkàn

pelican crossing (BRIT) n (AUT) 押しボタン式信号 oshíbotanshiki shìǹgō

pellet [pel'it] n (of paper, mud etc) 丸めた球 marúmeta tamà; (also: **shotgun pellet**) 散弾銃の弾 sandanjū no tamá

pelt [pelt] vt: **to pelt someone with something** ...に...を浴びせ掛ける ...ni ...wo abísekakerù
♦vi (rain) 激しく降る hagéshikù fúrù; (inf: run) 駆ける kakérù
♦n (animal skin) 毛皮 kegáwa

pelvis [pel'vis] n 骨盤 kotsúban

pen [pen] n (for writing: fountain pen, ballpoint pen) ペン péň; (: felt-tip pen etc) サインペン saíňpen; (enclosure: for sheep, pigs etc) 囲い kakói

penal [pi:'nəl] adj (colony, institution) 刑罰の keíbatsu no; (system, code, reform) 刑法の keíhō no

penalize [pi:'nəlaiz] vt (punish) 罰するbassúrù; (: SPORT) ...にペナルティーを科する ...ni penárutì wo kasúrù

penalty [pen'əlti:] n (punishment) 罰 bátsù; (fine) 罰金 bakkín; (SPORT) ペナルティー penárutì

penalty (kick) n (RUGBY, SOCCER) ペナルティーキック penárutì kikkù

penance [pen'əns] n 償い tsugúnai

pence [pens] pl of **penny**

pencil [pen'səl] n (for writing, drawing) 鉛筆 eńpitsu

pencil case n 筆入れ fudéìre

pencil sharpener n 鉛筆削り eńpitsukezúri, シャープナー shắpunā

pendant [pen'dənt] n ペンダント péňdanto

pending [pen'diŋ] prep ...を待つ間 ...wo mátsù aída
♦adj (business) 未決の mikétsu no; (lawsuit) 審理中の shińrichū no; (exam) 差迫った sashísemattà

pendulum [pen'dʒələm] n (of clock) 振子 furíko

penetrate [pen'itreit] vt (subj: person: enemy territory) ...に侵入する ...ni shińnyū suru; (forest etc) ...に入り込む ...ni haírikomù; (: water etc) 染込む shimíkomù; (: light) 通る tōru

penetrating [pen'itreitiŋ] adj (sound, glance, mind, observation) 鋭い surúdoì

penetration [penitrei'ʃən] n (action) 入り込む事 haírikomù kotó

penfriend [pen'frend] (BRIT) n = **pen pal**

penguin [pen'gwin] n ペンギン péňgin

penicillin [penisil'in] n ペニシリン peníshirin

peninsula [pənin'sələ] n 半島 hańtō

penis [pi:'nis] n 陰茎 iňkei, ペニス péňìs

penitent [pen'itənt] adj (person: very sorry) 後悔している kókai shite irù

penitentiary [peniten'tʃə:ri:] (US) n 刑務所 keímushò

penknife [pen'naif] n ペンナイフ peńnaìfu

pen name n ペンネーム peńnèmu

penniless [pen'i:lis] adj (person) 一文無しの ichímoňnashi no

penny [pen'i:] (pl **pennies** or BRIT **pence**) n (US) ペニ pénì, セント séňto;

(BRIT: after 1971: = one hundredth of a pound) ペニ péni

pen pal n ペンパル péñparu, ペンフレンド peñfureñdo

pension [pen'tʃən] n (state benefit) 年金 neñkin; (company pension etc) 恩給 oñkyū

pensioner [pen'tʃənə:r] (BRIT) n (old-age pensioner) 年金で生活する老人 neñkin dè seíkatsu surù rōjìn, 年金暮らしの人 neñkingurāshi no hitó

pension fund n 年金基金 neñkinkikiñ

pensive [pen'siv] adj (person, expression etc) 考え込んだ kañgaekoñda

pentagon [pen'təgɑ:n] n: the Pentagon (US: POL) 国防総省 kokúbōsōshō, ペンタゴン peñtàgon

Pentecost [pen'təkɔ:st] n 聖霊降臨祭 seíreikōriñsai

penthouse [pent'haus] n (flat) 屋上階 okújōkai

pent-up [pent'ʌp'] adj (feelings) たまった tamáttà

penultimate [pinʌl'təmit] adj 最後から2番目の saígo kara nibáñme no

people [pi:'pəl] npl (persons) 人々 hitóbìto; (inhabitants) 住民 jūmin; (citizens) 市民 shímìn; (POL): the people 国民 kokúmin
♦n (nation) 国民 kokúmin; (race) 民族 míñzoku

several people came 数人来ました sūnin kimashitá

people say that ... ...だと言われている ...da to iwárete irù, ...だそうだ ...da sō dà

pep [pep] (inf) n (energy, vigor) 元気 geñki

pepper [pep'ə:r] n (spice) こしょう koshō; (hot pepper) トウガラシ tōgarashi; (sweet pepper) ピーマン pīman
♦vt (fig): to pepper with ...を振掛ける ...wo furíkakerù

peppermint [pep'ə:rmint] n (sweet) ハッカあめ hakkáame

peptalk [pep'tɔ:k] (inf) n (encouraging talk) 激励演説 gekíreienzetsù

pep up vt (enliven) 活気付ける kakkízukerù

per [pə:r] prep (of amounts, prices etc: for each) ...につき ...ni tsukí

per day/person 1日〔1人〕につき ... ichínichi〔hitórì〕ni tsukí...

per annum 1年につき... ichínèn ni tsukí...

per capita [-kæp'itə] adj (income) 一人当りの hitóri atarì no
♦adv 一人当り hitóri atarì

perceive [pə:rsi:v'] vt (sound) 聞く kíkù; (light) 見る mírù; (difference) 認識する niñshiki suru; (notice) ...に気が付く ...ni ki ga tsukù; (realize, understand) 分かる wakárù

per cent n パーセント pásènto

percentage [pə:rsen'tidʒ] n (amount) 割合 waríai, 率 rítsù

perception [pə:rsep'ʃən] n (insight) 洞察力 dōsatsuryòku; (opinion, understanding) 理解 rikái; (faculty) 知覚 chikáku

perceptive [pə:rsep'tiv] adj (person) 洞察力のある dōsatsuryòku no árù, 鋭敏な eíbin na; (analysis, assessment) 鋭い surúdoì

perch [pə:rtʃ] n (for bird) 止り木 tomárigì; (fish) パーチ páchi ◊スズキに似た淡水魚 suzúki ni nità tañsuigyò
♦vi: to perch (on) (bird) (...に) 止る (...ni) tomárù; (person) (...に) 腰掛ける (...ni) koshíkakerù

percolator [pə:r'kəleitə:r] n (also: coffee percolator) パーコレーター pákorētā

percussion [pə:rkʌʃ'ən] n 打楽器 dagákki ◊総称 sōshō

peremptory [pəremp'tə:ri:] (pej) adj (person) 横柄な ōhei na; (order, instruction) 断固たる dañkotarù

perennial [pəren'i:əl] adj (flower, plant) 多年生の tanéñsei no; (fig: problem, feature etc) ありがちな arígachi na

perfect [adj, n pə:r'fikt vb pə:rfekt'] adj (without fault: person, weather, behavior etc) 完璧な kañpeki na; (utter: nonsense, stranger etc) 全くの mattáku no
♦n (also: perfect tense) 完了形 kañryōkei

♦*vt* (technique) 仕上げる shiágerù

perfection [pərfek'ʃən] *n* (faultlessness) 完璧さ kańpekisa

perfectionist [pərfek'ʃənist] *n* 完璧主義者 kańpekishugishà

perfectly [pər'fiktli:] *adv* (emphatic) 全く mattáku; (faultlessly: perform, do etc) 完璧に kańpeki ni; (completely: understand etc) 完全に kańzen ni

perforate [pər'fəreit] *vt* ...に穴を開ける ...ni aná wò akérù

perforations [pərfərei'ʃənz] *npl* (series of small holes) ミシン目 mishíñme

perform [pərfɔːrm'] *vt* (carry out: task, operation, ceremony etc) 行う okónaù, する surú; (piece of music) 演奏する eńsō suru; (play etc) 上演する jōén suru
♦*vi* (well, badly) する surú, やる yarú

performance [pərfɔːr'məns] *n* (of actor) 演技 eńgi; (of dancer) 踊り odóri; (of musician) 演奏 eńsō; (of singer) 歌い方 utáikata; (of play, show) 上演 jōén; (of car, engine) 性能 seínō; (of athlete, company, economy) 成績 seíseki

performer [pərfɔːr'mər] *n* (actor, dancer, singer etc) 芸能人 geínōjìn

perfume [pər'fjuːm] *n* (cologne, toilet water, essence) 香水 kōsui; (pleasant smell: of flowers etc) 香り kaórì

perfunctory [pərfʌŋk'tɔːriː] *adj* (kiss, remark etc) いい加減な iíkagen na

perhaps [pərhæps'] *adv* (maybe) たぶん ...だろう tábùn ...daró

peril [per'əl] *n* (great danger) 危険 kikén

perimeter [pərim'itər] *n* 周辺 shúhen

period [pir'iəd] *n* (length of time) 期間 kikáñ; (SCOL) 時限 jigén; (full stop) 終止符 shúshifù, ピリオド pírìodo; (MED) 月経 gekkéi, メンス méñsu, 生理 seíri
♦*adj* (costume, furniture) 時代の jidái no

periodic(al) [pi:ri:aːd'ik(əl)] *adj* (event, occurrence) 周期的な shúkiteki na, 定期的な teíkiteki na

periodical [pi:ri:aːd'ikəl] *n* (magazine) 雑誌 zasshí

periodically [pi:ri:aːd'ikli:] *adv* 定期的に teíkiteki ni

peripheral [pərif'ərəl] *adj* 二次的な nijíteki na; (on the edge: *also* COMPUT) 周辺の shúhen no
♦*n* (COMPUT) 周辺機器 shúhenkikì

periphery [pərif'ə:ri:] *n* (edge) 周辺 shúhen

periscope [per'iskoup] *n* 潜望鏡 seńbōkyō

perish [per'iʃ] *vi* (die) 死ぬ shinú; (die out) 滅びる horóbirù; (rubber, leather etc) 腐る kusárù

perishable [per'iʃəbəl] *adj* (food) いたみやすい itámiyasuì

perjury [pər'dʒə:ri:] *n* (LAW) 偽証 gishō

perk [pərk] (*inf*) *n* (extra) 役得 yakútokù

perk up *vi* (cheer up) 元気を出す géñki wo dásù

perky [pər'ki:] *adj* (cheerful) 朗らかな hogáraka na

perm [pərm] *n* (for hair) パーマ pàma

permanent [pər'mənənt] *adj* 永久的な eíkyūteki na

permeate [pər'miːeit] *vi* (pass through) 浸透する shińtō suru; (*fig*: spread) 広がる hirógarù
♦*vt* (subj: liquid) ...に染込む ...ni shimíkomù; (: idea) ...に広まる ...ni hirómarù

permissible [pərmis'əbəl] *adj* (action, behavior) 許される yurúsarerù

permission [pərmiʃ'ən] *n* (consent, authorization) 許可 kyókà

permissive [pərmis'iv] *adj* (person, behavior, society) 甘い amáì

permit [*n* pər'mit *vb* pərmit'] *n* (official authorization) 許可証 kyokáshō
♦*vt* (allow) 許可する kyókà suru; (make possible) 可能にする kanō ni surù

permutation [pərmjətei'ʃən] *n* 置換え okíkae

pernicious [pərniʃ'əs] *adj* (very harmful: attitude, influence etc) 有害な yúgai na; (MED) 悪性の akúsei no

perpendicular [pərrpəndik'jələr] *adj* (line, surface) 垂直の suíchoku no; (cliff, slope) 険しい kewáshiì

perpetrate [pər'pitreit] *vt* (commit: crime) 犯す okású

perpetual [pərrpetʃ'uːəl] *adj* (constant:

motion, darkness) 永久の eíkyū no;
(: noise, questions) 年がら年中の neñgaraneñjū no

perpetuate [pə:rpetʃ'u:eit] *vt* (situation, custom, belief etc) 永続させる eízoku saserù

perplex [pə:rpleks'] *vt* (person) まごつかせる magótsukaserù

persecute [pə:r'səkju:t] *vt* (harass, oppress; minorities etc) 迫害する hakúgai suru

persecution [pə:rsəkju:'ʃən] *n* (of minorities etc) 迫害 hakúgai

perseverance [pə:rsəvi:r'əns] *n* 根気 koñki

persevere [pə:rsəvi:r'] *vi* 辛抱強く続ける shiñbōzuyokù tsuzúkerù

Persian [pə:r'ʒən] *adj* ペルシアの pérùshia no

♦*n* ペルシア人 perúshiajìn
the (Persian) Gulf ペルシア湾 perúshiawàn

persist [pə:rsist'] *vi*: *to persist (in doing something)* (...をし)続ける (...wo shi)tsuzúkerù

persistence [pə:rsis'təns] *n* (determination) 根気強さ koñkizuyòsa

persistent [pə:rsis'tənt] *adj* (noise, smell, cough etc) いつまでも続く ítsùmademo tsuzúkù; (person: determined) 根気強い koñkizuyoì

person [pə:r'sən] *n* 人 hitó
in person (appear, sing, recite etc) 本人が hoñnin ga

personal [pə:r'sənəl] *adj* (belongings, phone etc) 個人の kojín no; (opinion, life, habits etc) 個人的な kojínteki na; (in person: visit) 本人自身の hoñninjishìn no

personal assistant *n* 秘書 hishó

personal call *n* (TEL) 私用の電話 shiyó no deñwa

personal column *n* 私信欄 shishínraǹ

personal computer *n* パーソナルコンピュータ pásonarukoñpyūta, パソコン pasókòn

personality [pə:rsənæl'iti:] *n* (character) 人格 jiñkaku; (famous person) 有名人 yūmeijìn

personally [pə:r'sənəli:] *adv* (for my etc part) 個人的には kojínteki ni wà; (in person) 本人が hoñnin ga
to take something personally ...を個人攻撃と受止める ...wo kojínkōgeki to ukétomerù

personal organizer *n* 予定帳 yotéichō

personify [pə:rsa:n'əfai] *vt* (evil) ...の権化である ...no góñge de árù; (good) ...の化身である ...no késhìn de árù

personnel [pə:rsənel'] *n* 職員 shokúin ◇総称 sōshō

perspective [pə:rspek'tiv] *n* (ARCHIT, ART) 遠近法 eñkinhō; (way of thinking) 見方 mikáta
to get something into perspective (fig) 事情を考えて...を見る jijō wò kañgaetè ...wo mírù

Perspex [pə:rs'peks] ® *n* アクリル ákùriru

perspiration [pə:rspərei'ʃən] *n* 汗 ásè

persuade [pə:rsweid'] *vt*: *to persuade someone to do something* ...する様に...を説き伏せる ...surú yò ni ...wo tokífuserù

persuasion [pə:rswei'ʒən] *n* (act) 説得 settóku; (creed) 信条 shiñjō

persuasive [pə:rswei'siv] *adj* (person, argument) 説得力のある settókuryòku no árù

pertaining [pə:rtein'iŋ]: *pertaining to prep* (relating to) ...に関する ...ni kañ suru

pertinent [pə:r'tənənt] *adj* (answer, remark) 適切な tekísetsu na

perturb [pə:rtə:rb'] *vt* (person) 不安にする fuán ni surù

Peru [pəru:'] *n* ペルー pérù

peruse [pəru:z'] *vt* (newspaper, documents etc) ...に目を通す ...ni mé wo tōsù

Peruvian [pəru:'vi:ən] *adj* ペルーの pérù no

♦*n* ペルー人 perújìn

pervade [pə:rveid'] *vt* (subj: smell, feeling) ...に充満する ...ni jūman suru

perverse [pə:rvə:rs'] *adj* (contrary: behavior) 天のじゃくの amá no jàku no

perversion [pə:rvə:r'ʒən] *n* (sexual) 変態

heñtai; (of truth) 曲解 kyokkái; (of justice) 悪用 akúyō

pervert [n pəːr'vəːrt vb pəːrvəːrt'] n (sexual pervert) 変態 heñtai

♦vt (person, mind) 堕落させる daráku saseru; (truth, someone's words) 曲解する kyokkái suru

pessimism [pes'əmizəm] n 悲観主義 hikánshùgi, ペシミズム peshímizùmu

pessimist [pes'əmist] n 悲観主義者 hikánshugisha, ペシミスト peshímisùto

pessimistic [pesəmis'tik] adj (person) 悲観的な hikánteki na, ペシミスティックな peshímisutikkù na

pest [pest] n (insect) 害虫 gaíchū; (fig: nuisance) うるさいやつ urúsai yatsù

pester [pes'təːr] vt (bother) 悩ませる nayámaserù

pesticide [pes'tisaid] n 殺虫剤 satchū́zài

pet [pet] n (domestic animal) 愛がん動物 aígandōbùtsu, ペット péttð

♦cpd (theory, hate etc) 十八番の oháko no

♦vt (stroke: person, animal) 愛ぶする aíbu suru

♦vi (inf: sexually) ペッティングする pettíngu suru

teacher's pet (favorite) 先生のお気に入り señsei nò o-kí ni irì

petal [pet'əl] n 花びら hanábirà

peter [pi:'təːr]: **peter out** vi (road, stream etc) だんだんなくなる dañdañ nakúnarù; (conversation, meeting) しりすぼまりに終る shirísubomarì ni owárù

petite [pətiːt'] adj (referring to woman: small) 小柄な kogára na

petition [pətiʃ'ən] n (signed document) 陳情書 chiñjōshò; (LAW) 請願 seígan

petrified [pet'rəfaid] adj (fig: terrified) 恐怖に駆られた kyófu ni karáretà

petrol [pet'rəl] (BRIT) n (fuel) ガソリン gasórin

two/four-star petrol レギュラー〔ハイオク〕ガソリン regyúrā〔haíoku〕gasórin

petrol can n ガソリン缶 gasóriñkan

petroleum [pətrou'li:əm] n 石油 sekíyu

petrol pump (BRIT) n (in garage) ガソリンポンプ gasórinpoñpu

petrol station (BRIT) n ガソリンスタンド gasórinsutañdo

petrol tank (BRIT) n ガソリンタンク gasórintañku

petticoat [pet'i:kout] n (underskirt) ペチコート péchìkōto

petty [pet'i:] adj (small, unimportant) さsいな sásài na; (small-minded) 狭量な kyóryō na

petty cash n (in office) 小口現金 kogúchigeñkin

petty officer n (in navy) 下士官 kashíkaǹ

petulant [pet'ʃələnt] adj せっかちな sekkáchi na

pew [pju:] n (in church) 長いす nagáisu

pewter [pju:'təːr] n しろめ shírðme

phallic [fæl'ik] adj (object, symbol) 陰茎状の iñkeijō no

phantom [fæn'təm] n (ghost) お化け o-báke

pharmaceutical [fɑːrməsuː'tikəl] adj 製薬の seíyaku no

pharmacist [fɑːr'məsist] n 薬剤師 yakúzaishì

pharmacy [fɑːr'məsi:] n 薬局 yakkyóku

phase [feiz] n (stage) 段階 dañkai

♦vt: **to phase something in/out** ...を段階的に取入れる〔なくす〕...wo dañkaiteki nì torírerù〔nakúsù〕

Ph.D. [pi:'eitʃ'di:'] abbr = **Doctor of Philosophy**

pheasant [fez'ənt] n キジ kijí

phenomena [finɑːm'ənə] npl of **phenomenon**

phenomenal [finɑːm'ənəl] adj 驚異的な kyóiteki na

phenomenon [finɑːm'ənɑːn] (pl **phenomena**) n 現象 geñshō

philanthropist [filæn'θrəpist] n 慈善家 jizénka

Philippines [fil'ipi:nz] npl: **the Philippines** フィリピン fírìpin

philosopher [filɑːs'əfəːr] n (scholar) 哲学者 tetsúgakushà

philosophical [filəsɑːf'ikəl] adj (ideas, conversation etc) 哲学的な tetsúgakuteki na; (fig: calm, resigned) 冷静な reísei na

philosophy [fiˈlɑsˈəfiː] *n* (SCOL) 哲学 tetsúgàku; (set of ideas: of philosopher) ...の哲学 ...no tetsúgàku; (theory: of any person) 考え方 kañgaekatà, 思想 shisố

phlegm [flem] *n* (substance) たん tañ

phlegmatic [flegmǽtik] *adj* (person) のろまな norốma na

phobia [fouˈbiːə] *n* (irrational fear: of insects, flying, water etc) 恐怖症 kyṓfushố

phone [foun] *n* (system) 電話 deñwa; (apparatus) 電話器 deñwakì
♦*vt* ...に電話を掛ける ...ni deñwa wò kakérù
to be on the phone (BRIT: possess a phone) 電話を持っている deñwa wò motté irù; (be calling) 電話中である deñwachū de arù

phone back *vt* ...に電話を掛け直す ...ni deñwa wò kakénaosù
♦*vi* 電話を掛け直す deñwa wò kakénaosù

phone book *n* (directory) 電話帳 deñwachō

phone booth *n* 電話ボックス deñwabokkùsu

phone box (BRIT) *n* 電話ボックス deñwabokkùsu

phone call *n* 電話 deñwa

phone-in [founˈin] (BRIT) *n* (RADIO, TV) 視聴者が電話で参加する番組 shichōsha ga deñwa dè sañka suru bañgumi

phonetics [fənetˈiks] *n* 音声学 oñseigàku

phone up *vt* ...に電話を掛ける ...ni deñwa wò kakérù
♦*vi* 電話を掛ける deñwa wò kakérù

phoney [founˈiː] *adj* (false: address) うその úso no; (: accent) 偽の nisé no; (person) 信用できない shiñ-yō dekinài

phonograph [founˈəgræf] (US) *n* 蓄音機 chikúonkì

phosphorus [fɑːsˈfərəs] *n* りん ríñ

photo [fouˈtou] *n* (photograph) 写真 shashín

photocopier [fouˈtəkɑːpiːəːr] *n* (machine) 写真複写機 shashínfukushakì, コピー機 kopíkì

photocopy [fouˈtəkɑːpiː] *n* コピー kópī
♦*vt* (picture, document etc) ...のコピーを取る ...no kópī wo tórù

photogenic [foutədʒenˈik] *adj* (person) 写真写りの良い shashín-utsurì no yóì

photograph [fouˈtəgræf] *n* 写真 shashín
♦*vt* (person, object, place etc) 撮影する satsúei suru

photographer [fətɑːgˈrəfəːr] *n* カメラマン kaméramàn

photographic [foutəgræfˈik] *adj* (equipment etc) 写真の shashín no

photography [fətɑːgˈrəfiː] *n* (art, subject) 写真撮影 shashínsatsùei

phrase [freiz] *n* (group of words, expression) 言方 iíkatà; (LING) 句 kú
♦*vt* (express) 表現する hyṓgen suru

phrase book *n* (foreign language aid) 表現集 hyṓgenshū

physical [fizˈikəl] *adj* (of the body: needs, punishment, exercise etc) 肉体的な nikútaiteki na; (properties, properties) 物理的な butsúriteki na; (world, universe, object) 自然の shizén no; (sciences) 物理学の butsúrigàku no

physical education *n* 体育 taíiku

physically [fizˈikliː] *adv* (fit, attractive) 肉体的に nikútaiteki ni

physician [fiziˈʃən] *n* (doctor) 医者 ishá

physicist [fizˈəsist] *n* 物理学者 butsúrigakushà

physics [fizˈiks] *n* 物理学 butsúrigàku

physiology [fiziɑːlˈədʒiː] *n* (science) 生理学 seírigàku; (functioning: of animal, plant) 生理 seíri

physiotherapy [fiziːouθeːrˈəpiː] *n* (MED) 物理療法 butsúriryōhō

physique [fizikˈ] *n* (build: of person) 体格 taíkaku

pianist [piːˈænist] *n* (MUS) ピアニスト piánisùto

piano [piːænˈou] *n* (MUS) ピアノ piáno

piccolo [pikˈəlou] *n* (MUS) ピッコロ pikkóro

pick [pik] *n* (tool: *also*: **pick-axe**) つるはし tsurúhàshi

◆*vt* (select) 選ぶ erábù; (gather: fruit, flowers) 摘む tsúmù; (remove, take) 取る tórù; (lock) こじ開ける kojíakerù

take your pick (choose) 選ぶ erábù

the pick of (best) ...からえり抜かれた物 ...kara erínukaretà mónò

to pick one's nose/teeth 鼻〔歯〕をほじる haná〔há〕wò hojírù

to pick a quarrel (with someone) (...に) けんかを売る (...ni) keñka wò urú

pick at *vt fus* (food) ちびちび食べる chíbichibi tabérù

picket [pik'it] *n* (in strike) ピケ piké

◆*vt* (factory, workplace etc) ...にピケを張る ...ni piké wò hárù

pickle [pik'əl] *n* (*also*: **pickles**: as condiment) ピクルス píkurusu; (*fig*: mess) 苦境 kukyő

◆*vt* (CULIN: in vinegar) 酢漬にする suzúke ni surù; (: in salt water) 塩漬にする shiózuke ni surù

pick on *vt fus* (person: criticize) 非難する hinán suru; (: treat badly) いじめる ijímerù

pick out *vt* (distinguish) 識別する shikíbetsu suru; (choose from a group) 選び出す erábidasù, ピックアップする pikkúappù suru

pickpocket [pik'pɑ:kit] *n* すり súrì

pick up *vi* (improve: health, economy, trade) 良くなる yőkù naru

◆*vt* (object: from floor) 拾う hiróu; (POLICE: arrest) 逮捕する taího suru; (collect: person, parcel etc) 引取る hikítorù; (AUT: passenger) 乗せる nosérù; (person: for sexual encounter) 引っ掛ける hikkákerù; (learn: language, skill etc) 覚える obőerù; (RADIO) 受信する jushín suru

to pick up speed 加速する kasóku suru

to pick oneself up (after falling etc) 起き上る okíagarù

pickup [pik'ʌp] *n* (small truck) ピックアップ pikkúappù

picnic [pik'nik] *n* (outdoor meal) ピクニック pikunikku

picture [pik'tʃər] *n* (painting, drawing, print) 絵 é; (photograph) 写真 shashín;

(TV) 画像 gaző; (film) 映画 eíga; (*fig*: description) 描写 byősha; (: situation) 事態 jítài

◆*vt* (imagine) 想像する sőzo suru

picture book *n* 絵本 ehőñ

pictures [pik'tʃərz] (*BRIT*) *npl*: *the pictures* (cinema) 映画 eíga

picturesque [piktʃəresk'] *adj* (place, building) 風情のある fúzei no árù

pie [pai] *n* (CULIN: vegetable, meat, fruit) パイ páî

piece [pi:s] *n* (bit or part of larger thing) かけら kákéra; (portion: of cake, chocolate, bread etc) 一切れ hitókìre; (length: of string, ribbon) 一本 íppòn; (item): *a piece of clothing/furniture/advice* 1つ hitótsu

◆*vt*: *to piece together* (information) 総合する sőgo suru; (parts of a whole) 継ぎ合せる tsugíawaserù

to take to pieces (dismantle) 分解する buñkai suru

piecemeal [pi:s'mi:l] *adv* (irregularly) 少しずつ sukóshizutsù

piecework [pi:s'wə:rk] *n* 出来高払いの仕事 dekídakabaràì no shigóto

pie chart *n* 円形グラフ eñkeiguràfu

pier [pi:r] *n* 桟橋 sañbashi

pierce [pi:rs] *vt* (puncture: surface, material, skin etc) 貫通する kañtsū suru

piercing [pi:rs'iŋ] *adj* (*fig*: cry) 甲高い kañdakaì; (: eyes, stare) 鋭い surúdoî; (wind) 刺す様な sásù yō na

piety [pai'əti:] *n* (REL) 信心 shiñjiñ

pig [pig] *n* (ZOOL) ブタ butá; (*pej*: unkind person) 畜生 chikúshō; (: greedy person) 欲張り目 yokúbarimè

pigeon [pidʒ'ən] *n* (bird) ハト hátò

pigeonhole [pidʒ'ənhoul] *n* (for letters, messages) 小仕切り koshíkiri

piggy bank [pig'i:-] *n* (money box) 貯金箱 chokíñbako

pigheaded [pig'hedid] (*pej*) *adj* (stubborn) 頑固な gañko na

piglet [pig'lit] *n* 子ブタ kobúta

pigment [pig'mənt] *n* 色素 shikíso

pigskin [pig'skin] *n* ブタのなめし革 butá no naméshigàwa

pigsty [pig'stai] *n* (on farm) ブタ小屋 bu-tágoya

pigtail [pig'teil] *n* (plait) お下げ o-ságe

pike [paik] *n* (fish) カワカマス kawáka-màsu, パイク páiku

pilchard [pil'tʃə:rd] *n* (fish) イワシ iwáshi

pile [pail] *n* (heap, stack) 山 yamá; (of carpet, cloth) 毛足 keáshi, パイル páiru
♦*vt* (*also*: **pile up**: objects) 積上げる tsu-míageru
♦*vi* (*also*: **pile up**: objects) 積重なる tsu-míkasanaru; (problems, work) たまる ta-máru

pile into *vt fus* (car) ...に乗込む ...ni no-ríkomu

piles [pailz] *npl* (MED) じ ji

pile-up [pail'ʌp] *n* (AUT) 衝突事故 shó-totsujikò

pilfering [pil'fə:riŋ] *n* (petty thieving) く すねる事 kusúneru kotó

pilgrim [pil'grim] *n* (REL) 巡礼者 juńrei-shā

pilgrimage [pil'grəmidʒ] *n* (REL) 巡礼 juńreì

pill [pil] *n* (MED: tablet) 錠剤 józai
the pill (contraceptive pill) 経口避妊薬 keíkōhinìñ-yaku, ピル pírù

pillage [pil'idʒ] *vt* (loot: house, town etc) 略奪する ryakúdatsu suru

pillar [pil'ə:r] *n* (ARCHIT) 柱 hashíra

pillar box (*BRIT*) *n* (MAIL) ポスト pó-sùto

pillion [pil'jən] *n*: **to ride pillion** (on motorcycle) 後ろに相乗りする ushíro nì aínori surù

pillory [pil'ə:ri:] *vt* (criticize strongly) 非 難する hínàn suru

pillow [pil'ou] *n* (cushion: for head) まく ら mákùra

pillowcase [pil'oukeis] *n* (cover: for pil-low) 枕カバー makúrakabà, ピロケース pírōkèsu

pilot [pai'lət] *n* (AVIAT) 操縦士 sójūshi, パイロット páirotto
♦*cpd* (scheme, study etc) 試験的な shikén-teki na
♦*vt* (aircraft) 操縦する sójū suru

pilot light *n* (on cooker, boiler, fire) 口 火 kuchíbi

pimp [pimp] *n* ポン引き poñbiki, ひも hi-mó

pimple [pim'pəl] *n* にきび níkibi

pin [pin] *n* (metal: for attaching, fasten-ing) ピン píñ
♦*vt* (fasten with pin) ピンで止める píñ de tomérù
pins and needles (in arms, legs etc) し びれが切れる事 shibíre gà kirérù kotó
to pin someone down (*fig*) ...に約束させ る ...ni yakúsoku saserù, ...にくぎを刺 す ...ni kugí wò sásù
to pin something on someone (*fig*) ...に ...のぬれぎぬを着せる ...ni ...no nuréginù wo kiserù

pinafore [pin'əfɔ:r] *n* (*also*: **pinafore dress**) エプロンドレス epúrondorèsu

pinball [pin'bɔ:l] *n* (game) スマートボー ル sumátobòru; (machine) スマートボール 機 sumátobōruki

pincers [pin'sə:rz] *npl* (TECH) やっとこ yattóko, ペンチ péñchi; (of crab, lobster etc) はさみ hasámi

pinch [pintʃ] *n* (small amount: of salt etc) 一つまみ hitótsùmami
♦*vt* (person: with finger and thumb) つね る tsunérù; (*inf*: steal) くすねる kusúne-rù
at a pinch 緊急の場合 kiñkyū nò baái

pincushion [pin'kuʃən] *n* (SEWING) 針 刺し harísashì

pine [pain] *n* (*also*: **pine tree**) マツ má-tsù; (wood) マツ材 matsúzài
♦*vi*: **to pine for** (person, place) 思い焦 がれる omóikogarerù

pineapple [pain'æpəl] *n* (fruit) パイナッ プル paínappùru

pine away *vi* (gradually die) 衰弱して死 ぬ suíjaku shite shinù

ping [piŋ] *n* (noise) ぴゅーんという音 pyūn to iú otò

ping-pong [piŋ'pɔ:ŋ] ® *n* (sport) 卓球 takkyū, ピンポン píñpon

pink [piŋk] *adj* ピンク色の piñkuiro no
♦*n* (color) ピンク色 piñkuiro; (BOT) ナ デシコ nadéshìko

pinnacle [pin'əkəl] *n* (of building, mountain) 天辺 teppéń; (*fig*) 頂点 chốteń

pinpoint [pin'pɔint] *vt* (discover) 発見する hakkén suru; (explain) 説明する setsúmei suru; (position of something) 正確に示す seíkaku nì shimésù

pint [paint] *n* (US: = 473 cc; BRIT: = 568 cc) パイント paíntó
a pint of beer, (BRIT: inf) a pint ビール1パイント bíru ichípaìnto

pin-up [pin'ʌp] *n* (picture) ピンナップ写真〔絵〕 pińnappushashiñ[e]

pioneer [paiəni:r'] *n* (initiator: of scheme, science, method) 先駆者 seńkushà, パイオニア paíonìa; (early settler) 開拓者 kaítakushà

pious [pai'əs] *adj* (person) 信心深い shińjiñbukai

pip [pip] *n* (seed of fruit) 種 tané; (BRIT: time signal on radio) 時報 jihō

pipe [paip] *n* (gen, also for smoking) パイプ paípu; (also: **water pipe**) 水道管 suídōkan; (also: **gas pipe**) ガス管 gasúkan
♦*vt* (water, gas, oil) パイプで運ぶ paípu de hakóbù

pipes [paipz] *npl* (also: **bagpipes**) バグパイプ bagúpaìpu

pipe cleaner *n* パイプクリーナー paípukurìnā

pipe down (*inf*) *vi* (be quiet) 黙る damárù

pipe dream *n* (hope, plan) 夢想 musố

pipeline [paip'lain] *n* (for oil, gas) パイプライン paípuraìn

piper [pai'pə:r] *n* (bagpipe player) バグパイプ奏者 bagúpaipu sòsha

piping [pai'piŋ] *adv*: **piping hot** (water, food, coffee) うんと熱い úñto atsúī

piquant [pi:'kənt] *adj* (food: spicy) ぴりっとした piríttò shitá; (*fig*: interesting, exciting) 興味深い kyómibùkai

pique [pi:k] *n* 立腹 rippúku

pirate [pai'rit] *n* (sailor) 海賊 kaízoku
♦*vt* (book, video tape, cassette etc) ...の海賊版を作る ...no kaízokubañ wo tsukúrù

pirate radio (BRIT) *n* 海賊放送 kaízokuhòsō

pirouette [piru:et'] *n* つま先旋回 tsumásakiseñkai

Pisces [pai'si:z] *n* (ASTROLOGY) 魚座 uózà

piss [pis] (*inf!*) *vi* (urinate) おしっこする oshíkkò suru

pissed [pist] (*inf!*) *adj* (US) 怒った okőttà; (BRIT: drunk) 酔っ払った yoppárattà

pistol [pis'təl] *n* けん銃 keñjū, ピストル pisútoru

piston [pis'tən] *n* ピストン písùton

pit [pit] *n* (hole in ground) 穴 aná; (in surface of something) くぼみ kubómi; (also: **coal pit**) 炭坑 tañkō; (quarry) 採石場 saísekijō
♦*vt*: *to pit one's wits against someone* ...と知恵比べをする ...to chiékuràbe wo suru

pitch [pitʃ] *n* (BRIT: SPORT: ground) グラウンド guráuñdo; (MUS) 調子 chōshi, ピッチ pitchi; (*fig*: level, degree) 度合 doai; (tar) ピッチ pítchì
♦*vt* (throw) 投げる nagérù
♦*vi* (fall forwards) つんのめる tsuńnomerù
to pitch a tent (erect) テントを張る téñto wo hárù

pitch-black [pitʃ'blæk'] *adj* (night, place) 真っ暗な makkúra na

pitched battle [pitʃt-] *n* (violent fight) 激戦 gekísen

pitchfork [pitʃ'fɔ:rk] *n* ホーク hóku

piteous [pit'i:əs] *adj* (sight, sound etc) 悲惨な hisán na

pitfall [pit'fɔ:l] *n* (difficulty, danger) 落し穴 otóshiàna, 危険 kikén

pith [piθ] *n* (of orange, lemon etc) わた watá

pithy [piθ'i:] *adj* (comment, saying etc) 中身の濃い nakámì no kôī

pitiful [pit'ifəl] *adj* (touching: appearance, sight) 哀れな awáre na

pitiless [pit'ilis] *adj* (person) 冷酷な reíkoku na

pits [pits] *npl* (AUT) ピット pitto

pittance [pit'əns] *n* (very small income) スズメの涙 suzúme no namída

pity [pit'i:] n (compassion) 哀れみ awáremì

♦vt 哀れむ awáremù

what a pity! (expressing disappointment) 残念だ zañnen da

pivot [piv'ət] n (TECH) 旋回軸 señkaijìku, ピボット píbðtto; (fig) 中心 chúshin

pizza [pi:t'sə] n ピッツァ píttsà, ピザ pízà

placard [plæk'ɑ:rd] n (sign: in public place) 看板 kañban; (: in march etc) プラカード purákàdo

placate [plei'keit] vt (person, anger) なだめる nadámerù

place [pleis] n (in general: point, building, area) 所 tokóro, 場所 bashó; (: position: of object) 位置 íchì; (seat) 席 sékì; (job, post etc) 職 shokú, ポスト pósùto; (home): **at/to his place** 彼の家で[へ] kárè no ié de(e); (role: in society, system etc) 役割 yakúwarì

♦vt (put: object) 置く okú; (identify: person) 思い出す omóidasù

to take place (happen) 起る okórù

out of place (not suitable) 場違いの bachígai no

in the first place (first of all) まず第一に mázù daíchi nì

to change places with someone ...と交代する ...to kōtai suru

to be placed (in race, exam) 入賞する nyūshō suru

place of birth n 出生地 shusséichì

placenta [pləsen'tə] n 胎盤 taíban

placid [plæs'id] adj (person) 穏和な oñwa na

plagiarism [plei'dʒə:rizəm] n ひょう窃 hyōsetsu, 盗作 tōsaku

plague [pleig] n (MED) 伝染病 deñsenbyō; (fig: of locusts etc) 異常発生 ijōhasséi

♦vt (fig: subj: problems, difficulties) 悩ます nayámasù

plaice [pleis] n inv (fish) カレイ kárèi

plaid [plæd] n (cloth) チェックの生地 chékkù no kíjì

plain [plein] adj (unpatterned) 無地の mújì no; (simple: dress, food) 質素な shíssò na; (clear, easily understood) 明白な meíhaku na; (not beautiful) 不器量な bukíryð na

♦adv (wrong, stupid etc) 全く mattáku

♦n (area of land) 平原 heígen

plain chocolate n ブラックチョコレート burákku chokorēto

plain-clothes [plein'klouz] adj (police officer) 私服の shifúku no

plainly [plein'li:] adv (obviously) 明白に meíhaku ni; (hear, see, smell: easily) はっきりと hakkírì to; (state: clearly) ざっくばらんに zákkùbaran ni

plaintiff [plein'tif] n (LAW) 原告 geñkoku

plaintive [plein'tiv] adj (cry, voice) 哀れっぽい awáreppoì

plait [plæt] n (of hair) お下げ o-ságe; (of rope, leather) 編みひも状の物 amíhimojð no monð

plan [plæn] n (scheme, project) 計画 keíkaku, プラン púràn; (drawing) 図面 zúmèn; (schedule) 予定表 yotéihyō

♦vt (work out in advance: crime, holiday, future etc) 計画する keíkaku suru

♦vi (think ahead) 計画する keíkaku suru

to plan to do ...しようと計画する ...shiyō tò keíkaku suru

plane [plein] n (AVIAT) 飛行機 híkòki; (MATH) 面 méñ; (fig: level) 段階 dañkai; (tool) かんな kanna; (also: **plane tree**) スズカケノキ suzúkake no ki, プラタナス purátanàsu

planet [plæn'it] n 惑星 wakúsei

plank [plæŋk] n (of wood) 板 ítà

planner [plæn'ə:r] n (gen) 計画をする人 keíkaku wo suru hitò; (also: **town planner**) 都市計画担当者 toshíkeikaku tantōshà; (of TV program, project) 計画者 keíkakushà

planning [plæn'iŋ] n (of future, project, event etc) 計画 keíkaku; (also: **town planning**) 都市計画 toshíkeìkaku

family planning 家族計画 kazókukeìkaku

planning permission n 建築許可 keñchikukyokà

plant [plænt] n (BOT) 植物 shokúbùtsu;

(machinery) 設備 sétsùbi; (factory) プラント puráñto

♦*vt* (seed, plant, sapling) 植える uérù; (field, garden) ...に植える ...ni uérù; (secretly: microphone, bomb, incriminating evidence etc) 仕掛ける shikákerù

plantation [plæntei'ʃən] *n* (of tea, rubber, sugar etc) 農園 nóeñ; (area planted out with trees) 植林地 shokúriñchi

plaque [plæk] *n* (commemorative plaque: on building etc) 銘板 meîban; (on teeth) 歯こう shîkō

plasma [plæz'mə] *n* 血清 kesséi

plaster [plæs'tə:r] *n* (for walls) しっくい shikkúî, (*also*: **plaster of Paris**) 石こう sekkô; (*BRIT*: *also*: **sticking plaster**) ばんそうこう bañsôkō

♦*vt* (wall, ceiling) ...にしっくいを塗る ...ni shikkúî wo nurú; (cover): *to plaster with* ...に...をべったり張る ...ni ...wo bettárî hárù

plastered [plæs'tə:rd] (*inf*) *adj* 酔っ払った yopparáttà

plasterer [plæs'tərə:r] *n* (of walls, ceilings) 左官屋 sakáñ-ya

plastic [plæs'tik] *n* 合成樹脂 gôseijushî, プラスチック purásuchikkù

♦*adj* (made of plastic: bucket, chair, cup etc) プラスチック製の purásuchikkusei no

plastic bag *n* ポリ袋 porîbùkuro

Plasticine [plæs'tisi:n] ® *n* 合成粘土 gôseineñdo

plastic surgery *n* 整形手術 seíkeishujùtsu

plate [pleit] *n* (dish) 皿 sará; (plateful of food, biscuits etc) 一皿 hitósàra; (in book: picture, photograph) 1ページ大の挿絵 ichípèjidai nò sashîè, プレート púrēto; (dental plate) 入れ歯 iréba

gold/silver plate 貴金属の食器類 kikínzoku no shokkírùi

plateau [plætou'] (*pl* **plateaus** *or* **plateaux**) *n* (GEO) 高原 kôgen

plate glass *n* (for window, door) 板ガラス itágaràsu

platform [plæt'fɔ:rm] *n* (at meeting, for band) 演壇 eñdan; (raised structure: for

landing, loading on etc) 台 dái; (RAIL) ホーム hômu; (*BRIT*: of bus) 踏段 fumídan, ステップ sutéppù; (POL) 綱領 kôryō

platinum [plæt'ənəm] *n* 白金 hakkín, プラチナ puráchina

platitude [plæt'ətu:d] *n* 決り文句 kimárimoñku

platonic [plətɑ:'nik] *adj* 純粋に精神的な juñsui ni seíshinteki na, プラトニックな purátonikkù na

platoon [plətu:n'] *n* 小隊 shôtai

platter [plæt'ə:r] *n* 盛皿 morízara

plausible [plɔ:'zəbəl] *adj* (theory, excuse, statement) もっともらしい mottómorashî; (person) 口先のうまい kuchísaki nò umaî

play [plei] *n* (THEATER, RADIO, TV) 劇 gékì

♦*vt* (subj: children: game) ...して遊ぶ ...shite asóbù; (football, tennis, chess) やる yarú; (compete against) ...と試合をする ...to shiái wò suru; (part, role: in play, film etc) 演ずる eñzurù, ...にふんする ...ni fuñsurù; (instrument, tune) 演奏する eñsō suru; (listen to: tape, record) 聞く kîkù

♦*vi* (children: on beach, swings etc) 遊ぶ asóbù; (MUS: orchestra, band) 演奏する eñsō suru; (: record, tape, radio) かかる kakárù

to play safe 大事を取る daîji wò tórù

playboy [plei'bɔi] *n* プレーボーイ purébòi

play down *vt* 軽く扱う karúku atsukaù

player [plei'ə:r] *n* (SPORT) 選手 séñshu, プレーヤー puréyà; (MUS) 奏者 sôsha; (THEATER) 役者 yakúsha

playful [plei'fəl] *adj* (person, animal) 遊び好きの asóbizuki no

playground [plei'graund] *n* (in park) 遊び場 asóbiba; (in school) 校庭 kôtei, 運動場 uñdōjô

playgroup [plei'gru:p] (*BRIT*) *n* 保育園 hoíkuèn

playing card [plei'iŋ-] *n* トランプ toráñpu

playing field *n* グラウンド guráundo

playmate [plei'meit] *n* 遊び友達 asóbitomòdachi

play-off [plei'ɔ:f] n (SPORT) 優勝決定戦 yūshōketteísen, プレーオフ puréofù

playpen [plei'pen] n ベビーサークル bebīsākuru

plaything [plei'θiŋ] n おもちゃ omóchà

playtime [plei'taim] n (SCOL) 休み時間 yasúmijikàn

play up vi (cause trouble: machine) 調子が悪くなる chōshi gà wárùku naru; (: children) 行儀を悪くする gyōgi wò wárùku suru

playwright [plei'rait] n 劇作家 gekísakka

plc [pi:elsi:'] abbr (= public limited company) 有限株式会社 yūgen kabushikigaishà

plea [pli:] n (request) 懇願 koñgan; (LAW) 申立て mōshitate

plead [pli:d] vt (LAW) 申立てる mōshitaterù; (give as excuse: ignorance, ill health etc) ...だと言い訳する ...dá tò iíwake surù

♦vi (LAW) 申立てる mōshitaterù; (beg): **to plead with someone** ...に懇願する ...ni koñgan suru

pleasant [plez'ənt] adj (agreeable, nice: weather, chat, smile etc) 気持の良い kimóchi no yoì; (agreeable: person) 愛想の良い aísō no yoì

pleasantries [plez'əntri:z] npl: **to exchange pleasantries** あいさつを交わす aísatsu wo kawásù

please [pli:z] excl (polite request) どうぞ dōzo, どうか dōka; (polite acceptance): **yes, please** ええ, 有難う eé, arígatō; (to attract someone's attention) 済みません sumímaseñ

♦vt (give pleasure or satisfaction to) 喜ばす yorókobasù

♦vi (give pleasure, satisfaction) 人を喜ばす hitó wò yorókobasù; (think fit): **do as you please** お好きな様にして下さい o-súki na yō ni shité kudasaì

please yourself! (inf) ご勝手に go-kátte nì

pleased [pli:zd] adj (happy, satisfied): **pleased (with)** (...で) 満足している

(...de) mañzoku shite irù

pleased to meet you 初めまして hajímemashìte

pleasing [pli:'ziŋ] adj (remark etc) 愉快な yúkài na, うれしい uréshiì; (picture) 楽しい tanóshiì; (person) 愛敬のある aíkyō no arù

pleasure [pleʒ'ə:r] n (happiness, satisfaction) 快楽 kaíraku; (activity of enjoying oneself, enjoyable experience) 楽しみ tanóshimì

it's a pleasure どういたしまして dō itáshimashitè

pleasure boat n 遊覧船 yūransen

pleat [pli:t] n ひだ hídà, プリーツ purītsù

pledge [pledʒ] n (promise) 約束 yakúsoku

♦vt (promise: money, support, help) 約束する yakúsoku suru

plentiful [plen'tifəl] adj (food, supply, amount) 豊富な hōfù na

plenty [plen'ti:] n: **plenty of** (much, many) 沢山の takúsan no; (sufficient) 十分な jūbun na

pleurisy [plur:'isi:] n ろく膜炎 rokúmakuèn

pliable [plai'əbəl] adj (material) しなやかな shináyàka na; (fig: person) 素直な súnào na

pliant [plai'ənt] adj = **pliable**

pliers [plai'ə:rz] npl ペンチ peñchi

plight [plait] n (of person, country) 苦境 kukyō

plimsolls [plim'səlz] (BRIT) npl 運動靴 uñdōgutsu, スニーカー suníkà

plinth [plinθ] n 台座 daíza

plod [plɑ:d] vi (walk) とぼとぼ歩く tóbòtobo arúkù; (fig) 何とかやる nán to ka yárù

plonk [plɑ:ŋk] (inf) n (BRIT: wine) 安ワイン yasúwaìn

♦vt: **to plonk something down** たたきつける物に...を置く tatákitsukeru yō ni ...wo ókù

plot [plɑ:t] n (secret plan) 陰謀 iñbō; (of story, play, film) 筋 sújì, プロット puróttò; (of land) 区画 kukáku

♦vt (sb's downfall etc) たくらむ takúra-

mù; (AVIAT, NAUT: position on chart) 地図 に 書込む chízù ni kakíkomu; (MATH: point on graph) グラフにする gúrafu ni suru
♦*vi* (conspire) 陰謀を企てる iṅbō wò kuwádaterù

plotter [plɑ:t'ə:r] *n* (instrument) 製図道具 seízudōgu

plough [plau] (*US also*: **plow**) *n* (AGR) すき sukí
♦*vt* (earth) 耕す tagáyasù
to plough money into (company, project etc) ...に金をつぎ込む ...ni kané wò tsugíkomù

ploughman's lunch [plau'mənz-] (BRIT) *n* 軽食 keíshoku ◇パブのランチで，パン，チーズ，ピクルスからなる pábù no ráṅchi de, páṅ, chízu, píkùrusu kara nárù

plough through *vt fus* (crowd) ...をかき分けて歩く ...wo kakíwakete arukù

plow [plau] (*US*) = **plough**

ploy [plɔi] *n* 策略 sakúryaku

pluck [plʌk] *vt* (fruit, flower, leaf) 摘む tsúmù; (musical instrument) つま弾く tsumábikù; (bird) ...の羽をむしる ...no hané wò mushírù; (remove hairs from: eyebrow) ...の毛を抜く ...no ké wò nukú
♦*n* (courage) 勇気 yúki
to pluck up courage 勇気を出す yúki wo dásù

plug [plʌg] *n* (ELEC) 差込み sashíkomi, プラグ púràgu; (stopper: in sink, bath) 栓 séṅ; (AUT: *also*: **spark(ing) plug**) スパークプラグ supákupuràgu
♦*vt* (hole) ふさぐ fuságù; (*inf*: advertise) 宣伝する seṅden suru

plug in *vt* (ELEC) ...のプラグを差込む ...no púràgu wo sashíkomù

plum [plʌm] *n* (fruit) プラム púràmu
♦*cpd* (*inf*): **plum job** 甘い汁を吸える職 amái shirù wo suérù shokú

plumage [plu:'midʒ] *n* 羽 hané ◇鳥の体を覆う羽の総称 torí nò karáda wo ōù hané no sōshō

plumb [plʌm] *vt*: **to plumb the depths** (*fig*) (of unpleasant emotion) 辛酸をなめ尽す shiṅsan wò namétsukusù; (of un-

pleasant expression) ...を極端に表現する ...wo kyokútan nì hyṓgen suru

plumber [plʌm'ə:r] *n* 配管工 haíkankō

plumbing [plʌm'iṅ] *n* (piping) 水道設備 suídōsetsubì; (trade, work) 配管業 haíkaṅgyō

plume [plu:m] *n* (of bird) 羽 hané; (on helmet, horse s head) 前立 maédate

plummet [plʌm'it] *vi*: **to plummet (down)** (bird, aircraft) 真っ直ぐに落下する massúgù ni rakká surù; (price, amount, rate) 暴落する bṓraku suru

plump [plʌmp] *adj* (person) ぽっちゃりした potchárî shita
♦*vi*: **to plump for** (*inf*: choose) 選ぶ erábù

plump up *vt* (cushion, pillow) 膨らませる fukúramaserù

plunder [plʌn'də:r] *n* (activity) 略奪 ryakúdatsu; (stolen things) 分捕り品 buṅdorihiṅ
♦*vt* (steal from: city, tomb) 略奪する ryakúdatsu suru

plunge [plʌndʒ] *n* (dive: of bird, person) 飛込み tobíkomi; (*fig*: of prices, rates etc) 暴落 bṓraku
♦*vt* (hand, knife) 突っ込む tsukkómù
♦*vi* (fall: person, thing) 落ちる ochírù; (dive: bird, person) 飛込む tobíkomù; (*fig*: prices, rates etc) 暴落する bṓraku suru
to take the plunge 冒険する bōken suru

plunger [plʌn'dʒə:r] *n* (for sink) プランジャー puráṅjā ◇長い棒の付いたゴムカップ nagáî bō no tsuitá gomúkappù

plunging [plʌn'dʒiṅ] *adj* (neckline) 切込みの深い kiríkomi no fukaî

pluperfect [plu:pə:r'fikt] *n* 過去完了形 kakókanryōkei

plural [plu:r'əl] *adj* 複数の fukúsū no
♦*n* 複数形 fukúsūkei

plus [plʌs] *n* (*also*: **plus sign**) 加符号 kafúgō, プラス púràsu
♦*prep* (MATH) ...に...を加算して ...ni ...wo kasán shite, ...に...を足して ...ni ...wo tashíte; (in addition to) ...に加えて ...ni kuwáete

2 plus 2 is 4 2足す2は4 ní tasù ní wà yóñ

ten/twenty plus (more than) 10〔20〕以上 jû(nijû)ijô

plush [plʌʃ] *adj* (car, hotel etc) 豪華な gô-ka na

plutonium [plu:tou'ni:əm] *n* プルトニウム purútoníumu

ply [plai] *vt* (a trade) 営む itónamù
♦*vi* (ship) 往復する ôfuku suru
♦*n* (of wool, rope) 太さ futósa
to ply someone with drink ...に強引に酒を勧める ...ni gôin nî saké wò susúmerù

plywood [plai'wud] *n* ベニヤ板 benîyaità

P.M. [pi:'em'] *abbr* = **Prime Minister**

p.m. [pi:'em'] *adv abbr* (= *post meridiem*) 午後 gôgò

pneumatic [nu:mæt'ik] *adj* (air-filled) 空気で膨らませた kûki dè fukúramasetà; (powered by air) 空気... kûki...

pneumatic drill *n* 空気ドリル kûkidorîru

pneumonia [nu:moun'jə] *n* 肺炎 haîen

poach [poutʃ] *vt* (steal: fish) 密漁する mitsúryô suru; (: animals, birds) 密猟する mitsúryô suru; (cook: egg) 落し卵にする otóshitamagò ni suru, ポーチエッグにする pôchitoeggù ni suru; (: fish) 煮る nirú
♦*vi* (steal: fish) 密漁する mitsúryô suru; (: animals, birds) 密猟する mitsúryô suru

poached [poutʃt] *adj*: **poached egg** 落し卵 otóshitamagò, ポーチエッグ pôchitoeggù

poacher [pou'tʃəːr] *n* (of fish) 密漁者 mitsúryôshà; (of animals, birds) 密猟者 mitsúryôshà

P.O. Box [pi:'ou-] *n abbr* = **Post Office Box**

pocket [pɑ:k'it] *n* (on jacket, trousers, suitcase, car door etc) ポケット pokéttò; (*fig*: small area) 孤立地帯 korítsuchitài
♦*vt* (put in one's pocket) ポケットに入れる pokéttò ni irérù; (steal) くすねる kusúnerù
to be out of pocket (*BRIT*) 損する sóñ suru

pocketbook [pɑ:k'itbuk] (*US*) *n* (wallet) 財布 saîfu; (handbag) ハンドバッグ hañdobaggù

pocket calculator *n* 電卓 deñtaku

pocket knife *n* ポケットナイフ pokéttonaîfu

pocket money *n* 小遣い kózùkai

pod [pɑ:d] *n* さや sáyà

podgy [pɑ:dʒ'i:] *adj* 小太りの kobûtòri no

podiatrist [pədai'ətrist] (*US*) *n* 足治療医 ashíchiryôi

poem [pou'əm] *n* 詩 shi

poet [pou'it] *n* 詩人 shijîn

poetic [pouet'ik] *adj* (relating to poetry) 詩の shi no; (like poetry) 詩的な shitéki na

poet laureate *n* 桂冠詩人 keikanshijin

poetry [pou'itri:] *n* (LITERATURE) 詩歌 shîika

poignant [pɔin'jənt] *adj* (emotion, look, grief etc) 痛ましい itámashiî

point [pɔint] *n* (*gen*) 点 teñ, ポイント poîñto; (sharp end: of needle, knife etc) せん端 señtan; (purpose) 目的 mokúteki; (significant part) 要点 yôteñ; (detail, aspect, quality) 特徴 tokúchō; (particular place or position) 地点 chitéñ; (moment) 時点 jítèn; (stage in development) 段階 dañkai; (score: in competition, game, sport) 得点 tokúten, 点数 tensû; (*BRIT*: ELEC: socket) コンセント kôñsento; (*also*: **decimal point**) 小数点 shôsûteñ; (in numbers): **2 point 3 (2.3)** 2点3 ní teñ sañ
♦*vt* (show, mark) 指す sásù; (gun etc): **to point something at someone** ...に...を向ける ...ni ...wo mukérù
♦*vi*: **to point at** (with finger, stick etc) ...を指す ...wo sásù

to be on the point of doing something ...をする所である ..wo suru tokoró de árù

to make a point of doing 努めて...する tsutómete ...surù

to get/miss the point 相手が言わんとする事が分かる〔分からない〕aîte gà iwáñ to suru kotŏ ga wakárù〔wakáranaî〕

to come to the point 要点を言う yôteñ

wò iú

there's no point (in doing) (...するの
は) 無意味だ (...surú no wà) muími dà

point-blank [pɔint'blæŋk'] *adv* (say,
ask) ずばり zubárì; (refuse) あっさり as-
sárì; (*also*: **at point-blank range**) 至近距
離で shikínkyorì de

pointed [pɔin'tid] *adj* (stick, pencil, chin,
nose etc) とがった togátta; (*fig*: remark)
辛らつな shíratsu na

pointedly [pɔin'tidli:] *adv* (reply etc) 意
味深長に ímìshinchō ni

pointer [pɔin'tə:r] *n* (on chart, machine)
針 hárì; (*fig*: piece of information or
advice) ヒント hínto

pointless [pɔint'lis] *adj* (useless, senseless) 無意味な muími na

point of view *n* (opinion) 観点 kánten

point out *vt* (in debate etc) ...を指摘する
...wo shitéki suru

points [pɔints] *npl* (AUT) ポイント poínto; (RAIL) 転てつ機 teñtetsukì, ポイント
poínto

point to *vt fus* (*fig*) ...を指摘する ...wo
shitéki suru

poise [pɔiz] *n* (composure) 落ち着き ochítsuki

poison [pɔi'zən] *n* (harmful substance)
毒 dokú

♦*vt* (person, animal: kill with poison) 毒
殺する dokúsatsu suru; (: give poison to)
...に毒を飲ませる ...ni dokú wò nomáserù

poisonous [pɔi'zənəs] *adj* 有毒な yúdoku
na, 毒... dokú...

poke [pɔuk] *vt* (jab with finger, stick etc)
つつく tsutsúkù; (put): **to poke something in(to)** ...の中へ...を突っ込む ...no
nákà e ...wo tsukkómù

poke about *vi* (search) 物色する busshóku suru

poker [pɔu'kə:r] *n* (metal bar) 火かき棒
hikákibò; (CARDS) ポーカー pōkà

poky [pɔu'ki:] *adj* (room, house) 狭苦し
い semákurushiì

Poland [pɔu'lənd] *n* ポーランド pōrando

polar [pɔu'lə:r] *adj* (GEO, ELEC) 極地の
kyókùchi no

polar bear *n* 北極グマ hokkyókugùma

polarize [pɔu'lə:raiz] *vt* 分裂させる buñretsu saserù

Pole [pɔul] *n* ポーランド人 pōrandojìn

pole [pɔul] *n* (post, stick) 棒 bő, さお sáò;
(GEO, ELEC) 極 kyókù

flag pole 旗ざお hatázao

telegraph/telephone pole 電柱 deñchū

pole bean (*US*) *n* (runner bean) インゲ
ン íñgen

police [pəli:s'] *n* (organization) 警察 keísatsu; (members) 警官 keíkan

♦*vt* (street, area, town) ...の治安を維持す
る ...no chián wò íjì suru

police car *n* パトカー patőkà

policeman [pəli:s'mən] (*pl* **policemen**) *n*
警官 keíkan

police state *n* (POL) 警察国家 keísatsu-
kokkà

police station *n* 警察署 keísatsusho

policewoman [pəli:s'wumən] (*pl* **police-
women**) *n* 婦人警官 fujínkeìkan, 婦警 fukéi

policy [pɑ:l'isi:] *n* (POL, ECON: set of
ideas, plans) 政策 seísaku; (*also*: **insurance policy**) 保険証券 hokénshòken

polio [pɔu'li:ou] *n* 小児麻ひ shőnimahì,
ポリオ pórìo

Polish [pɔu'liʃ] *adj* ポーランドの pőrando
no; (LING) ポーランド語の pőrando-
go no

♦*n* (LING) ポーランド語 pőrandogo

polish [pɑ:l'iʃ] *n* (*also*: **shoe polish**) 靴墨
kutsúzumi; (for furniture, floors etc) 光
沢剤 kőtakuzài; (shine: on shoes, floors,
furniture etc) 光沢 kőtaku; (*fig*: refinement) 洗練 señren

♦*vt* (put polish on, make shiny) 磨く
migáku

polished [pɑ:l'iʃt] *adj* (*fig*: person, style)
洗練された señren sareta

polish off *vt* (work) 仕上げる shiágerù;
(food) 平らげる taíragerù

polite [pəlait'] *adj* (person: well-
mannered) 礼儀正しい reígitadashiì;
(socially superior: company, society) 上
流の jőryū no

politeness [pəlait'nis] *n* 礼儀正しさ reígitadashisa

political [pəlit'ikəl] *adj* (relating to politics) 政治の seíji no; (person) 政治に関心ある seíji nì kańshin arù

politically [pəlit'ikli:] *adv* 政治的に seíjiteki ni

politician [pɑ:liti'ʃən] *n* 政治家 seíjika

politics [pɑ:'litiks] *n* (activity) 政治 seíji; (subject) 政治学 seíjigàku
♦*npl* (beliefs, opinions) 政治的思想 seíjitekishisō

poll [poul] *n* (*also*: **opinion poll**) 世論調査 yoróñchòsa; (political election) 選挙 señkyo
♦*vt* (in opinion poll) ...の意見を聞く ...no íkèn wo kikú; (number of votes) 獲得する kakútoku suru

pollen [pɑ:l'ən] *n* 花粉 kafún

polling day [pou'liŋ-] (*BRIT*) *n* 投票日 tóhyòbi

polling station (*BRIT*) *n* 投票所 tóhyòjo

pollute [pəlu:t'] *vt* (air, water, land) 汚染する osén suru

pollution [pəlu:'ʃən] *n* (process) 汚染 osén; (substances) 汚染物質 osénbusshìtsu

polo [pou'lou] *n* (sport) ポロ pórò

polo-necked [pou'lounekt] *adj* (sweater) とっくりえりの tokkúrierì no

poltergeist [poul'tə:rgaist] *n* けん騒霊 keñsōrei, ポルターガイスト porútāgaìsuto

polyester [pɑ:li:es'tə:r] *n* ポリエステル poríesùteru

polyethylene [pɑ:li:eθ'əli:n] (*US*) *n* ポリエチレン poríechirèn

polystyrene [pɑ:li:stai'ri:n] *n* ポリスチレン porísuchirèn

polytechnic [pɑ:li:tek'nik] *n* 科学技術専門学校 kagákugijùtsu senmongakkō ◊ 英国では大学レベルの高等教育機関 eíkoku de wà daígakurebèru no kótōkyòiku kikàn

polythene [pɑ:l'əθi:n] (*BRIT*) *n* = **polyethylene**

pomegranate [pɑ:m'əgrænit] *n* ザクロ zákùro

pomp [pɑ:mp] *n* 華やかさ hanáyàkasa

pompom [pɑ:m'pɑ:m] *n* ポンポン póñpon

pompon [pɑ:m'pɑ:n] *n* = **pompom**

pompous [pɑ:m'pəs] (*pej*) *adj* (person, piece of writing) もったい振った mottáibuttà

pond [pɑ:nd] *n* (natural, artificial) 池 iké

ponder [pɑ:n'də:r] *vt* 熟考する jukkō suru

ponderous [pɑ:n'də:rəs] *adj* (large and heavy) 大きくて重い ōkikute omóì; (speech, writing) 重苦しい omókurushiì

pong [pɔ:ŋ] (*BRIT*: *inf*) *n* 悪臭 akúshū

pontificate [pɑ:ntif'ikeit] *vi* (*fig*): **to pontificate (about)** (...について) もったい振って話す (...ni tsúite) mottáibuttè hanásù

pontoon [pɑ:ntu:n'] *n* (platform) ポンツーン poñtsūn; (for seaplane etc) フロート fúròto

pony [pou'ni:] *n* ポニー pónì

ponytail [pou'ni:teil] *n* (person's hairstyle) ポニーテール poníteru

pony trekking [-trek'iŋ] (*BRIT*) *n* 乗馬旅行 jóbaryokō

poodle [pu:'dəl] *n* プードル púdoru

pool [pu:l] *n* (*also*: **pool of water**) 水たまり mizútamari; (pond) 池 iké; (*also*: **swimming pool**) プール púru; (*fig*: of light, liquid) たまり tamári; (SPORT) 玉突 tamátsuki, ビリヤード birīyàdo
♦*vt* (money, knowledge, resources) 出し合う dashíaù, プールする púru suru
typing pool タイピストのプール taípisùto no púru

pools [pu:lz] *npl* (football pools) トトカルチョ totókarùcho

poor [pu:r] *adj* (not rich: person, place, country) 貧しい mazúshiì, 貧乏な bíñbō na; (bad) 粗末な sómàtsu na
♦*npl*: **the poor** 貧乏人 bíñbònin ◊ 総称 sōshō
poor in (resources etc) ...が不足している ...ga fusóku shite irù

poorly [pu:r'li:] *adj* (ill) 病気の byóki no
♦*adv* (badly: designed) 粗末に sómàtsu ni; (paid, furnished) 不十分に fujūbùn ni

pop [pɑ:p] *n* (MUS) ポップス póppùsu;

(fizzy drink) 炭酸飲料 tańsan-ińryō, ソー
ダ水 sốdasùi; (*inf*: father) 父ちゃんtố-
chan, パパ pápà; (sound) ぽんという音
pốń to iú otò
♦*vt* (put quickly) 突っ込む tsukkómù
♦*vi* (balloon) 破裂する harétsu suru;
(cork) 飛出す tobídasù

popcorn [pɑ:p'kɔ:rn] *n* ポップコーン
poppúkòn

pope [poup] *n* 法王 hốō

pop in *vi* 立寄る tachíyorù

poplar [pɑ:p'lər] *n* ポプラ pópùra

poplin [pɑ:p'lin] *n* ポプリン pópùrin

pop out *vi* 飛出る tobíderù

popper [pɑ:p'ər] (*BRIT*) *n* (for fasten-
ing) スナップ sunáppù

poppy [pɑ:p'i:] *n* ケシ keshí

Popsicle [pɑ:p'sikəl] (® *US*) *n* (ice lolly)
アイスキャンディー aísukyaǹdī

pop star *n* ポップスター poppúsutā

populace [pɑ:p'jələs] *n* 大衆 taíshū

popular [pɑ:p'jələr] *adj* (well-liked: person, place, thing) 人気のある niǹki no
arù; (of ordinary people: idea, belief) 一
般の ippán no, 流行の ryūkō no; (non-
academic) 一般向けの ippánmuke no;
(POL) 国民の kokúmin no

popularity [pɑ:pjəlær'iti:] *n* (of person,
thing, activity) 人気 niǹki

popularize [pɑ:p'jələraiz] *vt* (sport,
music, fashion) 普及させる fukyū sase-
rù; (science, ideas) 分かりやすくする wa-
káriyasukù suru

population [pɑ:pjəleiʃ'ən] *n* (inhabitants:
of country, area) 住民 júmin; (number of
inhabitants) 人口 jiǹkō

populous [pɑ:p'jələs] *adj* (country, city,
area) 人口の多い jiǹkō no ối

pop up *vi* 現れる aráwarerù

porcelain [pɔ:r'səlin] *n* 磁器 jíkì

porch [pɔ:rtʃ] *n* (ARCHIT: entrance) 玄
関 genkan; (*US*) ベランダ beránda

porcupine [pɔ:r'kjəpain] *n* ヤマアラシ
yamáarashi

pore [pɔ:r] *n* (ANAT) 毛穴 keána; (BOT)
気孔 kikố; (GEO) 小穴 koána
♦*vi*: to pore over (book, article etc) 熟
読する jukúdoku suru

pork [pɔ:rk] *n* 豚肉 butániku

pornographic [pɔ:rnəgræf'ik] *adj* (film,
book, magazine) わいせつな waísetsu
na, ポルノの poruno no

pornography [pɔ:rnɑ:'grəfi:] *n* (films,
books, magazines) ポルノ pórùno

porous [pɔ:r'əs] *adj* (soil, rock, clay etc)
小穴の多い koána nò ôi

porpoise [pɔ:r'pəs] *n* イルカ irúka

porridge [pɔ:r'idʒ] *n* オートミール ôto-
mīru

port [pɔ:rt] *n* (harbor) 港 mináto;
(NAUT: left side) 左げん sagén; (wine)
ポートワイン pốtowaìn
port of call 寄港地 kikốchì

portable [pɔ:r'təbəl] *adj* (television,
typewriter, telephone etc) 携帯用の keítai yố no, ポータブルの pốtaburu no

porter [pɔ:r'tər] *n* (for luggage) 赤帽 a-
kábō, ポーター pốtā; (doorkeeper) 門番
moñban

portfolio [pɔ:rtfou'li:ou] *n* (case) かばん
kabán; (POL) 大臣の職 daíjin no shokú;
(FINANCE) ポートフォリオ pốtoforìo;
(of artist) 代表作品集 daíhyōsakuhìnshū

porthole [pɔ:rt'houl] *n* げん窓 geńsō

portion [pɔ:r'ʃən] *n* (part) 部分 búbùn;
(helping of food) 一人前 ichíninmaè

portly [pɔ:rt'li:] *adj* (man) 太った futótta

portrait [pɔ:r'trit] *n* (picture) 肖像 shố-
zō, ポートレート pốtorèto

portray [pɔ:rtrei'] *vt* (subj: artist) 描く
egákù; (: actor) 演じる eńjirù

portrayal [pɔ:rtrei'əl] *n* (artist's: *also*
representation in book, film etc) 描写
byốsha; (actor's) 演技 eńgi

Portugal [pɔ:r'tʃəgəl] *n* ポルトガル porútogàru

Portuguese [pɔ:rtʃəgi:z'] *adj* ポルトガル
の porútogàru no; (LING) ポルトガル語
の porútogarugồ no
♦*n inv* ポルトガル人 porútogarujìn;
(LING) ポルトガル語 porútogarugồ

pose [pouz] *n* (posture) ポーズ pồzu
♦*vi* (pretend): *to pose as* ...を装う ...wo
yosóoù, ...の名をかたる ...no ná wò katárù
♦*vt* (question) 持出す mochídasù; (prob-

lem, danger) ...である ...de árù

to pose for (painting etc) ...のためにポーズを取る ...no tamé nì pôzu wo tórù

posh [pɑːʃ] (*inf*) *adj* (smart: hotel, restaurant etc) 高級な kốkyū na; (upper class: person, behavior) 上流階級の jốryūkaíkyū no

position [pəzíʃən] *n* (place: of house, thing, person) 位置 íchì; (of person's body) 姿勢 shiséi; (social status) 地位 chíì; (job) 職 shokù; (in race, competition) 第...位 daí ...i; (attitude) 態度 taído; (situation) 立場 tachíba

♦*vt* (person, thing) 置く okú

positive [pɑːzʼ ətiv] *adj* (certain) 確かな táshīka na; (hopeful, confident) 確信している kakúshin shite irú; (definite: decision, action, policy) 積極的な sekkyókuteki na

posse [pɑːsʼíː] (*US*) *n* 捜索隊 sôsakutai

possess [pəzesʼ] *vt* (have, own: car, watch, radio etc) 所有する shoyū suru, 保有する hoyū suru; (quality, ability) ...がある ...ga árù, ...を持っている ...wo móttè irú; (subj: feeling, belief) 支配する shíhài suru

possession [pəzeʃʼən] *n* (state of possessing) 所有 shoyū

to take possession of 占領する seńryō suru

possessions [pəzeʃʼənz] *npl* (belongings) 持物 mochímòno

possessive [pəzesʼiv] *adj* (of another person) ...の愛情を独占したがる ...no aíjō wò dokúsen shitagarù; (of things) 他人に使わせたがらない tanín nì tsukáwasetagaranài; (LING) 所有を表す shoyū wò aráwasu

possibility [pɑːsəbiĺʼ əti:] *n* 可能性 kanốsei; (possible event) 可能な事 kanố na kotð

possible [pɑːsʼəbəl] *adj* (which can be done) 可能な kanố na; (event, reaction) 有り得る aríurù; (candidate, successor) 成り得る naríurù

it's possible (may be true) そうかも知れない số ka mð shirénal

as fast as possible できるだけ早く de-

kíru dakè hayákù

possibly [pɑːsʼəbli:] *adv* (perhaps) あるいは arúiwa; (expressing surprise, shock, puzzlement) ...が考えられない ...ga kańgaerarenài; (emphasizing someone's efforts) できる限り dekíru kagirì

I cannot possibly come どう合っても私は行かれません dốatté mo watákushi wa ikáremaseñ

post [poust] *n* (*BRIT*: service, system) 郵便 yūbin; (: letters) 郵便(物) yūbin (bùtsu); (delivery) 配達 haítatsu ◊1回分の配達郵便を指す ikkáibun no haítatsuyūbin wo sásù; (pole) 柱 hashíra; (job, situation) 職 shokú; (MIL) 持場 mochíba

♦*vt* (*BRIT*: send by post) 郵送する yūsố suru; (: put in mailbox) 投かんする tốkan suru; (: appoint): *to post someone to* ...を...へ配置する ...wo ...e haíchi suru

postage [pous'tidʒ] *n* (charge) 郵便料金 yūbin ryốkin

postage stamp *n* (郵便)切手 (yūbin) kitté

postal [pous'təl] *adj* (charges, service, strike) 郵便の yūbin no

postal order *n* 郵便為替 yūbin kawàse

postbox [poust'bɑːks] (*BRIT*) *n* (郵便)ポスト (yūbin)pósùto

postcard [poust'kɑːrd] *n* (郵便)葉書 (yūbin) hagáki

postcode [poust'koud] (*BRIT*) *n* 郵便番号 yūbin bañgō

postdate [poust'deit] *vt* (check) ...に先の日付を付ける ...ni sakí nò hizúke wò tsukérù

poster [pous'təːr] *n* ポスター pósùtā

poste restante [poust res'tɑːnt] (*BRIT*) *n* 局留 kyokúdome

posterity [pɑːsteːr'iti:] *n* 後世 kốsei

postgraduate [poustgrædʒ'uːit] *n* 大学院生 daígakuiñsei

posthumous [pɑːs'tʃəməs] *adj* (award, publication) 死後の shígð no

postman [poust'mən] (*pl* **postmen**) *n* 郵便屋 yūbin-ya

postmark [poust'mɑːrk] *n* 消印 keshíin

post-mortem [poustmɔːr'təm] *n* 司法解剖 shihốkaibð, 検死解剖 keńshikaibð

post office n (building) 郵便局 yūbiñkyoku; (organization): *the Post Office* 郵政省 yūseíshō

Post Office Box n 私書箱 shishóbàko

postpone [poustpoun'] vt 延期する eñki suru

postscript [poust'skript] n 追伸 tsuíshin

posture [pɑːs'tʃəːr] n (position of body) 姿勢 shiséi; (fig) 態度 taído

postwar [poust'wɔːr] adj (building, period, politics) 戦後の señgo no

posy [pou'ziː] n 花束 hanátàba ◇小さい花束を指すと chiísaí hanátàba wo sásù

pot [pɑːt] n (for cooking) なべ nábè; (also: **teapot**) ティーポット típottò; (also: **coffeepot**) コーヒーポット kóhīpottò; (tea/coffee in pot) ティー〔コーヒー〕ポット一杯 tí〔kóhī〕pottò íppai; (bowl, container: for paint etc) つぼ tsubó; (flowerpot) 植木鉢 uékibàchi; (inf: marijuana) マリファナ maríffàna

◆vt (plant) 鉢に植える hachí nì uérù

to go to pot (inf: work, performance) 駄目になる damé ni narù

potato [pətei'tou] (pl **potatoes**) n ジャガイモ jagáimo

potato peeler [-piː'ləːr] n 皮むき器 kawámukikì

potent [pout'ənt] adj (powerful: weapon, argument, drink) 強力な kyōryoku na; (man) 性的能力のある seítekinōryoku no árù

potential [pəten'tʃəl] adj (candidate) 成り得る narúrù; (sales, success) 可能な kanō na; (danger etc) 潜在する señzai suru

◆n (talents, abilities) 潜在能力 señzaińryoku; (promise, possibilities) 将来性 shōraisei

potentially [pəten'tʃəliː] adv 潜在的に señzaiteki ni

pothole [pɑːt'houl] n (in road) 穴ぼこ anábòko; (BRIT: underground) 洞くつ dōkutsu

potholing [pɑːt'houliŋ] (BRIT) n: *to go potholing* 洞くつを探検する dōkutsu wo tañken suru

potion [pou'ʃən] n (of medicine, poison etc) 水薬 mizúgusùri

potluck [pɑːt'lʌk] n: *to take potluck* 有り合せの物で間に合せる aríawase no monò de ma ní awaserù

potted [pɑːt'id] adj (food) つぼ詰めの tsubózume no; (plant) 鉢植えの hachíue no; (abbreviated: account, biography etc) 要約した yōyaku shita

potter [pɑːt'əːr] n (pottery maker) 陶芸家 tōgeika

◆vi: *to potter around/about in the garden* (BRIT) ぶらぶらと庭いじりをする búrabura to niwáijiri wo suru

pottery [pɑːt'əːriː] n (pots, dishes etc) 陶器 tōki; (factory, workshop) 陶器製造所 tōkiseizōjo

potty [pɑːt'iː] adj (inf: mad) 狂った kurúttà

◆n (for child) おまる o-máru

pouch [pautʃ] n (for tobacco, coins etc) 小袋 kobúkuro; (ZOOL) 袋 fukúro

poultry [poul'triː] n (live chickens, ducks etc) 家きん kakíñ; (meat from chickens etc) 鳥肉 toríniku

pounce [pauns] vi: *to pounce on* (animal, person) ...に襲い掛る ...ni osóikakarù; (fig: mistake, idea etc) 攻撃する kōgeki suru

pound [paund] n (unit of weight) ポンド póñdo; (BRIT: unit of money) ポンド póñdo

◆vt (beat: table, wall etc) 強くたたく tsúyòku tatákù; (crush: grain, spice etc) 砕く kudákù

◆vi (heart) どきどきする dókìdoki suru

pound sterling n ポンド póñdo

pour [pɔːr] vt (tea, wine, cereal etc) つぐ tsugú

◆vi (water, blood, sweat etc) 流れ出る nagárederù

to pour someone a drink ...に酒をついでやる ...ni saké wò tsuíde yarù

pour away/off vt 流して捨てる nagáshite suterù

pour in vi (people) ぞろぞろと入って来る zórðzoro to haítte kurù; (information) 続々と入る zókùzoku to haíru

pouring [pɔːr'iŋ] adj: *pouring rain* 土砂

降りの雨 dosháburi no amè

pour out vi (people) ぞろぞろと出て来る zórózoro to deté kurù

♦vt (tea, wine etc) つぐ tsugú; (fig: thoughts, feelings, etc) せきを切った様に吐き出す sékì wo kittá yô ni hakídasù

pout [paut] vi 膨れっ面をする fukúrettsura wò suru

poverty [pɑːvˈəːrtiː] n 貧乏 bínbō

poverty-stricken [pɑːvˈəːrtiːstrikən] adj (people, town, country) 非常に貧しい hijō ní mazúshiì

powder [pauˈdəːr] n (tiny particles of solid substance) 粉 koná; (face powder) おしろい oshíroi, パウダー páùdā

♦vt: **to powder one's face** 顔におしろいをつける kaó nì oshíroi wò tsukérù

powder compact n コンパクト kónpakuto

powdered milk [pauˈdəːrd-] n 粉ミルク konámirùku

powder puff n パフ páfù

powder room n 化粧室 keshóshitsu

power [pauˈəːr] n (control: over people, activities) 権力 kénryoku; (ability, opportunity) 能力 nóryoku; (legal right) 権利 kénri; (of explosion, engine) 威力 íryòku; (electricity) 電力 dénryoku

to be in power (POL etc) 権力を握っている kénryoku wo nigítte irù

power cut (BRIT) n 停電 teíden

powered [pauˈəːrd] adj: **powered by** ...で動く ...de ugókù

power failure n 停電 teíden

powerful [pauˈəːrfəl] adj (person, organization) 権力のある yúryoku na; (body) 力強い chikárazuyoì; (blow, kick etc) 強力な kyóryoku na; (engine) 馬力の強い baríki no tsuyoí; (speech, piece of writing) 力強い chikárazuyoì

powerless [pauˈəːrlis] adj (without control or influence) 無力な múryòku na

powerless to do ...する力がない ...súrù chikára ga naì

power point (BRIT) n コンセント kónsento

power station n 発電所 hatsúdensho

p.p. [piːˈpiːˈ] abbr (= per procurationem):

p.p. J. Smith J.Smithの代理として jē sumísù no daíri tòshité; (= pages) ページ péji

PR [piːɑːrˈ] abbr = **public relations**

practicable [prækˈtikəbəl] adj (scheme, task, idea) 実用的な jitsúyoteki na

practical [prækˈtikəl] adj (not theoretical: difficulties, experience etc) 実際の jissái no; (person: sensible) 現実的な geñjitsuteki na; (: good with hands) 器用な kíyo na; (ideas, methods) 現実的な geñjitsuteki na; (clothes, things: sensible) 実用的な jitsúyoteki na

practicality [præktikælˈitiː] n (no pl) 現実主義 geñjitsushùgi; (of situation etc) 現実 geñjitsu

practical joke n 悪ふざけ warúfuzàke

practically [prækˈtikliː] adv (almost) ほとんど hotóñdo

practice [prækˈtis] n (habit) 習慣 shúkan; (of profession) 業務 gyómu; (REL) おきてを守る事 okíte wò mamóru kotò; (exercise, training) 練習 reńshū; (MED, LAW: business) 開業 kaígyo

♦vt (train at: musical instrument, sport etc) 練習する reńshū suru; (carry out: custom, craft etc) 行う okónaù; (religion) ...のおきてを守る ...no okite wo mamoru; (profession) ...に従事する ...ni jūji suru

♦vi (train) 練習する reńshū suru; (lawyer, doctor etc) ...の業務をする ...no gyómu wo suru

in practice (in reality) 実際には jissái ni wà

out of practice 腕が鈍って udé gà nibúttè

practicing [prækˈtisiŋ] (BRIT **practising**) adj (Christian etc) おきてを守っている okíte wò mamótte irù; (doctor, lawyer) 業務をしている gyómu wo shité irù

practise [prækˈtis] vt, vi (BRIT) = **practice**

practitioner [præktiˈʃənəːr] n (MED): **medical practitioner** 医者 ishá

pragmatic [prægmætˈik] adj (person, reason etc) 現実的な geñjitsuteki na

prairie [preːrˈiː] n 草原 sógen

praise [preiz] *n* (expression of approval, admiration) 賞賛 shōsan

♦*vt* (express approval, admiration: of person, thing, action etc) ほめる homérù

praiseworthy [preiz'wə:rði:] *adj* (person, act etc) ほめるべき homérùbeki

pram [præm] (*BRIT*) *n* 乳母車 ubágurùma

prance [præns] *vi* (person) 威張って歩く ibátte arùku; (horse) 躍る様に歩く odóru yō ni arúkù

prank [præŋk] *n* いたずら itázura

prawn [prɔ:n] *n* エビ ebí

pray [prei] *vi* (REL) 祈る inórù; (*fig*) 祈る inórù, 願う negáù

prayer [pre:r] *n* (REL: activity, words) 祈り inóri

preach [pri:tʃ] *vi* (REL) 説教する sékkyō suru; (*pej*: moralize) お説教する o-sékkyō suru

♦*vt* (peace, doctrine etc) 説く tókù

to preach a sermon 説教する sékkyō suru

preacher [pri:'tʃə:r] *n* (REL) 説教者 sekkyōshà

preamble [pri:'æmbəl] *n* (to spoken words) 前置き maéoki; (to written words) 前書 maégaki

precarious [prikeə:r'i:əs] *adj* (dangerous: position, situation) 不安定な fuántei na; (*fig*) 危険な kikén na

precaution [prikɔ:'ʃən] *n* 用心 yōjin

precede [prisi:d'] *vt* (event, period of time) ...の前に起る ...no máè ni okórù; (person) ...の前を歩く ...no máè wo arúkù; (sentence, paragraph, chapter) ...の前にある ...no máè ni árù

precedence [pres'idəns] *n* (priority) 優先 yūsen

precedent [pres'idənt] *n* (action, official decision) 判例 hañrei; (something that has happened before) 先例 señrei

preceding [prisi:'diŋ] *adj* (chapter, programme, day) ...の前の ...no máè no

precept [pri:'sept] *n* おきて okíte

precinct [pri:'siŋkt] *n* (*US*: part of city) 管区 káñku

pedestrian precinct (*BRIT*) 歩行者天

国 hokṓshateñgoku

shopping precinct (*BRIT*) ショッピングセンター shóppìngu señtā ◇車が閉出される kurúma gà shimédasarerù

precincts [pri:'siŋkts] *npl* (of a large building) 構内 kōnai

precious [preʃ'əs] *adj* (commodity: valuable, useful) 貴重な kichṓ na; (object, material) 高価な kōka na

precious stone *n* 宝石 hōseki

precipice [pres'əpis] *n* 断崖 dañgai

precipitate [prisip'iteit] *vt* (hasten) 早める hayámerù

precise [prisais'] *adj* (exact: time, nature etc) 正確な seíkaku na; (detailed: instructions, plans etc) 細かい komákaì

precisely [prisais'li:] *adv* (accurately) 正確に seíkaku ni; (exactly) その通り sonṓ tōri

precision [prisiʒ'ən] *n* 正確さ seíkakusa

preclude [priklu:d'] *vt* (action, event) 不可能にする fukánō ni suru

precocious [prikou'ʃəs] *adj* (child, talent) 早熟な sõjuku na

preconceived [pri:kənsi:vd'] *adj*:
preconceived idea 先入観 señnyūkan

precondition [pri:kəndiʃ'ən] *n* 前提条件 zeñteijṓken

precursor [prikə:r'sə:r] *n* (person) 先駆者 señkushà; (thing) 前触れ maébure

predator [pred'ətə:r] *n* 捕食者 hoshókushà

predecessor [pred'isesə:r] *n* (person) 前任者 zeñniñsha

predestination [pri:destinei'ʃən] *n* 予定説 yotéisètsu

predicament [pridik'əmənt] *n* 苦境 kukyṓ

predict [pridikt'] *vt* 予言する yogén suru

predictable [pridikt'əbəl] *adj* (event, behavior etc) 予知できる yóchì dekírù

prediction [pridik'ʃən] *n* 予言 yogén

predominantly [pridɑ:m'ənəntli:] *adv* 圧倒的に attṓteki ni

predominate [pridɑ:m'əneit] *vi* (person, thing) ...が圧倒的に多い ...ga attṓteki nî ṓì; (feature, quality) 目立つ medátsù

pre-eminent [pri:em'ənənt] *adj* (person,

thing) 優れた sugúretá

pre-empt [pri:'empt] *vt* (decision, action, statement) 先取りする sakídori suru

preen [pri:n] *vt*: **to preen itself** (bird) 羽繕いをする hazúkùroi wo suru

to preen oneself 得意がる tokúígaru

prefab [pri:'fæb] *n* プレハブ住宅 puréhabujútaku

prefabricated [pri:fæb'rikeitid] *adj* (buildings) プレハブの puréhabu no

preface [pref'is] *n* (in book) 前書 maégaki

prefect [pri:'fekt] (*BRIT*) *n* (in school) 監督生 kańtokuséi

prefer [prifə:r'] *vt* (like better: person, thing, activity) ...の方を好む ...no hố wò konómù

to prefer doing/to do ...する方が好きである ...suru hố gà sukí de arù

preferable [pref'ərəbəl] *adj* ...が望ましい ...ga nozómashìì

preferably [prifə:r'əbli:] *adv* できれば dekírèba

preference [pref'ə:rəns] *n* (liking) 好み konómi

to give preference to ...を優先的に扱う ...wo yűsenteki nì atsúkaù

preferential [prefəren'tʃəl] *adj*: **preferential treatment** 優先的な取扱い yűsenteki nà torítsatsukai

prefix [pri:'fiks] *n* 接頭辞 settốjì

pregnancy [preg'nənsi:] *n* (of woman, female animal) 妊娠 nińshin

pregnant [preg'nənt] *adj* (woman, female animal) 妊娠している nińshin shite irù

prehistoric [pri:histɔ:r'ik] *adj* (person, dwelling, monster etc) 有史以前の yűshiizèn no

prejudice [predʒ'ədis] *n* (unreasonable dislike) 偏見 heńken; (bias in favor) ひいき hííki

prejudiced [predʒ'ədist] *adj* (person: prejudiced against) ...に対して偏見のある ...ni táìshite heńken no arù; (: prejudiced in favor) ...をひいきにした ...wo hííki ni shitá

preliminary [prilim'əne:ri:] *adj* (action,

discussion) 予備的な yobíteki na

prelude [prei'lu:d] *n* (preliminary event) 前兆 zeńchō; (*MUS*) 序曲 jókyòku

premarital [pri:mær'itəl] *adj* 婚前の końzen no

premature [pri:mətʃu:r'] *adj* (earlier than expected: baby) 早産の sôzan no; (death, arrival) 早過ぎた hayásugita; (too early: action, event etc) 時期尚早の jíkìshōsō no

premature aging 早老 sốrō

premeditated [primed'əteitid] *adj* 計画的な keíkakuteki na

premier [primjir'] *adj* (best) 最良の saíryō no

♦*n* (*POL*) 総理大臣 sốridaìjin, 首相 shushố

première [primjir'] *n* (of film) 初公開 hatsúkōkai; (of play) 初演 shoén

premise [prem'is] *n* 前提 zeńtei

premises [prem'isiz] *npl* (of business, institution) 構内 kốnai

on the premises 構内で kốnai de

premium [pri:'mi:əm] *n* (*COMM*: extra sum of money) 割増金 warímashikin, プレミアム purémiamu; (: sum paid for insurance) 掛金 kakékin

to be at a premium (expensive) 高価である kôka de arù; (hard to get) 手に入りにくい té nì haírinikùi

premium bond (*BRIT*) *n* 割増金付き債券 warímashikintsukisaìken ◊抽選による賞金が付く chúsen ni yorù shốkin ga tsukù

premonition [preməniʃ'ən] *n* 予感 yokán

preoccupation [pri:a:kjəpei'ʃən] *n* (obsession) 専念する事 seńnen surù kotő; (worry) 気掛りな事 kigákàri na kotő

preoccupied [pri:a:k'jəpaid] *adj* (person) 上の空になった uwánosora ni nátta

prep [prep] *n* (*SCOL*: study) 勉強 beñkyō

prepaid [pri:peid'] *adj* (paid in advance) 支払い済みの shiháraizumi no

preparation [prepərei'ʃən] *n* (activity) 準備 júnbi; (food) 料理 ryőri; (medicine) 薬品 yakúhin; (cosmetic) 化粧品 keshốhin

preparations [prepərei'ʃənz] *npl* (arrangements) 準備 júnbi

preparatory [pripær'ətɔːriː] *adj* (report) 予備の yóbì no; (training) 準備の júnbi no

preparatory school *n* (*US*) 予備校 yobíkō; (*BRIT*) 私立小学校 shirítsu shōgakkō

prepare [pripeːr'] *vt* (make ready: plan, speech, meal etc) 準備する júnbi suru; (CULIN) 調理する chōri suru
◆*vi*: **to prepare for** (event, action) ...の 準備をする ...no júnbi wo suru
prepared to (willing) ...する用意がある ...surú yōi ga árù
prepared for (ready) ...の用意ができて いる ...no yōi ga dékìte irú

preponderance [pripɑːn'dərəns] *n* (of people, things) 大多数 daítasū

preposition [prepəziʃ'ən] *n* 前置詞 zeńchishi

preposterous [pripɑːs'tərəs] *adj* (suggestion, idea, situation) 途方もない tohōmonaì

prep school *n* = **preparatory school**

prerequisite [prirek'wizit] *n* 必要条件 hitsúyōjōken

prerogative [prərɑːg'ətiv] *n* (of person, group) 特権 tokkén

Presbyterian [prezbitiːr'iːən] *adj* 長老派 の chōrōha no
◆*n* 長老派の信者 chōrōha no shiñja

preschool [priː'skuːl'] *adj* (age, child, education) 就学前の shūgakumaè no

prescribe [priskraib'] *vt* (MED: medicine) 処方する shohō suru; (treatment) 命ずる meízurù

prescription [priskrip'ʃən] *n* (MED: slip of paper) 処方せん shohōsen; (: medicine) 処方薬 shohōyàku

presence [prez'əns] *n* (state of being somewhere) ...に居る事 ...ni irú kotò; (*fig*: strong personal quality) 風さい fūsai; (spirit, invisible influence) 霊 reí
in someone's presence ...の居る前で ...no irú maè de

presence of mind *n* 機転 kitén

present [*adj, n* prez'ənt *vb* prizent'] *adj* (current: person, thing) 現在の geñzai no; (in attendance) 出席している shussé-

ki shite irù
◆*n* (actuality): **the present** 現在 geñzai; (gift) 贈り物 okúrimono, プレゼント purézènto
◆*vt* (give: prize, award etc) 贈る okúrù; (cause, provide: difficulty, threat etc) ...になる ...ni nárù; (information) 与える atáerù; (describe: person, thing) 描写す る byōsha suru; (RADIO, TV) 提供する teíkyō suru; (formally introduce: person) 紹介する shōkai suru
to give someone a present ...にプレゼ ントを上げる ...ni purézènto wo agérù
at present 今の所 imá no tokoro

presentable [prizen'təbəl] *adj* (person) 人前に出られる hitómae nì derárerù

presentation [prezəntei'ʃən] *n* (of plan, proposal, report etc) 提出 teíshutsu; (appearance) 体裁 teísai; (formal ceremony) 贈呈式 zōteishìki

present-day [prez'əntdei'] *adj* 現代の geñdai no

presenter [prizen'tər] *n* (RADIO, TV) 司会者 shikáīsha

presently [prez'əntliː] *adv* (soon) 間もな く mamónàku; (now) 現在 geñzai

preservation [prezə·rvei'ʃən] *n* (act of preserving) 保存 hozón; (state of being preserved) 保存状態 hozónjōtai

preservative [prizə·r'vətiv] *n* (for food, wood, metal etc) 保存剤 hozónzai

preserve [prizə·rv'] *vt* (maintain: situation, condition) 維持する íjì suru; (: building, manuscript) 保存する hozón suru; (food) 保存する hozón suru
◆*n* (*often pl*: jam, marmalade) ジャム já-mù

preside [prizaid'] *vi*: **to preside (over)** (meeting, event etc) (...の) 議長をする (...no) gichō wò suru

presidency [prez'idənsiː] *n* (POL: post) 大統領職 daítōryōshokù; (: time in office) 大統領任期 daítōryō no nińki

president [prez'idənt] *n* (POL) 大統領 daítōryō; (of organization) ...長 ...chō

presidential [prezidən't'ʃəl] *adj* 大統領の daítōryō no

press [pres] *n*: **the Press** (newspapers)

報道機関 hódōkikàn; (journalists) 報道陣 hódōjìn; (printing press) 印刷機 ínsatsukì; (of switch, button, bell) 押す事 osú kotò
◆vt (hold one thing against another) 押付ける oshítsukerù; (button, switch, bell etc) 押す osú; (iron: clothes) ...にアイロンを掛ける ...ni áiron wò kakérù; (put pressure on: person) せき立てる sekítaterù; (insist): **to press something on someone** ...に ...を押付ける ...ni ...wo o-shítsukerù
◆vi (squeeze) 押える osáerù; (pressurize): **to press for** (improvement, change etc) ...のために働く ...no tamé nì határakù; (forcibly) 強要する kyóyō suru
we are pressed for time/money 時間〔金〕が足りない jíkàn〔kané〕ga tarínai

press agency n 通信社 tsúshìnsha
press conference n 記者会見 kishákaìken
pressing [pres'iŋ] adj (engagement, decision etc) 緊急の kíñkyū no
press on vi (despite problems etc) ひるまずに続ける hirúmazù ni tsuzúkerù
press stud (BRIT) n スナップ sunáppù
press-up [pres'ʌp] (BRIT) n 腕立て伏せ udétatefùse
pressure [preʃ'əːr] n (physical force: also fig) 圧力 atsúryòku; (also: **air pressure**) 気圧 kiátsu; (also: **water pressure**) 水圧 suíatsu; (also: **oil pressure**) 油圧 yuátsu; (stress) 圧迫 appáku, プレッシャー purésshā
to put pressure on someone (to do) (...する様に) ...に圧力を掛ける (...surú yò ni) ...ni atsúryòku wo kakérù
pressure cooker n 圧力ガマ atsúryoku-gàma
pressure gauge n 圧力計 atsúryokukei
pressure group n (POL) 圧力団体 atsúryokudañtai, プレッシャーグループ purésshāgurūpu
pressurized [preʃ'əraizd] adj (cabin, container, spacesuit) 気圧を一定に保った kiátsu wò ittéi ni tamottà
prestige [presti:ʒ'] n 名声 meísei
prestigious [prestidʒ'əs] adj 著名な cho-

méi na
presumably [prizu:'məbli:] adv たぶん tábùn, おそらく osóraku
presume [prizu:m'] vt: **to presume (that)** (suppose) (...だと) 推定する (...dá tò) suítei suru
presumption [prizʌmp'ʃən] n (supposition) 推定 suítei
presumptuous [prizʌmp'tʃu:əs] adj せん越な señ-etsu na
presuppose [pri:səpouz'] vt ...を前提とする ...wo zeñtei tò suru
pretence [pritens'] (US also: **pretense**) n (false appearance) 見せ掛け misékake
under false pretences うそを言って úsò wo itté
pretend [pritend'] vt (feign) ...の振りをする ...no furí wò suru
◆vi (feign) 見せ掛ける misékakerù
to pretend to do ...する振りをする ...suru furí wò suru
pretense [pritens'] (US) n = **pretence**
pretentious [priten'tʃəs] adj (claiming importance, significance: person, play, film etc) うぬぼれた unúboreta
pretext [pri:'tekst] n 口実 kójitsu
pretty [prit'i:] adj (person, thing) きれいな kírèi na
◆adv (quite) かなり kánàri
prevail [priveil'] vi (be current: custom, belief) はやる hayárù; (gain acceptance, influence: proposal, principle) 勝つ kátsù
prevailing [privei'liŋ] adj (wind) 卓越風 takúetsufù; (dominant: fashion, attitude etc) 一般の ippán no
prevalent [prev'ələnt] adj (common) 一般的な ippánteki na
prevent [privent'] vt: **to prevent someone from doing something** ...が...をするのを妨げる ...ga ...wo suru no wò samátagerù
to prevent something from happening ...が起るのを防ぐ ...ga okórù no wo fuségù
preventative [priven'tətiv] adj = **preventive**
prevention [priven'tʃən] n 予防 yobó

preventive [priven'tiv] *adj* (measures, medicine) 予防の yobō no

preview [pri:'vju:] *n* (of film) 試写会 shishákài; (of exhibition etc) 招待展示内覧 shōtaitenjinaîran

previous [pri:'vi:əs] *adj* (earlier: event, thing, period of time) 前の mâe no

previously [pri:'vi:əsli:] *adv* 前に mâe ni

pre-war [pri:'wɔːr'] *adj* 戦前の seńzen no

prey [prei] *n* 獲物 emôno
♦*vi*: **to prey on** (animal: feed on) ...を捕食する ...wo hoshóku suru
it was preying on his mind 彼はそれを気にしていた kâre wa soré wò ki ní shite itá

price [prais] *n* (amount of money) 値段 nedán; (*fig*) 代価 daíshō
♦*vt* (goods) ...に値段を付ける ...ni nedán wò tsukérù

priceless [prais'lis] *adj* 非常に貴重な hijō nì kichó na

price list *n* 値段表 nedáñhyð

prick [prik] *n* (short, sharp pain) ちくっとする痛み chikúttò suru itámi
♦*vt* (make hole in) 鋭い物で刺す surúdoì monó dè sású; (cause pain) ちくっと刺す chikúttò sásù
to prick up one's ears (listen eagerly) 耳を澄まして聞く mimí wò sumáshite kikú

prickle [prik'əl] *n* (of plant) とげ togé; (sensation) ちくちくする痛み chíkùchiku suru itámi

prickly [prik'li:] *adj* (plant) とげだらけの togédaràke no; (fabric) ちくちくする chíkùchiku suru

prickly heat *n* 汗も asémo

pride [praid] *n* (satisfaction) 誇り hokôri; (dignity, self-respect) 自尊心 jisôñshin, プライド puráido; (*pej*: feeling of superiority) 高慢 kôman
♦*vt*: **to pride oneself on** ...を誇りとする ...wo hokóri tð suru

priest [pri:st] *n* (Christian: Catholic, Anglican etc) 司祭 shisâî; (non-Christian) 僧侶 sôryo

priestess [pri:s'tis] *n* (non-Christian) みこ mîkð

priesthood [pri:st'hud] *n* (position) 司祭職 shisáishoku

prig [prig] *n* 気取り屋 kidóriyà

prim [prim] (*pej*) *adj* (formal, correct) 堅苦しい katákurushiî; (easily shocked) 上品ぶった jōhìnbutta

primarily [praimer:'ili:] *adv* (above all) 主に ômô ni

primary [prai'me:ri:] *adj* (first in importance) 主要な shuyō na
♦*n* (*US*: election) 予備選挙 yobíseñkyo

primary school *n* 小学校 shôgakkô

primate [prai'meit] *n* (ZOOL) 霊長類 reíchōrui

prime [praim] *adj* (most important) 最も重要な mottómò jûyô na; (best quality) 最上の saîjô no
♦*n* (of person's life) 盛り sakári
♦*vt* (wood) ...に下塗りをする ...ni shitánuri wò suru; (*fig*: person) ...に教え込む ...ni oshíekomù
prime example (typical) 典型的な例 teñkeiteki nà reí

Prime Minister *n* 総理大臣 sôridaljin, 首相 shushô

primeval [praimi:'vəl] *adj* (existing since long ago): *primeval forest* 原生林 geñseîrin; (feelings, tribe) 原始的な geñshiteki na

primitive [prim'ətiv] *adj* 原始的な geñshiteki na

primrose [prim'rouz] *n* ツキミソウ tsukímisò

primus (stove) [prai'məs-] (*BRIT*) *n* 石油こんろ sekíyukoñro

prince [prins] *n* (son of king etc) 王子 ôji; (son of Japanese emperor) 親王 shiñnô

princess [prin'sis] *n* (daughter of king etc) 王女 ôjo; (daughter of Japanese emperor) 内親王 naíshinnô

principal [prin'səpəl] *adj* (most important: reason, character, aim etc) 主要な shuyô na
♦*n* (of school) 校長 kôchô; (of college) 学長 gakúchô

principle [prin'səpəl] *n* (moral belief) 信念 shíñnen; (general rule) 原則 geñsoku; (scientific law) 法則 hôsoku *in principle* (theoretically) 原則として geńsoku tòshité

on principle (morally) 主義として shugí tòshité

print [print] *n* (letters and numbers on page) 印刷文字 ińsatsumojì; (ART) 版画 hańga; (PHOT) 陽画 yṑga、プリント purínto; (footprint) 足跡 ashíatò; (fingerprint) 指紋 shimón

♦*vt* (produce: book, newspaper, leaflet) 印刷する ińsatsu suru; (publish: story, article etc) 記載する kisái suru; (cloth) ...になっ染まる ...ni nassén suru; (write in capitals) 活字体で書く katsújitai dè kákù

out of print 絶版で zeppán de

printed matter [prin'tid-] *n* 印刷物 ińsatsubùtsu

printer [prin'tər] *n* (person, firm) 印刷屋 ińsatsuyà; (machine) 印刷機 ińsatsukì

printing [prin'tiŋ] *n* (act, art) 印刷 ińsatsu

printout [print'aut] *n* (COMPUT) プリントアウト puríntoaùto

prior [prai'ər] *adj* (previous: knowledge, warning, consent etc) 事前の jizén no; (more important: claim, duty) より重要な yorí jūyō na

prior to ...の前に ...no máè ni

priority [praio:r'iti:] *n* (most urgent task) 優先課題 yūseńkadài; (most important thing, task) 最重要課題 saíjūyōkadài

to have priority (over) (...に) 優先する (...ni) yūsen suru

prise [praiz] *vt*: *to prise open* こじ開ける kojíakerù

prism [priz'əm] *n* プリズム purízumu

prison [priz'ən] *n* (building) 刑務所 keímusho

♦*cpd* 刑務所の keímusho no

prisoner [priz'ənə:r] *n* (in prison) 囚人 shújin; (captured person) 捕虜 hóryò

prisoner of war *n* 戦争捕虜 seńsōhoryò

pristine [pris'ti:n] *adj* (condition: new) 真新しい maátarashiì; (: like new) 新品同様の shińpindōyō no

privacy [prai'vəsi:] *n* プライバシー puráibashì

private [prai'vit] *adj* (not public: property, club etc) 私有の shiyū no、プライベートの puráibēto no; (not state-owned: industry, service) 民間の mińkan no; (discussion, sitting etc) 非公開の hikṓkai no; (personal: activities, belongings) 個人の kojín no; (: thoughts, plans) 心の中の kokóro no naka no; (quiet: place) 奥まった okúmattà; (: person) 内気な uchíki na; (confidential) 内密の naímitsu no; (intimate) 部外者立入禁止の bugáisha tachíirikinshi no

♦*n* (MIL) 兵卒 heísotsu

「*private*」 (on envelope) 親展 shińten; (on door) 部外者立入禁止 bugáishà tachíirikinshi

in private 内密に naímitsu ni

private enterprise *n* (not state owned) 民間企業 mińkan kigyò; (owned by individual) 個人企業 kójin kigyò

private eye *n* 私立探偵 shirítsutañtei

private property *n* 私有地 shiyūchì

private school *n* (fee-paying) 私立学校 shirítsugakkṑ

privatize [prai'vətaiz] *vt* (government-owned company etc) 民間に払い下げる mińkan nì haráí sagerù

privet [priv'it] *n* イボタノキ ibótanoki

privilege [priv'əlidʒ] *n* (advantage) 特権 tokkén; (opportunity) 光栄な機会 kōei na kikaì

privileged [priv'əlidʒd] *adj* (having advantages) 特権のある tokkén no arù; (having special opportunity) 光栄な機会を得た kōei na kikaì wo etá

privy [priv'i:] *adj*: *to be privy to* 内々に関知している naínai nì káñchi shité irù

prize [praiz] *n* (reward) 賞 shō

♦*adj* (first class) 典型的な teńkeiteki na

♦*vt* 重宝する chṓhō suru

prize-giving [praiz'giviŋ] *n* 表彰式 hyṓshōshìki

prizewinner [praiz'winə:r] *n* 受賞者 jushṓshà

pro [prou] *n* (SPORT) 職業選手 shokúgyōseñshu、プロ púrò

♦prep (in favor of) ...に賛成して ...ni sańsei shite

the pros and cons 賛否両論 sáńpiryōron

probability [prɑːbəbil'əti:] *n* (likelihood): *probability of/that* ...の(...が起る)公算 ...no (...ga okórù) kōsan

in all probability たいてい taítei

probable [prɑːb'əbəl] *adj* (likely to happen) 起りそうな okórisō na; (likely to be true) ありそうな arísō na

probably [prɑːb'əbli:] *adv* たぶん tábùn, おそらく osóraku

probation [prəbei'ʃən] *n*: *on probation* (LAW) 保護観察で hogōkańsatsu de; (employee) 見習いで minárai de

probe [proub] *n* (MED) ゾンデ zóǹde; (SPACE) 探査衛星 tańsaeisèi; (enquiry) 調査 chósa

♦vt (investigate) 調査する chósa suru; (poke) ついって探る tsutsúite sagúrù

problem [prɑːb'ləm] *n* 問題 mońdai

problematic(al) [prɑːbləmæt'ik(əl)] *adj* 問題になる mońdai ni narú

procedure [prəsi:'dʒər] *n* (way of doing something) やり方 yaríkata; (ADMIN, LAW) 手続 tetsúzuki

proceed [prəsi:d'] *vi* (do afterwards): *to proceed to do something* ...をし始める ...wo shihájimerù; (continue): *to proceed (with)* (...を)続ける (...wo) tsuzúkerù; (activity, event, process: carry on) 続ける tsuzúkerù; (person: go) 行く ikú

proceedings [prəsi:'diŋz] *npl* (organized events) 行事 gyōji; (LAW) 訴訟手続き soshōtetsuzùki

proceeds [prou'si:dz] *npl* 収益 shūeki

process [prɑːs'es] *n* (series of actions: *also* BIOL, CHEM) 過程 katéi, プロセス purósèsu

♦vt (raw materials, food) 加工する kakō suru; (information) 処理する shórì suru

processing [prɑːs'esiŋ] *n* (PHOT) 現像 geńzō

procession [prəseʃ'ən] *n* 行列 gyóretsu

proclaim [prəkleim'] *vt* (announce) 宣言する señgen suru

proclamation [prɑːkləmei'ʃən] *n* 宣言 señgen

procrastinate [prəkræs'təneit] *vi* 先に延ばす sakí nì nobásù

procreation [proukri:ei'ʃən] *n* 生殖 seíshoku

procure [prəkjur'] *vt* 調達する chótatsu suru

prod [prɑːd] *vt* (push: with finger, stick, knife etc) つつく tsutsúkù

♦n (with finger, stick, knife etc) 一突き hitótsuki

prodigal [prɑːd'əgəl] *adj*: *prodigal son/daughter* 放とう息子(娘) hōtōmusùko (musùme)

prodigious [prədidʒ'əs] *adj* 巨大な kyódai na

prodigy [prɑːd'ədʒi:] *n* 天才 teńsai

produce [*n* prou'du:s *vb* prədu:s'] *n* (AGR) 農産物 nōsanbùtsu

♦vt (cause: effect, result etc) 起す okósù; (make, create: object) 作る tsukúrù; (BIOL: fruit, seeds) つける tsukérù, ...には...がなる ...ni wa ...ga narú; (: young) 産む umú; (CHEM) 作り出す tsukúridasù; (fig: evidence, argument) 示す shimésù; (: bring or take out) 取出す torídasù; (play, film, program) 製作する seísaku suru

producer [prədu:'sər] *n* (of film, play, program, record) 製作者 seísakushà, プロデューサー puródyūsà; (country: of food, material) 生産国 seísankòku; (company: of food, material) 生産会社 seísangaìsha

product [prɑːd'əkt] *n* (thing) 産物 sańbutsu; (result) 結果 kekká

production [prədʌk'ʃən] *n* (process of manufacturing, growing) 生産 seísan; (amount of goods manufactured, grown) 生産高 seísańdaka; (THEATER) 上演 jōen

electricity production 発電 hatsúden

production line *n* 工程ライン kōteiraìn, ライン ráìn

productive [prədʌk'tiv] *adj* (person, thing: *also fig*) 生産的な seísanteki na

productivity [prɑːdəktiv'əti:] *n* 生産能

力 seísannóryoku

profane [prəfein'] *adj* (secular, lay) 世俗
的な sezőkuteki na; (language etc) 下品
な gehín na

profess [prəfes'] *vt* (claim) 主張する shuchő suru; (express: feeling, opinion) 明言
する meígen suru

profession [prəfeʃ'ən] *n* (job requiring
special training) 知的職業 chitékishoku-
győ; (people) 同業者仲間 dőgyōshanakà-
ma

professional [prəfeʃ'ənəl] *adj* (skill,
organization, advice) 専門職の seímoñ-
shoku no; (not amateur: photographer,
musician etc) プロの púrò no; (highly
trained) 専門家の seímonka no; (of a
high standard) 本職らしい hoñshokura-
shiî

♦*n* (doctor, lawyer, teacher etc) 知的職
業者 chitékishokugyőshà; (SPORT) プロ
púrò; (skilled person) 玄人 kúròto

professor [prəfes'ə:r] *n* (US) 教師 kyő-
shi, 先生 seńsei; (BRIT) 教授 kyőju

proficiency [prəfiʃ'ənsi:] *n* 熟練 jukúren

proficient [prəfiʃ'ənt] *adj* 熟練した jukúren shita

profile [prou'fail] *n* (of person's face) 横
顔 yokőgaò; (fig: article) 経歴 keíreki

profit [pra:f'it] *n* (COMM) 利益 ríeki

♦*vi*: **to profit by/from** (fig) ...がために
なる ...ga tamé nì nárù

profitability [pra:fitəbil'əti:] *n* (ECON)
収益性 shúekisei

profitable [pra:f'itəbəl] *adj* (ECON) 利
益になる ríeki ni nárù

profound [prəfaund'] *adj* (great: shock,
effect) 強い tsuyóì; (intellectual: idea,
work) 深遠な shiñ-en na

profusely [prəfju:s'li:] *adv* (bleed) 多量に
taryő ni; (thank) 重ね重ね kasánegasàne

profusion [prəfju:'ʒən] *n* 大量 taíryō

prognoses [pra:gnou'si:z] *npl of* **prognosis**

prognosis [pra:gnou'səs] (*pl* **prognoses**)
n (forecast) 予想 yoső; (of illness) 予後
yőgð

program [prou'græm] (BRIT **programme**) *n* (of actions, events) 計画 keí-

kaku; (RADIO, TV) 番組 bañgumi; (leaflet) プログラム purőguràmu;
(COMPUT) プログラム purőguràmu

♦*vt* (machine, system) ...にプログラムを
入れる ...ni purőguràmu wo irérù

programing [prou'græmiŋ] (BRIT **programming**) *n* (COMPUT) プログラム作
成 purőguramu sakuseì, プログラミング
purőguramiñgu

programmer [prou'græmə:r] *n*
(COMPUT) プログラマー purőguràmā

progress [*n* pra:g'res *vb* pragres'] *n*
(process of getting nearer to objective)
前進 zeńshin; (changes, advances in society) 進歩 shíñpo; (development) 発展 hattén

♦*vi* (become more advanced, skilled) 進
歩する shíñpo suru; (become higher in
rank) 昇進する shőshin suru; (continue)
続く tsuzúkù

in progress (meeting, battle, match) 進
行中で shiñkőchū de

progression [pragreʃ'ən] *n* (gradual
development) 進展 shiñten; (series) 連続
reñzoku

progressive [pragres'iv] *adj* (person) 進
歩的な shiñpoteki na; (change) 段階的な
dañkaiteki na

prohibit [prouhib'it] *vt* (forbid, make illegal) 禁じる kiñjirù

prohibition [prouəbiʃ'ən] *n* (law, rule)
禁則 kiñsoku; (forbidding: of strikes,
alcohol etc) 禁止 kiñshi; (US): **Prohibition** 禁酒法時代 kiñshuhőjidài

prohibitive [prouhib'ətiv] *adj* (price etc)
法外な hő gai na, 手が出ない様な tế gầ
dénai yō na

project [*n* pra:dʒ'ekt *vb* pradʒekt'] *n*
(large-scale plan, scheme) 計画 keíkaku;
(SCOL) 研究テーマ keñkyűtēma

♦*vt* (plan) 計画する keíkaku suru; (estimate: figure, amount) 見積る mitsúmorù; (light) 投射する tősha suru; (film, picture) 映写する eísha suru

♦*vi* (stick out) 突出る tsukíderù

projectile [pradʒek'təl] *n* 弾丸 dañgan

projection [pradʒek'ʃən] *n* (estimate) 見
積り mitsúmori; (overhang) 突起 tokkí;

(CINEMA) 映写 eísha

projector [prədʒek'tə:r] n 映写機 eíshakì

proletarian [proulite:r'i:ən] adj 無産階級の musánkaìkyū no, プロレタリアの purôretarla no

proletariat [proulite:r'i:ət] n 無産階級 musánkaìkyū, プロレタリア purôretarla

proliferate [proulif'ə:reit] vi 急増する kyúzo suru

prolific [proulif'ik] adj (artist, composer, writer) 多作の tasáku no

prologue [prou'lɔːg] n (of play) 序幕 jomáku, プロローグ purôrồgu; (of book) 序言 jogén

prolong [prəlɔːŋ] vt (life, meeting, holiday) 引延ばす hikínobasù, 延長する eńchō suru

prom [prɑːm] n abbr = promenade; (US: ball) 学生舞踏会 gakúseibutòkai

promenade [prɑːməneid'] n (by sea) 海岸の遊歩道 kaígan nò yúhodồ

promenade concert (BRIT) n 立見席のある音楽会 tachímisèki no árù oñgakukài

prominence [prɑːm'ənəns] n (importance) 重要性 jūyōsei

prominent [prɑːm'ənənt] adj (important) 重要な jūyō na; (very noticeable) 目立つ medátsù

promiscuous [prəmis'kju:əs] adj (person) 相手構わずにセックスをする aíte kamawazù ni sékkùsu wo suru

promise [prɑːm'is] n (vow) 約束 yakúsoku; (talent) 才能 saínō; (hope) 見込み mikómi
♦vi (vow) 約束する yakúsoku suru
♦vt: to promise someone something, promise something to someone ...に ...を約束する ...ni ...wo yakúsoku suru
to promise (someone) to do something/that (...に) ...すると約束する (...ni) ...surú to yakúsoku suru

promising [prɑːm'isiŋ] adj (person, thing) 有望な yúbō na

promote [prəmout'] vt (employee) 昇進させる shôshin saserù; (product, pop star) 宣伝する señden suru; (ideas) 促進

する sokúshin suru

promoter [prəmou'tə:r] n (of event) 興業主 kôgyồshù, プロモーター purômồtầ; (of cause, idea) 推進者 suíshiñsha

promotion [prəmou'ʃən] n (at work) 昇進 shôshin; (of product, event, idea) 宣伝 señden

prompt [prɑːmpt] adj (rapid: reaction, response etc) 迅速な jiñsoku na
♦adv (exactly) 丁度 chôdo
♦n (COMPUT) プロンプト purôñputo
♦vt (cause) ...の原因となる ...no geñ-in tò narú; (when talking) ...に水を向ける ...ni mizú wò mukérù
to prompt someone to do something ...が...をするきっ掛けとなる ...ga ...wo suru kikkáke to narù

promptly [prɑːmpt'li:] adv (immediately) 直ちに tádàchi ni; (exactly) 丁度 chôdo

prone [proun] adj (lying face down) うつ伏せの utsúbuse no
prone to (inclined to) ...しがちな ...shigáchi na

prong [prɔːŋ] n (of fork) 歯 há

pronoun [prou'naun] n 代名詞 daímeìshi

pronounce [prənauns'] vt (word) 発音する hatsúon suru; (declare) 言言する señgen suru; (give verdict, opinion) 言渡す iíwatasù

pronounced [prənaunst'] adj (marked) 著しい ichíjirushiì

pronunciation [prənʌnsi:ei'ʃən] n 発音 hatsúon

proof [pru:f] n (evidence) 証拠 shôko; (TYP) 校正刷り kôseizuri, ゲラ gerá
♦adj: proof against ...に耐えられる ...ni taérarerù

prop [prɑːp] n (stick, support: also fig) 支え sasáe
♦vt (also: prop up) 支える sasáerù; (lean): to prop something against ...を...に立掛ける ...wo ...ni tatékakerù

propaganda [prɑːpəgæn'də] n 宣伝 señden, プロパガンダ purôpagañda

propagate [prɑːp'əgeit] vt (idea, information) 普及させる fukyů saserù

propel [prəpel'] vt (vehicle, boat,

machine) 推進する suíshin suru; (*fig*: person) 駆立てる karítaterù

propeller [prəpel'əːr] *n* プロペラ puróperà

propensity [prəpen'siti:] *n* 傾向 keíkō

proper [praːp'əːr] *adj* (real, authentic) ちゃんとした chánto shita; (correct) 正しい tadáshiì; (suitable) 適当な tekítō na; (socially acceptable) 社会の通念にかなった shákai no tsūnen ni kanáttà; (referring to place): *the village proper* 村そのもの murá sono monò

properly [praːp'əːrli:] *adv* (adequately: eat, study) 充分に júbun ni; (decently: behave) 正しく tadáshiku

proper noun *n* 固有名詞 koyúmeìshi

property [praːp'əːrti:] *n* (possessions) 財産 zaísan; (building and its land) 物件 bukkén; (land owned) 所有地 shoyúchì; (quality: of substance, material etc) 特性 tokúsei

property owner *n* 地主 jinúshi

prophecy [praːf'isi:] *n* 予言 yogén

prophesy [praːf'isai] *vt* (predict) 予言する yogén suru

prophet [praːf'it] *n* (REL) 予言者 yogénsha

prophetic [prəfet'ik] *adj* (statement, words) 予言的な yogénteki na

proportion [prəpɔːr'ʃən] *n* (part: of group, amount) 割合 waríai; (number: of people, things) 数 kázù; (ratio) 率 rítsù

proportional [prəpɔːr'ʃənəl] *adj*: *proportional (to)* (...に) 比例する (...ni) hiréi suru

proportional representation *n* 比例代表制 hiréidaihyōsei

proportionate [prəpɔːr'ʃənit] *adj*: *proportionate (to)* (...に) 比例する (...ni) hiréi suru

proposal [prəpou'zəl] *n* (plan) 提案 teían

a proposal (of marriage) 結婚の申込み kekkón nò móshikomi, プロポーズ purópòzu

propose [prəpouz'] *vt* (plan, idea) 提案する teían suru; (motion) 提出する teíshutsu suru; (toast) ...の音頭を取る ... no óndo wo tórù

♦*vi* (offer marriage) 結婚を申込む kekkón wò móshikomù, プロポーズする purópòzu suru

to propose to do ...するつもりでいる ...suru tsumóri de irù

proposition [praːpəziʃ'ən] *n* (statement) 主張 shuchő; (offer) 提案 teían

proprietor [prəprai'ətəːr] *n* (of hotel, shop, newspaper etc) 持主 mochínushi, オーナー ōnā

propriety [prəprai'əti:] *n* (seemliness) 礼儀正しさ reígitadashìsa

pro rata [-rɑː'tə] *adv* 比例して hiréi shite

prosaic [prouzei'ik] *adj* (person, piece of writing) 散文的な sañbunteki na

prose [prouz] *n* (not poetry) 散文 sañbun

prosecute [praːs'əkjuːt] *vt* (LAW) 訴追する sotsúi suru

prosecution [praːsəkjuː'ʃən] *n* (action) 訴追 sotsúi; (accusing side) 検察側 keñsatsugàwa

prosecutor [praːs'əkjuːtəːr] *n* (*also*: **public prosecutor**) 検察官 keñsatsukàn

prospect [praːs'pekt] *n* (possibility) 可能性 kanősei; (outlook) 見込み mikómi

♦*vi*: *to prospect (for)* (gold etc) (...を) 探鉱する (...wo) tañkō suru

prospecting [praːs'pektiŋ] *n* (for gold, oil etc) 探鉱 tañkō

prospective [prəspek'tiv] *adj* (son-in-law, customer, candidate etc) ...になろうとしている ...ni naró tò shité irù

prospects [praːs'pekts] *npl* (for work etc) 見込み mikómi

prospectus [prəspek'təs] *n* (of college, school, company) 要綱 yṓkō

prosper [praːs'pəːr] *vi* (person, business, city etc) 繁栄する hañ-ei suru

prosperity [praːsper'iti:] *n* 繁栄 hañ-ei

prosperous [praːs'pəːrəs] *adj* (person, city etc) 裕福な yúfuku na; (business etc) 繁盛している hañjō shite irù

prostitute [praːs'titutt] *n* (female) 売春婦 baíshuñfu; (male) 男娼 dañshō

prostrate [praːs'treit] *adj* (face down) うつ伏せの utsúbuse no

protagonist [proutæg'ənist] *n* (supporter) 支援者 shiénsha; (leading participant: in event, movement) リーダー格の人 rídākaku nò hitó; (THEATER) 主役 shuyáku; (in story etc) 主人公 shujínkō

protect [prətékt'] *vt* (person, thing) 守る mamórù, 保護する hógò suru

protection [prətek'ʃən] *n* 保護 hógò

protective [prətek'tiv] *adj* (clothing, layer, etc) 防護の bŏgò no; (gesture) 防衛の bŏei no; (person) 保護的な hogóteki na

protégé [prou'təʒei] *n* 偉い人のひいきを受ける人 erái hitó nò hiíki wò ukérù hitó

protein [prou'ti:n] *n* たんぱく質 taṅpakushitsu

protest [*n* prou'test *vb* prətest'] *n* (strong expression of disapproval, opposition) 抗議 kŏgi

♦*vi*: **to protest about/against/at** ...に抗議する ...ni kŏgi suru

♦*vt* (insist): **to protest (that)** (...だと) 主張する (...dá tò) shuchŏ suru

Protestant [prɑ:t'istənt] *adj* 新教の shiṅkyō no, プロテスタントの purótesùtanto no

♦*n* 新教徒 shiṅkyŏto, プロテスタント教徒 purótesùtanto kyŏto

protester [prətes'tə:r] *n* 抗議者 kŏgishà

protocol [prou'təkɔ:l] *n* 外交儀礼 gaíkōgirèi

prototype [prou'tətaip] *n* 原型 geṅkei

protracted [proutræk'tid] *adj* (absence, meeting etc) 長引いた nagábiita

protrude [proutru:d'] *vi* (rock, ledge, teeth etc) 突出る tsukéderù

proud [praud] *adj* (pleased): **proud of** ...を誇りとする ...wo hokóri tò suru; (dignified) プライドのある puráido no arù; (arrogant) 尊大な soṅdai na

prove [pru:v] *vt* (verify) 立証する risshŏ suru

♦*vi*: **to prove (to be) correct** *etc* 結局...が正しいと判明する kekkyóku ...ga tadáshii tò hafímei suru

to prove oneself 自分の才能を立証する jibún nò saínō wò risshŏ suru

proverb [prɑ:v'ə:rb] *n* ことわざ kotówaza

proverbial [prəvə:r'bi:əl] *adj* ことわざの kotówaza no

provide [prəvaid'] *vt* (give) 与える atáerù; (make available) 供給する kyŏkyū suru

to provide someone with something ...に...を供給する ...ni ...wo kyŏkyō suru

provided (that) [prəvaid'did-] *conj* ...という条件で ...tó iù jŏken de

provide for *vt fus* (person) ...の面倒を見る ...no meṅdō wò mírù

♦*vt* (future event) ...に備える ...ni sonáerù

Providence [prɑ:v'idəns] *n* 摂理 sétsùri

providing [prəvai'diŋ] *conj*: **providing (that)** ...という条件で ...tó iù jŏken de

province [prɑ:v'ins] *n* (of country) 県 kéñ; (*fig*) 管轄 kaṅkatsu

provincial [prəvin't'ʃəl] *adj* (town, newspaper etc) 地方の chihŏ no; (*pej*) 田舎じみた inákajimità

provision [prəviʒ'ən] *n* (supplying) 供給 kyŏkyū; (of contract, agreement) 規定 kitéi

provisional [prəviʒ'ənəl] *adj* (government, agreement, arrangement etc) 暫定的な zaṅteiteki na

provisions [prəviʒ'ənz] *npl* (food) 食料 shokúryō

proviso [prəvai'zou] *n* 規定 kitéi

provocation [prɑ:vəkei'ʃən] *n* 挑発 chŏhatsu

provocative [prəvɑ:k'ətiv] *adj* (remark, article, gesture) 挑発的な chŏhatsuteki na; (sexually stimulating) 扇情的な seṅjōteki na

provoke [prəvouk'] *vt* (annoy: person) 怒らせる okóraserù; (cause: fight, argument etc) 引起こす hikíokosù

prow [prau] *n* へさき hesáki, 船首 séṅshu

prowess [prau'is] *n* (outstanding ability) 手腕 shúwàn

prowl [praul] *vi* (*also*: **prowl about, prowl around**) うろつく urótsukù

♦*n*: **on the prowl** あさり歩いて asáriaruitè

prowler [prau'lə:r] *n* うろつく人 urótsuku hitó

proximity [prɑ:ksim'iti:] *n* 近さ chikása
proxy [prɑ:k'si:] *n*: **by proxy** 代理を通じて dafri wò tsújite
prude [pru:d] *n* 上品ぶる人 jóhiñburu hitó
prudence [pru:'dəns] *n* (care, sense) 慎重さ shiñchōsa
prudent [pru:'dənt] *adj* (careful, sensible) 慎重な shiñchō na
prune [pru:n] *n* 干しプラム hoshípuràmu
♦*vt* (bush, plant, tree) せん定する sefitei suru
pry [prai] *vi*: **to pry (into)** (...を) せん索する (...wo) sefisaku suru
PS [pi:es'] *abbr* = **postscript**
psalm [sɑ:m] *n* 詩編 shihén
pseudo- [su:'dou] *prefix* 偽... nisé...
pseudonym [su:'dənim] *n* 筆名 hitsúmei, ペンネーム peñnèmu
psyche [sai'ki:] *n* 精神 seíshin
psychiatric [saiki:æt'rik] *adj* (hospital, problem, treatment) 精神科の seíshinka no
psychiatrist [sikai'ətrist] *n* 精神科医 seíshinka-ì
psychiatry [sikai'ətri:] *n* 精神医学 seíshin-igàku
psychic [sai'kik] *adj* (person: *also*: **psychical**) 霊媒の reíbai no; (of the mind) 精神の seíshin no
psychoanalysis [saikouənæl'isis] *n* 精神分析 seíshinbuñseki
psychoanalyst [saikouæn'əlist] *n* 精神分析医 seíshinbunseki-ì
psychoanalyze [saikouæn'əlaiz] *vt* ...の精神分析をする ...no seíshinbuñseki wo suru
psychological [saikələ:dʒ'ikəl] *adj* (related to the mind: difference, problem etc) 精神的な seíshinteki na; (related to psychology: test, treatment etc) 心理的な shiñriteki na
psychologist [saikɑ:l'ədʒist] *n* 心理学者 shiñrigakùsha
psychology [saikɑ:l'ədʒi:] *n* (study) 心理学 shiñrigàku; (mind) 心理 shiñri
psychopath [sai'kəpæθ] *n* 精神病質者 seíshinbyōshitsushà

psychosomatic [saikousoumæt'ik] *adj* 精神身体の seíshinshiñtai no
psychotic [saikɑ:t'ik] *adj* 精神病の seíshinbyō no
PTO [pi:ti:'ou'] *abbr* (= *please turn over*) 裏面に続く rímen ni tsuzukù
pub [pʌb] *n* *abbr* (= *public house*) 酒場 sakába, パブ pábù
puberty [pju:'bə:rti:] *n* 思春期 shishúñki
pubic [pju:'bik] *adj*: **pubic hair** 陰毛 iñmō
public [pʌb'lik] *adj* (of people: support, opinion, interest) 国民の kokúmin no; (for people: building, service) 公共の kókyō no; (for people to see: statement, action etc) 公の ōyake no
♦*n*: **the public** (all people of country, community) 公衆 kōshū; (particular set of people) ...層 ...sō; (fans, supporters) 支持者 shijíshà
in public 公に ōyake ni, 人前で hitómaè de
to make public 公表する kōyō suru
public address system *n* 場内放送 (装置) jōnaihōsō(sōchi)
publican [pʌb'likan] *n* パブの亭主 pábù no teíshu
publication [pʌblikei'ʃən] *n* (act) 出版 shuppán; (book, magazine) 出版物 shuppáñbutsu
public company *n* 株式会社 kabúshiki-gaìsha
public convenience (*BRIT*) *n* 公衆便所 kōshūbeñjo
public holiday *n* 休日 kyújitsu
public house (*BRIT*) *n* 酒場 sakába, パブ pábù
publicity [pʌblis'əti:] *n* (information) 宣伝 señden; (attention) 広く知られる事 hírōku shiráreru kotò
publicize [pʌb'ləsaiz] *vt* (fact, event) 報道する hōdō suru
publicly [pʌb'likli:] *adv* 公に ōyake ni, 人前で hitómaè de
public opinion *n* 世論 yóròn
public relations *n* 広報活動 kōhōkatsu-dō, ピーアール píarù
public school *n* (*US*) 公立学校 kóritsu-

gakkō; (BRIT) 私立学校 shirítsugakkō

public-spirited [pʌb'likspir'itid] *adj* 公共心のある kókyōshin nò árù

public transport *n* 公共輸送機関 kókyō-yusōkikaǹ

publish [pʌb'liʃ] *vt* (book, magazine) 出版する shuppán suru, 発行する hakkō suru; (letter etc: in newspaper) 記載する kisái suru; (subj: person: article, story) 発表する happyō suru

publisher [pʌb'liʃə:r] *n* (person) 発行者 hakkōshà; (company) 出版社 shuppáǹsha

publishing [pʌb'liʃiŋ] *n* (profession) 出版業 shuppangyō

puce [pjuːs] *adj* 暗かっ色の aǹkasshoku no

pucker [pʌk'əːr] *vt* (part of face) ...をしかめる ...wo shikámerù; (fabric etc) ...にしわを寄せる ...ni shiwá wò yoserù

pudding [pud'iŋ] *n* (cooked sweet food) プディング púdìngu; (BRIT: dessert) デザート dezāto

black pudding ブラッドソーセージ buráddosōsèji

puddle [pʌd'əl] *n* (also: **a puddle of water**) 水溜まり mizutamari; (of blood etc) 溜まり tamari

puff [pʌf] *n* (of cigarette, pipe) 一服 ippúku; (gasp) あえぎ aégi; (of air, smoke) 一吹き hitófuki

♦*vt*: *to puff one's pipe* パイプをふかす pálpu wo fukásù

♦*vi* (breathe loudly) あえぐ aégù

puffed [pʌft] (inf) *adj* (out of breath) 息を切らせた íki wo kirásetà

puff out *vt* (fill with air: one's chest, cheeks) 膨らます fukúramasù

puff pastry *n* パイ皮 paíkawa

puffy [pʌf'iː] *adj* (eye) はれぼったい harébottaì; (face) むくんだ mukúǹda

pull [pul] *n* (tug): *to give something a pull* ...を引っ張る ...wo hippárù

♦*vt* (gen) 引く hikú; (tug: rope, hair etc) 引っ張る hippárù

♦*vi* (tug) 引く hikú, 引っ張る hippárù

to pull to pieces 引き裂く hikísakù

to pull one's punches 手加減する teká-

gen suru

to pull one's weight 仲間同様に働く nakámadōyo ni határakù

to pull oneself together 落着きを取り戻す ochítsuki wò torímodosù

to pull someone's leg (fig) ...をからかう ...wo karákaù

pull apart *vt* (break) ばらばらにする barábara nì suru

pull down *vt* (building) 取り壊す toríko-wasù

pulley [pul'iː] *n* 滑車 kasshá

pull in *vi* (AUT: at the curb) ...に停車する ...ni teísha suru; (RAIL) 到着する tō-chaku suru

pull off *vt* (take off: clothes etc) 脱ぐ núgù; (fig: difficult thing) ...に成功する ...ni seíkō suru

pull out *vi* (AUT: from curb) 発進する hasshín suru; (RAIL) 出発する shuppátsu suru

♦*vt* (extract) 取出す torídasù

pull over *vi* (AUT) 道路わきに寄せて停車する dōrowaki ni yosete teísha suru

pullover [pul'ouvə:r] *n* セーター sētā

pull through *vi* (MED) 治る naórù

pull up *vi* (AUT, RAIL: stop) 停車する teísha suru

♦*vt* (raise: object, clothing) 引上げる hi-kíagerù; (uproot) 引抜く hikínukù

pulp [pʌlp] *n* (of fruit) 果肉 kaníku

pulpit [pul'pit] *n* 説教壇 sekkyōdaǹ

pulsate [pʌl'seit] *vi* 脈動する myakúdō suru

pulse [pʌls] *n* (ANAT) 脈拍 myakúhaku; (rhythm) 鼓動 kodō; (BOT) 豆類 mamé-rùi

pulverize [pʌl'vəːraiz] *vt* (crush to a powder) 砕く kudákù; (fig: destroy) 破壊する hakái suru

puma [puː'mə] *n* ピューマ pyūma

pummel [pʌm'əl] *vt* 続け様にげんこつで打つ tsuzúkezama nì geǹkotsu de utsù

pump [pʌmp] *n* (for water, air, petrol) ポンプ póǹpu; (shoe) パンプス páǹpusu

♦*vt* (force: in certain direction: liquid, gas) ポンプで送る póǹpu de okúrù; (obtain supply of: oil, **water**, gas) ポンプ

で汲む pónpu de kúmù

pumpkin [pʌ́mp'kin] *n* カボチャ kabócha

pump up *vt* (inflate) ポンプで膨らます pónpu de fukúramasù

pun [pʌn] *n* しゃれ sharé

punch [pʌntʃ] *n* (blow) げんこつで打つ事 geñkotsu dè útsù kotó, パンチ páñchi; (tool: for making holes) パンチ páñchi; (drink) ポンチ póñchi

♦*vt* (hit): *to punch someone/something* げんこつで...を打つ geñkotsu de ...wo útsù

punchline [pʌntʃ'lain] *n* 落ち ochí

punch-up [pʌntʃ'ʌp] (*BRIT: inf*) *n* けんか keñka

punctual [pʌŋk'tʃuːəl] *adj* 時間を厳守する jíkàn wo geñshu suru

punctuation [pʌŋktʃuːei'ʃən] *n* 句読法 kutóhò

puncture [pʌŋk'tʃəːr] *n* パンク pañku

♦*vt* ...に穴を開ける ...ni aná wo akérù

pundit [pʌn'dit] *n* 物知り monóshiri

pungent [pʌn'dʒənt] *adj* (smell, taste) 刺激的な shigékiteki na

punish [pʌn'iʃ] *vt* (person, crime) 罰する bassúrù

punishment [pʌn'iʃmənt] *n* (act) 罰する事 bassúrù kotó; (way of punishing) 罰 bátsù

punk [pʌŋk] *n* (*also*: **punk rock**) パンクロック pañkurokkù; (*also*: **punk rocker**) パンクロッカー pañkurokkà; (*US: inf*: hoodlum) ちんぴら chíñpira

punt [pʌnt] *n* (boat) ボート bòto ◇底が平らでさおで川底を突いて進める物を指す sokó ga taira de sâò de kawázoko wo tsuitè susúmeru mono wò sásù

punter [pʌn'təːr] *n* (*BRIT*: gambler) ばくち打ち bakúchiùchi; (*inf*: client, customer) 客 kyakú

puny [pju:'ni:] *adj* (person, effort) ちっぽけな chippóke na

pup [pʌp] *n* (young dog) 子イヌ koínu

pupil [pju:'pəl] *n* (SCOL) 生徒 seíto; (of eye) どう孔 dókò

puppet [pʌp'it] *n* (doll) 操り人形 ayátsurinìñgyō; (*fig*: person) かいらい kaírai

puppy [pʌp'i:] *n* 子イヌ koínu

purchase [pəːr'tʃis] *n* (act of buying) 購入 kónyū; (item bought) 買い物 kaímono

♦*vt* (buy: house, book, car etc) 買う káù

purchaser [pəːr'tʃisəːr] *n* 買い手 kaíte

pure [pju:r] *adj* (not mixed with anything: silk, gold etc) 純粋な juñsui na; (clean, healthy: water, air etc) 清潔な seíketsu na; (*fig*: woman, girl) 純潔な juñketsu na; (complete, total: chance, bliss) 全くの mattáku no

purée [pjurei'] *n* (of tomatoes, potatoes, apples etc) ピューレ pyùre

purely [pju:r'li:] *adv* 単に táñ ni

purgatory [pəːr'gətɔ:ri:] *n* (REL) れん獄 reñgoku; (*fig*) 地獄 jigóku

purge [pəːrdʒ] *n* (POL) 粛正 shukúsei, パージ pàji

♦*vt* (organization) 粛正する shukúsei suru, パージする pàji suru

purify [pju:r'əfai] *vt* (air, water etc) 浄化する jòka suru

purist [pju:r'ist] *n* 純正主義者 juñseishugìshà

puritan [pju:r'itən] *n* 禁欲主義者 kiñ-yoku shugìshà

purity [pju:r'iti:] *n* (of silk, gold etc) 純粋さ juñsuisa; (of water, air etc) 清潔 seíketsu; (*fig*: of woman, girl) 純潔 juñketsu

purple [pəːr'pəl] *adj* 紫色の murásakiiro no

purport [pəːr'pɔ:rt] *vi*: *to purport to be/do* ...である〔...ができる〕と主張する ...de árù〔...ga dekírù〕to shuchô suru

purpose [pəːr'pəs] *n* (reason) 目的 mokúteki; (objective: of person) 目標 mokúhyō

on purpose 意図的に itóteki ni, わざと wáza to

purposeful [pəːr'pəsfəl] *adj* (person, look, gesture) 果敢な kakán na

purr [pəːr] *vi* (cat) ごろごろとのどを鳴らす gòrogoro to nódò wo narásù

purse [pəːrs] *n* (for money) 財布 saífu; (*US*: handbag) ハンドバッグ handobaggù

♦*vt* (lips) すぼめる subómerù

purser [pəːrˈsəːr] n (NAUT) 事務長 jimúchō, パーサー pāsā

pursue [pəˈrsuː] vt (follow: person, thing) 追う óu, 追跡する tsuíseki suru; (fig: activity, interest) 行う okonau; (: plan) 実行する jikkố suru; (: aim, result) 追い求める oímotomerù

pursuer [pəˈrsuːˈəːr] n 追跡者 tsuísekishà

pursuit [pəˈrsuːt] n (chase: of person, thing) 追跡 tsuíseki; (fig: of happiness, pleasure etc) 追求 tsuíkyū; (pastime) 趣味 shúmi

pus [pʌs] n うみ umí

push [puʃ] n 押す事 osú kotð
♦vt (press, shove) 押す osú; (promote) 宣伝する seńden suru
♦vi (press, shove) 押す osú; (fig: demand urgently): **to push for** 要求する yőkyū suru

push aside vt 押しのける oshínokerù

pushchair [puʃˈtʃeːr] (BRIT) n いす型ベビーカー isúgata bebíkā

pusher [puʃˈəːr] n (drug pusher) 売人 baínin

push off (inf) vi: **push off!** 消えうせろ kiéuserð

push on vi (continue) 続ける tsuzúkerù

pushover [puʃˈouvəːr] (inf) n: **it's a pushover** 朝飯前だ asámeshimaè da

push through vi (crowd etc) ...を押し分けて進む ...wo oshíwakete susumù
♦vt (measure, scheme etc) 押し通す oshítōsu

push up vt total, prices 押し上げる oshíagerù

push-up [puʃˈʌp] (US) n (press-up) 腕立て伏せ udétatefùse

pushy [puʃˈiː] (pej) adj 押しの強い oshí no tsuyoí

puss [pus] (inf) n ネコちゃん nékòchan

pussy(cat) [pusˈiː(kæt)] (inf) n ネコちゃん nékòchan

put [put] (pt, pp put) vt (place: thing) 置く okú; (: person: in institution etc) 入れる irérù; (express: idea, remark etc) 表現する hyőgen suru; (present: case, view) 説明する setsúmei suru; (ask: question) する súrù; (place: person: in state, situa-tion) 追込む oíkomù, 置く okú; (estimate) 推定する suítei suru; (write, type: word, sentence etc) 書く kákù

put about/around vt (rumor) 広める hirómerù

put across vt (ideas etc) 分からせる wakáraserù

put away vt (store) 仕舞っておく shimátte okú

put back vt (replace) 戻す modósù; (postpone) 延期する eñki suru; (delay) 遅らせる okúraserù

put by vt (money, supplies etc) 蓄えておく takúwaete okù

put down vt (on floor, table) 下ろす orósù; (in writing) 書く kákù; (riot, rebellion) 鎮圧する chiñ-atsu suru; (kill: animal) 安楽死させる afirakushi saserù; (attribute): **to put something down to** ...のせいにする ...wo ...no seí ni surù

put forward vt (ideas, proposal) 提案する teían suru

put in vt (application, complaint) 提出する teíshutsu suru; (time, effort) つぎ込む tsugíkomù

put off vt (delay) 延期する eñki suru; (discourage) いやにさせる iyá ni saserù

put on vt (shirt, blouse, dress etc) 着る kírù; (hat etc) かぶる kabúrù; (shoes, pants, skirt etc) はく hakú; (gloves etc) はめる hamérù; (make-up, ointment etc) つける tsukérù; (light etc) つける tsukérù; (play etc) 上演する jően suru; (brake) かける kakérù; (record, tape, video) かける kakérù; (kettle, dinner etc) 火にかける hí ni kakérù; (assume: look, behavior etc) 装う yosóoù; (gain): **to put on weight** 太る futórù

put out vt (fire, candle, cigarette, light) 消す kesú; (take out: rubbish, cat etc) 出す dásù; (one's hand) 伸ばす nobásù; (inf: person): **to be put out** 怒っている okótte irù

putrid [pjuˈtrid] adj 腐った kusáttà

putt [pʌt] n (GOLF) パット pátto

put through vt (TEL: person, call) つなぐ tsunágù; (plan, agreement) 成功させる seíkō saserù

putting green [pʌt'iŋ-] n (GOLF: smooth area around hole) グリーン gurîn; (: for practice) パット練習場 páttòreñshújō

putty [pʌt'iː] n パテ pátè

put up vt (build) 建てる tatérù; (raise: umbrella) 広げる hirógerù; (: tent) 張る hárù; (: hood) かぶる kabúrù; (poster, sign etc) 張る harú; (increase: price, cost) 上げる agérù; (accommodate) 泊める tomérù

put-up [put'ʌp]: **put-up job** (BRIT) n 八百長 yaôchô

put up with vt fus 我慢する gámàn suru

puzzle [pʌz'əl] n (question, game) なぞなぞ nazónazo; (toy) パズル pázùru; (mystery) なぞ nazô
♦vt 当惑させる tôwaku saserù
♦vi: **to puzzle over something** ...を思案する ...wo shîan suru

puzzling [pʌz'liŋ] adj (thing, action) 訳の分からない wákè no wakáranaî

pyjamas [pədʒɑːm'əz] (BRIT) npl = **pajamas**

pylon [pai'lɑːn] n (for electric cables) 鉄塔 tettô

pyramid [pir'əmid] n (ARCHIT) ピラミッド pirámiddô; (shape, object, pile) ピラミッド状の物 pirámiddojô no monô

Pyrenees [pir'əniːz] npl: **the Pyrenees** ピレネー山脈 pírènè sáñmyaku

python [pai'θɑːn] n ニシキヘビ nishíkihebì

Q

quack [kwæk] n (of duck) がーがー gàgā; (pej: doctor) やぶ医者 yabúisha

quad [kwɑːd] abbr = **quadrangle**; **quadruplet**

quadrangle [kwɑːd'ræŋgəl] n (courtyard) 中庭 nakániwa

quadruple [kwɑːdruː'pəl] vt (increase fourfold) 4倍にする yoñbai ni suru
♦vi 4倍になる yoñbai ni naru

quadruplets [kwɑːdrʌ'plits] npl 四つ子

yotsúgo

quagmire [kwæg'maiəːr] n (bog) 湿地 shitchí; (muddy place) ぬかるみ nukárumi

quail [kweil] n (bird) ウズラ uzúra
♦vi: **to quail at/before** (anger, prospect) ...の前でおじけづく ...no maè de ojíkezùku

quaint [kweint] adj (house, village) 古風で面白い kofû de omóshiroî; (ideas, customs) 奇抜な kimyô na

quake [kweik] vi (with fear) 震える furúeru
♦n abbr = **earthquake**

Quaker [kwei'kəːr] n クエーカー教徒 kuêkākyóto

qualification [kwɑːləfəkei'ʃən] n (often pl: training, degree, diploma) 資格 shikáku; (skill, quality) 能力 nōryòku; (reservation, modification) 限定 geñtei, 条件 jōken

qualified [kwɑːl'əfaid] adj (trained) 資格のある shikáku no aru; (fit, competent): **qualified to** ...する能力がある ...suru nōryòku ga aru; (limited) 条件付きの jôkentsuki no

qualify [kwɑːl'əfai] vt (make competent) ...に資格を与える ...ni shikáku wo ataerù; (modify) 限定する gentei suru
♦vi (pass examination(s)): **to qualify (as)** ...の資格を取る ...no shikáku wo torù; (be eligible): **to qualify (for)** (...の) 資格がある (...no) shikáku ga aru; (in competition): **to qualify (for)** (...に進む) 資格を得る (...ni susúmu) shikáku wo eru

quality [kwɑːl'itiː] n (standard: of work, product) 品質 hiñshitsu; (characteristic: of person) 性質 seîshitsu; (: of wood, stone etc) 特徴 tokúchō

qualm [kwɑːm] n (doubt) 疑問 gimón
qualms of conscience 良心のか責 ryôshin nò kasháku

quandary [kwɑːn'driː] n: **to be in a quandary** 途方に暮れる tohô ni kuréru

quantity [kwɑːn'titiː] n (amount: of uncountable thing) 量 ryô; (: of countable things) 数 kazù

quantity surveyor *n* 積算士 sekīsan-shi ◊工事などの費用を見積りで計算する人 kṓji nadð no hīyṓ wo mitsúmori dè keísan suru hitð

quarantine [kwɔːr'əntiːn] *n* (isolation) 隔離 kakúri

quarrel [kwɔːr'əl] *n* (argument) けんか keńka
◆*vi*: **to quarrel (with)** (...と) けんかする (...to) keńka suru

quarrelsome [kwɔːr'əlsəm] *adj* けんかっ早い keńkappayaí

quarry [kwɔːr'iː] *n* (for stone) 石切り場 ishíkiriba, 採石場 saísekijṓ; (animal) 獲物 emóno

quart [kwɔːrt] *n* クォート kwṓto

quarter [kwɔːr'təːr] *n* (fourth part) 4分の1 yońbun no ichi; (US: coin) 25セント玉 nijúgosentodamà; (of year) 四半期 shiháñki; (district) 地区 chíkù
◆*vt* (divide by four) 4等分する yońtōbun suru; (MIL: lodge) 宿泊させる shukúhaku saseru
a quarter of an hour 15分 jūgófun

quarter final *n* 準々決勝 juńjunkesshð

quarterly [kwɔːr'təːrliː] *adj* (meeting, payment) 年4回の nèn-yońkai no
◆*adv* (meet, pay) 年4回に nèn-yońkai ni

quarters [kwɔːr'təːrz] *npl* (barracks) 兵舎 heísha; (living quarters) 宿舎 shúkusha

quartet(te) [kwɔːrtet'] *n* (group: of instrumentalists) 四重奏団 shijūsṓdan, カルテット karútetto; (: of singers) 四重唱団 shijúshōdan, カルテット karútetto; (piece of music) 四重奏曲 shijúsōkyokù

quartz [kwɔːrts] *n* 水晶 suíshō

quash [kwɑːʃ] *vt* (verdict, judgement) 破棄する hakí suru

quasi- [kwei'zai] *prefix* 疑似... gijí...

quaver [kwei'vəːr] *n* (BRIT: MUS) 八分音符 hachíbùn ońpu
◆*vi* (voice) 震える furúeru

quay [kiː] *n* (also: **quayside**) 岸壁 gańpeki

queasy [kwiːˈziː] *adj* (nauseous) 吐気がする hakíkè ga suru

queen [kwiːn] *n* (monarch) 女王 joð; (king's wife) 王妃 ōhī; (ZOOL: also:

queen bee) 女王バチ joðbachi; (CARDS, CHESS) クイーン kuíñ

queen mother *n* 皇太后 kṓtaigð

queer [kwiːr] *adj* (odd) 変な heñ na
◆*n* (inf: homosexual) ホモ homó

quell [kwel] *vt* (opposition) 鎮める shizúmeru; (unease, fears) なだめる nadámeru, 静める shizúmeru

quench [kwentʃ] *vt*: **to quench one's thirst** のどの乾きをいやす nodð no kawákī wo iyásù

querulous [kweːr'ələs] *adj* (person, voice) 愚痴っぽい guchíppòi

query [kwiər'iː] *n* (question) 質問 shitsúmon
◆*vt* (question) ...に聞く ...ni kikú, ...に質問する ...ni shitsúmon suru

quest [kwest] *n* 探求 tańkyū

question [kwes'tʃən] *n* (query) 質問 shitsúmon; (doubt) 疑問 gimóñ; (issue) 問題 mońdai; (in test: problem) 問 toí
◆*vt* (ask) ...に聞く ...ni kikú, ...に質問する ...ni shitsúmon suru; (interrogate) 尋問する jińmon suru; (doubt) ...に疑問を投げ掛ける ...ni gimóñ wo nagékakeru
beyond question 疑いもなく utágai mo naku
out of the question 全く不可能で mattáku fúkanð de

questionable [kwes'tʃənəbəl] *adj* (doubtful) 疑わしい utágawashii

question mark *n* 疑問符 gimóñfu

questionnaire [kwestʃəneːr'] *n* 調査票 chōsáhyō, アンケート añkḗtð

queue [kjuː] *n* (BRIT) 列 retsù
◆*vi* (also: **queue up**) 列を作る retsù wo tsukúru

quibble [kwib'əl] *vi* 詰まらない議論をする tsumáranài giròn wo suru

quiche [kiːʃ] *n* キッシュ kisshù ◊パイの一種 paí no isshù

quick [kwik] *adj* (fast: person, movement, action etc) 早い hayáī; (agile) 素早い subáyai; (: mind) 理解の早い rikái no hayáī; (brief: look, visit) 短い mijíkài, ちょっとした chottó shita
◆*n*: **cut to the quick** (fig) ...の感情を害する ...no kańjō wo gaí sùru

be quick! 急いで isóîde

quicken [kwik'ən] vt (pace, step) 早める hayámeru
♦vi (pace, step) 早くなる hayáku naru

quickly [kwik'li:] adv 早く hayáku

quicksand [kwik'sænd] n 流土砂 ryúdosha, クイックサンド kuíkkùsando

quick-witted [kwik'wit'id] adj (alert) 機敏な kibín na

quid [kwid] (BRIT: inf) n inv ポンド poñdo

quiet [kwai't] adj (not loud or noisy) 静かな shizúka na; (silent) 何も言わない nanî mo iwánai; (peaceful: place) 平和な heiwa na; (calm: person) もの静かな monóshizuka na; (without fuss etc: ceremony) 簡単な kañtan na
♦n (peacefulness) 静けさ shizúkesa; (silence) 静かにする事 shizúka ni suru koto
♦vi (US: also: **quiet down**) (grow calm) 落着く ochitsuku; (grow silent) 静かになる shizúka ni naru
♦vt (person, animal) 落着かせる ochítsukaseru

quieten [kwai'itən] (BRIT) = **quiet** vi, vt

quietly [kwai'itli:] adv (speak, play) 静かに shizúka ni; (silently) 黙って damáttè

quietness [kwai'itnis] n (peacefulness) 静けさ shizúkesa; (silence) 静かにする事 shizúka ni suru koto

quilt [kwilt] n (covering) ベッドカバー beddôkabâ; (also: **continental quilt**) 掛布団 kakebuton, キルト kirúto

quin [kwin] n abbr = **quintuplet**

quinine [kwai'nain] n キニーネ kinînè

quintet(te) [kwintet'] n (group) 五重奏団 gojûsōdan, クインテット kuíñtetto; (piece of music) 五重奏曲 gojûsökyoku

quintuplets [kwintʌ'plits] npl 五つ子 itsútsugo

quip [kwip] n 警句 keíku

quirk [kwə:rk] n (unusual characteristic) 癖 kusé; (accident: of fate, nature) 気まぐれ kimágure

quit [kwit] (pt, pp **quit** or **quitted**) vt (smoking, grumbling) やめる yaméru;

(job) 辞める yaméru; (premises) ...から出ていく ...kara detè iku
♦vi (give up) やめる yaméru; (resign) 辞める yaméru

quite [kwait] adv (rather) かなり kanári; (entirely) 全く mattáku, 完全に kañzen ni; (following a negative: almost): **that's not quite big enough** それはちょっと小さい soré wa chottó chiisai
I saw quite a few of them 私はそれらをかなり沢山見ました watákushi wa soréra wo kanári takúsan mimashita
quite (so)! 全くその通り mattáku sonó tōri

quits [kwits] adj: **quits (with)** (...と)おあいこである (...to) o-áiko de aru
let's call it quits (call it even) おあいこにしましょう o-aíko ni shimáshō; (stop working etc) やめましょう yamémashō

quiver [kwiv'ə:r] vi (tremble) 震える furúerù

quiz [kwiz] n (game) クイズ kuîzu; (US: short test) 小テスト shótesùto
♦vt (question) 尋問する jiñmon suru

quizzical [kwiz'ikal] adj (look, smile) なぞめいた nazómeîta

quorum [kwɔ:r'əm] n (of members) 定足数 teísokusû

quota [kwou'tə] n 割当数〔量〕waríatesû〔ryô〕

quotation [kwoutei'ʃən] n (from book, play etc) 引用文 iñ-yöbuñ; (estimate) 見積り mitsúmori

quotation marks npl 引用符 iñyôfù

quote [kwout] n (from book, play etc) 引用文 iñyöbuñ; (estimate) 見積り mitsúmori
♦vt (sentence, proverb etc) 引用する iñyö suru; (figure, example) 引合いに出す hikfai ni dasù; (price) 見積る mitsúmorù
♦vi: **to quote from** (book, play etc) ...から引用する ...kara iñ-yö suru

quotes [kwouts] npl (quotation marks) 引用符 iñ-yôfù

quotient [kwou'ʃənt] n (factor) 指数 shisû

R

rabbi [ræb'ai] n ラビ rábî ◇ユダヤ教の聖
職者 yudáyakyō nò seíshokushà

rabbit [ræb'it] n ウサギ usági

rabbit hutch n ウサギ小屋 uságigoyà

rabble [ræb'əl] (pej) n 群衆 gunshū

rabies [rei'bi:z] n 恐犬病 kyōkeñbyō

RAC [ɑ:reisi:'] (BRIT) n abbr (= Royal
Automobile Club) 英国自動車連盟 eíko-
ku jidósha reñmei

raccoon [ræku:n'] n アライグマ aráigù-
ma

race [reis] n (species) 人種 jiñshu; (competition: for speed) 競走 kyósō, レース
rếsù; (: for power, control) 競争 kyósō;
(public gambling event: also: **horse race**)
競馬 keíba; (: also: **bicycle race**) 競輪 keírin; (: also: **motorboat race**) 競艇 kyótei
♦vt (horse) 競馬に出場させる keíba nì
shutsújó saserù; (compete against: person) ...と競走する ...to kyósō suru
♦vi (compete: for speed) 競走する kyósō
suru; (: for power, control) 競争する kyósō suru; (hurry) 急いで行く isóide ikù;
(pulse) どきどきする dókìdoki suru;
(engine) 空回りする karámawarì suru

race car (US) n レーシングカー rếshi-
ngukà

race car driver (US) n レーサー rếsā

racecourse [reis'kɔ:rs] n 競馬場 keíbajò

racehorse [reis'hɔ:rs] n 競走馬 kyósōba

racetrack [reis'træk] n (for people) ト
ラック torákkù; (for cars) サーキット sākitto

racial [rei'ʃəl] adj 人種の jiñshu no, 人種
... jiñshu...

racing [rei'siŋ] n (horses) 競馬 keíba;
(bicycles) 競輪 keírin; (motorboats) 競艇
kyótei; (cars) 自動車レース jidósharèsu;
(motorcycles) オートレース ótorèsu

racing car (BRIT) n = **race car**

racing driver (BRIT) n = **race car
driver**

racism [rei'sizəm] n 人種差別 jiñshusabètsu

racist [rei'sist] adj (statement, policy) 人
種差別的な jiñshusabetsuteki na
♦n 人種差別主義者 jiñshusabetsushugì-
shà

rack [ræk] n (also: **luggage rack**) 網棚
amídana; (shelf) 棚 taná; (also: **roof
rack**) ルーフラック rúfurakkù; (dish
rack) 水切りかご mizúkirikago
♦vt: **racked by** (pain, anxiety) ...でもだ
え苦しんで ...de modáekurushiñde
to rack one's brains 知恵を絞る chié
wò shibórù

racket [ræk'it] n (for tennis, squash etc)
ラケット rakéttò; (noise) 騒音 sóon;
(swindle) 詐欺 sági

racoon [ræku:n'] n = **raccoon**

racquet [ræk'it] n (for tennis, squash
etc) ラケット rakéttò

racy [rei'si:] adj きびきびした kíbìkibi
shita

radar [rei'dɑ:r] n レーダー rễdā

radial [rei'di:əl] adj (also: **radial-ply**) ラ
ジアルの rájìaru no

radiance [rei'di:əns] n (glow) 光 hikári

radiant [rei'di:ənt] adj (happy, joyful) 輝
く kagáyakù

radiate [rei'di:eit] vt (heat) 放射する hōsha suru; (emotion) ...で輝く ...de kagáyakù
♦vi (lines) 放射状に広がる hōshajō nì hirógarù

radiation [reidi:ei'ʃən] n (radioactive) 放
能 hōshanō; (from sun etc) 放射 hōsha

radiator [rei'di:eitər] n ラジエーター
rajiẽtā

radical [ræd'ikəl] adj (change etc) 抜本
的な bappónteki na; (person) 過激な ka-
géki na; (organization) 過激派の kagékiha no, 過激派... kagékiha...

radii [rei'di:ai] npl of **radius**

radio [rei'di:ou] n (broadcasting) ラジオ
放送 rajíohōsō; (device: for receiving
broadcasts) ラジオ rájìo; (: for transmit-
ting and receiving signals) 無線通信機
musếntsūshìñki
♦vt (person) ...と無線で通信する ...to mu-
sên dè tsúshin suru
on the radio ラジオで rájìo de

radioactive [reidi:ouæk'tiv] *adj* 放射性
の hōshasei no

radiography [reidi:ɑːg'rəfi:] *n* レントゲ
ン撮影 reńtogensatsuèi

radiology [reidi:ɑːl'ədʒi:] *n* 放射線医学
hōshasen-igàku

radio station *n* ラジオ放送局 rajío hō-
sōkyòku

radiotherapy [reidi:ouθe:r'əpi:] *n* 放射
線療法 hōshasenryōhō

radish [ræd'iʃ] *n* はつかだいこん hatsú-
kadaîkon

radius [rei'di:əs] (*pl* **radii**) *n* (of circle) 半
径 hańkei; (from point) 半径内の範囲 hań-
keinai nò háń-i

RAF [ɑːrieief'] *n abbr* = **Royal Air
Force**

raffle [ræf'əl] *n* 宝くじ takárakùji ◇当る
と金ではなく賞品をもらえる物を指す a-
tárù to kané de wa nakù shóhin wò
moráerù monó wò sásù

raft [ræft] *n* (craft) いかだ ikáda; (*also*:
life raft) 救命いかだ kyúmei ikàda

rafter [ræf'tə:r] *n* はり harí

rag [ræg] *n* (piece of cloth) ぞうきん ző-
kin; (torn cloth) ぼろ bórò; (*pej*: newspaper) 三流紙 sańryùshi; (*BRIT*: UNI-
VERSITY: for charity) 慈善募金運動 ji-
zénbokin-uñdō

rag-and-bone man [rægənboun'-]
(*BRIT*) *n* = **ragman**

rag doll *n* 縫いぐるみ人形 nuíguruminiñ-
gyō

rage [reidʒ] *n* (fury) 憤怒 fúndo
♦*vi* (person) 怒り狂う ikárikuruù;
(storm) 荒れ狂う arékuruù; (debate) 荒れ
る arérù

it's all the rage (very fashionable) 大
流行している daíryūkō shite irù

ragged [ræg'id] *adj* (edge) ぎざぎざの gi-
zágiza no; (clothes) ぼろぼろの boróboro
no; (appearance) 不ぞろいの fuzórði no

ragman [ræg'mæn] (*pl* **ragmen**) *n* くず
屋 kuzúya

rags [rægz] *npl* (torn clothes) ぼろぼろの
衣服 boróboro no ifúku

raid [reid] *n* (MIL) 襲撃 shūgeki; (criminal) 不法侵入 fuhốshiñnyù; (by police) 手

入れ teíre
♦*vt* (MIL) 襲撃する shūgeki suru; (crimi-
nally) ...に不法侵入する ...ni fuhốshiñnyū
suru; (subj: police) 手入れする teíre suru

rail [reil] *n* 手すり tesúri
by rail (by train) 列車で resshá de

railing(s) [rei'liŋ(z)] *n(pl)* (fence) さく
sakú

railroad [reil'roud] (*US*) *n* (track) 線路
séñro; (company) 鉄道 tetsúdō

railroader [reil'roudə:r] (*US*) *n* 鉄道員
tetsúdōìn

railroad line (*US*) *n* 鉄道線 tetsúdōsen

railroad station (*US*) *n* 駅 ékì

rails [reilz] *npl* (for train) レール rèru

railway [reil'wei] (*BRIT*) *n* = **railroad**
etc

railwayman [reil'weimən] (*BRIT*: *pl*
railwaymen) *n* = **railroader**

rain [rein] *n* 雨 ámè
♦*vi* 雨が降る ámè ga fúrù
in the rain 雨の中で ámè no nákà de
it's raining 雨が降っている ámè ga futté irù

rainbow [rein'bou] *n* にじ nijí

raincoat [rein'kout] *n* レーンコート rén-
kōto

raindrop [rein'drɑːp] *n* 雨の一滴 ámè no
ittéki

rainfall [rein'fɔːl] *n* 雨量 kőuryò

rainy [rei'ni:] *adj* 雨模様の amémoyô no

raise [reiz] *n* (payrise) 賃上げ chiń-age
♦*vt* (lift) 持上げる mochíagerù;
(increase: salary) 上げる agérù; (: production) 増やす fuyásù; (improve:
morale) 高める takámerù; (: standards)
引上げる hikíagerù; (produce: doubts,
question) 引起こす hikíokosù; (rear: cattle) 飼育する shiíku suru; (: family) 育て
る sodáterù; (cultivate: crop) 栽培する
saíbai suru; (get together: army, funds,
loan) 集める atsúmerù

to raise one's voice 声を大きくする
kôè wo ōkiku suru

raisin [rei'zin] *n* 干しぶどう hoshíbudô,
レーズン rězun

rake [reik] *n* (tool) レーキ rèki
♦*vt* (garden) レーキで...の土をならす rè-

ki de ...no tsuchí wò narásù; (leaves) か
き集める kakíatsumerù; (with machine
gun) 掃射する sōsha suru

rally [rˈælˈiː] n (POL etc) 集会 shūkai;
(AUT) ラリー rarī; (TENNIS etc) ラリ
ー rárī

♦vt (support) 集める atsúmerù

♦vi (sick person, Stock Exchange) 持直
す mochínaosù

rally round vt fus (fig: give support to)
...の支援に駆け付ける ...no shién nì kaké-
tsukerù

RAM [ræm] n abbr = **(random access
memory)** ラム rámù

ram [ræm] n (ZOOL) 雄ヒツジ osúhitsùji

♦vt (crash into) ...に激突する ...ni gekítotsu suru; (push: bolt, fist etc) 押込む oshíkomù

ramble [rˈæmbəl] n (walk) ハイキング
háikingu

♦vi (walk) ハイキングする háikingu suru; (talk: also: **ramble on**) だらだらしゃべる dárádara shabérù

rambler [rˈæmblər] n (walker) ハイカー háikā; (BOT) ツルバラ tsurúbara

rambling [rˈæmblɪŋ] adj (speech) 取留めのない torítome no naî; (house) だだっ広い dadáppiroì; (BOT) つる性の tsurúsei no

ramp [ræmp] n 傾斜路 keísharo

on/off ramp (US: AUT) 入口〔出口〕ランプ irîguchi(degúchi)ráñpu

rampage [rˈæmpeidʒ] n: **to be on the
rampage** 暴れ回っている abáremawatte irú

♦vi: **they went rampaging through
the town** 彼らは町中暴れ回った kárèra wa machíjū abaremawattà

rampant [rˈæmpənt] adj (crime) はびこる habíkorù; (disease) まん延する mañ-en suru

rampart [rˈæmpɑːrt] n (fortification) 城壁 jōheki

ramshackle [rˈæmʃækəl] adj (house, car, table) がたがたの gatágata no

ran [ræn] pt of **run**

ranch [ræntʃ] n 牧場 bokújō

rancher [rˈæntʃər] n 牧場主 bokújōshu

rancid [rˈænsid] adj (butter, bacon etc)
悪くなった wárùku natta

rancor [rˈæŋkər] (BRIT **rancour**) n 恨み urámi

random [rˈændəm] adj (arrangement,
selection) 手当り次第の teátarishidài no;
(COMPUT, MATH) 無作為の musákùi no

♦n: **at random** 手当り次第に teátarishidài ni

random access n (COMPUT) ランダムアクセス rañdamuakùsesu

randy [rˈændiː] (inf) adj セックスをしたがっている sékkùsu wo shitágatte irù

rang [ræŋ] pt of **ring**

range [reindʒ] n (also: **mountain range**)
山脈 sañmyaku; (of missile) 射程距離 shatéikyorî; (of voice) 声域 seíiki;
(series: of proposals, offers, products) 一連の... ichîren no ...; (MIL: also: **shooting range**) 射撃場 shagékijō; (also:
kitchen range) レンジ rêñji

♦vt (place) 歩き回る arúkimawarù;
(arrange) 並べる naráberù

♦vi: **to range over** (extend) ...にわたる
...ni watárù

to range from ... to ... ...から...までにわたる ...kárà ...mádè ni watárù

ranger [reindʒər] n 森林警備隊員 shiñrinkeibitaiin, レンジャー rêñjā

rank [ræŋk] n (row) 列 rétsù; (MIL) 階級 kaíkyū; (status) 地位 chíi; (BRIT: also:
taxi rank) タクシー乗場 takúshīnorîba

♦vi: **to rank among** ...のうちに数えられる ...no uchî nì kazóerarerù

♦adj (stinking) 臭い kusáì

the rank and file (fig: ordinary members) 一般の人 ippáñ no hitô, 一般人 ippánjin

rankle [rˈæŋkəl] vi (insult) わだかまる wadákamarù

ransack [rˈænsæk] vt (search) 物色する busshóku suru; (plunder) 略奪する ryakúdatsu suru

ransom [rˈænsəm] n (money) 身代金 minóshirokiñ

to hold to ransom (fig: nation, company, individual) ...に圧力を掛ける ...ni atsúryòku wo kakérù

rant [rænt] *vi* (rave) わめく wamékù

rap [ræp] *vt* (on door, table) たたく tatákù

rape [reip] *n* (of woman) 強かん gṓkan; (BOT) アブラナ abúranà

◆*vt* (woman) 強かんする gṓkan suru

rape(seed) oil [reip'(si:d)-] *n* ナタネ油 natáneabùra

rapid [ræp'id] *adj* (growth, development, change) 急速な kyū́soku na

rapidity [rəpid'iti:] *n* (speed) 速さ háyàsa

rapidly [ræp'idli:] *adv* (grow, develop, change) 急速に kyū́soku ni

rapids [ræp'idz] *npl* (GEO) 早瀬 hayáse

rapist [rei'pist] *n* 強かん者 gṓkansha

rapport [ræpɔːr'] *n* 親和関係 shiñwakañkei

rapture [ræp'tʃər] *n* (delight) 歓喜 káñki

rapturous [ræp'tʃərəs] *adj* (applause) 熱狂的な nekkyṓteki na

rare [re:r] *adj* (uncommon) まれな maré na; (unusual) 珍しい mezúrashìi; (CULIN: steak) レアの rêa no

rarely [reər'li:] *adv* (seldom) めったに...ない méttà ni ...náì

raring [re:r'iŋ] *adj*: **raring to go** (inf: keen) 意気込んでいる ikígonde irù

rarity [re:r'iti:] *n* (exception) 希有な物 kéù na monó; (scarcity) 希少性 kishṓsei

rascal [ræs'kəl] *n* (rogue) ごろつき gorótsuki; (mischievous child) いたずらっ子 itázurakkò

rash [ræʃ] *adj* (person) 向こう見ずの mukṓmìzu no; (promise, act) 軽率な keísotsu na

◆*n* (MED) 発しん hasshín; (spate: of events, robberies) 多発 tahátsu

rasher [ræʃ'ər] *n* (of bacon) 一切れ hitókìre

raspberry [ræz'be:ri:] *n* キイチゴ kiíchìgo

rasping [ræs'piŋ] *adj*: **a rasping noise** きしむ音 kishímù otó

rat [ræt] *n* ネズミ nezúmi

rate [reit] *n* (speed) 速度 sókùdo; (of change, inflation) 進行度 shiñkòdo; (ratio: also of interest) 率 rítsù; (price: at hotel etc) 料金 ryṓkin

◆*vt* (value, estimate) 評価する hyṓka suru

to rate someone/something as ...を...と評価する ...wo ...to hyṓka suru

rateable value [rei'təbəl-] (BRIT) *n* 課税評価額 kazéi hyōkagàku

ratepayer [reit'peiər] (BRIT) *n* 納税者 nōzéisha ◇固定資産税の納税者について言う kotéishisañzei no nōzéisha ni tsuítè iú

rates [reits] *npl* (BRIT: property tax) 固定資産税 kotéishisañzei; (fees) 料金 ryṓkin

rather [ræð'ər] *adv* (quite, somewhat) かなり kánari; (to some extent) 少し sukóshì; (more accurately): **or rather** 正確に言えば seíkaku nì iébà

it's rather expensive (quite) かなり値段が高い kánari nedán gà takáì; (too) 値段が高過ぎる nedán gà takásugirù

there's rather a lot かなり沢山ある kánari takúsan arù

I would rather go どちらかというと行きたいと思う dóchìra ka to iú tò ikítaì to omóù

ratify [ræt'əfai] *vt* (agreement, treaty) 批准する hijún suru

rating [rei'tiŋ] *n* (assessment) 評価 hyṓka; (score) 評点 hyṓten; (NAUT: BRIT: sailor) 海軍兵卒 kaígunheìsotsu

ratings [rei'tiŋz] *npl* (RADIO, TV) 視聴率 shichṓritsu

ratio [rei'ʃou] *n* 率 rítsù

in the ratio of 100 to 1 100に1つという割合で hyaku ni hitotsù to iu warái de

ration [ræʃ'ən] *n* (allowance: of food, petrol etc) 配給分 haíkyùbun

◆*vt* (food, petrol etc) 配給する haíkyū suru

rational [ræʃ'ənəl] *adj* (solution, reasoning) 合理的な gṓriteki na; (person) 訳の分かる wákè no wakárù

rationale [ræʃənæl'] *n* 根拠 kóñkyo

rationalize [ræʃ'ənəlaiz] *vt* (justify) 正当化する seítōka suru

rationally [ræʃ'ənəli:] *adv* (sensibly) 合理的な gôriteki ni

rationing [ræʃ'əniŋ] *n* (of food, petrol etc) 配給 haîkyū

rations [reiʃ'ənz] *npl* (MIL) 兵糧 hyôrō

rat race *n* 競争の世界 kyôsō nò sêkai

rattle [ræt'əl] *n* (of door, window) がたがたという音 gátàgata to iú oto; (of train, car, engine etc) ごう音 gôon; (of coins) じゃらじゃらという音 járàjara to iú oto; (of chain) がらがらという音 gáràgara to iú oto; (object: for baby) がらがら garágarà

♦*vi* (small objects) がらがら鳴る gáràgara narú; (car, bus): **to rattle along** がたがた走る gatagata hashírù

♦*vt* (unnerve) どぎまぎさせる dógìmagi sasérù

rattlesnake [ræt'əlsneik] *n* ガラガラヘビ garágarahebì

raucous [rɔː'kəs] *adj* しゃがれ声の shagáregoè no

ravage [ræv'idʒ] *vt* (damage) 荒す arásù

ravages [ræv'idʒiz] *npl* (of time, weather) 荒廃 kôhai

rave [reiv] *vi* (in anger) わめく wamékù; (with enthusiasm) ...をべたほめする ...wo betábòme suru; (MED) うわごとを言う uwágoto wò iú

raven [rei'vən] *n* ワタリガラス watárigaràsu

ravenous [ræv'ənəs] *adj* 猛烈におなかがすいた môretsu nì onáka ga suîta

ravine [rəvi:n'] *n* 渓谷 keîkoku

raving [rei'viŋ] *adj*: **raving lunatic** ど気違い dokíchigaì

ravishing [ræv'iʃiŋ] *adj* (beautiful) 悩殺する nôsatsu suru

raw [rɔː] *adj* (uncooked) 生の námà no; (not processed: cotton, sugar etc) 原料のままの genríyō no mamá no; (sore) 赤むけした akámuke shità; (inexperienced) 青二才の aónisai no; (weather, day) 肌寒い hadázamuî

raw deal (*inf*) *n* ひどい仕打 hidôî shiúchi

raw material *n* (coal, oil, gas etc) 原料 genríyō

ray [rei] *n* (*also*: **ray of light**) 光線 kôsen; (*also*: **ray of heat**) 熱線 nessén

the rays of the sun 太陽の光線 taîyō no kôsen

a ray of hope 希望のひらめき kibô nò hirámeki

rayon [rei'ɑːn] *n* レーヨン rêyon

raze [reiz] *vt* 根こそぎ破壊する nekôsògi hakái suru

razor [rei'zəːr] *n* (open razor) かみそり kamísorì; (safety razor) 安全かみそり afzenkamisòri; (electric razor) 電気かみそり defkikamisòri

razor blade *n* かみそりの刃 kamísorì no há

Rd *n abbr* = **road**

re [rei] *prep* (with regard to) ...に関して ...ni káñ shite

reach [riːtʃ] *n* (range: of arm) 手が届く範囲 tè gà todôku háñ-i; (scope: of imagination) 範囲 háñ-i; (stretch: of river etc) 区域 kûiki

♦*vt* (arrive at: place) ...に到着する ...ni tôchaku suru; (: conclusion, agreement, decision, end) ...に達する ...ni tassúrù; (be able to touch) ...に手が届く ...ni tè gà todôkù; (by telephone) ...に連絡する ...ni refíraku suru

♦*vi* (stretch out one's arm) 手を伸ばす tè wò nobásù

within reach 手の届く所に tè nò todôku tokôrð ni

out of reach 手の届かない所に tè nò todôkanaî tokôrð ni

within reach of the shops/station 商店街(駅)の近くに shôteñgai(êkî)no chikákù ni

「*keep out of the reach of children*」子供の手が届かない所に保管して下さい kodômo no tè gà todôkanaî tokôrð ni hokán shitè kudásaî

reach out *vt* (hand) 伸ばす nobásù

♦*vi* 手を伸ばす tè wò nobásù

to reach out for something ...を取ろうとして手を伸ばす ...wo torô tò shite tè wò nobásù

react [riːækt'] *vi* (CHEM): *to react (with)* (...と) 反応する (...to) hafíñō su

ru; (MED): **to react (to)** (...に対して)
副作用が起る (...ni táishite) fukusayò ga
okòrù; (respond): **to react (to)** (...に)
反応する (...ni) hañnô suru; (rebel): **to
react (against)** (...に) 反発する (...ni)
hañpatsu suru

reaction [ri:æk'∫ən] n (response): **reaction (to)** (...に対する) 反応 (...ni taísu-
rù) hañnô; (rebellion): **reaction
(against)** (...に対する) 反発 (...ni taí-
surù) hañpatsu; (belief in conservatism)
反動 hañdô; (CHEM) 反応 hañnô; (MED)
副作用 fukúsayò

reactionary [ri:æk'∫əneːri:] adj (forces,
attitude) 反動的な hañdôteki na

reactions [ri:æk'∫ənz] npl (reflexes) 反
応 hañnô

reactor [ri:æk'tə:r] n (also: **nuclear
reactor**) 原子炉 geñshirò

read [ri:d] (pt, pp read) vi (person, child)
...を読む ...wo yómù; (piece of writing,
letter etc) ...と書いてある ...to káîte árù
♦vt (book, newspaper, music etc) 読む
yómù; (mood, thoughts) 読取る yomíto-
rù; (meter, thermometer etc) 読む yómù;
(study: at university) 学ぶ manábù

readable [ri:'dəbəl] adj (writing) 読める
yomêrù; (book, author etc) 読ませる yo-
máserù

reader [ri:'də:r] n (of book, newspaper
etc) 読者 dókùsha; (book) リーダー rīdā;
(BRIT: at university) 助教授 jokyôjù
an avid reader 読書家 dokúshòka

readership [ri:'də:r∫ip] n (of newspaper
etc) 読者 dókùsha ◊総称 sôsho

readily [red'əli:] adv (willingly) 快く ko-
kôroyokù; (easily) たやすく tayásukù;
(quickly) 直ぐに súgù ni

readiness [red'i:nis] n (preparedness) 用
意ができている yôi ga dekite iru koto;
(willingness) ...する意志 ...suru ishi
in readiness (prepared) 用意ができて
yôi ga dekite

reading [ri:d'iŋ] n (of books, newspapers
etc) 読書 dokusho; (in church, as entertainment) 朗読 rôdoku; (on meter, thermometer etc) 記録 kiroku

readjust [ri:əd∫ʌst'] vt (alter: position,

knob, mirror etc) 調節する chôsetsu suru
♦vi (adapt): **to readjust (to)** (...に) な
れる (...ni) nareru

read out vt 朗読する rôdoku suru

ready [red'i:] adj (prepared) 用意ができ
ている yôi ga dekíte iru; (willing) ...する
意志がある ...surú ishi ga árù; (available)
用意されている yôi sarête irù
♦n: **at the ready** (MIL) 銃を構えて jù
wo kamáetè
to get ready
♦vi 支度する shitáku suru
♦vt 準備する júñbi suru

ready-made [red'i:meid'] adj 既製の ki-
sêi no

ready money n 現金 geñkiñ

ready reckoner [-rek'ənər] n 計算表
keísañhyō

ready-to-wear [red'i:təweːr'] adj 既製
の kiséi no

reaffirm [ri:əfə:rm'] vt 再び言明する futátabi geñmei suru

real [ri:l] adj (actual, true: reason, interest, result etc) 本当の hoñtô no; (not artificial: leather, gold etc) 本物の hoñmono
no; (not imaginary: life, feeling) 実際の
jissái no; (for emphasis): **a real idiot/
miracle** 正真正銘のばか〔奇跡〕shôshin-
shômei no bákà 〔kiséki〕
in real terms 事実は jíjitsu wa

real estate n 不動産 fudôsan

realism [ri:'əlizəm] n (practicality) 現実
主義 geñjitsushugì; (ART) リアリズム ri-
árizùmu

realist [ri:'əlist] n 現実的な人 geñjitsuteki nà hitó

realistic [ri:əlis'tik] adj (practical) 現実
的な geñjitsuteki na; (true to life) 写実的
な shajîtsuteki na

reality [ri:æl'iti:] n (actuality, truth) 事
実 jíjitsu
in reality 事実は jíjitsu wa

realization [ri:ələzei'∫ən] n (understanding: of situation) 実感 jikkán; (fulfilment: of dreams, hopes) 実現 jitsúgen;
(of asset) 現金化 geñkiñka

realize [ri:'əlaiz] vt (understand) 実感す

る jikkán suru; (fulfil: a dream, hope, project etc) 実現する jitsúgen suru; (COMM: asset) 現金に替える geńkiñ ni kaérù

really [riːˈəliː] *adv* (for emphasis) 実にjitsú ni, とても totémo; (actually): *what really happened* 実際に起った事は jissái nì okótta kotó wa

really? (indicating interest) そうですか sô desu ka; (expressing surprise) 本当ですか hoñtô desu kà

really! (indicating annoyance) うんもう! úñ mô!

realm [relm] *n* (of monarch) 王国 ôkoku; (fig: area of activity or study) 分野 búñya

realtor [ˈriːəltəːr] (*US*) *n* 不動産業者 fudôsangyôsha

reap [riːp] *vt* (crop) ...の刈入れをする ...no karírè wò suru; (fig: benefits, rewards) 収穫する shûkaku suru

reappear [riːəpiːˈr] *vi* 再び現れる futátabi arawererù

rear [riːr] *adj* (back) 後ろの ushíro no

♦*n* (back) 後ろ ushíro

♦*vt* (cattle) 飼育する shíku suru; (family) 育てる sodáterù

♦*vi* (also: **rear up**: animal) 後足で立ち上る atóashi de tachíagarù

rearguard [ˈriːrgɑːrd] *n* (MIL) 後衛 kôei

rearmament [riːɑːrmˈəmənt] *n* 再軍備 saíguñbi

rearrange [riːəreindʒˈ] *vt* 並べ直す narábenaosù

rear-view mirror [riːrˈvjuːˈ-] *n* (AUT) バックミラー bakkúmirà

reason [riːˈzən] *n* (cause) 理由 riyû; (ability to think) 理性 riséi

♦*vi: to reason with someone* ...の説得に当る ...no settóku nì atárù

it stands to reason that ...という事は当然である ...to iú kotò wa tôzen de arù

reasonable [riːˈzənəbəl] *adj* (sensible) 訳の分かる wákè no wakárù; (fair: number, amount) 程々の hodóhodo no; (: quality) まあまあの mâmā no; (: price) 妥当な datô na

reasonably [riːˈzənəbliː] *adv* (sensibly)

常識的に jôshikiteki ni; (fairly) 程々に hodóhodo ni

reasoned [riːˈzənd] *adj* (argument) 筋の通った súji no tôttà

reasoning [riːˈzəniŋ] *n* (process) 推理 suíri

reassurance [riːəʃuːrˈəns] *n* 安ど áñdo

reassure [riːəʃuːrˈ] *vt* (comfort) 安心させる añshin saserù

to reassure someone of ...に...だと安心させる ...ni...dá tò añshin saserù

reassuring [riːəʃuːrˈiŋ] *adj* (smile, manner) 安心させる añshin saserù

rebate [riːˈbeit] *n* (on tax etc) リベート ribétò

rebel [*n* rebˈəl *vb* ribelˈ] *n* (against political system) 反逆者 hañgyakushà; (against society, parents etc) 反抗分子 hañkôbuñshi

♦*vi* (against political system) 反乱を起す hañran wò okósù; (against society, parents etc) 反抗する hañkô suru

rebellion [ribelˈjən] *n* (against political system) 反乱 hañran; (against society, parents etc) 反抗 hañkô

rebellious [ribelˈjəs] *adj* (subject) 反逆者の hañgyakushà no; (child, behavior) 反抗的な hañkôteki na

rebirth [riːbəːrθˈ] *n* 復活 fukkátsu

rebound [*vb* riːbaundˈ *n* riːˈbaund] *vi* (ball) 跳ね返る hanékaerù

♦*n: on the rebound* (ball) 跳ね返った所を hanékaetta tokórò wo; (fig: person) ...した反動で ...shítà hañdô de

rebuff [ribʌfˈ] *n* 拒絶 kyozétsu

rebuild [riːbildˈ] (*pt, pp* **rebuilt**) *vt* (town, building etc) 建直す taténaosù; (economy, confidence) 立直す taténaosù

rebuke [ribjuːkˈ] *vt* しかる shikárù

rebut [ribʌtˈ] *vt* しりぞける shirízokerù

recalcitrant [rikælˈsitrənt] *adj* (child, behavior) 反抗的な hañkôteki na

recall [riːkɔːlˈ] *vt* (remember) 思い出す omóidasù; (parliament, ambassador etc) 呼戻す yobímodosù

♦*n* (ability to remember) 記憶 kióku; (of ambassador etc) 召還 shôkan

recant [rikæntˈ] *vi* 自説を取消す jisétsu

wǒ toríkesù

recap [ri:'kæp] vt (summarize) 要約する yōyaku suru

♦vi ...を要約する ...wo yōyaku suru

recapitulate [ri:kəpít∫'u:leit] vt, vi = **recap**

recapture [ri:kæp't∫ər] vt (town, territory etc) 奪環する dakkán suru; (atmosphere, mood etc) 取戻す torímodosù

rec'd abbr = **received**

recede [risid'] vi (tide) ひく hikú; (lights etc) 遠のく tōnokù; (memory) 薄らぐ usúragù; (hair) はげる hagérù

receding [risi:'diŋ] adj (hair) はげつつある hagétsutsu arù; (chin) 無いに等しい náì ni hitóshiì

receipt [risi:t'] n (document) 領収書 ryōshūsho; (from cash register) レシート reshítò; (act of receiving) 受取る事 ukétorù kotó

receipts [risi:ts'] npl (COMM) 収入 shūnyū

receive [risi:v'] vt (get: money, letter etc) 受け取る ukétorù; (criticism, acclaim) 受ける ukérù; (visitor, guest) 迎える mukáerù

to receive an injury けがする kegá surù

receiver [risi:'vər] n (TEL) 受話器 juwákì; (RADIO, TV) 受信機 jushíñki; (of stolen goods) 故買屋 kobáìya; (COMM) 管財人 kañzaìniñ

recent [ri:'sənt] adj (event, times) 近ごろの chikágòro no

recently [ri:'səntli:] adv 近ごろ chikágòro

receptacle [risep'təkəl] n 容器 yōkì

reception [risep'∫ən] n (in hotel, office, hospital etc) 受付 ukétsuke; (party) レセプション resépùshon; (welcome) 歓迎 kañgei; (RADIO, TV) 受信 jushín

reception desk n 受付 ukétsuke, フロント furóñto

receptionist [risep'∫ənist] n 受付係 ukétsukegakàri

receptive [risep'tiv] adj (person, attitude) 前向きの maémuki no

recess [ri:'ses] n (in room) 壁のくぼみ

kabé nò kubómi; (secret place) 奥深い所 okúfukaì tokórò; (POL etc: holiday) 休憩時間 kyūkeijikàn

recession [rise∫'ən] n 景気後退 keíkikòtai

recharge [ri:t∫a:rdʒ'] vt (battery) 充電する jūden suru

recipe [res'əpi:] n (CULIN) 調理法 chōrihō; (fig: for success) 秘けつ hikétsu; (: for disaster) やり方 yaríkata

recipient [risip'i:ənt] n (of letter, payment etc) 受取人 ukétorinìn

reciprocal [risip'rəkəl] adj (arrangement, agreement) 相互の sōgò no

recital [risait'əl] n (concert) リサイタル risáitaru

recite [risait'] vt (poem) 暗唱する añshō suru

reckless [rek'lis] adj (driving, driver) 無謀な mubō na; (spending) 無茶な múchà na

recklessly [rek'lisli:] adv (drive) 無謀に mubō ni; (spend) むやみに múyàmi ni

reckon [rek'ən] vt (calculate) 計算する keísan suru; (think): *I reckon that ...* ...だと思う ...dá tò omóù

reckoning [rek'əniŋ] n (calculation) 計算 keísan

reckon on vt fus (expect) 当てにする a-té nì suru

reclaim [rikleim'] vt (demand back) ...の返還を要求する ...no heñkan wò yōkyū suru; (land: by filling in) 埋め立てる umétaterù; (: by draining) 干拓する kañtaku suru; (waste materials) 再生する saísei suru

reclamation [rekləmei'∫ən] n (of land: by filling in) 埋め立て umétate; (: by draining) 干拓 kañtaku

recline [riklain'] vi (sit or lie back) もたれる motárerù

reclining [riklain'iŋ] adj: *reclining seat* リクライニングシート rikúrainingushìto

recluse [rek'lu:s] n 隠とん者 iñtoñsha

recognition [rekəgni∫'ən] n (of person, place) 認識 niñshiki; (of problem, fact) 意識 íshìki; (of achievement) 認める事

mitómeru kotő

transformed beyond recognition 見分けが付かない程変化した miwáke ga tsukanái hodo hếñka shita

recognizable [rekəgnaiˈzəbəl] *adj*: ***recognizable (by)*** (...で) 見分けが付く (...de) miwáke ga tsukù

recognize [rekˈəgnaiz] *vt* (person, place, attitude, illness) ...だと分かる...dá tồ wakárù; (problem, need) 意識する íshìki suru; (qualification, achievement) 認める mitómerù; (government) 承認する shónìn suru

to recognize by/as ...で〔として〕分かる ...de 〔toshìtě〕 wakárù

recoil [rikoilˈ] *vi* (person): ***to recoil from doing something*** ...するのをいやがる ...surú no wồ iyágarù

♦*n* (of gun) 反動 hañdō

recollect [rekəlektˈ] *vt* (remember) 思い出す omóidasù

recollection [rekəlekˈʃən] *n* (memory) 思い出 omóide; (remembering) 思い出す事 omóidasu kotồ

recommend [rekəmendˈ] *vt* (book, shop, person) 推薦する suísen suru; (course of action) 勧める susúmerù

recommendation [rekəmendeiˈʃən] *n* (of book, shop, person) 推薦 suísen; (of course of action) 勧告 kañkoku

recompense [rekˈəmpens] *n* (reward) 報酬 hốshū

reconcile [rekˈənsail] *vt* (two people) 仲直りさせる nakánaòri sasérù; (two facts, beliefs) 調和させる chốwa saserù

to reconcile oneself to something (unpleasant situation, misery etc) ...だとあきらめる ...dá tồ akíramerù

reconciliation [rekənsiliˈeiˈʃən] *n* (of people etc) 和解 wakái; (of facts etc) 調和 chốwa

recondition [riːkəndiˈʃən] *vt* (machine) 修理する shūri suru

reconnaissance [rikɑːnˈisəns] *n* (MIL) 偵察 teísatsu

reconnoiter [riːkənoiˈtəːr] (*BRIT* **reconnoitre**) *vt* (MIL: enemy territory) 偵察する teísatsu suru

reconsider [riːkənsidˈəːr] *vt* (decision, opinion etc) 考え直す kañgaenaosù

reconstruct [riːkənstrʌktˈ] *vt* (building) 建直す taténaosù; (policy, system) 練り直す nerínaosù; (event, crime) 再現する saígen suru

reconstruction [riːkənstrʌkˈʃən] *n* (of building, country) 再建 saíken; (of crime) 再現 saígen

record [*n* rekˈəːrd *vb* rekɔːrdˈ] *n* (gen) 記録 kiróku; (MUS: disk) レコード rekố-dồ; (history: of person, company) 履歴 riréki; (*also*: **criminal record**) 前科 zéñka

♦*vt* (write down) 記録する kiróku suru; (temperature, speed etc) 表示する hyốji suru; (MUS: song etc) 録音する rokúon suru

in record time 記録的速さで kirókuteki hayàsa de

off the record *adj* (remark) オフレコの ofúreko no

♦*adv* (speak) オフレコで ofúreko de

record card *n* (in file) ファイルカード faírukầdo

recorded delivery [rikɔːrˈdid-] (*BRIT*) *n* (MAIL) 簡易書留 kañ-i kakìtome

recorder [rikɔːrˈdəːr] *n* (MUS: instrument) リコーダー rikốdầ

record holder *n* (SPORT) 記録保持者 kiróku hojishầ

recording [rikɔːrˈdiŋ] *n* 録音 rokúon

record player *n* レコードプレーヤー rekốdopurềyầ

recount [rikauntˈ] *vt* (story, event etc) 述べる nobérù

re-count [*n* riːˈkaunt *vb* riːkauntˈ] *n* (POL: of votes) 数え直し kazóenaoshi

♦*vt* (votes etc) 数え直す kazốenaosù

recoup [rikuːpˈ] *vt*: ***to recoup one's losses*** 損失を取戻す sońshitsu wồ torímodosù

recourse [riːˈkɔːrs] *n*: ***to have recourse to*** ...を用いる ...wo mochíirù

recover [rikʌvˈəːr] *vt* (get back: stolen goods, lost items, financial loss) 取戻す torímodosù

♦*vi*: ***to recover (from)*** (illness) (...が)

治る (...ga) naórù; (operation, shock, experience) (...から) 立直る (...kará) tachínaorù

recovery [rikʌv'ə:ri:] n (from illness, operation: in economy etc) 回復 kaífuku; (of stolen, lost items) 取戻し torímodoshi

re-create [ri:kri:eit'] vt 再現する saígen suru

recreation [rekri:ei'ʃən] n (play, leisure activities) 娯楽 goráku

recreational [rekri:ei'ʃənəl] adj 娯楽の goráku no

recrimination [rikrimənei'ʃən] n 責合い seméai

recruit [rikru:t'] n (MIL) 新兵 shínpei; (in company, organization) 新入社〔会〕員 shínnyūsha(kai)ìn
♦vt 募集する boshū suru

recruitment [rikru:t'mənt] n 募集 boshū

rectangle [rek'tæŋgəl] n 長方形 chōhōkei

rectangular [rektæŋ'gjələ:r] adj (shape, object etc) 長方形の chōhōkei no

rectify [rek'təfai] vt (correct) 正す tadásù

rector [rek'tə:r] n (REL) 主任司祭 shunínshisài

rectory [rek'tə:ri:] n (house) 司祭館 shisáikan

recuperate [riku:'pə:reit] vi (recover: from illness etc) 回復する kaífuku suru

recur [rikə:r'] vi (error, event) 繰返される kuríkaesarerù; (illness, pain) 再発する saíhatsu suru

recurrence [rikə:r'əns] n (of error, event) 繰返し kuríkaeshi; (of illness, pain) 再発 saíhatsu

recurrent [rikə:r'ənt] adj 頻繁に起る hínpan nì okórù

red [red] n (color) 赤 ákà; (pej: POL) 過激派 kagékiha
♦adj 赤い akái
to be in the red (bank account, business) 赤字になっている akáji nì natté irù

red carpet treatment n 盛大な歓迎式 seídai nà kaṅgeishìki

Red Cross n 赤十字 sekíjūji

redcurrant [red'kʌr'ənt] n アカフサスグリ akáfusasugùri

redden [red'ən] vt (turn red) 赤くする akáku suru
♦vi (blush) 赤面する sekímen suru

reddish [red'iʃ] adj 赤っぽい akáppòi

redeem [ridi:m'] vt (fig: situation, reputation) 救う sukúù; (something in pawn, loan) 請出す ukédasù; (REL: rescue) 救う sukúù

redeeming [ridi:'miŋ] adj: **redeeming feature** 欠点を補う取柄 kettén wò ogínaù toríe

redeploy [ri:diplɔi'] vt (resources) 配置し直す haíchi shinaosù

red-haired [red'he:rd] adj 赤毛の akáge no

red-handed [red'hæn'did] adj: **to be caught red-handed** 現行犯で捕まる geńkōhan de tsukámarù

redhead [red'hed] n 赤毛の人 akáge no hitò

red herring n (fig) 本論から注意をそらす物 hoñron kara chūì wo sorásù monó

red-hot [red'hɑ:t'] adj (metal) 真っ赤に焼けた makká nì yakétà

redirect [ri:dərekt'] vt (mail) 転送する teñsō suru

red light n: **to go through a red light** (AUT) 信号無視をする shiṅgōmùshi wo suru

red-light district [red'lait-] n 赤線地区 akásenchikù

redo [ri:du:'] (pt redid pp redone) vt やり直す yarínaosù

redolent [red'ələnt] adj: **redolent of** (smell: also fig) ...臭い ...kusái

redouble [ri:dʌb'əl] vt: **to redouble one's efforts** 一層努力する issō doryóku suru

redress [ridres'] n (compensation) 賠償 baíshō
♦vt (error, wrong) 償う tsugúnaù

Red Sea n: **the Red Sea** 紅海 kōkai

redskin [red'skin] n (pej) インディアン ińdian

red tape n (fig) 形式的手続き keíshikiteki tetsuzúki

reduce [ridu:s'] vt (decrease: spending, numbers etc) 減らす herásù

to reduce someone to (begging, stealing) ...を余儀なくさせる ...wo yogínaku saserù

to reduce someone to tears 泣かせる nakáserù

to reduce someone to silence 黙らせる damáraserù

「*reduce speed now*」(AUT) 徐行 jokô

at a reduced price (goods) 割引で warîbiki de

reduction [ridʌk'ʃən] n (in price) 値下げ neságe; (in numbers etc) 減少 geñshô

redundancy [ridʌn'dənsi:] n (dismissal) 解雇 káiko; (unemployment) 失業 shitsugyô

redundant [ridʌn'dənt] adj (worker) 失業中の shitsúgyōchū no; (detail, object) 余計な yokéi na

to be made redundant 解雇される kâiko sarérù

reed [ri:d] n (BOT) ア シ ashî; (MUS: of clarinet etc) リード rîdo

reef [ri:f] n (at sea) 暗礁 añshô

reek [ri:k] vi: *to reek (of)* (...の) におい がぷんぷんする (...no) niôi ga púñpun suru

reel [ri:l] n (of thread, string) 巻 makî; (of film, tape: *also* on fishing-rod) リール rîru; (dance) リール rîru

♦vi (sway) よろめく yorómekù

reel in vt (fish, line) 手繰り寄せる tagúriyoserù

ref [ref] (inf) n abbr = **referee**

refectory [rifek'tə:ri:] n 食堂 shokúdō

refer [rifə:r'] vt (person, patient): *to refer someone to* ...を...に回す ...wo ...ni mawásù; (matter, problem): *to refer something to* ...を...に委託する ...wo ...ni itáku suru

♦vi: *to refer to* (allude to) ...に言及する ...ni geñkyū suru; (consult) ...を参照する ...wo sañshō suru

referee [refəri:'] n (SPORT) 審判員 shiñpan-in, レフェリー réferī; (BRIT: for job application) 身元保証人 mimótohoshōnìn

♦vt (football match etc) ...のレフェリー をやる ...no réferī wo yárù

reference [ref'ə:rəns] n (mention) 言及 geñkyū; (in book, paper) 引用文献 iñ-yō buñken; (for job application: letter) 推薦 状 suíseñjō

with reference to (COMM: in letter) ...に関しては ...ni kañshite wa

reference book n 参考書 sañkôsho

reference number n 整理番号 seíribañgō

referenda [refəren'də] npl of **referendum**

referendum [refəren'dəm] (pl **referenda**) n 住民投票 júmintôhyo

refill [vb ri:fil' n ri:'fil] vt (glass etc) ...にもう一杯つぐ ...ni mô ippaî tsugù; (pen etc) ...に...を詰替える ...ni ...wo tsumékaerù

♦n (of drink etc) お代り o-káwari; (for pen etc) スペアー supéâ

refine [rifain'] vt (sugar, oil) 精製する seísei suru; (theory, idea) 洗練する señren suru

refined [rifaind'] adj (person, taste) 洗練 された señren saretà

refinement [rifain'mənt] n (of person) 優雅さ yûgasa; (of system) 精度 seído

reflect [riflekt'] vt (light, image) 反射す る hañsha suru; (situation, attitude) 反映 する hañ-ei suru

♦vi (think) じっくり考える jikkúrî kañgaerù

it reflects badly/well on him それは 彼の悪い〔いい〕所を物語っている soré wa kárè no warúî 〔íi〕 tokórô wo monôgatatte irù

reflection [riflek'ʃən] n (of light, heat) 反射 hañsha; (image) 影 kágè; (of situation, attitude) 反映する hañ-ei suru monð; (criticism) 非難 hínàn; (thought) 熟考 jukkô

on reflection よく考えると yôkù kañgaerù to

reflector [riflek'tə:r] n 反射器 hañshakì

reflex [ri:'fleks] adj (action, gesture) 反 射的な hañshateki na

♦n (PHYSIOLOGY, PSYCH) 反射 hañsha

reflexive [riflek'siv] *adj* (LING) 再帰 の safki no

reform [rifɔːrm'] *n* (of sinner, character) 改心 kaíshin; (of law, system) 改革 kaíkaku

♦*vt* (sinner) 改心させる kaíshin saserù; (law, system) 改革する kaíkaku suru

Reformation [refəːrmei'ʃən] *n*: *the Reformation* 宗教改革 shúkyokaíkaku

reformatory [rifɔːr'mətɔːriː] (*US*) *n* 感化院 karíkaìn

refrain [rifrein'] *vi*: *to refrain from doing* ...をしない様にする ...wo shinái yò ni suru

♦*n* (of song) 繰返し kuríkaeshi, リフレイ ン rifúreìn

refresh [rifreʃ'] *vt* (subj: sleep, drink) 元 気付ける geñkizukerù

to refresh someone's memory ...に思い 出させる ...ni omóidasaserù

refresher course [rifreʃ'əːr-] (*BRIT*) *n* 研修会 keńshūkài

refreshing [rifreʃ'iŋ] *adj* (drink) 冷たく ておいしい tsumétakùte oíshiĩ; (sleep) 気 分をさわやかにする kíbùn wo sawáyàka ni suru

refreshments [rifreʃ'mənts] *npl* (food and drink) 軽食 keíshoku

refrigeration [rifridʒərei'ʃən] *n* (of food) 冷蔵 reízō

refrigerator [rifridʒ'əːreitəːr] *n* 冷蔵庫 reízōko

refuel [riːfjuːʼəl] *vi* 燃料を補給する neñryō wo hokyú suru

refuge [refʼjuːdʒ] *n* (shelter) 避難場所 hináñbasho

to take refuge in ...に避難する ...ni hínàn suru

refugee [refjudʒiːʼ] *n* 難民 nañmin

refund [*n* riːʼfʌnd *vb* rifʌnd'] *n* 払い戻し haráimodoshi

♦*vt* (money) 払い戻す haráimodosù

refurbish [riːfəːrʼbiʃ] *vt* (shop, theater) 改装する kaísō suru

refusal [rifjuːʼzəl] *n* 断り kotówari, 拒否 kyóhì

first refusal (option) オプション権 o-

púshoñken

refuse[1] [rifjuːzʼ] *vt* (request, offer, gift) 断る kotówarù; (invitation) 辞退する jítài suru; (permission, consent) 拒む kobámù

♦*vi* (say no) 断る kotówarù; (horse) 飛越 を拒否する hiétsu wò kyóhì suru

to refuse to do something ...するのを 拒む ...surú no wò kobámù

refuse[2] [refʼjuːs] *n* (rubbish) ごみ gomí

refuse collection *n* ごみ収集 gomíshū-shū

refute [rifjuːtʼ] *vt* (argument) 論破する roñpa suru

regain [rigein'] *vt* (power, position) 取戻 す torímodosù

regal [riːʼgəl] *adj* 堂々とした dódō to shi-tà

regalia [rigeiʼliːə] *n* (costume) 正装 seísō

regard [rigɑːrdʼ] *n* (gaze) 視線 shisén; (attention, concern) 関心 kañshin; (esteem) 尊敬 soñkei

♦*vt* (consider) 見なす mínàsu

to give one's regards to ...から...によろ しく伝える ...kará ...nì yoróshiku tsutáe-rù

with kindest regards 敬具 keígu

regarding, as regards, with regard to (with reference to, concerning) ...に関 して ...ni kañshitè

regardless [rigɑːrdʼlis] *adv* (carry on, continue) 構わずに kamáwazù ni

regardless of (danger, consequences) ...を顧みず ...wo kaérimizù

regatta [rigɑːtʼə] *n* ヨット〔ボート〕競技 会 yottó〔bóto〕kyōgikài

regenerate [riːdʒenʼəːreit] *vt* (inner cities, arts) よみがえらせる yomígaera-serù

regent [riːʼdʒənt] *n* 摂政 sesshő

regime [reiʒiːmʼ] *n* (system of government) 政治体制 seíjitaìsei

regiment [redʒʼəmənt] *n* (MIL) 連隊 reñtai

regimental [redʒəmenʼtəl] *adj* 連隊の reñtai no

region [riːʼdʒən] *n* (area: of land) 地区 chíkù; (: of body) ...部 ...bù; (administrative division of country) 行政区 gyṓseíku

in the region of (*fig*: approximately) 約 yákù

regional [ri:'dʒənəl] *adj* (organization, wine, geography) 地元の jimóto no; (provincial) 地方の chihṓ no

register [redʒ'istər] *n* (list: of births, marriages, deaths, voters) 登録簿 tṓrokùbo; (SCOL: of attendance) 出席簿 shussékibò; (MUS: of voice) 声域 seíki; (: of instrument) 音域 oñ-iki
♦*vt* (birth, death, marriage) 届出る todókederù; (car) 登録する tṓroku suru; (MAIL: letter) 書留にする kakítome nì suru; (subj: meter, gauge) 示す shimésù
♦*vi* (at hotel) チェックインする chekkúìn suru; (for work) 名前を登録する namáè wo tṓroku suru; (as student) 入学手続きをする nyūgakutetsuzuki wò suru; (make impression) ぴんと来る piñ tò kúrù

registered [redʒ'istərd] *adj* (MAIL: letter, parcel) 書留の kakítome no

registered trademark *n* 登録商標 tṓrokushṓhyō

registrar [redʒ'istrɑ:r] *n* (official) 戸籍係 kosékigakàri; (in college, university) 教務係 kyṓmugakàri; (*BRIT*: in hospital) 医務吏員 imúrìn

registration [redʒistrei'ʃən] *n* (*gen*) 登録 tṓroku; (of birth, death) 届出 todókede; (AUT: *also*: **registration number**) ナンバー náñbā

registry [redʒ'istri:] *n* 登記所 tṓkisho

registry office (*BRIT*) *n* 戸籍登記所 kosékitòkisho

to get married in a registry office 戸籍登記所で結婚する kosékitòkisho dè kekkón suru

regret [rigret'] *n* (sorrow) 悔み kuyámi
♦*vt* (decision, action) 後悔する kṓkai suru; (loss, death) 悔む kuyámù; (inability to do something) 残念に思う zafnen nì omóù; (inconvenience) 済まないと思う sumánài to omóù

regretfully [rigret'fəli:] *adv* (sadly) 残念ながら zañnen nagàra

regrettable [rigret'əbəl] *adj* (unfortunate: mistake, incident) あいにくの aínikù no

regular [reg'jələr] *adj* (even: breathing, pulse etc) 規則的な kisókuteki na; (evenly-spaced: intervals, meetings etc) 定期的な teíkiteki na; (symmetrical: features, shape etc) 対称的な taíshoteki na; (frequent: raids, exercise etc) 頻繁な hiñpan na; (usual: time, doctor, customer etc) 通常の tsūjō no; (soldier) 正規の seíki no; (LING) 規則変化の kisókuheñka no
♦*n* (client etc) 常連 jṓren

regularity [regjələr'iti:] *n* (frequency) 高頻度 kṓhìndo

regularly [reg'jələrli:] *adv* (at evenly-spaced intervals) 規則的に kisókuteki ni; (symmetrically: shaped etc) 対称的に taíshoteki ni; (often) 頻繁に hiñpan ni

regulate [reg'jəleit] *vt* (conduct, expenditure) 規制する kiséi suru; (traffic, speed) 調整する chṓsei suru; (machine, oven) 調節する chṓsetsu suru

regulation [regjəlei'ʃən] *n* (of conduct, expenditure) 規制 kiséi; (of traffic, speed) 調整 chṓsei; (of machine, oven) 調節 chṓsetsu; (rule) 規則 kisóku

rehabilitation [ri:həbilətei'ʃən] *n* (of criminal, addict) 社会復帰 shakáifukkì, リハビリテーション rihábiritḗshon

rehearsal [rihə:r'səl] *n* リハーサル rihā́saru

rehearse [rihə:rs'] *vt* (play, dance, speech etc) ...のリハーサルをする ...no rihā́saru wo suru

reign [rein] *n* (of monarch) 治世 chiséi; (*fig*: of terror etc) 支配 shíhài
♦*vi* (monarch) 君臨する kuñrin suru; (*fig*: violence, fear etc) はびこる habíkorù; (: peace, order etc) 行渡る ikíwatarù

reimburse [ri:imbə:rs'] *vt* (pay back) ...に弁償する ...ni beñshō suru

rein [rein] *n* (for horse) 手綱 tazúna

reincarnation [ri:inkɑ:rnei'ʃən] *n* (belief) 輪ね ríñne

reindeer [rein'di:r] *n inv* トナカイ tonákài

reinforce [ri:infɔːrs'] vt (strengthen: object) 補強する hokyố suru; (: situation) 強化する kyốka suru; (support: idea, statement) 裏付ける urázukerù

reinforced concrete [ri:infɔːrst'-] n 鉄筋コンクリート tekkín konkurītò

reinforcement [ri:infɔːrs'mənt] n (strengthening) 補強 hokyố

reinforcements [ri:infɔːrs'mənts] npl (MIL) 援軍 eñgun

reinstate [ri:insteit'] vt (worker) 復職させる fukúshoku saserù; (tax, law, text) 元通りにする motódōri ni surù

reiterate [ri:it'əreit] vt (repeat) 繰返す kuríkaesù

reject [n ri:'dʒekt vb ridʒekt'] n (COMM) 傷物 kizúmono
♦vt (plan, proposal etc) 退ける shirízokerù; (offer of help) 断る kotówarù; (belief, political system) 拒絶する kyozétsu suru; (candidate) 不採用にする fusáiyō ni suru; (coin) 受付けない ukétsukenài; (goods, fruit etc) 傷物として処分する kizúmono toshitè shóbùn suru

rejection [ridʒek'ʃən] n (of plan, proposal, offer of help etc) 拒否 kyóhì; (of belief etc) 拒絶 kyozétsu; (of candidate) 不採用 fusáiyō

rejoice [ridʒɔis'] vi: to rejoice at/over ...を喜ぶ ...wo yorókobù

rejuvenate [ridʒu:'vəneit] vt (person) 若返らせる wakágaeraserù

relapse [rilæps'] n (MED) 再発 saíhatsu

relate [rileit'] vt (tell) 話す hanásù; (connect) 結び付ける musúbitsukerù
♦vi: to relate to (person, subject, thing) ...に関係がある ...ni kañkei ga arù

related [rilei'tid] adj (person) 血縁がある ketsúen ga arù; (animal, language) 近縁の kiñ-en no
related to ...に関係がある ...ni kañkei ga arù

relating [rilei'tiŋ]: relating to prep ...に関する ...ni kañ suru

relation [rilei'ʃən] n (member of family) 親せき shiñseki; (connection) 関係 kañkei

relations [relei'ʃənz] npl (dealings) 関係

kañkei; (relatives) 親せき shiñseki

relationship [rilei'ʃənʃip] n (between two people, countries, things) 関係 kañkei; (also: family relationship) 親族関係 shiñzokukañkei

relative [rel'ətiv] n (member of family) 親類 shíñrui, 親せき shiñseki
♦adj (comparative) 相対的な sốtaiteki na; (connected): relative to ...に関する ...ni kañ suru

relatively [rel'ətivli:] adv (comparatively) 比較的 hikákuteki

relax [rilæks'] vi (person: unwind) くつろぐ kutsúrogù; (muscle) 緩む yurúmù
♦vt (one's grip) 緩める yurúmerù; (mind, person) くつろがせる kutsúrogaserù; (rule, control etc) 緩める yurúmerù

relaxation [ri:læksei'ʃən] n (rest) 休み yasúmi; (of muscle, grip) 緩み yurúmi; (of rule, control etc) 緩和 kañwa; (recreation) 娯楽 goráku

relaxed [rilækst'] adj (person) 落着いた ochítsuità; (discussion, atmosphere) くつろいだ kutsúroìda

relaxing [rilæks'iŋ] adj (holiday, afternoon) くつろいだ kutsúroìda

relay [ri:'lei] n (race) リレー rírè
♦vt (message, question) 伝える tsutáerù; (programme, signal) 中継する chúkei suru

release [rili:s'] n (from prison) 釈放 shakúhō; (from obligation) 免除 méñjo; (of gas, water etc) 放出 hōshutsu; (of film) 封切り fúkiri; (of book, record) 発売 hatsúbai
♦vt (prisoner: from prison) 釈放する shakúhō suru; (: from captivity) 解放する kaíhō suru; (gas etc) 放出する hōshutsu suru; (free: from wreckage etc) 救出する kyúshutsu suru; (TECH: catch, spring etc) 外す hazúsù; (book, record) 発売する hatsúbai suru; (film) 公開する kốkai suru; (report, news) 公表する kốhyō suru

relegate [rel'əgeit] vt (downgrade) 格下げする kakúsage suru; (BRIT: SPORT): to be relegated 格下げされる kakúsage sarerù

relent [rilent'] vi (give in) ...の態度が軟化

する ...no táîdo ga nańka suru

relentless [rilent'lis] *adj* (unceasing) 絶間ない taémanaî; (determined) 執念深い shúneñbukai

relevance [rel'əvəns] *n* (of remarks, information) 意義 ígî; (of question etc) 関連 kańren

relevant [rel'əvənt] *adj* (fact, information, question) 意義ある ígî árù
relevant to (situation, problem etc) ...に関連のある ...ni kańren no arù

reliability [rilaiəbil'əti:] *n* (of person, machine) 信頼性 shińraisei; (of information) 信ぴょう性 shiñpyōsei

reliable [rilai'əbəl] *adj* (person, firm) 信頼できる shińrai dekirù; (method, machine) 信頼性のある shiñraisei no arù; (news, information) 信用できる shiñyō dekirù

reliably [rilai'əbli:] *adv*: *to be reliably informed that ...* 確かな情報筋による と... táshîka na jôhōsùji ni yorú tò ...

reliance [rilai'əns] *n*: *reliance (on)* (...への) 依存 (...é nò) izón

relic [rel'ik] *n* (REL) 聖遺物 seíbùtsu; (of the past) 遺物 ibútsu

relief [rili:f'] *n* (from pain, anxiety etc) 緩和 kańwa; (help, supplies) 救援物資 kyûenbusshì; (ART) 浮彫 ukíbori, レリーフ rerífù; (GEO) 際立つ事 kiwádatsu kotò

relieve [rili:v'] *vt* (pain, fear, worry) 緩和する kańwa suru; (patient) 安心させる ańshin saserù; (bring help to: victims, refugees etc) ...に救援物資を届ける ...ni kyûenbusshì wo todókerù; (take over from: colleague, guard) ...と交替する ...to kôtai suru
to relieve someone of something (load) ...の ...を持って上げる ...no ...wo móttè agérù; (duties, post) ...を解任する ...wo kaínin suru
to relieve oneself 小便する shóben suru

religion [rilidʒ'ən] *n* 宗教 shúkyō

religious [rilidʒ'əs] *adj* (activities, faith) 宗教の shúkyō no; (person) 信心深い shiñjinbukai

relinquish [riliŋ'kwiʃ] *vt* (authority) ...から手を引く ...kara té wò hikú; (plan, habit) やめる yamérù

relish [rel'iʃ] *n* (CULIN) レリッシュ rerísshù; (enjoyment) 楽しみ tanóshimi
♦*vt* (enjoy: food, competition) 楽しむ tanóshimù
to relish the thought/idea/prospect of something/doing something ...を 〔...するのを〕心待ちに待つ ...wo 〔... surú nò wo〕 kokóromachi nì mátsù

relocate [ri:lou'keit] *vt* 移動させる idô saserù
♦*vi* 移動する idô suru

reluctance [riluk'təns] *n* (unwillingness) 気が進まない事 kí gà susúmanai kotò

reluctant [rilak'tənt] *adj* (unwilling) 気が進まない kí gà susúmanaî

reluctantly [rilak'təntli:] *adv* (unwillingly) いやいやながら iyáiyanagàra

rely on [rilai'-] *vt fus* (be dependent on) ...に頼る ...ni tayórù; (trust) ...を信用する ...wo shiń-yō suru

remain [rimein'] *vi* (survive, be left) 残る nokórù; (continue to be) 相変らず...である aíkawarazù ...de árù; (stay) とどまる todómarù

remainder [rimein'də:r] *n* (rest) 残り nokóri

remaining [rimei'niŋ] *adj* 残りの nokóri no

remains [rimeinz'] *npl* (of meal) 食べ残り tabénokori; (of building) 廃虚 haíkyo; (corpse) 遺体 itái

remand [rimænd'] *n*: *on remand* 拘置中で kôchichū de
♦*vt*: *to be remanded in custody* 拘置される kôchi sarerù

remand home (*BRIT*) *n* 少年院 shónen-ìn

remark [rimɑːrk'] *n* (comment) 発言 hatsúgen
♦*vt* (comment) 言う iú

remarkable [rimɑːr'kəbəl] *adj* (outstanding) 著しい ichíjirushiì

remarry [riːmærˈiː] *vi* 再婚する saíkon suru

remedial [rimiːˈdiːəl] *adj* (tuition, classes) 補修の hoshū no; (exercise) 矯正の kyōsei no

remedy [rem'idi:] *n* (cure) 治療法 chiryóhō

♦*vt* (correct) 直す naósù

remember [rimem'bər] *vt* (call back to mind) 思い出す omóidasù; (bear in mind) 忘れない様にする wasúrenai yō ni suru; (send greetings): *remember me to him* 彼によろしくお伝え下さい kárè ni yoróshikù o-tsútae kudasái

remembrance [rimem'brəns] *n* (memory: of dead person) 思い出 omóide; (souvenir: of place, event) 記念品 kinénhin

remind [rimaind'] *vt*: *to remind someone to do something* ...するのを忘れない様に...に注意する ...surú no wò wasúrenai yō ni ...ni chūí suru

to remind someone of something ...に...を思い出させる ...ni ...wo omóidasasèru

she reminds me of her mother 彼女を見ると彼女の母親を思い出す kánòjo wo mírù to kánòjo no haháoya wò omóidasù

reminder [rimaind'ər] *n* (souvenir) 記念品 kinénhin; (letter) 覚書 obóegaki

reminisce [remənis'] *vi* (about the past) 追憶する tsuíoku suru

reminiscent [remənis'ənt] *adj*: *to be reminiscent of something* ...を思い出させる ...wo omóidasasèru

remiss [rimis'] *adj* (careless) 不注意な fuchūí na

it was remiss of him 彼は不注意だった kárè wa fuchūí dáttà

remission [rimiʃ'ən] *n* (of debt) 免除 ménjo; (of prison sentence) 減刑 génkei; (of illness) 緩解 kańkai; (REL: of sins) 許し yurúshi

remit [rimit'] *vt* (send: money) 送金する sókin suru

remittance [rimit'əns] *n* (payment) 送金 sókin

remnant [rem'nənt] *n* (small part remaining) 残り nokóri; (of cloth) 切れ端 kiréhashi

ses) 補修の hoshū no; (exercise) 矯正の kyōsei no

remnants [rem'nənts] *npl* (COMM) 端切れ hagíre

remorse [rimɔːrs'] *n* (guilt) 後悔 kōkai

remorseful [rimɔːrs'fəl] *adj* (guilty) 後悔している kōkai shite irú

remorseless [rimɔːrs'lis] *adj* (*fig*: noise, pain) 絶間ない taémanaì

remote [rimout'] *adj* (distant: place, time) 遠い tōí; (person) よそよそしい yosóyososhiì; (slight: possibility, chance) かすかな kásùka na

remote control *n* 遠隔操作 eńkakusōsa, リモートコントロール rimótokontorōru

remotely [rimout'li:] *adv* (distantly) 遠くに tōku ni; (slightly) かすかに kásùka ni

remould [ri:'mould] (*BRIT*) *n* (tire) 再生タイヤ saíseitaiya

removable [rimu:'vəbəl] *adj* (detachable) 取外しのできる toríhazushi nò dekírù

removal [rimu:'vəl] *n* (taking away) 取除く事 torínozoku kotò; (of stain) 消し取る事 keshítoru kotò; (*BRIT*: from house) 引っ越し hikkóshi; (from office: dismissal) 免職 meńshoku; (MED) 切除 sétsùjo

removal van (*BRIT*) *n* 引っ越しトラック hikkóshi torakkù

remove [rimu:v'] *vt* (*gen*) 取除く torínozokù; (clothing) 脱ぐ núgù; (bandage etc) 外す hazúsù; (stain) 消し取る keshítorù; (employee) 解雇する kaíko suru; (MED: lung, kidney, appendix etc) 切除する sétsùjo suru

removers [rimu:'vərz] (*BRIT*) *npl* (company) 引っ越し屋 hikkóshiyà

remuneration [rimju:nərei'ʃən] *n* (payment) 報酬 hōshū

Renaissance [ren'isɑːns] *n*: *the Renaissance* ルネッサンス runéssànsu

render [ren'dəːr] *vt* (give: thanks, service) する surú; (make) させる sasérù

rendering [ren'dəːriŋ] *n* (MUS: instrumental) 演奏 eńsō; (: song) 歌い方 utáikatà

rendez-vous [rɑːn'deivuː] *n* (meeting) 待ち合せ machíawase; (place) 待ち合せの

場所 machíawase nò báshò

renegade [ren'əgeid] n 裏切者 urágirimono

renew [rinu:'] vt (resume) 再び始める futátabi hajimerù; (loan, contract etc) 更新
する kóshin suru; (negotiations) 再開す
る saíkai suru; (acquaintance, relationship) よみがえらせる yomígaeraserù

renewal [rinu:'əl] n (resumption) 再開
saíkai; (of license, contract etc) 更新 kóshin

renounce [rinauns'] vt (belief, course of
action) 捨てる sutérù; (claim, right, peerage) 放棄する hóki suru

renovate [ren'əveit] vt (building,
machine) 改造する kaízo suru

renovation [renəvei'ʃən] n 改造 kaízo

renown [rinaun'] n (fame) 名声 meísei

renowned [rinaund'] adj (famous) 有名
な yūmei na

rent [rent] n (for house) 家賃 yáchìn

♦vt (take for rent: house) 賃借する chín-
shaku suru; (: television, car) レンタルで
借りる rêntaru de karírù; (also: rent
out: house) 賃貸する chíntai suru; (: television, car) 貸出す kashídasù

rental [ren'təl] n (for television, car) レ
ンタル rêntaru

renunciation [rinʌnsi:ei'ʃən] n 放棄 hóki

reorganize [ri:ɔ:r'gənaiz] vt 再編成する
saíhensei suru

rep [rep] n abbr (COMM) = representative; (THEATER) = repertory

repair [ripe:r'] n (of clothes, shoes) 修繕
shúzen; (of car, road, building etc) 修理
shúri

♦vt (clothes, shoes) 修繕する shúzen suru; (car, engine, road, building) 修理する
shúri suru

in good/bad repair 整備が行届いてい
る(いない) seíbi gà ikítodoite irù (inài)

repair kit n 修理キット shúrikittò

repatriate [ri:pei'tri:eit] vt (refugee, soldier) 送還する sókan suru

repay [ripei'] (pt, pp repaid) vt (money,
debt, loan) 返済する heńsai suru; (person) ...に借金を返済する ...ni shakkíñ wo

heńsai suru; (sb's efforts) ...に答える ...ni
kotáerù; (favor) ...の恩返しをする ...no
ońgaeshi wò suru

repayment [ripei'mənt] n (amount of
money) 返済金 heńsaikiñ; (of debt, loan
etc) 返済 heńsai

repeal [ripi:l'] n (of law) 廃止する haíshi
suru

♦vt (law) 廃止 haíshi

repeat [ripi:t'] n (RADIO, TV) 再放送 saíhōsō

♦vt (say/do again) 繰返す kuríkaesù;
(RADIO, TV) 再放送する saíhōsō surù

♦vi 繰返す kuríkaesù

repeatedly [ripi:t'idli:] adv (again and
again) 再三 saísan

repel [ripel'] vt (drive away: enemy,
attack) 撃退する gekítai suru; (disgust:
subj: appearance, smell) ...に不快な感じ
を与える ...ni fukái na kańji wò atáerù

repellent [ripel'ənt] adj いやな iyá nà

♦n: insect repellent 虫よけ mushíyoke

repent [ripent'] vi: to repent (of) (sin,
mistake) (...を) 後悔する (...wo) kókai
suru

repentance [ripen'təns] n 後悔 kókai

repercussions [ri:pə:rkʌ'ʃənz] npl 反響
hańkyō

repertoire [rep'ə:rtwɑ:r] n レパートリー
repátòrī

repertory [rep'ə:rtɔ:ri:] n (also: repertory theater) レパートリー演劇 repáto-
rīeńgeki

repetition [repitiʃ'ən] n (repeat) 繰返し
kuríkaeshi

repetitive [ripet'ətiv] adj (movement,
work) 単純反復の tańjunhañpuku no;
(speech) くどい kudóì; (noise) 反復される
hańpuku sarerù

replace [ripleis'] vt (put back) 元に戻す
mótò ni modósù; (take the place of) ...に
代る ...ni kawárù

replacement [ripleis'mənt] n (substitution) 置き換え okíkae; (substitute) 代り
の物 kawári no monò

replay [ri:plei'] n (of match) 再試合 saí-
shiai; (of tape, film) 再生 saísei

replenish [riplen'iʃ] vt (glass) ...にもう一

杯つぐ ...in mố ippâi tsugú; (stock etc) 補充する hojú suru

replete [ripli:t'] *adj* (well-fed) 満腹の mañpuku no

replica [rep'ləkə] *n* (copy) 複製 fukúsei, レプリカ repúrîka

reply [riplai'] *n* (answer) 答え kotáè
♦*vi* (to question, letter) 答える kotáerù

reply coupon *n* 返信券 heñshinken ◊切手と交換できる券 kittè tð kồkan dekirù kén

report [ripɔːrt'] *n* (account) 報告書 hôkokushò; (PRESS, TV etc) 報道 hôdō; (BRIT: also: **school report**) レポート repốtò; (of gun) 銃声 jûsei
♦*vt* (give an account of: event, meeting) 報告する hôkoku suru; (PRESS, TV etc) 報道する hôdō suru; (theft, accident, death) 届け出る todókederù
♦*vi* (make a report) 報告する hôkoku suru; (present oneself): **to report (to someone)** (...に) 出頭する (...ni) shuttô suru; (be responsible to): **to report to someone** ...が直属の上司である ...ga chokúzoku nò jôshi de arù

report card (US, SCOTTISH) *n* 通知表 tsúchihyồ

reportedly [ripɔːr'tidli:] *adv* うわさによると uwása ni yoru tð

reporter [ripɔːr'tər] *n* (PRESS, TV etc) 記者 kishá

repose [ripouz'] *n*: **in repose** (face, mouth) 平常で heíjô de

reprehensible [reprihen'səbəl] *adj* (behavior) 不届きな futódòki na

represent [reprizent'] *vt* (person, nation) 代表する daíhyố suru; (view, belief) ...の典型的な例である ...no teñkeiteki nà rêî de arù; (symbolize: idea, emotion) ...のシンボルである ...no shíñboru de árù; (constitute) ...である ...de árù; (describe): **to represent something as** ...を...として描写する ...wo ...toshite byốsha suru; (COMM) ...のセールスマンである ...no sếrusumàn de arù

representation [reprizentei'ʃən] *n* (state of being represented) 代表を立てている事 daíhyõ wô tátète irú kotð; (pic-

ture) 絵 é; (statue) 彫像 chốzō; (petition) 陳情 chiñjô

representations [reprizentei'ʃənz] *npl* (protest) 抗議 kôgi

representative [reprizen'tətiv] *n* (of person, nation) 代表者 daíhyõsha; (of view, belief) 典型 teñkei; (COMM) セールスマン sếrusumàn; (US: POL) 下院議員 kaíngiìn
♦*adj* (group, survey, cross-section) 代表的な daíhyõteki na

repress [ripres'] *vt* (people, revolt) 抑圧する yokúatsu suru; (feeling, impulse) 抑制する yokúsei suru

repression [repreʃ'ən] *n* (of people, country) 抑圧 yokúatsu; (of feelings) 抑制 yokúsei

repressive [repres'iv] *adj* (society, measures) 抑圧的な yokúatsuteki na

reprieve [ripri:v'] *n* (LAW) 執行延期 shikkốeñki ◊特に死刑について言う tôku ni shikéi ni tsuitè iú; (fig: delay) 延期 eñki

reprimand [rep'rəmænd] *n* (official rebuke) 懲戒 chôkai
♦*vt* 懲戒する chôkai suru

reprint [*n* ri:'print *vb* ri:print'] *n* 復刻版 fukkốkuban
♦*vt* 復刻する fukkốku suru

reprisal [riprai'zəl] *n* 報復 hôfuku

reprisals [riprai'zəlz] *npl* (acts of revenge) 報復行為 hôfukukôi

reproach [riproutʃ'] *n* (rebuke) 非難 hínàn
♦*vt*: **to reproach someone for something** ...の...を非難する ...no ...wo hínàn suru

reproachful [riproutʃ'fəl] *adj* (look, remark) 非難めいた hinánmeìta

reproduce [ri:prədu:s'] *vt* (copy: document etc) 複製する fukúsei suru; (sound) 再生する saísei suru
♦*vi* (mankind, animal, plant) 繁殖する hañshoku suru

reproduction [ri:prədʌk'ʃən] *n* (copy: of document, report etc) 複写 fukúsha; (of sound) 再生 saísei; (of painting, furniture) 複製品 fukúseihin; (of mankind, animal etc) 繁殖 hańshoku

reproductive [ri:prəd∧k'tiv] *adj* (system, process) 繁殖の hańshoku no

reproof [ripru:f'] *n* しっ責 shisséki

reprove [ripru:v'] *vt*: **to reprove someone for something** ...の事で...をしっ責する ...no kotő dè ...wo shisséki suru

reptile [rep'tail] *n* は虫類 hachűrùi

republic [rip∧b'lik] *n* 共和国 kyőwakòku

republican [rip∧b'likən] *adj* (system, government etc) 共和国の kyőwakòku no; (US: POL): **Republican** 共和党の kyőwatő no

repudiate [ripju:'di:eit] *vt* (accusation, violence) 否定する hitéi suru

repugnant [rip∧g'nənt] *adj* 不愉快な fuyúkài na

repulse [rip∧ls'] *vt* (enemy, attack) 撃退する gekítai suru

repulsive [rip∧l'siv] *adj* (sight, idea) 不愉快な fuyúkài na

reputable [rep'jətəbəl] *adj* 評判の良い hyőban no yoî

reputation [repjətei'ʃən] *n* 評判 hyőban

reputed [ripju:'tid] *adj* (supposed) ...とされる ...to sarérù

reputedly [ripju:'tidli:] *adv* (supposedly) 人の言うには hitő nò iú ni wà

request [rikwest'] *n* (polite demand) 願い negái; (formal demand) 要望 yőbō; (RADIO, TV) リクエスト rikúesùto

♦*vt*: **to request something of/from someone** (politely) ...に ...をお願いする ...ni ...wo o-négai suru; (formally) ...に ...を要望する ...wo yőbō suru; (RADIO, TV) リクエストする rikúesùto suru

request stop (BRIT) *n* 随時停留所 zuíjiteiryûjo ◇乗降客がいる時だけバスが留る停留所 jőkōkyaku ga irú toki dakè básù ga tomárù teíryùjo

requiem [rek'wi:əm] *n* (REL) 死者のためのミサ shíshà no tamé nò mísà; (MUS) 鎮魂曲 chiñkoňkyoku, レクイエム rekúîemu

require [rikwaiə:r'] *vt* (need) ...が必要である ...ga hitsúyō de arù; (order): **to**

require someone to do something ...に ...する事を要求する ...ni ...surú kotő wo yőkyū suru

requirement [rikwaiə:r'mənt] *n* (need) 必要条件 hitsúyōjòken; (want) 要求 yőkyū

requisite [rek'wizit] *n* (requirement) 必要条件 hitsúyōjòken

♦*adj* (required) 必要な hitsúyō na

requisition [rekwizi'ʃən] *n*: **requisition (for)** (demand) (...の) 請求 (...no) seíkyū

♦*vt* (MIL) 徴発する chőhatsu suru

resale [ri:'seil] *n* 転売 teńbai

rescind [risind'] *vt* (law) 廃止する haíshi suru; (contract, order etc) 破棄する hákì suru

rescue [res'kju:] *n* (help) 救援 kyűen; (from drowning, accident) 人命救助 jińmeikyûjo

♦*vt*: **to rescue (from)** (person, animal) (...から) 救う (...kara) sukúù; (company) 救済する kyúsai suru

rescue party *n* 救援隊 kyűentai, レスキュー隊 resúkyûtai

rescuer [res'kju:ə:r] *n* 救助者 kyűjosha

research [risə:rtʃ'] *n* 研究 keńkyū

♦*vt* (story, subject) 研究する keńkyū suru; (person) ...について情報を集める ...ni tsuíte jőhō wò atsúmerù

researcher [risə:r'tʃə:r] *n* 研究者 keńkyūsha

resemblance [rizem'bləns] *n* (likeness) 似ている事 nité iru kotő

resemble [rizem'bəl] *vt* ...に似ている ...ni nité irù

resent [rizent'] *vt* ...に対して腹を立てる ...ni táìshite hará wò tatérù

resentful [rizent'fəl] *adj* 怒っている o-kőtte irù

resentment [rizent'mənt] *n* 恨み urámi

reservation [rezə:rvei'ʃən] *n* (booking) 予約 yoyáku; (doubt) 疑い utágai; (for tribe) 居留地 kyoryúchì

reserve [rizə:rv'] *n* (store) 備蓄 bichíku, 蓄え takúwae; (SPORT) 補欠 hokétsu; (game reserve) 保護区 hogőkù; (restraint) 遠慮 eńryo

♦vt (keep) 取って置く tóttè oku; (seats, table etc) 予約する yoyáku suru

in reserve 蓄えてあって takúwaete attè

reserved [rizə:rvd'] adj (restrained) 遠慮深い eńryobùkai

reserves [rizə:rvz'] npl (MIL) 予備軍 yobígùn

reservoir [rez'ə:rvwɑ:r] n (of water) 貯水池 chosúchìi

reshuffle [ri:ʃʌf'əl] n: **Cabinet reshuffle** (POL) 内閣改造 naíkakukaizồ

reside [rizaid'] vi (person: live) 住む súmù

residence [rez'idəns] n (formal: home) 住い sumáì; (length of stay) 滞在 taízai

residence permit (BRIT) n 在留許可 zaíryūkyokà

resident [rez'idənt] n (of country, town) 住民 júmin; (in hotel) 泊り客 tomárikyakù

♦adj (population) 現住の geńjū no; (doctor) レジデントの réjìdento no

residential [reziden'tʃəl] adj (area) 住宅の jútaku no; (course) 住込みの sumíkomi no; (college) 全寮制の zeńryōsei no

residue [rez'idu:] n (remaining part) 残留物 zańryùbutsu

resign [rizain'] vt (one's post) 辞任する jinín suru

♦vi (from post) 辞任する jinín suru

to resign oneself to (situation, fact) あきらめて...を認める akírametè ...wo mitómerù

resignation [rezignei'ʃən] n (post) 辞任 jinín; (state of mind) あきらめ akírame

resigned [rizaind'] adj (to situation etc) あきらめている akírameté irù

resilience [rizil'jəns] n (of material) 弾力 dańryoku; (of person) 回復力 kaffukuryòku

resilient [rizil'jənt] adj (material) 弾力のある dańryoku no arù; (person) 立直りの速い tachínaori nò hayáì

resin [rez'in] n 樹脂 júshì

resist [rizist'] vt 抵抗する teíkō suru

resistance [rizis'təns] n (gen) 抵抗 teíkō; (to illness, infection) 抵抗力 teíkōryòku

resolute [rez'əlu:t] adj (person) 意志の強

い íshì no tsuyóì; (refusal) 断固とした dáñko to shitá

resolution [rezəlu:'ʃən] n (decision) 決心 kesshíñ; (determination) 決意 kétsùi; (of problem, difficulty) 解決 kaíketsu

resolve [rizɑ:lv'] n (determination) 決意 kétsùi

♦vt (problem, difficulty) 解決する kaíketsu suru

♦vi: **to resolve to do** ...しようと決心する ...shiyó tò kesshíñ suru

resolved [rizɑ:lvd'] adj (determined) 決心している kesshíñ shité irù

resonant [rez'ənənt] adj 朗朗たる rórồ taru

resort [rizɔ:rt'] n (town) リゾート rizóto; (recourse) 利用 riyó

♦vi: **to resort to** ...を利用する ...wo riyó suru

in the last resort 結局 kekkyókù

resound [rizaund'] vi: **to resound (with)** (...の音が...中に) 鳴り響く (...no otó ga ...jū ni) naríhibikù

resounding [rizaun'diŋ] adj (noise) 響き渡る hibíkiwatarù; (fig: success) 完全な kańzen na

resource [ri:'sɔ:rs] n (raw material) 資源 shígen

resourceful [risɔ:rs'fəl] adj (quick-witted) やり手の yaríte no

resources [ri:'sɔ:rsiz] npl (coal, iron, oil etc) 天然資源 teńnenshigèn; (money) 財産 záìsan

respect [rispekt'] n (consideration, esteem) 尊敬 soñkei

♦vt 尊敬する soñkei suru

with respect to ...に関して ...ni káñ shite

in this respect この点では konó ten de wà

respectability [rispektəbil'əti:] n 名声 meísei

respectable [rispek'təbəl] adj (morally correct) 道理にかなった dóri nì kanáttà; (large: amount) かなりの kánàri no; (passable) まあまあの máầmà no

respectful [rispekt'fəl] adj (person, behavior) 礼儀正しい reígitadashiì

respective [rispek'tiv] *adj* (separate) それぞれの sorézòre no

respectively [rispek'tivli:] *adv* それぞれ sorézòre

respects [rispekts'] *npl* (greetings) あいさつ áīsatsu

respiration [respərei'ʃən] *n see* **artificial respiration**

respite [res'pit] *n* (rest) 休息 kyūsoku

resplendent [risplen'dənt] *adj* 華やかな hanáyàka na

respond [rispɑːnd'] *vi* (answer) 答える kotáerù; (react: to pressure, criticism) 反応する hañnō suru

response [rispɑːns'] *n* (answer) 答え kotáè; (reaction) 反応 hañnō

responsibility [rispɑːnsəbil'əti:] *n* (liability) 責任 sekínin; (duty) 義務 gímù

responsible [rispɑːn'səbəl] *adj* (liable): **responsible (for)** (...の) 責任がある (...no) sekínin gà árù; (character, person) 責任感のある sekíniñkan no aru; (job) 責任の重い sekínin nò omóí

responsive [rispɑːn'siv] *adj* (child, gesture) 敏感な biñkan na; (to demand, treatment) よく応じる yókù ōjírù

rest [rest] *n* (relaxation) 休み yasúmi; (pause) 休止 kyūshi; (remainder) 残り nokóri; (object: to support something) 台 dáì; (MUS) 休止符 kyūshifù

♦*vi* (relax) 休む yasúmù; (stop) 休止する kyūshi suru; **to rest on** (idea) ...に基づく ...ni motózukù; (weight, object) ...に置かれている ...ni okárete irù

♦*vt* (head, eyes, muscles) 休ませる yasúmaserù; (lean): **to rest something on/against** ...を...に置く〔寄り掛ける〕 ...wo ...ni okú (yoríkakerù)

the rest of them (people) 残りの人たち nokóri nò hitótàchi; (objects) 残りの物 nokóri no monò

it rests with him to ... ...するのは彼の責任だ ...surú no wà kárè no sekínin dà

restaurant [res'tə:rənt] *n* レストラン rē-sūtoran

restaurant car (*BRIT*) *n* 食堂車 shokūdōsha

restful [rest'fəl] *adj* 心を落着かせる ko-

kórò wo ochítsukaserù

rest home *n* 養老院 yōrōìn

restitution [restitu:'ʃən] *n*: **to make restitution to someone for something** (compensate) ...に対して...の弁償をする ...ni táìshite ...no beñshō wo surù

restive [res'tiv] *adj* (person, crew) 反抗的な hañkōteki na; (horse) 言う事を聞かない iú kotò wo kikánaì

restless [rest'lis] *adj* (person, audience) 落着かない ochítsukanaì

restoration [restərei'ʃən] *n* (of building etc) 修復 shūfuku; (of law and order, faith, health) 回復 kaífuku; (of something stolen) 返還 heñkan; (to power, former state) 復旧 fukkyū

restore [ristɔːr'] *vt* (building) 修復する shūfuku suru; (law and order, faith, health) 回復する kaífuku suru; (something stolen) 返す káèsu; (to power, former state) 元に戻す mótò ni modósù

restrain [ristrein'] *vt* (feeling, growth, inflation) 抑制する yokúsei suru; (person): **to restrain (from doing)** (...しない様に) 抑える (...shínaí yṓ ni) osáerù

restrained [ristreind'] *adj* (style, person) 控え目な hikáeme na

restraint [ristreint'] *n* (restriction) 抑制 yokúsei; (moderation) 程々 hodóhodo; (of style) 控え目な調子 hikáeme nà chṓshi

restrict [ristrikt'] *vt* (limit: growth, numbers etc) 制限する seígen suru; (: vision) 邪魔する jámà suru; (confine: people, animals) ...の動きを制限する ...no ugóki wò seígen suru; (: activities, membership) 制限する seígen suru

restriction [ristrik'ʃən] *n* (gen) 制限 seígen; (of vision) 妨げ samátagè; (limitation): **restriction (on)** (...の) 制限 (...no) seígen

restrictive [ristrik'tiv] *adj* (environment) 束縛的な sokúbakuteki na; (clothing) きつい kitsúí

restrictive practices *npl* (INDUSTRY) 制限的慣行 seígentekikañkō

rest room (*US*) *n* お手洗 o-téarài

restructure [ri:strʌk'tʃə:r] *vt* (business,

economy) 再編成する saíheñsei suru

result [rizʌlt'] n (of event, action) 結果 kekká; (of match) スコア sukóà; (of exam, competition) 成績 seíseki

◆vi (of event, action) ...に終る ...ni owárù

as a result of ...の結果 ...no kekká

resume [ri:zu:m'] vt (work, journey) 続ける tsuzúkerù

◆vi (start again) また始まる matá hàjimaru

résumé [rez'u:mei] n (summary) 要約 yōyaku; (US: curriculum vitae) 履歴書 rirékishò

resumption [rizʌmp'ʃən] n (of work, activity) 再開 saíkai

resurgence [risər'dʒəns] n 復活 fukkátsu

resurrection [rezərek'ʃən] n (of hopes, fears) よみがえらせる事 yomígaeraserù kotó; (REL): *the Resurrection* キリストの復活 kirísuto no fukkátsu

resuscitate [risʌs'əteit] vt (MED) そ生させる soséi saserù

resuscitation [risʌsətei'ʃən] n そ生 soséi

retail [ri:'teil] adj (trade, department, shop, goods) 小売の koúri no

◆adv 小売で koúri de

retailer [ri:'teilər] n (trader) 小売業者 koúrigyōsha

retail price n 小売価格 koúrikakàku

retain [ritein'] vt (keep) 保つ tamótsù

retainer [ritei'nər] n (fee) 依頼料 iráiryō

retaliate [ritæl'i:eit] vi: *to retaliate (against)* (attack, ill-treatment) (...に対して) 報復する (...ni taíshite) hőfuku suru

retaliation [ritæli:ei'ʃən] n 報復 hőfuku

retarded [ritɑr'did] adj (child) 知恵遅れの chiékùre no; (development, growth) 遅れた okúretà

retch [retʃ] vi むかつく mukátsukù

retentive [riten'tiv] adj (memory) 優れた sugúretà

reticent [ret'isənt] adj 無口な múkùchi na

retina [ret'ənə] n (ANAT) 網膜 mőmaku

retire [ritaiər'] vi (give up work: gen) 引

退する iñtai suru; (: at a certain age) 定年退職する teínentaìshoku suru; (withdraw) 引下がる hikísagarù; (go to bed) 寝る nérù

retired [ritaiər'd] adj (person: gen) 引退した iñtai shita; (: at a certain age) 定年退職した teínentaìshoku shita

retirement [ritaiər'mənt] n (giving up work: gen) 隠退 iñtai; (: at a certain age) 定年退職 teínentaìshoku

retiring [ritaiər'iŋ] adj (leaving) 退職する taíshoku suru; (shy) 内気な uchíki na

retort [ritɔrt'] vi しっぺ返しをする shippégaèshi wo suru

retrace [ri:treis'] vt: *to retrace one's steps* 来た道を戻る kitá michì wo modórù

retract [ritrækt'] vt (statement, offer) 撤回する tekkái suru; (claws, aerial etc) 引っ込める hikkómerù

retrain [ri:trein'] vt 再訓練する saíkuñren suru

retraining [ri:trei'niŋ] n 再訓練 saíkuñren

retread [ri:'tred] n (tire) 再生タイヤ saíseitaìya

retreat [ritri:t'] n (place) 隠れ家 kakúregà; (withdrawal) 避難 hínàn; (MIL) 退却 taíkyaku

◆vi (from danger, enemy) 避難する hínàn suru; (MIL) 退却する taíkyaku suru

retribution [retrəbju:'ʃən] n 天罰 teñbatsu

retrieval [ritri:'vəl] n (of object) 回収 kaíshū; (of situation) 繕う事 tsukúrou kotó; (of honor) ばん回 bañkai; (of error) 償い tsugúnaì; (loss) 取返し toríkaeshi

retrieve [ritri:v'] vt (object) 回収する kaíshū suru; (situation) 繕う tsukúroù; (honor) ばん回する bañkai suru; (error) 償う tsugúnaù; (loss) 取返す toríkaesù

retriever [ritri:'vər] n (dog) リトリーバ犬 ritórībakèn

retrograde [ret'rəgreid] adj 後戻りの atómodòri no

retrospect [ret'rəspekt] n: *in retrospect* 振返ってみると furíkaette miru tò

retrospective [retrəspek'tiv] adj (exhibition) 回顧的な kaíkoteki na; (feeling, opinion) 過去にさかのぼる kákò ni sakánoborù; (law, tax) そ及する sokyū́ suru

return [ritəːrn'] *n* (going or coming back) 帰り kaéri; (of something stolen, borrowed etc) 返還 heńkan; (FINANCE: from land, shares, investment) 利回り rímáwari

♦*cpd* (journey) 帰りの kaéri no; (BRIT: ticket) 往復の ốfuku no; (match) 雪辱の setsújoku no

♦*vi* (person etc: come or go back) 帰る kaérù; (feelings, symptoms etc) 戻る modórù; (regain): **to return to** (consciousness) ...を回復する ...wo kaífuku suru; (power) ...に返り咲く ...ni kaérizakù

♦*vt* (favor, love etc) 返す kaésù; (something borrowed, stolen etc) 返却する heńkyaku suru; (LAW: verdict) ...と答申する ...to tóshin suru; (POL: candidate) 選出する seńshutsu suru; (ball) 返す kaésù

in return (for) (...の) お返しに (...no) o-káeshi ni

by return of post 折返し郵便で orìkaeshiyūbin de

many happy returns (of the day)! お誕生日おめでとう o-tánjòbi omédetò

returns [ritəːrnz'] *npl* (COMM) 利益 ríèki

reunion [riːjuːn'jən] *n* (of family) 集いtsudói; (of school, class etc) 同窓会 dṓsōkai; (of two people) 再会 saíkai

reunite [riːjuːnait'] *vt* (bring or come together again) 元のさやに収めさせる mótò no sáyà ni osámesaserù; (reconcile) 和解させる wakái saserù

rev [rev] *n abbr* (AUT: = *revolution*) 回転 kaíten

♦*vt* (also: **rev up**: engine) ふかす fukású

revamp [riːvæmp'] *vt* (organization, company, system) 改革する kaíkaku suru

reveal [rivi:l'] *vt* (make known) 明らかにする akíràka ni suru; (make visible) 現すaráwasù

revealing [rivi:'liŋ] *adj* (action, statement) 手の内を見せる tè nò uchí wò misérù; (dress) 肌をあらわにする hádà

reveille [rev'əli:] *n* (MIL) 起床らっぱ kishṓ rappá

revel [rev'əl] *vi*: *to revel in something/ in doing something* (enjoy) ...を [...するのを] 楽しむ ...wo [...surú no wò] tanóshimù

revelation [revəlei'ʃən] *n* (fact, experience) 意外な新知識 igái nà shińchishìki

revelry [rev'əlri:] *n* どんちゃん騒ぎ dońchan sawàgi

revenge [rivendʒ'] *n* (for injury, insult) 復しゅう fukúshū

to take revenge on (enemy) ...に復しゅうする ...ni fukúshū suru

revenue [rev'ənu:] *n* (income: of individual, company, government) 収入 shū́nyū

reverberate [rivəːr'bəːreit] *vi* (sound, thunder etc: *also fig*) 響く hibíkù

reverberation [rivəːrbərei'ʃən] *n* (of sound, etc: *also fig*) 響き hibíki

revere [rivi:r'] *vt* 敬愛する keíai suru

reverence [rev'əːrəns] *n* 敬愛 keíai

Reverend [rev'əːrənd] *adj* (in titles) ...師 ...shī ○聖職者の名前に付ける敬称 seíshokushà no namáè ni tsukérù keíshō

reversal [rivəːr'səl] *n* (of order) 反転 hańten; (of direction) 逆戻り gyakúmodòri; (of decision, policy) 逆転 gyakúten; (of roles) 入れ代り irékawari

reverse [rivəːrs'] *n* (opposite) 反対 hańtai; (back) 裏 urá; (AUT: *also:* **reverse gear**) バック bákkù; (setback, defeat) 失敗 shippái

♦*adj* (opposite: order, direction, process) 反対の hańtai no, 逆の gyakú no; (: side) 裏の urá no

♦*vt* (order, position, direction) 逆にする gyakú ni surù; (process, policy, decision) 引っ繰り返す hikkúrikaèsu; (roles) 入れ替える irékaerù; (car) バックさせる bákkù saserù

♦*vi* (BRIT: AUT) バックする bákkù suru

reverse-charge call [rivəːrs'tʃəːrdʒ-] (BRIT) *n* 受信人払い電話 jushínninbarai deńwa

reversing lights [rivəːr'siŋ-] (BRIT)

npl (AUT) バックライト bakkúraìto

revert [rivə:rt'] *vi*: **to revert to** (former state) ...に戻る ...ni modórù; (LAW: money, property) ...に帰属する ...ni kizóku surù

review [rivju:'] *n* (magazine) 評論雑誌 hyőronzasshì; (MIL) 閲兵 eppéi; (of book, film etc) 批評 hihyő; (examination: of situation, policy etc) 再検討 saíkeñtō

♦*vt* (MIL) 閲兵する eppéi suru; (book, film etc) ...の批評を書く ...no hihyő wò kákù; (situation, policy etc) 再検討する saíkeñtō suru

reviewer [rivju:'ə:r] *n* (of book, film etc) 批評者 hihyőshà

revile [rivail'] *vt* (insult) 侮辱する bujóku suru

revise [rivaiz'] *vt* (manuscript) 修正する shűsei suru; (opinion, price, procedure) 変える kaérù

♦*vi* (BRIT: study) 試験勉強する shikénbeñkyō suru

revision [riviʒ'ən] *n* (amendment) 修正 shűsei; (for exam) 試験勉強 shikénbeñkyō

revitalize [ri:vai'təlaiz] *vt* ...に新しい活力を与える ...ni atárashiì katsúryòku wo atáerù

revival [rivai'vəl] *n* (recovery) 回復 kaífuku; (of interest, faith) 復活 fukkátsu; (THEATER) リバイバル ribáìbaru

revive [rivaiv'] *vt* (person) ...の意識を回復させる ...no íshìki wo kaífuku saserù; (economy, industry) 復興させる fukkő saserù; (custom, hope, courage) 復活させる fukkátsu saserù; (play) 再上演する saíjōen suru

♦*vi* (person: from faint) 意識を取戻す íshìki wo torímodosù; (: from ill-health) 元気になる géñki ni nárù; (activity, economy etc) 回復する kaífuku suru; (faith, interest etc) 復活する fukkátsu suru

revoke [rivouk'] *vt* 取消す toríkesù

revolt [rivoult'] *n* (rebellion) 反逆 hañgyaku

♦*vi* (rebel) 反逆する hañgyaku suru

♦*vt* (disgust) むかつかせる mukátsukaserù

revolting [rivoul'tiŋ] *adj* (disgusting) むかつかせる mukátsukaserù

revolution [revəlu:'ʃən] *n* (POL) 革命 kakúmei; (rotation: of wheel, earth etc: also AUT) 回転 kaíten

revolutionary [revəlu:'ʃəne:ri:] *adj* (method, idea) 革命的な kakúmeiteki na; (leader, army) 革命の kakúmei no

♦*n* (POL: person) 革命家 kakúmeika

revolutionize [revəlu:'ʃənaiz] *vt* (industry, society etc) ...に大変革をもたらす ...ni daíheñkaku wò motárasù

revolve [rivɑ:lv'] *vi* (turn: earth, wheel etc) 回転する kaíten suru; (life, discussion): **to revolve (a)round** ...を中心に展開する ...wo chűshin nì teñkai suru

revolver [rivɑ:l'və:r] *n* けん銃 keñjū, リボルバー ribórubā ◊ 回転式の物を指す kaítenshiki no monó wò sásù

revolving [rivɑ:l'viŋ] *adj* (chair etc) 回転式の kaítenshiki no

revolving door *n* 回転ドア kaíten doà

revue [rivju:'] *n* (THEATER) レビュー rébyù

revulsion [rivʌl'ʃən] *n* (disgust) 嫌悪 kéñ-o

reward [riwɔ:rd'] *n* (for service, merit, work) 褒美 hőbi; (money for capture of criminal, information etc) 賞金 shőkin

♦*vt*: **to reward (for)** (effort) (...のために) 褒美を与える (... no tamé nì) hőbi wò atáerù

rewarding [riwɔ:rd'iŋ] *adj* (*fig*: worthwhile) やりがいのある yarígai no arù

rewind [ri:waind'] (*pt*, *pp* **rewound**) *vt* (tape, cassette) 巻戻す makímodosù

rewire [ri:waiə:r'] *vt* (house) ...の電気配線をし直す ...no deñki haísen wo shínaosù

rewrite [ri:rait'] (*pt* **rewrote**, *pp* **rewritten**) *vt* 書き直す kakínaosù

rhapsody [ræp'sədi:] *n* (MUS) 狂詩曲 kyőshikyòku, ラプソディー rápùsodī

rhetorical [ritɔːr'ikəl] *adj* (question, speech) 修辞的な shűjiteki na

rheumatic [ru:mæt'ik] *adj* リューマチの ryűmachi no

rheumatism [ruː'mətizəm] n リューマチ ryū́machi

Rhine [rain] n: *the Rhine* ライン川 raíngawa

rhinoceros [rainɑːs'ərəs] n サイ saí

rhododendron [roudəden'drən] n シャクナゲ shakúnage

Rhone [roun] n: *the Rhone* ローヌ川 rő̄nùgawa

rhubarb [ruː'bɑːrb] n ルバーブ rubábù

rhyme [raim] n (of two words) 韻 iñ; (verse) 詩 shi; (technique) 韻を踏む事 iñ wò fumú kotò

rhythm [rið'əm] n リズム rízumu

rhythmic(al) [rið'mik(əl)] adj リズミカ ルな rizúmikàru na

rib [rib] n (ANAT) ろっ骨 rokkótsu
♦vt (tease) からかう karákaù

ribbon [rib'ən] n リボン ríbòn
in ribbons (torn) ずたずたになって zutázuta ni nattè

rice [rais] n (grain) 米 komé; (cooked) 御飯 góhàn

rice pudding n ライスプディング raísu pudiñgù ◊御飯にミルク，卵，砂糖などを加えたデザート góhàn ni mírùku, tamágo, satő nadò wo kuwáèta dezátò

rich [ritʃ] adj (person, country) 金持の kanémochi no; (clothes, jewels) 高価な kőka na; (soil) 肥えた koétà, 肥よくな hiyőku na; (food, diet) 濃厚な nőkō na; (color, voice, life) 豊かな yútàka na; (abundant): *rich in* (minerals, resources etc) ...に富んだ ...ni tóñda
♦npl: *the rich* 金持 kanémochi ◊総称 sőshō

riches [ritʃ'iz] npl (wealth) 富 tómì

richly [ritʃ'liː] adv (dressed, decorated) 豪華に gőka ni; (rewarded, deserved, earned) 十分に júbuñ ni

rickets [rik'its] n くる病 kurúbyō

rickety [rik'ətiː] adj (shaky) がたがたの gatágata no

rickshaw [rik'ʃɔː] n 人力車 jińrikìsha

ricochet [rikəʃei'] vi (bullet, stone) 跳ね飛ぶ hanétobù

rid [rid] (pt, pp **rid**) vt: *to rid someone of something* ...の...を取除く ...no ...wo torínozokù
to get rid of (something no longer required) 捨てる sutérù; (something unpleasant or annoying) ...を取除く ...wo torínozokù

ridden [rid'ən] pp of **ride**

riddle [rid'əl] n (conundrum) なぞなぞ nazónazo; (mystery) なぞ nazó
♦vt: *to be riddled with* ...だらけである ...dáràke de árù

ride [raid] n (in car, on bicycle, horse) 乗る事 norú kotò; (distance covered) 道のり michínori
♦vb (pt **rode**, pp **ridden**)
♦vi (as sport) 乗馬をする jőba wo suru; (go somewhere: on horse, bicycle, bus) 乗って行く notté ikù
♦vt (a horse, bicycle, motorcycle) ...に乗る ...ni norù; (distance) 行く ikú
to take someone for a ride (fig: deceive) ぺてんに掛ける petén nì kakérù
to ride a bicycle 自転車に乗る jitéñsha ni norú
to ride at anchor (NAUT) 停泊する teíhaku suru

rider [rai'dəːr] n (on horse) 乗り手 noríte; (on bicycle, motorcycle) 乗る人 norú hitò, ライダー ráìda

ridge [ridʒ] n (of hill) 尾根 őne; (of roof) 天辺 teppéñ; (wrinkle) うね uné

ridicule [rid'əkjuːl] n あざける azákerì
♦vt あざける azákerù

ridiculous [ridik'jələs] adj (foolish) ばかげた bakágetà

riding [rai'diŋ] n (sport, activity) 乗馬 jőba

riding school n 乗馬学校 jőbagakkő

rife [raif] adj: *to be rife* (bribery, corruption, superstition) はびこる habíkorù
to be rife with (rumors, fears) ...がはびこっている ...ga habíkotte irù

riffraff [rif'ræf] n (rabble) ろくでなしの連中 rokúdenashi no reñchū

rifle [rai'fəl] n (gun) ライフル ráìfuru
♦vt (steal from: wallet, pocket etc) ...の中身を盗む ...no nakámi wò nusúmù

rifle range n (for sport) 射撃場 shagékijò; (at fair) 射的 shatéki

rifle through vt fus (papers) ...を かき 回して捜す ...wo kakímawashite sagásù

rift [rift] n (split: in ground) 亀裂 kirétsu; (: in clouds) 切れ間 kiréma; (fig: disagreement) 仲たがい nakátagaì

rig [rig] n (also: **oil rig**) 油井掘削装置 yuséi kussaku sòchi

♦vt (election, game etc) 不正操作する fuséisòsa suru

rigging [rig'iŋ] n (NAUT) 索具 sakúgù

right [rait] adj (correct: answer, solution, size etc) 正しい tadáshiì; (suitable: person, clothes, time) 適当な tekítō na; (: decision etc) 適切な tekísetsu na; (morally good) 正当な seítō na; (fair, just) 公正な kòsei na; (not left) 右の migí no

♦n (what is morally right) 正義 seígi; (entitlement) 権利 keńri; (not left) 右 migí

♦adv (correctly: answer etc) 正しく tadáshìku; (properly, fairly: treat etc) 公正に kòsei ni; (not on the left) 右に migí ni; (directly, exactly): **right now** 今すぐ ímà súgù

♦vt (put right way up: ship, car etc) 起す okósù; (correct: fault, situation, wrong) 正す tadásù

♦excl では dé wà

to be right (person) ...の言う事が合っている ...no iú kotò ga atté irù; (answer) 正解である seíkai de arù; (clock, reading etc) 合っている atté irù

by rights 当然 tòzen

on the right 右に migí ni

to be in the right ...の方が正しい ...no hò gà tadáshiì

right away すぐに súgù ni

right in the middle 丁度真ん中に chódo mañnaka ni

right angle n (MATH) 直角 chokkáku

righteous [rai'tʃəs] adj (person) 有徳な yùtoku na; (anger) 当然な tòzen na

rightful [rait'fəl] adj (heir, owner) 合法の gòhō no; (place, share) 正当な seítō na

right-handed [rait'hændid] adj (person) 右利きの migíkiki no

right-hand man [rait'hænd'-] n 右腕 migíude

right-hand side n 右側 migígawa

rightly [rait'li:] adv (with reason) 当然 tòzen

right of way n (on path etc) 通行権 tsùkōken; (AUT) 先行権 seńkōken

right-wing [rait'wiŋ] adj (POL) 右翼の úyòku no

rigid [ridʒ'id] adj (structure, back etc) 曲らない magáranaì; (attitude, views etc) 厳格な geńkaku na; (: principle, control etc) 厳しい kibíshiì

rigmarole [rig'məroul] n (procedure) 手続 tetsúzùki

rigor [rig'ə:r] (BRIT **rigour**) n (strictness) 厳格さ geńkakusa; (severity): **rigors of life/winter** 生活〔冬〕の厳しさ seíkatsu〔fuyú〕nò kibíshisa

rigorous [rig'ə:rəs] adj (control, test) 厳密な geńmitsu na; (training) 厳しい kibíshiì

rig out (BRIT) vt: **to rig out as** ...の仮装をする ...no kasò wò suru

to rig out in ...を着る ...wo kírù

rig up vt 作り上げる tsukúriagerù

rile [rail] vt (annoy) ...を怒らせる ...wo okóraserù

rim [rim] n (of glass, dish) 縁 fuchí; (of spectacles) フレーム furèmù; (of wheel) リム rímù

rind [raind] n (of bacon, fruit, cheese) 皮 kawá

ring [riŋ] n (of metal, light, smoke) 輪 wá; (for finger) 指輪 yubíwà; (of spies, drug-dealers etc) 組織 sòshiki; (for boxing, of circus) リング ríngu; (bullring) 闘牛場 tògyūjō; (sound of bell) ベルの音 bérù no otó

♦vb (pt **rang**, pp **rung**)

♦vi (person: by telephone) 電話を掛ける deńwa wo kakérù; (telephone, bell, doorbell) 鳴る narú; (also: **ring out**: voice, words) 鳴り響く naríhibikù

♦vt (BRIT: TEL) ...に電話を掛ける ...ni deńwa wò kakérù; (bell etc) 鳴らす narásù

a ring of people 車座になった人々 kurúmaza ni nattà hitóbìto

a ring of stones 環状に並んだ石 kańjō-shì

ni naránda ishí

to give someone a ring (BRIT: TEL)
...に電話を掛ける ...ni deńwa wò kakérù

my ears are ringing 耳鳴りがする mimínari ga surù

ring back (BRIT) vt (TEL) ...に電話を
掛け直す ...ni deńwa wò kakénaosù

♦vi (TEL) 電話を掛け直す deńwa wò kakénaosù

ringing [riŋ'iŋ] n (of telephone, bell) 鳴
る音 narú otò; (in ears) 耳鳴り mimínari

ringing tone n (TEL) ダイヤルトーン
daíyarutòn

ringleader [riŋ'li:də:r] n (of gang) 主犯
shuhán

ringlets [riŋ'lits] npl (of hair) 巻き毛 makíge

ring off (BRIT) vi (TEL) 電話を切る
deńwa wò kírù

ring road (BRIT) n 環状線 kańjōsen

ring up (BRIT) vt (TEL) ...に電話を掛け
る ...ni deńwa wò kakérù

rink [riŋk] n (also: **ice rink**) スケートリ
ンク sukétorìnku

rinse [rins] n (of dishes, hands) すすぎ
susúgi; (of hair) リンスする事 ríńsu suru
kotò; (dye: for hair) リンス ríńsu

♦vt (dishes, hands etc) すすぐ susúgù;
(hair etc) リンスする ríńsu suru; (also:
rinse out: clothes) すすぐ susúgù;
(: mouth) ゆすぐ yusúgù

riot [rai'ət] n (disturbance) 騒動 sódō

♦vi (crowd, protestors etc) 暴動を起す
bódō wò okósù

a riot of colors 色取り取り irótoridòri

to run riot (children, football fans etc)
大騒ぎをする ōsawàgi wo suru

riotous [rai'ətəs] adj (mob, assembly
etc) 暴動的な bódōteki na; (behavior, living) 遊とうざんまい yútōzanmai; (party)
どんちゃん騒ぎの dońchan sawàgi no

rip [rip] n (tear) 破れ目 yabúremè

♦vt (paper, cloth) 破る yabúrù

♦vi (paper, cloth) 破れる yabúrerù

ripcord [rip'kɔːrd] n (on parachute) 引き
網 hikízùna

ripe [raip] adj (fruit, grain, cheese) 熟し
た jukú shità

ripen [rai'pən] vt (subj: sun) 熟させる jukú saserù

♦vi (fruit, crop) 熟する jukú suru

ripple [rip'əl] n (wave) さざ波 sazánami;
(of laughter, applause) ざわめき zawá-
meki

♦vi (water) さざ波が立つ sazánami gà
tátsù

rise [raiz] n (slope) 上り坂 nobórizaka;
(hill) 丘 oká; (increase: in wages: BRIT)
賃上げ chín-age; (: in prices, temperature) 上昇 jóshō; (fig: to power etc) 出世
shussé

♦vi (pt rose, pp risen) (prices, numbers)
上がる agárù; (waters) 水かさが増す mi-
zúkasa gà masú; (sun, moon) 昇る nobórù; (person: from bed etc) 起きる okírù;
(sound, voice) 大きくなる ōkiku nárù;
(also: **rise up**: tower, building) そびえる
sobíerù; (: rebel) 立ち上がる tachíagarù;
(in rank) 昇進する shóshin suru

to give rise to ...を起す ...wo okósù

to rise to the occasion 腕前を見せる
udémaè wo misérù

risen [riz'ən] pp of **rise**

rising [rai'ziŋ] adj (increasing: number,
prices) 上がる agárù; (tide) 満ちる michírù; (sun, moon) 昇る nobórù

risk [risk] n (danger) 危険 kikén;
(INSURANCE) リスク rísùku

♦vt (endanger) 危険にさらす kikén nì sarásù; (chance) ...の危険を冒す ...no kinén
wò okásù

to take/run the risk of doing ...する
危険を冒す ...súrú kikén wò okásù

at risk 危険にさらされて kikén nì sara-
sáretè

at one's own risk 自分の責任で jibún
nò sekínin de

risky [ris'ki:] adj (dangerous) 危険な kikén na

risqué [riskei'] adj (joke) わいせつがかっ
た waísetsugakattà

rissole [ris'ɑːl] n (of meat, fish etc) メン
チカツ meńchikatsù

rite [rait] n 儀式 gíshìki

last rites (REL) 終油の秘蹟 shúyu nò
hiséki

ritual [ritʃ'uːəl] *adj* (law, dance) 儀式的な gishíkiteki na
♦*n* 儀式 gíshìki

rival [rai'vəl] *n* ライバル ráìbaru
♦*adj* ライバルの ráìbaru no
♦*vt* (match) ...に匹敵する ...ni hittéki suru

rivalry [rai'vəlriː] *n* (competition) 競争 kyṓsō

river [riv'əːr] *n* 川 kawá
♦*cpd* (port, traffic) 川の kawá no
up/down river 川上〔下〕へ kawákami〔shimo〕e

riverbank [riv'əːrbæŋk] *n* 川岸 kawágishi

riverbed [riv'əːrbed] *n* 河原 kawára

rivet [riv'it] *n* (bolt) リベット ribéttò
♦*vt* (fig): *to rivet one's eyes/attention on* ...に注目する ...ni chūmoku suru

Riviera [riviːer'ə] *n: the (French) Riviera* リビエラ ribíèra
the Italian Riviera イタリアのリビエラ itária nò ribíèra

road [roud] *n* (gen) 道 michí, 道路 dṓro
♦*cpd* (accident, sense) 交通の kṓtsū no
major/minor road 優先〔非優先〕道路 yūsen(hiyūsen)dòro

roadblock [roud'blɑːk] *n* 検問所 keñmonjo

roadhog [roud'hɔːg] *n* マナーの悪いドライバー mánà no warúî doráìbā

road map *n* 道路地図 dṓrochizù

road safety *n* 交通安全 kṓtsūañzen

roadside [roud'said] *n* 道路脇 dṓrowakì

roadsign [roud'sain] *n* 道路標識 dṓrohyòshiki

road user *n* ドライバー doráìbā

roadway [roud'wei] *n* 車道 shadṓ

roadworks [roud'wəːrks] *npl* 道路工事 dṓrokòjì

roadworthy [roud'wəːrðiː] *adj* (car) 整備状態のいい seíbijòtai no íì

roam [roum] *vi* (wander) さまよう samáyoù

roar [rɔːr] *n* (of animal) ほえ声 hoégoè; (of crowd) どよめき doyómeki; (of vehicle, storm) とどろき todóroki
♦*vi* (animal) ほえる hoérù; (person) どな

る donárù; (crowd) どよめく doyómekù; (engine, wind etc) とどろく todórokù
a roar of laughter 大笑い ṓwarài
to roar with laughter 大笑いする ṓwarài suru
to do a roaring trade ...の商売が繁盛する ...no shṓbai gà hañjō suru

roast [roust] *n* (of meat) ロースト rṓsuto
♦*vt* (meat, potatoes) オーブンで焼く ṓbun de yakú; (coffee) いる írù

roast beef *n* ローストビーフ rṓsutobìfu

rob [rɑːb] *vt* (person, house, bank) ...から盗む ...kara nusúmù
to rob someone of something ...から...を盗む ...kará ...wo nusúmù; (fig: deprive) 奪う ubáù

robber [rɑːb'əːr] *n* 強盗 doróbō

robbery [rɑːb'əːriː] *n* (theft) 盗み nusúmi

robe [roub] *n* (for ceremony etc) ローブ rṓbu; (also: **bath robe**) バスローブ basúròbu; (US) ひざ掛け hizákake

robin [rɑːb'in] *n* コマドリ komádòri

robot [rou'bət] *n* ロボット robóttò

robust [roubʌst'] *adj* (person) たくましい takúmashiì; (economy) 健全な keñzen na; (appetite) おう盛な ṓsei na

rock [rɑːk] *n* (substance) 岩石 gañseki; (boulder) 岩 iwá; (US: small stone, pebble) 小石 koíshi; (BRIT: sweet) 氷砂糖 kṓrizatò
♦*vt* (swing gently: cradle) 優しく揺する yasáshiku yusurù; (: child) あやす ayásù; (shake: subj: explosion, waves etc) 激しく揺さぶる hagéshiku yusuburù
♦*vi* (object) 揺れる yurérù; (person) 震える furúerù
on the rocks (drink) オンザロックで oñzarokkù de; (marriage etc) 危ぶまれて ayábumaretè

rock and roll *n* ロックンロール rokkúnrōru

rock-bottom [rɑːk'bɑːt'əm] *adj* (fig: lowest point) 最低の saítei no

rockery [rɑːk'əːriː] *n* (in garden) 庭石 niwá-ishi ◇総称 sōshō

rocket [rɑːk'it] *n* (space rocket) ロケット rokéttò; (missile) ロケット弾 rokéttodañ; (firework) ロケット花火 rokétto hanábi

rocking chair [rɑ:k'iŋ-] n 揺り いす yu-ríisu

rocking horse n 揺り木馬 yurímokùba

rocky [rɑ:k'i:] adj (covered with rocks) 岩だらけの iwádaràke no; (unsteady: table) 不安定な fuántei na; (unstable: business, marriage) 危ぶまれている ayábumarete irù

rod [rɑ:d] n (pole) さお saó; (also: **fishing rod**) 釣ざお tsurízao

rode [roud] pt of **ride**

rodent [rou'dənt] n げっ歯類 gesshírùi

rodeo [rou'di:ou] n ロデオ ródèo

roe [rou] n (species: also: **roe deer**) ノロ ジカ norójìka; (of fish) 卵 tamágò
  hard roe 腹子 haráko
  soft roe 白子 shirákò

rogue [roug] n 野郎 yaró

role [roul] n 役 yakú

roll [roul] n (of paper, cloth etc) 巻き makí; (of banknotes) 札束 satsútabà; (also: **bread roll**) ロールパン rőrupàn; (register, list) 名簿 meíbo; (sound: of drums etc) とどろき todőroki
  ♦vt (ball, stone etc) 転がす korőgasù; (also: **roll up**: string) 巻く makú; (: sleeves) まくる makúrù; (cigarette) 巻く makú; (eyes) 白黒させる shírőkuro sasérù; (also: **roll out**: pastry) 延ばす nobásù; (flatten: lawn, road, surface) ならす narásù
  ♦vi (ball, stone etc) 転がる korőgarù; (drum) 鳴り響く naríhibikù; (vehicle: also: **roll along**) 走る hashírù; (ship) 揺れる yurérù

roll about/around vi 転がる korőgarù

roll by vi (time) 過ぎる sugírù

roll call n 点呼 téñko

roller [rou'lər] n (gen) ローラー rőrā; (for hair) カーラー kárā

roller coaster [-kous'tər] n ジェットコースター jettőkōsutā

roller skates npl ローラースケート rőrāsukèto

roll in vi (mail, cash) 大量に入る taíryō nì haírù

rolling [rou'liŋ] adj (landscape) うねりの

多い unéri no ōi

rolling pin n めん棒 méñbō

rolling stock n (RAIL) 車両 sharyő ◇総称 sőshō

roll over vi 寝返りを打つ negáeri wò útsù

roll up vi (inf: arrive) やって来る yatté kurù
  ♦vt (carpet, newspaper, umbrella etc) 巻く makú

ROM [rɑ:m] n abbr (COMPUT: = **read only memory**) ロム rőmù

Roman [rou'mən] adj ローマの rőma no

Roman Catholic adj ローマカトリックの rőmakatorikkù no
  ♦n ローマカトリック信者 rőmakatorikkù shiñja

romance [roumæns'] n (love affair) 恋愛 reñ-ai; (charm) ロマンス rőmànsu; (novel) 恋愛小説 reñ-ai shősetsu

Romania [roumei'ni:ə] n = **Rumania**

Roman numeral n ローマ数字 rőmasūji

romantic [roumæn'tik] adj ロマンチックな románchikkù na

Rome [roum] n ローマ rőma

romp [rɑ:mp] n 騒々しい遊び sőzōshiì asóbi
  ♦vi (also: **romp about**: children, dogs etc) はしゃぎ回る hashágimawarù

rompers [rɑ:m'pərz] npl ロンパース roñpásu

roof [ru:f] (pl **roofs**) n 屋根 yánè, ルーフ rúfu
  ♦vt (house, building etc) 屋根を付ける yánè wo tsukérù
  the roof of one's mouth 口がい kőgai

roofing [ru:'fiŋ] n 屋根ふき材 yanéfukizài

roof rack n (AUT) ルーフラック rúfurakkù

rook [ruk] n (bird) ミヤマガラス miyámagaràsu; (CHESS) ルック rúkkù

room [ru:m] n (in house, hotel etc) 部屋 heyá; (space) 空間 kúkan, 場所 bashó; (scope: for improvement, change etc) 余地 yóchì
  「*rooms for rent*」, 「*rooms to let*」 貸間

あり kashíma arí

single/double room シングル〔ダブル〕部屋 shínguru〔daburu〕beyà

rooming house [ru:'miŋ-] (*US*) *n* 下宿屋 geshúkuya

roommate [ru:m'meit] *n* ルームメート rūmuméto ◇寄宿舎などで同室に泊まる人 kishúkushà nádò de dōshitsu nì tomárù hitó

rooms [ru:mz] *npl* (lodging) 下宿 geshúku

room service *n* (in hotel) ルームサービス rūmusābisu

roomy [ru:'mi:] *adj* (building, car) 広々とした hiróbiro to shità; (garment) ゆったりした yuttári shità

roost [ru:st] *vi* (birds) ねぐらにつく negúra ni tsukù

rooster [ru:s'tə:r] *n* オンドリ oñdòri

root [ru:t] *n* (BOT) 根 né; (MATH) 根 kóñ; (of problem, belief) 根源 koñgen
◆*vi* (plant) 根を下ろす né wò orósù; (belief) 定着する teíchaku suru

the root of a hair 毛根 mōkon

the root of a tooth 歯根 shikón

root about *vi* (*fig*: search) かき回す kakímawasù

root for *vt fus* (support) ...を応援する ...wo óen surù

root out *vt* (find) 捜し出す sagáshidasù

roots [ru:ts] *npl* (family origins) ルーツ rūtsu

rope [roup] *n* (thick string) ロープ rōpu; (NAUT) 綱 tsuná; (for climbing) ザイル záiru
◆*vt* (tie) 縛る shibárù; (climbers: *also*: **rope together**) ザイルでつなぐ záiru de tsunágù; (an area: *also*: **rope off**) 縄で仕切る nawá dè shikírù

to know the ropes (*fig*: know how to do something) こつが分かっている kotsú gà wakátte irù

rope in *vt* (*fig*: person) 誘い込む sasóikomù

rope ladder *n* 縄ばしご nawábashigo

rosary [rou'zə:ri:] *n* ロザリオ rozário

rose [rouz] *pt of* **rise**
◆*n* (single flower) バラ bará; (shrub) バ

ラの木 bará nò kí; (on watering can) はす口 hasúkuchi

rosé [rouzei'] *n* ロゼワイン rozéwaìn

rosebud [rouz'bʌd] *n* バラのつぼみ bará nò tsubómi

rosebush [rouz'buʃ] *n* バラの木 bará no ki

rosemary [rouz'me:ri:] *n* ローズマリー rōzumarī

rosette [rouzet'] *n* ロゼット rozéttò

roster [ras'tə:r] *n*: *duty roster* 勤務当番表 kíñmutōbañhyō

rostrum [ras'trəm] *n* 演壇 eñdan

rosy [rou'zi:] *adj* (color) バラ色の bará-iro no; (face, cheeks) 血色のいい kesshókù no iî; (situation) 明るい akáruî

a rosy future 明るい見通し akáruì mitőshi

rot [rat] *n* (decay) 腐敗 fuhái; (*fig*: *pej*: rubbish) でたらめ detárame
◆*vt* (cause to decay: teeth, wood, fruit etc) 腐らす kusárasù
◆*vi* (decay: teeth, wood, fruit etc) 腐る kusárù

rota [rou'tə] (*BRIT*) *n* 勤務当番表 kíñmutōbañhyō

rotary [rou'tə:ri:] *adj* 回転式の kaíteñshiki no

rotate [rou'teit] *vt* (revolve) 回転させる kaíten saserù; (change round: jobs) 交替でやる kótai de yarù
◆*vi* (revolve) 回転する kaíten suru

rotating [rou'teitiŋ] *adj* (movement) 回転する kaíten suru

rotation [routei'ʃən] *n* (revolving) 回転 kaíten; (changing round: jobs) 交替 kótai; (of crops) 輪作 ríñsaku

rote [rout] *n*: *by rote* 暗記で añki de

rotor [rou'tə:r] *n* (*also*: **rotor blade**) 回転翼 kaíteñyoku, ローター rōtā

rotten [rat'ən] *adj* (decayed: fruit, meat, wood, eggs etc) 腐った kusáttà; (*fig*: person, situation) いやな iyá nà; (*inf*: bad) ひどい hidőì

a rotten tooth 虫歯 mushíba

to feel rotten (ill) 気分が悪い kíbùn ga warúì

rotund [routʌnd'] *adj* (person) 丸々と太

った marúmarù to futótta

rouble [ruː'bəl] (BRIT) n = **ruble**

rouge [ruːʒ] n ほお紅 hóbeni

rough [rʌf] adj (skin, surface, cloth) 粗い aráì; (terrain, road) 凸凹の dekóboko no; (voice) しゃがれた shagáretà; (person, manner: violent) 荒っぽい aráppoì; (: brusque) ぶっきらぼうな bukkírabò na; (treatment) 荒い aráì; (weather, sea) 荒れた arétà; (town, area) 治安の悪い chiánnò warúì; (plan, sketch) 大まかな ómaka na; (guess) 大よその óyoso no

♦n (GOLF): **in the rough** ラフに ráfù ni

to rough it 原始的な生活をする geńshiteki nà seíkatsu wò suru

to sleep rough (BRIT) 野宿する nójuku suru

roughage [rʌf'idʒ] n 繊維 séñ-i

rough-and-ready [rʌf'ənred'iː] adj 原始的な geńshiteki na

roughcast [rʌf'kæst] n (for wall) 小石を混ぜたしっくい koíshi wò mazétà shikkúì

rough copy n 下書き shitágaki

rough draft n 素案 soán

roughly [rʌf'liː] adv (handle) 荒っぽく aráppokù; (make) 大まかに ómaka ni; (speak) ぶっきらぼうに bukkírabò ni; (approximately) 大よそ óyoso

roughness [rʌf'nis] n (of surface) 荒さ arása; (of manner) がさつさ gasátsusa

roulette [ruːlet'] n ルーレット rúretto

Roumania [ruːmei'niːə] n = **Rumania**

round [raund] adj 丸い marúì; (figures, sum) 概数の gaísū no

♦n (BRIT: of toast) 一切 hitókire; (of policeman, milkman, doctor) 巡回 juñkai; (game: of cards) 一勝負 hitóshōbu; (: in competition) 一回戦 ...kaísen; (of ammunition) 一発 ippátsu; (BOXING) ラウンド ráundo; (also: **round of golf**) ラウンド ráundo; (of talks) 一連 ichíren

♦vt (corner) 回る mawárù

♦prep (surrounding): **round his neck/the table** 首(家)の回りに kubí[ié]nò mawári ni; (in a circular movement): **to move round the room** 部屋の中を一回りする heyá no nakà wo hitómawarì

suru: to sail round the world 世界一周の航海をする sékàisshū nò kókai chi suru; (in various directions): **to move round a room/house** 部屋(家)の中を動き回る heyá (ié)no nakà wo ugókimawarù; (approximately): **round about 300** 大よそ300 óyoso sañbyaku

♦adv: **all round** 回りに mawári ni

a round of golf ゴルフのワンラウンド górùfu no wañraundo

the long way round 遠回り tómawari

all the year round 一年中 ichínenjū

it's just round the corner (fig) 直ぐそこまで来ている súgù sokó madè kité irù

round the clock 24時間 nijú-yo jíkàn

to go round (revolve) 回る mawárù

to go round to someone's (house) ...のうちへ行く ...no uchí è ikú

to go round the back 裏に回る urá nì mawárù

to go round a house ある家を訪ねる árù ié wò tazúnerù

enough to go round みんなに足りる程 miñna nì tarírù hodó

a round of applause 拍手 hákùshu

a round of drinks/sandwiches みんなに一通りの飲み物(サンドウイッチ)をおごる事 miñna nì hitótōri nò nomímòno (sañdouicchì)wo ogórù kotó

roundabout [raund'əbaut] n (BRIT) (AUT) ロータリー rótarī; (at fair) メリーゴーラウンド meríggōraundo

♦adj (route) 遠回りの tómawàri no; (means) 遠回しの tómawàshi no

rounders [raun'dərz] npl (game) ラウンダーズ raúndāzu ◇野球に似た英国のゲーム yakyū ni nità eíkoku no gēmu

roundly [raund'liː] adv (fig: criticize) 厳しく kibíshikù

round off vt (speech etc) 終える oérù

round-shouldered [raund'ʃouldərd] adj ねこ背の nekózè no

round trip n 往復旅行 ófukuryokō

round up vt (cattle, people) 駆集める karíatsumerù; (price, figure) 概数にする gaísū ni suru

roundup [raund'ʌp] n (of news, information) まとめ matóme; (of animals) 駆集め karíatsume; (of criminals) 一斉逮捕

isséitaího

rouse [rauz] *vt* (wake up) 起す okósù; (stir up) 引起す hikíòkosù

rousing [rau'zíŋ] *adj* (cheer, welcome) 熱狂的な nekkyóteki na

rout [raut] *n* (MIL) 敗走 haísō
♦*vt* (defeat) 敗走させる haísō saserù

route [ru:t] *n* (way) ルート rūto; (of bus, train) 路線 rosén; (of shipping) 航路 kóro; (of procession) 通り道 tórimíchi

route map (*BRIT*) *n* (for journey) 道路 地図 dórochìzu

routine [ru:ti:n'] *adj* (work) 日常の nichíjō no; (procedure) お決りの o-kímari no
♦*n* (habits) 習慣 shúkan; (drudgery) 反復 作業 hañpukusagyō; (THEATER) お決 りの演技 o-kímari nò éñgi

rove [rouv] *vt* (area, streets) はいかいす る haíkai suru

row[1] [rou] *n* (line of people, things) 列 rétsu; (KNITTING) 段 dáñ; (in boat) こ ぐ事 kogú kotò
♦*vi* (in boat) こぐ kogú
♦*vt* (boat) こぐ kogú
in a row (*fig*) 一列に ichíretsu ni

row[2] [rau] *n* (racket) 騒ぎ sáwàgi; (noisy quarrel) 口論 kóron; (dispute) 論争 roñsō; (*BRIT inf*: scolding): *to give someone a row* ...に大目玉を食らわす ...ni ómedàma wo kuráwasù
♦*vi* (argue) 口論する kóron suru

rowboat [rou'bout] (*US*) *n* ボート bóto

rowdy [rau'di:] *adj* (person: noisy) 乱暴 な rañbō na; (occasion) 騒々しい sózōshìi

rowing [rou'iŋ] *n* (sport) ボートレース bótorèsu

rowing boat (*BRIT*) *n* = **rowboat**

royal [rɔi'əl] *adj* 国王〔女王〕の kokúō〔jó-ō〕no

Royal Air Force (*BRIT*) *n* 英国空軍 eíkokukúgun

royalty [rɔi'əlti:] *n* (royal persons) 王族 ōzoku; (payment to author) 印税 íñzei

rpm [ɑ:rpi:em'] *abbr* (= *revolutions per minute*) 毎分回転数 maífunkaiteñsū

RSVP [ɑ:resvi:pi:'] *abbr* (= *répondez s'il vous plaît*) 御返事を請う go-héñji wò kóù

Rt Hon. (*BRIT*) *abbr* (= *Right Honourable*) 閣下 kákkà

rub [rʌb] *vt* こする kosúrù
♦*n*: *to give something a rub* こする kosúrù
to rub one's hands (together) もみ手 をする momíde wò suru
to rub someone the wrong way (*US*) *or to rub someone up the wrong way* (*BRIT*) 怒らせる okóraserù

rubber [rʌb'əːr] *n* (substance) ゴム gómù; (*BRIT*: eraser) 消しゴム keshígomu

rubber band *n* 輪ゴム wagómu

rubber plant *n* ゴムの木 gómù no ki

rubbery [rʌb'əːri:] *adj* (material, substance) ゴムの様な gómù no yō na; (meat, food) 固い katáî

rubbish [rʌb'iʃ] *n* (waste material) ごみ gomí; (junk) 廃品 haíhin; (*fig: pej*: nonsense) ナンセンス náñsensu

rubbish bin (*BRIT*) *n* ごみ箱 gomíbako

rubbish dump *n* ごみ捨て場 gomísuteba

rubble [rʌb'əl] *n* (debris) がれき garéki; (CONSTR) バラス báràsu

ruble [ru:'bəl] (*BRIT* **rouble**) *n* (currency) ルーブル rūburu

rub off *vi* (paint) こすり取る kosúritorù

rub off on *vt fus* ...に移る ...ni utsúrù

rub out *vt* (erase) 消す késù

ruby [ru:'bi:] *n* ルビー rúbī

rucksack [rʌk'sæk] *n* リュックサック ryukkúsakkù

rudder [rʌd'əːr] *n* (of ship) かじ kají; (of plane) 方向かじ hókōda

ruddy [rʌd'i:] *adj* (face, complexion) 血 色の良い kesshóku no yoì; (*BRIT*: *inf*: damned) くそったれの kusóttarè no

rude [ru:d] *adj* (impolite: person, manners, word) 無礼な buréi na; (shocking: word, behavior) 下品な gehín na

rudeness [ru:d'nis] *n* (impoliteness) 無礼 buréi

rudimentary [ru:dəmen'təːri:] *adj* (equipment, knowledge) 原始的な geñshiteki na

rudiments [ru:'dəmənts] *npl* (basics) 基 本 kihón

rueful [ru:'fəl] *adj* 悲しい kanáshiì

ruffian [rʌf'iːən] *n* ごろつき gorótsuki

ruffle [rʌf'əl] *vt* (hair) 乱す midású; (clothes) しわくちゃにする shiwákucha ni surù; (*fig*: person) 怒らせる okóraserù

rug [rʌg] *n* (on floor) じゅうたん jūtan; (*BRIT*: blanket) ひざ掛け hizákake

rugby [rʌg'biː] *n* (*also*: **rugby football**) ラグビー rágúbī

rugged [rʌg'id] *adj* (landscape) 岩だらけ の iwádarake no; (features) ごつい gotsúì; (character) 無愛想な buáiso na

rugger [rʌg'əːr] (*BRIT*: *inf*) *n* ラグビー rágúbī

ruin [ruː'in] *n* (destruction: of building) 破壊 hakái; (: of hopes, plans) ざ折 zasétsu; (downfall) 失墜 shittsúi; (: bankruptcy) 破産 hasán; (remains: of building) 廃虚 haíkyo

♦*vt* (destroy: building) 破壊する hakái suru; (: hopes, plans, health) 損す kowásù; (: future) 台無しにする daínashi ni surù; (: person) 失墜させる shittsúi saserù; (: financially) 破産に追込む hasán ni oíkomù

ruinous [ruː'inəs] *adj* (expense, interest) 破滅的な hamétsuteki na

ruins [ruː'inz] *npl* (of building, castle etc) 廃虚 haíkyo

rule [ruːl] *n* (norm, regulation) 規則 kisóku; (government) 君臨 kuńrin; (ruler) 物差し monósashi

♦*vt* (country, person) 支配する shíhai suru

♦*vi* (leader, monarch etc) 君臨する kuńrin suru; (*LAW*) 裁定する saítei suru

as a rule 普通は futsū wà

ruled [ruːld] *adj* (paper) けい紙 keíshi

rule out *vt* (idea, possibility etc) 除外する jogái suru

ruler [ruː'ləːr] *n* (sovereign) 元首 génshu; (for measuring) 物差し monósashi

ruling [ruː'liŋ] *adj* 支配する shíhai suru

♦*n* (*LAW*) 決定 kettéi

ruling party 与党 yótṍ

ruling class 支配階級 shiháikaikyū

rum [rʌm] *n* ラム酒 ramúshu

Rumania [ruːmei'niːə] *n* ルーマニア rū́mania

Rumanian [ruːmei'niːən] *adj* ルーマニア の rū́mania no; (*LING*) ルーマニア語の rū́maniagō no

♦*n* (person) ルーマニア人 rū́maniajìn; (*LING*) ルーマニア語 rū́maniagō

rumble [rʌm'bəl] *n* ごう音 gṍon, とどろき todóroki

♦*vi* (make rumbling noise: heavy truck) ごう音を響かせて走る gṍon wò hibíkasète hashírù; (: stomach) 鳴る narú; (: pipes) ゴボゴボいう góbògobo íù; (: thunder) とどろく todórokù

rummage [rʌm'idʒ] *vi* (search) 引っかき回して捜す hikkákimawashitè sagásù

rumor [ruː'məːr] (*BRIT* **rumour**) *n* うわさ uwása

♦*vt*: **it is rumored that ...** ...だとうわさされている ...dá tò uwása sarete irù

rump [rʌmp] *n* (of animal) しり shirí; (of group, political party) 残党 zańtō

rump steak *n* ランプステーキ rañpusutḗki

rumpus [rʌm'pəs] *n* 騒ぎ sawági

run [rʌn] *n* (fast pace) 駆け足 kakéashi; (for exercise) ジョギング jogíñgu; (in car) ドライブ dóràibu; (distance traveled) 行程 kṍtei; (journey) 区間 kukán; (series) 継続 keízoku; (*SKI*) ゲレンデ gerénde; (*CRICKET*, *BASEBALL*) 得点 tokúten; (*THEATER*) 上演期間 jṍeñkikàn; (in tights, stockings) ほころび hokórobi

♦*vb* (*pt* **ran**, *pp* **run**)

♦*vt* (race, distance) 走る hashírù; (operate: business, hotel) 経営する keíei suru; (: competition, course) 行う okónaù; (: house) ...の切盛りをする ...no kirímori wò suru; (*COMPUT*) 走らせる hashíraserù; (: pass: hand) 通す tṍsu; (water) 出す dásù; (bath) ...に水をはる ...ni mizú wò hárù; (*PRESS*: feature) 載せる nosérù

♦*vi* (move quickly) 走る hashírù; (flee) 逃げる nigérù; (work: machine) 作動する sadṍ suru; (bus, train: operate) 動く ugókù; (: travel) 走る hashírù; (continue: play) 上演される jṍen sarerù; (: contract) 継続する keízoku suru; (flow: river, liquid) 流れる nagárerù; (colors) 落ちる ochírù; (washing) 色落ちする iróochi suru; (in election) 立候補する rikkōho suru; (nose) 鼻水が出る hanámizu ga derù

there was a run on ... (meat, tickets) 人々は...を買いに殺到した hitóbito wa ...wo kaí nì sattó shità

in the long run 行く行く(は) yukúyuku (wà)

on the run 逃亡中で tóbōchū de

I'll run you to the station 駅まで車で送ろう ékì made kurúma dè okúrō

to run a risk 危険を冒す kikén wò okásù

run about/around *vi* (children) はしゃぎ回る hashágimawarù

run across *vt fus* (find) 偶然に見付ける gūzen nì mitsúkerù

run away *vi* (from home, situation) 逃げる nigérù

runaway [rʌn'əwei] *adj* (horse, truck) 暴走の bōsō no; (person) 逃走中の tōsōchū no

run down *vt* (production, factory) ...の規模を縮小する ...no kíbò wo shukúshō suru; (AUT: person) ひく hikú; (criticize) けなす kenásù

to be run down (person: tired) へとへとになっている hetóheto nì natté irù

rung [rʌŋ] *pp of* ring

♦*n* (of ladder) 一段 ichídàn

run in (*BRIT*) *vt* (car) ...のならし運転をする ...no naráshiuñten wo suru

run into *vt fus* (meet: person, trouble) ...に出会う ...ni deáù; (collide with) ...にぶつかる ...ni butsúkarù

runner [rʌn'əːr] *n* (in race: person) 競走の選手 kyōsō nò sefishu, ランナー ráñnā; (: horse) 競走馬 kyōsōba; (on sledge) 滑り木 subérigi, ランナー ráñnā; (for drawer etc) レール rḗru

runner bean (*BRIT*) *n* サヤインゲン sayáiñgen

runner-up [rʌnəːrʌp'] *n* 第2位入賞者 daí ni-i nyūshōsha

running [rʌn'iŋ] *n* (sport) ジョギング jogíngu; (of business, organization) 経営 keféi

♦*adj* (water) 水道の suídō no

to be in/out of the running for something ...の候補者である〔でなくなっている〕...no kóhoshà de árù〔de nakúnatte irù〕

6 days running 連続6日間 reñzoku muikakàn

running commentary *n* 生中継 namáchūkei

running costs *npl* (of car, machine etc) 維持費 ijíhi

runny [rʌn'iː] *adj* (honey, egg) 緩い yurúi; (nose) 垂れる tarérù; (eyes) 目やにの出る meyáni nò dérù

run off *vt* (water) ...から流れ落ちる ...kara nagáreochirù; (copies) 印刷する iñsatsu suru

♦*vi* (person, animal) 逃げる nigérù

run-of-the-mill [rʌnəvðəmil'] *adj* (ordinary) ごく普通の gókù futsū no

run out *vi* (person) 走って出る hashítte derù; (liquid) 流れ出る nagárederù; (lease, passport) 切れる kirérù; (money) なくなる nakúnarù

run out of *vt fus* (money, time, ideas) ...がなくなる ...ga nakúnarù

run over *vt* (AUT) ひく hikú

♦*vt fus* (revise) おさらいする o-sárai suru

runt [rʌnt] *n* (animal) 未熟児 mijúkujì; (*pej*: person) どちび dochíbi

run through *vt fus* (instructions) ...に目を通す ...ni mé wo tōsu; (rehearse, practice; play) 一通り練習する hitótōri reñshū suru

run up *vt* (debt) ...がかさむ ...ga kasámù

to run up against (difficulties) ...にぶつかる ...ni butsúkarù

run-up [rʌn'ʌp] *n* (*BRIT*): *run-up to* (election etc) ...への準備期間 ...é nò juñbikikàn

runway [rʌn'wei] *n* (AVIAT) 滑走路 kassōrò

rupee [ruː'piː] *n* (currency) ルピー rúpī

rupture [rʌp'tʃəːr] *n* (MED) ヘルニア herúnia

rural [ruː'rəl] *adj* (area) 田舎の ináka no; (economy) 地方の chihō no

ruse [ruːz] *n* 策略 sakúryaku

rush [rʌʃ] n (hurry) 大急ぎ ōisogi; (COMM: sudden demand) 急激な需要 kyūgeki nà juyō; (of water, current) 奔流 hon̄ryū; (of feeling, emotion) 高まり takámari; (BOT) イグサ igúsa
♦vt (hurry) 急がせる isógaserù
♦vi (person) 急ぐ isógù; (air, water) 速く流れる háyaku nagárerù

rush hour n ラッシュアワー rasshúawà

rusk [rʌsk] n (biscuit) ラスク rásùku

Russia [rʌ̀ʃə] n ロシア róshìa

Russian [rʌ̀ʃən] adj ロシアの róshìa no; (LING) ロシア語の roshíagò no
♦n (person) ロシア人 roshíajìn; (LING) ロシア語 roshíagò

rust [rʌst] n さび sabí
♦vi (iron, machine etc) さびる sabírù

rustic [rʌ̀stik] adj (style, furniture) 田舎風の inákafū no

rustle [rʌ̀səl] vi (leaves) かさかさいう kásàkasa iú
♦vt (paper) かさかさ動かす kásàkasa ugókasù; (US: cattle) 盗む nusúmù

rustproof [rʌ̀stpru:f] adj (car, machine) さびない sabínaì

rusty [rʌ̀sti:] adj (car) さびた sábìta; (fig: skill) ...の勘が鈍くなった ...no kañ gà níbùku natta

rut [rʌt] n (groove) わだち wadáchi; (ZOOL: season) 発情期 hatsújòki
to be in a rut 型にはまっている katá nì hamátte irù

ruthless [ru:θlis] adj (person) 血も涙もない chí mò namída mò náì; (action) 残酷な zañkoku na

rye [rai] n (cereal) ライ麦 raímugì

rye bread n ライパン raípañ

S

Sabbath [sæb'əθ] n (Jewish) 土曜日 doyōbì; (Christian) 日曜日 nichíyòbi

sabbatical [səbæt'ikəl] n (also: sabbatical year) 一年休暇 ichínen kyūka ◇7年置きに大学教授などに与えられる1年の長期有給休暇 nanánen okí nì daígakukyòju nádò ni atáerarerù ichínen no chōkiyū-

kyūkyùka

sabotage [sæb'ətɑ:ʒ] n 破壊工作 hakái-kōsaku
♦vt (machine, building) 破壊する hakái suru; (plan, meeting) 妨害する bōgai suru

saccharin(e) [sæk'ə:rin] n サッカリン sakkárìn

sachet [sæʃei'] n (of shampoo, sugar, etc) 小袋 kobúkùro ◇一回分ずつのシャンプー，砂糖などを入れた小さな包 ikkáibun zutsu no shān̄pū, satō nádò wo iréta chiīsana tsutsúmi

sack [sæk] n (bag: for flour, coal, grain, etc) 袋 fukúro
♦vt (dismiss) 首にする kubí ni surù; (plunder) 略奪する ryakúdatsu suru
to get the sack 首になる kubí ni narù

sacking [sæk'iŋ] n (dismissal) 解雇 kái-ko; (material) ズック zúkkù

sacrament [sæk'rəmənt] n (ceremony: Protestant) 聖礼典 seíreiteñ; (: Catholic) 秘跡 hiséki

sacred [sei'krid] adj (of religion: music, history, writings) 宗教の shūkyo no; (holy: animal, building, memory) 神聖な shínsei na

sacrifice [sæk'rəfais] n (offering of someone/something) 犠牲 giséi; (thing/person offered) いけにえ ikénie
♦vt (animal) 殺す korósu; (fig: human lives, health, career) 犠牲にする giséi ni surù

sacrilege [sæk'rəlidʒ] n 冒とく bōtoku

sacrosanct [sæk'rousæŋkt] adj (also fig) 神聖な shínsei na

sad [sæd] adj (unhappy: person, day, story, news) 悲しい kanáshii; (: look) 悲しそうな kanáshisō na; (deplorable: state of affairs) 嘆かわしい nagékawa-shiì

saddle [sæd'əl] n (for horse) くら kurá; (of bicycle) サドル sadoru
♦vt (horse) ...にくらを付ける ...ni kurá wò tsukérù
to be saddled with (inf) ...の重荷を負わされる ...no omóni wò owásarerù

saddlebag [sæd'əlbæg] n (on bicycle) サ

ドルバッグ sadórubaggù

sadism [sei'dizəm] *n* サディズム sadízùmu

sadistic [sədis'tik] *adj* サディスティックな sadísutikkù na

sadly [sæd'li:] *adv* (unhappily) 悲しそうに kanáshisō ni; (unfortunately) 残念ながら zañneñnagara; (seriously: mistaken, neglected) ひどく hídòku

sadly lacking (in) 残念ながら (...が)ない zañneñnagara (...ga) náì

sadness [sæd'nis] *n* 悲しみ kanáshimi

sae [eseii:'] *abbr* (= *stamped addressed envelope*) 返信用封筒 heñshin-yō fūtō ◇ 宛先を書き, 切手を張った物を指す atésaki wò kákì, kitté wò hattá mono wò sásù

safari [səfɑ:'ri:] *n* サファリ sáfàri

safe [seif] *adj* (out of danger) 安全な場所にいる〔ある〕añzen na bashò ni irú 〔árù〕; (not dangerous, sure: place) 安全な añzen na; (unharmed: return, journey) 無事な bují na; (without risk: bet, subject, appointment) 安全な añzen na, 安心できる añshin dekirù; (: seat in parliament) 落選する恐れのない rakúsen suru osore nò náì

◆*n* (for valuables, money) 金庫 kíñko

safe from (attack) ...される心配のない場所にいる〔ある〕...sarèru shiñpai no náì bashò ni irú 〔árù〕

safe and sound (return, sleep, etc) 無事で bují de

(just) to be on the safe side 念のために neñ no tame nì

safe-conduct [seif'kɑːn'dʌkt] *n* (right to pass) 通行許可 tsūkōkyokà

safe-deposit [seif'dipə:zit] *n* (vault) 貸金庫室 kashíkiñkoshitsu; (*also:* **safe deposit box**) 貸金庫 kashíkiñko

safeguard [seif'gɑːrd] *n* 保護手段 hogóshudàn

◆*vt* 保護する hógò suru

safekeeping [seifki:'piŋ] *n* 保管 hokán

safely [seif'li:] *adv* (without risk: assume, say) 安心して añshin shite; (without mishap: drive) 安全に añzen ni; (arrive) 無事に bují ni

safety [seif'ti:] *n* 安全 añzen

safety belt *n* 安全ベルト añzenberùto, シートベルト shītoberùto

safety pin *n* 安全ピン añzeñpin

safety valve *n* 安全弁 añzeñben

saffron [sæf'rən] *n* (powder) サフラン sáfùran

sag [sæg] *vi* (breasts, hem) 垂れ下がる tarésagarù; (roof) 凹む kubómu

saga [sæg'ə] *n* (long story, *also fig*) 長編物語 chōhenmonogatàri

sage [seidʒ] *n* (herb) セージ sēji; (wise man) 賢人 keñjin

Sagittarius [sædʒite:r'i:əs] *n* (sign of Zodiac) 射手座 itézà

Sahara [səher:r'ə] *n*: *the Sahara (Desert)* サハラ砂漠 sahára sabàku

said [sed] *pt, pp of* **say**

sail [seil] *n* (on boat) 帆 hó; (trip): *to go for a sail* ヨットに乗る yóttò ni noru

◆*vt* (boat) 操縦する sōjū suru

◆*vi* (travel: ship) 航海する kōkai suru; (SPORT) ヨットに乗る yóttò ni norú; (begin voyage: ship) 出航する shukkō suru; (: passenger) 船で出発する fúnè de shuppátsu suru

they sailed into Copenhagen 彼らはコペンハーゲンに入港した kárèra wa kopénhàgen ni nyūkō shità

sailboat [seil'bout] (*US*) *n* ヨット yóttò

sailing [sei'liŋ] *n* (SPORT) ヨット遊び yottóasobì

to go sailing ヨットに乗る yóttò ni norú, ヨット遊びをする yottóasòbi wo suru

sailing boat *n* ヨット yóttò

sailing ship *n* 帆船 hañsen

sailor [sei'lər] *n* (seaman) 船乗り funánòri

sail through *vt fus* (*fig*. exams, interview etc) ...に楽々と合格する ...ni rakúraku to gōkaku suru

saint [seint] *n* (*also fig*) 聖人 sēijin

saintly [seint'li:] *adj* (person, life, expression) 聖人の様な sēijin no yō nà

sake [seik] *n*: *for the sake of someone/something* ...のために ...no tamé nì

salad [sæl'əd] *n* サラダ sáràda

salad bowl *n* サラダボール sarádabòru

salad cream (*BRIT*) *n* マヨネーズ ma-yónēzu

salad dressing *n* サラダドレッシング sarádadoresshìngu

salami [səlɑ:mi:] *n* サラミ sárami

salary [sæl'ə:ri:] *n* 給料 kyūryò

sale [seil] *n* (act of selling: commercial goods etc) 販売 hañbai; (: house, land etc) 売却 baíkyaku; (at reduced prices) 安売り yasúuri, セール sèru; (auction) 競売 kyóbai

「**for sale**」売物 urímono

on sale 発売中 hatsúbaichū

on sale or return (goods) 委託販売で itákuhañbai de

saleroom [seil'ru:m] *BRIT n* = **salesroom**

sales [seilz] *npl* (total amount sold) 売上 uríage

sales clerk (*BRIT* **sales assistant**) *n* 店員 teñ-in

salesman [seilz'mən] (*pl* **salesmen**) *n* (in shop) 男子店員 dañshiteñ-in; (representative) セールスマン sèrusumàn

salesroom [seilz'ru:m] (*US*) *n* 競売場 kyóbaijō

saleswoman [seilz'wumən] (*pl* **saleswomen**) *n* 女子店員 joshíteñ-in

salient [sei'li:ənt] *adj* (features, points) 重要な jūyò na

saliva [səlaiv'ə] *n* だ液 daéki

sallow [sæl'ou] *adj* (complexion) 血色の悪い kesshóku nò warúi

salmon [sæm'ən] *n inv* サケ sákè

salon [səlɑːn'] *n* (hairdressing salon, beauty salon) 美容院 biyóìn

saloon [səlu:n'] *n* (*US*: bar) 酒場 sakába; (*BRIT*: AUT) セダン sédàn; (ship's lounge) 広間 hírōma

salt [sɔ:lt] *n* 塩 shió

◆*vt* (preserve: fish, beef, etc) 塩漬にする shiózukè ni suru; (put salt on) ...に塩を掛ける ...ni shió wo kakérù

salt cellar *n* 塩入れ shió-ire

saltwater [sɔ:lt'wɔ:tər] *adj* (fish, plant) 海水の kaísui no

salty [sɔ:l'ti:] *adj* しょっぱい shoppáì

salutary [sæl'jətəːri:] *adj* (lesson, reminder) ためになる tamé ni narù

salute [səlu:t'] *n* (MIL) 敬礼 keírei; (with guns) 礼砲 reíhō; (*gen*: greeting) あいさつ áisatsu

◆*vt* (MIL) ...に敬礼する ...ni keírei suru; (*fig*) ...に敬意を表す ...ni kéìi wo aráwasù

salvage [sæl'vidʒ] *n* (action: *gen*) 救助作業 kyūjo sagyò; (: of shipwreck) 海難救助作業 kaínan kyūjo sagyò; (things saved) サルベージ sarúbèji, 救助された物 kyūjò sareta monó

◆*vt* 救助する kyūjo suru; (*fig*: situation etc) 収拾する shūshū suru

salvation [sælvei'ʃən] *n* (REL) 霊魂の救い rélkon no sukúi; (economic etc) 救済 kyūsai

Salvation Army *n* 救世軍 kyūseigùn

salvo [sæl'vou] *n* (in battle) 一斉射撃 isséishagèki; (ceremonial) 一斉祝砲 isséishukùhō

same [seim] *adj* 同じ onáji

◆*pron*: **the same** 同じ物 onáji monò

the same book as ...と同じ本 ...to onáji hoñ

at the same time (at the same moment) 同時に dōji ni; (yet) とはいえ なお wà ie

all/just the same それにしても soré ni shite mò

to do the same (as someone) (...と) 同じ事をする (...to) onáji koto wo suru

the same to you! お前もだ omáe mo dà ◇侮辱を返す時に言う bujóku wò kaésu toki nì iú

sample [sæm'pəl] *n* (MED: blood/urine sample) 検体 keñtai, サンプル sáñpuru; (of work, merchandise) 見本 mihòn, サンプル sáñpuru

◆*vt* (food) 試食する shishóku suru; (drink) 試飲する shiín suru

sanatoria [sænətɔːr'iːə] *npl of* **sanatorium**

sanatorium [sænətɔːr'iːəm] (*pl* **sanatoria**) *n* = **sanitarium**

sanctify [sæŋk'təfai] *vt* 神聖にする shiñsei ni surù

sanctimonious [sæŋktəmou'niːəs] *adj*

(person, remarks) 宗教心を装う shūkyōshiǹ wo yosóoù

sanction [sæŋk'(ə)n] n (approval) お墨付き osúmitsùki, 認可 níǹka
♦vt (give approval to) 認可する níǹka suru

sanctions [sæŋk'(ə)nz] npl (severe measures) 制裁処置 seísaishochì

sanctity [sæŋk'titi:] n 神聖さ shiǹseisa

sanctuary [sæŋk't∫u:eri:] n (also: **bird sanctuary**) 鳥類保護区 chōruihogokù, サンクチュアリ saǹkuchùari; (place of refuge) 避難所 hináǹjo; (REL: in church) 内陣 naíjin

sand [sænd] n (material, fine grains) 砂 suná; (beach: also: **sands**) 砂浜 sunáhama
♦vt (piece of furniture: also: **sand down**) 紙やすりで磨く kamíyasùri de migáku

sandal [sæn'dəl] n (shoe) サンダル saǹdaru

sandbox [sænd'bɑ:ks] US n (for children) 砂場 sunába

sandcastle [sænd'kæsəl] n 砂の城 suná no shirò

sand dune n 砂丘 sakyū

sandpaper [sænd'peipə:r] n 紙やすり kamíyasùri, サンドペーパー saǹdopèpà

sandpit [sænd'pit] (BRIT) n = **sandbox**

sandstone [sænd'stoun] n 砂岩 ságàn

sandwich [sænd'witʃ] n サンドイッチ saǹdoitchì
♦vt: **sandwiched between** ...の間に挟まれて ...no aída nì hasámarète
cheese/ham sandwich チーズ〔ハム〕サンドイッチ chízù〔hámù〕saǹdoitchì

sandwich course (BRIT) n サンドイッチコース saǹdoitchikòsu ◊勉強と現場実習を交互に行う課程 beńkyō tò geńbajisshū wo kōgō ni okónaù katéi

sandy [sæn'di:] adj (beach) 砂の suná no; (color) 砂色の suná-iro no

sane [sein] adj (person) 正気の shōki no; (sensible: action, system) 合理的な gōriteki na

sang [sæŋ] pt of **sing**

sanitarium [sæniter'i:əm] (US) n 療養所 ryōyōjo, サナトリウム sanátoriùmu

sanitary [sæn'iteri:] adj (system, arrangements, inspector) 衛生の eísei no; (clean) 衛生的な eíseiteki na

sanitary napkin (BRIT **sanitary towel**) n 生理用ナプキン seíriyō napùkin

sanitation [sæniteí'(ə)n] n (in house) 衛生設備 eíseisetsùbi; (in town) 下水道設備 gesúidōsetsùbi

sanitation department (US) n 清掃局 seísōkyoku

sanity [sæn'iti:] n (quality of being sane: of person) 正気 shōki; (common sense: of suggestion etc) 合理性 gōrisei

sank [sæŋk] pt of **sink**

Santa Claus [sæn'tə klɔ:z] n サンタクロース saǹtakurōsu

sap [sæp] n (of plants) 樹液 juéki
♦vt (strength, confidence) 失わせていく ushínawasete ikù

sapling [sæp'liŋ] n 苗木 naégi

sapphire [sæf'aiə:r] n サファイア safáìa

sarcasm [sɑ:r'kæzəm] n 皮肉 hiníku

sarcastic [sɑːrkæs'tik] adj (person) いやみ好きな iyámizùki na; (remark, smile) 皮肉な hiníku na

sardine [sɑːrdiːn'] n イワシ iwáshi

Sardinia [sɑːrdin'i:ə] n サルディニア島 sarúdiniatò

sardonic [sɑːrdɑn'ik] adj (smile) あざける様な azákeru yō na

sari [sɑː'riː] n サリー sárì

sash [sæʃ] n (Western) サッシュ sásshù; (Japanese) 帯 óbì

sat [sæt] pt, pp of **sit**

Satan [sei'tən] n 大魔王 daímaò, サタン sátàn

satchel [sætʃ'əl] n (child's) かばん kabán

satellite [sæt'əlait] n (body in space) 衛星 eísei; (communications satellite) 通信衛星 tsūshin-eisei

satellite dish n パラボラアンテナ parábora aǹtena

satin [sæt'ən] n サテン sátèn
♦adj サテンの sátèn no

satire [sæt'aiə:r] n (form of humor) 風刺 fūshi; (novel) 風刺小説 fūshishōsetsu; (play) 風刺劇 fūshigekì

satirical [sətir'ikəl] adj (remarks, draw-

ings etc) 風刺の fúshi no
satisfaction [sætisfæk'ʃən] *n* (pleasure)
満足 mánzoku; (refund, apology etc) 謝
罪 shazái
satisfactory [sætisfæk'tə:ri:] *adj* (patient's condition) 良い yóí; (results, progress) 満足できる mánzoku dekíru
satisfy [sæt'isfai] *vt* (please) 満足させる
mánzoku saserù; (meet: needs, demand)
...に応じる ...ni ōjirù; (convince) 納得させ
る nattóku saserù
satisfying [sæt'isfaiiŋ] *adj* (meal, job,
feeling) 満足な mánzoku na
saturate [sætʃ'ə:reit] *vt*: *to saturate
(with)* (*also fig*) (...で)一杯にする (...de)
ippái ni surù
saturation [sætʃərei'ʃən] *n* (*also fig*) 飽
和状態 hōwajōtai
Saturday [sæt'ə:rdei] *n* 土曜日 doyōbì
sauce [sɔ:s] *n* (sweet, savory) ソース sōsù
saucepan [sɔ:s'pæn] *n* ソースパン sōsu-
pañ
saucer [sɔ:'sə:r] *n* 受皿 ukézàra, ソーサ
ー sōsā
saucy [sɔ:s'i:] *adj* (cheeky) ずうずうしい
zūzūshiì
Saudi [sau'di:]: *Saudi Arabia n* サウジ
アラビア saújiaràbia
Saudi (Arabian) *adj* サウジアラビアの
saújiaràbia no
sauna [sɔ:'nə] *n* サウナ sáùna
saunter [sɔ:n'tə:r] *vi* のんびりと歩く noñ-
birì to árùku
sausage [sɔ:'sidʒ] *n* ソーセージ sōséji
sausage roll *n* ソーセージパン sōséjipañ
sauté [sɔ:tei'] *adj*: *sauté potatoes* フラ
イポテト furáipotèto
savage [sæv'idʒ] *adj* (cruel, fierce: dog)
どうもうな dōmō na; (: attack) 残忍な
zañnin na; (primitive: tribe) 未開な mikái na
♦*n* 野蛮人 yabáñjiñ
savagery [sæv'idʒri:] *n* 残忍さ zanninsa
save [seiv] *vt* (rescue, someone, someone's
life, marriage) 救う sukúu; (economize
on: money, time) 節約する setsúyaku suru; (put by: receipts etc) 取って置く tóttè
oku; (: money) 蓄える takúwaeru;

(COMPUT) 格納する kakúnō suru, セー
ブする sēbu suru; (avoid: work, trouble)
省く habúkù; (keep: seat) 確保する kákùho suru; (SPORT: shot, ball) セーブす
る sēbu suru
♦*vi* (*also*: save up) 貯金する chokín suru
♦*n* (SPORT) セーブ sēbu
♦*prep* (except) (...を)除いて (...wo) nozóite
saving [sei'viŋ] *n* (on price etc) 節約 setsúyaku
♦*adj*: *the saving grace of something*
...の唯一の長所 ...no yuíitsu no chōsho
savings [sei'viŋz] *npl* (money) 貯金 chokín
savings account *n* 普通預金口座 futsú-
yokinkōza
savings bank *n* 普通銀行 futsúgiñkò
savior [seiv'jə:r] (*BRIT* **saviour**) *n* (*gen*)
救い主 sukúinùshi; (REL) 救世主 kyūseī-
shu
savor [sei'və:r] (*BRIT* **savour**) *vt* (food,
drink, experience) 味わう ajíwaù
savory [sei'və:ri:] (*BRIT* **savoury**) *adj*
(dish: not sweet: spicy) ぴりっとした pi-
ríttò shita; (: salt-flavored) 塩味の shióa-
ji no
saw [sɔ:] *n* (tool) のこぎり nokógìri
♦*vt* (*pt* sawed, *pp* sawed *or* sawn) のこ
ぎりで切る nokógìri de kírù
♦*pt* of see
sawdust [sɔ:'dʌst] *n* のこくず nokókuzù
sawed-off [sɔ:d'ɔ:f] *n* (*US*): *sawed-off
shotgun* 短身散弾銃 tañshin sandanjū ◊
のこぎりで銃身を短く切った散弾銃 no-
kógìri de jūshin wò mijíkaku kittà sañ-
danjū
sawmill [sɔ:'mil] *n* 製材所 seízaisho
sawn-off [sɔ:n'ɔ:f] *adj* (*BRIT*) = sawed-
off
saxophone [sæk'səfoun] *n* サキソホーン
sakísohòn
say [sei] *n*: *to have one's say* 意見を言
う íkèn wo iú
♦*vt* (*pt*, *pp* said) 言う iú
to have a/some say in something ...に
ついてある程度の発言権がある ...ni tsuí-
te áru teidō no hatsúgeñken ga árù

to say yes/no 承知する〔しない〕shóchi suru〔shinaí〕

could you say that again? もう一度言ってくれませんか mó ichidò itté kuremaseñ ka

that is to say つまり tsúmari

that goes without saying それは言うまでもない soré wà iú made mo naí

saying [sei'iŋ] *n* (proverb) ことわざ kotówaza; (words of wisdom) 格言 kakúgen; (often repeated phrase) 愛用の言葉 aíyō no kotoba

scab [skæb] *n* (on wound) かさぶた kasábuta; (*pej:* strike-breaker) スト破り sutóyabùri

scaffold [skæf'əld] *n* (for execution) 死刑台 shikéidai; (for building etc) = **scaffolding**

scaffolding [skæf'əldiŋ] *n* 足場 ashíba

scald [skɔːld] *n* やけど yakédo ◊熱湯や蒸気などによるやけどを指す nettó yà jókì nado ni yórù yakédo wò sásù

♦*vt* (burn: skin) やけどさせる yakédo saserù

scale [skeil] *n* (*gen:* set of numbers) 目盛 memóri; (of salaries, fees etc) 表 hyő; (of fish) うろこ uróko; (MUS) 音階 oñkai; (of map, model) 縮尺 shukúshōrìtsu; (size, extent) 規模 kíbò

♦*vt* (mountain, tree) 登る nobórù

on a large scale 大規模で daíkibò de

scale of charges 料金表 ryőkinhyò

scale down *vt* 縮小する shukúshō suru

scales [skeilz] *npl* (for weighing) 量り hakári

scallop [skɑːl'əp] *n* (ZOOL) ホタテガイ hotátegài; (SEWING) スカラップ sukárappù

scalp [skælp] *n* 頭の皮膚 atáma no hifù, 頭皮 tōhi

♦*vt* ...の頭皮をはぐ ...no tőhî wo hágù

scalpel [skæl'pəl] *n* メス mésù

scamper [skæm'pəːr] *vi:* *to scamper away/off* (child, animal) ぱたぱた走って行く pátàpata hashítte ikù

scampi [skæm'piː] *npl* エビフライ ebífuràì

scan [skæn] *vt* (examine: horizon) 見渡す miwátasu; (glance at quickly: newspaper) ...にさっと目を通す ...ni sáttò mé wò tősù; (TV, RADAR) 走査する sósa suru

♦*n* (MED) スキャン sukyán

scandal [skæn'dəl] *n* (shocking event) 醜聞 shúbun, スキャンダル sukyáñdaru; (defamatory: reports, rumors) 陰口 kagéguchi; (gossip) うわさ uwása; (*fig:* disgrace) 恥ずべき事 hazúbeki kotő

scandalize [skæn'dəlaiz] *vt* 憤慨させる fuñgai saserù

scandalous [skæn'dələs] *adj* (disgraceful, shocking: behavior etc) 破廉恥な harénchi na

Scandinavian [skændənei'viːən] *adj* スカンディナビアの sukándinabìa no

scant [skænt] *adj* (attention) 不十分な fujúbùn na

scanty [skæn'tiː] *adj* (meal) ささやかな sasáyàka na; (underwear) 極めて小さい kiwámète chíìsaí

scapegoat [skeip'gout] *n* 身代り migáwari

scar [skɑːr] *n* (on skin: *also fig*) 傷跡 kizúato

♦*vt* (*also fig*) 傷跡を残す kizúato wò nokósu

scarce [skers] *adj* (rare, not plentiful) 少ない sukúnaí

to make oneself scarce (*inf*) 消えうせる kiéuserù

scarcely [skers'liː] *adv* (hardly) ほとんど...ない hotőndo ...náì; (with numbers: barely) わずかに wázùka ni

scarcity [sker'sitiː] *n* (shortage) 不足 fusóku

scare [sker] *n* (fright) 恐怖 kyőfu; (public fear) 恐慌 kyőkō

♦*vt* (frighten) 怖がらす kowágarasù

bomb scare 爆弾騒ぎ bakúdan sawàgi

to scare someone stiff ...に怖い思いをさせる ...ni kowái omoî wo saserù

scarecrow [sker'krou] *n* かかし kakáshi

scared [skerd] *adj:* *to be scared* 怖がる kowágarù

scare off/away *vt* おどかして追払う odōkashite oiharaù

scarf [skɑːrf] (*pl* **scarfs** *or* **scarves**) *n* (long) マフラー máfūrā; (square) スカーフ sukáfù

scarlet [skɑːrˈlit] *adj* (color) ひ色 hífro

scarlet fever *n* しょう紅熱 shōkōnetsu

scarves [skɑːrvz] *npl of* **scarf**

scary [skeːrˈiː] (*inf*) *adj* 怖い kowáī

scathing [skeiˈðiŋ] *adj* (comments, attack) 辛らつな shíñratsu na

scatter [skætˈəːr] *vt* (spread: seeds, papers) まき散らす makíchirasù; (put to flight: flock of birds, crowd of people) 追散らす oíchirasù

♦*vi* (crowd) 散る chírù

scatterbrained [skætˈəːrbreind] (*inf*) *adj* (forgetful) おつむの弱い o-tsúmù no yowáī

scavenger [skævˈindʒəːr] *n* (person) くず拾い kuzúhiròi

scenario [sinerˈiːou] *n* (THEATER, CINEMA) 脚本 kyakúhon, シナリオ shinárĭo; (*fig*) 筋書 sujígaki

scene [siːn] *n* (THEATER, *fig*) 場 ba, シーン shíñ; (of crime, accident) 現場 geñba; (sight, view) 景色 késhĭki; (fuss) 騒ぎ sáwàgi

scenery [siːˈnəːriː] *n* (THEATER) 大道具 ōdōgu; (landscape) 景色 késhĭki

scenic [siːˈnik] *adj* (picturesque) 景色の美しい késhĭki no utsúkushiī

scent [sent] *n* (pleasant smell) 香り kaóri; (track) 通った後のにおい tōtta átò no niōī; (*fig*) 手がかり tegákàri; (liquid perfume) 香水 kōsui

scepter [sepˈtəːr] (*BRIT* **sceptre**) *n* しゃく shaku

sceptic [skepˈtik] (*BRIT*) *n* = **skeptic** *etc*

schedule [skedʒˈuːl] *n* (of trains, buses) 時間割 jikáñwari; (list of events and times) 時刻表 jikókuhyō; (list of prices, details etc) 表 hyō

♦*vt* (timetable, visit) 予定する yotéi suru

on schedule (trains, buses) 定刻通りに teíkokudòri ni; (project etc) 予定通りに yotéídòri ni

to be ahead of schedule 予定時間より

早い yotéijikàn yórī hayáī

to be behind schedule 予定時間に遅れる yotéijikàn ni okúrerù

scheduled flight [skedʒˈuːld-] *n* 定期便 teíkibin

schematic [skiːmætˈik] *adj* (diagram etc) 模式的な moshíkiteki na

scheme [skiːm] *n* (personal plan, idea) もくろみ mokúromi; (dishonest plan, plot) 陰謀 iñbō; (formal plan: pension plan etc) 計画 keíkaku, 案 áñ; (arrangement) 配置 háīchi

♦*vi* (intrigue) たくらむ takúramù

scheming [skiːˈmiŋ] *adj* 腹黒い haráguroī

♦*n* たくらむ事 takúramù kotó

schism [skizˈəm] *n* 分裂 buñretsu

schizophrenic [skitsəfrenˈik] *adj* 精神分裂症の seíshinbunretsushō no

scholar [skɑːlˈəːr] *n* (pupil) 学習者 gakúshūsha; (learned person) 学者 gakúsha

scholarly [skɑːlˈəːrliː] *adj* (text, approach) 学問的な gakúmonteki na; (person) 博学的な hakúgakuteki na

scholarship [skɑːlˈəːrʃip] *n* (academic knowledge) 学問 gakúmòn; (grant) 奨学金 shōgakukìn

school [skuːl] *n* (place where children learn: *gen*) 学校 gakkō; (*also*: **elementary school**) 小学校 shōgakkō; (*also*: **secondary school**: lower) 中学校 chūgakkō; (: higher) 高(等学)校 kō(tōgak)kō; (*US*: university) 大学 daígaku

♦*cpd* 学校の gakkō no

school age *n* 学齢 gakúrei

schoolbook [skuːlˈbuk] *n* 教科書 kyōkashò

schoolboy [skuːlˈbɔi] *n* 男子生徒 dañshiseìto

schoolchildren [skuːlˈtʃildrən] *npl* 生徒 seìto

schooldays [skuːlˈdeiz] *npl* 学校時代 gakkōjidài

schoolgirl [skuːlˈgəːrl] *n* 女子生徒 joshíseìto

schooling [skuːˈliŋ] *n* (education at school) 学校教育 gakkōkyōiku

schoolmaster [skuːlˈmæstəːr] *n* 教師

kyōshi, 教員 kyōin, 先生 seńsei ◇男子教員 dańshikyōin

schoolmistress [sku:l'mistris] *n* 教師 kyōshi, 教員 kyōin, 先生 seńsei ◇女子教員 joshíkyōin

schoolteacher [sku:l'ti:tʃəːr] *n* 教師 kyōshi, 教員 kyōin, 先生 seńsei ◇男女を問わず使う dáñjo wo tówàzu tsukáù

schooner [sku:'nəːr] *n* (ship) 帆船 hańsen

sciatica [saiæt'ikə] *n* 座骨神経痛 zakótsushinkeītsū

science [sai'əns] *n* (study of natural things) 科学 kágaku; (branch of such knowledge) ...学 ...gàku

science fiction *n* 空想科学物語 kūsōkagakumonogatāri, SF esuefu

scientific [saiəntif'ik] *adj* (research, instruments) 科学の kágaku no

scientist [sai'əntist] *n* 科学者 kagákushà

scintillating [sin'təleitiŋ] *adj* (fig: conversation, wit, smile) 輝く様な kagáyakù yō na

scissors [siz'əːrz] *npl* (*also*: **a pair of scissors**) はさみ hasámi

scoff [skɑ:f] *vt* (BRIT: inf: eat) がつがつ食う gátsùgatsu kúù
♦*vi*: **to scoff (at)** (mock) ...をあざける ...wo azákerù

scold [skould] *vt* しかる shikárù

scone [skoun] *n* スコーン sukóñ ◇小さなホットケーキの一種 chíisa na hottókèki no ísshū

scoop [sku:p] *n* (measuring scoop: for flour etc) スコップ sukóppù; (for ice cream) サーバー sābā; (PRESS) スクープ sukúpu

scoop out *vt* すくい出す sukúidasù

scoop up *vt* すくい上げる sukúiagerù

scooter [sku:'təːr] *n* (*also*: **motor scooter**) スクーター sukútā; (toy) スクーター sukútā ◇片足を乗せて走る遊び道具 katáashi wo nosetè hashírù asóbidōgu

scope [skoup] *n* (opportunity) 機会 kikái; (range: of plan, undertaking) 範囲 háñ-i; (: of person) 能力 nōryoku

scorch [skɔːrtʃ] *vt* (clothes) 焦がす kogásù; (earth, grass) 枯らす karásù

score [skɔːr] *n* (total number of points etc) 得点 tokúten, スコア sukóa; (MUS) 楽譜 gakúfu; (twenty) 20 nījū
♦*vt* (goal, point, mark) 取る tórù; (achieve: success) 収める osámerù
♦*vi* (in game) 得点する tokúten suru; (FOOTBALL etc) トライする toráì suru; (keep score) 得点を記録する tokúten wo kirókù suru

scores of (very many) 多数の tasū no

on that score その点に関して sonó teñ ni kañshitè

to score 6 out of 10 10回中6回成功する jukkáichū rokkaī seíkō suru

scoreboard [skɔːr'bɔːrd] *n* スコアボード sukóabòdo

score out *vt* 線を引いて消す séñ wo hifte kesù

scorn [skɔːrn] *n* 軽べつ keíbetsu
♦*vt* 軽べつする keíbetsu suru

scornful [skɔːrn'fəl] *adj* (laugh, disregard) 軽べつ的な keíbetsuteki na

Scorpio [skɔːr'pi:ou] *n* (sign of Zodiac) さそり座 sasórizà

scorpion [skɔːr'pi:ən] *n* サソリ sasóri

Scot [skɑːt] *n* スコットランド人 sukóttorandojìn

Scotch [skɑːtʃ] *n* (whisky) スコッチ sukótchī

scotch [skɑːtʃ] *vt* (end: rumor) 消し止める keshítomerù; (plan, idea) 没にする bótsù ni suru

scot-free [skɑːt'fri:'] *adv*: **to get off scot-free** (unpunished) 何の罰も受けない náñ no bátsù mo ukénaì

Scotland [skɑːt'lənd] *n* スコットランド sukóttoraňdo

Scots [skɑːts] *adj* (accent, people) スコットランドの sukóttorando no

Scotsman [skɑːts'mən] (*pl* **Scotsmen**) *n* スコットランドの男性 sukóttorando no dansei

Scotswoman [skɑːts'wumən] (*pl* **Scotswomen**) *n* スコットランドの女性 sukóttorando no joséi

Scottish [skɑːt'iʃ] *adj* (history, clans, people) スコットランドの sukóttoraňdo no

scoundrel [skaun'drəl] n 悪党 akútồ

scour [skaur] vt (search: countryside etc) くまなく捜し回る kumánàku sagáshimawarù

scourge [skəːrdʒ] n (cause of trouble: also fig) 悩みの種 nayámi no tanè

scout [skaut] n (MIL) 斥候 sekkố; (also: **boy scout**) ボーイスカウト bốisukaùto

girl scout (US) ガールスカウト gấrusukaùto

scout around vi 捜し回る sagáshimawarù

scowl [skaul] vi 顔をしかめる káồ wo shikámerù

to scowl at someone しかめっつらをして...をにらむ shikámettsura wồ shité ...wo nirámù

scrabble [skræb'əl] vi (claw): *to scrabble (at)* (...を)引っかく (...wo) hikkákù; (also: **scrabble around**: search) 手探りで探す teságùri de sagásù

◆n: *Scrabble* ® スクラッブル sukúrabbùru ◇単語作りゲーム tañgozukurigềmu

scraggy [skræg'iː] adj (animal, body, neck etc) やせこけた yasékoketà

scram [skræm] (inf) vi (get away fast) うせる usérù

scramble [skræm'bəl] n (difficult climb) よじ上り yojínobori; (struggle, rush) 奪い合い ubáiai

◆vi: *to scramble out/through* 慌てて出る〔通る〕 awátete derù〔tồru〕

to scramble for ...の奪い合いをする ...no ubáiai wo surù

scrambled eggs [skræm'bəld-] npl いり卵 iritamago, スクランブルエッグ sukúranburu eggù

scrap [skræp] n (bit: of paper, material etc) 切れ端 kiréhashi; (: of information) 少し sukóshì; (fig: of truth) 欠けら kakéra; (fight) けんか keñka; (also: **scrap iron**) くず鉄 kuzútetsu

◆vt (discard: machines etc) くず鉄にする kuzútetsu ni surù; (fig: plans etc) 捨てる sutérù

◆vi (fight) けんかする keñka suru

scrapbook [skræp'buk] n スクラップブック sukúrappubukkù

scrap dealer n くず鉄屋 kuzútetsuyà

scrape [skreip] n (fig: difficult situation) 窮地 kyúchì

◆vt (scrape off: potato skin etc) むくmukú; (scrape against: hand, car) こする kosúrù

◆vi: *to scrape through* (exam etc) ...をどうにか切抜ける ...wo dồ ni ka kirínukerù

scrape together vt (money) かき集める kakíatsumerù

scrap heap n (fig): *on the scrap heap* 捨てられて sutérarete

scrap merchant n (BRIT) = **scrap dealer**

scrap paper n 古い紙 furúì kamí, 古紙 kóshì, ほご hốgồ

scrappy [skræp'iː] adj (piece of work) 雑な zatsú na

scraps [skræps] npl (leftovers: food, material etc) くず kúzù

scratch [skrætʃ] n (cut: on body, furniture: also from claw) かき傷 kakíkizu

◆cpd: *scratch team* 寄集めチーム yoséatsumechìmu

◆vt (rub: one's nose etc) かく kákù; (damage: paint, car) 傷付ける kizútsukerù; (with claw, nail) ひっかく hikkákù

◆vi (rub one's body) ...をかく ...wo kákù

to start from scratch 何もない所から始める naní mo naì tokóro karà hajímerù

to be up to scratch いい線をいっている íì sêñ wo itté irù

scrawl [skrɔːl] n なぐり書き nagúrigaki

◆vi なぐり書きする nagúrigaki suru

scrawny [skrɔː'niː] adj (person, neck) やせこけた yasékoketà

scream [skriːm] n 悲鳴 himéi

◆vi 悲鳴を上げる himéi wo agerù

scree [skriː] n 岩くず iwákuzu ◇崩れ落ちてたい積した岩くずを指す kuzúreochitè taíseki shità iwákuzu wo sasù

screech [skriːtʃ] vi (person) 金切り声を出す kanákirigoè wo dásù; (bird) きーきー声で鳴く kíkìgoè de nákù; (tires, brakes) きーきーと鳴る kíkì to nárù

screen [skriːn] n (CINEMA) スクリーン

sukúrìn; (TV, COMPUT) ブラウン管 buráunkan; (movable barrier) ついたて tsuítate; (fig: cover) 幕 makú

♦vt (protect, conceal) 覆い隠す ốikakusù; (from the wind etc) ...の...よけになる ...no...yoké ni narù; (film) 映写する eísha suru; (television program) 放映する hốei suru; (candidates etc) 審査する shínsa suru

screening [skri:'niŋ] n (MED) 健康診断 keñkōshìñdan

screenplay [skri:n'plei] n 映画脚本 eígakyakùhon

screw [skru:] n (for fixing something) ねじ néjì

♦vt (fasten) ねじで留める neji de tomérù

screwdriver [skru:'draivə:r] n ねじ回し nejímawashì

screw up vt (paper etc) くしゃくしゃにする kushákùsha ni suru

to screw up one's eyes 目を細める mé wò hosómerù

scribble [skrib'əl] n 走り書き hashírigakì

♦vt (write carelessly: note etc) 走り書きする hashírigaki suru

♦vi (make meaningless marks) 落書する rakúgaki suru

script [skript] n (CINEMA etc) 脚本 kyakúhon, スクリプト sukúripùto; (system of writing) 文字 mójì

scripture(s) [skrip't∫ə:r(z)] n(pl) (holy writing(s) of a religion) 聖典 seíten

scroll [skroul] n (official paper) 巻物 makímono

scrounge [skraundʒ] vt (inf): *to scrounge something off/from someone* ...に...をねだる ...ni...wo nedárù

♦n: *on the scrounge* たかって takáttè

scrub [skrʌb] n (land) 低木地帯 teíbokuchitaì

♦vt (rub hard: floor, hands, pan, washing) ごしごし洗う goshígoshi aráù; (inf: reject: idea) 取り止める toríyamerù

scruff [skrʌf] n: *by the scruff of the neck* 首筋をつかんで kubísuji wò tsukáñde

scruffy [skrʌf'i:] adj (person, object, appearance) 薄汚い usúgitanaì

scrum(mage) [skrʌm('idʒ)] n (RUGBY) スクラム sukúramu

scruple [skru:'pəl] n (gen pl) 良心のとがめ ryőshìn no togáme

scrupulous [skru:'pjələs] adj (painstaking: care, attention) 細心の saíshin no; (fair-minded: honesty) 公正な kősei na

scrutinize [skru:'tənaiz] vt (examine closely) 詳しく調べる kuwáshikù sharáberù

scrutiny [skru:'təni:] n (close examination) 吟味 gíñmi

to keep someone under scrutiny ...を監視する ...wo kañshi suru

scuff [skʌf] vt (shoes, floor) すり減らす suríherasù

scuffle [skʌf'əl] n (fight) 乱闘 rañtō

sculptor [skʌlp'tə:r] n 彫刻家 chőkokuka

sculpture [skʌlp't∫ə:r] n 彫刻 chōkoku

scum [skʌm] n (on liquid) 汚い泡 kitánaì awà; (pej: people) 人間のくず niñgen nò kúzù

scupper [skʌp'ə:r] (BRIT: inf) vt (plan, idea) 邪魔して失敗させる jamá shitè shippái saserù

scurrilous [skə:r'ələs] adj 口汚い kuchígitanaì

scurry [skə:r'i:] vi ちょこちょこ走る chốkòchoko hashíru

scurry off vi ちょこちょこ走って行く chốkòchoko hashítte ikù

scuttle [skʌt'əl] n (also: coal scuttle) 石炭入れ sekítan-ire

♦vt (ship) 沈没させる chíñbotsu saserù

♦vi (scamper): *to scuttle away/off* ちょこちょこ走っていく chốkòchoko hashítte ikù

scythe [saið] n 大がま őgamà ◇柄も刃も長いかま é mò há mò nagáî kámà

sea [si:] n 海 úmì; (fig: very many) 多数 tasū; (: very much) 多量 taryō

♦cpd (breeze, bird, air etc) 海の úmì no

by sea (travel) 海路で kaíro de

on the sea (boat) 海上で kaíjō de; (town) 海辺の umíbe no

out to/at sea 沖に okí ni
to be all at sea (fig) 頭が混乱している
atáma gà kofiran shite irú
a sea of faces (fig) 顔の海 kaó nò úmí
seaboard [siːˈbɔːrd] n 海岸 kaígan
seafood [siːˈfuːd] n 魚介類 gyokáiruì, シーフード shífūdo ◇料理に使う魚介類を指す ryōri ni tsukáù gyokáiruì wo sású
seafront [siːˈfrʌnt] n 海岸 kaígan ◇海辺の町などの海沿いの部分を指す umíbe nò machí nadò no umízoi no bubùn wo sású
sea-going [siːˈgouiŋ] adj (ship) 遠洋航用の efi-yōkōkaiyò no
seagull [siːˈgʌl] n カモメ kamóme
seal [siːl] n (animal) アザラシ azárashi ◇セイウチを除いて全てのひれ足類を含む sefuchì wo nozóìte súbète no hiréashiruì wo fúkumù; (official stamp) 印章 ifishō; (closure) 封印 fūin
◆vt (close: envelope) ...の封をする ...no fū wò suru; (: opening) 封じる fújirù
in season (fruit, vegetables) しゅんで shúñ de
out of season (fruit, vegetables) 季節外れで kisétsuhàzure de
seasonal [siːˈzənəl] adj (work) 季節的な kisétsuteki na
seasoned [siːˈzənd] adj (fig: traveler) 経験豊かな keíken yutàka na
seasoning [siːˈzəniŋ] n 調味料 chōmiryò, 薬味 yakúmi
season ticket n (RAIL) 定期券 teíkikèn; (THEATER) シーズン入場券 shízun nyūjōken
seat [siːt] n (chair) いす isú; (in vehicle, theater: place) 席 sékì; (PARLIAMENT) 議席 giséki; (buttocks: also of trousers) しり shirí
◆vt (place: guests etc) 座らせる suwáraserù; (subj: table, theater: have room for) ...人分の席がある ...nífibun no sékì ga árù
to be seated 座る suwárù
seat belt n シートベルト shítoberùto
sea water n 海水 kaísui
seaweed [siːˈwiːd] n 海草 kaísō
seaworthy [siːˈwərːðiː] adj (ship) 航海に耐えられる kōkai nì taérarerù
sec. abbr = **second(s)**
secluded [siklúːˈdid] adj (place) 人里離れた hitózato hanaretà; (life) 隠とんの ifi-

ton no

seclusion [siklu:'ʒən] n 隔離 kákùri

second [sek'ənd] adj (after first) 第二 (の) dái ní (no)

♦adv (come, be placed: in race etc) 二番 に níbàn ni; (when listing) 第二に dái ní ni

♦n (unit of time) 秒 byǒ; (AUT: also: **second gear**) セカンド sekándo; (COMM: imperfect) 二流品 niryúhìn; (BRIT: SCOL: degree) 2級優等卒業学位 níkyū yūtō sotsugyō gakùi ¶ see also **first**

♦vt (motion) ...に支持を表明する ...ni shíjì wo hyǒmei suru; (BRIT: worker) 派遣 する hakén suru

secondary [sek'ənde:ri:] adj (less important) 二次的な nijíteki na

secondary school n 中等高等学校 chútōkōtōgakkò

second-class [sek'əndklæs'] adj (hotel, novel, work) 二流の niryū no; (tickets, transport) 2等の nitō no

♦adv (travel) 2等で nitō de

secondhand [sek'əndhænd'] adj (clothing, car) 中古の chūko no

second hand n (on clock) 秒針 byóshìn

secondly [sek'əndli:] adv 2番目に nibánme ni

secondment [sek'əndmənt] (BRIT) n 派遣 hakén

second-rate [sek'əndreit'] adj (film etc) 二流の niryū no

second thoughts npl ためらい tamérai

on second thought (US) or **thoughts** (BRIT) 気が変って ki gá kawatté

secrecy [si:'krisi:] n: **to swear someone to secrecy** ...に秘密を誓わせる ...ni himítsu wò chikáwaserù

secret [si:'krit] adj (plan, passage, agent) 秘密の himítsu no; (admirer, drinker) ひ そかな hisókà na

♦n 秘密 himítsu

in secret 内密に naímitsu ni

secretarial [sekriter:r'i:əl] adj (work, course, staff, studies) 秘書の hishó no

secretariat [sekriter:r'i:ət] n 事務局 jimúkyòku

secretary [sek'rite:ri:] n (COMM) 秘書 hishó; (of club) 書記 shokí

Secretary of State (for) (BRIT: POL) (...)大臣 (...)dáijin

secretion [sikri:'ʃən] n (substance) 分泌 物 buńpitsubùtsu

secretive [si:'kritiv] adj 秘密主義の himítsushùgi no

secretly [si:'kritli:] adv (tell, marry) 内密 に naímitsu ni

sect [sekt] n 宗派 shúha

sectarian [sekte:r'i:ən] adj (riots etc) 宗 派間の shúhakàn no

section [sek'ʃən] n (part) 部分 búbùn; (department) ...部 ...bù; (of document) 章 shǒ; (of opinion) 一部 ichíbù; (cross-section) 断面図 dańmenzù

sector [sek'tə:r] n (part) 部門 búmòn; (MIL) 戦闘地区 señtōchikù

secular [sek'jələ:r] adj (music, society etc) 世俗の sezóku no; (priest) 教区の kyóku no

secure [sikju:r'] adj (safe: person) 安全な 場所にいる añzen na bashó ni irú; (: money) 安全な場所にある añzen na bashô ni árù; (: building) 防犯対策完備の bóhantaisakukañbi no; (firmly fixed, strong: rope, shelf) 固定された kotéi saretà

♦vt (fix: rope, shelf etc) 固定する kotéi suru; (get: job, contract etc) 確保する kákùho suru

security [sikju:r'iti:] n (protection) 警備 kéĩbi; (for one's future) 保証 hoshǒ; (FINANCE) 担保 táñpo

sedan [sidæn'] (US) n (AUT) セダン sédàn

sedate [sideit'] adj (person, pace) 落着い た ochítsuità

♦vt (MED: with injection) ...に鎮静剤を 注射する ...ni chiñseizài wo chūshà suru; (: with pills etc) ...に鎮静剤を飲ませる ...ni chiñseizài wo nomáserù

sedation [sidei'ʃən] n (MED): **under sedation** 薬で鎮静されて kusúri dè chiñsei saretè

sedative [sed'ətiv] n 鎮静剤 chiñseizài

sedentary [sed'ənte:ri:] adj (occupation,

work) 座ってする suwátte surú

sediment [sed'əmənt] *n* (in bottle) おり orí; (in lake etc) 底のたい積物 sokó nò taísekibútsu

seduce [sidu:s'] *vt* (entice: *gen*) 魅了する miryố suru; (: sexually) 誘惑する yūwaku suru, たらし込む tāráshikomù

seduction [sidʌk'ʃən] *n* (attraction) 魅惑 miwáku; (act of seducing) 誘惑 yūwaku

seductive [sidʌk'tiv] *adj* (look, voice, *also fig* offer) 誘惑的な yūwakuteki na

see [si:] (*pt* **saw**, *pp* **seen**) *vt* (*gen*) 見る mírù; (accompany): *to see someone to the door* ...を戸口まで送る ...wo tốgùchi mádè okúrù; (understand) 分かる wakárù

♦*vi* (*gen*) 見える miérù; (find out) 調べる shiráberù

♦*n* (REL) 教区 kyŏkù

to see that someone does something ...が...する様に気を付ける ...ga...surú yŏ ni kí wo tsukérù

see you soon! またね matá nè

see about *vt fus* ...の問題を調べて片付ける ...no mońdai wò shirábete katazù keru

seed [si:d] *n* (of plant, fruit) 種 tánè; (sperm) 精液 seíeki; (*fig*: *gen* pl) 種 tánè; (TENNIS) シード shído

to go to seed (plant) 種ができる tánè ga dekírù; (*fig*) 衰える otóroerù

seedling [si:d'liŋ] *n* 苗 náè

seedy [si:'di:] *adj* (shabby: person, place) 見すぼらしい misúborashiǐ

seeing [si:'iŋ] *conj*: *seeing (that)* ...だから ...dákàra

seek [si:k] (*pt*, *pp* **sought**) *vt* (truth, shelter, advice, post) 求める motómerù

seem [si:m] *vi* ...に見える ...ni miérù

there seems to be ... ...がある様です ...ga árù yŏ desù

seemingly [si:'miŋli:] *adv* ...らしく ...rashíkù

seen [si:n] *pp* of **see**

see off *vt* ...を見送る ...wo miókurù

seep [si:p] *vi* (liquid, gas) 染み透る shimítòru

seesaw [si:'sɔ:] *n* シーソー shísŏ

seethe [si:ð] *vi* (place: with people/things) 騒然としている sốzen to shite irù

to seethe with anger 怒りで煮え繰り返る ikári dè niékurikaerù

see through *vt* 最後までやり通す saígo made yaríỏsu

♦*vt fus* 見抜く minúkù

see-through [si:'θru:] *adj* (blouse etc) すけすけルックの sukésukerukkù no

see to *vt fus* ...の世話をする ...no sewá wò suru

segment [seg'mənt] *n* (part: *gen*) 一部 ichíbù; (of orange) ふさ fusá

segregate [seg'rəgeit] *vt* 分ける wakérù

seismic [saiz'mik] *adj* (activity) 地震の jishín no

seize [si:z] *vt* (grasp) つかむ tsukámù; (take possession of: power, control, territory) 奪う ubáù; (: hostage) 捕まえる tsukámaerù; (opportunity) 捕える toráerù

seize up *vi* (TECH: engine) 焼き付く yakétsukù

seize (up)on *vt fus* ...に飛付く ...ni tobítsukù

seizure [si:'ʒə:r] *n* (MED) 発作 hossá; (LAW) 没収 bosshū; (: of power) 強奪 gốdatsu

seldom [sel'dəm] *adv* めったに...ない méttà ni...náǐ

select [silekt'] *adj* (school, group, area) 一流の ichíryū no

♦*vt* (choose) 選ぶ erábù

selection [silek'ʃən] *n* (being chosen) 選ばれる事 erábareru kotò; (COMM: range available) 選択 seńtaku

selective [silek'tiv] *adj* (careful in choosing) 選択的な seńtakuteki na; (not general: strike etc) 限られた範囲の kagírareta háń-i no

self [self] (*pl* **selves**) *n*: *the self* 自我 jígà

♦*prefix* 自分で(の)... jibún de (no) ...

self-assured [self'əʃu:rd'] *adj* 自信のある jishín no arù

self-catering [self'kei'tə:riŋ] *adj* (BRIT: holiday, apartment) 自炊の jisúi no

self-centered [self'sen'tə:rd] (BRIT **self-centred**) *adj* 自己中心の jikóchūshinno

self-colored [self'kʌl'ə:rd] (*BRIT* **self-coloured**) *adj* (of one color) 単色の tañshoku na

self-confidence [self'ka:n'fidəns] *n* 自信 jishín

self-conscious [self'ka:n'tʃəs] *adj* (nervous) 照れる terérù

self-contained [self'kənteind'] (*BRIT*) *adj* (flat) 設備完備の setsúbikañbi no

self-control [self'kəntroul'] *n* 自制 jiséi

self-defense [self'difens'] (*BRIT* **self-defence**) *n* 自己防衛 jikóbōei
in self-defense 自己防衛で jikóbōei de

self-discipline [self'dis'əplin] *n* 気力 kíryòku

self-employed [self'imploid'] *adj* 自営業の jiéigyò no

self-evident [self'ev'idənt] *adj* 自明の jiméi no

self-governing [self'gʌv'ə:rniŋ] *adj* 独立の dokúritsu no

self-indulgent [self'indʌl'dʒənt] *adj* 勝手気ままな kattékimama na

self-interest [self'in'trist] *n* 自己利益 jikórièki

selfish [sel'fiʃ] *adj* 身勝手な migátte na

selfishness [sel'fiʃnis] *n* 利己主義 rikóshùgi

selfless [self'lis] *adj* 献身的な keñshinteki na

self-made [self'meid'] *adj*: *self-made man* 自力でたたき上げた人 jiríki dè tatákiageta hitò

self-pity [self'pit'i:] *n* 自己れんびん jikóreñbin

self-portrait [self'po:r'trit] *n* 自画像 jigázò

self-possessed [self'pəzest'] *adj* 落着いた ochítsuità

self-preservation [self'prezə:rvei'ʃən] *n* 本能的自衛 hoñnōtekijièi

self-respect [self'rispekt'] *n* 自尊心 jisóñshin

self-righteous [self'rai'tʃəs] *adj* 独善的な dokúzenteki na

self-sacrifice [self'sæk'rəfais] *n* 献身 keñshin

self-satisfied [self'sæt'isfaid] *adj* 自己満足の jikómañzoku no

self-service [self'sə:r'vis] *adj* (shop, restaurant, service station) セルフサービスの serúfusābisu no

self-sufficient [self'səfiʃ'ənt] *adj* (farm, country) 自給自足の jikyūjisòku no; (person) 独立独歩の dokúritsudoppò no

self-taught [self'to:t'] *adj* 独学の dokúgàku no

sell [sel] (*pt*, *pp* **sold**) *vt* (gen) 売る urú; (*fig*: idea) 売込む uríkomù
♦*vi* (goods) 売れる urérù
to sell at/for $10 値段は10ドルである nedán wà 10 dòrù de árù

sell-by date [sel'bai-] (*BRIT*) *n* 賞味期限 shōmikigèn

seller [sel'ə:r] *n* 売手 uríte

selling price [sel'iŋ-] *n* 値段 nedán

sell off *vt* 売払う urfharaù

sell out *vi* (use up stock): *to sell out (of something)* (...が)売切れる (...ga) uríkirerù
the tickets are sold out 切符は売切れた kippú wà uríkire da

sellotape [sel'əteip] ® (*BRIT*) *n* セロテープ serótēpu

selves [selvz] *pl of* **self**

semaphore [sem'əfɔ:r] *n* 手旗 tebáta

semblance [sem'bləns] *n* 外観 gaíkan

semen [si:'mən] *n* 精液 seíeki

semester [simes'tə:r] (*US*) *n* 学期 gakkí

semi... [sem'i:] *prefix* 半分の... hañbùn no ...

semicircle [sem'i:sə:rkəl] *n* 半円形 hañeñkei

semicolon [sem'i:koulən] *n* セミコロン semíkoròn

semiconductor [semi:kəndʌk'tə:r] *n* 半導体 hañdōtai

semidetached (house) [semi:ditætʃt'] (*BRIT*) *n* 二戸建て住宅 nikódate jùtaku

semifinal [semi:fai'nəl] *n* 準決勝 juñkesshò

seminar [sem'əna:r] *n* セミナー sémīnà

seminary [sem'əne:ri:] *n* (REL) 神学校 shiñgakkō

semiskilled [semi:skild'] *adj* (work,

worker) 半熟練の hanjukùren no

senate [sen'it] n 上院 jōin

senator [sen'ətə:r] n 上院議員 jōingiìn

send [send] (pt, pp **sent**) vt (dispatch) 送る okúrù; (transmit: signal) 送信する sōshin suru

send away vt (letter, goods) 送る okúrù; (unwelcome visitor) 追払う oíharaù

send away for vt fus 郵便で注文する yūbin dè chūmon suru

send back vt 送り返す okúrikaesù

sender [send'ə:r] n 差出人 sashídashinìn

send for vt fus (thing) 取寄せる toríyoseru; (person) 呼寄せる yobíyoserù

send off vt (goods) 送る okúrù; (BRIT: SPORT: player) 退場させる taíjō saserù

send-off [send'ɔ:f] n: **a good send-off** 素晴らしい送別 subárashiì sōbetsu

send out vt (invitation) 送る okúrù; (signal) 発信する hasshín suru

send up vt (price, blood pressure) 上昇させる jōshō saserù; (astronaut) 打上げる uchíagerù; (BRIT: parody) 風刺する fūshi suru

senile [si:'nail] adj 老いぼれた oíboretà, ぼけた bōkèta; (MED) 老人性の rōjinsei no

senior [si:n'jə:r] adj (older) 年上の toshíue no; (on staff: position, officer) 幹部の kánbu no; (of higher rank: partner) 上級の jōkyū no

senior citizen n 老人 rōjin, 高齢者 kōreisha

seniority [si:njo:r'iti:] n (in service) 年功 nénkō

sensation [sensei'ʃən] n (feeling) 感覚 kańkaku; (great success) 大成功 daíseikō

sensational [sensei'ʃənəl] adj (wonderful) 素晴らしい subárashiì; (causing much interest: headlines) 扇情的な señjōteki na; (: result) センセーショナルな señsēshōnaru na

sense [sens] n (physical) 感覚 kańkaku; (feeling: of guilt, shame etc) 感じ kanji; (good sense) 常識 jōshiki; (meaning: of word, phrase etc) 意味 ímì

♦vt (become aware of) 感じる kanjirù

it makes sense (can be understood) 意味が分かる ímì ga wakáru; (is sensible) 賢明だ keńmei dà

sense of humor ユーモアを解する心 yūmòa wo kaí surù kokórð, ユーモアのセンス yūmòa no sénsu

senseless [sens'lis] adj (pointless: murder) 無意味な muími na; (unconscious) 気絶した kizétsu shitá

sensible [sen'səbəl] adj (person) 利口な rikō na; (reasonable: price, advice) 合理的な gōriteki na; (: decision, suggestion) 賢明な keńmei na

sensitive [sen'sətiv] adj (understanding) 理解のある ríkai no árù; (nerve, skin) 敏感な bíñkan na; (instrument) 高感度の kōkando no; (fig: touchy: person) 怒りっぽい okórippòi; (: issue) 際どい kiwádoì

sensitivity [sensitiv'əti:] n (understanding) 理解 ríkai; (responsiveness: to touch etc) 敏感さ bíñkansa; (: of instrument) 感度 káñdo; (touchiness: of person) 怒りっぽさ okóripposà; (delicate nature: of issue etc) 際どさ kiwádosà

sensual [sen'ʃu:əl] adj (of the senses: rhythm etc) 官能的な kańnōteki na; (relating to sexual pleasures) 肉感的な nikkánteki na

sensuous [sen'ʃu:əs] adj (lips, material etc) 官能的な kańnōteki na

sent [sent] pt, pp of **send**

sentence [sen'təns] n (LING) 文 búñ; (LAW) 宣告 señkoku

♦vt: *to sentence someone to death/5 years in prison* ...に死刑〔懲役5年〕の判決を言渡す ...ni shikéi〔chōeki gonèn〕nò hańketsu wò iíwatasù

sentiment [sen'təmənt] n (tender feelings) 感情 kañjō; (opinion, also pl) 意見 íkèn

sentimental [sentəmen'təl] adj (song) 感傷的な kańshōteki na, センチメンタルな seńchimeñtaru na; (person) 情にもろい jō nì moróì

sentry [sen'tri:] n 番兵 bañpei

separate [adj sep'rit vb sep'əreit] adj (distinct: piles, occasions, ways, rooms) 別々の betsúbetsu no

♦*vt* (split up: people, things) 分ける wakérù; (make a distinction between: twins) 見分ける miwákerù; (: ideas etc) 区別する kubétsu suru

♦*vi* (split up, move apart) 分かれる wakárerù

separately [sep'ritli:] *adv* 別々に betsúbetsu ni

separates [sep'rits] *npl* (clothes) セパレーツ separētsu

separation [sepərei'ʃən] *n* (being apart) 分離 bunri; (time spent apart) 別れ別れ になっている期間 wakárewakáre ni natté irú kikáñ; (LAW) 別居 bekkyó

September [septem'bə:r] *n* 9月 kúgatsu

septic [sep'tik] *adj* (wound, finger etc) 感染した kañsen shita

septic tank *n* 浄化槽 jókasò

sequel [si:'kwəl] *n* (follow-up) 後日談 gojítsudàn; (of film, story) 続編 zokúhen

sequence [si:'kwins] *n* (ordered chain) 連続 reñzoku; (also: **dance sequence, film sequence**) 一場面 ichíbamèn, シークエンス shíkueñsu

sequin [si:'kwin] *n* シークイン shíkuìn, スパンコール supáñkòru

serene [səri:n'] *adj* (smile, expression etc) 穏やかな odáyàka na

serenity [səren'iti:] *n* 穏やかさ odáyàkasa

sergeant [sɑːr'dʒənt] *n* (MIL etc) 軍曹 gúñsò; (POLICE) 巡査部長 juñsabùchò

serial [si:r'i:əl] *n* 連続物 reñzokumono

serialize [si:r'i:əlaiz] *vt* (in newspaper, magazine) 連載する reñsai suru; (on radio, TV) 連続物として放送する reñzokumono toshitè hósò suru

serial number *n* 製造番号 seízōbañgò

series [si:r'i:z] *n inv* (group) 一連 ichíren; (of books, TV programs) シリーズ shiri̥zù

serious [si:r'i:əs] *adj* (person, manner) 真剣な shiñken na; (important: matter) 大事な daíji na; (grave: illness, condition) 重い omóì

seriously [si:r'i:əsli:] *adv* (talk, take) 真剣に shiñken ni; (hurt) ひどく hídòku

seriousness [si:r'i:əsnis] *n* (of person,

manner) 真剣さ shiñkensa; (importance) 重大さ júdaisa; (gravity) 重さ omósa

sermon [sə:r'mən] *n* (also *fig*) 説教 sekkyó

serrated [se:rei'tid] *adj* (edge, knife) の こぎり状の nokógirijō no

serum [si:r'əm] *n* 血清 kesséi

servant [sə:r'vənt] *n* (gen) 召使い meshítsukài; (*fig*) 人に仕える物 hitó nì tsukáerù monó

serve [sə:rv] *vt* (gen: company, country) 仕える tsukáerù; (in shop: goods) 売る urú; (: customer) ...の用をうかがう ...no yó wò ukágaù; (subj: train) ...の足になる ...no ashí nì naru; (apprenticeship) 務める tsutómerù

♦*vi* (at table) 給仕する kyúji suru; (TENNIS) サーブする sábu suru; (be useful):

to serve as/for ...として役に立つ ...toshíte yakú ni tatsù

♦*n* (TENNIS) サーブ sábu

to serve to do ...をするのに役に立つ ...wo suru nò ni yakú ni tatsù

it serves him right 自業自得だ jigójitòku da

to serve a prison term 服役する fukúeki suru

serve out/up *vt* (food) 出す dásù

service [sə:r'vis] *n* (gen: help) 役に立つ事 yakú ni tatsù koto; (in hotel) サービス sábisu; (REL) 式 shikí; (AUT) 整備 seíbi; (TENNIS) サーブ sábu; (plates, dishes etc) 一そろい hitósoroì; (also: **train service**) 鉄道の便 tetsúdō nò bén; (also: **plane service**) 空の便 sórà no bén

♦*vt* (car, washing machine) 整備する seíbi suru

military/national service 兵役 heíeki

to be of service to someone ...に役に立つ ...ni yakú ni tatsù

serviceable [sə:r'visəbəl] *adj* 役に立つ yakú ni tatsù

service area *n* (on motorway) サービス エリア sábisu erìa

service charge (*BRIT*) *n* サービス料 sábisuryò

serviceman [sə:r'vismæn] (*pl* **servicemen**) *n* (MIL) 軍人 guñjin

Services [sər'visiz] *npl*: *the Services* (army, navy etc) 軍隊 gúntai

service station *n* ガソリンスタンド gasórinsutàndo; (*BRIT*: on motorway) サービスエリア sábisu erìa

serviette [sər'vi:et'] (*BRIT*) *n* 紙ナプキン kamínapùkin

servile [sər'vail] *adj* (person, obedience) おもねる様な omóneru yō na

session [sef'ən] *n* (period of activity: recording/drinking session) ...するために集まる事 ...surú tame nì atsúmaru kotð

to be in session (court) 開廷中である kaíteichū de arù; (Parliament etc) 開会中である kaíkaichū de arù

set [set] *n* (collection of things) 一そろい hitósoroì, 一式 isshíki, セット séttð; (radio set) ラジオ rájìo; (TV set) テレビ térèbi; (TENNIS) セット séttð; (group of people) 連中 reńchù; (MATH) セット séttð; (CINEMA, THEATER) 舞台装置 butáisòchi, セット séttð; (HAIRDRESSING) セット séttð

◆*adj* (fixed: rules, routine) 決りの kimári no; (ready) 用意ができた yōì ga dekíta

◆*vb* (*pt, pp* set)

◆*vt* (place) 置く ðkù; (fix, establish: time, price, rules etc) 決める kimérù; (: record) 作る tsukúrù; (adjust: alarm, watch) セットする séttð suru; (impose: task) 命ずる meízurù; (: exam) 作る tsukúrù

◆*vi* (sun) 沈む shizúmù; (jam, jelly, concrete) 固まる katámarù; (broken bone) 治る nåðru

to set the table 食卓の用意をする shokútaku nð yōì wo suru

to be set on doing something どうしても...をすると決めている dōshite mo ... wo suru tð kiméte irù

to set to music ...に曲を付ける ...ni kyokú wð tsukérù

to set on fire ...に火を付ける ...ni hí wð tsukérù

to set free 放してやる hanáshite yarù, 自由にする jiyú ni surù

to set something going ...を始めさせる

...wo hajímesaserù

to set sail 出航する shukkố suru

set about *vt fus* (task) 始める hajímerù

set aside *vt* (money etc) 取って置く tótte oku; (time) 空けておく akéte okù

set back *vt* (cost): *to set someone back $5* 5ドル払わなければならない go dórù haráwànakereba naránaì; (in time): *to set someone back (by)* ...を (...) 遅らせる ...wo (...) okúraserù

setback [set'bæk] *n* (hitch) 苦難 kúnàn

set menu *n* 定食メニュー teíshokumenyū

set off *vi* 出発する shuppátsu suru

◆*vt* (bomb) 爆発させる bakúhatsu saserù; (alarm) 鳴らす narásù; (chain of events) ...の引金となる ...no hikígane to narù; (show up well: jewels) 引立たせる hikítataserù

set out *vi* (depart) 出発する shuppátsu suru

◆*vt* (arrange: goods etc) 並べて置く narábete okù; (state: arguments) 述べる nobérù

to set out to do something ...をするつもりである ...wo suru tsumori de arù

settee [seti:'] *n* ソファー sófà

setting [set'iŋ] *n* (background) 背景 haíkei; (position: of controls) セット séttð; (of jewel) はめ込み台 hamékomidài

the setting of the sun 日没 nichíbotsu

settle [set'əl] *vt* (argument, matter) ...に決着を付ける ...ni ketcháku wð tsukérù; (accounts) 清算する seísan suru; (MED: calm: person) 落着かせる ochítsukaserù

◆*vi* (*also*: **settle down**) 一カ所に落着く ikkáshò ni ochítsukù; (bird) 降りる orírù; (dust etc) つく tsukú; (calm down: children) 静まる shizúmarù

to settle for something ...で我慢する ...de gámàn suru

to settle on something ...に決める ...ni kimérù

settle in *vi* 新しい所に落着く atárashiî tokórò ni ochítsukù

settle up *vi*: *to settle up with someone* ...に借金を返す ...ni shakkín wo káèsu

settlement [set'əlmənt] n (payment) 清算 seísan; (agreement) 和解 wakái; (village etc) 集落 shúraku

settler [set'lə:r] n 入植者 nyúshokushà

set up vt (organization) 設立する setsúritsu suru

setup [set'ʌp] n (organization) 機構 kikó; (situation) 様子 yósu, 状況 jókyō

seven [sev'ən] num 七(の) nánà (no), 七つ(の) nanátsù (no)

seventeen [sev'əntiːn'] num 十七(の) júnanà (no)

seventh [sev'ənθ] num 第七(の) dái nanà (no)

seventy [sev'əntiː] num 七十(の) nanájù (no)

sever [sev'ə:r] vt (artery, pipe) 切断する setsúdan suru; (relations) 切る kírù, 断つ tátsù

several [sev'ə:rəl] adj (things) 幾つかの íkùtsu ka no; (people) 幾人かの íkùnin ka no

◆pron 幾つか íkùtsu ka
several of us 私たちの中から幾人か watákushitàchi no nákà kara íkùnin ka

severance [sev'ə:rəns] n (of relations) 断交 dańkō

severance pay n 退職金 taíshokukìn

severe [sivir'] adj (serious: pain) 激しい hageshíì; (: damage) 大きな ókì na; (: shortage) 深刻な shiñkoku na; (hard: winter, climate) 厳しい kibíshiì; (stern) 厳格な geńkaku na; (plain: dress) 簡素な kánso na

severity [siver'iti:] n (seriousness: of pain) 激しさ hageshisa; (: of damage) 大きさ ókisa; (: of shortage) 深刻さ shiñkokusa; (bitterness: of winter, climate) 厳しさ kibíshisa; (sternness) 厳格さ geńkakusa; (plainness: of dress) 簡素さ kánsosa

sew [sou] (pt **sewed**, pp **sewn**) vt 縫う núù

sewage [suː'idʒ] n (waste) 汚水 osúì

sewer [suː'ə:r] n 下水道 gesúìdō

sewing [sou'iŋ] n (activity) 裁縫 saíhō; (items being sewn) 縫物 nuímono

sewing machine n ミシン míshìn

sewn [soun] pp of **sew**

sew up vt (item of clothing) 縫い合せる nuíawaserù

sex [seks] n (gender) 性別 seíbetsu; (lovemaking) セックス sékkùsu
to have sex with someone ...とセックスをする ...to sékkùsu wo suru

sexist [seks'ist] adj 性差別の seísabètsu no

sextet [sekstet'] n (group) セクステット sekúsutettò

sexual [sek'ʃuəl] adj (of the sexes: reproduction) 有性の yúsei no; (: equality) 男女の dáñjo no; (of sex: attraction) 性的な seíteki na; (: relationship) 肉体の nikútai no

sexy [sek'si:] adj (pictures, underwear etc) セクシーな sékùshī na

shabby [ʃæb'i:] adj (person, clothes) 見すぼらしい misúborashiì; (trick, treatment) 卑劣な hirétsu na

shack [ʃæk] n バラック barákkù

shackles [ʃæk'əlz] npl (on foot) 足かせ ashíkasè; (on hands) 手かせ tékàse; (fig) 束縛 sokúbaku

shade [ʃeid] n (shelter) 日陰 hikáge; (also: **lampshade**) ランプのかさ ráñpu no kásà; (of colour) 色合 iróaì; (small quantity): *a shade too large* ちょっと大き過ぎる chottó ōkisugirù
◆vt (shelter) ...の日よけになる ...no hiyóke ni narù; (eyes) ...に手をかざす ...ni té wò kazásù
in the shade 日陰に hikáge ni
a shade more もうちょっと mó chottò

shadow [ʃæd'ou] n 影 kágè
◆vt (follow) 尾行する bikó suru

shadow cabinet (BRIT) n (POL) 影の内閣 kágè no naíkaku

shadowy [ʃæd'oui:] adj (in shadow) 影の多い kágè no óì; (dim: figure, shape) 影の様な kágè no yó nà

shady [ʃei'di:] adj (place) 日陰のある hikáge no arù; (trees) 日よけになる hiyóke ni narù; (fig: dishonest: person, deal) いかがわしい ikágawashiì

shaft [ʃæft] n (of arrow) 矢柄 yagára; (of spear) 柄 e; (AUT, TECH) 回転軸 kaíteñjiku, シャフト sháfùto; (of mine) 縦坑 ta-

tēkō; (of elevator) 通路 tsúrŏ
a shaft of light 一条の光 ichíjō no
hikarī

shaggy [ʃægˈiː] *adj* (appearance, beard,
dog) ぼさぼさの bosábosa no

shake [ʃeik] (*pt* **shook**, *pp* **shaken**) *vt*
(*gen*) 揺すぶる yusúburù; (bottle) 振る fú-
rù; (cocktail) シェイクする shéìkù suru;
(building) 揺るがす yurúgasù; (weaken:
beliefs, resolve) ぐらつかせる gurátsu-
kaserù; (upset, surprise) ...にショックを
与える ...ni shókkù wo atáerù
♦*vi* (tremble) 震える furúerù
to shake one's head (in refusal, dismay) 頭を振る atáma wò fúrù
to shake hands with someone ...と握
手をする ...to ákushu wo suru

shaken [ʃeiˈkən] *pp* of **shake**

shake off *vt* (lit) 振り落す furíotosù;
(*fig*: pursuer) まく makú

shake up *vt* (lit: ingredients) よく振る
yókù furu; (*fig*: organization) 一新する
isshín suru

shaky [ʃeiˈkiː] *adj* (hand, voice) 震える furúerù; (table, building) ぐらぐらする gú-
ragura suru

shall [ʃæl] *aux vb*: *I shall go* 行きます
ikímasù
shall I open the door? ドアを開けま
しょうか dőà wo akémashō ka
I'll get some, shall I? 少し取ってきま
しょうか sukóshì totté kimashō ka

shallow [ʃælˈou] *adj* (water, box, breathing) 浅い asáì; (*fig*: ideas etc) 浅薄な señpaku na

sham [ʃæm] *n* いんちき íñchiki
♦*vt* ...の振りをする ...no furí wò suru

shambles [ʃæmˈbəlz] *n* 大混乱 daíkoñran

shame [ʃeim] *n* (embarrassment) 恥 hají;
(disgrace) 不面目 fuméñboku
♦*vt* 辱める hazúkashimerù
it is a shame that ... ...であるのは残
念だ ...de árù no wa zañneñ da
it is a shame to do ... ...するのはもっ
たいない ...surú no wà mottáinaì
what a shame! 残念だ zañneñ da

shamefaced [ʃeimˈfeist] *adj* 恥ずかしそ
うな hazúkashisŏ na

shameful [ʃeimˈfəl] *adj* (disgraceful) 恥
ずべき hazúbeki

shameless [ʃeimˈlis] *adj* (liar, deception)
恥知らずの hajíshirazù no

shampoo [ʃæmpuːˈ] *n* シャンプー sháñpū
♦*vt* シャンプーする sháñpū suru
shampoo and set シャンプーとセット
sháñpū to séttő

shamrock [ʃæmˈrɑːk] *n* ツメクサ tsumé-
kusa, クローバー kurőbā

shandy [ʃænˈdiː] *n* シャンディー sháñdī ◇
ビールをレモネードで割った飲物 bíru
wo remőnĕdo de wattá nomimonŏ

shan't [ʃænt] = **shall not**

shanty town [ʃænˈtiː-] *n* バラック集落
barákkushūraku

shape [ʃeip] *n* (form, outline) 形 katáchi
♦*vt* (fashion, form) 形作る katáchizuku-
rù; (someone's ideas, life) 方向付ける hő-
kōzukerù
to take shape (painting) 段々格好がつ
く dañdañ kakkő ga tsukù; (plan) 具体化
してくる gutáika shite kurù

-shaped [ʃeipt] *suffix*: *heart-shaped* ハ
ート形の hátògata no

shapeless [ʃeipˈlis] *adj* 不格好な bukákkō na

shapely [ʃeipˈliː] *adj* (woman, legs) 美し
い utsúkushiì

shape up *vi* (events) 具体化してくる gutáika shite kurù; (person) 期待通りに進
歩する kitáidŏri ni shiñpo suru

share [ʃeːr] *n* (part received) 分け前 wa-
kémaè; (part contributed) 持分 mochíbun,
負担分 futáñbun; (COMM) 株 kabú
♦*vt* (books, toys, room) 共用する kyőyō
suru; (cost) 分担する buñtan suru; (one's
lunch) 分けてやる wakéte yarù; (have in
common: features, qualities etc) ...の点
で似ている ...no tén de nité irù

shareholder [ʃeːrˈhouldəːr] *n* 株主 kabú-
nùshi

share out *vi* 分配する buñpai suru

shark [ʃɑːrk] *n* サメ samé

sharp [ʃɑːrp] *adj* (razor, knife) よく切れ
る yókù kirérù; (point, teeth) 鋭い surúdoì; (nose, chin) とがった togátta; (outline) くっきりした kukkíri shità; (pain)

鋭い surúdoì; (cold) 身を切る様な mí wò kírù yō na; (taste) 舌を刺す様な sásù yō na; (MUS) ピッチが高過ぎる pítchì ga takásugirù; (contrast) 強い tsuyóì; (increase) 急な kyú na; (voice) 甲高い kańdakaì; (person: quick-witted) 抜け目のない nukéme no naì; (dishonest: practice etc) 不正な fuséi na

◆n (MUS) えい音記号 eíonkigò, シャープ shápù

◆adv (precisely): **at 2 o'clock sharp** 2時きっかりに nííì kikkárì ni

sharpen [ʃɑːr'pən] vt (stick etc) とがらせる togáraserù; (pencil) 削る kezúrù; (fig: appetite) そそる sosórù

sharpener [ʃɑːr'pənəːr] n (also: **pencil sharpener**) 鉛筆削り eńpitsukezùri

sharp-eyed [ʃɑːrp'aid] adj 目の鋭い mé nò surudoì

sharply [ʃɑːrp'liː] adv (turn, stop) 急にkyú ni; (stand out) くっきりと kukkírì to; (contrast) 強く tsuyókù; (criticize, retort) 辛らつに shińratsu ni

shatter [ʃæt'əːr] vt (break) 割る warú, 木っ端みじんにする kóppàmijin ni suru; (fig: ruin) 台無しにする daínashi ni surù; (: upset) がっくりさせる gakkúrì sasérù

◆vi (break) 割れる warérù

shave [ʃeiv] vt (person, face, legs etc) そる sórù

◆vi ひげをそる higé wò sórù

◆n: **to have a shave** (at barber's) ひげをそってもらう higé wò sóttè moráù; (oneself) ひげをそる higé wò sórù

shaver [ʃei'vəːr] n (also: **electric shaver**) 電気かみそり deńkikamisori

shaving [ʃei'viŋ] n (action) ひげをそる事 higé wò sórù kotó

shaving brush n シェービングブラシ shēbinguburàshi

shaving cream, shaving foam n シェービングクリーム shēbingukurímu

shavings [ʃei'viŋz] npl (of wood etc) かんなくず kańnakuzù

shawl [ʃɔːl] n 肩掛 katákàke, ショール shōrù

she [ʃiː] pron 彼女は〔が〕 kánòjo wa 〔ga〕

sheaf [ʃiːf] (npl **sheaves**) n (of corn, papers)

束 tábà

shear [ʃiːr] (pt **sheared**, pp **shorn**) vt (sheep) ...の毛を刈る ...no kế wò karú

shear off vi 折れる orérù

shears [ʃiːrz] npl (for hedge) はさみ hasámi

sheath [ʃiːθ] n (of knife) さや sáyà; (contraceptive) コンドーム końdōmu, スキン sukíñ

sheaves [ʃiːvz] npl of **sheaf**

she-cat [ʃiː'kæt] n 雌ネコ mesúneko

shed [ʃed] n 小屋 koyá

◆vt (pt, pp **shed**) (leaves, fur, hair etc) 落す otósù; (skin) 脱皮する dappí suru; (tears) 流す nagásù

to shed blood 人を殺す hitó wò korósù

to shed a load (subj: truck etc) 荷崩れを起す nikúzure wo okósù

she'd [ʃiːd] = **she had**; **she would**

sheen [ʃiːn] n つや tsuyá

sheep [ʃiːp] n inv ヒツジ hitsúji

sheepdog [ʃiːp'dɔːg] n 牧用犬 bokúyōken

sheepish [ʃiː'piʃ] adj 恥ずかしそうな hazúkashisò na

sheepskin [ʃiː'pskin] n ヒツジの毛皮 hitsúji nò kegáwa, シープスキン shīpusukiñ

sheer [ʃiːr] adj (utter) 全くの mattáku no; (steep) 垂直の suíchoku no; (almost transparent) ごく薄手の gokú usúde no

◆adv (straight up: rise) 垂直に suíchoku ni

sheet [ʃiːt] n (on bed) シーツ shítsù; (of paper, glass, metal) 一枚 ichímaì

a sheet of ice アイスバーン aísubàn

sheik(h) [ʃiːk] n 首長 shuchó

shelf [ʃelf] (pl **shelves**) n 棚 taná

shell [ʃel] n (on beach) 貝殻 kaígara; (of egg, nut etc) 殻 kará; (explosive) 弾丸 dańgan; (of building) 外壁 sotókabe

◆vt (peas) むく múkù; (MIL: fire on) 砲撃する hốgeki suru

she'll [ʃiːl] = **she will**; **she shall**

shellfish [ʃel'fiʃ] n inv (crab) カニ kaní; (prawn, shrimp etc) エビ ebí; (lobster) ロブスター robúsùtā; (scallop, clam etc) 貝 kái ◇料理用語として殻のある海の生物を指す ryốriyōgo toshite kará no arù úmi no séibutsu wo sásù

shelter [ʃel'tər] n (building) シェルター
shérùtā; (protection: for hiding) 隠れ場
所 kakúrebashò; (: from rain) 雨宿りの
場所 amáyàdori no bashó
♦vt (protect) 守る mamórù; (give lodging to: homeless, refugees) ...に避難の場
所を提供する ...ni hínan no bashó wò
teíkyō surù; (: wanted man) かくまう
kakúmaù
♦vi (from rain etc) 雨宿りをする amáyàdori wo surù; (from danger) 避難する
hínan suru; (hide) 隠れる kakúrerù

sheltered [ʃel'tərd] adj (life) 世間の荒波
から守られた sékèn no aránami karà
mamóraretà; (spot) 雨風を避けられる á-
mèkaze wo sakérarerù
sheltered housing 老人・身障者用住宅
rójìn, shínshōshayō jùtaku

shelve [ʃelv] vt (fig: plan) 棚上げにする
taná-age ni surù

shelves [ʃelvz] npl of shelf

shepherd [ʃep'ərd] n ヒツジ飼い hitsúji-
kài
♦vt (guide) 案内する afinai suru

shepherd's pie (BRIT) n シェパードパ
イ shepádopaì ◇ひき肉にマッシュポテト
を乗せて焼いた料理 hikíniku nì masshú-
potèto wo noséte yaità ryòri

sheriff [ʃer'if] (US) n 保安官 hoáñkan

sherry [ʃer'i:] n シェリー酒 sheríshù

she's [ʃi:z] = she is; she has

Shetland [ʃet'lənd] n (also: the Shet-
lands, the Shetland Isles) シェットラン
ド諸島 shettórando shotò

shield [ʃi:ld] n (MIL) 盾 tátè; (SPORT:
trophy) 盾型トロフィー tatégata toròfī;
(protection) ...よけ ...yokè
♦vt: to shield (from) ...の(...)よけにな
る ...no (...) yokè ni narù

shift [ʃift] n (change) 変更 heñkō; (work-
period) 交替 kótai; (group of workers) 交
替組 kótaigùmi
♦vt (move) ...の位置を変える ...no íchì
wo kaérù; (remove: stain) 抜く nukú
♦vi (move: wind, person) 変る kawárù

shiftless [ʃift'lis] adj (person) ろくでなし
の rokúdenashi no

shift work n 交替でする作業 kótai de
suru sagyò

shifty [ʃif'ti:] adj (person, eyes) うさん臭
い usáñkusaì

shilling [ʃil'iŋ] (BRIT) n シリング shírìn-
gu ◇かつての英国の硬貨でポンドの1/20
kátsùte no eíkoku no kòka de póñdo no
nijùbun no ichí

shilly-shally [ʃil'i:ʃæli:] vi ぐずぐずする
gúzùguzu suru

shimmer [ʃim'ər] vi ちらちら光る chíra-
chira hikárù

shin [ʃin] n 向こうずね mukózune

shine [ʃain] n つや tsuyá
♦vb (pt, pp shone)
♦vi (sun) 照る térù; (torch, light, eyes) 光
る hikárù; (fig: person) 優れる sugúrerù
♦vt (glasses) ふく fukú; (shoes) 磨く mi-
gákù
to shine a torch on something ...を懐
中電燈で照す ...wo kaíchūdeñtō de terásù

shingle [ʃiŋ'gəl] n (on beach) 砂利 jarí

shingles [ʃiŋ'gəlz] n (MED) 帯状ヘルペス
taíjōherupèsu

shiny [ʃai'ni:] adj (coin) ぴかぴかの piká-
pika no; (shoes, hair, lipstick) つやつや
の tsuyátsuya no

ship [ʃip] n 船 fúnè
♦vt (transport by ship) 船で運ぶ fúnè de
hakóbù; (send: goods) 輸送する yusó suru

shipbuilding [ʃip'bildiŋ] n 造船 zósen

shipment [ʃip'mənt] n (goods) 輸送貨物
yusókamòtsu

shipper [ʃip'ər] n 送り主 okúrinùshi

shipping [ʃip'iŋ] n (transport of cargo)
運送 uñsō; (ships collectively) 船舶 séñ-
paku

shipshape [ʃip'ʃeip] adj きちんとした kichíñ to shita

shipwreck [ʃip'rek] n (event) 難破 nañpa; (ship) 難破船 nañpasen
♦vt: to be shipwrecked 難破する nañpa
suru

shipyard [ʃip'jɑːrd] n 造船所 zósenjo

shire [ʃaiəːr] (BRIT) n 郡 gúñ

shirk [ʃəːrk] vt (work, obligations) 怠る

okótarù

shirt [ʃəːrt] n (man's) ワイシャツ waíshatsu; (woman's) シャツブラウス shatsúburaùsu

in (one's) shirt sleeves 上着を脱いで uwági wo núide

shit [ʃit] (*inf!*) excl くそっ kusót

shiver [ʃívːəːr] n (act of shivering) 身震い mibúrui

♦vi 震える furúerù

shoal [ʃoul] n (of fish) 群れ muré; (*fig: also:* **shoals**) 大勢 ōzeì

shock [ʃɑːk] n (start, impact) 衝撃 shógeki; (ELEC) 感電 kańden; (emotional) 打撃 dagéki, ショック shókkù; (MED) ショック shókkù

♦vt (upset, offend) ...にショックを与える ...ni shókkù wo atáerù

shock absorber n 緩衝器 kańshōkì

shocking [ʃɑːkʲiŋ] adj (awful: standards, accident) ひどい hidóì; (outrageous: play, book) 衝撃的な shógekiteki na

shod [ʃɑːd] pt, pp of **shoe**

shoddy [ʃɑːdʲiː] adj (goods, workmanship) 粗雑な sozátsu na

shoe [ʃuː] n (for person) 靴 kutsú; (for horse) てい鉄 teítetsu

♦vt (pt, pp **shod**) (horse) ...にてい鉄を付ける ...ni teítetsu wò tsukérù

shoebrush [ʃuːˈbrʌʃ] n 靴ブラシ kutsúburàshi

shoelace [ʃuːˈleis] n 靴ひも kutsúhìmo

shoe polish n 靴磨き kutsúmigàki

shoeshop [ʃuːˈʃɑːp] n 靴屋 kutsúyà

shoestring [ʃuːˈstriŋ] n (*fig*): *on a shoestring* わずかの金で wázùka no kané de

shone [ʃoun] pt, pp of **shine**

shoo [ʃuː] excl しっ shítt ◇動物を追っ払う時に言う言葉 dóbutsu wò oíharaù toki ni iú kotoba

shook [ʃuk] pt of **shake**

shoot [ʃuːt] n (on branch, seedling) 若枝 wakáèda

♦vb (pt, pp **shot**)

♦vt (gun) 撃つ útsù; (arrow) 射る írù; (kill: bird, robber etc) 撃ち殺す uchíkorosù; (wound) そ撃する sogéki suru; (execute) 銃殺する júsatsu suru; (film) 撮

影する satsúei suru

♦vi (with gun/bow): *to shoot (at)* (...を目掛けて) 撃つ〔射る〕 (...wo megákete) útsù 〔írù〕; (SOCCER) シュートする shúto suru

shoot down vt (plane) 撃ち落とす uchíotosù

shoot in/out vi (rush) 飛込む〔飛出す〕 tobíkomù 〔tobídasù〕

shooting [ʃuːˈtiŋ] n (shots) 発砲事件 happójikèn; (HUNTING) 狩猟 shuryō

shooting star n 流れ星 nagárebòshi

shoot up vi (*fig*) 急上昇する kyújōshō suru

shop [ʃɑːp] n (selling goods) 店 misé; (*also:* **workshop**) 作業場 sagyóbà

♦vi (*also:* **go shopping**) 買物する kaímono suru

shop assistant (*BRIT*) n 店員 teń-in

shop floor (*BRIT*) n 労働側 ródōgawa

shopkeeper [ʃɑːpˈkiːpəːr] n 店主 ténshu

shoplifting [ʃɑːpˈliftiŋ] n 万引 mańbiki

shopper [ʃɑːpˈəːr] n (person) 買物客 kaímonokyàku

shopping [ʃɑːpˈiŋ] n (goods) 買物 kaímono

shopping bag n ショッピングバッグ shoppíngubaggù

shopping center (*BRIT* **shopping centre**) n ショッピングセンター shoppíngusentà

shop-soiled [ʃɑːpˈsɔild] adj (goods) 棚ざらしの tanázaràshi no

shop steward (*BRIT*) n (INDUSTRY) 職場代表 shokúbadaihyō

shop window n ショーウインドー shóuiñdò

shore [ʃɔːr] n 岸 kishí

♦vt: *to shore up* 補強する hokyó suru

on shore 陸に rikú ni

shorn [ʃɔːrn] pp of **shear**

short [ʃɔːrt] adj (not long) 短い mijíkaì; (person: not tall) 背の低い sé nò hikúì; (curt) ぶっきらぼうな bukkírabô na; (insufficient) 不足している fusóku shite irù

to be short of something ...が不足している ...ga fusóku shite irù

in short 要するに yó surù ni

short of doing ... ...をしなければ ...wo shinákerèba

it is short for それは...の短縮形です soré wà ... no tañshukukei desu

to cut short (speech, visit) 予定より短くする yotéi yorì mijíkakù suru

everything short of ... ...を除いて何でも ...wo nozóìte náñ de mo

to fall short of ...に達しない ...ni tasshínaì

to run short of ...が足りなくなる ...ga tarínakunarù

to stop short (while walking etc) 急に立止まる kyǘ ni tachidomarù; (while doing something) 急にやめる kyǘ ni yamerù

to stop short of ...まではしない ...mádè wa shináì

shortage [ʃɔːr'tidʒ] *n*: *a shortage of* ...不足 ...busóku

shortbread [ʃɔːr'bred] *n* ショートブレッド shótobureddò ◇小麦粉，バター，砂糖で作った菓子 komúgiko, bátà, satő dè tsukútta kashì

short-change [ʃɔːrt'tʃeindʒ] *vt* ...に釣銭を少なく渡す ...ni tsurísen wò sukúnakù watásù

short-circuit [ʃɔːrtsəːr'kit] *n* (ELEC) ショート shóto

shortcoming [ʃɔːrt'kʌmiŋ] *n* 欠点 kettéñ

short(crust) pastry [ʃɔːrt'(krʌst)-](*BRIT*) *n* パイ生地 páikijì

shortcut [ʃɔːrt'kʌt] *n* 近道 chikámichi

shorten [ʃɔːr'tən] *vt* (clothes, visit) 短くする mijíkakù suru

shortfall [ʃɔːrt'fɔːl] *n* 不足 fusóku

shorthand [ʃɔːrt'hænd] *n* 速記 sokkí

shorthand typist (*BRIT*) *n* 速記もできるタイピスト sokkí mo dekirù taípisùto

shortlist [ʃɔːrt'list] (*BRIT*) *n* (for job) 予備審査の合格者リスト yobíshiǹsa no gőkakusha risùto

short-lived [ʃɔːrt'livd'] *adj* つかの間の tsuká no ma no

shortly [ʃɔːrt'liː] *adv* 間もなく ma mő nàku

shorts [ʃɔːrts] *npl*: *(a pair of) shorts* (short trousers) 半ズボン hañzùbon;

(men's underwear) パンツ páñtsu

short-sighted [ʃɔːrt'sai'tid] (*BRIT*) *adj* 近眼の kíñgan no; (*fig*) 先見の明のない señken no meí no nai

short-staffed [ʃɔːrt'stæft'] *adj*: *to be short-staffed* 人手不足である hitódebùsoku de aru

short story *n* 短編小説 tañpenshősetsu

short-tempered [ʃɔːrt'tempəːrd] *adj* 短気な táñki na

short-term [ʃɔːrt'təːrm] *adj* (effect, borrowing) 短期の táñki no

shortwave [ʃɔːrt'weiv'] *n* (RADIO) 短波 táñpa

shot [ʃɑːt] *pt, pp of* **shoot**
◆*n* (of gun) 発砲 happő; (try, *also* SOCCER etc) シュート shúto; (injection) 注射 chúsha; (PHOT) ショット shóttò

a good/poor shot (person) 射撃のうまい〔下手な〕人 shagéki no umaì〔hetá na〕hitő

like a shot (without any delay) 鉄砲玉の様に teppődama no yő ni

shotgun [ʃɑːt'gʌn] *n* 散弾銃 sañdañjū

should [ʃud] *aux vb*: *I should go now* もうおいとましなくては wa mő o-ítoma shinakute wà

he should be there now 彼は今あそこにいるはずです kárè wa ímà asőko nì irú hazù desu

I should go if I were you 私だったら，行きますよ watákushi dattàra, ikímasu yő

I should like to ... ...をしたいと思いますが ...wo shitái tò omóimasù ga

shoulder [ʃoul'dəːr] *n* (ANAT) 肩 kátà
◆*vt* (*fig*: responsibility, blame) 負う őù

shoulder bag *n* ショルダーバッグ shorúdābaggù

shoulder blade *n* 肩甲骨 keñkőkotsu

shoulder strap *n* ショルダーストラップ shorúdasutorappù

shouldn't [ʃud'ənt] = **should not**

shout [ʃaut] *n* 叫び声 sakébigoè
◆*vt* 大声で言う őgoè de iú
◆*vi* (*also*: **shout out**) 叫ぶ sakébù

shout down *vt* (speaker) どなって黙らせる donáttè damáraserù

shouting [ʃaut'iŋ] n 叫び声 sakébigoè

shove [ʃʌv] vt 押す osú; (inf: put): **to shove something in** …を …に 押込む …wo …ni oshíkomù

shovel [ʃʌv'əl] n (gen) スコップ sukóppù, シャベル shábèru; (mechanical) パワーシャベル pawáshabèru

♦vt (snow) かく kákù; (coal, earth) すくう sukúù

shove off vi: **shove off!** (inf) うせろ usérò

show [ʃou] n (demonstration: of emotion) 表現 hyógen; (semblance) 見せ掛け misékake; (exhibition: flower show etc) 展示会 teńjikài, ショー shó; (THEATER, TV) ショー shó

♦vb (pt showed, pp shown)

♦vt (indicate) 示す shimésù, 見せる misérù; (exhibit) 展示する teńji suru; (courage etc) 示す shimésù; (illustrate, depict) 描写する byósha suru; (film: in movie theater) 上映する jóei suru; (program, film: on television) 放送する hósō suru

♦vi (be evident) 見える miérù; (appear) 現れる aráwarerù

for show 格好だけの kakkó dake no

on show (exhibits etc) 展示中 teńjichū

show business n 芸能界 geínōkai

showdown [ʃou'daun] n 対決 taíketsu

shower [ʃau'əːr] n (of rain) にわか雨 niwákaamè; (of stones etc) …の雨 …no ámè; (for bathing in) シャワー sháwà

♦vi 降ってくる futté kurù

♦vt: **to shower someone with** …の上に …を降らす …no ué nì …wo furásù

to have a shower シャワーを浴びる sháwà wo abírù

showerproof [ʃau'əːrpruːf] adj 防水の bósui no ◇にわか雨程度なら耐えられるが強い雨にはぬれてしまうコートなどについて言う niwákaamè téído nara taérarerù ga tsuyói amè ni wa nuréteshimau kòto nado ni tsúìte iú

show in vt (person) 中へ案内する nákà e añnai suru

showing [ʃou'iŋ] n (of film) 上映 jóei

show jumping [-dʒʌmp'iŋ] n (of horses) 障害飛越 shógaihietsu

shown [ʃoun] pp of **show**

show off vi (pej) 気取る kidóru

♦vt (display) 見せびらかす misébirakasù

show-off [ʃou'ɔːf] (inf) n (person) 自慢屋 jimán-yà

show out vt (person) 出口へ案内する déguchi e añnaì suru

showpiece [ʃou'piːs] n (of exhibition etc) 立派な見本 rippá nà mihón

showroom [ʃou'ruːm] n ショールーム shórūmu

show up vi (stand out) 目立つ medátsù; (inf: turn up) 現れる aráwarerù

♦vt (uncover: imperfections etc) 暴露する bákùro suru

shrank [ʃræŋk] pt of **shrink**

shrapnel [ʃræp'nəl] n 弾丸の破片 dañgan nò hahén

shred [ʃred] n (gen pl) 切れ端 kiréhashi

♦vt (gen) ずたずたにする zutázuta ni surù; (CULIN) 刻む kizámù

shredder [ʃred'əːr] n (vegetable shredder) 削り器 kezúrikì; (document shredder) シュレッダー shuréddà

shrewd [ʃruːd] adj (businessman) 抜け目のない nukéme no naì; (assessment) 賢明な keńmei na

shriek [ʃriːk] n 金切り声 kanákirigoè

♦vi 金切り声を出す kanákirigoè wo dásù

shrill [ʃril] adj (cry, voice) 甲高い kańdakaì

shrimp [ʃrimp] n (shellfish) えび ebí

shrine [ʃrain] n (place of worship) 礼拝堂 reíhaidō; (for relics) 聖遺物容器 seíbutsuyòki; (fig: building) 殿堂 deńdō; (: place) 聖地 seíchi

shrink [ʃriŋk] (pt shrank, pp shrunk) vi (cloth) 縮む chijímù; (be reduced: profits, audiences) 減る herú; (move: also: **shrink away**) 縮こまって逃げる chijíkomattè nigérù

♦vt (cloth) 縮める chijímerù

♦n (inf: pej: psychiatrist) 精神科医 seíshinka-ì

to shrink from (doing) something …を(するのを)いやがる …wo (surú no wò) iyágarù

shrinkage [ʃriŋk'idʒ] n 縮まる分 chijímarù bún

shrinkwrap [ʃriŋk'ræp] vt ラップで包む ráppù de tsutsúmù

shrivel [ʃriv'əl] (also: **shrivel up**) vt しおれさせる shióresaserù
♦vi しおれる shiórerù

shroud [ʃraud] n 覆い ói
♦vt: **shrouded in mystery** なぞに包まれて nazó nì tsutsúmaretè

Shrove Tuesday [ʃrouv-] n 謝肉祭の火曜日 shaníkusài no kayóbi

shrub [ʃrʌb] n 低木 teíboku

shrubbery [ʃrʌb'əːri:] n 植込み uékomi

shrug [ʃrʌg] n 肩をすくめる事 kátà wo sukúmerù kotó
♦vt, vi: **to shrug (one's shoulders)** 肩をすくめる kátà wo sukúmerù

shrug off vt (criticism) 受流す ukénagasù; (illness) 無視する múshì suru

shrunk [ʃrʌŋk] pp of **shrink**

shudder [ʃʌd'əːr] n 身震い mibúrùi
♦vi (person: with fear, revulsion) 身震いする mibúrùi suru

shuffle [ʃʌf'əl] vt (cards) 混ぜる mazérù
♦vi (walk) 足を引きずって歩く ashí wò hikízutte arukù

to shuffle (one's feet) (while standing, sitting) 足をもぞもぞ動かす ashí wò mózòmozo ugókasù

shun [ʃʌn] vt (publicity, neighbors etc) 避ける sakérù

shunt [ʃʌnt] vt (train) 分岐線に入れる buńkisen ni irerù; (object) 動かす ugókasù

shut [ʃʌt] (pt, pp **shut**) vt (door) 閉める shimérù; (shop) しまう shimáù; (mouth, eyes) 閉じる tojírù
♦vi (door, eyes, shop) 閉る shimárù

shut down vt (for a time) 休業させる kyúgyo saserù; (forever) 閉鎖する heísa suru
♦vi (for a time) 休業する kyúgyo surù; (forever) 閉鎖になる heísa ni narù

shut off vt (supply etc) 遮断する shadán suru

shutter [ʃʌt'əːr] n (on window: also PHOT) シャッター sháttà

shuttle [ʃʌt'əl] n (plane etc) シャトル

shátoru; (also: **space shuttle**) スペースシャトル supésushatoru; (also: **shuttle service**) 折り返し運転 oríkaeshi uñten

shuttlecock [ʃʌt'əlka:k] n シャトルコック shattórukokkù

shut up vi (inf: keep quiet) 黙る damáru
♦vt (close) しまう shimau; (silence) 黙らせる damáraseru

shy [ʃai] adj (timid: animal) 臆病な okúbyo na; (reserved) 内気な uchíki na

shyness [ʃai'nis] n (timidity: of animal) 臆病 okúbyò; (reservedness) 内気 uchíki

Siamese [saiəmi:z'] adj: **Siamese cat** シャムネコ shamúneko

Siberia [saibi:'ri:ə] n シベリア shibéria

sibling [sib'liŋ] n 兄弟 kyódai ◇男兄弟にも女兄弟 (姉妹) にも使う otókokyòdai ni mo ońnakyòdai (shímài) ni mo tsukáù

Sicily [sis'ili:] n シチリア shichíria

sick [sik] adj (ill) 病気の byóki no; (nauseated) むかついた mukátsuita; (humor) 病的な byóteki na; (vomiting): **to be sick** 吐く hákù

to feel sick むかつく mukátsukù

to be sick of (fig) ...にうんざりしている ...ni uñzari shite irù

sick bay n (on ship) 医務室 imúshìtsu

sicken [sik'ən] vt むかつかせる mukátsukaserù

sickening [sik'əniŋ] adj (fig) 不快な fukái na

sickle [sik'əl] n かま kámà

sick leave n 病気休暇 byókikyùka

sickly [sik'li:] adj (child, plant) 病気がちな byókigachi na; (causing nausea: smell) むかつかせる mukátsukaserù

sickness [sik'nis] n (illness) 病気 byóki; (vomiting) おう吐 ôto

sick pay n 病気手当 byókiteàte

side [said] n (of object) 横 yokó; (of body) 脇腹 wakíbara; (of lake) 岸 kishí; (aspect) 側面 sokúmen; (team) 側 gawá
♦adj (door, entrance) 横の yokó no
♦vi: **to side with someone** ...の肩を持つ ...no kátà wo mótsù

the side of the road 路肩 rokáta

the side of a hill 山腹 sańpuku

by the side of ...の横に ...no yokó ni

side by side 横に並んで yokó ni naraǹde

from side to side 左右に sáyǔ ni

from all sides 四方八方から shihóhappō kara

to take sides (with) (...に)味方する (...ni) mikáta suru

sideboard [said'bɔːrd] *n* 食器戸棚 shokkítódana、サイドボード saídobōdo

sideboards [said'bɔːrdz] (*BRIT*) *npl* = **sideburns**

sideburns [said'bəːrnz] *npl* もみあげ momíage

side drum *n* (MUS) 小太鼓 kodáiko

side effect *n* (MED, *fig*) 副作用 fukúsayō

sidelight [said'lait] *n* (AUT) 車幅灯 shafúkutō

sideline [said'lain] *n* (SPORT) サイドライン saídoraìn; (*fig*: supplementary job) 副業 fukúgyō

sidelong [said'lɔːŋ] *adj*: *to give someone/something a sidelong glance* ...を横目で見る ...wo yokóme de mirù

sidesaddle [said'sædəl] *adv*: *to ride sidesaddle* 馬に横乗りする umá nì yokónori surù

side show *n* (stall at fair, circus) 見世物屋台 misémonoyatài

sidestep [said'step] *vt* (*fig*) 避けて通る sakétetòru

side street *n* わき道 wakímichi

sidetrack [said'træk] *vt* (*fig*) ...の話を脱線させる ...no hanáshi wò dassén saserù

sidewalk [said'wɔːk] (*US*) *n* 歩道 hodō

sideways [said'weiz] *adv* (go in) 横向きに yokómuki ni; (lean) 横へ yokó e

siding [sai'diŋ] *n* (RAIL) 側線 sokúsen

sidle [sai'dəl] *vi*: *to sidle up (to)* (...に)こっそり近寄る (...ni) kossórì chikáyorù

siege [siːdʒ] *n* (*gen*, MIL) 包囲 hóī

siesta [siːes'tə] *n* 昼寝 hirúne

sieve [siv] *n* ふるい furúi

♦*vt* ふるう furúu

sift [sift] *vt* (*fig*: *also*: **sift through**: information) ふるい分ける furúiwakerù; (sieve) ふるう furúu

sigh [sai] *n* ため息 taméikì

♦*vi* ため息をつく taméikì wo tsukú

sight [sait] *n* (faculty) 視覚 shikáku; (spectacle) 光景 kókei; (on gun) 照準器 shójunki

♦*vt* 見掛ける mikákerù

in sight 見える所に miérù tokóro ni

on sight (shoot) 見付け次第 mitsúkeshidài

out of sight 見えない所に miénaì tokóro ni

sightseeing [sait'siːiŋ] *n* 名所見物 meíshokeǹbutsu

to go sightseeing 名所見物に行く meíshokeǹbutsu ni ikú

sign [sain] *n* (with hand) 合図 aízu; (indication: of present condition) しるし shirúshi; (: of future condition) 兆し kizáshi; (notice) 看板 kaǹban; (written) 張紙 harígami

♦*vt* (document) ...に署名〔サイン〕する ...ni shoméi 〔sáìn〕 suru; (player) 雇う yatóù

to sign something over to someone ...を...に譲渡する ...wo...ni jốtò suru

signal [sig'nəl] *n* (*gen*) 信号 shingō; (equipment on highway, railway) 信号機 shingốki

♦*vi* (make signs: *also* AUT) 合図をする aízu wo suru

♦*vt* (person) ...に合図をする ...ni aízu wo suru; (message) ...する様に合図をする ...suru yō ni aizu wo suru

signalman [sig'nəlmən] (*pl* **signalmen**) *n* (RAIL) 信号手 shingốshu

signature [sig'nətʃəːr] *n* 署名 shoméi、サイン sáìn

signature tune *n* テーマ音楽 tếmaoǹgaku

signet ring [sig'nit-] *n* 印章指輪 iǹshōyubiwà

significance [signif'əkəns] *n* (importance) 重要性 jũyōsei

significant [signif'ikənt] *adj* (full of meaning: look, smile) 意味深い imíbukài; (important: amount, discovery) 重要な jũyō na

signify [sig'nəfai] *vt* 意味する ímì suru

sign language *n* 手話 shūwà

sign on vi (MIL) 入隊する nyū́tai surù; (BRIT: as unemployed) 失業手当を請求する shitsúgyōteàte wo seíkyū suru; (for course) 受講手続をする jukótetsuzùki wo suru

♦vt (MIL: recruits) 入隊させる nyū́tai saserù; (employee) 雇う yatóù

signpost [sain'poust] n 案内標識 aññai-hyōshiki

sign up vi (MIL) 入隊する nyū́tai suru; (for course) 受講手続をする jukótetsuzùki wo suru

silence [sai'ləns] n (of person) 沈黙 chímoku; (of place) 静けさ shizúkesà

♦vt (person, opposition) 黙らせる damáraserù

silencer [sai'lənsə:r] n (on gun) 消音器 shóoñki, サイレンサー saíreñsā; (BRIT: AUT) 消音器 shóoñki, マフラー máfūrā

silent [sai'lənt] adj (person) 黙っているdamátte irù; (place) しんとした shiñtó shitá; (machine) 音のない otó no naì; (film) 無声の muséi no

to remain silent 黙っている damátte irù

silent prayer 黙とう mokútō

silent partner n (COMM) 出資者 shusshísha ◇資本金の一部を出すが、業務に直接関与しない社員について言う shihóñkin no ichíbù wo dásù ga, gyómu ni chokúsetsu kañyo shináī shá-ìn ni tsuite iú

silhouette [silu:et'] n シルエット shírùetto

silicon chip [sil'ikən-] n シリコンチップ shfrikonchippù

silk [silk] n 絹 kínù

♦adj (scarf, shirt) 絹の kínù no

silky [sil'ki:] adj (material, skin) 絹の様な kínù no yố nà

silly [sil'i:] adj (person, idea) ばかな bákà na

silo [sai'lou] n (on farm, for missile) サイロ saíro

silt [silt] n (in harbor, river etc) 沈泥 chíñdei

silver [sil'və:r] n (metal) 銀 gíñ; (coins) 硬貨 kốkà; (items made of silver) 銀製品 giñseíhin

♦adj (color) 銀色の gíñ-iro no; (made of silver) 銀の gíñ no

silver paper (BRIT) n 銀紙 gíñgami

silver-plated [sil'və:rplei'tid] adj 銀めっきの giñmekkī no

silversmith [sil'və:rsmiθ] n 銀細工師 giñzaikushī

silvery [sil'və:ri:] adj (like silver) 銀の様な gíñ no yố nà

similar [sim'ələ:r] adj: *similar (to)* (...に)似た (...ni) nitá

similarity [siməlær'iti:] n 似ている事 nité irù kotó

similarly [sim'ələ:rli:] adv 同じ様に onáji yố ni

simile [sim'əli:] n 例え tatóè

simmer [sim'ə:r] vi (CULIN) ぐつぐつ煮える gútsùgutsu niérù

simpering [sim'pə:riŋ] adj (person) ばかみたいな作り笑いをする bákàmitai na tsukúriwarài wo suru

a simpering smile ばかみたいな作り笑い bákàmitai na tsukúriwarài

simple [sim'pəl] adj (easy) 簡単な kañtan na; (plain: dress, life) 素朴な sobóku na, シンプルな shíñpuru na; (foolish) ばかな bákà na; (COMM: interest) 単純な tañjun na

simplicity [simplis'əti:] n (ease) 簡単さ kañtansa; (plainness) 素朴さ sobókusa; (foolishness) 白痴 hakuchi

simplify [sim'pləfai] vt 簡単にする kañtan ni surù

simply [sim'pli:] adv (in a simple way: live) 素朴に sobóku ni; (talk) 平易に héī ni; (just, merely) 単に tán ni

simulate [sim'jəleit] vt (enthusiasm, innocence) 装う yosóoù

simulated [sim'jəleitid] adj (hair, fur) 偽の nisé no, 人工の jinkó no; (nuclear explosion) 模擬の mógí no

simultaneous [saiməltei'ni:əs] adj (translation, broadcast) 同時の dójî no

simultaneously [saiməltei'ni:əsli:] adv 同時に dójì ni

sin [sin] n 罪 tsúmì

♦vi 罪を犯す tsúmì wo okásù

since [sins] *adv* それ以来 soré irài
♦*prep* ...以来 ...írài
♦*conj* (time) ...して以来 ...shité irài;
(because) ...ので ...nódè
since then, ever since それ以来 soré
irài

sincere [sinsi:r'] *adj* 誠実な seíjitsu na

sincerely [sinsi:r'li:] *adv*: *yours sincerely* (in letters) 敬具 keígu

sincerity [sinser'iti:] *n* 誠実さ seíjitsusa

sinew [sin'ju:] *n* (of person, animal) けん
kéñ, 筋 sújì

sinful [sin'fəl] *adj* (thought, person) 罪深
い tsumíbukaì

sing [siŋ] (*pt* **sang**, *pp* **sung**) *vt* 歌う utáù
♦*vi* (gen) 歌う utáù; (bird) 鳴く nakú

Singapore [siŋ'gəpɔ:r] *n* シンガポール
shiñgapòru

singe [sindʒ] *vt* 焦がす kogásù

singer [siŋ'ə:r] *n* 歌手 káshù

singing [siŋ'iŋ] *n* (noise: of people) 歌声
utágoè; (: of birds) 鳴声 nakígoè; (art) 声
楽 seígaku

single [siŋ'gəl] *adj* (individual) 一つ一つ
の hitótsuhitotsù no; (unmarried) 独身の
dokúshin no; (not double) 一つだけの hitótsu dake nò
♦*n* (BRIT: *also*: **single ticket**) 片道乗車
券 katámichijòshakèn; (record) シングル
盤 shiñguruban

single-breasted [siŋ'gəlbres'tid] *adj*
(jacket, suit) シングルの shiñguru no

single file *n*: *in single file* 一列縦隊で
ichíretsujùtai de

single-handed [siŋ'gəlhæn'did] *adv*
(sail, build something) 一人で hitórì de

single-minded [siŋ'gəlmain'did] *adj* 一
つだけの目的を追う hitótsu dake nò mo-
kúteki wò oú

single out *vt* (choose) 選び出す erábidasù; (distinguish) 区別する kúbetsu suru

single room *n* シングル部屋 shiñguru-
beya

singles [siŋ'gəlz] *n* (TENNIS) シングル
ス shiñgurusu

singly [siŋ'gli:] *adv* (alone, one by one:
people) 一人ずつ hitóri zutsu; (: things)
一つずつ hitótsu zutsu

singular [siŋ'gjələ:r] *adj* (odd: occurrence) 変った kawátta; (outstanding:
beauty) 著しい ichíjirushiì; (LING) 単数
の tañsū no
♦*n* (LING) 単数 tañsū

sinister [sin'istə:r] *adj* 怪しげな ayáshigè na

sink [siŋk] *n* 流し nagáshi
♦*vb* (*pt* **sank**, *pp* **sunk**)
♦*vt* (ship) 沈没させる chiñbotsu saserù;
(well, foundations) 掘る hórù
♦*vi* (ship) 沈没する chiñbotsu suru;
(heart, spirits) しょげる shogérù; (ground)
沈下する chíñka suru; (*also*: **sink back**, **sink
down**: into chair) 身を沈める mí wò shizúmerù; (: to one's knees etc) しゃがみ込
む shágamikomù; (: head etc) うなだれる
unádarerù
to sink something into (teeth, claws
etc) ...に...を食込ませる ...ni...wo kuíko-
maserù

sink in *vi* (*fig*: words) 理解される ríkài
sarérù, 身にしみる mí nì shimírù

sinner [sin'ə:r] *n* 罪人 tsumíbito

sinus [sai'nəs] *n* (ANAT) 副鼻こう fukú-
bikò

sip [sip] *n* 一口 hitókuchi
♦*vt* ちびりちびり飲む chibírìchibiri nómù

siphon [sai'fən] *n* サイホン sáihon

siphon off *vt* (liquid) サイホンで汲み出
す sáihon de kumídasù; (money etc) ほか
へ回す hoká è mawásù

sir [sə:r] *n* ◇男性に対する丁寧な呼び掛
け.日本語では表現しない dañsei ni tai
surù teínei na yobíkake. nihóñgo de wa
hyógen shinaì
Sir John Smith ジョン・スミス卿 jóñ
sumísukyò
yes sir はい háì

siren [sai'rən] *n* サイレン sáiren

sirloin [sə:r'lɔin] *n* (*also*: **sirloin steak**)
サーロインステーキ sároinsutèki

sissy [sis'i:] (*inf*) *n* 弱虫 yowámushi

sister [sis'tə:r] *n* (relation: *gen*) 女きょう
だい ofinakyòdai, 姉妹 shímài; (*also*:
older sister) 姉 anê, 姉さん nêèsan; (*also*:

younger sister) 妹 imóto; (nun) 修道女 shūdōjo; (BRIT: nurse) 婦長 fuchō

sister-in-law [sis'tə:rinlɔ:] (pl **sisters-in-law**) n (older) 義理の姉 girí nò ané; (younger) 義理の妹 girí nò imóto

sit [sit] (pt, pp **sat**) vi (sit down) 座る suwáru, 腰掛ける koshíkakerù; (be sitting) 座っている suwátte irù, 腰掛けている koshíkakete irù; (assembly) 会期中である kaíkichū de arù; (for painter) モデルになる móderu ni nárù
♦vt (exam) 受ける ukérù

sitcom [sit'kɑːm] n abbr (= situation comedy) 連続放送コメディー reńzoku hōsōkomèdī

sit down vi 座る suwáru, 腰掛ける koshíkakerù

site [sait] n (place) 場所 bashó; (also: **building site**) 用地 yōchì
♦vt (factory, cruise missiles) 置く ókù

sit-in [sit'in] n (demonstration) 座り込み suwárikomi

sit in on vt fus (meeting) 傍聴する bōchō suru

sitting [sit'iŋ] n (of assembly etc) 開会 kaíkai; (in canteen) 食事の時間 shokúji nò jikan

we have two sittings for lunch 昼食は2交代で出されます chūshoku wà nikōtai de dasáremasù

sitting room n 居間 imá

situated [sitʃ'u:eitid] adj ...にある ...ni árù

situation [sitʃu:ei'ʃən] n (state) 状況 jōkyō; (job) 職 shokú; (location) 立地条件 ritchíjōken

「**situations vacant**」(BRIT) 求人 kyūjin ◇新聞などの求人欄のタイトル shiñbun nadò no kyūjinran no táitoru

sit up vi (after lying) 上体を起す jōtai wò okósù; (straight) きちんと座る kichíñto suwárù; (not go to bed) 起きている ókìte irú

six [siks] num 六 (の) rokú (no), 六つ (の) múttsù (no)

sixteen [siks'ti:n'] num 十六 (の) jūroku (no)

sixth [siksθ] num 第六 (の) dái roku (no)

sixty [siks'ti:] num 六十 (の) rokújū (no)

size [saiz] n (gen) 大きさ ōkisa; (extent: of project etc) 規模 kíbo; (of clothing, shoes) サイズ sáìzu; (glue) サイズ sáìzu ◇紙のにじみ止め kamí nò nijímidome

sizeable [sai'zəbəl] adj (crowd, income etc) かなり大きい kánari ōkìi

size up vt (person, situation) 判断する handan suru

sizzle [siz'əl] vi (sausages etc) じゅうじゅうと音を立てる jūjū to otó wò tatérù

skate [skeit] n (ice skate) スケート sukḕto; (roller skate) ローラースケート rṓrāsukèto; (fish) エイ eí
♦vi スケートをする sukḗto wo suru

skateboard [skeit'bɔːrd] n スケートボード sukḗtobòdo

skater [skei'tə:r] n スケートをする人 sukḗto wo suru hito, スケーター sukḗtā

skating [skei'tiŋ] n (SPORT) スケート sukḗto

skating rink n スケートリンク sukḗtoriñku

skeleton [skel'itən] n (bones) がい骨 gáìkotsu; (TECH: framework) 骨組 honégumi; (outline) 骨子 kósshì

skeleton staff n 最小限度の人員 saíshōgeñdo no jiñ-in

skeptic [skep'tik] (US) n 疑い深い人 utágaibukaì hitó

skeptical [skep'tikəl] (US) adj 疑っている utagátte irù, 信用しない shiñ-yō shinaì

skepticism [skep'tisizəm] (US) n 疑問 gímòn

sketch [sketʃ] n (drawing) スケッチ sukétchì; (outline) 骨子 kósshì; (THEATER, TV) 寸劇 suńgeki, スキット sukíttò
♦vt スケッチする sukétchì suru; (also: **sketch out**: ideas) ...のあらましを言う ...no arámashi wò iú

sketchbook [sketʃ'buk] n スケッチブック sukétchibukkù

sketchy [sketʃ'i:] adj (coverage, notes etc) 大雑把な ōzappà na

skewer [skju:'ə:r] n くし kushí

ski [ski:] n スキー sukī

♦vi スキーをする sukī wo surú

ski boot n スキー靴 sukígùtsu

skid [skid] n (AUT) スリップ suríppù

♦vi (gen, AUT) スリップする suríppu suru

skier [ski:'ə:r] n スキーヤー sukíyà

skiing [ski:'iŋ] n スキー sukī

ski jump n スキージャンプ sukíjànpu

skilful [skil'fəl] (BRIT) adj = **skillful**

ski lift n スキーリフト sukírifùto

skill [skil] n (ability, dexterity) 熟練 jukúren; (work requiring training: computer skill etc) 技術 gíjùtsu

skilled [skild] adj (able) 上手な jōzu na; (worker) 熟練の jukúren no

skillful [skil'fəl] (BRIT: skilful) adj 上手な jōzu na

skim [skim] vt (milk) ...の上澄みをすくい取る ...no uwázumi wò sukúitorù; (glide over) ...すれすれに飛ぶ ...surésure nì tobú

♦vi: **to skim through** (book) ...をざっと読む ...wo záttő yómù

skimmed milk [skimd-] n 脱脂乳 dasshínyù

skimp [skimp] vt (also: **skimp on**: work) いいかげんにする iíkagen nì suru; (: cloth etc) けちる kechírù

skimpy [skim'pi:] adj (meager: meal) 少な過ぎる sukúnasugirù; (too small: skirt) 短過ぎる mijíkasugirù

skin [skin] n (gen: of person, animal) 皮膚 hífù; (: of fruit) 皮 kawá; (complexion) 顔の肌 kaó nò hádà

♦vt (fruit etc) ...の皮をむく ...no kawá wò múkù; (animal) ...の皮を剝ぐ ...no kawá wò hágù

skin-deep [skin'di:p'] adj (superficial) 表面だけの hyṓmen daké no

skin-diving [skin'daiviŋ] n スキンダイビング sukíndaìbingu

skinny [skin'i:] adj (person) やせた yasétà

skintight [skin'tait] adj (jeans etc) 体にぴったりの karáda nì pittárì no

skip [skip] n (movement) スキップ sukíppù; (BRIT: container) ごみ箱 gomíbàko

♦vi (jump) スキップする sukíppù suru; (with rope) 縄跳びする nawátobi suru

♦vt (pass over: boring parts) とばす tobásù; (miss: lunch) 抜く nukú; (: lecture) すっぽかす suppókasù

ski pants npl スキーズボン sukízubòn

ski pole n スキーストック sukísutokkù

skipper [skip'ə:r] n (NAUT) 船長 senchō; (SPORT) 主将 shushō, キャプテン kyápùten

skipping rope [skip'iŋ-] (BRIT) n 縄跳びの縄 nawátobi nò nawá

skirmish [skə:r'miʃ] n (also MIL) こぜりあい kozérìai

skirt [skə:rt] n スカート sukátò

♦vt (fig: go round) 避けて通る sákète tórù

skirting board [skə:r'tiŋ-] (BRIT) n 幅木 habáki

ski slope n ゲレンデ gerénde

ski suit n スキー服 sukífùku

skit [skit] n スキット sukíttò

skittle [skit'əl] n スキットルのピン sukíttòru no pín

skittles [skit'əlz] n (game) スキットル sukíttòru ◇9本のピンを木のボールで倒すボーリングに似た遊び kyúhòn no pín wo kí no bṓru de taosu bṓringu ni nita asobi

skive [skaiv] (BRIT: inf) vi サボる sabórù

skulk [skʌlk] vi うろつく urótsukù

skull [skʌl] n (ANAT) 頭がい骨 zugáikotsu

skunk [skʌŋk] n (animal) スカンク sukánku

sky [skai] n 空 sórà

skylight [skai'lait] n 天窓 teñmado

skyscraper [skai'skreipə:r] n 摩天楼 maténrō

slab [slæb] n (stone) 石板 sekíban; (of cake, cheese) 厚い一切れ atsúi hitokìre

slack [slæk] adj (loose: rope, trousers etc) たるんでいる tarúnde irù; (slow: period) 忙しくない isógashikunaì; (careless: security, discipline) いい加減な iíkagen na

slacken [slæk'ən] (also: **slacken off**) vi

(demand) 減る herú; (speed) 落ちる ochírù

♦vt (trousers) 緩める yurúmerù; (speed) 緩める yurúmerù, 落す otósù

slacks [slæks] npl ズボン zubón, スラックス surákkùsu

slag heap [slæg-] n ぼた山 botáyama

slag off (BRIT: inf) vt (criticize) ...の悪口を言う ...no warúgùchi wo iú

slain [slein] pp of slay

slalom [slɑ́:ləm] n 回転競技 kaítenkyồgi, スラローム surárồmu

slam [slæm] vt (door) ばたんと閉める batán to shimérù; (throw) 投付ける nagétsukerù; (criticize) 非難する hínàn suru

♦vi (door) ばたんと閉まる batán to shimárù

slander [slǽndəːr] n 中傷 chúshō

slang [slæŋ] n (informal language) 俗語 zokúgo, スラング suráŋgu; (jargon: prison slang etc) 符丁 fuchố

slant [slænt] n (sloping: position) 傾斜 keísha; (fig: approach) 見方 mikáta

slanted [slǽntid] adj (roof) 傾斜のある keísha no arù; (eyes) つり上った tsuríshagattà

slanting [slǽntiŋ] adj = slanted

slap [slæp] n (hit) 平手打ち hiráteuchi, びんた bíntà

♦vt (child, face) ぴしゃりと打つ pishárì to útsù

♦adv (directly) まともに matómo nì

to slap something on something (paint etc) ...を...にいい加減に塗り付ける ...wo ...ni iíkagen nì nurítsukerù

slapdash [slǽpdæʃ] adj (person, work) いい加減な iíkagen na

slapstick [slǽpstik] n (comedy) どたばた喜劇 dotábata kigèki

slap-up [slǽpʌp] adj: **a slap-up meal** (BRIT) 御馳走 gochísō

slash [slæʃ] vt (cut: upholstery, wrists etc) 切る kírù ◇特に長くて深い切傷を付けるという意味で使う tókù ni nágàkute fukáì kiríkizu wo tsukérù to iú imì de tsukáù; (fig: prices) 下げる sagérù

slat [slæt] n (of wood, plastic) 板 ítà ◇百葉箱に使われる様な薄くて細い板を指す

hyakúyōbàko ni tsukáwareru yò na usúkùte hosóì ítà wo sásù

slate [sleit] n (material) 粘板岩 neñbañgan; (piece: for roof) スレート surétò

♦vt (fig: criticize) けなす kenásù

slaughter [slɔ́ːtəːr] n (of animals) と殺 tosátsu; (of people) 虐殺 gyakúsatsu

♦vt (animals) と殺する tosátsu suru; (people) 虐殺する gyakúsatsu suru

slaughterhouse [slɔ́ːtəːrhaus] n と殺場 tosátsujō

Slav [slɑːv] adj スラブ民族の surábumiñzoku no

slave [sleiv] n 奴隷 doréi

♦vi (also: **slave away**) あくせく働く ákùseku határakù

slavery [sléivəːri:] n (system) 奴隷制度 doréiseìdo; (condition) 奴隷の身分 doréi no mībùn

slavish [sléiviʃ] adj (obedience) 卑屈な hikútsu na; (copy) 盲目的な mốmokuteki na

slay [slei] (pt slew, pp slain) vt 殺す korósù

sleazy [slíːziː] adj (place) 薄汚い usúgitanaì

sledge [sledʒ] n そり sórì

sledgehammer [sledʒhæməːr] n 大づち ổzùchi

sleek [sliːk] adj (shiny, smooth: hair, fur etc) つやつやの tsuyátsuyà no; (car, boat etc) 優雅な yúga na

sleep [sliːp] n 睡眠 suímin

♦vi (pt, pp slept) (gen) 眠る nemúrù, 寝る nerú; (spend night) 泊る tomárù

to go to sleep (person) 眠る nemúrù, 寝る neru

sleep around vi 色々な人とセックスをする iróiro na hito tò sékkùsu wo suru

sleeper [slíːpəːr] n (BRIT: RAIL: on track) まくら木 makúragi; (: train) 寝台列車 shiñdairesshà

sleep in vi (oversleep) 寝坊する nebố suru

sleeping bag [slíːpiŋ-] n 寝袋 nebúkùro

sleeping car n (RAIL) 寝台車 shiñdaishà

sleeping partner (BRIT) n (COMM)

= **silent partner**

sleeping pill n 睡眠薬 suímiñ-yaku

sleepless [sliːpˈlis] adj: *a sleepless night* 眠れない夜 nemúrenai yorù

sleepwalker [sliːpˈwɔːkəːr] n 夢遊病者 muyúbyòshà

sleepy [sliːˈpiː] adj (person) 眠い nemúi; (fig: village etc) ひっそりとした hissórì to shita

sleet [sliːt] n みぞれ mizóre

sleeve [sliːv] n (of jacket etc) そで sodé; (of record) ジャケット jáketto

sleeveless [sliːvˈlis] adj (garment) そでなしの sodénashi no, スリーブレスの suríburèsu no

sleigh [slei] n そり sórì

sleight [slait] n: *sleight of hand* 奇術 kíjutsu

slender [slenˈdəːr] adj (slim: figure) ほっそりした hossórì shita, スリムな súrìmu na; (small: means, majority) わずかな wázùka na

slept [slept] pt, pp of **sleep**

slew [sluː] vi (BRIT) = **slue**

♦pt of **slay**

slice [slais] n (of meat, bread, lemon) スライス suráìsu; (utensil: fish slice) フライ返し furáigaèshi; (: cake slice) ケーキサーバー kékisàbā

♦vt (bread, meat etc) スライスする suráìsu suru

slick [slik] adj (skillful: performance) 鮮やかな azáyàka na; (clever: salesman, answer) 抜け目のない nukéme no naì

♦n (also: **oil slick**) 油膜 yumáku

slid [slid] pt, pp of **slide**

slide [slaid] n (downward movement) 下落 geráku; (in playground) 滑り台 subéridài; (PHOT) スライド suráìdo; (BRIT: also: **hair slide**) 髪留 kamídòme, ヘアクリップ heákurìppu

♦vb (pt, pp **slid**)

♦vt 滑らせる subéraserù

♦vi (slip) 滑る subérù; (glide) 滑る様に動く subéru yỏ ni ugókù

slide rule n 計算尺 keísanjaku

sliding [slaiˈdiŋ] adj: *sliding door* 引戸 hikídò

sliding scale n スライド制 suráidosei

slight [slait] adj (slim: figure) やせ型のyaségata no; (frail) か弱い kayówaì; (small: increase, difference) わずかな wázùka na; (error, accent, pain etc) ちょっとした chóttò shita; (trivial) ささいな sásài na

♦n (insult) 侮辱 bujóku

not in the slightest 少しも...ない sukóshì mo ...náì

slightly [slaitˈliː] adv (a bit, rather) 少し sukóshì

slim [slim] adj (person, figure) ほっそりした hossórì shita; (chance) わずかな wázùka na

♦vi (lose weight) やせる yasérù

slime [slaim] n ぬるぬるした物 núrùnuru shita monó

slimming [slimˈiŋ] n (losing weight) そう身 sóshin

slimy [slaiˈmiː] adj (pond) ぬるぬるした物に覆われた núrùnuru shita monó nì ówaretà

sling [sliŋ] n (MED) 三角きん sañkakùkin; (for baby) 子守り帯 komóriòbi; (weapon) 石投げ器 ishínagekì

♦vt (pt, pp **slung**) (throw) 投げる nagérù

slip [slip] n (while walking) 踏み外し fumíhazushi; (of vehicle) スリップ suríppù; (mistake) 過ち ayámachì; (underskirt) スリップ suríppù; (also: **slip of paper**) 一枚の紙 ichímài no kamí ◇通常メモ用紙, 伝票などの様な小さい紙を指す tsújô memoyòshi, deñpyô nadò no yỏ nà chíìsaì kamí wò sásù

♦vt (slide) こっそり...を...にやる kossóri ...wo ...ni yarú

♦vi (slide) 滑る subérù; (lose balance) 踏外す fumíhazusù; (decline) 悪くなる wárùku nárù; (move smoothly): *to slip into/out of* (room etc) そっと入る〔出て行く〕sóttò háìru 〔détè iku〕

to give someone the slip ...をまく ...wo mákù

a slip of the tongue うっかり言ってしまう事 ukkárì itté shimaù kotó

to slip something on/off さっと...を着る〔脱ぐ〕sáttò ...wo kírù 〔nugu〕

slip away *vi* (go) そっと立ち去る sóttò tachísaru

slip in *vt* (put) こっそり入れる kossórì irérù

♦*vi* (errors) いつの間にか入ってしまう ítsu no ma ni kà haítte shimaù

slip out *vi* (go out) そっと出て行く sóttò détè ikú

slipped disc [slipt-] *n* つい間板ヘルニア tsuíkañbanherunìa

slipper [slip'əɪr] *n* (carpet slipper) スリッパ suríppà

slippery [slip'əːriː] *adj* (road) 滑りやすい subériyasuì; (fish etc) つかみにくい tsukáminikuì

slip road (*BRIT*) *n* (on motorway: access road) 入路 nyúro; (: exit road) 出口 deguchi

slipshod [slip'ʃɑːd] *adj* いい加減な iíkagen na

slip up *vi* (make mistake) 間違いをする machígai wò suru

slip-up [slip'ʌp] *n* (error) 間違い machígaì

slipway [slip'wei] *n* 造船台 zósendài

slit [slit] *n* (cut) スリット suríttò; (opening) すき間 sukíma

♦*vt* (*pt, pp* slit) 切り開く kiríhirakù

slither [sliðʾəːr] *vi* (person) 足を取られながら歩く ashí wò torárenagara arukù; (snake etc) はう háu

sliver [sliv'əːr] *n* (of glass, wood) 破片 hahéñ; (of cheese etc) 一切れ hitókìre

slob [slɑːb] (*inf*) *n* (man) だらしない野郎 daráshinai yaró; (woman) だらしないあま daráshinai áma

slog [slɑːg] (*BRIT*) *vi* (work hard) あくせく働く ákùseku határakù

♦*n*: **it was a hard slog** 苦労した kuró shita

slogan [slou'gən] *n* スローガン surógàn

slop [slɑːp] *vi* (*also*: **slop over**) こぼれる kobórerù

♦*vt* こぼす kobósù

slope [sloup] *n* (gentle hill) 坂道 sakámìchi; (side of mountain) 山腹 sañpuku; (ski slope) ゲレンデ geréñde; (slant) 傾斜 keísha

♦*vi*: **to slope down** 下り坂になる kudárizaka ni narù

slope up *vi* 上り坂になる nobórizaka ni narù

sloping [slou'piŋ] *adj* (ground, roof) 傾斜になっている keísha ni natte irù; (handwriting) 斜めの nanáme no

sloppy [slɑːp'iː] *adj* (work, appearance) だらしない daráshinai

slot [slɑːt] *n* (in machine) 投入口 tónyūguchi, スロット suróttò

♦*vt*: **to slot something into ...** (のスロットに)...を入れる ... (no suróttò nado) ni ...wo irérù

sloth [slɔːθ] *n* (laziness) 怠惰 táìda

slot machine *n* (*BRIT*: vending machine) 自動販売機 jidóhanbaikì; (for gambling) スロットマシーン suróttomashìn

slouch [slautʃ] *vi* (person) だらしない姿勢で...する daráshinaì shisei dè ... suru

slovenly [slʌv'ənliː] *adj* (dirty: habits, conditions) 汚い kitánaì; (careless: piece of work) だらしない daráshinaì

slow [slou] *adj* (music, journey) ゆっくりした yukkúrì shita; (service) 遅い osóì, のろい noróì; (person: not clever) 物覚えの悪い monóobðe no warúì; (watch, clock): **to be slow** 遅れている okúrete irù

♦*adv* ゆっくりと yukkúrì to, 遅く osókù

♦*vt* (*also*: **slow down, slow up**: vehicle) ...のスピードを落す ...no supído wo otósù; (: business etc) 低迷させる teímei saserù

♦*vi* (*also*: **slow down, slow up**: vehicle) スピードを落す supído wo otósù; (: business etc) 下火になる shitábi nì narù

「**slow**」 (road sign) 徐行 jokó

slowly [slou'liː] *adv* ゆっくりと yukkúrì to, 遅く osókù

slow motion *n*: **in slow motion** スローモーションで surómòshon de

sludge [slʌdʒ] *n* (mud) へどろ hedóro

slue [sluː] (*US* veer) *vi* スリップする suríppù suru

slug [slʌg] *n* (creature) なめくじ namékujì; (bullet) 弾丸 dáñgan, 鉄砲玉 teppódama

sluggish [slʌgˈiʃ] *adj* (stream, engine, person) 緩慢な kańman na; (COMM: trading) 不活発な fukáppatsu na

sluice [sluːs] *n* (*also*: **sluicegate**) 水門 suímon; (channel) 水路 suíro

slum [slʌm] *n* (house) 汚い家 kitánaì ié; (area) 貧民街 hińmiǹgai, スラム súramu

slump [slʌmp] *n* (economic) 不景気 fukéiki; (COMM) スランプ suráňpu
♦*vi* (fall: person) 崩れ落ちる kuzúreochirù; (: prices) 暴落する bóraku suru

slung [slʌŋ] *pt*, *pp* *of* **sling**

slur [sləːr] *n* (*fig*): **slur (on)** (...の)悪口 (...no) warúkùchi
♦*vt* (words) 口ごもって言う kuchígomottě iú

slush [slʌʃ] *n* (melted snow) 溶けかかった雪 tokékakattà yukí

slush fund *n* 裏金用資金 uráganeyōshikiǹ

slut [slʌt] (*inf!*) *n* ぱいた baíta

sly [slai] *adj* (smile, expression, remark) 意味ありげな imífarige na; (person: clever, wily) ずるい zurúì

smack [smæk] *n* (slap) 平手打ち hiráteuchi; (on face) びんた bíñta
♦*vt* (hit: man) ぶつ bútsù; (: child) 平手で打つ hiráte de útsù; (: on face) ...にびんたを食らわす ...ni bíñta wo kurawásù
♦*vi*: **to smack of** (smell of) ...くさい ...kusáì; (remind one of) ...を思わせる ...wo omówaserù

small [smɔːl] *adj* (person, object) 小さい chíīsaì; (child: young) 幼い osánaì; (quantity, amount) 少しの sukóshì no

small ads *npl* (*BRIT*) 分類広告 buńruikōkoku

small change *n* 小銭 kozéni

small fry *npl* (unimportant people) 下っ端 shitáppa

smallholder [smɔːlˈhouldəːr] (*BRIT*) *n* 小作農 shójisakunō

small hours *npl*: **in the small hours** 深夜に shíñya ni

smallpox [smɔːlˈpɑːks] *n* 天然痘 teńnentō

small talk *n* 世間話 sekénbanàshi

smart [smɑːrt] *adj* (neat, tidy) きちんとした kichíñ to shitá; (fashionable: clothes etc) しゃれた sharéta, いきな ikí na, スマートな sumátò na; (: house, restaurant) しゃれた shareta, 高級な kōkyū na; (clever) 頭がいい atáma ga iì; (quick) 早い hayáì
♦*vi* しみる shimírù; (*fig*) 悔しがる kuyáshigarù

smarten up [smɑːrˈtən-] *vi* 身なりを直す mínàri wo naósù
♦*vt* きれいにする kírèi ni suru

smash [smæʃ] *n* (collision: *also*: **smash-up**) 衝突 shótotsu; (smash hit) 大ヒット daíhittò
♦*vt* (break) めちゃめちゃに壊す mechámecha ni kowásù; (car etc) 衝突してめちゃめちゃにする shótotsu shitě mechámecha ni surù; (SPORT: record) 破る yabúrù
♦*vi* (break) めちゃめちゃに壊れる mechámecha nì kowárerù; (against wall etc) 激突する gekítotsu suru

smashing [smæʃˈiŋ] (*inf*) *adj* 素晴らしい subárashiì

smattering [smætˈəːriŋ] *n*: **a smattering of** ...をほんの少し ...wo hoñno sukoshì

smear [smiˈəːr] *n* (trace) 染み shimí; (MED) スミア sumía
♦*vt* (spread) 塗る nurú; (make dirty) 汚す yogósù

smear campaign *n* 中傷作戦 chúshōsakuseñ

smell [smel] *n* (odor) におい niói; (sense) 臭覚 kyúkaku
♦*vb* (*pt*, *pp* **smelt** *or* **smelled**)
♦*vt* (become aware of odor) ...のにおいがする ...no nioi ga suru; (sniff) かぐ kagú
♦*vi* (*pej*) におう nióù, 臭い kusáì; (food etc) ...においがする ...nióì ga suru
to smell of ...のにおいがする ...no nióì ga suru

smelly [smelˈiː] *adj* (cheese, socks) 臭い kusáì

smile [smail] *n* ほほえみ hohóemi
♦*vi* ほほえむ hohóemù

smirk [smə:rk] n にやにや笑い niyániya warài

smithy [smiθ'i:] n 鍛冶屋の仕事場 kajíyà no shigótobà

smock [smɑːk] n (gen) 上っ張り uwáppari, (children's) スモック sumókkù; (US: overall) 作業着 sagyṓgì

smog [smɔːg] n スモッグ sumóggù

smoke [smouk] n 煙 kemúri
♦vi (person) タバコを吸う tabáko wò súù; (chimney) 煙を出す kemúri wò dásù
♦vt (cigarettes) 吸う súù

smoked [smoukt] adj (bacon etc) 薫製の kuńsei no; (glass) いぶした ibúshita

smoker [smou'kə:r] n (person) タバコを吸う人 tabáko wò súù hito, 喫煙者 kitsúeñsha; (RAIL) 喫煙車 kitsúeñsha

smokescreen [smouk'skri:n] n (also fig) 煙幕 éñmaku

smoking [smou'kiŋ] n (act) 喫煙 kitsúen
「**no smoking**」(sign) 禁煙 kiń-en

smoky [smou'ki:] adj (atmosphere, room) 煙い kemúî; (taste) 薫製の (様な) kuńsei no (yṓ na)

smolder [smoul'də:r] (US) vi (fire: also fig: anger, hatred) くすぶる kusúburù

smooth [smuːð] adj (gen) 滑らかな naméràka na; (sauce) つぶつぶのない tsubútsubu no naì; (flat: sea) 穏やかな odáyaka na; (flavor, whisky) まろやかな maróyàka na; (movement) 滑らかな naméràka na; (pej: person) 口先のうまい kuchísaki nò umáî
♦vt (also: **smooth out**: skirt, piece of paper etc) ...のしわを伸ばす ...no shiwá wò nobásù; (: creases) 伸ばす nobásù; (: difficulties) 取除く torínozokù

smother [smʌð'ə:r] vt (fire) ...に...をかぶせて消す ...ni ...wo kabúsete kesù; (suffocate: person) 窒息させる chissóku saserù; (repress: emotions) 抑える osáerù

smoulder [smoul'də:r] (BRIT) vi = **smolder**

smudge [smʌdʒ] n 汚れ yogóre
♦vt 汚す yogósù

smug [smʌg] adj 独り善がりの hitóriyogarì no

smuggle [smʌg'əl] vt (diamonds etc) 密

輸する mitsúyu suru; (refugees) 密入国させる mitsúnyūkoku saserù

smuggler [smʌg'lə:r] n 密輸者 mitsúyushà

smuggling [smʌg'liŋ] n (traffic) 密輸 mitsúyu

smutty [smʌt'i:] adj (fig: joke, book) わいせつな waísetsu na

snack [snæk] n (light meal) 軽食 keíshoku; (food) スナック sunákkù

snack bar n スナックバー sunákkubà, スナック sunákkù

snag [snæg] n 障害 shṓgai

snail [sneil] n カタツムリ katátsumùri ◇一般に水生の巻貝をも指す ippán nì suísei nò makígai wo mo sásù

snake [sneik] n (gen) ヘビ hébì

snap [snæp] n (sound) ぱちっという音 pachíttò iú otò; (photograph) 写真 shashín
♦adj (decision etc) 衝動的な shṓdōteki na
♦vt (break) 折る órù; (fingers) 鳴らす narásù
♦vi (break) 折れる orérù; (fig: person: speak sharply) 辛らつな事を言う shiñratsu na kotð wo iú
to snap shut (trap, jaws etc) がちゃっと閉まる gacháttð shimárù

snap at vt fus (subj: dog) かみつこうとする kamítsukð to suru

snap off vi (break) 折れる orérù ◇折れて取れる場合に使う órète torérù baái nì tsukáù

snappy [snæp'i:] (inf) adj (answer, slogan) 威勢のいい iséi no iî
make it snappy (hurry up) 早くしなさい háyàku shinásaî

snapshot [snæp'ʃɑːt] n 写真 shashín

snap up vt (bargains) すぐ買う súgù káù

snare [sne:r] n わな wánà

snarl [snɑːrl] vi (animal) うなる unárù; (person) どなる donárù

snatch [snætʃ] n (small piece: of conversation, song etc) 断片 dañpeñ
♦vt (snatch away: handbag, child etc) ひったくる hittákurù; (fig: opportunity) 利用する riyṓ suru; (: look, some sleep etc)

急いでやる isóide yarù

sneak [sni:k] (*pt, pp* **sneaked** *also US* **snuck**) *vi*: *to sneak in/out* こっそり入る〔出る〕kossórì háiru〔deru〕

♦*n* (*inf*) 告げ口するひと tsugéguchi suru hitò

to sneak up on someone ...に忍び寄る ...ni shinóbiyorù

sneakers [sni:'kə:rz] *npl* 運動靴 uñdōgutsu, スニーカー suníkà

sneer [sni:r] *vi* (laugh nastily) 冷笑する reíshō suru; (mock): *to sneer at* ...をあざわらう ...wo azáwaraù

sneeze [sni:z] *n* くしゃみ kushámì

♦*vi* くしゃみをする kushámì wo suru

sniff [snif] *n* (sound) 鼻をくんくん鳴らす音 haná wò kúñkun narásù otò; (smell: by dog, person) くんくんかぐ事 kúñkun kagú kotò

♦*vi* (person: when crying etc) 鼻をくんくん鳴らす haná wò kúñkun narásù

♦*vt* (*gen*) かぐ kagú; (glue, drugs) 鼻で吸う haná dè súù

snigger [snig'ə:r] *vi* くすくす笑う kúsùkusu waráù

snip [snip] *n* (cut) はさみで切る事 hasámi dè kírù koto; (*BRIT: inf*: bargain) 掘出し物 horídashimonò

♦*vt* (cut) はさみで切る hasámi dè kírù

sniper [snai'pə:r] *n* そ撃兵 sogékihèi

snippet [snip'it] *n* (of information, news) 断片 dañpen

snivelling [sniv'əliŋ] *adj* (whimpering) めそめそ泣く mésòmeso nakú

snob [sna:b] *n* 俗物 zokúbutsu

snobbery [sna:b'ə:ri:] *n* 俗物根性 zokúbutsukoñjō

snobbish [sna:b'iʃ] *adj* 俗物的な zokúbutsuteki na

snooker [snuk'ə:r] *n* ビリヤード biríyàdo

snoop [snu:p] *vi*: *to snoop about* こっそりのぞき回る kossórì nozókimawarù

snooty [snu:'ti:] *adj* (person, letter, reply) 横柄な ōhèi na

snooze [snu:z] *n* 昼寝 hirúne

♦*vi* 昼寝する hirúne suru

snore [snɔ:r] *n* いびき ibíki

♦*vi* いびきをかく ibíki wò kákù

snorkel [snɔ:r'kəl] *n* (for swimming) シュノーケル shunōkèru

snort [snɔ:rt] *n* 鼻を鳴らす事 haná wò narásù koto

♦*vi* (animal, person) 鼻を鳴らす haná wò narásù

snout [snaut] *n* ふん fúñ

snow [snou] *n* 雪 yukí

♦*vi* 雪が降る yukí gà fúrù

snowball [snou'bɔ:l] *n* 雪のつぶて yukí nò tsubúte

♦*vi* (*fig*: problem, campaign) どんどん大きくなる dóñdon ōkiku nárù

snowbound [snou'baund] *adj* (people) 雪に閉じ込められた yukí ni tojíkomerarèta; (vehicles) 雪で立ち往生した yukí dè tachíōjō shita

snowdrift [snou'drift] *n* 雪の吹きだまり yukí nò fukídamarì

snowdrop [snou'dra:p] *n* 雪の花 yukíno-hanà

snowfall [snou'fɔ:l] *n* (amount) 降雪量 kōsetsuryō; (a fall of snow) 降雪 kōsetsu

snowflake [snou'fleik] *n* 雪のひとひら yukí nò hitóhìra

snowman [snou'mæn] (*pl* **snowmen**) *n* 雪だるま yukídaruma

snowplow [snou'plau] (*BRIT* **snowplough**) *n* 除雪車 josétsushà

snowshoe [snou'ʃu:] *n* かんじき kañjiki

snowstorm [snou'stɔ:rm] *n* 吹雪 fúbùki

snub [snʌb] *vt* (person) 鼻であしらう haná dè ashíraù

♦*n* 侮辱 bujóku

snub-nosed [snʌb'nouzd] *adj* 鼻先の反った hanásaki nò sottá

snuck [snʌk] (*US*) *pt, pp of* **sneak**

snuff [snʌf] *n* かぎタバコ kagítabàko

snug [snʌg] *adj* (sheltered: person, place) こじんまりした kojínmarì shita; (person) 心地好い kokóchiyoì; (well-fitting) ぴったりした pittárì shita

snuggle [snʌg'əl] *vi*: *to snuggle up to someone* ...に体を擦付ける ...ni karáda wò surítsukerù

KEYWORD

so [sou] *adv* **1** (thus, likewise) そう số, その通り sonố tồri

so saying he walked away そう言って彼は歩き去った số ittè kárè wa arúki-sattà

while she was so doing, he ... 彼女がそれをやっている間彼は... kánòjo ga sorè wo yattè iru aĭda kárè wa...

if so だとすれば dấ tò suréba

do you enjoy soccer? if so, come to the game フットボールが好きですか、だったら試合を見に来て下さい futtồbồru ga sukí desù ká, dáttàra shiái wồ mi ní kite kudasaì

I didn't do it - you did so! やったのは私じゃない -いや、お前だ yattá no wa watákushi ja naì -iyá, omáe dà

so do I, so am I etc 私もそうです watákushi mồ sồ desù

I like swimming - so do I 私は水泳が好きです -私もそうです watákushi wầ suíei gầ sukí desù -watákushi mồ sồ desù

I'm still at school - so am I 私はまだ学生です -私もそうです watákushi wầ mádầ gakúsei desù -watákushi mồ sồ desù

I've got work to do - so has Paul 私には仕事がありますから -ポールもそうですよ watákushi ni wầ shigótò gầ arímasu karầ -pồru mo sồ desù yồ

it's 5'o'clock - so it is! 5時です -あっ、そうですね gójì desu -át, sồ desù nế

I hope so そう希望します sồ kibồ shimasù

I think so そうだと思います sồ da tồ omóimasù

so far これまで korế mầdè

how do you like the book so far? これまでその本はどうでしたか korế mầdè sonố hoñ wa dồ deshìta ka

so far I haven't had any problems ここまでは問題はありません kokó mầdè wa mofidai wầ arímaseñ

2 (in comparisons etc: to such a degree) そんなに sofina nì

so quickly (that) (...がある程) 素早く (...ga árù hodo) subáyầku, とても素早く (...したので...) totémo subáyầku (...shitá no dè ...)

so big (that) (...がある程) 大きな (...ga árù hodo) ồkina, とても大きい (ので...) totémo ồkii (nố dè ...)

she's not so clever as her brother 彼女は兄さん程利口ではない kánòjo wa niísañ hodo rìkồ de wa naì

we were so worried 私たちはとても心配していましたよ watákushitầchi wa totémo shifipai shite imashìta yồ

I wish you weren't so clumsy あなたの不器用さはどうにかなりませんかね anátà no bukíyồsầ wa dồ nì kà narímasen kầ nế

I'm so glad to see you あなたを見てほっとしました anátà wo mítề hồttồ shi-máshità

3: so much *adv* そんなに沢山で sofina nì takúsañ de

♦*adj* そんなに沢山の sofina nì takúsañ de

I've got so much work 私は仕事が山程あります watákushi wầ shigótò gầ yamá hodồ arímasù

I love you so much あなたを心から愛しています anátà wo kokórồ kara áì shite imasu

so many そんなに沢山 (の) sofina nì takúsañ (no)

there are so many things to do する事が山程あります surú kotồ ga yamá hodồ arímasù

there are so many people to meet 私が会うべき人たちは余りにも大勢です watákushi gầ áùbeki hitótầchi wa amári ni mồ ồzei desù **4** (phrases): *10 or so* 10匹ぐらい júkkồ gurai

so long! (*inf*: goodbye) じゃね já nề, またね matá nề

♦*conj* **1** (expressing purpose): *so as to do* ...する様 [ため] に ...surú yồ [tamề] ni

we hurried so as not to be late 遅れない様に急いで行きました okúrenai yồ ni isồĭde ikímashìta

so (that) ...する様 [ため] に ...surú yồ

〔tamḕ〕ni
I brought it so (that) you could see it あなたに見せるために持ってきました anátā ni misérū tame ni motté kimashíta

2 (expressing result) ...であるから......、...で árū kara ...、...の で...nő dḕ ...

he didn't arrive so I left 彼が来なかったので私は帰りました kárē ga kónàkatta nő de watákushi wà kaérimashìta

so I was right after all 結局私の言った通りでした kekkyőkù watákushi nò ittá tòri deshìta

so you see, I could have gone ですから ね、行こうと思えば行けたんです désù kara né, ikő tò omóebà ikétan desù

---

soak [souk] *vt* (drench) ずぶぬれにする zubúnure nì suru; (steep in water) 水に漬ける mizú nì tsukéru
♦*vi* (dirty washing, dishes) 漬かる tsukárū

soak in *vi* (be absorbed) 染み込む shimíkomù

soak up *vt* (absorb) 吸収する kyūshū surù

soap [soup] *n* 石けん sekkén

soapflakes [soup'fleiks] *npl* フレーク石けん furékusekkèn ◇洗濯用の固形石けんをフレークにした物を指す sentakuyő no kokéisekkèn wo furékù ni shitá monò wo sásù

soap opera *n* メロドラマ meródorama ◇テレビやラジオの連続物を指す térèbi ya rájìo no renzókumonð wo sásù

soap powder *n* 粉石けん konásekkèn

soapy [sou'pi:] *adj* (hands etc) 石けんのついた sekkén no tsuità
soapy water 石けん水 sekkénsui

soar [sɔːr] *vi* (on wings) 舞上がる maíagarù; (rocket) 空中に上がる kűchū nì agárù; (price, production, temperature) 急上昇する kyūjōshō suru; (building etc) そびえたつ sobíetatsù

sob [sɑːb] *n* しゃくり泣き shakúrinaki
♦*vi* 泣きじゃくる nakíjakurù

sober [sou'bəːr] *adj* (serious) まじめな majíme na; (dull: color, style) 地味な ji-

mí na; (not drunk) しらふの shírafu no

sober up *vt* ...の酔いを覚ます ...no yoí wò samásù
♦*vi* 酔いが覚める yoí gà samérù

so-called [sou'kɔ:ld'] *adj* (friend, expert) いわゆる iwáyurù ◇多くの場合不信や軽べつなどを表す őkù no baái fushín yà keíbetsu nadð wo aráwasù

soccer [sɑ:k'əːr] *n* サッカー sákkà

sociable [sou'ʃəbəl] *adj* 愛想の良い aíso no yoì

social [sou'ʃəl] *adj* (gen: history, structure, background) 社会の shákāi no; (leisure: event, life) 社交的な shakőteki na; (sociable: animal) 社会性のある shakáisei no arù
♦*n* (party) 懇親会 końshinkai

social club *n* 社交クラブ shakőkuràbu

socialism [sou'ʃəlizəm] *n* 社会主義 shakáishugī

socialist [sou'ʃəlist] *adj* 社会主義の shakáishugī no
♦*n* 社会主義者 shakáishugishà

socialize [sou'ʃəlaiz] *vi*: *to socialize (with)* (...と) 交際する (...to) kősai suru

socially [sou'ʃəli:] *adv* (visit) 社交的に shakőteki ni; (acceptable) 社会的に shakáiteki ni

social security (*BRIT*) *n* 社会保障 shakáihoshō

social work *n* ソーシャルワーク sősharuwàku

social worker *n* ソーシャルワーカー sősharuwākà

society [səsai'əti:] *n* (people, their lifestyle) 社会 shákaì; (club) 会 kaî; (*also*: *high society*) 上流社会 jőryūshakài

sociologist [sousi:ɑ:l'ədʒist] *n* 社会学者 shakáigakùsha

sociology [sousi:ɑ:l'ədʒi:] *n* 社会学 shakáigaku

sock [sɑ:k] *n* 靴下 kutsúshita

socket [sɑ:k'it] *n* (gen: cavity) 受け口 ukégùchi; (ANAT: of eye) 眼か gánka; (ELEC: for light bulb) ソケット sokéttð; (*BRIT*: ELEC: wall socket) コンセント kónsento

sod [sɑːd] n (of earth) 草の生えた土 kusá nò háèta tsuchí; (BRIT: inf!) くそ kusó

soda [souˈdə] n (CHEM) ナトリウム化合物 natóriùmu kagóbutsu ◇一般にか性ソーダ, 重曹などを指す ippán nì kaséisòda, jūsō nadò wo sásù; (also: **soda water**) ソーダ水 sōdàsui; (US: also: **soda pop**) 清涼飲料 seíryòinryō

sodden [sɑːdˈən] adj びしょぬれの bishónure no

sodium [souˈdiːəm] n ナトリウム natóriùmu

sofa [souˈfə] n ソファー sófà

soft [sɔːft] adj (not hard) 柔らかい yawárakaì; (gentle, not loud: voice, music) 静かな shízùka na; (not bright: light, color) 柔らかな yawárakà na; (kind: heart, approach) 優しい yasáshii

soft drink n 清涼飲料水 seíryòinryōsui

soften [sɔːfˈən] vt (gen: make soft) 柔らかくする yawárakàku suru; (effect, blow, expression) 和らげる yawárageru
♦vi (gen: become soft) 柔らかくなる yawárakaku narù; (voice, expression) 優しくなる yasáshiku narù

softly [sɔːftˈliː] adv (gently) 優しく yasáshiku; (quietly) 静かに shízùka ni

softness [sɔːftˈnis] n (gen) 柔らかさ yawárakasa; (gentleness) 優しさ yasáshisa

soft spot n: **to have a soft spot for someone** ...が大好きである ...ga dáìsuki de árù

software [sɔːftˈweːr] n (COMPUT) ソフトウエア sofútoueà

soggy [sɑːgˈiː] adj (ground, sandwiches etc) ぐちゃぐちゃの guchágucha no

soil [soil] n (earth) 土壌 dójò; (territory) 土地 tochí
♦vt 汚す yogósù

solace [sɑːlˈis] n 慰め nagúsame

solar [souˈlər] adj (eclipse, power etc) 太陽の táìyō no

sold [sould] pt, pp of **sell**

solder [sɑːdˈər] vt はんだ付けにする hañdazuke nì suru
♦n はんだ hañda

soldier [soulˈdʒər] n (in army) 兵隊 heítai; (not a civilian) 軍人 guñjin

sold out adj (COMM: goods, tickets, concert etc) 売切れで uríkire de

sole [soul] n (of foot) 足の裏 ashí nò urá; (of shoe) 靴の底 kutsú nò sokó; (fish: pl inv) シタビラメ shitábiràme
♦adj (unique) 唯一の yuíitsu no

solely [soulˈliː] adv ...だけ ...dáke

solemn [sɑːlˈəm] adj (person) 謹厳な kiñgen na; (music) 荘重な sōchō na; (promise) 真剣な shíñken na

sole trader n (COMM) 自営業者 jiéigyòsha

solicit [səlisˈit] vt (request) 求める motómerù
♦vi (prostitute) 客引きする kyakúbiki suru

solicitor [səlisˈitər] (BRIT) n (for wills etc, in court) 弁護士 beñgoshì

solid [sɑːlˈid] adj (not hollow) 中空でない chūkū de naí; (not liquid) 固形の kokéi no; (reliable: person, foundations etc) しっかりした shikkárì shita; (entire) まる... marú...; (pure: gold etc) 純粋の juñsui no
♦n (solid object) 固体 kotái

solidarity [sɑːlidæˈriti:] n 団結 dañketsu

solidify [səlidˈəfai] vi (fat etc) 固まる katámarù

solids [sɑːlˈidz] npl (food) 固形食 kokéishòku

solitaire [sɑːlˈiteːr] n (gem) 一つはめの宝石 hitótsuhame nò hōseki; (game) 一人遊び hitóriasobì

solitary [sɑːlˈiteːriː] adj (person, animal, life) 単独の tañdoku no; (alone: walk) 一人だけでする hitórì dake de suru; (isolated) 人気のない hitóke no naí; (single: person) 一人だけの hitórì dake no; (: animal, object) 一つだけの hitótsu dake no

solitary confinement n 独房監禁 dokúbō kañkin

solitude [sɑːlˈətuːd] n 人里を離れている事 hitózato wò hanárete iru kotò

solo [souˈlou] n (piece of music, performance) 独奏 dokúsō
♦adv (fly) 単独で tañdoku de

soloist [souˈlouist] n 独奏者 dokúsōshà

soluble [sɑːlˈjəbəl] adj (aspirin etc) 溶ける tokérù

solution [səlu:'ʃən] *n* (of puzzle, problem, mystery: answer) 解決 kaíketsu; (liquid) 溶液 yṓeki

solve [sɑ:lv] *vt* (puzzle, problem, mystery) 解決する kaíketsu suru

solvent [sɑ:l'vənt] *adj* (COMM) 支払い能力のある shiháraiṅōryoku no aru
♦*n* (CHEM) 溶剤 yṓzai

somber [sɑ:m'bə:r] (*BRIT* **sombre**) *adj* (dark: color, place) 暗い kuráì; (serious: person, view) 陰気な íṅki na

---KEYWORD---

some [sʌm] *adj* **1** (a certain amount or number of) 幾らかの íkùraka no, 幾つかの íkùtsuka no, 少しの sukóshì no

some tea/water/biscuits お茶〔水，ビスケット〕 o-chá(mizú, bisúkettò) ◊この用法では日本語で表現しない場合が多い konó yōhō de wa nihóngo dè hyṓgen shinaí baái ga ṓi

some children came 何人かの子供が来た nánninka no kodómo gà kítà

there's some milk in the fridge 冷蔵庫にミルクがあります reízòko ni mírùku ga arímasu

he asked me some questions 彼は色々な事を聞きました kárè wa iróiro na kotò wo kikímashìta

there were some people outside 数人の人が外に立っていた súnìn no hitó gà sótò ni tatté ità

I've got some money, but not much 金はあるにはありますが，少しだけです kané wà árù ni wa arímasù gá, sukóshì dake désù

2 (certain: in contrasts) ある árù

some people say that ... ...と言っている人がいます ...tò itté irù hitó ga imasù

some people hate fish, while others love it 魚の嫌いな人もいれば大好きな人もいます sakána nò kiráì na hitó mo irébà daísuki na hitó mo imásù

some films were excellent, but most were mediocre 中には優れた映画もあったが，大半は平凡な物だった nákà ni wa sugúreta eígà mo attá gà, taíhan wa heíbon na monò dáttà

3 (unspecified) 何かの nánìka no, だれかの dáreka no

some woman was asking for you だれか女の人があなたを訪ねていましたよ dáreka oṅna no hitò ga anátà wo tazúnete imashìta yó

he was asking for some book (or other) 彼は何かの本を捜していました kárè wa nánìka no hóṅ wo sagáshite imashìta

some day いつか ítsùka, そのうち sonó uchì

we'll meet again some day そのうちまた会うチャンスがあるでしょう sonó uchì matá áù cháṅsu ga árù deshō

shall we meet some day next week? 来週のいつかに会いましょうか raíshū nò ítsùka ni aímashò ká

♦*pron* **1** (a certain number) 幾つか íkùtsuka

I've got some (books etc) 私は幾つか持っています watákushi wà íkùtsuka móttè imasu

some (of them) have been sold 数個は売れてしまいました sūkò wa uréte shimaimashìta

some went for a taxi and some walked 何人かはタクシーを拾いに行ったが，残りの人は歩いた nánninka wa tákùshī wo hiróì ni itta gà, nokóri nò hitó wà arúìta

2 (a certain amount) 幾分か ikúbun kà

I've got some (money, milk) 私は幾分か持っています watákushi wà ikúbun kà móttè imasu

some was left 少し残っていた sukóshì nokótte ità

could I have some of that cheese? そのチーズを少しもらっていいかしら sonó chīzu wo sukóshì moráttè íì kashírà

I've read some of the book その本の一部を読みました sonó hoṅ no ichíbù wo yomímashìta

♦*adv*: *some 10 people* 10人ぐらい júnìn gurai

somebody [sʌm'bɑ:di:] *pron* = **someone**
somehow [sʌm'hau] *adv* (in some way)

何とかして nánĭ to ka shite; (for some reason) どういう訳か dṓ iu wákĕ ka

KEYWORD

someone [sʌmˈwʌn] *pron* だれか dárĕka, 人 hitŏ

there's someone coming 人が来ます hitŏ gă kimásŭ

I saw someone in the garden だれか庭にいました dárĕka niwá nĭ imáshĭta

someplace [sʌmˈpleis] (*US*) *adv* = **somewhere**

somersault [sʌmˈəːrsɔːlt] *n* とんぼ返り toñbogaèri

◆*vi* (person, vehicle) とんぼ返りする toñbogaèri suru

KEYWORD

something [sʌmˈθiŋ] *pron* 何か nánĭka

something nice 何かいい物 nánĭka íi mono

something to do 何かする事 nánĭka suru kotŏ

there's something wrong 何かおかしい nánĭka okáshĭĭ

would you like something to eat/drink? 何か食べません〔飲みません〕か nánĭka tabémaseñ〔nomímaseñ〕ká

sometime [sʌmˈtaim] *adv* (in future) いつか ítsŭka; (in past): *sometime last month* 先月のいつか señgetsu no ítsŭka

sometimes [sʌmˈtaimz] *adv* 時々 tokídoki

somewhat [sʌmˈwʌt] *adv* 少し sukóshĭ

KEYWORD

somewhere [sʌmˈweːr] *adv* (be) どこかに〔で〕dókŏka ni〔de〕; (go) どこかへ dókŏka e

I must have lost it somewhere どこかに落した様です dókŏka ni otóshĭta yŏ desu

it's somewhere or other in Scotland スコットランドのどこかにあります sukóttoraǹdo no dókŏka ni arímasŭ

somewhere else (be) どこか外の所に

〔で〕dókŏka hoká no tokorŏ ni〔de〕; (go) どこか外の所へ dókŏka hoká no tokorŏ e

son [sʌn] *n* 息子 musúko

sonar [souˈnɑːr] *n* ソナー sónǎ

song [sɔːŋ] *n* (MUS) 歌 utá; (of bird) さえずり saézurì

sonic [sɑːˈnik] *adj*: *sonic boom* ソニックブーム soníkkubūmu

son-in-law [sʌnˈinlɔː] (*pl* **sons-in-law**) *n* 義理の息子 girí no musuko

sonnet [sɑːˈnit] *n* ソネット sonéttŏ

sonny [sʌnˈiː] (*inf*) *n* 坊や bŏya

soon [suːn] *adv* (in a short time) もうすぐ mŏ sugù; (a short time after) 間もなく mamónaku; (early) 早く hayákù

soon afterwards それから間もなく soré karà mamónaku ¶ *see also* **as**

sooner [suˈnəːr] *adv* (time) もっと早く móttŏ háyàku; (preference): *I would sooner do that* 私はむしろあれをやりたい watákushi wà múshĭro aré wò yarítaĭ

sooner or later 遅かれ早かれ osókare hayákàre

soot [sut] *n* すす súsù

soothe [suːð] *vt* (calm: person, animal) 落着かせる ochítsukaserù; (reduce: pain) 和らげる yawáragerù

sophisticated [səfisˈtikeitid] *adj* (woman, lifestyle, audience) 世慣れた yonárèta; (machinery) 精巧な seíkŏ na; (arguments) 洗練された señren sarèta

sophomore [sɑːˈfəmɔːr] (*US*) *n* 2年生 ninéñsei

soporific [sɑːpərifˈik] *adj* (speech) 眠気を催させる nemúke wò moyŏosaserù; (drug) 睡眠の suímin no

sopping [sɑːpˈiŋ] *adj*: *sopping (wet)* (hair, clothes etc) びしょぬれの bishónure no

soppy [sɑːpˈiː] (*pej*) *adj* (sentimental) センチな señchi na

soprano [səprænˈou] *n* (singer) ソプラノ sopúrano

sorcerer [sɔːrˈsərər] *n* 魔法使い mahŏtsukaì

sordid [sɔːrˈdid] *adj* (dirty: bed-sit etc) 汚らしい kitánarashiì; (wretched: story etc) 浅ましい asámashiì, えげつない egétsunaì

sore [sɔːr] *adj* (painful) 痛い itáì
♦*n* (shallow) ただれ tadáre; (deep) かいよう kaíyō

sorely [sɔːrˈli:] *adv*: *I am sorely tempted to* よほど...しようと思っている yohódo ...shiyō to omótte irù

sorrow [sɑːrˈou] *n* (regret) 悲しみ kanáshimi

sorrowful [sɑːrˈoufəl] *adj* (day, smile etc) 悲しい kanáshiì

sorrows [sɑːrˈouz] *npl* (causes of grief) 不幸 fúkō

sorry [sɑːrˈi:] *adj* (regretful) 残念な zańneñ na; (condition, excuse) 情けない nasákenaì
sorry! (apology) 済みません sumímaseñ
sorry? (pardon) はい？ haí？◇相手の言葉を聞取れなかった時に言う aíte no kotòba wo kikítorenakatta tokì ni iú
to feel sorry for someone ...に同情する ...ni dōjō suru

sort [sɔːrt] *n* (type) 種類 shúrui
♦*vt* (*also*: **sort out**: papers, mail, belongings) より分ける yorí wakerù; (: problems) 解決する kaíketsu suru

sorting office [sɔːrˈtiŋ-] *n* 郵便物振分け場 yūbinbutsufuriwakejò

SOS [esoues˺] *n* エスオーエス esú ō esù

so-so [sou˺sou˺] *adv* (average) まあまあ maámaà

soufflé [su:flei˺] *n* スフレ súfùre

sought [sɔːt] *pt, pp of* **seek**

soul [soul] *n* (spirit etc) 魂 támashiì; (person) 人 hitó

soul-destroying [soul˺distrɔiiŋ] *adj* (work) ぼけさせる様な bokésaseru yō na

soulful [soul˺fəl] *adj* (eyes, music) 表情豊かな hyōjō yutàka na

sound [saund] *adj* (healthy) 健康な keńkō na; (safe, not damaged) 無傷の múkizu no; (secure: investment) 安全な ańzen na; (reliable, thorough) 信頼できる shińrai dekirù; (sensible: advice) 堅実な keńjitsu na

♦*adv*: *sound asleep* ぐっすり眠って gussúrì nemútte
♦*n* (noise) 音 otó; (volume on TV etc) 音声 óñsei; (GEO) 海峡 kaíkyo
♦*vt* (alarm, horn) 鳴らす narásù
♦*vi* (alarm, horn) 鳴る narú; (*fig*: seem) ...の様である ...no yō de arù
to sound like ...の様に聞える ...no yō ni kikőerù

sound barrier *n* 音速障害 ońsokushṑgai

sound effects *npl* 音響効果 ońkyōkòka

soundly [saund˺li:] *adv* (sleep) ぐっすり gussúrì; (beat) 手ひどく tehídoku

sound out *vt* (person, opinion) 打診する dashín suru

soundproof [saund˺pru:f] *adj* (room etc) 防音の bőon no

soundtrack [saund˺træk] *n* (of film) サウンドトラック saúndotorakkù

soup [su:p] *n* スープ sűpu
in the soup (*fig*) 困って komáttè

soup plate *n* スープ皿 sűpuzarà

soupspoon [su:p˺spu:n] *n* スープスプーン sűpusupùn

sour [sau˺ər] *adj* (bitter) 酸っぱい suppáì; (milk) 酸っぱくなった suppákù náttà; (*fig*: bad-tempered) 機嫌の悪い kigén no waruì
it's sour grapes (*fig*) 負け惜しみだ makéoshimi da

source [sɔːrs] *n* (*also fig*) 源 minámoto

south [sauθ] *n* 南 minámi
♦*adj* 南の minámi no
♦*adv* (movement) 南へ minámi e; (position) 南に minámi ni

South Africa *n* 南アフリカ minámi afùrika

South African *adj* 南アフリカの minámi afùrika no
♦*n* 南アフリカ人 minámi afurikajìn

South America *n* 南米 nańbei

South American *adj* 南米の nańbei nò
♦*n* 南米人 nańbeijìn

south-east [sauθi:st˺] *n* 南東 nańtō

southerly [sʌð˺əːrli:] *adj* (to/towards the south: aspect) 南への minámi e nò; (from the south: wind) 南からの minámi kara nò

southern [sʌð'ə:rn] *adj* (in or from the south of region) 南 の minámi no; (to/towards the south) 南向きの minámimuki no

the southern hemisphere 南半球 mínámiháñkyū

South Pole *n* 南極 nańkyoku

southward(s) [sauθ'wə:rd(z)] *adv* 南 へ minámi e

south-west [sauθwest'] 南西 nańsei

souvenir [su:vəni:r'] *n* (memento) 記念品 kinéñhin

sovereign [sɑ:v'rin] *n* (ruler) 君主 kúñshu

sovereignty [sɑ:v'rənti:] *n* 主権 shukéñ

soviet [sou'vi:it] *adj* ソビエトの sobíetò no

the Soviet Union ソ連 sóren

sow[1] [sau] *n* (pig) 牝豚 mesúbùta

sow[2] [sou] (*pt* **sowed**, *pp* **sown**) *vt* (*gen*: seeds) まく mákù; (*fig*: spread: suspicion etc) 広める hirómerù

soy [sɔi] (*BRIT* **soya**) *n*: **soy bean** 大豆 dáìzu

soy sauce しょう油 shóyù

spa [spɑ:] *n* (*also*: **spa town**) 鉱泉町 kōseñmachi; (*US*: *also*: **health spa**) ヘルスセンター herúsuseñtā

space [speis] *n* (gap) すき間 sukíma, ギャップ gyáppù; (place) 空所 kū̀sho, 余白 yoháku; (room) 空間 kū̀kan; (beyond Earth) 宇宙空間 uchū̀kūkan, スペース supḗsu; (interval, period) 間 ma

♦*cpd* 宇宙... úchū...

♦*vt* (*also*: **space out**: text, visits, payments) 間隔を置く kañkaku wò okú

spacecraft [speis'kræft] *n* 宇宙船 uchū̀sen

spaceman [speis'mæn] (*pl* **spacemen**) *n* 宇宙飛行士 uchū̀hikōshi

spaceship [speis'ʃip] *n* = **spacecraft**

spacewoman [speis'wumən] (*pl* **spacewomen**) *n* 女性宇宙飛行士 joséi uchū̀hikōshi

spacing [speis'siŋ] *n* (between words) スペース supḗsu

spacious [speis'ʃəs] *adj* (car, room etc) 広

い hirói

spade [speid] *n* (tool) スコップ sukóppù; (child's) おもちゃのスコップ omóchà no sukóppù

spades [speidz] *npl* (CARDS: suit) スペード supēdo

spaghetti [spəget'i:] *n* スパゲッティ supágettì

Spain [spein] *n* スペイン supéìn

span [spæn] *n* (of bird, plane) 翼長 yokúchō; (of arch) スパン supáñ; (in time) 期間 kikán

♦*vt* (river) ...にまたがる ...ni matágarù; (*fig*: time) ...に渡る ...ni watárù

Spaniard [spæn'jə:rd] *n* スペイン人 supéinjìn

spaniel [spæn'jəl] *n* スパニエル supánièru

Spanish [spæn'iʃ] *adj* スペインの supéìn no; (LING) スペイン語の supéingo no

♦*n* (LING) スペイン語 supéingo

♦*npl*: *the Spanish* スペイン人 supéinjìn ◇総称 sōshō

spank [spæŋk] *vt* (someone, someone's bottom) ...のしりをたたく ...no shirí wò tatákù

spanner [spæn'ə:r] (*BRIT*) *n* スパナ supánà

spar [spɑ:r] *n* (pole) マスト másùto

♦*vi* (BOXING) スパーリングする supárìngu suru

spare [spe:r] *adj* (free) 空きの akí no; (surplus) 余った amáttà

♦*n* = **spare part**

♦*vt* (do without: trouble etc) ...なしで済ます ...náshì de sumásù; (make available) 与える atáerù; (refrain from hurting: person, city etc) 助けてやる tasúkete yarù

to spare (surplus: time, money) 余った amáttà

spare part *n* 交換用部品 kōkan-yōbuhiñ

spare time *n* 余暇 yókà

spare wheel *n* (AUT) スペアタイア supéataià

sparing [spe:r'iŋ] *adj*: *to be sparing with* ...を倹約する ...wo keñ-yaku suru

sparingly [spe:r'iŋli:] *adv* (use) 控え目に

hikáeme ni

spark [spɑːrk] *n* 火花 híbàna, スパーク supákù; (*fig*: of wit etc) ひらめき hirámekì

spark(ing) plug [spɑːrk'(iŋ)-] *n* スパークプラグ supákùpurágu

sparkle [spɑːr'kəl] *n* きらめき kirámekì
♦*vi* (shine: diamonds, water) きらめく kirámekù

sparkling [spɑːr'kliŋ] *adj* (wine) 泡立つ awádatsù; (conversation, performance) きらめく様な kirámeku yố na

sparrow [spær'ou] *n* スズメ suzúme

sparse [spɑːrs] *adj* (rainfall, hair, population) 少ない sukúnaì

spartan [spɑːr'tən] *adj* (*fig*) 簡素な kánso na

spasm [spæz'əm] *n* (MED) けいれん keíren

spasmodic [spæzmɑːd'ik] *adj* (*fig*: not continuous, irregular) 不規則な fukísoku na

spastic [spæs'tik] *n* 脳性麻ひ患者 nốseimahikañja

spat [spæt] *pt, pp of* **spit**

spate [speit] *n* (*fig*): *a spate of* (letters, protests etc) 沢山の takúsañ no

spatter [spæt'əːr] *vt* (liquid, surface) ...を...にはねかす ...wo ...ni hanékasù

spatula [spætʃ'ələ] *n* (CULIN, MED) へら hérà

spawn [spɔːn] *vi* (fish etc) 産卵する sañran suru
♦*n* (frog spawn etc) 卵 tamágò

speak [spiːk] (*pt* **spoke**, *pp* **spoken**) *vt* (language) 話す hanásù; (truth) 言う iú
♦*vi* (use voice) 話す hanásù; (make a speech) 演説する eñzetsu suru

to speak to someone ...に話し掛ける ...ni hanáshikakerù

to speak to someone of/about something ...に...のことを話す ...ni ...no kotó wò hanásù

speak up! もっと大きな声で話しなさい móttò ốkìna kóè de hanáshi nasaì

speaker [spiː'kəːr] *n* (in public) 演説者 eñzetsushà; (*also*: **loudspeaker**) スピーカー supíkằ; (POL): *the Speaker* (US,

BRIT) 下院議長 ka-íngichồ

spear [spiːr] *n* (weapon) やり yarí
♦*vt* 刺す sásù

spearhead [spiːr'hed] *vt* (attack etc) ...の先頭に立つ ...no señtố nì tátsù

spec [spek] (*inf*) *n*: *on spec* 山をかけて yamá wo kakète

special [speʃ'əl] *adj* 特別な tokúbetsu na
special delivery 速達 sokútatsu
special school (*BRIT*) 特殊学校 tokúshugakkồ
special adviser 特別顧問 tokúbetsukomòn
special permission 特別許可 tokúbetsukyokà

specialist [speʃ'əlist] *n* (*gen*) 専門家 señmonka; (MED) 専門医 señmoñ-i

speciality [speʃiːæl'əti:] *n* = **specialty**

specialize [speʃ'əlaiz] *vi*: *to specialize (in)* (...を) 専門的にやる (...wo) señmonteki ni yarù

specially [speʃ'əliː] *adv* (especially) 特に tókù ni; (on purpose) 特別に tokúbetsu ni

specialty [speʃ'əltiː] *n* (dish) 名物 mếibutsu; (study) 専門 señmon

species [spiː'ʃiːz] *n inv* 種 shú

specific [spisif'ik] *adj* (fixed) 特定の tokútei no; (exact) 正確な seíkaku na

specifically [spisif'ikliː] *adv* (especially) 特に tókù ni; (exactly) 明確に meíkaku ni

specification [spesəfəkei'ʃən] *n* (TECH) 仕様 shiyố; (requirement) 条件 jốkeñ

specifications [spesəfəkei'ʃənz] *npl* (TECH) 仕様 shiyố

specify [spes'əfai] *vt* (time, place, color etc) 指定する shitéi suru

specimen [spes'əmən] *n* (single example) 見本 mihóñ; (sample for testing, *also* MED) 標本 hyóhon

speck [spek] *n* (of dirt, dust etc) 粒 tsúbù

speckled [spek'əld] *adj* (hen, eggs) 点々模様の teñteñmoyố no

specs [speks] (*inf*) *npl* 眼鏡 mégàne

spectacle [spek'təkəl] *n* (scene) 光景 kốkei; (grand event) スペクタクル supékùtakuru

spectacles [spek'tək_{al}z] *npl* 眼 鏡 mégane

spectacular [spektæk'jələr] *adj* (dramatic) 劇的な gekíteki na; (success) 目覚しい mezámashiì

spectator [spek'teitər] *n* 観 客 kañkyaku

specter [spek'tər] (*US*) *n* (ghost) 幽 霊 yūrei

spectra [spek'trə] *npl of* **spectrum**

spectre [spek'tər] (*BRIT*) = **specter**

spectrum [spek'trəm] (*pl* **spectra**) *n* (color/radio wave spectrum) スペクトル supékùtoru

speculate [spek'jəleit] *vi* (FINANCE) 投機をする tōki wo suru; (try to guess): *to speculate about* ...についてあれこれと憶測する ...ni tsuíte arékòre to okúsoku suru

speculation [spekjəlei'ʃən] *n* (FINANCE) 投機 tōki; (guesswork) 憶測 okúsoku

speech [spi:tʃ] *n* (faculty) 話す能力 hanásu nōryoku; (spoken language) 話し言葉 hanáshikotòba; (formal talk) 演説 eñzetsu, スピーチ supíchi; (THEATER) せりふ seŕífù

speechless [spi:tʃ'lis] *adj* (be, remain etc) 声も出ない kóè mo denái

speed [spi:d] *n* (rate, fast travel) 速度 sókùdo, スピード supídò; (haste) 急ぎ isógi; (promptness) 素早さ subáyasà
at full/top speed 全速力で zeńsokuryòku de

speed boat *n* モーターボート mótābòto

speedily [spi:'dili:] *adv* 素早く subáyakù

speeding [spi:'diŋ] *n* (AUT) スピード違反 supído-ihàn

speed limit *n* 速度制限 sokúdoseìgen

speedometer [spi:da:m'itər] *n* 速度計 sokúdokèi

speed up *vi* (*also fig*) 速度を増す sókùdo wo masú
♦*vt* (*also fig*) ...の速度を増す ...no sókùdo wo masú, 速める hayámerù

speedway [spi:d'wei] *n* (sport) オートレース ōtorèsu

speedy [spi:'di:] *adj* (fast: car) スピードの出る supídò no dérù; (prompt: reply, recovery, settlement) 速い hayáì

spell [spel] *n* (*also*: *magic spell*) 魔法 mahō; (period of time) 期間 kikáñ
♦*vt* (*pt, pp* **spelled** *or* (*Brit*) **spelt**) (*also*: **spell out**) ...のつづりを言う ...no tsuzúri wò iú; (*fig*: advantages, difficulties) ...の兆しである ...no kizáshi de arù
to cast a spell on someone ...に魔法を掛ける ...ni mahō wò kakérù
he can't spell 彼はスペルが苦手だ kárè wa supérù ga nigáte dà

spellbound [spel'baund] *adj* (audience etc) 魅せられた miséraretà

spelling [spel'iŋ] *n* つづり tsuzúri, スペリング supéringu

spend [spend] (*pt, pp* **spent**) *vt* (money) 使う tsukáù; (time, life) 過す sugósù

spendthrift [spend'θrift] *n* 浪費家 rōhikà

spent [spent] *pt, pp of* **spend**

sperm [spə:rm] *n* 精子 seíshi

spew [spju:] *vt* 吐き出す hakídasù

sphere [sfi:r] *n* (round object) 球 kyū; (area) 範囲 hañ-i

spherical [sfe:r'ikəl] *adj* (round) 丸い marúì

sphinx [sfiŋks] *n* スフィンクス sufíñkusu

spice [spais] *n* 香辛料 kốshiñryō, スパイス supáìsu
♦*vt* (food) ...にスパイスを入れる ...ni supáìsu wo irérù

spick-and-span [spik'ənspæn'] *adj* きちんときれいな kichíñ to kírèi na

spicy [spai'si:] *adj* (food) スパイスの利いた supáìsu no kiítà

spider [spai'dər] *n* クモ kúmò

spike [spaik] *n* (point) くい kuí; (BOT) 穂 hố

spill [spil] (*pt, pp* **spilt** *or* **spilled**) *vt* (liquid) こぼす kobósù
♦*vi* (liquid) こぼれる kobórerù

spill over *vi* (liquid: *also fig*) あふれる afúrerù

spin [spin] *n* (trip in car) ドライブ doráìbu; (AVIAT) きりもみ kirímomi; (on ball) スピン supíñ
♦*vb* (*pt, pp* **spun**)

♦*vt* (wool etc) 紡ぐ tsumúgù; (ball, coin) 回転させる kaíten saserù

♦*vi* (make thread) 紡ぐ tsumúgù; (person, head) 目が回る mé gà mawárù

spinach [spin'itʃ] *n* (plant, food) ホウレンソウ hőreñsô

spinal [spai'nəl] *adj* (injury etc) 背骨の sebőne no

spinal cord *n* せき髄 sekízùi

spindly [spind'li:] *adj* (legs, trees etc) か細い kabősoì

spin-dryer [spindrai'ə:r] (*BRIT*) *n* 脱水機 dassúikì

spine [spain] *n* (ANAT) 背骨 sebőne; (thorn: of plant, hedgehog etc) とげ togé

spineless [spain'lis] *adj* (fig) 意気地なしの ikújinàshi no

spinning [spin'iŋ] *n* (art) 紡績 bőseki

spinning top *n* こま kőmà

spinning wheel *n* 紡ぎ車 tsumúgigurùma

spin-off [spin'ɔ:f] *n* (fig: by-product) 副産物 fukúsañbutsu

spin out *vt* (talk, job, money, holiday) 引延ばす hikínobasù

spinster [spin'stə:r] *n* オールドミス őrudomisù

spiral [spai'rəl] *n* ら旋形 raséñkei

♦*vi* (fig: prices etc) うなぎ登りに上る unáginobòri ni nobórù

spiral staircase *n* ら旋階段 rasénkaidàn

spire [spai'ə:r] *n* せん塔 señtō

spirit [spir'it] *n* (soul) 魂 támàshii; (ghost) 幽霊 yűrei; (energy) 元気 géñki; (courage) 勇気 yűki; (frame of mind) 気分 kíbùn; (sense) 精神 seíshin

in good spirits 気分上々で kíbùn jőjō de

spirited [spir'itid] *adj* (performance, retort, defense) 精力的な seíryokuteki na

spirit level *n* 水準器 suíjuñki

spirits [spir'its] *npl* (drink) 蒸留酒 jőryūshu

spiritual [spir'itʃu:əl] *adj* (of the spirit: home, welfare, needs) 精神的な seíshinteki na; (religious: affairs) 霊的な reíteki na

♦*n* (*also*: **Negro spiritual**) 黒人霊歌 kokújinreìka

spit [spit] *n* (for roasting) 焼きぐし yakígushi; (saliva) つばき tsubáki

♦*vi* (*pt, pp* **spat**) (throw out saliva) つばを吐く tsubá wo hákù; (sound: fire, cooking) じゅうじゅういう jūjū iu; (rain) ばらつく parátsukù

spite [spait] *n* 恨み urámi

♦*vt* (person) ...に意地悪をする ...ni ijíwarù wo suru

in spite of ...にもかかわらず ...ní mò kakáwarazù

spiteful [spait'fəl] *adj* (child, words etc) 意地悪な ijíwarù na

spittle [spit'əl] *n* つばき tsubáki

splash [splæʃ] *n* (sound) ざぶんという音 zabún to iú otò; (of color) 派手なはん点 hadé nà hañten

♦*vt* はね掛ける hanékakerù

♦*vi* (*also*: **splash about**) ぴちゃぴちゃ水をはねる pichápìcha mizú wò hanérù

spleen [spli:n] *n* (ANAT) ひ臓 hiző

splendid [splen'did] *adj* (excellent: idea, recovery) 素晴らしい subárashì; (impressive: architecture, affair) 立派な rippá nà

splendor [splen'də:r] (*BRIT* **splendour**) *n* (impressiveness) 輝き kagáyakì

splendors [splen'də:rz] *npl* (features) 特色 tokúshoku

splint [splint] *n* 副木 fukúboku

splinter [splin'tə:r] *n* (of wood, glass) 破片 hahéñ; (in finger) とげ togé

♦*vi* (bone, wood, glass etc) 砕ける kudákerù

split [split] *n* (crack) 割れ目 waréme; (tear) 裂け目 sakéme; (fig: division) 分裂 buñretsu; (: difference) 差異 sá-ì

♦*vb* (*pt, pp* **split**)

♦*vt* (divide) 割る wárù, 裂く sákù; (party) 分裂させる buñretsu saserù; (share equally: work) 手分けしてやる tewáke shite yarù; (: profits) 山分けする yamáwake suru

♦*vi* (divide) 割れる warérù

split up *vi* (couple) 別れる wakárerù;

(group, meeting) 解散する kaísan suru

splutter [splʌt'əːr] vi (engine etc) ぱちぱち音を立てる páchìpachi otó wò tatérù; (person) どもる domórù

spoil [spɔil] (pt, pp **spoilt** or **spoiled**) vt (damage, mar) 台無しにする daínashi ni surù; (child) 甘やかす amáyakasù

spoils [spɔilz] npl (loot: also fig) 分捕り品 buńdorihìn

spoilsport [spɔil'spɔːrt] n 座を白けさせる人 zá wò shirákesaserù hitó

spoke [spouk] pt of **speak**

♦n (of wheel) スポーク supókù

spoken [spou'kən] pp of **speak**

spokesman [spouks'mən] (pl **spokesmen**) n スポークスマン supókusumàn

spokeswoman [spouks'wumən] (pl **spokeswomen**) n 女性報道官 joséi hōdōkan, 女性スポークスマン joséi supókusumàn

sponge [spʌndʒ] n (for washing with) スポンジ supóñji; (also: **sponge cake**) スポンジケーキ supóñjikèki

♦vt (wash) スポンジで洗う supóñji de aráù

♦vi: **to sponge off/on someone** ...にたかる ...ni takárù

sponge bag (BRIT) n 洗面バッグ seńmenbaggù ◊洗面道具を入れて携帯するバッグ seńmendōgu wo irète keitai surù bággù

sponsor [spɑn'səːr] n (of player, event, club, program) スポンサー supóñsà; (of charitable event etc) 協賛者 kyōsañsha; (for application) 保証人 hoshőnin; (for bill in parliament etc) 提出者 teíshutsushà

♦vt (player, event, club, program etc) ...のスポンサーになる ...no supóñsà ni nárù; (charitable event etc) ...の協賛者になる ...no kyōsañsha ni nárù; (applicant) ...の保証人になる ...no hoshőnin ni nárù; (proposal, bill etc) 提出する teíshutsu suru

sponsorship [spɑn'səːrʃip] n (financial support) 金銭的の援助 kiñsentekieñjo

spontaneous [spɑntei'niːəs] adj (unplanned: gesture) 自発的な jihátsuteki

na

spooky [spuː'kiː] (inf) adj (place, atmosphere) お化けが出そうな o-báke gà desō nà

spool [spuːl] n (for thread) 糸巻 itómàki; (for film, tape etc) リール rīru

spoon [spuːn] n さじ sají, スプーン supún

spoon-feed [spuːn'fiːd] vt (baby, patient) スプーンで食べさせる supún de tabésaserù; (fig: students etc) ...に一方的に教え込む ...ni ippőteki nì oshíekomù

spoonful [spuːn'ful] n スプーン一杯分 supún ippáibun

sporadic [spɔːræd'ik] adj (glimpses, attacks etc) 散発的な sańpatsuteki na

sport [spɔːrt] n (game) スポーツ supőtsu; (person) 気さくな人 kisáku nà hitó

♦vt (wear) これみよがしに身に付ける korémiyogàshi ni mi ni tsukérù

sporting [spɔːr'tiŋ] adj (event etc) スポーツの supőtsù no; (generous) 気前がいい kimáé ga íì

to give someone a sporting chance ...にちゃんとしたチャンスを与える ...ni chañtò shita cháñsu wo atáerù

sport jacket (US) n スポーツジャケット supőtsujakettò

sports car [spɔːrts-] n スポーツカー supőtsukà

sports jacket (BRIT) n = **sport jacket**

sportsman [spɔːrts'mən] (pl **sportsmen**) n スポーツマン supőtsumàn

sportsmanship [spɔːrts'mənʃip] n スポーツマンシップ supőtsumanshippù

sportswear [spɔːrts'weəːr] n スポーツウエア supőtsuueà

sportswoman [spɔːrts'wumən] (pl **sportswomen**) n スポーツウーマン supőtsuùman

sporty [spɔːr'tiː] adj (good at sports) スポーツ好きの supőtsuzuki no

spot [spɑt] n (mark) 染み shimí; (on pattern, skin etc) はん点 hañten; (place) 場所 bashó; (RADIO, TV) コーナー kőnà; (small amount): **a spot of** 少しの sukőshì no

♦vt (notice: person, mistake etc) ...に気

が付く ...ni kí gà tsúkù
on the spot (in that place) 現場に genba ni; (immediately) その場で sonó ba de, 即座に sókùza ni; (in difficulty) 困って komátte

spot check n 抜取り検査 nukítorikensa

spotless [spɑːtˈlis] adj (shirt, kitchen etc) 清潔な seíketsu na

spotlight [spɑːtˈlait] n スポットライト supóttoraìto

spotted [spɑːtˈid] adj (pattern) はん点模様の hañtenmoyō no

spotty [spɑːtˈiː] adj (face, youth: with freckles) そばかすだらけの sobákasudaràke no; (: with pimples) にきびだらけの nikíbidaràke no

spouse [spaus] n (male/female) 配偶者 haígùsha

spout [spaut] n (of jug) つ ぎ 口 tsugígùchi; (of pipe) 出口 dégùchi
♦vi (flames, water etc) 噴出す fukídasù

sprain [sprein] n ねんざ neñza
♦vt: **to sprain one's ankle/wrist** 足首〔手首〕をねんざする ashíkùbi〔tékùbi〕wo neñza suru

sprang [spræŋ] pt of **spring**

sprawl [sprɔːl] vi (person: lie) 寝そべる nesóberù; (: sit) だらしない格好で座る daráshinai kakkō de suwárù; (place) 無秩序に広がる muchítsujo ni hirógarù

spray [sprei] n (small drops) 水煙 mizúkemùri; (sea spray) しぶき shíbùki; (container: hair spray etc) スプレー supúrè; (garden spray) 噴霧器 fuñmukì; (of flowers) 小枝 koéda
♦vt (sprinkle) 噴霧器で...に...を掛ける fuñmukì de ...ni ...wo kakérù; (crops) 消毒する shōdoku suru

spread [spred] n (range, distribution) 広がり hirógari; (CULIN: for bread) スプレッド supúreddò; (inf: food) ごちそう gochísō
♦vb (pt, pp **spread**)
♦vt (lay out) 並べる naráberù; (butter) 塗る nurù; (wings, arms, sails) 広げる hirógerù; (workload, wealth) 分配する buñpai suru; (scatter) まく mákù
♦vi (disease, news) 広がる hirógarù;

(also: **spread out**: stain) 広がる hirógarù

spread-eagled [spredˈiːgəld] adj 大の字に寝た daí no jì ni netá

spread out vi (move apart) 散らばる chirábarù

spreadsheet [spredˈʃiːt] n (COMPUT) スプレッドシート supúreddoshìto

spree [spriː] n: **to go on a spree** ...にふける ...ni fukérù

sprightly [spraitˈliː] adj (old person) かくしゃくとした kakúshaku to shitá

spring [spriŋ] n (leap) 跳躍 chōyaku; (coiled metal) ばね bánè; (season) 春 hárù; (of water) 泉 izúmi
♦vi (pt **sprang**, pp **sprung**) (leap) 跳ぶ tobú

in spring (season) 春に hárù ni

springboard [spriŋˈbɔːrd] n スプリングボード supúringubòdo

spring-cleaning [spriŋˈkliːˈniŋ] n 大掃除 ōsōji ◊春とは関係なく言う hárù to wa kañkeinakù iú

springtime [spriŋˈtaim] n 春 hárù

spring up vi (thing: appear) 現れる aráwarerù

sprinkle [spriŋˈkəl] vt (scatter: liquid) まく mákù; (: salt, sugar) 振り掛ける furíkakerù

to sprinkle water on, sprinkle with water ...に水をまく ...ni mizú wò mákù

sprinkler [spriŋˈklər] n (for lawn, to put out fire) スプリンクラー supúrinkurà

sprint [sprint] n (race) 短距離競走 tañkyorikyōsō, スプリント supúrìnto
♦vi (gen: run fast) 速く走る háyàku hashírù; (SPORT) スプリントする supúrìnto suru

sprinter [sprintˈər] n スプリンター supúrìntā

sprout [spraut] vi (plant, vegetable) 発芽する hatsúga suru

sprouts [sprauts] npl (also: **Brussels sprouts**) 芽キャベツ mekyábètsu

spruce [spruːs] n inv (BOT) トウヒ tóhì
♦adj (neat, smart) スマートな sumátò na

sprung [sprʌŋ] pp of **spring**

spry [sprai] adj (old person) かくしゃく

とした kakúshaku to shitá

spun [spʌn] *pt, pp of* **spin**

spur [spəːr] *n* 拍車 hakúsha; (*fig*) 刺激 shigéki

♦*vt* (*also*: **spur on**) 激励する gekírei suru

on the spur of the moment とっさに tossá ni

spurious [spjuːr'iːəs] *adj* (false: attraction) 見せ掛けの misékake no; (: argument) 間違った machígattà

spurn [spəːrn] *vt* (reject) はねつける hanétsukerù

spurt [spəːrt] *n* (of blood etc) 噴出 fúnshutsu; (of energy) 奮発 fúnpatsu

♦*vi* (blood, flame) 噴出す fukídasù

spy [spai] *n* スパイ supáì

♦*vi*: *to spy on* こっそり見張る kossóri mihárù

♦*vt* (see) 見付ける mitsúkerù

spying [spai'iŋ] *n* スパイ行為 supáikòi

sq. *abbr* = **square**

squabble [skwɑ:b'əl] *vi* 口げんかする kuchígeňka suru

squad [skwɑːd] *n* (MIL, POLICE) 班 háñ; (SPORT) チーム chímu

squadron [skwɑːd'rən] *n* (MIL) 大隊 daítai

squalid [skwɑːl'id] *adj* (dirty, unpleasant: conditions) 汚らしい kitánarashiì; (sordid: story etc) えげつない egétsunaì

squall [skwɔːl] *n* (stormy wind) スコール sukóru

squalor [skwɑːl'əːr] *n* 汚い環境 kitánai kaňkyō

squander [skwɑːn'dəːr] *vt* (money) 浪費する rṓhi suru; (chances) 逃す nogásù

square [skweːr] *n* (in shape) 正方形 seíhōkei; (in town) 広場 híròba; (*inf*: person) 堅物 katábutsu

♦*adj* (in shape) 正方形の seíhōkei no; (*inf*: ideas, tastes) 古臭い furúkusaì

♦*vt* (arrange) ...を...に一致させる ...wo ...ni itchí saserù; (MATH) 2乗する nijṓ suru; (reconcile) ...を...と調和させる ...wo ...to chṓwa saserù

all square 貸し借りなし kashíkàri náshì

a square meal 十分な食事 júbùn na shokúji

2 meters square 2メーター平方 ni mḗtā heíhō

2 square meters 2平方メーター ni heíhō mḗtā

squarely [skweːr'liː] *adv* (directly: fall, land etc) まともに matómo nì; (fully: confront) きっぱりと kippárì to

squash [skwɑːʃ] *n* (*US*: marrow etc) カボチャ kabócha; (*BRIT*: drink): *lemon/orange squash* レモン〔オレンジ〕スカッシュ remón〔oréñji〕sukasshù; (SPORT) スカッシュ sukásshù

♦*vt* つぶす tsubúsù

squat [skwɑːt] *adj* ずんぐりした zuňguri shita

♦*vi* (*also*: **squat down**) しゃがむ shagámù

squatter [skwɑːt'əːr] *n* 不法居住者 fuhṓkyojūsha

squawk [skwɔːk] *vi* (bird) ぎゃーぎゃー鳴く gyågyā nakú

squeak [skwiːk] *vi* (door etc) きしむ kishímù; (mouse) ちゅーちゅー鳴く chūchū nakú

squeal [skwiːl] *vi* (children) きゃーきゃー言う kyåkyā iú; (brakes etc) キーキー言う kíkī iú

squeamish [skwiː'miʃ] *adj* やたら...に弱い yatára ...ni yowáì

squeeze [skwiːz] *n* (*gen*: of hand) 握り締める nigírishimerù kotó; (ECON) 金融引締め kiñ-yūhikishime

♦*vt* (*gen*) 絞る shibórù; (hand, arm) 握り締める nigírishimerù

squeeze out *vt* (juice etc) 絞り出す shibóridasù

squelch [skweltʃ] *vi* ぐちゃぐちゃ音を立てる gúchàgucha otó wò tatérù

squid [skwid] *n* イカ iká

squiggle [skwig'əl] *n* のたくった線 notákuttà séñ

squint [skwint] *vi* (have a squint) 斜視である sháshì de árù

♦*n* (MED) 斜視 sháshì

squire [skwai'əːr] (*BRIT*) *n* 大地主 ṓjinùshi

squirm [skwəːrm] *vi* 身もだえする mimõdàe suru

squirrel [skwə:r'əl] n リス rísù

squirt [skwə:rt] vi 噴出す fukídasù
♦vt 噴掛ける fukíkakerù

Sr abbr = **senior**

St abbr = **saint; street**

stab [stæb] n (with knife etc) ひと刺し hitósàshi; (inf: try): **to have a stab at (doing) something** ...をやってみる ...wo yatté mirù
♦vt (person, body) 刺す sásù
a stab of pain 刺す様な痛み sásù yō na itámi

stability [stəbil'əti:] n 安定 aftei

stabilize [stei'bəlaiz] vt (prices) 安定させる aftei saserù
♦vi (prices, one's weight) 安定する aftei suru

stable [stei'bəl] adj (prices, patient's condition) 安定した aftei shita; (marriage) 揺るぎない yurúgi naì
♦n (for horse) 馬小屋 umágoya

staccato [stəkɑ:'tou] adv スタッカート sutákkāto

stack [stæk] n (pile) ...の山 ...no yamá
♦vt (pile) 積む tsumú

stadium [stei'di:əm] n 競技場 kyógijō, スタジアム sutájiamu

staff [stæf] n (work force) 職員 shokúin; (BRIT: SCOL) 教職員 kyóshokuin
♦vt ...の職員として働く ...no shokúin toshite határakù

stag [stæg] n 雄ジカ ójìka

stage [steidʒ] n (in theater etc) 舞台 bútai; (platform) 台 dái; (profession): **the stage** 俳優業 haíyūgyō; (point, period) 段階 dañkai
♦vt (play) 上演する jóen suru; (demonstration) 行う okónaù
in stages 少しずつ sukóshi zutsù

stagecoach [steidʒ'koutʃ] n 駅馬車 ekíbashà

stage manager n 舞台監督 butáikàntoku

stagger [stæg'ə:r] vi よろめく yorómekù
♦vt (amaze) 仰天させる gyóten saserù; (hours, holidays) ずらす zurásù

staggering [stæg'ə:riŋ] adj (amazing) 仰天させる gyóten saserù

stagnant [stæg'nənt] adj (water) よどんだ yodóñda; (economy etc) 停滞した teítai shita

stagnate [stæg'neit] vi (economy, business, person) 停滞する teítai suru; (person) だれる darérù

stag party n スタッグパーティ sutággupàti

staid [steid] adj (person, attitudes) 古めかしい furúmekashiì

stain [stein] n (mark) 染み shimí; (coloring) 着色剤 chakúshokuzai, ステイン sutéin
♦vt (mark) 汚す yogósù; (wood) ...にステインを塗る ...ni sutéin wo nûrù

stained glass window [steind-] n ステンドグラスの窓 suténdoguràsu no mádò

stainless steel [stein'lis-] n ステンレス sutéñrèsu

stain remover [-rimu:'və:r] n 染み抜き shimínuki

stair [ste:r] n (step) 段 dáñ, ステップ sutéppù

staircase [ste:r'keis] n 階段 kaídan

stairs [ste:rz] npl (flight of steps) 階段 kaídan

stairway [ste:r'wei] n = **staircase**

stake [steik] n (post) くい kúì; (COMM: interest) 利害関係 rigáikañkei; (BETTING: gen pl) 賞金 shókin
♦vt (money, life, reputation) かける kakérù
to stake a claim to ...に対する所有権を主張する ...ni taí surù shoyúken wo shuchó suru
to be at stake 危ぶまれる ayábumarerù

stalactite [stəlæk'tait] n しょう乳石 shónyūseki

stalagmite [stəlæg'mait] n 石じゅんせ kíjun

stale [steil] adj (bread) 固くなった katáku nattá; (food, air) 古くなった fúrùku natta; (air) よどんだ yodóñda; (smell) かび臭い kabíkusaì; (beer) 気の抜けた kí nð nukétà

stalemate [steil'meit] n (CHESS) ステールメート sutérumèto; (fig) 行き詰り ikízumari

stalk [stɔ:k] n (of flower, fruit) 茎 kukí
♦vt (person, animal) ...に忍び寄る ...ni shinóbiyorù

stalk off vi 威張って行く ibátte ikù

stall [stɔ:l] n (in market) 屋台 yátài; (in stable) 馬房 babó
♦vt (AUT: engine, car) エンストを起す eñsuto wò okósù; (fig: delay: person) 引止める hikítomerù; (: decision etc) 引延ばす hikínobasù
♦vi (AUT: engine, car) エンストを起す eñsuto wò okósù; (fig: person) 時間稼ぎをする jikánkasegì wò suru

stallion [stæl'jən] n 種ウマ tanéuma

stalls [stɔ:lz] (BRIT) npl (in cinema, theater) 特別席 tokúbetsusèki

stalwart [stɔ:l'wərt] adj (worker, supporter, party member) 不動の fudő no

stamina [stæm'inə] n スタミナ sutámina

stammer [stæm'ə:r] n どもり dómòri
♦vi どもる domórù

stamp [stæmp] n (postage stamp) 切手 kitté; (rubber stamp) スタンプ sutáñpu; (mark, also fig) 特徴 tokúchō
♦vi (also: stamp one's foot) 足を踏み鳴らす ashí wò fumínarasù
♦vt (letter) ...に切手を張る ...ni kitté wò harú; (mark) 特徴付ける tokúchōzukerù; (with rubber stamp) ...にスタンプを押す ...ni sutáñpu wo osú

stamp album n 切手帳 kittéchō

stamp collecting [-kələk'tiŋ] n 切手収集 kittéshūshū

stampede [stæmpi:d'] n (of animal herd) 暴走 bōsō; (fig: of people) 殺到 sattő

stance [stæns] n (way of standing) 立っている姿勢 tatté irù shiséi; (fig) 姿勢 shiséi

stand [stænd] n (position) 構え kámàe; (for taxis) 乗場 noríba; (hall, music stand) 台 dái; (SPORT) スタンド sutáñdo; (stall) 屋台 yátài
♦vb (pt, pp stood)
♦vi (be: person, unemployment etc) ...になっている ...ni natté irù; (be on foot) 立つ tátsù; (rise) 立ち上る tachíagarù; (remain: decision, offer) 有効である yúkō de arù; (in election etc) 立候補する rikkőho suru
♦vt (place: object) 立てる tatérù; (tolerate, withstand: person, thing) ...に耐える ...ni taérù; (treat, invite to) おごる ogőrù

to make a stand (fig) 立場を執る tachíba wò tórù

to stand for parliament (BRIT) 議員選挙に出馬する giíneñkyo ni shutsúba suru

standard [stæn'də:rd] n (level) 水準 suíjun; (norm, criterion) 基準 kijűn; (flag) 旗 hatá
♦adj (normal: size etc) 標準的な hyőjunteki na; (text) 権威のある kéñ-i no árù

standardize [stæn'də:rdaiz] vt 規格化する kikákuka suru

standard lamp (BRIT) n フロアスタンド furóasutañdo

standard of living n 生活水準 seíkatsusuijùn

standards [stæn'də:rdz] npl (morals) 道徳基準 dőtoku kijùn

stand by vi (be ready) 待機する táiki suru
♦vt fus (opinion, decision) 守る mamórù; (person) ...の力になる ...no chikára ni narù

stand-by [stænd'bai] n (reserve) 非常用の物 hijőyō no monő

to be on stand-by 待機している táiki shité irù

stand-by ticket n (AVIAT) キャンセル待ちの切符 kyañserumachi nò kippú

stand down vi (withdraw) 引下がる hikísagarù

stand for vt fus (signify) 意味する ímì suru; (represent) 代表する daíhyō suru; (tolerate) 容認する yőnin suru

stand-in [stænd'in] n 代役 daíko

stand in for vt fus (replace) ...の代役を務める ...no daíyaku wò tsutómerù

standing [stæn'diŋ] adj (on feet: ovation) 立ち上ってする tachíagatte surù; (permanent: invitation) 持続の jizóku no, 継続の keízoku no

♦*n* (status) 地位 chíi

of many years' standing 数年前から続いている sūnen maè kara tsuzúite irù

standing joke *n* お決りの冗談 o-kímari nò jṓdañ

standing order (*BRIT*) *n* (at bank) 自動振替 jidṓfurīkae ◇支払額が定額である場合に使う shiháraìgaku ga teígaku de arù bāaì ni tsukáù

standing room *n* 立見席 tachímisèki

stand-offish [stændɔ:f'iʃ] *adj* 無愛想な buáìso na

standpoint [stænd'pɔint] *n* 観点 kañteñ

standstill [stænd'stil] *n*: *at a standstill* (*also fig*) 滞って todókōtte

to come to a standstill 止ってしまう tomátte shimaù

stand up *vi* (rise) 立ち上る tachíagarù

stand up for *vt fus* (defend) 守る mamórù

stand up to *vt fus* (withstand: *also fig*) ...に立向かう ...ni tachímukaù

stank [stæŋk] *pt of* **stink**

staple [stei'pəl] *n* (for papers) ホチキスの針 hóchìkisu no hárì

♦*adj* (food etc) 主要の shuyṓ no

♦*vt* (fasten) ホチキスで留める hóchìkisu de tomérù

stapler [stei'plə:r] *n* ホチキス hóchìkisu

star [stɑ:r] *n* (in sky) 星 hoshí; (celebrity) スター sutā

♦*vi*: *to star in* ...で主演する ...de shuén suru

♦*vt* (THEATER, CINEMA) 主役とする shuyáku to surù

starboard [stɑ:r'bə:rd] *n* 右げん úgeñ

starch [stɑ:rtʃ] *n* (for shirts etc) のり norí; (CULIN) でんぷん deñpun

stardom [stɑ:r'dəm] *n* スターの身分 sutā no mibùn

stare [ste:r] *n* じろじろ見る事 jíròjiro mírù koto

♦*vi*: *to stare at* じろじろ見る jíròjiro mírù

starfish [stɑ:r'fiʃ] *n* ヒトデ hitode

stark [stɑ:rk] *adj* (bleak) 殺風景な sappūkèi na

♦*adv*: *stark naked* 素っ裸の suppádàka no

starling [stɑ:r'liŋ] *n* ムクドリ mukúdòri

starry [stɑ:r'i:] *adj* (night, sky) 星がよく見える hoshí gà yókù miérù

starry-eyed [stɑ:r'i:aid] *adj* (innocent) 天真らん漫な teñshinranman na

stars [stɑ:rz] *npl*: *the stars* (horoscope) 星占い hoshíuranaì

start [stɑ:rt] *n* (beginning) 初め hajíme; (departure) 出発 shuppátsu; (sudden movement) ぎくっとする事 gikúttò suru kotò; (advantage) リード rīdo

♦*vt* (begin) 始める hajímerù; (cause) 引起こす hikíokosù; (found: business etc) 創立する sṓritsu suru; (engine) かける kakérù

♦*vi* (begin) 始まる hajímarù; (with fright) ぎくっとする gikúttò suru; (train etc) 出発する shuppátsu suru

to start doing/to do something ...をし始める ...wo shihájimerù

starter [stɑ:r'tə:r] *n* (AUT) スターター sutātā; (SPORT: official) スターター sutātā; (*BRIT*: CULIN) 最初の料理 saísho no ryōri

starting point [stɑ:r'tiŋ-] *n* 出発点 shuppátsuteñ

startle [stɑ:r'təl] *vt* 驚かす odórokasù

startling [stɑ:r'liŋ] *adj* (news etc) 驚く様な odórokù yṓ na

start off *vi* (begin) 始める hajímerù; (begin moving) 出発する shuppátsu suru

start up *vi* (business etc) 開業する kaígyò suru; (engine) かかる kakárù; (car) 走り出す hashíridasù

♦*vt* (business etc) 創立する sṓritsu suru; (engine) かける kakérù; (car) 走らせる hashíraserù

starvation [stɑ:rvei'ʃən] *n* 飢餓 kígà

starve [stɑ:rv] *vi* (*inf*: be very hungry) おなかがぺこぺこである onáka gà pekópeko de árù; (*also*: **starve to death**) 餓死する gáshì suru

♦*vt* (person, animal: not give food to) 飢えさせる uésaserù; (: to death) 餓死させる gáshì sasérù

state [steit] n (condition) 状態 jōtai; (government) 国 kuní
♦vt (say, declare) 明言する meígen suru
to be in a state 取乱している torímidashite irú

stately [steit'li:] adj (home, walk etc) 優雅な yūga na

statement [steit'mənt] n (declaration) 陳述 chíñjutsu

States [steits] npl: **the States** 米国 beíkoku

statesman [steits'mən] (pl **statesmen**) n リーダー格の政治家 rídākaku nò seíjikà

static [stæt'ik] n (RADIO, TV) 雑音 zatsúon
♦adj (not moving) 静的な seíteki na

static electricity n 静電気 seídeñki

station [stei'ʃən] n (RAIL) 駅 ékì; (police station etc) 署 shó; (RADIO) 放送局 hōsōkyoku
♦vt (position: guards etc) 配置する haíchi suru

stationary [stei'ʃəneːri:] adj (vehicle) 動いていない ugóite inaì

stationer [stei'ʃənəːr] n 文房具屋 buñbōguya

stationer's (shop) [stei'ʃənəːrz-] n 文房具店 buñbōguteñ

stationery [stei'ʃəneːri:] n 文房具 buñbōgu

stationmaster [stei'ʃənmæstəːr] n (RAIL) 駅長 ekíchō

station wagon (US) n ワゴン車 wagóñsha

statistic [stətis'tik] n 統計値 tōkeichì

statistical [stətis'tikəl] adj (evidence, techniques) 統計学的な tōkeigakuteki na

statistics [stətis'tiks] n (science) 統計学 tōkeigàku

statue [stætʃ'u:] n 像 zō

stature [stætʃ'əːr] n 身長 shíñchō

status [stei'təs] n (position) 身分 míbùn; (official classification) 資格 shikáku; (importance) 地位 chíi
the status quo 現状 geñjō

status symbol n ステータスシンボル sutétasushiñboru

statute [stætʃ'u:t] n 法律 hóritsu

statutory [stætʃ'u:tɔːri:] adj (powers, rights etc) 法定の hōtei no

staunch [stɔːntʃ] adj (ally) 忠実な chújitsu na

stave off [steiv-] vt (attack, threat) 防ぐ fuségù

stay [stei] n (period of time) 滞在期間 taízaikikàn
♦vi (remain) 居残る inókorù; (with someone, as guest) 泊る tomárù; (in place: spend some time) とどまる todómarù
to stay put とどまる todómarù
to stay the night 泊る tomárù

stay behind vi 居残る inókorù

stay in vi (at home) 家に居る ié nì irú

staying power [stei'iŋ-] n 根気 koñki

stay on vi 残る nokórù

stay out vi (of house) 家に戻らない ié nì modóranaì

stay up vi (at night) 起きている ókìte irú

stead [sted] n: **in someone's stead** ...の代りに ...no kawári ni
to stand someone in good stead ...の役に立つ ...no yakú ni tatsù

steadfast [sted'fæst] adj 不動の fudō no

steadily [sted'ili:] adv (firmly) 着実に chakújitsu ni; (constantly) ずっと zuttő; (fixedly) じっと jittő; (walk) しっかりと shikkárì to

steady [sted'i:] adj (constant: job, boyfriend, speed) 決った kimátta, 変らない kawáranaì; (regular: rise in prices) 着実な chakújitsu na; (person, character) 堅実な keñjitsu na; (firm: hand etc) 震えない furúenaì; (calm: look, voice) 落着いた ochítsùita
♦vt (stabilize) 安定させる añtei saserù; (nerves) 静める shizúmerù

steak [steik] n (also: **beefsteak**) ビーフステーキ bífusutèki; (beef, fish, pork etc) ステーキ sutéki

steal [sti:l] (pt **stole**, pp **stolen**) vt 盗む nusúmù
♦vi (thieve) 盗む nusúmù; (move secretly) こっそりと行く kossórì to ikú

stealth [stelθ] *n*: **by stealth** こっそりと kossórì to

stealthy [stel'θi:] *adj* (movements, actions) ひそかな hisókà na

steam [sti:m] *n* (mist) 水蒸気 suíjòki; (on window) 曇り kumóri
♦*vt* (CULIN) 蒸す músù
♦*vi* (give off steam) 水蒸気を立てる suíjòki wo tatérù

steam engine *n* 蒸気機関 jókikikàn

steamer [sti:'mə:r] *n* 汽船 kisén

steamroller [sti:m'roulə:r] *n* ロードローラー rốdoròrā

steamship [sti:m'ʃip] *n* = **steamer**

steamy [sti:'mi:] *adj* (room) 湯気でもうもうの yúge de mốmô no; (window) 湯気で曇った yúge de kumóttà; (heat, atmosphere) 蒸暑い mushíatsuì

steel [sti:l] *n* 鋼鉄 kótetsu
♦*adj* 鋼鉄の kótetsu no

steelworks [sti:l'wə:rks] *n* 製鋼所 seíkōjo

steep [sti:p] *adj* (stair, slope) 険しい kewáshiì; (increase) 大幅の ốhaba na; (price) 高い takái
♦*vt* (fig: soak) 浸す hitásù

steeple [sti:'pəl] *n* せん塔 sefitō

steeplechase [sti:'pəltʃeis] *n* 障害レース shốgairèsu

steer [sti:r] *vt* (vehicle) 運転する ufiten suru; (person) 導く michíbikù
♦*vi* (maneuver) 車を操る kurúma wò ayátsurù

steering [sti:r'iŋ] *n* (AUT) ステアリング sutéaringu

steering wheel *n* ハンドル hafidoru

stem [stem] *n* (of plant) 茎 kukí; (of glass) 足 ashí
♦*vt* (stop: blood, flow, advance) 止める tomérù

stem from *vt fus* (subj: condition, problem) ...に由来する ...ni yurái suru

stench [stentʃ] *n* 悪臭 akúshū

stencil [sten'səl] *n* (lettering) ステンシルで書いた文字 sutéñshiru de káita mójì; (pattern used) ステンシル sutéñshiru
♦*vt* (letters, designs etc) ステンシルで書く sutéñshiru de kákù

stenographer [stənɑːg'rəfə:r] (*US*) *n* 速記者 sokkísha

step [step] *n* (footstep, *also fig*) 一歩 íppò; (sound) 足音 ashfoto; (of stairs) 段 dáñ, ステップ sutéppù
♦*vi* **to step forward** 前に出る máè ni dérù **to step back** 後ろに下がる ushíro nì sagárù
in/out of step (with) (...と) 歩調が合って〔ずれて〕(...to) hochố ga attè〔zurète〕

stepbrother [step'brʌðə:r] *n* 異父〔異母〕兄弟 ífù〔íbò〕kyốdaì

stepdaughter [step'dɔ:tə:r] *n* まま娘 mamámusùme

step down *vi* (*fig*: resign) 辞任する jinín suru

stepfather [step'fɑ:ðə:r] *n* まま父 mamáchichi

stepladder [step'lædə:r] *n* 脚立 kyatátsu

stepmother [step'mʌðə:r] *n* まま母 mamáhaha

step on *vt fus* (something: walk on) 踏む fumú

stepping stone [step'iŋ-] *n* 飛石 tobíishi

steps [steps] (*BRIT*) *npl* = **stepladder**

stepsister [step'sistə:r] *n* 異父〔異母〕姉妹 ífù〔íbò〕shímài

stepson [step'sʌn] *n* まま息子 mamámusùko

step up *vt* (increase: efforts, pace etc) 増す masú

stereo [ster'i:ou] *n* (system) ステレオ sutéreo; (record player) レコードプレーヤー rekốdopurèyā
♦*adj* (*also*: **stereophonic**) ステレオの sutéreo no

stereotype [ster'i:ətaip] *n* 固定概念 kotéigaìnen

sterile [ster'əl] *adj* (free from germs: bandage etc) 殺菌した sakkín shita; (barren: woman, female animal) 不妊の funín no; (: man, male animal) 子供を作れない kodómo wò tsukúrenaì; (land) 不毛の fumó no

sterilize [ster'əlaiz] *vt* (thing, place) 殺菌する sakkín suru; (woman) ...に避妊手術をする ...ni hinínshujùtsu wo suru

sterling [stəːr'liŋ] *adj* (silver) 純銀の juŋgin no
♦*n* (ECON) 英国通貨 eíkokutsūka
one pound sterling 英貨1ポンド eíka ichí poňdo

stern [stəːrn] *adj* (father, warning etc) 厳しい kibíshiì
♦*n* (of boat) 船尾 seňbi

stethoscope [steθ'əskoup] *n* 聴診器 chôshiňki

stew [stuː] *n* シチュー shichū
♦*vt* (meat, vegetables) 煮込む nikómù; (fruit) 煮る nirú

steward [stuː'əːrd] *n* (on ship, plane, train) スチュワード suchūwādo

stewardess [stuː'əːrdis] *n* (especially on plane) スチュワーデス suchūwādesu

stick [stik] *n* (gen: of wood) 棒 bô; (as weapon) こん棒 koňbō; (walking stick) つえ tsúe
♦*vb* (*pt, pp* **stuck**)
♦*vt* (with glue etc) 張る harú; (*inf:* put) 置く okú; (: tolerate) ...の最後まで我慢する ...no sáigo made gámàn suru; (thrust): *to stick something into* ...の中へ...を突っ込む ...no nákà e ...wo tsukkómù
♦*vi* (become attached) くっつく kuttsúkù; (be immovable) 引っ掛る hikkákarù; (in mind etc) 焼付く yakítsukù

a stick of dynamite ダイナマイト1本 dainamaito ippon

sticker [stik'əːr] *n* ステッカー sutékkà

sticking plaster [stik'iŋ-] *n* ばんそうこう baňsōkō

stickler [stik'ləːr] *n*: *to be a stickler for* ...に対してやかましい ...ni káň shite yakámashiì

stick out *vi* (ears etc) 突出る tsukíderù

stick up *vi* (hair etc) 立つ tátsù

stick-up [stik'ʌp] (*inf*) *n* ピストル強盗 pisútoru gôtō

stick up for *vt fus* (person) ...の肩をもつ ...no kátà wo mótsù; (principle) 守る mamórù

sticky [stik'iː] *adj* (messy: hands etc) べたべたしている bétàbeta shité irù; (label) 粘着の neńchaku no; (*fig:* situation) 厄介な yákkài na

stiff [stif] *adj* (hard, firm: brush) 堅い katáì; (hard: paste, egg-white) 固まった katámattà; (moving with difficulty: arms, legs, back) こわばった kowábattà; (: door, zip etc) 堅い katáì; (formal: manner, smile) 堅苦しい katágurushiì; (difficult, severe: competition, sentence) 厳しい kibíshiì; (strong: drink, breeze) 強い tsuyóì; (high: price) 高い takáì
♦*adv* (bored, worried, scared) ひどく hídòku

stiffen [stif'ən] *vi* (body, muscles, joints) こわばる kowábarù

stiff neck *n* 首が回らない事 kubí gà mawáranaì kotó

stifle [stai'fəl] *vt* (cry, yawn) 抑える osáerù; (opposition) 抑圧する yokúatsu suru

stifling [staif'liŋ] *adj* (heat) 息苦しい ikígurushiì

stigma [stig'mə] *n* (*fig:* of divorce, failure, defeat etc) 汚名 ômèi

stile [stail] *n* 踏段 fumídan ◇牧場のさくの両側に設けられ、人間が越えられるが家畜が出られない様にした物 bokújō nò sakú nò ryôgawa nì mókerarè, niŋgen gà koérarerù ga kachíku dè derárenai yô ni shitá monò

stiletto [stilet'ou] (*BRIT*) *n* (*also:* **stiletto heel**) ハイヒール haíhìru

still [stil] *adj* (person, water, air) 動かない ugókanaì; (place) 静寂な seíjaku na
♦*adv* (up to this time, yet) まだ mádà; (even) 更に sárà ni; (nonetheless) それにしても soré ni shite mò

stillborn [stil'bɔːrn] *adj* 死産の shízàn no

still life *n* 静物画 seíbutsugà

stilt [stilt] *n* (pile) 脚柱 kyakúchū; (for walking on) 竹馬 takéuma

stilted [stil'tid] *adj* (behavior, conversation) 堅苦しい katákurushiì

stimulant [stim'jələnt] *n* 覚せい剤 kakúseizaì

stimulate [stim'jəleit] *vt* (person, demand) 刺激する shigéki suru

stimulating [stim'jəleitiŋ] *adj* (conversation, person, experience) 刺激的な shigékiteki na

stimuli [stim'jəlai] *npl of* **stimulus**

stimulus [stim'jələs] (*pl* **stimuli**) *n* (encouragement, *also* MED) 刺激 shigéki

sting [stiŋ] *n* (wound) 虫刺され mushísasarè; (pain) 刺す様な痛み sásù yō na itámi; (organ) 針 hárì
◆*vb* (*pt, pp* **stung**)
◆*vt* (insect, plant etc) 刺す sásù; (*fig*) 傷付ける kizútsukerù
◆*vi* (insect, plant etc) 刺す sásù; (eyes, ointment etc) しみる shimírù

stingy [stin'dʒi:] *adj* けちな kéchì na

stink [stiŋk] *n* (smell) 悪臭 akúshū
◆*vi* (*pt* **stank**, *pp* **stunk**) (smell) におう nióù

stinking [stiŋ'kiŋ] (*inf*) *adj* (*fig*) くそったれの kusóttàre no

stint [stint] *n* 仕事の期間 shigóto no kikañ
◆*vi*: **to stint on** (work, ingredients etc) ...をけちる ..wo kechírù

stipulate [stip'jəleit] *vt* ...の条件を付ける ...no jōken wò tsukérù

stir [stəːr] *n* (*fig*: agitation) 騒ぎ sáwàgi
◆*vt* (tea etc) かき混ぜる kakímazerù; (*fig*: emotions) 刺激する shigéki suru
◆*vi* (move slightly) ちょっと動く chóttò ugókù

stirrup [stəːr'əp] *n* あぶみ abúmi

stir up *vt* (trouble) 引起こす hikíokosù

stitch [stitʃ] *n* (SEWING, MED) 一針 hitóhàri; (KNITTING) ステッチ sutétchì; (pain) わき腹のけいれん wakíbara nò keíren
◆*vt* (sew: *gen*, MED) 縫う núù

stoat [stout] *n* てん téñ

stock [stɑːk] *n* (supply) 資源 shígèn; (COMM) 在庫品 zaíkohìn; (AGR) 家畜 kachíku; (CULIN) 煮出し汁 nidáshijìru、ストック sutókkù; (descent) 血統 kettō; (FINANCE: government stock etc) 株式 kabúshìki
◆*adj* (*fig*: reply, excuse etc) お決りの o-kímàri no
◆*vt* (have in stock) 常備する jōbì suru
stocks and shares 債券 saíken
in/out of stock 在庫がある〔ない〕zaíko gà árù〔nai〕
to take stock of (*fig*) 検討する keñtō suru

stockbroker [stɑːk'broukəːr] *n* 株式仲買人 kabúshikinakagainìn

stock cube (*BRIT*) *n* 固形スープの素 kokéi sūpu no moto

stock exchange *n* 株式取引所 kabúshikitorihikijò

stocking [stɑːk'iŋ] *n* ストッキング sutókkiñgu

stockist [stɑːk'ist] (*BRIT*) *n* 特約店 tokúyakutèn

stock market *n* 株式市場 kabúshikishijò

stock phrase *n* 決り文句 kimárimoñku

stockpile [stɑːk'pail] *n* 備蓄 bichíku
◆*vt* 貯蔵する chozō suru

stocktaking [stɑːk'teikiŋ] (*BRIT*) *n* (COMM) 棚卸し tanáoroshi

stock up with *vt* ...を仕入れる ...wo shiírérù

stocky [stɑːk'i:] *adj* (strong, short) がっしりした gasshírì shita; (short, stout) ずんぐりした zuñgurì shita

stodgy [stɑːdʒ'i:] *adj* (food) こってりした kottérì shita

stoical [stou'ikəl] *adj* 平然とした heízen tò shita

stoke [stouk] *vt* (fire, furnace, boiler) ...に燃料をくべる ...ni neñryō wo kubérù

stole [stoul] *pt of* **steal**
◆*n* ストール sutórù

stolen [stou'lən] *pp of* **steal**

stolid [stɑːl'id] *adj* (person, behavior) 表情の乏しい hyōjō no tobóshiì

stomach [stʌm'ək] *n* (ANAT) 胃 i; (belly) おなか onáka
◆*vt* (*fig*) 耐える taérù

stomachache [stʌm'əkeik] *n* 腹痛 fukútsū

stone [stoun] *n* (rock) 石 ishí; (pebble) 小石 koíshi; (gem) 宝石 hōseki; (in fruit) 種 táne; (MED) 結石 kessēki; (*BRIT*: weight) ストーン sutőñ ◇体重の単位, 約 6.3 kg taíjū no tañ-i, yákù 6.3 kg
◆*adj* (pottery) ストーンウエアの sutőñ-ueä no

◆*vt* (person) ...に石を投付ける ...ni ishi wo nagetsukeru; (fruit) ...の種を取る ...no táne wo tórù

stone-cold [stoun'kould'] *adj* 冷え切った hiékittà

stone-deaf [stoun'def'] *adj* かなつんぼの kanátsuñbo no

stonework [stoun'wə:rk] *n* (stones) 石造りの物 ishízukùri no mono

stony [stou'ni:] *adj* (ground) 石だらけの ishídaràke no; (*fig*: glance, silence etc) 冷淡な reítan na

stood [stud] *pt, pp of* **stand**

stool [stu:l] *n* スツール sutsúrù

stoop [stu:p] *vi* (*also*: **stoop down**: bend) 腰をかがめる koshí wò kagámerù; (*also*: **have a stoop**) 腰が曲っている koshí gà magátte irù

stop [sta:p] *n* (halt) 停止 teíshi; (short stay) 立寄り tachíyori; (in punctuation: *also*: **full stop**) ピリオド píriòdo; (bus stop etc) 停留所 teíryūjo

◆*vt* (break off) 止める tomérù; (block: pay, check) ...の支払を停止させる ...no shiháraì wò teíshi saserù; (prevent: *also*: **put a stop to**) やめさせる yamésaserù

◆*vi* (halt: person) 立ち止る tachídomarù; (: watch, clock) 止まる tomárù; (end: rain, noise etc) やむ yamú

to stop doing something ...するのをやめる ...surú no wò yamérù

stop dead *vi* 急に止る kyū ní tomárù

stopgap [sta:p'gæp] *n* (person/thing) 間に合せの人〔物〕 ma ní awase nò hitó 〔monó〕

stop off *vi* 立寄る tachíyorù

stopover [sta:p'ouvə:r] *n* (*gen*) 立寄って泊る事 tachíyottè tomáru kotò; (AVIAT) 給油着陸 kyúyuchakùriku

stoppage [sta:p'idʒ] *n* (strike) ストライキ sutóraìki; (blockage) 停止 teíshi

stopper [sta:p'ə:r] *n* 栓 séñ

stop press *n* 最新ニュース saíshinnyùsu

stop up *vt* (hole) ふさぐ fuságù

stopwatch [sta:p'wa:tʃ] *n* ストップウオッチ sutóppuuotchì

storage [stɔːr'idʒ] *n* 保管 hokán

storage heater *n* 蓄熱ヒーター chikú-

netsuhītā ◇深夜など電気需要の少ない時に熱を作って蓄え，昼間それを放射するヒーター shíñ-ya nádò defikijuyò no sukúnai tokì ni netsú wo tsukuttè takúwaè, hirúma soré wò hōsha suru hītā

store [stɔ:r] *n* (stock) 蓄え takúwaè; (depot) 倉庫 sōko; (*BRIT*: large shop) デパート depātò; (*US*) 店 misé; (reserve) 備蓄 bichíku

◆*vt* (provisions, information etc) 蓄える takúwaerù

in store 未来に待構えて mírài ni machíkamaetè

storeroom [stɔ:r'ru:m] *n* 倉庫 sōko

stores [stɔ:rz] *npl* (provisions) 物資 bússhi

store up *vt* (nuts, sugar, memories) 蓄える takúwaerù

storey [stɔ:r'i:] (*BRIT*: floor) *n* = **story**

stork [stɔ:rk] *n* コウノトリ kōnotòri

storm [stɔ:rm] *n* (bad weather) 嵐 áràshi; (*fig*: of criticism, applause etc) 爆発 bakúhatsu

◆*vi* (*fig*: speak angrily) どなる donárù

◆*vt* (attack: place) 攻撃する kōgeki suru

stormy [stɔ:r'mi:] *adj* (weather) 荒れ模様の arémoyò no; (*fig*: debate, relations) 激しい hagéshiì

story [stɔ:r'i:] *n* (*gen*: *also*: **history**) 物語 monógatàri; (lie) うそ úsò; (*US*) 階 kái

storybook [stɔ:r'i:buk] *n* 童話の本 dōwa no hoñ

stout [staut] *adj* (strong: branch etc) 丈夫な jōbu na; (fat) 太った futóttà; (resolute: friend, supporter) 不動の fudō no

◆*n* (beer) スタウト sutáùto

stove [stouv] *n* (for cooking) レンジ réñji; (for heating) ストーブ sutóbù

stow [stou] *vt* (*also*: **stow away**) しまう shimáù

stowaway [stou'əwei] *n* 密航者 mikkṓshà

straddle [stræd'əl] *vt* (chair, fence etc: *also fig*) ...にまたがる ...ni matágarù

straggle [stræg'əl] *vi* (houses etc) 散在する sañzai suru; (people etc) 落ごする rakúgo suru

straggly [stræg'li:] *adj* (hair) ぼさぼさし

た bósàbosa shita

straight [streit] *adj* (line, road, back, hair) 真っ直ぐの massúgù no; (honest: answer) 正直な shójiki na; (simple: choice, fight) 簡潔な kańketsu na

♦*adv* (directly) 真っ直ぐに massúgù ni; (drink) ストレートで sutórèto de

to put/get something straight (make clear) 明らかにする akíràka ni suru

straight away, straight off (at once) 直ちに tádàchi ni

straighten [streítən] *vt* (skirt, bed etc) 整える totónoerù

straighten out *vt* (*fig*: problem, situation) 解決する kaíketsu suru

straight-faced [streit'feist] *adj* まじめな顔をした majíme nà kaó wo shità

straightforward [streitfɔ:r'wə:rd] *adj* (simple) 簡単な kańtan na; (honest) 正直な shójiki na

strain [strein] *n* (pressure) 負担 fután; (TECH) ひずみ hizúmi; (MED: tension) 緊張 kińchō; (breed) 血統 kettő

♦*vt* (back etc) 痛める itámerù; (stretch: resources) ...に負担をかける ...ni fután wò kakérù; (CULIN: food) こす kosú

back strain (MED) ぎっくり腰 gikkúri-gòshi

strained [streind] *adj* (back, muscle) 痛めた itámetà; (relations) 緊迫した kińpaku shità

a strained laugh 作り笑い tsukúriwaràì

strainer [strei'nə:r] *n* (CULIN) こし器 koshíkì

strains [streinz] *npl* (MUS) 旋律 seńritsu

strait [streit] *n* (GEO) 海峡 kaíkyō

strait-jacket [streit'dʒækit] *n* 拘束衣 kősokuì

strait-laced [streit'leist] *adj* しかつめらしい shikátsumerashiì

straits [streits] *npl*: *to be in dire straits* (*fig*) 困り果てている komárihatete irù

strand [strænd] *n* (of thread, hair, rope) 一本 íppòn

stranded [stræn'did] *adj* (holiday-makers) 足留めされた ashídome saretà

strange [streindʒ] *adj* (not known) 未知の míchì no; (odd) 変な hếñ na

strangely [streindʒ'li:] *adv* (act, laugh) 変った風に kawátta fū ni ¶ *see also* **enough**

stranger [strein'dʒə:r] *n* (unknown person) 知らない人 shíránai hitò; (from another area) よそ者 yosómono

strangle [stræŋ'gəl] *vt* (victim) 絞殺する shimékorosù; (*fig*: economy) 圧迫する appáku suru

stranglehold [stræŋ'gəlhould] *n* (*fig*) 抑圧 yokúatsu

strap [stræp] *n* 肩ひも katáhimo, ストラップ sutórappù

strapping [stræp'iŋ] *adj* たくましい takúmashiì

strata [stræt'ə] *npl of* **stratum**

stratagem [stræt'ədʒəm] *n* 策略 sakúryàku

strategic [strəti:'dʒik] *adj* (positions, withdrawal, weapons etc) 戦略的な seńryakuteki na

strategy [stræt'idʒi:] *n* (plan, *also* MIL) 作戦 sakúsen

stratum [strei'təm] (*pl* **strata**) *n* (*gen*) 層 ső; (in earth's surface) 地層 chiső; (in society) 階層 kaísō

straw [strɔ:] *n* (dried stalks) わら wárà; (drinking straw) ストロー sutórő

that's the last straw! もう我慢できない mő gámàn dekínaì

strawberry [strɔ:'be:ri:] *n* イチゴ ichígo

stray [strei] *adj* (animal) のら ... norá...; (bullet) 流れ ... nagáre...; (scattered) 点在する teńzai suru

♦*vi* (children, animals) はぐれる hagúrerù; (thoughts) 横道にそれる yokómichi nì sorérù

streak [stri:k] *n* (stripe: *gen*) 筋 sújì

♦*vt* ...に筋を付ける ...ni sújì wo tsukérù

♦*vi*: *to streak past* 猛スピードで通り過ぎる mősupìdo de tőrisugirù

stream [stri:m] *n* (small river) 小川 ogáwa; (of people, vehicles, smoke) 流れ nagáre; (of questions, insults etc) 連続 reńzoku

♦vt (SCOL: students) 能力別に分ける nṓryokubetsu ni wakérù
♦vi (water, oil, blood) 流れる nagárerù
to stream in/out (people) 流れ込む〔出る〕 nagárekomù〔derù〕

streamer [stri:'mə:r] *n* 紙テープ kamítèpu

streamlined [stri:m'laind] *adj* 流線形の ryū́senkei no

street [stri:t] *n* 道 michí

streetcar [stri:t'kɑ:r] (*US*) *n* 路面電車 roméndeǹsha

street lamp *n* 街灯 gaítō

street plan *n* 市街地図 shigáichizu

streetwise [stri:t'waiz] (*inf*) *adj* 裏町の悪知恵を持っている urámachi no warújie wò motté irù

strength [streŋkθ] *n* (physical) 体力 taíryoku; (of girder, knot etc) 強さ tsúyòsa; (*fig*: power, number) 勢力 seíryoku

strengthen [streŋk'θən] *vt* (building, machine) 補強する hokyṓ suru; (*fig*: group, argument, relationship) 強くする tsúyòku suru

strenuous [stren'ju:əs] *adj* (energetic: exercise) 激しい hagéshiì; (determined: efforts) 精力的な seíryokuteki na

stress [stres] *n* (force, pressure, *also* TECH) 圧力 atsúryòku; (mental strain) ストレス sutórèsu; (emphasis) 強調 kyṓchō
♦vt (point, importance etc) 強調する kyṓchō suru; (syllable) ...にアクセントを置く ...ni ákùsento wo okú

stretch [stretʃ] *n* (area: of sand, water etc) 一帯 ittái
♦vi (person, animal) 背伸びする sénòbi suru; (extend): *to stretch to/as far as* ...まで続く ...máde tsuzúkù
♦vt (pull) 伸ばす nobásù; (subj: job, task: make demands of) ...に努力を要求する ...ni dóryòku wo yōkyū́ suru

stretcher [stretʃ'ə:r] *n* 担架 tánka

stretch out *vi* 体を伸ばす karáda wò nobásù
♦vt (arm etc) 伸ばす nobásù; (spread) 広げる hirógerù

strewn [stru:n] *adj*: *strewn with* ...が散らばっている ...ga chirábatte irù

stricken [strik'ən] *adj* (person) 打ちひしがれた uchíhishigaretà; (city, industry etc) 災いに見舞われた wazáwai nì mimáwaretà
stricken with (arthritis, disease) ...にかかっている ...ni kakátte irù

strict [strikt] *adj* (severe, firm: person, rule) 厳しい kibíshiì; (precise: meaning) 厳密な geńmitsu na

strictly [strikt'li:] *adv* (severely) 厳しく kibíshikù; (exactly) 厳密に geńmitsu ni

stridden [strid'ən] *pp* of **stride**

stride [straid] *n* (step) 大またの一歩 ṓmàta no íppò
♦vi (*pt* **strode**, *pp* **stridden**) 大またに歩く ṓmàta ni arúkù

strident [straid'ənt] *adj* (voice, sound) 甲高い kańdakaì

strife [straif] *n* 反目 hańmoku

strike [straik] *n* (of workers) ストライキ sutóraìki; (of bird etc) 発見 hakkén; (MIL: attack) 攻撃 kṓgeki
♦vb (*pt*, *pp* **struck**)
♦vt (hit: person, thing) 打つ útsù; (*fig*: subj: idea, thought) ...の心に浮ぶ ...no kókòro ni ukábù; (oil etc) 発見する hakkén suru; (bargain, deal) 決める kimérù
♦vi (go on strike) ストライキに入る sutóraìki ni haíru; (attack: soldiers) 攻撃する kṓgeki suru; (: illness) 襲う osóù; (: disaster) 見舞う mimáù; (clock) 鳴る narú
on strike (workers) ストライキ中で sutóraikichū de
to strike a match マッチを付ける mátchì wo tsukérù

strike down *vt* (kill) 殺す korósù; (harm) 襲う osóù

striker [strai'kə:r] *n* (person on strike) ストライキ参加者 sutóraikisaǹkashà; (SPORT) 攻撃選手 kṓgekiseńshu

strike up *vt* (MUS) 演奏し始める eńsō shihajimerù; (conversation) 始める hajímerù; (friendship) 結ぶ musúbù

striking [strai'kiŋ] *adj* (noticeable) 目立つ medátsù; (attractive) 魅力的な miryókuteki na

string [strɪŋ] *n* (thin rope) ひも himő; (row: of beads etc) 数珠つなぎの物 juzútsunăgi no monő; (: of disasters etc) 一連 ichíren; (MUS) 弦 geñ

♦*vt* (*pt*, *pp* **strung**): **to string together** つなぐ tsunăgu

a string of islands 列島 rettő

to pull strings (*fig*) コネを利用する kőne wo riyő suru

to string out 一列に並べる ichíretsu nǐ naráberù

string bean *n* さや豆 sayámame

string(ed) instrument [strɪŋ(d)-] *n* (MUS) 弦楽器 geñgakkì

stringent [strɪnˈdʒənt] *adj* (rules, measures) 厳しい kibíshiì

strings [strɪŋz] *npl*: **the strings** (MUS): section of orchestra) 弦楽器 geñgakkì

strip [strɪp] *n* (gen) 細長い切れ hosónagaì kiré; (of land, water) 細長い一帯 hosónagaì ittái

♦*vt* (undress) 裸にする hadáka ni surù; (paint) はがす hagásù; (*also*: **strip down**: machine) 分解する buñkai suru

♦*vi* (undress) 裸になる hadáka ni narù

strip cartoon *n* 四こま漫画 yoñkoma mañga

stripe [straip] *n* (gen) しま shima; (MIL, POLICE) そで章 sodéshō

striped [straipt] *adj* しま模様の shimámoyô no

strip lighting *n* 蛍光灯 keíkōtō

stripper [stripˈəːr] *n* ストリッパー sutórippā

striptease [stripˈtiːz] *n* ストリップショー sutórippushō

strive [straiv] (*pt* **strove**, *pp* **striven**) *vi*: **to strive for something/to do something** ...しようと努力する ...shiyő tò dőryòku suru

striven [strivˈən] *pp* of **strive**

strode [stroud] *pt* of **stride**

stroke [strouk] *n* (blow) 一撃 ichígeki; (SWIMMING) ストローク sutórōku; (MED) 脳卒中 nősotchú; (of paintbrush) 筆の運び fudé nò hakóbi

♦*vt* (caress) なでる nadérù

at a stroke 一気に íkkì ni

stroll [stroul] *n* 散歩 sañpo

♦*vi* 散歩する sañpo suru

stroller [strouˈləːr] (*US*) *n* (pushchair) いす型ベビーカー isúgata bebíkā

strong [strɔːŋ] *adj* (person, arms, grasp) 強い tsuyői; (stick) 丈夫な jőbu na; (wind) 強い tsuyői; (imagination) 想像力のある sőzōryoku no árù; (personality) 気性の激しい kishő nò hagéshiì; (influence) 強い tsuyői; (nerves) 頑丈な gañjō na; (smell) 強烈な kyőretsu na; (coffee) 濃い kőî; (taste) 際立った kiwádattà

they are 50 strong 50人いる gojűnîn irú

stronghold [strɔːŋˈhould] *n* とりで toríde; (*fig*) 根城 néjìro

strongly [strɔːŋˈliː] *adv* (solidly: construct) 頑丈に gañjō ni; (with force: push, defend) 激しく hagéshikù; (deeply: feel, believe) 強く tsúyòku

strongroom [strɔːŋˈruːm] *n* 金庫室 kiñkoshîtsu

strove [strouv] *pt* of **strive**

struck [strʌk] *pt*, *pp* of **strike**

structural [strʌkˈtʃəːrəl] *adj* (damage, defect) 構造的な kőzoteki na

structure [strʌkˈtʃəːr] *n* (organization) 組織 sőshìki; (building) 構造物 kőzōbùtsu

struggle [strʌgˈəl] *n* 闘争 tősō

♦*vi* (try hard) 努力する dőryòku suru; (fight) 戦う tatákaù

strum [strʌm] *vt* (guitar) つま弾く tsumábikù

strung [strʌŋ] *pt*, *pp* of **string**

strut [strʌt] *n* (wood, metal) 支柱 shichú

♦*vi* 威張って歩く ibátte arukù

stub [stʌb] *n* (of check, ticket etc) 控え hikáè; (of cigarette) 吸殻 suígara

♦*vt*: **to stub one's toe** つま先をぶつける tsumásaki wò butsúkerù

stubble [stʌbˈəl] *n* (AGR) 切株 kiríkàbu; (on chin) 不精ひげ bushőhìge

stubborn [stʌbˈəːrn] *adj* (child, determination) 頑固な gáñko na

stub out *vt* (cigarette) もみ消す momíkesù

stuck [stʌk] *pt*, *pp* of **stick**

♦*adj* (jammed) 引っ掛っている hikká-katte iru

stuck-up [stʌk'ʌp'] (*inf*) *adj* 天ぐになっている teñgu nì natté irù

stud [stʌd] *n* (on clothing etc) 飾りボタン kazáribotàn; (earring) 丸玉 marúdamà (on sole of boot) スパイク supáìku; (*also*: **stud farm**) 馬の繁殖牧場 umá nò hañshokubokujò; (*also*: **stud horse**) 種馬 tanéùma

♦*vt* (*fig*): **studded with** ...をちりばめた ...wo chiríbametà

student [stu:'dənt] *n* (at university) 学生 gakúsei; (at lower schools) 生徒 seíto

♦*adj* (nurse, life, union) 学生の gakúsei no

student driver (*US*) *n* 仮免許運転者 karímenkyo unteñsha

studies [stʌd'i:z] *npl* (subjects studied) 勉強の科目 beñkyō nò kamóku

studio [stu:'di:ou] *n* (TV etc) スタジオ sutájìo; (sculptor's etc) アトリエ atórìe

studio apartment (*BRIT* **studio flat**) *n* ワンルームマンション wañrūmu máñshon

studious [stu:'di:əs] *adj* (person) 勉強家の beñkyōka no; (careful: attention) 注意深い chūibukaì

studiously [stu:'di:əsli:] *adv* (carefully) 注意深く chūibukakù

study [stʌd'i:] *n* (activity) 勉強 beñkyō; (room) 書斎 shosái

♦*vt* (learn about: subjects) 勉強する beñkyō suru; (examine: face, evidence) 調べる shiráberù

♦*vi* 勉強する beñkyō suru

stuff [stʌf] *n* (thing(s)) 物 monó, 事 kotó; (substance) 素質 soshítsu

♦*vt* (soft toy: *also* CULIN) ...に詰める ...ni tsumérù; (dead animals) はく製にする hakúsei ni surù; (*inf*: push: object) 差込む sashíkomù

stuffing [stʌf'iŋ] *n* (gen, CULIN) 詰物 tsumémono

stuffy [stʌf'i:] *adj* (room) 空気の悪い kúki nò waruì; (person, ideas) 古臭い furúkusaì

stumble [stʌm'bəl] *vi* つまづく tsumázuku

to stumble across/on (*fig*) ...に出くわす ...ni dekúwasù

stumbling block [stʌm'bliŋ-] *n* 障害 shōgai

stump [stʌmp] *n* (of tree) 切株 kiríkàbu; (of limb) 断端 dañtan

♦*vt*: **to be stumped** まごつく magótsukù

stun [stʌn] *vt* (subj: news) あ然とさせる azen to sasérù; (: blow on head) 気絶させる kizetsu sasérù

stung [stʌŋ] *pt, pp* of **sting**

stunk [stʌŋk] *pp* of **stink**

stunning [stʌn'iŋ] *adj* (*fig*: news, event) 仰天させる gyōten saserù; (: girl, dress) 美しい utsúkushiì

stunt [stʌnt] *n* (in film) スタント sutáñto; (*also*: **publicity stunt**) 宣伝用のトリック señden-yō no toríkkù

stunted [stʌn'tid] *adj* (trees, growth etc) 成長を阻害された seíchō wò sogái saretà

stuntman [stʌnt'mən] (*pl* **stuntmen**) *n* スタントマン sutáñtoman

stupefy [stu:'pəfai] *vt* ぼう然とさせる bōzen ni saserù

stupendous [stu:pen'dəs] *adj* 途方もない tohōmonaì

stupid [stu:'pid] *adj* (person, question etc) ばかな bákà na

stupidity [stu:pid'iti:] *n* 愚かさ orókasà

stupor [stu:'pər] *n* 前後不覚 zéñgofukáku

sturdy [stər'di:] *adj* (person, thing) がっちりした gatchírī shita

stutter [stʌt'ə:r] *n* どもり dómòri

♦*vi* どもる domórù

sty [stai] *n* (*also*: **pigsty**) 豚小屋 butágoya

stye [stai] *n* (MED) ものもらい monómorài

style [stail] *n* (way, attitude) やり方 yaríkata; (elegance) 優雅さ yūgàsa; (design) スタイル sutáìru

stylish [stai'liʃ] *adj* 優雅な yūgà na

stylus [stai'ləs] *n* (of record player) 針 harí

suave [swɑːv] *adj* 物腰の丁寧な monógoshi no teínei na

subconscious [sʌbkɑːn'tʃəs] *adj* (desire etc) 潜在意識の señzaiishíki no

subcontract [sʌbkəntrækt'] *vt* 下請に出す shitáuke nì dásù

subdivide [sʌbdivaid'] *vt* 小分けする kowáke suru

subdue [səbduː'] *vt* (rebels etc) 征服する seífuku suru; (passions) 抑制する yokúsei suru

subdued [səbduːd'] *adj* (light) 柔らかな yawárakà na; (person) 落込んだ ochíkoñda

subject [*n* sʌb'dʒikt *vb* səbjekt'] *n* (matter) 話題 wadái; (SCOL) 学科 gakká; (of kingdom) 臣民 shiñmiñ; (GRAMMAR) 主語 shúgo

♦*vt: to subject someone to something* ...を...にさらす ...wo ...ni sarásù

to be subject to (law) ...に服従しなければならない ...ni fukújù shinakerèba naránaì; (heart attacks) ...が起りやすい ...ga okóriyasuì

to be subject to tax 課税される kazéi sarerù

subjective [səbdʒek'tiv] *adj* 主観的な shukáñteki na

subject matter *n* (content) 内容 naíyō

subjugate [sʌb'dʒəgeit] *vt* (people) 征服する seífuku suru

subjunctive [səbdʒʌŋk'tiv] *n* 仮定法 katéihō

sublet [sʌb'let] *vt* また貸しする matágashi suru

sublime [səblaim'] *adj* 素晴らしい subárashiì

submachine gun [sʌbməʃiːn'-] *n* 軽機関銃 keíkikañjū

submarine [sʌb'məriːn] *n* 潜水艦 señsuikan

submerge [səbmə:rdʒ'] *vt* 水中に沈める suíchū nì shizúmerù

♦*vi* (submarine, sea creature) 潜る mogúrù

submission [səbmiʃ'ən] *n* (state) 服従 fukújù; (claim) 申請書 shiñseishò; (of plan) 提出 teíshutsu

submissive [səbmis'iv] *adj* 従順な jújun na

submit [səbmit'] *vt* (proposal, application etc) 提出する teíshutsu suru

♦*vi: to submit to something* ...に従う ...ni shitágaù

subnormal [sʌbnɔːr'məl] *adj* (below average: temperatures) 通常以下の tsújōikà no

subordinate [səbɔːr'dənit] *adj* 二次的な nijíteki na

♦*n* 部下 búkà

subpoena [səpi:'nə] *n* (LAW) 召喚状 shōkañjō

subscribe [səbskraib'] *vi: to subscribe to* (opinion) ...に同意する ...ni dóì suru; (fund) ...に寄付する ...ni kífu suru; (magazine etc) ...を購読する ...wo kódoku suru

subscriber [səbskraib'ə:r] *n* (to periodical, telephone) 購読者 kódokushà; (to telephone) 加入者 kanyúshà

subscription [səbskrip'ʃən] *n* (to magazine etc) 購読契約 kódokukeiyàku

subsequent [sʌb'səkwənt] *adj* (following) その後の sonó atò no; (resulting) その結果として起る sonó kekkà toshite okórù

subsequently [sʌb'səkwəntli:] *adv* その後 sonó atò

subside [səbsaid'] *vi* (feeling) 収る osámarù; (flood) ひく hikú; (wind) やむ yamú

subsidence [səbsaid'əns] *n* (in road etc) 陥没 kañbotsu

subsidiary [səbsid'i:e:ri:] *adj* (question, details) 二次的な nijíteki na

♦*n* (also: **subsidiary company**) 子会社 kogáisha

subsidize [sʌb'sidaiz] *vt* (education, industry etc) ...に補助金を与える ...ni hojókìn wo atáerù

subsidy [sʌb'sidi:] *n* 補助金 hojókìn

subsistence [səbsis'təns] *n* (ability to live) 最低限度の生活水準 saíteigeñdo no seíkatsusuijùn

subsistence allowance (*BRIT*) *n* (advance payment) 支度金 shitákukìn;

(for expenses etc) 特別手当 tokúbetsu teáte

substance [sʌb'stəns] n (product, material) 物質 busshítsu

substantial [səbstæn'tʃəl] adj (solid) 頑丈な gañjō na; (fig: reward, meal) 多い ói

substantially [səbstæn'tʃəli:] adv (by a large amount) 大いに ói ni; (in essence) 本質的に hoñshitsuteki ni

substantiate [səbstæn'tʃi:eit] vt 裏付けする urázukerù

substitute [sʌb'stitu:t] n (person) 代人 daínin; (thing) 代用品 daíyōhìn
♦vt: **to substitute A for B** Bの代りにAを置く B nò kawári nì A wò okú

substitution [sʌbstitu:'ʃən] n (act of substituting) 置換え okíkae; (SOCCER) 選手交代 señshukōtai

subterfuge [sʌb'tə:rfju:dʒ] n 策略 sakúryàku

subterranean [sʌbtərei'ni:ən] adj 地下の chiká no

subtitle [sʌb'taitəl] n 字幕スーパー jimákusūpā

subtle [sʌt'əl] adj (slight: change) 微妙な bimyṓ na; (indirect: person) 腹芸のうまい harágèi no umáì

subtlety [sʌt'əlti:] n (small detail) 微妙な所 bimyṓ na tokórò; (art of being subtle) 腹芸 harágeì

subtotal [sʌbtou'təl] n 小計 shṓkei

subtract [səbtrækt'] vt ...から ...を引く ...kárà ...wò hikú

subtraction [səbtræk'ʃən] n 引算 hikízan

suburb [sʌb'ə:rb] n 都市周辺の自治体 toshíshūhen no jichítai

suburban [səbə:r'bən] adj (train, lifestyle etc) 郊外の kṓgai no

suburbia [səbə:r'bi:ə] n 郊外 kṓgai

suburbs [sʌb'ə:rbz] npl: **the suburbs** (area) 郊外 kṓgai

subversive [səbvə:r'siv] adj (activities, literature) 破壊的な hakáiteki na

subway [sʌb'wei] n (US: underground railway) 地下鉄 chikátetsu; (BRIT: underpass) 地下道 chikádṑ

succeed [səksi:d'] vi (plan etc) 成功する

seíkō suru; (person: in career etc) 出生する shusshṓ suru
♦vt (in job) ...の後任になる ...no kṓnin ni narù; (in order) ...の後に続く ...no átò ni tsuzúkù
to succeed in doing ...する事に成功する ...surú kotò ni seíkō suru

succeeding [səksi:'diŋ] adj (following) その後の sonó atò no

success [səkses'] n (achievement) 成功 seíkō; (hit, also person) 大ヒット daíhittò

successful [səkses'fəl] adj (venture) 成功した seíkō shita; (writer) 出生した shusshṓ shita
to be successful 成功する seíkō suru
to be successful in doing ...する事に成功する ...surú kotò ni seíkō suru

successfully [səkses'fəli:] adv (complete, do) うまく úmàku

succession [səkses'ʃən] n (series) 連続 reñzoku; (to throne etc) 継承 keíshō
in succession 立続けに tatétsuzuke ni

successive [səkses'iv] adj 連続の reñzoku no

successor [səkses'ə:r] n 後任 kṓnin

succinct [səksiŋkt'] adj 簡潔な kañketsu na

succulent [sʌk'jələnt] adj 汁が多くておいしい shírù ga ṓkùte oíshiì

succumb [səkʌm'] vi (to temptation) 負ける makérù; (to illness: become very ill) ...で倒れる ...de taórerù; (: die) ...で死ぬ ...de shinú

such [sʌtʃ] adj (emphasizing similarity) この(その、あの)様な konó (sonó, anó) yṓ na; (of that kind): **such a book** そんな本 soñna hoñ; (so much): **such courage** そんな勇気 soñna yūki
♦adv こんな(そんな、あんな)に konna (soñna, añna)nì
such books そんな本 soñna hoñ
such a long trip あんなに長い旅行 añna ni nagái ryokō
such a lot of そんなに沢山の soñna nì takúsan no
such as (like) ...の様な ...no yṓ na
as such その物 sonó monò

such-and-such [sʌtʃ'ənsʌtʃ] *adj* しかじ
かの shikájìka no

suck [sʌk] *vt* (*gen*: ice-lolly etc) なめる
namérù; (bottle, breast) 吸う súù

sucker [sʌk'əːr] *n* (ZOOL) 吸盤 kyúban; (*inf*: easily cheated person) かも kámò

suction [sʌk'ʃən] *n* 吸引 kyúin

Sudan [su:dæn'] *n* スーダン sũdan

sudden [sʌd'ən] *adj* (unexpected, rapid:
increase, shower, change) 突然の totsúzen no

all of a sudden (unexpectedly) 突然
totsúzen

suddenly [sʌd'ənli:] *adv* (unexpectedly)
突然 totsúzen

suds [sʌdz] *npl* 石けんの泡 sekkén no a-
wà

sue [su:] *vt* ...を相手取って訴訟を起こす
...wo aítedottè soshő wő okósù

suede [sweid] *n* スエード suédò

suet [su:'it] *n* 脂肪 shibő◇料理に使うウ
シやヒツジの堅い脂肪を指す ryőrì ni
tsukáù ushí yà hitsúji nò katáì shibő wo
sásù

Suez [su:'ez] *n*: **the Suez Canal** スエズ
運河 suézu uñga

suffer [sʌf'əːr] *vt* (undergo: hardship etc)
経験する keíken suru; (bear: pain, rude-
ness) 我慢する gáman suru

♦*vi* (be harmed: person, results etc) 苦し
む kurúshimù; (results etc) 悪くなる wárùku nárù

to suffer from (illness etc) ...の病気にか
かっている ...no byőkì ni kakátte irù

sufferer [sʌf'əːrəːr] *n* (MED) 患者 kañja

suffering [sʌf'əːriŋ] *n* (hardship) 苦しみ
kurúshimi

suffice [səfais'] *vi* 足りる tarírù

sufficient [səfiʃ'ənt] *adj* 十分な júbùn na

sufficiently [səfiʃ'əntli:] *adv* 十分に júbùn ni

suffix [sʌf'iks] *n* 接尾辞 setsúbijì

suffocate [sʌf'əkeit] *vi* 窒息する chissóku suru

suffocation [sʌfəkei'ʃən] *n* 窒息 chissóku

suffrage [sʌf'ridʒ] *n* (right to vote) 参政
権 sañseikèn

suffused [səfju:zd'] *adj*: **suffused with**
(light, color, tears) ...で満たされた ...de
mitásaretà

sugar [ʃug'əːr] *n* 砂糖 satő

♦*vt* (tea etc) ...に砂糖を入れる ...ni satő
wő irérù

sugar beet *n* サトウダイコン satődaìkon

sugar cane *n* サトウキビ satőkìbi

suggest [səgdʒest'] *vt* (propose) 提案する
teían suru; (indicate) 示唆する shísa suru

suggestion [səgdʒes'tʃən] *n* (proposal)
提案 teían; (indication) 示唆 shísà

suggestive [səgdʒes'tiv] (*pej*) *adj* (remarks, looks) 卑わいな hiwái na

suicide [su:'isaid] *n* (death, *also fig*) 自殺
jisátsu; (person) 自殺者 jisátsushà ¶ *see
also* **commit**

suit [su:t] *n* (man's) 背広 sebíro; (woman's)
スーツ sũtsu; (LAW) 訴訟 soshő;
(CARDS) 組札 kumífùda

♦*vt* (*gen*: be convenient, appropriate)
...に都合がいい ...ni tsugő ga iî; (color,
clothes) ...に似合う ...ni niáù; (adapt): **to
suit something to** ...を...に合せる ...wo
...ni awáserù

well suited (well matched: couple) お似
合いの o-níaì no

suitable [su:'təbəl] *adj* (convenient: time,
moment) 都合のいい tsugő no iî; (appro-
priate: person, clothes etc) 適当な tekítò
na

suitably [su:'təbli:] *adv* (dressed) 適当に
tekítò ni; (impressed) 期待通りに kitái-
dőri ni

suitcase [su:t'keis] *n* スーツケース sũtsu-
kềsu

suite [swi:t] *n* (of rooms) スイートルーム
suítorùmu; (MUS) 組曲 kumíkyòku;
(furniture): **bedroom / dining room
suite** 寝室〔食堂〕用家具の一そろい shiñ-
shitsu(shokúdō)yő kágù no hitósòroi

suitor [su:'təːr] *n* 求婚者 kyúkoñsha

sulfur [sʌl'fəːr] (*US*) *n* 硫黄 iő

sulk [sʌlk] *vi* すねる sunérù

sulky [sʌl'ki:] *adj* (child, silence) すねた
sunétà

sullen [sʌl'ən] *adj* (person, silence) すね
た sunétà

sulphur [sʌl'fər] n = sulfur

sultan [sʌl'tən] n サルタン sárutan ◇ イスラム教国の君主 isúramukyŏkoku no kúńshu

sultana [sʌltæn'ə] n (fruit) 白いレーズン shiróī rḗsun

sultry [sʌl'tri:] adj (weather) 蒸暑い mushíatsuì

sum [sʌm] n (calculation) 計算 keísan; (amount) 金額 kiñgaku; (total) 合計 gŏkei

summarize [sʌm'əraiz] vt 要約する yŏyaku suru

summary [sʌm'əri:] n 要約 yŏyaku

summer [sʌm'ər] n 夏 natsú
♦adj (dress, school) 夏の natsú no
in summer 夏に natsú ni

summer holidays npl 夏休み natsúyasùmi

summerhouse [sʌm'əːrhaus] n (in garden) 東屋 azúmayà

summertime [sʌm'əːrtaim] n (season) 夏 natsú

summer time n (by clock) サマータイム samátaìmu

summer vacation (US) n 夏休み natsúyasùmi

summit [sʌm'it] n (of mountain) 頂上 chŏjo; (also: **summit conference/meeting**) 首脳会議 shunŏkaìgi, サミット samíttŏ

summon [sʌm'ən] vt (person, police, help) 呼ぶ yobú; (to a meeting) 召集する shŏshu suru; (LAW: witness) 召喚する shŏkan suru

summons [sʌm'ənz] n (LAW) 召喚書 shŏkansho; (fig) 呼出し yobídashi
♦vt (JUR) 召喚する shŏkan suru

summon up vt (strength, energy, courage) 奮い起す furúiokosù

sump [sʌmp] (BRIT) n (AUT) オイルパン oírupaǹ

sumptuous [sʌmp'tʃu:əs] adj 豪華な gŏkà na

sum up vt (describe) 要約する yŏyaku suru
♦vi (summarize) 要約する yŏyaku suru

sun [sʌn] n (star) 太陽 taíyŏ; (sunshine) 日光 níkkŏ

sunbathe [sʌn'beið] vi 日光浴する nikkŏyoku suru

sunburn [sʌn'bəːrn] n (painful) 日焼け hiyáke

sunburnt [sʌn'bəːrnt] adj (tanned) 日に焼けた hi ní yaketà; (painfully) ひどく日焼けした hídoku hiyáke shita

Sunday [sʌn'dei] n 日曜日 nichíyŏbi

Sunday school n 日曜学校 nichíyŏgakkŏ

sundial [sʌn'dail] n 日時計 hidókèi

sundown [sʌn'daun] n 日没 nichíbotsu

sundries [sʌn'dri:z] npl (miscellaneous items) その他 sonó tà

sundry [sʌn'dri:] adj (various) 色々な iróiro na
all and sundry だれもかも dárè mo ká mò

sunflower [sʌn'flauəːr] n ヒマワリ hímáwàri

sung [sʌŋ] pp of **sing**

sunglasses [sʌn'glæsiz] npl サングラス sañguràsu

sunk [sʌŋk] pp of **sink**

sunlight [sʌn'lait] n 日光 níkkŏ

sunlit [sʌn'lit] adj 日に照らされた hi ní terasaretà

sunny [sʌn'i:] adj (weather, day) 晴れた háreta; (place) 日当りの良い hiátari no yoì

sunrise [sʌn'raiz] n 日の出 hi nó de

sun roof n (AUT) サンルーフ sañrùfu

sunset [sʌn'set] n 日没 nichíbotsu

sunshade [sʌn'ʃeid] n (over table) パラソル párasoru

sunshine [sʌn'ʃain] n 日光 níkkŏ

sunstroke [sʌn'strouk] n 日射病 nisshábyō

suntan [sʌn'tæn] n 日焼け hiyáke

suntan lotion n 日焼け止めローション hiyákedome rŏshon

suntan oil n サンタンオイル sañtan oirù

super [su:'pəːr] (inf) adj 最高の saíkō no

superannuation [su:pəːræniu:ei'ʃən] n 年金の掛金 neñkin nò kakékiǹ

superb [su:pəːrb'] adj 素晴らしい subárashiĩ

supercilious [su:pə:rsil'i:əs] *adj* (disdainful, haughty) 横柄な ōhei na

superficial [su:pə:rfiʃ'əl] *adj* (wound) 浅い asái; (knowledge) 表面的な hyṓmenteki na; (shallow: person) 浅はかな asáhàka na

superfluous [su:pə:r'flu:əs] *adj* 余計な yokéi na

superhuman [su:pə:rhju:'mən] *adj* 超人的な chṓjinteki na

superimpose [su:pə:rimpouz'] *vt* 重ね合せる kasáneawaserù

superintendent [su:pə:rinten'dənt] *n* (of place, activity) …長 …chṓ; (POLICE) 警視 keíshi

superior [səpi:r'i:ə:r] *adj* (better) (より) すぐれた (yorí) sugúretà; (more senior) 上位の jōi no; (smug) 偉ぶった erábuttà
◆*n* 上司 jōshi

superiority [səpi:ri:ɔ:r'iti:] *n* 優位性 yūīsei

superlative [səpə:r'lətiv] *n* (LING) 最上級 saíjōkyū

superman [su:'pə:rmæn] (*pl* **supermen**) *n* 超人 chōjin

supermarket [su:'pə:rma:rkit] *n* スーパー sūpà

supernatural [su:pə:rnætʃ'ə:rəl] *adj* (creature, force etc) 超自然の chṓshizen no
◆*n*: **the supernatural** 超自然の現象 chōshizen no geñshō

superpower [su:pə:rpau'ə:r] *n* (POL) 超大国 chṓtaikoku

supersede [su:pə:rsi:d'] *vt* …に取って代る …ni tóttè kawárù

supersonic [su:pə:rsɑ:n'ik] *adj* (flight, aircraft) 超音速の chṓonsoku no

superstar [su:'pə:rstɑ:r] *n* (CINEMA, SPORT etc) スーパースター sūpàsutā

superstition [su:pə:rstiʃ'ən] *n* 迷信 meíshin

superstitious [su:pə:rstiʃ'əs] *adj* (person) 迷信深い meíshinbùkai; (practices) 迷信的な meíshinteki na

supertanker [su:'pə:rtæŋkə:r] *n* スーパータンカー sūpàtaṅkā

supervise [su:'pə:rvaiz] *vt* (person, activ-

ity) 監督する kañtoku suru

supervision [su:pə:rviʒ'ən] *n* 監督 kañtoku

supervisor [su:'pə:rvaizə:r] *n* (of workers, students) 監督 kañtoku

supine [su:'pain] *adj* 仰向きの aōmuki no

supper [sʌp'ə:r] *n* (early evening) 夕食 yūshoku; (late evening) 夜食 yashóku

supplant [səplænt'] *vt* (person, thing) …に取って代る …ni tóttè kawárù

supple [sʌp'əl] *adj* (person, body, leather etc) しなやかな shináyàka na

supplement [*n* sʌp'ləmənt *vb* sʌp'ləment] *n* (additional amount, e.g. vitamin supplement) 補給品 hokyúhìn; (of book) 補遺 hóì; (of newspaper, magazine) 付録 furóku
◆*vt* 補足する hosóku suru

supplementary [sʌpləmən'tə:ri:] *adj* (question) 補足的な hosókuteki na

supplementary benefit (*BRIT*) *n* 生活保護 seíkatsuhogò

supplier [səplai'ə:r] *n* (COMM: person, firm) 供給業者 kyṓkyūgyòsha

supplies [səplaiz'] *npl* (food) 食料 shokúryō; (MIL) 軍需品 guñjuhìn

supply [səplai'] *vt* (provide) 供給する kyṓkyū suru; (equip): **to supply (with)** (…を) 支給する (…wo) shikyū suru
◆*n* (stock) 在庫品 zaíkohìn; (supplying) 供給 kyṓkyū

supply teacher (*BRIT*) *n* 代行教師 daíkōkyòshi

support [səpɔ:rt'] *n* (moral, financial etc) 支援 shién; (TECH) 支柱 shichū
◆*vt* (morally: football team etc) 支援する shién suru; (financially: family etc) 養う yashínaù; (TECH: hold up) 支える sasáerù; (sustain: theory etc) 裏付ける urázukerù

supporter [səpɔ:r'tə:r] *n* (POL etc) 支援者 shiénshà; (SPORT) ファン fáñ

suppose [səpouz'] *vt* (think likely) …だと思う …dá tò omóù; (imagine) 想像する sōzō suru; (duty): **to be supposed to do something** …する事になっている …surú kotò ni natté irù

supposedly [səpou'zidli:] *adv* …だとされ

て ...dá tò sarétè

supposing [səpou'ziŋ] *conj* も し ... mó-shǐ...

suppress [səpres'] *vt* (revolt) 鎮圧する chiń-atsu suru; (information) 隠す kakú-sù; (feelings, yawn) 抑える osáerù

suppression [səpreʃ'ən] *n* (of revolt) 鎮圧 chiń-atsu; (of information) 隠ぺい inpei; (of feelings etc) 抑制 yokúsei

supremacy [səprem'əsiː] *n* 優越 yúetsu

supreme [səpriːm'] *adj* (in titles: court etc) 最高の saíkō no; (effort, achievement) 最上の saíjō no

surcharge [səːr'tʃɑːrdʒ] *n* (extra cost) 追加料金 tsuíkaryòkin

sure [ʃuːr] *adj* (definite, convinced) 確信している kakúshin shite irù; (aim, remedy) 確実な kakújitsu na; (friend) 頼りになる táyòri ni nárù

to make sure of something ...を確かめる ...wo tashíkamerù

to make sure that ...だと確かめる ...dá tò tashíkamerù

sure! (of course) いいとも fi to mo

sure enough 案の定 ań no jō

sure-footed [ʃuːr'fut'id] *adj* 足のしっかりした ashí nò shikkárì shita

surely [ʃuːr'liː] *adv* (certainly: *US: also:* **sure**) 確かに táshìka ni

surety [ʃuːr'ətiː] *n* (money) 担保 tánpo

surf [səːrf] *n* 打寄せる波 uchíyoseru namì

surface [səːr'fis] *n* (of object) 表面 hyómen; (of lake, pond) 水面 suímen

♦*vt* (road) 舗装する hosō suru

♦*vi* (fish, person in water: *also fig*) 浮上する fujō suru

surface mail *n* 普通郵便 futsúyùbin

surfboard [səːrf'bɔːrd] *n* サーフボード sáfubòdo

surfeit [səːr'fit] *n*: *a surfeit of* ...の過剰 ...no kajō

surfing [səːr'fiŋ] *n* サーフィン sáfìn

surge [səːrdʒ] *n* (increase: *also fig*) 高まり takámarì

♦*vi* (water) 波打つ namíutsù; (people, vehicles) 突進する tosshín suru; (emotion) 高まる takámarù

surgeon [səːr'dʒən] *n* 外科医 gekấ-ì

surgery [səːr'dʒəːriː] *n* (treatment) 手術 shújùtsu; (*BRIT*: room) 診察室 shińsatsushìtsu; (: *also*: **surgery hours**) 診療時間 shińryō jikàn

surgical [səːr'dʒikəl] *adj* (instrument, mask etc) 外科用の gekáyō no; (treatment) 外科の geká no

surgical spirit (*BRIT*) *n* 消毒用アルコール shōdokuyō arúkòru

surly [səːr'liː] *adj* 無愛想な buáìsō na

surmount [səːrmaunt'] *vt* (*fig*: problem, difficulty) 乗越える noríkoerù

surname [səːr'neim] *n* 名字 myōji

surpass [səːrpæs'] *vt* (person, thing) しのぐ shinógù

surplus [səːr'pləs] *n* (extra, *also* COMM, ECON) 余剰分 yojóbùn

♦*adj* (stock, grain etc) 余剰の yojō no

surprise [səːrpraiz'] *n* (unexpected) 思い掛け無い事 omóigakenaì monó; (astonishment) 驚き odóroki

♦*vt* (astonish) 驚かす odórokasù; (catch unawares: army, thief) ...の不意を突く ...no fuí wò tsukú

surprising [səːrprai'ziŋ] *adj* 驚くべき odórokubèki

surprisingly [səːrprai'ziŋliː] *adv* (easy, helpful) 驚く程 odóroku hodò

surrealist [səːriː'əlist] *adj* (paintings etc) 超現実主義の chōgenjitsushùgi no

surrender [səren'dəːr] *n* 降伏 kōfuku

♦*vi* (army, hijackers etc) 降伏する kōfuku suru

surreptitious [səːrəptiʃ'əs] *adj* ひそかな hisōka na

surrogate [səːr'əgit] *n* 代理の daíri no

surrogate mother *n* 代理母 daírihahà

surround [səraund'] *vt* (subj: walls, hedge etc) 囲む kakómù; (MIL, POLICE etc) 包囲する hōi suru

surrounding [səraun'diŋ] *adj* (countryside) 周囲の shūi no

surroundings [səraun'diŋz] *npl* 周辺 shūhen

surveillance [səːrveiˈləns] *n* 監視 kańshi

survey [*n* səːr'vei *vb* səːrvei'] *n* (examination: of land, house) 測量 sokúryō;

(investigation: of habits etc) 調査 chốsa
♦vt (land, house etc) 測量する sokúryō suru; (look at: scene, work etc) 見渡す miwátasù

surveyor [sə:rvei'ə:r] n (of land, house) 測量技師 sokúryōgishi

survival [sə:rvai'vəl] n (continuation of life) 生存 seízon; (relic) 遺物 ibútsu

survive [sə:rvaiv'] vi (person, thing) 助かる tasúkarù; (custom etc) 残る nokórù
♦vt (outlive: person) ...より長生きする ...yóri nagáikì suru

survivor [sə:rvai'və:r] n (of illness, accident) 生存者 seízoñsha

susceptible [səsep'təbəl] adj: *susceptible (to)* (affected by: heat, injury) (...に) 弱い (...ni) yowáì; (influenced by: flattery, pressure) (...に) 影響されやすい (...ni) eíkyō sareyasuì

suspect [adj, n sʌs'pekt vb səspekt'] adj 怪しい ayáshiì
♦n 容疑者 yōgishà
♦vt (person) ...が怪しいと思う ...ga ayáshiì to omóù; (think) ...ではないかと思う ...dé wà naî ka to omóù

suspend [səspend'] vt (hang) つるす tsurúsù; (delay, stop) 中止する chūshì suru; (from employment) 停職処分にする teíshokushobùn ni suru

suspended sentence [səspen'did-] n (LAW) 執行猶予付きの判決 shikkốyūyotsuki no haňketsu

suspender belt [səspen'də:r-] n ガーターベルト gátāberùto

suspenders [səspen'də:rz] npl (US) ズボンつり zubôñtsuri; (BRIT) ガーターベルトのストッキング留め gátāberùto no sutókkingudôme

suspense [səspens'] n (uncertainty) 気掛り kigákarì; (in film etc) サスペンス sásùpensu
to keep someone in suspense はらはらさせる háràhara saséru

suspension [səspen'tʃən] n (from job, team) 停職 teíshoku; (AUT) サスペンション sasúpeñshon; (of driver's license, payment) 停止 teíshi

suspension bridge n つり橋 tsurībàshi

suspicion [səspiʃ'ən] n (distrust) 疑いutágai; ((bad) feeling) 漠然とした感じ bakúzen to shitä kañji

suspicious [səspiʃ'əs] adj (suspecting: look) 疑い深い utágaibukaì; (causing suspicion: circumstances) 怪しげな ayáshigè na

sustain [səstein'] vt (continue: interest etc) 維持する íjì suru; (subj: food, drink) ...に力を付ける ...ni chikára wò tsukérù; (suffer: injury) 受ける ukérù

sustained [səsteind'] adj (effort, attack) 絶間ない taémanaì

sustenance [sʌs'tənəns] n 食物 shokúmòtsu

swab [swɑ:b] n (MED) 綿球 meňkyū

swagger [swæg'ə:r] vi 威張って歩く ibátte arukù

swallow [swɑ:l'ou] n (bird) ツバメ tsubáme
♦vt (food, pills etc) 飲込む nomíkomù; (fig: story) 信じ込む shiňjikomù; (: insult) ...に黙って耐える ...ni damáttè taérù; (one's pride, one's words) 抑える osáerù

swallow up vt (savings etc) 飲込む nomíkomù

swam [swæm] pt of **swim**

swamp [swɑ:mp] n 沼地 numáchi
♦vt (with water etc) 水没させる suíbotsu saserù; (fig: person) 圧倒する attố suru

swan [swɑ:n] n ハクチョウ hakúchō

swap [swɑ:p] n 交換 kốkan
♦vt: *to swap (for)* (exchange (for)) (...) と交換する (...to) kốkan suru; (replace (with)) (...と) 取替える (...to) toríkaerù

swarm [swɔ:rm] n (of bees) 群れ muré; (of people) 群衆 guñshū
♦vi (bees) 群れで巣別れする muré dè suwákarè suru; (people) 群がる murágarù; (place): *to be swarming with* ...に...がうじゃうじゃいる ...ni ...ga újauja irú

swarthy [swɔ:r'ði:] adj 浅黒い aságuroì

swastika [swɑ:s'tikə] n かぎ十字 kagíjūji

swat [swɑ:t] vt (insect) たたく tatákù

sway [swei] vi (person, tree) 揺れる yuré-

rù
♦*vt* (influence) 揺さぶる yusáburù

swear [swe'ər] (*pt* **swore**, *pp* **sworn**) *vi* (curse) 悪態をつく akútai wò tsukú
♦*vt* (promise) 誓う chikáù

swearword [swe:r'wə:rd] *n* 悪態 akútai

sweat [swet] *n* 汗 áse
♦*vi* 汗をかく áse wo kákù

sweater [swet'ə:r] *n* セーター séta

sweatshirt [swet'ʃə:rt] *n* トレーナー torénà

sweaty [swet'i:] *adj* (clothes, hands) 汗ばんだ asébañda

Swede [swi:d] *n* スウェーデン人 suúēdenjìn

swede [swi:d] (*BRIT*) *n* スウェーデンカブ suúēdeñkabu

Sweden [swi:d'ən] *n* スウェーデン suúēden

Swedish [swi:'diʃ] *adj* スウェーデンのsuúēden no; (LING) スウェーデン語の suúēdeñgo no
♦*n* (LING) スウェーデン語 suúēdeñgo

sweep [swi:p] *n* (act of sweeping) 掃く事 hákù kotó; (*also*: **chimney sweep**) 煙突掃除夫 eñtotsusōjìfu
♦*vb* (*pt*, *pp* **swept**)
♦*vt* (brush) 掃く hákù; (with arm) 払う haráù; (*subj*: current) 流す nagásù
♦*vi* (hand, arm) 振る furú; (wind) 吹きまくる fukímakurù

sweep away *vt* 取除く torínozokù

sweeping [swi:'piŋ] *adj* (gesture) 大振りな ōburi na; (generalized: statement) 十把一からげの jíppàhitókàrage no

sweep past *vi* (at great speed) 猛スピードで通り過ぎる mōsupído de tōrisugirù; (majestically) 堂々と通り過ぎる dódò tò tōrisugiru

sweep up *vi* 掃き取る hakítorù

sweet [swi:t] *n* (candy) あめ amé; (*BRIT*: pudding) デザート dezáto
♦*adj* (not savory: taste) 甘い amáì; (*fig*: air, water, smell, sound) 快い kokóroyoì; (: kind) 親切な shíñsetsu na; (attractive: baby, kitten) かわいい kawáiì

sweetcorn [swi:t'kɔ:rn] *n* トウモロコシ tōmoròkoshi

sweeten [swi:t'ən] *vt* (add sugar to) 甘くする amáku surù; (soften: temper) なだめる nadámerù

sweetheart [swi:t'hɑ:rt] *n* (boyfriend/girlfriend) 恋人 koíbito

sweetness [swi:t'nis] *n* (amount of sugar) 甘さ amása; (*fig*: of air, water, smell, sound) 快さ kokóroyosà; (kindness) 親切 shíñsetsu; (attractiveness: of baby, kitten) かわいさ kawáisà

sweetpea [swi:t'pi:] *n* スイートピー suítopì

swell [swel] *n* (of sea) うねり unéri
♦*adj* (*US*: *inf*: excellent) 素晴らしい subárashì
♦*vi* (*pt* **swelled**, *pp* **swollen** *or* **swelled**) (increase: numbers) 増える fuérù; (get stronger: sound, feeling) 増す masú; (*also*: **swell up**: face, ankle etc) はれる harérù

swelling [swel'iŋ] *n* (MED) はれ haré

sweltering [swel'tə:riŋ] *adj* (heat, weather, day) うだる様な udáru yō na

swept [swept] *pt*, *pp* *of* **sweep**

swerve [swə:rv] *vi* (person, animal, vehicle) それる sorérù

swift [swift] *n* (bird) アマツバメ amátsubàme
♦*adj* (happening quickly: recovery) じん速な jíñsoku na; (moving quickly: stream, glance) 早い hayáì

swiftly [swift'li:] *adv* (move, react, reply) 早く háyàku

swig [swig] (*inf*) *n* (drink) がぶ飲み gabúnomi

swill [swil] *vt* (*also*: **swill out**, **swill down**) がぶがぶ飲む gábùgabu nómù

swim [swim] *n*: **to go for a swim** 泳ぎに行く oyógi nì ikú
♦*vb* (*pt* **swam**, *pp* **swum**)
♦*vi* (person, animal) 泳ぐ oyógù; (head, room) 回る mawárù
♦*vt* (the Channel, a length) 泳いで渡る oyóìde watárù

swimmer [swim'ə:r] *n* 泳ぐ人 oyógù hitó

swimming [swim'iŋ] *n* 水泳 suíei

swimming cap *n* 水泳用の帽子 suíeiyō no bōshi

swimming costume (*BRIT*) *n* 水着 mizúgi

swimming pool *n* 水泳プール suíeipūru

swimming trunks *npl* 水泳パンツ suíeipaǹtsu

swimsuit [swim'su:t] *n* 水着 mizúgi

swindle [swin'dəl] *n* 詐欺 ságì

♦*vt* ぺてんにかける peten nî kakérù

swine [swain] (*inf!*) *n* 畜生め chikúshōme

swing [swiŋ] *n* (in playground) ぶらんこ búranko; (movement) 揺れ yuré; (change: in opinions etc) 変動 heǹdō; (MUS: also rhythm) スイング suíngu

♦*vb* (*pt, pp* swung)

♦*vt* (arms, legs) 振る furú; (also: swing round: vehicle etc) 回す mawásù

♦*vi* (pendulum) 揺れる yurérù; (on a swing) ぶらんこに乗る búranko ni norú; (also: swing round: person, animal) 振向く furímukù; (: vehicle) 向きを変える múkì wo kaérù

to be in full swing (party etc) たけなわである takénawa de arù

swing bridge *n* 旋回橋 seǹkaikyō

swingeing [swin'dʒiŋ] (*BRIT*) *adj* (blow, attack) 激しい hagéshiì; (cuts) 法外な hốgai na

swinging door [swiŋ'iŋ-] (*BRIT* swing door) *n* 自在ドア jizáidòa

swipe [swaip] *vt* (hit) たたく tatákù; (*inf*: steal) かっ払う kappáraù

swirl [swə:rl] *vi* (water, smoke, leaves) 渦巻く uzúmakù

swish [swiʃ] *vt* (tail etc) 音を立てて振る otó wò tátète furú

♦*vi* (clothes) 衣ずれの音を立てる kinúzure nò otó wò tatérù

Swiss [swis] *adj* スイスの suísu no

♦*n inv* スイス人 suísujìn

switch [switʃ] *n* (for light, radio etc) スイッチ suítchì; (change) 取替え toríkae

♦*vt* (change) 取替える toríkaerù

switchboard [switʃ'bɔːrd] *n* (TEL) 交換台 kốkandai

switch off *vt* (light, radio) 消す kesú; (engine, machine) 止める tomérù

switch on *vt* (light, radio, machine) つ

ける tsukérù; (engine) かける kakérù

Switzerland [swit'sə:rlənd] *n* スイス suísu

swivel [swiv'əl] *vi* (also: swivel round) 回る mawárù

swollen [swou'lən] *pp of* swell

swoon [swu:n] *vi* 気絶する kizétsu suru

swoop [swu:p] *n* (by police etc) 手入れ te-íre

♦*vi* (also: swoop down: bird, plane) 舞降りる maíorirù

swop [swɑ:p] = swap

sword [sɔ:rd] *n* 刀 katána

swordfish [sɔ:rd'fiʃ] *n* メカジキ mekájìki

swore [swɔ:r] *pt of* swear

sworn [swɔ:rn] *pp of* swear

♦*adj* (statement, evidence) 宣誓付きの seǹseitsuki no; (enemy) 年来の neǹrai no

swot [swɑ:t] *vi* がり勉する garíben suru

swum [swʌm] *pp of* swim

swung [swʌŋ] *pt, pp of* swing

sycamore [sik'əmɔːr] *n* カエデ kaéde

syllable [sil'əbəl] *n* 音節 oǹsetsu

syllabus [sil'əbəs] *n* 講義概要 kốgigaìyō

symbol [sim'bəl] *n* (sign, abbreviation) 記号 kigố; (representation) 象徴 shốchō

symbolic(al) [simbɑːl'ik(əl)] *adj* 象徴的な shốchōteki na

symbolism [sim'bəlizəm] *n* 象徴的意味 shốchōteki imì

symbolize [sim'bəlaiz] *vt* 象徴する shốchō suru

symmetrical [simet'rikəl] *adj* 対称的な taíshōteki na

symmetry [sim'itri:] *n* 対称 taíshō

sympathetic [simpəθet'ik] *adj* (showing understanding) 同情的な dốjōteki na; (likeable: character) 人好きのする hitózuki no surù; (showing support): *sympathetic to(wards)* ...に好意的である ...ni kốiteki de arù

sympathies [sim'pəθi:z] *npl* (support, tendencies) 支援 shién

sympathize [sim'pəθaiz] *vi*: *to sympathize with* (person) ...に同情する ...ni dốjō suru; (feelings, cause) ...に共感する ...ni kyốkan suru

sympathizer [sim'pəθaizə:r] n (POL) 支援者 shiénsha

sympathy [sim'pəθi:] n (pity) 同情 dójo
with our deepest sympathy 心からお悔みを申上げます kokórò kara o-kúyami wò mōshiagemasù
in sympathy (workers: come out) 同情して dójō shite

symphony [sim'fəni:] n 交響曲 kókyòkyoku

symposia [simpou'zi:ə] npl of **symposium**

symposium [simpou'zi:əm] (pl **symposiums** or **symposia**) n シンポジウム shiñpojiùmu

symptom [simp'təm] n (indicator: MED) 症状 shójo; (: gen) しるし shirúshi

synagogue [sin'əgɑ:g] n ユダヤ教会堂 yudáyakyōkaidō

synchronize [siŋ'krənaiz] vt (watches, sound) 合せる awáserù

syncopated [siŋ'kəpeitid] adj (rhythm, beat) シンコペートした shiñkopēto shita

syndicate [sin'dəkit] n (of people, businesses, newspapers) シンジケート shiñjikèto

syndrome [sin'droum] n (also MED) 症侯群 shókogun

synonym [sin'ənim] n 同意語 dóigo

synopses [sinɑ:p'si:z] npl of **synopsis**

synopsis [sinɑ:p'sis] (pl **synopses**) n 概要 gaíyō

syntax [sin'tæks] n (LING) 統語法 tógohò, シンタックス shiñtakkùsu

syntheses [sin'θəsi:z] npl of **synthesis**

synthesis [sin'θəsis] (pl **syntheses**) n (of ideas, styles) 総合する sógō suru

synthetic [sinθet'ik] adj (man-made: materials) 合成の gósei no

syphilis [sif'əlis] n 梅毒 baídoku

syphon [sai'fən] = **siphon**

Syria [si:r'i:ə] n シリア shírìa

Syrian [si:r'i:ən] adj シリアの shírìa no
♦n シリア人 shiríàjin

syringe [sərindʒ'] n 注射器 chúshakì

syrup [sir'əp] n シロップ shiróppù

system [sis'təm] n (organization) 組織 sóshìki; (POL): **the system** 体制 taísei;

(method) やり方 yaríkata; (the body) 身体 shíntai
the digestive system (MED) 消化器系 shōkakikèi
the nervous system (MED) 神経系 shiñkeikèi

systematic [sistəmæt'ik] adj (methodical) 組織的な soshíkiteki na

system disk n (COMPUT) システムディスク shisútemu disùku

systems analyst [sis'təmz-] n システムアナリスト shisútemu anarisùto

T

ta [tɑ:] (BRIT: inf) excl (thanks) どうも dómo

tab [tæb] n (on file etc) 耳 mimí; (on drinks can etc) プルタブ purútàbu, プルトップ purútoppù; (label: name tab) 名札 nafúda
to keep tabs on (fig) 監視する kañshi suru

tabby [tæb'i:] n (also: **tabby cat**) とら毛のネコ toráge nò nékò

table [tei'bəl] n (piece of furniture) テーブル tébùru; (MATH, CHEM etc) 表 hyő
♦vt (BRIT: motion etc) 上程する jótei suru; (US: put off: proposal etc) 棚上げにする taná-age ni surù
to lay/set the table 食卓に皿を並べる shokútaku nì sará wò naráberù

tablecloth [tei'bəlklɔ:θ] n テーブルクロス tébùrukurosù

table d'hôte [tæb'əl dout'] adj (menu, meal) 定食の teíshoku no

table lamp n 電気スタンド deñki sutañdo

tablemat [tei'bəlmæt] n (for plate) テーブルマット tébùrumattò; (for hot dish) なべ敷 nabéshìki

table of contents n 目次 mokúji

tablespoon [tei'bəlspu:n] n (type of spoon) テーブルスプーン tébùrusupùn; (also: **tablespoonful**: as measurement) 大さじ一杯 ósaji ippài

tablet [tæb'lit] n (MED) 錠剤 józai

a stone tablet 石板 sekíban

table tennis n 卓球 takkyū́

table wine n テーブルワイン tḗburuwaìn

tabloid [tæb'lɔid] n (newspaper) タブロイド新聞 tabúroido shiñbun

taboo [tæbu:'] n (religious, social) タブー tabū́

◆*adj* (subject, place, name etc) タブーの tabū́ no

tabulate [tæb'jəleit] vt (data, figures) 表にする hyṓ ni surù

tacit [tæs'it] adj (agreement, approval etc) 暗黙の añmoku no

taciturn [tæs'itə:rn] adj (person) 無口な múkuchi na

tack [tæk] n (nail) びょう byṑ; (fig) やり方 yaríkata

◆*vt* (nail) びょうで留める byṑ de toméru; (stitch) 仮縫する karínui suru

◆*vi* (NAUT) 間切る magírù

tackle [tæk'əl] n (gear: fishing tackle etc) 道具 dṓgu; (for lifting) ろくろ rókuro, 滑車 kássha; (FOOTBALL, RUGBY) タックル tákkuru

◆*vt* (deal with: difficulty) ...と取組む ...to toríkumù; (challenge: person) ...に掛合う ...ni kakéaù; (grapple with: person, animal) ...と取組む ...to toríkumù; (FOOTBALL, RUGBY) タックルする tákkùru suru

tacky [tæk'i:] adj (sticky) べたべたする bétàbeta suru; (pej: of poor quality) 安っぽい yasúppoì

tact [tækt] n 如才なさ josáinasà

tactful [tækt'fəl] adj 如才ない josáinaì

tactical [tæk'tikəl] adj (move, withdrawal, voting) 戦術的な señjutsuteki na

tactics [tæk'tiks] n 用兵学 yṓheigàku

◆*npl* 駆引き kakéhìki

tactless [tækt'lis] adj 気転の利かない kitén no kikanaì

tadpole [tæd'poul] n オタマジャクシ otámajakùshi

taffy [tæf'i:] (US) n (toffee) タフィー táfī ◇あめの一種 amé nò ísshu

tag [tæg] n (label) 札 fudá

tag along vi ついて行く tsuíte ikú

tail [teil] n (of animal) しっ尾 shíppò; (of plane) 尾部 bíbù; (of shirt, coat) すそ susò

◆*vt* (follow: person, vehicle) 尾行する bikṓ suru

tail away/off vi (in size, quality etc) 次第に減る shídai ni herù

tailback [teil'bæk] (BRIT) n (AUT) 交通渋滞 kṓtsūjūtai

tail end n 末端 mattán

tailgate [teil'geit] n (AUT: of hatchback) 後尾ドア kōbidòa

tailor [tei'lə:r] n 仕立屋 shitáteya

tailoring [tei'lə:riŋ] n (cut) 仕立て方 shitátekata; (craft) 仕立職 shitáteshòku

tailor-made [tei'lə:rmeid] adj (suit) あつらえの atsúraè no; (fig: part in play, person for job) おあつらえ向きの o-átsuraemuki no

tails [teilz] npl (formal suit) えん尾服 eñbifùku

tailwind [teil'wind] n 追風 oíkaze

tainted [teint'id] adj (food, water, air) 汚染された osén saretà; (fig: profits, reputation etc) 汚れた yogóretà

Taiwan [tai'wɑ:n'] n 台湾 taíwàñ

take [teik] (pt **took**, pp **taken**) vt (photo, notes, holiday etc) とる tórù; (shower, walk, decision etc) する surú; (grab: someone's arm, hand etc) 取る tórù; (gain: prize) 得る érù; (require: effort, courage, time) ...が必要である ...ga hitsúyō de arù; (tolerate: pain etc) 耐える taérù; (hold: passengers etc) 収容する shūyō suru; (accompany, bring, carry: person) 連れて行く tsuréte ikù; (: thing) 持って行く mottè ikù; (exam, test) 受ける ukérù

to take something from (drawer etc) ...を...から取出す ...wo ...kárà torídasù; (steal from: person) ...を...から盗む ...wo ...kárà nusúmù

I take it that ... ...だと思っていいですね ...dá tò omótte iì desu né

take after vt fus (resemble) ...に似ている ...ni nité irù

take apart vt 分解する buñkai suru

take away vt (remove) 下げる sagérù; (carry off) 持って行く mottè ikù; (MATH) 引く hikú

takeaway [tei'kəwei] (*BRIT*) *n* = **take-out**

take back *vt* (return) 返す kaésù; (one's words) 取消す toríkesù

take down *vt* (dismantle: building) 解体する kaítai suru; (write down: letter etc) 書き取る kakítorù

take in *vt* (deceive) だます damásù; (understand) 理解する rikái suru; (include) 含む fukúmù; (lodger) 泊める tomérù

take off *vi* (AVIAT) 離陸する ríriku suru; (go away) 行ってしまう itté shimaù
♦*vt* (remove) 外す hazúsù

takeoff [teik'ɔːf] *n* (AVIAT) 離陸 ríriku

take on *vt* (work) 引受ける hikíukerù; (employee) 雇う yatóù; (opponent) ...と戦う ...to tatákaù

take out *vt* (invite) 外食に連れて行く gaíshoku nì tsurétè ikù; (remove) 取出す torídasù

takeout [teik'aut] (*US*) *n* (shop, restaurant) 持帰り料理店 mochíkaeriryōritèn; (food) 持帰り料理 mochíkaeriryòri

take over *vt* (business, country) 乗っ取る nottórù
♦*vi*: **to take over from someone** ...と交替する ...to kótai suru

takeover [teik'ouvəːr] *n* (COMM) 乗っ取り nottóri

take to *vt fus* (person, thing, activity) 気に入る ki ní irù, 好きになる sukí ni narù; (engage in: hobby etc) やり出す yarídasù

take up *vt* (a dress) 短くする mijíkakù suru; (occupy: post, time, space) ...につく ...ni tsukú; (: time) ...がかかる ...ga kakárù; (engage in: hobby etc) やり出す yarídasù
to take someone up on something (offer, suggestion) ...に応じる ...ni ójirù

takings [tei'kiŋz] *npl* 売上金 uríage

talc [tælk] *n* (*also*: **talcum powder**) タルカムパウダー tarúkamupaùda

tale [teil] *n* (story, account) 物語 monógatàri
to tell tales (*fig*: to teacher, parents etc) 告げ口する tsugéguchi suru

talent [tæl'ənt] *n* 才能 saínō

talented [tæl'əntid] *adj* 才能ある saínō arù

talk [tɔːk] *n* (a prepared speech) 演説 eñzetsu; (conversation) 話 hanáshi; (gossip) うわさ uwása
♦*vi* (speak) 話す hanásù; (give information) しゃべる shabérù
to talk about ...について話す ...ni tsuíte hanásù
to talk someone into doing something ...する様に...を説得する ...surú yò ni ...wo settóku suru
to talk someone out of doing something ...しない様に...を説得する ...shinái yò ni ...wo settóku suru
to talk shop 仕事の話をする shigóto nò hanáshi wo surù

talkative [tɔː'kətiv] *adj* おしゃべりな o-shábèri na

talk over *vt* (problem etc) 話し合う hanáshiaù

talks [tɔːks] *npl* (POL etc) 会談 kaídan

talk show *n* おしゃべり番組 o-shábèri bañgumi

tall [tɔːl] *adj* (person) 背が高い sé gà takáì; (object) 高い takáì
to be 6 feet tall (person) 身長が6フィートである shinchō gà 6 fítò de árù

tall story *n* ほら話 horábanàshi

tally [tæl'iː] *n* (of marks, amounts of money etc) 記録 kiróku
♦*vi*: **to tally (with)** (subj: figures, stories etc) (...と) 合う (...to) áù

talon [tæl'ən] *n* かぎづめ kagízume

tambourine [tæm'bəriːn] *n* タンバリン táñbarin

tame [teim] *adj* (animal, bird) なれた nárèta; (*fig*: story, style) 平凡な heíbon na

tamper [tæm'pəːr] *vi*: **to tamper with something** ...をいじる ...wo ijírù

tampon [tæm'pɑːn] *n* タンポン táñpon

tan [tæn] *n* (*also*: **suntan**) 日焼け hiyáke
♦*vi* (person, skin) 日に焼ける hi ní yakerù
♦*adj* (color) 黄かっ色の ókasshòku no

tandem [tæn'dəm] *n*: **in tandem** (together) 2人で futári dè

tang [tæŋ] *n* (smell) 鼻をつくにおい haná wò tsukú nióì; (taste) ぴりっとした味 piríttò shita ají

tangent [tæn'dʒənt] *n* (MATH) 接線 sessén

to go off at a tangent (*fig*) わき道へそれる wakímichi e sorérù

tangerine [tændʒəri:n'] *n* ミカン míkàn

tangible [tæn'dʒəbəl] *adj* (proof, benefits) 具体的な gutáiteki na

tangle [tæŋ'gəl] *n* もつれ motsúre

to get in(to) a tangle (*also fig*) もつれる motsúrerù

tank [tæŋk] *n* (*also*: **water tank**) 貯水タンク chosúitañku; (for fish) 水槽 suísō; (MIL) 戦車 sénsha

tanker [tæŋk'ə:r] *n* (ship) タンカー táñkā; (truck) タンクローリー tañkurōrī

tanned [tænd] *adj* (skin) 日に焼けた hi ní yaketá

tantalizing [tæn'təlaiziŋ] *adj* (smell, possibility) 興味をそそる kyómi wò sosórù

tantamount [tæn'təmaunt] *adj*: *tantamount to* ...も同然である ...mo dốzen de arù

tantrum [tæn'trəm] *n* かんしゃく kañshaku

tap [tæp] *n* (on sink etc) 蛇口 jagúchi; (*also*: **gas tap**) ガスの元栓 gásù no motósen; (gentle blow) 軽くたたく事 karúku tatakù kotó

♦*vt* (hit gently) 軽くたたく karúku tatakù; (resources) 利用する riyő suru; (telephone) 盗聴する tốchō suru

on tap (*fig*: resources) いつでも利用できる ítsùdemo riyő dekirù

tap-dancing [tæp'dænsiŋ] *n* タップダンス tappúdañsu

tape [teip] *n* (*also*: **magnetic tape**) 磁気テープ jikítēpu; (cassette) カセットテープ kaséttotēpu; (sticky tape) 粘着テープ nefíchakutēpu; (for tying) ひも himó

♦*vt* (record: sound) 録音する rokúon suru; (: image) 録画する rokúga suru; (stick with tape) テープで張る tēpu de harú

tape deck *n* テープデッキ tếpudekkì

tape measure *n* メジャー méjā

taper [tei'pə:r] *n* (candle) 細いろうそく hosóî rốsokù

♦*vi* (narrow) 細くなる hósòku narù

tape recorder *n* テープレコーダー tếpurekồdā

tapestry [tæp'istri:] *n* (object) タペストリー tapésutorî; (art) ししゅう shishú

tar [tɑːr] *n* コールタール kốrutāru

tarantula [təræn'tʃələ] *n* タランチュラ taráñchura

target [tɑːr'git] *n* (thing aimed at, *also fig*) 的 matô

tariff [tær'if] *n* (tax on goods) 関税 kañzei; (BRIT: in hotels, restaurants) 料金表 ryőkiñhyo

tarmac [tɑːr'mæk] *n* (BRIT: on road) アスファルト asúfarùto; (AVIAT) エプロン épùron

tarnish [tɑːr'niʃ] *vt* (metal) さびさせる sabísaserù; (*fig*: reputation etc) 汚す yogósù

tarpaulin [tɑːrpɔː'lin] *n* シート shíto

tarragon [tær'əgən] *n* タラゴン táràgon ◇香辛料の一種 kốshiñryō no ísshù

tart [tɑːrt] *n* (CULIN) タルト tárùto ◇菓子の一種 káshî no ísshù; (BRIT: *inf*: prostitute) ばいた báìta

♦*adj* (flavor) 酸っぱい suppâî

tartan [tɑːr'tən] *n* タータンチェック tấtanchekkù

♦*adj* (rug, scarf etc) タータンチェックの tấtanchekkù no

tartar [tɑːr'tə:r] *n* (on teeth) 歯石 shiséki

tartar(e) sauce [tɑːr'tə:r-] *n* タルタルソース tarútarusōsu

tart up (BRIT) *vt* (*inf*: object) 派手にする hadé nì suru

to tart oneself up おめかしをする o-mékashi wò suru

task [tæsk] *n* 仕事 shigóto

to take to task ...の責任を問う ...no sekínin wò tôù

task force *n* (MIL, POLICE) 機動部隊 kidốbutai

Tasmania [tæzmei'ni:ə] *n* タスマニア tasúmanìa

tassel [tæs'əl] *n* 房 fusá

taste [teist] n (also: **sense of taste**) 味覚 mikáku; (flavor: also: **aftertaste**) 味 ajî; (sample) 一口 hitókuchi; (fig: glimpse, idea) 味わい ajíwaî
♦vt (get flavor of) 味わう ajíwaù; (test) 試食する shishóku suru
♦vi: **to taste of/like** (fish etc) …の味がする …no ajî ga surù
you can taste the garlic (in it) (含まれている) ニンニクの味がする (fukúmarete irù) nínniku nò ajî ga surù
in good/bad taste 趣味がいい〔悪い〕 shúmî ga íi〔warúî〕

tasteful [teist'fəl] adj (furnishings) 趣味の良い shúmî no yôî

tasteless [teist'lis] adj (food) 味がない ajî ga naî; (remark, joke, furnishings) 趣味の悪い shúmî no warúî

tasty [teis'ti:] adj (food) おいしい oíshiî

tatters [tæt'əːrz] npl: **in tatters** (clothes, papers etc) ずたずたになって zutázuta ni nattè

tattoo [tætuː'] n (on skin) 入れ墨 irézumi; (spectacle) パレード parédò
♦vt (name, design) …の入れ墨をする …no irézumi wò suru

tatty [tæt'i:] (BRIT: inf) adj (inf) 薄汚い usúgitanaî

taught [tɔːt] pt, pp of **teach**

taunt [tɔːnt] n あざけり azákerî
♦vt あざける azákerù

Taurus [tɔːr'əs] n 牡牛座 oúshizà

taut [tɔːt] adj ぴんと張った pín tò hattá

tavern [tæv'əːrn] n (old) 酒場 sakába

tax [tæks] n 税金 zeíkin
♦vt (earnings, goods etc) …に税金をかける …ni zeíkin wò kakérù; (fig: test: memory) 最大限に使う saídaîgen ni tsukáù; (patience) 試練にかける shírèn ni kakérù

taxable [tæk'səbəl] adj (income) 課税される kazéi sarerù

taxation [tæksei'ʃən] n (system) 課税 kazéi; (money paid) 税金 zeíkin

tax avoidance [-əvoi'dəns] n 節税 setsúzei

tax disc (BRIT) n (AUT) 納税ステッカー nōzeisutekkā

tax evasion n 脱税 datsúzei

tax-free [tæks'fri:'] adj (goods, services) 免税の meñzei no

taxi [tæk'si:] n タクシー tákùshī
♦vi (AVIAT: plane) 滑走する kassō suru

taxi driver n タクシーの運転手 tákùshī no uñteñshu

taxi rank (BRIT) n = **taxi stand**

taxi stand n タクシー乗場 takúshīnorî-ba

tax payer [-pei'əːr] n 納税者 nōzeishà

tax relief n 減税 geñzei

tax return n 確定申告書 kakúteishiñ-kokushò

TB [ti:bi:'] n abbr = **tuberculosis**

tea [ti:] n (drink: Japanese) お茶 o-chá; (: English) 紅茶 kōchá; (BRIT: meal) おやつ o-yátsù
high tea (BRIT) 夕食 yūshoku◊夕方早目に食べる食事 yūgata hayáme nì tabérù shokúji

tea bag n ティーバッグ tíbaggù

tea break (BRIT) n 休憩 kyūkei

teach [ti:tʃ] (pt, pp **taught**) vt (gen) 教える oshíerù; (be a teacher of) …(の)教師をする …(no)kyōshi wò suru
♦vi (be a teacher: in school etc) 教師をする kyōshi wò suru

teacher [ti:'tʃəːr] n 教師 kyōshi, 先生 señseî

teaching [ti:'tʃiŋ] n (work of teacher) 教職 kyōshoku

tea cosy n お茶帽子 o-chábōshi

tea cup n (Western) ティーカップ tíkappù; (Japanese) 湯飲み茶碗 yunómijawàn, 湯飲み yunómi

teak [ti:k] n チーク chíku

tea leaves npl 茶殻 chagára

team [ti:m] n (of people: gen, SPORT) チーム chímu; (of animals) 一組 hitókumi

teamwork [ti:m'wəːrk] n チームワーク chímuwàku

teapot [ti:'pɑːt] n きゅうす kyūsu

tear¹ [teːr] n (hole) 裂け目 sakéme
♦vb (pt **tore**, pp **torn**)
♦vt (rip) 破る yabúrù
♦vi (become torn) 破れる yabúrerù

tear² [tiːr] n (in eye) 涙 námìda
in tears 泣いている naîte irù

tear along *vi* (rush) 猛スピードで走って行く môsupîdò de hashîtte ikù

tearful [tir'fəl] *adj* (family, face) 涙ぐんだ namídaguñda

tear gas *n* 催涙ガス saíruigasù

tearoom [ti:'ru:m] *n* 喫茶店 kissáteñ

tear up *vt* (sheet of paper etc) ずたずたに破る zutázuta nì yabúrù

tease [ti:z] *vt* からかう karákaù

tea set *n* 茶器セット chakísettò

teaspoon [ti:'spu:n] *n* (type of spoon) ティースプーン tîsupùn; (also: **teaspoonful**: as measurement) 小さじ一杯 kosáji ippái

teat [ti:t] *n* (ANAT) 乳首 chikúbì; (also: **bottle teat**) ほ乳瓶の乳首 honyúbìn no chikúbì

teatime [ti:'taim] *n* おやつの時間 o-yátsù no jikáñ

tea towel (*BRIT*) *n* ふきん fukíñ

technical [tek'nikəl] *adj* (terms, advances) 技術の gíjùtsu no

technical college (*BRIT*) *n* 高等専門学校 kôtōseñmoñgakkô

technicality [teknikæl'iti:] *n* (point of law) 法律の専門的細目 hôritsu nò señmonteki saimòku; (detail) 細かい事 komákaì kotó

technically [tek'nikli:] *adv* (strictly speaking) 正確に言えば seíkaku nì iébà; (regarding technique) 技術的に gíjùtsuteki ni

technician [tek'nikəl] *n* 技術者 gijútsushà

technique [tekni:k'] *n* 技術 gíjùtsu

technological [teknələ:dʒ'ikəl] *adj* 技術的な gijútsuteki na

technology [teknɑ:l'ədʒi:] *n* 科学技術 kagákugijùtsu

teddy (bear) [ted'i:-] *n* クマのぬいぐるみ kumá nò nuígurumi

tedious [ti:'di:əs] *adj* (work, discussions etc) 退屈な taíkutsu na

tee [ti:] *n* (GOLF) ティー tî

teem [ti:m] *vi*: **to teem with** (visitors, tourists etc) ...がぞろぞろ来ている ...ga zôrðzoro kité irù

it is teeming (with rain) 雨が激しく降っている ámè ga hagéshikù futté irù

teenage [ti:n'eidʒ] *adj* (children, fashions etc) ティーンエージャーの tîn-êjà no

teenager [ti:n'eidʒə:r] *n* ティーンエージャー tîn-êjà

teens [ti:nz] *npl*: **to be in one's teens** 年齢は10代である neñrei wà júdài de árù

tee-shirt [ti:'ʃə:rt] *n* = **T-shirt**

teeter [ti:'tə:r] *vi* (also fig) ぐらつく gurátsukù

teeth [ti:θ] *npl of* **tooth**

teethe [ti:ð] *vi* (baby) 歯が生える há gà haérù

teething ring [ti:'ðiŋ-] *n* おしゃぶり o-shábùri ◊リング状の物を指す riñgujô no monó wò sásù

teething troubles *npl* (fig) 初期の困難 shókì no kôñnan

teetotal [ti:tout'əl] *adj* (person) 酒を飲まない saké wò nománaì

telecommunications [teləkəmju:nikei'ʃənz] *n* 電気通信 deñkitsûshin

telegram [tel'əgræm] *n* 電報 deñpō

telegraph [tel'əgræf] *n* (system) 電信 deñshin

telegraph pole *n* 電柱 deñchū

telepathic [teləpæθ'ik] *adj* テレパシーの terépàshī no

telepathy [təlep'əθi:] *n* テレパシー terépàshī

telephone [tel'əfoun] *n* 電話 deñwa
♦*vt* (person) ...に電話をかける ...ni deñwa wò kakérù; (message) 電話で伝える deñwa dè tsutáerù

on the telephone (talking) 電話中で deñwachū de; (possessing phone) 電話を持っている deñwa wò môtte irù

telephone booth *n* 電話ボックス deñwabokkùsu

telephone box (*BRIT*) *n* = **telephone booth**

telephone call *n* 電話 deñwa

telephone directory *n* 電話帳 deñwachō

telephone number *n* 電話番号 deñwabañgō

telephonist [telə'founist] (*BRIT*) *n* 電話交換手 deñwakōkañshu

telescope [tel'əskoup] n 望遠鏡 bōenkyō

telescopic [teliskɑ:p'ik] adj (lens) 望遠の bōen no; (collapsible: tripod, aerial) 入れ子式の irékoshǐki no

television [tel'əviʒən] n (all senses) テレビ térèbi

on television テレビで térèbi de

television set n テレビ受像機 terébijuzōki

telex [tel'eks] n テレックス terékkùsu
♦vt (company) ...にテレックスを送る ...ni terékkùsu wo okúrù; (message) テレックスで送る terékkùsu de okúrù

tell [tel] (pt, pp **told**) vt (say) ...に言う ...ni iú; (relate: story) 述べる nobérù; (distinguish): **to tell something from** ...から...を区別する ...kará ...wò kúbètsu suru
♦vi (talk): **to tell (of)** ...について話す ...ni tsúîte hanásù; (have an effect) 効果的である kōkateki de arù

to tell someone to do something ...に...する様に言う ...ni ...surú yō ni iú

teller [tel'ə:r] n (in bank) 出納係 suítōgakàri

telling [tel'iŋ] adj (remark, detail) 意味深い imíbukài

tell off vt: **to tell someone off** しかる shikaru

telltale [tel'teil] adj (sign) 証拠の shōko no

telly [tel'i:] (BRIT: inf) n abbr = **television**

temerity [təme:r'iti:] n ずうずうしさ zūzūshìsà

temp [temp] n abbr (= temporary) 臨時職員 riñjishokuiñ

temper [tem'pə:r] n (nature) 性質 seíshitsu; (mood) 機嫌 kigéñ; (fit of anger) かんしゃく kañshaku
♦vt (moderate) 和らげる yawáragerù

to be in a temper 怒っている okótte irù

to lose one's temper 怒る okórù

temperament [tem'pə:rəmənt] n (nature) 性質 seíshitsu

temperamental [tempə:rəmen'təl] adj (person, fig: car) 気まぐれな kimágùre na

temperate [tem'pə:rit] adj (climate, country) 温暖な oñdan na

temperate zone n 温帯 oñtai

temperature [tem'pə:rətʃə:r] n (of person, place) 温度 óñdo

to have/run a temperature 熱がある netsú ga arù

tempest [tem'pist] n 嵐 áràshi

tempi [tem'pi:] npl of **tempo**

temple [tem'pəl] n (building) 神殿 shiñden; (ANAT) こめかみ komékami

tempo [tem'pou] (pl **tempos** or **tempi**) n (MUS) テンポ téñpo; (fig: of life etc) ペース pēsu

temporarily [tempəre:r'ili:] adv 一時的に ichíjiteki ni

temporary [tem'pə:re:ri:] adj (passing) 一時的な ichíjiteki na; (worker, job) 臨時の riñji no

tempt [tempt] vt 誘惑する yūwaku suru

to tempt someone into doing something ...する様に...を誘惑する ...surú yō ni ...wo yūwaku suru

temptation [temptei'ʃən] n 誘惑 yūwaku

tempting [temp'tiŋ] adj (offer) 魅惑的な miwákuteki na; (food) おいしそうな ofshisō na

ten [ten] num 十 (の) jū (no)

tenacity [tənæs'iti:] n (of person, animal) 根気強さ koñkizùyosa

tenancy [ten'ənsi:] n (possession of room, land etc) 賃借 chiñshaku; (period of possession) 賃借期間 chiñshakukikàn

tenant [ten'ənt] n (rent-payer) 店子 tanáko, テナント tenáñto

tend [tend] vt (crops, sick person) ...の世話をする ...no sewá wò suru
♦vi: **to tend to do something** ...しがちである ...shigáchi de arù

tendency [ten'dənsi:] n (of person, thing) 傾向 keíkō

tender [ten'də:r] adj (person, heart, care) 優しい yasáshìi; (sore) 触ると痛い sawáru tò itáì; (meat) 柔らかい yawárakaì; (age) 幼い osánaì
♦n (COMM: offer) 見積り mitsúmori; (money): **legal tender** 通貨 tsúkà

♦*vt* (offer, resignation) 提出する teíshutsu suru

to tender an apology 陳謝する chínsha suru

tenderness [ten'də:rnis] *n* (affection) 優しさ yasáshisà; (of meat) 柔らかさ yawárakasà

tendon [ten'dən] *n* けん kén

tenement [ten'əmənt] *n* 安アパート yasúapàto

tenet [ten'it] *n* 信条 shiñjō

tennis [ten'is] *n* テニス téñisu

tennis ball *n* テニスボール tenísubòru

tennis court *n* テニスコート tenísukòto

tennis player *n* テニス選手 tenísuseñshu

tennis racket *n* テニスラケット tenísurakettò

tennis shoes *npl* テニスシューズ tenísushùzu

tenor [ten'ə:r] *n* (MUS) テノール tenórù

tenpin bowling [ten'pin-] *n* ボウリング bóriñgu

tense [tens] *adj* (person, smile, muscle) 緊張した kiñchō shita; (period) 緊迫した kíñpaku shita

♦*n* (LING) 時制 jiséi

tension [ten'ʃən] *n* (nervousness) 緊張 kiñchō; (between ropes etc) 張力 chōryoku

tent [tent] *n* テント téñto

tentacle [ten'təkəl] *n* (of octopus etc) あし ashí

tentative [ten'tətiv] *adj* (person, step, smile) 自信のない jishín no naì; (conclusion, plans) 差し当っての sashíatattè no

tenterhooks [ten'tə:rhuks] *npl* : *on tenterhooks* はらはらして hárahara shite

tenth [tenθ] *num* 第十 (の) dáìjū (no)

tent peg *n* テントのくい téñto no kuí

tent pole *n* テントの支柱 téñto no shichū

tenuous [ten'ju:əs] *adj* (hold, links, connection etc) 弱い yowái

tenure [ten'jə:r] *n* (of land, buildings etc) 保有権 hoyúken; (of office) 在職期間 zaíshokukikàn

tepid [tep'id] *adj* (tea, pool etc) ぬるい

nurúì

term [tə:rm] *n* (word, expression) 用語 yōgo; (period in power etc) 期間 kikáñ; (SCOL) 学期 gakkí

♦*vt* (call) ...と言う ...to iú

in the short/long term 短〔長〕期間で tañ〔chō〕kikàn de

terminal [tə:r'mənəl] *adj* (disease, cancer, patient) 末期の mákkì no

♦*n* (ELEC) 端子 táñshi; (COMPUT) 端末機 tañmatsukì; (*also*: **air terminal**) ターミナルビル tāminarubìru; (BRIT: *also*: **coach terminal**) バスターミナル basútāminaru

terminate [tə:r'məneit] *vt* (discussion, contract, pregnancy) 終らせる owáraserù, 終える oérù; (contract) 破棄する hákì suru; (pregnancy) 中絶する chúzetsu suru

termini [tə:r'məni:] *npl of* **terminus**

terminology [tə:rmənɑ:l'ədʒi:] *n* 用語 yōgo ◇総称 sōshō

terminus [tə:r'mənəs] (*pl* **-mini**) *n* (for buses, trains) ターミナル tāminaru

terms [tə:rmz] *npl* (conditions: *also* COMM) 条件 jōken

to be on good terms with someone ...と仲がいい ...to nákà ga íi

to come to terms with (problem) ...と折合いがつく ...to oríaì ga tsukú

terrace [te:r'əs] *n* (BRIT: row of houses) 長屋 nagáyà; (patio) テラス téràsu; (AGR) 段々畑 dañdanbatàke

terraced [te:r'əst] *adj* (house) 長屋の nagáyà no; (garden) ひな壇式の hinádañshiki no

terraces [te:r'əsiz] (BRIT) *npl* (SPORT): *the terraces* 立見席 tachímisèki

terracotta [te:rəkɑ:t'ə] *n* テラコッタ terácottà

terrain [tərein'] *n* 地面 jímèn

terrible [te:r'əbəl] *adj* ひどい hidóì

terribly [te:r'əbli:] *adv* (very) とても totémo; (very badly) ひどく hídòku

terrier [te:r'i:ə:r] *n* テリア térìa

terrific [tərif'ik] *adj* (very great: thunderstorm, speed) 大変な taíhen na; (wonderful: time, party) 素晴らしい subárashiî

terrify [te:r'əfai] vt おびえさせる obîesaserù

territorial [te:ritɔ:r'i:əl] adj (waters, boundaries, dispute) 領土の ryôdò no

territory [te:r'itɔ:ri:] n (gen) 領土 ryôdò; (fig) 縄張 nawâbarî

terror [te:r'ər] n (great fear) 恐怖 kyôfu

terrorism [te:r'ərizəm] n テロ térò

terrorist [te:r'ərist] n テロリスト terôrisùto

terrorize [te:r'əraiz] vt おびえさせる obîesaserù

terse [tə:rs] adj (style) 簡潔な kañketsu na; (reply) そっけない sokkénaî ◇言葉数が少なく無愛想な返事などについて言う kotôbakazù ga sukúnakù buâîsō na heñji nadò ni tsûîte iú

Terylene [te:r'əli:n] ® n テリレン térîren ◇人工繊維の一種 jiñkōseñ-i no ísshū

test [test] n (trial, check: also MED, CHEM) テスト tésùto; (of courage etc) 試練 shîren; (SCOL) テスト tésùto; (also: **driving test**) 運転免許の試験 uñtenmeñkyo no shikêñ
♦vt (gen) テストする tésùto suru

testament [tes'təmənt] n 証拠 shôko
the Old/New Testament 旧〔新〕約聖書 kyû(shiñ)yaku seisho

testicle [tes'tikəl] n こう丸 kôgan

testify [tes'təfai] vi (LAW) 証言する shôgen suru
to testify to something ...が...だと証言する ...ga ...dá tò shôgen suru

testimony [tes'təmouni:] n (LAW: statement) 証言 shôgen; (clear proof) 証拠 shôko

test match n (CRICKET, RUGBY) 国際戦 kokúsaisen, 国際試合 kokúsaijiâi

test pilot n テストパイロット tesútopairottô

test tube n 試験管 shikéñkan

tetanus [tet'ənəs] n 破傷風 hashôfū

tether [teð'ə:r] vt (animal) つなぐ tsunágù
♦n: *at the end of one's tether* 行き詰って ikízumattè

text [tekst] n 文書 búñsho

textbook [tekst'buk] n 教科書 kyôkasho

textiles [teks'tailz] npl (fabrics) 織物 orímòno; (textile industry) 織物業界 orîmonogyôkai

texture [teks'tʃə:r] n (of cloth, skin, soil, silk) 手触り tezáwàri

Thailand [tai'lənd] n タイ tâî

Thames [temz] n: *the Thames* テムズ川 têmùzugawa

KEYWORD

than [ðæn] conj (in comparisons) ...より (も) ...yóri(mo)
you have more than 10 あなたは10個以上持っています anátà wa júkkò îjô móttè imasu
I have more than you/Paul 私はあなた〔ポール〕より沢山持っています watákushi wà anátà〔pôrù〕yori takúsañ móttè imasu
I have more pens than pencils 私は鉛筆よりペンを沢山持っています watákushi wà eñpitsu yorì péñ wo takúsañ móttè imasu
she is older than you think 彼女はあなたが思っているより年ですよ kánòjo wa anátà ga omótte irù yôrì toshî desù yó
more than once 数回 sûkài

---

thank [θæŋk] vt (person) ...に感謝する ...ni káñsha suru
thank you (very much) (大変)有難うございました (taîhen) arígātō gozáimashìtà
thank God! ああ良かった ā yókàtta

thankful [θæŋk'fəl] adj: *thankful (for)* (...を) 有難く思っている (...wo) arígatakù omótte irù

thankless [θæŋk'lis] adj (task) 割の悪い warî no waruî

thanks [θæŋks] npl 感謝 káñsha
♦excl (also: **many thanks**, **thanks a lot**) 有難う arígatô

Thanksgiving (Day) [θæŋksgiv'iŋ-] n 感謝祭 kañshasaî

thanks to prep ...のおかげで ...no o-kágge dè

KEYWORD

that [ðæt] (*demonstrative adj, pron: pl* **those**) *adj* (demonstrative) その sonó, あの anó

that man/woman/book その[あの]男性[女性, 本] sonó [anó] dañsei [jòsei, hoñ]

leave those books on the table その本をテーブルの上に置いていって下さい sonó hoñ wo tēburu no uē nì oíte ittè kudásaî

that one それ sorè, あれ arê

that one over there あそこにある物 asóko nì árù monó

I want this one, not that one 欲しいのはこれです、あれは要りません hoshíi no wà koré desù, aré wà irímaseñ

♦*pron* **1** (demonstrative) それ sorè, あれ arê

who's/what's that? あれはだれですか[何ですか] aré wà dárè desu ká[náñ desu ká]

is that you? あなたですか anátà desu ká

I prefer this to that あれよりこちらの方が好きです aré yorì kochíra no hō ga sukí desù

will you eat all that? あれを全部食べるつもりですか aré wò zénbu tabérù tsumóri desù ká

that's my house 私の家はあれです watákushi nò iê wà aré desù

that's what he said 彼はそう言いましたよ kárè wa sô iimashìta yó

what happened after that? それからどうなりましたか soré karà dô narimashìta ká

that is (to say) つまり tsúmàri, すなわち sunáwàchi

2 (relative): *the book (that) I read* 私の読んだ本 watákushi nò yóñda hóñ

the books that are in the library 図書館にある本 toshókàn ni árù hóñ

the man (that) I saw 私の見た男 watákushi nò mítà otóko

all (that) I have 私が持っているだけ watákushi gà móttè irú dàke

the box (that) I put it in それを入れた箱 sorè wò iréta hakò

the people (that) I spoke to 私が声を掛けた人々 watákushi gà kôè wo kákèta hitóbìto

3 (relative: of time): *the day (that) he came* 彼が来た日 kárè ga kitá hì

the evening/winter (that) he came to see us 彼が私たちの家に来た夜[冬] kárè ga watákushitàchi no iê ni kitá yorù[fuyù]

♦*conj* ...だと ...dá tò

he thought that I was ill 私が病気だと彼は思っていました watákushi gà byōkì dá tò kárè wa omótte imashìta

she suggested that I phone you あなたに電話する様にと彼女は私に勧めました anátà ni deñwa suru yô ni to kánòjo wa watákushi nì susúmemashìta

♦*adv* (demonstrative) それ程 soré hodò, あれ程 aré hodò, そんなに soñna nì, あんなに añna nì

I can't work that much あんなに働けません añna nì határakemaseñ

I didn't realize it was that bad 事態があれ程悪くなっているとは思っていませんでした jítai ga aré hodò wárùku nattè irù to wa omótte imaseñ deshìta

that high あんなに高い añna nì takáì

the wall's about that high and that thick 塀はこれぐらい高くてこれぐらい厚い heî wà koré gurài tákàkute koré gurài atsúì

thatched [θætʃt] *adj* (roof, cottage) わらぶきの warábuki no

thaw [θɔ:] *n* 雪解けの陽気 yukídokè no yôkì

♦*vi* (ice) 溶ける tokérù; (food) 解凍される kaítō sarerù

♦*vt* (food: *also*: **thaw out**) 解凍する kaítō suru

KEYWORD

the [ðə] *def art* **1** (*gen*) その sonó ◊ 通常日本語では表現しない tsújō nihóngo de wà hyôgen shinaî

the history of France フランスの歴史

furánsu nò rekíshi

the books/children are in the library 本〔子供たち〕は図書館にあります〔います〕hón〔kodómotàchi〕wa toshòkàn ni arímasù〔imásù〕

she put it on the table/gave it to the postman 彼女はテーブルに置きました〔郵便屋さんにあげました〕kánòjo wa tèburu ni okímashìta〔yùbin-yasan nì agémashìta〕

he took it from the drawer 彼は引出しから取り出しました kárè wa hikídashi karà torídashimashìta

I haven't the time/money 私にはそれだけの時間〔金〕がありません watákushi ni wa soré dakè no jikán〔kanè〕gà arímasèn

to play the piano/violin ピアノ〔バイオリン〕をひく piáno〔baíorin〕wo hikú

the age of the computer コンピュータの時代 kofipyùta no jidái

I'm going to the butcher's/the cinema 肉屋に〔映画を見に〕行って来ます nikùyà ni〔eíga wò mí nì〕itté kimasù

2 (+ adjective to form noun)

the rich and the poor 金持と貧乏人 kanémochì to bífbònin

the wounded were taken to the hospital 負傷者は病院に運ばれた fushóshà wa byóìn ni hakóbaretà

to attempt the impossible 不可能な事をやろうとする fukánó na kotò wo yaró to surù

3 (in titles): *Elizabeth the First* エリザベス1世 erízabèsu ísséi

Peter the Great ピョートル大帝 pyótòru taítei

4 (in comparisons): *the more he works the more he earns* 彼は働けば働く程もうかる kárè wa határakèba határaku hodò mókarù

the more I look at it the less I like it 見れば見る程いやになります mírèba míru hodò iyá ni narimasù

theater [θi:'ətər] (*BRIT* **theatre**) *n* (building with stage) 劇場 gekíjò; (art form) 演劇 efigeki; (*also*: **lecture thea-**

ter) 講義室 kógishìtsu; (MED: *also*: **operating theater**) 手術室 shujútsushìtsu

theater-goer [θi:'ətə:rgouə:r] *n* 芝居好き shibáizùki

theatrical [θi:æt'rikəl] *adj* (event, production) 演劇の efigeki no; (gestures) 芝居みた shibáijimìta

theft [θeft] *n* 窃盗 settó

their [ðe:r] *adj* 彼らの kárèra no ¶ *see also* **my**

theirs [ðe:rz] *pron* 彼らの物 kárèra no monó ¶ *see also* **mine**

them [ðem] *pron* (direct) 彼らを kárèra wo; (indirect) 彼らに kárèra ni; (stressed, after prep) 彼ら kárèra ¶ *see also* **me**

theme [θi:m] *n* (main subject) 主題 shudái, テーマ tèma; (MUS) テーマ tèma

theme park *n* テーマ遊園地 témayuènchi

theme song *n* 主題歌 shidáìka

themselves [ðəmselvz'] *pl pron* (reflexive) 彼ら自身を kárèra jishìn wo; (after prep) 彼ら自身 kárèra jishìn ¶ *see also* **oneself**

then [ðen] *adv* (at that time) その時(に) sonó tokì (ni); (next, later, and also) それから soré karà

◆*conj* (therefore) だから dá kàra

◆*adj*: *the then president* 当時の大統領 tójì no daítòryò

by then (past) その時 sonó tokì; (future) その時になったら sonó tokì ni nattárà

from then on その時から sonó tokì kara

theology [θi:ɑ:l'ədʒi:] *n* 神学 shifigaku

theorem [θi:r'əm] *n* 定理 teíri

theoretical [θi:əret'ikəl] *adj* (biology, possibility) 理論的な rirónteki na

theorize [θi:'ə:raiz] *vi* 学説を立てる gakúsetsu wò tatérù

theory [θi:ə:r'i:] *n* (all senses) 理論 ríròn

in theory 理論的には rirónteki ni wà

therapeutic(al) [θe:rəpju:'tik(əl)] *adj* 治療の chiryó no

therapist [θe:r'əpist] *n* セラピスト serápisùto

therapy [θeːrˈəpiː] *n* 治療 chiryō

KEYWORD

there [ðeːr] *adv* 1: *there is, there are* …がある〔いる〕…ga árù〔irú〕

there are 3 of them (things) 3つあります míttsu arímasù; (people) 3人います saṅniṅ imásù

there is no one here だれもいません dáre mo imásèn

there is no bread left パンがなくなりました páṅ ga nakúnarimashìta

there has been an accident 事故があI りました jíkò ga arímashìta

there will be a meeting tomorrow 明日会議があります asú káìgi ga arímasù

2 (referring to place) そこに〔で、へ〕sokó nì〔dè, e〕, あそこに〔で、へ〕asokó nì〔dè, e〕

where is the book? - it's there 本はどこにありますか−あそこにあります hóṅ wa dókò ni arímasù ká - asóko nì arímasù

put it down there そこに置いて下さい sokó nì oíte kudasaí

he went there on Friday 彼は金曜日に行きました kárè wa kiṅ-yōbi ni ikímashìta

I want that book there そこの本が欲しい sokó nò hóṅ ga hoshíi

there he is! いました imáshìta

3: *there, there* (especially to child) よしよし yóshì yóshì

there, there, it's not your fault/don't cry よしよし、お前のせいじゃないから〔泣かないで〕yóshì yóshì, omáe nò seí ja naì kara〔nakánaìde〕

thereabouts [ðeːrˈəbauts] *adv* (place) そこら辺 sokórahèn; (amount) それぐらい soré guraì

thereafter [ðeːræfˈtəːr] *adv* それ以来 soré iraì

thereby [ðeːrˈbai] *adv* それによって soré ni yotté

therefore [ðeːrˈfɔːr] *adv* だから dá kàra

there's [ðeːrz] = there is; there has

thermal [θəːrˈməl] *adj* (underwear) 防寒

用の bôkan-yô no; (paper) 感熱の kaṅnetsu no; (printer) 熱式の netsúshìki no

thermal spring 温泉 oṅsen

thermometer [θəːrmɑːmˈitəːr] *n* (for room/body temperature) 温度計 oṅdokèi

Thermos [θəːrˈməs] ® *n* (also: **Thermos flask**) 魔法瓶 mahôbìn

thermostat [θəːrˈməstæt] *n* サーモスタット sāmosutattò

thesaurus [θisɔːrˈəs] *n* シソーラス shisôràsu

these [ðiːz] *pl adj* これらの korérà no
♦*pl pron* これらは〔を〕 korérà wa〔wo〕

theses [θiːsˈiːz] *npl of* thesis

thesis [θiːsˈis] (*pl* theses) *n* (for doctorate etc) 論文 roṅbun

they [ðei] *pl pron* 彼らは〔が〕 kárèra wa〔ga〕

they say that … (it is said that) …と言われている …to iwárete irù

they'd [ðeid] = they had; they would

they'll [ðeil] = they shall, they will

they're [ðeːr] = they are

they've [ðeiv] = they have

thick [θik] *adj* (in shape: slice, jersey etc) 厚い atsúi; (line) 太い futói; (in consistency: sauce, mud, fog etc) 濃い kôi; (: forest) 深い fukáì; (stupid) 鈍い nibúì
♦*n*: *in the thick of the battle* 戦いのさなかに tatákai nò sáṅàka ni

it's 20 cm thick 厚さは20センチだ atsúsa wà nijússeṅchi da

thicken [θikˈən] *vi* (fog etc) 濃くなる kôkù naru; (plot) 込入ってくる komíitte kurù
♦*vt* (sauce etc) 濃くする kôkù suru

thickness [θikˈnis] *n* 厚み atsúmi

thickset [θikˈset] *adj* (person, body) がっちりした gatchírì shita

thickskinned [θikˈskind] *adj* (fig: person) 無神経な mushíṅkei na

thief [θiːf] (*pl* thieves) *n* 泥棒 doróbō

thieves [θiːvz] *npl of* thief

thigh [θai] *n* 太もも futómomo

thimble [θimˈbəl] *n* 指抜き yubínuki

thin [θin] *adj* (gen) 薄い usúi; (line) 細い hosóì; (person, animal) やせた yasétà;

(crowd) まばらな mabára na

♦vt: **to thin (down)** (sauce, paint) 薄める usúmerù

thing [θiŋ] n (gen) 物事 monógòto; (physical object) 物 monó; (matter) 事 kotó:
to have a thing about someone/something (mania) ...が大嫌いである ...ga dáîkirai de árù; (fascination) ...が大好きである ...ga dáîsuki de árù
poor thing かわいそうに kawáisō ni
the best thing would be to ... ...するのが一番いいだろう ...surú nò ga ichíban iî darō
how are things? どうですか dô desu ká

things [θiŋz] npl (belongings) 持物 mochímòno

think [θiŋk] (pt, pp **thought**) vi (reflect) 考える kañgaerù; (believe) 思う omóù
♦vt (imagine) ...だと思う ...dá tò omóù
what did you think of them? 彼らの事をどう思いましたか kárèra no kotó wo dô omóimashità ka
to think about something/someone ...について考える ...ni tsúîte kañgaerù
I'll think about it 考えておくね kañgaete okù nè
to think of doing something ...しようと思う ...shiyô tò omóù
I think so/not そうだ〔違う〕と思う số dà〔chigáù〕to omóù
to think well of someone ...に対して好感を持つ ...ni táîshite kōkan wò mótsù

think over vt (offer, suggestion) よく考える yókù kañgaerù

think tank n シンクタンク shiñkutañku

think up vt (plan, scheme, excuse) 考え出す kañgaedasù

thinly [θin'li:] adv (cut, spread) 薄く usúkù

third [θə:rd] num 第三 (の) dáî san (no)
♦n (fraction) 3分の1 sañbun no ichí; (AUT: also: **third gear**) サードギヤ sádogiyà; (BRIT: SCOL: degree) 3級優等卒業学位 sañkyū yūtō sotsugyō gakùi
¶ see also **first**

thirdly [θə:rd'li:] adv 第三に dáî san ni

third party insurance (BRIT) n 損害倍償保険 soñgaibaishōhokèn

third-rate [θə:rd'reit'] adj 三流の sañryū no

Third World n: *the Third World* 第三世界 dáî san sékài

thirst [θə:rst] n 渇き kawáki

thirsty [θə:rs'ti:] adj (person, animal) のどが渇いた nódò ga kawáita; (work) のどが渇く nódò ga kawákù
to be thirsty (person, animal) のどが渇いている nódò ga kawáite irù

thirteen [θə:r'ti:n'] num 十三 (の) jū̀san (no)

thirty [θə:r'ti:] num 三十 (の) sáñjū (no)

KEYWORD

---

this [ðis] (pl **these**) adj (demonstrative) この konó
this man/woman/book この男性〔女性, 本〕konó dansei(josei, hon)
these people/children/records この人たち〔子供たち, レコード〕konó hitotàchi(kodomotàchi, rekòdo)
this one これ koré
it's not that picture but this one that I like 私が好きなのはあの絵ではなくて、この絵です watákushi gà sukí na no wà anó e de wa nakùte, konó e desù
♦pron (demonstrative) これ koré
what is this? これは何ですか koré wà náñ desu ká
who is this? この方はどなたですか konó katà wa dónàta desu ká
I prefer this to that 私はあれよりこの方が好きです watákushi wà aré yorí konó hô ga sukí desù
this is where I live 私の住いはここです watákushi no sumài wa kokó desù
this is what he said 彼はこう言いました kárè wa kô iimashìta
this is Mr Brown (in introductions/photo) こちらはブラウンさんです kochíra wà buráûnsan desu; (on telephone) こちらはブラウンですが kochíra wà burá-

ùn desu ga

◆*adv* (demonstrative): *this high/long* 高さ〔長さ〕はこれぐらいで tákàsa〔nágàsa〕wa koré gùrai de

it was about this big 大きさはこれぐらいでした ōkìsa wa korégùrai deshita

the car is this long 車の長さはこれぐらいです kurúma no nagàsa wa koré gùrai desu

we can't stop now we've gone this far ここまで来たらやめられません kokò madè kitàrà yaméraremaseǹ

---

thistle [θisˈəl] *n* アザミ azámi

thong [θɔːŋ] *n* バンド bândo

thorn [θɔːrn] *n* とげ togé

thorny [θɔːrˈniː] *adj* (plant, tree) とげの多い togé no ōi; (problem) 厄介な yákkai na

thorough [θəːrˈou] *adj* (search, wash) 徹底的な tettéiteki na; (knowledge, research) 深い fukái; (person: methodical) きちょうめんな kichōmen na

thoroughbred [θəːrˈoubred] *adj* (horse) サラブレッド sarábureddò

thoroughfare [θəːrˈoufeːr] *n* 目抜き通り menúkidòri

「*no thoroughfare*」通行禁止 tsúkōkinshi

thoroughly [θəːrˈouliː] *adv* (examine, study, wash, search) 徹底的に tettéiteki ni; (very) とても totémo

those [ðouz] *pl adj* それらの sorérà no, あれらの arérà no

◆*pl pron* それらを sorérà wo, あれらを arérà wo

though [ðou] *conj* ...にもかかわらず ...ní mò kakáwarazù

◆*adv* しかし shikáshì

thought [θɔːt] *pt, pp of* **think**

◆*n* (idea, reflection) 考え kañgaè; (opinion) 意見 íkèn

thoughtful [θɔːtˈfəl] *adj* (person: deep in thought) 考え込んでいる kañgaekonde irù; (: serious) 真剣な shiñken na; (considerate: person) 思いやりのある omóiyari no arù

thoughtless [θɔːtˈlis] *adj* (inconsiderate:

behavior, words, person) 心ない kokóronaì

thousand [θauˈzənd] *num* 千 (の) séñ (no)

two thousand 二千 (の) niséñ (no)

thousands of 何千もの... nañzeñ mo no ...

thousandth [θauˈzəndθ] *num* 第千 (の) dáí sen (no)

thrash [θræʃ] *vt* (beat) たたく tatákù; (defeat) ...に快勝する ...ni kaíshō suru

thrash about/around *vi* のたうつ notáutsu

thrash out *vt* (problem) 討議する tōgi suru

thread [θred] *n* (yarn) 糸 ítò; (of screw) ねじ山 nejíyama

◆*vt* (needle) ...に糸を通す ...ni ítò wo tōsù

threadbare [θredˈbeːr] *adj* (clothes, carpet) 擦切れた suríkiretà

threat [θret] *n* (*also fig*) 脅し odóshi; (*fig*) 危険 kikén

threaten [θretˈən] *vi* (storm, danger) 迫る semárù

◆*vt*: *to threaten someone with/to do* ...で〔...すると言って〕...を脅す ...de 〔...surú tò ittê〕...wo odósù

three [θriː] *num* 三 (の) sañ (no)

three-dimensional [θriːˈdimenˈtʃənəl] *adj* 立体の rittái no

three-piece suit [θriːˈpiːs-] *n* 三つぞろい mitsúzorði

three-piece suite *n* 応接三点セット ōsetsu santensettò

three-ply [θriːˈplai] *adj* (wool) 三重織りの sañjūori no

thresh [θreʃ] *vt* (AGR) 脱穀する dakkóku suru

threshold [θreʃˈould] *n* 敷居 shikíi

threw [θruː] *pt of* **throw**

thrift [θrift] *n* 節約 setsúyaku

thrifty [θrifˈtiː] *adj* 節約家の setsúyakukà no

thrill [θril] *n* (excitement) スリル súrìru; (shudder) ぞっとする事 zottó suru kotð

◆*vt* (person, audience) わくわくさせる wákùwaku sasérù

to be thrilled (with gift etc) 大喜びである ốyoròkobi de árù

thriller [θril'ʔ:r] *n* (novel, play, film) スリラー surírầ

thrilling [θril'iŋ] *adj* (ride, performance, news etc) わくわくさせる wákùwaku saserù

thrive [θraiv] (*pt* **throve**, *pp* **thrived** or **thriven**) *vi* (grow: plant) 生茂る oíshigerù; (: person, animal) よく育つ yókù sodátsù; (: business) 盛んになる sakán ni narù; (do well): *to thrive on something* ...で栄える ...de sakáerù

thriven [θraivən] *pp of* **thrive**

thriving [θraiv'iŋ] *adj* (business, community) 繁盛している háñjō shité irù

throat [θrout] *n* のど nódò

to have a sore throat のどが痛い nódò ga itáî

throb [θrɑ:b] *n* (of heart) 鼓動 kodố; (of wound) うずき uzúki; (of engine) 振動 shíndō

♦*vi* (heart) どきどきする dókìdoki suru; (head, arm: with pain) ずきずきする zúkìzuki suru; (machine: vibrate) 振動する shíndō suru

throes [θrouz] *npl*: *in the throes of* (war, moving house etc) ...と取組んでいるさなかに ...to toríkunde irù sánàka ni

thrombosis [θrɑ:mbou'sis] *n* 血栓症 kessénshō

throne [θroun] *n* 王座 ōzà

throng [θrɔ:ŋ] *n* 群衆 guńshū

♦*vt* (streets etc) ...に殺到する ...ni sattố suru

throttle [θrɑ:t'əl] *n* (AUT) スロットル surốttòru

♦*vt* (strangle) ...ののどを絞める ...no nódò wo shimérù

through [θru:] *prep* (space) ...を通って ...wo tốttè; (time) ...の間中 ...no aídà jū; (by means of) ...を使って ...wo tsukáttè; (owing to) ...が原因で ...ga geñ-in dè

♦*adj* (ticket, train) 直通の chokútsū no

♦*adv* 通して tốshite

to put someone through to someone (TEL) ...を...につなぐ ...wo ...ni tsunágù

to be through (TEL) つながれる tsuná-

garerù; (relationship: finished) 終る owárù

「*no through road*」(*BRIT*) 行き止り ikídomarî

throughout [θru:aut'] *prep* (place) ...の至る所に ...no itárù tokoro ni; (time) ...の間中 ...no aídà jū

♦*adv* 至る所に itárù tokoro ni

throve [θrouv] *pt of* **thrive**

throw [θrou] *n* (gen) 投げる事 nagérù kotő

♦*vt* (*pt* **threw**, *pp* **thrown**) (object) 投げる nagérù; (rider) 振り落す furíotosù; (*fig*: person: confuse) 迷わせる mayówaserù

to throw a party パーティをやる pátî wo yárù

throw away *vt* (rubbish) 捨てる sutérù; (money) 浪費する rốhi suru

throwaway [θrou'awei] *adj* (toothbrush) 使い捨ての tsukáisùte no; (line, remark) 捨てぜりふ染みた sutézerifujimîta

throw-in [θrou'in] *n* (SPORT) スローインsurốîn

throw off *vt* (get rid of: burden, habit) かなぐり捨てる kanágurisuterù; (cold) ...が治る ...ga naốrù

throw out *vt* (rubbish, idea) 捨てる sutérù; (person) ほうり出す hốridasù

throw up *vi* (vomit) 吐く hákù

thru [θru:] (*US*) = **through**

thrush [θrʌʃ] *n* (bird) つぐみ tsugúmi

thrust [θrʌst] *n* (TECH) 推進力 suíshiñryoku

♦*vt* (*pt*, *pp* **thrust**) (person, object) 強く押す tsúyòku osú

thud [θʌd] *n* ばたんという音 batáñ to iú otō

thug [θʌg] *n* (*pej*) ちんぴら chiñpira; (criminal) 犯罪者 hańzaīsha

thumb [θʌm] *n* (ANAT) 親指 oyáyubi

♦*vt*: *to thumb a lift* ヒッチハイクする hitchíhaìku suru

thumbtack [θʌm'tæk] (*US*) *n* 画びょう gabyố

thumb through *vt fus* (book) 拾い読みする hiróiyomi suru

thump [θʌmp] *n* (blow) 一撃 ichígeki; (sound) どしんという音 doshíñ to iú otó
◆*vt* (person, object) たたく tatákú
◆*vi* (heart etc) どきどきする dókìdoki suru

thunder [θʌn'də:r] *n* 雷 kamínari
◆*vi* 雷が鳴る kamínari ga narú; (*fig*: train etc): **to thunder past** ごう音を立てて通り過ぎる góon wo tátète tōrisugirù

thunderbolt [θʌn'də:rboult] *n* 落雷 rakúrai

thunderclap [θʌn'də:rklæp] *n* 雷鳴 raímei

thunderstorm [θʌn'də:rstɔ:rm] *n* 雷雨 ráîu

thundery [θʌn'də:ri:] *adj* (weather) 雷が鳴る kamínari ga narú

Thursday [θə:rz'dei] *n* 木曜日 mokúyòbi

thus [ðʌs] *adv* (in this way) こうして kō shíte; (consequently) 従って shitágattè

thwart [θwɔ:rt] *vt* (person, plans) 邪魔する jamá suru

thyme [taim] *n* タイム táîmu

thyroid [θai'rɔid] *n* (*also*: **thyroid gland**) 甲状腺 kōjōsen

tiara [ti:ær'ə] *n* ティアラ tíàra

Tibet [tibet'] *n* チベット chibéttò

tic [tik] *n* チック chíkkù

tick [tik] *n* (sound: of clock) かちかち káchìkachi; (mark) 印 shirúshi; (ZOOL) だに daní; (*BRIT*: *inf*): **in a tick** もうすぐ mō sugú
◆*vi* (clock, watch) かちかちいう káchìkachi iú
◆*vt* (item on list) ...に印を付ける ...ni shirúshi wò tsukérù

ticket [tik'it] *n* (for public transport, theater etc) 切符 kippú; (in shop: on goods) 値札 nefúda; (for raffle, library etc) チケット chikéttò; (*also*: **parking ticket**) 駐車違反のチケット chūsha-ihàn no chikéttò

ticket collector *n* 改札係 kaísatsugakàri

ticket office *n* (RAIL, theater etc) 切符売場 kippú urība

tickle [tik'əl] *vt* (person, dog) くすぐる

kusúguru
◆*vi* (feather etc) くすぐったい kusúguttai

ticklish [tik'liʃ] *adj* (person) くすぐったがる kusúguttagarù; (problem) 厄介な yákkài na

tick off *vt* (item on list) ...に印を付ける ...ni shirúshi wò tsukérù; (person) しかる shikárù

tick over *vi* (engine) アイドリングする aídoriñgu suru; (*fig*: business) 低迷する teímei suru

tidal [taid'əl] *adj* (force) 潮の shió no; (estuary) 干満のある kañman no arù

tidal wave *n* 津波 tsunámi

tidbit [tid'bit] (*US*) *n* (food) うまいもの一口 umái monò hitókuchi; (news) 好奇心をあおり立てるうわさ話 kókishiñ wo aóritaterù uwásabanàshi

tiddlywinks [tid'li:wiŋks] *n* おはじき ohájìki

tide [taid] *n* (in sea) 潮 shió; (*fig*: of events, fashion, opinion) 動向 dōkō
high/low tide 満(干)潮 mañ(kañ)chō

tide over *vt* (help out) ...の一時的な助けになる ...no ichíjiteki nà tasúke ni narù

tidy [tai'di:] *adj* (room, dress, desk, work) きちんとした kichíñ to shita; (person) きれい好きな kiréìzuki na
◆*vt* (*also*: **tidy up**: room, house etc) 片付ける katázukerù

tie [tai] *n* (string etc) ひも himó; (*BRIT*: *also*: **necktie**) ネクタイ nékùtai; (*fig*: link) 縁 éñ; (SPORT: even score) 同点 dóten
◆*vt* (fasten: parcel) 縛る shibárù; (: shoelaces, ribbon) 結ぶ musúbù
◆*vi* (SPORT etc) 同点になる dóten nì narù
to tie in a bow ちょう結びにする chō-musùbi ni suru
to tie a knot in something ...に結び目を作る ...ni musúbime wò tsukúrù

tie down *vt* (*fig*: person: restrict) 束縛する sokúbaku suru; (: to date, price etc) 縛り付ける shibáritsukerù

tier [ti:r] *n* (of stadium etc) 列 rétsù; (of cake) 層 sō

tie up vt (parcel) ...にひもを掛ける ...ni himó wò kakérù; (dog, boat) つなぐ tsunagu; (prisoner) 縛る shibárù; (arrangements) 整える totónoerù

to be tied up (busy) 忙しい isógashiî

tiger [tai'gəːr] n トラ torá

tight [tait] adj (firm: rope) ぴんと張った piñ tò hattá; (scarce: money) 少ない sukúnaî; (narrow: shoes, clothes) きつい kitsúî; (bend) 急な kyū na; (strict: security, budget, schedule) 厳しい kibíshiî; (inf: drunk) 酔っ払った yoppárattà
♦adv (hold, squeeze, shut) 堅く katákù

tighten [tait'ən] vt (rope, screw) 締める shimérù; (grip) 固くする katáku suru; (security) 厳しくする kibíshikù suru
♦vi (grip) 固くなる katáku narù; (rope) 締る shimárù

tightfisted [tait'fis'tid] adj けちな kéchi na

tightly [tait'li:] adv (grasp) 固く katákù

tightrope [tait'roup] n 綱渡りの綱 tsunáwatàri no tsuná

tights [taits] npl タイツ táitsu

tile [tail] n (on roof) かわら kawára; (on floor, wall) タイル táiru

tiled [taild] adj (roof) かわらぶきの kawárabuki no; (floor, wall) タイル張りの taírubari no

till [til] n (in shop etc) レジの引出し réji no hikídashi
♦vt (land: cultivate) 耕す tagáyasù
♦prep, conj = **until**

tiller [til'əːr] n (NAUT) だ柄 dahéi, チラー chírà

tilt [tilt] vt 傾ける katámukerù
♦vi 傾く katámukù

timber [tim'bəːr] n (material) 材木 zaímoku; (trees) 材木用の木 zaímokuyð no kí

time [taim] n (gen) 時間 jíkàn; (epoch: often pl) 時代 jidái; (by clock) 時刻 jíkòku; (moment) 瞬間 shuñkan; (occasion) 回 kâi; (MUS) テンポ téñpo
♦vt (measure time of: race, boiling an egg etc) ...の時間を計る ...no jíkàn wo hakárù; (fix moment for: visit etc) ...の時期を選ぶ ...no jíkì wo erábù; (remark

etc) ...のタイミングを合せる ...no taímiñgu wo awáserù

a long time 長い間 nagái aidà

for the time being 取りあえず toríaezù

4 at a time 4つずつ yottsú zùtsu

from time to time 時々 tokídoki

at times 時には tokí ni wà

in time (soon enough) 間に合って ma ní attè; (after some time) やがて yagátè; (MUS) ...のリズムに合せて ...no rízùmu ni awásetè

in a week's time 1週間で isshúkàn de

in no time 直ぐに súgù ni

any time いつでも ítsù de mo

on time 間に合って ma ní attè

5 times 5 5かける5 gó kakerù gó

what time is it? 何時ですか náñji desu ká

to have a good time 楽しむ tanóshimù

time bomb n 時限爆弾 jigénbakùdan

time lag n 遅れ okúre

timeless [taim'lis] adj 普遍的な fuhénteki na

time limit n 期限 kígèn

timely [taim'li:] adj (arrival, reminder) 時宜を得た jígì wo étà, 丁度いい時の chōdo ii tokí no, タイムリーな táimurī na

time off n 休暇 kyúka

timer [tai'məːr] n (time switch) タイムスイッチ taímusuitchì; (in cooking) タイマー táimà

time scale (BRIT) n 期間 kíkàn

time-share [taim'ʃeːr] n リゾート施設の共同使用権 rizótoshisètsu no kyódòshiyòken

time switch n タイムスイッチ taímusuitchì, タイマー taimà

timetable [taim'teibəl] n (RAIL etc) 時刻表 jikókuhyō; (SCOL etc) 時間割 jikánwari

time zone n 時間帯 jikántai

timid [tim'id] adj (shy) 気が小さい ki gá chíisaì; (easily frightened) 臆病な okúbyò na

timing [tai'miŋ] n (SPORT) タイミング taímingu

the timing of his resignation 彼の辞

退のタイミング kárè no jítài no taímingu

timpani [tim'pəni:] *npl* ティンパニー tímpanī

tin [tin] *n* (material) すず súzù; (*also:* **tin plate**) ブリキ buríki; (container: biscuit tin etc) 箱 hakó; (: *BRIT:* can) 缶 káñ

tinfoil [tin'fɔil] *n* ホイル hôìru

tinge [tindʒ] *n* (of color) 薄い色合 usúí iróaì; (of feeling) 気味 kimí
♦*vt:* **tinged with** (color) ...の色合を帯びた ...no iróaì wo óbìta; (feeling) ...の気味を帯びた ...no kimí wò óbìta

tingle [tiŋ'gəl] *vi* (person, arms etc) ぴりぴりする bíríbiri suru

tinker [tiŋk'ə:r]: **to tinker with** *vt fus* いじくる ijíkurù

tinned [tind] (*BRIT*) *adj* (food, salmon, peas) 缶詰の kañzume no

tin opener [-ou'pənə:r] (*BRIT*) *n* 缶切り kañkirī

tinsel [tin'səl] *n* ティンセル tíñseru

tint [tint] *n* (color) 色合い iróaì; (for hair) 染毛剤 señmōzai

tinted [tin'tid] *adj* (hair) 染めた sométa; (spectacles, glass) 色付きの irótsuki no

tiny [tai'ni:] *adj* 小さな chíìsa na

tip [tip] *n* (end: of paintbrush etc) 先端 señtan; (gratuity) チップ chíppù; (*BRIT:* for rubbish) ごみ捨て場 gomí suteba; (advice) 助言 jogén
♦*vt* (waiter) ...にチップをあげる ...ni chíppù wo agérù; (tilt) 傾ける katámukerù; (overturn: *also:* **tip over**) 引っ繰り返す hikkúrikaesù; (empty: *also:* **tip out**) 空ける akérù

tip-off [tip'ɔ:f] *n* (hint) 内報 naíhō

tipped [tipt] (*BRIT*) *adj* (cigarette) フィルター付きの firútātsuki no

Tipp-Ex [tip'eks] (R) *BRIT*) *n* 修正ペン shúseipeñ ◇白い修正液の出るフェルトペン shiróì shúseieki no derú ferútopeñ

tipsy [tip'si:] (*inf*) *adj* 酔っ払った yoppárattà

tiptoe [tip'tou] *n*: **on tiptoe** つま先立って tsumásakidattè

tiptop [tip'tɑ:p] *adj*: **in tiptop condition** 状態が最高で jōtai gà saíkō dè

tire [taiə:r'] *n* (*BRIT* **tyre**) タイヤ tâìya
♦*vt* (make tired) 疲れさせる tsukáresaserù
♦*vi* (become tired) 疲れる tsukárerù; (become wearied) うんざりする uñzarì suru

tired [taiə:rd'] *adj* (person, voice) 疲れた tsukáretà
to be tired of something ...にうんざりしている ...ni uñzarì shité irù

tireless [taiə:r'lis] *adj* (worker) 疲れを知らない tsukáre wò shiránaì; (efforts) たゆまない tayúmanaī

tire pressure *n* タイヤの空気圧 tâìya no kûkiatsù

tiresome [taiə:r'səm] *adj* (person, thing) うんざりさせる uñzarì sasérù

tiring [taiə:r'iŋ] *adj* 疲れさせる tsukáresaserù

tissue [tiʃ'u:] *n* (ANAT, BIO) 組織 sóshìki; (paper handkerchief) ティッシュ tísshù

tissue paper *n* ティッシュペーパー tisshúpēpā

tit [tit] *n* (bird) シジュウカラ shijúkàra
to give tit for tat しっぺ返しする shippégaèshi suru

titbit [tit'bit] *n* = **tidbit**

titillate [tit'əleit] *vt* 刺激する shigéki suru ◇特に性的描写などについて言う tókù ni seíteki byōsha nádò ni tsúìte iú

title [tait'əl] *n* (of book, play etc) 題名 daí; (personal rank etc) 肩書 katágaki; (BOXING etc) タイトル tâìtoru

title deed *n* (LAW) 権利証書 keñrishôsho

title role *n* 主役 shuyáku

titter [tit'ə:r] *vi* くすくす笑う kusúkusu waraù

TM [ti:em'] *abbr* = **trademark**

KEYWORD

to [tu:] *prep* **1** (direction) ...へ...é
to go to France/London/school/the station フランス〔ロンドン，学校，駅〕へ行く furánsu〔rôñdon, gakkô, ékì〕e ikù
to go to Claude's/the doctor's クロー

ドの家〔医者〕へ行く kurōdo no ié〔ishá〕e ikù

the road to Edinburgh エジンバラへの道 ejínbara é nò michí

to the left/right 左〔右〕へ hidári〔migí〕e

2 (as far as) ...まで ...madè

from here to London ここからロンドンまで kokó karà róñdon madè

to count to 10 10まで数える jū madè kazóerù

from 40 to 50 people 40ないし50人の人 yóñjū náishi gojúniñ no hitó

3 (with expressions of time): **a quarter to 5** 5時15分前 gójì jūgofun máè

it's twenty to 3 3時20分前です sáñji nijúppuñ máè desu

4 (for, of) ...の ...no

the key to the front door 玄関のかぎ géñkan no kagí

she is secretary to the director 彼女は所長の秘書です kánòjo wa shochō nò hishó desù

a letter to his wife 妻への手紙 tsúmà e no tegámi

5 (expressing indirect object) ...に ...ni

to give something to someone ...に...を与える ...ni ...wò atáerù

to talk to someone ...に話す ...ni hanásù

I sold it to a friend 友達にそれを売りました tomódachi nì soré wò urímashìta

to cause damage to something ...に損害を与える ...ni soñgai wò atáerù

to be a danger to someone/something ...を危険にさらす ...wò kikén nì sarásù

to carry out repairs to something ...を修理する ...wò shūrì suru

you've done something to your hair あなたは髪型を変えましたね anáta wa kamígata wò kaémashìta né

6 (in relation to) ...に対して ...ni táishite

A is to B as C is to D A対Bの関係はC対Dの関係に等しい A táì B no kañkei wà C táì D no kañkei nì hitóshiì

...als to 2 スコアは3対2 sukóà wa ...áì 2

30 miles to the gallon ガソリン1ガロンで30マイル走れる gasórin ichígaròn de sañjūmaìru hashírerù

7 (purpose, result): **to come to someone's aid** ...を助けに来る ...wò tasúke nì kúrù

to sentence someone to death ...に死刑の宣告を下す ...ni shikéi nò señkoku wò kudásù

to my surprise 驚いた事に odóroita kotò ni

♦**with vb 1** (simple infinitive): **to go/eat** 行く〔食べる〕事 ikú〔tabérù〕kotò

2 (following another verb): **to want to do** ...したい ...shitái

to try to do ...をしようとする ...wò shiyō tò suru

to start to do ...をし始める ...wò shihájimerù

3 (with vb omitted): **I don't want to** それをしたくない soré wò shitákùnai

you ought to あなたはそうすべきです anáta wa sō sùbeki desu

4 (purpose, result) ...するために ...surú tamè ni, ...する様に ...surú yō ni, ...しに ...shí nì

I did it to help you あなたを助け様と思ってそれをしました anáta wo tasúke-yō to omóttè soré wì shímashìta

he came to see you 彼はあなたに会いに来ました kárè wa anáta ni áì ni kimáshìta

I went there to meet him 彼に会おうとしてあそこへ行きました kárè ni aō tò shite asóko e ikímashìta

5 (equivalent to relative clause): **I have things to do** 色々とする事があります iróiro tò suru kotò ga arímasù

he has a lot to lose if ... ...が起れば、彼は大損をするだろう ...gà okórèba, kárè wa ōzòn wo suru darō

the main thing is to try 一番大切なのは努力です ichíban taísetsu ná no wà dóryòku desu

6 (after adjective etc): **ready to go** 行く準備ができた ikú juñbi ga dékìta

too old/young to ... ...するのに年を取り過ぎている〔若過ぎる〕...surú no nì to-

shí wǒ torísugite irù(wakásugirù)
it's too heavy to lift 重くて持上げられ
ません omókùte mochíageraremasèñ
♦*adv: push/pull the door to* ドアを閉
める dóawo shimérù ◇ぴったり閉めない
場合に使う pittárì shimériai baái nì tsukáù

toad [toud] n ヒキガエル hikígaèru

toadstool [toud'stu:l] n キノコ kínòko

toast [toust] n (CULIN) トースト tósuto;
(drink, speech) 乾杯 kañpai
♦*vt* (CULIN: bread etc) 焼く yákù;
(drink to) ...のために乾杯する ...no tamé
nì kañpai suru

toaster [tous'tə:r] n トースター tósutā

tobacco [təbæk'ou] n タバコ tabáko

tobacconist [təbæk'ənist] n タバコ売り
tabákoùri

tobacconist's (shop) [təbæk'ənists-] n
タバコ屋 tabákoya

toboggan [təba:g'ən] n (also child's) ト
ボガン tobógañ

today [tədei'] adv (also fig) 今日(は) kyó
(wà)
♦n 今日 kyó; (fig) 現在 géñzai

toddler [ta:d'lə:r] n 幼児 yójì

to-do [tədu:'] n (fuss) 騒ぎ sáwàgi

toe [tou] n (of foot) 足指 ashíyùbi; (of
shoe, sock) つま先 tsumásaki
♦*vt: to toe the line* (fig) 服従する fukújū suru

toenail [tou'neil] n 足のつめ ashí no tsu-
mè

toffee [tɔ:f'i:] n = **taffy**

toffee apple (BRIT) n タフィー衣のり
んご tafígoromo no riñgo

toga [tou'gə] n トーガ tóga

together [tu:geð'ə:r] adv (to/with each
other) 一緒に fsshò ni; (at same time) 同
時に dóji ni
together with ...と一緒に ...to ísshò ni

toil [tɔil] n 労苦 rókù
♦*vi* あくせく働く ákùseku határakù

toilet [tɔi'lit] n (apparatus) 便器 béñki,
トイレ tóìre; (room with this apparatus)
便所 beñjo, お手洗い o-téarài, トイレ tóìre

toilet bag (for woman) 化粧バッグ ke-
shóbaggù; (for man) 洗面バッグ señmen-
baggù

toilet paper n トイレットペーパー toí-
rettopèpā

toiletries [tɔi'litri:z] npl 化粧品 keshóhìn

toilet roll n トイレットペーパーのロー
ル tofrettopèpā no rórù

toilet soap n 化粧石けん keshósekkèn

toilet water n 化粧水 keshósùi

token [tou'kən] n (sign, souvenir) 印 shirúshi; (substitute coin) コイン kóīn
♦*adj* (strike, payment) 名目の meí-
moku no
book/record/gift token (BRIT) 商品
券 shóhiñkèn

Tokyo [tou'ki:jou] n 東京 tókyō

told [tould] pt, pp of **tell**

tolerable [ta:l'ə:rəbəl] adj (bearable) 我
慢できる gámàn dekírù; (fairly good) ま
あまあの mámà no

tolerance [ta:l'ə:rəns] n (patience) 寛容
kañ-yō; (TECH) 耐久力 taíkyūryòku

tolerant [ta:l'ə:rənt] adj: *tolerant (of)*
(...に) 耐えられる ...ni taérarerù

tolerate [ta:l'ə:reit] vt (pain, noise, injustice) 我慢する gámàn suru

toll [toul] n (of casualties, deaths) 数 kázù; (tax, charge) 料金 ryókin
♦*vi* (bell) 鳴る narú

tomato [təmei'tou] (pl **tomatoes**) n トマ
ト tómàto

tomb [tu:m] n 墓 haká

tomboy [ta:m'bɔi] n お転婆 o-téñba

tombstone [tu:m'stoun] n 墓石 haká-ishi

tomcat [ta:m'kæt] n 雄ネコ osúneko

tomorrow [təmɔ:r'ou] adv (also fig) 明
日 asú, あした ashíta
♦n (also fig) 明日 asu, あした ashíta
the day after tomorrow あさって a-
sáttè
tomorrow morning あしたの朝 ashíta
nò ásà

ton [tʌn] n トン tóñ ◇BRIT = 1016 kg;
US = 907 kg
tons of (inf) ものすごく沢山の monósu-
gòku takúsan no

tone [toun] n (of voice) 調子 chóshi; (of

instrument) 音色 ne-íro; (of color) 色調 shikíchō

♦*vi* (colors: *also*: **tone in**) 合う áu

tone-deaf [toun'def] *adj* 音痴の ónchi no

tone down *vt* (color, criticism, demands) 和らげる yawárageru; (sound) 小さくする chíisakù suru

tone up *vt* (muscles) 強くする tsúyòku suru

tongs [tɔ:ŋz] *npl* (*also*: **coal tongs**) 炭ば さみ sumíbasàmi; (curling tongs) 髪ごて kamígote

tongue [tʌŋ] *n* (ANAT) 舌 shitá; (CULIN) タン táñ; (language) 言語 géñgo

tongue in cheek (speak, say) からかっ て karákàtte

tongue-tied [tʌŋ'taid] *adj* (*fig*) ものも言 えない monó mò iénai

tongue-twister [tʌŋ'twistə:r] *n* 早口言 葉 hayákuchi kotobà

tonic [tɑ:n'ik] *n* (MED, *also fig*) 強壮剤 kyósōzai; (*also*: **tonic water**) トニックウ オーター toníkkuuòtā

tonight [tənait'] *adv* (this evening) 今日 の夕方 kyó no yūgata; (this night) 今夜 kóñ-ya

♦*n* (this evening) 今日の夕方 kyó no yūgata; (this night) 今夜 kóñ-ya

tonnage [tʌn'idʒ] *n* (NAUT) トン数 toñsū

tonsil [tɑ:n'səl] *n* へんとうせん heñtōsen

tonsillitis [tɑ:nsəlai'tis] *n* へんとうせん 炎 heñtōsen-èn

too [tu:] *adv* (excessively) あまりに...過ぎ る amári nì ...sugírù; (*also*) ...も (また) ...mo (matá)

too much adv あまり沢山で amári takusañ de

♦*adj* あまり沢山の amári takusañ no

too many adv あまり沢山の amári takusañ no

♦*pron* あまり沢山 amári takusañ

took [tuk] *pt of* **take**

tool [tu:l] *n* 道具 dógù

tool box *n* 道具箱 dōgubàko

toot [tu:t] *n* (of horn) ぷーぷー púpū; (of whistle) ぴーぴー pípī

♦*vi* (with car-horn) クラクションを鳴ら す kurákùshon wo narásù

tooth [tu:θ] (*pl* **teeth**) *n* (ANAT, TECH) 歯 há

toothache [tu:θ'eik] *n* 歯の痛み há nò i-támi, 歯痛 shitsū

toothbrush [tu:θ'brʌʃ] *n* 歯ブラシ habúràshi

toothpaste [tu:θ'peist] *n* 歯磨き hamigaki

toothpick [tu:θ'pik] *n* つまようじ tsumáyōji

top [tɑ:p] *n* (of mountain, tree, head, ladder) 天辺 teppéñ; (page) 頭 atáma; (of cupboard, table, box) ...の上 ...no ué; (of list etc) 筆頭 hittó; (lid: of box, jar, bottle) ふた futá; (blouse etc) トップ tóppù; (toy) こま kómà

♦*adj* (highest: shelf, step) 一番上の ichíban ue no; (: marks) 最高の saíkò no; (in rank: salesman etc) ぴかーの pikā-ichí no

♦*vt* (be first in: poll, vote, list) ...の首位 に立つ ...no shúi ni tátsù; (exceed: estimate etc) 越える koérù

on top of (above) ...の上に ...no ué nì; (in addition to) ...に加えて ...ni kuwáetè

from top to bottom 上から下まで ué kara shitá madè

top floor *n* 最上階 saíjōkai

top hat *n* シルクハット shirúkuhattò

top-heavy [tɑ:p'hevi] *adj* (object) 不安 定な fuáñtei na; (administration) 幹部の 多過ぎる káñbu no ósugirù

topic [tɑ:p'ik] *n* 話題 wadái

topical [tɑ:p'ikəl] *adj* 時事問題の jijímoñdai no

topless [tɑ:p'lis] *adj* (bather, waitress, swimsuit) トップレスの tóppùresu no

top-level [tɑ:p'lev'əl] *adj* (talks, decision) 首脳の shunó no

topmost [tɑ:p'moust] *adj* (branch etc) 一 番上の ichíban ue no

top off (*US*) *vt* = **top up**

topple [tɑ:p'əl] *vt* (government, leader) 倒す taósù

♦*vi* (person, object) 倒れる taórerù

top-secret [tɑ:p'si:'krit] *adj* 極秘の gokúhi no

topsy-turvy [tɑ:p'si:tə:r'vi:] *adj* (world) はちゃめちゃの háchàmecha no
♦*adv* (fall, land etc) 逆様に sakásama ni

top up *vt* (bottle etc) 一杯にする ippái ni surú

torch [tɔ:rtʃ] *n* (with flame) たいまつ táimatsu; (*BRIT*: electric) 懐中電とう kaíchūdeñtō

tore [tɔ:r] *pt of* **tear**

torment [*n* tɔ:r'ment *vb* tɔ:rment'] *n* 苦しみ kurúshimì
♦*vt* (subj: feelings, guilt etc) 苦しませる kurúshimaserù, 悩ませる nayámaserù; (*fig*: annoy: subj: person) いじめる ijímerù

torn [tɔ:rn] *pp of* **tear**

tornado [tɔ:rnei'dou] (*pl* **tornadoes**) *n* 竜巻 tatsúmaki

torpedo [tɔ:rpi:'dou] (*pl* **torpedoes**) *n* 魚雷 gyorái

torrent [tɔ:r'ənt] *n* (flood) 急流 kyúryū; (*fig*) 奔流 hoñryū

torrential [tɔ:ren'tʃəl] *adj* (rain) 土砂降りの doshábùri no

torrid [tɔ:r'id] *adj* (sun) しゃく熱の shakúnetsu no; (love affair) 情熱的な jónetsuteki na

torso [tɔ:r'sou] *n* 胴 dố

tortoise [tɔ:r'təs] *n* カメ kámè

tortoiseshell [tɔ:r'təʃel] *adj* べっ甲の bekkố no

tortuous [tɔ:r'tʃu:əs] *adj* (path) 曲りくねった magárikunettà; (argument) 回りくどい mawárikudoì; (mind) 邪悪な jaáku na

torture [tɔ:r'tʃə:r] *n* (*also fig*) 拷問 gốmon
♦*vt* (*also fig*) 拷問にかける gốmon nì kakérù

Tory [tɔ:r'i:] (*BRIT*) *adj* 保守党の hoshútō no
♦*n* 保守党員 hoshútōin

toss [tɔ:s] *vt* (throw) 投げる nagérù; (one's head) 振る furú
to toss a coin コインをトスする kóin wo tósù suru
to toss up for something コインをトスして...を決める kóin wo tósù shité ...wò

kimérù
to toss and turn (in bed) ころげ回る korógemawarù

tot [tɑ:t] *n* (*BRIT*: drink) おちょこ一杯 ochóko íppài; (child) 小さい子供 chiísaì kodómo

total [tout'əl] *adj* (complete: number, workforce etc) 全体の zeñtai no; (: failure, wreck etc) 完全な kañzen na
♦*n* 合計 gốkei
♦*vt* (add up: numbers, objects) 合計する gốkei suru; (add up to: X dollars/ pounds) 合計は...になる gốkei wà ...ni nárù

totalitarian [toutælite:r'i:ən] *adj* 全体主義の zeñtaishùgi no

totally [tou'təli:] *adv* (agree, write off, unprepared) 全く mattáku

totter [tɑ:t'ə:r] *vi* (person) よろめく yorómekù

touch [tʌtʃ] *n* (sense of touch) 触覚 shokkáku; (contact) 触る事 sawárù kotó
♦*vt* (with hand, foot) ...に触る ...ni sawárù; (tamper with) いじる ijiru; (make contact with) ...に接触する ...ni sesshóku suru; (emotionally) 感動させる kañdō saserù
a touch of (*fig*: frost etc) 少しばかり sukóshi bakàri
to get in touch with someone ...に連絡する ...ni reñraku suru
to lose touch (friends) ...との連絡が途絶える ...tó nò reñraku gà todáerù

touch-and-go [tʌtʃ'əngou'] *adj* 危ない abúnai

touchdown [tʌtʃ'daun] *n* (of rocket, plane: on land) 着陸 chakúriku; (: on water) 着水 chakúsui; (*US FOOTBALL*) タッチダウン tatchídaùn

touched [tʌtʃt] *adj* (moved) 感動した kañdō shita

touching [tʌtʃ'iŋ] *adj* 感動的な kañdōteki na

touchline [tʌtʃ'lain] *n* (*SPORT*) サイドライン saídoraìn

touch on *vt fus* (topic) ...に触れる ...ni furérù

touch up *vt* (paint) 修正する shúsei suru

touchy [tʌtʃ'iː] *adj* (person) 気難しいki-múzukashii

tough [tʌf] *adj* (strong, hard-wearing: material) 丈夫な jóbu na; (meat) 固いka-tái; (person: physically) 頑丈な ganjō na; (: mentally) 神経が太い shińkei gà futói; (difficult: task, problem, way of life) 難しい muzúkashiī; (firm: stance, negotiations, policies) 譲らない yuzúranaī

toughen [tʌf'ən] *vt* (someone's character) 強くする tsúyoku suru; (glass etc) 強化する kyōka suru

toupée [tuːpeiʔ] *n* かつら katsúra ◇男性のはげを隠す小さな物を指す dańsei no hagè wo kakúsù chíisa na monò wo sásù

tour [tuːr] *n* (journey) 旅行 ryokō; (*also*: **package tour**) ツアー tsúā; (of town, factory, museum) 見学 keńgaku; (by pop group etc) 巡業 juńgyō

◆*vt* (country, city, factory etc) 観光旅行する kańkōryokō suru; (city) 見物する keńbutsu suru; (factory etc) 見学する keńgaku suru

tourism [tuːr'izəm] *n* (business) 観光 kań-kō

tourist [tuːr'ist] *n* 観光客 kańkōkyaku

◆*cpd* (attractions etc) 観光の kańkō no

tourist class (on ship, plane) ツーリストクラス tsúrisutokurāsu

tourist office *n* 観光案内所 kańkōan-naisho

tournament [tuːr'nəmənt] *n* トーナメント tóńamento

tousled [tau'zəld] *adj* (hair) 乱れた midá-retā

tout [taut] *vi*: **to tout for business** (business) 御用聞きする goyókìki suru

◆*n* (*also*: **ticket tout**) だふ屋 dafúyà

tow [tou] *vt* (vehicle, caravan, trailer) 引く hikú, けん引する keń-in suru

「**in (US *or* BRIT) on tow**」(AUT) けん引中 keń-ińchū

toward(s) [tɔːrd(z)] *prep* (direction) ...の方へ ...no hố è; (attitude) ...に対して ...ni táíshite; (purpose) ...に向かって ...ni mu-kátte; (in time) ...のちょっと前に ...no chóttò mâe ni

towel [tau'əl] *n* (hand/bath towel) タオル tãoru

towelling [tau'əliŋ] *n* (fabric) タオル地 tãorujì

towel rack (BRIT: **towel rail**) *n* タオル掛け tãorukàke

tower [tau'əːr] *n* 塔 tố

tower block (BRIT) *n* 高層ビル kốsōbi-rù

towering [tau'əːriŋ] *adj* (buildings, trees, cliffs) 高くそびえる tákàku sobíe-rù; (figure) 体の大きな karáda nò ốkī na

town [taun] *n* 町 machí

to go to town 町に出掛ける machí nì dekákerù; (*fig*: on something) 思い切りやる omóikiri yarù, 派手にやる hadé nì yárù

town center *n* 町の中心部 machí nò chúshińbu

town council *n* 町議会 chốgikài

town hall *n* 町役場 machíyakùba

town plan *n* 町の道路地図 machí nò dố-rochizù

town planning *n* 開発計画 kaíhatsuke-ikàku

towrope [tou'roup] *n* けん引用ロープ keń-in-yō rốpù

tow truck (US) *n* (breakdown lorry) レッカー車 rekkáshā

toxic [tɑːk'sik] *adj* (fumes, waste etc) 有毒の yúdoku no

toy [tɔi] *n* おもちゃ omóchà

toyshop [tɔi'ʃɑːp] *n* おもちゃ屋 omócha-yà

toy with *vt fus* (object, food) いじくり回す ijíkurimawasù; (idea) ...しようかなと考えてみる ...shiyó kà na to kańgaete mirù

trace [treis] *n* (sign) 跡 átò; (small amount) 微量 biryō

◆*vt* (draw) トレースする torésù suru; (follow) 追跡する tsuíseki suru; (locate) 見付ける mitsúkerù

tracing paper [trei'siŋ-] *n* トレーシングペーパー torēshingupēpà

track [træk] *n* (mark) 跡 átò; (path: *gen*) 道 michí; (: of bullet etc) 弾道 dáńdō; (: of suspect, animal) 足跡 ashíatò; (RAIL) 線路 señro; (on tape, record: *also* SPORT)

トラック torákkù

♦vt (follow: animal, person) 追跡する tsuíseki suru

to keep track of ...を監視する ...wo kańshi suru

track down vt (prey) 追詰める otsumerù; (something lost) 見付ける mitsúkerù

tracksuit [træk'suːt] n トレーニングウエア toréningu ueà

tract [trækt] n (GEO) 地帯 chitái; (pamphlet) 論文 roñbun

traction [træk'ʃən] n (power) けん引力 keń-iñryoku; (MED): *in traction* けん引療法中 keń-iñryōchū

tractor [træk'təːr] n トラクター torákutā

trade [treid] n (activity) 貿易 bóeki; (skill) 技術 gíjùtsu; (job) 職業 shokúgyō

♦vi (do business) 商売する shóbai suru

♦vt (exchange): *to trade something (for something)* (...と) ...を交換する (...to) ...wò kókan suru

trade fair n トレードフェアー torédofeà

trade in vt (old car etc) 下取に出す shitádori nì dásù

trademark [treid'mɑːrk] n 商標 shóhyō

trade name n 商品名 shóhiñmei

trader [trei'dəːr] n 貿易業者 bóekigyōsha

tradesman [treidz'mən] (pl **tradesmen**) n 商人 shónin

trade union n 労働組合 ródōkumìai

trade unionist [-ju:n'jənist] n 労働組合員 ródōkumiaìn

tradition [trədiʃ'ən] n 伝統 deńtō

traditional [trədiʃ'ənəl] adj (dress, costume, meal) 伝統的な deńtōteki na

traffic [træf'ik] n (movement: of people, vehicles) 往来 órai; (: of drugs etc) 売買 báibai; (air traffic, road traffic etc) 交通 kótsū

♦vi: *to traffic in* (liquor, drugs) 売買する báibai suru

traffic circle (US) n ロータリー rótarī

traffic jam n 交通渋滞 kótsūjūtai

traffic lights npl 信号(機) shíñgō(kì)

traffic warden n 違反駐車取締官 ihán-

chūsha toríshimarikàn

tragedy [trædʒ'idi:] n 悲劇 higéki

tragic [trædʒ'ik] adj (death, consequences) 悲劇的な higékiteki na; (play, novel etc) 悲劇の higéki no

trail [treil] n (path) 小道 kómichi; (track) 足跡 ashíàtò; (of smoke, dust) 尾 ó

♦vt (drag) 後に引く átò ni hikú; (follow: person, animal) 追跡する tsuíseki suru

♦vi (hang loosely) 後ろに垂れる ushíro nì tarérù; (in game, contest) 負けている makéte irù

trail behind vi (lag) 遅れる okúrerù

trailer [trei'ləːr] n (AUT) トレーラー torérā; (US: caravan) キャンピングカー kyañpingukā; (CINEMA) 予告編 yokókuheñ

trailer truck (US) n トレーラートラック torérātorakkù

train [trein] n (RAIL) 列車 resshá; (underground train) 地下鉄 chikátetsu; (of dress) トレイン toréin

♦vt (educate: mind) 教育する kyóiku suru; (teach skills to: apprentice, doctor, dog etc) 訓練する kuñren suru; (athlete) 鍛える kitáerù; (point: camera, hose, gun etc): *to train on* 向ける mukérù

♦vi (learn a skill) 訓練を受ける kuñren wò ukérù; (SPORT) トレーニングする toréningu suru

one's train of thought 考えの流れ kañgaè no nagáre

trained [treind] adj (worker, teacher) 技術が確かな gíjùtsu ga táshika na; (animal) 訓練された kuñren saretà

trainee [treini:'] n (apprentice: hairdresser etc) 見習 mínàrai; (teacher etc) 実習生 jisshūsei

trainer [trei'nəːr] n (SPORT: coach) コーチ kóchi; (: shoe) スニーカー suníkà; (of animals) 訓練師 kuñreñshi

training [trei'niŋ] n (for occupation) 訓練 kuñren; (SPORT) トレーニング toréniñgu

in training トレーニング中 toréniñgu-chū

training college n (gen) 職業大学 shokúgyōdaigàku; (for teachers) 教育大学

kyốikudaigàku

training shoes npl スニーカー sunîkằ

traipse [treips] vi 足を棒にして歩き回る ashí wò bố ni shitè arúkimawarù

trait [treit] n 特徴 tokúchō

traitor [trei'tə:r] n 裏切り者 urágirimðno

tram [træm] (BRIT) n (also: **tramcar**) 路面電車 roméndeńsha

tramp [træmp] n (person) ルンペン rúñpen; (inf: pej: woman) 浮気女 uwákioňna
♦vi どしんどしん歩く doshíňdoshin arúkù

trample [træm'pəl] vt: to trample (underfoot) 踏み付ける fumítsukerù

trampoline [træmpəli:n'] n トランポリン toráňporin

trance [træns] n (gen) こん睡状態 koñsuijỗtai; (fig) ぼう然とした状態 bốzen to shità jỗtai

tranquil [træŋ'kwil] adj (place, old age) 平穏な heíon na; (sleep) 静かな shízùka na

tranquillity [træŋkwil'iti:] n 平静さ heíseisà

tranquillizer [træŋ'kwəlaizə:r] n (MED) 鎮静剤 chińseĭzai

transact [trænsækt'] vt: to transact business 取引する toríhìki suru

transaction [trænsæk'ʃən] n (piece of business) 取引 toríhìki

transatlantic [trænsətlæn'tik] adj (trade, phone-call etc) 英米間の eíbeikàn no

transcend [trænsend'] vt 越える koérù

transcript [træn'skript] n (of tape recording etc) 記録文書 kiróku buňsho

transfer [træns'fə:r] n (moving: of employees etc) 異動 idỗ; (: of money) 振替 furíkaè; (POL: of power) 引継ぎ hikítsugi; (SPORT) トレード torédò; (picture, design) 写し絵 utsúshiè
♦vt (move: employees) 転任させる teńnin saserù; (: money) 振替える furíkaerù; (: power) 譲る yuzúrù
to transfer the charges (BRIT: TEL) コレクトコールにする korékutokồru ni suru

transform [træn'sfɔ:rm] vt 変化させる

hếňka sasérù

transformation [trænsfə:rmei'ʃən] n 変化 hếňka

transfusion [trænsfju:'ʒən] n (also: **blood transfusion**) 輸血 yukétsu

transient [træn'ʃənt] adj 一時的な ichíjiteki na

transistor [trænzis'tə:r] n (ELEC) トランジスタ toráňjisùta; (also: **transistor radio**) トランジスタラジオ toráňjisuta rajìo

transit [træn'sit] n: in transit (people, things) 通過中の tsúkachū no

transition [trænzi'ʃən] n 移行 ikỗ

transitional [trænzi'ʃənəl] adj (period, stage) 移行の ikỗ no

transitive [træn'sətiv] adj (LING): transitive verb 他動詞 tadốshi

transit lounge n (at airport etc) トランジットラウンジ toráňjitto raùnji

transitory [træn'sitɔ:ri:] adj つかの間の tsuká no ma nò

translate [trænz'leit] vt (word, book etc) 翻訳する hoń-yaku suru

translation [trænzlei'ʃən] n (act/result of translating) 訳 yákù

translator [trænslei'tə:r] n 訳者 yákùsha

transmission [trænsmiʃ'ən] n (of information, disease) 伝達 deńtatsu; (TV: broadcasting, program broadcast) 放送 hỗsō; (AUT) トランスミッション toráňsumisshòn

transmit [trænsmit'] vt (message, signal, disease) 伝達する deńtatsu suru

transmitter [trænsmit'ə:r] n (piece of equipment) トランスミッタ toráňsumittà

transparency [trænsper'ənsi:] n (of glass etc) 透明度 tốmeĭdo; (PHOT: slide) スライド suráĭdo

transparent [trænsper:r'ənt] adj (seethrough) 透明の tỗmei no

transpire [trænspaiə:r'] vi (turn out) 明らかになる akíràka ni nárù; (happen) 起る okórù

transplant [vb trænzplænt' n trænz'plænt] vt (seedlings: also: MED: organ)

移植する ishóku suru
♦*n* (MED) 移植 ishóku

transport [*n* trǽns'pɔ:rt *vb* trænspɔ:rt'] *n* (moving people, goods) 輸送 yusō; (*also*: **road/rail transport** *etc*) 輸送機関 yusōkikan; (car) 車 kurúma
♦*vt* (carry) 輸送する yusō suru

transportation [trænspə:rtei'ʃən] *n* (transport) 輸送 yusō; (means of transport) 輸送機関 yusōkikan

transport café (*BRIT*) *n* トラック運転手向きのレストラン torákkuunteñshu mukí no resútoraň

transvestite [trænsves'tait] *n* 女装趣味の男性 josōshùmi no dañsei

trap [træp] *n* (snare, trick) わな wánà; (carriage) 軽馬車 keíbashà
♦*vt* (animal) わなで捕える wánà de toraérù; (person: trick) わなにかける wánà ni kakérù; (: confine: in bad marriage, burning building): **to be trapped** 逃げられなくなっている nigérarenakù natté irù

trap door *n* 落し戸 otóshidò

trapeze [træpi:z'] *n* 空中ぶらんこ kūchūburañko

trappings [træp'iŋz] *npl* 飾り kazári

trash [træʃ] *n* (rubbish: *also pej*) ごみ gomí; (: nonsense) でたらめ detárame

trash can (*US*) *n* ごみ入れ gomíirè

trauma [trɔ:'mə] *n* 衝撃 shōgeki, ショック shókkù

traumatic [trɔ:mæt'ik] *adj* 衝撃的な shōgekiteki na

travel [træv'əl] *n* (traveling) 旅行 ryokō
♦*vi* (person) 旅行する ryokō suru; (news, sound) 伝わる tsutáwarù; (wine etc): **to travel well/badly** 運搬に耐えられる〔耐えられない〕uñpan nì taérarerù〔taérarenaì〕
♦*vt* (distance) 旅行する ryokō suru

travel agency *n* 旅行代理店 ryokōdairitèn

travel agent *n* 旅行業者 ryokōgyòsha

traveler [træv'ələr] (*BRIT* **traveller**) *n* 旅行者 ryokōshà

traveler's check [træv'ələrz-] (*BRIT* **traveller's cheque**) *n* トラベラーズチェ

ック toráberāzuchekkù

traveling [træv'əliŋ] (*BRIT* **travelling**) *n* 旅行 ryokō

travels [træv'əlz] *npl* (journeys) 旅行 ryokō

travel sickness *n* 乗物酔い norímonoyoì

travesty [træv'isti:] *n* パロディー párodī

trawler [trɔ:'lə:r] *n* トロール漁船 torōrugyòsen

tray [trei] *n* (for carrying) お盆 o-bón; (on desk) デスクトレー desúkutorè

treacherous [tretʃ'ə:rəs] *adj* (person, look) 裏切り者の urágirimòno no; (ground, tide) 危険な kikén na

treachery [tretʃ'ə:ri:] *n* 裏切り urágirì

treacle [tri:'kəl] *n* 糖みつ tōmitsu

tread [tred] *n* (step) 歩調 hochō; (sound) 足音 ashíotò; (of stair) 踏面 fumízùra; (of tire) トレッド toréddò
♦*vi* (*pt* **trod**, *pp* **trodden**) 歩く arúkù

tread on *vt fus* 踏む fumú

treason [tri:'zən] *n* 反逆罪 hañgyakuzài

treasure [treʒ'ə:r] *n* (gold, jewels etc) 宝物 takáramono; (person) 重宝な人 chōhō nà hitó
♦*vt* (value: object) 重宝する chōhō suru; (: friendship) 大事にしている daíji nì shité irù; (: memory, thought) 心に銘記する kokórò ni meíki suru

treasurer [treʒ'ə:rə:r] *n* 会計 kaíkei

treasures [treʒ'ə:rz] *npl* (art treasures etc) 貴重品 kichōhìn

treasury [treʒ'ə:ri:] *n*: (*US*) **the Treasury Department**, (*BRIT*) **the Treasury** 大蔵省 ōkurashō

treat [tri:t] *n* (present) 贈物 okúrimono
♦*vt* (handle, regard: person, object) 扱う atsúkaù; (MED: patient, illness) 治療する chiryō suru; (TECH: coat) 処理する shōrì suru

to treat someone to something ...に...をおごる ...ni ...wo ogórù

treatment [tri:t'mənt] *n* (attention, handling) 扱い方 atsúkaikata; (MED) 治療 chiryō

treaty [tri:'ti:] *n* 協定 kyōtei

treble [treb'əl] *adj* 3倍の sañbai no;

(MUS) 高音部の kōonbu no
♦vt 3倍にする saṅbai nǐ suru
♦vi 3倍になる saṅbai ni narù

treble clef n (MUS) 高音部記号 kōonbu-kigō

tree [tri:] n 木 kī

tree trunk n 木の幹 kī nò mīkì

trek [trek] n (long difficult journey: on foot) 徒歩旅行 tohóryokō; (: by car) 自動車旅行 jidōsharyokō; (tiring walk) 苦しい道のり kurúshiǐ michínori

trellis [trel'is] n (for climbing plants) 棚 taná

tremble [trem'bəl] vi (voice, body, trees: with fear, cold etc) 震える furúeru; (ground) 揺れる yurérù

tremendous [trimen'dəs] adj (enormous: amount etc) ばく大な bakúdai na; (excellent: success, holiday, view etc) 素晴らしい subárashiǐ

tremor [trem'ə:r] n (trembling: of excitement, fear: in voice) 震え furúê; (also: **earth tremor**) 地震 jishín

trench [trentʃ] n (channel) 溝 mizó; (for defense) ざんごう zaṅgō

trend [trend] n (tendency) 傾向 keíkō; (of events) 動向 dṓkō; (fashion) トレンド toréňdo

trendy [tren'di:] adj (idea, person, clothes) トレンディな toréňdi na

trepidation [trepidei'ʃən] n (apprehension) 不安 fuáń

trespass [tres'pæs] vi: **to trespass on** (private property) ...に不法侵入する ...ni fuhṓshiňnyū suru
「no trespassing」立入禁止 tachíirikiň-shi

trestle [tres'əl] n (support for table etc) うま umá

trial [trail] n (LAW) 裁判 saíban; (test: of machine etc) テスト tésùto
on trial (LAW) 裁判に掛けられて saíban ni kakérareté
by trial and error 試行錯誤で shikṓsakùgo de

trial period n テスト期間 tesúto kikàn

trials [trailz] npl (unpleasant experiences) 試練 shírèn

triangle [trai'æŋgəl] n (MATH) 三角 sáň-kaku; (MUS) トライアングル toráiaṅ-guru

triangular [traiæŋ'gjələ:r] adj 三角形の saňkakkèi no

tribal [trai'bəl] adj (warrior, warfare, dance) 種族の shúzoku no

tribe [traib] n 種族 shúzoku

tribesman [traibz'mən] (pl **tribesmen**) n 種族の男性 shúzoku no dańsei

tribulations [tribjəlei'ʃənz] npl 苦労 kúrō, 苦難 kúnan

tribunal [traibju:'nəl] n 審判委員会 shiňpan iiňkai

tributary [trib'jəte:ri:] n 支流 shiryú

tribute [trib'ju:t] n (compliment) ほめの言葉 homé no kotobà
to pay tribute to ...をほめる ...wò homérù

trice [trais] n: **in a trice** あっという間に áttó iú ma nì

trick [trik] n (magic trick) 手品 téjìna; (prank, joke) いたずら itázura; (skill, knack) こつ kotsú; (CARDS) トリック toríkkù
♦vt (deceive) だます damásù
to play a trick on someone ...にいたずらをする ...ni itázura wò suru
that should do the trick これでいいはずだ koré de iǐ hazú dà

trickery [trik'ə:ri:] n 計略 keíryaku

trickle [trik'əl] n (of water etc) 滴り shi-tátari
♦vi (water, rain etc) 滴る shitátarù

tricky [trik'i:] adj (job, problem, business) 厄介な yákkài na

tricycle [trai'sikəl] n 三輪車 saṅrinsha

trifle [trai'fəl] n (small detail) ささいな事 sásài na ◇(CULIN) トライフル toráǐfuru ◇カステラにゼリー、フルーツ、プリンなどをのせたデザート kasútera nǐ zérì, furútsù, púrìn nádò wo nosétà dezádò
♦adv: **a trifle long** ちょっと長い chóttò nagáì

trifling [traif'liŋ] adj (detail, matter) ささいな sásài na

trigger [trig'ə:r] n (of gun) 引金 hikígane

trigger off vt (reaction, riot) ...の引金
となる ...no hikígane tò nárù

trigonometry [trigənə:m'ətri:] n 三角法
sañkakuhō

trill [tril] vi (birds) さえずる saézurù

trim [trim] adj (house, garden) 手入れの
行届いた teíre nò ikítodoità; (figure) すっ
らっとした suráttò shitá

♦n (haircut etc) 刈る事 karú kotò; (on
car) 飾り kazári

♦vt (cut: hair, beard) 刈る karú; (decorate): **to trim (with)** (...で) 飾る (...de)
kazárù; (NAUT: a sail) 調節する chốse-
tsu suru

trimmings [trim'iŋz] npl (CULIN) お決
りの付け合せ o-kímàri no tsukéawase

trinket [triŋ'kit] n (ornament) 安い置物
yasúì okímono; (piece of jewellery) 安い
装身具 yasúì sōshìngu

trio [tri:'ou] n (gen) 三つ組 mitsúgumi;
(MUS) トリオ tórìo

trip [trip] n (journey) 旅行 ryokō; (outing) 遠足 eńsoku; (stumble) つまずき tsu-
mázuki

♦vi (stumble) つまずく tsumázukù; (go
lightly) 軽快に歩く keíkai nì arúkù

on a trip 旅行中で ryokóchū de

tripe [traip] n (CULIN) トライプ toráì-
pu ◇ウシ、ブタなどの胃の料理 ushí, bu-
tá nadò no i no ryốri; (pej: rubbish) 下ら
ない物 kudaranai mono ◇特に人の発言
や文書について言う tókù ni hitó nò hatsúgen yà búñsho ni tsúìte iú

triple [trip'əl] adj (ice cream, somersault
etc) トリプルの torípùru no

triplets [trip'lits] npl 三つ子 mitsúgo

triplicate [trip'ləkit] n: **in triplicate** 三
通で sañtsū de

tripod [trai'pɑːd] n 三脚 sañkyaku

trip up vi (stumble) つまずく tsumázukù

♦vt (person) つまずかせる tsumázukase-
rù

trite [trait] adj 陳腐な chíñpu na

triumph [trai'əmf] n (satisfaction) 大満
足 daímañzoku; (great achievement) 輝
かしい勝利 kagáyakashiì shốrì

trigger off vt (reaction, riot) ...の引金
◆vi: **to triumph (over)** (...に) 打勝つ
(...ni) uchíkatsù

triumphant [traiʌm'fənt] adj (team,
wave, return) 意気揚々とした íkìyōyō to
shitá

trivia [triv'i:ə] npl 詰まらない事 tsumá-
ranai kotò

trivial [triv'i:əl] adj (unimportant) 詰ま
らない tsumáranaì; (commonplace) 平凡
な heíbon na

trod [trɑːd] pt of **tread**

trodden [trɑːd'ən] pp of **tread**

trolley [trɑːl'iː] n (for luggage, shopping,
also in supermarkets) 手車 tegúruma;
(table on wheels) ワゴン wágòn; (also:
trolley bus) トロリーバス torórìbàsu

trombone [trɑːmboun'] n トロンボーン
toróñbōn

troop [truːp] n (of people, monkeys etc)
群れ muré

troop in/out vi ぞろぞろと入って来る
〔出て行く〕zóròzoro to haítte kurù
〔détè iku〕

trooping the color [truː'piŋ-] (BRIT)
n (ceremony) 軍旗敬礼の分列行進 kuñki-
keírei no buñretsu kōshin

troops [truːps] npl (MIL) 兵隊 heítai

trophy [trou'fiː] n トロフィー toróñfī

tropic [trɑː'pik] n 回帰線 kaíkisèn
the tropics 熱帯地方 nettái chihō

tropical [trɑː'pikəl] adj (rain forest etc)
熱帯 (地方) の nettái(chihō) no

trot [trɑːt] n (fast pace) 小走り kobáshī-
ri; (of horse) 速足 hayáàshi, トロット toróttò

♦vi (horse) トロットで駆ける toróttò de
kakérù; (person) 小走りで行く kobáshìri
de ikú

on the trot (BRIT: fig) 立続けに tatétsuzuke ni

trouble [trʌb'əl] n (difficulty) 困難 koñ-
nan; (worry) 心配 shiñpai; (bother,
effort) 苦労 kúrò; (unrest) トラブル torábùru; (MED): **heart etc trouble** ...病
...byō

♦vt (worry) ...に心配を掛ける ...ni shiñpai wò kakérù; (person: disturb) 面倒を
かける meñdō wo kakérù

♦vi: *to trouble to do something* わざ わざ...する wázàwaza ...suru

to be in trouble (*gen*) 困っている ko mátte irù; (ship, climber etc) 危険にあっ ている kikén ni atte irù

it's no trouble! 迷惑ではありませんか ら mē*waku de wa arímasen karà

what's the trouble? (with broken tele vision etc) どうなっていますか dō natté imasù ká; (doctor to patient) いかがです か ikága desù ká

troubled [trʌb'əld] *adj* (person, country, life, era) 不安な fuán na

troublemaker [trʌb'əlmeikə:r] *n* トラブ ルを起す常習犯 torábùru wo okósù jō shūhan; (child) 問題児 moñdaìji

troubles [trʌb'əlz] *npl* (personal, POL etc) 問題 moñdai

troubleshooter [trʌb'əlʃu:tə:r] *n* (in con flict) 調停人 chōteinìn

troublesome [trʌb'əlsəm] *adj* (child, cough etc) 厄介な yákkai na

trough [trɔ:f] *n* (*also*: **drinking trough**) 水入れ mizúirè; (feeding trough) えさ入 れ esá-irè; (depression) 谷間 taníma

troupe [tru:p] *n* (of actors, singers, dancers) 団 dán

trousers [trau'zə:rz] *npl* ズボン zubón

short trousers 半ズボン hañzubòn

trousseau [tru:'sou] (*pl* **trousseaux** *or* **trousseaus**) *n* 嫁入り道具 yomé-iri dōgu

trout [traut] *n inv* マス masu

trowel [trau'əl] *n* (garden tool) 移植ごて ishókugòte; (builder's tool) こて koté

truant [tru:'ənt] (*BRIT*) *n*: *to play tru ant* 学校をサボる gakkō wo sabórù

truce [tru:s] *n* 休戦 kyūsen

truck [trʌk] *n* (*US*) トラック torákkù; (RAIL) 台車 daísha

truck driver *n* トラック運転手 torákku unteñshu

truck farm (*US*) *n* 野菜農園 yasáinòen

trudge [trʌdʒ] *vi* (*also*: **trudge along**) と ぼとぼ歩く tóbòtobo arúkù

true [tru:] *adj* (real: motive) 本当の hofitō no; (accurate: likeness) 正確な seíkaku na; (genuine: love) 本物の hofimono no; (faithful: friend) 忠実な chūjitsu na

to come true (dreams, predictions) 実現 される jitsúgen sarerù

truffle [trʌf'əl] *n* (fungus) トリュフ tō ryùfu; (sweet) トラッフル toráffùru ◇菓 子の一種 káshī no ísshū

truly [tru:'li:] *adv* (really) 本当に hofitō ni; (truthfully) 真実に shífijitsu ni; (faith fully) *yours truly* (in letter) 敬具 kēígu

trump [trʌmp] *n* (*also*: **trump card**: *also fig*) 切札 kirífùda

trumped-up [trʌmpt'ʌp'] *adj* (charge, pretext) でっち上げた detchíagetà

trumpet [trʌm'pit] *n* トランペット torán petto

truncheon [trʌn'tʃən] *n* 警棒 keíbō

trundle [trʌn'dəl] *vt* (push chair etc) ご ろごろ動かす górògoro ugókasù

♦vi: *to trundle along* (vehicle) 重そう に動く omósō ni ugókù; (person) ゆっく り行く yukkúrì ikú

trunk [trʌŋk] *n* (of tree, person) 幹 míkì; (of person) 胴 dō; (of elephant) 鼻 haná; (case) トランク toráñku; (*US*: AUT) ト ランク toráñku

trunks [trʌŋks] *npl* (*also*: **swimming trunks**) 水泳パンツ suíei pañtsu

truss [trʌs] *n* (MED) ヘルニアバンド he rúnia bañdo

truss (up) *vt* (CULIN) 縛る shibárù

trust [trʌst] *n* (faith) 信用 shifi-yō; (responsibility) 責任 sekínin; (LAW) 信 託 shifitaku

♦vt (rely on, have faith in) 信用する shif-yō suru; (hope) きっと...だろうね kittó ...dárò né; (entrust): *to trust something to someone* ...を...に任せる ...wo ...ni makáserù

to take something on trust (advice, information) 証拠なしで...を信じる shō ko nashī de ...wo shiñjirù

trusted [trʌs'tid] *adj* (friend, servant) 信 用された shifi-yō saretà

trustee [trʌsti:'] *n* (LAW) 受託者 jutáku shà; (of school etc) 理事 ríjī

trustful/trusting [trʌst'fəl/trʌs'tiŋ] *adj* (person, nature, smile) 信用する shifi yō suru

trustworthy [trʌst'wə:rði:] *adj* (person,

report) 信用できる shiń-yō dekirù

truth [tru:θ] n (true fact) 真実 shíñjitsu; (universal principle) 真理 shíñri

truthful [tru:θ'fəl] adj (person, answer) 正直な shṓjiki na

try [trai] n (attempt) 努力 dóryòku; (RUGBY) トライ toráì

♦vt (attempt) やってみる yatté mirù; (test: something new: also: **try out**) 試す tamésù; (LAW: person) 裁判にかける sáìban ni kakérù; (strain: patience) ぎりぎりまで追込む girígiri madè oíkomù

♦vi (make effort, attempt) 努力する dóryòku suru

to have a try やってみる yatté mirù

to try to do something (seek) ...をしようとする ...wo shíyò to suru

trying [trai'iŋ] adj (person) 気難しい kimúzukashìì; (experience) 苦しい kurúshiì

try on vt (dress, hat, shoes) 試着する shicháku suru

tsar [zɑːr] n ロシア皇帝 roshía kòtei

T-shirt [ti:'ʃəːrt] n Tシャツ tíshatsu

T-square [ti:'skweːr] n T定規 tíjōgi

tub [tʌb] n (container: shallow) たらい taraí; (: deeper) おけ ókè; (bath) 湯舟 yúbùne

tuba [tu:'bə] n チューバ chūba

tubby [tʌb'i:] adj 太った futóttà

tube [tu:b] n (pipe) 管 kúdà; (container, in tire) チューブ chūbu; (BRIT: underground) 地下鉄 chikátetsu

tuberculosis [tu:bəːrkjəlou'sis] n 結核 kekkáku

tube station (BRIT) n 地下鉄の駅 chikátetsu nò ékì

tubular [tu:'bjələːr] adj (furniture, metal) 管状の kañjō no; (furniture) パイプ製の paípusei no

TUC [ti:ju:si:'] n abbr (BRIT: = Trades Union Congress) 英国労働組合会議 eíkoku rōdōkumiai kaìgi

tuck [tʌk] vt (put) 押込む oshíkomù

tuck away vt (money) 仕舞い込む shimáikomù; (building): _to be tucked away_ 隠れている kakúrete irù

tuck in vt (clothing) 押込む oshíkomù;

(child) 毛布にくるんで寝かせる mṓfù ni kurúñde nekáserù

♦vi (eat) かぶりつく kabúritsukù

tuck shop (BRIT) n 売店 baíten ◊学校内でお菓子などを売る売店を指す gakkṓnaì de o-káshi nadò wo urú baíten wò sásù

tuck up vt (invalid, child) 毛布にくるんで寝かせる mṓfù ni kurúñde nekáserù

Tuesday [tu:z'dei] n 火曜日 kayṓbì

tuft [tʌft] n (of hair, grass etc) 一房 hitófùsa

tug [tʌg] n (ship) タグボート tagúbòto

♦vt 引っ張る hippárù

tug-of-war [tʌg'əvwɔːr] n (SPORT) 綱引き tsunáhiki; (fig) 競り合い seríaì ◊二者間の競り合いを指す nishákàn no seríaì wo sásù

tuition [tu:iʃ'ən] n (BRIT) 教授 kyṓjù; (: private tuition) 個人教授 kojíñkyòju; (US: school fees) 授業料 jugyṓryō

tulip [tu:'lip] n チューリップ chūrippu

tumble [tʌm'bəl] n (fall) 転ぶ事 koróbu kotò

♦vi (fall: person) 転ぶ koróbù; (water) 落ちる ochírù

to tumble to something (inf) ...に気が付く ...ni ki gá tsukù

tumbledown [tʌm'bəldaun] adj (building) 荒れ果てた aréhatetà

tumble dryer (BRIT) n 乾燥機 kañsōki

tumbler [tʌm'bləːr] n (glass) コップ koppú

tummy [tʌm'i:] (inf) n (belly, stomach) おなか onákà

tumor [tu:'məːr] (BRIT **tumour**) n しゅよう shuyṓ

tumult [tu:'məlt] n 大騒ぎ ōsawàgi

tumultuous [tu:mʌl'tʃuːəs] adj (welcome, applause etc) にぎやかな nigíyàka na

tuna [tu:'nə] n inv (also: **tuna fish**) マグロ maguro; (in can, sandwich) ツナ tsúnà

tune [tu:n] n (melody) 旋律 señritsu

♦vt (MUS) 調律する chṓritsu suru; (RADIO, TV) 合せる awáserù; (AUT) チューンアップする chūn-appù suru

to be in/out of tune (instrument, singer)

調子が合って〔外れて〕いる chōshi gà atte〔hazúreteiru〕

to be in/out of tune with (fig) ...と気が合っている〔いない〕...to ki gá atte irù〔inái〕

tuneful [tu:n'fəl] adj (music) 旋律のきれいな seńritsu nò kírèi na

tuner [tu:'nər] n: *piano tuner* 調律師 chōritsushì

tune in vi (RADIO, TV): *to tune in (to)* (...を) 聞く (...wo) kikú

tune up vi (musician, orchestra) 調子を合せる chōshi wò awáserù

tunic [tu:'nik] n チュニック chuníkkù

Tunisia [tu:ni:'ʒə] n チュニジア chuníjìa

tunnel [tʌn'əl] n (passage) トンネル tońneru; (in mine) 坑道 kṓdo
♦vi トンネルを掘る tońneru wo hórù

turban [tə:r'bən] n ターバン tábàn

turbine [tə:r'bain] n タービン tábìn

turbulence [tə:r'bjələns] n (AVIAT) 乱気流 rańkiryù

turbulent [tə:r'bjələnt] adj (water) 荒れ狂う arékuruù; (fig: career) 起伏の多い kífùku no ōĭ

tureen [təri:n'] n スープ鉢 sūpubàchi, チューリン chūrin

turf [tə:rf] n (grass) 芝生 shibáfu; (clod) 芝土 shibátsuchi
♦vt (area) 芝生を敷く shibáfu wò shikú

turf out (inf) vt (person) 追出す oídasù

turgid [tə:r'dʒid] adj (speech) 仰々しい gyōgyōshiì

Turk [tə:rk] n トルコ人 torúkojìn

Turkey [tə:r'ki:] n トルコ tórùko

turkey [tə:r'ki:] n (bird, meat) 七面鳥 shichímenchò, ターキー tákì

Turkish [tə:r'kiʃ] adj トルコの tórùko no; (LING) トルコ語の torúkogò no
♦n (LING) トルコ語 torúkogò

Turkish bath n トルコ風呂 torúkobùro

turmoil [tə:r'mɔil] n 混乱 końran

in turmoil 混乱して końran shitè

turn [tə:rn] n (change) 変化 héñka; (in road) カーブ kábù; (tendency: of mind, events) 傾向 keíkō; (performance) 出し物 dashímòno; (chance) 番 báñ; (MED) 発作 hossá

♦vt (handle, key) 回す mawásù; (collar, page) めくる mekúrù; (steak) 裏返す urágaesù; (change): *to turn something into* ...を...に変える ...wo ...ni kaérù

♦vi (object) 回る mawárù; (person: look back) 振向く furímukù; (reverse direction: in car) Uターンする yūtàn suru; (: wind) 向きが変る múkì ga kawárù; (milk) 悪くなる wárùku nárù; (become) なる nárù

a good turn 親切 shíñsetsu

it gave me quite a turn ああ、怖かった ā, kowákattà

「*no left turn*」(AUT) 左折禁止 sasétsukiñshi

it's your turn あなたの番です anáta nò báñ desu

in turn 次々と tsugítsugi tò

to take turns (at) 交替で (...を) する kṓtai dè (...wo) suru

turn away vi 顔をそむける kaó wò somúkerù
♦vt (applicants) 門前払いする moñzenbarài suru

turn back vi 引返す hikíkaesù
♦vt (person, vehicle) 引返させる hikíkaesaserù; (clock) 遅らせる okúraserù

turn down vt (refuse: request) 断る kotówarù; (reduce: heating) 弱くする yówàku suru; (fold: bedclothes) 折返す oríkaesù

turn in vi (inf: go to bed) 寝る nerú
♦vt (fold) 折込む oríkomù

turning [tə:r'niŋ] n (in road) 曲り角 magárikadò

turning point n (fig) 変り目 kawárimè

turnip [tə:r'nip] n カブ kábù

turn off vi (from road) 横道に入る yokómichi nì háiru
♦vt (light, radio etc) 消す kesú; (tap) ...の水を止める ...no mizú wò tomérù; (engine) 止める tomérù

turn on vt (light, radio etc) つける tsukérù; (tap) ...の水を出す ...no mizú wò dásù; (engine) かける kakérù

turn out vt (light, gas) 消す kesú; (produce) 作る tsukúrù
♦vi (voters) 出る dérù

to turn out to be (prove to be) 結局...で あると分かる kekkyóku ...de árù to wakaru

turnout [təːrnˈaut] *n* (of voters etc) 人出 hitódè

turn over *vi* (person) 寝返りを打つ negáeri wò utsù

♦*vt* (object) 引っ繰り返す hikkúrikaesu; (page) めくる mekúrù

turnover [təːrnˈouvəːr] *n* (COMM: amount of money) 売上高 uríagedàka; (: of goods) 回転率 kaíteñritsu; (: of staff) 異動率 idórìtsu

turnpike [təːrnˈpaik] (*US*) *n* 有料道路 yúryōdōro

turn round *vi* (person) 振り向く furímukù; (vehicle) Uターンする yútàn suru; (rotate) 回転する kaíten suru

turnstile [təːrnˈstail] *n* ターンスタイル táñsutaìru

turntable [təːrnˈteibəl] *n* (on record player) ターンテーブル táñtēburu

turn up *vi* (person) 現れる aráwarerù; (lost object) 見付かる mitsúkarù

♦*vt* (collar) 立てる tatérù; (radio, stereo etc) ...のボリュームを上げる ...no boryúmu wò agérù; (heater) 強くする tsúyòku suru

turn-up [təːrnˈʌp] (*BRIT*) *n* (on trousers) 折返し oríkaeshi

turpentine [təːrˈpəntain] *n* (*also*: **turps**) テレビン油 terébiñ-yu

turquoise [təːrˈkɔiz] *n* (stone) トルコ石 torúkoìshi

♦*adj* (color) 青みどりの aómidòri no

turret [təːrˈit] *n* (on building) 小塔 shótō; (on tank) 旋回砲塔 señkaihōtō

turtle [təːrˈtəl] *n* カメ kámè

turtleneck (sweater) [təːrˈtəlnek-] *n* タートルネック tátorunekkù

tusk [tʌsk] *n* きば kíbà

tussle [tʌsˈəl] *n* (fight, scuffle) 取っ組み合い tokkúmiài

tutor [tuːˈtəːr] *n* (SCOL) チューター chùtā; (private tutor) 家庭教師 katéikyòshi

tutorial [tuːtɔːrˈiːəl] *n* (SCOL) 討論授業 tőronjugyð

tuxedo [tʌksiːˈdou] (*US*) *n* タキシード takíshìdo

TV [tiːviː] *n abbr* = **television**

twang [twæŋ] *n* (of instrument) びゅんという音 byùn to iú otò; (of voice) 鼻声 hanágoè

tweed [twiːd] *n* ツイード tsuídò

tweezers [twiːˈzəːrz] *npl* ピンセット píñsetto

twelfth [twelfθ] *num* 第十二の dái jūni no

twelve [twelv] *num* 十二 (の) jûnî (no)

at twelve (o'clock) (midday) 正午に shógò ni; (midnight) 零時に reíji ni

twentieth [twenˈtiːiθ] *num* 第二十の dái níjū no

twenty [twenˈtiː] *num* 二十 (の) níjù (no)

twice [twais] *adv* 2回 nikái

twice as much ...の二倍 ...no nibái

twiddle [twidˈəl] *vt* いじくる ijíkurù

♦*vi*: *to twiddle (with) something* ...を いじくる ...wo ijíkurù

to twiddle one's thumbs (*fig*) 手をこまねく té wò kománekù

twig [twig] *n* 小枝 koéda

♦*vi* (*inf*: realize) 気が付く ki gá tsukù

twilight [twaiˈlait] *n* 夕暮 yûgure

twin [twin] *adj* (sister, brother) 双子の futágo no; (towers, beds etc) 対の tsúî no, ツインの tsuíñ no

♦*n* 双子の一人 futágo nò hitórì

♦*vt* (towns etc) 姉妹都市にする shimáitoshi ni suru

twin-bedded room [twinˈbedid-] *n* ツインルーム tsuíñrūmu

twine [twain] *n* ひも himó

♦*vi* (plant) 巻付く makítsukù

twinge [twindʒ] *n* (of pain) うずき uzúki; (of conscience) かしゃく kasháku; (of regret) 苦しみ kurúshimì

twinkle [twiŋˈkəl] *vi* (star, light, eyes) きらめく kirámekù

twirl [twəːrl] *vt* くるくる回す kúrùkuru mawásù

♦*vi* くるくる回る kúrùkuru mawárù

twist [twist] *n* (action) ひねり hinéri; (in road, coil, flex) 曲り magári; (in story) ひねり hinéri

♦vt (turn) ひ ね る hinérù; (injure: ankle etc) ねんざする neñza suru; (weave) より 合さる yoríawasarù; (roll around) 巻付け る makítsukerù; (fig: meaning, words) 曲げる magérù

♦vi (road, river) 曲りくねる magárikunerù

twit [twit] (inf) n ばか bákà

twitch [twitʃ] n (pull) ぐいと引く事 guí tò hikú kotò; (nervous) 引きつり hikítsuri

♦vi (muscle, body) 引きつる hikítsurù

two [tu:] num 二 (の) ní (no), 二つ (の) futátsù (no)

to put two and two together (fig) あ れこれを総合してなぞを解く arékore wo sốgō shitè nazó wò tókù

two-door [tu:'dɔ:r] adj (AUT) ツードア の tsúdoà no

two-faced [tu:'feist] (pej) adj (person) 二 枚舌の nimáijita no

twofold [tu:'fould] adv: *to increase twofold* 倍になる baí ni narù

two-piece (suit) [tu:'pi:s-] n ツーピース の服 tsúpìsu no fukú

two-piece (swimsuit) n ツーピースの 水着 tsúpìsu no mizúgi

twosome [tu:'səm] n (people) 二 人 組 futárigùmi

two-way [tu:'wei] adj: *two-way traffic* 両方向交通 ryóhōkōkòtsū

tycoon [taiku:n'] n: (business) tycoon 大物実業家 ōmonojitsugyōka

type [taip] n (category, model, example) 種類 shúruì; (TYP) 活字 katsúji

♦vt (letter etc) タイプする taípu suru

type-cast [taip'kæst] adj (actor) はまり 役の hamáriyaku no

typeface [taip'feis] n 書体 shotái

typescript [taip'skript] n タイプライタ ーで打った原稿 taípuraìta de úttà geñkò

typewriter [taip'raitə:r] n タイプライタ ー taípuraìta

typewritten [taip'ritən] adj タイプライ ターで打った taípuraìta de úttà

typhoid [tai'fɔid] n 腸チフス chốchifùsu

typhoon [taifu:n'] n 台風 taífū

typical [tip'ikəl] adj 典型的な teñkeiteki

na

typify [tip'əfai] vt ...の典型的な例である ...no teñkeiteki nà reí de arù

typing [tai'piŋ] n タイプライターを打つ 事 taípuraìta wo útsù kotó

typist [tai'pist] n タイピスト taípisùto

tyranny [ti:r'əni:] n 暴政 bōsei

tyrant [tai'rənt] n 暴君 bōkun

tyre [taiə:r'] (BRIT) n = **tire**

tzar [zɑ:r] n = **tsar**

U

U-bend [ju:'bend] n (in pipe) トラップ toráppù

ubiquitous [ju:bik'witəs] adj いたる所に ある itáru tokoro nì aru

udder [ʌd'ə:r] n 乳房 chibúsa ◇ ウシ、ヤ ギなどについて言う ushí, yagí nado ni tsuite iú

UFO [ju:efou'] n abbr (= unidentified flying object) 未確認飛行物体 mikákunin hikōbuttài, ユーフォー yūfō

Uganda [ju:gæn'də] n ウガンダ ugáñda

ugh [ʌ] excl おえっ oét

ugliness [ʌg'li:nis] n 醜さ miníkusà

ugly [ʌg'li:] adj (person, dress etc) 醜い miníkuì; (dangerous: situation) 物騒な bussố nà

UK [ju:'kei] n abbr = **United Kingdom**

ulcer [ʌl'sə:r] n かいよう kaíyō

Ulster [ʌl'stə:r] n アルスター arùsutā

ulterior [ʌlti:r'i:ə:r] adj: *ulterior motive* 下心 shitágokòro

ultimate [ʌl'təmit] adj (final: aim, destination, result) 最後の saìgo no; (greatest: insult, deterrent, authority) 最大の saídai no

ultimately [ʌl'təmitli:] adv (in the end) やがて yagáte; (basically) 根本的に koñponteki ni

ultimatum [ʌltimei'təm] n 最後通ちょう saígotsūchō

ultrasound [ʌl'trəsaund] n (MED) 超 音 波 chốoñpa

ultraviolet [ʌltrəvai'əlit] adj (rays, light) 紫外線の shigáisen no

umbilical cord [ʌmbil'ikəl-] *n* へその緒 hesó no o

umbrella [ʌmbrel'ə] *n* (for rain) 傘 kasá, 雨傘 amágasà; (for sun) 日傘 higása, パラソル parásoru

umpire [ʌm'paiə:r] *n* (TENNIS, CRICKET) 審判 shinpan, アンパイア añpaìa
◆*vt* (game) ...のアンパイアをする ...no añpaìa wo suru

umpteen [ʌmp'ti:n'] *adj* うんと沢山の uñto takusan no

umpteenth [ʌmp'ti:nθ'] *adj*: **for the umpteenth time** 何回目か分からないが nañkaime kà wakáranaì ga

UN [juː'en'] *n abbr* = **United Nations**

unable [ʌnei'bəl] *adj*: **to be unable to do something** ...する事ができない ...surú koto gà dekínai

unaccompanied [ʌnəkʌm'pəni:d] *adj* (child, woman) 同伴者のいない dóhañsha no inai; (luggage) 別送の bessó no; (song) 無伴奏の mubáñsò no

unaccountably [ʌnəkaunt'əbli:] *adv* 妙に myó nì

unaccustomed [ʌnəkʌs'təmd] *adj*: **to be unaccustomed to** (public speaking, Western clothes etc) ...になれていない ...ni naréte inai

unanimous [juːnæn'əməs] *adj* (vote) 満場一致の mañjòitchi no; (people) 全員同意の zeñ-indòi no

unanimously [juːnæn'əməsli:] *adv* (vote) 満場一致で mañjòitchi de

unarmed [ʌnɑː:rmd'] *adj* 武器を持たない búkì wo motánaì, 丸腰の marúgoshi no **unarmed combat** 武器を使わない武術 búkì wo tsukáwanaì bújùtsu

unashamed [ʌnəʃeimd'] *adj* (greed) 恥知らずの hajíshiràzu no; (pleasure) 人目をはばからない hitóme wo habákaranài

unassuming [ʌnəsuː'miŋ] *adj* (person, manner) 気取らない kidóranai

unattached [ʌnətætʃt'] *adj* (person) 独身の dokúshìn no; (part etc) 遊んでいる asónde iru

unattended [ʌnəten'did] *adj* (car, luggage, child) ほったらかしの hottáraka-

shi no

unattractive [ʌnətræk'tiv] *adj* (person, character) いやな iyá na; (building, appearance, idea) 魅力のない miryóku no nai

unauthorized [ʌnɔ:θ'ə:raizd] *adj* (visit, use, version) 無許可の mukyókà no

unavoidable [ʌnəvɔi'dəbəl] *adj* (delay) 避けられない sakérarenài

unaware [ʌnəwer'] *adj*: **to be unaware of** ...に気が付いていない ...ni ki gá tsuìte inai

unawares [ʌnəwe:rz'] *adv* (catch, take) 不意に fuí ni

unbalanced [ʌnbæl'ənst] *adj* (report) 偏った katáyottà; (mentally) 狂った kurúttà

unbearable [ʌnbe:r'əbəl] *adj* (heat, pain) 耐えられない taérarenài; (person) 我慢できない程いやな gamán dekínaì hodo iyá na

unbeatable [ʌnbi:'təbəl] *adj* (team) 無敵の mutéki no; (quality) 最高の saíkò no; (price) 最高に安い saíkò ni yasúì

unbeknown(st) [ʌnbinoun(st)'] *adv*: **unbeknown(st) to me/Peter** 私(ピーター)に気付かれずに watákushi [pītà]ni kizúkarezù ni

unbelievable [ʌnbili:'vəbəl] *adj* 信じられない shiñjirarenái

unbend [ʌnbend'] (*pt, pp* **bent**) *vi* (relax) くつろぐ kutsúrogù
◆*vt* (wire) 真っ直ぐにする massúgù ni suru

unbiased [ʌnbai'əst] *adj* (person, report) 公正な kósei na

unborn [ʌnbɔ:rn'] *adj* (child, young) おなかの中の onáka no nakà no

unbreakable [ʌnbrei'kəbəl] *adj* (glassware, crockery etc) 割れない warénai; (other objects) 壊れない kowárenai

unbroken [ʌnbrou'kən] *adj* (seal) 開けてない akéte naì; (silence, series) 続く tsuzúku; (record) 破られていない yabúrarète inai; (spirit) くじけない kujíkenài

unbutton [ʌnbʌt'ən] *vt* ...のボタンを外す ...no botán wo hazúsu

uncalled-for [ʌnkɔ:ld'fɔ:r] *adj* (remark)

余計な yokéi na; (rudeness etc) いわれの ない iwáre no nai

uncanny [ʌnkˈænˈiː] *adj* (silence, resemblance, knack) 不気味な bukìmi na

unceasing [ʌnsiːˈsiŋ] *adj* 引っ切り無しの hikkírinashì ne

unceremonious [ʌnseːrəmouˈniːəs] *adj* (abrupt, rude) ぶしつけな bushítsuke na

uncertain [ʌnsəːˈtən] *adj* (hesitant: voice, steps) 自信のない jishín no nai; (unsure) 不確実な fukákùjitsu na

uncertainty [ʌnsəːˈtənti] *n* (not knowing) 不確実さ fukákùjitsusa; (also *pl*: doubts) 疑問 gimón

unchanged [ʌntʃeindʒˈd] *adj* (condition) 変っていない kawátte inai

unchecked [ʌntʃektˈ] *adv* (grow, continue) 無制限に muséigen ni

uncivilized [ʌnsivˈilaizd] *adj* (gen: country, people) 未開の mikái no; (fig: behavior, hour etc) 野蛮な yabán na

uncle [ʌŋˈkəl] *n* おじ ojí

uncomfortable [ʌnkʌmfˈtəbəl] *adj* (physically, *also* furniture) 使い心地の悪い tsukáigokochi nð warúĩ; (uneasy) 不安な fuán na; (unpleasant: situation, fact) 厄介な yakkái na

uncommon [ʌnkaːmˈən] *adj* (rare, unusual) 珍しい mezúrashii

uncompromising [ʌnkaːmˈprəmaiziŋ] *adj* (person, belief) 融通の利かない yūzū no kikánai

unconcerned [ʌnkənsəːrndˈ] *adj* (indifferent) 関心がない kañshin ga naĩ; (not worried) 平気な heíki na

unconditional [ʌnkəndiʃˈənəl] *adj* 無条件の mujókèn no

unconscious [ʌnkaːnˈtʃəs] *adj* (in faint, *also* MED) 意識不明の ishíkifumei no; (unaware): **unconscious of** ...に気が付かない ...ni kí ga tsukánaĩ
◆*n:* **the unconscious** 潜在意識 señzaiishìki

unconsciously [ʌnkaːnˈtʃəsli] *adv* (unawares) 無意識に muíshìki ni

uncontrollable [ʌnkəntrouˈləbəl] *adj* (child, animal) 手に負えない te nĩ oénai; (temper) 抑制のきかない yokúsei no ki-

kánai; (laughter) やめられない yaméra-renái

unconventional [ʌnkənven'tʃənəl] *adj* 型破りの katáyabùri no

uncouth [ʌnkuːθ] *adj* 無様な buzáma na

uncover [ʌnkʌvˈəːr] *vt* (take lid, veil etc off) ...の覆いを取る ...no oĩ wo torù; (plot, secret) 発見する hakkén suru

undecided [ʌndisaiˈdid] *adj* (person) 決定していない kettéi shite inai; (question) 未決定の mikettéi no

undeniable [ʌndinaiˈəbəl] *adj* (fact, evidence) 否定できない hitéi dekínaĩ

under [ʌnˈdəːr] *prep* (beneath) ...の下に ...no shitá ni; (in age, price: less than) ...以下に ...ikà ni; (according to: law, agreement etc) ...によって ...ni yottè; (someone's leadership) ...のもとに ...no motð ni
◆*adv* (go, fly etc) ...の下に〔で〕...no shitá ni〔de〕
under there あそこの下に〔で〕asóko no shitá ni〔de〕
under repair 修理中 shūrĩchū

under... *prefix* 下の... shitá no...

under-age [ʌndəreidʒ'] *adj* (person, drinking) 未成年の miséinen no

undercarriage [ʌndəˈrkæriˈidʒ] (*BRIT*) *n* (AVIAT) 着陸装置 chakúrikusōchi

undercharge [ʌnˈdəːrtʃaːrdʒ] *vt* ...から正当な料金を取らない ...kara séitō na ryōkìn wo toránai

underclothes [ʌnˈdəːrklouz] *npl* 下着 shitági

undercoat [ʌnˈdəːrkout] *n* (paint) 下塗り shitánuri

undercover [ʌndəːrkʌvˈəːr] *adj* (work, agent) 秘密の himítsu no

undercurrent [ʌnˈdəːrkəːrənt] *n* (fig: of feeling) 底流 teíryū

undercut [ʌnˈdəːrkʌt] (*pt, pp* **undercut**) *vt* (person, prices) ...より低い値段で物を売る ...yorî hikûî nedán de monð wo urú

underdog [ʌnˈdəːrdɔːg] *n* 弱者 jakûsha

underdone [ʌnˈdəːrdʌn] *adj* (CULIN) 生焼けの namáyake no

underestimate [ʌndəːresˈtəmeit] *vt* (person, thing) 見くびる mikúbiru

underexposed [ʌndə:riksˈpouzd'] *adj* (PHOT) 露出不足の roshútsubusoku no

underfed [ʌndə:rˈfed'] *adj* (person, animal) 栄養不足の eíyōbusòku no

underfoot [ʌndə:rˈfut'] *adv* (crush, trample) 脚の下に〔で〕ashí no shitá ni〔de〕

undergo [ʌndə:rˈgou'] (*pt* **underwent** *pp* **undergone**) *vt* (test, operation, treatment) 受ける ukérù

to undergo change 変る kawárù

undergraduate [ʌndə:rˈgrædʒ'u:it] *n* 学部の学生 gakúbu no gakúsei

underground [ʌnˈdə:rgraund] *n* (BRIT: railway) 地下鉄 chikátetsu; (POL) 地下組織 chikásoshiki

♦*adj* (car park) 地下の chiká no; (newspaper, activities) 潜りの mogúrì no

♦*adv* (work) 潜りで mogúrì de; (fig): *to go underground* 地下に潜る chiká ni mogúrù

undergrowth [ʌnˈdə:rgrouθ] *n* 下生え shitábae

underhand [ʌnˈdə:rhænd] *adj* (fig) ずるい zurúi

underhanded [ʌnˈdə:rhæn'did] *adj* = **underhand**

underlie [ʌndə:rˈlai'] (*pt* **underlay** *pp* **underlain**) *vt* (fig: be basis of) ...の根底になっている ...no końtei ni nattè iru

underline [ʌnˈdə:rlain] *vt* 下線する kasén suru, ...にアンダーラインを引く ...ni ańdārain wo hikú; (fig) 強調する kyóchō suru

underling [ʌnˈdə:rliŋ] (*pej*) *n* 手下 teshíta

undermine [ʌnˈdə:rmain] *vt* (confidence) 失わせる ushínawaseru; (authority) 弱める yowámerù

underneath [ʌndə:rniːˈθ'] *adv* 下に〔で〕shitá ni〔de〕

♦*prep* ...の下に〔で〕...no shitá ni〔de〕

underpaid [ʌndə:rˈpeid'] *adj* 安給料の yasúkyūryò no

underpants [ʌnˈdə:rpænts] *npl* パンツ pańtsu

underpass [ʌnˈdə:rpæs] (BRIT) *n* 地下道 chikádō

underprivileged [ʌndə:rpriv'əlidʒd] *adj*

(country, race, family) 恵まれない megúmarenai

underrate [ʌndə:reit'] *vt* (person, power etc) 見くびる mikúbirù; (size) 見誤る miáyamarù

undershirt [ʌnˈdə:rʃə:rt] (US) *n* アンダーシャツ ańdāshatsù

undershorts [ʌnˈdə:rʃɔːrts] (US) *npl* パンツ pańtsu

underside [ʌnˈdə:rsaid] *n* (of object) 下側 shitágawa; (of animal) おなか onáka

underskirt [ʌnˈdə:rskə:rt] (BRIT) *n* アンダースカート ańdāsukātò

understand [ʌndə:rstænd'] (*pt*, *pp* **understood**) *vt* 分かる wakárù, 理解する rikái suru

♦*vi* (believe): *I understand that* ...だそうですね ...da sódesù ne, ...だと聞いていますが ...da tò kifte imasu gà

understandable [ʌndə:rstæn'dəbəl] *adj* (behavior, reaction, mistake) 理解できる rikái dekírù

understanding [ʌndə:rstæn'diŋ] *adj* (kind) 思いやりのある omóiyari no aru

♦*n* (gen) 理解 rikái; (agreement) 合意 góì

understatement [ʌndə:rsteit'mənt] *n* (of quality) 控え目な表現 hikáeme na hyógen

that's an understatement! それは控え目過ぎるよ sore wa hikáemesugírù yo

understood [ʌndə:rstud'] *pt*, *pp* of **understand**

♦*adj* (agreed) 合意された góì sareta; (implied) 暗黙の ańmoku no

understudy [ʌnˈdə:rstʌdi] *n* (actor, actress) 代役 daíyaku

undertake [ʌndə:rteik'] (*pt* **undertook** *pp* **undertaken**) *vt* (task) 引受ける hikífukerù

to undertake to do something ...する事を約束する ...surú koto wo yakúsoku suru

undertaker [ʌnˈdə:rteikə:r] *n* 葬儀屋 sógiyà

undertaking [ʌnˈdə:rteikiŋ] *n* (job) 事業 jigyō; (promise) 約束 yakúsoku

undertone [ʌnˈdə:rtoun] *n*: *in an undertone* 小声 kogóe

underwater [ˌʌndə'rwɔ:t'ə:r] *adv* (use) 水中に〔で〕suíchū ni(de); (swim) 水中に潜って suíchū ni mogútte
♦*adj* (exploration) 水中の suíchū no; (camera etc) 潜水用の sénsuiyō no

underwear [ˌʌn'də:rweːr] *n* 下着 shítagi

underworld [ˌʌn'də:rwə:rld] *n* (of crime) 暗黒街 afíkokugai

underwriter [ˌʌn'də:raitə:r] *n* (INSURANCE) 保険業者 hokéngyōshà

undesirable [ˌʌndiziaiə:r'əbəl] *adj* (person, thing) 好ましくない konómashikunai

undies [ʌn'di:z] (*inf*) *npl* 下着 shítagi ◇女性用を指す joséiyō wo sasù

undisputed [ˌʌndispju:'tid] *adj* (fact) 否定できない hitéi dekinaî; (champion etc) 断トツの dañtotsu no

undo [ʌndu:'] (*pt* **undid** *pp* **undone**) *vt* (unfasten) 外す hazúsu; (spoil) 台無しにする daínashi ni suru

undoing [ʌndu:'iŋ] *n* 破滅 hamétsu

undoubted [ʌndau'tid] *adj* 疑う余地のない utágau yochî no naî

undoubtedly [ʌndau'tidli:] *adv* 疑う余地なく utágau yochî naku

undress [ʌndres'] *vi* 服を脱ぐ fukú wo nugù

undue [ʌndu:'] *adj* (excessive) 余分な yobún na

undulating [ʌn'dʒəleitiŋ] *adj* (countryside, hills) 起伏の多い kifúku no ōî

unduly [ʌndu:'li:] *adv* (excessively) 余分に yobún ni

unearth [ʌnə:rθ'] *vt* (skeleton etc) 発掘する hakkútsu suru; (*fig*: secrets etc) 発見する hakkén suru

unearthly [ʌnə:rθ'li:] *adj* (hour) とんでもない tofíde mo naî

uneasy [ʌni:'zi:] *adj* (person: not comfortable) 窮屈な kyúkutsu na; (: worried: *also* feeling) 不安な fuán na; (peace, truce) 不安定な fuáñtei na

uneconomic(al) [ˌʌni:kənɑ:m'ik(əl)] *adj* 不経済な fukéìzai na

uneducated [ˌʌned'ʒu:keitid] *adj* (person) 教育のない kyóiku no nai

unemployed [ˌʌnemplɔid'] *adj* (worker) 失業中の shitsúgyōchū no
♦*npl*: **the unemployed** 失業者 shitsúgyōshà ◇総称 sōshō

unemployment [ˌʌnemplɔi'mənt] *n* 失業 shitsúgyō

unending [ʌnen'diŋ] *adj* 果てし無い hatéshí naî

unerring [ʌnə:r'iŋ] *adj* (instinct etc) 確実な kakújitsu na

uneven [ʌni:'vən] *adj* (not regular: teeth) 不ぞろいの fuzórôi no; (performance) むらのある murá no aru; (road etc) 凸凹の dekôboko no

unexpected [ˌʌnikspek'tid] *adj* (arrival) 不意の fuî no; (success etc) 思い掛けない omóigakenaî, 意外な igài na

unexpectedly [ˌʌnikspek'tidli:] *adv* (arrive) 不意に fuî ni; (succeed) 意外に igài ni

unfailing [ʌnfei'liŋ] *adj* (support, energy) 尽きる事のない tsukíru koto no naî

unfair [ʌnfe:r'] *adj*: **unfair (to)** (...に対して) 不当な (...ni taishite) futô na

unfaithful [ʌnfei'θfəl] *adj* (lover, spouse) 浮気な uwáki na

unfamiliar [ʌnfəmil'jə:r] *adj* (place, person, subject) 知らない shiránai
to be unfamiliar with ...を知らない ...wo shiránai

unfashionable [ʌnfæʃ'ənəbəl] *adj* (clothes, ideas, place) はやらない hayáranaî

unfasten [ʌnfæs'ən] *vt* (undo) 外す hazúsu; (open) 開ける akéru

unfavorable [ʌnfei'və:rəbəl] (*BRIT* **unfavourable**) *adj* (circumstances, weather) 良くない yokúnai; (opinion, report) 批判的な hiháñteki na

unfeeling [ʌnfi:'liŋ] *adj* 冷たい tsumétai, 冷酷な reîkoku na

unfinished [ʌnfin'iʃt] *adj* (incomplete) 未完成の mikáñsei no

unfit [ʌnfit'] *adj* (physically) 運動不足の uñdōbusoku no; (incompetent): **unfit (for)** (...に) 不向きな (...ni fumúki na
to be unfit for work 仕事に不向きである shigóto ni fumúki de aru

unfold [ʌnfould'] vt (sheets, map) 広げる hirōgeru

♦vi (situation) 展開する teñkai suru

unforeseen [ʌnfɔːrsiːn'] adj (circumstances etc) 予期しなかった yokî shinákatta, 思い掛けない omōigakenaī

unforgettable [ʌnfərget'əbəl] adj 忘れられない wasúrerarenaī

unforgivable [ʌnfəːrgivˈəbəl] adj 許せない yurúsenai

unfortunate [ʌnfɔːrˈtʃənit] adj (poor) 哀れな awāre na; (event) 不幸な fukô na; (remark) まずい mazúi

unfortunately [ʌnfɔːrˈtʃənitliː] adv 残念ながら zañneñnagara

unfounded [ʌnfaun'did] adj (criticism, fears) 根拠のない koñkyo no nāi

unfriendly [ʌnfrend'liː] adj (person, behavior, remark) 不親切な fushîñsetsu na

ungainly [ʌngeinˈliː] adj ぎこちない gikôchinaī

ungodly [ʌngɑːdˈliː] adj (hour) とんでもない toñdemonaī

ungrateful [ʌngreitˈfəl] adj (person) 恩知らずの ofishirâzu no

unhappiness [ʌnhæpˈiːnis] n 不幸せ fushîawâse, 不幸 fukô

unhappy [ʌnhæpˈiː] adj (sad) 悲しい kanáshii; (unfortunate) 不幸な fukô na; (childhood) 恵まれない megúmarenaī; (dissatisfied): **unhappy about/with** (arrangements etc) ...に不満がある ...nī fumán ga aru

unharmed [ʌnhɑːrmd'] adj 無事な bují na

unhealthy [ʌnhelˈθiː] adj (person) 病弱な byôjaku na; (place) 健康に悪い keñkōni warúī; (fig: interest) 不健全な fukéñzen na

unheard-of [ʌnhəːrdˈəv] adj (shocking) 前代未聞の zeñdaimimon no; (unknown) 知られていない shirárete inaī

unhurt [ʌnhəːrt'] adj 無事な bují na

unidentified [ʌnaidenˈtəfaid] adj 未確定の mikákùtei no ¶ see also **UFO**

uniform [juːˈnəfɔːrm] n 制服 seífuku, ユニフォーム yunífōmù

♦adj (length, width etc) 一定の ittéi no

uniformity [juːnəfɔːrˈmitiː] n 均一性 kiñitsusei

unify [juːˈnəfai] vt 統一する tōîtsu suru

unilateral [juːnəlætˈəːrəl] adj (disarmament etc) 一方的な ippôteki na

uninhabited [ʌninhæbˈitid] adj (island etc) 無人の mujín no; (house) 空き家になっている akíya ni nattê iru

unintentional [ʌninten'tʃənəl] adj 意図的でない itôteki de naī

union [juːnˈjən] n (joining) 合併 gappéi; (grouping) 連合 reñgô; (also: **trade union**) 組合 kumíai

♦cpd (activities, leader etc) 組合の kumíai no

Union Jack n 英国国旗 eíkokukòkki, ユニオンジャック yunîonjakkù

unique [juːniːk'] adj 独特な dokútoku na, ユニークな yunîkù na

unisex [juːˈniseks] adj (clothes, hairdresser etc) ユニセックスの yunísekkusu no

unison [juːˈnisən] n: **in unison** (say) 一同に ichídō ni; (sing) 同音で dôon de, ユニゾンで yunîzon de

unit [juːˈnit] n (single whole, also measurement) 単位 tañ-i; (section: of furniture etc) ユニット yunîtto; (team, squad) 班 hàn

kitchen unit 台所用ユニット daídokoroyô yunîtto

unite [juːnait'] vt (join: gen) 一緒にする isshô ni suru, 一つにする hitôtsu ni suru; (: country, party) 結束させる kessokusaseru

♦vi 一緒になる isshô ni naru, 一つになる hitôtsù ni naru

united [juːnaiˈtid] adj (gen) 一緒になった isshô ni natta, 一つになった hitôtsù ni natta; (effort) 団結した dañketsu shita

United Kingdom n 英国 eíkoku

United Nations (Organization) n 国連 kokúren

United States (of America) n (アメリカ) 合衆国 (amérika)gasshùkoku

unit trust (BRIT) n ユニット型投資信託 yunîttogata tôshishiñtaku

unity [juː'niti] n 一致 itchí

universal [juːnəvəːr'səl] adj 普遍的な fuhénteki na

universe [juː'nəvəːrs] n 宇宙 uchū

university [juːnəvəːr'siti] n 大学 daígaku

unjust [ʌndʒʌst'] adj 不当な futó na

unkempt [ʌnkempt'] adj (appearance) だらしのない daráshi no naí; (hair, beard) もじゃもじゃの mojámoja no

unkind [ʌnkaind'] adj (person, behavior, comment etc) 不親切な fushínsetsu na

unknown [ʌnnoun'] adj 知られていない shiráretè inái

unlawful [ʌnlɔː'fəl] adj (act, activity) 非合法な higóhō na

unleash [ʌnliːʃ'] vt (fig: feeling, forces etc) 爆発させる bakúhatsu saseru

unless [ʌnles'] $conj$ ...しなければ〔でなければ〕 ...shínakereba〔denákereba〕
  unless he comes 彼が来なければ karè ga konákereba

unlike [ʌnlaik'] adj (not alike) 似ていない nité inaì; (not like) 違った chigátta
  ◆*prep* (different from) ...と違って ...to chigátte

unlikely [ʌnlaik'liː] adj (not likely) ありそうもない arísō mo naì; (unexpected: combination etc) 驚くべき odórokubeki

unlimited [ʌnlim'itid] adj (travel, wine etc) 無制限の muséīgen no

unlisted [ʌnlis'tid] (*BRIT* ex-directory) adj (ex-directory) 電話帳に載っていない deńwachō ni notté inaì

unload [ʌnloud'] vt (box, car etc) ...の積荷を降ろす ...no tsumíni wo orósù

unlock [ʌnlɑːk'] vt ...のかぎを開ける ...no kagí wo akéru

unlucky [ʌnlʌk'iː] adj (person) 運の悪い uń no warúi; (object, number) 縁起の悪い eńgi no warúi
  to be unlucky (person) 運が悪い uń ga warúi

unmarried [ʌnmæ'riːd] adj (person) 独身の dokúshin no; (mother) 未婚の mikón no

unmask [ʌnmæsk'] vt (reveal: thief etc) ...の正体を暴く ...no shōtaì wo abákù

unmistakable [ʌnmistei'kəbəl] adj (voice, sound, person) 間違え様のない machígaeyō no naì

unmitigated [ʌnmit'əgeitid] adj (disaster etc) 紛れもない magíre mò naí

unnatural [ʌnnætʃ'əːrəl] adj 不自然な fushízen na

unnecessary [ʌnnes'iseːri:] adj 不必要な fuhítsuyō na

unnoticed [ʌnnou'tist] adj: (*to go/pass*) *unnoticed* 気付かれない kizúkàrenai

UNO [uː'nou] n $abbr$ = **United Nations Organization**

unobtainable [ʌnəbtei'nəbəl] adj (item) 手に入らない te nì haíranaì; (*TEL*): *this number is unobtainable* この電話番号は現在使用されていません konó deñwabangō wa geńzai shiyō sarete imásèn

unobtrusive [ʌnəbtruː'siv] adj (person) 遠慮がちな eńryogachi na; (thing) 目立たない medátanaì

unofficial [ʌnəfiʃ'əl] adj (news) 公表されていない kóhyō sarete inaì; (strike) 公認されていない kóñin sarete inaì

unorthodox [ʌnɔːr'θədɑːks] adj (treatment) 通常でない tsújō de nai; (*REL*) 正統でない seítō de nai

unpack [ʌnpæk'] vi 荷物の中身を出して片付ける nimótsu no nakámi wo dashíte katázukerù
  ◆*vt* (suitcase etc) ...の中身を出して片付ける ...no nakámi wo dashíte katázukerù

unpalatable [ʌnpæl'ətəbəl] adj (meal) まずい mazúi; (truth) 不愉快な fuyúkai na

unparalleled [ʌnpær'əleld] adj (unequalled) 前代未聞の zeńdaimimon no

unpleasant [ʌnplez'ənt] adj (disagreeable: thing) いやな iyà na; (: person, manner) 不愉快な fuyúkài na

unplug [ʌnplʌg'] vt (iron, TV etc) ...のプラグを抜く ...no purágu wo nukú

unpopular [ʌnpɑːp'jələːr] adj (person, decision etc) 不評の fuhyō no

unprecedented [ʌnpres'identid] adj 前代未聞の zeńdaimimon no

unpredictable [ʌnpridik'təbəl] adj

(weather, reaction) 予測できない yosóku dekínaì; (person): *he is unpredictable* 彼のする事は予測できない karè no suru koto wa yosóku dekínai

unprofessional [ʌnprəfeʃ'ənəl] *adj* (attitude, conduct) 職業倫理に反する shokúgyōrìnri ni hań suru

unqualified [ʌnkwa:l'əfaid] *adj* (teacher, nurse etc) 資格のない shikáku no nai; (complete: disaster) 全くの mattáku no, 大... daì...; (: success) 完全な kańzen na, 大... daì...

unquestionably [ʌnkwes'tʃənəbli:] *adv* 疑いもなく utágai mò naku

unravel [ʌnræv'əl] *vt* (ball of string) ほ ぐす hogúsù; (mystery) 解明する kaímei suru

unreal [ʌnri:l'] *adj* (not real) 偽の nisé no; (extraordinary) うその様なuső no yō na

unrealistic [ʌnri:əlis'tik] *adj* (person, project) 非現実的な higénjitsuteki na

unreasonable [ʌnri:'zənəbəl] *adj* (person, attitude) 不合理な fugőrì na; (demand) 不当な futő na; (length of time) 非常識な hijőshìki na

unrelated [ʌnrilei'tid] *adj* (incident) 関係 のない kańkei no naì, 無関係の mukáńkei na; (family) 親族でない shińzoku de naì

unrelenting [ʌnrilen'tiŋ] *adj* 執念深い shúnenbukai

unreliable [ʌnrilai'əbəl] *adj* (person, firm) 信頼できない shińrai dekinaì; (machine, watch, method) 当てにならな い até ni naranaì

unremitting [ʌnrimit'iŋ] *adj* (efforts, attempts) 絶間ない taéma naì

unreservedly [ʌnrizə:r'vidli:] *adv* 心か ら kokórò kara

unrest [ʌnrest'] *n* (social, political, industrial etc) 不安 fuáń

unroll [ʌnroul'] *vt* 広げる hirőgeru

unruly [ʌnru:'li:] *adj* (child, behavior) 素 直でない sunáo de nai, 手に負えない te nì oénaì; (hair) もじゃもじゃの mojámoja no

unsafe [ʌnseif'] *adj* (in danger) 危険にさ

らされた kinkén ni sarásareta; (journey, machine, bridge etc) 危険な kikén na, 危 ない abúnai

unsaid [ʌnsed'] *adj*: *to leave something unsaid* ...を言わないでおく ...wo iwánai- de okù

unsatisfactory [ʌnsætisfæk'tə:ri:] *adj* (progress, work, results) 不満足な fumáńzoku na

unsavory [ʌnsei'və:ri:] (*BRIT* **unsavoury**) *adj* (*fig*: person, place) いかが わしい ikágawashiì

unscathed [ʌnskeiðd'] *adj* 無傷の mukízu no

unscrew [ʌnskru:'] *vt* (bottletop etc) ね じって開ける nejítte akéru; (sign, mirror etc) ...のねじを抜く ...no nejî wo nukú

unscrupulous [ʌnskru:p'jələs] *adj* (person, behavior) 悪徳... akútoku...

unsettled [ʌnset'əld] *adj* (person) 落付か ない ochítsukanaì; (weather) 変りやすい kawáriyasuì

unshaven [ʌnʃei'vən] *adj* 不精ひげの bushőhìge no

unsightly [ʌnsait'li:] *adj* (mark, building etc) 醜い miníkuì, 目障りな mezáwàri na

unskilled [ʌnskild'] *adj* (work, worker) 未熟練の mijúkuren no

unspeakable [ʌnspi:'kəbəl] *adj* (indescribable) 言語に絶する geńgo ni zéssuru, 想像を絶する sőzō wo zéssurù; (awful) ひどい hidőì

unstable [ʌnstei'bəl] *adj* (piece of furniture) ぐらぐらする gurágura suru; (government) 不安定な fuántei na; (mentally) 情緒不安定な jőchofuántei na

unsteady [ʌnsted'i:] *adj* (step, legs) ふら ふらする furáfura suru; (hands, voice) 震 える furúeru; (ladder) ぐらぐらする gurágura suru

unstuck [ʌnstʌk'] *adj*: *to come unstuck* (label etc) 取れてしまう toréte shimaù; (*fig*: plan, idea etc) 失敗する shippái suru

unsuccessful [ʌnsəkses'fəl] *adj* (attempt) 失敗した shippái shita; (writer) 成功しない seíkō shinaì, 売れない uréna- i; (proposal) 採用されなかった saíyō sa- rénakatta *to be unsuccessful* (in attempting something) 失敗する shippai suru; (application) 採用されない saíyō sarènai

unsuccessfully [ʌnsəkses'fəli:] *adv* (try) 成功せずに seíkō sezu ni

unsuitable [ʌnsu:'təbəl] *adj* (inconvenient: time, moment) 不適当な futékìtō na; (inappropriate: clothes) 場違いの bachígaì no; (: person) 不適当な futékìtō na

unsure [ʌnʃu:r'] *adj* (uncertain) 不確実な fukákùjitsu na

unsure about ...について確信できない ...ni tsuìte kakúshin dekìnaì

to be unsure of oneself 自信がない jishín ga nai

unsuspecting [ʌnsəspek'tiŋ] *adj* 気付いていない kizúite inai

unsympathetic [ʌnsimpəθet'ik] *adj* (showing little understanding) 同情しない dōjō shinai; (unlikeable) いやな iyà na

untapped [ʌntæpt'] *adj* (resources) 未開発の mikáìhatsu no

unthinkable [ʌnθiŋk'əbəl] *adj* 考えられない kañgaerarenaì

untidy [ʌntai'di:] *adj* (room) 散らかった chírakatta; (person, appearance) だらしない daráshi nai

untie [ʌntai'] *vt* (knot, parcel, ribbon) ほどく hodókù; (prisoner) ...の縄をほどく ...no nawá wo hodókù; (parcel, dog) ...のひもをほどく ...no himó wo hodókù

until [ʌntil'] *prep* ...まで ...madè

◆*conj* ...するまで ...suru madè

until he comes 彼が来るまで karè ga kurù made

until now 今まで imámadè

until then その時まで sonó toki madè

untimely [ʌntaim'li:] *adj* (inopportune: moment, arrival) 時機の悪い jikī no warúì

an untimely death 早死に hayájini, 若死に wakájini

untold [ʌntould'] *adj* (story) 明かされていない akásarete inai; (joy, suffering, wealth) 想像を絶する sōzō wo zessúru

untoward [ʌntɔ:rd'] *adj* 困った komáttà

unused [ʌnju:zd'] *adj* (not used: clothes, portion etc) 未使用の mishíyō no

unusual [ʌnju:'ʒu:əl] *adj* (strange) 変った kawátta; (rare) 珍しい mezúrashiì; (exceptional, distinctive) 並外れた namíhazureta

unveil [ʌnveil'] *vt* (statue) ...の除幕式を行う ...no jomákushiki wo okónau

unwanted [ʌnwɔ:n'tid] *adj* (clothing etc) 不要の fuyō no; (child, pregnancy) 望まれなかった nozómarenakatta

unwavering [ʌnwei'vərŋ] *adj* (faith) 揺るぎ無い yurúginaì; (gaze) じっとした jittō shita

unwelcome [ʌnwel'kəm] *adj* (guest) 歓迎されない kañgeisarenaì; (news) 悪い warúì

unwell [ʌnwel'] *adj*: *to feel unwell* 気分が悪い kibùn ga warúì

to be unwell 病気である byóki de aru

unwieldy [ʌnwi:l'di:] *adj* (object, system) 大きくて扱いにくい ōkíkute atsúkaini-kuì

unwilling [ʌnwil'iŋ] *adj*: *to be unwilling to do something* ...するのをいやがっている ...surú no wo iyagatte iru

unwillingly [ʌnwil'iŋli:] *adv* いやがって iyágatte

unwind [ʌnwaind'] (*pt*, *pp* **unwound**) *vt* (undo) ほどく hodókù

◆*vi* (relax) くつろぐ kutsúrogù

unwise [ʌnwaiz'] *adj* (person) 思慮の足りない shiryō no tarínai; (decision) 浅はかな asáhàka na

unwitting [ʌnwit'iŋ] *adj* (victim, accomplice) 気付かない kizúkànai

unworkable [ʌnwə:r'kəbəl] *adj* (plan) 実行不可能な jikkófukanō nà

unworthy [ʌnwə:r'ði:] *adj* ...の値打がない ...no neúchi ga naî

unwrap [ʌnræp'] *vt* 開ける akéru

unwritten [ʌnrit'ən] *adj* (law) 慣習の kañshū no; (agreement) 口頭での kōtō de no

---

KEYWORD

---

up [ʌp] *prep*: *to go up something* ...を登る ...wo nobóru

to be up something ...の上に（登って）いる ...no ué ni nobotte iru

he went up the stairs/the hill 彼は階段〔坂〕を登った karè wa kaídan〔sakà〕wo nobótta

the cat was up a tree ネコは木の上にいた nekò wa ki nò ué ni ita

we walked/climbed up the hill 私たちは丘を登った watákushitachi wa oká wo nobótta

they live further up the street 彼らはこの道をもう少し行った所に住んでいます karèra wa konó michi wo mő sukoshi ittá tokoro ni suǹde imasu

go up that road and turn left この道を交差点まで行って左に曲って下さい konó michi wo kõsaten màde itte hidári ni magátte kudásaì

♦*adv* **1** (upwards, higher) 上に〔で, へ〕 ué ni〔de, e〕

up in the sky/the mountains 空〔山の上〕に sorà〔yamá no ué〕ni

put it a bit higher up もう少し高い所に置いて下さい mő sukoshì takáî tokoro ni oíte kudásaì

up there あの上に anó ue ni

what's the cat doing up there? ネコは何であの上にいるのかしら nekò wa naǹde anó ue nì irú no kashira

up above 上の方に〔で〕ué no hő nì〔de〕

there's a village and up above, on the hill, a monastery 村があって, その上の丘に修道院がある murá ga atte, sonő ue no oká ni shūdőin ga aru

2: *to be up* (out of bed) 起きている okíte iru; (prices, level) 上がっている agátte iru; (building) 建ててある tatéte aru, 立っている tattè iru; (tent) 張ってある hatté aru

3: *up to* (as far as) ...まで ...made

I've read up to p.60 私は60ページまで読みました watákushi wa rokújupèji madè yomímashita

the water came up to his knees 水深は彼のひざまでだった suíshin wa karè no hizà madè datta

up to now 今〔これ〕まで imà〔korè〕madè

I can spend up to $10 10ドルまで使えます júdòru made tsukáemasu

4: *to be up to* (depending on) ...の責任である ...no sekínin de aru, ...次第である ...shídai de aru

it's up to you あなた次第です anàta shídai desu

it's not up to me to decide 決めるのは私の責任ではない kiméru no wa watákushi no sekínin de wa naì

5: *to be up to* (equal to) ...に合う ...ni aù

he's not up to it (job, task etc) 彼にはその仕事は無理です karè ni wa sonő shigoto wa murî desu

his work is not up to the required standard 彼の仕事は基準に合いません karè no shigóto wa kijún ni aìmasen

6: *to be up to* (inf: be doing) やっている yatté iru

what is he up to? (showing disapproval, suspicion) あいつは何をやらかしているんだろうね aítsu wa nanì wo yarákushite irún darő nè

♦*n*: *ups and downs* (in life, career) 浮き沈み ukíshizumi

we all have our ups and downs だれだっていい時と悪い時がありますよ darè datte iî toki to warû toki ga arimasu yo

his life had its ups and downs, but he died happy 彼の人生には浮き沈みが多かったが, 死ぬ時は幸せだった karè no jiǹsei ni wa ukíshizumi ga ōkattà ga, shinú toki wa shiáwase datta

---

upbringing [ʌp'briŋiŋ] *n* 養育 yőiku

update [ʌpdeit'] *vt* (records, information) 更新する kőshin suru

upgrade [ʌp'greid'] *vt* (improve: house) 改築する kaíchiku suru; (job) 格上げする kakúage suru; (employee) 昇格させる shőkaku saseru

upheaval [ʌphi:'vəl] *n* 変動 heǹdő

uphill [*adj* ʌp'hil *adv* ʌp'hil'] *adj* (climb) 上りの nobőri no; (fig: task) 困難な koǹnan na

♦*adv*: *to go uphill* 坂を上る sakà wo nobóru

uphold [ʌphould'] (*pt*, *pp* **upheld**) *vt* (law, principle, decision) 守る mamőrù

upholstery [ʌphoul'stə:ri:] *n* いすに張っ

た生地 isú ni hattá kijí

upkeep [ʌp'kiːp] n (maintenance) 維持 ijí

upon [əpɑːn'] prep ...の上に〔で〕...no ué ni 〔de〕

upper [ʌp'əːr] adj 上の方の ué no hō nò
◆n (of shoe) 甲皮 kōhi

upper-class [ʌp'əːrklæs'] adj (families, accent) 上流の jōryū no

upper hand n: **to have the upper hand** 優勢である yūsei de aru

uppermost [ʌp'əːrmoust] adj 一番上の i-chíban ue no
what was uppermost in my mind 私が真っ先に考えたのは watákushi ga massákì ni kaígaèta no wa

upright [ʌp'rait] adj (straight) 直立の chokúritsu no; (vertical) 垂直の suíchoku no; (fig: honest) 正直な shōjiki na

uprising [ʌp'raiziŋ] n 反乱 hañran

uproar [ʌp'rɔːr'] n (protests, shouts) 大騒ぎ ōsawàgi

uproot [ʌpruːt'] vt (tree) 根こそぎにする nekósogi ni suru; (fig: family) 故郷から追出す kokyō kara oídasù

upset [n ʌp'set vb ʌpset'] (pt, pp **upset**) n (to plan etc) 失敗 shippái
◆vt (knock over: glass etc) 倒す taósù; (routine, plan) 台無しにする daínashi ni suru; (person: offend, make unhappy) 動転させる dōten saseru
◆adj (unhappy) 動転した dōten shita
to have an upset stomach 胃の具合が悪い i nò gúai ga warúì

upshot [ʌp'ʃɑːt] n 結果 kekká

upside down [ʌp'said-] adv (hang, hold) 逆様に〔で〕sakásama ni〔de〕
to turn a place upside down (fig) 家中を引っかき回す iéjū wo hĩkkakímawasu

upstairs [ʌp'steːrz] adv (be) 2階に〔で〕nikái ni〔de〕; (go) 2階へ nikái e
◆adj (window, room) 2階の nikái no
◆n 2階 nikái

upstart [ʌp'stɑːrt] n 横柄な奴 ōhèi na yatsú

upstream [ʌp'striːm] adv 川上に〔で、へ〕kawákami ni〔de, e〕, 上流に〔で、へ〕jōryū ni〔de, e〕

uptake [ʌp'teik] n: **to be quick/slow on**

the uptake 物分かりがいい〔悪い〕monówakàri ga iì〔warui〕

uptight [ʌp'tait'] adj ぴりぴりした pirípiri shita

up-to-date [ʌp'tədeit'] adj (most recent: information) 最新の saíshin no; (person) 最新の情報に通じている saíshin no jōhō ni tsūjite irú

upturn [ʌp'təːrn] n (in luck) 好転 kōten; (COMM: in market) 上向き uwámuki

upward [ʌp'wəːrd] adj (movement, glance) 上への ué e no

upwards [ʌp'wəːrdz] adv (move, glance) 上の方へ ué no hō è; (more than): **upward(s) of** ...以上の ...ijō no

uranium [jurei'niːəm] n ウラン uràn, ウラニウム urániumù

urban [əːr'bən] adj 都会の tokái no

urbane [əːrbein'] adj 上品な jōhin na

urchin [əːr'tʃin] n (child) がき gakí; (waif) 浮浪児 furóji

urge [əːrdʒ] n (need, desire) 衝動 shōdō
◆vt: **to urge someone to do something** ...する様に...を説得する ...surú yō ni ...wo settóku suru

urgency [əːr'dʒənsiː] n (importance) 緊急性 kíñkyūseì; (of tone) 緊迫した調子 kíñpaku shita chōshi

urgent [əːr'dʒənt] adj (need, message) 緊急な kíñkyū na; (voice) 切迫した seppáku shita

urinal [juːr'ənəl] n 小便器 shōbeñki

urinate [juːr'əneit] vi 小便をする shōben wo suru

urine [juːr'in] n 尿 nyō, 小便 shōben

urn [əːrn] n (container) 骨つぼ kotsútsubo; (also: **coffee/tea urn**) 大型コーヒー〔紅茶〕メーカー ōgátakōhī(kōcha)mèkā

Uruguay [juː'rəgwei] n ウルグアイ urùguai

us [ʌs] pron 私たちを〔に〕watákushitachi wo〔ni〕¶ see also **me**

US(A) [juː'es'(ei')] n abbr = **United States (of America)**

usage [juː'sidʒ] n (LING) 慣用 kañyō

use [n juːs vb juːz] n (using) 使用 shíyō; (usefulness, purpose) 役に立つ事 yakú ni tatsu koto 利益 ríeki

◆*vt* (object, tool, phrase etc) 使う tsukáu, 用いる mochíirù, 使用する shíyō suru
in use 使用中 shíyōchū
out of use 廃れて sutáretè
to be of use 役に立つ yakú ni tatsu
it's no use (not useful) 使えません tsukáemasen; (pointless) 役に立ちません yakú ni tachimasen, 無意味です muímì desu
she used to do it 前は彼女はそれをする習慣でした maè wa kanòjo wa soré wo suru shúkan deshita
to be used to ...に慣れている ...ni narète iru

used [juːzd] *adj* (object) 使われた tsukáwareta; (car) 中古の chūkò no

useful [juːsˈfəl] *adj* 役に立つ yakú ni tatsu, 有益な yúeki na, 便利な benìrí na

usefulness [juːsˈfəlnis] *n* 実用性 jitsúyōsei

useless [juːsˈlis] *adj* (unusable) 使えない tsukáenai, 役に立たない yakú ni tatanai; (pointless) 無意味な múimì na, 無駄な mudá na; (person: hopeless) 能無しの nōnashi no, 役に立たない yakú ni tatanai

user [juːˈzəːr] *n* 使用者 shiyōsha

user-friendly [juːˈzəːrfrend'liː] *adj* (computer) 使いやすい tsukáiyasuī, ユーザーフレンドリーな yúzafuréndorī na

use up *vt* 全部使ってしまう zeňbu tsukátte shimaù, 使い尽す tsukáitsukusù

usher [ʌʃˈəːr] *n* (at wedding) 案内係 aňnaigakàri

usherette [ʌʃəret'] *n* (in cinema) 女性案内係 josèi aňnaigakàri

USSR [juːesesaːr'] *n: the USSR* ソ連 sorén

usual [juːˈʒuːəl] *adj* (time, place etc) いつもの itsùmo no
as usual いつもの様に itsùmo no yō ni

usually [juːˈʒuːəliː] *adv* 普通は futsū wa

usurp [juːsəːrpˈ] *vt* (title, position) 強奪する gōdatsu suru

utensil [juːtenˈsəl] *n* 器具 yōgu
kitchen utensils 台所用具 daídokoro yōgu

uterus [juːˈtəːrəs] *n* 子宮 shikyū

utility [juːtilˈitiː] *n* (usefulness) 有用性 yúyōsei, 実用性 jitsúyōsei; (*also:* **public utility**) 公益事業 kōekijigyō

utility room *n* 洗濯部屋 señtakubeya

utilize [juːˈtəlaiz] *vt* (object) 利用する riyō suru, 使う tsukáu

utmost [ʌtˈmoust] *adj* 最大の saídai no
◆*n: to do one's utmost* 全力を尽す zeňryoku wo tsukusù

utter [ʌtˈəːr] *adj* (total: amazement, fool, waste, rubbish) 全くの mattáku no
◆*vt* (sounds) 出す dasú, 発する hassúru; (words) 口に出す kuchí ni dasú, 言う iù

utterance [ʌtˈəːrəns] *n* 発言 hatsúgen, 言葉 kotóba

utterly [ʌtˈəːrliː] *adv* 全く mattáku

U-turn [juːˈtəːrn] *n* Uターン yútāñ

V

v. *abbr* = **verse; versus; volt;** (= **vide**) ...を見よ ...wo mìyo

vacancy [veiˈkənsiː] *n* (*BRIT*: job) 欠員 ketsúin; (room) 空き部屋 akíbeya

vacant [veiˈkənt] *adj* (room, seat, toilet) 空いている aíte iru; (look, expression) うつろの utsúro no

vacant lot (*US*) *n* 空き地 akíchi

vacate [veiˈkeit] *vt* (house, one's seat) 空ける akéru; (job) 辞める yaméru

vacation [veikeiˈʃən] *n* (*esp US*: holiday) 休暇 kyúka; (SCOL) 夏休み natsúyasumì

vaccinate [vækˈsəneit] *vt: to vaccinate someone (against something)* ...に (...の) 予防注射をする ...ni (...no) yobōchūshà wo suru

vaccine [vækˈsiːn] *n* ワクチン wakúchin

vacuum [vækˈjuːm] *n* (empty space) 真空 shiňkū

vacuum cleaner *n* (真空) 掃除機 (shiňkū)sōjikì

vacuum-packed [vækˈjuːmpækt'] *adj* 真空パックの shiňkūpakkù no

vagabond [vægˈəbɑːnd] *n* 浮浪者 furōshà, ルンペン ruňpen

vagina [vədʒaiˈnə] *n* ちつ chitsú

vagrant [veiˈgrənt] *n* 浮浪者 furōshà, ルンペン ruňpen

vague [veig] *adj* (blurred: memory, outline) ぼんやりとした boñ-yarì to shita; (uncertain: look, idea, instructions) 漠然とした bakúzen to shita; (person: not precise) 不正確な fuseìkaku na; (: evasive) 煮え切らない nièkiranài

vaguely [veig'li:] *adv* (not clearly) ぼんやりとして boñ-yarì to shite; (without certainty) 漠然と bakúzen to, 不正確に fuseìkaku ni; (evasively) あいまいに aìmai ni

vain [vein] *adj* (conceited) うぬぼれた unúboreta; (useless: attempt, action) 無駄な mudá na

in vain 何のかいもなく nañ no kaí mo nakù

valentine [væl'əntain] *n* (*also:* **valentine card**) バレンタインカード baréntaiñkàdo; (person) バレンタインデーの恋人 baréntaiñdè no koìbito

valet [vælei'] *n* 召使い meshítsukài

valiant [væl'jənt] *adj* (attempt, effort) 勇敢な yūkan na

valid [væl'id] *adj* (ticket, document) 有効な yūkō na; (argument, reason) 妥当な datō na

validity [vəlid'iti:] *n* (of ticket, document) 有効性 yūkōseì; (of argument, reason) 妥当性 datōseì

valley [væl'i:] *n* 谷(間) taní(ma)

valor [væl'ə:r] (*BRIT* **valour**) *n* 勇ましさ isámashisà

valuable [væl'ju:əbəl] *adj* (jewel etc) 高価な kōka na; (time, help, advice) 貴重な kichō na

valuables [væl'ju:əbəlz] *npl* (jewellery etc) 貴重品 kichōhin

valuation [vælju:ei'ʃən] *n* (worth: of house etc) 価値 kachì; (judgment of quality) 評価 hyōka

value [væl'ju:] *n* (financial worth) 価値 kachì, 価格 kakáku; (importance, usefulness) 価値 kachì

◆*vt* (fix price or worth of) ...に値を付ける ...ni ne wő tsukérù; (appreciate) 大切にする taísetsu ni suru, 重宝する chōhō suru

values [væl'ju:z] *npl* (principles, beliefs)

価値観 kachíkañ

value added tax [-æd'id-] (*BRIT*) *n* 付加価値税 fukákachizèi

valued [væl'ju:d] *adj* (appreciated: customer, advice) 大切な taísetsu na

valve [vælv] *n* 弁 beñ, バルブ barúbu

vampire [væm'paiə:r] *n* 吸血鬼 kyúketsùki

van [væn] *n* (AUT) バン bañ

vandal [væn'dəl] *n* 心無い破壊者 kokóronaì hakáisha

vandalism [væn'dəlizəm] *n* 破壊行動 hakáikōdō

vandalize [væn'dəlaiz] *vt* 破壊する hakái suru

vanguard [væn'gɑ:rd] *n* (*fig*): *in the vanguard of* ...の先端に立って ...no señtan ni tattè

vanilla [vənil'ə] *n* バニラ baníra

vanilla ice cream *n* バニラアイスクリーム baníra aísukurīmu

vanish [væn'iʃ] *vi* (disappear suddenly) 見えなくなる miénàku narù, 消える kiéru

vanity [væn'iti:] *n* (of person: unreasonable pride) 虚栄心 kyoéishiñ

vantage point [væn'tidʒ-] *n* (lookout place) 観察点 kañsatsuten; (viewpoint) 有利な立場 yūri na tachíba

vapor [vei'pə:r] (*BRIT* **vapour**) *n* (gas) 気体 kitái; (mist, steam) 蒸気 jōki

variable [ve:r'i:əbəl] *adj* (likely to change: mood, quality, weather) 変りやすい kawáriyasuì; (able to be changed: temperature, height, speed) 調節できる chōsetsu dekírù

variance [ve:r'i:əns] *n*: *to be at variance (with)* (people) (...と) 仲たがいしている (...to) nakátagài shité iru; (facts) (...と) 矛盾している (...to) mujúñ shité iru

variation [ve:ri:ei'ʃən] *n* (change in level, amount, quantity) 変化 heñka, 変動 heñdō; (different form: of plot, musical theme etc) 変形 heñkei

varicose [vær'əkous] *adj*: *varicose veins* 拡張蛇行静脈 kakúchōdakòjōmyaku

varied [ver'i:d] *adj* (diverse: opinions, reasons) 様々な sámàzama na; (full of changes: career) 多彩な tasái na

variety [vərai'əti:] *n* (degree of choice, diversity) 変化 heñka, バラエティー baráetī; (varied collection, quantity) 様々な物 sámàzama na mono; (type) 種類 shurûi

variety show *n* バラエティーショー baráetīshō

various [ver'i:əs] *adj* 色々な iróiro na

varnish [va:r'niʃ] *n* (product applied to surface) ニス nisù
◆*vt* (apply varnish to: wood, piece of furniture etc) ...にニスを塗る ...ni nisù wo nuru; (: nails) ...にマニキュアをする ...ni maníkyua wo suru
nail varnish マニキュア maníkyua

vary [ver'i:] *vt* (make changes to: routine, diet) 変える kaéru
◆*vi* (be different: sizes, colors) ...が色々ある ...ga iróiro aru; (become different): *to vary with* (weather, season etc) ...によって変る ...ni yótte kawáru

vase [veis] *n* 花瓶 kabín

Vaseline [væs'əli:n]® *n* ワセリン wasérin

vast [væst] *adj* (wide: area, knowledge) 広い hiróì; (enormous: expense etc) ばく大な bakúdai na

VAT [væt] *n abbr* = **value added tax**

vat [væt] *n* 大おけ ōokè

Vatican [væt'ikən] *n*: *the Vatican* (palace) バチカン宮殿 bachíkan kyûdeñ; (authority) ローマ法王庁 rôma hōōchō

vault [vɔ:lt] *n* (of roof) 丸天井 marûteñjō; (tomb) 地下納骨堂 chikánôkotsudô; (in bank) 金庫室 kiñkoshitsú
◆*vt* (*also*: **vault over**) 飛越える tobíkoerù

vaunted [vɔ:n'tid] *adj*: *much-vaunted* ご自慢の go-jíman no

VCR [vi:si:ɑ:r'] *n abbr* = **video cassette recorder**

VD [vi:di:'] *n abbr* = **venereal disease**

VDU [vi:di:ju:'] *n abbr* = **visual display unit**

veal [vi:l] *n* 子ウシ肉 koúshiniku

veer [vi:r] *vi* (vehicle, wind) 急に向きを変える kyû ni mukî wo kaéru

vegetable [vedʒ'təbəl] *n* (BOT) 植物 shokúbutsu; (edible plant) 野菜 yasái
◆*adj* (oil etc) 植物性の shokúbutsusei no

vegetarian [vedʒiter:r'i:ən] *n* 菜食主義者 saíshokushugishà
◆*adj* (diet etc) 菜食主義の saíshokushugi no

vegetate [vedʒ'iteit] *vi* 無為に暮す muî ni kurású

vegetation [vedʒiteiʃ'ən] *n* (plants) 植物 shokúbutsu ◇総称 sôshō

vehement [vi:'əmənt] *adj* (strong: attack, passions, denial) 猛烈な môretsu na

vehicle [vi:'ikəl] *n* (machine) 車 kurúma; (*fig*: means of expressing) 手段 shudàn

veil [veil] *n* ベール bēru

veiled [veild] *adj* (*fig*: threat) 隠された kakúsarèta

vein [vein] *n* (ANAT) 静脈 jômyaku; (of ore etc) 脈 myakú
vein of a leaf 葉脈 yômyaku

velocity [vəlɑ:s'iti:] *n* 速度 sokúdo

velvet [vel'vit] *n* ビロード birôdo, ベルベット berúbetto
◆*adj* ビロードの birôdo no, ベルベットの berúbettò no

vendetta [vendet'ə] *n* 復しゅう fukúshū

vending machine [ven'diŋ-] *n* 自動販売機 jidôhanbaiki

vendor [ven'də:r] *n* (of house, land) 売手 urîte; (of cigarettes, beer etc) 売子 urîko

veneer [vəni:r'] *n* (on furniture) 化粧張り keshôbari; (*fig*: of person, place) 虚飾 kyoshôku

venereal [vəni:r'i:əl] *adj*: *venereal disease* 性病 seîbyō

Venetian blind [vəni:'ʃən-] *n* ベネシャンブラインド benéshanburaindô

Venezuela [venizwei'lə] *n* ベネズエラ benézuèra

vengeance [ven'dʒəns] *n* (revenge) 復しゅう fukúshū
with a vengeance (*fig*: to a greater extent) 驚く程 odôròku hodo

venison [ven'isən] *n* シカ肉 shikániku

venom [ven'əm] *n* (of snake, insect) 毒 dokú; (bitterness, anger) 悪意 ákui

venomous [ven'əməs] *adj* (poisonous: snake, insect) 毒... dokú...; (full of bitterness: look, stare) 敵意に満ちた tekíi ni michíta

vent [vent] *n* (*also*: **air vent**) 通気孔 tsúkikō; (in jacket) ベンツ beñtsu
♦*vt* (*fig*: feelings, anger) ぶちまける buchímakeru

ventilate [ven'təleit] *vt* (room, building) 換気する kañki suru

ventilation [ventəlei'ʃən] *n* 換気 kañki

ventilator [ven'təleitə:r] *n* (TECH) 換気装置 kañkisōchi, ベンチレーター beñchirētā; (MED) 人工呼吸器 jiñkōkokyūkì, レスピレタ resúpiretà

ventriloquist [ventril'əkwist] *n* 腹話術師 fukúwajùtsushi

venture [ven'tʃə:r] *n* (risky undertaking) 冒険 bōken
♦*vt* (opinion) おずおず言う ozùozu iú
♦*vi* (dare to go) おずおず行く ozùozu ikú
business venture 投機 tōki

venue [ven'ju:] *n* (place fixed for something) 開催地 kaísaichi

veranda(h) [vəræn'də] *n* ベランダ beránda

verb [və:rb] *n* 動詞 dōshi

verbal [və:r'bəl] *adj* (spoken: skills etc) 言葉の kotóba no; (: translation etc) 口頭の kōtō no; (of a verb) 動詞の dōshi no

verbatim [və:rbei'tim] *adj* 言葉通りの kotóbadòri no
♦*adv* 言葉通りに kotóbadòri ni

verbose [və:rbous'] *adj* (person) 口数の多い kuchíkazu no ōi; (speech, report etc) 冗長な jōchō na

verdict [və:r'dikt] *n* (LAW) 判決 hañketsu; (*fig*: opinion) 判断 hañdan

verge [və:rdʒ] *n* (BRIT: of road) 路肩 rokáta
「*soft verges*」(BRIT: AUT) 路肩軟弱 rokáta nanjaku
to be on the verge of doing something ...する所である ...surú tokoro dè arù

verge on *vt fus* ...同然である ...dōzen de arù

verify [ve:r'əfai] *vt* (confirm, check) 確認する kakúnin suru

veritable [ve:r'itəbəl] *adj* (reinforcer: = real) 全くの mattáku no

vermin [və:r'min] *npl* (animals) 害獣 gaíjū; (fleas, lice etc) 害虫 gaíchū

vermouth [və:rmu:θ'] *n* ベルモット berúmottò

vernacular [və:rnæk'jələ:r] *n* (language) その土地の言葉 sonó tochi no kotóba

versatile [və:r'sətəl] *adj* (person) 多才の tasái no; (substance, machine, tool etc) 使い道の多い tsukáimichi no ōi

verse [və:rs] *n* (poetry) 詩 shi; (one part of a poem: *also* in bible) 節 setsù

versed [və:rst] *adj*: *(well-)versed in* ...に詳しい ...ni kuwáshii

version [və:r'ʒən] *n* (form: of design, production) 型 katá; (: of book, play etc) ...版...bañ; (account: of events, accident etc) 説明 setsúmei

versus [və:r'səs] *prep* ...対... ...tai ...

vertebra [və:r'təbrə] *(pl vertebrae)* *n* せきつい sekítsùi

vertebrae [və:r'təbrei] *npl of* **vertebra**

vertebrate [və:r'təbreit] *n* せきつい動物 sekítsuidōbutsu

vertical [və:r'tikəl] *adj* 垂直の suíchoku no

vertigo [və:r'təgou] *n* めまい memái

verve [və:rv] *n* (vivacity) 気迫 kiháku

very [ve:r'i:] *adv* (+ adjective, adverb) とても totémo, 大変 taíhen, 非常に hijō ni
♦*adj*: *it's the very book he'd told me about* 彼が話していたのは正にその本だ karè ga hanáshite ita no wà masá ni sonó hon dà
the very last 正に最後の masá ni saígo no
at the very least 少なくとも sukunàkutomo
very much 大変 taíhen

vessel [ves'əl] *n* (NAUT) 船 funè; (container) 容器 yōki *see* **blood**

vest [vest] *n* (US: waistcoat) チョッキ chókki; (BRIT) アンダーシャツ añdā shatsù

vested interests [ves'tid-] *npl* 自分の利益 jibún no rièki, 私利 shirì

vestige [ves'tidʒ] *n* 残り nokóri

vet [vet] (*BRIT*) *n abbr* = **veterinary surgeon**
♦*vt* (examine: candidate) 調べる shirábe-rù

veteran [vet'əːrən] *n* (of war) ...戦争で戦った人 ...seńsō de tatákatta hito; (former soldier) 退役軍人 taíekigunjin; (old hand) ベテラン betéran

veterinarian [vetəːrənəːr'iːən] (*US*) *n* 獣医 jūī

veterinary [vet'əːrəneːriː] *adj* (practice, care etc) 獣医の jūī no

veterinary surgeon (*BRIT*) *n* = **veterinarian**

veto [viː'tou] (*pl* **vetoes**) *n* (right to forbid) 拒否権 kyohìken; (act of forbidding) 拒否権の行使 kyohìken no kōshì
♦*vt* ...に拒否権を行使する ...ni kyohìken wo kōshì suru

vex [veks] *vt* (irritate, upset) 怒らせる o-kóraserù

vexed [vekst] *adj* (question) 厄介な yakkài na

via [vai'ə] *prep* (through, by way of) ...を経て ...wo hetè, ...経由 ...keìyu

viable [vai'əbəl] *adj* (project) 実行可能な jikkókanō na; (company) 存立できる soñritsu dekirù

viaduct [vai'ədʌkt] *n* 陸橋 rikkyô

vibrant [vai'brənt] *adj* (lively) 力強い chikárazuyoì; (bright) 生き生きした ikíkì shita; (full of emotion: voice) 感情のこもった kañjō no komótta

vibrate [vai'breit] *vi* (house, machine etc) 振動する shiñdō suru

vibration [vaibrei'ʃən] *n* 振動 shiñdō

vicar [vik'əːr] *n* 主任司祭 shuníñshisaì

vicarage [vik'əːridʒ] *n* 司祭館 shisáikañ

vicarious [vaikeːr'iːəs] *adj* (pleasure) 他人の身になって感じる taníñ no mi ní nattè kañjirù

vice [vais] *n* (moral fault) 悪徳 akútoku; (TECH) 万力 mañriki

vice- [vais] *prefix* 副... fukú...

vice-president [vais'prez'idənt] *n* (*US* POL) 副大統領 fukúdaitōryō

vice squad *n* 風俗犯罪取締班 fūzokuhañzai toríshimarihań

vice versa [vais'vəːr'sə] *adv* 逆の場合も同じ gyakú no baái mo onáji

vicinity [visin'əti] *n* (area): *in the vicinity (of)* (...の) 近所に (...no) kiñjo ni

vicious [viʃ'əs] *adj* (violent: attack, blow) 猛烈な mōretsu na; (cruel: words, look) 残酷な zañkoku na; (horse, dog) どう猛な dōmō na

vicious circle *n* 悪循環 akújuñkan

victim [vik'tim] *n* (person, animal, business) 犠牲者 giséìsha

victimize [vik'təmaiz] *vt* (strikers etc) 食い物にする kuímono nì suru

victor [vik'təːr] *n* 勝利者 shōrìsha

Victorian [viktour'iːən] *adj* ヴィクトリア朝の bikútoriachō no

victorious [viktɔːr'iːəs] *adj* (triumphant: team, shout) 勝ち誇る kachíhokoru

victory [vik'təːriː] *n* 勝利 shōrì

video [vid'iːou] *cpd* ビデオの bideo no
♦*n* (video film) ビデオ bidèo, ビデオ映画 bidèo eìga; (*also:* **video cassette**) ビデオカセット bidéokasettð; (*also:* **video cassette recorder**) ビデオテープレコーダー bidéo tēpùrekōdā, VTR buitíāru

video tape *n* ビデオテープ bidéotēpù

vie [vai] *vi:* *to vie (with someone)(for something)* (...のために)(...と) 競り合う (...no tamé ni) (...to) seríaù

Vienna [viːen'ə] *n* ウィーン uiîñ

Vietnam [viːetnɑːm'] *n* ベトナム betónamu

Vietnamese [viːetnɑːmiːz'] *adj* ベトナムの betónamu no; (LING) ベトナム語の betónamugō no
♦*n inv* (person) ベトナム人 betónamujiñ; (LING) ベトナム語 betónamugō

view [vjuː] *n* (sight) 景色 keshìki; (outlook) 見方 mikáta; (opinion) 意見 ikèn
♦*vt* (look at: *also fig*) 見る mirù
on view (in museum etc) 展示中 teñjichū
in full view (of) (...の) 見ている前で (...no) mitè iru maè de

in view of the weather こういう天気だから kō īu teñki da karà

in view of the fact that ...だという事を考えて ...da tō iu koto wo kañgaetè

in my view 私の考えでは watákushi no kañgae de wà

viewer [vjuː'əːr] *n* (person) 見る人 mirù hito

viewfinder [vjuː'faindəːr] *n* ファインダー faíndā

viewpoint [vjuː'pɔint] *n* (attitude) 考え方 kañgaekata, 見地 keñchi; (place) 観察する地点 kañsatsu suru chitén

vigil [vidʒ'əl] *n* 不寝番 fushíñban

vigilance [vidʒ'ələns] *n* 用心 yōjin

vigilant [vidʒ'ələnt] *adj* 用心する yōjin suru

vigor [vig'əːr] (*BRIT* **vigour**) *n* (energy: of person, campaign) 力強さ chikárazuyosà

vigorous [vig'əːrəs] *adj* (full of energy: person) 元気のいい geñki no iì; (: action, campaign) 強力な kyóryoku na; (: plant) よく茂った yokù shigéttà

vile [vail] *adj* (evil: action) 下劣な gerétsu na; (: language) 下品な gehìn na; (unpleasant: smell, weather, food, temper) ひどい hidoì

villa [vil'ə] *n* (country house) 別荘 bessð; (suburban house) 郊外の屋敷 kōgài no yashikí

village [vil'idʒ] *n* 村 murá

villager [vil'idʒəːr] *n* 村民 sofimíñ

villain [vil'in] *n* (scoundrel) 悪党 akútō; (in novel) 悪役 akúyaku; (*BRIT*: criminal) 犯人 hañnin

vindicate [vin'dikeit] *vt* (person: free from blame) ...の正しさを立証する ...no tadashìsa wo risshṓsuru; (action: justify) ...が正当である事を立証する ...ga seítō de arù koto wo risshṓ suru

vindictive [vindik'tiv] *adj* (person) 執念深い shúnenbukaì; (action etc) 復しゅう心による fukúshūshìn ni yoru

vine [vain] *n* (climbing plant) ツル tsurù; (grapevine) ブドウの木 budó no ki

vinegar [vin'əgəːr] *n* 酢 su

vineyard [vin'jəːrd] *n* ブドウ園 budóen

vintage [vin'tidʒ] *n* (year) ブドウ収穫年 budṓ shūkakuneñ

♦*cpd* (classic: comedy, performance etc) 典型的な teñkeiteki na

vintage car *n* クラシックカー kurashìkku kā

vintage wine *n* 当り年のワイン atáridoshi no waìn

vinyl [vai'nil] *n* ビニール binírù

viola [viːou'lə] *n* (MUS) ビオラ bìora

violate [vai'əleit] *vt* (agreement, peace) 破る yaburù; (graveyard) 汚す kegasù

violation [vaiəlei'ʃən] *n* (of agreement etc) 違反 iháñ

violence [vai'ələns] *n* (brutality) 暴力 bōryòku; (strength) 乱暴 rañbō

violent [vai'ələnt] *adj* (brutal: behavior) 暴力の bōryòku no, 乱暴な rañbō na; (intense: debate, criticism) 猛烈な mōrétsu na

a violent death 変死 heñshi

violet [vai'əlit] *adj* 紫色の murásakiiro no

♦*n* (color) 紫 murasàki; (plant) スミレ sumíre

violin [vaiəlin'] *n* バイオリン baíorin

violinist [vaiəlin'ist] *n* バイオリン奏者 baíorinsōsha, バイオリニスト baíorinisuto

VIP [viːaipiː'] *n abbr* (= *very important person*) 要人 yōjìn, 貴賓 kihìn, ブイアイピー buíaipī, ビップ bíppù

viper [vai'pəːr] *n* クサリヘビ kusárihebì

virgin [vəːr'dʒin] *n* (person) 処女 shojð, バージン bājìn

♦*adj* (snow, forest etc) 処女... shojð...

virginity [vəːrdʒin'əti:] *n* (of person) 処女 shojð

Virgo [vəːr'gou] *n* (sign) 乙女座 otomèza

virile [vir'əl] *adj* 男らしい otókorashiì

virility [vəril'əti:] *n* (sexual power) 性的能力 seítekinōryoku; (*fig*: masculine qualities) 男らしさ otókorashisà

virtually [vəːr'tʃuːəli:] *adv* (almost) 事実上 jijítsujō

virtue [vəːr'tʃuː] *n* (moral correctness) 徳 tokú, 徳行 tokkṓ; (good quality) 美徳 bitóku; (advantage) 利点 ritén, 長所 chōshŏ

by virtue of ...である事で ... de arù ko-tŏ de

virtuosi [vəːrtʃuːou'ziː] npl of **virtuoso**

virtuoso [vəːrtʃuːou'zou] (pl **virtuosos** or **virtuosi**) n 名人 meíjin

virtuous [vəːr'tʃuːəs] adj (displaying virtue) 良心的な ryōshínteki na, 高潔な kōkétsu na, 敬けんな keíken na

virulent [vir'jələnt] adj (disease) 悪性の akúsei no 危険な kiken na; (actions, feelings) 憎悪に満ちた zōō ni michíta

virus [vai'rəs] n ウイルス uírusu

visa [viː'zə] n 査証 sashŏ, ビザ bízà

vis-à-vis [viːzaːviː'] prep (compared to) ...と比べて ...to kurábete; (in regard to) ...に関して ...ni kań shite

viscose [vis'kouz] n ビスコース人絹 bísúkōsùjìnkeñ, ビスコースレーヨン bisúkō-sùrēyòn

viscous [vis'kəs] adj ねばねばした nebàneba shita

visibility [vizəbil'əti:] n 視界 shikái

visible [viz'əbəl] adj (able to be seen or recognized: also fig) 目に見える me nī mierù

vision [viʒ'ən] n (sight: ability) 視力 shiryòku; (: sense) 視覚 shikáku; (foresight) ビジョン bijòn; (in dream) 幻影 geń-ei

visit [viz'it] n (to person, place) 訪問 hŏmon
◆vt (person: US also: visit with) 訪問する hŏmon suru, 訪ねる tazúnerù, ...の所へ遊びに行く ...no tokóro e asóbi ni ikú; (place) 訪問する hŏmon suru, 訪ねる tazúneru

visiting hours [viz'itiŋ-] npl (in hospital etc) 面会時間 meñkaijikan

visitor [viz'itəːr] n (person visiting, invited) 客 kyakú; (tourist) 観光客 kañkōkyàku

visor [vai'zəːr] n (of helmet etc) 面 meñ; (of cap etc) ひさし hisáshi; (AUT: also: **sun visor**) 日よけ hiyóke

vista [vis'tə] n (view) 景色 keshìki

visual [viʒ'uːəl] adj (arts etc) 視覚の shikáku no

visual aid n 視覚教材 shikákukyōzai

visual display unit n モニター monítā, ディスプレー disúpurè

visualize [viʒ'uːəlaiz] vt (picture, imagine) 想像する sŏzō suru

vital [vait'əl] adj (essential, important, crucial) 重要な jūyŏ na; (full of life: person) 活発な kappátsu na; (necessary for life: organ) 生命に必要な seímei ni hitsúyō na

vitality [vaitæl'iti:] n (liveliness) 元気geñki

vitally [vai'təliː] adv: **vitally important** 極めて重要な kiwámète jūyŏ na

vital statistics npl (of population) 人口動態統計 jiñkōdōtaitōkei; (inf: woman's measurements) スリーサイズ surísaizù

vitamin [vai'təmin] n ビタミン bitámin

vivacious [vivei'ʃəs] adj にぎやかな nigiyàka na

vivid [viv'id] adj (clear: description, memory) 鮮明な seímei na; (bright: color, light) 鮮やかな azáyàka na; (imagination) はつらつとした hatsúratsu to shitá

vividly [viv'idliː] adv (describe) 目に見える様に me nī mierù yō ni; (remember) はっきりと hakkírì to

vivisection [vivisek'ʃən] n 生体解剖 seítaikaibō

V-neck [viː'nek] n (also: **V-neck jumper/pullover**) Vネックセーター buínekkusètā

vocabulary [voukæb'jələːriː] n (words known) 語い goì

vocal [vou'kəl] adj (of the voice) 声の koè no; (articulate) はっきり物を言う hakkírì monò wo iú

vocal c(h)ords npl 声帯 seítai

vocation [voukei'ʃən] n (calling) 使命感 shiméikan; (chosen career) 職業 shokugyŏ

vocational [voukei'ʃənəl] adj (training etc) 職業の shokugyŏ no

vociferous [vousif'əːrəs] adj (protesters, demands) やかましい yakámashii, しつこい shitsúkoì

vodka [vɑd'kə] n ウォッカ uókkà

vogue [voug] n 流行 ryūkŏ

の hōshí no

voice [vɔis] n (of person) 声 koé
♦*vt* (opinion) 表明する hyōmei suru

void [vɔid] n (emptiness) 空虚 kūkyo;
(hole) 穴 aná, 空間 kūkan
♦*adj* (invalid) 無効の mukō no; (empty):
void of ...が全くない ...ga mattáku naí

volatile [vɑ:'lətəl] adj (liable to change:
situation) 不安定な fuántei na; (: person)
気まぐれな kimágure na; (: liquid) 揮発
性の kihátsusei no

volcanic [vɑ:lkæn'ik] adj (eruption) 火山
の kazán no; (rock etc) 火山性の kazán-
sei no

volcano [vɑ:lkei'nou] (pl **volcanoes**) n 火
山 kazán

volition [vouli'ʃən] n: **of one's own**
volition 自発的に jihátsuteki ni, 自由意
志で jiyúishí de

volley [vɑ:l'i:] n (of stones etc) 一斉に投
げられる ... isséi ni nagérareru ...; (of
questions etc) 連発 reñpatsu; (TENNIS
etc) ボレー boré
a volley of gunfire 一斉射撃 isséishagèki

volleyball [vɑ:l'i:bɔ:l] n バレーボール ba-
rébōru

volt [voult] n ボルト borúto

voltage [voul'tidʒ] n 電圧 deñ-atsu

voluble [vɑ:l'jəbəl] adj (person) 口達者な
kuchídasshà na; (speech etc) 流ちょうな
ryūchō na

volume [vɑ:l'ju:m] n (space) 容積 yōsèki;
(amount) 容量 yōryō; (book) 本 hoñ;
(sound level) 音量 oñryō, ボリューム bo-
ryūmu
Volume 2 第2巻 daínikan

voluminous [vəlu:'minəs] adj (clothes)
だぶだぶの dabúdabu no; (correspondence, notes) 大量の taíryo no, 多数のta-
sù no

voluntarily [vɑ:lənteːr'ili:] adv (willingly) 自発的に jihátsuteki ni, 自由意志でji-
yúishi de

voluntary [vɑ:l'ənteːri:] adj (willing,
done willingly: exile, redundancy) 自発
的な jihátsuteki na, 自由意志による jiyú-
ishi ni yoru; (unpaid: work, worker) 奉仕

volunteer [vɑ:ləntiːr'] n (unpaid helper)
奉仕者 hōshísha, ボランティア boráñtia;
(to army etc) 志願者 shigáñsha
♦*vt* (information) 自発的に言う jihátsuteki ni iú, 提供する teíkyo suru
♦*vi* (for army etc) ...への入隊を志願する
...e no nyūtai wo shigán suru
to volunteer to do ...しようと申出る
...shiyōto mōshíderu

voluptuous [vəlʌp'tʃuːəs] adj (movement, body, feeling) 官能的な kañnōteki
na, 色っぽい iróppoi

vomit [vɑ:m'it] n 吐いた物 haíta monó,
反吐 hedó
♦*vt* 吐く hakù
♦*vi* 吐く haku

vote [vout] n (method of choosing) 決議
hyōketsu; (indication of choice, opinion)
投票 tōhyō; (votes cast) 投票数 tōhyōsū;
(also: **right to vote**) 投票権 tōhyōkèn
♦*vt* (elect): *to be voted chairman etc*
座長に選出される zachō ni señshutsu saréru; (propose): *to vote that* ...という事
を提案する ...to iú koto wo teían suru
♦*vi* (in election etc) 投票する tōhyō suru
vote of thanks 感謝決議 kañshaketsu-
gì

voter [vou'təːr] n (person voting) 投票者
tōhyōshà; (person with right to vote) 有
権者 yūkeñsha

voting [vou'tiŋ] n 投票 tōhyō

vouch for [vautʃ-] *vt fus* (person, quality etc) 保証する hoshō suru

voucher [vau'tʃəːr] n (for meal: also:
luncheon voucher) 食券 shokkén; (with
petrol, cigarettes etc) クーポン kūpon;
(also: **gift voucher**) ギフト券 gifútokeñ

vow [vau] n 誓い chikái
♦*vt: to vow to do/that* ...する事 (...だと
いう事) を誓う ...surú koto (...da to iú
koto) wo chikáu

vowel [vau'əl] n 母音 boín

voyage [vɔi'idʒ] n (journey: by ship,
spacecraft) 旅 tabí, 旅行 ryokō

V-sign [vi:'sain] (*BRIT*) n V サイン buì-
sain ◇手の甲を相手に向けると軽べつの
サイン；手のひらを向けると勝利のサイ

ン té no kō wo aíte ni mukéru to keíbetsu no saín; te nó hirá wo mukéru to shōrí no saín

vulgar [vʌl'gər] *adj* (rude: remarks, gestures, graffiti) 下品な gehín na; (in bad taste: decor, ostentation) 野暮な yabô na

vulgarity [vʌlgær'iti:] *n* (rudeness) 下品な言葉 gehín na kotóba; (ostentation) 野暮ったい事 yabóttaì kotó

vulnerable [vʌl'nə:rəbəl] *adj* (person, position) やられやすい yaráreyasuǐ, 無防備な mubôbi na

vulture [vʌl'tʃə:r] *n* ハゲタカ hagétaka

W

wad [wɑːd] *n* (of cotton wool, paper) 塊 katámari; (of banknotes etc) 束 tabà

waddle [wɑːd'əl] *vi* (duck, baby) よちよち歩く yochíyochi arúkù; (fat person) よたよた歩く yotáyota arúkù

wade [weid] *vi*: **to wade through** (water) ...の中を歩いて通る ...no nakâ wo arúîte tōrù; (fig: a book) 苦労して読む kurồ shité yomù

wafer [wei'fə:r] *n* (biscuit) ウエハース uèhàsu

waffle [wɑː'f'əl] *n* (CULIN) ワッフル waffùru; (empty talk) 下らない話 kudáranai hanáshi
♦*vi* (in speech, writing) 下らない話をする kudáranai hanáshi wo suru

waft [wæft] *vt* (sound, scent) 漂わせる tadayowaseru
♦*vi* (sound, scent) 漂う tadáyou

wag [wæg] *vt* (tail, finger) 振る furù
♦*vi*: **the dog's tail was wagging** イヌはしっぽを振っていた inú wà shippô wo futté ità

wage [weidʒ] *n* (*also*: **wages**) 賃金 chíngin, 給料 kyúryō
♦*vt*: **to wage war** 戦争をする sensô wo suru

wage earner [-əːr'nəːr] *n* 賃金労働者 chíngínrōdōsha

wage packet *n* 給料袋 kyúryōbukùro

wager [wei'dʒəːr] *n* かけ kaké

waggle [wæg'əl] *vt* (hips) 振る furu; (eyebrows etc) ぴくぴくさせる pikùpiku saséru

wag(g)on [wæg'ən] *n* (*also*: **horse-drawn wag(g)on**) 荷馬車 nibáshà; (*BRIT*: RAIL) 貨車 kashá

wail [weil] *n* (of person) 泣き声 nakígoè; (of siren etc) うなり unári
♦*vi* (person) 泣き声をあげる nakígoè wo agéru; (siren) うなる unarù

waist [weist] *n* (ANAT, *also* of clothing) ウエスト uésùto

waistcoat [weist'kout] (*BRIT*) *n* チョッキ chókki, ベスト besùto

waistline [weist'lain] *n* (of body) 胴回り dômawàri, ウエスト uésùto; (of garment) ウエストライン uésùtoraìn

wait [weit] *n* (interval) 待ち時間 machí jikan
♦*vi* 待つ matsù
to lie in wait for ...を待伏せする ...wo machíbuse suru
I can't wait to (fig) 早く...したい hayáku ...shitái
to wait for someone/something ...を待つ ...wo matsu

wait behind *vi* 居残って待つ inokotte matsù

waiter [wei'tə:r] *n* (in restaurant etc) 給仕 kyūjī, ウエーター uétā, ボーイ bôi

waiting [wei'tiŋ] *n*: 「**no waiting**」(*BRIT*: AUT) 停車禁止 teísha kínshi

waiting list *n* 順番待ちの名簿 junbanmachi no meíbo

waiting room *n* (in surgery, railway station) 待合室 machíaìshitsu

wait on *vt fus* (people in restaurant) ...に給仕する ...ni kyūjī suru

waitress [wei'tris] *n* ウエートレス uétòresu

waive [weiv] *vt* (rule) 適用するのをやめる tekíyō suru no wð yaméru; (rights etc) 放棄する hōkî suru

wake [weik] (*pt* **woke** *or* **waked**, *pp* **woken** *or* **waked**) *vt* (*also*: **wake up**) 起す okósù
♦*vi* (*also*: **wake up**) 目が覚める me gá samérù

♦n (for dead person) 通夜 tsuyà, tsúya; (NAUT) 航跡 kóseki

waken [wei'kən] vt, vi = **wake**

Wales [weilz] n ウェールズ uéruzu

the Prince of Wales プリンスオブウェールズ puríñsu obu uéruzu

walk [wɔːk] n (hike) ハイキング haíkingu; (shorter) 散歩 sañpo; (gait) 歩調 hochō; (in park, along coast etc) 散歩道 sañpomichì, 遊歩道 yúhodō

♦vi (go on foot) 歩く arúkù; (for pleasure, exercise) 散歩する sañpo suru

♦vt (distance) 歩く arúkù; (dog) 散歩に連れて行く sañpo ni tsuréte ikú

10 minutes' walk from here ここから徒歩で10分の所に kokó karà tohò do juppùn no tokóro ni

people from all walks of life あらゆる身分の人々 aráyurù mibùn no hitóbìto

walker [wɔː'kəːr] n (person) ハイカー haíkā

walkie-talkie [wɔː'kiːtɔː'kiː] n トランシーバー toráñshībā

walking [wɔː'kiŋ] n ハイキング haíkingu

walking shoes npl 散歩靴 sañpogutsu

walking stick n ステッキ sutékkì

walk out vi (audience) 出て行く deté ikú; (workers) ストライキをする sutóraìki wo suru

walkout [wɔːk'aut] n (of workers) ストライキ sutóraìki

walk out on (inf) vt fus (family etc) 見捨てる misúteru

walkover [wɔːk'ouvəːr] (inf) n (competition, exam etc) 朝飯前 asámeshimaè

walkway [wɔːk'wei] n 連絡通路 refirakutsúrō

wall [wɔːl] n (gen) 壁 kabé; (city wall etc) 城壁 jōheki

walled [wɔːld] adj (city) 城壁に囲まれた jōheki ni kakómareta; (garden) 塀をめぐらした heí wo megúrashita

wallet [wɑː'lit] n 札入れ satsúire, 財布 saífu

wallflower [wɔːl'flauəːr] n ニオイアラセイトウ nióiaraseitō

to be a wallflower (fig) だれもダンスの相手になってくれない daré mo dañsu no aíte ni nattè kurénai, 壁の花である kabé no hana de arù

wallop [wɑː'ləp] (inf) vt ぶん殴る buñnaguru

wallow [wɑː'lou] vi (animal: in mud, water) ころげ回る korógemawarù; (person: in sentiment, guilt) ふける fukérù

wallpaper [wɔːl'peipəːr] n 壁紙 kabégami

♦vt (room) ...に壁紙を張る ...ni kabégami wo harú

wally [wei'liː] (BRIT: inf) n ばか bakā

walnut [wɔːl'nʌt] n (nut) クルミ kurúmi; (also: **walnut tree**) クルミの木 kurúmi no ki; (wood) クルミ材 kurúmizaì

walrus [wɔːl'rəs] (pl **walrus** or **walruses**) n セイウチ seíuchi

waltz [wɔːlts] n (dance, MUS) 円舞曲 eñbukyòku, ワルツ warútsu

♦vi (dancers) ワルツを踊る warútsu wo odóru

wan [wɑːn] adj (person, complexion) 青白い aójiroi; (smile) 悲しげな kanáshigenà

wand [wɑːnd] n (also: **magic wand**) 魔法の棒 mahō no bō

wander [wɑːn'dəːr] vi (person) ぶらぶら歩く burábura arúkù; (attention) 散漫になる safiman ni narù; (mind, thoughts: here and there) さまよう samáyoù; (: to specific topic) 漂う tadáyoù

♦vt (the streets, the hills etc) ...をぶらぶら歩く ...wo burùbura arúkù

wane [wein] vi (moon) 欠ける kakérù; (enthusiasm, influence etc) 減る herú

wangle [wæŋ'gəl] (inf) vt うまい具合に獲得する umái guái ni kakútoku suru

want [wɑːnt] vt (wish for) 望む nozómu, ...が欲しい ...ga hoshiì; (need, require) ...が必要である ...ga hitsúyō de arù

♦n: *for want of* ...がないので ...ga naí no de

to want to do ...したい ...shitái

to want someone to do something ...に...してもらいたい ...ni...shité moraitaì

wanted [wɑːnt'id] adj (criminal etc) 指名手配中の shiméitehàichū no 「**wanted**」(in advertisements) 求む motómù

wanting [wɑː'tiŋ] adj: **to be found wanting** 期待を裏切る kitái wo urágirù

wanton [wɑːn'tən] adj (gratuitous) 理由のない riyú no naì; (promiscuous) 浮気な uwáki na

wants [wɑːnts] npl (needs) 必要とする物 hitsúyō to suru monó, ニーズ nīzu

war [wɔːr] n 戦争 sénsō
to make war (on) (also fig) …と戦う …to tatákau

ward [wɔːrd] n (in hospital) 病棟 byőtō; (POL) 区 ku; (LAW: child: also: **ward of court**) 被後見人 hikőkennin

warden [wɔːr'dən] n (of park, game reserve, youth hostel) 管理人 kañrinìn; (of prison etc) 所長 shochő; (BRIT: also: **traffic warden**) 交通監視官 kõtsűkanshikañ

warder [wɔːr'dəːr] n (BRIT) 看守 kañshu

ward off vt (attack, enemy) 食止める kuítomerù; (danger, illness) 防ぐ fuségù

wardrobe [wɔːrd'roub] n (for clothes) 洋服だんす yőfukudañsu; (collection of clothes) 衣装 ishő; (CINEMA, THEATER) 衣装部屋 ishőbeya

warehouse [weːr'haus] n 倉庫 sőkò

wares [weːrz] npl 商品 shőhin, 売物 urímono

warfare [wɔːr'feːr] n 戦争 sénsō

warhead [wɔːr'hed] n 弾頭 dañtō

warily [weːr'iliː] adv 用心深く yőjínbukakù

warlike [wɔːr'laik] adj (nation) 好戦的な kősenteki na; (appearance) 武装した busőshita

warm [wɔːrm] adj (meal, soup, day, clothes etc) 暖かい atátakaì; (thanks) 心からの kokóro kara no; (applause, welcome) 熱烈な netsúretsu na; (person, heart) 優しい yasáshiì, 温情のある oñjō no arù
it's warm (just right) 暖かい atátakaì; (too warm) 暑い atsúì
I'm warm 暑い atsúì
warm water ぬるま湯 murúmayù

warm-hearted [wɔːrm'hɑːr'tid] adj 心の優しい kokóro no yasáshiì

warmly [wɔːrm'liː] adv (applaud, welcome) 熱烈に netsúretsu ni
to dress warmly 厚着する atsúgi suru

warmth [wɔːrmθ] n (heat) 暖かさ atátakasa; (friendliness) 温かみ atátakami

warm up vi (person, room, soup, etc) 暖まる atátamarù; (weather) 暖かくなる atátakaku narù; (athlete) 準備運動をする juñbiundő wo suru, ウォーミングアップをする uőminguappù suru
♦vt (hands etc) 暖める atátamerù; (engine) 暖気運転する dañkiuñten suru

warn [wɔːrn] vt (advise): **to warn someone of/that** …に…があると〔…だと〕警告する …ni …ga arù to 〔…da to〕keíkoku suru
to warn someone not to do …に…しないよう警告する …ni …shináì yō keíkoku suru

warning [wɔːr'niŋ] n 警告 keíkoku

warning light n 警告灯 keíkokutō

warning triangle n (AUT) 停止表示板 teíshihyőjiban

warp [wɔːrp] vi (wood etc) ゆがむ yugámu
♦vt (fig: character) ゆがめる yugámeru

warrant [wɔːr'ənt] n (voucher) 証明書 shőmeìsho; (LAW: for arrest) 逮捕状 taíhojő; (: search warrant) 捜索令状 sősakureijő

warranty [wɔːr'əntiː] n (guarantee) 保証 hoshő

warren [wɔːr'ən] n (also: **rabbit warren**) ウサギ小屋 uságigoya; (fig: of passages, streets) 迷路 meíro

warrior [wɔːr'iːəːr] n 戦士 señshi

Warsaw [wɔːr'sɔː] n ワルシャワ warúshawa

warship [wɔːr'ʃip] n 軍艦 guñkan

wart [wɔːrt] n いぼ ibő

wartime [wɔːr'taim] n: **in wartime** 戦時中 señjichū

wary [weːr'iː] adj 用心深い yőjinbukaì

was [wʌz] pt of **be**

wash [wɔːʃ] vt (gen) 洗う aráu; (clothes etc) 洗濯する señtaku suru

♦vi (person) 手を洗う te wò aráu; (sea etc): *to wash over/against something* ...に打寄せる ...ni uchíyoseru, ...を洗う ...wo aráu

♦n (clothes etc) 洗濯物 señtakumono; (washing program) 洗い aráī; (of ship) 航跡の波 kōseki no namí

to have a wash 手を洗う te wò aráu

to give something a wash ...を洗う ...wo aráu

washable [wɔːʃʻəbəl] *adj* 洗濯できる señtaku dekirù

wash away *vt* (stain) 洗い落す araioto-su; (subj: flood, river etc) 流す nagasu

washbasin [wɔːʃʻbeisin] (*US also:* **wash-bowl**) *n* 洗面器 señmeñki

washcloth [wɔːʃʻklɔːθ] (*US*) *n* (face cloth) フェースタオル fésutaorù

washer [wɔːʃʻəːr] *n* (TECH: metal) 座金 zagáne, ワッシャー wasshá; (machine) 洗濯機 señtakuki

washing [wɔːʃʻiŋ] *n* (dirty, clean) 洗濯物 señtakumono

washing machine *n* 洗濯機 señtakuki

washing powder (*BRIT*) *n* 洗剤 señzai

washing-up [wɔːʃʻiŋʌpʻ] (*BRIT*) *n* (action) 皿洗い saráaraì; (dirty dishes) 汚れた皿 yogóretà sará

washing-up liquid (*BRIT*) *n* 台所用洗剤 daídokoroyō senzai

wash off *vi* 洗い落される aráiotosàreru

wash-out [wɔːʃʻaut] (*inf*) *n* (failed event) 失敗 shippái

washroom [wɔːʃʻruːm] (*US*) *n* お手洗い o-téaraì

wash up *vi* (*US*) 手を洗う te wò aráu; (*BRIT*) 皿洗いをする saráaraì wo suru

wasn't [wʌzʻənt] = **was not**

wasp [wɑːsp] *n* アシナガバチ ashínagabàchi ◇スズメバチなど肉食性のハチの総称 suzúmebàchi nado nikúshokuseì no hachi no sōshō

wastage [weisʻtidʒ] *n* (amount wasted, loss) 浪費 rōhi

natural wastage 自然消耗 shizénshōmō

waste [weist] *n* (act of wasting: life, money, energy, time) 浪費 rōhi; (rubbish)

廃棄物 haíkibutsu; (*also:* **household waste**) ごみ gomí

♦*adj* (material) 廃棄の haíki no; (left over) 残り物の nokórimono no; (land) 荒れた aréta

♦*vt* (time, life, money, energy) 浪費する rōhi suru; (opportunity) 失う ushínau, 逃す nogásù

to lay waste (destroy: area, town) 破壊する hakái suru

waste away *vi* 衰弱する suíjaku suru

waste disposal unit (*BRIT*) *n* ディスポーザー disúpōzā

wasteful [weistʻfəl] *adj* (person) 無駄使いの多い mudázùkai no ōì; (process) 不経済な fukeízai na

waste ground (*BRIT*) *n* 空き地 akíchi

wastepaper basket [weistʻpeipəːr-] *n* くずかご kuzúkàgo

waste pipe *n* 排水管 haísuìkan

wastes [weists] *npl* (area of land) 荒れ野 aréno

watch [wɑːtʃ] *n* (*also:* **wristwatch**) 腕時計 udédokeì; (act of watching) 見張り mihári; (vigilance) 警戒 keíkai; (group of guards: MIL, NAUT) 番兵 bañpei; (NAUT: spell of duty) 当直 tōchoku, ワッチ watchī

♦*vt* (look at: people, objects, TV etc) 見る mírù; (spy on, guard) 見張る mihárù; (be careful of) ...に気を付ける ...ni ki wó tsukerù

♦*vi* (look) 見る mírù; (keep guard) 見張る miháru

watchdog [wɑːtʃʻdɔːg] *n* (dog) 番犬 bañken; (*fig*) 監視者 kañshisha, お目付け役 o-métsukeyaku

watchful [wɑːtʃʻfəl] *adj* 注意深い chúibukaì

watchmaker [wɑːtʃʻmeikəːr] *n* 時計屋 tokéiya

watchman [wɑːtʃʻmən] (*pl* **watchmen**) *see* **night**

watch out *vi* 気を付ける ki wó tsukerù, 注意する chūi suru

watch out! 危ない! abúnai!

watch strap *n* 腕時計のバンド udédokeì no bañdo

water [wɔːˈtər] n (cold) 水 mizú; (hot) (お) 湯 (o)yú

♦vt (plant) ...に 水 を やる ...ni mizú wo yarú

♦vi (eyes) 涙 が 出 る namída ga derù; (mouth) よだれが出る yodáre ga derù

in British waters 英国領海に〔で〕eíkokuryōkai ni〔de〕

water cannon n 放水砲 hósuihō

water closet (*BRIT*) n トイレ toíre

watercolor [wɔːˈtərkʌlər] n (picture) 水彩画 suísaiga

watercress [wɔːˈtərkres] n クレソン kuréson

water down vt (milk etc) 水で 薄 める mizú de usúmeru; (*fig*: story) 和らげる yawáragerù

waterfall [wɔːˈtərfɔːl] n 滝 takí

water heater n 湯沸器 yuwákashikì

watering can [wɔːˈtəriŋ-] n じょうろ jōró

water level n 水位 suíi

water lily n スイレン suíren

waterline [wɔːˈtərlain] n (NAUT) 喫水線 kissúisen

waterlogged [wɔːˈtərlɔːgd] adj (ground) 水浸しの mizúbitashi no

water main n 水道本管 suídōhonkaǹ

watermelon [wɔːˈtərmelən] n スイカ suíka

waterproof [wɔːˈtərpruːf] adj (trousers, jacket etc) 防水の bósui no

watershed [wɔːˈtərʃed] n (GEO: natural boundary) 分水界 buńsuikaì; (: high ridge) 分水嶺 buńsuìrei; (*fig*) 分岐点 buńkitèn

water-skiing [wɔːˈtərskiːiŋ] n 水上スキー suíjōsukī

watertight [wɔːˈtərtait] adj (seal) 水密の suímitsu no

waterway [wɔːˈtərwei] n 水路 suíro

waterworks [wɔːˈtərwərks] n (building) 浄水場 jōsuijō

watery [wɔːˈtəriː] adj (coffee) 水っぽい mizúppoì; (eyes) 涙ぐんだ namídagundà

watt [wɑːt] n ワット wattò

wave [weiv] n (of hand) 一振り hitófuri; (on water) 波 namí; (RADIO) 電波 deǹpæ; (in hair) ウェーブ uébù; (*fig*: surge) 高まり takámarì, 急増 kyūzō

♦vi (signal) 手 を 振る te wò furù; (branches, grass) 揺れる yuréru; (flag) なびく nabíkù

♦vt (hand, flag, handkerchief) 振る furù; (gun, stick) 振り回す furímawasù

wavelength [weivˈleŋkθ] n (RADIO) 波長 hachō

on the same wavelength (*fig*) 気が合って ki gà attè

waver [weiˈvər] vi (voice) 震 え る furúeru; (love) 揺らぐ yurágu; (person) 動揺する dóyō suru

his gaze did not waver 彼 は 目 を 反らさなかった kárè wa mé wò sorásanakattà

wavy [weiˈviː] adj (line) くねくねした kunékune shita; (hair) ウェーブのある uébù no aru

wax [wæks] n (polish, for skis) ワックス wakkùsu; (*also*: **earwax**) 耳 あ か mimífakà

♦vt (floor, car, skis) ...にワックスを掛ける ...ni wakkùsu wo kakérù

♦vi (moon) 満ちる michírù

waxworks [wæksˈwərks] npl (models) ろう 人形 rōníngyō

♦n (place) ろう人形館 rōníngyōkan

way [wei] n (route) ...へ 行 く 道 ...e ikú michí; (path) 道 michí; (access) 出 入 口 deíriguchi; (distance) 距 離 kyórì; (direction) 方向 hókō; (manner, method) 方法 hóhō; (habit) 習慣 shūkan

which way? - this way どちらへ ? - こちらへ dochìra é ? - kochíra e

on the way (en route) 途中で tochū de

to be on one's way 今向かっている imá mukátte irù, 今途中である imá tochū de arù

to be in the way (*also fig*) 邪魔である jamá de arù

to go out of one's way to do something わざわざ...する wazàwasa ...suru

under way (project etc) 進行中で shińkōchū de

to lose one's way 道に迷う michí ni mayóù

in a way ある意味では arù imì de wa

in some ways ある面では arù men de wa

no way! (*inf*) 絶対に駄目だ zettái ni damé dà

by the way ... ところで tokóro dè

「*way in*」(*BRIT*) 入口 iríguchi

「*way out*」(*BRIT*) 出口 degùchi

the way back 帰路 kírò

「*give way*」(*BRIT*: *AUT*) 進路譲れ shìnro yuzúre

waylay [weilei'] (*pt, pp* **waylaid**) *vt* 待伏 せする machíbuse suru

wayward [wei'wəːrd] *adj* (behavior, child) わがままな wagamáma na

W.C. [dʌb'əlju:si:'] (*BRIT*) *n* トイレ toíre

we [wi:] *pl pron* 私たちは〔が〕 watákushitàchi wa〔ga〕

weak [wi:k] *adj* (*gen*) 弱い yowáì; (dollar, pound) 安い yasúì; (excuse) 下手な hetá nà; (argument) 説得力のない settókuryoku no naì; (tea) 薄い usúi

weaken [wi:'kən] *vi* (person, resolve) 弱る yowárù; (health) 衰える otóroerù; (influence, power) 劣る otórù

♦*vt* (person, government) 弱くする yowákù suru

weakling [wi:k'liŋ] *n* (physically) 虚弱児 kyojákuji; (morally) 骨無し honénashi

weakness [wi:k'nis] *n* (frailty) 弱さ yowàsa; (fault) 弱点 jakúteǹ

to have a weakness for ... ...に目がない ...ni me gà naì

wealth [welθ] *n* (money, resources) 富 tomì, 財産 zaísan; (of details, knowledge etc) 豊富さ hőfu_na

wealthy [wel'θi:] *adj* (person, family, country) 裕福な yūfùku na

wean [wi:n] *vt* (baby) 離乳させる rinyū saséru

weapon [wep'ən] *n* 武器 bukì

wear [we:r] *n* (use) 使用 shiyő; (damage: through use) 消耗 shőmō; (clothing): *sportswear* スポーツウェア supőtsùuea

♦*vb* (*pt* **wore**, *pp* **worn**)

♦*vt* (shirt, blouse, dress etc) 着る kirú; (hat etc) かぶる kabúrù; (shoes, pants, skirt etc) はく hakú; (gloves **etc**) はめる

haméru; (make-up) つける tsukérù; (damage: through use) 使い古す tsukáifurusù

♦*vi* (last) 使用に耐える shiyő ni taérù; (rub through etc: carpet, shoes, jeans) すり減る suríheru

babywear 幼児ウェア yōjìuea

evening wear イブニングウェア ibúningu ueà

wear and tear *n* 消耗 shőmō

wear away *vt* すり減らす suríherasu

♦*vi* (inscription etc) すり減って消える suríhette kíeru

wear down *vt* (heels) すり減らす suríherasu; (person, strength) 弱くする yowákù suru, 弱らせる yowáraserù

wear off *vi* (pain etc) なくなる nakúnaru

wear out *vt* (shoes, clothing) 使い古す tsukáifurusù; (person) すっかり疲れさせる sukkárì tsukáresaséru; (strength) 尽くす nakúsu

weary [wi:r'i:] *adj* (tired) 疲れ果てた tsukárehatetà; (dispirited) がっかりした gakkárì shita

♦*vi*: *to weary of ...*に飽きる ...ni akírù

weasel [wi:'zəl] *n* イタチ itáchi

weather [weð'əːr] *n* 天気 teñki, 天候 teñkō

♦*vt* (storm, crisis) 乗切る noríkirù

under the weather (*fig*: ill) 気分が悪い kíbun ga warúì

weather-beaten [weð'əːrbiːtən] *adj* (face, skin, building, stone) 風雪に鍛えられた fúsetsu ni kitáeraretà

weathercock [weð'əːrkɑ:k] *n* 風見鶏 kazámidòri

weather forecast *n* 天気予報 teñkiyohō

weatherman [weð'əːrmæn] (*pl* **weathermen**) *n* 天気予報係 teñkiyohōgakarì

weather vane [-vein] *n* = **weathercock**

weave [wi:v] (*pt* **wove**, *pp* **woven**) *vt* (cloth) 織る orù; (basket) 編む amù

weaver [wi:'vəːr] *n* 機織職人 hatáorishokunin

weaving [wi:'viŋ] *n* (craft) 機織 hatáori

web [web] *n* (*also:* **spiderweb**) クモの巣 kumó no su; (on duck's foot) 水かき mizúkaki; (network, *also fig*) 網 amí

we'd [wi:d] = **we had; we would**

wed [wed] (*pt, pp* **wedded**) *vt* (marry) ...と結婚する ...to kekkón suru
♦*vi* 結婚する kekkón suru

wedding [wed'iŋ] *n* 結婚式 kekkónshiki
silver/golden wedding (anniversary) 銀〔金〕婚式 giñ〔kiñ〕kóñshiki

wedding day *n* (day of the wedding) 結婚の日 kekkón no hi; (*US*: anniversary) 結婚記念日 kekkón kineñbi

wedding dress *n* 花嫁衣装 hanáyome ishō, ウエディングドレス uédingudoŕèsu

wedding present *n* 結婚祝い kekkón iwaí

wedding ring *n* 結婚指輪 kekkón yubíwa

wedge [wedʒ] *n* (of wood etc) くさび kusábi; (of cake) 一切れ hitókirè
♦*vt* (jam with a wedge) くさびで留める kusábi dè toméru; (pack tightly: of people, animals) 押込む oshíkomù

Wednesday [wenz'dei] *n* 水曜日 suíyōbì

wee [wi:] (*SCOTTISH*) *adj* (little) 小さい chiísaí

weed [wi:d] *n* 雑草 zassō
♦*vt* (garden) ...の草むしりをする ...no kusámushìri wo suru

weedkiller [wi:d'kilər] *n* 除草剤 josózai

weedy [wi:'di:] *adj* (man) 柔そうな yawásō na

week [wi:k] *n* 週間 shūkan
a week today/on Friday 来週の今日〔金曜日〕raíshū no kyō〔kiñ-yōbì〕

weekday [wi:k'dei] *n* (*gen*, COMM) 平日 heíjitsu, ウイークデー uíkùdē

weekend [wi:k'end] *n* 週末 shūmátsu, ウイークエンド uíkùendo

weekly [wi:k'li:] *adv* (deliver etc) 毎週 maíshū
♦*adj* (newspaper) 週刊の shūkan no; (payment) 週払いの shūbarai no; (visit etc) 毎週の maishū no
♦*n* (magazine) 週刊誌 shūkanshi; (newspaper) 週刊新聞 shūkanshínbun

weep [wi:p] (*pt, pp* **wept**) *vi* (person) 泣く naku

weeping willow [wi:'piŋ-] *n* シダレヤナギ shidáreyanàgi

weigh [wei] *vt* ...の重さを計る ...no omósa wo hakáru
♦*vi* ...の重さは...である ...no omósa wa ...de arù
to weigh anchor いかりを揚げる ikári wo agéru

weigh down *vt* (person, pack animal etc) ...の重さで動きが遅くなる ...no omósa de ugóki ga osóku narù; (*fig*: with worry): *to be weighed down* ...で沈み込む ...de shizúmikomu

weight [weit] *n* (metal object) 重り omóri; (heaviness) 重さ omósa
to lose/put on weight 体重が減る〔増える〕taíjū ga herú〔fueru〕

weighting [wei'tiŋ] (*BRIT*) *n* (allowance) 地域手当 chíìkiteatè

weightlifter [weit'liftər] *n* 重量挙げ選手 jūryōage señshu

weighty [wei'ti:] *adj* (heavy) 重い omói; (important: matters) 重大な jūdai na

weigh up *vt* (person, offer, risk) 評価する hyōka suru

weir [wi:r] *n* せき sekí

weird [wi:rd] *adj* 奇妙な kimyō na

welcome [wel'kəm] *adj* (visitor, suggestion, change) 歓迎すべき kangeisubeki; (news) うれしい ureshii
♦*n* 歓迎 kañgei
♦*vt* (visitor, delegation, suggestion, change) 歓迎する kañgei suru; (be glad of: news) うれしく思う uréshìku omóù
thank you - you're welcome! どうも有難う - どういたしまして dōmò arígàtò - dō.itáshimashitè

weld [weld] *n* 溶接 yōsetsu
♦*vt* 溶接する yōsetsu suru

welfare [wel'fe:r] *n* (well-being) 幸福 kōfuku, 福祉 fukúshī; (social aid) 生活保護 seíkatsuhogò

welfare state *n* 福祉国家 fukúshikokkà

welfare work *n* 福祉事業 fukúshijigyò

well [wel] *n* (for water) 井戸 idò; (*also:* oil well) 油井 yuséi

♦*adv* (to a high standard, thoroughly: *also* for emphasis with adv, adj or prep phrase) よく yokù

♦*adj*: **to be well** (person: in good health) 元気である geńkì de árù

♦*excl* そう、ねえ sồ, nē

as well (in addition) も mo

as well as (in addition to) ...の外に ...no hoká ni

well done! よくやった yokù yattá

get well soon! 早く治ります様に hayáku naõrimasu yō nĩ, お大事に o-dáiji ni

to do well (person) 順調である juńchō de arù; (business) 繁盛する hańjō suru

we'll [wi:l] = **we will; we shall**

well-behaved [wel'bihcivd'] *adj* (child, dog) 行儀の良い gyồgi no yoí

well-being [wel'bi:'iŋ] *n* 幸福 kồfuku, 福祉 fukúshi

well-built [wel'bilt'] *adj* (person) 体格の良い taīkaku no yoí

well-deserved [wel'dizə:rvd'] *adj* (success, prize) 努力相応の doryòkusōô no

well-dressed [wel'drest'] *adj* 身なりの良い minári no yoí

well-heeled [wel'hi:ld'] (*inf*) *adj* (wealthy) 金持の kanémochì no

wellingtons [wel'iŋtənz] *npl* (*also*: **wellington boots**) ゴム長靴 gomúnagagutsu

well-known [wel'noun'] *adj* (famous: person, place) 有名な yūmei na

well-mannered [wel'mæn'ə:rd] *adj* 礼儀正しい reīgitádashii

well-meaning [wel'mi:'niŋ] *adj* (person) 善意の zeń-i no; (offer etc) 善意に基づく zeń-i ni motózukù

well-off [wel'ɔ:f'] *adj* (rich) 金持の kanémochi no

well-read [wel'red'] *adj* 博学の hakúgaku no

well-to-do [wel'tədu:'] *adj* 金持の kanémochì no

well up *vi* (tears) こみ上げる komíageru

well-wisher [wel'wiʃə:r] *n* (friends, admirers) 支持者 shijísha, ファン faň

Welsh [welʃ] *adj* ウェールズの uěruzu no; (LING) ウェールズ語の uěruzugo no

♦*n* (LING) ウェールズ語 uěruzugo

Welsh *npl*: **the Welsh** ウェールズ人 uěruzujin

Welshman/woman [welʃ'mən/wumən] (*pl* **Welshmen/women**) *n* ウェールズ人の男性〔女性〕uěruzujin no dańsei〔joséi〕

Welsh rarebit [-re:r'bit] *n* チーズトースト chīzùtōsùto

went [went] *pt of* **go**

wept [wept] *pt, pp of* **weep**

we're [wi:r] = **we are**

were [wə:r] *pt of* **be**

weren't [wə:r'ənt] = **were not**

west [west] *n* (direction) 西 nishí; (part of country) 西部 seību

♦*adj* (wing, coast, side) 西の nishí no, 西側の nishígawa no

♦*adv* (to/towards the west) 西へ nishí e

west wind 西風 nishíkaze

West *n*: **the West** (POL: US plus western Europe) 西洋 seīyō

West Country: **the West Country** (*BRIT*) *n* 西部地方 seībuchihō

westerly [wes'tə:rli:] *adj* (point) 西寄りの nishíyori no; (wind) 西からの nishí kara no

western [wes'tə:rn] *adj* (of the west) 西の nishí no; (POL: of the West) 西洋の seīyō no

♦*n* (CINEMA) 西部劇 seībugeki

West Germany *n* 西ドイツ nishídoitsu

West Indian *adj* 西インド諸島の nishíindoshotō nð

♦*n* 西インド諸島の人 nishíindoshotō no hitð

West Indies [-in'di:z] *npl* 西インド諸島 nishíindoshotō

westward(s) [west'wə:rd(z)] *adv* 西へ nishí e

wet [wet] *adj* (damp) 湿った shimétta; (wet through) ぬれた nuréta; (rainy: weather, day) 雨模様の amémòyō no

♦*n* (*BRIT*: POL) 穏健派の人 onkénha no hitð

to get wet (person, hair, clothes) ぬれる nuréru

「*wet paint*」ペンキ塗立て peńki nurítate

to be a wet blanket (*fig*) 座を白けさせ

る za wo shirákesaseru

wet suit n ウェットスーツ uéttòsūtsu

we've [wi:v] = **we have**

whack [wæk] vt たたく tatákù

whale [weil] n (ZOOL) クジラ kujíra

wharf [wɔːrf] (pl **wharves**) n 岸壁 gañ-peki

wharves [wɔːrvz] npl of **wharf**

KEYWORD

---

what [wʌt] adj 1 (in direct/indirect questions) 何の nán no, 何... nánì...

what size is it? サイズは幾つですか sáìzu wa íkutsu desu ká

what color is it? 何色ですか nánì iro desu ká

what shape is it? 形はどうなっていますか katáchi wà dó nattè imásù ká

what books do you need? どんな本がいりますか dóñna hóñ wo irú ká

he asked me what books I needed 私にはどんな本がいるかと彼は聞いていました watákushi ni wà dóñna hóñ ga irú kà to kárè wa kiítè imáshìta

2 (in exclamations) 何て... náñte...

what a mess! 何て有様だ náñte arísama dà

what a fool I am! 私は何てばかだ watákushi wà náñte bákà da

♦pron 1 (interrogative) 何 nánì, 何 náñ

what are you doing? 何をしていますか nánì wo shité imasù ká

what is happening? どうなっていますか dó nattè imásù ká

what's in there? その中に何が入っていますか sonó nakà ni nánì ga háìtte imasu ká

what is it? - it's a tool 何ですか-道具です náñ desu ká - dógu desu

what are you talking about? 何の話ですか náñ no hanáshì desu ká

what is it called? これは何と言いますか kórè wa náñ to iímasù ká

what about me? 私はどうすればいいんですか watákushi wà dó surèba íín desu ká

what about doing ...? ...しませんか ...shimáseñ ká

2 (relative): *is that what happened?* 事件は今話した通りですか jíkèn wa íma hanáshita tòri desu ká

I saw what you did/was on the table あなたのした事(テーブルにあった物)を見ました anátà no shitá kotò(tébu-ru ni attá monò)wo mimáshìta

he asked me what she had said 彼は彼女の言った事を私に尋ねた kárè wa kánòjo no ittá kotò wo watákushi nì tazúnetà

tell me what you're thinking about 今何を考えているか教えて下さい íma nánì wo kañgaete irù ká oshíete kudasai

what you say is wrong あなたの言っている事は間違っています anátà no itté iru kotò wa machígattè imásù

♦excl (disbelieving) 何 nánì

what, no coffee! 何、コーヒーがないんだって？ nánì, kóhì gà naíñ datté?

I've crashed the car - what! 車をぶつけてしまった-何? kurúma wò butsú-kete shimattà - nañ?

---

whatever [wʌtev'ə:r] adj: *whatever book* どんな本でも dóñna hoñ de mo

♦pron: *do whatever is necessary/you want* 何でも必要〔好き〕な事をしなさい nañ de mo hitsúyò(sukí)na koto wò shínásai

whatever happens 何が起っても naní ga okótte mo

no reason whatever/whatsoever 全く理由がない mattáku riyû ga nai

nothing whatever 全く何もない mattá-ku nanî mo nai

whatsoever [wʌtsouev'ə:r] adj = **what-ever**

wheat [wi:t] n 小麦 komúgi

wheedle [wi:d'əl] vt: *to wheedle some-one into doing something* ...を口車に乗せて...させる ...wo kuchíguruma ni no-séte ...sasèru

to wheedle something out of some-one 口車に乗せて...を...からだまし取る kuchíguruma ni noséte ...wo ...karà da-máshitorù

wheel [wi:l] n (of vehicle etc) 車 kurúma,

車輪 sharín, ホイール hoîru; (also: **steering wheel**) ハンドル hañdoru; (NAUT) だ輪 darín

♦*vt* (pram etc) 押す osú

♦*vi* (birds) 旋回する señkai suru; (also:- **wheel round**: person) 急に向き直る kyū nì mukínaorù

wheelbarrow [wi:l'bærou] *n* 一輪車 i-chírìnsha, ネコ車 nekóguruma

wheelchair [wi:l'tʃe:r] *n* 車いす kurúma-isù

wheel clamp *n* (AUT) ◊違反駐車の自動車車輪に付けて走れなくする金具 ihánchūsha no jidốshàsharin ni tsukéte hashírenaku surù kanágu

wheeze [wi:z] *vi* (person) ぜいぜいいう zeîzei iú

─────────────────
KEYWORD
─────────────────

when [wen] *adv* いつ ítsù

when did it happen? いつ起ったんですか ítsù okóttañ desu ká

I know when it happened いつ起ったかはちゃんと分かっています ítsù okótta kà wa cháňto wakátte imásù

when are you going to Italy? イタリアにはいつ行きますか itáría ni wa ítsù ikímasù ká

when will you be back? いつ帰って来ますか ítsù kaétte kimasù ká

♦*conj* 1 (at, during, after the time that) ...する時 ...surú tokì, ...すると ...surú tò, ...したら ...shitárà, ...してから ...shité karà

she was reading when I came in 私が部屋に入った時彼女は本を読んでいた watákushi gà heyá nì háìtta toki kánòjo wa hôñ wo yôñde imáshìta

when you've read it, tell me what you think これを読んだらご意見を聞かせて下さい kórè wo yóñdara go-íkèn wo kikásete kudasaì

be careful when you cross the road 道路を横断する時には気を付けてね dốro wo ốdàn suru tokì ni wa kí wò tsukétè né

that was when I needed you あなたにいて欲しかったのはその時ですよ aná-tà ni ité hoshikattà no wa sonó tokì desu yó

2: (on, at which): *on the day when I met him* 彼に会った日は kárè ni áttà hí wà

one day when it was raining 雨が降っていたある日 ámè ga futté ità árù hí

3 (whereas): *you said I was wrong when in fact I was right* あなたは私が間違っていると言いましたが，事実は間違っていませんでした anátà wa watákushi gà machígatte irù to iímashìta gà, jíjïtsu wa machígattè imásen deshìta

why did you buy that when you can't afford it? 金の余裕がないのになぜあれを買ったんですか kané nò yoyū gà náì no ni názè aré wò kattáñ desu ká

─────────────────

whenever [wenev'ə:r] *adv* いつか ítsù ka

♦*conj* (any time) ...するといつも... ...surú to itsùmo...; (every time that) ...する度に ...surú tabì ni

where [we:r] *adv* (place, direction) どこ(に，で) dokò (ni, de)

♦*conj* ...の所に〔で〕 ...no tokóro ni〔de〕

this is where ... これは...する所です kórè wa ... surù tokoro desu

whereabouts [we:r'əbauts] *adv* どの辺に donò hen ni

♦*n: nobody knows his whereabouts* 彼の居場所は不明だ karè no ibásho wa fuméi da

whereas [we:ræz'] *conj* ...であるのに対して ...de arù no ni taîshite

whereby [we:rbai'] *pron* それによって soré ni yottè

whereupon [we:rəpɑ:n'] *conj* すると surú to

wherever [we:rev'ə:r] *conj* (no matter where) どこに〔で〕...しても dokò ni〔de〕...shite mo; (not knowing where) どこに...か知らないが dokò ni ...ká shiranai ga

♦*adv* (interrogative: surprise) 一体全体どこに〔で〕 ittái zentai dokò ni〔de〕

wherewithal [we:r'wiθɔ:l] *n* 金 kané

whet [wet] *vt* (appetite) そそる sosóru

whether [weð'ə:r] *conj* ...かどうか ...ka dố kà

I don't know whether to accept or not 引受けるべきかどうかは分からない hikúkerubeki kà dó kà wa wakáranài

whether you go or not 行くにしても行かないにしても ikú nì shité mò ikánai nì shité mò

it's doubtful whether he will come 彼はたぶん来ないだろう karè wa tabùn konài darō

KEYWORD

which [wítʃ] *adj* **1** (interrogative: direct, indirect) どの dónò, どちらの dóchìra no

which picture do you want? どちらの絵がいいんですか dóchìra no é gà iíñ desu ká

which books are yours? あなたの本はどれとどれですか anátà no hóñ wa dórè to dórè desu ká

tell me which picture/books you want どの絵〔本〕が欲しいか言って下さい dónò é〔hóñ〕gà hoshíí kà itté kudasaì

which one? どれ dórè

which one do you want? どれが欲しいんですか dórè ga hoshíìñ desu ká

which one of you did it? あなたたちのだれがやったんですか anátà tachi no dárè ga yattáñ desu ká

2: *in which case* その場合 sonó baài

the train may be late, in which case don't wait up 列車が遅れるかもしれないが, その場合先に寝て下さい résshà ga okúreru ka mò shirénaì ga, sonó baài sakí ni netè kudasaì

by which time その時 sonó tokì

we got there at 8 pm, by which time the cinema was full 映画館に着いたのは夜の8時でしたが, もう満席になっていました eígakàn ni tsuíta no wa yórùno hachíjì deshita ga, mó mañseki ni natté imashìta

◆*pron* **1** (interrogative) どれ dórè

which (of these) are yours? どれとどれがあなたのですか dórè to dórè ga anátà no monó desù ká

which of you are coming? あなたたちのだれとだれが一緒に来てくれますか anátàtachi no dárè to dárè ga ísshò ni

kité kuremasù ká

here are the books/files - tell me which you want 本〔ファイル〕はこれだけありますが, どれとどれが欲しいんですか hóñ〔fàîru〕wa koré dakè arímasù ga, dórè to dórè ga hoshíìñ desu ká

I don't mind which どれでもいいんですよ dórè de mo iíñ desu yó

2 (relative): *the apple which you ate/which is on the table* あなたの食べた〔テーブルにある〕りんご anátà no tábèta〔têburu ni árù〕riñgo

the meeting (which) we attended 私たちが出席した会議 watákushitàchi ga shusséki shità kâîgi

the chair on which you are sitting あなたが座っているいす anátà ga suwátte irù ísú

the book of which you spoke あなたが話していた本 anátà ga hanáshite ità hóñ

he said he knew, which is true/I feared 彼は知っていると言ったが, その通りでした〔私の心配していた通りでした〕 kárè wa shitté irù tò ittá gà, sonó tòri deshita〔watákushi nò shiñpai shite ita tòri deshita〕

after which その後 sonó atò

---

whichever [wítʃévˈəːr] *adj*: *take whichever book you prefer* どれでもいいから好きな本を取って下さい doré de mo iî kara sukí nà hon wo tottè kudasaì

whichever book you take あなたがどの本を取っても anátà ga donò hon wo tottè mo

whiff [wíf] *n* (of perfume, gasoline, smoke) ちょっと...のにおいがすること chottò ...no nióî ga suru koto

while [wáîl] *n* (period of time) 間 aída

◆*conj* (at the same time as) ...する間 ...surú aida; (as long as) ...する限りは ...surú kagìri wa; (although) ...するにもかかわらず ...surú nì mo kakáwarazu

for a while しばらくの間 shibáràku no aída

while away *vt* (time) つぶす tsubúsu

whim [wím] *n* 気まぐれ kimágure

whimper [wim'pə:r] n (cry, moan) 哀れっぽい泣き声 awáreppoĭ nakígoè
♦vi (child, animal) 哀れっぽいなき声を出す awáreppoĭ nakígoè wo dasù

whimsical [wim'zikəl] adj (person) 気まぐれな kimágure na; (poem) 奇抜な kibátsu na; (look, smile) 変な heñ na

whine [wain] n (of pain) 哀れっぽいなき声 awáreppoĭ nakígoè; (of engine, siren) うなり unári
♦vi (person, animal) 哀れっぽいなき声を出す awáreppoĭ nakígoè wo dasù; (engine, siren) うなる unárù; (fig: complain) 愚痴をこぼす guchí wo kobósù

whip [wip] n (lash, riding whip) むち muchĭ; (POL) 院内幹事 iñnaikañji
♦vt (person, animal) むち打つ muchíutsù; (cream, eggs) 泡立てる awádaterù, ホイップする hoíppù suru; (move quickly): to whip something out/off さっと取出す〔はずす, 脱ぐ〕sattó torídasu 〔hazúsu, nugù〕

whipped cream [wipt-] n ホイップクリーム hoíppukurīmù

whip-round [wip'raund] (BRIT) n 募金 bokín

whirl [wə:rl] vt (arms, sword etc) 振回す furímawasù
♦vi (dancers) ぐるぐる回る gurùguru mawáru; (leaves, water etc) 渦巻く uzúmakù

whirlpool [wə:rl'pu:l] n 渦巻 uzúmàki

whirlwind [wə:rl'wind] n 竜巻 tatsúmaki

whir(r) [we:r] vi (motor etc) うなり unári

whisk [wisk] n (CULIN) 泡立て器 awádatekĭ
♦vt (cream, eggs) 泡立てる awádaterù
to whisk someone away/off ...を素早く連去る ...wo subáyakù tsurésarù

whiskers [wis'kə:rz] npl (of animal, man) ひげ higé

whiskey [wis'ki:] (BRIT whisky) n ウイスキー uísukĭ

whisper [wis'pə:r] n (low voice) ささやき sasáyaki
♦vi ささやく sasáyakù

♦vt ささやく sasáyakù

whist [wist] n ホイスト hoísuto

whistle [wis'əl] n (sound) 口笛 kuchíbue; (object) 笛 fué
♦vi (person) 口笛を吹く kuchíbue wo fukù; (bird) ぴーぴーさえずる pĭpĭ saézurù; (bullet) ひゅーとうなる hyǔ to unárù; (kettle) ぴゅーと鳴る pyǔ to narú

white [wait] adj (color) 白い shiróĭ; (pale: person, face) 青白い aójiroĭ; (with fear) 青ざめた aózamèta
♦n (color) 白 shiró; (person) 白人 hakújin; (of egg) 白身 shirómĭ

white coffee (BRIT) n ミルク入りコーヒー mirúkuirikōhī

white-collar worker [wait'kɑ:l'ə:r-] n サラリーマン sarárīmàn, ホワイトカラー howáitokarà

white elephant n (fig) 無用の長物 muyố no chōbutsu

white lie n 方便のうそ hōben no usò

white paper n (POL) 白書 hakùsho

whitewash [wait'wɑ:ʃ] n (paint) のろ noró ◇石灰, 白亜, のりを水に混ぜた塗料 sekkài, hakùa, norí wo mizú ni mazèta toryố
♦vt (building) ...にのろを塗る ...ni norố wo nurú; (fig: happening, career, reputation) ...の表面を繕う ...no hyốmeñ wo tsukúroù

whiting [wai'tiŋ] n inv (fish) タラ tarà

Whitsun [wit'sən] n 聖霊降臨節 seíreikōrinsetsu

whittle [wit'əl] vt: to whittle away, whittle down (costs: reduce) 減らす herásu

whiz(z) [wiz] vi: to whizz past/by (person, vehicle etc) ぴゅーんと通り過ぎる byún to tốrisugirù

whiz(z) kid (inf) n 天才 teñsai

KEYWORD
---

who [hu:] pron 1 (interrogative) だれ dárè, どなた dónàta
who is it?, who's there? だれですか dárè desu ká
who are you looking for? だれを捜しているんですか dárè wo sagáshite irúñ

desu ká

I told her who I was 彼女に名乗りました kánòjo ni nanórimashìta

I told her who was coming to the party パーティの出席予定者を彼女に知らせました páti no shussékiyoteìsha wo kánòjo ni shirásemashìta

who did you see? だれを見ましたか dárè wo mimáshìta ká

2 (relative): *my cousin who lives in New York* ニューヨークに住んでいるいとこ nyúyòku ni súnde iru itókò

the man/woman who spoke to me 私に話しかけた男性〔女性〕watákushi nì hanáshikaketà dañsei〔joséi〕

those who can swim 泳げる人たち oyógerù hitótàchi

whodunit [hu:dʌn'it] (*inf*) *n* 探偵小説 tañteishōsetsu

whole [houl] *adj* (entire) 全体の zeñtai no; (not broken) 無傷の mukīzu no
♦*n* (entire unit) 全体 zeñtai; (all): *the whole of* 全体の zeñtai no
the whole of the town 町全体 machízeñtai
on the whole, as a whole 全体として zeñtai toshite

whole food(s) [houl'fu:d(z)] *n*(*pl*) 無加工の食べ物 mukákō no tabémonò

wholehearted [houl'hɑr'tid] *adj* (agreement etc) 心からの kokóro kàra no

wholemeal [houl'mi:l] *adj* (bread, flour) 全粒の zeñryū no, 全麦の zeñbaku no

wholesale [houl'seil] *n* (business) 卸 oróshi, 卸売 oróshiuri
♦*adj* (price) 卸の oróshi nò; (destruction) 大規模の daíkibò no
♦*adv* (buy, sell) 卸で oróshi dè

wholesaler [houl'seilə:r] *n* 問屋 toñ-ya

wholesome [houl'səm] *adj* (food, climate) 健康に良い keñkō ni yoì; (person) 健全な keñzen na

wholewheat [houl'wi:t] *adj* = wholemeal

wholly [houl'i:] *adv* (completely) 完全に kañzen ni

whom [hu:m] *pron* 1 (interrogative) だれを dárè wo, どなたを dónàta wo
whom did you see? だれを見ましたか dárè wo mimáshìta ká
to whom did you give it? だれに渡しましたか dárè ni watáshimashìta ká
tell me from whom you received it だれに〔から〕それをもらったかを教えて下さい dárè ni〔kárà〕sorè wò morátta kà wo oshíete kudasaì

2 (relative): *the man whom I saw/to whom I spoke* 私が見た〔話し掛けた〕男性 watákushi gà mítà〔hanáshikaketà〕dañsei
the lady with whom I was talking 私と話していた女性 watákushi tò hanáshite itá joséi

whooping cough [wu:'piŋ-] *n* 百日ぜき hyakúnichizèki

whore [hɔ:r] (*inf*: *pej*) *n* 売女 baíta

whose [hu:z] *adj* 1 (possessive: interrogative) だれの dárè no, どなたの dónàta no
whose book is this?, whose is this book? これはだれの本ですか koré wà dárè no hốñ desu ká
whose pencil have you taken? だれの鉛筆を持ってきたんですか dárè no eñpitsu wò motté kitañ desu ká
whose daughter are you? あなたはどなたの娘さんですか anátà wa dónàta no musúme-sañ desu ká
I don't know whose it is だれの物か私には分かりません dárè no monó kà watákushi ni wà wakárimaseñ

2 (possessive: relative): *the man whose son you rescued* あなたが助けた子供の父親 anátà ga tasúketa kodomò no chíchíoya
the girl whose sister you were speaking to あなたと話していた女性の妹 anátà to hanáshite itá joséi no imốtò
the woman whose car was stolen 車を盗まれた女性 kurúma wò nusúmaretà

josei

◆*pron* だれの物 dáre no monó, どなたの物 dónàta no monó

whose is this? これはだれのですか kóre wa dáre no desu ká

I know whose it is だれの物か知っています dáre no monó kà shitté imasù

whose are these? これらはだれの物ですか korérà wa dáre no monó desù ká

KEYWORD

why [wai] *adv* なぜ náze, どうして dóshìte

why is he always late? どうして彼はいつも遅刻するのですか dóshìte kárè wa ítsùmo chikóku suru nò desu ká

why don't you come too? あなたも来ませんか anátà mo kimáseñ ká

I'm not coming - why not? 私は行きません-どうしてですか watákushi wà i-kímaseñ - dóshìte desu ká

fancy a drink? - why not? 一杯やろうか-いいね íppài yaró ká - íi né

why not do it now? 今すぐやりませんか ímà súgù yarímaseñ ka

◆*conj* なぜ náze, どうして dóshìte

I wonder why he said that どうしてそんな事を言ったのかしら dóshìte soñna kotó wo ittá nò kashira

the reason why 理由 riyú

that's not (the reason) why I'm here 私が来たのはそのためじゃありません watákushi gà kitá no wà sonó tamè ja arímaseñ

◆*excl* (expressing surprise, shock, annoyance etc)◇日本語では表現しない場合が多い nihóngo de wà hyógeñ shinaí baái gà ói

why, it's you! おや，あなたでしたか oyá, anátà deshita ká

why, that's impossible/quite unacceptable! そんな事はできません[認められません] soñna kotó wà dekímaseñ [mitómeraremaseñ]

I don't understand - why, it's obvious! 訳が分かりません-ばかでも分かる事だよ wákè ga wakárimaseñ - bákà de

mo wakárù kotó dà yó

---

whyever [waiev'ə:r] *adv* 一体 なぜ ittai náze

wicked [wik'id] *adj* (crime, man, witch) 極悪の gokúaku no; (smile) 意地悪そうな ijíwarusó nà

wickerwork [wik'ə:rwə:rk] *adj* (basket, chair etc) 籐編みの tóami no, 枝編みの edáami no

◆*n* (objects) 籐編み細工品 tóamizaikuhin, 枝編み細工品 edáamizaikuhin

wicket [wik'it] *n* (CRICKET: stumps) 三柱門 sañchúmòn, ウイケット uíkètto; (: grass area) ピッチ pitchĭ

◇2つのウイケット間のグランド futátsu nò uíkettokàn no gurándo

wide [waid] *adj* (gen) 広い hirói; (grin) 楽しげな tanóshige na

◆*adv: to open wide* (window etc) 広く開ける hiróku akéru

to shoot wide ねらいを外す nerái wo hazúsu

wide-angle lens [waid'æŋ'gəl-] *n* 広角レンズ kókaku reñzu

wide-awake [waid'əweik'] *adj* すっかり目が覚めた sukkárì me gà saméta

widely [waid'li:] *adv* (gen) 広く hiróku; (differing) 甚だしく hanáhadashikù

widen [wai'dən] *vt* (road, river, experience) 広くする hiróku suru, 広げる hirógeru

◆*vi* (road, river, gap) 広くなる hiróku narù, 広がる hirógaru

wide open *adj* (window, eyes, mouth) 大きく開けた ókìku akéta

widespread [waidspred'] *adj* (belief etc) はびこった habíkottà

widow [wid'ou] *n* 未亡人 mibójìn, 後家 goké

widowed [wid'oud] *adj* (mother, father) やもめになった yamóme ni nattá

widower [wid'ouə:r] *n* 男 や も め otóko-yamóme

width [widθ] *n* (distance) 広さ hirósa; (of cloth) 幅 habá

wield [wi:ld] *vt* (sword, power) 振るう fu-rúu

wife [waif] (*pl* **wives**) *n* (*gen*) 妻 tsumà; (one's own) 家内 kanài; (someone else's) 奥さん okùsan

wig [wig] *n* かつら katsúra

wiggle [wig'əl] *vt* (hips) くねらす kunérasù; (ears etc) ぴくぴく動かす pikùpiku ugókasù

wild [waild] *adj* (animal, plant) 野生の yaséi no; (rough: land) 荒れ果てた aréhatèta; (: weather, sea) 荒れ狂う arékuruù; (person, behavior, applause) 興奮した kőfun shita; (idea) 突飛な toppí na; (guess) 当てずっぽうの atézuppó no

wilderness [wil'də:rnis] *n* 荒野 kőyà, 原野 geñ-ya, 未開地 mikáichì

wild-goose chase [waild'gu:s'-] *n* (*fig*) 無駄な捜索 mudá na sősaku

wildlife [waild'laif] *n* (animals) 野生動物 yaséidōbùtsu

wildly [waild'li:] *adv* (behave) 狂った様に kurúttā yō ni; (applaud) 熱狂的に nekkyőteki ni; (hit) めくら滅法に mekúra-meppő ni; (guess) 当てずっぽうに atézuppó ni; (happy) 最高に saíkō ni

wilds [waildz] *npl* 荒野 kőyà, 原野 geñ-ya, 未開地 mikáichì

wilful [wil'fəl] (*US also*: **willful**) *adj* (obstinate: child, character) わがままな wagámamà na; (deliberate: action, disregard etc) 故意の koī no

---

KEYWORD

will [wil] (*vt: pt, pp* **willed**) *aux vb* **1** (forming future tense): *I will finish it tomorrow* 明日終ります ashíta owárimasù

I will have finished it by tomorrow 明日にでもなれば終るでしょう asú ni dè mo nárèba owárù deshő

will you do it? - yes I will/no I won't やりますか - はい，やります[いいえ，やりません] yarímasù ká - háì, yarímasù[iíè, yarímaseñ]

when will you finish it? いつ終りますか ítsù owárimasù ká

2 (in conjectures, predictions): *he will/he'll be there by now* 彼はもう着いているでしょう kárè wa mő tsuíte irú de-

shő

that will be the postman 郵便屋さんでしょう yűbinya-san deshő

this medicine will help you この薬なら効くでしょう konő kusuri narà kikú deshő

this medicine won't help you この薬は何の役にも立ちません konő kusuri wà nañ no yakú ni mò tachímaseñ

3 (in commands, requests, offers): *will you be quiet!* 黙りなさい damárinasaî

will you come? 来てくれますか kitè kuremasù ká

will you help me? 手伝ってくれますか tetsúdattè kurémasù ká

will you have a cup of tea? お茶をいかがですか o-chá wo ikága desu ká

I won't put up with it! 我慢できません gámàn dekímaseñ

♦*vt: to will someone to do something* 意志の力で…に…をさせようとする íshì no chikára dè …ni …wò saséyő tò suru

he willed himself to go on 彼は精神力だけで続けようとした kárè wa seíshinryòku dakè dè tsuzúkeyő tò shita

♦*n* (volition) 意志 íshì; (testament) 遺言 yuígon

---

willful [wil'fəl] (*US*) *adj* = **wilful**

willing [wil'iŋ] *adj* (with goodwill) 進んで…する susúnde …surù; (enthusiastic) 熱心な nesshín na

he's willing to do it 彼はそれを引き受けてくれるそうです karè wa sorè wo hikíukète kureru sō dèsu

willingly [wil'iŋli:] *adv* 進んで susúnde

willingness [wil'iŋnis] *n* 好意 kőī

willow [wil'ou] *n* ヤナギ yanági

willpower [wil'pauə:r] *n* 精神力 seíshiñryòku

willy-nilly [wil'i:nil'i:] *adv* 否応なしに iyáō nashì ni

wilt [wilt] *vi* (flower, plant) 枯れる karéru

wily [wai'li:] *adj* (fox, move, person) ずる賢い zurúgashikoî

win [win] *n* (in sports etc) 勝利 shőrì, 勝ち kachí

♦vb (pt, pp won)

♦vt (game, competition) ...で勝つ ...de katsú; (election) ...で当選する ...de tōsen suru; (obtain: prize, medal) もらう moráu, 受ける ukérù; (money) 当てる atérù; (support, popularity) 獲得する kakútoku suru

♦vi 勝つ katsù

wince [wins] vi 顔がこわばる kaó ga kowábaru

winch [wintʃ] n ウインチ uíñchi

wind¹ [wind] n (air) 風 kazé; (MED) 呼吸 kokyū; (breath) 息 ikì

♦vt (take breath away from) ...の息を切らせる ...no ikì wo kiráserù

wind² [waind] (pt, pp **wound**) vt (roll: thread, rope) 巻く makú; (wrap: bandage) 巻付ける makítsukerù; (clock, toy) ...のぜんまいを巻く ...no zeñmai wo makú

♦vi (road, river) 曲りくねる magárikunerù

windfall [wind'fɔːl] n (money) 棚ぼた tanábota

winding [wain'diŋ] adj (road) 曲りくねった magárikunettà; (staircase) らせん状の rasénjō no

wind instrument n (MUS) 管楽器 kañgakki

windmill [wind'mil] n 風車 kazágurùma

window [win'dou] n 窓 madò

window box n ウインドーボックス uíndōbokkùsu

window cleaner n (person) 窓ふき職人 madófukishokùnin

window envelope n 窓付き封筒 madótsukifūtò

window ledge n 窓下枠 madóshitawàku

window pane n 窓ガラス madógarasu

window-shopping [win'douʃɑːpiŋ] n ウインドーショッピング uíndōshoppìngu

windowsill [win'dousil] n 窓下枠 madóshitawàku

windpipe [wind'paip] n 気管 kikán

windscreen [wind'skriːn] (BRIT) n = **windshield**

windshield [wind'ʃiːld] (US) n フロント

ガラス furóntogaràsu, ウインドシールド uíndoshīrùdo

windshield washer n ウインドシールドワシャー uíndoshīrùdowashà

windshield wiper [-waip'əːr] n ワイパー waìpā

windswept [wind'swept] adj (place) 吹きさらしの fukísarashi no; (person) 風で髪が乱れた kazé de kamí gá midárèta

wind up vt (clock, toy) ...のぜんまいを巻く ...no zeñmai wo makú; (debate) 終りにする owári ni suru

windy [win'diː] adj (weather, day) 風の強い kazé no tsuyoì
it's windy 風が強い kazé ga tsuyoì

wine [wain] n ブドウ酒 budóshu, ワイン waìn

wine bar n ワインバー waìnbā

wine cellar n ワインの地下貯蔵庫 waìn no chikáchozōkò

wine glass n ワイングラス waínguràsu

wine list n ワインリスト waìnrisùto

wine merchant n ワイン商 waínshò

wine waiter n ソムリエ somúrie

wing [wiŋ] n (of bird, insect, plane) 羽根 hané, 翼 tsubása; (of building) 翼 yokú; (BRIT: AUT) フェンダー feñdā

winger [wiŋ'əːr] n (SPORT) ウイング uíñgu

wings [wiŋz] npl (THEATER) そで sodé

wink [wiŋk] n (of eye) ウインク uíñku
♦vi (with eye) ウインクする uíñku suru; (light etc) 瞬く matátakù

winner [win'əːr] n (of prize, race, competition) 勝者 shōshà

winning [win'iŋ] adj (team, competitor, entry) 勝った kattà; (shot, goal) 決勝の kesshō no; (smile) 愛敬たっぷりの aíkyō tappúrì no

winnings [win'iŋz] npl 賞金 shōkin

win over vt (person: persuade) 味方にする mikáta ni suru

win round (BRIT) vt = **win over**

winter [win'təːr] n (season) 冬 fuyú
in winter 冬には fuyú nì wa

winter sports npl ウインタースポーツ uíntasupōtsù

wintry [win'triː] adj (weather, day) 冬ら

しい fuyúrashiî

wipe [waip] *n*: *to give something a wipe* ...をふく ...wo fukú

♦*vt* (rub) ふく fukú; (erase: tape) 消す kesú

wipe off *vt* (remove) ふき取る fukítorù

wipe out *vt* (debt) 完済する kańsai suru; (memory) 忘れる wasúreru; (destroy: city, population) 滅ぼす horóbosù

wipe up *vt* (mess) ふき取る fukítorù

wire [wai'əːr] *n* (metal etc) 針金 harígane; (ELEC) 電線 deńsen; (telegram) 電報 deńpō

♦*vt* (house) ...の配線工事をする ...no haísenkōjì wo suru; (*also*: **wire up**: electrical fitting) 取付ける torítsukerù; (person: telegram) ...に電報を打つ ...ni deńpō wo utsú

wireless [wai'əːrlis] (*BRIT*) *n* ラジオ rajío

wiring [waiər'iŋ] *n* (ELEC) 配線 haísen

wiry [waiə·r'iː] *adj* (person) やせて強じんな yasé de kyōjin na; (hair) こわい kowáî

wisdom [wiz'dəm] *n* (of person) 知恵 chié; (of action, remark) 適切さ tekísetsusa

wisdom tooth *n* 親知らず oyáshirazù

wise [waiz] *adj* (person, action, remark) 賢い kashíkoî, 賢明な keńmei na

...wise *suffix*: *timewise/moneywise etc* 時間[金銭]的に jikán(kińsen)teki ni

wisecrack [waiz'kræk] *n* 皮肉な冗談 hiníku na jōdań

wish [wiʃ] *n* (desire) 望み nozómi, 希望 kibō; (specific) 望みの物 nozómi no mono

♦*vt* (want) 望む nozómù, 希望する kibō suru

best wishes (for birthday, etc) おめでとう omédetō

with best wishes (in letter) お体をお大事に o-kárada wo o-dáiji ni

to wish someone goodbye ...に別れのあいさつを言う ...ni wakáre no aísatsu wo iu, ...にさよならを言う ...ni sayónarà wo iu

he wished me well 彼は「成功を祈る」と言いました karè wa "seíkō wo inórù"to iímashìta

to wish to do ...したいと思う ...shitaî to omóù

to wish someone to do something ...に...してもらいたいと思う ...ni ...shité moraitaì to omóù

to wish for ...が欲しいと思う ...ga hoshíî to omóù

wishful [wiʃ'fəl] *adj*: *it's wishful thinking* その考えは甘い sonó kangaè wa amaí, それは有り得ない事だ soré wa aríenaì kotó dà

wishy-washy [wiʃ'iːwɑːʃiː] (*inf*) *adj* (color) 薄い usúi; (ideas, person) 迫力のない hakúryoku no naî

wisp [wisp] *n* (of grass, hair) 小さな束 chiísana tabà; (of smoke) 一筋 hitósùji

wistful [wist'fəl] *adj* (look, smile) 残念そうな zańnensō na

wit [wit] *n* (wittiness) ユーモア yūmòa, ウィット uíttò; (intelligence: *also*: **wits**) 知恵 chié; (person) ウィットのある人 uíttò no aru hito

witch [witʃ] *n* 魔女 majò

witchcraft [witʃ'kræft] *n* 魔術 majútsu

witch-hunt [witʃ'hʌnt] *n* (*fig*) 魔女狩り majógari

KEYWORD

with [wiθ] *prep* **1** (accompanying, in the company of) ...と ...to, ...と一緒に ...to ísshò ni

I was with him 私は彼と一緒にいました watákushi wà kárè to ísshò ni imáshìta

we stayed with friends 私たちは友達の家に泊りました watákushitàchi wa tomódachi nò ié nì tomárimashìta

we'll take the children with us 子供たちを一緒に連れて行きます kodómotàchi wo ísshò ni tsuréte ikimasù

mix the sugar with the eggs 砂糖を卵に混ぜて下さい satō wò tamágo nì mázète kudásaî

I'll be with you in a minute 直ぐ行きますからお待ち下さい súgù ikímasu karà o-máchi kudasaî

I'm with you (I understand) 分かります wakárimasù

to be with it (*inf*: up-to-date) 現代的で
ある gendaiteki de arù; (: alert) 抜け目が
ない nukéme gà náì
2 (descriptive): *a room with a view* 見
晴らしのいい部屋 mihárashi nò íì heyá
the man with the grey hat/blue eyes
灰色の帽子をかぶった〔青い目の〕男 haíi-
ro nò bóshì wò kabútta〔aóì mé nò〕otó-
ko
3 (indicating manner, means, cause):
with tears in her eyes 目に涙を浮かべ
ながら mé nì námìda wo ukábènagara
to walk with a stick つえをついて歩く
tsúè wo tsuíte arùku
red with anger 怒りで顔を真っ赤にし
て ikári dè kaó wò makká nì shité
to shake with fear 恐怖で震える kyófu dè furúerù
to fill something with water ...を水で
一杯にする ...wò mizú de íppáì nì surù
you can open the door with this key
このかぎでドアを開けられます konó ka-
gí dè dóà wo akéraremasù

withdraw [wiðdrɔː'] (*pt* **withdrew** *pp*
withdrawn) *vt* (object) 取出す torídasu;
(offer, remark) 取消す toríkesu, 撤回す
る tekkái suru
♦*vi* (troops) 撤退する tettái suru; (person) 下がる sagárù
to withdraw money (from the bank) 金
を引出す kané wo hikídasù

withdrawal [wiðdrɔː'əl] *n* (of offer,
remark) 撤回 tekkái; (of troops) 撤退
tettái; (of services) 停止 teíshi; (of participation) 取りやめる事 toríyameru koto;
(of money) 引出し hikídashi

withdrawal symptoms *n* (MED) 禁断
症状 kíndanshōjō

withdrawn [wiðdrɔːn'] *adj* (person) 引っ
込みがちな hikkómigachi na

wither [wið'əːr] *vi* (plant) 枯れる karéru

withhold [wiθhould'] (*pt*, *pp* **withheld**)
vt (tax etc) 源泉徴収する gensenchōshū
suru; (permission) 拒む kobámù; (information) 隠す kakúsù

within [wiðin'] *prep* (inside: referring to
place, time, distance) ...以内に〔で〕...inài

ni〔de〕
♦*adv* (inside) 中の nakà no
within reach (of) (...に) 手が届く所
に〔で〕 (...ni) té gà todókù tokoro ni〔de〕
within sight (of) (...が) 見える所に
〔で〕 (...ga) miérù tokoro ni〔de〕
within the week 今週中に konshúchū
ni
within a mile of ...の1マイル以内に
...no ichímairu inài ni

without [wiðaut'] *prep* ...なしで ...nashì
de
without a coat コートなしで kótò nashì de
without speaking 何も言わないで naní
mo iwanàìde
to go without something ...なしで済ま
す ...nashì de sumásù

withstand [wiθstænd'] (*pt*, *pp* **with-
stood**) *vt* (winds, attack, pressure) ...に
耐える ...ni taérù

witness [wit'nis] *n* (person who sees) 目
撃者 mokúgekishà; (person who counter-
signs document: *also* LAW) 証人 shónìn
♦*vt* (event) 見る mirù, 目撃する mokúge-
ki suru; (document) 保証人として...にサ
インする hoshónin toshite ...ni saín suru
to bear witness to (*fig*: offer proof of)
...を証明する ...wo shómei suru

witness stand (*BRIT* **witness box**) *n*
証人席 shónìnseki

witticism [wit'əsizəm] *n* (remark) 冗談
jódañ

witty [wit'iː] *adj* (person) ウイットのある
uíttò no arù; (remark etc) おどけた odó-
keta

wives [waivz] *npl of* **wife**

wizard [wiz'əːrd] *n* 魔法使い mahótsu-
kài

wk *abbr* = **week**

wobble [wɑːb'əl] *vi* (legs) よろめく yorómekù; (chair) ぐらぐらする gurágura su-
ru; (jelly) ぶるぶるする purùpuru suru

woe [wou] *n* 悲しみ kanáshimi

woke [wouk] *pt of* **wake**

woken [wou'kən] *pp of* **wake**

wolf [wulf] (*pl* **wolves**) *n* オオカミ ōkami

wolves [wulvz] *npl of* **wolf**

woman [wum'ən] (pl **women**) n 女 ońna, 女性 joséi

woman doctor n 女医 joí

womanly [wum'ənli:] adj (virtues etc) 女性らしい joséirashii

womb [wu:m] n (ANAT) 子宮 shikyū́

women [wim'ən] pl of **woman**

women's lib [wim'ənzlib'] (inf) n ウーマンリブ úmanribù

won [wʌn] pt, pp of **win**

wonder [wʌn'də:r] n (miracle) 不思議 fushígi; (feeling) 驚異 kyōī

♦vi: **to wonder whether/why** ...かしら〔なぜ...かしら〕と思う ...ka shira〔nazè ...ka shira〕to omóù

to wonder at (marvel at) ...に驚く ...ni odórokù

to wonder about ...の事を考える ...no kotó wò kangaèru

it's no wonder (that) ... (という事) は不思議ではない ...(to iú koto) wà fushígi de wà naí

wonderful [wʌn'də:rfəl] adj (excellent) 素晴らしい subárashiì; (miraculous) 不思議な fushígi na

wonderfully [wʌn'də:rfli:] adv (excellently) 素晴らしく subárashikù; (miraculously) 不思議に fushígi ni

won't [wount] = **will not**

woo [wu:] vt (woman) ...に言い寄る ...ni iíyorù; (audience etc) ...にこびる ...ni kobírù

wood [wud] n (timber) 木材 mokúzai, 木 ki; (forest) 森 morí, 林 hayáshi, 木立 kodàchi

wood carving n (act, object) 木彫 kibóri

wooded [wud'id] adj (slopes, area) 木の茂った kí nò shigéttà

wooden [wud'ən] adj (object) 木でできた kí dè dekita, 木製の mokúsei no; (house) 木造の mokúzō no; (fig: performance, actor) でくの坊の様な dekúnobō no yō nà

woodpecker [wud'pekə:r] n キツツキ kitsútsukì

woodwind [wud'wind] npl (MUS) 木管楽器 mokkángakkì

woodwork [wud'wə:rk] n (skill) 木材工芸 mokúzaikōgèi

woodworm [wud'wə:rm] n キクイムシ kikúimùshi

wool [wul] n (material, yarn) 毛糸 keíto, ウール úrù

to pull the wool over someone's eyes (fig) ...をだます ...wo damásù

woolen [wul'ən] (BRIT **woollen**) adj (socks, etc) 毛糸の keíto no, ウールの úrù no

the woolen industry 羊毛加工業界 yōmōkakōgyōkài

woolens [wul'ənz] npl 毛糸衣類 keítoiruì

wooly [wul'i:] (BRIT **woolly**) adj (socks, hat etc) 毛糸の keíto no, ウールの úrù no; (fig: ideas) 取留めのない torítome no naí; (person) 考え方のはっきりしない kańgaekatà no hakkírì shinái

word [wə:rd] n (unit of language: written, spoken) 語 go, 単語 tańgo, 言葉 kotóba; (promise) 約束 yakúsoku; (news) 知らせ shiráse, ニュース nyūsù

♦vt (letter, message) ...の言回しを選ぶ ...no iímawashi wo erábù

in other words 言替えると iíkaerù to

to break/keep one's word 約束を破る〔守る〕yakúsoku wo yabúrù(mamórù)

to have words with someone ...と口げんかをする ...to kuchígeñka wo suru

wording [wə:r'diŋ] n (of message, contract etc) 言回し iímawashi

word processing n ワードプロセシング wādopuroseshìngu

word processor [-prɑː'sesə:r] n ワープロ wāpuro

wore [wɔ:r] pt of **wear**

work [wə:rk] n (gen) 仕事 shigóto; (job) 職 shokú; (ART, LITERATURE) 作品 sakúhin

♦vi (person: labor) 働く határaku; (mechanism) 動く ugókù; (be successful: medicine etc) 効く kikú

♦vt (clay, wood etc) 加工する kakó suru; (land) 耕す tagáyasù; (mine) 採掘する saíkutsu suru; (machine) 動かす ugókasù; (cause: effect) もたらす motárasù; (: miracle) 行う okónau *to be out of work* 失業中である shitsú-gyōchū de arù

to work loose (part) 緩む yurúmù; (knot) 解ける tokérù

workable [wəːrˈkəbəl] *adj* (solution) 実行可能な jikkōkanō na

workaholic [wəːrkəhɑːˈlik] *n* 仕事中毒の人 shigótochūdòku no hito, ワーカホリック wākahorīkku

worker [wəːrˈkəːr] *n* 労働者 rōdōshà

workforce [wəːkˈfɔːrs] *n* 労働人口 rōdō-jinkò

working class [wəːrˈkiŋ-] *n* 労働者階級 rōdōshakaìkyū

working-class [wəːrˈkiŋklæs] *adj* 労働者階級の rōdōshakaìkyū no

working order *n*: *in working order* ちゃんと動く状態で chańto ugokù jōtai de

workman [wəːrkˈmən] (*pl* **workmen**) *n* 作業員 sagyōìn

workmanship [wəːrkˈmənʃip] *n* (skill) 腕前 udémae

work on *vt fus* (task) ...に取組む ...ni toríkumu; (person: influence) 説得する settóku suru; (principle) ...に基づく ...ni motōzukù

work out *vi* (plans etc) うまくいく umáku iku

◆*vt* (problem) 解決する kaíketsu suru; (plan) 作る tsukúrù

it works out at $100 100ドルになる hyakúdòru ni narù

works [wəːrks] *n* (BRIT: factory) 工場 kōjō

◆*npl* (of clock, machine) 機構 kikō

worksheet [wəːrkˈʃiːt] *n* ワークシート wākushītò

workshop [wəːrkˈʃɑːp] *n* (at home, in factory) 作業場 sagyōjō; (practical session) ワークショップ wākushoppù

work station *n* ワークステーション wākusutēshòn

work-to-rule [wəːrkˈtəːruːl] (BRIT) *n* 順法闘争 juńpōtōsō

work up *vt*: *to get worked up* 怒る okőrù

world [wəːrld] *n* 世界 sekài

◆*cpd* (champion) 世界 ... sekài...; (power, war) 国際的... kokúsaiteki..., 国際... kokúsai...

to think the world of someone (fig: admire) ...を高く評価する ...wo takáku hyōkà suru; (: love) ...が大好きである ...ga daìsuki de arù

worldly [wəːrldˈliː] *adj* (not spiritual) 世俗的な sezőkuteki na; (knowledgeable) 世才にたけた sesái ni takèta

worldwide [wəːrldˈwaid] *adj* 世界的な sekáiteki na

worm [wəːrm] *n* (also: **earthworm**) ミミズ mimízu

worn [wɔːrn] *pp* of **wear**

◆*adj* (carpet) 使い古した tsukáifurushi-tà; (shoe) 履き古した hakífurushità

worn-out [wɔːrnˈaut] *adj* (object) 使い古した tsukáifurushità; (person) へとへとに疲れた hetóheto ni tsukáretà

worried [wəːrˈiːd] *adj* (anxious) 心配している shiñpai shite irù

worry [wəːrˈiː] *n* (anxiety) 心配 shíñpai

◆*vt* (person) 心配させる shiñpai saserù

◆*vi* (person) 心配する shiñpai surù

worrying [wəːrˈiːiŋ] *adj* 心配な shíñpai na

worse [wəːrs] *adj* 更に悪い sarà ni wáruì

◆*adv* 更に悪く sarà ni warùku

◆*n* 更に悪い事 sarà ni warùi koto

a change for the worse 悪化 akká

worsen [wəːrˈsən] *vt* 悪くする warùku suru

◆*vi* 悪くなる warùku naru

worse off *adj* (financially) 収入が減った shúñyū ga hettà; (fig): *you'll be worse off this way* そんな事は得策ではない soñna koto wa tokúsaku de wa naì

worship [wəːrˈʃip] *n* (act) 礼拝 reíhai

◆*vt* (god) 礼拝する reíhai suru; (person, thing) 崇拝する sūhái suru

Your Worship (BRIT: to mayor, judge) 閣下 kakká

worst [wəːrst] *adj* 最悪の saíaku no

◆*adv* 最もひどく mottómo hidòku

◆*n* 最悪 saíaku

at worst 最悪の場合 saíaku no baái

worth [wəːrθ] *n* (value) 価値 kachì

♦*adj: to be worth $100* 価格は100ドルである kakáku wa hyakúdoru de arù
it's worth it やる価値がある yarú kachì ga aru
to be worth one's while (to do) (...する事は) ...のためになる (...surú koto wa) ...no tamé ni naru

worthless [wəːrθ'lis] *adj* (person, thing) 価値のない kachí no nai

worthwhile [wəːrθ'wail'] *adj* (activity, cause) ためになる tamé ni naru

worthy [wəːr'ðiː] *adj* (person) 尊敬すべき sonkeisubeki; (motive) 良い yoì
worthy of ...にふさわしい ...ni fusáwashiì

KEYWORD

would [wud] *aux vb* **1** (conditional tense): *if you asked him he would do it* 彼にお願いすればやってくれるでしょう kárè ni o-négai surèba yatté kureru deshô
if you had asked him he would have done it 彼に頼めばやってくれた事でしょう kárè ni tanómebà yatté kuretà kotó deshô
2 (in offers, invitations, requests): *would you like a biscuit?* ビスケットはいかがですか bisúkettò wa ikágà desu ká
would you ask him to come in? 彼に入ってもらって下さい kárè ni háitte morátte kudasaì
would you open the window please? 窓を開けてくれますか mádò wo akéte kuremasù ká
3 (in indirect speech): *I said I would do it* 私はやってあげると約束しました watákushi wà yatté agerù to yakúsoku shimashìta
he asked me if I would go with him 一緒に行ってくれと彼に頼まれました isshó ní itté kurè to kárè ni tanómaremashìta
4 (emphatic): *it WOULD have to snow today!* 今日に限って雪が降るなんてなあ kyó nì kagíttè yukí gà fúrù nánte nâ

you WOULD say that, wouldn't you! あんたの言いそうな事だ ánta no iísò na kotó dà
5 (insistence): *she wouldn't behave* あの子はどうしても言う事を聞いてくれない anó kò wa dô shite mò iú kotó wo kiíte kurenaì
6 (conjecture): *it would have been midnight* だとすれば夜中の12時という事になります dà tò surèbâ yonáka nò jûnijì to iú kotó ni narímasù
it would seem so そうらしいね só rashiì né
7 (indicating habit): *he would go there on Mondays* 彼は毎週月曜日にそこへ行く事にしていました kárè wa maíshu getsúyòbi ni sokó è ikú kotó ni shité imashìta
he would spend every day on the beach 彼は毎日浜でごろごろしていました kárè wa maínichi hamá dè górògoro shite imáshìta

---

would-be [wud'biː'] *(pej) adj* ...志望の ...shibô no
wouldn't [wud'ənt] = **would not**
wound[1] [waund] *pt, pp* of **wind**
wound[2] [wuːnd] *n* 傷 kizú
♦*vt* ...に傷を負わせる ...ni kizú wo owáseru, 負傷させる fushô saséru
wove [wouv] *pt* of **weave**
woven [wou'vən] *pp* of **weave**
wrangle [ræŋ'gəl] *n* 口論 kôron
wrap [ræp] *n* (stole) 肩掛 katakake, ストール sutôrù; (cape) マント mantò, ケープ kēpù
♦*vt* (cover) 包む tsutsúmù; (pack: *also*: **wrap up**) こん包する konpô suru; (wind: tape etc) 巻付ける makítsukerù
wrapper [ræp'əːr] *n* (on chocolate) 包み tsutsúmi; (*BRIT*: of book) カバー kabâ
wrapping paper [ræp'iŋ-] *n* (brown) クラフト紙 kuráfùtoshi; (fancy) 包み紙 tsutsúmigami
wrath [ræθ] *n* 怒り ikári
wreak [riːk] *vt* (havoc) もたらす motárasù
to wreak vengeance on ...に復しゅうす

る ...ni fukúshū suru

wreath [ri:θ] n (funeral wreath) 花輪 ha-náwa

wreck [rek] n (vehicle) 残がい zañgai; (ship) 難破船 nañpasen; (pej: person) 変り果てた人 kawárihatetá hitó
♦vt (car etc) めちゃめちゃに壊す mechá-mecha ni kowásù; (fig: chances) 台無しにする daínashi ni suru

wreckage [rek'idʒ] n (of car, plane, ship, building) 残がい zañgai

wren [ren] n (ZOOL) ミソサザイ misósa-zài

wrench [rentʃ] n (TECH: adjustable) スパナ supánà; (: fixed size) レンチ reñchi; (tug) ひねり hinéri; (fig) 心痛 shíntsū
♦vt (twist) ひねる hinérù

to wrench something from someone ...から...をねじり取る ...kara...wo nejíri-torù

wrestle [res'əl] vi: *to wrestle (with someone)* (fight) (...と) 格闘する (...to) kakútō suru; (for sport) (...と) レスリングする (...to) resúringu suru

to wrestle with (fig) ...と取組む ...to to-ríkumu, ...と戦う ...to tatákau

wrestler [res'lər] n レスラー resúrā

wrestling [res'liŋ] n レスリング resúrin-gu

wretched [retʃ'id] adj (poor, unhappy) 不幸な fukó na; (inf: very bad) どうしようもない dō shiyó mo nai

wriggle [rig'əl] vi (also: **wriggle about**: person, fish, snake etc) うねうねする u-néune suru

wring [riŋ] (pt, pp **wrung**) vt (wet clothes) 絞る shibórù; (hands) もむ mo-mú; (bird's neck) ひねる hinérù; (fig): *to wring something out of someone* ...に ...を吐かせる ...ni ...wo hákaserù

wrinkle [riŋ'kəl] n (on skin, paper etc) しわ shiwá
♦vt (nose, forehead etc) ...にしわを寄せる ...ni shiwá wo yosérù
♦vi (skin, paint etc) しわになる shiwá ni naru

wrist [rist] n 手首 tekúbi

wristwatch [rist'wɑːtʃ] n 腕時計 udédo-kèi

writ [rit] n 令状 reíjō

write [rait] (pt **wrote**, pp **written**) vt 書く kakù
♦vi 書く kakù

to write to someone ...に手紙を書く ...ni tegámi wo kakù

write down vt 書く kakù, 書留める ka-kítomeru

write off vt (debt) 帳消しにする chóke-shi ni suru; (plan, project) 取りやめる to-ríyameru

write-off [rait'ɔːf] n 修理不可能な物 shūrífukánō na mono

writer [rai'tər] n (author) 著者 chóshà; (professional) 作家 sakká; (person who writes) 書手 kakíte

write up vt (report, minutes etc) 詳しく書く kuwáshiku kakù

writhe [raið] vi 身もだえする mimódàe suru

writing [rai'tiŋ] n (words written) 文字 mojì, 文章 buñshō; (handwriting) 筆跡 hisséki; (of author) 作品 sakúhin, 作風 sakúfū; (activity) 書物 kakímono

in writing 書面で shomén de

writing paper n 便せん biñsen

written [rit'ən] pp of **write**

wrong [rɔːŋ] adj (bad) 良くない yokúnai; (incorrect: number, address etc) 間違った machígatta; (not suitable) 不適当な futékìtō na; (reverse: side of material) 裏側の urágawa no; (unfair) 不正な fuséi na
♦adv 間違って machígatte, 誤って ayá-mattè
♦n (injustice) 不正 fuséi
♦vt (treat unfairly) ...に悪い事をする ...ni warúi koto wo surù

you are wrong to do it それは不正な事です sore wa fuséi na koto desù

you are wrong about that, you've got it wrong それは違います soré wa chigáimasù

to be in the wrong 間違っている ma-chígattè iru

what's wrong? どうしましたか dō shi-máshita ká

to go wrong (person) 間違う machígaù; (plan) 失敗する shippái suru; (machine) 狂う kurúù

wrongful [rɔ:ŋ'fəl] *adj* (imprisonment, dismissal) 不当な futô na

wrongly [rɔ:ŋ'li:] *adv* 間違って machígattè

wrote [rout] *pt of* **write**

wrought [rɔ:t] *adj*: **wrought iron** 練鉄 refitetsu

wrung [rʌŋ] *pt, pp of* **wring**

wry [rai] *adj* (smile, humor, expression) 皮肉っぽい hiníkuppoì

wt. *abbr* = **weight**

X

Xmas [eks'mis] *n abbr* = **Christmas**

X-ray [eks'rei] *n* (ray) エックス線 ekkúsusen; (photo) レントゲン写真 refitogefishashin
♦*vt* ...のレントゲンを撮る ...no refitogefi wo torú

xylophone [zai'ləfoun] *n* 木琴 mokkín

Y

yacht [jɑ:t] *n* ヨット yottò

yachting [jɑ:t'iŋ] *n* ヨット遊び yottóasobi

yachtsman [jɑ:ts'mən] (*pl* **yachtsmen**) *n* ヨット乗り yottónori

Yank [jæŋk] (*pej*) *n* ヤンキー yafikī

Yankee [jæŋk'i:] (*pej*) *n* = **Yank**

yap [jæp] *vi* (dog) きゃんきゃんほえる kyafikyan hoérù

yard [jɑ:rd] *n* (of house etc) 庭 niwá; (measure) ヤード yādò

yardstick [jɑ:rd'stik] *n* (*fig*) 尺度 shakúdò

yarn [jɑ:rn] *n* (thread) 毛糸 keíto; (tale) ほら話 horábanashi

yawn [jɔ:n] *n* あくび akúbi
♦*vi* あくびする akúbi suru

yawning [jɔ:n'iŋ] *adj* (gap) 大きな ōkína

yd. *abbr* = **yard(s)**

yeah [je] (*inf*) *adv* はい haì

year [ji:r] *n* 年 nefi, toshí, 1年 ichínèn
to be 8 years old 8才である hassái de aru
an eight-year-old child 8才の子供 hassái no kodómo

yearly [ji:r'li:] *adj* 毎年の maínen no, maítoshi no
♦*adv* 毎年 maínen, maítoshi

yearn [jə:rn] *vi*: **to yearn for something** ...を切に望む ...wo setsù ni nozómu
to yearn to do ...をしたいと切に望む ...wo shitái to setsù ni nozómu

yeast [ji:st] *n* 酵母 kōbò, イースト īsùto

yell [jel] *n* 叫び sakébi
♦*vi* 叫ぶ sakébù

yellow [jel'ou] *adj* 黄色い kiíroi

yelp [jelp] *n* (of animal) キャンと鳴く事 kyafi to nakú koto; (of person) 悲鳴 himéi
♦*vi* (animal) きゃんと鳴く kyafi to nakú; (person) 悲鳴を上げる himéi wò agérù

yeoman [jou'mən] (*pl* **yeomen**) *n*: **yeoman of the guard** 国王の親衛隊員 kokúō no shifi-eitaiìfi

yes [jes] *adv* はい haì
♦*n* はいという返事 haì to iú hefiji
to say/answer yes 承諾する shódaku suru

yesterday [jes'tə:rdei] *adv* 昨日 kinô, sakújìtsu
♦*n* 昨日 kinô, sakújìtsu
yesterday morning/evening 昨日の朝〔夕方〕kinô no asà〔yūgata〕
all day yesterday 昨日一日 kinô ichínichi

yet [jet] *adv* まだ madà; (already) もう mô
♦*conj* がしかし ga shikáshì
it is not finished yet まだできていない madà dekîte inái
the best yet これまでの物で最も良い物 koré madè no mono dè mottómo yoì mono
as yet まだ madà

yew [ju:] *n* (tree) イチイ ichíi

Yiddish [jid'iʃ] *n* イディッシュ語 idísshugo

yield [ji:ld] *n* (AGR) 収穫 shūkaku; (COMM) 収益 shūeki

♦*vt* (surrender: control, responsibility) 譲る yuzúru; (produce: results, profit) もたらす motárasù

♦*vi* (surrender) 譲る yuzúru; (*US*: AUT) 道を譲る michí wo yuzúru

YMCA [waiemsi:ei'] *n abbr* (= *Young Men's Christian Association*) キリスト教青年会 kirísutokyōseínnenkai, ワイエムシ ー エー waíemushìe

yog(h)ourt [jou'gə:rt] *n* ヨーグルト yō-gurúto

yog(h)urt [jou'gə:rt] *n* = **yog(h)ourt**

yoke [jouk] *n* (of oxen) くびき kubíki; (*fig*) 重荷 omóni

yolk [jouk] *n* 卵黄 rañ-ō, 黄身 kimí

KEYWORD

you [ju:] *pron* **1** (subj: *sing*) あなたは〔が〕anátā wa〔ga〕; (: *pl*) あなたたちは〔が〕anátātàchi wa〔ga〕

you are very kind あなたはとても親切ですね anátā wa totémo shíñsetsu desu ne, ご親切に有難うございます go-shíñsetsu ni arígàtō gozáimasù

you Japanese enjoy your food あなたたち日本人は食べるのが好きですね anátatàchi nihóñjìn wa tabérù no ga sukí desù nè

you and I will go あなたと私が行く事になっています anátā to watákushi gà ikú kotò ni natté imasù

2 (obj: direct, indirect: *sing*) あなたを〔に〕anátā wo〔ni〕; (: : *pl*) あなたたちを〔に〕anátātàchi wo〔ni〕

I know you 私はあなたを知っています watákushi wà anátā wo shitté imasù

I gave it to you 私はそれをあなたに渡しました watákushi wà soré wò anátā ni watáshimashìta

3 (stressed): *I told YOU to do it* やれというのはあなたに言ったんですよ yaré tò iú no wà anátā ni ittáñ desu yó

4 (after prep, in comparisons)

it's for you あなたのためです anátā no tamé desù

can I come with you? 一緒に行っていいですか isshó nì itté íi desu ká

she's younger than you 彼女はあなたより若いです kánòjo wa anátā yori wakái desu

5 (impersonal: one)

fresh air does you good 新鮮な空気は健康にいい shíñsen nà kúkì wa keñkō ni íi

you never know どうなるか分かりませんね dō narù ka wakárimaseñ nè

you can't do that! それはいけませんよ soré wà ikémaseñ

---

you'd [ju:d] = **you had**; **you would**

you'll [ju:l] = **you will**; **you shall**

young [jʌŋ] *adj* (person, animal, plant) 若い wakái

♦*npl* (of animal) 子 ko; (people): *the young* 若者 wakámono

younger [jʌŋ'gə:r] *adj* (brother etc) 年下の toshíshita no

youngster [jʌŋ'stə:r] *n* 子供 kodómo

your [ju:r] *adj* (singular) あなたの anáta no; (plural) あなたたちの anátatàchi no ¶ *see also* **my**

you're [ju:r] = **you are**

yours [ju:rz] *pron* (singular) あなたの物 anátà no mono; (plural) あなたたちの物 anátatàchi no mono ¶ *see also* **mine**; **faithfully**; **sincerely**

yourself [ju:rself'] *pron* あなた自身 anáta jishìn ¶ *see also* **oneself**

yourselves [ju:rselvz'] *pl pron* あなたたち自身 anátatàchi jishìn ¶ *see also* **oneself**

youth [ju:θ] *n* (young days) 若い時分 wakái jibun; (young man: *pl* **youths**) 少年 shōnen

youth club *n* 青少年クラブ seíshōnèn kurábu

youthful [ju:θ'fəl] *adj* (person) 若い wakái; (looks) 若々しい wakáwakashìi; (air, enthusiasm) 若者独特の wakámono-dokútoku no

youth hostel *n* ユースホステル yūsúhosùteru

Youth Training (*BRIT*) 職業訓練 shokúgyōkunreǹ ◇失業青少年のためのもの shitsúgyōseishōnen no tamé no monò

you've [ju:v] = **you have**

Yugoslav [ju:'gouslɑ:v] *adj* ユーゴスラビアの yūgosurabīa no
♦*n* ユーゴスラビア人 yūgosurabiajin

Yugoslavia [ju:'gouslɑ:'vi:ə] *n* ユーゴスラビア yūgosurabīa

yuppie [jʌp'i:] (*inf*) *n* ヤッピー yappì
♦*adj* ヤッピーの yappì no

YWCA [waidʌbəlju:siei'] *n abbr* (= *Young Women's Christian Association*) キリスト教女子青年会 kirísutokyōjoshìseńnenkai, ワイダブリューシーエー waídaburyūshīē

Z

Zambia [zæm'bi:ə] *n* ザンビア zańbia

zany [zei'ni:] *adj* (ideas, sense of humor) ばかげた bakágeta

zap [zæp] *vt* (COMPUT: delete) 削除する sakùjo suru

zeal [zi:l] *n* (enthusiasm) 熱情 netsújō; (*also*: **religious zeal**) 狂信 kyōshín

zealous [zel'əs] *adj* 熱狂的な nekkyóteki na

zebra [zi:'brə] *n* シマウマ shimáuma

zebra crossing (*BRIT*) *n* 横断歩道 ōdánhodò

zenith [zi:'niθ] *n* 頂点 chōtèn

zero [zi:'rou] *n* 零点 reíten, ゼロ zerò

zest [zest] *n* (for life) 熱意 netsùi; (of orange) 皮 kawá

zigzag [zig'zæg] *n* ジグザグ jigùzagu
♦*vi* ジグザグに動く jigùzagu ni ugókù

Zimbabwe [zimbɑ:'bwei] *n* ジンバブウェ jińbabùue

zinc [ziŋk] *n* 亜鉛 aèn

zip [zip] *n* (*also*: **zip fastener**) = **zipper**
♦*vt* (*also*: **zip up**) = **zipper**

zip code (*US*) *n* 郵便番号 yūbinbańgō

zipper [zip'ə:r] (*US*) *n* チャック chakkù, ジッパー jippā, ファスナー fasùnā
♦*vt* (*also*: **zipper up**) ...のチャックを締める ...no chakkù wo shimérù

zodiac [zou'di:æk] *n* 十二宮図 jūníkyừzu

zombie [zɑ:m'bi:] *n* (*fig*): **like a zombie** ロボットの様に〔な〕robőttð no yõ ni 〔na〕

zone [zoun] *n* (area, *also* MIL) 地帯 chitái

zoo [zu:] *n* 動物園 dőbutsùen

zoologist [zoua:l'ədʒist] *n* 動物学者 dőbutsugakùsha

zoology [zoua:l'ədʒi:] *n* 動物学 dőbutsugàku

zoom [zu:m] *vi*: **to zoom past** 猛スピードで通り過ぎる mősupìdo de tōrísugiru

zoom lens *n* ズームレンズ zūmureñzu

zucchini [zu:ki:'ni:] (*US*) *n inv* ズッキーニ zukkìnì

SUPPLEMENT

NUMBERS

Cardinal numbers:

1	一	ichi	11	十一	jūichi	21	二十一	nijūichi
2	二	ni	12	十二	jūni	22	二十二	nijūni
3	三	san	13	十三	jūsan	etc		
4	四	yon/shi	14	十四	jūyon/jūshi	30	三十	sanjū
5	五	go	15	十五	jūgo	40	四十	yonjū
6	六	roku	16	十六	jūroku	50	五十	gojū
7	七	nana/shichi	17	十七	jūnana/jūshichi	60	六十	rokujū
8	八	hachi	18	十八	jūhachi	70	七十	nanajū/shichijū
9	九	ku/kyū	19	十九	jūku/jūkyū	80	八十	hachijū
10	十	jū	20	二十	nijū	90	九十	kyūjū

Note: the alternative forms given for 4, 7, 9 etc are not necessarily interchangeable. The choice is determined by usage.

100	百	hyaku	1,000	千	sen, 一千 issen	10,000	一万	ichiman
200	二百	nihyaku	2,000	二千	nisen	20,000	二万	niman
300	三百	sanbyaku	3,000	三千	sanzen	etc		
400	四百	yonhyaku	4,000	四千	yonsen			
500	五百	gohyaku	5,000	五千	gosen			
600	六百	roppyaku	6,000	六千	rokusen			
700	七百	nanahyaku	7,000	七千	nanasen			
800	八百	happyaku	8,000	八千	hassen			
900	九百	kyūhyaku	9,000	九千	kyūsen			

Alternate set of numbers:

These are used often for counting, particularly for counting things without "counters" (see below), and for expressing the age of children.

1	一つ	hitotsu	6	六つ	muttsu
2	二つ	futatsu	7	七つ	nanatsu
3	三つ	mittsu	8	八つ	yattsu
4	四つ	yottsu	9	九つ	kokonotsu
5	五つ	itsutsu	10	十	tō

Ordinal numbers:

"The first," "the second" etc are expressed by the formula 第 x 番目 *dai x banme*, where x is the cardinal number and *dai, banme* or *me* can be variously omitted. Thus "the third" can be expressed by any of the following:

第三番目　daisanbanme
三番目　sanbanme
三番　sanban
第三　daisan

The alternate cardinal numbers from 1 to 9 can also be made into ordinal numbers by the addition of 目 *me* alone: "the third" = 三つ目 *mittsume*.

Days of the month:

The days of the month are written straightforwardly by a cardinal number plus the character for day 日. But the reading is not straightforward and needs to be learned.

一日	tsuitachi	七日	nanoka
二日	futsuka	八日	yōka
三日	mikka	九日	kokonoka
四日	yokka	十日	tōka
五日	itsuka	二十日	hatsuka
六日	muika		

Days 11 to 19 and 21 to 31 are expressed straightforwardly by a cardinal number + *nichi*. Thus the 18th day of the month is *jūhachinichi*.

Fractions:

In Japanese you express fractions by the formula y分のx *y bun no x*, where *y* is the DENOMINATOR, not the numerator. In other words, in Japanese you say the denominator first, then the numerator, thus:

1/2　二分の一　nibun no ichi
2/3　三分の二　sanbun no ni
3/4　四分の三　yonbun no san

Counters:

As in English we often say "2 *head* of cattle", "a *bunch* of grapes", "a *flock* of geese", Japanese uses counters for almost all everyday things, including people. There are many counters, some common, some exotic (like using the same counter for "rabbit" as you would for "bird"). Here is a list of counters you will need for your daily life.

counter:		used for:
人	nin	people
名	mei	people (interchangeable with *nin* except in set phrases)
匹	hiki	animals in general, except birds
頭	tō	relatively large animals
羽	wa	birds
個	ko	3-dimensional, relatively rounded objects: balls, stones, apples, cups
枚	mai	thin, flat things: pieces of paper, computer disks, handkerchiefs, blankets, dishes
本	hon	long things: pencils, ropes, sticks
冊	satsu	books and things bound like books: notebooks, diaries
台	dai	cars, trucks, bicycles, large machines
足	soku	shoes, socks etc that come in matched pairs
歳	sai	age of living things in years
杯	hai	containers full of something: cupful, glassful, spoonful

Like the use in English of "an" instead of "a" before words that begin with a vowel, Japanese makes pronunciation changes depending on the last syllable of the cardinal number and the first letter of a counter. Here are the most important.

1. Counters beginning with "h"

   一本, 一匹 ippon, ippiki
   二本, 二匹 nihon, nihiki
   三本, 三匹 sanbon, sanbiki
   四本, 四匹 yonhon, yonhiki
   五本, 五匹 gohon, gohiki
   六本, 六匹 roppon, roppiki
   七本, 七匹 nanahon, nanahiki
   八本, 八匹 happon, happiki
   九本, 九匹 kyūhon, kyūhiki
   十本, 十匹 juppon, juppiki

2. Counters beginning with unvoiced consonants (k, s, t, ch) double the consonant after the numbers 1 and 10.

   一個, 一歳 ikko, issai
   十個, 十歳 jukko, jussai

3. "k" also doubles after 6.

   六個 rokko

4. The voiced consonants g, z, d, m, n, r, w generally do not change.

5. The counter 人 *nin* for persons has an atypical pronunciation for 1 and 2.

一人 hitori

二人 futari

6. The counter 歳 *sai* for age has an atypical pronunciation for 20 years of age.

二十歳 hatachi

DEMONSTRATIVES

Japanese demonstratives begin with 4 prefixes: *ko-*, *so-*, *a-*, and *do-*. *Ko-* expresses nearness to the speaker; *so-* expresses distance from the speaker but nearness to the listener; *a-* expresses distance from both speaker and listener; and *do-* forms interrogatives.

kō	like this	sō	like that	aa	like that	dō	how ?
kono	this	sono	that	ano	that	dono	which ?
kore	this (one)	sore	that (one)	are	that (one)	dore	which (one) ?
koko		soko		asoko		doko	
kotchi	here	sotchi	there	atchi	there	dotchi	where ?
kochira		sochira		achira		dochira	
konna	such a	sonna	such a	anna	such a	donna	what kind of ?

UNDERSTANDING JAPANESE

Japanese has certain characteristics not always found in the European family of languages. This shows up in particular in the way the subject of the sentence is expressed (or unexpressed, as we shall see), and in the numerous particles which take the place of declensions, prepositions, auxiliaries etc in Western languages. Although it may take years to learn to use these characteristics like a native, being aware of their existance can serve as a shortcut to a fuller understanding of Japanese.

1. The hidden subject

Consider the following sentence. It is the opening line to Yasunari Kawabata's Nobel Prize-winning "Snow Country".

国境の長いトンネルを抜けると雪国であった。kokkyō no nagai tonneru wo nukeru to yukiguni de atta.

My translation would be:

"When your train emerged from the long tunnel beneath the border, you suddenly found yourself in the snow-bound countryside."

Notice that there is no "train" or "your" or "you" expressed in the original.

Japanese prefers not to express words that are apparent from the context or the choice of expression. This happens most frequently with the grammatical subject of the sentence, not only in literature, but especially in daily conversation.

A: どちらへお出かけですか dochira e o-dekake desu ka

B: 郵便局へ手紙を出しに行きます yūbinkyoku e tegami wo dashi ni ikimasu

Here there is no need for an *anata wa* in A or a *watashi wa* in B. The choice of words (the polite *dochira* with *o-...*) contains the "you" in A, and makes an "I" in B's answer superfluous.

In Japanese the verbal part of the sentence is the most important, and normally comes at the end. In a long sentence the listener has to wait till the end of the sentence in order to grasp the meaning. In English, the grammatical subject is the most important part, and is expressed at the beginning of the sentence, and auxiliary information about the subject is imparted gradually. This makes for great clarity of meaning, whereas Japanese sentences can often produce ambiguities. But this is a product of the Japanese culture, where reticence is considered virtue and outspokenness vice.

2. Particles

Japanese uses particles to make clear the relationship among words in a sentence. English frequently relies on position of words in the sentence for this. In a simple example, the meaning of A below is reversed if you reverse the position of the words, as in B.

A. John hit Sue.

B. Sue hit John.

On the other hand, consider the following example and its literal Japanese translation.

She gave me a book.

彼女は私に1冊の本をくれました.

kanojo *wa* watashi *ni* issatsu *no* hon *wo* kuremashita.

This is a standard translation. But the following are also possible, in context, without changing the meaning.

watashi *ni* kanojo *wa* issatsu *no* hon *wo* kuremashita.

issatsu *no* hon *wo* kanojo *wa* watashi *ni* kuremashita.

kuremashita, kanojo *wa* watashi *ni* issatsu *no* hon *wo*.

In other words, the particles make the meaning clear without regard to the position of the various sentence elements, even when the position is somewhat unnatural. On the other hand, if you confuse the particles, your speech becomes unintelligible. To say that someone's train of thought is illogical or contradictory, the Japanese have an old metaphor.

てにをはが合わない。 te-ni-wo-ha ga awanai.

Literally, "his particles are all mixed up." This underscores the correct use of particles, even for a native speaker of Japanese.

The Japanese classify their particles as follows.

Case particles: Added to nouns and pronouns, they indicate relation to other words in the sentence: no, ga, wo, ni, e, to, yori, kara, de.

Adverbial particles: They are added to nouns, pronouns, and adverbs and restrict the meaning of the verbal parts of the sentence : sae, made, bakari, dake, hodo, kurai, nado, nanka, nante, yara, zo, ka, zutsu.

Modifying particles: They add their own meaning to the word they follow and also modify the verbal parts of the sentence: wa, mo, koso, demo (also written "de mo"), shika, datte.

Sentence particles: They conclude a sentence and indicate interrogation, exclamation, emotion, prohibition etc: ka, kai, kashira, na, zo, ze, tomo (to mo), tte, no, ne, sa, ya, yo.

Parenthetical particles: They are placed at the end of phrases and clauses and are used to adjust sentence rhythm or to express emotion, emphasis etc: na, ne, sa.

Connecting particles: They are appended to various verbal phrases and clauses to indicate their connection with what follows: ba, to, te mo (de mo), keredo (keredomo), ga, no ni, no de, kara, shi, te (de), nagara.

The following illustrate typical Japanese usage of the more important particles. The translations given show one way, but not necessarily the only way, of expressing the concept in English.

a. Case particles

§ **の no**: indicates possession, location etc

父の本　chichi no hon "my father's book" —possession

海の風　umi no kaze "a sea breeze" —location

大学の教授　daigaku no kyōju "a university professor" —affiliation

紫の花　murasaki no hana "a purple flower" —attribute

小説家の川端氏　shōsetsuka no kawabatashi "Mr. Kawabata the novelist" —apposition

§ **が ga**: follows nouns or pronouns

私が行きます　watashi ga ikimasu "I will go." —indicates subject

メロンが好きだ　meron ga suki da "I like melons." —indicates object of desire, ability, likes and dislikes etc

それがね、本当なんだよ　sore ga ne, hontō nan da yo "The thing is, the story is true." —attached to a demonstrative like a connecting particle

§ を wo: follows nouns or pronouns

本を読む　hon wo yomu "to read a book" —indicates object of an action verb

歩道を歩く　hodō wo aruku "to walk on the sidewalk" —indicates location with a verb of movement

この半年を堪え忍んだ　kono hantoshi wo taeshinonda "I have suffered in silence for the past 6 months." —indicates duration of an action

朝９時に家を出る　asa kuji ni ie wo deru "to leave the house at 9 o'clock" —indicates the place where an action commences

§ に ni: indicates the person or thing to which an action extends

朝５時に起床する　asa goji ni kishō suru "to get up at 5 a. m." —indicates time

空に虹が出る　sora ni niji ga deru "A rainbow appears in the sky." —indicates place

仕事に熱中する　shigoto ni netchū suru "to concentrate on one's work" —indicates the object of an action

会社にたどりつく　kaisha ni tadoritsuku "to reach one's office" —indicates destination or direction

悪夢にうなされる　akumu ni unasareru "to be tormented by a nightmare" —indicates cause

１週間に２日はお休み　isshūkan ni futsuka wa o-yasumi "We have 2 days a week off." —indicates ratio, proportion etc

犬に吠えられる　inu ni hoerareru "to be barked at by a dog" —indicates the agent of an action

大人になる　otona ni naru "to become an adult" —indicates the result of change

ぴかぴかに光る　pikapika ni hikaru "to shine brightly" —indicates manner

§ へ e:

西へ進む　nishi e susumu "to advance toward the west" —indicates the direction of an action

君への思い　kimi e no omoi "my longing for you" —indicates the object of an action

学校へ着く　gakkō e tsuku "to arrive at school" —indicates destination

兄がすぐそこへ来ています　ani ga sugu soko e kite imasu "My brother is right near here." —indicates location of an action

§ と to:

友人と話す　yūjin to hanasu "to talk with friends" —expresses the idea of "with"

以前と同じやり方　izen to onaji yarikata "the same manner as before" —indicates a term of comparison

政治家となる　seijika to naru "to become a politician" —indicates the result of change

開催地は山梨と決定した　kaisaichi wa Yamanashi to kettei shita "We decided to hold the meeting in Yamanashi." —indicates the content of an action or state

延々と続く　en-en to tsuzuku "to go on endlessly" —indicates the manner of an action or state

§ より yori:

父より背が高い　chichi yori se ga takai "I am taller than my father." —indicates a term of comparison

5時より前に帰る　goji yori mae ni kaeru "to be back before 5" —indicates a limit

§ から kara: used after nouns and pronouns, and indicates point of departure, or cause

明日から夏休み　myōnichi kara natsuyasumi "Summer vacation starts tomorrow." —indicates a spatial or temporal point of departure

窓から西日が差す　mado kara nishibi ga sasu "The western sun shines in through the window." —expresses the idea of "passing through"

何から何までお世話になりました　nani kara nani made o-sewa ni narimashita "You took wonderful care of me." —indicates extent

母から聞いた話　haha kara kiita hanashi "something I heard from my mother" —indicates a source

ビールは麦から作る　bīru wa mugi kara tsukuru "Beer is made from grain." —indicates constituent materials etc

§ で de:

プールで泳ぐ　pūru de oyogu "to swim in the pool" —indicates the location of an action.

ペンで書く　pen de kaku "to write with a pen" —indicates instrument, means, material etc

病気で死ぬ　byōki de shinu "to die from a sickness" —indicates cause, reason, motive

b. Adverbial particles

§ まで made: used after nouns and pronouns, and connects them with verbal parts or other particles

東京から北海道まで旅する　tōkyō kara hokkaidō made tabi suru "to travel from Tōkyō to Hokkaidō" —indicates the outer limits of an action in space or time

あくまで計画を実行する　aku made keikaku wo jikkō suru "to push a plan through to the finish" —expresses final extent of an action

§ だけ **dake:** expresses the limits of something

2 人だけで話したい　futari dake de hanashitai "I want to talk to you alone." —indicates a limit

あれだけ食べたら満腹です　are dake tabetara manpuku desu "I'm full after eating all that." —expresses the idea of "that much"

§ ほど **hodo:** used after various noun and verb forms

後 5 枚ほど必要です　ato gomai hodo hitsuyō desu "I need about 5 more sheets of paper." —expresses an approximation of number or quantity

かわいそうなほどしょんぼりしている　kawaiasō na hodo shonbori shite iru "He's looking so depressed I can't help feeling sorry for him." —expresses an action or state resulting from some characteristic

悪い奴ほど手が白い　warui yatsu hodo te ga shiroi "The evilest men have the whitest hands." —indicates 2 items, the second of which changes in direct proportion to change in the first

c. Modifying particles

§ は **wa:** used after many kinds of words. The original use was to single out one item of a group.

勉強はもう済んだ　benkyō wa mō sunda "I have finished my homework." —here singles out one item from a group of things to do

象は鼻が長い　zō wa hana ga nagai "The elephant has a long trunk." —singles out an item of subject matter about which some information is given

行きはよいよい, 帰りは恐い　iki wa yoi yoi, kaeri wa kowai "Going is easy, but getting back is the problem." —expresses 2 or more contrasting judgments

君とは絶交だ　kimi to wa zekkō da "I want nothing more to do with you." —indicates emphasis

◇ **Note:** in modern Japanese, wa is frequently used to express a word that corresponds to the grammatical subject of a sentence in English.

§ も **mo:** used after many kinds of words

花も実もある男　hana mo mi mo aru otoko "a man in both looks and deeds" —coordinates 2 or more concepts

料理もろくにできない　ryōri mo roku ni dekinai "She can't even cook properly." —singles out one among many other implied concepts

兄も病気になった　ani mo byōki ni natta "My older brother got sick too." —expresses the concept of "also"

そして誰もいなくなった　soshite dare mo inakunatta "And then there was no one." —used with a negative to express the idea of "nothing, no one"

§ しか shika:

生き残ったのは1人しかいない　ikinokotta no wa hitori shika inai "Only one person was left alive." —used with a negative to express the idea of "only"

d. Sentence particles

§ か ka: expresses a variety of questions

君はだれですか　kimi wa dare desu ka "Who are you?"

本当に行くのか　hontō ni iku no ka "Are you really going?"

散歩に行きませんか　sanpo ni ikimasen ka "How about going for a walk?"

こんなことができないのか　konna koto ga dekinai no ka "Can't you even do something as simple as this?"

そうか、失敗だったのか　sō ka, shippai datta no ka "Oh, so it ended in failure, eh?"

§ ね ne: used at the end of a sentence

まあ、きれいな花ね　maa, kirei na hana ne "Oh, look at the pretty flower!" —expresses an exclamation

この本は君のですね　kono hon wa kimi no desu ne "This is your book, right?" —expresses a tag question

遅れてごめんなさいね　okurete gomen nasai ne "Do forgive me for being late." —expresses a request for the listener's understanding, sympathy, agreement etc

e. Parenthetical particles

§ ね ne: appended to words or phrases as a transition word, or to adjust sentence rhythm etc

そうですね、考えておきましょう　sō desu ne, kangaete okimashō "Well, let me think about it."

私ね、その秘密知っているの　watashi ne, sono himitsu shitte iru no "Listen, I know the secret behind that."

f. Connecting particles

§ ば ba

雨が降れば、旅行は中止　ame ga fureba, ryokō wa chūshi "If it rains, the trip is off." —expresses a possible condition

消息筋によれば、また株価が下がるらしい　shōsokusuji ni yoreba, mata kabuka ga sagaru rashii "According to a knowledgeable source, stock prices are going to fall again." —indicates the basis for a statement

日が沈めば夜になる　hi ga shizumeba yoru ni naru "Night comes when the sun sets." —expresses an invariable cause and effect relationship

5年前を思えば、随分楽になった　gonen mae wo omoeba, zuibun raku ni natta "Compared with 5 years ago, I am quite well off now." —indicates a past time for comparison with the present

§ **と to:** used after the present tense form of verbs

庭へ出ると、桜が咲いていた　niwa e deru to, sakura ga saite ita "When you went into the garden, you could see the cherry trees in bloom." —joins two contemporaneous actions

本を置くと、すぐ出て行った　hon wo oku to, sugu dete itta "He put down the book and left the room." —joins two successive actions

話が始まると、静かになった　hanashi ga hajimaru to, shizuka ni natta "When the lecture began, the audience became silent and listened." —expresses the beginning or cause etc of an action

はっきり言うと、それは失敗です　hakkiri iu to, sore wa shippai desu "Frankly, it's a failure." —expresses a preamble to what follows

§ **ても te mo** (with certain verbal forms it becomes でも *de mo*): used to express permission etc

果物なら食べてもいいですよ　kudamono nara tabete mo ii desu yo "Fruit is all right for you to eat."

§ **けれども keredomo:** used after verbs and -ii adjectives

貧しいけれども、心は豊かだった　mazushii keredomo, kokoro wa yutaka datta "He was poor materially, but rich in spirit." —expresses some sort of contrast

勝手な言い分ですけれども、帰らせて下さい　katte na iibun desu keredomo, kaerasete kudasai "I'm sorry to do so at this point, but I really must leave." —joins a preamble to the main point of the sentence

レコード持ってきたけれども、聞いてみる　rekōdo motte kita keredomo, kiite miru? "I brought a record along. Do you want to hear it?" —simply joins two clauses

§ **が ga:** used after verbs and -ii adjectives

ご存知のことと思いますが、一応説明します　go-zonji no koto to omoimasu ga, ichiō setsumei shimasu "I'm sure you are already familiar with the problem, but I'll run through it briefly for you anyway." —joins a preamble to the main part of the sentence

驚いて振り向いたが、もはやだれの姿もなかった　odoroite furimuita ga, mohaya dare no sugata mo nakatta "In surprise I wheeled around to look back, but whoever it was had already disappeared." —expresses a temporal relationship between two clauses

見かけは悪いが，たいへん親切な男　mikake wa warui ga, taihen shinsetsu na otoko "He doesn't look it, but he's really a very kind man." —expresses contrast

§ **のに no ni:** expresses dissatisfaction, unexpectedness etc

待っていたのに，来なかった　matte ita no ni, konakatta "I waited and waited, but he didn't come."

§ **ので no de:** expresses cause, reason, basis etc

分からないので，質問しました wakaranai no de, shitsumon shimashita "I didn't understand, so I asked."

§ **から kara**

暑いから，のどが渇いた　atsui kara, nodo ga kawaita "It was hot, and I became very thirsty." —expresses cause, reason, basis etc

決心したからには，やり通そう　kesshin shita kara ni wa, yaritōsō "We have made the decision, so let's see it through to the end." —expresses the notion of "having done such and such, it follows that..."

DAILY JAPANESE

Here we present a selection of very typical and idiomatic Japanese words and phrases. These examples occur with a high frequency in daily life in Japan. The English translations given in boldface provide an idea of the meaning, but are not absolute. A number of translations are possible, depending on the context, tone of voice, person speaking or spoken to, etc.

Some words occur in the examples which have no English equivalent, or are unintelligible to a person unfamiliar with Japan. Foreigners living in Japan often prefer to use these as loan words in conversation, rather than resorting to some clumsy translation. Such words are marked with an asterisk (∗) in the translation, and are explained in a short glossary at the end of the section.

1. Indispensable words

私　watashi **I**

(Note: slightly formal: 私 watakushi; familiar: male: 僕 boku; female: あたし atashi; very familiar/rough/vulgar, usually male: おれ ore)

あなた anata **you**

(Note: familiar/affectionate: 君 kimi; very familiar/rough/vulgar: お前 omae; rough/vulgar: てめえ temē; insulting: きさま kisama)

彼　kare **he**

彼女　kanojo **she**

はい　hai **yes**

いいえ　iie **no**

どうぞ　dōzo **please**

ありがとう（ございます）arigatō (gozaimasu) **Thank you.**

どういたしまして　dō itashimashite **You're welcome./Don't mention it.**

いいえ，結構です　iie, kekkō desu **No, thank you.**

すみません　sumimasen **excuse me/pardon me/I'm sorry**

2. Greetings

General

お早うございます　o-hayō gozaimasu **Good morning.**

今日は　konnichi wa **Good morning./Good afternoon./Hello.** (said from about 10 a.m. to early evening)

今晩は　konban wa **Good evening.**

お休みなさい　o-yasumi nasai **Good night.**

ご機嫌いかがですか　go-kigen ikaga desu ka **How are you?** (very formal)

お元気ですか　o-genki desu ka **How are you?** (less formal)

ありがとう．とても元気です　arigatō. totemo genki desu **I'm fine, thank you.**

よいお天気ですね　yoi o-tenki desu ne **Nice weather, isn't it?**

今日は寒いですね　kyō wa samui desu ne **It's cold today, isn't it?**

さようなら　sayōnara **Goodbye.**

行って参ります　itte mairimasu (no English equivalent; said when leaving for a destination with the intention of returning)

行っていらっしゃい　itte irasshai (no English equivalent; said in response to the above)

ただ今　tadaima **I'm home./I'm back.**

お帰りなさい　o-kaeri nasai **Welcome home./Welcome back.** (said in response to the above, but the order may also be reversed)

Visiting

ごめん下さい　gomen kudasai **Hello./Anybody home?**

いらっしゃいませ　irasshaimase **Welcome.**

おじゃまします　o-jama shimasu (no English equivalent; said when entering a place)

どうぞこちらへ　dōzo kochira e **This way, please.**

ちょっとお待ち下さい　chotto o-machi kudasai **One moment, please.**

お掛け下さい　o-kake kudasai **Have a seat.**

お目にかかれてうれしいです　o-me ni kakarete ureshii desu **Pleased to meet you.**

長いことおじゃまいたしました　nagai koto o-jama itashimashita **Thank you for your time.**

この辺で失礼いたします　kono hen de shitsurei itashimasu **I'll be going now.**

明日またお会いしましょう　myōnichi mata o-ai shimashō **See you again tomorrow.**

Meals

お上がり下さい　o-agari kudasai **Help yourself** (literally, "please eat")

いただきます　itadakimasu (no English equivalent; said when beginning to eat or drink)

ごちそうさまでした　gochisōsama deshita **I enjoyed the meal./Thanks for the meal.**

3. Introducing oneself

私は日本人（オーストラリア人）です　watashi wa nihonjin (ōsutorariajin) desu **I am Japanese/Australian.**

名前は鈴木花子です　namae wa suzuki hanako desu **My name is Hanako Suzuki.**

私は学生です　watashi wa gakusei desu **I am a university student.**

京都からきました　kyōto kara kimashita **I come from Kyoto.**

22才です　nijūnissai desu **I am 22 years old.**

兄が2人妹が1人います　ani ga futari imōto ga hitori imasu **I have 2 older brothers and a younger sister.**

父は建築家です　chichi wa kenchikuka desu **My father is an architect.**

私は外国に行ったことがありません　watashi wa gaikoku ni itta koto ga arimasen **I have never been to a foreign country.**

私は少ししか英語を話せません　watashi wa sukoshi shika eigo wo hanasemasen **I can only speak a little English.**

趣味は音楽鑑賞です　shumi wa ongaku kanshō desu **My favorite pastime is listening to music.**

. . . が好きではありません　...ga suki de wa arimasen **I don't like ....**

私は水泳が得意です　watashi wa suiei ga tokui desu **I am a good swimmer.**

. . . が苦手です　...ga nigate desu **I am not very good at....**

4. Questions and requests

これは何ですか　kore wa nan desu ka **What is this?**

あの人はだれですか　ano hito wa dare desu ka **Who is that ?**

いつですか　itsu desu ka **When (is it etc) ?**

どこから来ましたか　doko kara kimashita ka **Where did you come from/where are you from ?**

どうなりましたか　dō narimashita ka **What happened/what is the matter ?**

どのぐらい遠いですか　donogurai tōi desu ka **How far (away) is it ?**

いくらですか　ikura desu ka **How much is it ?**

何をしているのですか　nani wo shite iru no desu ka **What are you doing ?**

何がほしいのですか　nani ga hoshii no desu ka **What do you want ?**

... がありますか　...ga arimasu ka **Is there a .../do you have ... ?**

... を持っていますか　...wo motte imasu ka **Do you have a ... ?**

これをいただいてもよろしいですか　kore wo itadaite mo yoroshii desu ka **May I have this ?**

... がほしい　...ga hoshii **I want a ....**

... がほしくない　...ga hoshikunai **I don't want ....**

... を取って下さい　...wo totte kudasai **Take ....**

5. Manners

ごめんなさい　gomen nasai **I'm sorry./Pardon me./Forgive me.**

失礼します　shitsurei shimasu **Excuse me./pardon me.**

すみません　sumimasen **Excuse me.** (used to get attention when seeking information, calling a waiter etc)

お手数掛けてすみません　o-tesū kakete sumimasen **I'm sorry to trouble you like this.**

よろしくお願いします　yoroshiku o-negai shimasu (no English equivalent; rather like a very formal "please")

ご迷惑でしょうか　go-meiwaku deshō ka **Is it too much trouble ?**

心配いりません　shinpai irimasen **Don't worry.**

かまいません　kamaimasen **It doesn't matter.**

よろしいんですよ　yoroshiin desu yo **That's all right.**

何とおっしゃいましたか　nan to osshaimashita ka **What did you say ?**

もう一度言って下さい　mō ichido itte kudasai **Please say that again.**

ゆっくり話して下さい　yukkuri hanashite kudasai **Please speak slowly.**

急いでいます　isoide imasu **I'm in a hurry.**

用意ができています　yōi ga dekite imasu **I'm ready.**

ちょっとお待ち下さい　chotto o-machi kudasai **Just a moment, please.**

6. Conveying information

私はあの少年を知っています　watashi wa ano shōnen wo shitte imasu **I know that boy.**

その人を知りません　sono hito wo shirimasen **I never heard of him/her.**

はっきりとは分かりません　hakkiri to wa wakarimasen **I really don't know for certain.**

覚えています　oboete imasu **(Yes,) I remember.**

忘れました　wasuremashita **I forgot.**

私はとても怒っています　watashi wa totemo okotte imasu **I am very angry.**

私はたいへん不愉快です　watashi wa taihen fuyukai desu **I am very upset.**

気分は最高です　kibun wa saikō desu **I feel great.**

とても幸せです　totemo shiawase desu **I feel very happy.**

残念です　zannen desu **That's too bad.**

家族と／が離ればなれで寂しい　kazoku to／ga hanarebanare de sabishii **I miss my family.**

それは正しいと思います　sore wa tadashii to omoimasu **That's correct.**

あなたは間違っています　anata wa machigatte imasu **You're mistaken.**

あなたの言う通りです　anata no iu tōri desu **It's as you say.**

一生懸命に働きます　isshōkenmei ni hatarakimasu **I'm going to work hard.**

7. Eating out

a. getting seats

私はとても空腹です　watashi wa totemo kūfuku desu **I'm very hungry.**

私はのどが渇きました　watashi wa nodo ga kawakimashita **I'm thirsty.**

食事に行きましょう　shokuji ni ikimashō **Let's go someplace to eat.**

安い店を紹介してくれませんか　yasui mise wo shōkai shite kuremasen ka **Do you know some inexpensive place ?**

角のてんぷら屋がおいしいと評判です　kado no tenpuraya ga oishii to hyōban desu **They say the tempura* place on the corner is pretty good.**

1時にテーブルを予約して下さい　ichiji ni tēburu wo yoyaku shite kudasai **Reserve a table for one o'clock, will you please ?**

3人連れですが、空いているテーブルありますか　sanninzure desu ga, aite iru tēburu arimasu ka **Do you have a table for 3 ?**

満席です　manseki desu **Sorry, we're all filled up.**

昼時はどこも混んでいます　hirudoki wa doko mo konde imasu **At noontime everywhere you go it's crowded.**

禁煙席にお願いします　kin-enseki ni o-negai shimasu **We want a non-smoking** table, please.

b. ordering

メニューを見せていただけますか　menyū wo misete itadakemasu ka **Can we see a menu, please?**

定食はありますか　teishoku wa arimasu ka **Do you have set meals?**

本日のおすすめ料理は何ですか　honjitsu no o-susume ryōri wa nan desu ka **What's today's specialty?**

この地方の名物は何ですか　kono chihō no meibutsu wa nan desu ka **What's the local specialty?**

何を食べたいですか　nani wo tabetai desu ka **What do you feel like eating?**

これは何の料理ですか　kore wa nan no ryōri desu ka **What is this?**

... を食べて見ませんか　...wo tabete mimasen ka **How about trying the ...?**

私は... にしたい　watashi wa ...ni shitai **I want the ....**

私は魚が大好きです　watashi wa sakana ga daisuki desu **I just love fish.**

私は肉は嫌いです　watashi wa niku wa kirai desu **I hate meat.**

私はピーマンは食べられません　watashi wa pīman wa taberaremasen **I can't eat green peppers.**

おいしいです　oishii desu **It's delicious.**

これはまずい　kore wa mazui **It tastes awful.**

もう少しパンを下さい　mō sukoshi pan wo kudasai **Can we have some more bread, please?**

ご飯のおかわりを下さい　gohan no o-kawari wo kudasai **Another bowl of rice, please.**

塩を取って下さい　shio wo totte kudasai **Please pass the salt.**

スープがまだきていません　sūpu ga mada kite imasen **We didn't get our soup yet.**

味が薄い　aji ga usui **This needs more seasoning.**

辛すぎます　karasugimasu **It's too salty.**

おなかがいっぱいになりました　onaka ga ippai ni narimashita **I'm full.**

c. drinks

飲物は何になさいますか　nomimono wa nani ni nasaimasu ka **What will you have to drink?**

生ビールを下さい　namabīru wo kudasai **We'll have draft beer.**

ブランディーはありますか　burandī wa arimasu ka **Do you have any brandy?**

ミルクティーを2つ下さい　mirukutī wo futatsu kudasai **Two teas with milk,** please.

ダイエットをしているので砂糖はいりません　daietto wo shite iru no de satō wa irimasen **I'm on a diet, so no sugar, please.**

コーヒーのおかわりを下さい　kōhī no o-kawari wo kudasai **More coffee, please.**

水をもういっぱい下さい　mizu wo mō ippai kudasai **More water, please.**

このお茶は少し熱い　kono o-cha wa sukoshi atsui **This tea is too hot.**

d. paying

勘定をお願いします　kanjō wo o-negai shimasu **Can I have the bill, please?**

伝票を調べて下さい。間違っていると思います　denpyō wo shirabete kudasai. machigatte iru to omoimasu **Check this bill, will you? I think there's a mistake on it.**

サラダは取っていません　sarada wa totte imasen **I didn't order any salad.**

伝票を別々にしてくれませんか　denpyō wo betsubetsu ni shite kuremasen ka **Will you give us separate bills, please?**

e. restaurant words

レストラン　resutoran **restaurant**

軽食　keishoku **light lunches**

メニュー　menyū **menu**

勘定(書)　kanjō(gaki) **bill/check**

化粧室　keshōshitsu **restroom(s)**

ウエイトレス　ueitoresu **waitress**

ウエイター　ueitā **waiter**

板前　itamae **cook**

茶碗(ﾜﾝ)　chawan **rice bowl/teacup (for Japanese tea)**

湯呑み　yunomi **teacup (for Japanese tea)**

カップ　kappu **cup/teacup/coffee cup (with handle)**

箸(ﾊｼ)　hashi **chopsticks**

つまようじ　tsumayōji **toothpick**

灰皿　haizara **ashtray**

たばこ　tabako **cigarette**

日本酒　nihonshu **sake***

銚子(ﾁｮｳ)／とっくり　chōshi*/tokkuri* **(no English equivalent; see glossary)**

熱燗(ﾝ)　atsukan **hot sake**

水　mizu **water**

ミルク　miruku **milk**

砂糖　satō **sugar**

紅茶　kōcha **tea**

日本茶　nihoncha **Japanese tea**

塩　shio **salt**

こしょう　koshō **pepper**

芥子(からし)　karashi **mustard**

油　abura **oil**

酢　su **vinegar**

正油(しょうゆ)　shōyu **soy sauce**

どんぶり　donburi **bowl**

味噌(みそ)　miso **miso***

わさび　wasabi **wasabi***

f. some Japanese dishes

すき焼き　sukiyaki　beef cooked at table with green onions, tofu, and leafy vegetables

寿司(すし)　sushi　cooked rice seasoned with vinegar and served in various forms with a topping of fish, shellfish, and vegetables

てんぷら　tenpura　fish, shellfish, and vegetables coated with batter and fried in deep fat

天丼(てんどん)　tendon　a bowl of rice topped with tempura* dipped in broth

豆腐　tōfu　white soya-bean curd with a soft, cheeselike consistency

梅干　umeboshi　ume* pickled with salt and a pungent seasoning

刺身　sashimi　fish and shellfish sliced and eaten raw with soy sauce and wasabi*

納豆　nattō　fermented soy beans

うどん　udon　wheat-flour noodles

そば – soba　buckwheat noodles

味噌(みそ)汁　misoshiru　soup flavored with miso

お握(にぎ)り　o-nigiri　rice compacted into a ball or other shape for carrying on outings, to work etc

餅(もち)　mochi　glutinous rice steamed, pounded into a paste, shaped into patties, and allowed to harden

赤飯　sekihan　glutinous rice steamed with red beans

たくあん　takuan　radish pickled in salt and rice bran

お好み焼き　okonomiyaki　a sort of hotcake made from wheat flour batter to which have been added various vegetables and other ingredients and fried on a hot plate

ところてん　tokoroten　a jelly made from a species of seaweed and eaten as a refreshing dish in summer

おでん　oden　various fish and vegetable preparations stewed in a light broth

ようかん　yōkan　a jellied confection made from highly sweetened beans

雑煮　zōni　a soup with vegetables, fish, and meat to which mochi are added: a traditional New Year's dish

おせち　o-sechi　an assortment of New Year's dishes prepared several days beforehand from ingredients that will not spoil; the idea is to give the womenfolk a degree of respite from the drudgery of kitchen work on the greatest feast of the year

煎餅(せんべい)　senbei　fried crackers made from rice flour

Shopping
a. going out

私は帽子が買いたい　watashi wa bōshi ga kaitai **I need a new hat.**

どのお店が一番よいですか　dono o-mise ga ichiban yoi desu ka **Do you know a good store?**

駅のそばの果物屋は安いので有名です　eki no soba no kudamonoya wa yasui no de yūmei desu **The fruit store near the station is known for its low prices.**

デパートで今セールをやっています　depāto de ima sēru wo yatte imasu **They're having a sale at the department store today.**

一緒に買い物に行きましょう　issho ni kaimono ni ikimashō **How about coming shopping with me?**

… はどこで買えますか　...wa doko de kaemasu ka **Where can you buy a ... ?**

一番近い本屋はどこですか　ichiban chikai hon-ya wa doko desu ka **Where's the closest bookstore?**

靴売場はどこですか　kutsu uriba wa doko desu ka **Where is the shoe department?**

b. picking things out

店員さん、これを見せて下さい　ten-insan, kore wo misete kudasai **Excuse me, Miss, could you let me examine this item?**

… を売っていますか　...wo utte imasu ka **Do you sell ... here?**

… を買いたいのです　...wo kaitai no desu **I'm looking for ....**

こちらはいかがでしょう　kochira wa ikaga deshou **How about this one?**

何色がよろしいのですか　nani-iro ga yoroshii no desu ka **What color would you like?**

きれいな色ですね　kirei na iro desu ne **That's a pretty color, isn't it?**

これが気に入りました　kore ga ki ni irimashita **I like this one.**

あちらの方が好きです　achira no hō ga suki desu **I like that one.**

この色はあまり好きではありません　kono iro wa amari suki de wa arimasen **I don't like this color.**

別な色のものがありますか　betsu na iro no mono ga arimasu ka **Do you have this in a different color?**

別の品物を見せて下さい　betsu no shinamono wo misete kudasai **Show me something else.**

もっと安いものはありませんか　motto yasui mono wa arimasen ka **Do you have something cheaper?**

予算は1万円です　yosan wa ichiman en desu **My spending limit is 10,000 yen.**

予算の枠内で買いたいのです　yosan no wakunai de kaitai no desu **I don't want to go over my limit.**

サイズはいくらですか　saizu wa ikura desu ka **What size do you take?**

これはどのサイズですか　kore wa dono saizu desu ka **What size is this?**

サイズ... を下さい　saizu... wo kudasai **Give me a size ....**

もっと大きいものがありますか　motto ōkii mono ga arimasu ka **Do you have something bigger?**

大きすぎる　ōkisugiru **It's too big.**

高すぎる　takasugiru **It's too expensive.**

c. in various stores
clothing and shoes

セーターを見せて下さい　sētā wo misete kudasai **Show me some sweaters.**

ウインドーにあるのが好きです　uindō ni aru no ga suki desu **I like the one in the window.**

その着物は実に豪華ですね　sono kimono wa jitsu ni gōka desu ne **That kimono is really gorgeous.**

残念ながら着物は1人で着られません　zannennagara kimono wa hitori de kiraremasen **It's unfortunate, but a kimono is hard to put on by oneself.**

黒い絹の手袋がほしい　kuroi kinu no tebukuro ga hoshii **I want a pair of black silk gloves.**

試着していいですか　shichaku shite ii desu ka **Can I try it on?**

胸まわりは... です　munemawari wa ...desu **My bust/chest measures ....**

ウエストは... です　uesuto wa ...desu **My waist measures ....**

襟(衿)のサイズは... です　eri no saizu wa ...desu **My collar size is....**

この色は今年の流行です　kono iro wa kotoshi no ryūkō desu **This color is in fashion this year.**

このスタイルは好きではありません　kono sutairu wa suki de wa arimasen **I don't like this style.**

コート売り場はどこですか　kōto uriba wa doko desu ka **Where do you sell coats?**

このネクタイは実におしゃれです　kono nekutai wa jitsu ni o-share desu **This necktie is really stylish.**

靴下を２足ほしい　kutsushita wo nisoko hoshii **I want 2 pairs of socks.**

ビーチサンダルがほしい　bīchisandaru ga hoshii **I want a pair of beach sandals.**

このかかとは高すぎる　kono kakato wa takasugiru **The heels are too high.**

food and drink

パンを１個下さい　pan wo ikko kudasai **One loaf of bread, please.**

冷凍食品コーナーはどこですか　reitōshokuhin kōnā wa doko desu ka **Where are the frozen foods?**

… を１キロ下さい　...wo ichikiro kudasai **Give me one kilo of ....**

牛乳を１瓶下さい　gyūnyū wo hitobin kudasai **Give me a bottle of milk.**

それは新鮮ですか　sore wa shinsen desu ka **Is that fresh?**

これは古くなっている　kore wa furuku natte iru **This isn't fresh any more.**

賞味期間を過ぎている　shōmikikan wo sugite iru **The date on this has expired.**

これは悪くなっている　kore wa waruku natte iru **This has gone bad.**

medicines

ばんそうこうを下さい　bansōkō wo kudasai **I'd like a roll of adhesive tape.**

バンドエイドを下さい　bandoeido wo kudasai **Give me a box of Band-Aids®.**

日焼け止めの薬ありますか　hiyakedome no kusuri arimasu ka **Have you got something to prevent sunburn?**

消化不良にきく薬を下さい　shōkafuryō ni kiku kusuri wo kudasai **Give me something for indigestion, please.**

のどが痛みます。トローチを下さい　nodo ga itamimasu. torōchi wo kudasai **I have a sore throat; give me a box of cough drops.**

虫刺されにきく薬をくれませんか　mushisasare ni kiku kusuri wo kuremasen ka **Can you give me something for insect bites?**

総合ビタミン剤を下さい　sōgōbitaminzai wo kudasai **I want a bottle of vitamin tablets.**

この処方箋（せん）を調合していただけますか　kono shohōsen wo chōgō shite itadakemasu ka **Can I have this prescription filled, please ?**

小さな救急箱はありますか   chiisana kyūkyūbako wa arimasu ka **Do you have a small first-aid kit ?**

アスピリンを1瓶下さい   asupirin wo hitobin kudasai **Give me a bottle of aspirin, please.**

newspapers, books, stationery

英字新聞は売っていますか   eijishinbun wa utte imasu ka **Do you carry English-language newspapers ?**

市街地図はありますか   shigaichizu wa arimasu ka **Do you have a city map ?**

... 著の本がありますか   ...cho no hon ga arimasu ka **Do you have any books by ... ?**

ノートを2冊とボールペンを1本下さい   nōto wo nisatsu to bōrupen wo ippon kudasai **Two notebooks and a ballpoint, please.**

横書きの便せんはありますか   yokogaki no binsen wa arimasu ka **Have you got letter paper for writing left to right ?**

d. paying for things

これはいくらですか   kore wa ikura desu ka **How much is this ?**

全部でいくらになりますか   zenbu de ikura ni narimasu ka **How much all together ?**

勘定をお願いします   kanjō wo o-negai shimasu **Can I have the bill, please ?**

アメリカの通貨で売ってくれますか   amerika no tsūka de utte kuremasu ka **Can I pay in American money ?**

トラベラーズチェックで受けてくれますか   toraberāzuchekku de ukete kuremasu ka **Will you take traveler's checks ?**

少し高いですね   sukoshi takai desu ne **That's rather expensive, isn't it ?**

割引きしてくれますか   waribiki shite kuremasu ka **Can you give me a discount ?**

ここのレジは混んでいます   koko no reji wa konde imasu **The line at this check-out counter is too long.**

レシートをいただけますか   reshīto wo itadakemasu ka **Can I have a receipt ?**

おつりが間違っています   o-tsuri ga machigatte imasu **You gave me the wrong change.**

e. complaints

責任者に会いたい   sekininsha ni aitai **I want to speak to your superior.**

昨日これを買いました　sakujitsu kore wo kaimashita **I bought this yesterday.**

これは汚れている（破れている，壊れている，ひびが入っている，不良品だ）　kore wa yogorete iru (yaburete iru, kowarete iru, hibi ga haitte iru, furyōhin da) **This is stained (torn, broken, cracked, defective).**

この本には落丁があります　kono hon ni wa rakuchō ga arimasu **This book has pages missing.**

この薬は全く効果がありません　kono kusuri wa mattaku kōka ga arimasen **This medicine doesn't have any effect at all.**

店員の態度が悪い　ten-in no taido ga warui **I don't like your clerk's manners.**

これを取り替えて下さいませんか　kore wo torikaete kudasaimasen ka **Can I exchange this, please?**

お金を払い戻して下さいませんか　o-kane wo haraimodoshite kudasaimasen ka **Can I have my money back, please?**

f. repairing and mending

時計が壊れてしまいました　tokei ga kowarete shimaimashita **My watch is broken.**

修理できますか　shūri dekimasu ka **Can it be fixed?**

これを直して下さい　kore wo naoshite kudasai **Can you fix this?**

残念ながらそれはもはや修理できません　zannennagara sore wa mohaya shūri dekimasen **I'm sorry, but it's beyond repair.**

靴のかかとを新しいのとつけ替えていただけますか　kutsu no kakato wo atarashii no to tsukekaete itadakemasu ka **Can you put new heels on these shoes?**

待っている間にやってくれますか　matte iru aida ni yatte kuremasu ka **Can you do it while I wait?**

いつできますか　itsu dekimasu ka **How soon can you have it done?**

どのぐらい時間がかかりますか　dono gurai jikan ga kakarimasu ka **How long will it take?**

このジャケットのシミは抜けないでしょうか　kono jaketto no shimi wa nukenai deshō ka **Can you remove the stain on this jacket?**

このズボンのすそがほつれているので繕っていただけますか　kono zubon no suso ga hotsurete iru no de tsukurotte itadakemasu ka **The cuffs on these pants are worn. Can you mend them?**

…の具合が悪いのでみていただけますか　...no guai ga warui no de mite itadakemasu ka **The ... is out of order. Could you have a look at it, please?**

できるだけ早く直していただきたい　dekiru dake hayaku naoshite itadakitai **I want** this fixed as soon as possible.

費用はいくらですか　hiyō wa ikura desu ka **How much will it cost?**

9. Postal and Telephone Service

a. the post office

一番近い郵便局はどこですか　ichiban chikai yūbinkyoku wa doko desu ka **Where is the nearest post office?**

郵便局は何時まで開いていますか　yūbinkyoku wa nanji made aite imasu ka **What time does the post office close?**

ポストはどこにありますか　posuto wa doko ni arimasu ka **Do you know where there's a mailbox?**

ちょうど記念切手を売り出しているところです　chōdo kinenkitte wo uridashite iru tokoro desu **They have just issued a new commemorative stamp.**

カナダまで葉書はいくらですか　kanada made hagaki wa ikura desu ka **How much is a postcard to Canada?**

アメリカまで航空便はいくらですか　amerika made kōkūbin wa ikura desu ka **How much is an air mail letter to America?**

イギリスまで船便ではいくらですか　igirisu made funabin de wa ikura desu ka **How much is surface mail to Britain?**

この小包をお願いします　kono kozutsumi wo o-negai shimasu **I want to mail this package.**

この手紙を速達で送りたい　kono tegami wo sokutatsu de okuritai **I want to send this letter by express mail.**

この手紙を書留にしたい　kono tegami wo kakitome ni shitai **I want to send this letter by registered mail.**

官製葉書を10枚下さい　kanseihagaki wo jūmai kudasai **Ten government postcards*, please.**

大体何日頃届きますか　daitai nannichi goro todokimasu ka **Do you know how many days it will take to get there?**

b. telephones and telegrams

一番近い電話ボックスはどこですか　ichiban chikai denwabokkusu wa doko desu ka **Where is the nearest telephone booth?**

電話を掛けたい　denwa wo kaketai **I want to make a phone call.**

オーストラリアに電話したい　ōsutoraria ni denwa shitai **I want to make a phone call to Australia.**

小銭が不足しています．テレフォンカードをお持ちですか　kozeni ga fusoku shite

imasu. terefonkādo wo o-mochi desu ka **I don't have enough small change. Do you have a telephone card?**

コレクトコールにしたい　korekutokōru ni shitai **I want to make a collect call.**

もしもし... さんですか　moshimoshi ...san desu ka **Hello. Is this Mr. ...?**

どちら様ですか　dochirasama desu ka **Who is this calling, please?**

内線... 番をお願いします　naisen ...ban wo o-negai shimasu **Give me extension ..., please.**

そのままお待ち下さい　sono mama o-machi kudasai **Please hold the line a moment.**

... はただ今外出中です　...wa tadaima gaishutsuchū desu **... is out at the moment.**

... はいつお戻りですか　...wa itsu o-modori desu ka **When will ... be back?**

伝言をお願いできますか　dengon wo o-negai dekimasu ka **Will you take a message, please?**

... より電話があったと彼に伝えて下さい　...yori denwa ga atta to kare ni tsutaete kudasai **Please tell him that ... called.**

後ほどお電話します　nochihodo o-denwa shimasu **I'll call again later.**

私に電話するように伝えて下さい　watashi ni denwa suru yō ni tsutaete kudasai **Please tell him to call me.**

話し中です　hanashichū desu **The line is busy.**

電話番号が間違っています　denwabangō ga machigatte imasu **You have the wrong number.**

留守番電話にメッセージが入っています　rusubandenwa ni messēji ga haitte imasu **There's a message on the answering machine.**

電報を打ちたい　denpō wo uchitai **I want to send a telegram.**

1語あたりいくらですか　ichigo atari ikura desu ka **How much is it for each word?**

祝電(弔電)を打ちたい　shukuden (chōden) wo uchitai **I want to send a telegram of congratulation [condolence].**

10. Transport

a. trains

駅はどこにありますか　eki wa doko ni arimasu ka **Where is the train station?**

新幹線のホームはどこですか　shinkansen no hōmu wa doko desu ka **Where are the shinkansen* tracks?**

切符は自動発券機で買えます　kippu wa jidōhakkenki de kaemasu **You can buy your ticket at the automatic ticket machine.**

新幹線の座席指定はこの用紙に必要事項を記入します　shinkansen no zaseki shitei wa kono yōshi ni hitsuyōjikō wo kinyū shimasu **You have to fill out this form to get a reserved seat on the shinkansen*.**

9：30分発京都行きの特急に乗りたいのですが　kujisanjippunhatsu kyōtoyuki no tokkyū ni noritai no desu ga **I want a ticket on the 9:30 special express to Kyōto, please.**

禁煙席を希望します　kin-enseki wo kibō shimasu **If possible I want a non-smoking seat.**

往復の切符を買いたい　ōfuku no kippu wo kaitai **I want a round-trip ticket.**

寝台車を予約したい　shindaisha wo yoyaku shitai **I want to reserve a berth on a sleeping car.**

寝台車はいくらですか　shindaisha wa ikura desu ka **How much does a sleeping car ticket cost?**

急行列車ですか、それとも普通列車ですか　kyūkōressha desu ka, soretomo futsūressha desu ka **Do you want the express train or the local train?**

この電車は…へ行きますか　kono densha wa ..e ikimasu ka **Does this train go to ...?**

もっと早くでる列車はありますか　motto hayaku deru ressha wa arimasu ka **Isn't there an earlier train?**

この列車には食堂車がありますか　kono ressha ni wa shokudōsha ga arimasu ka **Is there a dining car on this train?**

… まで片道 3 枚下さい　...made katamichi sanmai kudasai **Three one-way tickets to ..., please.**

この切符は何日間有効ですか　kono kippu wa nannichikan yūkō desu ka **How long is this ticket valid?**

この列車は何時に発車しますか　kono ressha wa nanji ni hassha shimasu ka **What time does this train leave?**

… 行きの列車は何番ホームから発車しますか　...yuki no ressha wa nanban hōmu kara hassha shimasu ka **Where do I get the train for ...?**

… には何時に到着しますか　...ni wa nanji ni tōchaku shimasu ka **What time does the train get to ...?**

… からの列車は何時に到着しますか　...kara no ressha wa nanji ni tōchaku shimasu ka **What time does the train from ... get in?**

この列車は…に停まりますか　kono ressha wa .. ni tomarimasu ka **Does this train stop at ...?**

この列車は遅れていますか　kono ressha wa okurete imasu ka **Is this train running late?**

指定券を持っています　shiteiken wo motte imasu **I have a reservation.**

車掌が検札に来ました　shashō ga kensatsu ni kimashita **The conductor is here to check the tickets.**

この席は空いていますか　kono seki wa aite imasu ka **Is this seat taken ?** (literally, "Is this seat open ?")

どこで乗換えですか　doko de norikae desu ka **Where do I transfer ?**

時刻表はどこにありますか　jikokuhyō wa doko ni arimasu ka **Where is the time-table ?**

近ごろは自動改札が増えました　chikagoro wa jidōkaisatsu ga fuemashita **Nowa-days you see more and more automatic wickets.**

b. buses

バス停はどこですか　basutei wa doko desu ka **Where is the bus stop ?**

... 行きのバスの発着所はどこですか　...yuki no basu no hatchakujo wa doko desu ka **Where do I get the bus for ... ?**

このバスは... に停まりますか　kono basu wa ...ni tomarimasu ka **Does this bus stop at ... ?**

... までどのぐらい時間がかかりますか　...made dono gurai jikan ga kakarimasu ka **How long does it take to get to ... ?**

定期観光バスに乗りたい　teiki kankōbasu ni noritai **I want to ride a scheduled sightseeing bus.**

そのバスは何時に... に着きますか　sono basu wa nanji ni ...ni tsukimasu ka **What time does the bus reach ... ?**

そのバスは何時に発車しますか　sono basu wa nanji ni hassha shimasu ka **What time does the bus leave ?**

このバスはどのぐらいの間隔で出ていますか　kono basu wa donogurai no kankaku de dete imasu ka **How often does this bus leave ?**

次のバスは何時ですか　tsugi no basu wa nanji desu ka **What time is the next bus ?**

... の近くを通りますか　...no chikaku wo tōrimasu ka **Does the bus pass near ... ?**

... 行きのバスはどれですか　...yuki no basu wa dore desu ka **Which is the bus for ... ?**

... まで行きたい　...made ikitai **I want to go to ....**

どこで降りたらいいでしょうか　doko de oritara ii deshō ka **Where should I get off ?**

最終バスは出てしまいましたか　saishūbasu wa dete shimaimashita ka **Has the last** bus already left ?

c. taxis

タクシー乗り場はどこですか　takushīnoriba wa doko desu ka **Where is the taxi stand ?**

空車が来ました　kūsha ga kimashita **Here comes an empty taxi.**

... ホテルまで行って下さい　...hoteru made itte kudasai **Take me to the ... Hotel.**

遅れているので少し急いでくれませんか　okurete iru no de sukoshi isoide kuremasen ka **I'm late, so could you go a little faster ?**

ここで止って下さい　koko de tomatte kudasai **Stop here, please.**

待っていて下さい　matte ite kudasai **Wait for me, please.**

名所旧跡がみたい　meishokyūseki ga mitai **I want to go sightseeing.**

そこは遠いですか　soko wa tōi desu ka **Is it very far from here ?**

... までどのぐらいの時間ですか　...made dono gurai no jikan desu ka **How long does it take to get there ?**

いくらですか　ikura desu ka **How much is it ?**

d. airplanes

航空会社の営業所はどこにありますか　kōkūgaisha no eigyōsho wa doko ni arimasu ka **Where is the airline office ?**

日曜日の午後の便で... まで3席予約したい　nichiyōbi no gogo no bin de ...made sanseki yoyaku shitai **I want 3 tickets to ... on the Sunday afternoon flight.**

金曜日に... までの便がありますか　kinyōbi ni ...made no bin ga arimasu ka **Is there a flight to ... on Friday ?**

その便は何時に発ちますか　sono bin wa nanji ni tachimasu ka **What time does that flight leave ?**

その便は何時に到着しますか　sono bin wa nanji ni tōchaku shimasu ka **What time does that flight arrive ?**

... の予約をキャンセルして下さい　...no yoyaku wo kyanseru shite kudasai **Please cancel my reservation for ...**

予約を変更したい　yoyaku wo henkō shitai **I want to change my reservation.**

次の便は何時ですか　tsugi no bin wa nanji desu ka **When is the next flight ?**

市内から空港までのバスがありますか　shinai kara kūkō made no basu ga arimasu ka **Is there a bus from the city center to the airport ?**

e. boats

その船は何時に出航ですか　sono fune wa nanji ni shukkō desu ka **What time does the boat leave?**

次の出航は何時ですか　tsugi no shukkō wa nanji desu ka **When does the next boat leave?**

その船はどこに入港ですか　sono fune wa doko ni nyūkō desu ka **What stops does the boat make?**

その船は...に寄港しますか　sono fune wa ...ni kikō shimasu ka **Does the boat stop at ...?**

...まで船便がありますか　...made funabin ga arimasu ka **Is there a boat to ...?**

この船でどのぐらい時間がかかりますか　kono fune de dono gurai jikan ga kakarimasu ka **How much time does this boat take to get there?**

一人用船室を予約できますか　hitoriyō senshitsu wo yoyaku dekimasu ka **Can I reserve a single stateroom?**

部屋にはいくつ寝台がありますか　heya ni wa ikutsu shindai ga arimasu ka **How many beds are there in the stateroom?**

いつ入港しますか　itsu nyūkō shimasu ka **When will we reach port?**

何時に乗船しなければなりませんか　nanji ni jōsen shinakereba narimasen ka **By what time do we have to be on board?**

港にどのぐらい停泊しますか　minato ni dono gurai teihaku shimasu ka **How long will the boat stay in port?**

f. cars

運転免許証を持っています　unten menkyoshō wo motte imasu **I have a driver's license.**

友人とドライブに出かけましょう　yūjin to doraibu ni dekakemashō **Let's go for a drive with some friends.**

いい車ですね. 自家用車ですか　ii kuruma desu ne. jikayōsha desu ka **Nice car. Is it yours?**

いいえ, レンタカーです　iie. rentakā desu **No, it's rented.**

どこで車を借りられますか　doko de kuruma wo kariraremasu ka **Where can I rent a car?**

レンタカーは1時間いくらですか　rentakā wa ichijikan ikura desu ka **What's the fee per hour to rent this car?**

一番近いガソリンスタンドはどこですか　ichiban chikai gasorinsutando wa doko desu ka **Where is the nearest gas station?**

満タンにして下さい　mantan ni shite kudasai **Fill it up, please.**

ガソリン，リッターあたりいくらですか　gasorin, rittā atari ikura desu ka **How much is gasoline per liter ?**

洗車して下さい　sensha shite kudasai **Wash the car, please.**

道路地図はありますか　dōrochizu wa arimasu ka **Do you have a road map ?**

駐車場はどこですか　chūshajō wa doko desu ka **Where is the parking lot ?**

ここは駐車禁止ですか　koko wa chūsha kinshi desu ka **Is this a no parking zone ?**

今どこでしょうか　ima doko deshō ka **Where are we now ?**

地図で示して下さい　chizu de shimeshite kudasai **Show me on the map.**

次のドライブインで昼食にしましょう　tsugi no doraibuin de chūshoku ni shimashō **Let's have lunch at the next drive-in.**

... にはどう行けばいいですか　...ni wa dō ikeba ii desu ka **How do you get to ... ?**

... はどこにありますか　...wa doko ni arimasu ka **Where is ... ?**

... への自動車道にはどう行けばいいですか　...e no jidōshadō ni wa dō ikeba ii desu ka **How do you get to the expressway for ... ?**

... へはどの道を行けば一番いいですか　...e wa dono michi wo ikeba ichiban ii desu ka **What's the best road to ... ?**

... までどのぐらいの距離がありますか　...made dono gurai no kyori ga arimasu ka **How far is it to ... ?**

... に夕刻までには着くのでしょうか　...ni yūkoku made ni wa tsuku no deshō ka **Will we reach ... by evening ?**

高速道路は混んでいます　kōsokudōro wa konde imasu **The expressway is clogged with heavy traffic.**

渋滞に巻き込まれました　jūtai ni makikomaremashita **I got caught in heavy traffic.**

抜け道がありますか　nukemichi ga arimasu ka **Is there a back road to get around the traffic ?**

このまま5キロほどまっすぐ行って下さい　kono mama 5 kiro hodo massugu itte kudasai **Go straight along this road for 5 kilometers.**

次の信号を右に曲って下さい　tsugi no shingō wo migi ni magatte kudasai **Turn right at the next signal.**

車の鍵(㊭)をなくさないように　kuruma no kagi wo nakusanai yō ni **Don't lose your car keys.**

some road signs

右側通行　migigawa tsūkō **keep right**

一方通行道路　ippōtsūkōdōrò **one way**

迂回　ukai **detour**

駐車禁止　chūsha kinshi **no parking**

追い越し禁止　oikoshi kinshi **no passing**

進入禁止　shinnyū kinshi **no entry**

前方道路工事中　zenpō dōro kōjichū **construction ahead**

11. Hotels

安くてよいホテルを紹介して下さい　yasukute yoi hoteru wo shōkai shite kudasai
Can you tell me the name of a hotel that is good and also cheap?

今夜部屋はありますか　kon-ya heya wa arimasu ka **Do you have a vacancy for
tonight?**

2人で泊まれる部屋がありますか　futari de tomareru heya ga arimasu ka **Do you
have a room for two?**

シングルの部屋を3室予約します　shinguru no heya wo sanshitsu yoyaku shimasu **I
would like to reserve 3 single rooms.**

その部屋は何階にありますか　sono heya wa nangai ni arimasu ka **What floor is
that room on?**

2階の部屋は空いていますか　nikai no heya wa aite imasu ka **Do you have a
room on the second floor?**

この部屋にします　kono heya ni shimasu **I'll take this room.**

別の部屋がありませんか　betsu no heya ga arimasen ka **Don't you have some
other room?**

ツインしかありません　tsuin shika arimasen **We only have a twin room.**

空き室はこれだけです　akishitsu wa kore dake desu **This is the only vacancy we
have.**

和室の部屋はありますか　washitsu no heya wa arimasu ka **Do you have a Japa-
nese-style room?**

この部屋は1泊いくらですか　kono heya wa ippaku ikura desu ka **What's the
rate for this room?**

もっと安い部屋はありませんか　motto yasui heya wa arimasen ka **Don't you
have something cheaper?**

明朝7：30分に起して下さい　myōchō shichiji sanjuppun ni okoshite kudasai **Please
wake me up at 7:30 tomorrow morning.**

私の部屋にはタオルがありません　watashi no heya ni wa taoru ga arimasen **There
are no towels in my room.**

シーツが汚れています　shītsu ga yogorete imasu **The sheets are dirty.**

トイレの水が流れません　toire no mizu ga nagaremasen **The toilet won't flush.**

シャワーの出がよくありません　shawā no de ga yoku arimasen **There's no pressure in the shower.**

窓が空きません．開けて下さい　mado ga akimasen. akete kudasai **I can't get the window open. Please open it.**

暑すぎます　atsusugimasu **It's too hot in here.**

暖房を強くできますか　danbō wo tsuyoku dekimasu ka **Can you turn up the heat?**

冷房がきいていません　reibō ga kiite imasen **The air conditioning isn't working.**

鍵(ぎ)を下さい　kagi wo kudasai **Give me my key, please.**

私宛のメッセージがありますか　watashi ate no messēji ga arimasu ka **Are there any messages for me?**

この洋服を洗濯してほしい　kono yōfuku wo sentaku shite hoshii **I want to get this dress cleaned.**

このスーツにアイロンを掛けてほしい　kono sūtsu ni airon wo kakete hoshii **I want to get this suit pressed.**

明日の午前中までにできますか　myōnichi no gozenchū made ni dekimasu ka **Can you have it done by tomorrow morning?**

食堂はどこですか　shokudō wa doko desu ka **Where is the dining room?**

明後日の朝立ちます　asatte no asa tachimasu **I'll be leaving the day after tomorrow in the morning.**

勘定書きを用意してくれますか　kanjōgaki wo yōi shite kuremasu ka **Will you get my bill ready, please?**

荷物を下におろしていただけますか　nimotsu wo shita ni oroshite itadakemasu ka **Can you have my luggage taken downstairs, please?**

10時にタクシーを1台呼んでいただけますか　jūji ni takushī wo ichidai yonde itadakemasu ka **Will you call me a taxi for 10 o'clock, please?**

お世話になりました　o-sewa ni narimashita **I enjoyed my stay.**

12. Leisure time

a. sightseeing

名所旧跡を見物しましょう　meishokyūseki wo kenbutsu shimashō **Let's go sightseeing.**

ガイドブックを持ってきましたか　gaidobukku wo motte kimashita ka **Did you bring the guidebook?**

当地の見所は何ですか　tōchi no midokoro wa nan desu ka **What is there to see** around here?

この建物は何ですか　kono tatemono wa nan desu ka **What is this building?**

いつ建てられましたか　itsu tateraremashita ka **When was it built?**

誰(が)が建てましたか　dare ga tatemashita ka **Who built it?**

このお寺は何と言いますか　kono o-tera wa nan to iimasu ka **What's the name of this temple?**

これは美術館ですか　kore wa bijutsukan desu ka **Is this an art museum?**

... は何時に開きますか　...wa nanji ni akimasu ka **What time does ... open?**

何曜日が休館ですか　nanyōbi ga kyūkan desu ka **What days is it closed on?**

入場料はいくらですか　nyūjōryō wa ikura desu ka **How much is the entrance fee?**

切符はどこで買えますか　kippu wa doko de kaemasu ka **Where do they sell the tickets?**

カメラを持ってきましたか　kamera wo motte kimashita ka **Did you bring your camera?**

写真をとって下さい　shashin wo totte kudasai **Take a picture of that.**

写真をとってもいいですか　shashin wo totte mo ii desu ka **Is it all right to take pictures?**

撮影は禁止です　satsuei wa kinshi desu **Picture-taking is forbidden.**

ガイドさんについて行って下さい　gaidosan ni tsuite itte kudasai **Follow the guide.**

ガイドは英語を話せますか　gaido wa eigo wo hanasemasu ka **Can the guide speak English?**

ガイドはいりません　gaido wa irimasen **I don't need a guide.**

少し足をのばしてみましょう　sukoshi ashi wo nobashite mimashō **Let's walk on a little further.**

城に行くのはどのバスですか　shiro ni iku no wa dono basu desu ka **Which is the bus that goes to the castle?**

... に行く道はこれですか　...ni iku michi wa kore desu ka **Is this the road that goes to ...?**

... に行くにはどう行ったらよいですか　...ni iku ni wa dō ittara yoi desu ka **How can I get to ...?**

歩いて行けますか　aruite ikemasu ka **Is it close enough to walk?**

当地の名物料理は何ですか　tōchi no meibutsuryōri wa nan desu ka **What kind of cooking is this place known for?**

有名なお店を教えて下さい　yūmei na o-mise wo oshiete kudasai **Can you tell me the names of important stores in this area?**

土産には何を買ったらいいですか　miyage ni wa nani wo kattara ii desu ka **What kind of souvenirs should I buy to take home with me?**

民芸品のお店を紹介して下さい　mingeihin no o-mise wo shōkai shite kudasai **Can you direct me to a place that sells folk art?**

b. sports

プロ野球の観戦に行きたい　puroyakyū no kansen ni ikitai **I want to go to a professional baseball game.**

一番安い席はいくらですか　ichiban yasui seki wa ikura desu ka **How much is the cheapest ticket?**

何時に始まりますか　nanji ni hajimarimasu ka **What time does the game start?**

テニスをやりたい　tenisu wo yaritai **I want to play tennis.**

この海岸で泳げますか　kono kaigan de oyogemasu ka **Can you swim at this beach?**

水泳禁止です　suiei kinshi desu **It's a no swimming zone.**

私は美容のためにヨガとエアロビクスをやっています　watashi wa biyō no tame ni yoga to earobikusu wo yatte imasu **I do yoga and aerobics for beauty care.**

相撲は日本の国技です　sumō wa nippon no kokugi desu **Sumo is the Japanese national sport.**

兄は柔道5段剣道2段です　ani wa jūdō godan kendō nidan desu **My older brother holds a fifth dan in judo and a second dan in kendo.**

釣りに行きませんか　tsuri ni ikimasen ka **Would you like to go fishing with me?**

ボートを借りられますか　bōto wo kariraremasu ka **Can we rent a boat?**

なかなかゴルフの腕前が上がりません　nakanaka gorufu no udemae ga agarimasen **I don't seem to make any progress at golf.**

私はマリンスポーツが得意です　watashi wa marin supōtsu ga tokui desu **I specialize in marine sports.**

運動し過ぎて体じゅうの筋肉が痛い　undō shisugite karadajū no kinniku ga itai **I exercised too hard, and all my muscles are sore.**

子供とキャッチボールをします　kodomo to kyatchibōru wo shimasu **I play catch with my son.**

家族と一緒にアウトドアスポーツを楽しみました　kazoku to issho ni autodoa spōtsu wo tanoshimimashita **I had fun playing outdoors with my family.**

c. events

映画館で何かおもしろいものをやっていますか　eigakan de nanika omoshiroi mono

wo yatte imasu ka **Is there some good movie playing at the theater now ?**

コンサートがありますか　konsāto ga arimasu ka **Are there any concerts scheduled ?**

... デパートで生け花展があります　...depāto de ikebanaten ga arimasu **There is an ikebana* exhibition at the ... Department Store.**

... ホールで明晩オペラがあります　...hōru de myōban opera ga arimasu **There is an opera tomorrow night at the ... Hall.**

S席のチケットを2枚ほしい　esu-seki no chiketto wo nimai hoshii **I want 2 S tickets*, please.**

来週の火曜日の席を予約したい　raishū no kayōbi no seki wo yoyaku shitai **I want a reserved seat for next Tuesday.**

前売り券は明日から売り出します　maeuriken wa myōnichi kara uridashimasu **Advance tickets go on sale tomorrow.**

開演は何時ですか　kaien wa nanji desu ka **What time does the play start ?**

演目は何ですか　enmoku wa nan desu ka **What's the title of the play ?**

指揮者は誰ですか　shikisha wa dare desu ka **Who is the conductor ?**

配役を教えて下さい　haiyaku wo oshiete kudasai **Tell me the names of the actors.**

プログラムを2部下さい　puroguramu wo nibu kudasai **Two programs, please.**

日本の古典芸能に関心がありますか　nippon no kotengeinō ni kanshin ga arimasu ka **Do you have any interest in classical Japanese theater ?**

歌舞伎は見たことがありますか　kabuki wa mita koto ga arimasu ka **Have you ever been to see Kabuki* ?**

能はまだ一度も見たことがありません　nō wa mada ichido mo mita koto ga arimasen **I have never seen a Noh* play.**

13. Sickness and Accidents

a. sickness

病院へ行きたいのですが、どこがいいでしょうか　byōin e ikitai no desu ga, doko ga ii deshō ka **I want to get medical attention. Can you recommend a good hospital ?**

お医者さんを呼んで下さい　o-ishasan wo yonde kudasai **Please call a doctor.**

救急車を呼んで下さい　kyūkyūsha wo yonde kudasai **Please call an ambulance.**

私は病気です　watashi wa byōki desu **I am sick.**

とても気分が悪い　totemo kibun ga warui **I feel terrible.**

吐き気がする　hakike ga suru **I feel nauseated.**

頭ががんがん痛い　atama ga gangan itai **I have a splitting headache.**

視力が急に落ちた　shiryoku ga kyū ni ochita **My eyesight has gotten bad all of a sudden.**

耳なりがひどいのです　miminari ga hidoi no desu **I have a terrible ringing in my ears.**

虫歯が痛くてたまりません　mushiba ga itakute tamarimasen **I have a terrible toothache.**

歯医者さんへ行かなければなりませんか　haishasan e ikanakereba narimasen ka **Do you need to see a dentist ?**

食あたりをしたようです　shokuatari wo shita yō desu **I must've eaten something that didn't agree with me.**

胃をこわしました　i wo kowashimashita **I've got an upset stomach.**

消化不良を起こしました　shōkafuryō wo okoshimashita **I've got indigestion.**

風邪をひきました　kaze wo hikimashita **I have a cold.**

息苦しい　ikigurushii **I have trouble breathing.**

目まいがする　memai ga suru **I feel dizzy.**

私はずっと糖尿病を煩っています　watashi wa zutto tōnyōbyō wo wazuratte imasu **I have had diabetes for a long time.**

全く食欲がありません　mattaku shokuyoku ga arimasen **I have no appetite.**

熟睡できません　jukusui dekimasen **I have trouble sleeping.**

寒気がします　samuke ga shimasu **I'm getting chills.**

咳(ﾀ)が止まりません　seki ga tomarimasen **I can't stop coughing.**

持病の... が悪化したようです　jibyō no ...ga akka shita yō desu **His chronic ... has gotten worse.**

足首を捻挫(ﾈ)した　ashikubi wo nenza shita **I sprained my ankle.**

右腕を骨折した　migiude wo kossetsu shita **I broke my right arm.**

やけどをした　yakedo wo shita **I burnt myself.**

切り傷をした　kirikizu wo shita **I cut myself.**

いつからそんな状態ですか　itsu kara sonna jōtai desu ka **How long have you been like this ?**

昨日からこんな状態です　sakujitsu kara konna jōtai desu **I've been like this since yesterday.**

どこが痛いですか　doko ga itai desu ka **Where do you hurt ?**

寝ていないといけませんか　nete inai to ikemasen ka **Do I absolutely have to stay in bed ?**

絶対安静が必要です　zettai ansei ga hitsuyō desu **You need absolute rest.**

口を開けなさい　kuchi wo akenasai **Open your mouth.**

舌を出しなさい　shita wo dashinasai **Stick out your tongue.**

横になりなさい　yoko ni narinasai **Lie down.**

息を吸いなさい〔吐きなさい〕　iki wo suinasai 〔hakinasai〕 **Breathe in 〔out〕.**

薬局にこの処方箋(ﾌﾞ)を持って行きなさい　yakkyoku ni kono shohōsen wo motte ikinasai **Take this prescription to a pharmacy.**

1日に3回これを飲んで下さい　ichinichi ni sankai kore wo nonde kudasai **Take this 3 times a day.**

注射しましょう　chūsha shimashō **I'll give you an injection.**

袖(ﾌﾞ)をまくりなさい　sode wo makuri nasai **Roll up your sleeve.**

少し気分がよくなりました　sukoshi kibun ga yoku narimashita **I feel a little better now.**

おかげさまですっかり元気になりました　o-kagesama de sukkari genki ni narimashita **Thanks to you, I am completely cured.**

b. accidents and disasters

交番はどこですか　kōban wa doko desu ka **Is there a police box* around here ?**

警察を呼んで下さい　keisatsu wo yonde kudasai **Call the police.**

大至急110番して下さい　daishikyū hyakutōban shite kudasai **Quick, dial 110.**

領事館に知らせて下さい　ryōjikan ni shirasete kudasai **Please inform my consulate.**

私のカバンが盗まれました　watashi no kaban ga nusumaremashita **My briefcase has been stolen.**

財布をすられました　saifu wo suraremashita **A pickpocket stole my wallet.**

パスポートがなくなりました　pasupōto ga nakunarimashita **My passport is missing.**

交通事故にあいました　kōtsūjiko ni aimashita **I have had a traffic accident.**

... に車をぶつけました　...ni kuruma wo butsukemashita **I crashed my car into a ....**

駅の階段から落ちました　eki no kaidan kara ochimashita **I fell down the stairs in the station.**

雪道で滑りました　yukimichi de suberimashita **I slipped on the snowy street.**

大けがをしました. 救急車を呼んで下さい　ōkega wo shimashita. kyūkyūsha wo yonde kudasai **I am badly hurt. Please call an ambulance.**

重傷です. そっと担架に乗せて下さい　jūshō desu. sotto tanka ni nosete kudasai **He is badly hurt. Go easy when you put him on the stretcher.**

意識を失っています. 大丈夫でしょうか　ishiki wo ushinatte imasu. daijōbu deshō ka **She's unconscious. Will she be okay ?**

火事だ！火事だ！　kaji da! kaji da! **Fire! Fire!**

消火器はどこですか　shōkaki wa doko desu ka **Where's the fire extinguisher ?**

今朝の地震にはびっくりしました　kesa no jishin ni wa bikkuri shimashita **The earthquake this morning was frightening.**

台風の大雨で床下浸水になりました　taifū no ōame de yukashita shinsui ni narimashita **The heavy rains of the typhoon flooded my house almost up to floor level.**

家の前の川が反乱しました　ie no mae no kawa ga hanran shimashita **The river in front of my house overflowed its banks.**

... が行方不明です　...ga yukuefumei desu **...is missing.**

山で遭難しました．救助隊を呼んで下さい　yama de sōnan shimashita. kyūjotai wo yonde kudasai **We've had a bad accident on the mountain. Please call out the rescue squad.**

仕事の現場で事故にあいました　shigoto no genba de jiko ni aimashita **He had an accident at the construction site.**

補償はどうなるのでしょうか　hoshō wa dō naru no deshō ka **What does he have to do to get compensation ?**

14. At the office

新入社員の... です．よろしく　shinnyūshain no ...desu. yoroshiku **I have just joined the company and my name is .... I am happy to meet you.**

今日からアルバイトをする事になった... です　kyō kara arubaito wo suru koto ni natta ...desu **My name is ... and I have started today as a part-timer here.**

会社の中を案内しましょうか　kaisha no naka wo annai shimashō ka **Shall I show you around the place ?**

名刺をいただけませんか　meishi wo itadakemasen ka **Could I have your card, please ?**

私のデスクはどこですか　watashi no desuku wa doko desu ka **Which is my desk ?**

初めに何をしたらいいですか　hajime ni nani wo shitara ii desu ka **What's the first thing I need to do ?**

この小包を出してきて下さい　kono kozutsumi wo dashite kite kudasai **Go mail this package, will you ?**

会議室はどこですか　kaigishitsu wa doko desu ka **Where is the conference room ?**

会議を始めます　kaigi wo hajimemasu **The meeting will now come to order.**

食事に行きます　shokuji ni ikimasu **I'm going out to lunch.**

毎日忙しい　mainichi isogashii **Every day is a busy one for me.**

残業をしなければなりません　zangyō wo shinakereba narimasen **I have to work overtime today.**

お先に失礼します　o-saki ni shitsurei shimasu (no English equivalent; said when going home ahead of one's colleagues)

お疲れさまでした　o-tsukaresama deshita (no English equivalent; said as a polite goodbye in response to the above)

忙しくていやになります　isogashikute iya ni narimasu **I'm so busy it isn't funny.**

昨日も終電で帰ったのです　kinō mo shūden de kaetta no desu **Yesterday also I worked till it was time for the last train.**

ストレスがたまっています　sutoresu ga tamatte imasu **I'm all stressed out.**

ファックスは今使っています　fakkusu wa ima tsukatte imasu **The fax machine is busy now.**

コンピュータ通信ができる人はだれですか　konpyūtatsūshin ga dekiru hito wa dare desu ka **Is there someone here who knows how to send electronic mail?**

コピーをして下さい　kopī wo shite kudasai **Make me a copy of this, please.**

ワープロを打って下さい　wāpuro wo utte kudasai **Type this out on the word processor, will you?**

ファックスを送って下さい　fakkusu wo okutte kudasai **Fax this out, will you please?**

これ，すぐお願いできますか　kore, sugu o-negai dekimasu ka **Can you handle this right away, please?**

今，ちょっと忙しいんだけど　ima, chotto isogashiin da kedo **Sorry, I'm terribly busy right now.**

この件，すぐに調べて下さい　kono ken, sugu ni shirabete kudasai **Will you look into this right away, please?**

これから課長と打ち合わせです　kore kara kachō to uchiawase desu **I've got a meeting with the manager now.**

出張で大阪へ行ってきました　shutchō de ōsaka e itte kimashita **I just got back from Osaka on a business trip.**

もうじき人事異動があります　mō jiki jinjiidō ga arimasu **There's going to be some personnel changes soon.**

根回しがうまくいっていません　nemawashi ga umaku itte imasen **The prearrangements* aren't going well.**

忘年会はだれが幹事ですか　bōnenkai wa dare ga kanji desu ka **Who's in charge of the bonenkai*?**

二次会はどこに決まりましたか　nijikai wa doko ni kimarimashita ka **Where are** you going for the nijikai* ?

彼は企画部のベテランです　kare wa kikakubu no beteran desu **He's a veteran employee of the planning department.**

この資料に目を通して下さい　kono shiryō ni me wo tōshite kudasai **I want you to read through this material, would you ?**

このパソコンの操作を教えて下さい　kono pasokon no sōsa wo oshiete kudasai **Can you show me how to run this computer ?**

... さんを応接室へお通し下さい　...san wo ōsetsushitsu e o-tōshi kudasai **Show ... to the reception room, please.**

帰りにいっぱい飲みませんか　kaeri ni ippai nomimasen ka **How about a drink on the way home ?**

もういっぱいいかがですか　mō ippai ikaga desu ka **Have another drink ?**

ちょっと酔ったからタクシーで帰ります　chotto yotta kara takushī de kaerimasu **I'm drunk, so I'll take a taxi home.**

仕事にやっと慣れました　shigoto ni yatto naremashita **I've finally gotten used to my work.**

昇進おめでとうございます　shōshin omedetō gozaimasu **Congratulations on your promotion.**

... についてご意見を聞かせて下さい　...ni tsuite go-iken wo kikasete kudasai **We'd like to hear your opinion on this matter.**

会社を辞めることにしました　kaisha wo yameru koto ni shimashita **I have decided to leave the company.**

転職することに決めました　tenshoku suru koto ni kimemashita **I have decided to look for a new job.**

15. Calendar events

a. January

日本のお正月は初めてです　nihon no o-shōgatsu wa hajimete desu **This is my first experience of the New Year's celebration in Japan.**

明けましておめでとうございます　akemashite omdetō gozaimasu **Happy New Year !**

初詣(½)では人がいっぱいでした　hatsumōde wa hito ga ippai deshita **The temples and shrines were crowded with people out for the first prayers of the year.**

みんなで百人一首をやりませんか　minna de hyakuninisshu wo yarimasen ka **How about all of us playing hyakunin-isshu* ?**

雑煮とお節料理を召し上がれ　zōni to o-sechíryōri wo meshiagare **Help yourself to** the zoni* and New Year's dishes.

年賀状がたくさん来ました　nengajō ga takusan kimashita **I received a whole lot of New Year's cards.**

b. February

2月3日は節分です　nigatsu mikka wa setsubun desu **February 3 is the setsubun* festivity.**

冬が終わって新春を迎える日です　fuyu ga owatte shinshun wo mukaeru hi desu **It is the day for celebrating the end of winter and the advent of spring.**

豆まきをして家の中に福を呼び込みます　mamemaki wo shite ie no naka ni fuku wo yobikomimasu **People throw beans and invoke happiness on their households.**

バレンタインデーは憂鬱(ろ)です　barentaindē wa yūutsu desu **I hate Valentine's Day.**

どうしてチョコレート売り場に女性が殺到するのか不思議です　dōshite chokorēto uriba ni josei ga sattō suru no ka fushigi desu **I never cease to wonder at all those women and girls crowding the chocolate candy counters.**

c. March

3月3日は桃の節句です　sangatsu mikka wa momo no sekku desu **March 3 is the peach blossom festival.**

女の子のいる家ではお雛(な)様を飾ります　onna no ko no iru ie de wa o-hinasama wo kazarimasu **In households with female children they set up a display of dolls.**

そろそろお花見のシーズンですね　sorosoro o-hanami no shīzun desu ne **It's about time for the cherry blossom season.**

桜の花が満開になりました　sakura no hana ga mankai ni narimashita **The cherry trees are in full blossom.**

卒業式帰りの女子大生をよく見かけます　sotsugyōshikigaeri no joshigakusei wo yoku mikakemasu **A conspicuous sight is women university students returning from their graduation ceremony.**

d. April

エープリルフールで以前ひどいいたずらをされました　ēpurirufūru de izen hidoi itazura wo saremashita **I once had a terrible prank played on me on April Fools' Day.**

新入生がお母さんの手に引かれて学校へ行きます　shinnyūsei ga o-kaasan no te ni

hikarete gakkō e ikimasu **Little children walk hand in hand with their mothers to their first day of school.**

会社も新しい社員が入って活気に満ちています　kaisha mo atarashii shain ga haitte kakki ni michite imasu **Companies are busy welcoming their new employees.**

---

e. May

5月5日は端午の節句です　gogatsu itsuka wa tango no sekku desu **May 5 is the Boys' Festival.**

男の子のいる家では鯉 (こい) のぼりを飾ります　otoko no ko no iru ie de wa koinobori wo kazarimasu **Households with male children fly big cloth carps on a pole.**

まちにまったゴールデンウイークの到来　machi ni matta gōruden-uīku no tōrai **Now comes the long-awaited Golden Week*.**

今年は何連休ですか　kotoshi wa nanrenkyū desu ka **How many days off will we have this year ?**

どこへ行っても混んでいるから家でゴロゴロします　doko e itte mo konde iru kara ie de gorogoro shimasu **Everywhere you go it will be crowded, so I'm just going to lie around at home.**

f. June

梅雨に入りました　tsuyu ni hairimashita **The rainy season has started.**

毎日雨ばかりでうっとうしいですね　mainichi ame bakari de uttōshii desu ne **Isn't it dreary, all this rain day in and day out ?**

g. July

7月7日は七夕です　shichigatsu nanoka wa tanabata desu **July 7 is the Star Festival.**

何か星に願いをかけましょうか　nanika hoshi ni negai wo kakemashō ka **Shall we pray to the stars for something ?**

ようやく梅雨が上がり暑さがきびしくなりました　yōyaku tsuyu ga agari atsusa ga kibishikunarimashita **The rainy season has ended and the heat has become oppressive.**

土用の丑 (うし) の日には夏ばて防止にウナギを食べる習慣です　doyō' no ushi no hi ni wa natsubate bōshi ni unagi wo taberu shūkan desu **On the day of the Ox in the dog days of summer, people customarily eat eel so as not to succumb to the heat.**

夏休みの計画は立てましたか　natsuyasumi no keikaku wa tatemashita ka **Have you made your plans for the summer vacation?**

h. August

海水浴に行きませんか　kaisuiyoku ni ikimasen ka **Do you care to go to the beach with me?**

お盆の帰省ラッシュのピークはいつですか　o-bon no kisei rasshu no pīku wa itsu desu ka **When is the back-to-the-country rush going to reach its peak during this o-bon*?**

盆踊りを見に行きましょう　bon-odori wo mi ni ikimashō **Let's go watch the bon-odori*.**

花火大会があります　hanabi taikai ga arimasu **There is going to be a fireworks display.**

金魚すくいはなかなか難しい　kingyōsukui wa nakanaka muzukashii **It's hard to catch goldfish with these paper nets.**

i. September

新学期が始まります　shingakki ga hajimarimasu **The new school term starts.**

今夜は仲秋の名月です　kon-ya wa chūshū no meigetsu desu **This is the night of the harvest moon.**

今年は台風が多いです　kotoshi wa taifū ga ōi desu **There are a lot of typhoons this year.**

j. October

あちこちで運動会があります　achikochi de undōkai ga arimasu **Many schools are having Field Day.**

芸術の秋です．美術館を散策します　geijutsu no aki desu. bijutsukan wo sansaku shimasu **Autumn is the season for art. I like to visit art museums at this time.**

食欲の秋です．また焼き芋(芋)を買ってしまった　shokuyoku no aki desu. mata yaki-imo wo katte shimatta **The autumn air stimulates the appetite. I bought some roasted sweet potatoes again.**

公園の樹々が見事に紅葉しています　kōen no kigi ga migoto ni kōyō shite imasu **The trees in the park are beautiful in their autumn colors.**

k. November

だんだん寒くなってきました　dandan samuku natte kimashita **It is gradually**

getting colder.
あちこちの大学で学園祭が催されます　achikochi no daigaku de gakuensai ga moyōsaremasu **Many universities are holding their school festival.**

l. December

師走は何となく気ぜわしい月です　shiwasu wa nan to naku kizewashii tsuki desu **Somehow December always makes me feel restless.**

クリスマスのプレゼントはもう買いましたか　kurisumasu no purezento wa mō kaimashita ka **Have you finished your Christmas shopping ?**

クリスマスイブは誰 (だれ) と過ごしますか　kurisumasuibu wa dare to sugoshimasu ka **Who are you going to spend Christmas Eve with ?**

年賀状はもう書きましたか　nengajō wa mō kakimashita ka **Have you written your New Year's cards yet ?**

忘年会が続いて少し胃がもたれました　bōnenkai ga tsuzuite sukoshi i ga motaremashita **I have been to so many year-end parties that my stomach feels queasy.**

m. Japanese public holidays

Jan. 1 元旦 gantan **New Year's Day**
Jan. 15 成人の日 seijin no hi **Coming-of-Age Day**
Feb. 11 建国記念日 kenkoku kinenbi **National Foundation Day**
March 20 春分の日 shunbun no hi **Spring Equinox**
April 29 緑の日 midori no hi **Nature Day**
May 3 憲法記念日 kenpō kinenbi **Constitution Day**
May 4 国民の休日 kokumin to kyūjitsu **Citizens' Day**
May 5 子供の日 kodomo no hi **Children's Day**
Sept. 15 敬老の日 keirō no hi **Senior Citizens' Day**
Sept 23 秋分の日 shunbun no hi **Autumn Equinox**
Oct. 10 体育の日 taiiku no hi **Sports Day**
Nov. 3 文化の日 bunka no hi **Culture Day**
Nov. 23 勤労感謝の日 kinrō kansha no hi **Labor Day**
Dec. 23 天皇誕生日 tennō tanjōbi **The Emperor's Birthday**
振替休日 furikae kyūjitsu **substitute holiday***

16. Dates and Times

日 hi/nichi **day**
朝 asa **morning**

昼 hiru **noon/daytime**

夕方 yūgata **evening**

夜 yoru **night**

午前 gozen **morning** (from daybreak to noon)

正午 shōgo **12 noon**

午後 gogo **afternoon**

真夜中 mayonaka **midnight**

今朝 kesa **this morning**

午前中 gozenchū **during the morning**

深夜 shin-ya **late at night**

今日 kyō **today**

昨日 kinō/sakujitsu **yesterday**

明日 ashita/asu/myōnichi **tomorrow**

明後日 asatte/myōgonichi **the day after tomorrow**

一昨日 ototoi/issakujitsu **the day before yesterday**

週 shū **week**

今週 konshū **this week**

先週 senshū **last week**

来週 raishū **next week**

日曜日 nichiyōbi **Sunday**

月曜日 getsuyōbi **Monday**

火曜日 kayōbi **Tuesday**

水曜日 suiyōbi **Wednesday**

木曜日 mokuyōbi **Thursday**

金曜日 kin-yōbi **Friday**

土曜日 doyōbi **Saturday**

月 tsuki/getsu **month**

今月 kongetsu **this month**

先月 sengetsu **last month**

来月 raigetsu **next month**

1月 ichigatsu **January**

2月 nigatsu **February**

3月 sangatsu **March**

4月 shigatsu **April**

5月 gogatsu **May**

6月 rokugatsu **June**

7月 shichigatsu **July**

8月 hachigatsu **August**

9月 kugatsu **September**

10月 jūgatsu **October**

11月 jūichigatsu **November**

12月 jūnigatsu **December**

年 nen/toshi **year**

今年 kotoshi/konnen **this year**

去年 kyonen **last year**

昨年 sakunen **last year**

来年 rainen **next year**

西暦 seireki **Western calendar year**

1993年 senkyūhyakukyūjūsannen **nineteen ninety-three**

年号 nengō **Japanese calendar year name**

平成5年 heisei gonen **the fifth year of Heisei (= 1993)**

季節 kisetsu **season**

四季 shiki **the four seasons**

春 haru **spring**

夏 natsu **summer**

秋 aki **autumn/fall**

冬 fuyu **winter**

閏年 uruudoshi **leap year**

今日は何日ですか kyō wa nannichi desu ka **What's today's date?**

3月3日です sangatsu mikka desu **It's March (the) third.**

今日は何曜日ですか kyō wa nan-yōbi desu ka **What day of the week is it today?**

水曜日です suiyōbi desu **It's Wednesday.**

今年は何年ですか kotoshi wa nannen desu ka **What year is it?**

1993年です senkyūhyakukyūjūsannen desu **It's nineteen ninety-three.**

今何時ですか ima nanji desu ka **What time is it?**

8時15分です hachiji jūgofun desu **It's eight fifteen.**

10時15分前です jūji jūgofun mae desu **It's fifteen to ten.**

いつ来ましたか itsu kimashita ka **When did you get here?**

お昼過ぎです o-hirusugi desu **A little after noon.**

GLOSSARY

bon-odori: A community dance held on certain evenings around the time of the o-bon festival.

bonenkai: A traditional party held at the end of the year by various work and social groups to bring the year to a happy end.

choshi: A tokkuri (see below) full of sake (see below).

Golden Week: Seven or more days, usually beginning April 29, during which 4 national holidays and 1 or 2 weekends occur.

government postcards: Postcards issued by the government on which the postage has been prepaid, so that no further postage is necessary; said in contrast to picture postcards etc which require a postage stamp.

hyakunin-isshu: A card game played at New Year's.

ikebana: The Japanese art of flower arranging.

Kabuki: A form of classical Japanese drama based on popular legends, with male actors in both male and female roles.

miso: Fermented bean paste.

nijikai: An informal drinking party taking place after a more formal party or banquet.

Noh: A form of classical Japanese drama based on religious or mythical themes and featuring very stylized dancing.

o-bon: The festival of the dead, held to commemorate one's ancestors. It is marked in modern times by a great exodus from the cities as people return to their ancestral homes in the country for the celebration. In most regions it is held on August 13, 14, and 15.

police box: A small local police station manned by 2 or more policemen 24 hours a day. It usually consists of a small office with toilet and sleeping facilities. In the cities there may be one every several hundred meters, depending on the population density.

prearrangements: Also called by their Japanese name, *nemawashi*, such arrangements usually consist of informal, often secret meetings with individual members of some decision-making committee etc to argue one's case before the full committee meets.

S tickets: Tickets to the S seats, i.e., the best reserved seats in the house in a theater or concert hall.

sake: A kind of wine made from fermented rice and often drunk hot.

setsubun: A festivity where people throw beans toward the outside of their houses to ward off devils.

shinkansen: The Japanese name for the so-called "bullet trains" that run at great speeds on wide, elevated tracks.

substitute holiday: The name given to a Monday observed as a holiday following a national holiday that fell on a Sunday.

tempura: Fish, shellfish, and vegetables dipped in batter and fried in deep fat. Spelled with an *n* in romaji, but with an *m* as an English loan word.

tokkuri: A small bottle for heating sake (see above).

ume: A green, very sour relative of the plum, used for various kinds of pickles and flavorings. Its tree, also called ume, is also cultivated for its beautiful white, pink, or red blossoms, which open in very early spring.

wasabi: A kind of horseradish, cultivated in cold mountain streams, and used as a pungent spice.

zoni: A broth containing vegetables and mochi (see page 605) and eaten at New Year's.